Stitz

The Gospel According to St. Mark

The Greek Text
with Introduction,
Notes, and Indexes

Vincent Taylor

SECOND EDITION

D0167525

BAKER BOOK HOUSE
Grand Rapids, Michigan 49506

8229936

PHOTOLITHOPRINTED BY CUSHING - MALLOY, INC.
ANN ARBOR, MICHIGAN, UNITED STATES OF AMERICA

PREFACE

THIS commentary was begun in the earlier years of the War, and, in its first stages, was sometimes written in circumstances when access to books was not easy, in the conviction that the time had come to attempt to harvest the rich gains which have gradually accumulated through the labours of many scholars in Markan fields. Over half a century has passed since the great commentary of Henry Barclay Swete was first published by the House of Macmillan, and, although other commentators have written learned works, no British commentary on the same scale has been attempted. The reason is not far to seek. The literature on questions of introduction, text, language, theology, and exegesis, in English, German, French, and Swedish, in encyclopaedias, monographs, and learned journals, is immense. Indeed, a would-be commentator might easily spend the whole of his life in reading and evaluating these contributions and find at the end that he had scarcely begun to write a line of his commentary; for, in addition to other inquiries, he must follow the history of criticism in general and the development of modern theology, the exegesis of the Old Testament, the Apocrypha and Pseudepigrapha, the Rabbinical writings, the main currents of Hellenistic thought, the history and fortunes of primitive Christianity, the problems of science, religion, and philosophy. No knowledge, in fact, pertaining to literature, art, history, liturgiology, and theology, is out of place in such an undertaking.

It may be suspected, however, that not only the scale of the necessary reading has led scholars to pause, but also the risk of appearing to presume to write a *definitive* commentary on St. Mark, when many vital questions are still the subject of debate. Can we yet say that the time has come when, in the words of Mark iv. 29, we must put forth the sickle because the harvest is come? I believe we can, provided we recognize that in due course other harvests will be reaped, perhaps richer and more varied still.

v

I hasten to say that in this work I have no thought of attempting to write a definitive commentary. I am content rather to report progress and perhaps to stimulate others to essay the task. It is not by one commentary, but by a series, that we are most likely to make real progress. And, for the encouragement of others, I may say that there is no task so rewarding. When we write monographs on such questions as the Parables, the Kingdom of God, or the Son of Man, we read everything germane to such inquiries, but other subjects, which do not make the same appeal, have perforce to be passed by. In writing a commentary this method is not possible. Every theme that arises must be followed, and every line of inquiry into which it opens. The commentator is compelled to be catholic in his sympathies, international in his outlook, hospitable in his interests.

Since no one can be adequately equipped for such an undertaking, I feel it incumbent upon me to indicate to the reader fields in which he must look for better guidance than that which I can give ; and two in particular, patristic studies and the question of Semitisms. On the side of patristic studies I have little to offer, partly because I have no special competence in this field, and partly because the need is so fully met in the classical commentaries of Swete and Lagrange. The question of Semitisms has interested me for many years, and I have followed the most important discussions carefully ; but, while not without knowledge of the subject, I am not in any sense a Semitic specialist. The subject cannot be omitted in a modern commentary, and I have therefore submitted all that I have written on this topic to the scrutiny of my friends, Dr. Wilbert F. Howard, Dr. Norman H. Snaith, and Dr. Matthew Black. For their friendly and faithful criticisms and suggestions I am most grateful, but, of course, the final responsibility for what I have written is my own.

Among many valuable commentaries I am especially indebted to those of Swete, J. Weiss, Lagrange, Rawlinson, and Lohmeyer. A commentary like that of Swete, which has guided the studies of two generations of British students, acquires a new interest in the eyes of anyone who tries to follow in his footsteps. If we allow for the want of adequate guidance in historical questions, of which Swete was fully aware, as the comments in the Prefaces to his second and third editions show, it is impossible to exaggerate the value of this monumental work, and especially its contributions to linguistic studies, patristic interpretations, and exegetical discussions. In some sense it is the greatness of Swete's work which has stood in the way of his successors. If, with some courage, but with humility, I venture to follow in his steps, it is because historical questions can no longer be ignored and because a wealth of discussion is available such as did not obtain in his day.

In this commentary a special interest has been taken in the obscure period which lies behind the composition of the Gospel. I hope I have given adequate consideration to the invaluable Papias tradition, which is so sound that, if we did not possess it, we should be compelled to postulate something very much like it. But the Gospel is not to be explained by the simple hypothesis of an Apostolic eyewitness. More than a single generation lies between it and the events and sayings of the historic Ministry of Jesus, and in many important respects the Gospel reflects the worship, theology, and cate-chetical interests of a living Christian Church. In spite of its manifest defects Form Criticism has forced this conviction upon us, and, although the criticism of Bultmann and others is excessively radical, much is to be learnt that is positive and constructive. I hope that in my treatment nothing merely polemical, still less discourteous, has been allowed to appear, for we learn most from those from whom we are compelled to differ.

The commentary is based on a modified form of the text of Westcott and Hort. Subsequent discoveries, especially those of the Washington Codex, Codex Koridethi, the Sinaitic Syriac MS., and the Chester Beatty Papyri, and further study of the Western and Caesarean texts and the Georgian and Armenian versions, have established a widely held conviction that many of Hort's readings need revision ; and in this matter I have felt it right to continue the first steps taken by Swete so long ago. I have fully used the extensive critical apparatus in S. C. E. Legg's *Nouum Testamentum Graece*. For this reason I have not attempted to provide a critical apparatus of my own, but have fully discussed many important textual variants, especially when they bear on questions of exegesis. Professor T. W. Manson has been kind enough to read what I have written and to examine the text, and I have profited greatly by his criticisms and suggestions. In questions of Jewish interest I have frequently used the massive *Kommentar* of H. L. Strack and P. Billerbeck, and in considering points of New Testament theology I have freely drawn upon the rich resources of G. Kittel's *Theologisches Wörterbuch*. The grammatical works of Blass, Debrunner, Moulton, Howard, and Robertson have been constantly used as well as Moulton and Milligan's *Vocabulary of the Greek Testament* and that mine of theological knowledge, Moulton and Geden's *Concordance to the Greek Testament*.

The methods I have followed may be briefly indicated. In the Introduction I have discussed the critical, grammatical, theological, and historical questions, and, in this way, have sought to avoid the need of discussing repeatedly the same points later. In the Commentary the text is treated in larger divisions, and then in sections containing the several narratives and sayings-groups. To all these, short introductions are provided and special questions are discussed in detached notes. At the end of the volume additional notes are supplied on larger questions to which the answers must necessarily be of a more general and speculative character. In this way I have tried to make the Commentary serviceable to readers who hold different views from mine, for I recognize that a commentator succeeds when he stimulates others to reach better results than his own. An asterisk is appended to lists of Markan passages recording the full use of a particular Greek word, and two asterisks when the complete New Testament record is given. When other commentaries and well-known works are mentioned, only the page number is supplied and abbreviations when more than one book is in question. For these references the Bibliography will serve as a key. Other abbreviations, I hope, will cause no difficulty. In general, I have supplied the data for discussion fully, especially when the issues are evenly balanced. At the same time I have expressed personal opinions in the belief that the reader has the right to know what the commentator thinks ; but I need hardly add that these opinions have no more authority than belongs to prolonged and careful study.

I gladly take the opportunity to express my deep gratitude to a few friends who have assisted me in various ways. In addition to those I have mentioned earlier I am indebted to my colleagues, the Rev. Dr. H. Watkin-Jones and the Rev. A. Raymond George, M.A., who were kind enough to read the typescript of the section on the Theology of the Gospel and Note B on the Twelve and the Apostles, and the Rev. Owen E. Evans, M.A., B.D., who has compiled the Index of Proper Names; and to the Revs. Dr. H. G. Meecham, Dr. C. Leslie Mitton, and C. Kingsley Barrett, M.A., B.D., who have shared with me the laborious task of correcting the proof-sheets. For the help so generously given I am deeply grateful, but of course the final responsibility for errors which may remain is my own. I wish also gratefully to acknowledge the courtesy and skill of the staff of Messrs. R. and R. Clark, of Edinburgh, whose accuracy is known the world over. In the hope that I may have contributed a little to reveal further the significance and meaning of St. Mark's Gospel I bring my work of a decade to an end. I count it an immeasurable privilege to have been permitted to write a commentary on a Gospel which is one of the greatest treasures of the Church and one of the most influential and astounding books in the world.

VINCENT TAYLOR

WESLEY COLLEGE,
HEADINGLEY, LEEDS
16th Dec. 1950

CONTENTS

xi

SELECT BIBLIOGRAPHY [1]

(1) COMMENTARIES

ST. MARK'S GOSPEL

ALLEN, W. C., *The Gospel according to Saint Mark*. London, 1915.
BACON, B. W., *The Gospel of Mark*. U.S.A., 1925.
The Beginnings of Gospel Story. U.S.A., 1909; third printing, 1925.
BARTLET, J. V., *St. Mark* (Century Bible). Edinburgh, 1922.
BLUNT, A. W. F., *The Gospel according to Saint Mark* (The Clarendon Bible). Oxford, 1929.
BRANSCOMB, B. H., *The Gospel of Mark* (The Moffatt New Testament Commentary). London, 1937.
BRUCE, A. B., *The Synoptic Gospels* (The Expositor's Greek Testament, i). London, 1897.
GOULD, E. P., *The Gospel according to Saint Mark* (The International Critical Commentary). Edinburgh, 1896.
HOLTZMANN, H. J., *Die Synoptiker* (*Hand-Commentar zum Neuen Testament*). Tübingen, 1901.
HUNTER, A. M., *The Gospel according to Saint Mark* (The Torch Bible Commentaries). London, 1948.
KLOSTERMANN, E., *Das Markusevangelium* (*Handbuch zum Neuen Testament*). Tübingen, 2nd ed., 1926.
LAGRANGE, M.-J., *Évangile selon Saint Marc*. Paris, 5th ed., 1929.
LOHMEYER, E., *Das Evangelium des Markus*. Göttingen, 1937.
LOISY, A., *Les Évangiles synoptiques*. Ceffonds, Paris, 1907, two vols.
L'Évangile selon Marc. Paris, 1912.
MENZIES, A., *The Earliest Gospel*. London, 1901.
MONTEFIORE, C. G., *The Synoptic Gospels*. London, 2nd ed., 1927, two vols.
PLUMMER, A., *The Gospel according to St. Mark* (Cambridge Greek Testament for Schools and Colleges). Cambridge, 1914.
RAWLINSON, A. E. J., *The Gospel according to St. Mark* (Westminster Commentaries). London, 7th ed., 1949.
SCHNIEWIND, J., *Das Evangelium nach Markus* (*Das Neue Testament Deutsch*). Göttingen, 4th ed., 1947.
STRACK, H. L., and BILLERBECK, P., *Kommentar zum Neuen Testament aus Talmud und Midrasch*, i-iv. München, 1922-8. Cited as Billerbeck.
SWETE, H. B., *The Gospel according to St. Mark*. London, 1898, 3rd ed., 1909, reprinted, 1920.
TURNER, C. H., *The Gospel according to St. Mark* (reprinted from *A New Commentary on Holy Scripture*, edited by C. Gore, H. L. Goudge, and A. Guillaume). London, 1928.

[1] Except where otherwise indicated, these works are cited by the page number after the author's name.

xiii

WEISS, B., *Die Evangelien des Markus und Lukas* (*Kritisch-exegetischer Kommentar über das Neue Testament*, edited by H. A. W. Meyer). Göttingen, 1901.

WEISS, J., *Das älteste Evangelium*. Göttingen, 1903.

Das Markusevangelium (in *Die Schriften des Neuen Testaments*, vol. i, 3rd ed. revised by W. Bousset). Göttingen, 1917. Cited as *Die Schr.* or *die Schr.*[4]

WELLHAUSEN, J., *Das Evangelium Marci*. Berlin, 2nd ed., 1909.

WOHLENBERG, G., *Das Evangelium des Markus*. Leipzig, 1910.

WOOD, H. G., *Mark* (in Peake's *Commentary on the Bible*). London, 1920.

OTHER COMMENTARIES

ALLEN, W. C., *The Gospel according to S. Matthew* (The International Critical Commentary). Edinburgh, 1907.

BERNARD, J. H., *The Gospel according to St. John* (The International Critical Commentary). Edinburgh, 1928.

CREED, J. M., *The Gospel according to St. Luke*. London, 1930.

EASTON, B. S., *The Gospel according to St. Luke*. Edinburgh, 1926.

LAGRANGE, M.-J., *Évangile selon Saint Luc*. Paris, 2nd ed., 1921. Cited as *St. Luke*.

Évangile selon Saint Matthieu. Paris, 1923. Cited as *St. Matt.*

Évangile selon Saint Jean. Paris, 3rd ed., 1927. Cited as *St. John*.

LIGHTFOOT, J. B., *Saint Paul's Epistle to the Galatians*. London, 1865, 9th ed., 1887.

Saint Paul's Epistle to the Philippians. London, 1868, 4th ed., 1878, reprint of 1900.

Saint Paul's Epistles to the Colossians and to Philemon. London, 1875, 9th ed., 1890.

LUCE, H. K., *The Gospel according to S. Luke* (Cambridge Greek Testament). Cambridge, 1933.

MCNEILE, A. H., *The Gospel according to St. Matthew*. London, 1915.

PLUMMER, A., *The Gospel according to S. Luke* (International Critical Commentary). Edinburgh, 4th ed., reprint of 1908.

ROBINSON, J. A., *St. Paul's Epistle to the Ephesians*. London, 2nd ed., reprint of 1941.

ROBINSON, T. H., *The Gospel of Matthew* (The Moffatt New Testament Commentary). Edinburgh, 1928.

SANDAY, W., and HEADLAM, A. C., *The Epistle to the Romans* (The International Critical Commentary). Edinburgh, 5th ed., 1902, reprint of 1914.

SELWYN, E. G., *The First Epistle of St. Peter*. London, 1946.

SMITH, B. T. D., *The Gospel according to S. Matthew* (Cambridge Greek Testament). Cambridge, 1927.

WELLHAUSEN, J., *Das Evangelium Matthaei*. Berlin, 1904.

Das Evangelium Lucae. Berlin, 1904.

Das Evangelium Johannis. Berlin, 1908.

(2) WORKS OF REFERENCE

BAUER, W., *Griechisch-deutsches Wörterbuch zu den Schriften des Neuen Testaments*. Giessen, 2nd ed., 1928, 4th ed., 1950.

BLASS, F., *Grammar of New Testament Greek*. Eng. Tr. by H. St. John Thackeray. London, 2nd ed., 1905.

BURTON, E. DE WITT, *Syntax of the Moods and Tenses of New Testament Greek*. Edinburgh, 3rd ed., 1898.

CHARLES, R. H., *The Apocrypha and Pseudepigrapha of the Old Testament in English* (ed. R. H. Charles). Oxford, 1913.

CHEYNE, T. K., and BLACK, J. S., *Encyclopaedia Biblica*, i-iv. London, 1899–1903. Cited as *EB*.

DALMAN, G., *The Words of Jesus*. Eng. Tr. by D. M. Kay. Edinburgh, 1902.

Jesus-Jeshua. Eng. Tr. by P. P. Levertoff. London, 1929. Cited as *JJ*.

Sacred Sites and Ways. Eng. Tr. by P. P. Levertoff. London, 1935. Cited as *SSW*.

DANBY, H., *The Mishnah*. Eng. Tr., Oxford, 1933.

DEBRUNNER, A., *Friedrich Blass' Grammatik des neutestamentlichen Griechisch*. Göttingen, 7th ed., 1943.

DEISSMANN, A., *Light from the Ancient East*. Eng. Tr. by L. R. M. Strachan. London, 2nd ed. (4th German ed.), 1927.

Bible Studies. Eng. Tr. by A. Grieve. Edinburgh, 1901. Cited as *BS*.

EDERSHEIM, A., *The Life and Times of Jesus the Messiah*, i, ii. London, 1883.

FIELD, F., *Notes on the Translation of the New Testament*. Cambridge, 1899.

GOODWIN, W. W., *Syntax of the Moods and Tenses of the Greek Verb*. London, 1897.

HASTINGS, J., *A Dictionary of the Bible*, i-v. Edinburgh, 1904.

A Dictionary of Christ and the Gospels, i, ii. Edinburgh, 1906. Cited as *DCG*.

HATCH, E., and REDPATH, H. A., *A Concordance to the Septuagint*, i, ii. Oxford, 1897.

HORT, F. J. A., and WESTCOTT, B. F., *The New Testament in the Original Greek*, Introduction and Appendix. Cambridge and London, 1882. Cited as Hort.

HOWARD, W. F., *Appendix on Semitisms in the New Testament* in Moulton's *Grammar*.

HUCK, A., *A Synopsis of the First Three Gospels*. English ed. (from the 9th German ed.) by F. L. Cross. Tübingen, 1936.

KENNEDY, H. A. A., *Sources of New Testament Greek*. Edinburgh, 1895.

KITTEL, G., *Theologisches Wörterbuch zum Neuen Testament*. Stuttgart, 1933–. Cited as *KThW*.

LEGG, S. C. E., *Nouum Testamentum Graece: Euangelium secundum Marcum*. Oxford, 1935.

LIDDELL, H. G., and SCOTT, R., *A Greek-English Lexicon*, i, ii. New ed. by Sir Henry Stuart Jones and R. McKenzie. Oxford, 1925–40.

MEECHAM, H. G., *Light from Ancient Letters*. London, 1923.
The Letter of Aristeas. Manchester, 1935.
The Epistle to Diognetus. Manchester, 1949.
MOULTON, J. H., and HOWARD, W. F., *A Grammar of New Testament Greek. Prolegomena*, 3rd ed., Edinburgh, 1908. Vol. ii, 1929.
Einleitung in die Sprache des Neuen Testaments, translated, with additions, from *Proleg.* Heidelberg, 1911.
MOULTON, J. H., and MILLIGAN, G., *The Vocabulary of the Greek Testament.* London, 1914–29.
MOULTON, W. F., and GEDEN, A. S., *A Concordance to the Greek Testament.* Edinburgh, 2nd ed., reprinted, 1906.
RADERMACHER, L., *Neutestamentliche Grammatik.* Tübingen, 2nd ed., 1925.
ROBERTSON, A. T., *A Grammar of the Greek New Testament.* New York, 3rd ed., 1919.
ROBERTSON, A. T., and DAVIS, W. H., *A New Short Grammar of the Greek Testament.* London, 1931.
SANDAY, W., *Sacred Sites of the Gospels.* Oxford, 1903.
SCHÜRER, E., *A History of the Jewish People in the Time of Jesus Christ*, i–vi. Eng. Tr. by S. Taylor and P. Christie. Edinburgh, 1901.
SHARP, D. S., *Epictetus and the New Testament.* London, 1914.
SMITH, G. A., *The Historical Geography of the Holy Land.* London, 25th ed., 1932. Cited as *HG*.
SOUTER, A., *The Text and Canon of the New Testament.* London, 1913.
A Pocket Lexicon to the Greek New Testament. Oxford, 1917.
THACKERAY, H. ST. J., *A Grammar of the Old Testament in Greek*, i. Cambridge, 1909.
TISCHENDORF, C., *Novum Testamentum Graece.* 8th ed., 1869.
TURNER, C. H., Articles on 'Markan Usage' in the *Journal of Theological Studies*, xxv–xxix, 1924–8.
WINER, G. B., *A Treatise on the Grammar of New Testament Greek*, translated from the German by W. F. Moulton. Edinburgh, 3rd ed., 1882.

(3) OTHER LITERATURE

ABRAHAMS, I., *Studies in Pharisaism and the Gospels.* Cambridge. First Series, 1917 ; Second Series, 1924.
ALBERTZ, M., *Die synoptischen Streitgespräche.* Berlin, 1921.
BACON, B. W., *Is Mark a Roman Gospel?* Cambridge, 1919.
Studies in Matthew. New York, 1930.
BARRETT, C. K., *The Holy Spirit and the Gospel Tradition.* London, 1947.
BERTRAM, G., *Die Leidensgeschichte Jesu und der Christuskult.* Göttingen, 1922.
BLACK, M., *An Aramaic Approach to the Gospels and Acts.* Oxford, 1946.
BOUSSET, W., *Kyrios Christos.* Göttingen, 3rd ed., 1926.
BOWMAN, J. W., *The Intention of Jesus.* London, 1945.

BULTMANN, R., *Die Geschichte der synoptischen Tradition.* Göttingen, 2nd ed., 1931.
Jesus and the Word. Eng. Tr. by L. P. Smith and E. Huntress. London, 1935.
BURKITT, F. C., *The Gospel History and its Transmission.* Edinburgh, 3rd ed., 1911.
Christian Beginnings. London, 1924.
BURNEY, C. F., *The Aramaic Origin of the Fourth Gospel.* Oxford, 1922.
The Poetry of our Lord. Oxford, 1925.
BUSSMANN, W., *Synoptische Studien.* Halle, 1925–31. Three Parts.
CADBURY, H. J., *The Style and Literary Method of Luke.* Cambridge, U.S.A., i, 1919: ii, 1920. Also articles in *The Beginnings of Christianity* (Lake and Foakes Jackson).
CADOUX, A. T., *The Parables of Jesus.* London, 1930.
The Sources of the Second Gospel. London, 1935.
The Theology of Jesus. London, 1940.
CADOUX, C. J., *The Historic Mission of Jesus.* London, 1941.
CLARK, A. C., *The Primitive Text of the Gospels and Acts.* Oxford, 1914.
COLWELL, E. C., *The Greek of the Fourth Gospel.* Chicago, 1931.
CRUM, J. M. C., *St. Mark's Gospel. Two Stages of its Making.* Cambridge, 1936.
DIBELIUS, M., *From Tradition to Gospel.* Eng. Tr. (from *Die Formgeschichte des Evangeliums*[2]) by B. L. Woolf. London, 1934.
DODD, C. H., *The Parables of the Kingdom.* London, 1935.
The Bible and the Greeks. London, 1935.
The Apostolic Preaching and its Developments. London, 1936.
History and the Gospel. London, 1938.
EASTON, B. S., *The Gospel before the Gospels.* London, 1928.
Christ in the Gospels. New York and London, 1930.
FASCHER, E., *Die formgeschichtliche Methode.* Giessen, 1924.
FIEBIG, P., *Der Erzählungsstil der Evangelien.* Leipzig, 1925.
FLEMINGTON, W. F., *The New Testament Doctrine of Baptism.* London, 1948.
FLEW, R. N., *The Idea of Perfection.* Oxford, 1934.
Jesus and His Church. London, 1938, 2nd ed., 1943.
GLASSON, T. F., *The Second Advent.* London, 1945.
GLOEGE, G., *Reich Gottes und Kirche.* Gütersloh, 1929.
GOGUEL, M., *The Life of Jesus.* Eng. Tr. by O. Wyon. London, 1933.
Jean-Baptiste. Paris, 1928.
GRANT, F. C., *The Growth of the Gospels.* New York, 1933.
Form Criticism. Chicago, 1934.
The Earliest Gospel. New York, 1943.
HARNACK, A., *The Date of the Acts and of the Synoptic Gospels.* London, 1911.
HAWKINS, J. C., *Horae Synopticae.* Oxford, 2nd ed., 1909. See also *Studies in the Synoptic Problem* (ed. W. Sanday).
HOSKYNS, E., and DAVEY, N., *The Riddle of the New Testament.* London, 1931, 3rd ed., 1947.

HOWARD, W. F., *The Fourth Gospel in Recent Criticism and Interpretation.* London, 1931, 3rd ed., 1947.
Christianity according to St. John. London, 1943.
The Romance of New Testament Scholarship. London, 1949.
JAMES, M. R., *The Apocryphal New Testament.* Oxford, 1924.
JEREMIAS, J., *Die Abendmahlsworte Jesu.* Göttingen, 1935, 2nd ed., 1949.
Jesus als Weltvollender. Gütersloh, 1930.
JÜLICHER, A., *Die Gleichnisreden Jesu.* Tübingen, 1899, 2nd ed., 1910.
KENYON, F. G., *Recent Developments in the Textual Criticism of the Greek Bible.* London, 1933.
The Chester Beatty Biblical Papyri. London, 1933–6.
The Text of the Greek Bible. London, 1937.
KILPATRICK, G. D., *The Origins of the Gospel according to St. Matthew.* Oxford, 1946.
KLAUSNER, J., *Jesus of Nazareth.* London, 1929.
KNOX, J., *Christ the Lord.* Chicago, 1945.
KNOX, W. L., *Some Hellenistic Elements in Primitive Christianity.* London, 1944.
LAKE, K., and FOAKES JACKSON, F. J., *The Beginnings of Christianity,* i-v. London, 1920–33.
LIGHTFOOT, R. H., *History and Interpretation in the Gospels.* London, 1935.
Locality and Doctrine in the Gospels. London, 1938.
The Gospel Message of St. Mark. Oxford, 1950.
MACKINNON, J., *The Historic Jesus.* London, 1931.
MANSON, T. W., *The Teaching of Jesus.* Cambridge, 1931.
The Sayings of Jesus (Bk. II of *The Mission and Message of Jesus,* 1937), published separately. London, 1949.
MANSON, W., *Jesus the Messiah.* London, 1943.
MARSH, H. G., *The Origin and Significance of the New Testament Baptism.* Manchester, 1941.
MEYER, A., *Die Entstehung des Markusevangeliums (Festgabe f. A. Jülicher).* Tübingen, 1927.
MEYER, ED., *Ursprung und Anfänge des Christentums,* i-iii. Stuttgart and Berlin, 1921–3.
MICKLEM, E. R., *Miracles and the New Psychology.* Oxford, 1922.
MOFFATT, J., *Introduction to the Literature of the New Testament.* Edinburgh, 3rd ed., 1918.
MOORE, G. F., *Judaism,* i-iii. Cambridge, U.S.A.. 1927–30.
OESTERLEY, W. O. E., *The Jewish Background of the Christian Liturgy.* Oxford, 1925.
The Gospel Parables in the Light of their Jewish Background. London, 1936.
OTTO, R., *Reich Gottes und Menschensohn.* München, 1934.
Eng. Tr., *The Kingdom of God and the Son of Man,* by F. V. Filson and B. L. Woolf. London, 1938.
PALLIS, A., *Notes on St. Mark and St. Matthew.* London, 1932.

PATTON, C. S., *Sources of the Synoptic Gospels.* New York, 1915.
RAMSEY, A. M., *The Resurrection of Christ.* London, 2nd ed., 1946.
The Glory of God and the Transfiguration of Christ. London, 1949.
RICHARDSON, A., *The Miracle Stories of the Gospels.* London, 1941.
Christian Apologetics. London, 1948.
SANDAY, W., *Studies in the Synoptic Problem* (ed. W. Sanday). Oxford, 1911.
The Life of Christ in Recent Research. London, 1908.
SCHMIDT, K. L., *Der Rahmen der Geschichte Jesu.* Berlin, 1919.
SCHOFIELD, J. N., *The Historical Background of the Bible.* London. 1938.
The Religious Background of the Bible. London, 1944.
SCHWEITZER, A., *The Quest of the Historical Jesus.* Eng. Tr. by W. Montgomery of *Von Reimarus zu Wrede,* 1906. London, 2nd ed., 1911.
Later German ed., *Die Geschichte der Leben-Jesu-Forschung,* 1913.
The Mystery of the Kingdom of God. Eng. Tr. by W. Lowrie of *Das Messianitäts- und Leidensgeheimnis. Eine Skizze des Lebens Jesu,* 1901. London, 1925.
SHARMAN, H. B., *Son of Man and Kingdom of God.* New York and London, 1943.
SMITH, B. T. D., *The Parables of the Synoptic Gospels.* Cambridge, 1937.
SNAITH, N. H., *The Jewish New Year Festival.* London, 1947.
STANTON, V. H., *The Gospels as Historical Documents,* i-iii. Cambridge, 1903–20.
STREETER, B. H., *The Four Gospels: A Study of Origins.* London, 1924.
SUNDWALL, J., *Die Zusammensetzung des Markusevangeliums.* Åbo, 1934.
TAYLOR, V., *Behind the Third Gospel.* Oxford, 1926.
The Gospels: A Short Introduction. London, 6th ed., 1948.
Jesus and His Sacrifice. London, 1937, 1948.
TORREY, C. C., *The Four Gospels: A New Translation.* London, n.d.
Our Translated Gospels. London, n.d.
WEISS, J., *The History of Primitive Christianity,* i, ii. Eng. Tr. of *Das Urchristentum,* 1917, by F. C. Grant, A. H. Forster, P. S. Kramer, S. E. Johnson. London, 1937.
WELLHAUSEN, J., *Einleitung in die drei ersten Evangelien.* Berlin, 2nd ed., 1911.
WENDLING, E., *Ur-Marcus.* Tübingen, 1905.
Die Entstehung des Marcus-Evangeliums. Tübingen, 1908.
WERNER, M., *Der Einfluss paulinischer Theologie im Markusevangelium.* Giessen, 1923.
WILLIAMS, N. P., *Studies in the Synoptic Problem* (ed. W. Sanday).
WREDE, W., *Das Messiasgeheimnis in den Evangelien.* Göttingen, 1901, 2nd ed., 1913.
ZAHN, TH., *Introduction to the New Testament,* i-iii. Eng. Tr. of the 3rd German ed. by M. W. Jacobus and others. Edinburgh, 1909.

(4) JOURNALS

AJT = *American Journal of Theology.*
ATR = *Anglican Theological Review.*
CNT = *Coniectanea Neotestamentica.*
CQR = *Church Quarterly Review.*
ET = *Expository Times.*
Exp = *Expositor.*
HTR = *Harvard Theological Review.*
JBL = *Journal of Biblical Literature.*
JR = *Journal of Religion.*
JTS = *Journal of Theological Studies.*
LQR = *London Quarterly and Holborn Review.*
RB = *Revue biblique.*
Th = *Theology.*
ThLZ = *Theologische Literaturzeitung.*
ThR = *Theologische Rundschau.*
ZNTW = *Zeitschrift für die neutestamentliche Wissenschaft.*

ABBREVIATIONS

Aq. = Aquila.
BDB = Brown, Driver, Briggs (Heb. Lex.).
ERE = *Encyclopaedia of Religion and Ethics.*
HDB = Hastings' *Dictionary of the Bible.*
HR = Hatch, Redpath (*Concordance to LXX*).
HS = *Horae Synopticae* (J. C. Hawkins).
JE = *Jewish Encyclopaedia.*
LS = Liddell and Scott (Greek Lex.).
SH = Sanday and Headlam.
Th. = Theodotion.
TR = Textus Receptus.
WM = Winer-Moulton (*Grammar of NT Greek*).
v. = ' see ' or ' verse '.
v.l. = *varia lectio.*

INTRODUCTION

I

THE HISTORY OF THE GOSPEL IN THE EARLY CHURCH

WE are fortunate in possessing statements regarding the Gospel which carry us back to the beginning of the second century. The earliest is that of Papias, Bishop of Hierapolis, in his *Exegesis of the Lord's Oracles* (*c.* A.D. 140), a lost work from which important quotations are made by Eusebius in his *Historia Ecclesiastica*. Papias not only speaks of Mark himself, but also quotes the testimony of an Elder who is generally supposed to have been the Elder John, an older contemporary. Only a little later we have the disputed reference of Justin Martyr to Peter's ' Memoirs ' and the statement of a Prologue to the Gospel recently discussed and recognized as Anti-Marcionite. Next follows a brief mutilated statement in the Muratorian Canon, which may be dated A.D. 170–90. To the same period belong the words of Irenaeus in his *Adversus Haereses*, and somewhat later those of Clement of Alexandria in his *Hypotyposes*. From the first half of the third century comes the testimony of Origen, and finally the statement of Jerome in his Commentary on Matt. at the close of the fourth century.

Signs of a knowledge of Mark in the Epistle of Barnabas (A.D. 130), the Epistle of Clement of Rome to the Corinthians (A.D. 95), the *Shepherd* of Hermas (? A.D. 145), and the Epistle of Polycarp to the Philippians (A.D. 135) are uncertain, and cannot be regarded as affording more than a knowledge of Synoptic tradition. Cf. *The NT in the Apostolic Fathers*, by a committee of the Oxford Society of Historical Theology ; P. N. Harrison, *Polycarp's Two Epistles to the Philippians*, 285-8.

I. PAPIAS

As quoted by Eus. *HE*, iii. 39. 15, his words are as follows :

Καὶ τοῦθ' ὁ πρεσβύτερος ἔλεγε· Μάρκος μέν, ἑρμηνευτὴς

Πέτρου γενόμενος, ὅσα ἐμνημόνευσεν ἀκριβῶς ἔγραψεν, οὐ μέντοι
τάξει, τὰ ὑπὸ [τοῦ] κυρίου ἢ λεχθέντα ἢ πραχθέντα. οὔτε γὰρ
ἤκουσε τοῦ κυρίου οὔτε παρηκολούθησεν αὐτῷ· ὕστερον δέ, ὡς
ἔφην, Πέτρῳ, ὃς πρὸς τὰς χρείας ἐποιεῖτο τὰς διδασκαλίας, ἀλλ'
οὐχ ὥσπερ σύνταξιν τῶν κυριακῶν ποιούμενος λογίων. ὥστε
οὐδὲν ἥμαρτε Μάρκος, οὕτως ἔνια γράψας ὡς ἀπεμνημόνευσεν·
ἑνὸς γὰρ ἐποιήσατο πρόνοιαν, τοῦ μηδὲν ὧν ἤκουσε παραλιπεῖν
ἢ ψεύσασθαί τι ἐν αὐτοῖς.

' And the Elder said this also : Mark, having become the interpreter of Peter, wrote down accurately all that he remembered of the
things said and done by the Lord, but not however in order. For
neither did he hear the Lord, nor did he follow Him, but afterwards,
as I said, Peter, who adapted his teachings to the needs (of the
hearers), but not as though he were drawing up a connected account
of the Lord's oracles. So then Mark made no mistake in thus recording some things just as he remembered them, for he made it his
one care to omit nothing that he had heard and to make no false
statement therein.'

The Elder's statement ends with the first sentence, the
rest being the opinion of Papias himself. Mark's office was
that of an interpreter, but it is reasonable to suppose that his
duties included those of an attendant, such as he fulfilled
when he accompanied Saul and Barnabas on the missionary
journey recorded in Acts xiii-xiv. From the Gospel itself we
should infer that he was also a teacher, but this is not stated
by the Elder. The reference to Peter recalls 1 Pet. v. 13,
Ἀσπάζεται ὑμᾶς ἡ ἐν Βαβυλῶνι συνεκλεκτὴ καὶ Μάρκος ὁ υἱός
μου, which is ' a natural expression of affection between
Apostle and pupil ' (Selwyn, 244). Cf. Swete, xxv : ' We
catch a glimpse of St. Mark's work at Rome during St.
Peter's residence in the city '.

While the Elder claims that Mark wrote accurately, he
is impressed by a difference between his order and that of
other accounts known to him. Probably he is thinking of
John (cf. Moffatt, 187 ; Streeter, 20) rather than Matt.,
though possibly he has both in mind (cf. Grant, 99) or oral
teaching (cf. Bacon, 30). In any case he is on the defensive.
Mark's order had been criticized at Ephesus. The rest of
the statement is the opinion of Papias himself. Papias
explains that Mark was neither a hearer nor a disciple of
Jesus ; he was dependent on Peter who addressed his teaching
to practical needs. The force with which he affirms that Mark

'made no mistake' shows that he too feels it necessary to defend Mark against current criticism and that he puts a high value on the Elder's testimony. The Papias tradition has been widely accepted, and with good reason, but it ought not to be taken as covering everything contained in Mark, and not necessarily the greater part of the Gospel, for there are clear signs that the Evangelist used other traditions in both narratives and sayings.

2. THE ANTI-MARCIONITE PROLOGUE

It has long been known that prefaces to many of the Epistles were current from an early date written in opposition to the views of Marcion, who first drew up a canon of the books he recognized as genuine and Apostolic. But since 1928 the researches of Dom Donatien de Bruyne [1] have shown that similar prologues were attached to the Gospels and are found in many Old Latin MSS. The preface to Matt. has not yet been recovered and that belonging to Mark lacks its beginning. The fragment is as follows:

. . . *Marcus adseruit, qui colobodactylus est nominatus, ideo quod ad ceteram corporis proceritatem digitos minores habuisset. iste interpres fuit Petri, post excessionem ipsius Petri descripsit idem hoc in partibus Italiae evangelium.*

'. . . Mark declared, who is called "stump-fingered", because he had rather small fingers in comparison with the stature of the rest of his body. He was the interpreter of Peter. After the death of Peter himself he wrote down this same gospel in the regions of Italy.'

In part this statement appears to be dependent on the Papias tradition, but it adds new information. The tradition that Mark had small fingers has hitherto been known only from later writers, Hippolytus and the author of the preface to codex Toletanus of the Vulgate, but the recognition that the Anti-Marcionite Prologues date back to the second century adds weight to the tradition. There is no reason to

---

[1] 'Les plus anciens prologues latines des Évangiles', *Revue Bénédictine*, xl. 193-214 (July 1928). Harnack was convinced that de Bruyne is right in dating the prologues A.D. 160–80. Cf.

Howard, *ET*, xlvii. 534-8, *Christianity according to St. John*, 11 f.

Colobodactylus, a transliteration of κολοβοδάκτυλος, is one of the indications that the Prologues were originally written in Greek.

trace the physical peculiarity to mutilation or to explain
the word as meaning ' deserter ' (so Tregelles, *v*. Swete,
xxvii) ; a natural defect seems implied. More important is
the statement that Mark wrote the Gospel in Italy after the
death of Peter. This is earlier testimony than that of Irenaeus
and confirms the view that by μετὰ τὴν τούτων ἔξοδον (*v. infra*)
the latter means the deaths of Peter and Paul. Earlier testimony is also given to the Roman origin of the Gospel.

3. JUSTIN MARTYR

Justin does not mention the Gospel directly, but speaks
of certain Ἀπομνημονεύματα Πέτρου which contained the
words ὄνομα Βοανεργές, ὅ ἐστιν υἱοὶ βροντῆς, or their equivalent,
found only in Mark iii. 17 (*Dial.* 106). Further, in *Dial.* 88,
apparently with reference to Mark vi. 3, he has the phrase
τέκτονος νομιζομένου. Cf. also *Apol.* i. 66, *Dial.* 103, and
see the tables in Sanday, *The Gospels in the Second Century*,
91 ff., 113 ff. It has been held that by Peter's ' Memoirs '
Justin means the *Gospel of Peter*, but this view is effectively
refuted by V. H. Stanton, i. 93-102. Cf. Lagrange, xxi f.
Stanton dates the *First Apology* A.D. 145-6, the *Second* a
little later, and the *Dialogue* before A.D. 161.

4. IRENAEUS

The testimony of Irenaeus is given in a section in which
he speaks of all the Gospels (*Adv. Haer.* iii. 1. 2). After
stating that Matthew wrote while Peter and Paul were preaching the gospel and founding the Church in Rome, he says :

Μετὰ δὲ τὴν τούτων ἔξοδον Μάρκος, ὁ μαθητὴς καὶ ἑρμηνευτὴς Πέτρου, καὶ αὐτὸς τὰ ὑπὸ Πέτρου κηρυσσόμενα ἐγγράφως
ἡμῖν παραδέδωκεν.

' And after the death of these Mark, the disciple and interpreter
of Peter, also transmitted to us in writing the things preached by
Peter.'

It has been argued by Dom J. Chapman, *JTS*, vi. 563 ff.,
Harnack, 130 f., W. C. Allen, 2, and others that Irenaeus
wished to show that the teaching of the Apostles did not
perish with their death, and that therefore his words do not

contradict the tradition of Clement of Alexandria (*v. infra*) that Mark was written during Peter's lifetime. But this is an unnatural interpretation of the words of Irenaeus and is contrary to the statement of the Anti-Marcionite Prologue. Irenaeus uses ἔξοδος as in Luke ix. 31 of departure in the sense of death, thus giving chronological information regarding the date of composition. The reference to Rome (ἐν Ῥώμῃ) in the context implies that the Gospel was composed there.

5. THE MURATORIAN CANON

Published by L. A. Muratori in 1740, the Canon is given in a badly mutilated fragment from a corrupt Bobbio MS. (vii–viii A.D.) in the Ambrosian Library at Milan. Cf. Souter, *TC*, 208 f. It contains the books recognized in Rome in the period A.D. 170–90. The opening sentence, obviously incomplete, clearly refers to Mark since it is followed by the words *Tertium euangelii librum secundum Lucam.* It reads:

. . . (*ali?*)*quibus tamen interfuit et ita posuit.*
' At some things he was present, and so he recorded them.'

It is a reasonable surmise that the broken phrase was preceded, as in the Papias tradition, by a reference to Peter's teaching. Lagrange, xxii f., conjectures that before *quibus* stood the words *sed iuxta quod audierat a Petro in concionibus*, and says that in this way *tamen* is well explained. Many scholars think that *quibus* is the second half of *aliquibus* ; *v.* Swete, xxxiii ; Rawlinson, xxvii.

6. CLEMENT OF ALEXANDRIA

Three passages from the writings of Clement call for notice, two quoted by Eusebius and a third current in Latin.

(1) Τοῦ Πέτρου δημοσίᾳ ἐν Ῥώμῃ κηρύξαντος τὸν λόγον καὶ πνεύματι τὸ εὐαγγέλιον ἐξειπόντος, τοὺς παρόντας, πολλοὺς ὄντας, παρακαλέσαι τὸν Μάρκον, ὡς ἂν ἀκολουθήσαντα αὐτῷ πόρρωθεν καὶ μεμνημένον τῶν λεχθέντων, ἀναγράψαι τὰ εἰρημένα· ποιήσαντα δέ, τὸ εὐαγγέλιον μεταδοῦναι τοῖς δεομένοις αὐτοῦ· ὅπερ ἐπιγνόντα τὸν Πέτρον προτρεπτικῶς μήτε κωλῦσαι μήτε προτρέψασθαι.—(Eus. *HE*, vi. 14. 6 f.)

' When Peter had preached the word publicly in Rome and

announced the gospel by the Spirit, those present, of whom there were many, besought Mark, since for a long time he had followed him and remembered what had been said, to record his words. Mark did this and communicated the gospel to those who made request of him. When Peter knew of it, he neither actively prevented nor encouraged the undertaking.'

(2) Γνόντα δὲ τὸ πραχθέν φασι τὸν ἀπόστολον, ἀποκαλύψαντος αὐτῷ τοῦ πνεύματος, ἡσθῆναι τῇ τῶν ἀνδρῶν προθυμίᾳ, κυρῶσαί τε τὴν γραφὴν εἰς ἔντευξιν ταῖς ἐκκλησίαις.—(Eus. HE, ii. 15. 2.)

' They say that, when the Apostle knew what had been done, the Spirit having revealed it to him, he was pleased with the zeal of the men, and ratified the writing for reading in the Churches.'

(3) *Marcus Petri sectator palam praedicante Petro evangelium Romae coram quibusdam Caesareanis equitibus et multa Christi testimonia preferente, petitus ab eis ut possent quae dicebantur memoriae commendare, scripsit ex his quae Petro dicta sunt evangelium quod secundum Marcum vocitatur.—(Adumbr. in 1 Pet. v. 13.)*

' Mark, the follower of Peter, while Peter was preaching publicly the gospel at Rome in the presence of certain of Caesar's knights and was putting forward many testimonies concerning Christ, being requested by them that they might be able to commit to memory the things which were being spoken, wrote from the things which were spoken by Peter the Gospel which is called according to Mark.'

These passages, especially the second and third, illustrate the development of the Petrine tradition. That Mark wrote in answer to requests is probable enough, in view of his knowledge of Peter's preaching, but that he did so during Peter's lifetime is improbable in the light of the testimony of Irenaeus and the Anti-Marcionite Prologue.

7. ORIGEN

Describing the composition of the four Gospels, Origen reaffirms the Papias tradition and supports it by citing 1 Pet. v. 13 :

Δεύτερον δὲ τὸ κατὰ Μάρκον, ὡς Πέτρος ὑφηγήσατο αὐτῷ, ποιήσαντα, ὃν καὶ υἱὸν ἐν τῇ καθολικῇ ἐπιστολῇ διὰ τούτων ὡμολόγησεν φάσκων· ἀσπάζεται ὑμᾶς ἡ ἐν Βαβυλῶνι συνεκλεκτὴ καὶ Μάρκος ὁ υἱός μου.—(Eus. HE, vi. 25. 5.)

' And second, that according to Mark, who did as Peter instructed him, whom also he acknowledged as a son in the Catholic

Epistle in these words, " She that is in Babylon, elect together with you, saluteth you, and Mark my son " '.

8. JEROME

Jerome, *Comm. in Matt.*, *Prooemium*, 6, writes :

Secundus Marcus interpres apostoli Petri et Alexandrinae ecclesiae primus episcopus, qui dominum quidem salvatorem ipse non vidit, sed ea quae magistrum audierat praedicantem iuxta fidem magis gestorum narravit quam ordinem.

' Second, Mark, the interpreter of the Apostle Peter and the first Bishop of the Church of Alexandria, who himself did not see the Lord the Saviour, but narrated those things which he heard his master preaching, with fidelity to the deeds rather than to their order.'

This testimony manifestly depends on the Papias tradition. The new point is the tradition that Mark was the first Bishop of Alexandria. This tradition is not mentioned by Papias, Irenaeus, Clement, and Origen ; and it is impossible to harmonize it with the Roman tradition which these writers attest, especially since Jerome and later writers say that Mark died in the eighth year of Nero's reign (A.D. 54–68) at Alexandria, that is, before the deaths of Peter and Paul. Cf. Jerome, *de Vir. Ill.* 8, *mortuus est autem octavo Neronis anno et sepultus Alexandriae succedente sibi Anniano* ; Eus. *HE*, ii. 16 and 24 ; *Const. Ap.* vii. 46 ; Epiph. *Haer.* li. 6. Cf. Swete, xxvii, who says that Jerome's statement ' seems to be merely an unsound inference from the Eusebian date for the succession of Annianus '. See also Lagrange, xxiv f.

SUMMARY

In sum, we may say that, from the beginning of the second century, the external evidence agrees in ascribing the authorship of the Gospel to Mark, ' the interpreter of Peter ', and, despite later opinions which fixed on Alexandria, in assigning its place of composition to Rome. On the question of its date different traditions arose, but the weight of evidence favours a date after Peter's martyrdom rather than during his lifetime. The external evidence is far from suggesting that Peter was

Mark's sole source of information, but, as is not surprising, the tendency was to emphasize this connexion and make it more direct. Nevertheless, in the earliest references it is not disguised that from a very early date the Gospel was not accorded an unqualified welcome and was criticized for its want of order. In candour and sobriety of tone the earliest references to the Papias tradition make a favourable impression, and down to modern times it has been widely accepted. It becomes vulnerable only when too much is based upon it, and when regard is not paid to the probability that other sources of information were open to the Evangelist, not only from the testimony of individuals, but in the life and worship of a living Church.

II

THE HISTORY OF THE GOSPEL
IN MODERN CRITICISM

WE are justified in beginning the story of critical opinion in the opening decades of the nineteenth century because, after its early popularity and wide dissemination, Mark was neglected for centuries. The favourite Gospel in the early Church was Matthew, and from the time of Augustine the opinion ruled that Mark was merely the lackey and abbreviator of Matthew : *Marcus eum subsecutus tanquam pedisequus et breviator eius videtur*, Aug. *de Consensu Evangelistarum*, i. 2 (4). In the fifth century Victor of Antioch says that he had not been able to find the work of an earlier commentator, and the next of whom we know is the Venerable Bede three centuries later. Commentaries were written in the Middle Ages and after the Reformation, but it was not until the priority of Mark was demonstrated, little more than a hundred years ago, that its supreme value for purposes of historical criticism was recognized.

At the beginning of the nineteenth century three main theories held the field. The Original-Gospel Hypothesis was maintained by J. G. Eichhorn (*Einleitung in das Neue Testament*, 1804). A short written sketch, it was held, of the more important elements in the Story of Jesus was supplied to Christian missionaries for use in instruction, and, independently, the first three Evangelists embodied this sketch in their Gospels. F. D. Schleiermacher (*Über die Schriften des Lukas. Ein kritischer Versuch*, 1817) posited the existence of several sources or fragments written on tablets or leaves of papyrus which contained a few sayings or the account of a single incident or an episode in the Gospel Story, of which the Evangelists made use. Thus, Schleiermacher suggested what has come to be known as the Fragment-Hypothesis, a view which afterwards he abandoned, but to which there is at least a partial return in the recent work of Martin Albertz (*Die synoptischen Streitgespräche*, 1921). The third hypothesis was the popular Tradition-Hypothesis supported by J. L. Gieseler in his *Historisch-kritischer Versuch über die Entstehung und die frühesten Schicksale der schriftlichen Evangelien*, 1818. This view presumes the existence of an original Gospel tradition received from the Apostles and committed to the earliest Christian missionaries and teachers, which subsequently attained a written form in the Gospels. It long maintained its appeal in Great Britain, being defended by Westcott, A. Wright, and G. Salmon. As late as 1908 the opinion is expressed in Salmon's *Human Element in the Gospels*, ' The most probable explanation of the fact that we have now three histories of our Lord's life, so like one another, yet in many parts so independent, is that we have preserved for us the oral Gospel as delivered at three different centres ', p. 27.

In Germany the *Leben Jesu* of D. F. Strauss, published in 1835, shook confidence in the oral theory and stimulated the further study of the Synoptic Problem. The possibility of giving a mythical interpretation to the events in the life of Jesus showed only too clearly how precarious the critical foundations were. A better interpretation of the Synoptic Problem was, however, reached by a closer study of the Gospels. In the same year that Strauss published his ' Life of Jesus ' C. Lachmann first formulated the solution which has stood the test of all subsequent investigation. In an epoch-making observation he wrote : ' There is not so much diversity in the order of the Gospel tales as most people imagine. It is indeed very great if you compare the Synoptic Gospels indiscriminately together, or compare Luke with Matthew ; but if you compare Mark with both the others separately the diversity is inconsiderable.' [1] Thus was suggested the hypothesis of the priority of Mark and its use by Matthew and Luke, which was developed by C. G. Wilke [2] and C. H. Weisse [3] and established by B. Weiss [4] and H. J. Holtzmann.[5]

It is not necessary to describe further this great achievement of German scholarship nor the steps by which Holtz-

---

[1] *Studien und Kritiken* (1835), 574, quoted by F. C. Burkitt, 37.
[2] *Der Urevangelist*, 1838.
[3] *Die evangelische Geschichte*, 1838.

[4] *V. Lehrbuch der Einl. in das NT* (1886), 473-555.
[5] *V. Die Synoptiker* (1901), 10-20.

mann combined it with the hypothesis of the sayings-source Q. As Dibelius [1] has said, the Two Source Theory ' is still the sure foundation of the criticism of the Synoptics '.

1900 TO 1914

In the opening years of the century the Two Document Hypothesis was accepted and developed by the scholars of many countries : in Great Britain by Sir John C. Hawkins,[2] V. H. Stanton,[3] W. Sanday,[4] J. Moffatt,[5] A. S. Peake,[6] and others ; in France by A. Loisy [7] and M. Goguel [8] ; in the United States by E. de Witt Burton,[9] C. S. Patton,[10] and B. W. Bacon.[11] Significant of the stability of critical opinion is the fact that, in a modern commentary, it is no longer necessary to prove the priority of Mark.[12] The extensive parallels to Mark in Matt. (90 per cent of Mark's verses) and in Luke (over 50 per cent), the high average of verbal agreement (about 51 per cent in Matt. and 53 per cent in Luke), the relative agreement in order, the stylistic and grammatical improvements in the later Gospels, the softening or omission of bold Markan statements, and the vivid character of Mark's Story, all combine to make it certain that Mark is our earliest Gospel used as a source by Matthew and Luke.

In this country the discussions were decisive, but it was some time before the results of criticism were seen in the commentaries. The great commentary of H. B. Swete, invaluable still for its linguistic notes and penetrating exegesis,

[1] *ET*, xli. 537.
[2] *Horae Synopticae*[2], 1909.
[3] *HDB*, ii. 234-49; *The Gospels as Historical Documents*, ii (1909).
[4] *Exp.*[4] iii. 81 f., 177 f., 302 f., 345 f., 411 f.; *Oxford Studies in the Synoptic Problem* (ed. 1911).
[5] *Introduction*[3], 1918.
[6] *Introduction*, 1909.
[7] *Les Évangiles syn.*, 1907.
[8] *Introduction*, i, 1923.
[9] *Introduction to the Gospels*, 1904.
[10] *Sources of the Synoptic Gospels*, 1915.
[11] *The Beginnings of Gospel Story*, 1909; *The Gospel of Mark*, 1925. Cf. also H. J. Cadbury, *The Style and Literary Method of Luke*, 1919-20,

and articles in *The Beginnings of Christianity*, i-v, 1920–33; B. S. Easton, *The Gospel according to St. Luke*, 1926; *The Gospel before the Gospels*, 1928; *Christ in the Gospels*, 1930; F. C. Grant, *The Growth of the Gospels*, 1933; *The Earliest Gospel*, 1943.
[12] This must be said despite the able but isolated plea for a revision of the Synoptic Problem in H. G. Jameson's *Origin of the Synoptic Gospels*, 1932. The Four Document Hypothesis of B. H. Streeter, *The Four Gospels: A Study of Origins*, 1924, is not a departure in principle from the Two Document Hypothesis, but an extension based on a still closer study of the evidence.

was first published in 1898 ; but, although it treats the personal history of Mark and the history of the Gospel in the
Early Church, it is almost completely silent about modern
criticism, and the later editions and reprints make few changes.
A footnote on p. lxv concurs in the rejection of the Ur-Markus
hypothesis, but makes the tantalizing remark that the author
is not prepared to express an opinion about the nature and
extent of the editorial revision which the Gospel has undergone.   More critical discussion was provided by the commentaries of A. B. Bruce in the *Expositor's Greek Testament*
(i, 1897) and E. P. Gould in the *International Critical Commentary* on St. Mark (1896), who refer to the views of H. A. W.
Meyer, B. Weiss, W. Beyschlag, H. J. Holtzmann, and others.
New interest also was stirred by the historical study made by
A. Menzies in *The Earliest Gospel* (1901).   Here more than
fifty pages of Introduction discuss the origin of the Gospels,
the motives which affected the formation of the tradition, its
state before Mark wrote, the nature of the Gospel, its sources,
order, treatment, readers, and date, and the early testimonies
to its authorship.   Liberal in spirit, the commentary contains
many striking observations, but despite allusions to the
opinions of continental critics, generally in footnotes, it is
very independent in treatment and is based on the English
text.   The commentaries of A. Plummer (1914) and W. C.
Allen (1915) belong to the Swete tradition, the former containing many valuable exegetical notes, the latter maintaining
the Aramaic origin of the Gospel.   But a full treatment of
the historical and critical problems is still wanting.   Not until
Rawlinson's commentary (1925) did the vital questions of
Introduction receive adequate treatment.   Thus, we have the
curious situation that, for a quarter of a century, while British
scholars were making classical contributions to the Synoptic
Problem, the commentators proceeded almost as if the
critical question did not exist.

Meantime, the debate continued, especially in Germany.
In this summary it is not possible to describe fully all the
issues that were raised and discussed.   The Ur-Markus
theory will be considered in the section [1] on the Sources, and
the claim that the Gospel is based on an Aramaic original or

[1] See later, pp. 68-72.

on Aramaic sources in the chapter [1] on the Semitic background of Mark. Here it will be best to consider the discussions which have turned on focal points : the theory of the ' Messianic Secret ' advocated by W. Wrede, the views of the extreme eschatological school, represented chiefly by J. Weiss and A. Schweitzer, and the contributions made by J. Weiss, J. Wellhausen, A. Loisy, and B. W. Bacon to questions of interpretation, especially as regards the alleged ' Paulinism ' of Mark, and the claim that what he records is *Gemeindetheologie*, a precipitate of the theology of the earliest Christian community.[2] These topics will bring us to the time of the First Great War, after which they continued to be discussed along with Form Criticism.

Looking back we can see that one of the most important turning-points was reached in the publication of W. Wrede's *Das Messiasgeheimnis in den Evangelien* in 1901, first introduced to English readers in the comments and criticisms of W. Sanday in his *Life of Christ in Recent Research* (1908).[3] Wrede maintained that it was not until after the Resurrection that the Messianic dignity of Jesus was affirmed in the Christian community, and that, in consequence, the many injunctions to observe secrecy in Mark are a literary device to account for the silence of the earliest tradition.[4] This important question must be considered later.[5] Meantime, reference must be made to the views of A. Schweitzer in his important works, *Das Messianitäts- und Leidensgeheimnis. Eine Skizze des Lebens Jesu* (1901), published in the same year as Wrede's work, and his *Von Reimarus zu Wrede* (1906),

[1] See later, pp. 55-66.

[2] The phrase, *der Niederschlag der Theologie der Urgemeinde*, is used by W. Bousset in his *Kyrios Christos*[3] (1926), 10. How living the question is, is shown by the observation of J. Schniewind in *Das Evangelium nach Markus* (1947), 166, that the question of the genuineness of the sayings in Mark xiii is a question of second rank, since each saying has such a stamp as is possible only from the ' actuality ' of Jesus : *Jedes einzelne Wort hat eine solche Prägung, wie sie nur von der Wirklichkeit 'Jesus' her möglich ist, und damit wird die Frage der ' Echt-*

heit' eine Frage zweiten Ranges. Whether such a position is possible without losing confidence in the historical character of the Gospel tradition, is one of the vital issues of our time.

[3] Pp. 69-76. See the comments of R. H. Lightfoot, *History and Interpretation in the Gospels*, 17.

[4] Wrede holds that the idea of the Messianic Secret was not invented by Mark, and must have been current in certain circles to which he belonged.

[5] See pp. 122-4.

familiar to English readers in W. Montgomery's translation, *The Quest of the Historical Jesus* (1911).

Schweitzer describes the relation between Wrede's views and his own as a contrast between 'thoroughgoing scepticism' and 'thoroughgoing eschatology'.[1] With Wrede he shares the view that the cast-iron 'Markan Hypothesis' is completely discredited,[2] but is much more positive in his estimate of the historical value of the Markan tradition, going so far as to say that the progressive recognition of the eschatological character of the teaching and acts of Jesus 'carries with it a progressive vindication of the evangelical tradition'.[3] Of particular interest is his interpretation of the narratives of the Feeding of the Five Thousand and the Last Supper as 'eschatological sacraments'. 'The feeding', he says, 'was more than a love-feast, a fellowship-meal. It was from the point of view of Jesus a sacrament of salvation.'[4] Schweitzer also attaches great importance to the Mission of the Twelve, the failure of the expected Parousia, the withdrawal beyond Galilee, the teaching concerning Messianic suffering, the Transfiguration and the confession of Peter, and is not afraid to admit the presence of dogmatic ideas in the mind of Jesus Himself.[5] All these interpretations of the Markan Story are bound up with his extreme doctrine of 'consistent eschatology', but are not, I think, so indissolubly connected with that teaching that it is impossible to hold the one without the other.

Two other scholars must be mentioned here whose work has left a deep impression on modern Markan studies, Julius Wellhausen and Johannes Weiss. The first edition of Wellhausen's commentary *Das Evangelium Marci* appeared in 1903 (2nd ed., 1909) and in the next five years was followed

---

[1] *The Quest of the Historical Jesus*, 329.

[2] *Op. cit.* 332 : 'There is a station at the end of each section of the narrative, and the connexions are not guaranteed'.

[3] *Op. cit.* 285.

[4] *Op. cit.* 375.

[5] *Op. cit.* 348 : 'For, after all, why should not Jesus think in terms of doctrine, and make history in action, just as well as a poor Evangelist can do it on paper, under the pressure of the theological interests of the primitive community?'. With reference to Wrede's claim that the resolve to suffer and die is dogmatic and therefore unhistorical, he says : 'But the thoroughgoing eschatological school says they are dogmatic, and therefore historical; because they find their explanation in eschatological conceptions', *op. cit.* 385.

by his commentaries on Matt., Luke, and John, and his *Einleitung in die drei ersten Evangelien* (1905, 2nd ed., 1911).
Coming to the closer study of the Gospels after more than half
a lifetime devoted to Old Testament research, Wellhausen
has much to contribute to the investigation of the Aramaic
element in Mark and its Jewish background, and J. M. Creed[1]
is justified in saying that in his discussions are to be found
the seeds of the more important developments of recent years.
But the commentaries are very short, and Wellhausen's
pregnant observations are in consequence announced rather
than discussed. In contrast with Schweitzer, his tendency is
to reduce the emphasis on the eschatological element, to lay
greater stress on the teaching ministry of Jesus as a whole,
and to attach great importance in the formation of the primitive tradition to the activity of the early Christian community,
in this respect anticipating the views of the Form Critics.
Frequent references will be made to his views in the present
commentary, especially as regards the Kingdom of God, the
Son of Man, the Mission of the Twelve, the Feeding of the
Five Thousand, and the present ending of the Gospel.

The work of Johannes Weiss is liberal in spirit and outlook, but is more constructive and suggestive than that of
Wellhausen His earliest work, *Die Predigt Jesu vom Reiche
Gottes* (1892, 2nd ed., 1900), in which the Kingdom is described as
wholly future and transcendental, was greeted with enthusiasm
by Schweitzer, but does not call for discussion at this point.[2]
More relevant for our immediate purpose are his *Das älteste
Evangelium* (1903), his commentary on Mark in *Die drei
älteren Evangelien* (4th ed., 1929), and his unfinished *magnum
opus, Das Urchristentum*, now available in the English translation, *The History of Primitive Christianity* (1937).[3] The
first of these works is of absorbing interest. It has links with
the past in the not infrequent references Weiss makes to the
Apostolic Source, consisting of sayings and narratives, which
his revered father, Bernhard Weiss, posited as a source used

---

[1] *The Gospel according to St. Luke*,
vii. See the very different estimates
of Wellhausen's work in Sanday's *Life
of Christ in Recent Research*, 154-61,
and R. H. Lightfoot's *History and
Interpretation in the Gospels*, 22-6.

[2] In the second edition, increased
from 67 to 214 pages, the treatment is
less radical.

[3] Translated by F. C. Grant, A. H.
Forster, P. S. Kramer, and S. E.
Johnson.

by Mark in addition to the reminiscences of Peter. It rests also on a modified form of the Ur-Markus hypothesis, in that frequently elements peculiar to Mark are attributed to the *Bearbeiter* or redactor. Wrede's hypothesis is strongly criticized and the emphasis on secrecy in the commands to maintain silence is traced to that idea of hardening, which we find also in John xii. 37-40, a passage which might almost be said to form a motto for the first part of Mark, and which reflects the ideas of the Pauline circle. The treatment of the Markan sources, apart from the full recognition of Petrine tradition, anticipates in some respects the work of the Form Critics,[1] since Weiss distinguishes (1) Petrine narratives, (2) controversial stories (*Schul- und Streitgespräche*), (3) Sayings with or without a historical framework, and (4) secondary popular traditions. Weiss leaves open the question whether Mark is to be identified with the John Mark of Acts xii. 12, 25, xv. 37, inclining to a negative answer in view of what he considers to be the defectiveness of the Jerusalem tradition in the Gospel and the uncertainty of early testimony about the identity of Mark.

While the views of Wrede, Wellhausen, and Weiss have proved influential and suggestive, the same cannot be said to the same degree of the works of Loisy and B. W. Bacon. In *Les Évangiles synoptiques* (1907) Loisy seeks to distinguish between an original Mark (Proto-Mark), in which the author uses reminiscences of Peter's preaching, and the secondary expansions of a later redactor. The present Gospel is held to be an anonymous compilation strongly reflecting the influence of primitive Christianity and Pauline teaching in particular. Bacon, in *The Beginnings of Gospel Story* (1909), refers to the extraordinary degree of coincidence in the results attained by Loisy and himself. Mark is held to be a Paulinist and a strong redactional element is to be found in his Gospel. In his essay, *Is Mark a Roman Gospel?* (1919) he argues that Mark represents the point of view of 'the strong', of whom St. Paul speaks in Rom. xiv, and that his attitude is anti-Judaic. In *The Gospel of Mark* (1925) he discusses the Pauline

---

[1] 'Every narrative that has been preserved, every saying that has survived, is evidence of some particular interest on the part of this primitive church', *The History of Primitive Christianity*, 12. Cf. the comments of F. C. Grant, *op. cit.* 8 n., 11 n., 77 n., 121 n.

and Markan Christology. He doubts whether the Evangelist knew the Pauline Epistles but thinks that we cannot account for the Gospel without the life, the thought, and the teaching of Paul. ' Mark shows a direct, but not a literary dependence on the teaching of the great Apostle to the Gentiles.' [1] In this work he maintains that a ' prophecy ', first formulated in the year A.D. 40 in connexion with the threat of Caligula to profane the Temple, was re-interpreted in A.D. 50 as ' a word of the Lord ' in the Thessalonian Epistles owing to the changed circumstances under Claudius, and was used by Mark in the composition of the Little Apocalypse in Mark xiii.

1918 TO 1939

In discussing the work of Bacon I have overstepped the stage reached in my account of the story of critical opinion. The prevailing interest was literary criticism, with signs of a growing concern for doctrine and its connexion with tradition. In spite of the war of 1914–18 much thought was devoted to this question, and immediately afterwards it manifested itself in a rapid output of creative work.

The Markan outline, assailed by Wrede and Schweitzer, was made the subject of a penetrating investigation by K. L. Schmidt in *Der Rahmen der Geschichte Jesu* published in 1919. In the opinion of many Schmidt has completely shattered the Synoptic framework. He recognizes traces of a connected story in some of the Markan sections, as, for example, in iv. 35-v. 43, but claims that as a whole the outline is a purely artificial construction. Towards the Markan material his attitude is conservative, especially as regards place names and topographical and temporal statements in the several narratives, but his final conclusion tolls like a passing bell announcing the death of long cherished beliefs. ' But as a whole there is no life of Jesus in the sense of an evolving biography, no chronological sketch of the Story of Jesus, but only single stories, *pericopae*, which are put into a framework.' [2] This conclusion, I think, is too sweeping,

---

[1] *Op. cit.* 271.

[2] *Aber im ganzen gibt es kein Leben Jesu im Sinne einer sich entwickelnden Lebensgeschichte, keinen chronologi-* *schen Aufriss der Geschichte Jesu, sondern nur Einzelgeschichten, Perikopen, die in ein Rahmenwerk gestellt sind, op. cit.* 317.

though it is undoubtedly true that Schmidt has shown that
the Markan outline is much less firm than had commonly
been supposed.[1] This important question is discussed later,
pp. 145-9.

In the same year in which Schmidt's book appeared Form
Criticism was brought to the notice of New Testament
scholars in a slim volume published by M. Dibelius of Heidelberg under the title *Die Formgeschichte des Evangeliums*.[2]
The basic assumption of the new discipline was that during
the oral period the tradition consisted in the main of isolated
units which could be classified according to their form and
traced from their origin in preaching and teaching to the
point when they were committed to writing in the Gospels.
The fundamental thesis is described by Fascher [3] in the words
Am Anfang war die Predigt, ' In the beginning was the
sermon '. The exception was the Passion Narrative, which
both Schmidt and Dibelius agreed was the earliest part of
the tradition to assume written form.   Dibelius takes a decisive step when he distinguishes *Paradigmen*, the short
stories which culminate in a saying of Jesus, from *Novellen*,
the more broadly conceived narratives in which scenes are
presented in greater detail, though we may doubt whether
he was justified in tracing the former exclusively to the work
of preachers and the latter to a special class of story-tellers
who provided models for Christian exorcists and healers.
Less satisfying also is his treatment of *Myths*, or stories which
record the actions of a divine being, and *Legends*, which tell
of the deeds of sainted persons, since these are historical
labels which do not describe distinctive narrative forms.   In
the second edition of his book Dibelius gives increased attention to the sayings.   These, he suggests, were collected for
hortatory purposes by teachers ' to give the Churches advice,

---

[1] See the important article of C. H.
Dodd, *ET*, xliii. 396-400, who concludes with the opinion that, while we
shall not place in the Markan order the
implicit confidence it once enjoyed
there is good reason to think that in
broad lines it represents ' a genuine
succession of events, within which
movement and development can be
traced '.

[2] The second edition, revised and
extended in 1933, is translated by
Bertram Lee Woolf in *From Tradition
to Gospel* (1934).

[3] *Die formgeschichtliche Methode*
(1924), 54. Dibelius writes : *Die Mission bot den Anlass, die Predigt das
Mittel zur Verbreitung dessen, was die
Schüler Jesu als Erinnerung bewahr-
ten, op. cit.* 6.

help, and commandment by means of the Master's words '.[1]
In the main, his treatment of the tradition is constructive.
It is especially attractive that the inquiry is pressed beyond
the work of Evangelists dealing with sources into the many-
sided life of the earliest communities. Inevitably in such
investigations the inquiry extends beyond ' forms ', and Form
Criticism becomes a branch of historical criticism.

The limitations of Form Criticism are still more apparent
in Bultmann's *Die Geschichte der synoptischen Tradition*
(1921, 2nd ed., 1931). Instead of *Paradigmen* Bultmann
speaks of *Apophthegmata* (' Apothegms '), distinguishing
controversial and biographical stories, and instead of *Novellen*
he prefers the better term *Wundergeschichten* (' Miracle-
stories '). The sayings are classified as: (1) Logia or
Wisdom-words, (2) Prophetic and apocalyptic words, (3) Law-
words and community-rules, (4) ' I-words ' or sayings in
the first person singular, and (5) Parables. These distinctions
are based on subject-matter rather than form.[2] Many of
Bultmann's observations on the sayings and Apothegms are
acute and suggestive, but the tendency of his criticism is
radical in the extreme.[3] Most of the historical narratives,
which he examines in great detail, are held to be legendary
and Hellenistic in origin. In a measure his scepticism is the
anxiety of a critic to do full justice to the influence on the
tradition of a community which rested upon, and appealed
to, the words of Jesus. This fact appears in his later essay,
Die Erforschung der synoptischen Evangelien (1930), in
which he says that, while the investigation of the sayings of
Jesus leads to a considerable uncertainty, it does not end
in complete scepticism,[4] and still more in his *Jesus* (1925),[5]
in which, as through a transparent veil, ' community-sayings '
disclose a virile picture of the teaching of Jesus. As compared
with Bultmann, Albertz makes a positive and constructive
study of the ' controversy-stories ' in *Die synoptischen Streitgespräche* (1921), but Bertram's *Die Leidensgeschichte Jesu*

---

[1] *From Tradition to Gospel*, 246.
[2] Cf. Easton, *The Gospel before the Gospels*, 74.
[3] Albertz speaks of his ' brazen scepticism ', *Die synoptischen Streit-gespräche*, v.

[4] *Op. cit.* 32. See F. C. Grant's translation in *Form Criticism*, 60.
[5] See the translation by L. P. Smith and E. Huntress in *Jesus and the Word* (1935); also *ET*, xliii. 489 f.

und der Christuskult (1922) and Sundwall's *Die Zusammen-setzung des Markusevangeliums* (1934) are negative to a degree.[1]

Fascher's contention is that Form Criticism is a new and finer instrument, but one among many,[2] and Koehler maintains that the problem of the New Testament is finally, not a form-critical issue, but a historical question.[3] These judgments are very sound. None the less, Form Criticism has made a real contribution to the discussion. It has pressed home the necessity of tracing the *Sitz im Leben* of the Gospel tradition to the life and needs of the primitive communities, and in Apothegms (or Pronouncement-stories) and in Miracle-stories it has detected ' forms ' which differ in kind from stories about Jesus in general. It has also shown that collections of these ' forms ' were made in the pre-Gospel period and that the Passion Narrative is the earliest connected narrative to be compiled. Qualifications will need to be made later when the historical value of Mark is considered[4]; but meantime it must be recognized that Form Criticism has made positive contributions to the study of the Gospels, and of Mark in particular.

While the work of the Form Critics was in full course, less spectacular, but solid, investigations were also in progress In his long and detailed work, *Synoptische Studien* (i, 1925 ; ii, 1929 ; iii, 1931), W. Bussmann has argued that Mark was compiled in three stages (G, B, and E)[5] and that Q includes two sources (R and T), and by continental scholars his conclusions have been widely accepted. In Great Britain A. T. Cadoux, *The Sources of the Second Gospel* (1935), claimed

---

[1] Later discussions include : M. Dibelius, *Stilkritisches zur Apostelgeschichte* (*Eucharisterion, Festschrift für H. Gunkel* (1923)), ii. 27-49 ; K. L. Schmidt, *Die Stellung der Evangelien in der allgemeinen Literaturgeschichte, ibid.* 50-134 ; H. Windisch, *Der johanneische Erzählungsstil, ibid.* 174-213 ; L. Brun, *Die Auferstehung Christi* (1925) ; P. Fiebig, *Der Erzählungsstil der Evangelien* (1925) ; L. Koehler, *Das formgeschichtliche Problem des Neuen Testaments* (1927) ; K. Kundsin, *Das Urchristentum im Lichte der Evangelienforschung* (1928) ; M.

Goguel, *La Vie de Jésus* (1932, Eng. Tr., *The Life of Jesus*, 1933) ; V. Taylor, *The Formation of the Gospel Tradition* (1933) ; R. H. Lightfoot, *History and Interpretation in the Gospels* (1935) ; A. W. F. Blunt, *The Gospels and the Critic* (1936) ; E. B. Redlich, *Form Criticism* (1939).

[2] *Op. cit.* 228.

[3] *Op. cit.* 41 ; *Denn das Problem des Neuen Testamentes ist nicht ein formgeschichtliches, sondern ein geschichtkritisches.*

[4] See pp. 130-49.

[5] See pp. 70-2.

that Mark used three written sources, and J. M. C. Crum, *St. Mark's Gospel* (1936), traced two stages in the making of the Gospel. The fascinating search for sources was also pursued in the first volume of Ed. Meyer's *Ursprung und Anfänge des Christentums* (i-iii, 1921–3), but this work has much wider interests in that it investigates the Gospels, the development of Judaism and Jesus of Nazareth, and the Acts together with the beginnings of Christianity, in the belief that the treatment of these themes is ' one of the greatest tasks which confronts the historian '. To the same period belong the commentaries of Rawlinson (1925) and Bartlet (1922), the first volumes of *The Beginnings of Christianity* (i-v, 1920–33), edited by Lake and Foakes Jackson, F. C. Burkitt's *Christian Beginnings* (1924), and the third edition of Bousset's *Kyrios Christos* (1926). During the years 1924–8 appeared the invaluable linguistic studies of C. H. Turner and his Seminar in the *Journal of Theological Studies*, xxv-xxix, which are reflected in Turner's commentary on Mark, reprinted after his death in 1930 from Gore's *A New Commentary on Holy Scripture*. In 1929 the appearance of M.-J. Lagrange's *Évangile selon Saint Marc*, in its fifth and enlarged edition, placed in the hands of scholars its learned author's mature conclusions on the Semitic element in Mark, the history of criticism, and many detailed points of exegesis.

The steady stream of the twenties became in the thirties a river in spate, for now many discussions on special themes were added to works more directly concerned with Mark. The two books of C. C. Torrey, *The Four Gospels* (n.d.) and *Our Translated Gospels* (n.d.), claimed that behind Mark lay an Aramaic original. T. W. Manson's *Teaching of Jesus* (1931) opened new avenues to the study of the problem of the Son of Man. F. C. Grant's *Growth of the Gospels* (1933) and B. S. Easton's *Christ in the Gospels* (1930) showed how the relevant literary and historical problems were being treated in the United States. A. T. Cadoux' *The Parables of Jesus* (1930), C. H. Dodd's *The Parables of the Kingdom* (1935), and B. T. D. Smith's *The Parables of the Synoptic Gospels* (1937) carried forward the classical discussions of Jülicher's *Die Gleichnisreden Jesu* (1889–1910). Rudolf Otto's *Reich Gottes und Menschensohn* (1934, Eng. Tr., *The Kingdom of*

God and the Son of Man, 1938), following upon Gerhard Gloege's *Reich Gottes und Kirche* (1929), broke new paths into the study of familiar themes. B. H. Branscomb's commentary on Mark in the *Moffatt New Testament Commentary* (1937) and R. H. Lightfoot's *Locality and Doctrine in the Gospels* (1938) strongly reflected the influence of continental discussions. In 1937 appeared the commentaries of J. Schniewind and E. Lohmeyer, both of which have strong theological interests, notably as regards the ' Messianic Secret ' in Mark, with a constant reference to eschatology in the case of Lohmeyer and a much higher appreciation of the historical element in the treatment of Schniewind.

In addition to the works already described others must be mentioned which have greatly influenced, though less directly, the study of Mark. Especially important are the works of Gustaf Dalman. His *Words of Jesus*, the English translation of his *Worte Jesu*,[1] was published in 1902, and has profoundly influenced all subsequent discussions of such fundamental questions as the Sovereignty of God and the use of the titles ' Son of Man ', ' Son of God ', ' Christ ' ' Son of David ', ' Lord ', and ' Master '. *Jesus-Jeshua* (1929)[2] discussed the three languages of Palestine in the time of Christ and the sayings connected with the Passover Meal and the Cross. His powerful argument in favour of identifying the Last Supper with the Passover Meal is supported by the similar arguments of Joachim Jeremias in his detailed essay *Die Abendmahlsworte Jesu* (1935, 2nd ed., 1949). Later Dalman's *Sacred Sites and Ways* (1935)[3] gave a most valuable account of the historical geography of the Holy Land, supplementing in this respect the earlier works of Sir George Adam Smith, *The Historical Geography of the Holy Land* (1894)[4] and *Jerusalem* (1907), and W. Sanday's *Sacred Sites of the Gospels* (1903).

An outstanding feature of the period is the help afforded in studying the Jewish background of the Gospel provided by G. F. Moore's *Judaism* (1927), the monumental commentary of H. L. Strack and P. Billerbeck, *Kommentar zum*

[1] I, 1898.
[2] Translated from *Jesus-Jeschua*, 1922, with additional notes by the author.
[3] Translated from the third edition of *Orte und Wege Jesu*, 1924, also with additional matter.
[4] 25th ed., 1932.

Neuen Testament aus Talmud und Midrasch, i-iv (1922–8), and H. Danby's *The Mishnah* (1933). Jewish scholars have also made invaluable contributions, including I. Abrahams, *Studies in Pharisaism and the Gospels* (i, 1917; ii, 1924), C. G. Montefiore in the second and enlarged edition of his *Synoptic Gospels* (1927), in which with candour and sympathy the comments of a Liberal Jew are made on the work of German, British, French, and American commentators and critics, and J. Klausner in his able and interesting study of the life, times, and teaching of Jesus in *Jesus of Nazareth* (1929). The grammarians also have enlarged our understanding of Mark's language and style. Important works, which have taken account of the Koine and the Septuagint, include H. St. John Thackeray's *A Grammar of the Old Testament in Greek* (1909), A. T. Robertson's *Grammar of New Testament Greek in the Light of Historical Research* (1914, 3rd ed., 1919), the revised edition of Blass' *Grammar of New Testament Greek* by A. Debrunner (6th ed., 1931) now in its 7th ed., the *Neutestamentliche Grammatik* of L. Radermacher (2nd ed., 1925), the *Grammaire du grec biblique* of F. M. Abel (1927), and the second volume of J. H. Moulton's *Grammar of New Testament Greek* (1929), with its invaluable Appendix on ' Semitisms in the New Testament ' by W. F. Howard. To these must be added an older work, still indispensable to every serious student, *Notes on the Translation of the New Testament* (1899), by F. Field, and J. H. Moulton and G. Milligan's *Vocabulary of the Greek Testament* (1914–1929), which presents and discusses the linguistic evidence of the papyri and other non-literary sources. On the textual side new interest has been created by Streeter's *Four Gospels* (1924), and F. G. Kenyon's *Recent Developments in the Textual Criticism of the Greek Bible* (1933), his *Text of the Greek Bible* (1937), and his *Chester Beatty Biblical Papyri* (1932–6), and by *Fragments of an Unknown Gospel* (1935) published by H. I. Bell and T. C. Skeat. A. J. Wensinck, of Leyden, has illustrated the close connexion between textual criticism and the study of the Aramaic element in the Gospels,[1] and a very full critical apparatus has been supplied by S. C. E. Legg in *Nouum Testamentum Graece: Euangelium secundum*

[1] Cf. M. Black, *An Aramaic Approach to the Gospels and Acts* (1946).

Marcum (1935).[1] From every side contributions have furthered the study of Mark; indeed, the wealth of relevant literature is the inspiration and the despair of the student. For, in addition to the works cited above, there are many important contributions in the Biblical Encyclopaedias [2] and articles too numerous to catalogue in the learned journals. It may safely be said that no work of the size of Mark has given rise to so much discussion.

THE PRESENT SITUATION

It is too early to discuss the contribution which books published since 1940 are likely to make to the study of Mark. The one exception which may be permitted is *The Historic Mission of Jesus* (1941) by the late C. J. Cadoux, which is not only a mine of information, but also contains many fruitful and positive suggestions which bear on the Story of Jesus and therefore, indirectly, upon the interpretation of Mark. In particular, the emphasis on the importance of the political factors and the recognition of a process of development in the mind of Jesus during His ministry, are sure to stimulate discussion. Indiscriminate condemnation of the Liberal Jesus School ought by now to have served its purpose.

From our survey of recent critical opinion it will be seen that, broadly speaking, there has been a steady and progressive movement of interest from the literary and critical aspects of the Gospel to its theological importance. We shall not be wrong if we trace this interest to the influence of *The Riddle of the New Testament* (1931) by the late Sir Edwyn Hoskyns and Noel Davey, and of Canon Alan Richardson's *Miracle-Stories of the Gospels* (1941). But the movement has deeper causes, to which Form Criticism in general and the work of Rudolf Bultmann in particular have contributed. Form Criticism sought to go behind sources to the living movement of communal activity out of which they emerged.

---

[1] But see the criticisms of G. D. Kilpatrick, *JTS*, xliii. 30-4 and T. W. Manson, *JTS*, xliii. 83-92.

[2] The works edited by J. Hastings: *A Dictionary of the Bible* (1898-1904), *A Dictionary of Christ and the Gos-* *pels* (1906-8); *Encyclopaedia Biblica*, edited by T. K. Cheyne and J. S. Black (1899–1903); *Theologisches Wörterbuch zum Neuen Testament*, edited by G. Kittel and G. Friedrich (1933–).

If negative conclusions were often reached, there does not appear to be any compelling reason why this should prove to be the case. The religious beliefs of the earliest communities naturally called for illustration and support from the historic tradition, and, if the beliefs coloured the tradition — a thesis to which full justice has been done — it is no less true that the beliefs were rooted in the tradition and did not emerge *ex nihilo* warmed by the winds of Hellenism and watered by the dews of the Orient.

Something more will be said upon this question in the section on the Theology of Mark. Here a caveat is necessary. No greater disservice to the study of the Gospel can be done than by a neglect of literary and historical criticism and of linguistic and textual studies in the supposed interests of theology. It is incredible folly to suppose that the day of the critical commentary is past, or that in a busy age students for the Ministry may be spared the necessity of acquiring a sound knowledge of New Testament Greek. Such a policy is against the true interests of theology, and can only result in a new Gnosticism, with the necessity of fighting the battle of the Epistle to the Colossians over again. The lesson of this survey is that syntax, criticism, and theology are an indissoluble whole, not to be broken without peril. Let Theology flourish, but not forget the rock from whence it is hewn and the hole of the pit from which it has been dug!

III

THE AUTHORSHIP, DATE, AND PLACE OF COMPOSITION

AUTHORSHIP

THERE can be no doubt that the author of the Gospel was Mark, the attendant of Peter. This is the unbroken testimony of the earliest Christian opinion from Papias onwards. In an age when the tendency of Christian tradition was to assign the authorship of the Gospels to Apostles, Mark is not likely to have been named as the author unless there was very good reason to make that claim.[1]

But was Mark the John Mark of the Acts and the companion of Paul? To-day this view is held almost with complete unanimity and it may be accepted as sound.

While not prepared to renounce this opinion, Johannes Weiss hesitates to assert it on two grounds: the identity of Mark and John Mark is not mentioned until the time of Jerome, and then somewhat tentatively; and, it is claimed, there are difficulties in believing that the Evangelist was a native of Jerusalem.[2] Weiss concedes that names like Bethphage, Bethany, Gethsemane, and Golgotha, and the references to the court of the high priest in xiv. 54, 66, and 68, reveal local knowledge, but suggests that the knowledge is due simply to the Petrine tradition and not to the author. Many other details in the Gospel, it is held, may have been added by the redactor.[3] And, in any case, these details are no substitute for a more adequate account of the trial of Jesus which a Jerusalemite, although only a youth, who had personal knowledge of those days, could have supplied. Moreover, could John Mark have described the Last Supper as a Passover Meal?

<hr/>

[1] ' The burden of proof is on those who would assert the traditional authorship of Matthew and John and on those who would deny it in the case of Mark and Luke ', Streeter, *The Four Gospels*, 562.

[2] *Das älteste Evangelium*, 382-414.
[3] E.g. in xi. 4, 16, 27, xii. 41, xiii. 3, xv. 8, 16, which are wanting in Matt. and Luke, and in xv. 7, which may be influenced by Luke xxiii. 19. *Op. cit.* 383.

It cannot be said that these arguments have made much impression upon critical opinion in general. It is certainly strange that as late as the end of the fourth century, commenting on the reference to Mark in Philem. 24, Jerome offers the conjecture, ' whom I think to be the writer of the Gospel ' [1] ; but the silence of earlier writers may well be due to the fact that they assumed Mark to be John Mark, as people have done down to the present day. On the historical side, the appeal of Weiss to the Petrine tradition does not account for the much greater detail in the Passion Narrative as compared with the Galilean sections, while to attribute picturesque passages to a redactor is arbitrary. We cannot safely suppose that John Mark would have had greater knowledge of the trial scenes than that which is shown in the Gospel accounts, or that it was impossible for him to accept the strongly held Roman tradition that the Supper was the Passover Meal. The presumption, therefore, is that Mark and John Mark are the same person. The identification, it is true, is not a matter of vital importance, since the historical value of the Gospel depends mainly on the material it contains. It might indeed be argued that, if the author is a Roman Christian, the signs of Gentile tradition in the Gospel are more easily explained, especially the echoes of catechetical teaching. But these features are no less credibly explained if John Mark is the author, in view of his long absence from Jerusalem and his interest in the missionary expansion of the Church. This view is raised to relative certainty if, on examination, it seems improbable that the references to John Mark and to Mark point to different persons.

John Mark

The name ' John Mark ' is somewhat of a misnomer, since he is never so described in the New Testament. In the Acts Luke three times speaks of him as ' John whose surname was Mark '. In xii. 12 he says that, on his release from prison, Peter went to the house of Mary, ' the mother of John whose other name was Mark ' (RSV). The house has a door in the gateway, and the door is attended by a female slave named Rhoda. The presumption is that Mary was a widow and a

---

[1] *Marcum . . . quem puto evangelii conditorem*, Migne, xxvi. 618.

woman of substance, and, further, that her house was a
rendezvous for the first Christians in Jerusalem. It is natural
to suppose that the 'upper room' (ὑπερῷον), where the
disciples foregathered after the Ascension (i. 13), was at this
house, and that it was the 'large upper room' (ἀνάγαιον μέγα)
where the Last Supper was celebrated (Mark xiv. 15, Luke
xxii. 12). But these are speculations which cannot be made
the basis of an argument, and they are discounted by the fact
that a still further speculation is necessary, namely that the
'householder' (Mark xiv. 14) had died in the short interval
between the Supper and the Ascension, since we never hear
of him again, but only of Mary. There is indeed no decisive
evidence that 'John Mark' was in any way connected with
the Supper, and, if he is the Evangelist, the bare account in
xiv. 17-25 suggests the contrary. All that we know is that
he was the son of an influential widow in Jerusalem.

Luke's second allusion is in Acts xii. 25. Here it is said
that, when Barnabas and Saul returned from Jerusalem,
after the famine visit, they brought with them 'John whose
other name was Mark'. From Acts xv. 37-9, where the
phrase 'John called Mark' is used, we learn that Mark
accompanied the Apostles on the so-called First Missionary
Journey, but withdrew from them in Pamphylia. The statement in Acts xiii. 13 is 'John left them (at Perga) and returned
to Jerusalem'. Ramsay [1] points out that he had not been
sent, like Barnabas and Saul, by the Spirit or the Church,
and suggests that he turned back because the proposal to go
into the country north of the Taurus was new and unexpected.
Apparently Barnabas did not take exception to his withdrawal, for when the second journey was projected he wanted
to take Mark with them again. Nothing is said of Mark's
duties, but it may reasonably be supposed they had to do
with travel arrangements, food and lodging, messages, inter-
views, and the like.[2] Paul, however, judged otherwise. To
him Mark's departure from Perga appeared in the light of a
defection. He thought it best not to take with them 'one
who had withdrawn from them in Pamphylia, and had not
gone with them to the work' (Acts. xv. 38). Thus arose the

---

[1] *The Church in the Roman Empire*, 61 f.; *St. Paul the Traveller and the
Roman Citizen*, 90.
                                                    [2] Cf. Swete, xvi.

well-known 'sharp contention', Barnabas taking Mark with him to Cyprus and Paul departing to Syria and Cilicia with Silas. Such are the circumstances recorded by Luke.

Paul himself refers to Mark in Col. iv. 10, Philem. 24, and in 2 Tim. iv. 11, but does not mention the name John. In Col. iv. 10 he conveys to the Colossian Church the greetings of Mark, whom he describes as the cousin (ἀνεψιός) of Barnabas. This is one of the 'undesigned coincidences' between the Pauline Epistles and the Acts and raises to virtual certainty the identification of Mark and John. The special interest taken in Mark by Barnabas, and their departure to Cyprus, are due to their family relationship and mutual esteem. The words of Paul, 'concerning whom you have received instructions ; if he come unto you, receive him ', were clear enough to the Colossians, but to us can be only a matter for conjecture. The simplest construction to put upon them is that Mark's arrival was uncertain, that information to this effect had been sent to the Colossians, with instructions about his reception. The suggestion that the Pauline Churches were aware of the estrangement and might not be ready to give a very hearty welcome to Mark,[1] is highly uncertain. No less conjectural is the suggestion of Swete,[2] that the visit was abandoned for Mark's visit to Egypt. What is certain is that at the time of writing Mark was with Paul and Aristarchus, and that a reconciliation must have taken place. This inference is confirmed by Philem. 24, written at the same time : ' Epaphras, my fellow-prisoner in Christ Jesus, sends greetings to you, and so do Mark, Aristarchus, Demas, and Luke, my fellow workers ' (οἱ συνεργοί μου). If these letters were written from Ephesus,[3] the date is c. A.D. 55, only five or six years after Paul's departure to Syria and Cilicia ; if from Rome, Mark's projected journey to Colossae belongs to the period c. A.D. 62.

The last Pauline reference to Mark is in the genuine note embedded in 2 Timothy : ' Take Mark, and bring him with you ; for he is useful to me in serving me ' (iv. 11). This message is very touching in its simplicity and pathos, and is fully in harmony with the kind of service presupposed by the

[1] Cf. T. K. Abbott, *ICC, Eph. and Col.* 300.
[2] *Op. cit.* xix.
[3] Cf. G. S. Duncan, *St. Paul's Ephesian Ministry*, 1929.

Acts. That it was answered, who can doubt ? So Mark comes to Rome, if indeed he had not worked there two or three years before.

The remaining New Testament reference, to which attention has already been drawn,[1] is 1 Pet. v. 13 : ' She who is in Babylon, elect together with you, saluteth you ; and so does Mark my son '. The relationship, which is tender and personal, extends backwards to the first days of the Church in Jerusalem, but, if the Epistle is Petrine, the allusion is to Peter's association with Mark in Rome about A.D. 64 or a little earlier. It is no doubt strange that one who in the Acts and Pauline Epistles is so closely associated with Paul should here be described in such intimate relationships with Peter. But the Acts brings Peter into close association with the house of Mary, Mark's mother, and there is nothing strange in the supposition that in the earliest Jerusalem days Mark heard the Apostle tell of the events of the ministry and death of Jesus. If we deny this relationship, we lose our right to say anything of value concerning personal contacts in the earliest community. Considerations of probability, the Papias tradition, and the content of Mark coincide in their testimony to the contact of Mark with Peter. This conclusion stands, even when the Petrine authorship of 1 Peter is denied,[2] but it is strengthened further if, as is probable, the Apostle wrote the Epistle. In this case, at the end as well as at the beginning, the two are in daily association. Nor is there anything in the strong tradition which connects Mark with Paul which throws doubt on this view. The evidence already considered shows that Mark's duties were administrative ; only in Philem. 24 is he called a συνεργός. Moreover, it will be argued later that,[3] while he shares many religious ideas with Paul, he is not a ' Paulinist ' in any strict sense of the word. He cannot therefore be so closely associated with a Pauline group in the Church as to exclude an intimate connexion with Peter.

The later traditions regarding Mark are without support in the New Testament. On the whole his alleged connexion with Alexandria must remain doubtful. The tradition that he was ' stump-fingered '[4] may well be a genuine reminis-

---

[1] See earlier, p. 2.   [2] Cf. F. W. Beare, *The First Epistle of Peter*, 1947.
        [3] See pp. 125-9.   [4] See pp. 3-4.

cence. The claim that he suffered as a martyr, attested in the
Paschal Chronicle and in the apocryphal Acts of Mark,[1] is late
and in the opinion of Swete cannot be traced back farther
than the fourth or fifth century.

DATE

It is generally agreed that Mark wrote during the decade
A.D. 60–70. Attempts to date the Gospel earlier are precarious. The view of C. C. Torrey,[2] that it was composed
in A.D. 39–40, is based upon the suggestion that the words
' the Abomination of Desolation standing where he ought not '
(xiii. 14) must have been written just before the assassination
of the Emperor Caligula on 24th January A.D. 41. This
hypothesis is uncertain in itself and in any case would not
compel us to date the Gospel so early. The date supported
by Harnack,[3] the sixth decade of the first century, is a further
inference from his doubtful hypothesis that the Acts of the
Apostles was written shortly after the two years mentioned
in xxviii. 30 f. and before the death of St. Paul.

The considerations which have led most scholars to date
the Gospel later are : the testimony of Irenaeus [4] and of the
Anti-Marcionite Prologue,[5] to the effect that Mark wrote
after the deaths of Peter and Paul ; the probability that the
Apocalyptic Discourse of Mark xiii reflects the situation of
A.D. 64–6, before the investment of Jerusalem ; the emphasis
Mark lays on suffering and persecution [6] ; and his interest
in the question of Gentile freedom.[7] How wide is the consensus of opinion may be seen from the following summary.
The Gospel is dated c. 65 by J. Weiss, Zahn, Streeter, and
Bartlet ; 65–7 by Rawlinson and Blunt ; 65–70 by Stanton,
Plummer, Peake, Burkitt, and McNeile ; 67–70 by Swete ;
c. 70 by Menzies, Gould, and Montefiore. The decade
subsequent to the Fall of Jerusalem (A.D. 70) is suggested
by Wellhausen, Bacon, and Branscomb, but this period is
unnecessarily late, and against it is the strong objection that

---

[1] Cf. Swete, xxvii f.
[2] See Bacon's discussion in *The
Gospel of Mark*, 54-63.
[3] *The Date of the Acts and the
Synoptic Gospels*, 126-33.

[4] See pp. 4-5.
[5] See pp. 3-4.
[6] Cf. viii. 34-8, x. 38 f., xiii. 9-13 ;
viii. 31, ix. 31, x. 33 f., 45.
[7] Cf. vii. 17-23, 26 f., xiii. 10.

xiii. 14 is not more explicit.   On the whole there is most to
be said for the date 65–7.

THE PLACE OF COMPOSITION

The Gospel was probably written for the use of the Church
in Rome.

The testimony of Chrysostom,[1] that the Gospel was composed in Egypt, cannot be reconciled with the words of
Clement of Alexandria [2] and Origen,[3] and is probably due to
a misunderstanding of an ambiguous statement of Eusebius :
' They say that Mark who was sent to Egypt first preached
the Gospel which in fact he committed to writing '.[4]   Without the support of a much stronger Church it is not likely
that Mark would have had a standing so authoritative that
Matthew and Luke could use it as a source.[5]

The case for Antioch is stronger.   In favour of this view
Bartlet [6] mentions several considerations : the fact that Papias
cites the testimony of John the Presbyter who lived in the
East ; the connexion of Peter with Antioch ; the reference
(xv. 21) to Simon of Cyrene (Acts xi. 20, xiii. 1) ; the use of
Aramaic words in Mark ; the place of Antioch as a centre
of Roman culture ; the early use of Mark by Matthew and
Luke ; the use of Galilean and Judaean place-names without
explanation ; the want of early testimony to the Roman
origin of the Gospel.

None of these arguments is conclusive and the case for
Rome is much stronger.   In favour of this view is the testimony of the Anti-Marcionite Prologue, of Irenaeus, and of
Clement of Alexandria, the evidence which points to Gentile
readers (vii. 3 f., xi. 13, xii. 42), including the explanations
of Aramaic words, the allusions to suffering and persecution
(viii. 34-8, x. 38 f., xiii. 9-13), and the relative frequency of
Latinized words and forms of speech.[7]

---

[1] καὶ Μάρκος δὲ ἐν Αἰγύπτῳ τῶν
μαθητῶν παρακαλεσάντων αὐτὸν αὐτὸ
τοῦτο ποιῆσαι (sc. συνθεῖναι τὸ εὐαγγέλιον), Prooem. in Matt.

[2] See pp. 5-6.

[3] See pp. 6-7.

[4] Hist. Eccl. ii. 16. Probably συν-
εγράψατο means ' had composed '.

[5] Burkitt points out that Alexan-
drine Christianity stood almost completely aloof from the main current of
Church life for more than a century
and a half after Christ, JTS, x.
169.

[6] St. Mark, 36 f.

[7] See later, p. 45.

THE TEXT

THE principal authorities are as follows.[1]

GREEK MANUSCRIPTS

Uncial MSS.

א	Sinaiticus.	The whole Gospel.	London, Brit. Mus.	iv.
A	Alexandrinus.	The whole Gospel.	London, Brit. Mus.	v.
B	Vaticanus.	The whole Gospel.	Rome, Vatican.	iv.
C	Ephraemi.	Contains i. 17-vi. 31, viii. 5-xii. 29, xiii. 18-xvi. 20.	Paris, Bibl. nat.	v.
D	Bezae.	The whole Gospel.	Cambridge, Univ. Lib.	v.
L	Regius.	Lacks x. 16-30, xv. 2-20.	Paris, Bibl. nat.	viii.
M	Campianus.	The whole Gospel.	Paris, Bibl. nat.	ix.
N	Purpureus Petropolitanus.	Contains v. 20-vii. 4, vii. 20-viii. 32, ix. 1-x. 43, xi. 7-xii. 19, xiv. 25-xv. 23, xv. 33-42.	Leningrad, Patmos, Paris, London, and Vienna.	vi.
U	Nanianus.	The whole Gospel.	Venice, S. Mark's.	ix or x.
W	Washington.	Lacks xv. 13-38.	Washington.	v.
Δ	Sangallensis.	The whole Gospel.	S. Gallen.	ix or x.
Θ	Koridethi.	The whole Gospel.	Tiflis.	vii–ix ?.
Π	Petropolitanus.	Lacks xvi. 18-20.	Leningrad.	ix.
Σ	Rossanensis.	Lacks xvi. 14-20.	Rossano.	vi.
Φ	Beratinus.	Lacks xiv. 62-xvi. 20.	Berat.	vi.
Ψ	Laurensis.	Contains ix. 5-xvi. 20.	Athos.	viii or ix.

Papyrus

P45.   Chester Beatty.   Contains : iv. 36-40, v. 15-26, 38-vi. 3,   iii.
vi. 16-25, 36-50, vii. 3-15, 25-viii. 1,
viii. 10-26, 34-ix. 8, ix. 18-31, xi.
27-33, xii. 1, 5-8, 13-19, 24-8.

Minuscules

Fam. 1.   Including : 1 Basle, 118 Oxford,   x–xv.
131 Rome, 209 Venice ; also 22
Paris, 1582 Athos Batopedi.

---

[1] For a fuller list *v.* Legg, *Nouum Testamentum Graece.*

Fam. 13.	Including: (a) 13 Paris, 346 Milan, 543 Michigan, 826 and 828 Grotta Ferrata; (b) 69 Leicester, 124 Vienna, 788 Athens; (c) 983 Athos, 1689 Serres.	xii–xv.
28.	Paris, Bibl. nat.	xi–xii.
33.	Paris, Bibl. nat.	ix–x.
157.	Rome, Vatican.	xii.
565.	Leningrad.	ix.
579.	Paris, Bibl. nat.	xiii.
700.	London, Brit. Mus.	xi–xii.
892.	London, Brit. Mus.	ix–x.
1071.	Athos, Laura.	xii.
1342.	Jerusalem.	xi.
1424.	Drama.	ix.

THE LATIN VERSIONS

(a) *The Old Latin* (it)

a	Vercellensis.	Lacks i. 22-34, iv. 17-24, 26-v. 19, xv. 15-xvi. 20.	Vercelli.	iv.
b	Veronensis.	The whole Gospel.	Verona.	v.
c	Colbertinus.	The whole Gospel.	Paris.	xii.
d	The Latin side of D.	The whole Gospel. Shares readings with a and k.	Cambridge.	v.
e	Palatinus.	Contains i. 20-iv. 8, iv. 19-vi. 9, xii. 37-40, xiii. 2 f., 24-7, 33-6. Akin in text to k.	Vienna. (? Trent.)	v.
f	Brixianus.	Lacks xii. 5-xiii. 32, xiv. 70-xvi. 20.	Brescia.	vi.
ff²	Corbeiensis II.	The whole Gospel.	Paris.	v–vi.
g¹	Sangermanensis I.	The whole Gospel.	Paris.	ix.
g²	Sangermanensis II.	The whole Gospel.	Paris.	x.
i	Vindobonensis.	Contains ii. 17-iii. 29, iv. 4-x. 1, x. 33-xiv. 36, xv. 33-40.	Naples.	v–vi.
k	Bobiensis.	Contains viii. 8-11, 14-16, 19-xvi. 8, and shorter ending.	Turin.	iv–v.
l	Rehdigeranus.	The whole Gospel.	Breslau.	viii.
m	*Speculum.*	Wrongly attributed to Augustine. Contains only xi. 25 f.		

n	Fragmenta Sangallensia.	Contains vii. 13-31, viii. 32-ix. 10, xiii. 2-20, xv. 22-xvi. 13. Text closely akin to a.	Chur, S. Gallen.	iv–v.
o	Fragmentum Sangallense.	Contains xvi. 14-20.	Chur, S. Gallen.	vii.
q	Monacensis.	Lacks i. 7-22, xv. 5-36.	Munich.	vii.
r¹	Usserianus I.	Lacks xiv. 58-xv. 4.	Dublin.	vii.
r²	Usserianus II.	Lacks iii. 24-iv. 19, v. 31-vi. 13, xv. 17-41.	Dublin.	vii.
δ	The Latin side of Δ.	The whole Gospel.	Chur, S. Gallen.	ix–x.
aur.	Aureus.	The whole Gospel.	Stockholm.	

(b) *The Vulgate* (vg).

WW = the ed. of J Wordsworth and H. J. White

THE SYRIAC VERSIONS

sy^s	Sinaiticus.	Contains i. 12-44, ii. 21-iv. 17, iv. 41- v. 26, vi. 5-xvi. 8.	Mon. of S. Catherine, Mt. Sinai.	iv.
sy^c	Curetonianus.	Contains only xvi. 17-20.	British Museum.	v.
sy^pe	Peshitta.	Contains the whole Gospel in many MSS. Ed. P. E. Pusey and G. H. Gwilliam, Oxford, 1901.		v.
sy^hl	Harclean.	Contains the whole Gospel. Marginal readings cited as sy^hl mg. Ed. J. White, Oxford, 1778.		vii.
sy^hier	Jerusalem or Palestinian.	Nearly all Gospel lectionaries. Ed. A. S. Lewis and M. D. Gibson, *A Palestinian Syriac Lectionary of the Gospels*, Cambridge,		vi

1899, and A. S.
Lewis, *Codex Cli-
maci Rescriptus,*
Cambridge, 1909.

THE EGYPTIAN VERSIONS

sa	Sahidic.	Ed. G. W. Horner, Oxford, 1911. Fragments and MSS. from the fourth century to the fourteenth.	iii–iv.
bo	Bohairic.	Ed. G. W. Horner, Oxford, 1898. Closer to Alexandrian text than Sahidic.	vi.

THE GEORGIAN VERSION

geo[1]	Adysh.	Omits xvi. 9-20.	ix.
geo[2]	A = Athos. B = Leningrad.—	Omits xvi. 9-20.	x.

THE ARMENIAN VERSION

arm Kenyon (*Text of the Greek Bible,* 126) says that three   v.
early MSS. examined by Conybeare at Edschmiadzin
omit xvi. 9-20. Another MS., which has these
verses, adds ' of the elder Ariston '.

THE AETHIOPIC VERSION

aeth Oldest MS. perhaps of thirteenth century. Cf. Souter,   ? v.
Text and Canon, 73.

ECCLESIASTICAL WRITERS

Ambr.	Ambrose of Milan.	iv.
Aphr.	Aphraates.	iv.
Ath.	Athanasius.	iv.
Aug.	Augustine.	iv–v.
Bas.	Basil of Caesarea.	iv.
Chrys.	Chrysostom.	iv–v.
Clem.	Clement of Alexandria.	ii–iii.
Cyp.	Cyprian.	iii.
Cyr. Alex.	Cyril of Alexandria.	iv–v.
Cyr. Hier.	Cyril of Jerusalem.	iv.
Ephr.	Ephraem Syrus.	iv.

Epiph.	Epiphanius.	iv.
Eus.	Eusebius of Caesarea.	iv.
Greg. Naz.	Gregory of Nazianzum.	iv.
Greg. Nys.	Gregory of Nyssa.	iv.
Hil.	Hilary.	iv.
Hip.	Hippolytus.	iii.
Iren.	Irenaeus.	ii.
Iren.*int.*	Latin tr. of the works of Iren.	iv.
Jer.	Jerome.	iv–v.
Just.	Justin Martyr.	ii.
Or.	Origen.	iii.
Or.*int.*	Latin tr. of the works of Or.	iv–v.
Tat.	Tatian.	ii.
Tert.	Tertullian.	ii–iii.
Vict.	Victor of Antioch.	v.

CLASSIFICATION OF MSS.

In accordance with Streeter's regrouping of the a, β, γ, and δ texts of WH, the following families may be distinguished [1]:

Alexandria	B; ℵ L sa bo; C 33 Δ Ψ; 579 892; Or Cyr. Alex.
Antioch	sy^s; sy^c; sy^pe; sy^hl sy^hier.
Caesarea	Θ 565; P^45 fam. 1 fam. 13 28 700 W^v.31-xvi geo; 1424 N Σ Φ; 1071 arm; Or Eus.
Italy and Gaul	D; b a; ff² i r; ff g l q; Tat Iren.
Carthage	k; W ^i-v.30 e; c; m; Cyp.

Streeter's 'Caesarean Family' is showing signs of partition into at least two families. See, for example, the work of T. Ayuso, in *Biblica*, xvi (1935), 369-415, who distinguishes (a) a Pre-Caesarean (Egyptian) group, containing P^45 W^v.31-xvi fam. 1 fam. 13 28, and (b) the Caesarean proper, represented by Θ 565 700.

THE MARKAN TEXT

The high value of the Westcott and Hort text and of the textual theory on which it is based is widely recognized, but, in view of subsequent discoveries, notably those of the MSS. W, Θ, sy^s, and P^45, and further study of the versions and of the Western and Eastern texts, it is generally agreed that this noble revision, now over sixty years old, is in need

---

[1] *The Four Gospels*, 108.

of considerable modification, especially in Mark. In this connexion the discussions of H. von Soden, E. Nestle, F. C. Burkitt, C. H. Turner, B. H. Streeter, K. Lake, G. W. Horner, R. P. Blake, F. G. Kenyon, and others are of the greatest value, and, while many points remain *sub judice*, considerable progress has been made towards the attainment of an older and better text.

The Western Text

In particular, the Western text is more highly valued, and is distinguished from the Eastern text represented by sy^{sc}, Θ, and other authorities. In an important article, ' W and Θ : Studies in the Western Text of St. Mark ', *JTS*, xvii. 1-21, F. C. Burkitt discussed important Western readings in Mark iii. 21 f., v. 33, vi. 13, 29, 35, vii. 31, viii. 10, ix. 49, xiii. 2, giving special attention to vi. 53 f., his main interest being to exhibit ' the " Western " tendency to paraphrase and unscientific harmonization '. A more positive appreciation of the value of the Western text can be seen in two valuable articles by C. H. Turner, *JTS*, xxviii. 145-58, xxix. 1-16. The first article takes the form of a textual commentary on Mark i and shows a decided preference for the readings of D a e k. Among the readings Turner accepted may be listed : υἱοῦ θεοῦ (i. 1), δέρριν (6), the omission of καὶ ζώνην δερματίνην περὶ τὴν ὀσφὺν αὐτοῦ (6), φωνή, without ἐγένετο (11), μετὰ δέ (14), [τῆς βασιλείας] (14), λέγων, without καί (15), ἐδίδασκεν εἰς τὴν συναγωγήν (21), ἔχων, οὐχ (22), λέγων (25), αὐτούς (27), ἐξελθόντες ἦλθον (29), τὰ δαιμόνια λαλεῖν and the omission of Χριστὸν εἶναι (34), κἀκεῖ (38), ἦν κηρύσσων (39), καὶ γονυπετῶν (40), δύνῃ (40), ὀργισθείς (41), εἰς πόλιν φανερῶς (45). In all, Turner lists sixteen differences between his text and that of WH.[1] The second article, ' Western Readings in the Second Half of St. Mark's Gospel ', discusses twenty-eight Western readings in viii. 8-xvi. 8. In eighteen (viii. 26, ix. 18, 38, x. 1, 2, 9, 22, 29, xi. 31, 32, xii. 6, 23, xiii. 15, xiv. 65, xv. 25, 34a, 34b, 43) he accepts the Western reading ; in eight (viii. 38, ix. 5, 19, x. 19, xiii. 22, xiv. 22, xv. 39, xvi. 1) he thinks it has the better claim ; in two (xii. 14, xiii. 2) he

---

[1] Six agree with WHmg and in eight cases Turner's mg agrees with the WH text.

regards the issue as doubtful. No better example could be given of the greater value assigned to Western readings as compared with the depreciatory estimate of WH.[1] Turner assigns the errors of the Alexandrian tradition mainly to assimilation, but also to the desire for grammatical correctness and the elimination of tautological expressions (*v.* xii. 23, xiii. 15). Especial value is assigned to k, and of the other Latin MSS. a and i are held to be ' definitely the best '. Of D Turner says that, however erratic it may be on occasion, it contains a very valuable text. The Eastern witnesses, sy[s], Θ, 565, fam. 1, fam. 13, and 28, in his judgment supply important evidence, without being decisive. ' The Western and the Alexandrian texts are primary : each of them may be right against all the rest. I doubt if the Eastern texts are ever, I am sure they are not often, right against the Western and Alexandrian texts combined. Their value comes in in cases where the Western texts are divided.' These opinions are of much interest in the light of later discussions, especially of the Caesarean text.[2]

The article of P.-L. Couchoud, ' *Notes de critique verbale sur St. Marc et St. Matthieu* ', *JTS*, xxxiv. 113-38, is of much interest because it examines many of the conjectures advanced by A. Pallis (*Notes on St. Mark and St. Matthew*, Oxford, 1932) in the light of the African Latin MSS. e and k. Many of Couchoud's brilliant suggestions are excessively speculative, but his treatment of many passages is of real value. Among these may be mentioned : ii. 21, where αἴρει τὸ πλήρωμα τὸ καινὸν ἀπὸ τοῦ παλαιοῦ is read with D and e ; viii. 26, μηδενὶ εἴπῃς εἰς τὴν κώμην ((D) and k) ; viii. 31 f., ἀναστῆναι καὶ παρρησίᾳ τὸν λόγον λαλεῖν (k) ; ix. 13, ᾿Ηλίας ἤδη ἦλθεν (C W) καὶ ἐποίησεν ὅσα ἔδει αὐτὸν ποιῆσαι (k) καθὼς γέγραπται ἐπ᾽ αὐτόν ; x. 40, ἄλλοις instead of ἀλλ᾽ οἷς (a b d ff k sy[s]) ; xiv. 51, om. ἐπὶ γυμνοῦ (W c k sy[s] sa) ; xv. 39, ὅτι οὕτως ἔκραξεν (k, D κράξαντα, A C W Θ κράξας). In some of these cases it is probable that the Western reading should be preferred.

The Caesarean Text

The Caesarean family has come to be recognized as a subdivision of the Eastern text mainly through the work of

---

[1] Apart, of course, from the value they assign to ' Western non-interpolations '.

[2] For the question whether Matthew and Luke used a Western text of Mark see T. F. Glasson, *ET*, lv. 180-4, lvii. 53 f., and C. S. C. Williams, *ET*, lvi. 41-5.

K. Lake [1] and B. H. Streeter,[2] not without hesitations on the part of other scholars. In a review of Streeter's *Four Gospels*, Burkitt [3] objected that the term ' Caesarean text ' gives apparent definiteness to a set of various readings which are ' obstinately disparate and amorphous ' ; and to this objection Streeter [4] replied that he was not thinking of a group derived from a single ancestor, but of the text which would have been found in an *average* MS. in a definite locality. In particular, he pointed out that in Mark i there are 102 cases in which one or more of the members of the Θ group give a non-Byzantine reading, but only five in which the members of the family differ from one another in a non-Byzantine reading. To the further objection that in cases of alleged textual corruption the true reading is rarely supported by family Θ alone, Streeter replied [5] that the Caesarean text preserves a correct reading even though it may be supported by other families.[6] Burkitt, however, maintained his view that its MSS. form one group along with sy[s], and that of this ' Eastern text ' sy[s] is the earliest and best witness. Further study of the quotations of Origen and Clement of Alexandria [7] and of the text of P[45] [8] has developed the case for presuming the existence of the Caesarean text,[9] though its relation to the Byzantine text still remains a problem for further investigation.[10] It is also a matter for discussion whether this

---

[1] From a close study of Codex 1 and its allies, Lake showed that Θ, fam. 1, fam. 13, 28, 565, 700 constitute a family presenting a common text equidistant between those represented by B and D. Cf. *Codex 1 of the Gospels and its Allies, Texts and Studies, Cambridge*, vii. 3, 1902 ; *HTR*, July 1923 ('The Text of the Gospels and the Koridethi Codex'), *HTR*, Oct. 1928 ('The Caesarean Text of the Gospel of Mark ').

[2] *The Four Gospels*, 1924, pp. 79-108.

[3] *JTS*, xxvi. 278-94. See also P. L. Hedley, *CQR*, cxviii. 23-39, 188-230.

[4] *JTS*, xxvi. 373-8, to which Burkitt's reply is appended.

[5] Besides citing Mark xiv. 62 and Matt. xxvii. 60 ; cf. *FG*, 324.

[6] The same is true of the list of 28 Western readings mentioned earlier on p. 38, for in more than half the variants discussed the Western reading is supported by fam. Θ.

[7] See the article of R. V. G. Tasker, ' The Quotations from the Synoptic Gospels in Origen's *Exhortation to Martyrdom* ', *JTS*, xxxvi. 60-5 (also xxxvii. 147 f.) and Streeter's rejoinder, *JTS*, xxxvi. 178-80.

[8] *V. infra.*

[9] Cf. F. G. Kenyon, *Recent Developments in the Textual Criticism of the Greek Bible*, 49 : ' As a result, therefore, of the investigations of Lake and Streeter von Soden's classification of his I family must, it would seem, be abandoned. The Western group (D and the Old Latin) must be definitely separated from the group, headed by Θ, which has been isolated as the text of Caesarea ' ; *The Text of the Greek Bible*, 211-13.

[10] See the articles by C. C. Tarelli on the Chester Beatty Papyrus mentioned below.

text originated in Caesarea or whether Origen brought it there from Alexandria.[1]

The Chester Beatty Papyrus P[45]

The discovery of the Chester Beatty Papyri, announced in *The Times* of November 19th, 1931, is for textual reasons an event of first importance, because they testify to the use of the codex form as early as the beginning of the third century, and because eleven of the MSS. contain Biblical texts, three of the NT (P[45], P[46], P[47]) and eight of the OT. P[45] contains portions of all the Gospels and the Acts, including Mark iv. 36-ix. 31, xi. 27-33, xii. 1-28. The text is Caesarean, but it contains also Alexandrian, Western, and Byzantine elements. According to Kenyon, its closest affinities are with W, then with fam. 13, then 565, fam. 1, and Θ, and then 700, while, as regards other witnesses, it is slightly closer to A than to D, and definitely less close to B and **ℵ**.[2]

The early date of P[45] (the first half of the third century), and the readings which it shares with B [3] and D, etc.,[4] suggest that it is an early representative of the Caesarean text, or is even pre-Caesarean, while its affinities with A [5] may point to the early existence of variants hitherto regarded as Byzantine.[6] In spite of many doubtful variants,[7] P[45], in agreement with Caesarean and Western MSS., attests some readings [8] which deserve preference over the WH text:

iv. 36* αφιουσιν . . . και	D W Θ P[45] fam. 13 28 543 565 700 b c e ff i r¹ sy[pe] sa geo.
iv. 40* + ουτως	A C W P[45] fam. 1 fam. 13 28 33 157 543 1071 sy[pe hl] geo aeth arm.

---

[1] Cf. Kenyon, *Recent Developments*, 48 f.

[2] Cf. *op. cit.* 57.

[3] Cf. Mark v. 43 (γνοι), vi. 23 (οτι εαν), 36 (τι φαγωσιν), 37 (δωσομεν), vii. 4 (Om. και κλινων), viii. 17 (Om. ετι), 37 (τι γαρ), 38 (γαρ εαν), ix. 21 (εως), 24 (Om. μετα δακρυων).

[4] Cf. vi. 2 (+επι τη διδαχη αυτου), vii. 5 (οι μαθηται σου ου περιπατ.), viii. 13 (εις το πλοιον), etc.

[5] Cf. vi. 2 (εν τη συναγωγη διδασκειν), 45 (απολυση), 48 (ειδεν), vii. 35 (+ευ-

θεως, διηνοιχθησαν), 29 (το δαιμονιον εκ της θυγατρος σου), etc.

[6] On this and other points connected with P[45] see the articles of C. C. Tarelli, *JTS*, xxxix. 254-9, xl. 46-55, 382-7, xliii. 19-25.

[7] E.g. vii. 5 (και ανιπτοις), vii. 31 (και σιδωνος), viii. 10 (μεγεδαν), 15 (των ηρωδιανων), 38 (και), and probably, in the above list, v. 22, ix. 2, 29. For the unfavourable estimate of Lietzmann, *JR*, xvi. 97 ('a text " gone to weeds " ') see *PC, suppl.* 23.

[8] Marked with an asterisk.

v. 19	διαγγειλον	D W P⁴⁵ fam. 1 fam. 13 28 543 700.
v. 22	+ιδου	A C N W Π Σ Φ P⁴⁵ minusc. *plur.* c f sy^hl geo^I *et* B arm.
v. 42b*	Om. ευθυς	A D N W Θ Π Σ Φ P⁴⁵ minusc. *plur.* it vg sy^pe hl sa geo arm.
vi. 3	ο του τεκτονος	P⁴⁵ fam. 13 33 543 565 579 700 a b c e r² aur vg aeth.
vi. 23*	+πολλα	D Θ P⁴⁵ 565 700 a b ff i q vg arm.
vi. 47*	+παλαι	D P⁴⁵ fam. 1 28 a b d ff g² i.
vii. 5*	+λεγοντες	D W Δ Θ P⁴⁵ fam. 13 28 543 565 700 a c ff i r¹ aur vg (*aliq.*) sa sy^s.
vii. 28*	Om. ναι	D W Θ P⁴⁵ 13 28 69 543 565 700 b c ff i arm.
vii. 28*	+λεγουσα	D W Θ P⁴⁵ 13 28 69 565 700 a f i n q sy^s sa arm.
viii. 17	+ολιγοπιστοι	W Θ Φ P⁴⁵ fam. 13 28 565 700 sy^hl mg geo^I.2 sa arm.
viii. 18	+ουπω νοειτε	Θ P⁴⁵ 565 arm.
viii. 18	ουδε μνημονευετε	D Θ P⁴⁵ 565 1342 it vg arm.
viii. 35*	την ψυχην αυτου	ℵ A C D* L W Δ Θ Π Σ Φ P⁴⁵ minusc. *omn.* Bas.
viii. 35	Om. εμου και	D P⁴⁵ 28 700 a b i n sy^s aeth arm Or.
ix. 2	εν τω προσευχεσθαι αυτους (αυτον)	W (Θ) P⁴⁵ fam. 13 (28) (472) 543 (565).
ix. 19*	και (instead of ο δε)	D W Θ P⁴⁵ fam. 1 fam. 13 28 543 565 it sy^hier bo aeth. Om. sy^s pe arm.
ix. 19*	+και διεστραμμενη	W P⁴⁵ fam. 13 543.
ix. 23	Om. το	D K M U Θ Π Φ P⁴⁵ fam. 13 28 543 565 1071 it (exc. a) vg sy^s pe hl geo.
ix. 28	προσηλθον	W Θ P⁴⁵ fam. 13 (exc. 124) 28 543 565 700
ix. 29	+και νηστεια	Unc. *omn.* (exc. ℵ* B) P⁴⁵ (*ut vid. propter spatium*) minusc. *omn.* it (exc. k) vg sy^s pe hl sa bo (*pler.*) geo² Bas.
ix. 30*	παρεπορευοντο	Unc. *pler.* P⁴⁵ minusc. *pler.* b d i k l q r^1.2 vg.
xii. 15*	+υποκριται	F G N W Θ Σ P⁴⁵ fam. 1 fam. 13 28 33 543 565 579 q sy^hl sa geo arm.

Modifications of the WH Text

In the Commentary alternative readings to the WH text

are adopted in the following passages : i. 1, 11, 14, 15, 21, 29, 34, 39, 40, 41 ; ii. 7, 12, 17, 21, 23 ; iii. 7, 8, 14, 16 ; iv. 8, 20, 28, 32, 36, 40 ; v. 19, 21, 22, 23, 42b ; vi. 3, 9, 14, 22, 23, 32, 33, 37, 39, 41, 45, 47 ; vii. 5, 9, 14, 16, 24, 28 ; viii. 1, 3, 26, 35, 38 ; ix. 5, 10, 12, 19, 30, 38, 41 ; x. 2, 9, 12, 19, 26, 29 ; xi. 19, 31, 32 ; xii. 23, 28, 43 ; xiii. 8, 15, 22 ; xiv. 4, 51, 62, 65, 68, 70 ; xv. 10, 12, 16, 34, 39, 43.

There are probably other passages in which the WH text needs modification, but, except in respect of variants where new evidence is strong, it has seemed best not to make further changes in the printed text, but to discuss the textual problems fully in the Commentary. In many cases where there are variants the best text is that of WH, for often fam. Θ, including P^{45}, supports B and its allies, and in other cases, of which v. 22, ix. 28, and ix. 41 are examples, conjecture may be necessary. Problems of especial difficulty arise when well attested Markan variants (e.g. vi. 3, viii. 35, ix. 2, 42, and xiv 62) agree with Matt. or Luke. In these instances the agreement may be due to assimilation. This is the explanation usually given, and there is much to be said for it. But it is also possible to maintain that the text of Matt. or Luke shows the Markan variant to be original. Whatever decision is taken by the commentator will be open to challenge. It would appear that the only sound course is to consider whether the Matthaean or Lukan reading is likely to have arisen if the accepted Markan text is read, to register an opinion, and to leave the issue for further expert discussion.

THE VOCABULARY, SYNTAX, AND STYLE

SWETE, xlvii, computes that, excluding proper names, 1270 separate words are used by Mark. Of these 79 are found nowhere else in the New Testament, but 41 of them appear in the Septuagint. Of the rest 7 are *hapax legomena*, including ἐκπερισσῶς (xiv. 31), ἔννυχα (i. 35), ἐπιράπτω (ii. 21), ἐπισυντρέχω (ix. 25), κεφαλιόω (xii. 4), προμεριμνάω (xiii. 11), and ὑπερπερισσῶς (vii. 37).

Hawkins, 12 f., gives a well-known and most useful list of 41 words and phrases which appear at least three times in Mark, and are either not found in Matt. or Luke or more often in Mark than in Matt. and Luke together. Of these ' characteristic words and phrases ' the most notable are: ἀπὸ μακρόθεν, διαστέλλομαι, ἐκθαμβέομαι, ἔρχεται or ἔρχονται used as historic presents, εὐαγγέλιον, εὐθύς, θαμβέομαι, κεντυρίων, κράβαττος, κύκλῳ, μάστιξ, μεθερμηνεύομαι, ξηραίνω, ὅ ἐστιν, οἰκία and οἶκος used without reference to the owner, ὅτι = ' why ? ', πάλιν, παρίστημι (intr.), περιβλέπομαι, πολλά used adverbially, πρωί, σιωπάω, συνζητέω, φέρω. Other words frequently found in Mark include ἐπερωτάω, ἤρξα(ν)το, and καί instead of δέ.

In contrast with the usage of Matt. and Luke φέρω is frequently used in the sense of ' bring '; cf. i. 32, ii. 3, vi. 27 f., etc.; and, as in the papyri, εἰς is often used in place of ἐν; cf. i. 9, 21, 39, ii. 1, etc. Cf. Turner, *JTS*, xxvi. 12-20. In line with the frequency of asyndeta in Mark (*v.* pp. 49 f.) is the absence or virtual absence of such particles as ναί (? vii. 28*), οὖν (xiii. 35, xv. 12*), and ἰδού in narrative passages. On all these points Turner's *Notes* (*JTS*, xxviii. 19-22) are of the greatest interest and importance, as well as his discussion of ὅτι interrogative (xxvii. 58-62), ὅτι recitative (xxviii. 9-15), and ἀποστερέω, κεφαλιόω, προδοῦναι, πυγμῇ, ἀλλά, (πρὸς) ἐαυτούς, ἐκ, ἀπό, πάλιν, ὑπάγω, and πορεύεσθαι with its compounds (xxix. 275-89). See Commentary *in loc.*

Special interest belongs to Mark's use of diminutives and

' Latin ' words. The diminutives are θυγάτριον (v. 23, vii. 25*), ἰχθύδιον (viii. 7*), κοράσιον (v. 41, etc.), κυνάριον (vii. 27 f.*), παιδίον (v. 39, etc.), πλοιάριον (iii. 9*), σανδάλιον (vi. 9*), ψιχίον (vii. 28*), and ὠτάριον (xiv. 47*). We may agree that Mark's use of ὠτάριον is not intended to suggest that the high priest's servant's ear was a particularly small one, and that Mark uses it because he is fond of that kind of word. The usage is colloquial and the words are not necessarily diminutive in sense. Cf. Turner, xxix. 349-52. Nevertheless, in view of its context, it is hard to think that κυνάριον is not used as a real diminutive, and possibly also πλοιάριον in iii. 9. The ' Latin ' words are : δηνάριον, κεντυρίων, κῆνσος, κοδράντης, κράβαττος, λεγιών, ξέστης, σπεκουλάτωρ, and the phrase ἱκανὸν ποιεῖν = satis facere. Of these words δηνάριον, κῆνσος, κοδράντης, κράβαττος, and λεγιών are found in other Gospels, but κεντυρίων, ξέστης, σπεκουλάτωρ, and ἱκανὸν ποιεῖν (cf. λαβόντες τὸ ἱκανόν, Acts xvii. 9, = satis accipere) are peculiar to Mark. The presence of almost all [1] these words in the papyri shows that they belonged to the Koine, but their frequency in Mark suggests that the Evangelist wrote in a Roman environment.

SYNTAX

Common Markan Constructions

1. *The Use of* εἰμί *followed by a Participle.*—As examples of the imperf. with the pres. participle Howard, ii. 452, cites : i. 13, ii. 6, 18, iv. 38, v. 5, 11, ix. 4, x. 22, 32 (*bis*), xiv. 4, 40, 49, 54, xv. 40, 43 ; that is, 16 instances as compared with Matt. (3), Luke (28), John (10), Acts (24), Paul (4), and 1 Pet. ii. 25. Add, with Turner, *JTS*, xxviii. 349-51, i. 22 and i. 39 (A C D W it sy⁸), also cases of ἦν c. perf. ptcp. i. 6, 33, vi. 52, xv. 7, 26, 46, and of the fut. c. pres. ptcp. xiii. 13, 25 (but *v.* Howard, ii. 451). Cf. also cases of ἐγένετο c. pres. ptcp. i. 4, ix. 3, 7. Turner thinks it might almost be said that the construction is for Mark, as for us, the real imperfect, and that his use of the imperf. is little, if at all, removed from his use of the aorist. It is doubtful, however, if this explanation is adequate. For the question of Semitic usage see pp. 62-3.

---

[1] κοδράντης is not illustrated in *VGT*. For ξέστης *v.* Moulton, ii. 155.

2. *A Multiplication of Participles.*—Swete, xlviii, cites
i. 21 προσελθὼν ἤγειρεν . . . κρατήσας, 41 σπλαγχνισθεὶς ἐκτείνας . . . ἥψατο, v. 25 ff. οὖσα . . . καὶ παθοῦσα . . . καὶ
δαπανήσασα . . . καὶ μηδὲν ὠφεληθεῖσα ἀλλὰ . . . ἐλθοῦσα,
ἀκούσασα . . . ἐλθοῦσα ἥψατο, xiv. 67 ἰδοῦσα . . . ἐμβλέψασα
λέγει, xv. 43 ἐλθὼν . . . τολμήσας εἰσῆλθεν.[1]

3. *Examples of ἄν followed by the Indicative.*—Cf. iii. 11
ὅταν αὐτὸν ἐθεώρουν, vi. 56a ὅπου ἂν εἰσεπορεύετο, 56b ὅσοι
ἂν ἥψαντο αὐτοῦ, xi. 19 ὅταν ὀψὲ ἐγένετο, 25 ὅταν στήκετε
προσευχόμενοι. These examples illustrate the weakening of
the connexion between compounds of ἄν and the subjunctive.
Moulton, i. 168, observes that the papyri yield only a small
number of parallels, showing that in general the grammatical
tradition held.

4. *The Use of Double Negatives.*—Cf. i. 44 Ὅρα μηδενὶ
μηδὲν εἴπῃς, v. 3 καὶ οὐδὲ ἀλύσει οὐκέτι οὐδεὶς ἐδύνατο αὐτὸν
δῆσαι, xvi. 8 καὶ οὐδενὶ οὐδὲν εἶπαν. Cf. also ii. 2, iii. 20, 27,
v. 37, vi. 5, vii. 12, ix. 8, xi. 14, xii. 14, xiv. 25, 60, 61, xv.
4, 5, etc. For the use of οὐ μή cf. Moulton, i. 187-92, who
points out that the construction is quite as rare in the NT as
it is in the papyri, apart from passages from the OT and
sayings of Christ, two classes which account for 90 per cent
of the whole. Moulton traces the usage to ' a feeling that
inspired language was fitly rendered by words of a peculiarly
decisive tone ', *op. cit.* 192. In Mark there are 8 examples
of the use of οὐ μή, all in sayings. Cf. xvi. [18].

5. *The Frequent Use of the Historic Present.*—Hawkins,
143-9, gives a list of 151 examples in Mark of which 72 are
cases of λέγει or λέγουσιν. Cf. Matt. (78, 59 involving λέγει,
λέγουσιν, and φησίν), with 15 additional examples in parables ;
Luke (4 or 6), with 5 in parables ; Acts (13) ; John (162). In
the LXX (337) the construction is ' by no means common '
(Hawkins), except in 1 Kgdms. (1 Sam.) where it appears
151 times. Cf. Hawkins, 213 f. It is evident that this vernacular usage (found also in Cl. Gk) is highly characteristic
of Mark's style, and only its over-use in Mark and John
raises the possibility of Aramaic influence. It is to be noted

---

[1] Swete also mentions the use of the
article with infinitives and sentences,
but these constructions are not unusually frequent in Mark. Cf. Robertson, 1426. The three perf. infins. after
διὰ τό in v. 4 are exceptional.

that, even in indirect narration the pres. (ii. 1) and the perf. (xv. 44, 47, xvi. 4) are used to express the speaker's point of view. Swete, xlix, indeed, claims that Mark uses his tenses with notable freedom, and cites v. 15 ff., vi. 14 ff., vii. 35, ix. 15, xv. 44.[1] The last example is striking : Pilate wondered εἰ ἤδη τέθνηκεν, but asked εἰ ἤδη ἀπέθανεν.

6. *The Impersonal Plural.*—Cf. Turner, *JTS*, xxv. 378-386. The use of a plural verb with no subject other than the quite general one ' people ' is common in Aramaic as a substitute for the passive, and is found in Mark in i. 22, 30, 32, 45, ii. 3, 18, iii. 2, 32, v. 14, 35, vi. 14, 33, 43, 54, vii. 32, viii. 22, x. 2, 13, 49, xiii. 9, 11, xiv. 12. To these Turner would add iii. 21, xiv. 1, xv. 10. Cf. also xiii. 26, xv. 27. Turner shows how drastically Matthew and Luke amend the Markan passages, either by inserting a subject or by substituting a passive, and claims that ' the evidence shows conclusively that the idiom is a regular and common one in Mark's narrative ', *op. cit.* 383. Lagrange thinks that in i. 30, iii. 2, v. 14 the plur. is not truly impersonal, and in x. 2 and xv. 10 adopts readings which contain a plur. subject.

Turner, *JTS*, xxvi. 228-31, also gives a list of so-called ' impersonal plurals ' followed by the sing., in which the third plur. replaces the first plur. in the account of an eyewitness, e.g. in i. 21 εἰσπορεύονται implies ' We entered into (Capernaum) '. The term is misleading since in each case the subject, though unexpressed, is personal ; but the examples are characteristic of Mark if they will bear the meaning suggested. The list is i. 21, 29 f., v. 1 f., 38, vi. 53 f., viii. 22, ix. 14 f., 30, 33, x. 32, 46, xi. 1, 11 (Θ i k), 12, 15, 19-21, 27, xiv. 18, 22, 26 f., 32. Where the passages are not omitted, the tendency of the later Synoptists is to use the singular. In very many of these cases the suggestion is attractive and cogent, but in each case it is the content of the story rather than the construction itself which supports it. How little one can argue from the construction is seen in xi. 12, 19-21 where it appears in the legend of the withered fig tree. The subjects are not named, not necessarily because Mark is replacing the first

---

[1] Swete further suggests that Mark frequently used the imperf. in a sense that conveys the impression of an eye- witness describing events which passed under his own eye (cf. v. 18, vii. 17, x. 17, xii. 41, xiv. 55).

person plur. by the third, but because it is clear to his mind
who are meant. The same explanation covers other lists
Turner gives of sing. verbs followed by a reference to the disciples, the Twelve, or the crowd, and of the use of the phrases
' His disciples ' and ' the crowd '. But it would be fair to
claim that these usages suggest that Mark stands nearer to
primitive testimony than Matthew or Luke.

For the connexion of the true impersonal plurals with
Aramaic tradition see p. 62.

7. *The Use of* ἤρξα(ν)το *as an Auxiliary Verb.*—Much
discussion has turned upon the question how far this construction is Semitic. The question is considered on pp. 63-4.
Meantime there can be no doubt that its use is characteristic
of Mark's style. It is found in Mark no less than 26 times :
i. 45, ii. 23, iv. 1, v. 17, 20, vi. 2, 7, 34, 55, viii. 11, 31, 32, x. 28,
32, 41, 47, xi. 15, xii. 1, xiii. 5, xiv. 19, 33, 65, 69, 71, xv. 8, 18.
Cf. Matt. (9, and in other tenses, in sayings, 2, and xiv. 30) ;
Luke (19 + 5 in sayings of Jesus or the Baptist) ; Acts (5) ;
John (1). Cf. Howard, ii. 455. J. W. Hunkin, *JTS*, xxv.
394, adds Luke xiv. 29, xxi. 28, xxiii. 30. In a few of the
Markan examples it may be argued that ἤρξα(ν)το means
' began ' ; Hunkin mentions x. 47, xiv. 33 ; Lagrange, xciii,
viii. 31, xiv. 19, 33, xv. 8. In the rest, Lagrange suggests,
the beginning of an action is more vaguely expressed, and
he compares the idiom *se mettre à* with the infin. Hunkin
lists 20 examples as doubtful in meaning, but recognizes
vi. 7, x. 32, xiii. 5 as ' more definitely quasi-auxiliary '. On
the whole it seems best, with the few possible exceptions
mentioned above, to regard ἤρξα(ν)το in the Markan passages as a redundant auxiliary verb. Cf. Turner, *JTS*,
xxviii. 352 f. The later Evangelists were plainly uneasy
about the Markan examples. Of the 26 Matthew takes over
6 only, and Luke 2. Their other examples must have been
taken in most cases from other sources. Q appears to have
contained 2 ; cf. Luke vii. 24 = Matt. xi. 7, Luke xii. 45 = Matt.
xxiv. 49 ; and L 20 or 23 examples.

Sentence Construction : 1. *Parataxis*

Parataxis, or the simple co-ordination of clauses with καί,
instead of the use of participles or subordinate clauses, is

one of the most noticeable characteristics of Mark's style. Hawkins, 151, points out that of the 88 sections in the WH text 80 begin with καί and only 6 have δέ as the second word, while in Matt. (159 sections) the numbers are 38 and 54 respectively and in Luke (145) 53 and 83. In fact, δέ is found in Mark only about 156 times, which is less than half the number we should expect if it was used as freely as in Matt. or Luke. This frequent use of καί is abundantly illustrated in the Greek papyri (*VGT*, 314; Deissmann, *LAE*, 131-6) and in Aramaic (Black, *AA*, 44-51). Moulton, i. 12, thinks that ' in itself the phenomenon proves nothing more than would a string of " ands " in an English rustic's story ', that is, elementary culture, not the literal rendering of a foreign idiom ; but in *VGT*, 314, it is recognized that ' it is impossible to deny that the use of καί in the LXX for the Heb. ייַ influenced the Johannine usage '. For the possibility of Aramaic influence in Mark, see pp. 57-8. It should be noted that there are cases of hypotactic parataxis in Mark as in the other Synoptics : possibly conditional parataxis of the imperative as in viii. 34 (' Then he will be my disciple '), temporal in xv. 25 (' when they crucified him '), and circumstantial in i. 19 and iv. 27.

2. *Asyndeta*

Cases of asyndeton or want of the connecting links supplied by particles and conjunctions, foreign to the spirit of Greek (except in rhetorical passages), but highly characteristic of Aramaic (cf. Black, *AA*, 38), are much more frequent in Mark (and John) than in Matt. or Luke. Turner, *JTS*, xxviii. 15-19, gives 38 examples and says that his list is probably not at all exhaustive. He shows that out of some 25 cases where both Matt. and Luke have parallels, Luke retains the asyndeton twice and Matthew never. Black's list [1] of 37 examples includes : iii. 35, iv. 28, v. 39b, vi. 26 (D), viii. 29b, ix. 24 (D), x. 9 (D), 25, 27, 28, 29, 41 (D), xi. 14 (D), xii. 9, 20, 23, 24, 27, 29, 31, 32, 36, 37, xiii. 6, 7b, 8b, 8c, 9b, 15, 17 (D), 34, xiv. 3b, 6c, 8, 19, xvi. 6bc. The com-

---

[1] Black, *AA*, 40, explains that he has not included natural Greek asyndeta, e.g. in commands or admonitions, at the opening of a continuous passage or speech or where a sentence begins with a demonstrative, or of asyndeta where there is no connexion between sentences (e.g. ii. 21).

ments of Lagrange, lxx f., are especially interesting. He mentions viii. 19, 29, ix. 24, 38, x. 27, 28, 29, xii. 24, 29, xiv. 3, and claims that in xiv. 19 the effect is like a silence in a conversation which has touched on a delicate point, and that in v. 39, x. 14, xii. 27, xiii. 7, xiv. 6 the effect is to emphasize the authority of Jesus. Many of the asyndeta naturally appear in sayings, but in Black's list 17 are examples apart from sayings. It is evident that they are characteristic of Mark's style as well as of the sayings. See further, p. 58.

3. *Anacolutha*

Cases of broken or incomplete construction, which are either altered or avoided in Matt. and Luke, are characteristic of Mark. Hawkins, 135-7, gives thirteen examples (iii. 16 f., iv. 31 f., v. 23, vi. 8 f., xi. 32, xii. 19, 38-40, xiii. 14, xiv. 49, including four of imperfect construction, iii. 8, iv. 8, vii. 19, x. 29 f.) and, in addition, three in which there is no parallel in Matt. or Luke, iv. 26, vii. 2-5, xiii. 34. Some of these passages are merely cases of parenthesis, e.g. the explanatory passage about Jewish rites of cleansing (vii. 3 f.), the comment ' making all meats clean ' (vii. 19), and ' they feared the people ' (xi. 32), while the masc. participle in xiii. 14 (ἑστηκότα) is used *ad sensum* (cf. ἰδών in ix. 20) and ἵνα ἐπιθῇς in v. 23 is imperatival. The remaining examples, as well as the parentheses, illustrate the popular character of Mark's Greek, and, as in the case of St. Paul, are due to the rapidity of the movement of thought and action. The parenthetical clauses have been carefully studied by Turner, *JTS*, xxvi. 145-56, who discusses no less than 19 examples : i. 1-4, ii. 10 f., 15 f., 22, 26b, iii. 22-30, vi. 14 f., vii. 2, 3 f., 18 f., 25-6a, viii. 15, 38-41, xii. 12a, xiii. 10, 14 (ὁ ἀναγινώσκων νοείτω), xiv. 36 (ὁ πατήρ), xvi. 3 f. (καὶ ἀναβλέψασαι . . . ὁ λίθος), 7 (ἐκεῖ αὐτὸν ὄψεσθε). For various reasons (*v.* Comm.) it is doubtful if i. 2 f., ii. 26b, iii. 22-30, viii. 15, and xvi. 7 ought to be included in this list, but there can be no doubt that parenthetical clauses are a feature of Mark's style.

4. *Pleonasms*

Apart from the use of the double negative and of such phrases as ἐκ παιδιόθεν and ἀπὸ μακρόθεν, Mark's sentences contain many redundant, or apparently redundant, expressions. But they are of different kinds. The following temporal and local statements add precision : i. 28 πανταχοῦ εἰς ὅλην τὴν περίχωρον τῆς Γαλιλαίας, 32 ὀψίας δὲ γενομένης, ὅτε ἔδυσεν ὁ ἥλιος, 35 πρωὶ ἔννυχα λίαν, 38 ἀλλαχοῦ εἰς τὰς ἐχομένας κωμοπόλεις, 45 ἔξω ἐπ᾽ ἐρήμοις τόποις, ii. 20 τότε νηστεύσουσιν ἐν ἐκείνῃ τῇ ἡμέρᾳ, x. 30 νῦν ἐν τῷ καιρῷ τούτῳ, xiii. 29 γινώσκετε ὅτι ἐγγύς ἐστιν ἐπὶ θύραις, xvi. 2 λίαν πρωί . . . ἀνατείλαντος τοῦ ἡλίου. The following work out the thought more fully : i. 42 ἀπῆλθεν ἀπ᾽ αὐτοῦ ἡ λέπρα, καὶ ἐκαθερίσθη, iv. 39 σιώπα, πεφίμωσο, v. 19 εἰς τὸν οἶκόν σου πρὸς τοὺς σούς, 39 τί θορυβεῖσθε καὶ κλαίετε ;, vi. 4 πατρίδι . . . συγγενεῦσιν . . . οἰκίᾳ, viii. 17 οὔπω νοεῖτε οὐδὲ συνίετε ; (Lagrange, lxxiv, adds iv. 40, xiv. 6, 15). In the following cases distinctions and picturesque details are apparent : v. 19 ὅσα ὁ κύριός σοι πεποίηκεν καὶ ἠλέησέν σε, 23 ἵνα σωθῇ καὶ ζήσῃ, vi. 25 εὐθὺς μετὰ σπουδῆς, x. 22 ὁ δὲ στυγνάσας ἐπὶ τῷ λόγῳ ἀπῆλθεν λυπούμενος, xii. 44 πάντα ὅσα εἶχεν ἔβαλεν, ὅλον τὸν βίον αὐτῆς, xiv. 30 σήμερον ταύτῃ τῇ νυκτί.

Lagrange, lxxiii, instances the following as true pleonasms :

ii. 25	χρείαν ἔσχεν καὶ ἐπείνασεν.
iii. 26	οὐ δύναται στῆναι ἀλλὰ τέλος ἔχει.
iv. 2	καὶ ἐδίδασκεν αὐτούς . . . καὶ ἔλεγεν αὐτοῖς ἐν τῇ διδαχῇ αὐτοῦ.
iv. 5	τὸ πετρῶδες ὅπου οὐκ εἶχεν γῆν πολλήν.
v. 15	τὸν δαιμονιζόμενον . . . τὸν ἐσχηκότα τὸν λεγιῶνα.
vii. 15	ἔξωθεν . . . εἰσπορευόμενον.
vii. 21	ἔσωθεν γὰρ ἐκ τῆς καρδίας.
vii. 33	ἀπὸ τοῦ ὄχλου κατ᾽ ἰδίαν.
ix. 2	κατ᾽ ἰδίαν μόνους.
xiv. 1	τὸ πάσχα καὶ τὰ ἄζυμα.
xiv. 43	εὐθὺς ἔτι αὐτοῦ λαλοῦντος.
xiv. 61	ἐσιώπα καὶ οὐκ ἀπεκρίνατο οὐδέν.
xv. 26	ἡ ἐπιγραφή . . . ἐπιγεγραμμένη.

It will be observed that in this list of 13 passages 5 appear in sayings and are illustrations of the parallelisms characteristic of Semitic speech ; cf. ii. 25, iii. 26, iv. 5, vii. 15, 21. The title in xiv. 1 corresponds with Jewish usage (v. Comm.) and there is a Jewish ring in the positive followed by the negative in xiv. 61. Further, the repetition τὸν ἐσχηκότα τὸν λ. (v. 15) has dramatic force, and there is a certain deliberate emphasis in vii. 33, ix. 2, xiv. 43. It is therefore open to question whether too much has not been made of the alleged redundancies of Mark's style. Rarely can they be called cases of prolixity of expression and often the tone is Semitic. The examples which Allen, *ET*, xiii. 328 ff., gave of redundancies which are due to translation from Aramaic deserve further study. Without going so far, Lagrange, lxxv, sees signs of the Semitic genius in v. 12, vi. 3, vii. 13, xiii. 19, 20, xiv. 18, especially when the verb seems to complete the substantive.

v. 12   Πέμψον ἡμᾶς εἰς τοὺς χοίρους, ἵνα εἰς αὐτοὺς εἰσέλθωμεν.
vi. 3   ὧδε πρὸς ἡμᾶς.
vii. 13   τῇ παραδόσει ὑμῶν ᾗ παρεδώκατε.
xiii. 19   ἀπ᾽ ἀρχῆς κτίσεως ἣν ἔκτισεν ὁ θεός.
xiii. 20   ἀλλὰ διὰ τοὺς ἐκλεκτοὺς οὓς ἐξελέξατο.
xiv. 18   καὶ ἀνακειμένων αὐτῶν καὶ ἐσθιόντων.

STYLE

Mark's Gospel is written in a relatively simple and popular form of Greek which has striking affinities with the spoken language of everyday life as it is revealed to us in the papyri and inscriptions. In this respect it differs profoundly from the masterpieces of Attic prose and even from the more cultured language of certain parts of Luke and Acts, the Epistle of James, the Epistle to the Hebrews, and the First and Second Epistles of Peter. Cf. Moulton, ii. 1-34. Perhaps the most obvious characteristic feature of Mark's Greek is his frequent use of καί paratactic, and correspondingly his failure to use the longer Greek period with its particles, conjunctions, and subordinating participles. Of the latter the one exception, pointed out by Wellhausen, *Einl.*[2] 13, is the description of the woman with the issue of blood in v. 25-7. The threefold use of διά with the perf. infin. in v. 4, in the description of the Gerasene demoniac, is also exceptional. It is possible, however, to overstress the ' barbarous ' character of Mark's Greek, for attention has already been drawn (*v.* p. 47) to Swete's examples of a careful use of tenses. Notable in this connexion are the descriptions of the demoniac in v. 15 and 18 (τὸν δαιμονιζόμενον, τὸν ἐσχηκότα τὸν λεγιῶνα, and ὁ δαιμονισθείς) and the distinction between πεποίηκεν and ἠλέησεν in v. 19, and also the conative imperfects in ix. 38 and xv. 23.

It is misleading to claim the numerous vivid details in Mark as illustrative of the Evangelist's style. The many concrete phrases peculiar to the Gospel (v. pp. 135-9), the frequent use of numbers, and the descriptions of the emotional reactions of individuals to the situations described, belong to the tradition he records and are not illustrations of his creative art. Several considerations favour this view : (1) the notable contrast between vividly told stories, based apparently on testimony, and other narratives constructed by Mark himself (v. the list on p. 83); (2) the frequent anacolutha and parentheses (p. 50); (3) the abrupt beginning in many narratives drastically edited by Luke (cf. H. J. Cadbury, *The Style and Literary Method of Luke*, 105-15). There is very much to be said for the view of Dibelius, 3, so far at least as Mark is concerned, that the Synoptists 'are principally collectors, vehicles of tradition, editors'. Cf. the remark of Lagrange, lxxv, on many of the Markan details : *ils sont dans le récit, parce qu'ils ont été dans la nature*. It is a further sign of the limitations of Mark's art as a writer that, in describing a new scene, he sometimes repeats on an extensive scale words and phrases he has used in an earlier narrative. Thus, the story of the Four Thousand is modelled on that of the Five Thousand, and, as shown in detail in the Commentary, the account of the Blind Man near Bethsaida on that of the Cure of the Deaf Mute and, above all, the story of Preparations for the Passover on that of the Entry into Jerusalem. Cf. viii. 22 f. and vii. 32-4; xiv. 13-16 and xi. 1-6; also iv. 39, 41 and i. 25, 27; vi. 1 f. and i. 21 f., 27. Finally, the same phrases are used repeatedly ; e.g. περιβλεψά-μενος (v. iii. 5, etc.), προσκαλεσάμενος with reference to the disciples (v. vi. 7, etc.) or the crowd (v. vii. 14, etc.); references to entering a house (vii. 17, ix. 28, 33, x. 10) and to incidents and discussions 'in the way' (viii. 27, ix. 33, x. 32). The impression we receive is that Mark records tradition very much as he finds it. If this observation detracts from his skill as a writer, it is more than compensated for by the importance it gives to the personal and communal tradition of which he is the bearer.

P.-L. Couchoud [1] has maintained that the Gospel was originally written in Latin, and that codex k is a badly executed fragment of the lost original. F. C. Burkitt, *JTS*, xxix. 375-81, observes that the hypothesis is not altogether beyond the region of possibility, but that Couchoud's examples do not prove his case. Composition in Greek at Rome is the best explanation. See further, Blass, 4, 76; Moulton, i. 20 f.; Robertson, 108-11. Much more important is the Aramaic element in the Gospel. There can be no doubt that it exists, and the question for discussion is its extent and character.

[1] 'Was the Gospel of Mark written in Latin?', reprinted from the *Crozer* *Quarterly*, Jan. 1928, translated by M. S. Enslin.

VI

THE SEMITIC BACKGROUND OF THE GOSPEL

THE Semitic background of Mark is unmistakable and the only questions for consideration are whether the Gospel is a translation of an Aramaic original or whether the Greek suggests dependence on Aramaic tradition. Although the former view has been strongly maintained by C. C. Torrey and in part by Wellhausen, Nestle, and, as regards the sayings of Jesus, by Dalman, the general tendency of New Testament scholars is to reject the hypothesis of direct translation, but to recognize that Mark's Greek is ' translation-Greek ' or at least is strongly coloured by Aramaic tradition. In this connexion the views of J. H. Moulton are highly significant. Although mainly concerned to support the contention of Deissmann, that the New Testament was written in the *lingua franca* of the first century, his published opinions [1] ' will reveal a progressive tendency to do full justice to the influence of translation where Semitic originals may be posited with good reason '.[2] W. F. Howard's judgment is in agreement with that of Lagrange : ' His (Mark's) Greek is always Greek, yet translation Greek ; not that he translates an Aramaic writing, but because he reproduces an Aramaic κατήχησις '.[3] More recently M. Black has concluded a detailed study of the whole question with the opinion that ' an Aramaic sayings-source or tradition lies behind the Synoptic Gospels ', especially as regards the words of Jesus, but that ' whether that source was written or oral, it is not possible from the evidence to decide '.[4] In the parables, he maintains, we cannot speak of ' translation-Greek ' in all cases, with the exception of the Sower in Mark and the Well-behaved Guest in the Bezan text of Matt. xx. 28. In the

[1] In successive editions of the *Prolegomena*, in articles in *Cambridge Biblical Essays*, and in Peake's Commentary.

[2] W. F. Howard in Moulton's *Grammar*, ii. 413.

[3] *Op. cit.* ii. 481.

[4] *An Aramaic Approach to the Gospels and Acts*, 206.

narrative element in Mark and its non-dominical sayings and dialogue, the Evangelist's monopoly of asyndeton in narrative, his excessive use of the paratactic construction, and of the Aramaic proleptic pronoun in narrative ' may conceivably be construed as evidence of the kind of Greek which an Aramaic-speaking Jew would write '.[1] His suggested mistranslation of πιστικός in xiv. 3 is held to be too conjectural to have any cogency as proof of source. The evidence of iv. 41 and ix. 38 ' is more convincing, and may be decisive ', but both examples appear in reported speech. ' Certainly what evidence we do possess makes the assumption of Aramaic sources for the Marcan narrative much less difficult than for the non-Marcan narrative portions of Matthew and Luke.' [2] This cautious and judicial opinion may be held to indicate the present position in scholarly judgment. We have very good reason to speak of an Aramaic background to the Greek of the Gospel ; there are grounds for suspecting the existence of Aramaic sources, which may, however, be oral ; and we can speak of the Evangelist's use of a tradition which ultimately is Aramaic ; but to say more is speculation.

In these matters we are dependent on a small band of Aramaic experts, and other students of the New Testament naturally hesitate to express opinions. Further, the specialists disagree among themselves,[3] especially where questions of mistranslation arise, and the whole question has been widened in its scope by the necessity, emphasized by A. J. Wensinck and M. Black, of taking textual evidence into increased account. Source criticism too, as has long been seen, has an important bearing on the inquiry, not only as regards Q, Mark, M, and L, but also in connexion with the sources, or source-strata, which underlie Mark. Again, as will be seen, the question of distribution is also very important. If ' Semitisms ', or what appear to be such, appear in some narratives or types of narratives more than in others, the evidence may have an important bearing on the historical character and origins of Mark. If it be objected that this is a case of *obscurum per obscurius*, we can at least be aware

---

[1] *Op. cit.* 206. [2] *Op. cit.* 207.
Cf. E. C. Colwell, *The Greek of the Fourth Gospel* (1931), 96-131.

of the peril and of the need to give more critical attention to the ' results '.

With these qualifications some account may be attempted of the ' secondary Semitisms ' in Mark, first as regards sentence construction, then in the several parts of speech, and finally in the matter of ' mistranslations '.

STYLE AND SENTENCE-STRUCTURE

The Order of Words.—Wellhausen, *Einl.*[2] 10 f. ; Howard, ii. 416-18 ; Black, 33 f. The verb is frequently found at the beginning of sentences, as may be seen from Kieckers's analysis mentioned by Howard, in which initial, middle, and end positions are distinguished (in comparable sections). The figures for Mark are 40/66/24, as compared with those for Herodotus, 47/165/71, but they are less striking than in Luke, 63/55/31, and John, 71/48/25, in which Howard describes the predominance of the initial position as remarkable. He reminds us, however, of the considerable number of verbs of saying in the Gospel, which regularly stand at the beginning.

Parallelism.—Burney, *PL*, 63-99 ; Howard, ii. 418 f. ; Black, 105-17. Naturally the evidence concerns mainly the sayings of Jesus, but Black points out that it is to be seen also in the sayings of the Baptist (i. 7 f.) and in dialogue in xi. 9 f., 28, xii. 14, xiii. 4, and xv. 29. He also cites examples of alliteration, assonance, and paronomasia in the parables of the Sower, the Seed growing Secretly, and the Mustard Seed, when these parables are translated back into Aramaic, in the sayings of ix. 38-45, and in many other sections in Matt. and Luke. Ultimate connexion with Aramaic tradition is unmistakable.

Tautology.—Allen, *ET*, xiii. 328-30 ; Lagrange, lxxii-lxxv ; Howard, ii. 419 f. See earlier, pp. 50-2. Here we receive the same impression. It is to be noted that of the six passages printed on p. 52, while three are sayings of Jesus, two, v. 12 and vi. 3, are the sayings of others, and xiv. 18 appears in narrative.

Parataxis.—Howard, ii. 420-3 ; Black, 44-51. Everyone notices the excessive use in Mark of καί in the simple co-ordination clauses, and it is difficult to decide whether it is simply a sign of elementary culture (cf. Moulton, i. 12) or of the influence of Aramaic where it is much more common than in Greek. To draw the latter conclusion is rarely safe unless other and clearer signs of Aramaic usage can be seen in a sentence or narrative. A special case is presented by the parable of the Sower (iv. 3-9), where, in contrast with other parables, there is no instance of a hypotactic aor. ptcp. Cf. Black, 45. Black doubts if paratactic imperatives without a connecting particle (ii. 11 ἔγειρε, ἆρον, iv. 39 σιώπα, πεφίμωσο) can be described as ' un-Greek ', but observes that they are certainly more

common in Hebrew or Aramaic. Wellhausen's suggestion, *Einl.*[1]
25 (*Einl.*[2] 13), that viii. 34 is an example of conditional parataxis
(' Then he will be my disciple '), is attractive, but one can hardly say
more. For the possibility of temporal καί in xv. 25 *v.* Comm. *in loc.*
On the whole question Black, 51, observes : ' The high proportion
. . . of instances of parataxis in the Gospels and the Acts cannot
be set down as unliterary Greek only ; Aramaic influence must have
been a contributory factor '.

  Casus Pendens followed by the Redundant Pronoun.—Howard,
ii. 423-5 ; Black, 34-8. Cf. i. 34 (D) καὶ τοὺς δαιμόνια ἔχοντας ἐξέβαλεν αὐτὰ ἀπ' αὐτῶν, vi. 16 ὃν ἐγὼ ἀπεκεφάλισα Ἰωάνην, οὗτος
ἠγέρθη, vii. 20 τὸ ἐκ τοῦ ἀνθρώπου ἐκπορευόμενον, ἐκεῖνο κοινοῖ
τὸν ἄνθρωπον, xiii. 11 ἀλλ' ὃ ἐὰν δοθῇ ὑμῖν . . . τοῦτο λαλεῖτε.
This construction is found in Cl. Gk and in the papyri, but is
especially characteristic of Hebrew and Aramaic. Cf. Burney,
AO, 64 f. It is also very common in John. Black draws attention
to the allied construction in Mark vii. 2 καὶ ἰδόντες τινὰς τῶν
μαθητῶν αὐτοῦ ὅτι κοιναῖς χερσίν . . ., xi. 32, xii. 34, and gives
an attractive explanation of the confused passage in viii. 24 βλέπω
τοὺς ἀνθρώπους, ὅτι ὡς δένδρα ὁρῶ περιπατοῦντας. His conclusion is that, although these constructions are not specially Semitic,
' their preponderance in the sayings of Jesus supports the view
that a translation Greek tradition is to be found there '.

  Asyndeta.—Black, 38-43. See earlier, pp. 49-50. No one who
works through the 38 examples discussed by Turner, *JTS*, xxviii.
15-19, can fail to be impressed ; but even more impressive are
Black's examples, which omit those which are natural in Greek, and
include 17 apart from sayings. He concludes that the greater
frequency of asyndeta in Mark ' may point to translation of an
Aramaic narrative tradition about Jesus '. This conclusion is very
cogent, although naturally we do not know at what point behind
Mark the translation is to be set.

  Misrenderings of dᵉ in Subordinate Clauses.—Burney, *AO*, 70,
PL, 145 n. ; Howard, ii. 434-7 ; Black, 52-64. In Aramaic *dᵉ* can
be a relative pronoun, the sign of the genitive, or a conjunction, and
can therefore be rendered by ὅς, ὅτι = ' because ', ὅτι *recitativum*,
ὅτε, or ὥστε. By many scholars it is held to be the cause of mistranslation in the Gospels. This possibility arises in ix. 38, where the
B ℵ text reads ὅτι οὐκ ἀκολουθεῖ ἡμῖν, whereas D A *et al.* read ὅς and
place the clause after δαιμόνια. Cf. Black, 53 and *v.* Comm. *in loc.*
A second case is iv. 41 τίς ἄρα οὗτός ἐστιν, ὅτι καὶ ὁ ἄνεμος καὶ
ἡ θάλασσα ὑπακούει αὐτῷ, where apparently ὅτι is used to avoid
ᾧ . . . αὐτῷ. This suggestion of Wellhausen, *Einl.*[2] 15, was
accepted by Moulton, *Einl.* 332 ; *v.* Howard, ii. 436. The parallels
to iv. 22 in Matt. x. 26 and Luke xii. 2 are explained by Wellhausen,
Einl.[2] 15, and Burney, *AO*, 76, in the same way. Cf. Black, 58 ;
Allen, 48, 50. On the possibility that ἵνα in Mark iv. 12 is due to a

misunderstanding of d^e = 'who' v. Manson, TJ, 76-80, and the points made by Black, 153-8. See also Black's discussion of xiv. 68 (v. Comm. *in loc.*), and his reference to the possibility that the D text in vi. 2 (ἵνα καί) may be rendered as a consecutive clause, ' so that even such miracles are done by his hand ', AA, 61 f. He concludes that there may be genuine instances of mistranslation, but that in most cases it is rather a matter of deliberate (and legitimate) interpretations. Besides a written or oral tradition of the sayings, the Evangelists, and especially Mark, ' may have possessed an Aramaic tradition of the dialogue and speeches of Jesus's many interlocutors ', AA, 66.

Circumstantial Clauses.—Wellhausen, 36; Howard, ii. 423; Black, 62-4. The clauses in question are introduced by καί paratactic. Cf. i. 19 καὶ αὐτοὺς ἐν τῷ πλοίῳ καταρτίζοντας τὰ δίκτυα, iv. 27 καὶ ὁ σπόρος βλαστᾷ καὶ μηκύνηται. J. T. Hudson, ET, liii. 266, adds i. 6, 11, iv. 38, v. 21, vii. 30, and Black instances vi. 45 (D) αὐτὸς δὲ ἀπολύει τὸν ὄχλον. Cf. the Hebrew and Aramaic use of *Waw* followed by a noun or pronoun and a verb. It is not necessary, however, to explain the passages in this way. In i. 19, for example, the construction, while loose, is not ungrammatical, and if we judge the parable of the Seed growing Secretly (iv. 26-9) to be based on a Semitic original, it is largely on other grounds.

Before passing on to consider the several parts of speech, we may claim that the evidence supplied by the structure of Markan sentences is insufficient in itself to prove that Mark is a translation of an Aramaic original, but that the use of Aramaic tradition, and possibly sources, is strongly suggested. In what follows only the more important points are treated. For a detailed study of the parts of speech v. Howard, ii. 430-70.

SEMITIC USAGES IN THE SEVERAL PARTS OF SPEECH

The Definite Article.—Wellhausen, 19; Howard, ii. 430 f.; Moulton, i. 81 f.; Black, 68-70. In several instances in Mark (and other Gospels) the article is inserted or omitted in an anomalous manner. Insertions: ii. 7 (D) τὰς ἁμαρτίας, iii. 26 (D) τὸ τέλος, vi. 55 (om. D W Θ fam. 1 28 fam. 13 (exc. 124) 543 565) τοῖς κραβάττοις, viii. 11 (D) τὸ σημεῖον, ix. 36 (D) τὸ παιδίον, x. 25 (B) διὰ τῆς τρυμαλίας τῆς ῥαφίδος, xii. 1 (D) τοῖς γεωργοῖς. Omissions: ii. 21 σχίσμα, vi. 35 (D) τόπος, ix. 15 (D) πᾶς ὄχλος, xiv. 62 (D) δυνάμεως. But it is uncertain whether these anomalies are Semitisms (cf. Black, 68 f.) and the value of D in its treatment of the article is dubious (cf. Howard, ii. 430 f.).

The Proleptic Pronoun.—Wellhausen, 19; Howard, ii. 431;

Black, 70-4. Sometimes an apparently redundant pronoun is used in an anticipatory sense for emphasis as in Aramaic. Cf. v. 16 (D) αὐτῷ τῷ δαιμονιζομένῳ, vi. 17 αὐτὸς γὰρ ῾Ηρῴδης, vi. 18 (D) αὐτὴν γυναῖκα τοῦ ἀδελφοῦ σου, vi. 22 (A C) αὐτῆς τῆς ῾Ηρῳδιάδος. See Black's comment, 73, on viii. 38 ἐν τῇ δόξῃ τοῦ πατρὸς αὐτοῦ, ' in his glory (namely that) of his Father '. He also adds v. 15 (D) αὐτὸν τὸν δαιμονιζόμενον, Luke iv. 43 (D), x. 7, Acts vii. 52 (D), and explains the construction as ' a genuine Aramaism '.

The Relative followed by a Resumptive Pronoun.—Wellhausen, 15; Blass, 175; Moulton, i. 94 f., 237, 249; Howard, ii. 434 f.; Black, 75. Cf. i. 7 οὗ οὐκ εἰμὶ ἱκανὸς κύψας λῦσαι τὸν ἱμάντα τῶν ὑποδημάτων αὐτοῦ, vii. 25 ἧς εἶχεν τὸ θυγάτριον αὐτῆς πνεῦμα ἀκάθαρτον. Cf. Matt. iii. 12, x. 11 (D), xviii. 20 (D), Luke viii. 12 (D), xii. 43 (D), John i. 27, 33, ix. 36 (?), xiii. 26, xviii. 9. This usage may be a sign of elementary culture (cf. Moulton's example from Dickens, ' Which her name is Mrs. Harris '), but it corresponds closely with the parallel use of d^e in Aramaic, and Black urges that its distribution in the Gospels ' gives clear proof of its Semitic origin '. Cf. Apoc. iii. 8, vii. 2, 9, xii. 6, 14, xiii. 8, 12, xvii. 9, xx. 8.

The Reflexive Pronoun.—Wellhausen, 23; Moulton, i. 87; Howard, ii. 432; Black, 75-8. In Aramaic the place of the reflexive pronoun is taken by the ethic dative. This usage may be reflected in Mark vii. 4 (D) ἃ παρέλαβον αὐτοῖς τηρεῖν, x. 26 (D) λέγοντες πρὸς ἑαυτούς, ' did them say ', and xiv. 4 ἦσαν δέ τινες ἀγανακτοῦντες πρὸς ἑαυτούς, ' some were indeed vexed '. Moulton points out that in translations from Semitic originals a periphrasis with ψυχή may be used instead of ἑαυτόν, and compares viii. 36 τὴν ψυχὴν αὐτοῦ (cf. Luke ix. 25 ἑαυτόν). Black, 76, describes the use of ψυχή as a reflexive ' a pure Semitism '.

The Indefinite Pronoun.—Wellhausen, 20; Howard, ii. 432 f.; Moulton, i. 96 f. For εἷς = τις see v. 22, x. 17, xii. 42, xiv. 47 (ℵ A L), 66, and for ἀπὸ τῶν ἰχθύων used as the equivalent of the plur. see vi. 43. For ἄνθρωπος = quidam (vii. 11) see Black, JTS, xlix. 161.

Numerals and Distributives.—Moulton, i. 95 f., 237; Howard, ii. 439 f.; Black, 90. The use of the cardinal for the ordinal is illustrated in xvi. 2 τῇ μιᾷ τῶν σαββάτων. The usage is Jewish Greek, but its distribution in the NT (Matt. xxviii. 1, Luke xxiv. 1, John xx. 1, 19, Acts xx. 7, 1 Cor. xvi. 2) suggests that it may be quasi-technical. With greater confidence the use of the cardinal in an adverbial sense in iv. 8 (D) ἐν τριάκοντα καὶ ἐν ἑξήκοντα καὶ ἐν ἑκατόν can be claimed as a Semitism, implying ḥadh ' one '. Cf. Allen, ET, xiii. 330; Black, 90. V. Comm. Possibly the distributives should be so regarded in vi. 7 δύο δύο, vi. 39 συμπόσια συμπόσια, vi. 40 πρασιαὶ πρασιαί, and xiv. 19 εἷς κατὰ εἷς. Lagrange, 150, holds that we cannot see in δύο δύο a pure Semitism, in view of μίαν μίαν in Sophocles (v. Moulton, 97) and the evidence of the papyri and MGk (v. Deissmann, LAE, 122 f.;

VGT, 173, 533, 598, 640 f.) ; but Black, 90, thinks the case against Semitisms is ' not very impressive '.

Degrees of Comparison.—Wellhausen, 21 ; Howard, ii. 441-3 ; Black, 86 f. In Semitic languages (Arabic excepted) there are no special forms for the comparative and superlative, and the positive is used for both. This usage is apparently without parallel in the Koine, although the comparative is there used for the superlative. There is good reason, therefore, to find Semitisms in ix. 43, 45, 47 καλόν, and xiv. 21 καλόν. Cf. Matt. ii. 16 (D), xxii. 36, Luke v. 39, ix. 48, xvi. 10 (D), John i. 15, ii. 10.

The Interrogative Particle.—A. J. Wensinck, *Semitismus*, 20, and Black, 87-9, find Aramaisms, corresponding to the Semitic use of the interrogative particle expressing wonder or indignation, in the following : ii. 7 (' Why ! '), 8 (' Can it be that . . . ? '), 24 (' Are they then . . . ? '), iv. 40, viii. 12, x. 18, xv. 34. Cf. Luke xii. 49, Matt. vii. 14 (Old Lat. and Syr.). ' The predominance of the Semitic idiom in Mark is significant ', Black, 89. All the suggested examples are in sayings. With these may be compared the use of the interrogative ὅτι in ii. 7 (B), 16, viii. 12 (C Or), ix. 11, 28.

Constructions which correspond to the Use of the Hebrew Infinitive Absolute.—Thackeray, 48 f. ; Dalman, 34 f. ; Howard, ii. 443-5. These constructions, which are extremely rare in Aramaic (Howard, ii. 443), are found mainly in sayings of Jesus containing Biblical quotations. Thus, as in the LXX, the dat. of the cognate noun is used with the finite verb in vii. 10 θανάτῳ τελευτάτω. But see also v. 42, in narrative, καὶ ἐξέστησαν εὐθὺς ἐκστάσει μεγάλῃ (RSV, ' they were overcome with amazement '). Alternatively, the finite verb is used with the participle in iv. 12 ἵνα βλέποντες βλέπωσιν . . . καὶ ἀκούοντες ἀκούωσιν. Cf. also the use of the cognate accusative to strengthen the force of the verb, found both in Hebrew and Aramaic, and sometimes in the LXX (cf. Gen. xxvii. 33). See iv. 41 καὶ ἐφοβήθησαν φόβον μέγαν, a passage otherwise open to the suggestion of containing a Semitism (ὅτι = d^e = ὦ, *v. supra*).

The Adverbial Use of προστίθημι.—Thackeray, 52 f. ; Allen, 169 ; Deissmann, *BS*, 67 n. ; Moulton, i. 233 ; Howard, ii. 445 f. Thackeray shows that in the LXX the Hiph. of יסף ' to add ' c. infin. is represented by προσέθετο λαβεῖν (109 times), προσέθετο καὶ ἔλαβεν (9), and προσθεὶς ἔλαβεν (6). With the first cf. xiv. 8 προέλαβεν μυρίσαι, xiv. 25 (D) οὐ μὴ προσθῶ πεῖν. *V.* Comm. *in loc.*

πολλά *Adverbial.*—Wellhausen, 21 ; Howard, ii. 446. See the note on i. 45. For the use of πολλά in Cl. Gk in the sense of ' very much ' *v.* LS, 1443. Howard observes that its disproportionate use in Mark (9 times, *v. HS*, 35) is ' a Markan mannerism which may be due to Aramaic influence ', ii. 446. Cf. Allen, 19 (' about 13 times ').

The Adverbs πάλιν *and* εὐθύς.—See the notes on ii. 1 and i. 10. Black, 82, submits that in xv. 13 πάλιν cannot be iterative, and, against Moffatt and *VGT*, 476, translates: ' They thereupon shouted ', thus supporting Wellhausen's suggestion, *Einl.*[2] 21, that πάλιν represents *tubh*, ' then ', ' thereupon '. *V.* Howard, ii. 446. Many suggestions have been made about the Aramaic counterpart of εὐθύς. *V.* Black, 79 n.

The Infrequency of the Passive with ὑπό.—Wellhausen, 18; Allen, *St. Matt.* xxiii; Howard, ii. 447. The distribution in the Gospels and Acts is: Mark (7), Matt. (22), Luke (22), John (1), Acts (36). Allen gives a list of 13 instances in which Matthew has changed an active or a middle verb in Mark into a passive. The Markan usage coincides with the avoidance of the passive in Aramaic when the subject of the action is named. See also the next two paragraphs.

The Impersonal Plural.—Wellhausen, 18; Howard, ii. 447 f.; Black, 91. See the account of this characteristic Markan usage on pp. 47-8. Black claims that the distribution of this construction in the Gospels confirms Wellhausen's view that it is to be traced to the influence of Aramaic.

The Use of the Intransitive Verb in Place of the Passive.—Wellhausen, 18; Howard, ii. 448; Lagrange, xcii; Black, *JTS*, xlix. 163. Cf. iv. 21 μήτι ἔρχεται ὁ λύχνος; vii. 19 ἐκπορεύεται (Matt. xv. 17 ἐκβάλλεται), ix. 43 ἀπελθεῖν εἰς τὴν γέενναν (in 45 and 47 βληθῆναι, cf. Matt. xviii. 8 f.), xiv. 21 ὑπάγει (in the sense of אזל, *discedere a vita*, *mori*). Cf. Black.

The Use of the Infinitive after εἶπεν *in the Sense of* ' *to command* '.—Allen, 50; Howard, ii. 450; Black, *JTS*, xlix. 162. Cf. v. 43 καὶ εἶπεν δοθῆναι αὐτῇ φαγεῖν, viii. 7 καὶ εὐλογήσας αὐτὰ εἶπεν καὶ ταῦτα παρατιθέναι, Luke xii. 13, xix. 15. Cf. also v. 8 ἔλεγεν γὰρ αὐτῷ, Ἔξελθε (cf. Luke viii. 29). Allen compares the use of אמר + ל c. infin. in late Hebrew and Aramaic. The same usage, however, is found in the papyri (*VGT*, 372). *V.* Comm. *in loc.*

The Use of ἐν τῷ *c. Infin.*—Moulton, i. 14, 215, 249; Howard, ii. 450 f. This construction is common in the LXX to render ב c. infin. Dalman, 33, claims that it was wanting in spoken Aramaic. Influenced by the argument of E. A. Abbott, that the construction with the meaning *during* is non-existent or very rare in Thucydides, Moulton came to describe it as belonging to the category of ' possible but unidiomatic Greek ', i. 249. Although very common in Luke (32 times), the idiom is found twice only in Mark: in iv. 4 ἐν τῷ σπείρειν, where, as often, it appears along with the καὶ ἐγένετο construction, in a parable strongly marked by Semitic influence, and in vi. 48 ἐν τῷ ἐλαύνειν.

Periphrastic Tenses.—Moulton, i. 226 f.; Blass, 202-5; Howard, ii. 451 f.; Black, 94 f. See the account of this characteristic Markan usage on p. 45. Moulton describes the periphrastic imperfect as a ' secondary Semitism ' in the Synoptics and Acts i-xii; cf. i. 226. The construction is classical and is fairly frequent in the LXX and is illustrated (in the pres., perf., and fut. perf.) in the papyri (*VGT*, 184 f.). For γίνομαι with the participle *v*. Allen, *ET*, xiii. 328; Black, 94. Black also draws attention to the use of the participle as an indicative, which, while occasionally found in the Koine, is especially characteristic of Aramaic; cf. Moulton, i. 224; D. Daube in an Appended Note in Selwyn's *First Ep. of St. Pet.* 471 ff. Cf. Mark i. 13 (D), iii. 6 (D), vii. 25 (D), ix. 26 (D); Matt. xxvii. 41 (D) = Mark xv. 31. Cf. Lagrange, xc.

The Redundant Use of the Participle.—Dalman, 20-6; Lagrange, xcii f.; Allen, *ET*, xiii. 330; Moulton, i. 14, 230 f., 241; Howard, ii. 452-4. The participles in question include: ἐλθών (v. 23, vii. 25, xii. 42, xiv. 40, 45, xvi. 1), ἀφείς (iv. 36, viii. 13, xii. 12, xiv. 50), ἀναστάς (i. 35, ii. 14, vii. 24, x. 1), ἀποκριθεὶς εἶπεν (or, λέγει) (iii. 33, vi. 37, vii. 28, viii. 29, ix. 5, 19, x. 3, 24, 51, xi. 14, 22, 33, xii. 35 (ἔλεγεν), xiv. 48, xv. 2, 12 (ἔλεγεν), λέγων (viii. 28, xii. 26). Howard recognizes a Semitic flavour in these examples, which are found also in other Gospels, but points out that it is hard to say when the participle is really pleonastic. It may be doubted if any of the examples of the use of ἐλθών or ἀφείς is pleonastic. In i. 35, vii. 24, and x. 1 ἀναστάς seems redundant, and probably, though not necessarily, in ii. 14. The force of ἀποκριθείς is not easy to assess. Howard thinks it is strictly redundant only in ix. 5, xi. 14, xii. 35. Lagrange finds no more than the idiom *il prit la parole* in ix. 5, x. 24, 51, xi. 14, xii. 35, xiv. 48, xv. 12. Dalman's view, that its counterpart is quite unknown in later Jewish Aramaic, needs correction in consequence of our increasing knowledge of first century Aramaic; cf. *JTS*, xlix. 159. To Howard's examples (*v. supra*) we ought perhaps to add x. 24, 51, xiv. 48, xv. 12 (cf. Lagrange), but the participle has force in iii. 33, vi. 37, vii. 28, viii. 29, ix. 19, x. 3, xi. 22, 33, that is, in 8 examples out of the 16 instances. λέγοντες after εἶπαν in viii. 28 and λέγων in xii. 26 are probably redundant like the Heb. לאמר.

The Redundant Auxiliary Verb ἤρξα(ν)το *c. Infin.*—Allen, 49 f.; Moulton, i. 14 f.; Howard, ii. 455 f.; Hunkin, *JTS*, xxv. 390-402; Black, 91. For this common Markan construction see earlier, p. 48. Allen traces the construction to the use of שׁרי in Aramaic as an auxiliary verb; cf. Dalman, 27. Thackeray, *JTS*, xxx. 370, who questions whether it is legitimate to speak of ἤρξα(ν)το *c.* infin. as an Aramaism, admits the possibility of Aramaic influence in Mark and Josephus, and attributes its frequency in Mark to the fact that it happened to correspond to a common Semitic phrase. Hunkin, also, while unwilling to allow that the sources used by Matthew and Luke were written in Aramaic, recognizes that the loose and somewhat pleonastic way in which ' begin ' is used in Mark and some of the sayings is consistent with the fact that Jesus and Mark were familiar with Aramaic. These guarded opinions show how difficult it is to deny the Aramaic origin of the construction in Mark. We may question whether its frequency in Proto-Luke (about 13 times) is without significance.

The Use of the Aorist to render the Semitic Perfect.—Moulton, i. 134 f. ; Howard, ii. 458 ; Black, 93. While ἐν σοι εὐδόκησα in i. 11 may be described as a summary aorist (G. G. Findlay) or as an aorist expressing what has *just happened* (Moulton), it is more likely, in view of Isa. xlii. 1 (in which the Heb. stative perfect is rendered by the aorist in the LXX) to be a rendering of the Semitic perfect. Cf. Allen, *St. Matt.* 29. Probably also ἐβάπτισα in i. 8 (cf. Matt. iii. 11 βαπτίζω) should be explained in the same way.

Prepositions.—Moulton, i. 61-8 ; Howard, ii. 460 f. ; Black, 83-6. The following usages may be noted. βλέπειν ἀπό (viii. 15, xii. 28) is effectively illustrated in the papyri ; *v.* Comm. *in loc.* The use of εἰς c. acc. to form the predicate appears in Mark only in quotations (x. 8, xii. 10). Moulton points to a similar use of εἰς expressing direction and cites M. Aurelius vi. 42 (' Marcus at any rate will not be suspected of Semitism ! '). But he allows Semitic influence in passages found in translation, where it has the advantage of being a literal rendering. ἐσθίειν ἀπό (מן אכל), vii. 28, may be explained in the same way. Here it is not a question of a quotation, and ἀπό may either replace the partitive genitive (as in later Greek) or reveal Aramaic tradition shining through the narrative. The latter seems the more probable explanation. πιστεύω ἐν (i. 15), σκανδαλίζομαι ἐν (vi. 3), and ἐργάζομαι ἐν (xiv. 6) appear to reflect the influence of ב. For πρὸς ἡμᾶς (vi. 3) *v.* Howard, ii. 467, and for κατέναντι (vi. 41 (D), xi. 2, xii. 41, xiii. 3) *v.* Howard, ii. 465 ; Black, 85. A possible reflection of Semitic idiom is suggested by Black in the repetition of the preposition before every noun in a series which it governs in iii. 8, vi. 56, xi. 1, and in D in v. 1, vi. 26, 36, viii. 31, xiv. 43.

Conjunctions and Particles.—Moulton, i. 241 ; Howard, ii. 468-470 ; Black, 57 f. The parallel use of ἀλλά and ἐὰν μή in iv. 22 and the textual variants ἀλλά and εἰ μή in ix. 8 may point to the Aramaic אלא, which is both exceptive and adversative. For x. 40 *v.* Moulton, i. 241. In viii. 12 εἰ *negandi* corresponds to אם in 1 Sam. xiv. 45.

Vocabulary.—See Black's comments on the following (most of which are noticed in the Comm.) : ἀπέχει (xiv. 41), ἐξῆλθεν (i. 28), ἐμβριμάομαι (i. 43), ἐπιφώσκω (with reference to xvi. 2), θάλασσα (i. 16), ποιέω (iv. 32, *JTS,* xlix. 162 f.), κορβάν (vii. 11), ὄρος (iii. 13), παραδίδωμι (iv. 29), πιστικός (xiv. 3), πλήρωμα (ii. 21), ποτήριον (x. 38, *JTS,* xlix. 159), ὑπάγω (xiv. 21, *JTS,* xlix. 163).

MISTRANSLATIONS

Mistranslations which can be shown to be credible supply strong evidence of the use of Semitic originals. Unfortunately, the experts often disagree, largely from uncertainty concerning the Aramaic of the first century A.D. Thus Black, 8 f., rejects Torrey's examples of mistranslation in vii. 3 and xiv. 3; *v*. Comm. He lays down the sound criteria that ' the mistranslations must be at least credible; and the conjectured Aramaic must be possible ', *AA*, 7. He claims the possibility of mistranslation in iv. 4, 22, 41, vii. 4, viii. 24, ix. 38, xiv. 3, 41, 68 (besides examples in other Gospels). See also his discussion of ἵνα in iv. 12 (*AA*, 153-7), where he prefers the explanation of the *interpretation* of an Aramaic saying rather than the hypothesis of mistranslation, of vi. 8 f., where a similar view is taken, and of iv. 29, where παραδοῖ is rendered ' is ready '. It seems unlikely that the argument from mistranslations will conflict with the inferences already drawn above; they confirm the view that Aramaic originals lie behind the sayings of Jesus and that we must allow for the probability that in many narratives Mark is dependent on Aramaic sources or tradition.

SUMMARY

Whether we consider the evidence afforded by the Markan style and sentence forms, the several parts of speech, or the hypothesis of mistranslation, we are brought to the same result — distrust of the claim that Mark was first written in Aramaic, confidence that its sayings and many of its narratives stand near Semitic tradition. This is a result of first importance. We cannot adopt without critical scrutiny the principle that the presence of an Aramaic element or atmosphere in Mark's Greek guarantees, without more ado, the historical character of what is recorded, for the possibility of mistakes and misunderstandings exists even in the higher waters of the stream of Gospel tradition. But we can certainly conclude that a Gospel so deeply coloured by Semitic usages must, in the main, bear a high historical value. And we can look with increased suspicion on critical theories which attribute to it corruptions traced to the impact of Hellenistic influences. The sympathies of Mark are Gentile in their range, but his tradition is Jewish Christian to the core.

If this conclusion is accepted, further inferences may be justified. Already the bearings of textual criticism on Semitisms are manifest. Can Semitisms also be significant in source criticism? The study of their *distribution* has not yet been seriously adventured. A tentative contribution to this question is made in the Note on the Construction of the Passion and Resurrection Narrative at the end of this volume, and, to a lesser degree, in the Note on the Compilation of the Apocalyptic Discourse. It is natural to ask if anything is to be gained by applying similar methods to earlier Markan sections. Probably the distribution of Semitisms may add something to the claim that the Feeding of the Five Thousand and the Feeding of the Four Thousand are doublets derived from different sources. If we mark possible Semitisms in the former by asterisks, the result is as follows : vi. 35*, 36, 37*, 38, 39*, 40*, 41, 42, 43**, 44 ; if in the latter : viii. 1* (?), 2, 3*, 4, 5, 6, 7, 8, 9. This is a very rough test, but its further development may show that vi. 35-44 has a Semitic basis and that viii. 1-9 is non-Semitic. If the results are less striking in other parts of i-xii, this may be because so much in these chapters rests on Aramaic tradition.

THE MARKAN SOURCES

THE success which has followed the attempt to determine
the sources used by Matthew and Luke naturally encouraged the hope that Mark's sources could also be traced.
That Mark did use earlier sources is suggested by the presence
of doublets in his Gospel, the account of the Feeding of the
Four Thousand and its sequel (viii. 1-26) as compared with
the story of the Five Thousand and the events which followed
(vi. 30-vii. 37), the presence of ' extracts ' from a sayings-
source (e.g. iv. 21-5, viii. 34-ix. 1, and ix. 42-50), the peculiar
character of the Apocalyptic Discourse in xiii, the signs of
strata in the Passion Narrative, and the absence of a parallel
to vi. 45-viii. 26 in Luke. To determine the sources is another
matter. In the later Gospels we can compare Matt. with
Luke, but we can compare sections of Mark only with other
sections in the same Gospel and consider the use the later
Synoptists have made of them. In the main the investigation
has taken the form of attempts to recover an earlier draft, the
Ur-Markus, or Original Mark, largely with negative results.
But the inquiry has in no way proved barren. If we cannot
recover Proto-Mark, we may learn much from the Gospel
itself about the tradition as Mark found it ; and, if this hope
is realized, the results will be far more valuable than the
recovery of what could only be a hypothetical draft.

Some account of the many forms of the Ur-Markus
Hypothesis must be given first. It would not be profitable
to discuss all its protean forms, especially those in which the
suggested original is longer than our canonical Mark,[1] and
since selection is necessary, we cannot do better than consider
the views of H. von Soden, E. Wendling, and W. Bussmann.
In addition to these theories some account must also be given
of Redaction and Compilation Hypotheses.

[1] Moffatt, *Introduction*, 192, mentions Ewald, Weisse, Schenkel, and
Réville.

THE UR-MARKUS HYPOTHESIS

H. von Soden

The views of von Soden are set out in his *Die wichtigsten Fragen im Leben Jesu*[2], 1907, and are discussed by C. S. Patton in his *Sources of the Synoptic Gospels* (1915). The principles by which the Ur-Markus is recovered are mainly matters of subject-matter and style. Thus, two kinds of narrative are distinguished : the first, and the earliest, consists of narratives in which attention is concentrated upon the words of Jesus ; the second, in which interest is taken in the events themselves. Mark ii. 1-iii. 6 is an example of the former; iv. 35-v. 43 of the latter. The *Kernstücke* are : i. 4-11, 16-20, 21-39; ii. 1-iii. 6; iii. 13-19, 20-35; iv. 1-8, 26-32; vi. 1-16; vii. 24-30 (?); viii. 27-ix. 1; ix. 33-40; x. 13-31; xii. 13-44; xiii. 1-6, 28-37. These passages, it is held, belong to the original Petrine tradition and Mark has interwoven other material into them. The stories are strikingly fresh and colourful ; everything breathes the odour of Palestine ; theological motifs are wanting ; the figure of Jesus is virile and human.

It will be seen that von Soden's distinction between narratives concerned with the words of Jesus and others in which the interest is centred in events, anticipates the work of the Form Critics, and of Dibelius in particular. He also makes acute observations about individual narratives. Thus, he distinguishes vii. 32-7 and viii. 22-6 from ii. 1-12 and iii. 1-6. In the former the healing is the main interest ; in the latter the real theme is not the miracle, but forgiveness and the law of the Sabbath. But his attempt to recover an earlier edition of Mark must be held to fail. Many of the more broadly depicted narratives have as much right to be regarded as Petrine as the favoured *Kernstücke*. For example, vii. 32-7 and viii. 22-6, mentioned above, are more primitive than the stories of ii. 1-iii. 6, which, by concentration on a theme, have attained their present form by a process of attrition. Thus, by the adoption of different principles of selection a totally different Ur-Markus could be posited. In short, the method adopted is highly subjective. Moreover, the manifest unity of the Markan style constitutes a formidable objection to all forms of the Ur-Markus Hypothesis.

VII]   INTRODUCTION   69

E. Wendling

Wendling's hypothesis is elaborated in his *Ur-Markus*
(1905) and more fully in his *Die Entstehung des Markusevangeliums* (1908), and is discussed by Patton, *op. cit.* 77-87 ;
Moffatt, *Introduction*, 227 f. ; N. P. Williams, *Oxford Studies*,
389-421 ; and Lagrange, *Évangile selon Saint Marc*, xlv f.
Three stages are distinguished in the formation of the Gospel,
M¹, M², and M³. The primitive draft resembles that presupposed by von Soden, but the method by which the stages
are delimited is somewhat different. Two strands are distinguished in chapter iv, namely 1-9 + 26-33 and 10-25. The
latter is redactional and by comparison with it other passages,
e.g. iii. 22-30, are also held to be insertions. In all, two
separate blocks of later elements are isolated, and in this way
the threefold structure is exposed. M¹ is the work of an
historian, M² of a poet, M³ of a theologian. The thesis is
brilliantly maintained and is supported by linguistic and
doctrinal arguments. The support of Wrede's theory of ' the
Messianic Secret ' is enlisted and the doctrinal motives are
held to be operative in the process of compilation. Nevertheless, the hypothesis evokes admiration rather than conviction.
Less perhaps than in the case of von Soden's analysis, but
just as certainly, assumptions and subjective considerations
supply a thin and unsubstantial mortar for an edifice unable
to withstand the winds of criticism. Particularly vulnerable
is the distinction between the historian, the poet, and the
theologian. ' Might not the same man ', asks Stanton, *The
Gospels as Historical Documents*, ii. 177, ' have a little in
him of all three ? ' The most characteristic Pauline ideas are
wanting in the supposed work of ' the theologian ', and the
distinctive Markan style and the Evangelist's favourite words
and phrases appear with perplexing impartiality in M¹, M²,
and M³. Finally we are left to account for the order of the
Gospel, which, if less precise than older commentators supposed, is strange in a building of different stones, different
colours, and different styles of architecture.[1]

Wendling's hypothesis might be treated under the heading

---

[1] For the contents of M¹, M², and   by Moffatt, *op. cit.* 227, or the analysis
M³ see the convenient summary given   of Williams, *op. cit.* 390-7.

of Redactional Hypotheses, but since M¹, or M¹ + M², constitutes an ' original Mark ', it is best classified along with von
Soden's theory. The same also may be said of W. Bussmann's
even more elaborate hypothesis, to which we now turn.

W. Bussmann

Mention has already been made of Bussmann's *Synoptische Studien*, which appeared in three parts during the
years 1925 to 1931. Little has been said of this work in Great
Britain (cf. Manson, *SJ*, 20 f., and two reviews by the present
writer, *HJ*, xxix. 757-60, xxx. 378-80), but on the continent
it has been received with considerable favour (cf. the observations of Otto, *KGSM*, 83-5 ; Schniewind, *ThR*, 1930, pp.
137 f.). The first part of this considerable volume entitled *Zur
Geschichtsquelle* concerns us here. In general it is a ' three
stage hypothesis ', like Wendling's, but supported by different
methods and arguments. The earliest stage, represented by
the symbol G, is Mark as it was known to Luke, the second
stage B is G expanded by a Galilean redactor, used as a source
by Matthew ; the final form E is B as it emerged from the
hands of a Roman editor, in short, the canonical Mark.

In substance, the hypothesis is not new. In this country
similar suggestions were put forward independently in 1911
by N. P. Williams and W. W. Holdsworth. In rejecting
Wendling's views, N. P. Williams [1] suggested that Mark was
current in at least three recensions during the period A.D.
70–100. (1) The original form which lacked both vi. 45-
viii. 26 and xiii ; (2) a form without vi. 45-viii. 26 used by
Luke ; (3) the canonical Mark used by Matthew. Holdsworth's hypothesis [2] embodies suggestions made earlier by
A. Wright,[3] and is even nearer to Bussmann's theory. Thus,
he distinguishes (1) an early Palestinian edition, used by
Luke, which lacked vi. 45-viii. 26 ; (2) a second edition for
Jews of the Dispersion used by Matthew ; (3) Mark in its
present form, prepared by the Evangelist for the Gentile
Church at Rome, which included smaller additions wanting
in Matt. and Luke.

---

[1] *Oxford Studies in the Synoptic*
Problem, 389-421.
[2] *The Christ of the Gospels*, 59-73.
[3] *Synopsis²*, p. lviii, *The Gospel of
St. Luke*, 83.

Bussmann's principal argument is his rejection of the explanation advanced by P. Feine,[1] H. J. Holtzmann,[2] and others, that Luke's fear of doublets accounts for his omission of large parts of Mark. Bussmann argues that Luke has most doublets of all the Synoptists [3] and that the absence from Luke of considerable parts of Mark is due to the fact that they were not present in the form of Mark which he used.[4] Similarly, the many smaller additional statements, wanting in Luke and Matt., such as personal names, numbers, Aramaic words, explanatory comments, Latin words, local and temporal statements, cannot have stood in the B form used by Matt., but must have been added in E by Mark.[5]

For several reasons Bussmann's case is unconvincing. (1) The presence of many doublets in Luke is due to the Evangelist's use of several sources, Mark, Q, L, and the Birth Stories, and in no way excludes the possibility that he might omit Markan stories and smaller details because he had parallels in other sources. (2) Fear of doublets is by no means the only reason which critics have suggested for Luke's omission of Markan passages. For example, Hawkins [6] suggests, as causes which account for the absence of vi. 45-viii. 26 from Luke, (a) the desire to avoid miracles achieved by material means (vii. 32-7, viii. 22-6), (b) the wish to prevent undue repetition, (c) a tendency to omit anti-Pharisaic controversy (vii. 1-23), and (d) the intention to ' spare the Twelve '. (3) The improbability that the many vivid details in Mark, names, numbers, and the like, are redactional. One has only to read the text of Bussmann's G to be convinced that it is an artificial construction which never existed in fact. (4) The possibility (or probability) that Luke used Mark, not as his principal source, but as a supplementary source, supplies the simplest explanation of the want of so much of Mark in Luke.

The last point is especially important. It has been too little recognized that Bussmann's hypothesis and the Proto-

[1] *Einleitung in das NT*, 1913, p. 138, where Feine expressly says, *Dupletten vermeidet er fast durchgängig*.

[2] *Die Synoptiker*[3], 1901, p. 19: *Wiederholungen geht Lc grundsätzlich aus dem Wege, ohne sie darum, bei der Doppelheit seiner Quellen, ganz vermeiden zu können*.

[3] *L hat meisten Dupletten von allen Synoptikern, soweit ist er von Dupletenfurcht entfernt, op. cit.* 57.

[4] *Op. cit.* 105.

[5] *Op. cit.* 100 f.

[6] *Oxford Studies*, 66-74.

Luke hypothesis are independent, and mutually exclusive, attempts to explain the same Synoptic data.[1] It may be argued that the latter is the sounder explanation, and, in this case, Bussmann's hypothesis receives its deathblow; but, even apart from this contention, the points made above are sufficient to show that it is unsound. If further refutation is called for, it is supplied by the fact that however Mark is subdivided, its sundered parts have linguistic homogeneity, and by the probability that the minor agreements of Matt. and Luke against Mark are very often cases of textual assimilation.[2]

REDACTION HYPOTHESES

Ur-Markus hypotheses might with reason be included under the present heading, but inasmuch as their aim is to recover an earlier form of Mark, they differ from hypotheses which, to a greater or less degree, accept our Mark as the Gospel which the Evangelist wrote, but seek to distinguish in it later redactional elements.

J. Weiss

The views of J. Weiss in *Das älteste Evangelium* (1903) might be included under either class. He doubts whether Mark as we now know it was read by Matt. and Luke and frequently assigns passages to a redactor (*Bearbeiter*). His view therefore is a form of the Ur-Markus hypothesis [3]; but he expressly observes that, in his view, the redactor has not altered the total form (*Gesamtaufriss*) of the original work, and his main interest is in the different kinds of material Mark used.

J C. Hawkins

Hawkins in *Horae Synopticae*[2], 152, rejects the idea of an Ur-Markus and claims that Mark as it stands is the source used by Matt. and Luke, but adds the comment, ' Almost; but not quite '. He sees an editor's hand in i. 1 (' Jesus Christ '), ix. 41 (' Christ's '); probably in the insertion of

---

[1] This point is made in my *Formation of the Gospel Tradition*, 200.

[2] Streeter, *The Four Gospels*, 295-321.

[3] He refers with approval (*op. cit.* 4) to the views of C. Weizsäcker in *Untersuchungen über die evangelische Geschichte* (1864).

' the gospel ' and ' persecutions ' in viii. 35 and x. 29 f. ; perhaps also in the reference to ' the Jews ' in vii. 3 ; and again in the numerals 200 and 300 in vi. 37 and xiv. 5 ; and possibly in 2000 in v 13 and the disagreement of the witnesses in xiv. 56, 59.

V. H. Stanton

Stanton's list of editorial expansions is fuller. Cf. *The Gospels as Historical Documents*, ii. 142-5, 156-69. His list of smaller differences includes : the use of ' gospel ' absolutely in i. 1, i. 14 f., viii. 35, x. 29 ; ' the carpenter ' in vi. 3 ; the reference to anointing with oil in vi. 13 ; the saying ' The Sabbath was made for man ' in ii. 27 ; the saying on being servant of all in ix. 35 ; the phrase ' for all the Gentiles ' in xi. 17 ; the temporal statements in iv. 35 f. ; the words ' He would not that any man should know it ' and ' for he taught his disciples ' in ix. 30, 31a ; ' twice ' in xiv. 30, 72 ; and perhaps ' in the days of Abiathar the high priest ' in ii. 26 and the reference to ' scribes ' in ix. 14. He further suggests that the form of Mark known to Luke lacked iii. 22-30, iv. 13b, 24b, 26-34, vi. 45-vii. 23, viii. 1-10, 14, 16-21, ix. 41-50, x. 2-12, xi. 11b-14, 19-25, xiii. 10, 34-7, and xiv. 3-9.

These are large concessions on the part of a scholar who rejects the hypotheses of von Soden and Wendling. In general one may say that there can be no objection in principle to redaction hypotheses. But, where textual questions do not arise, the detection of later elements necessarily becomes conjectural, and when carried beyond a certain point, redaction hypotheses become indistinguishable from Ur-Markus theories, and are then open to all the objections and criticisms to which the latter are exposed.[1]

COMPILATION HYPOTHESES

Compilation hypotheses attempt to show how the Evangelist has used written sources in the construction of the Gospel. They differ from redaction hypotheses in that the

---

[1] Bacon's views in *The Beginnings of Gospel Story* (1909) amount to a compilation hypothesis since the redactor is the Evangelist, a Paulinist who has left a doctrinal stamp upon primitive Christian tradition much of which is ultimately Petrine.

Redactor and the Evangelist are one and the same person. The interest centres, not in the fate of the Gospel after it was written, but in the process by which it was put together. The most notable examples in recent times are the views put forward by Ed. Meyer, A. T. Cadoux, and J. M. C. Crum.

Ed. Meyer

In *Ursprung und Anfänge des Christentums*, i-iii (1921–1923), Meyer draws attention to the very frequent references to the disciples in Mark, in the phrase ' His disciples ', and side by side with these, but distinct from them, the allusions to ' the Twelve ' in iii. (14), 16 (?), iv. 10, vi. 7, ix. 35, x. 32, xi. 11, xiv. 10, 17, 20, 43. He suggests that Mark has used two main sources : a ' disciple-source ', which embodies a uniform tradition and contains many Petrine narratives, and a ' Twelve-source ', not of Petrine origin, and used in the sections in which the Twelve are expressly mentioned, namely, iii. 15-19, iv. 10b-12, vi. 7-13 (30), ix. 33-50, x. 32b-45, xiv. 1 f., 10 f., 17-24, and to which Luke ix. 52-5 belongs. Mark has also used a special source in xiii and parallel accounts of the same tradition in vi. 30-vii. 37 and viii. 1-26. The most doubtful part of this hypothesis is the ' Twelve-source '. The allusions to the Twelve in Mark are peculiar and raise a difficult historical problem. Several of the narratives in which they are mentioned appear to be ' Markan constructions '[1] rather than units of pre-Markan tradition, and there is no reason to trace them to a documentary source. It is difficult to agree with C. H. Turner[2] in the view that from Caesarea Philippi onwards ' the disciples ' are practically identical with ' the Twelve '. There is greater reason to think that, at the time when Mark wrote, the term was

---

[1] See later, pp. 82-5.

[2] *JTS*, xxviii. 22-30. Referring to the words ' And he called the Twelve ' (ix. 35), Turner asks if it is reasonable to think that one set of persons had been discussing who was greatest (ix. 33 f.) and that the moral was pointed to a different set. This argument has force if ix. 33-7 is an original unit of tradition, but not if, as many commentators think, it is an artificial compilation of genuine fragments. Again, ' in the house ' (x. 10) suggests a limited number, but not necessarily twelve. And can we base much on tradition connected with the legend of the fig tree (xi. 11) ? Certainly in x. 32 and xiv. 17 the Twelve are in question, but it is still a large assumption that when Mark says ' His disciples ' or ' the Twelve ', he means same thing.

somewhat of an archaism, since after the Galilean Mission
(vi. 7-13) the Twelve were merged into the general body of
the disciples. The sporadic use of the term in Mark is some
confirmation of this view, as well as the fact that, with the
exception of the incident narrated in xiv. 12-16 (17), the
Twelve never again fulfil distinctive functions comparable
to those described in iii. 13-19 and vi. 7-13.

A. T. Cadoux

Compilation hypotheses are always exposed to the danger
of over-running the evidence. The suggestions offered may
be valid, but so also may other suggestions. This criticism
applies to Meyer's ' Twelve-source ', and it applies also to
A. T. Cadoux' more elaborate hypothesis. In his learned
discussion in *The Sources of the Second Gospel* (1935) Dr.
Cadoux suggests that the Evangelist has used three sources :
a Palestinian Gospel, which he calls A, written in Aramaic
about A.D. 40, perhaps under the authority of Peter ; a
Gospel of the Dispersion B, written by Mark about A.D. 67
in Alexandria, less Petrine but with a pro-Jewish bent ; a
Gentile Gospel C, written about A.D. 50 for the work of St.
Paul among the Gentiles. The hypothesis is held to account
for the many inconsequences, discrepancies, and harsh col-
locations in Mark. It is offered also as explaining the many
repetitions and variant traditions in the Gospel : e.g. the three
descriptions of Judas in xiv. 10, 20, and 43 ; the names of the
women at the Tomb in xv. 40 and 47 ; the use of ' Joses ' in
xv. 40, 47 and of ' Joseph ' in xv. 43, 45 ; the three accounts
of opinions concerning Jesus in vi. 14, 16, and viii. 28 ; three
strands of material in iv ; the two feeding stories in vi. 35-44
and viii. 1-9 ; and the three prophecies of the Passion in viii.
31, ix. 31, and x. 33 f. Many other points are assembled in
valuable Notes as well as linguistic and doctrinal arguments.
For all who appreciate the importance of studying the pre-
Markan tradition the value of Dr. Cadoux' work is very
great, but his hypothesis is carried to a point where it becomes
excessively conjectural. To mention only two examples : can
one feel any confidence in assigning the three sayings at the
Supper to different sources, xiv. 22 to A, 24 to B, and 25 to C,
and in attributing xvi. 2a and 8b to A, the rest of xvi. 1-8

to B, and the Eusebian text of Matt. xxviii. 18-20 to C ? The linguistic arguments also are far from conclusive.[1] The real value of the discussion is that it reveals the great variety of the oral tradition as the Evangelist found it, and it is to this situation, rather than to very hypothetical written sources, that attention should be directed.

J. M. C. Crum

Precisely the same conclusion is suggested by a study of Canon Crum's stimulating work, *St. Mark's Gospel: Two Stages of its Making* (1936). Here two strata are distinguished : Mark I, a Gospel story which might have been told by a man who grew up in close contact with Peter from A.D. 30 to 60 ; and Mark II, a second writing which works over and amplifies Mark I, written about A.D. 65, reflecting a later Christology, using the language of the Septuagint, and drawing upon a document closely related to ' Q '. Many valuable comments bring home to the mind that Mark is not simply an account of Peter's memoirs, and that behind the Gospel lies the experience of a living Church. This twofold tradition may have been reduced to writing, but we cannot hope to recover the sources with precision, and probability favours the conjecture that they were many and comparatively brief.

CONCLUSIONS

The study of the hypotheses which have been examined is barren if it ends with purely negative results. We may feel compelled to reject all known forms of the Ur-Markus Hypothesis, but there is something unseemly in an investigation which ends with *Requiescat Urmarcus*.[2] The same also may be said of the rejection of redactional and compilation hypotheses. There is no failure in Synoptic criticism, for, if we reject a particular suggestion worked out with great learning

[1] In a review (*Methodist Recorder*, Dec. 12th, 1935) W. F. Howard points out that the alleged Semitisms claimed by specialists are distributed in the suggested documents as follows: A 43, B 67, C 46.

[2] Cf. Williams, *op. cit.* 421. See also Turner, *JTS*, xxvi. 346: ' One more nail has been driven into the coffin of that old acquaintance of our youth, *Ur-Marcus*. He did enough harm in his time, but he is dead and gone: let no attempts be made to disinter his skeleton.'

and ability, we are compelled to reconsider the evidence on which it is based and seek a better explanation, knowing that a later critic may light upon a hypothesis sounder and more comprehensive still.

The only source for which a fairly general support can be claimed is the Markan sayings-collection, and on this question there are differences of opinion regarding its nature, identity, and unity.[1] The importance of the hypotheses which have been reviewed is their common assumption that the Evangelist has used several sources. This view remains highly probable even if the sources are not the literary entities described by Wendling, Bussmann, Meyer, and their successors. It is necessary, therefore, to study the Markan material afresh; to see what different types of tradition it includes; to consider their character, topical or otherwise; and to ask to what extent the narratives, or groups of narratives, consist of historical reminiscences, and to what degree they have been influenced by current catechetical and doctrinal interests. These questions will be considered in the following sections.

[1] See later, pp. 87 f.

THE MARKAN MATERIAL

THE material contained in Mark is of different kinds. The distinction between narratives and sayings, while primary, is not sufficient to cover the variety of the material, and a more detailed description must be attempted.

1. PRONOUNCEMENT-STORIES

These are the short narratives in which everything is subordinated to the desire to give a saying of Jesus which was of interest and importance to the earliest Christian communities. They belong to the type which Bultmann has described as Apothegms and Dibelius as Paradigms. It is in the isolating and description of this kind of narrative that Form Criticism has achieved its greatest success, but it is not wise to limit the formative influences to which they owe their peculiar character to preaching or to discussions within the community or to describe the type too narrowly. A pronouncement-story gains its form at a certain stage in its evolution, but there may also be narratives which have not yet reached this stage or have been modified in various ways. The distinctive feature of these stories is that they are popular in origin rather than personal narratives communicated by an eyewitness. To this type some twenty Markan narratives appear to belong.

The list is as follows [1] :

1.	ii. 5-10a.	On Forgiveness.	11.
2.	ii. 16 f.	On Eating with Taxgatherers and Sinners.	13.
3.	ii. 18-20.	On Fasting.	14.
4.	ii. 23-6.	On the Sabbath (Cornfields).	16.
5.	iii. 1-6.	On the Sabbath (Man with the Withered Hand).	18.
6.	iii. 22-6.	On Collusion with Satan.	22.
7.	iii. 31-5.	On the True Kindred of Jesus.	24.

[1] The numbers on the right are the section numbers in the Comm.

Possibly other narratives ought to be included in this list : (64) On Eternal Life, (65) On Riches, (66) On Rewards. But, on the whole, it is probable that these narratives are classified better as stories about Jesus which, at the time when Mark wrote, had not yet gained the rounded form of pronouncement-stories.

It is characteristic of these stories that most of them fall into groups arranged topically. This is true of the first five stories in ii. 1-iii. 6 and the five (13-17) in xi. 27-xii. 37 ; and again in 6 and 7, 8 and 9, and 11 and 12. No. 10 is embedded in a group of sayings in ix. 37-50 ; 18 follows the sayings on devouring widows' houses in xii. 40, and 19 stands at the beginning of the Apocalyptic Discourse in xiii. It is reasonable, therefore, to infer that the arrangement of these stories reflects catechetical interests.

2. MIRACLE-STORIES

Miracle-stories are those in which the main interest is the account of the miracle itself. Such stories normally have a threefold form in which the circumstances, the wonder itself, and the effect produced are successively described. A form of this kind is the natural manner in which miracles are recorded, but it will be found that many of the Markan narratives contain fuller details than is usual in the so-called ' form ' and which have reached the Evangelist along more personal channels. Even so, these narratives differ from other stories about Jesus in their content and their disposal in the Gospel. Seventeen of these narratives may be listed :

As in the pronouncement-stories the grouping of several of these narratives is noteworthy, but with the important difference that the stories in the groups are linked together by geographical and temporal statements. This is the case in i. 23-34 (Nos. 1-3) and iv. 35-v. 43 (Nos. 6-9). Apart from a few exceptions (4, 13, 15) the stories are connected with definite localities mentioned within the narrative or its immediate context. Vivid details, many of which are peculiar to Mark, set these narratives in striking contrast to the bare undated narratives in the earlier list, and suggest that for these incidents Mark had information at his command more direct than the common oral tradition of the Church.

3. STORIES ABOUT JESUS

Like the miracle-stories, but differing from them in subject-matter, are other stories vivid and colourful in character, but with no distinctive form. Of these narratives Form Criticism can give no useful account, for terms like ' legends ' and ' myths ' are characterizations which beg the question in advance. The value of the narratives can be judged only in accordance with the ordinary principles of historical criticism. Mark appears to have received these stories as existing units of tradition. In this respect they differ from narratives which he appears to have constructed on the basis of tradition, even when we allow for the fact that in the former he has introduced editorial modifications. Some twenty-nine narratives of the kind can be distinguished, twelve of which belong to the Passion Narrative.

The list is as follows :

1.	i. 1-8.	John the Baptist.	1.
2.	i. 9-11.	The Baptism of Jesus.	2.
3.	i. 12 f.	The Temptation.	3.
4.	i. 16-20.	The Call of the First Disciples.	5.
5.	i. 35-9.	The Departure to a Lonely Place.	9.
6.	ii. 13 f.	The Call of Levi.	12.
7.	vi. 1-6a.	The Rejection at Nazareth.	36.
8.	vii. 24-30.	The Syro-Phoenician Woman.	47.
9.	viii. 11-13.	The Demand for a Sign.	50.
10.	viii. 27-33.	The Confession of Peter.	53.
11.	ix. 2-8.	The Transfiguration.	55.
12.	x. 17-22.	The Rich Man's Question.	64.
13.	x. 23-7.	The Conversation on Riches.	65.
14.	x. 28-31.	The Question of Rewards.	66.
15.	x. 35-40.	The Request of James and John.	68.
16.	xi. 1-11.	The Entry into Jerusalem.	71.
17.	xi. 15-19.	The Cleansing of the Temple.	73.
18.	xiv. 3-9.	The Anointing.	92.
19.	xiv. 12-16.	The Preparations for the Supper.	94.
20.	xiv. 22-5.	The Last Supper.	96.
21.	xiv. 32-42.	Gethsemane.	98.
22.	xiv. 43-52.	The Arrest.	99.
23.	xiv. 53-65.	The Trial before the Priests.	100.
24.	xiv. 66-72.	The Denial.	101.
25.	xv. 1-15.	The Trial before Pilate.	102.
26.	xv. 16-20.	The Mockery by the Soldiers.	103.
27.	xv. 21-41.	The Crucifixion.	104.
28.	xv. 42-7.	The Burial.	105.
29.	xvi. 1-8.	The Visit to the Tomb.	106.

The account of the Death of John (vi. 17-29) is of the same type, but its subject is not Jesus. The Passion stories stand in close relation to one another and are discussed separately in Note J.

Most of the stories listed above are self-contained narratives. The Departure to a Lonely Place is an exception and is connected closely with the three miracle-stories in i. 21-39. The Conversation on Riches (13) and the Question of Rewards (14) are pendants to the Rich Man's Question (12) in the series x. 17-31. The rest are complete in themselves.

It is natural to suppose that these picturesque stories were known to Mark through personal informants, Peter and others. Not all the stories are Petrine, for some of them can have been known to the Evangelist from primitive Christian tradition, notably Nos. 1-3, and others describe incidents when Peter was not present, e.g. Nos. 8, 23, 25, 26, 27, 28, and 29. There is, however, good reason to trace to his testimony the Call of the First Disciples, the Departure to a Lonely Place, the Call of Levi, the Rejection at Nazareth, the Confession of Peter, the Transfiguration, the Rich Man's Question (and the two narratives attached to it), the Request of James and John, the Entry, the Cleansing, the Anointing, Gethsemane, the Arrest, and the Denial. Mark also may be indebted to Peter's reminiscences for many of the miracle-stories, and for some of the traditions in the narratives the Evangelist himself appears to have constructed. All these possibilities call for close consideration in the introductory notes to the several narratives. All that is claimed here is that the form and general character of the miracle-stories and the stories about Jesus are in harmony with the Papias tradition.

4. MARKAN CONSTRUCTIONS

In addition to the narratives listed above there are others which lack the vivid characteristics of these stories and appear to have been constructed by Mark himself (or a predecessor) from current fragmentary tradition. At the time when Mark wrote they did not exist as self-contained narratives, traceable directly or indirectly to informants. The tradition they contain is *given*, but the narratives are *constructed*. Some of them are little more than records of sayings or conversations with a brief narrative introduction. In this respect they resemble the Greek *Chriae* described by Dibelius, 152-64, which consist of ' the reproduction of a sharp pointed saying of general significance, originating in a definite person and arising out of a definite situation ', but, unlike the *Chriae*, they record, not wise or witty maxims, but sayings with a narrative interest and a religious purpose. These narratives include the following :

The bounds between these narratives and the previous group cannot be precisely drawn. In the broader sense of the term, all are stories about Jesus, and perhaps Nos. 1, 2, 4, 5, 6, and 7 differ from the rest only in being based less directly upon testimony. There is, however, a certain degree of artificiality in the construction of these narratives, as if Mark lacked fuller information. The Appointment of the Twelve, for example, refers vaguely to 'the mountain' (or 'hill country'), and relates only that Jesus chose and appointed twelve to be with Him and to be sent forth as heralds and exorcists. Even if we do not accept Ed. Meyer's theory, that in this story two separate accounts have been fused (*v.* Comm.), there is sufficient evidence to suggest that fragmentary traditions have been combined. The story of the Fears of the Family of Jesus is told in common Markan phrases and only records that the relatives of Jesus went out to apprehend Him in the belief that He was beside Himself. Similarly, the account of the Mission is told in familiar words and gains its vividness mainly from the Mission Charge. The narrative of Herod's Fears relates only popular impressions and the conviction of the tetrarch that the ministry of Jesus is the story of the Baptist all over again. The Return of the Twelve has no details which suggest a special tradition, and the Landing at Gennesaret has the appearance of a concluding summary. The Mystery of the Loaves mentions a well-remembered occasion when a failure to provision the boat prompted the warning against the leaven of the Pharisees and of Herod, and is followed by a severe rebuke which appears to have the readers in mind as much as the disciples and a distinction between two instances of miraculous feeding which it is difficult to accept as historical. The Priests' Plot merely mentions a negative decision and the Treachery of Judas little more than the fell purpose of the betrayer.

In the remaining stories brief references to the appropriate circumstances introduce sayings. The difficult saying on parables is spoken when Jesus is alone and the Twelve ask about the parables. The conversation about Elijah takes place ' as they were coming down from the mountain ' and is accompanied by a characteristically Markan charge to maintain silence. Preceded by a summary reference to a journey through Galilee, the Second Prophecy of the Passion is introduced by the simple caption, ' For he taught his disciples and said unto them '. In like manner the Third Prophecy follows a descriptive passage about the journey to Jerusalem and is preceded by the words, ' And he took again the Twelve and began to tell them the things that were to happen unto him '. The narrative about True Greatness consists of three sayings, each introduced by a brief reference to the circumstances, the third of which appears to be violently annexed from the sayings-collection drawn upon in ix. 37-50. Finally, the barest narrative elements are found in the Rebuke to the Ten, the Prophecy of the Betrayal, and the Prophecy of the Denial.

It cannot escape notice that no less than seven of these Markan constructions (Nos. 1, 3, 4, 6, 11, 12, 13) have to do with the Twelve, a fact which coheres with other indications that in Mark the tradition concerning them has become a somewhat distant memory. Cf. the note on iii. 13-19a and Note B.

It would be a hasty generalization to conclude that these narratives necessarily stand on a lower historical level than the rest of the Markan tradition. On any intelligent understanding of the Papias tradition it must be recognized that Mark is not limited to Petrine sources and, further, that the

Petrine tradition itself is not of one mould. If Mark is indebted to Peter, it is to be expected that some narratives will
stand at a short remove from his testimony, but that others
will stand at a greater remove. Any suggestion of the pupil
listening to his master note-book in hand is absurd ; but, if
he is dependent on memory, some memories will be faint.
Whether any of the Markan constructions have a Petrine
basis can neither be assumed nor ignored, but a decision,
where it is possible, will depend on an estimate of each
narrative in question.

5. SUMMARY STATEMENTS

Besides narratives, the Gospel contains a number of
summary statements (*Sammelberichte*) which describe the
activity over a period and give an outline to the course of
events. Two of the most important of these are i. 14 f., which
defines the opening of the public ministry and the theme of
the preaching of Jesus, and iii. 7-12, which describes the
external features of the ministry, the crowds, the use of the
boat, and the many sick who sought to touch Jesus and
the demoniacs who proclaimed Him as the Son of God. But
in addition to these sections (4 and 19) there are other
summary passages which introduce or conclude groups of
narratives or are attached to individual narratives : i. 21, 28,
39, 45, ii. 1 f., 13, iii. 6, iv. 1 f., 33 f., vi. 1, 6b, 7, 12 f., 30,
53, 56, vii. 1 f., 24, 31, viii. 1, 10, 22a, 27, ix. 2, 30, 33, x. 1,
32, 46, xi. 1, 11, 12, 15, 19, 20, 27, xiii. 1, 3, xiv. 1, 3, 12, 26,
32, 53, xv. 1.   C. H. Dodd, *ET*, xliii. 398 f., maintains that
a reliable account of the early ministry is provided by combining the summary passages in i. 14 f., 21 f., 39, ii. 13, iii.
7b-19, vi. 7, 12 f., 30, and claims that, in addition to materials
in pericopic form, Mark had an outline itself also traditional,
to which he attempted to work with incomplete success.
There is much to be said for this suggestion, provided it is
recognized that many geographical and temporal statements
belong to the narratives in which they appear.   References
to Capernaum, Dalmanutha, Caesarea Philippi, Jericho, and
Jerusalem are cases in point.
The use made of i. 14 f. and iii. 7-12 reveals an attempt

to introduce longer sections within the Gospel, but subsequently this endeavour breaks down and summary statements merely preface groups or describe the general progress of events in the course of journeys, especially the journey to Jerusalem.

6. THE SAYINGS AND PARABLES

The view that for this material Mark was dependent on Q has been decisively refuted by Streeter, 191. Where Markan sayings can be compared with the parallel Q version, the differences are too great to be explained by the use of a common source. Moreover, it is not easy to explain why, if Mark used Q, he made so small a use of that source, while the existence of parallel versions of sayings in the great Churches of primitive Christianity is highly probable. It is in every way likely that Mark drew upon a collection of sayings in the Church at Rome. But is ' collection ' the right word ? Was the source something more ?

At first sight the material set out in the table is bewildering in its variety. But this initial impression is largely due to the fact that the table gives the sayings in the order in which they appear in Mark. In many cases they are appended to other material : to pronouncement-stories in the cases of Nos. 1, 2, 3, 10, 13, and 16 ; and to other narratives in Nos. 11, 12, 14, and 15. If, then, this material has been taken from a collection, we do not know its original order, nor if it is derived from a single collection. In particular, it has long been held that the Apocalyptic Discourse in xiii is based on a separate document supplemented by sayings. See Note E. But closer study of Mark reveals signs of compilation. For example, iv. 21-5 has every appearance of being an ' excerpt ', or perhaps two associated ' excerpts ', from a collection. The same is true of the first four sayings in viii. 34-ix. 1, still more in the case of ix. 37-50 in which sayings are strung together by the aid of catchwords (v. Comm.), and again, in xi. 23-5, where the arrangement is

topical. Signs of a catechetical motive are manifest. A
Christian teacher has compiled groups of sayings by mnemonic
methods and on the basis of subject-matter.

Other indications point in the same direction. The
parable of the Sower has been furnished with a commentary
(iv. 13-20) and the teaching on Defilement with a list, shown
by its vocabulary to be of later date, of the things which defile
a man (vii. 21-3). Further, with some degree of exactitude,
it is possible to infer the period to which the compilation
belongs. Mark xiii. 9-13, or at least 12 f., probably reflects
the Neronic persecution (v. Comm.); and the expository
passages iv. 13-20 and vii. 21-3 would be well placed in the
same period. Equally, the themes selected in the excerpts
suit a time when Christian fidelity is challenged. Heroic
virtues are necessary (cf. viii. 24-7). A settled community
knows the problems of personal relationships among its
members (cf. iv. 18 f., ix. 37-50). Christianity has cut loose
from Judaism (cf. ii. 21 f., 27 f., vii. 27) and there is a strong
consciousness of standing on the threshold of the Parousia
(cf. viii. 38, xiii.).

These characteristics raise the question whether the term
'sayings-collection' is an adequate description of the material.
A Christian 'Vade Mecum' would be a better name. The
sayings are made serviceable for instruction. Christian
catechesis is on the way. We should, therefore, suppose that
the form and ordering of the material belong to the period
c. A.D. 65, and that the sayings have been extracted from
the Lesson Book of the Roman community.

SUMMARY

The facts set out above show the great variety of the
Markan material and how impossible it is to characterize it
in unqualified statements which treat it as if it were of one
stamp and kind. The nature of the material varies from
narratives and sayings which stand at a short remove from
the original eyewitnesses to tradition which has been shaped,
and to some extent adapted, for catechetical purposes, and
which in a measure reflects the hopes and fears of the second
generation of early Christianity. In its extent the former

is the greater and the latter has not lost touch with what was said and done in the historic ministry.   But it would be misleading to adopt Justin's phrase and describe Mark's Gospel as the Memoirs of Peter.   The Papias tradition stands, but the material warns us that it does not tell the full story.   It is probable that the Papias tradition has suffered in critical estimation from its friends more than from its enemies, and that it would be more justly esteemed if we did not stretch it on the Procrustean bed of impatient apologetics.   A clear need is revealed for a closer study of the historical value of the Gospel ; but this task must be deferred until its literary structure has been examined.

THE LITERARY STRUCTURE OF THE GOSPEL

THE many groups in which most of the narratives are found are of great interest and importance. The most obvious groups, i. 21-39, ii. 1-iii. 6, and iv. 35-v. 43, have long been observed; but there are other complexes in i. 1-13, iii. 19b-35, iv. 1-34, vi. 30-56, vii. 1-23, vii. 24-37, viii. 1-26, viii. 27-ix. 29, ix. 30-50, x. 1-31, x. 32-52, xi. 1-25, xi. 27-xii. 44, xiii. 5-37, and xiv. 1-xvi. 8. In some of these groups the material is arranged topically and in others with a narrative interest. The reason for this difference is one of the problems to be considered. It is also important to ask whether the groups are pre-Markan, and what part, if any, the Evangelist has taken in their compilation. These considerations bear closely upon the historical value and theological character of the Gospel.

THE SMALL COMPLEXES

1. *i. 1-13*

This section serves as the Introduction to the Gospel. Its basis is the association of the Preaching of John, the Baptism, and Temptation in the earliest tradition. In Mark the complex is constructed by the simplest of editorial links in 9 (' And it came to pass in those days ') and 12 (' And straightway '). No precise temporal statements are supplied and the place names belong to the individual narratives.

The section is followed by the summary passage i. 14 f. which mentions the circumstances in which Jesus began His mission and the good news He preached. The Call of the First Disciples (i. 16-20) is a self-contained narrative inserted at this point to prepare the way for i. 21-39.

2. *i. 21-39*

This group consists of the Demoniac in the Synagogue

(21-8), the Healing of Peter's Wife's Mother (29-31), Healings in the Evening (32-4), and the Departure to a Lonely Place (35-9). Closely linked together, the stories cover a period of twenty-four hours. Several features suggest that the complex is pre-Markan : the initial reference to Capernaum fixes the locality of all that follows ; the temporal and topographical links make the section a literary whole ; while i. 21 f., 28, and 39 may be editorial passages added when the Gospel was written, they can equally well belong to an original complex ; the reference to ' the door ' in 33 points back to ' the house ' mentioned in 29, and the final narrative forms the sequel to the whole. Everywhere we receive the impression of a vividly remembered whole.

There is good reason to think that the compiler was Mark himself. The vocabulary and style are his and the idea of ' the Messianic Secret ' is characteristic of the Gospel. The firm chronology of the complex cannot have been constructed by him. For this he must have been indebted to existing traditions. Otherwise, as Schmidt observes, it would have been easy for him to introduce into the group the account of the cure of the leper which appears as an isolated story in i. 40-5. Mark's practice, he holds, is not to invent topographical and chronological links for himself.[1] The complex therefore may have been the work of an earlier compiler, but, on the whole, it is best conceived as the work of Mark himself before he wrote his Gospel.

3. *ii. 1-iii. 6*

The distinctive character of this complex has long been recognized. Dibelius, 219, and Albertz, 5-16, describe it as a primitive collection of conflict-stories compiled by Mark or an earlier collector in order to show how Jesus came to His death through conflict with the Rabbis. The section consists of five pronouncement-stories : On Forgiveness (ii. 5-10a), On Eating with Taxgatherers and Sinners (ii. 15-17), On Fasting (ii. 18-20), On the Sabbath (Cornfields, ii. 23-6), On the Sabbath (The Man with the Withered Hand, iii. 1-6). Within it the Call of Levi (ii. 14) has been inserted as an introduction to ii. 15-17, and sayings from a collection in

---

[1] *Der Rahmen der Geschichte Jesu*, 67 f. ; Dibelius, 42, 219.

ii. 21 f. and 27 f. At the beginning (ii. 1-4, 10b-12) and the end (iii. 1-5) Petrine tradition appears to have been used. The arrangement is topical and, apart from ii. 13, there are no connecting-links between the narratives.

In the complex there is a steady mounting of the opposition from the silent criticism of ii. 6, the question to the disciples in ii. 16, the challenge to Jesus in ii. 18 and 24, the hostile watching in iii. 2, to the climax in the death-plot between the Pharisees and the Herodians in iii. 6. This arrangement is artificial, since, as J. Weiss, 154, observes, the charge of blasphemy is the weightiest indictment, and, relatively speaking, the last controversy is the lightest. Nevertheless, for catechetical purposes, the complex is skilfully arranged.

Albertz, 5, denies that the collection was made by Mark on four grounds : iii. 6 comes too early in the Markan plan ; the term ' Son of Man ' lacks the eschatological meaning which it bears from viii. 31 onwards ; the use of the further conflict-story in iii. 22-6 is strange after iii. 6 ; the allusion to the death of Jesus in ii. 20 does not harmonize with Mark's intention in viii. 31. These arguments strongly suggest that the complex is pre-Markan ; but they do not exclude the possibility that the compiler was Mark. The objection that the complex has not been adapted to suit the outline of the Gospel exists even if it is the work of a predecessor, but it is less cogent if Mark is the author. The use of sources often causes obscurities in a later narrative, and perhaps to a greater degree when an author is copying himself. With some confidence we may conclude that Mark compiled ii. 1-iii. 6 before he wrote his Gospel.[1] In this case, the interpreter of Peter was probably a teacher in the Roman community.

4. *iii. 19b-35*

Again the section is topical. A brief story in which Jesus is said to be beside Himself (19b-21) precedes a second in which He is accused of possession by Beelzebul and collusion with Satan (22-6). This story is followed by the sayings concerning the binding of the Strong Man and blasphemy

[1] Cf. Dibelius, 219.

against the Holy Spirit (27-30), and finally, in line with
19b-21, the narrative about the true kindred of Jesus (31-5)
is loosely appended.　There are no connecting-links in the
complex and the subject-matter is the same throughout.
The intention is to describe the charges to which Jesus was
exposed and the manner in which He met them.　The complex
met a need which must have been felt in the oral period and
which at that time could well be supplied.　An occasion for
its insertion in the Gospel was offered at iii. 10-12 by the
reference to the unclean spirits which fell down before Jesus
and hailed Him as the Son of God.　But we account best for
its presence in Mark if it had a previous existence, for its
insertion accounts for the anticlimax which arises after the
death plot in iii. 6.　Mark is not writing freely, but is using
another group of conflict-stories which he desires to preserve
intact.

There is good reason to think that, while topical, the
complex is not artificially constructed.　Manson, *SJ*, 85,
points out that Mark iii. 31-5 and Luke xi. 27 f. (' Blessed
is the womb that bare thee ') occupy the same relative positions at the end of a series of sayings on daemon possession,
and that both have a common sentiment, the doing of the
will of God.[1]　' This suggests the possibility that Mark iii.
20-35 was already a closed section before it was incorporated
in the Gospel ; and that Luke xi. 17-28 is a similar complete
section.'

5. *iv. 1-34*

Here again the arrangement is topical.　The series includes the Parable of the Sower (3-9), a saying on the purpose
of parables (11 f.), an explanation of the Sower (13-20), a
group of sayings (21-5), the Parable of the Seed Growing
Secretly (26-9), the Parable of the Mustard Seed (30-2), and a
statement on the use of parables (33 f.).　The grouping cannot
be primitive, and it is not surprising that various parts have
been held to be insertions : 10-12 by Wellhausen, 31 ; 10-20
by Klostermann, 45 ; 10-25 by J. Weiss, *Die Schr.*[4] 109-14.
It is possible that the three parables, with the explanation

[1] Cf. Mark iii. 35, ' Whosoever shall　28, ' Blessed are they that hear the
do the will of God . . .', and Luke xi.　word of God, and keep it '.

of the Sower, stood together in his sayings-source, and that Mark added 10-12 and 21-5 in the belief that these sayings were relevant to the meaning of parables.

But a further possibility is open. There is much to be said for the view that Mark inserted into the historical outline, visible in iii. 7-12 + iv. 1-9, 33 f. + iv. 35-v. 43, the material in iv. 10-32 from his sayings-source, together with iii. 13-19a (the Appointment of the Twelve) and the group iii. 19b-35 (*v. supra*). In this way we can explain why the boat mentioned in iii. 9, and used in iv. 1 f., is lost in iv. 10-34, to reappear suddenly in iv. 35 for the purpose of crossing the lake. A further point of interest is that iv. 1-34, though topical, like ii. 1-iii. 6 begins with a narrative element, thus suggesting a combined use of tradition and catechetical material.

6. *iv. 35-v. 43*

This complex consists of four narratives : the Storm on the Lake, the Gerasene Demoniac, the Raising of the Daughter of Jairus, and the Cure of the Woman with the Issue of Blood. Unlike the last three groups, but precisely as in i. 21-39, a narrative interest binds the whole together. Connecting links in iv. 35, v. 1, 21, the vivid character of the narratives, and the interweaving of the third and fourth, suggest that Mark is recording the incidents of a journey as he had been wont to hear of it from an eyewitness, presumably Peter (cf. v. 37). Nevertheless, it is strange that four miracle-stories should follow in immediate succession within a period of twenty-four hours. It is possible that the temporal succession is foreshortened, and that, despite the connecting-links, there are gaps before v. 1 and 21.[1] If so, the section is a historical series with a secondary topical interest, and in this manner it may have been current from the first.

The fuller story is a matter for conjecture. Apparently, it was during the late afternoon that Jesus crossed the lake, and soon after the storm night must have fallen.[2] It is not likely that the stay among the Gerasenes was only a matter

---

[1] Cf. Schmidt, 135-52.
[2] Lagrange suggests that the dis-   ciples may have spent the night in   fishing, landing the following morning.

of hours. The demoniac knew something of Jesus before he ran shrieking to meet him and the later events must have covered an appreciable interval of time. Further, the meeting with Jairus may not have happened immediately after the recrossing of the lake or necessarily at the place of landing. The complex is not discredited if a more varied series of events is telescoped, for this may happen even in the report of an eyewitness. Apart altogether from the question whether a miraculous interpretation is given to the stilling of the storm and the raising of the maid, there is good reason to trace iv. 35-v. 43 to the recollections of Peter.

7. *vi. 30-56*

Before this group there are three isolated stories: the Rejection at Nazareth (vi. 1-6a), the Mission Charge to the Twelve (vi. 6b-13), and Herod's Fears (vi. 14-16); and, as a pendant to the third, the account of the Death of the Baptist (vi. 17-29). These narratives do not form a complex, for there are no connecting-links and there is no common theme.

In contrast, vi. 30-56, which records the Feeding of the Five Thousand (35-44), the Crossing (45-52), and the Landing at Gennesaret (53-6), is a compact whole, to which Mark provides an introduction in the story of the Return of the Disciples (30-4), which points back to the Mission Charge (6b-13). Since vii. 1-23 is a topical complex (*v. infra*), the question arises whether vii. 24-37 is not a continuation of vi. 30-56, and a further issue, often debated, is whether vi. 30-vii. 37 and viii. 1-26 form a doublet.[1] Meantime, it is of advantage to examine vi. 30-56, vii. 1-23, and viii. 1-26 separately, since the first is historical in form, the second topical, and the third didactic.

In vi. 30-56, the story of the Feeding is vaguely connected with ' a wilderness place ' (31 and 35), but is closely articulated with the Crossing by the reference to the constraint which Jesus puts upon His disciples and to Bethsaida (45). The crossing is linked to its sequel by the words : ' And when they had crossed over, they came to the land unto Gennesaret, and moored to the shore ' (53). Here again we have the same

---

[1] This last question is treated in Note C.

historical continuity as in i. 21-39 and iv. 35-v. 43, in strong contrast with the topical sections, ii. 1-iii. 6, iii. 19b-35, iv. 1-34, and vii. 1-23.

8. *vii. 1-23*

The complex is topical. It consists of two pronouncement-stories, On the Washing of Hands (5-8) and On Qorban (9-13), and three groups of sayings on defilement (14 f., 17-19, 20-3), and is preceded by a brief narrative introduction (1 f.) and an explanation of the Jewish customs concerning cere-monial washings (3 f.). The remaining narrative elements are the editorial links in 9, 14, and 20. The complex appears to have been compiled for purposes of Christian instruction. Two additional features point in this direction — the com-ment in 19, ' making all meats clean ', and the list of sins in 21-3 expressed in the vocabulary of the Epistles.[1] The motive for the insertion of the complex at this point appears to be the desire to provide an introduction for vii. 24-37 and viii. 1-26, which are conceived by Mark as suggesting a Gentile ministry. On the whole, it is probable that he has used an existing complex for this purpose composed before the Gospel was written. It deals with a burning issue between Judaism and early Christianity and its teaching must have been con-genial to Mark's mind. The greatest importance must have been attached to the saying : ' There is nothing from without the man, that going into him can defile him ; but the things which proceed out of the man are those that defile the man ' (15). The question had far more than an academic interest, for the answer given to it decided the issue whether Christianity was capable of becoming a world religion.

9. *vii. 24-37*

As already suggested, this section may be a continua-tion of vi. 30-56. It describes the withdrawal of Jesus across the border of Galilee into the region of Tyre (24), the in-cident of the Syro-Phoenician Woman (25-30), the journey to Decapolis (31), and the Cure of the Deaf Mute (32-7). The geographical statements are detailed though obscure and the narratives are vivid. Personal testimony must be re-

[1] *V.* Comm. *in loc.*

sponsible for them, but at what remove we cannot tell. The
section resembles i. 21-39, iv. 35-v. 43, and vi. 30-56.

10. *viii. 1-26*

This group includes the Feeding of the Four Thousand
and the Crossing to Dalmanutha (1-10), the Demand for a
Sign (11-13), the Mystery of the Loaves (14-21), and the Cure
of the Blind Man (22-6). Introduced by the vague phrase
' In those days ', the complex makes precise references to
Dalmanutha and to Bethsaida. The contention of Schmidt,[1]
that Mark must have found these names in the tradition, is
sound, for otherwise we cannot explain why place-names are
so rare in Mark. The first three stories lack the vividness of
the fourth, but all are based ultimately on historical tradition.

While, however, the basis of the complex is historical,
liturgical and didactic interests have influenced its formation.
It is difficult not to think that the compiler has in mind a
community, like the Church at Corinth, which had failed to
understand the significance of the Eucharist. In these
circumstances he tells the story of the Feeding of the Four
Thousand and the events that followed. While, of old, no
sign had been given to the Pharisees, the disciples had received the sign of the loaves, which pointed forward to the
Eucharist. Preoccupied with material cares, they had not
understood the sign, and to them had been addressed the
reproachful question, ' Do ye not yet understand ? '. But, as
in the days of His flesh, Jesus was still the Giver of Light.
Not once, but twice, had He laid His hands on a blind man
near Bethsaida who at first saw men only as trees walking,
but in the end was restored and saw all things clearly. So
it had been with the disciples ; so it would be again.

Such appears to be the situation to which the complex
belongs. Catechesis is older than the Gospels and a catechetical interest accounts for the form and order of the
narratives. It explains the very severe form of the refusal
to give a sign to the Pharisees,[2] the over-emphasis upon the
disciples' stupidity, and the use of the Cure of the Blind Man
with its distinctive features. Loisy was mistaken in explaining
this narrative as a symbolic picture of the education of the

---

[1] *Op. cit.* 182 f., 207.   [2] As compared with Luke xi. 29.

disciples, but he rightly divined its catechetical value for the compiler. Probably the complex already existed before the Gospel was written, and the vocabulary, style, and ideas [1] suggest that the compiler was Mark.

11. *viii. 27-ix. 29*

This group reflects both narrative and topical interests. It is a combination of vivid narratives and sayings : the Confession of Peter and the First Prophecy of the Passion (27-33), Sayings on Crossbearing, Sacrifice, and the Kingdom (viii. 34-ix. 1), the Transfiguration (ix. 2-8), the Conversation during the Descent (9-13), and the Cure of the Epileptic Lad (14-29). The first narrative, connected with ' the villages of Caesarea Philippi ', is composite : the confession of Peter and the strong rebuke addressed to him are linked together by a prophecy of Messianic suffering, and sayings are loosely appended by the editorial passage, ' And he called unto him the multitude with his disciples, and said unto them ' (viii. 34a). The last saying (ix. 1) prepares the way for the story of the Transfiguration ' after six days ', the conversation takes place ' as they were coming down from the mountain ' (ix. 9), and the story of the Epileptic Lad is introduced by the statement, ' And when they came to the disciples, they saw a great multitude about them, and scribes questioning with them ' (ix. 14). In some respects the group differs from i. 21-39, iv. 35-v. 43, and vi. 30-56 in that we have to allow for Mark's editorial activity as well as his use of a traditional series of events. He may be using an existing complex but, as it stands, the group owes its form to the process of Gospel compilation.

12. *ix. 30-50*

In ix. 30-50 Mark has introduced material derived from his sayings-source by the Second Prophecy of the Passion (30-2) and the composite narrative on True Greatness (33-7). The first narrative is prefaced by the statement : ' And they went forth from thence, and passed through Galilee ; and he would not that any man should know it ' (30), and the second by the words : ' And they came to Capernaum ' (33).

[1] Cf. viii. 26.

Since Mark does not introduce such statements arbitrarily, it is fair to assume that he drew them from information at his disposal. But it is also clear that he had very little detailed knowledge concerning this journey.

We have already classified 33-7 as a ' Markan construction ', since it consists of fragments of tradition awkwardly assembled. Probably 37 was taken from the long excerpt from the sayings-source, in which the pronouncement-story On Helpers who are not Disciples (38 f.) was also embedded, and possibly other parts of 33-7 were derived from the same source. In any case, there are clear signs that Mark, or a predecessor, has given narrative form to an existing group of sayings. The same features present themselves as in iv. 1-34, and in the collection of pronouncement-stories in ii. 1-iii. 6, namely, sayings-material topically arranged, with a narrative element at the beginning.

13. *x. 1-31*

Like the last section, this complex begins with a topographical statement : ' And he arose from thence, and cometh into the borders of Judaea and beyond Jordan '. A reference to multitudes and teaching introduces two pronouncement-stories : On Divorce (2-9), with kindred sayings attached (10-12), and On Children (13-16), with a similar saying inserted (15). Then follows the Rich Man's Question (17-22), with its two pendants, the Conversation on Riches (23-7) and the Question of Rewards (28-31). The narrative elements are the statement that Jesus met the rich man ' as he was going forth into the way ' (17), the reference to the look of Jesus (23), and the remark that it was Peter who began to say, ' Lo, we have left all, and have followed thee ' (28). Thus, teaching on allied themes, marriage, children, and wealth, is given a narrative framework. Mark may be the compiler, but he may be using a traditional series used in Christian teaching. Again, as in ix. 30-50, he has no detailed information about the journey. The narrative frame is editorial, but apparently fragments of historical tradition still clung to the catechetical series. The process of compilation is not mere guesswork ; otherwise the two pronouncement-stories would not have been left bare. The presumption is that Mark is using scanty information and refrains from creating a more detailed record.

14. *x. 32-52*

The same characteristics appear in x. 32-52. The brief opening statement says that ' they were in the way going up to Jerusalem ', and is followed by the reference to amazement and awe, when Jesus takes the lead, as if the disciples felt the situation to be uncanny. Then follow the Third Prophecy of the Passion (32b-4), the Request of James and John (35-40), to which the Rebuke of the Ten is attached (41-5), and, finally, the story of the Cure of Bartimaeus (46-52), which is expressly connected with Jericho (46). A doctrinal interest marks the complex, reaching its climax in 45, but how little this interest is in sole control is seen by the addition of the story of the blind man, which has no justification for its presence save that it happened at Jericho and records a Messianic cry. The only sign of an earlier catechetical use of the material is in the teaching on true greatness in the Rebuke of the Ten. Mark has composed his account on the basis of the information at his command with the heightened consciousness that the shadow of the cross is drawing nearer.

15. *xi. 1-25*

The section consists of two stories about Jesus, the Entry into Jerusalem (1-11) and the Cleansing of the Temple (15-19), a miracle-story, the Cursing of the Fig Tree (12-14, 20-2), and an excerpt from the sayings-source on faith and prayer (23-5). An unwonted precision distinguishes the complex. The events described fall into a three-day period. Successively, we are told what happened ' on the morrow ' (12), ' when evening came ' (19), and ' in the morning ' (20). Apparently, an attempt has been made to set xi. 1-xiii. 37 in a chronological frame, along with the Passion Narrative, xiv. 1-xvi. 8, in order to obtain a day to day account of the events of the last tragic week. If this view is sound, xi. 1-25 differs from i. 21-39, iv. 35-v. 43, and vi. 30-56 + vii. 24-37, and the presumption is that Mark, who otherwise does not use editorial devices, has followed an arrangement already current in the Church at Rome.

16. *xi. 27-xii. 44*

Albertz [1] has given good reasons for the view that this section is based on a pre-Markan complex, xi. 15-17 + 27-33 + xii. 13-40, comparable to ii. 1-iii. 6, which included the Cleansing and the five pronouncement-stories, On Authority, On Tribute to Caesar, On the Resurrection, On the First Commandment, and On David's Son, and a small group of sayings on the scribes (xii. 38-40). With scarcely any connecting-links,[2] the narratives are arranged topically, in order to illustrate the conflicts of Jesus with the scribes, and it is very probable that some of the incidents belong to earlier periods in the ministry of Jesus. Mark has enlarged the group by inserting in it the Parable of the Wicked Husbandmen (xii. 1-12) and adding the story of the widow's almsgiving (xii. 41-4). As in ii. 1-iii. 6, the vocabulary and style suggest that Mark himself is the compiler. In this case, there is again reason to infer that, previous to the composition of the Gospel, he had combined episodes from the life of Jesus for catechetical purposes.

17. *xiii. 5-37*

The foundation of the discourse may be an apocalyptic prophecy concerning the Parousia in 5-8 + 24-7, but for the most part, and perhaps wholly, the material has been drawn from the sayings-source. Its contents, and the fact that it unduly crowds the third day referred to in xi. 20, suggest that it had an earlier existence and was composed shortly before the Gospel. See Note E.

18. *xiv. 1-xvi. 8*

In Note J it is maintained that in the pre-Gospel period the Passion Narrative was preceded by a shorter version which later was supplemented by Mark by Petrine traditions.

SUMMARY

It will be seen that the groups differ considerably in character. At least three types may be distinguished, all of which, in different ways, bear upon the question of the composition of the Gospel.

---

[1] *Die synoptischen Streitgespräche*, 16-36.   [2] Cf. xii. 28, 35, 38.

Groups of Narratives and Sayings formed on the Basis of Existing Tradition

The Introduction i. 1-13 (No. 1) and the four groups in ix. 30-xi. 25 (Nos. 12-15) are of this character, and the presumption is that they were formed in the process of writing the Gospel. Even so, they point to primitive groupings of material in the oral period. Thus, it was customary to think of the Gospel Story as beginning with the Preaching of John (cf. Acts i. 22, x. 37), and with this theme the Baptism and Temptation of Jesus were connected. More characteristic of the groups in question are ix. 30-50 (No. 12), in which sayings-material is given a narrative setting, x. 1-31 (No. 13), in which themes associated in Christian teaching (marriage, children, wealth) appear in a narrative frame, x. 32-52 (No. 14), which suggests a combination of historical and doctrinal interests, and xi. 1-25 (No. 15), which appears to represent an earlier attempt to give a temporal framework to the events leading to the Passion. Perhaps viii. 27-ix. 29 (No. 11) should be classified in this group, but on the whole there is more reason to include it in the next group where Petrine narratives appear in complexes.

Groups of Narratives based on Personal Testimony, probably that of Peter

To this class belong i. 21-39 (No. 2), iv. 35-v. 43 (No. 6), vi. 30-56 (No. 7), vii. 24-37 (No. 9), and viii. 27-ix. 29 (No. 11). These are all groups of vividly told narratives linked together by temporal and topographical statements. It is possible that some of them may have been committed to writing by Mark before he wrote the Gospel. In this case, when writing his Gospel, he copied himself. In any case, the groups were first oral cycles of tradition for which he was indebted to the recollections of an eyewitness. In its present form the Passion Narrative, xiv. 1-xvi. 8 (No. 18) is of the same type. See Note J. The structure of viii. 1-26 (No. 10) is similar to that of the other groups, but its didactic character, and the probability that it is in some sense a doublet of vi. 30-vii. 37, suggest that its connexion with Petrine testimony is more remote.

*Groups of Narratives topically arranged consisting of Sayings
   and Pronouncement-stories*

These include ii. 1-iii. 6 (No. 3), iii. 19b-35 (No. 4), iv.
1-34 (No. 5), vii. 1-23 (No. 8), xi. 27-xii. 44 (No. 16), and
xiii. 1-37 (No 17). The distinguishing feature of these groups
is the kind of tradition they contain and the want of connecting-links between the several narratives. Essentially
they belong to the sayings-tradition. Obvious as this fact is
in the case of the sayings and parables, it is no less true of
the narratives which are told for the sake of a significant
saying of Jesus to which all else is subordinated. It is not
to be denied that ultimately these narratives go back to the
tradition of eyewitnesses. Indeed, significantly enough, at
the beginning and end of ii. 1-iii. 6, and at the beginning of
iv. 1-34, there is a narrative element which suggests that Mark
has historical information at his disposal additional to that
supplied by the sayings-tradition. But the groups themselves
are manifestly of another order and origin than i. 21-39,
iv. 35-v. 43, and other complexes of the kind previously
listed. They consist of narratives in which the dominating
interest is a word of Jesus, and the groups are compiled, not
to describe a series of events, but to make known His mind
on issues of vital importance to the Christian community.
Hence, the want of vivid details, temporal statements, and
place-names. Sometimes the interest is purely topical as in
iv. 1-34, vii. 1-23, and xiii. 1-37. At other times there is a
secondary historical interest as when ii. 1-iii. 6 and xi. 27-
xii. 44 describe the conflicts of Jesus with the scribes and the
Jewish hierarchy, or when iii. 19b-35 reveals the kind of
charges to which Jesus was exposed. But the main concern
is what Jesus taught. Thus, these groups have a longer
history than the Petrine cycles; they have been compiled
earlier to meet the needs of the Christian society either by
Mark himself or a predecessor. In either case when Mark
took up his pen the groups were fixed cycles of oral tradition.

If the classification attempted above is relatively sound,
it has a most important bearing upon the composition of the
Gospel. As through a glass darkly, we can see the Evangelist
at work and in the background many others to whom he is

debtor. His equipment consisted of far more than a notebook and retentive memory. Behind him lay the teaching activity of a living Church. In it he had shared and upon it he was dependent. We may say more, for teaching is based on reflection and reflection on testimony. Mark's predecessors were not only teachers, but also preachers and evangelists, men who had received, reflected upon, and proclaimed the good news of the Kingdom of God. His Gospel is far more than a private undertaking ; it is a product of the life of the Church inspired by the Spirit of God.

X

THE PLAN AND ARRANGEMENT OF THE GOSPEL

IN writing his Gospel the Evangelist has used the complexes which have been examined, together with isolated narratives and summary statements, to form the larger divisions of his work. This aim has been attempted, but has not been completely fulfilled; for the Gospel is not a carefully planned literary composition, but a popular writing conditioned by the state of the existing tradition and by the fact that the Gospel was a new undertaking. In emphasizing the non-literary character of the Gospel, some scholars have not sufficiently appreciated the limitations imposed on the Evangelist by the earlier groupings of Gospel material. Anxious to retain the pre-Markan complexes unbroken, especially if some of them were his own compositions, the Evangelist was not in a position to write freely, disposing of his material at will and in accordance with a pre-arranged plan of his own. He could develop the broad outlines of his Story, in line with his knowledge of the course of events, but he was constrained to find room for existing short collections of episodes and catechetical material familiar to himself and his readers. If we have regard to these circumstances we shall be saved from the danger of acquiescing in some of the cavalier estimates which have been expressed regarding the nature and merits of his work. Although the Gospel does not conform to the model of the ancient biography, and can only be compared to its disadvantage with such works as the *Memorabilia* of Xenophon and the *Vita Apollonii* of Philostratus, it is something more than one of the popular cult-books of primitive Christianity.[1] It is, as i. 1 shows, an attempt to tell how the Good News concerning Jesus Christ, the Son of God, began, and thus to serve historical as well as religious ends.

[1] The term used by the Form Critics is *kultische Volksbücher*. Cf. K. L. Schmidt, *Die Stellung der Evangelien in der allgemeinen Literatur-geschichte, Eucharisterion*, ii. 50-134; Bultmann, 398 f.; Dibelius, 39 f.; Fascher, 228-31.

THE LARGER DIVISIONS

The Gospel begins with a short introduction in i. 1-13, which tells the stories of the Preaching of John the Baptist, the Baptism, and the Temptation of Jesus, as preparatory to the account of the Galilean Ministry.

Two major divisions relate the story of the Ministry. The first begins with the summary statement of i. 14 f., which tells how Jesus came into Galilee, preaching the gospel of God, after the delivering up of John, and summarizes the substance of His message. This division reaches its climax in the account of the hostile counsel of the Pharisees and the Herodians mentioned in iii. 6. The second division begins with the summary statement of iii. 7-12. Where this division ends is not easy to decide. Every possible answer has been given : iv. 34, v. 43, vi. 6, vi. 13, vii. 23, viii. 26, ix. 50. This variety of opinion suggests that the Evangelist's intentions cannot be determined with certainty ; and, in consequence, the limits of the division must be fixed by considerations of geography and the progress of the Story. From this stand-point, as K. L. Schmidt suggests,[1] there is most to be said for vi. 13. The Galilean Ministry has reached its climax with the rejection at Nazareth and the mission of the Twelve. The two stories which follow, Herod's Fears (vi. 14-16) and the Death of John (vi. 17-29), form a kind of interlude leading to the fourth division.

After iii. 7-12 there are no comparable summary statements introducing a division, but there are passages which introduce a new stage in the course of events, namely, viii. 27, xi. 1, and xiv. 1. These passages may be held to mark divisions. The fourth division, beginning at vi. 14, extends to viii. 26, and is mainly concerned with the ministry outside Galilee. The fifth division, viii. 27-x. 52, describes the journey to Jerusalem, and the sixth, xi. 1-xiii. 37, the ministry in Jerusalem. The final division, xiv. 1-xvi. 8, contains the Passion and Resurrection Narrative. To this climax the whole Gospel moves.[2]

---

[1] *Der Rahmen der Geschichte Jesu*, 171 f.

[2] Bultmann, 396, quotes the saying of M. Kähler, that the Gospels may be called Passion Stories with a circumstantial introduction, *Der sog. histor.* *Jesus*, 80, and the remark of A. Schlatter, that for every Evangelist the Gospel was the account of the progress of Jesus to the Cross, *Der Glaube im NT*[4], 477.

THE PLAN AND ARRANGEMENT OF THE GOSPEL

I. INTRODUCTION. i. 1-13.

(1)	John the Baptizer.	i. 1-8.
(2)	The Baptism of Jesus.	i. 9-11.
(3)	The Temptation.	i. 12 f.

II. THE GALILEAN MINISTRY. i. 14-iii. 6.

(4)	Opening Summary Statement.	i. 14 f.
(5)	The Call of the First Disciples.	i. 16-20.

(a) *The Ministry at Capernaum.* *i. 21-39*

(6)	The Demoniac in the Synagogue.	i. 21-8.
(7)	The Healing of Peter's Wife's Mother.	i. 29-31.
(8)	Healings in the Evening.	i. 32-4.
(9)	The Departure to a Lonely Place.	i. 35-9.

(10)	The Cure of a Leper.	i. 40-5.

(b) *Conflicts with the Scribes.* *ii. 1-iii. 6*

(11)	The Paralytic and Forgiveness.	ii. 1-12.
(12)	The Call of Levi.	ii. 13 f.
(13)	On Eating with Taxgatherers and Sinners.	ii. 15-17.
(14)	On Fasting.	ii. 18-20.
(15)	Sayings on Patches and Wineskins.	ii. 21 f.
(16)	On the Sabbath (Cornfields).	ii. 23-6.
(17)	Sayings on the Sabbath.	ii. 27 f.
(18)	On the Sabbath (Man with Withered Hand).	iii. 1-6.

III. THE HEIGHT OF THE GALILEAN MINISTRY. iii. 7-vi. 13

(19)	Summary Statement: Crowds by the Lake.	iii. 7-12.
(20)	The Appointment of the Twelve.	iii. 13-19a.

(a) *Charges brought against Jesus.* *iii. 19b-35*

(21)	The Fears of the Family of Jesus.	iii. 19b-21.
(22)	On Collusion with Satan.	iii. 22-6.
(23)	Sayings on the Strong Man and on Blasphemy.	iii. 27-30.
(24)	On the True Kindred of Jesus.	iii. 31-5.

(b) *Parabolic Teaching.* *iv. 1-34*

(25)	The Parable of the Sower.	iv. 1-9.
(26)	The Purpose of Parables.	iv. 10-12.

(c) *The Resurrection. xvi. 1-8 (9-20)*

(106) The Visit of the Women to the xvi. 1-8.
Empty Tomb.
(The Appearance to Mary Magda- (xvi. 9-11.)
lene.)
(The Appearance to Two Travellers.) (xvi. 12 f.)
(The Appearance to the Eleven.)　　(xvi. 14-18.)
(The Ascension and the Session on (xvi. 19 f.)
High.)

The table printed above illustrates the place of the smaller complexes already discussed within the larger divisions of the Gospel.

The plan reveals the scanty character of the tradition contained in the groups i. 1-13, ix. 30-50, x. 1-31, x. 32-52, and xi. 1-25. Many of the several narratives contained in these sections belong to the best tradition, but of the course of events Mark's knowledge is manifestly fragmentary. For his Introduction (i. 1-13) he wrote what everyone knew, although, as the Commentary will show, his account bears the impress of his ideas and beliefs. For the long journey to Jerusalem from Caesarea Philippi (ix. 30-x. 52) he had little precise information at his command beyond that which might be inferred from single narratives. The same also must be said of the Jerusalem ministry, which was of much longer duration than his account would lead us to suppose. Here apparently he was handicapped by earlier but unsatisfactory attempts to set in a chronological frame the events leading to the Passion (xi. 1-25).

In contrast with these sections the continuous narrative complexes in i. 21-39, iv. 35-v. 43, vi. 30-56, vii. 24-37, and viii. 27-ix. 29, in the construction of which Mark had the advantage of fuller information, stand out from the rest. How far this estimate is justified will depend on the closer study of the sections, but even from the table it is apparent how much they contribute to the outline of the Gospel. The same impression is left by the summary of the contents of the Passion Narrative. Here beyond question special knowledge is at Mark's disposal. The contrast between these complexes and those in ix. 30-xi. 25 (*v. supra*) gives point to this conclusion.

Lastly, the table gives visual support to the view that

ii. 1-iii. 6, iii. 19b-35, iv. 1-34, vii. 1-23, xi. 27-xii. 44 are pre-Markan collections of discourse material. It can be seen at a glance how these complexes halt, interrupt, or break the course of events, and in some cases (e.g. vii. 1-23) anticipate what follows. Invaluable in itself, iii. 19b-35 creates a literary anticlimax after ii. 1-iii. 6, and this section, so far as iii. 6 is concerned, appears too early in the outline. Mark iv. 1-34 is manifestly overloaded with kindred material; vii. 1-23 severs vi. 30-56 from its natural sequel in vii. 24-37; had xi. 27-xii. 44 been disintegrated some of its narratives could readily and with advantage have been placed in the Galilean period; while xiii. 1-37, with its abundance of sayings and parables, crowds the stage. A more gifted writer would have arranged things differently, as the later Evangelists have done, possibly to the advantage of the general reader, but certainly to the loss of the student and the historian. In the sections under review the arrangement of the material is best understood if it is seen that Mark is preserving, more or less intact, didactic complexes already familiar to his first readers.

MARK'S METHODS

Mark's methods as a writer throw light upon the importance of his Gospel. Among the conclusions which can be drawn from the investigations of the preceding chapters the following may be mentioned.

(1) First, it is apparent that, when Mark takes over an isolated story from the tradition, he is content to leave it almost as he finds it. He finds a place for it in his outline, but uses the simplest of editorial links, and sometimes none at all. This usage can be observed in i. 16-20, i. 40-5, iii. 13-19a, vi. 1-6a, vi. 6b-13, vi. 14-16, and vi. 17-29.

(2) Secondly, he leaves previously existing complexes almost intact. In consequence, it is possible for the modern student to appreciate the conditions which obtained in the oral period and to learn much about the life of the primitive Christian communities.

(3) Thirdly, he rarely comments upon his material, but allows it to speak for itself. The exceptions are vii. 3 f. and 19b. This fact justifies caution in estimating the elements

often traced to his editorial activity, e.g. his treatment of the idea of the ' Messianic Secret '.[1]

(4) Fourthly, Mark does not attempt to impose a narrative form on the topical complexes already in existence in the tradition. In this respect he differs completely from Matthew, and the explanation must be found in himself and in the fact that primitive groups of sayings-tradition had a certain standing derived from their use in teaching.

(5) When Mark finds doublets in the tradition, he uses both elements, instead of selecting one or conflating the two. The two Feeding stories illustrate this tendency, if criticism is right in regarding them as a doublet. He uses both because one is familiar to him through oral tradition and the other through catechetical teaching, though doubtless he believes that two incidents are described.

If the qualities mentioned above are negative, they are none the less virtues. Historical knowledge owes a great deal to Mark's restraint.

A positive appreciation of Mark's qualities as a writer depends on a detailed examination of his work. His selection of material is influenced by his interest in exorcisms, crowds, and miraculous events, in the Gentile Mission of his day, in contemporary apocalyptic, and, above all, in the redemptive work and mission of Jesus. Many of these interests he shared with the Church of his day. It is necessary, therefore, to examine the theology of his Gospel and the degree to which he is faithful to historical tradition.

[1] See pp. 122-4.

XI

THE THEOLOGY OF THE GOSPEL

IT will be useful to consider the theology of the Gospel
before treating its historical value, inasmuch as, in modern
discussions, the Evangelist's theology is held to condition his
writing. It is not necessary to examine the theology of all
the Gospel material, but only its distinctive features and the
special interests of Mark. The points for inquiry are the
Kingdom of God as Mark understands it, his eschatology,
his christology, particularly as it is revealed by the names and
titles of Jesus which he uses, his soteriology, and the doctrines
which he shares with Paul.

THE KINGDOM OF GOD

The basic idea of the βασιλεία τοῦ θεοῦ is that of the ' Rule '
or ' Reign ' of God, corresponding to the Aramaic *malkuth*,
' kingship ', ' kingly rule ', ' reign ', ' sovereignty '. Recent
discussion [1] has strongly emphasized the idea of the Kingly
Rule of God, and with good reason. But while the Rule of
God is the primary idea, that of a domain [2] or community is
also necessarily implied (cf. ix. 47).

Jesus spoke of the *Basileia* as future (xiv. 25, Luke xi.
2, etc.), but also as present in Himself and in His ministry
(cf. Luke vii. 18-23, x. 23 f., xi. 20, 31 f.). In a true sense,
therefore, He taught a ' realized eschatology ',[3] and is Himself
αὐτοβασιλεία.[4] It may be doubted, however, if these very
distinctive ideas find clear expression in Mark, for in this
Gospel the main emphasis lies upon the Kingdom as future

---

[1] Cf. G. Gloege, *Reich Gottes und
Kirche*, 49-54; T. W. Manson, *TJ*, 116-
284; R. Otto, *The Kingdom of God and
the Son of Man*, 72-93; K. L. Schmidt,
Art. βασιλεία, *KThW*, i. 579-92, *Theology*, May, 1927; R. N. Flew, *The Idea
of Perfection*, 8-40, *Jesus and His
Church*, 27-47; C. H. Dodd, *The
Parables of the Kingdom*, 34-80.

[2] Cf. Flew, *Jesus and His Church*,
34.

[3] Cf. Dodd, *op. cit.* 51.

[4] Cf. Schmidt, *op. cit.* i. 591. This
may also be suggested by the concurrence of ἔρχεσθαι πρός με and ἡ βασιλεία
τοῦ θεοῦ in x. 14, and of ἕνεκεν ἐμοῦ
and ἕνεκεν τοῦ εὐαγγελίου in x. 29.

and, indeed, imminent, and as the community in which God's will is done.

The thought of the imminence of the Kingdom appears in i. 15 and ix. 1. In the former (*v.* Comm.) Jesus announces that the Kingdom is ' at hand '; in the latter He declares that some of His hearers will live to see it come. In the parables of the Sower (iv. 3-9), the Seed Growing Secretly (iv. 26-9), and the Mustard Seed (iv. 30-2), the Kingdom is present in the situation in which Jesus finds Himself, as Professor Dodd maintains, and the same conception is implicit in the words spoken to the scribe : ' Thou art not far from the kingdom of God ' (xii. 34). It is uncertain, however, how far Mark had entered into this conception. From the sayings in Mark we should gather rather the impression that he thinks of the Kingdom mainly eschatologically, as a community shortly to be established by God. The saying about receiving the Kingdom ' as a little child ' (x. 15) suggests the idea of a divine gift which a man can receive here and now, but those which speak of *entering into* the Kingdom (ix. 47, x. 15b, 23 f.) can have either a present or a future meaning, but probably the latter in Mark's estimation, especially in ix. 47 where there is a contrast with βληθῆναι εἰς τὴν γέενναν. In these sayings the thought of a domain is also implied, the realm in which God's sovereignty prevails. The reference to drinking new wine in the *Basileia* (xiv. 25) and the description of Joseph as looking for it (xv. 43) are manifestly eschatological ; they point forward to a time when God's will is perfectly fulfilled. On the whole, then, we must say that Mark's view of the Kingdom is eschatological, and that he does not record, and perhaps has not assimilated, the more distinctive elements in the teaching of Jesus, implicit in Markan sayings but more clearly evident in Q (cf. Luke xi. 20, xvii. 20 f., Matt. xxi. 31) and in such parables as the Leaven (Luke xiii. 20 f.), Treasure Hid in a Field (Matt. xiii. 44), and the Pearl Merchant (Matt. xiii. 45 f.). This inference agrees with his emphasis on the Parousia and his use of the apocalyptic forecast in xiii. 5-8 + 24-7. There is no sign in Markan teaching of the conception of the Kingdom as an earthly or political institution. Supernatural in character, the Kingdom has greater affinity with the teaching of the Book of Daniel, although nothing is said of a general resurrection of the dead and the final judgment and of the Parousia in connexion with it. These negative characteristics suggest the presence of an original element in the teaching of Jesus which emerges only partially in Mark.

ESCHATOLOGY

Inevitably in discussing Mark's teaching concerning the Kingdom of God it has been necessary to speak of his Eschatology. Two points, however, call for further notice. (1) Mark's eschatology has a strong apocalyptic cast. Not only is the Parousia the object of his earnest expectation, but the events leading up to it and its spectacular character are strongly emphasized. The End will be preceded by discernible signs, wars, earthquakes, famines, heavenly portents, and the Son of Man will visibly appear in clouds (xiii. 5-8, 24-7). Mark writes to insist that ' the End is not yet ' (xiii. 7, 10), but he has no doubt that it is imminent and that it will be seen. In this teaching Mark is influenced by beliefs tenaciously held in the Church of his day (cf. Acts iii. 19-21, 1 Thess. iv. 13-18, 2 Thess. ii. 1-17), and it is probable that his account of the teaching of Jesus is thereby coloured and to some extent distorted. Jesus affirmed that the prophecy of Dan. vii. 13 would be fulfilled (xiv. 62), and probably spoke of His return, but the strong contrast between the eschatological teaching in Q [1] and L and that found in Mark and in M suggests that in the primitive tradition His teaching was seen out of focus. (2) Secondly, Mark nowhere brings the teaching concerning the Parousia into connexion with the idea of Messianic suffering. The Son of Man comes without scars, and when it is foretold that He will rise again after three days, it is not said in the same saying that He will come in glory. This independence in the two series of sayings presents a difficult problem. To identify the prophecies of resurrection with those of the Parousia is probably too easy a solution, but to reject the prophecies of suffering in the interests of the Parousia sayings is too violent an expedient. The latter is the solution favoured by Bultmann. The Parousia sayings,

[1] Cf. T. W. Manson, 262, *SJ*, 143.

he maintains, are older than the prophecies of suffering and resurrection, which are *vaticinia ex eventu*.[1] This explanation is unsatisfactory, for while x. 33 f. reflects a knowledge of the Passion story, the prophecies of suffering as a whole are too deeply rooted in Mark and L to be disposed of so summarily. In point of fact both series are coloured by Christian beliefs and hopes ; but neither can be sacrificed to the other. The best solution is the view outlined above, that in Mark the Parousia sayings are original but are out of focus, that Jesus undoubtedly prophesied His suffering and death, but spoke of His return in terms less explicit and apocalyptic than viii. 38 and xiii. 26 would suggest.

CHRISTOLOGY

The character of Mark's Christology can be seen best from his use of the names and titles of Jesus.

Jesus

Under this personal name (found 81 times) Jesus is frequently mentioned. ' Jesus Christ ' is used once only (i. 1), ' Lord Jesus ' only in the spurious ending (xvi. 19), and ' Christ Jesus ' never. The adjective ' Nazarene ' is added in i. 24, x. 47, xiv. 67, and xvi. 6. These facts reveal the primitive character of Mark, for nothing in the Gospel suggests the use of ' Jesus ' as a cult-name. Cf. A. Deissmann, in *Mysterium Christi*, 3-27. Even more frequently Mark speaks of Jesus without any designation, as ' He ' or ' Him '. It is taken for granted who is meant. Cf. Lohmeyer, 1.

Christ

In seven instances only is this term found : i. 1, viii. 29, ix. 41, xii. 35, xiii. 21, xiv. 61, xv. 32, and in none does Jesus use it of Himself. Failure to use this title is bound up with the question of His Messiahship and is a further illustration of the primitive character of Mark.

Son of David

This Messianic title is applied to Jesus twice in the

---

[1] *Theologie des Neuen Testaments* (1948), i. 30.

narrative of Bartimaeus (x. 47 f.). It is also used once by
Jesus in controversy with the scribes (xii. 35), but not with
direct reference to Himself. In contrast Matthew has the
title in six additional cases.

Son of Mary

Mark vi. 3 is the only New Testament passage in which
this name is applied to Jesus, and there it is textually suspect.
V. Comm. in loc. There is no sign that Mark was aware of
the Virgin Birth tradition. On the other hand, Jesus is not
described, as in Luke iii. 23, iv. 22, John i. 45, vi. 42, as ' the
son of Joseph '. In vi. 3 He is spoken of as ' the carpenter ',
but more probably, ' the son of the carpenter ', as in
Matt., should be read.

Lord

Mark has κύριε (' Sir ') once, appropriately enough in
the words of the Syro-Phoenician woman (vii. 28), and
possibly also in i. 40 and x. 51. ὁ κύριος appears in xi. 3,
probably with no more significance than ' Master ' or
' Teacher '; it lacks that deeper reverential meaning which
it bears in the 16 or 17 instances in Luke, and in John subsequently to the Resurrection. It is possible, indeed, that in
xi. 3 it refers to the owner of the colt. With reference to
κύριος, Burkitt, CB, 47 f., observes that its sparing use in
the Synoptic Gospels is one of the many evidences that the
tradition is based ultimately on reminiscence and not upon
creative fancy. ' And here, as elsewhere,' he adds, ' the good
historical tradition is mainly due to the influence of the
Gospel of Mark: it was not indeed itself much read, but it
moulded the language of the more popular gospels according
to Matthew and Luke.'

Rabbi, Teacher

These are the common designations by which Jesus is
addressed in Mark. Rabbi means, literally, ' My great one ',
the nearest English equivalent being ' Sir ',[1] and Rabboni
has much the same meaning. They are terms of respect

---

[1] Cf. Burkitt, op. cit. 42.

addressed to Jewish teachers of the Law. In Mark Rabbi is used three times: in ix. 5, xi. 21, and xiv. 45. Rabboni is read in x. 51, but Rabbi by important MSS. *V.* Comm. Much more common, however, is ' Teacher ', διδάσκαλος, which is used 11 times (10 in the voc.), and by Jesus Himself in xiv. 14. Mark employs it as an equivalent to Rabbi for the benefit of His Gentile readers.

Prophet

Mark vi. 15 and viii. 28 show that Jesus was looked upon as a prophet, and implicitly He spoke of Himself as such in vi. 4. Mark himself does not use it as a title for Jesus.

Son of Man

'Ο υἱὸς τοῦ ἀνθρώπου is a rendering, almost unintelligible to a Greek, of the Aramaic *bar nasha*, literally ' man ', but capable of conveying the sense ' the man ', and so of being used in a Messianic sense. For the Old Testament background of the name *v.* Comm. on ii. 10. Found exclusively in the Gospels, with the exception of Acts vii. 56, the title appears 14 times in Mark and, apart from ii. 10, 28, subsequently to the challenge ' Who say ye that I am ? ' (viii. 29): ii. 10, 28, viii. 31, 38, ix. 9, 12, 31, x. 33, 45, xiii. 26, xiv. 21 (*bis*), 41, 62*. Cf. Q (11), M (6), L (6), John (12), and editorial examples in Matt. xvi. 13, 28, xxiv. 39 (?), xxvi. 2.

The possibility that the title was used in a communal sense arises in ii. 10 and 28, but for the most part, and perhaps entirely, this usage lies behind Mark, where ' Son of Man ' is used, exclusively by Jesus, as a personal Messianic term. In nine Markan passages (viii. 31, ix. 9, 12, 31, x. 33, 45, xiv. 21 (*bis*), 41) it is re-interpreted in terms of the Suffering Servant of Yahweh (Isa. lii. 13-liii) ; in three it is used eschatologically to describe the Son of Man as depicted in Dan. vii and the Book of Enoch. The Servant conception lies behind the words of the Divine Voice in i. 11, ' Thou art my Son ; my Beloved, in thee I am well pleased ', although not the idea of the Suffering Servant. This idea appears, subsequently to ' Caesarea Philippi ', in the sayings listed above. Whether the Son of Man was interpreted Messianically in pre-Christian times,[1] and whether the idea of the Suffering Messiah was then current,[2] are moot points ; but there can be no doubt that Jesus is the originator of the doctrine, in the sense that He gave it life and made it determinative in His teaching and action. The attempt to trace its origin to the Christian community [3] has not succeeded because the identification is a work of creative genius and because it appears exclusively in sayings of Jesus. The three eschatological sayings raise difficulties. Mark xiv. 62 can be credibly explained as a genuine utterance of Jesus (*v.* Comm.) and His teaching probably lies behind viii. 38 and xiii. 26 ; but a comparison of viii. 38 with the parallel saying in Q (Luke xii. 8 f. = Matt. x. 32 f.), and the apocalyptic context in which xiii. 26 appears, strongly suggest later developments in the Markan tradition influenced by the Advent Hope of the Christian community

Son of God

Beyond question this title represents the most fundamental element in Mark's Christology. The name appears five times : at the beginning in i. 1,[4] in the confession of the demoniacs (iii. 11, v. 7), in the high priest's question (xiv. 61, ' the Son of the Blessed '), and at the end in the centurion's cry (xv. 39). But to these must be added the words of the Divine Voice at the Baptism, ' Thou art my Son ' (i. 11), and in the narrative of the Transfiguration, ' This is my Beloved Son : hear ye him ' (ix. 7), and in the phrase ' neither the Son ' in the saying concerning the Day (xiii. 32).

In the Old Testament the term is applied to angels (Gen. vi. 2, Job i. 6, xxxviii. 7), to Israel (Hos. xi. 1, Exod. iv. 22), and to the king (2 Sam. vii. 14, Psa. ii. 7, lxxxix. 26) ; and in later Jewish literature to the Messiah (? cf. 4 Ezra vii. 28) and to the righteous Israel (Ecclus. iv. 10, Psa. Sol. xiii. 8, xvii. 30, xviii. 4). But none of these usages really elucidates the Markan title. Even the idea of the Son of God

---

[1] Formerly widely accepted, the view that the Son of Man is the Messiah is now disputed. Cf. H. H. Rowley, *The Relevance of Apocalyptic*, 55 f. But see also W. D. Davies, *Paul and Rabbinic Judaism*, 279 f. ; J. Bowman, *ET*, lix.

287 f. ; M. Black, *ET*, lx. 14 f.
[2] Cf. W. Manson, *Jesus the Messiah*, 173 f. ; W. D. Davies, *op. cit.* 276-84 ; M. Black, *op. cit.* 14 f.
[3] Cf. Bousset, *Kyrios Christos*.
[4] *V.* Comm.

as the Messiah has to be stretched and expanded and given a significance which it had never borne before. The Markan Son of God is a Divine Being who appears in human form, whose *dynamis* is manifest in His bearing and speech and in His mighty works, and yet whose humanity is real so that He is deeply moved in the presence of human suffering (i. 43), angry with hypocrisy and grieved at the blindness of men's hearts (iii. 5), astonished at unbelief (vi. 6), indignant with stupidity and want of feeling (x. 14), limited in knowledge (xiii. 32), filled with shuddering awe at the approach of death (xiv. 33), silent in the presence of injustice (xiv. 60, xv. 4), ignominy (xiv. 65, xv. 16-20), and railing (xv. 29-32), royal in death (xv. 39). The sheer humanity of the Markan portraiture catches the eye of the most careless reader ; and yet, it is but half seen if it is not perceived that this Man of Sorrows is also a Being of supernatural origin and dignity, since He is the Son of God. The same conception lies behind the use of the title Son of Man, for He is not only the Suffering Servant, but also the One who will sit at God's right hand and come with power upon the clouds of heaven (xiv. 62). Mark's christology is a high christology, as high as any in the New Testament, not excluding that of John. It may be held that ultimately it implies a doctrine of pre-existence, but this idea is nowhere suggested in Mark. The claim that, according to Mark, Jesus becomes the Son of God by adoption has often been made, but it probably rests upon a superficial reading of the Gospel. The Evangelist's idea is rather that Jesus is by nature the Son of God, and that the Voice at the Baptism declares Him to be such. Mark has no theory of the Incarnation, but his assumption appears to be that Jesus is *Deus absconditus*, the Hidden God. This view is not docetism, since the humanity of Christ is conceived as real. It is rather the view that, behind a fully human life, Deity is concealed, but is visible for those who have eyes to see, in His personality, teaching, and deeds. In so describing this christology we are probably expressing it with a precision greater than that in which it appeared to the mind of the Evangelist. It is uncertain, indeed, whether he had reflected upon it at all, and no more can be claimed than that this is the character of the christology which is implied. Its nature will appear more clearly if we consider what is meant by ' the Messianic Secret ' in Mark.

The Messianic Secret

This conception, presented in a particularly challenging form by W. Wrede in *Das Messiasgeheimnis in den Evangelien* (1901), has powerfully affected all subsequent discussion of the Markan christology. In the form in which Wrede presented it, the theory has been widely rejected,[1] but it continues to exert a great influence, and therefore calls for reconsideration in a modern commentary.

Wrede's hypothesis is based on significant data within the Gospel. The daemons who seek to make Jesus known are silenced (i. 25, 34, iii. 11 f.), and silence is enjoined after notable miracles (i. 44, v. 43, vii. 36, viii. 26), after Peter's confession (viii. 30), and at the descent from the Mount of Transfiguration (ix. 9). Jesus withdraws from the crowd on secret journeys (vii. 24, ix. 30) and gives private instruction to His disciples on ' the mystery of the kingdom of God ' (iv. 10-12), on ' that which defiles a man ' (vii. 17-23), on prayer (ix. 28 f.), Messianic suffering (viii. 31, ix. 31, x. 33 f.), and the Parousia (xiii. 3-37). Jesus, it is represented, keeps His Messiahship a secret so long as He is upon earth, and while He reveals Himself to His disciples (as distinct from the people), He remains unintelligible even to them (ix. 32). Only with His Resurrection does the true perception of what He is begin.[2] The warp of the Gospel is shot through by a strong weft of dogmatic ideas, and its outline is full of contradictions and inherent improbabilities.

In opposition to Wrede it has been argued that Jesus would never have been confessed as its Messiah after the Resurrection unless He had been recognized as such during

---

[1] See, for example, the criticisms of Jülicher, *Neue Linien in der Kritik der evangelischen Überlieferung*; J. Weiss, *Das älteste Evangelium*, 52-60; Schweitzer, *The Quest of the Historical Jesus*, 336-48; Sanday, *The Life of Christ in Recent Research*, 69-76; Burkitt, *AJT* (1911), xv. No. 2, 175-93; Peake, Art. ' The Messiah and the Son of Man ', *Bulletin of the John Rylands Library*, vol. 8, No. 1, Jan. 1924; La-

grange, xli f.; Rawlinson, 258-62.

[2] *Beiden Gedanken, die vielfach ineinander übergehen, liegt die gemeinsame Anschauung zu Grunde, dass die wirkliche Erkenntnis dessen, was er ist, erst mit seiner Auferstehung beginnt, op. cit.* 114. It should be added that Wrede holds that the idea of the Messianic Secret was not invented by Mark, but was current in certain circles to which he belonged. *Op. cit.* 145.

His ministry; that His crucifixion is unintelligible unless He was condemned as a Messianic pretender; and that otherwise the first preachers would not have incurred the odium of preaching a Crucified Messiah. Moreover, it is claimed, the inscription on the cross and the narratives of Peter's Confession, the Entry into Jerusalem, and the Trial before the Sanhedrin strongly attest the presence of Messianic tension during the ministry of Jesus. These are powerful arguments. All the more remarkable, therefore, is the persistence of Wrede's influence in modern criticism.[1] 'The citadel has caved in; but the flag still flies.' The explanation must be that, while the idea of the Messianic Secret is untenable as Wrede presented it, none the less it is of great historical and theological importance. The view that Jesus enjoined silence in order to avert the danger of revolution [2] is sound as far as it goes, but it is perilously near the suggestion of playing for safety. The data call for a fuller explanation. In fact, the Messianic Secret lies behind almost every narrative in Mark, particularly the Healing of the Paralytic, the Feeding of the Five Thousand, the Entry into Jerusalem, and the Trial scenes. But it is not a hypothesis imposed on the records from without, but an element integral to the tradition itself. Jesus imposed silence because of the nature of Messiahship as He conceived it to be. To Him it was not primarily a matter of status but of action. In His own estimation Jesus is Messiah in His works of healing, His exorcisms, His victory over Satanic powers, His suffering, dying, rising, and coming with the clouds of heaven. Messiahship is a destiny; it is that which He does, that which the Father is pleased to accomplish in Him and which He fulfils in filial love. It is for this reason that He silences the demoniacs and commands His disciples to tell no man His secret till after the Resurrection. The Messiah already, He would not be the Messiah until His destiny was fulfilled. We may agree that it is necessary to read the Story in terms of doctrine; but the doctrine is that of Jesus Himself. This view of the Messianic Secret is in line with the Markan

---

[1] Cf. R. H. Lightfoot, *History and Interpretation in the Gospel*, 16-22; Dibelius, 223; Bultmann, 371; and the commentaries of Schniewind and Lohmeyer.
[2] Cf. Peake, *op. cit.* 66.

christology and soteriology. The agreement is too astonishing to be the work of art ; it is the reflection of historical reality.

SOTERIOLOGY

With the christology of Mark its soteriology is indissolubly joined. The latter cannot be tacked on to the former ; what Jesus does arises out of, and can only be understood in terms of, what He is. As the Suffering Servant who is the Son of Man, He must suffer, die, rise again, be exalted to God's right hand, and come in glory. This unity is the final argument which justifies the rejection of the view that the prophecies of the Passion are the dogmatic ideas of the Christian community read back into the Story of Jesus. It need not be disputed that viii. 31, ix. 31, and x. 33 f., especially the last, are to some extent modified by a knowledge of the Crucifixion narrative. The point which survives the most searching criticism is the conviction of Jesus that, as the Son of Man, He must suffer many things, and be rejected, and be killed, and rise again. This idea emerges again in ix. 12b and is elucidated in x. 45 and xiv. 24. These sayings are discussed in detail in the Commentary. Here, it is enough to say that, if they are genuine, as there is good reason to believe them to be, they show that Jesus faced suffering and death with a clear understanding of the purpose which it was the Father's will for Him to fulfil.

No saying in Mark, or in any of the Gospels, suggests that Jesus interpreted His death as a means of revealing the love of God. In all that He does, the Father's love is a basic assumption,[1] but the redemptive activity itself is otherwise conceived. The two metaphors in x. 45 and xiv. 24 are of decisive importance. His life is given as ' a ransom for many ' and as surrendered is ' the blood of the covenant '. Both ideas are sacrificial. The ' ransom ' is the price paid to effect deliverance from sin and from judgment. The ' blood of the covenant ' ratifies a covenant bond between God and men, a relationship of fellowship and obedience, which is based upon forgiveness, redemption, and reconciliation. These metaphors are not worked out in the Markan sayings into

[1] Cf. John iii. 16, 1 John iii. 16, Rom. v. 8.

anything approaching a doctrinal synthesis, but, none the less, they are determinative ideas in an articulated cycle of thought. They imply that Jesus thought of His surrendered life as a dedicated self-offering to God in the name of men and for their sake. Pagan ideas of appeasement are foreign to this conception. The self-offering is a means of approach to God, representative and communal in character, made available for men. A relationship of faith union is implied, but this idea is not expressed in any Markan saying. These sayings concentrate rather on the redemptive work of Christ Himself by which His Messianic task is fulfilled. In particular, the ἐκθαμβεῖσθαι καὶ ἀδημονεῖν of xiv. 33, and the death cry of xv. 34, reveal that experience of sinbearing which inalienably belongs to the destiny of the Suffering Son of Man. Ultimately, the Markan representation belongs to the cycle of ideas which is worked out in the Epistle to the Hebrews, but it has closer affinities with the Pauline doctrine of *In Christo*. Nevertheless, it is far indeed from being developed into a theological hypothesis, but remains rooted in the black soil of factual experience and deed. Germane to the question whether it represents the ideas of Jesus Himself, or is a later construction reflecting early Christian beliefs, is this historical realism and the fact that at no point are we compelled to take a step outside the circle of Jewish beliefs. ' Ransom ', ' covenant ', and ' sinbearing ', are distinctive Old Testament ideas, and recourse to the suggestion of the infiltration of Hellenistic concepts is entirely unnecessary. What we find in Mark is no superimposed dogmatic construction, but the virile ideas of Jesus Himself.

AFFINITIES WITH PAULINE TEACHING

The Paulinism of Mark has been hotly debated for nearly a century, since the time when, in opposition to the Tübingen School, G. Volkmar contended that the Gospel was an allegorical presentation of Pauline teaching in the form of a narrative. In more recent times the Pauline character of Mark has been maintained by Loisy [1] and Bacon,[2] and

---

[1] *Les Évangiles synoptiques*, i. 116.
[2] *The Beginnings of Gospel Story*, xxvii f., *The Gospel of Mark*, 221-71.

strongly denied by A. Schweitzer,[1] P. Wernle,[2] and M. Werner.[3] The whole question is surveyed by Lagrange, clivclxiv, and admirably summarized by Rawlinson, xliii-xlv. Whether Mark was familiar with the Pauline Epistles, and to what extent, if any, he was influenced by Pauline teaching, can be decided only by examining his vocabulary and the nature of the affinity between characteristic elements in his theology and the distinctive ideas of Paul :

Vocabulary

It is not surprising that there should be a common element in the vocabulary of Mark and Paul. The problem is its extent and implications. Among the more important points the following may be noted :

δύναμις is used 10 times in Mark to describe divine power and the works of power wrought by Jesus ('mighty works'). In the Pauline Epistles it is found in both senses, and especially the power of God, no less than 44 times. Cf. vi. 14 ἐνεργοῦσιν αἱ δυνάμεις ἐν αὐτῷ and Gal. iii. 5 ὁ . . . ἐνεργῶν δυνάμεις ἐν ὑμῖν.

εἰρηνεύω, ix. 50*, Rom. xii. 18, 2 Cor. xiii. 11, 1 Thess. v. 13**.

εὐαγγέλιον (7), Paul (56). Cf. τὸ εὐαγγέλιον τοῦ θεοῦ in i. 14 and Rom. i. 1, xv. 16, 2 Cor. xi. 7, 1 Thess. ii. 2, etc. Lagrange questions if Mark would have used the word if he had not lived in Paul's company.

καρποφορέω, iv. 20, 28*, Matt. (1), Luke (1), Paul (4)**.

κηρύσσω (12), Matt. (9), Luke (9), Acts (8), Paul (16), Rest (4)**.

λόγος is used in Mark in various senses, but sometimes, as in Luke, Acts, and Paul of the Christian message. Cf. iv. 16 (τὸν λόγον) εὐθὺς μετὰ χαρᾶς λαμβάνουσιν αὐτόν and 1 Thess. i. 6 δεξάμενοι τὸν λόγον . . . μετὰ χαρᾶς.

μεταμορφόω, ix. 2*, Matt. xvii. 2, Rom. xii. 2, 2 Cor. iii. 18**.

μυστήριον, iv. 11*, cf. Rom. xi. 25, xvi. 25, 1 Cor. ii. 1, iv. 1, Eph. iii. 3 f., 9, vi. 19, Col. i. 26 f., ii. 2, iv. 3. Note τοὺς ἔξω in Col. iv. 5 and τοῖς ἔξω in Mark iv. 11.

παράπτωμα, xi. 25*, Matt. vi. 14 f., Paul (16)**.

πώρωσις, iii. 5*, Rom. xi. 25, Eph. iv. 18 (διὰ τὴν πώρωσιν τῆς καρδίας αὐτῶν)**. Also πωρόω, vi. 52, viii. 17*, John xii. 40, Rom. xi. 7, 2 Cor. iii. 14**.

σοφία, vi. 2*, Paul (28). As Mark speaks of a wisdom 'given', so in Gal. ii. 9 and 1 Cor. iii. 10 Paul speaks of grace.

φρονέω, viii. 33*, Matt. xvi. 23, Acts xxviii. 22, Paul (22), 1 Tim. vi. 17**.

---

[1] *The Quest*, 348.   [2] *Die synoptische Frage*, 199 f.
[3] *Der Einfluss paulinischer Theologie im Markusevangelium* (1923).

ἐν ὀνόματι, ὅτι Χριστοῦ ἐστέ, ix. 41, cf. 1 Cor. i. 12 Ἐγὼ δὲ Χριστοῦ.

Note also the Pauline vocabulary of vii. 21-3, especially πορνεία Paul (10), πλεονεξία Paul (6), ἀσέλγεια Paul (4), ἀφροσύνη Paul (3).

From this list it would be hazardous to infer more than that Mark may have lived in a Pauline environment and possibly knew Romans and 1 Thessalonians. No deep influence of the Epistles is suggested, especially in view of the different emphasis on πίστις by Paul and the absence of λύτρον and λυτροῦμαι and their cognates from his Epistles (ἀντίλυτρον, 1 Tim. ii. 6), and, further, the absence from Mark of such distinctive Pauline words as δικαιοσύνη, δικαιόω, δοκιμάζω, δόκιμος, οἰκόνομος, πιστός, σωτηρία, ταπεινόω, φρόνιμος, and φῶς and σκότος used metaphorically.

Ideas

Mark has doctrinal affinities with Pauline teaching in respect of christology, soteriology, the universality of salvation, the hardening or reprobation of the Jews, and the Law. In christology the most notable agreement is in the use of the terms Son of God and the Son. This usage, however, is characteristic of primitive Christianity as a whole. Moreover, there are important differences between the Son of Man christology of Mark and the Wisdom-Logos christology of Paul. Paul does not describe Jesus as the superhuman Son of Man, although he has affinities with this conception in his doctrine of the Second Adam and the Man from heaven (1 Cor. xv. 47); and, on the other hand, Mark does not represent Him as ' the image of the invisible God ' or show knowledge of the doctrines of pre-existence and kenosis. As regards soteriology the affinities are greater, but Paul uses analogies other than that of a ' ransom ', and is not influenced to the same degree by sacrificial ideas and the idea of the Suffering Servant, while his emphasis on the death of Christ ' for our sins ', and as the commendation of the love of God Himself, is less apparent in Mark. The Markan and Pauline accounts of the institution of the Eucharist probably represent different primitive liturgical traditions, and it is a disputed point whether Mark xiv. 24 (' This is my blood of the cove-

nant ') or I Cor. xi. 25 (' This cup is the new covenant in my
blood ') is the earlier.

In Mark's day the universality of salvation (cf. xiii. 10,
xiv. 9) was a commonly accepted Christian belief, present
already in Paul's Epistles, but not necessarily derived from
him. Mark's πρῶτον in vii. 27 calls to mind Paul's Ἰουδαίῳ
τε πρῶτον καὶ Ἕλληνι (Rom. i. 16, ii. 9 f.), but it was not Paul's
idea that the Gospel should be preached to the Gentiles only
after Jews had been satisfied.[1] It may well be that it was
in a Pauline environment that Mark came to realize to the
full the blindness and hardheartedness of the Jews [2] and the
fact of their rejection by God, and that in this matter, and in
the teaching concerning offences, we are to see the influence
of Rom. ix-xi. But it is also clear that these ideas belonged
to the earliest tradition, and are even more strongly expressed
in Matt. xxi. 43 and John xii. 37-41, while Pauline teaching
on the ultimate restoration of Israel (Rom. xi. 13-36) has no
echo in Mark. At the most, therefore, the debt to Paul is
indirect and partial rather than direct and complete. The
same also may be said of the attitude to the Law in Mark and
in Paul's Epistles. Both are rooted in the teaching of Jesus
Himself. In ii. 27 f. the law of the Sabbath is re-interpreted
in a broader and more humane sense, but it is not abrogated,
and in xii. 29-31 the highest principles of the Law, the love
of God and of one's neighbour, are commended. The teaching on divorce (x. 2-12) goes beyond what is taught in the
Law, in placing man and woman on the same plane, but in
this matter there is no need to invoke the influence of Paul.
In general, we may say that it is ' the teaching of the elders '
rather than the Law that is repudiated, and that the impulse
to give this representation comes from Jesus. The utmost
that we are entitled to claim is that the emphasis on freedom
may well reflect a Pauline environment. Most of all do we
receive this impression in the Markan comment in vii. 19,
' making all meats clean ', in the list of vices in vii. 21-3, and
in the reference to the *velum scissum* in xv. 38. Here Mark
writes as a Pauline Christian would write, underlining and
commenting upon teaching congenial to his mind.

---

[1] Cf. Lagrange, clxi.
[2] Cf. iii. 5 πώρωσις, x. 5 σκληροκαρδία, cf. iv. 11 f.

The study of doctrine carries us no farther than the inferences suggested by the vocabulary. Parallel to the want of distinctive Pauline words is the absence from Mark of the great Pauline ideas of justification by faith, faith union with Christ, and life in the Spirit. A Pauline atmosphere, Pauline influence, possibly a knowledge of the Epistles, all these are credible suggestions ; but the suggestion of a recast of the primitive Gospel in terms of Paulinism is a wild and unsubstantial hypothesis. Least of all can we share the view which detects partizan elements in Mark, which sees an allusion to the Apostle in the story of the unauthorized exorcist (ix. 38-40), or in the declaration that the seats on the right hand and the left are for those for whom they have been prepared (x. 40), in the strong rebukes addressed to the disciples for their want of intelligence (viii. 17-21), or in the infant set in the midst and caressed by Jesus. For these perceptions the eyes of a Loisy are necessary.

Werner's conclusion [1] is that, where Mark and Paul agree, the tradition consists of primitive Christian ideas, that distinctive Pauline ideas are wanting in Mark or are differently presented, and that, accordingly, the suggestion of the influence of Pauline theology must be dismissed. There is great force in these contentions, but a fully balanced estimate must take account of Bacon's question : ' Can we imagine a gospel such as Mark taking form in a community ignorant of the teaching of Paul ? '.[2] Bacon answers with ' a decided No '. One respects a decided No, but a qualified negative represents more truly the actual position. Mark wrote with the pen of a Roman Christian, but he has neither recast nor obscured the historic tradition. His Jesus is the Jesus of Galilee.

[1] *Op. cit.* 209.   [2] *Op. cit.* 271.

XII

THE HISTORICAL VALUE OF THE GOSPEL

HOW far does the Gospel give a reliable account of the teaching of Jesus, His person and work, and the course of His ministry?

In judging an ancient writer like Mark, it would not be right to apply to his work modern standards of accuracy, but neither would it be just to judge him by the freer standards of the best Greek historians.[1] Mark was not seeking to write history and is not a historian. His purpose was simpler. He wanted to tell how the Good News concerning Jesus Christ, God's Son, began. Familiar with the Gospel Message of his day, he wished to tell the story of its beginnings in Galilee and Judaea, all the more since he had been associated with Peter and remembered his teaching. The motives which led him to write must have been those which influenced all the Synoptic writers — the delay of the Parousia, the passing away of eyewitnesses, and the desire to preserve the oral teaching of the primitive communities. Other motives, apologetic, liturgical, catechetical, must also have guided his undertaking. If we are justified in tracing behind his Gospel smaller complexes of evangelic material, both topical and narrative in form, the desire to combine these, and make them as far as possible a whole, will have been present, especially if already he had expanded a short Roman account of the Passion by the aid of Petrine reminiscences. The need for such an account must have been felt from a very early time, if the tragic fate of Jesus crowned by the glory of the Resurrection was to be understood, and this inference is sustained, not only by the Passion Narrative itself, but also by the existence of such oral or written collections as ii. 1-iii. 6 and xi. 15-17 + 27-33 + xii. 13-40, of which the former

[1] Like Thucydides, who says that he put into the mouth of each speaker the sentiments proper to the occasion, as he thought they would be likely to express them, while seeking to give the general purport of what was actually said, i. 22.

ends with a reference to the death plot hatched against Jesus by the Pharisees and Herodians. If these primitive collections had been made, either by Mark or a predecessor, what design could be more natural than that of prefacing the Story of the Passion by an account of the historic ministry beginning with the Preaching of John and the Baptism of Jesus ?

It is entirely wrong to explain the Gospel as a simple transcript of the recollections of Peter. The supreme advantage of being able to use his testimony is one of Mark's greatest qualifications, but the contents of the Gospel show that Peter was not his only source of information and that the Petrine reminiscences vary considerably from detailed narratives to fragmentary tradition. In addition to Petrine narratives, forms of Church tradition, including pronouncement-stories and sayings, were used by the Evangelist. The historical value of the Gospel depends on the nature and the use made of these sources of information.

MOTIVES VISIBLE IN THE GOSPEL

Apologetic Aims

It cannot be said that apologetic aims have deeply affected the Evangelist's work. He certainly emphasizes the reality of the humanity of Jesus, but we do not receive the impression that he is opposing docetic tendencies or answering objections. In this respect Mark differs from Matt. and John. In the broader sense of the term an apologetic interest is doubtless to be seen in the claim that Jesus is the Messiah, and the Son of God, that He is the Victor over Satan and all his powers, that He suffered, died, and was buried, and that He rose victorious over death ; but Mark's interest lies rather in confirming the faith of his readers than in a desire to confute opponents and establish the truth. An interest in the Old Testament is visible in the Passion Narrative, determining the language and possibly, in the case of some of the taunts addressed to the Crucified, adding details to the story ; but this interest is not deep or creative, and there is nothing corresponding to the desire of Matthew to show that certain events happened ' in order that it might be fulfilled which was

spoken by the prophets '. The words found in many MSS.
and versions in xv. 28, ' And the scripture was fulfilled,
which saith . . .', are manifestly a later addition, and it is not
excluded that xiv. 49, ' that the scriptures may be fulfilled ',
is part of the saying of Jesus, or, since the phrase is not in
Mark's manner, a scribal comment.　Other apologetic
features, as, for example, the statement about the Temple
veil, are better considered as doctrinal.　Similarly, the insistence upon the necessity of preaching the gospel ' unto all
the nations ' (xiii. 10) is hortatory and catechetical rather
than apologetic.

Liturgical Interests

These interests may perhaps be seen in the allusions to
fasting (ii. 20), anointing (vi. 13), and prayer (ix. 29, xi. 24 f.),
that is, in matters of religious practice.　An interest in the
worship of the Church comes out more plainly in the attention
given to the institution of the Eucharist (xiv. 22-5) and its
association with the Passover (xiv. 16-20).　The narrative
of the Last Supper is liturgical in the sense that all the interest
lies in the declaratory words of Jesus.　It is just such an
account as might have been current in the usage of a primitive
Church ; it lacks the detail and the interest in secondary
features which might have appeared in a Petrine story.
Everything is concentrated in what Jesus does and says.　The
same interest appears in the stories of Miraculous Feeding,
especially in vi. 41 and viii. 6 f., and perhaps also in other
stories which have to do with bread, as, for example, vii.
25-30 and viii. 14-21.　Both the selection and the use of the
tradition are those of one who highly valued this central rite
of primitive worship.　The historical bearings of this liturgical
interest will doubtless be variously estimated.　Those who
see the simple teaching of Jesus being transformed into a
cult will estimate it as a sign of the darkening of the primitive
tradition ; but those who trace the prophetic symbolism in
the story to Jesus Himself will feel that the liturgical interests
have acted conservatively in preserving primitive tradition.
This view is strongly supported by the Palestinian character
of the tradition, its Jewish ideas and Aramaic idioms, which
suggest that it was brought to Rome, and not formed there.

Catechetical Motives

Many indications suggest that Mark reflects the catechesis of the Church for which it was written. The topical complexes, ii. 1-iii. 6, iv. 1-34, vii. 1-23, the topical and mnemonic principles by which sayings appear to have been compiled, notably in iv. 21-5, viii. 34-ix. 1, ix. 37-50, and xi. 23-5, the succession of allied themes in x. 1-31, the use that appears to have been made of viii. 1-26, and the interests met by the Apocalyptic Discourse, disclose the life and teaching of a settled Christian community in the pre-Gospel period. Here again is a factor which affects the historical value, and in different ways. On the one hand, teachers may colour tradition by expressing it in a new idiom and a later vocabulary; on the other hand, with practical Christian interests at stake, they will wish to provide catechumens with genuine tradition. Both tendencies can be seen in Mark, the former in iv. 13-30, vii. 19b, 21-3, xiii. 10, 12 f., the latter in the general trustworthiness of the sayings-tradition. Catechetical interests are also shown in frequent explanatory clauses introduced by γάρ, the translation of Aramaic words, and the explanation of Jewish terms (vii. 11, xii. 42, xv. 42) and customs (vii. 3 f.). In sum, the tendency of these interests is to elucidate the tradition rather than to obscure its original meaning.

Doctrinal Motives

Our earlier discussion of Mark's theology and his Pauline affinities strongly supports the historical worth of the Gospel. Both in its christology and soteriology primitive beliefs are grounded in the tradition, and, in spite of claims to the contrary, reflect the thoughts of Jesus. This is particularly evident when the names and titles of Jesus are considered, since in recording the Story of Jesus it is easy to reveal the standpoint of a later time. Contrary to the views of Wrede, Mark's treatment of the idea of the Messianic Secret, so far from being a doctrinal construction, preserves, as no other Gospel does, an original element in the thought of Jesus, and the same must be said of the Evangelist's emphasis upon the idea of Messianic suffering. It is undoubtedly true that

Mark's Gospel reflects the ideas of the primitive Christian *Kerygma*,[1] but it does this because the earliest preaching rested upon what Jesus had done and taught. Nevertheless, Mark writes a generation after the historic ministry, and it would be strange indeed if his Gospel lacked the watermarks of his time. In three respects a later interest can be seen. First, in the confession that Jesus is the Son of God ascribed to daemons and to the heathen centurion by the cross. That Jesus was conscious of a unique filial relationship to God is implied by the story of the Baptism, His conception of Messiahship, and His sayings (xiii. 32, Luke x. 21 f., etc.). We require, however, much stronger evidence than we possess that ' Son of God ' was a generally recognized Messianic title, if we are to reject the view that iii. 11 is a Christianized version of the cries of the demoniacs. And the same must be said of the centurion's confession. Mark read more into these confessions than was actually said because he saw these incidents with Christian eyes. We must also interpret in the same way his account of the Divine Voice at the Transfiguration. A conviction gained by the three intimate disciples is here expressed in direct speech. Secondly, a contemporary interest also appears in the reference to the Rent Veil in xv. 38. An irresistible conviction of the new way opened between God and man here clothes itself in a legendary development of the tradition, which is carried much farther in Matt. The same view will also be taken of the nature-miracles in Mark by those who believe that the basis of these narratives is to be found in non-miraculous events. A third contemporary interest appears in the apocalyptic enhancement of the sayings-tradition in Mark. The Apocalyptic Discourse in xiii is the clearest example of this tendency, but it is seen also in viii. 38 when this passage is compared with its parallel in Q, Luke xii. 8 f. = Matt. x. 32 f. As previously maintained, ' realized eschatology ' is implicit in the Markan parables and in the Messiahship of Jesus, but it is not present in Mark with the clarity in which it appears in Q because Mark's main emphasis is on the ' unrealized eschatology ' of the Advent Hope of primitive Christianity. The dénouement

---

[1] Cf. Dodd, *The Apostolic Preaching*, 38-43; Bultmann, 373, 398 f.; Schniewind, *ThR* (1930), 142, 158 f.. 179-88.

lies ahead when the Son of Man comes with the clouds of heaven. In this representation Mark is faithful to the teaching of Jesus, but he sees it through the veil of apocalyptic. The time of the Parousia, though near, is unknown (xiii. 32), but the Day will be preceded by visible signs, war, earthquake, famine, persecution, and celestial signs, and the Son of man will gather His elect from the four winds. All this is so different from Luke xvii. 22 ff., that we are entitled to suspect the transposition of the original tradition into another key.[1]

The extent to which the various interests discussed above affect the historical value of Mark will be variously estimated. To the present writer they do not seem to detract from its worth to any serious degree if allowance is made for them in exegesis.

THE OBJECTIVITY OF THE GOSPEL

If the vivid details in Mark are original, they are of the greatest importance in assessing its historical value. In themselves lifelike touches are not a sure criterion, since they may be due to the exercise of a vivid imagination, but they present data on which a judgment may be based, especially if their character and distribution are considered. Among the more important elements peculiar to Mark the following may be noted in chapters i-vi.

i. 7.	' Stooping down.'
i. 10.	' Rent ' (Matt. and Luke ' opened '), of the heavens, and ' into (Jesus) ' used of the Spirit (Matt. and Luke ' upon ').
i. 12.	' Driveth ' (of the Spirit). Matt. and Luke ' brought '.
i. 13.	' And he was with the wild beasts.'
i. 20.	' With the hired servants.'
i. 23.	' An unclean spirit.'
i. 29.	' And of Andrew, with James and John.'
i. 33.	' And the whole city was gathered together at the door.'
i. 35.	' And in the morning, a great while before day . . and there prayed.'
i. 36.	' And Simon and they that were with him.' ' Tracked him down.'
i. 41.	' And being moved with compassion' (*v.l.* ' being angry ')
i. 43.	' And he strictly charged him ' (or ' was deeply moved ').'

[1] See T. W. Manson, *TJ*, 262, *SJ*, 336.

i. 45.   ' Insomuch that Jesus could no more enter openly into a city.'

ii. 1 f.   The reference to Capernaum ' after some days ', and the report that he was ' indoors ', with the explanation that there was no room even about the door, while ' He spoke the word to them '.

ii. 3.   ' Borne of four.'

ii. 4.   ' And when they could not come nigh unto him ', they ' uncovered the roof where he was ', and ' broke it up '.

ii. 8.   ' In his spirit.'

ii. 13.   References to the sea-side, the crowd, and to teaching.

ii. 14.   ' Levi the son of Alphaeus.'

ii. 16.   ' The scribes of the Pharisees.'

ii. 18.   The statement that John's disciples ' and the Pharisees ' were fasting.

ii. 23.   ' As they went.'

ii. 26.   ' When Abiathar was high priest.'

iii. 4.   ' But they held their peace.'

iii. 6.   ' With the Herodians.'

iii. 7 f.   ' To the sea ', ' from Galilee ', ' and from Idumaea, and beyond Jordan ', ' hearing what great things he did '.

iii. 9.   The little boat which attends upon Jesus because of the crowd.

iii. 10 f.   The reference to people with plagues pressing upon Jesus, and to those with unclean spirits falling down and crying, ' Thou art the Son of God '.

iii. 13.   ' Whom he would.'

iii. 14.   ' That they might be with him ', and preach, and cast out devils.

iii. 17.   ' Boanerges, which is, Sons of thunder.'

iii. 30.   ' Because they said, He hath an unclean spirit.'

iii. 31.   ' They sent unto him, calling him.'

iii. 34.   ' And looking round on them which sat round about him.'

iv. 1.   ' And again he began to teach ', ' in the sea ', ' by the sea on the land '.

iv. 10.   ' And when he was alone ', ' they that were about him with the twelve '.

iv. 33 f.   ' As they were able to hear it ', ' but privately to his own disciples he expounded all things '.

iv. 35.   ' And on that day, when even was come.'

iv. 36.   ' And leaving the multitude, they take him with them, even as he was ', ' and other boats were with him '.

iv. 37.   The waves ' beat into ' the boat ' now ' filling.

iv. 38.   ' In the stern ', ' on the cushion ', ' carest thou not . . . ? '.

iv. 39.   ' Peace, be still.'

iv. 40.   ' Have ye not yet (faith) ? '

iv. 41.	' (They feared) exceedingly.'
v. 1.	' Of the sea ', Gerasenes (Mark and Luke, Gadarenes Matt.).
v. 2.	' Out of the boat ', ' straightway ', ' an unclean spirit '.
v. 3-5.	The passage gives a graphic description of the demoniac who could not be bound, ' no, not with a chain ', who broke his chains and fetters, but could not be tamed. ' And always, night and day, in the tombs and in the mountains, he was crying out, and cutting himself with stones.'
v. 6.	' From afar ', ' ran ', ' worshipped '.
v. 7.	' I adjure thee by God.'
v. 10.	' Out of the country ' (Luke ' into the abyss ').
v. 11.	' A great (herd).'
v. 13.	' Unclean spirits ', ' in number about two thousand '.
v. 15.	' Him that was possessed with devils ', ' even him that had the legion '.
v. 16.	' And concerning the swine.'
v. 18.	' He that had been possessed with (devils).'
v. 19.	' And he suffered him not ', ' unto thy friends ', ' the Lord ', ' and how he had mercy on thee '.
v. 20.	' Decapolis ', ' and all men did marvel '.
v. 21.	The reference to crossing over again ' in the boat unto the other side ', the gathering of a ' great ' multitude, and the fact that ' he was by the sea '.
v. 23.	' At the point of death ' (Matt. ' even now dead ').
v. 26.	The description of the woman who had suffered many things at the hands of the doctors, and was no better, but rather grew worse. Cf. Luke ' could not be healed of any '.
v. 27.	' Having heard the things concerning Jesus.'
v. 29.	' She felt in her body that she was healed of her plague.'
v. 30.	The statement that Jesus was aware of the loss of the power proceeding from him.
v. 31.	The remonstrance of the disciples who repeat the question, ' Who touched me ? '.
v. 32.	' And he looked round about to see her that had done this thing.' Cf. Matt. ' And seeing her '.
v. 33.	' Fearing ', ' knowing what had been done to her ', ' all the truth '.
v. 35.	' They come ', ' any further '.
v. 36.	' Not heeding the word spoken.'
v. 37.	' The brother of James.'
v. 39.	' Why make ye a tumult, and (weep) ? '
v. 40.	' Where the child was.'
v. 41.	' Talitha cumi ; which is, being interpreted, Damsel, I say unto thee, Arise.'
v. 42.	' With a great amazement.'

v. 43.	'That no man should know this.' The charge to give the child food. So Luke.
vi. 1.	'And his disciples follow him.'
vi. 3.	'Here.'
vi. 4.	'And among his own kin.'
vi. 5 f.	The statement that He could do no mighty work, save lay His hands on a few sick people, and that He marvelled because of their unbelief. Contrast Matt.
vi. 7.	'By two and two.' Cf. Luke x. 1 (of the Seventy).
vi. 8 f.	The permission of a staff and sandals.
vi. 12 f.	The references to repentance, exorcisms, and anointing.
vi. 14.	'For his name had become known.'
vi. 17.	'For he had married her.'
vi. 19.	'And Herodias set herself against him.'
vi. 20.	'Knowing that he was a righteous man and a holy, and kept him safe ', ' and when he heard him ', ' and he heard him gladly '.
vi. 21.	'His lords, and the high captains, and the chief men of Galilee.'
vi. 22 f.	'Ask of me whatsoever thou wilt, and I will give it thee ', ' unto the half of my kingdom '.
vi. 24 f.	The conference with the mother and the quick return of the girl.
vi. 26.	'Exceeding sorry ', ' he would not reject her '.
vi. 27.	'An executioner ', ' to bring his head '.
vi. 29.	'And laid it (his corpse) in a tomb.'
vi. 30.	'(And the apostles) gather themselves together unto Jesus ', ' all things ', ' and whatsoever they had taught '.
vi. 31.	'And he saith unto them, Come ye yourselves apart into a wilderness place, and rest a while. For there were many coming and going, and they had no leisure so much as to eat.'
vi. 33.	The statement that the crowd outran them.
vi. 34.	'As sheep not having a shepherd ' (cf. Matt. ix. 36), ' and he began to teach them many things '.
vi. 35.	'Now far spent.'
vi. 37.	The disciples' ironical question, ' Shall we go and buy two hundred pennyworth of bread, and give them to eat ? '.
vi. 38.	The inquiry, ' How many loaves have ye ? ', the command to go and see, and the sequel.
vi. 39 f.	'By companies ' (cf. Luke), ' the green grass ', ' in ranks ', ' by hundreds ' (cf. Luke).
vi. 41.	'And the two fishes divided he among them all.'
vi. 45.	'To Bethsaida ' (cf. Luke ix. 10).
vi. 46.	The reference to taking leave of the crowd.

vi. 47.   ' On the land.'

vi. 48.   ' And seeing them distressed in rowing ' (Matt. speaks of the boat). ' And he would have passed by them.'

vi. 49 f.   ' Supposed ', ' for they all saw him '.

vi. 51.   ' Sore amazed in themselves.'

vi. 52.   ' For they understood not concerning the loaves, but their heart was hardened ' (or ' blinded ').

vi. 53.   ' And moored to the shore.'

vi. 54.   ' And when they were come out of the boat, straightway the people (knew him).'

vi. 55.   The sick carried on pallets ' where they heard he was '.

vi. 56.   ' And wheresoever he entered, into villages, or into cities, or into the country, they laid the sick in the market-places ', ' if it were but ', ' him '.

It would be profitable to continue the summary in chapters vii-xvi, but enough evidence is provided to show the significance of the Markan wealth of detail.

Some of these passages may be the result of inference and imagination. The following appear to be editorial: i. 45, ii. 13, iii. 7 f., iv. 10, 33 f., vi. 12 f., 34. Explanatory passages include : i. 23 (' an unclean spirit '), ii. 8 (' in his spirit '), iii 17 (' Boanerges '), 30 (' because they said, He hath an un-clean spirit '), v. 37 (' the brother of James '), vi. 14, 17, 19, 20, 31b, 52. To decide what is imaginative is more specula-tive. It seems probable, however, that details are visualized and imaginatively described in i. 7 (' stooping '), the descrip-tion of the rending of the heavens in i. 10, the allusion to the constraint of the Spirit in i. 12, the picture of Jesus with the wild beasts in i. 13, the reference to the whole city (i. 33), the portrayal of the people with plagues and the unclean spirits falling down and crying, ' Thou art the Son of God ' (iii. 10 f.), possibly the allusions to amazement (v. 20, 42), the naming of the guests (vi. 21), and the account of the king's offer (vi. 22 f.) which recalls details in the story of Esther. There may be other passages of the kind, but the great majority of the items in the list have rather the appearance of graphic details recorded because they were given in the tradition. What point, for example, is there in mentioning ' the hired servants ' (i. 20), the fact that the paralytic was ' borne of four ' (ii. 3), the description of the breaking up of the roof (ii. 4), the statement that the disciples plucked the

ears of corn ' as they went ' (ii. 23), the reference to the little
boat (iii. 9), ' other boats ' (iv. 36), ' the cushion ' (iv. 38),
the desperate cry, ' Carest thou not . . . ? ' (iv. 38), the
ironical repetition of the question, ' Who touched me ? '
(v. 31), the place ' where the child was ' (v. 40), ' the executioner ' (vi. 27), the half sarcastic question about buying two
hundred pennyworth of bread (vi. 37), ' companies ', ' green
grass ', and ' ranks ' (vi. 39 f.), His passing by the disciples
(vi. 48), mooring (vi. 53), and other details, unless these things
were known and remembered ? It must be borne in mind
that the same features are found throughout the whole Gospel,
including the Passion Narrative.

If this argument is questioned, not only in this detail and
that, but as a whole, it is necessary to account for the relative
want of vivid details in the narratives already classified as
' Markan Constructions '.[1] Why, for example, is the account
of the appointment of the Twelve (iii. 13-19b) so bare ? Why
is the place so vaguely characterized as ' the mountain ', and
why is only a statement of the purpose of the choice given
and a mere list of names ? Why are there no imaginative
touches in the Fears of the Family of Jesus (iii. 21), the
Purpose of Parables (iv. 10-12), the Mission Charge (vi. 6b-
13), the Descent from the Mount (ix. 9-13), and the Rebuke of
the Ten (x. 41-5) ? How comes it that Mark has missed the
opportunity of embellishing such dramatic scenes as the
Priests' Plot (xiv. 1 f.) and the Treachery of Judas (xiv. 10 f.) ;
and why are the narratives of True Greatness (ix. 33-7) and
the Mystery of the Loaves (viii. 14-21) so ill constructed ?
The explanation can only be that for these narratives Mark
was dependent on fragmentary tradition and did not attempt
to colour it, that he is not a creative writer comparable to
Luke or John. But if so, the limitations of Mark point to
his fidelity to tradition. In his stories about Jesus and his
miracle-stories the wealth of detail is given, not created. His
objectivity is a sign of the high historical value of the Gospel.

THE MIRACULOUS ELEMENT IN THE GOSPEL

How far is the historical value of Mark affected by the

---

[1] See earlier, pp. 82-5.

presence of legendary elements, particularly in the nature-miracles? This question raises the further inquiry whether legendary elements are present, and whether the distinction between the healing-miracles and the so-called nature-miracles is valid. There can be little doubt that there is a profound difference between the healing-miracles and the alleged parallels in modern psychotherapy. Jesus uses methods like those of the psychologist, but in His works of healing He exercises a super-human *dynamis* which belongs to His person and for which modern psychiatry can supply no adequate parallel. Many readers of Mark feel that the same explanation accounts for the nature-miracles. In short, when Jesus stills the storm, multiplies loaves, walks upon water, and destroys the fig tree, He is releasing divine power resident in Him in the circumstances of His earthly mission. To this view there is no valid objection on philosophical grounds. The idea of nature as a closed system, obedient to fixed and immutable laws, is no longer tenable in the light of modern conceptions of matter and atomic power. The so-called ' laws ' summarize what is observable in the world of nature under the normal conditions of daily life ; but they do not preclude the emergence of unusual phenomena, granted the presence of a sufficient cause which, for all we know to the contrary, may be spiritual.

Many theologians, whose views command respect, accept all the Gospel miracles on the grounds stated above and because Jesus is the incarnation of divine power and love.[1] In reality, however, these arguments are prolegomena to the inquiry ; they dispose of the objection that, on scientific and philosophical grounds, miracles are impossible ; but they leave open the historical question, whether the nature-miracles happened, and the theological question, whether they cohere with a true doctrine of the Incarnation. The nature-miracles differ from the healing-miracles in that they are not wrought upon living persons, and, for reasons stated below, it appears probable, on both historical and doctrinal grounds, that a miraculous interpretation has been super-imposed upon the original tradition. The case of the raising of the daughter of Jairus occupies a border line position, and

[1] Cf. A. Richardson, *The Miracle Stories of the Gospels.*

a decision here must be made on historical grounds and the impression which the narrative makes upon us.

In the first place, it is difficult not to recognize a legendary element in miracle-stories where the action of Jesus is not in question, such as the Baptism, the Transfiguration, and the Visit to the Tomb. In modern criticism it is widely held that the Baptism was an event highly significant in the consciousness of Jesus, and that there was no actual rending of the heavens and no voice heard by others. It may be doubted, however, if this is what Mark means, and certainly in the later tradition visible and audible phenomena are described.[1] A similar element is also present in the Transfiguration, in the references to Moses and Elijah, the Voice from the cloud, and the use of $\mu\epsilon\tau\alpha\mu\rho\phi\delta\omega$. In the narrative of the Visit to the Tomb, quite apart from the question of the Empty Tomb, there are imaginative details in the statement that the women came to anoint Jesus, the question ' Who will roll away the stone for us from the door of the tomb ? ', the angel's message, and the explanation that, being afraid, they said nothing to anyone.[2] If this legendary development is recognized, the possibility of its presence in the accounts of the nature-miracles cannot be foreclosed.

Secondly, elements within these narratives are capable of a non-miraculous interpretation. Few commentators accept the historical character of the cursing of the fig tree. By wide consent it is agreed that the basis of the story is a spoken parable or a legend which had grown up in connexion with a withered tree Jesus was said to have passed on His way from Bethany to Jerusalem. As regards the stilling of the storm, the walking on the water, and the multiplication of the loaves, the distinction between what really happened and the interpretation placed on the facts by the Evangelist, or even by the eyewitnesses, is a relevant consideration. Jesus may have addressed the winds without thinking of controlling their power (cf. xi. 14, 23), and the exclamation, ' Who then is this, that even the wind and the sea obey him ? ', may be a natural, but mistaken comment. In the account of the meal in the wilderness only the numbers and the statement that

---

[1] Cf. Luke iii. 21 f., John i. 32.
[2] These points are discussed in detail in the Commentary.

all ate and were filled suggest a miracle, while vi. 41 points
to a eucharistic meal ; and in the story of the crossing of the
lake the disciples thought they saw an apparition. Similar
features are present in the story of Jairus' daughter : Jesus
took no notice of the tidings of death, the saying, ' The
child is not dead, but sleeps ', is ambiguous, and ἀνέστη may
mean no more than that she arose from a trance-like sleep.[1]

Thirdly, it is difficult to give a satisfactory account of the
purpose of these incidents. In the narratives there is no
suggestion that the miracles were wrought to demonstrate
the Messiahship of Jesus or to convince men of His supernatural claims. If the incidents happened as they are
reported, they must have been exceptional acts of compassion. Compassion can easily be seen in the raising of the
little maid, but were there not many bereaved parents in
Galilee, and was Jesus accustomed to raise the dead ? Storms
on the lake were frequent, and in the disciples' extremity
Jesus might well rely on the providential care of the
Father, all the more since He believed that His hour was
not yet come. But what special circumstances called for
the control of winds and power to walk upon waves ? And
were the five thousand in such an extremity of hunger that
a creative act was necessary ? There may be answers to
these questions, but all the known answers breathe an air of
strain.

Lastly, the christology of the nature-miracles is different
from that implicit in the Markan tradition as a whole. The
christology of the latter is that of a *Deus absconditus*, who
fully accepts the limitations of a human life and remains
hidden save to the eyes of faith ; the christology of the nature-
miracles is that of a *Deus revelatus*, the God who throws off
all disguise and is not bound by the conditions of human
existence. Both representations appear in Mark, and it is
for this reason that Dibelius [2] is able to speak paradoxically
of the Gospel as ' a book of secret epiphanies ' ; but we shall
do well to hesitate before we accept this representation as
historical, partly because the ' epiphanies ' turn out to be
legends, and more because we may find ourselves well on

[1] For the several questions raised in this summary *v*. Comm. *in loc.*
[2] *Op. cit.* 94 f., 229 f.

the way to a docetic view of the person of Christ.   Religiously
and theologically, an Incarnation doctrine which takes Paul's
' being found in fashion as a man ' seriously is of greater
value than one which suggests the Greek idea of a demi-god,
and the quick returns of such a christology are small com-
pensation for the loss of the abiding wonder which sees the
Godhead ' veiled in flesh ' and finds its true glory expressed
in the lines :

> ' He laid His glory by,
>   He wrapped Him in our clay ;
> Unmarked by human eye,
>   The latent Godhead lay '.

This theological argument will doubtless be differently
evaluated ; but the case as a whole is strongly in favour of
the conclusion that the beliefs and presuppositions of the first
century have left their mark on the records of the Gospel
miracles and particularly the nature-miracles.

If the view outlined above is accepted, the question arises
how far it compromises the otherwise high estimate we have
formed of the Markan tradition.   The answer, I suggest, is
that this estimate is not appreciably diminished, since it stands
on its own grounds, unless we sigh for infallibility and distort
the truth of the Papias tradition.   Light still shines when
refraction is recognized.   The surprising thing about the
Gospel of Mark is not that it contains legendary elements,
but the small amount of these features, and this fact can be
explained only by the restraint of the Evangelist and his use
of early and valuable tradition.

The best defence of the nature-miracles, as of the miracles generally, is Canon Alan Richardson's *The Miracle Stories of the Gospels*
(1941). Canon Richardson takes the view that ' the miracle-stories
are a part of the Gospel itself ' (p. 126), that Christ is ' the manifestation of the power of God in the world ', and that ' His mighty
deeds are the signs of the effectual working of that power '.   He
claims that, if we accept the Gospel proclaimed by the Evangelists,
' we accept the history they record ', and that, if we reject it, ' we
shall inevitably reject the view that Jesus performed miracles ',
or we shall seek to explain them away.   This argument unduly
simplifies the problem ; it does not take account of a possible difference between the original facts and the form in which the Evangelists
record them ; and for its justification it would require something

like the theory of verbal inspiration. Canon Richardson is conscious of the danger of over-simplification, and later he observes that the problem of the history of each recorded miracle remains open for critical and historical discussion. In the end it is admitted that ' each reader of the Gospels must, on the basis of his own studies and insights, make his own estimate of the historical probability of any particular episode for himself ', and that ' he will not wish to press his own conclusions upon others ' (p. 130). This is well and finely said ; but, if it is true, the basic theological claim, that ' the miracle-stories form an essential and inseparable part of the Gospel tradition ' (p. 1), is open to qualification, and should be replaced by the more modest principle : ' Some miracle-stories, but not necessarily all, are a part of the Gospel itself '. See further, the strong and forceful argument of D. S. Cairns in *The Faith that Rebels* (1928).

THE MARKAN OUTLINE

The last question to be considered is how far the Markan outline supplies a credible account of the course of the ministry of Jesus. The widespread view of many continental scholars is that, in *Der Rahmen der Geschichte Jesu*, K. L. Schmidt has shown that the outline is irretrievably broken, apart from fragmentary episodes in some of the smaller complexes and in the Passion Narrative.[1] This question must now be considered more closely.

Some account of the main outline must first be recalled. The Gospel is rightly characterized as a Passion Narrative with an introduction. If it is so judged, and not as a more ambitious historical record, many objections are met. It must also be recognized that much of Mark's material had for various purposes already been arranged in groups and in some cases probably by himself. He does not write with complete literary freedom ; he copies others and himself.

The Evangelist begins where primitive Christianity began, with the Preaching of John, the Baptism, and Temptation. He does not describe a preliminary Judaean ministry. If, then, we accept the testimony of the Fourth Gospel, as we have good reason to do, there is a gap in the outline at the beginning. Nevertheless, Mark appropriately fixes on the imprisonment of the Baptist as the decisive moment for the opening of

[1] See earlier, pp. 17-18.

the Galilean ministry, on the imminence of the Kingdom
as its distinctive message, and the call of the disciples as its
first step.   It is soon manifest that he has no day to day
account of the progress of the mission, but he shows good
historical judgment in using an impressive record of a typical
day in the life of Jesus (i. 21-39), followed by the account of
the cure of a leper.   Before the reference to Capernaum in
ii. 1 there is a further gap in the phrase ' after some days ',
and use is then made of a topically arranged pre-Markan
group of conflict-stories (ii. 1-iii. 6), which causes the allusion
to the death plot of the Pharisees and the Herodians to appear
too early in the outline.   The description in iii. 7-12 of the
crowds, the healings, the anxiety of the sick to touch Jesus,
and the silencing of the demoniacs, gives a vivid picture of
the enthusiastic and tumultuous scenes which attended the
mission, but it is only a summary account.   The narrative
of the appointment of the Twelve is undated and the account of the charges of collusion with Satan and the fears
of the family of Jesus is taken over from an existing complex.

There is clearly no ordered sequence in the early part of
the story of events apart from i. 21-39 and possibly iii. 19b-35.
If, however, we have regard to history in the broader sense,
we must recognize that Mark brings out the main points, the
announcement of the Kingdom, the choice and appointment
of the Twelve, the healing ministry, the conflicts with the
Pharisees, and the charges brought against Jesus.   In iv. 1-34
the teaching by the lake side comes to the fore, but, after the
narrative passage in 1 f., as often where sayings are in question, the arrangement is editorial.   It is notable how particular
days stand out.   This day appears to be remembered, not
only for the teaching, but also for the crossing and recrossing
of the lake, and a series of events, perhaps telescoped, but
given in chronological order (iv. 34-v. 43).   At the beginning
of vi there is a want of precision, but Mark intends to recount
that, after the Mission of the Twelve, which followed the Rejection at Nazareth, Jesus withdrew first with His disciples (vi.
30-4), and subsequently alone (vii. 24), into retirement.   We
receive this impression, not so much from what is actually said,[1]

[1] Cf. vii. 24, 31.

as from the course of the story as a whole, especially if
vi. 30-56 + vii. 24-37 and viii. 1-26 cover the same period, since
in this case the incident near Caesarea Philippi follows soon
after the withdrawal to Tyre and Sidon and the return to
Bethsaida.[1] In spite of what has been said to the contrary,[2]
the Confession of Peter is a watershed in the Markan Story.
With that event begins the teaching that the Son of Man
' must suffer ', and from this point onwards, although from
time to time Jesus teaches the multitude,[3] He more frequently
instructs His disciples.[4] ' Six days ' after Peter's Confession
the Transfiguration follows, and with ix. 30 begins the
journey through Galilee and Judaea (x. 1) and Jericho (x. 46)
to Jerusalem. As we have seen,[5] for the details of this journey
Mark has little information and is compelled to use fragmentary tradition. The events in and around Jerusalem are
also narrated in a very summary fashion, and a comparison
with John (cf. x. 40-2, xi. 54-7) shows how much longer and
more varied this period was. Step by step the sacred drama
moves to its climax in the story of the betrayal, arrest, trials,
crucifixion, death, and resurrection of Jesus.

If we consider this outline along with the various groups
examined earlier, we shall see the truth of Schmidt's estimate
as well as its limitations. Mark's Gospel is a collection of
self-contained narratives, many of which are grouped topically and others chronologically; but it is not a heap of
unstrung pearls. On the contrary, the Evangelist has a true
sense of the course of events, knows the issues involved, and
the points on which the Story turns. His framework is
factual rather than chronological in the full sense. He writes,
as it were, on an even plane, so that it is vain to argue that
his account implies a ministry of twelve months or less,
in contrast with the two to three years covered by John;
but the plane has contours and dividing ridges which imply
a broad knowledge of the course of events as well as of

---

[1] See Note D on pp. 632-6.

[2] Cf. Bultmann, 375, who, following
Wrede, rejects the view that viii. 27-33
is a new turn in the Story, and says
that, in reality, it is an epoch for the
reader, not for the life of Jesus. Cf.
also Schweitzer, *The Quest of the Historical Jesus*, 329-34.

[3] The crowd is mentioned in viii. 34,
ix. 14, x. 1, 46, xi. 18, xii. 37, and
public teaching in x. 1, xi. 17, xii. 35,
xiv. 49.

[4] Cf. viii. 31-3, ix. 9-13, 28 f., 31-50,
x. 23-45, xi. 22-5, xiii. 1-37.

[5] See earlier, pp. 98-100.

details.[1] What Schmidt has destroyed is the cast-iron Markan hypothesis, which posits a fixed historical scheme, biographical in kind. In fact, the outline is partial and broken, like a river which at times in its course disappears from sight, but the Story has movement and direction, again like a river which reaches the sea. We shall not use the outline with the confidence of many earlier critics, contemptuously dismissing other tradition because it is not Markan and does not fall obviously within the scheme; but any attempt to tell the Story of Jesus even broadly, showing how beginning from the earliest preaching the Kingdom of God it ends in death and victory, must use, and is justified in using, the Markan outline.

SUMMARY

In sum we may say that in Mark we have an authority of first rank for our knowledge of the Story of Jesus. Separated at the time of writing by little more than a generation from the death of Jesus, its contents carry us back farther into the oral period before Mark wrote to the tradition first of the Palestinian community and subsequently that of the Gentile Church at Rome. The historical value of Mark depends on the Evangelist's fidelity to that tradition, including his special advantages as a hearer of Peter's preaching. Whether we judge his work by a consideration of the various influences which affected it, those of defence, worship, teaching, and doctrine, or whether we consider its objective character, we

[1] Cf. W. F. Howard, *LQR* (July 1927), 79: 'The verisimilitude of the development of the ministry as given in Mark is a miracle of artistry if it cannot be traced back to the coherent memory of a writer who recorded the story as he had heard it from one who was himself no small part in the developing drama'; C. H. Dodd, *ET*, xliii (June 1932), 400: 'It is hazardous to argue from the precise sequence of the narrative in detail; yet there is good reason to believe that in broad lines the Marcan order does represent a genuine succession of events, within which movement and development can be traced'; F. C. Burkitt, *JTS* (April 1935), xxxvi. 187 f.: 'In opposition to the opinion of many scholars I feel that Mark *is* a Biography, if by Biography we mean the chief outlines of a career, rather than a static characterization. In Mark there is movement and progression. . . . It does not sound to me like *Gemeindetheologie*, the unconscious secretion of a community of believers. Nothing but a strong element of personal reminiscence could have produced it. And therefore I still hold to the belief that it embodies the private reminiscences of Peter, supplemented for the last week by the reminiscences of the young Mark himself.'

reach the same conclusion that here is a writing of first-rate historical importance. Its relatively few legendary elements and its apocalyptic tendencies, and the gaps in its outline of the course of events, qualify but do not undermine this estimate. We may say of the Gospel what St. Paul says of the first missionaries ; we have this treasure in earthen vessels, that the exceeding greatness of the power may be of God (2 Cor. iv. 7). Without this Gospel, which is not only invaluable in itself, but is also one of the most important sources upon which all the Gospels depend, it is impossible to account for the history of primitive Christianity, or to imagine the perils from which it was preserved ; for it sets at the centre the personality of Jesus Himself and His redemptive work for men.

KATA MAPKON

I

Mk. i. 1-13 INTRODUCTION

THE first thirteen verses of the Gospel form a closely connected section which serves as an introduction to the whole. In the arrangement of Westcott and Hort, who leave a space after i. 8, this unity is somewhat concealed. There is no real break at this point.[1] After stating his theme in i. 1, the Evangelist's intention is to describe summarily the preaching of John the Baptist and the baptism and temptation of Jesus as a prelude to his account of the Galilean Mission. In this respect he was following an existing tradition, for it is clear from Ac. i. 22, 'beginning from the baptism of John', that the earliest Christian preaching began in this manner. His aim is to set the reader at the right point of view for an understanding of the story of Jesus as a whole. It cannot be surprising therefore if his theology has left its stamp upon the material he has derived from Christian tradition. To what extent he used existing narratives in the section is uncertain, but it is to be expected that he would select and arrange his material in order to show how 'the Good News about Jesus Christ, the Son of God' began.

Mk. i. 1-8   1. JOHN THE BAPTIZER   Cf. Mt. iii. 1-12
                                                    Lk. iii. 1-18

In recording this story Mark has used existing tradition. K. L. Schmidt, 18, finds an original unit in 4-8, to which apparently Mark added 1-3, the phrase 'in the wilderness' (4), and the description of John (6). In this way, he suggests, a story about a Jordan-baptizer was adapted to that of a wilderness-preacher. Bultmann, 261, agrees, but finds further additions in 7 f. Lohmeyer, 10, 12, sees signs of earlier tradition in the absolute use of ἡ ἔρημος (i. 3 f., 12 f.; v. Comm.), in ἔσθων (here only in Mk), the unusual periphrastic tenses in i. 4, 6, the tense of ἐβάπτισα, and the initial position of the verbs.

The narrative is composed by a process of selection and emphasis. Mark could have reported more concerning John. He knows that he gathered round him a body of disciples (ii. 18, vi. 29), that he was put to death by Antipas (vi. 14-29), and that his great success was an embarrassment to the chief priests (xi. 27-33). Believing John to be Elijah *redivivus* (ix. 13), he here relates that his coming was in fulfilment of prophecy (i. 2 f.), and describes his prophet's clothing (i. 6), his ministry and repen-

---

[1] Cf. R. H. Lightfoot, 61-3.

151

tance-baptism (i. 4 f.), concentrating attention upon the advent of the Mightier One and the baptism he will dispense (i. 7 f.). His immediate purpose leads him to omit a fuller account of John's preaching and his announcement of impending doom (cf. Mt. iii. 7-12, Lk. iii. 7-14, 17). The narrative is not that of a historian, but of a Christian believer deeply interested in John's eschatological message and its relation to the ministry of Jesus.

I. 1 ΑΡΧΗ τοῦ εὐαγγελίου Ἰησοῦ Χριστοῦ υἱοῦ θεοῦ.

1. Ἀρχὴ τοῦ εὐαγγελίου Ἰησοῦ Χριστοῦ υἱοῦ θεοῦ. ἀρχή, x. 6, xiii. 9, 19*, 'beginning'. Rawlinson, 6, translates 'starting-point'. Cf. Hos. i. 2, Ἀρχὴ λόγου κυρίου ἐν Ὡσῆε, Prov. i. 1, Eccl. i. 1, Cant. i. 1. εὐαγγέλιον, i. 14 f., viii. 35, x. 29, xiii. 10, xiv. 9, xvi. [15]*; Mt (4), Lk (0); 'Good News'. In Cl. Gk the word originally meant 'the reward of good tidings', but it is rarely found outside the NT and early Christian literature. In the sense of 'good tidings' the plur. appears in an inscription (c. 9 B.C.) with reference to the birthday of Augustus (VGT, 259). Characteristic of Mk (Hawkins, 12), and freely used by St. Paul, the word is employed here, not of a book or generally, but of the Apostolic message of salvation in Christ (cf. J. Weiss, 29-42). See 1 Thess. iii. 2, 2 Cor. ix. 13, Gal. i. 7, Phil. i. 27. Ἰησοῦ Χριστοῦ, here only in Mk, is a personal name. The gen. is objective : 'the good news about Jesus Christ'; cf. Holtzmann, 111; J. Weiss, 26 f.; Lagrange, 2; Swete, 1; Plummer, 51; Gould, 3. υἱοῦ θεοῦ is omitted by א* Θ 28 syhier geo¹ arm Iren Or, and by the WH text. There are strong reasons, however, for accepting the phrase as original, in view of its attestation (אa B D L W it vg sype hl sa bo geo² arm (3 best MSS.) Iren Orint. Aug), its possible omission by homoioteleuton, and the use of the title in Mark's Christology (v. Intr. 120 f.). For the Patristic evidence v. Turner, JTS, xxviii. 150. See also Lagrange, 3, and Rawlinson, 4 f.

Elsewhere in Mk Jesus is spoken of as 'the Son of God' (iii. 11, v. 7, xv. 39), 'My beloved Son' (i. 11, ix. 7),

'the Son of the Blessed' (xiv. 61). The idea is not simply Messianic. A supernatural being is described, but not with the precision of Phil. ii. 6 or Lk. i. 35. Cf. J. Weiss, Die Schr.⁴ 76-9; Bultmann, ThNT, i. 129-32.

The verse is probably intended by Mark as a title, as the absence of the article before ἀρχή may indicate (cf. Moulton, i. 82; Robertson, 781, 793), with reference either to the account of the Baptist's ministry (cf. Gould, 2), or to the entire Gospel (Zahn, ii. 458 ff.; Swete, 1; Klostermann, 4; Montefiore, i. 3; Plummer, 51). The second alternative is to be preferred. No other narrative in Mk is preceded by a title. The words, moreover, point far beyond the story of the Fore-runner and admirably sum up the substance of the Gospel. Mark proposes to relate how the good news about Jesus Christ the Son of God began.

If this view is taken, a full stop should be placed, as in WH, after i. 1. So RV and RSV. This view is preferable to that of Turner, JTS, xxvi. 146, who treats 2 f. as a parenthesis. Cf. Rawlinson, 6, 250 f. : 'The starting-point of the Good News about Jesus Christ (in accordance with scriptural words of the Prophet Isaiah, "The voice of a man crying in the desert, Make ye ready the way of the Lord, Make straight his paths "), was John, who baptized in the desert, and proclaimed a baptism of repentance with a view to the remission of sins'. This suggestion is attractive, but it obscures the character of i. 1 as a title and tends to subordinate the importance of the quotation of Isa. xl. 3.

Καθὼς γέγραπται ἐν τῷ Ἡσαίᾳ τῷ προφήτῃ   2
Ἰδοὺ ἀποστέλλω τὸν ἄγγελόν μου πρὸ προσώπου σου,
ὃς κατασκευάσει τὴν ὁδόν σου·
φωνὴ βοῶντος ἐν τῇ ἐρήμῳ   3
Ἑτοιμάσατε τὴν ὁδὸν Κυρίου·

2. Καθώς stands at the beginning of a new sentence as in Lk. xi. 30, xvii. 26, Jn. iii. 14, and 1 Cor. ii. 9. The common formula of citation καθὼς γέγραπται (LXX, 4 Kgdms. xiv. 6, etc.) is found here only in Mk. But cf. ix. 13, xiv. 21. The perf., expressing past action with abiding results, is best rendered by 'stands written'; cf. vii. 6, ix. 12 f., xi. 17, xiv. 21, 27. In x. 4 f., xii. 19 the aor. is used. Ἡσαίας, vii. 6*. προφήτης, vi. 4, 15, viii. 28, xi. 32*. The reading ἐν τοῖς προφήταις (A W fam. 13 28 118 543 579 et al.) is an attempt to meet the difficulty that the first quotation is not from Isa.

ἰδού, iii. 32, iv. 3, x. 28, 33, xiv. 41 f. καὶ ἰδού, common in Mt and Lk, is not found in Mk. ἀποστέλλω, 20 times*, v. iii. 14. ἄγγελος, i. 13 (q.v.), viii. 38, xii. 25, xiii. 27, 32*. Here only in Mk in the sense of the messenger of God (KThW, i. 82). πρόσωπον, xii. 14, xiv. 65*, 'face'; Cl., LXX, Pap. In the papyri, as also in Cl. Gk, it is further used of the 'outward appearance' and in the sense of 'person.' (VGT, 553). κατασκευάζω*.

The first part of the quotation agrees verbatim with Ex. xxiii. 20a, καὶ ἰδοὺ ἐγὼ ἀποστέλλω τὸν ἄγγελόν μου πρὸ προσώπου σου; the second part with the Heb. of Mal. iii. 1 ('. . . and he shall prepare the way before me') rather than with the LXX (καὶ ἐπιβλέψεται ὁδὸν πρὸ προσώπου μου),[1] but differs from both in reading τὴν ὁδόν σου. Mark's version is manifestly a re-interpretation of the prophecy in a Messianic sense. The same combination appears in Mt. xi. 10 = Lk. vii. 27 (with the addition of ἔμπροσθέν σου), which is either the text of Q or a Matthaean addition to that source (cf. T. W. Manson, SJ, 69). In agreement with Holtzmann, 111 f., Lagrange, 4,

and Rawlinson, 6, explain the quotation as a copyist's gloss, and there are good reasons for this view. (1) The quotation is wanting in the parallel narratives; (2) It breaks the natural connexion between the reference to Isaiah and the quotation from Isa. xl. 3 in Mk. i. 3; (3) the same combination of Ex. xxiii. 20a and the Heb. of Mal. iii. 1 appears in Mt. xi. 10 and Lk. vii. 27. These arguments are not equally forcible. Matthew and Luke may have deliberately omitted the quotation in i. 2, and Mark may have inadvertently introduced it from a collection of Messianic proof-texts. It is very difficult, however, to suppose that all the Synoptists found it in the same form, and, on the whole, it is best to regard the quotation in i. 2 as a later insertion, despite the fact that there is no textual evidence against it.

3. The second quotation is taken almost verbatim from the LXX text of Isa. xl. 3, the only difference being that Mark replaces τοῦ θεοῦ ἡμῶν by αὐτοῦ. Again Mark interprets the prophecy Messianically. So also the Rabbis; cf. Billerbeck, i. 96 f. The Heb. connects 'in the wilderness' with 'prepare'. φωνή, i. 11, 26, v. 7, ix. 7, xv. 34, 37*; βοάω, xv. 34; ἔρημος, i. 4, 12 f., ἔρημος τόπος, i. 35, 45, vi. 31 f., 35*. The 'wilderness' is the wild uncultivated country to the west of the Dead Sea, but the phrase may be used generally in harmony with the prophecy.

ἑτοιμάζω, x. 40, xiv. 12, 15 f., xv. 1 (?)*. κύριος is used 15 times in Mk, and twice in the title ὁ κύριος in the spurious ending. Here it used of God, as in v. 19, xi. 9, xii. 11, 29 f., 36, xiii. 20, but it is possible that Mark has the Messiah in mind; cf. xii. 36 f., xiii. 35. All the more remarkable is

---

[1] The LXX appears to have read panah rather than pinnah; cf. Lohmeyer, 11.

εὐθείας ποιεῖτε τὰς τρίβους αὐτοῦ,

4 ἐγένετο Ἰωάνης ὁ βαπτίζων ἐν τῇ ἐρήμῳ κηρύσσων βάπτισμα

the fact that he never uses κύριος of Jesus, except in the voc. in vii. 28, and, with the article once in xi. 3, possibly in the sense of ' the Master '. In ii. 28 it is used in the predicate : ' The Son of Man is lord even of the Sabbath '; in xii. 9 of ' the lord of the vineyard '; and in xiii. 35 in the phrase ' the lord of the house '. These facts illustrate the primitive character of Mark's usage. In Lk ὁ κύριος is found 16 or 17 times. Matthew's usage agrees with that of Mk, while John probably restricts the title to the Risen Christ (cf. Bernard, *St. Jn*, 55 f., 132). With τὴν ὁδὸν κυρίου cf. τὴν ὁδὸν τοῦ θεοῦ (xii. 14). In εὐθείας ποιεῖτε τὰς τρίβους αὐτοῦ, εὐθύς is used as an adj.*. τρίβος* is a beaten track ; so Herodotus viii. 140 and Pap. (*VGT*, 641).

After the quotation Swete has a full stop, but it is better to use a comma, with WH, Nestle, Plummer, and Lagrange, or a semi-colon with the RV. This punctuation brings the quotation into close relation with i. 4. Mark's intention appears to be to assert that, just as Scripture told of a Voice *crying in the wilderness*, so John came *preaching in the wilderness*.

4. Ἰωάνης (of the Baptist), 16 times*. Mark takes great interest in John; cf. i. 6, 9, 14, ii. 18, vi. 14-25, viii. 28, xi. 30, 32. He does not describe his birth and parentage, but presents him as the Fore-runner of Jesus. Emphasis is laid on his emergence in accordance with the divine purpose. Hence the use of ἐγένετο. The word may be taken with κηρύσσων, thus forming a periphrastic tense ; cf. ix. 3, 7, and see Howard, ii. 452 ; but it may stand alone, as in Jn. i. 6, 2 Pet. ii. 1, 1 Jn. ii. 18, with a Semitic emphasis. Cf. Lohmeyer, 12 n. See also RSV. βαπτίζω, i. 5, 8 (*bis*), 9, vi. 14, 24, x. 38 (*bis*), 39 (*bis*), xvi. [16]*, ' to dip ', 'plunge', is the intensive form of βάπτω; Cl., LXX (4), Pap. (*VGT*, 102). Cf. Flemington, 11 f. κηρύσσω, i. 7,

14, 38 f., 45, iii. 14, v. 20, vi. 12, vii. 36, xiii. 10, xiv. 9, xvi. [15, 20]*, ' to proclaim ' (<κῆρυξ) ; Cl., LXX, Pap. Here, as in vi. 14, 24*, John is described as ὁ βαπτίζων ; in vi. 25 and viii. 28* as ὁ βαπτιστής, the form exclusively used in Mt (7) and Lk (3), and by Josephus. In Mk the two are almost synonymous, but there is a greater emphasis in ὁ βαπτίζων on the action. If καί is read before κηρύσσων, the Gk may be read ' the baptizer and preacher ' (cf. Swete, 3), or ' who was baptizing and preaching '; but καί should be omitted with B 33 73 579 892 sa bo, and ὁ βαπτίζων treated as a noun. Cf. J. Weiss, 127 n. ; Gould, 6 ; Lagrange, 5 ; Turner, *JTS*, xxviii. 150. The fact that John is introduced without any further description shows that Mk was written for readers to whom his work and ministry were well known.

In βάπτισμα μετανοίας εἰς ἄφεσιν ἁμαρτιῶν every word is important. βάπτισμα, x. 38 f., xi. 30*, Mt (2), Lk (4), Ac (6), Pl (3), 1 Pet. iii. 21**, is the distinctive NT word for ' baptism '. Here it is characterized by the gen. of quality μετανοίας, ' a repentance-baptism '. μετάνοια*, <μετανοέω. As the derivation shows, the noun denotes ' a change of mind ', but in the NT it is used in a deeper sense, indicating a deliberate turning (cf. the Heb. שׁוּב), ' a coming to one's senses, resulting in a change of conduct ' (*VGT*, 404). The baptism has for its end (εἰς) the remission of sins. ἄφεσις, iii. 29*, is ' remission '. The deeper sense of ' forgiveness ', as the restoration of broken relationships, is the product of Christian thought and experience. Cf. Taylor, *Forgiveness and Reconciliation*, 1-23. Both ἁμαρτία, i. 5, ii. 5, 7, 9 f.*, and ἁμάρτημα, iii. 28 f.*, are derived from ἁμαρτάνω, ' to miss the mark ', ' to sin '. The latter denotes a specific act of sin, the former both an act of sin (in the Synoptics) and a state of mind hostile to

μετανοίας εἰς ἄφεσιν ἁμαρτιῶν. καὶ ἐξεπορεύετο πρὸς αὐτὸν 5
πᾶσα ἡ Ἰουδαία χώρα καὶ οἱ Ἱεροσολυμεῖται πάντες, καὶ ἐβαπτίζοντο ὑπ' αὐτοῦ ἐν τῷ Ἰορδάνῃ ποταμῷ ἐξομολογούμενοι τὰς
ἁμαρτίας αὐτῶν. καὶ ἦν ὁ Ἰωάνης ἐνδεδυμένος τρίχας καμήλου 6
καὶ ζώνην δερματίνην περὶ τὴν ὀσφὺν αὐτοῦ, καὶ ἔσθων ἀκρίδας

God and an evil power to which man is exposed (Jn and the Pauline Epp.). Cf. G. Stählin, *KThW*, i. 297-9. Baptism does not take place *ex opere operato* (cf. Lagrange, 6), but it is not a mere picturesque symbol. Repentance is essential, but in harmony with the OT idea of prophetic representative action (cf. I Kgs. xxii. II, Isa. xx. 2, Jer. xix. 10, xxviii. 10, Ezek. iv. 3; also Mk. xiv. 22, 24, Ac. xxi. 11), baptism gives expression to the act of repentance, and thereby becomes an effective action leading to the remission of sins. Mark's phrase is expressed in the vocabulary of primitive Christianity (cf. Ac. ii. 38, v. 31, x. 43, Eph. i. 7, Col. i. 14), but gives a historical account of John's baptism. The fundamental ideas are derived from the OT and there is no need to trace their origin to Hellenistic influences.

5. ἐκπορεύομαι, vi. 11, vii. 15, 19, 20 f., 23, x. 17, 46, xi. 19, xiii. 1*, Mt (5), Lk (3), Ac (3), Pl (1), Apoc (8)**. The word is characteristic of Mk; cf. Hawkins, 12. Ἰουδαία, iii. 7, x. 1, xiii. 14*. χώρα, v. 1, 10, vi. 55*. Ἱεροσολυμεῖτης, Jn. vii. 25**. There is a touch of hyperbole in Mark's reference to all the land of Judaea and all the people of Jerusalem, but there is no doubt that John's ministry aroused the greatest interest. The correct use of the two imperfects, ἐξεπορεύετο and ἐβαπτίζοντο, gives a vivid effect and illustrates a careful use of tenses. In certain respects John's baptism resembled Jewish proselyte-baptism (*tebilah*), but differed from it in that it was not an act of self-baptism and was administered to Jews, and that the action was an eschatological sacrament anticipatory of the in-breaking of the Kingdom of God. Cf. H. H. Rowley, *Hebrew Union College Annual* (Cin-

cinnati), xv (1940) 313-34. For the view that the *tebilah* goes back to the first century A.D. see Billerbeck, i. 102 ff.; Oepke, *KThW*, i. 533; Rowley, *op. cit.* 320. Marsh, 9-14; Flemington, 4-11. For the sacred associations of the Jordan *v.* Abrahams, i. 33; Marsh, 36-8. Connected with the ministries of Elijah and Elisha, above all in the story of Naaman (2 Kings v), the Jordan is the natural scene of John's baptism. Ἰορδάνης, i. 9, iii. 8, x. 1*; ποταμός*. ἐξομολογέω*, ' to acknowledge ', ' confess ', ' avow openly '; LXX, Pap. (*VGT*, 224). The verb belongs to later Gk. In the LXX it is mainly used in the sense of giving thanks or offering praise (but *v.* Dan. ix. 20), as in Mt. xi. 25 = Lk. x. 21. Here presumably the confession takes place before or during the act of baptism.

6. The clothing and food of John are now described. ἐνδύω (-δύνω), vi. 9, xv. 20*; Cl., LXX, Pap. The periphrastic tense ἦν . . . ἐνδεδυμένος denotes habitual action, ' was clothed (as his custom was) ', and is not simply the equivalent of the aor. pass. See *VGT*, 212. For the periphrastic imperf., (ἦν) . . . ἔσθων, so freely used by Mark, see the Intr. 45. The construction is probably a ' secondary Semitism '. When using Mk, Matthew usually omits it. Luke has many examples in L. ἔσθω is an earlier form of ἐσθίω; cf. Moulton, ii. 238.

The words which follow are either *hapax leg.* or rare in Mk: θρίξ*; κάμηλος, x. 25*; ζώνη, vi. 8*; δερμάτινος*, Mt. iii. 4**; ὀσφύς*; περί c. acc. (9)*. The internal accs. τρίχας and ζώνην are used regularly after the pass. of the verb of clothing. For the acc. of the person (external) and of the thing (internal) after the active *v.* xv. 17. Probably a garment woven of camel's hair is

7 καὶ μέλι ἄγριον.   καὶ ἐκήρυσσεν λέγων Ἔρχεται ὁ ἰσχυρότερός

meant. The reference to the girdle is probably intended to recall the description of Elijah in 4 Kgdms. i. 8, Ἀνὴρ δασὺς καὶ ζώνην δερματίνην περιεζωσμένος τὴν ὀσφὺν αὐτοῦ. D reads δέρρην (δέρριν) and a *pellem*, a reading which Turner, *JTS*, xxviii. 151, accepts instead of τρίχας, but it seems more probable that Moulton and Milligan are right in explaining it as a corruption derived from Zech. xiii. 4 (*VGT*, 142). The phrase καὶ ζώνην δερματίνην περὶ τὴν ὀσφὺν αὐτοῦ is wanting in D a b d ff r¹ t vg (1 MS.), and Turner, 12, *JTS*, xxviii. 151, thinks it may be a copyist's addition from Mt. iii. 4. While this is a possible explanation, it is more likely that the phrase is deliberately introduced by Mark, who believes that John belongs to the prophetic order and is Elijah, whose coming is foretold in Mal. iii. 1, iv. 5 f. (cf. Mk. ix. 9-13). For the belief that Elijah would be the precursor of the Messiah see Moore, ii. 357-62.

John's food is described as consisting of locusts and wild honey. ἀκρίς*, Mt. iii. 4, Apoc. ix. 3, 7**; μέλι*, Mt. iii. 4, Apoc. x. 9 f.**; ἄγριος*, Mt. iii. 4, Ju. 13**. The Bedouins are said to eat locusts roasted or salted. Wild honey is either the honey found in rocks or possibly the sap of certain trees. Cf. Billerbeck, i. 98-101; Lagrange, 7; Lohmeyer, 16; Gould, 8 (' wilderness food ').

Matthew's stylistic alterations are of much interest. The periphrastic constructions are replaced by εἶχεν τὸ ἔνδυμα αὐτοῦ and ἡ δὲ τροφὴ ἦν αὐτοῦ ἀκρίδες καὶ μ. α. (iii. 4). In 1-3 the variations affect the substance of the story : the wilderness is identified as ' the wilderness of Judaea '; John's message is μετανοεῖτε· ἤγγικεν γὰρ ἡ βασιλεία τῶν οὐρανῶν (iii. 2); Isa. xl. 3 is directly applied to him and the reference to a repentance-baptism is omitted. Luke probably uses another

source, but shows his knowledge of Mk in reproducing βάπτισμα μετανοίας εἰς ἄφεσιν ἁμαρτιῶν (iii. 3). To the description of John's clothing and food he has no parallel.

7. Mark's account of the Baptist's preaching is very brief. He has nothing corresponding to the sayings in Q (Mt. iii. 7-10 = Lk. iii. 7-9, 17) about the wrath to come, the axe laid at the root of the trees, the fan in the hands of the Coming One, the threshing floor, and the burning of the chaff in unquenchable fire. Neither does he record the exhortations to the multitudes, the taxgatherers, and the soldiers (Lk. iii. 10-14). Everything is concentrated on the prophecy of the coming of the Mightier One and the baptism which, in contrast to his own baptism by water, the Messiah will dispense.

The present ἔρχεται sounds the note of immediacy. ὁ ἰσχυρός (iii. 27) has a long history behind it (cf. Isa. xlix. 25, liii. 12). It is applied in various ways to Satan (iii. 27), to powerful oppressors (Apoc. vi. 15, xix. 18), to angels (Apoc. x. 1, xviii. 21), and to God (Apoc. xviii. 8, 1 Cor. x. 22). Here, as by implication in iii. 27, and more directly in Lk. xi. 22, it describes the expected eschatological deliverer and judge. The idea implies a primitive Christology which W. Grundmann, *KThW*, iii. 404 f., believes goes back to Jesus Himself. John speaks of the Mighty One as stronger than himself, ὁ ἰσχυρότερός μου, which may suggest a consciousness of standing at the beginning of the unfolding of the eschatological drama. It is perhaps a refinement when Lohmeyer, 18, interprets ὀπίσω μου¹ of the slave-master relationship, thus suggesting the startling paradox that this One who follows after is none the less the Judge and Saviour of the End Time; for while ὀπίσω in the LXX frequently denotes place, it is also used of succession in

¹ μου is omitted by B Or and Turner, *JTS*, xxviii. 151, with much doubt, puts it in brackets. The omission of κύψας in a number of MSS. (*v.* Legg) is probably accidental or due to assimilation.

μου ὀπίσω [μου], οὗ οὐκ εἰμὶ ἱκανὸς κύψας λῦσαι τὸν ἱμάντα τῶν
ὑποδημάτων αὐτοῦ· ἐγὼ ἐβάπτισα ὑμᾶς ὕδατι, αὐτὸς δὲ βαπτίσει 8
ὑμᾶς πνεύματι ἁγίῳ.

time (cf. HR, especially 3 Kgdms. i. 6,
Neh. iii. 17, xi. 8, Dan. (Theod.) ii. 39,
vii. 6 f.). For ὀπίσω (i. 17, 20, viii. 33 f.,
xiii. 16*), a later form of ὄπισθεν (v.
27*), which is used in the LXX, the
NT, and MGk, as a prep. c. gen., like
the Heb. אַחֲרֵי, see Moulton, i. 99;
VGT, 453.

For this Deliverer John confesses his
unworthiness to perform the mean
duties of a slave. For examples in
Rabbinic literature of the loosing or
bearing (Mt. iii. 11) of shoes see Billerbeck, i. 121, ii. 1. ἱκανός, x. 46, xv.
15*, 'fit', 'sufficient', and (with
numbers) 'much', 'many'. Mark
alone has κύψας*. ἱμάς*, Lk. iii. 16,
Jn. i. 27, Ac. xxii. 25**, is the 'thong'
or 'strap' for fastening sandals or
binding prisoners (VGT, 304). ὑπόδημα*, 'sandal'; Cl., LXX, Pap.
(VGT, 657). For the redundant αὐτοῦ
after οὗ οὐκ εἰμὶ ἱκανός v. Intr. 60, and
cf. vii. 25 (ix. 3 and xiii. 19). Its presence, with other constructions already
noted, marks the Semitic tone of the
narrative.

8. In the second saying John draws
a sharp contrast between his baptism
and that of the Coming One, marked
by the emphatic use of the pronouns
ἐγώ and αὐτός. ἐβάπτισα may be 'the
aorist of the thing just happened' (cf.
Howard, ii. 458 f.), but more probably
represents the Heb. stative perf.
'baptize'. See Intr. 64. Matthew
has βαπτίζω (iii. 11).

πνεύματι ἁγίῳ is used of the Holy
Spirit.[1] In i. 10, 12 the form is τὸ
πνεῦμα, and in iii. 29, xii. 36, xiii. 11

τὸ πνεῦμα τὸ ἅγιον. In view of NT
usage as a whole it seems doubtful if
we ought to read 'with holy spirit'
here. In Q (Mt. iii. 11 = Lk. iii. 16)
the corresponding phrase is ἐν πνεύματι
ἁγίῳ καὶ πυρί, 'with the Holy Spirit
and with fire'. The question therefore
arises whether the original contrast
was with a baptism with fire, that is,
of judgment; cf. Amos vii. 4, Isa.
xxxi. 9, Mal. iii. 2, 1 Cor. iii. 13, 2
Thess. i. 7 f. So Wellhausen, Mt, in
loc.; J. Weiss, 125, Die Schr.⁴ i. 74;
Bultmann, 116 n.; Creed, 54; Manson, SJ, 41; Flemington, 19. This
view is strongly supported by the saying about the fan, the wheat, and the
chaff, which immediately follows in Q.
In this context a reference to the fire
of judgment is natural. Probably,
then, the reference to the Holy Spirit
has been introduced under the influence of the Christian practice of baptism. It is true that the outpouring of
the Spirit was expected in the last
times; cf. Joel ii. 28 f., Isa. xliv. 3,
Ezek. xxxvi. 26 f., Test. Levi xviii;
but the Spirit is not described as the
gift of the Messiah. Cf. Lagrange, 8:
Il n'était pas question dans ces passages
d'un intermédiaire. An alternative
suggestion is that the original phrase
was 'with wind and fire'. This conjectural rendering would be in harmony with the later reference to the
fan and the fire, while πνεύματι would
suggest to Christian readers a reference to the Spirit. Cf. R. Eisler, The
Messiah Jesus and John the Baptist,
275 f.; C. K. Barrett, 126.

DETACHED NOTE ON JOSEPHUS'S REFERENCE TO JOHN THE BAPTIST

Josephus, Ant. xviii. 5. 2, describes John as a good man who exhorted
the Jews to practise virtue, to display righteousness towards one another,

---

[1] ἐν before πνεύματι should probably be omitted with B L b vg geo Aug.

to show piety towards God, and to come together in baptism.[1] Baptism, he explains, would be acceptable to God, if it served, not[2] for the remission of certain sins, but for the purifying of the body, provided that the soul had first been purified by righteousness. Josephus mentions the profound effect exerted by John's preaching upon the people. Indeed, it is to this fact that he attributes Herod's act in arresting John and executing him later in the fortress of Machaerus. He thought it far better to take the initiative and put him to death ' lest, if a riot actually took place, he might himself be involved in trouble and have cause to regret it '. The account is not one which could be attributed to a Christian writer, and with some confidence it may be accepted as authentic.[3] Like Mark, but for different reasons, Josephus makes no reference to John's eschatological preaching, and he does not mention his announcement of the coming of the Messiah (cf. Mk. i. 7). ' This may be due to ignorance, but it seems more probable that his evidence has been influenced and altered by his pre-conceived purpose to be silent on the subject of Messianism.'[4]

Mk. i. 9-11   2. THE BAPTISM OF JESUS   Cf. Mt. iii. 13-17
                                                         Lk. iii. 21 f.

This Story about Jesus is based on the earliest tradition, as its vocabulary and ideas show. Without denying that the baptism of Jesus by John is historical, Bultmann, 264, describes the narrative as a faith-legend (*Glaubenslegende*), and Dibelius, 271, speaks of it as a myth, that is, according to his definition, a story about the actions of a divine being. Neither of these terms indicates a narrative-form and each suggests a depreciatory estimate which is not warranted. Schmidt, 29, thinks that the narrative existed as a separate item of tradition. With additions in the phrases ' in those days ' and ' straightway ', Mark has used a narrative which was current independently of i. 1 (4)-8. Wendling and von Soden, he reminds us, take the opposite view ; they find in the introduction a continuous whole, the former in i. 4-14, the latter in i. 1-15. Perhaps both views are true. There are traces of separate accounts of the Baptism in Mk, Mt. iii. 14 f., and possibly Lk. iii. 21 f., while still another form was current in the *Gospel according to the Hebrews* (*v.* M. R. James, 5). Mark may have used an existing account, but he has integrated it so closely into i. 1-13 that this section is a whole. It is probable that he regarded 9-11 and 12 f. as a single narrative, for no Markan pericope ends so abruptly as 9-11, and the action of the Spirit begun in 10 is continued in 12.

In considering the story the Evangelist's narrative and the experience of Jesus should be treated separately. What can be said of the experience is discussed in Note A at the end of the volume. This distinction throws into relief the fact that Mark is not writing creatively, but is recording historical tradition. This judgment is suggested by the ideas which lie behind the narrative, as the Commentary will show.

---

[1] So the ambiguous βαπτισμῷ συνιέναι is rendered by Goguel, *Jean-Baptiste*, 19 ; Marsh, 64 ; Barrett, 32 ; Flemington, 24.   Creed, 312, reads ' to come to baptism '.
[2] Goguel, *LJ*, 265, reads ' not only '.
[3] Cf. Abrahams, i. 30-5.   Abrahams thinks that Josephus means to represent John as an Essene. Goguel, *LJ*, 268 f., observes that none of the practices of the Essenes (the worship of angels, prayer at sunrise, the daily lustration, the white robe) is adopted by John.   His baptism was effective once for all.
[4] Goguel, 266.

The parallel narratives confirm this view. In Lk the second person (cf. Mk. i. 11) is preserved, but the descent of the Spirit is apparently visible to all (cf. Lk. iii. 22, ' in bodily form '). In Mt a later development of the tradition is shown by the use of the third person, by the earlier omission of the phrase ' the baptism of repentance for the remission of sins ', and by the story of the Baptist's hesitation (iii. 14 f.) which indicates a sense of the need to explain how Jesus came to submit to baptism. In Jn the Baptism is not narrated at all; only the statement is made that John had seen the Spirit descending upon Jesus and abiding upon Him (i. 32-4). A still greater development is visible in the *Gospel according to the Hebrews*, in which Jesus says : ' Wherein (what) have I sinned, that I should go and be baptized of him ? unless peradventure this very thing that I have said is a sin of ignorance.' The Markan narrative antedates these difficulties, which are not even felt by the Evangelist. Having described John's baptism as for the remission of sins, he can say objectively that Jesus ' was baptized by John '. The difficulty has not occurred to him. His account clearly belongs to a point nearer the original facts. It is not possible to accept the argument of Lagrange, 13 : *Jésus reçoit l'appel de Dieu, et en même temps Dieu l'autorise par des signes extérieurs*, for it is not accidental that a public manifestation is described by the later narratives and an assurance to Jesus by the earliest. Mark's account must undoubtedly be preferred. Its value is attested by the Palestinian ideas it contains and by the original use of Scripture it reflects.

⌜ΚΑΙ ΕΓΕΝΕΤΟ⌝ ἐν ἐκείναις ταῖς ἡμέραις ἦλθεν Ἰησοῦς ἀπὸ 9
Ναζαρὲτ τῆς Γαλιλαίας καὶ ἐβαπτίσθη εἰς τὸν Ἰορδάνην ὑπὸ

9 Ἐγένετο

9. The vague expression of time ἐν ἐκείναις ταῖς ἡμέραις, found also in viii. I, xiii. 17, 24*, appears to be editorial. Mark wishes to indicate that the baptism of Jesus happened in the course of the Baptist's ministry. The καὶ ἐγένετο construction is rare in Mk. In Lk-Acts it is found frequently in the three forms : (a) καὶ ἐγένετο (ἐγένετο δὲ) ἦλθεν, (b) καὶ ἐγένετο (ἐγένετο δὲ) καὶ ἦλθεν, (c) ἐγένετο δὲ (καὶ ἐγένετο) ἐλθεῖν. Of these the first is used in Mk here and in iv. 4*; the second not at all; and the third in ii. 15, 23*. Here, along with ἐν ἐκείναις ταῖς ἡμέραις, καὶ ἐγένετο . . . ἦλθεν has a Semitic flavour. Cf. Ex. ii. 11, Lk. ii. 1, etc. Ἰησοῦς is a transcription of the Hebrew ישׁוּע (Jeshua), a shortened form of ' Jehoshua ' (Joshua), ' He whose salvation is Yahweh ' or ' God's salvation '. Significantly, the name is introduced without any explanation or statement of parentage, as in the case

of John. For the first readers of the Gospel an explanation was not necessary. For the use of the name as a proof of the historicity of Jesus v.; Deissmann, *Mysterium Christi*, 26 ; Foerster, *KThW*, iii. 294. ἀπὸ Ναζαρὲτ τῆς Γαλιλαίας marks the place of departure. It is not mentioned in the OT, nor by Josephus, nor in the Talmud. The panoramic view of the plain of Esdraelon from the hills by which it is surrounded has often been described; cf. G. A. Smith, 432 f.; G. Dalman, *SSW*, 57-78; J. N. Schofield, 15-17. The baptism is described in the simplest possible manner in the words καὶ ἐβαπτίσθη εἰς τὸν Ἰορδάνην ὑπὸ Ἰωάνου. For εἰς as practically the equivalent of ἐν in Hellenistic Gk v. Moulton, i. 62 f., 234, 245; Swete, 8; Lagrange, 9; Turner, *JTS*, xxvi. 14-20. No sense of embarrassment is present in the Markan account such

10 Ἰωάνου. καὶ εὐθὺς ἀναβαίνων ἐκ τοῦ ὕδατος εἶδεν σχιζομένους
τοὺς οὐρανοὺς καὶ τὸ πνεῦμα ὡς περιστερὰν καταβαῖνον εἰς αὐτόν·

as is evident in the story of John's hesitation added by Matthew (iii. 14 f.). Luke's reference is made in a participial clause in which prayer is also mentioned, καὶ Ἰησοῦ βαπτισθέντος καὶ προσευχομένου (iii. 21).

10. εὐθύς, Mk (41), Mt (18), Lk (7), Jn (6), 'immediately', 'at once', 'shortly', 'so then'. The meaning 'immediately' is illustrated in the papyri (VGT, 262). Sometimes, however, the word is used as an inferential conjunction, 'so then'. Howard, ii. 446, instances i. 21, 23, 29, 30; cf. Lagrange, xcviii f. See also Intr. 61 f. ἀναβαίνων (iii. 13, iv. 7 f., 32, vi. 51, x. 32 f., xv. 8*) is circumstantial. The subject of εἶδεν is Jesus. So Mt. iii. 16. It is difficult to decide whether Mark means to describe a vision or objective phenomena. Probably the latter is meant, but he does not suggest that the rending of the heavens was visible to others. σχιζομένους (xv. 38*) describes action in progress. Matthew and Luke use ἀνοίγω,[1] and probably by assimilation D it vg syhier sa geo support ἠνυγμένους in Mk. The rending of the heavens is a common feature of apocalyptic thought, the underlying idea being that of a fixed separation of heaven from earth only to be broken in special circumstances. Cf. Apoc. Bar. xxii. 1, Test. Levi ii. 6, v. 1, xviii. 6, Test. Jud. xxiv. 2, and in the NT Jn. i. 51, Ac. vii. 56, Apoc. iv. 1, xi. 19, xix. 11. That the idea is old is shown by Isa. lxiv. 1, ἐὰν ἀνοίξῃς τὸν οὐρανόν.

At the rending of the heavens Jesus sees the Spirit descending to Him as a dove. τὸ πνεῦμα (i. 12*) is a Christian term; cf. Jn. 1. 32 f., Ac. x. 19, xi. 12, Rom. viii. 16, 26 f., etc. In Jewish literature it would have sug-

gested rather a daemon or the wind (cf. Dalman, 203), the more Jewish terms being πνεῦμα θεοῦ (Mt. iii. 16) and τὸ πνεῦμα τὸ ἅγιον (Lk. iii. 22). But if the vocabulary is Christian, the ideas are Jewish. The apocalyptic passages mentioned above all connect the rending of the heavens with revelation, and 1 En. xlix. 3, lxii. 2, Psa. Sol. xvii. 42, Test. Levi xviii. 6 f., and Test. Jud. xxiv. 2 f. associate the gift of the Spirit with the Messiah, an idea which goes back ultimately to Isa. lxi. 1. Cf. Barrett, 42-4; Davies, 205, 215 f. Nevertheless, Mark's account is distinctive. He does not speak of endowment with the Spirit, but of the Spirit coming down to Jesus. Cf. Lohmeyer, 23, ' Not a gift, but a form '. καταβαίνω, used absolutely in iii. 22, ix. 9, xiii. 15,[2] xv. 30, 32*, is here followed by εἰς αὐτόν, in the sense of ' to him ', as in Jn. ii. 12, Ac. xiv. 25, xvi. 8, xviii. 22, xxv. 6.[3] Mt and Lk have ἐπ' αὐτόν, and in Mk this reading is attested in most MSS., but εἰς αὐτόν is certainly original in view of its strong attestation (B D fam. 13 543 837 a d g[1] t) and because it is the more difficult reading. That εἰς here means ' to ' and not ' into ' is suggested by εἶδεν and the immediate action taken by the Spirit when the divine voice is heard. In Mark's account Jesus is not constrained by an internal impulse but by an external power.

The Spirit is seen ὡς περιστερὰν (xi. 15*). The expression is metaphorical, ' as a dove '. Luke adds σωματικῷ εἴδει, ' in bodily form '. The origin of the dove imagery is obscure. Rabbinic literature takes the dove as an emblem of Israel. The Targum to Cant. ii. 12 compared the voice of the turtle-dove to ' the voice of the Holy Spirit of

---

[1] The agreement of Mt and Lk against Mk in using ἀνοίγω and ἐπί instead of εἰς (Mk. i. 10) suggests that Q, as well as Mk, may have contained an account of the Baptism. Cf. Streeter, 188.
[2] Here, if εἰς τὴν οἰκίαν is read, the meaning is ' into '.
[3] In the remaining examples, Ac. vii. 15 (?), viii. 38, Rom. x. 17**, εἰς=' into '. In the NT generally εἰς often has the meaning ' to ' after a verb of motion. The cases where it means ' into ' are more numerous, but this meaning is determined by the context and the frequent use of εἰσέρχομαι and sometimes by ἐμβαίνω.

καὶ φωνὴ ἐκ τῶν οὐρανῶν   Σὺ εἶ ὁ υἱός μου ὁ ἀγαπητός, ἐν σοὶ 11
εὐδόκησα.

11 ἐγένετο *post* φωνή

salvation ', but the evidence is late and is discounted by Billerbeck, i. 125. The best explanation is that the imagery is connected with the picture of the Spirit of God brooding or hovering creatively over the primaeval waters (Gen. i. 2). Cf. the words of Ben Zoma, a younger contemporary of the Apostles, in *B. Ḥag.* 15a: ' I was considering the space between the upper waters and the lower waters, and there is only between them a mere three fingers' breadth, as it is said, And the Spirit of God was brooding on the face of the waters like a dove which broods over her young but does not touch them '. In support of Ben Zoma Abrahams, i. 49 f., quotes Rashi, and says, ' Even without the Ben Zoma analogue one could hardly doubt that the Synoptists must have had Gen. i. 2 in mind '. Cf. Lagrange, 13 ; Creed, 57 ; Bartlet, 92 ; Barrett, 38 f. This view is much to be preferred to those which speak of the dove as a type of gentleness (Mt. x. 16), or of the divine wisdom (Philo, *Quis rer. div. her.* 127) or of the grace of God shown in the dove which brought tidings to Noah (Gen. viii. 8-11).[1]

11. καὶ φωνὴ ἐκ τῶν οὐρανῶν. The phrase is very abrupt, for probably ἐγένετο should be omitted. It is wanting in א* D ff t vg (1 MS.), and the omission is implied by ἠκούσθη (*post* οὐρανῶν) read by Θ 28 565 g¹ geo¹ syhier, and by Mt. iii. 17, καὶ ἰδοὺ φωνή . . . λέγουσα. The reading may be an assimilation to Lk. iii. 22, γενέσθαι. Cf. Turner, *JTS*, xxviii. 151 f. The word is omitted by Ti, put in brackets by WH and Nestle, but read by Souter, Swete, and Lagrange. Lohmeyer, 20 n., omits it. The need for a supple-

ment was clearly felt by scribes from a very early period, and ' there was ' or ' came ' must be understood by the modern reader. It may be conjectured that the absence of a verb is due to over literal translation of an Aramaic original.

The nearest analogue to the divine voice at the Baptism is the *Bath qol* (literally ' daughter of the voice ') frequently mentioned in the Rabbinical literature. See the numerous examples cited by Billerbeck, i. 125-32. The Tosaphist on *Sanh.* 11a explains it as a sound proceeding from another, ' as when a man strikes a powerful blow and a second sound is heard '. Thus the *Bath qol* is an echo. Sometimes it is compared with the muttering or chirping of a bird. Cf. Abrahams, i. 47 f. In *B. Berach.* 3a it is likened to the moaning of a dove. Abrahams suggests that this association of the bird and the heavenly voice illustrates and authenticates the symbolism of the Synoptists. It is another question whether this interesting analogue adequately explains the experience of Jesus Himself.

The words Σὺ εἶ ὁ υἱός μου ὁ ἀγαπητός, ἐν σοὶ εὐδόκησα are addressed to Jesus Himself. So Lk. iii. 22. Mt. iii. 17 has the third person, Οὗτός ἐστιν, etc., and ἐν ᾧ which appears also in Mk as an inferior *v.l.* in A W *et al.* 124 579 1071 b d g¹ Jer. ἀγαπητός, ix. 7, xii. 6*, is used in the sense of μονογενής, *unicus*, ' only ', ' sole '. Cf. Swete, 10 ; Turner, 13, *JTS*, xxvii. 113-29 ; Souter, *JTS*, xxviii. 59 f. ; Lagrange, 10, who says : *Dans l'A.T. il n'y a pas grande différence entre ' chéri ' et ' unique '.* Like ἐβάπτισα in i. 8, εὐδόκησα* can be regarded as a summary

[1] Gunkel, *Das Märchen im AT*, 147-51, and Gressmann, ' Die Sage von der Taufe Jesu und die vorderoriental. Taubengöttin ', *Arch. f. Religionswissenschaft*, 20 (1920-1), 1-40, 323-59, explain the dove by the legendary motif in which the choice of a king is determined by a bird ; but, as Bultmann, 265, observes, this motif is manifestly strange to the Markan story. He rejects also as too bold the further suggestion of Gressmann, that the dove is derived from a myth in which a goddess in the form of a dove chooses an aspirant to kingship to be her son or lover. For a discussion of the attempt of Leisegang, *Pneuma Hagion*, 80-95, to connect the descent of the Spirit as a dove with the Hellenistic idea of divine begetting, see Barrett, 36 f.

or timeless aor. (cf. Moulton, i. 134 f.). It is unlikely that it refers to the earthly life of Jesus, ' I came to take pleasure ' (Gould, 12). W. C. Allen, *St. Mt*, 29, suggests that it may be modelled on the aors. of Isa. xlii. 1, ' which were probably interpreted as implying the divine election of Israel, and so here the divine election of the Messiah '. If so, the aor. cannot be pressed; it probably represents the Heb. stative perf. and may be rendered : ' I am well pleased '. So RV and RSV. Cf. Moffatt : ' In thee is my delight '. See further, Intr. 64.

The importance of i. 11 cannot be exaggerated. The language recalls that of Psa. ii. 7, Υἱός μου εἶ σύ, ἐγὼ σήμερον γεγέννηκά σε, and Isa. xlii. 1, Ἰσραὴλ ὁ ἐκλεκτός μου, προσεδέξατο αὐτὸν ἡ ψυχή μου, but it is not a quotation and contains echoes of other OT passages : Gen. xxii. 2, τὸν υἱόν σου τὸν ἀγαπητόν, Isa. xliv. 2, μὴ φοβοῦ, παῖς μου Ἰακώβ, καὶ ὁ ἠγαπημένος Ἰσραήλ, lxii. 4, ὅτι εὐδόκησεν κύριος ἐν σοί. J. Weiss, 133, suggests that the Markan version is secondary to that of the Western text of Lk. iii. 22 (cf. Psa. ii. 7) : ' Thou art my Son; this day have I begotten thee '. In this case the primitive tradition was an adoption-formula which Mark modified in consequence of the Pauline belief that Jesus was the pre-existent Son. But, not only is this view extremely speculative, it also fails to account for the

striking and original combination of ideas in i. 11. Here the idea of the Messianic Son is combined with that of the Servant, and while it is possible that this fusion was effected earlier in certain circles (*v*. Intr. 119 f.), it is to be traced to the mind and experience of Jesus rather than to the Evangelist. It is to be noted that Bultmann, 267 f., who assigns the origin of the story to the Hellenistic community, recognizes that the words of i. 11 (or Lk. iii. 22, D) could have been applied to Jesus in Palestinian Christianity, since they do not necessarily imply metaphysical Sonship. The ideas, indeed, are fundamentally Jewish, although they are combined in a new and creative way. The terms of the announcement do not include the more obvious Messianic expressions. Jesus, for example, is not addressed as ' the Christ '. What is expressed is a new and vital relationship to God which transcends Messiahship as it was understood in Jewish thought. Mk. i. 11 gives strong support to the contention of Harnack that ' our Lord's consciousness of Sonship must have preceded in time his consciousness of Messiahship, must indeed have formed a stepping-stone to the latter '.[1] The fundamental note in the saying is the filial status of Jesus ; and the words are best understood as an assurance, or confirmation, of this relationship, rather than a disclosure or revelation. Cf. C. J. Cadoux, 52.

Mk. i. 12 f.   3. THE TEMPTATION   Cf. Mt. iv. 1-11
                                                                          Lk. iv. 1-13

This narrative is surprisingly brief and bare. Lohmeyer, 26, points out that it differs from 1-8, and probably also from 9-11, in content and style. The subject stands at the beginning of the clauses and the verb follows, and the historic present appears for the first time. There is also a rhythmical structure which may be represented as a b/a b. Cf. J. Weiss, 135 ; Lohmeyer, 26 f. Bultmann, 270 f., suggests that the narrative is a residue of an earlier detailed legend about Jesus, or, more probably, a nature-myth like that of the conflict of Marduk with the Chaos-dragon, or a story about the temptation of the Buddha, or Zarathustra, or later Christian saints. The words ' being tempted of Satan ' may be a sub-

[1] *The Sayings of Jesus*, 245.

sequent addition to a story which perhaps originally told of life in Paradise before man lived at enmity with the beasts. Of these suggestions it may be said that, while all things are possible, less speculative explanations are to be preferred. Either Mark knew the more detailed story in Q, and could assume a knowledge of it on the part of his readers [1]; or, as seems more probable, he did not know this narrative which, presumably, he would have been glad to use, but was familiar only with the fact of the temptation by Satan as part of the catechetical tradition of the Church, a possibility favoured by the rhythmical form of the narrative. Less probable is the suggestion that he wished to avoid the details of the Q narrative,[2] for he does not shrink from stating that Jesus was tempted by Satan. Moreover, the fuller story in Q would have enabled him to describe the victory of the Son of God over the Adversary, a theme which interests him greatly; cf. iii. 22-6, 27, viii. 33.

As previously noted, the narrative is closely connected with the Baptism. Bultmann, 270, thinks the connexion secondary. We may suppose, on the contrary, that it was because this association was already firmly established in the tradition that Mark included the Temptation in his Introduction. Rawlinson, 12, observes that the story had cate-chetical value: ' The newly baptized Christian must be ready, like his Lord, to face immediately the onset of the Tempter '. An imaginative element is present in the references to the wild beasts and the angels, but the basic idea that Jesus was tempted is bound up with His conception of Messiahship and is historical.

Καὶ εὐθὺς τὸ πνεῦμα αὐτὸν ἐκβάλλει εἰς τὴν ἔρημον. καὶ ἦν   12
ἐν τῇ ἐρήμῳ τεσσεράκοντα ἡμέρας πειραζόμενος ὑπὸ τοῦ   13

12. For τὸ πνεῦμα and εὐθύς v. i. 10. ἐκβάλλω, 17 times* and xvi. [17]. Swete, 10 f., thinks that such render-ings as *expellit* (vg), ' driveth ' (AV) or ' driveth forth ' (RV) are perhaps too strong in this context. ' At the most ', he says, ' the word denotes here only a pressure upon the spirit (Victor: ἕλκει), not an irresistible power.' This explanation does not seem satisfactory in view of Mark's usage, since he uses the verb eleven times of the expulsion of daemons, the removal of an eye (ix. 47), the cleansing of the Temple (xi. 15), and the casting out of the heir from the vineyard (xii. 8). Used here with εὐθύς (' immediately '), the verb appears to indicate strong, if not vio-lent, propulsion, as compared with ἀν-ήχθη (Mt. iv. 1) and ἤγετο (Lk. iv. 1). Cf. Rawlinson, 12. Swete, 11, appears

to distinguish the wilderness from that mentioned in i. 4 (cf. Klostermann, 13), but there is no indication of this in the text, and probably the allusion is quite general to the wilderness as the home of evil powers. Cf. G. Kittel, *KThW*, ii. 655. Note the vivid use of the his-toric present (ἐκβάλλει) which is char-acteristic of Mark's style (Hawkins, 143-9): Mk (151), Mt (93), Lk (9), Jn (164); v. Intr. 46 f.

13. ἦν . . . πειραζόμενος may be a periphrastic imperf. (v. Intr. 45, 62 f.), but the parallelism with καὶ οἱ ἄγγελοι δι-ηκόνουν αὐτῷ suggests that the participle is used independently. The acc. of dura-tion of time, τεσσεράκοντα ἡμέρας, is used generally. The phrase recalls the experiences of Moses (Ex. xxxiv. 28) and Elijah (1 Kings xix. 8); cf. also Ac. i. 3. πειράζω, viii. 11, x. 2, xii. 15*, is

---

[1] Cf. Rawlinson, 12; J. Weiss, 133 f., *Die Schr.* 75.
[2] Cf. J. Weiss, 134.

Σατανᾶ, καὶ ἦν μετὰ τῶν θηρίων, καὶ οἱ ἄγγελοι διηκόνουν αὐτῷ.

used of testing with hostile intent. ὁ Σατανᾶς,[1] iii. 23, 26, iv. 15, viii. 33*, is a transliteration of the Aramaic אֲטֽנָא. Q has ὁ διάβολος. With Paul (διάβολος, Eph. iv. 27, vi. 11*), Mark shows a preference for the term ὁ Σατανᾶς. In the OT Satan (שָׂטָן, 'the accuser', 'adversary') is mentioned rarely and in late books, as an angel whose duty it is to accuse men in Job i, ii and Zech. iii. 1 f., and as an evil power in 1 Chron. xxi. 1. Derived apparently from Persian sources, the idea is developed and appears frequently in the later Jewish writings, especially the apocryphal books and the Rabbinical literature, where under various names, Beliar, Sammael, Mastema, Satan is the prince of evil, the opponent of God, and antichrist. Cf. Charles, Apoc. ii. 76-87; Billerbeck, i. 136-49; W. Foerster, KThW, ii. 74-80.

θηρίον*, dimin. of θήρ 'a wild beast'. Wild beasts may be mentioned to emphasize the loneliness of the place; cf. Swete, 11. 'For hours, as you travel across these hills, you may feel no sign of life, except the scorpions and vipers which your passage startles, in

the distance a few wild goats or gazelles, and at night the wailing of the jackal and the hyena's howl. He was alone with the wild beasts', G. A. Smith, 317. A further explanation is that the presence of wild beasts is traditionally associated with OT pictures of evil powers (Psa. xxii. 11-21, Ezek. xxxiv. 5, 8, 25) and with the triumph of righteousness (Job v. 22 f., Isa. xi. 6-9). In Test. Napht. viii. 4 the flight of the devil, the fear of the wild beasts, and the support of angels are mentioned together, and in Psa. xci. 11-13 dominion over wild beasts is mentioned along with the promise of service by angels. It may even be that there is an implicit contrast between Adam and the victorious Messiah. We do not know what ideas the first Christians read into the narrative, but it is probable that, while the language is pictorial and imaginative, the ideas are religious and theological.

διακονέω, i. 31, x. 45, xv. 41*, 'to serve'. The imperf. διηκόνουν has the augment as if the verb were compound. Cf. Blass, 39; Moulton, ii. 303. See also i. 31 and xv. 41.

II

Mk. i. 14-iii. 6   THE OPENING OF
THE GALILEAN MINISTRY

A new section begins with the summary statement in i. 14 f. and continues to the end of iii. 6. After i. 14 f. an isolated story, the Call of the First Disciples (i. 16-20) follows, then a closely connected group of stories describing a day in the ministry of Jesus (i. 21-39). To this group the Cure of the Leper (i. 40-5) is appended, and this is followed by a second complex of loosely connected Pronouncement-stories (ii. 1-iii. 6) which show how Jesus came into conflict with the scribes and Pharisees, reaching their climax in the death plot mentioned in iii. 6. For the construction of these groups see Intr. 90-2. The purpose of the section is to describe the opening period of the Galilean Ministry. Since the same theme is continued in iii. 7 ff., it is a point for inquiry why the note of tragedy is struck so early and decisively in iii. 6.

---

[1] In the NT Semitic names ending in ας or ᾶς take their gen. in a or ᾶ. Cf. Moulton, ii. 146.

Mk. i. 14 f.   4. OPENING SUMMARY   Cf. Mt. iv. 12-17
                         STATEMENT   Lk. iv. 14 f.

This passage, like iii. 7-12, is one of the summary statements (*Sammel-berichte*) which determine the outline of the Gospel. Unlike similar passages which introduce or complete a particular narrative (i. 45, ii. 1, etc.) or appear to belong to an earlier complex (i. 21 f., 28, 39, ii. 1 f., iii. 6, etc.), i. 14 f. is intended to cover the period ending with iii. 6. The passage describes the opening of the public ministry, beginning with the arrest of John the Baptist and the message Jesus proclaimed. The Evangelist does not tell us when, or where, or in what circumstances the ministry began, apart from the bare reference to John. Clearly, he was not interested in such matters. His chronology is controlled by the preaching praxis of the Church. As J. Weiss, 136, says, it is a *heils-geschichtliche Chronologie*. Mark began where the first missionary preachers began, describing ' the event which happened, throughout all Judaea, beginning from Galilee *after the baptism which John preached*' (Ac. x. 37, Lake's rendering). It may be that he did not know of an earlier activity side by side with that of the Baptist. There is, as Schmidt observes, 34, a gap between i. 13 and 14, in which there is room for the special tradition on which the Fourth Evangelist drew. In any case, Mark rightly fixes on the arrest of John as the decisive moment for the beginning of the ministry.[1] Matthew goes farther than his source in saying : ' Now when he heard (ἀκούσας) that John was delivered up, he withdrew into Galilee ' (iv. 12).

Mark does not say to what place Jesus went. Unlike Matthew (iv. 12) and Luke (iv. 16), he does not mention Nazareth, nor does he speak of a later departure to Capernaum. He mentions Galilee, and at once we find ourselves by the lake side.

The message of Jesus described in i. 15 is a summary of what Jesus proclaimed. Cf. Wellhausen, 7 ; Bultmann, 124 ; Schmidt, 33 ; J. Weiss, 137 ; Rawlinson, 13. There is force in the observation of Wellhausen, that Jesus did not go about constantly repeating the same formula, but taught according to the circumstances of the moment ; but Mark rightly catches the eschatological note in the preaching of Jesus. Many parables of the Kingdom, in addition to those recorded in Mk, and some of the ' Son of Man sayings ' in Q, may well belong to this period.

Μετὰ δὲ τὸ παραδοθῆναι τὸν Ἰωάνην ἦλθεν ὁ Ἰησοῦς εἰς τὴν 14

14. καὶ μετά is read by B D a ff syˢ bo geo², but μετὰ δέ is attested by ℵ A L Δ Θ W *al. plur.* minusc. *omn.* syᵖᵉ ʰˡ it vg sa geo¹ arm Eus Aug, and probably should be read here, Mark's intention being to indicate a turning-point in the Story, as at vii. 24, x. 32, xiv. 1. Cf. Turner, *JTS*, xxviii. 152 ; R. H. Lightfoot, 62 f. μετά c. infin.

(aor.), xiv. 28, xvi. [19]*. The articu-lar infin. is found 15 times in Mk, 11 c. prep. Cf. Robertson, 1426 f. παραδί-δωμι, 20 times*, ' to deliver up ' ; here sc. εἰς φυλακήν. The absolute use of the verb carries with it the idea of a delivering up which is God's will, cf ix. 31, etc., and in this sense is char-acteristic of Mark's theology.

[1] ' He begins with the moment when Jesus appeared in Galilee as a new star ', says Weiss, 136. ' So ', he adds, ' can Peter have begun his narrative.'

15 Γαλιλαίαν, κηρύσσων τὸ εὐαγγέλιον τοῦ θεοῦ καὶ λέγων ὅτι

For ὁ Ἰησοῦς v. i. 9; Γαλιλαία i. 9; κηρύσσω i. 4; εὐαγγέλιον i. 1. The gen. in τὸ εὐαγγέλιον τοῦ θεοῦ is variously explained as objective ('about God'; cf. Rawlinson, 14) or subjective ('from God'; cf. Lagrange, 16; Swete, 13; J. Weiss, *Die Schr.*⁴ 79; Gould, 15; Branscomb, 25). Rawlinson mentions the latter as an alternative and it is probably the better view. The theme of the preaching is the Good News from God. The phrase is Pauline; cf. 1 Thess. ii. 2, 8 f., Rom. i. 1, xv. 16, 2 Cor. xi. 7. Many MSS. insert τῆς βασιλείας before τοῦ θεοῦ (A D W *et al.* fam. 13 (exc. 69) 22 28ᵐᵍ 118 700 1071 *al. pler.* a c f r¹·² vg syᵖᵉ bo aeth). The reading is favoured by Turner, *JTS*, xxviii. 153, but seems best explained as a scribal addition to the unusual Markan phrase.

15. καὶ λέγων (om. אּ* c vg (1 MS.) syˢ Or) is placed in square brackets by WH and omitted by Ti, but should be read with B L W Δ Θ minusc. *pler.* vg syᵖᵉ ʰˡ bo geo. The real question, says Turner, *JTS*, xxviii. 153, is the genuineness of καί, which is more widely omitted (v. Legg), and he suggests that here and in i. 40 it is perhaps easier to understand its insertion rather than its omission. λέγειν ὅτι is found in Mk some 38 times (cf. Turner, *JTS*, xxviii. 9-15; Lagrange, ci), and in most cases the participle is used (i. 15, 40, ii. 12, iii. 11, v. 23, 35, viii. 28, xiii. 6, xiv. 57 f.) or the imperfect (iii. 21 f., iv. 21, v. 28, vi. 4, 14 f., 18, 35, vii. 20, ix. 31). Sometimes, instead of indirect speech, which Mark avoids, the construction is used for what is said repeatedly (cf. ii. 12, iii. 11, v. 28) or summarily (cf. iii. 22, vii. 20, xiii. 6), but this cannot be inferred from the construction itself; the context must decide. Cf. viii. 31, καὶ ἤρξατο διδάσκειν αὐτοὺς ὅτι. καιρός, x. 30, xi. 13, xii. 2, xiii. 33*, 'time', 'season', 'opportunity' (*VGT*, 315). For the idea of 'the appointed time' cf. Ezek. vii. 12, Dan. xii. 4, 9, Zeph. i. 12, etc.; Gal.

iv. 4, Eph. i. 10. In the sayings of Jesus the idea appears in Mk. xiii. 33, 'Ye know not when the time is', Mt. xxvi. 18, 'My time is at hand', Lk. xix. 44, 'the time of thy visitation', xxi. 8, 'The time is at hand', 24, 'the times of the Gentiles'. πληρόω, xiv. 49*. The idea is eschatological. The time is one determined in the counsels of God.

βασιλεία, 20 times*, 14 in the phrase ἡ βασιλεία τοῦ θεοῦ, i. 15, iv. 11, 26, 30, ix. 1, 47, x. 14 f., 23 f., 25, xii. 34, xiv. 25, xv. 43. Corresponding to the Aramaic *malkuth*, the phrase means 'the kingly rule' of God, His 'reign' or 'sovereignty'. For the detailed discussion of this dominating idea see Intr. 114-16, where it is held that, while 'the rule of God' is the primary emphasis, the thought of a community is necessarily implied. Jesus spoke of the *Basileia* as future (xiv. 25, Lk. xi. 2, etc.), but also as present in Himself and His ministry (Lk. vii. 18-23, x. 23 f., xi. 20, 31 f.). In a true sense, therefore, He taught a 'realized eschatology' (Dodd, 51), but how far this idea is supported by the present verse is open to question.

ἐγγίζω, xi. 1, xiv. 42*, 'to come near'. *VGT*, 178, says: 'This verb is not so common as we might have expected'. ἤγγικεν is usually translated 'is at hand', 'has drawn near'. Cf. Swete, 13; Rawlinson, 13; Bartlet, 100; Wood, 682; Lagrange, 16 f., translates *proche*, but supports *est arrivé*; Wellhausen, 7; J. Weiss, 137; Klostermann, 14; C. J. Cadoux, 198 f.; B. T. D. Smith, 78 n.; Oesterley, *GP*, 46; H. V. Martin, *ET*, lii. 271-3. Professor C. H. Dodd, 44, strongly contends for the translation 'has come'. So Lohmeyer, 30; cf. H. Preisker, *KThW*, ii. 329-32. He argues, *ET*, xlviii. 140, that ἐγγίζω is used in various tenses in the LXX to translate *naga'* (Aramaic, *meṭa*), 'to reach', 'arrive', and that in Jer. xxviii. (li.) 9 B has the perf. (אּ A have

Πεπλήρωται ὁ καιρὸς καὶ ἤγγικεν ἡ βασιλεία τοῦ θεοῦ· μετανοεῖτε καὶ πιστεύετε ἐν τῷ εὐαγγελίῳ.

the aor.). See the important discussions of J. Y. Campbell and J. M. Creed, *ET*, xlviii. 91-4, 184 f. Professor Dodd maintains that in six out of eight cases the meaning is clearly that of arrival : so *naga'* in Jon. iii. 6, Jer. xxviii. (li.) 9 (B), Psa. xxxi. (xxxii.) 6, cvi. (cvii.) 18, and *meṭa* in Dan. iv. 8, 19; while the meaning of the Heb. is weakened perhaps in Sir. li. 6 and Psa. lxxxvii. 4 (lxxxviii. 3), but possibly that of the Gk is strengthened. Thus, he concludes, ἐγγίζω ' could be used to translate Hebrew and Aramaic verbs meaning " arrive " without being untrue to their meaning ', *ET*, xlviii. 141. It is difficult to accept this argument. Of the examples cited the only certain case appears to be Jon. iii. 6, ' And the tidings reached the king of Nineveh '. Moreover, in a number of cases ἐγγίζω is used to translate *qarab* ' to approach '. While, then, the translation ' has come ' may be possible, it seems more likely that ἤγγικεν should be rendered ' is at hand ' or ' has drawn near ', as in Rom. xiii. 12, Jas. v. 8, and 1 Pet. iv. 7 (cf. Mt. xxvi. 45 f., Lk. xxi. 8, 20). The difference, of course, is not great, since only a negligible interval is meant, and there is clear evidence (*v. supra*) that Jesus believed the *Basileia* to be present in Himself and His ministry.

On the basis of the announcement Jesus calls for repentance and belief in the Good News. μετανοέω, vi. 12*, is used in the LXX to translate *niḥam*,

Ni. ' to be sorry ', ' repent ', but in the NT is represented better by *shubh* ' to turn back ' (cf. J. Kosnetter, *Die Taufe Jesu*, cited by Flew, *JC*, 50 f.). See the note on i. 4. πιστεύω, v. 36, ix. 23 f., 42, xi. 23 f., 31, xiii. 21, xv. 32, xvi. [13 f., 16 f.]*, ' to believe ', ' have faith in '. Here only in the NT is the verb used with ἐν, for neither Jn. iii. 15 (Bernard, 116) nor Eph. i. 13 (Abbott, 22) is a real parallel. The construction is best explained as translation Greek; cf. Howard, ii. 464. Cf. LXX, Psa. cv. (cvi.) 12, Jer. xii. 6. The phrase is rendered best, not by the too literal translation ' believe in the Gospel ', but more simply by ' believe the Good News '. If εὐαγγέλιον is taken in this sense, there is no reason why the words should not be regarded as authentic. Rawlinson, 251, suggests that Jesus may have used an Aramaic phrase expressive of ' good tidings ' or have quoted Isa. lxi. 1 (cf. Mt. xi. 5, Lk. iv. 18, vii. 22). Cf. Lagrange, 18. Many commentators, however, feel that the word belongs to the vocabulary of Mark, in the sense of ' the Christian Message '; cf. Wellhausen, 7; J. Weiss, 137; Klostermann, 4 f.; Branscomb, 25. Probably this is the meaning in i. 1, viii. 35, xiii. 10, and xiv. 9; but it is inapposite here. The reference to the imminence of the coming of the Kingdom suggests that εὐαγγέλιον means ' good news '; cf. Bartlet, 101. Although the word belongs to Mark's vocabulary, it correctly describes the substance of the Galilean preaching.

Mk. i. 16-20   5. THE CALL OF THE FIRST   Cf. Mt. iv. 18-22
DISCIPLES   (Lk. v. 1-11)

Strictly speaking, this story includes two narratives, 16-18 and 19 f., and to these the Call of Levi, ii. 14, forms a third. Between i. 14 f. and 16-20 there is a gap, as also between i. 20 and 21. Cf. Schmidt, 43. The story is introduced to prepare the way for the group i. 21-39, in which the disciples play an important part, but it is told also for its own sake and in order to emphasize the necessity of ' following Jesus '. The Evangelist has the call of Elisha (1 Kings xix. 19-21) in mind, although there is no reason to think that he has modelled his narrative on this story. He strongly emphasizes the fact that the disciples left all and followed Jesus, and probably the story gained this significance from its use in Christian preaching. There is good reason to describe it as a Petrine Story, that is, a narrative which rests ultimately upon the reminiscences of Peter. Cf. Bartlet, 102 ; Ed. Meyer, i. 99. On this view we do justice to the presence of picturesque details like the references to the mending of the nets and Zebedee with the hired servants, and also to the fact that the story is told from the standpoint of the fishermen on the lake who saw Jesus passing by. Cf. J. Weiss, 138. The somewhat schematic character of i. 16-18, 19 f., and ii. 14 is due to constant repetition in the primitive tradition, and, on this account, the survival of the details noted above is all the more remarkable. ' With this narrative ', says Schmidt, 44, ' we are brought within the circle of the first disciples of Jesus themselves.' This explanation of the genesis of the story is much to be preferred to that of Bultmann, 26 f., who classifies the narrative as a Biographical Apothegm which presents an ' ideal scene ', perhaps spun out of the metaphor about ' fishers of men '. Dibelius, 111 f., develops a similar view. Lohmeyer, 31-3, explains it as an epiphany-story belonging to a cycle which told of the appearing of Jesus as the Son of Man. It is astonishing how widely appraisals of the story can differ. Proof is clearly impossible and decision a matter of literary and historical judgment.

16   Καὶ παράγων παρὰ τὴν θάλασσαν τῆς Γαλιλαίας εἶδεν Σίμωνα
καὶ Ἀνδρέαν τὸν ἀδελφὸν Σίμωνος ἀμφιβάλλοντας ἐν τῇ θα-

16. παράγω, ii. 14, xv. 21*, ' to pass by '. παράγων παρά is certainly unusual. Probably παρὰ τὴν θάλασσαν τῆς Γαλιλαίας is the Evangelist's addition to the original oral story. Mark has the full phrase here and in vii. 31, elsewhere he has ἡ θάλασσα alone ; cf. ii. 13, iii. 7, iv. 1, v. 1, 13, 21. Black, 96, observes that θάλασσα in the sense of λίμνη is thoroughly Semitic. Luke uses λίμνη and speaks of the ' Lake of Gennesaret ' (v. 1), and, using a later name, John twice calls it ' the Sea of Tiberias ' (vi. 1, xxi. 1). Twelve miles long and six miles across at its widest point, the lake provided a natural highway between Galilee and Peraea and between many towns and fishing villages on its western and northern shores, including Bethsaida Julias, Capernaum, Magdala, and Tiberias. For descriptive details see G. A. Smith, 439-63 ; Dalman, 121 f. ; Schofield, 18 f.

As Jesus passes by He sees Simon and Andrew his brother. Mark uses

Σίμων seven times in speaking of the Apostle (i. 16 (bis), 29 f., 36, iii. 16, xiv. 37). He never uses the name ' Simon Peter ', but has Πέτρος 19 times. Proportionately to its size Mk mentions the Apostle more frequently than Mt or Lk. Σίμων is a later form of Συμεών, Heb. Shimeon (Gen. xxix. 33, Lk. ii. 25, etc.). The name is used by Jesus when He addresses the Apostle (xiv. 37, Mt. xvi. 17, xvii. 25, Lk. xxii. 31), and notably when his weakness is apparent (xiv. 37, Lk. xxii. 31). Συμεών is found in Ac. xv. 14 and 2 Pet. i. 1 (א A), but Σίμων in Ac. x. 5, 18, 32, and 2 Pet. i. 1 (B). These names seem to indicate a greater degree of intimacy. The vividness with which the personality of the Apostle is presented in Mk is characteristic of the Gospel and is in harmony with the Papias tradition (v. Intr. 1-3).

Ἀνδρέας, i. 29, iii. 18, xiii. 3*, is a Greek name. Swete, 14, cites Herodotus vi. 126. In contrast with Peter, Andrew is a lay figure in Mk. We

λάσσῃ, ἦσαν γὰρ ἁλεεῖς· καὶ εἶπεν αὐτοῖς ὁ Ἰησοῦς Δεῦτε ὀπίσω 17
μου, καὶ ποιήσω ὑμᾶς γενέσθαι ἁλεεῖς ἀνθρώπων. καὶ εὐθὺς 18
ἀφέντες τὰ δίκτυα ἠκολούθησαν αὐτῷ. Καὶ προβὰς ὀλίγον εἶδεν 19

learn nothing of him except that he was Peter's brother, that he lived with Peter at Capernaum, that he was one of the Twelve, and that he is one of the four addressed on the Mount of Olives.

ἀμφιβάλλω** is used absolutely of the casting of a net. In Cl. Gk the verb is used of putting on clothes or of embracing. A use similar to that of Mk is illustrated in Pap. Flor. ii. 119. 3 (*VGT*, 28), but owing to the defectiveness of the MS., it is not possible to be sure that it is used absolutely. Matthew adds ἀμφίβληστρον*, a casting net (iv. 18). The prep. in ἐν τῇ θαλάσσῃ illustrates the loss of the distinction between ἐν and εἰς in popular speech. ἁλιεύς, i. 17*, Mt. iv. 18 f., Lk. v. 2**, <ἅλς, the sea. The form ἁλεεῖς is by dissimilation for ἁλιεῖς as in the LXX and the papyri. Cf. Moulton, ii. 76, 142.

17. To the two disciples Jesus gives the command ' Come ye after me ' and promises that He will make them to become ' fishers of men '. δεῦτε (= δεῦρο ἴτε), vi. 31, xii. 7*, is used as the plur. of the adv. δεῦρο (x. 21*) regarded as an imperative ; Cl., LXX, Pap. (*VGT*, 143) ; ' Hither ! ', ' Come ! '. Cf. Moulton, i. 172 ; Blass, 208. For ὀπίσω v. i. 7. The idea of following Jesus is prominent in Mk and is expressed in various ways : with ἀπέρχεσθαι ὀπίσω in i. 20 ; ἔρχεσθαι ὀπίσω in viii. 34 ; and ἀκολουθεῖν c. dat. in ii. 14 f., viii. 34b, etc. Matthew omits γενέσθαι. The metaphor ' fishers of men ' appears in Jer. xvi. 16 : ' Behold, I will send for many fishers, saith the Lord, and they shall fish them ', but here as a threat of judgment. Cf. Amos iv. 2, Hab. i. 14-17, Ezek. xxix. 4 f. The words of Jesus summon Simon and Andrew to become disciples and heralds of the Kingdom of God. The metaphor can quite naturally have been suggested by the daily occupation of

the brothers and there is no need to trace it to a current logion.

18. The response is immediate. For εὐθύς v. i. 10. Many commentators point out that it is more intelligible if Simon and Andrew had previously had contact with Jesus, as Jn. i. 35-42 indicates. Cf. McNeile, 46 ; Bartlet, 103 ; Branscomb, 28. ἀφίημι is frequently used in Mk in the sense of ' leave ', ' abandon ', some 15 times in all. For the meaning ' suffer ', ' permit ' (10 times) v. i. 34, v. 19, xi. 16, etc., for ' forgive ' (9 times) v. ii. 5, etc., and ' utter ' xv. 37. In the picturesque reference to the leaving of the nets the decisiveness of the response is intentionally stressed. δίκτυον, i. 19*, is a net of any kind, in contrast with ἀμφίβληστρον (Mt. iv. 18) ' a casting net ', and σαγήνη (Mt. xiii. 47) ' a drag net '. In all the Gospels ἀκολουθέω is used freely, sometimes absolutely, but generally c. dat., to describe attachment to the person of Jesus, personal surrender to His summons, and acceptance of His leadership (viii. 34). See i. 17.

19. Next follows the parallel story of the calling of James and John. προβαίνω *, ' to go forward ', ' advance ' (in years, Lk. i. 7, etc.) ; Cl., LXX, Pap. (*VGT*, 537). ὀλίγον is used as an adv. of space and time (vi. 31). Ἰάκωβος is the name of James the son of Zebedee here and in i. 29, iii. 17 (*bis*), v. 37 (*bis*), ix. 2, x. 35, 41, xiii. 3, xiv. 33*. For James the brother of Jesus v. vi. 3, James the son of Alphaeus iii. 18, James the Less xv. 40. All that we learn from Mk is that James was the son of Zebedee, probably the elder son, that he was one of the Twelve belonging to the inner circle present at the raising of the daughter of Jairus, the Transfiguration, and the discourse on the Mount of Olives, and the Agony, and that he shared with John a desire for precedence at the Parousia (x. 35).

Ἰάκωβον τὸν τοῦ Ζεβεδαίου καὶ Ἰωάνην τὸν ἀδελφὸν αὐτοῦ,
20 καὶ αὐτοὺς ἐν τῷ πλοίῳ καταρτίζοντας τὰ δίκτυα, καὶ εὐθὺς
ἐκάλεσεν αὐτούς. καὶ ἀφέντες τὸν πατέρα αὐτῶν Ζεβεδαῖον ἐν
τῷ πλοίῳ μετὰ τῶν μισθωτῶν ἀπῆλθον ὀπίσω αὐτοῦ.

Ζεβεδαῖος, i. 20, iii. 17, x. 35*, is mentioned only in connexion with his sons. Ἰωάνης: for the references to John see those associated with James above, also ix. 38 in the story of the unauthorized exorcist.

καὶ αὐτοὺς ἐν τῷ πλοίῳ καταρτίζοντας τὰ δίκτυα is a circumstantial clause, Semitic in character, but not exclusively so. Cf. Howard, ii. 423; Black, 63, 66. Cf. also iv. 27, καὶ ὁ σπόρος . . . μηκύνηται, and see Intr. 59. Mt. iv. 21 omits the superfluous καὶ αὐτούς. καταρτίζω*, to render ἄρτιος, 'fit', 'complete'; here of the mending of nets. VGT, 332, cites an example of the verb used of garments prepared as a gift, and cites Wynne, Exp. VII. viii. 282 ff., who suggests that in Mk the idea is that of folding the nets to be ready for use. In the more general sense of making complete or perfecting the verb is used by St. Paul in Rom. ix. 22, 1 Cor. i. 10, 2 Cor. xiii. 11, Gal. vi. 1, 1 Thess. iii. 10 (cf. Lightfoot in loc.). See also Lk. vi. 40, Heb. x. 5, xi. 3, xiii. 21, 1 Pet. v. 10**. The definite article in ἐν τῷ πλοίῳ indicates the thing appropriate to the circumstances; cf. 'the bushel' and 'the lampstand' in iv. 21. As might be expected in a Gospel which often mentions the lake, πλοῖον is used frequently in Mk (17 times).

20. Here εὐθύς (v. i. 10) means 'immediately'. Mt. iv. 22 connects εὐθέως with ἀφέντες, but Mark's intention appears to be to suggest that Jesus summoned James and John as soon as He saw them. καλέω, ii. 17, iii. 31, xi. 17*, is used less frequently in Mk than might be expected. The completeness of the response is expressed by saying that they left their father Zebedee in the boat with the hired servants and went away after Jesus. μισθωτός, Jn. x. 12 f.**, 'a hired servant'. The phrase, peculiar to Mk, is best explained as a reminiscence. It does not necessarily mean that James and John belonged to a higher social station. In Lk. v. 10 the disciples are described as 'partners', and probably none of them should be regarded as poor men. For ἀπῆλθον ὀπίσω αὐτοῦ v. i. 17. Mark appears to have in mind a lifelong response, possibly exaggerating the actual facts, since in iv. 1 and 35 Peter's boat seems to be available. This representation probably reflects a catechetical interest. The comment of J. Weiss, 140, is very much to the point, that Peter himself, like Paul in Gal. i, ii, may have forgotten the gradual growing of his enthusiasm for Jesus, while only the one moment, in which the words of Jesus marked the final decision, remained for him unforgettable.

(a) Mk. i. 21-39   THE MINISTRY AT CAPERNAUM

This well-knit section, which is associated with Capernaum and its neighbourhood, includes four narratives, as follows:

(6) i. 21-8.   The Demoniac in the Synagogue.
(7) i. 29-31. The Healing of Peter's Wife's Mother.
(8) i. 32-4.   Healings in the Evening.
(9) i. 35-9.   The Departure to a Lonely Place.

For the narrative character of the complex, as compared with ii. 1-iii. 6, v. Intr. 90-2. The group stands apart from others in that it is based on the

earliest personal testimony, being comparable in this respect only with
iv. 35-v. 43, vi. 30-56, vii. 24-37, and the Passion Narrative. Of it Johannes
Weiss writes, ' This self-contained character of the group is best explained
by the view that so Peter was wont to relate of the day in which Jesus
came forward in his native town for the first time with words and deeds
of which a number took place in his house ', *Die Schr.* 78.[1]

| Mk. i. 21-8 | 6. THE DEMONIAC IN THE | Cf. Mt. vii. 28 f. |
| | SYNAGOGUE | Lk. iv. 31-7 |

The narrative is a Miracle-story (Bultmann, 223 f.), but it lacks the
rounded form to which Form Critics assign this name. Probably this is
the reason why Dibelius, 43, classifies it as a ' Paradigm of a less pure type ',
and why Bultmann pares away so much from the existing narrative.
Thus, he attributes the four opening words in 21, the whole of 22, the
phrase about a new teaching with authority in 27, and 28 to the Evangelist.
There is, however, another way of explaining the facts. The form of the
narrative *precedes* that of the Miracle-story proper. In it we see a stage
before it has become a popular narrative, one nearer to the original eyewitnesses. In this way we account best for the description of the impression made by the teaching of Jesus (22), the comments of the hearers (27),
the picture of the demoniac (23), his bold words and divided personality
(24). Probably 21 f. and 28 are integral to the whole, or at least to the
complex to which it belongs. So the story was told and so Mark recorded
it ! The narrative abounds in primitive features. No embarrassment is
felt in recording a story of exorcism, such as led the Fourth Evangelist to
exclude this type of narrative from his Gospel. Jesus shares the ideas
of his time, but so far transcends them that by a commanding word alone,
without the use of magical practices, He casts out the unclean spirit. He
Himself is the subject of the story. His teaching and accent of authority,
the supernatural aura of His person, His reaction to evil, His ringing
command and sentence of expulsion — these are the points which arrest
the attention of the reader. The story has this character, not because
Mark has embellished a shorter oral version current in the community,
but because he records a tradition which preserves the colour and detail
of the actual event. The contrary view of Wrede, 22-32, who sees the
influence of dogmatic ideas in the knowledge shown by the daemons of
the Messianic dignity of Jesus, is rejected by J. Weiss, 143-6, who asks,
' What in these events is incredible ? '. The only scientific and critical
view, he claims, is that here we have a piece of very original tradition, not
derived from ideas, but fixed in respect of time and place and accredited
through personal reminiscence.

Καὶ εἰσπορεύονται εἰς Καφαρναούμ. Καὶ εὐθὺς τοῖς σάββασιν 21

21. καὶ εἰσπορεύονται εἰς Καφαρναούμ.
Om. sys. εἰσπορεύομαι, iv. 19, v. 40, vi.
56, vii. 15, 18 f., xi. 2* (*HS²*, 12). For
the historic pres. *v.* i. 12. Καφαρναούμ,
ii. 1, ix. 33*, is one of the rare place

names in Mk. The town is not mentioned in the OT. By most modern
scholars it is identified with *Tell Ḥûm*
on the north-west shore of the lake
about two miles from the entrance of

[1] This passage is wanting in the later editions revised after Weiss's death by W. Bousset and
W. Heitmüller ; *v.* 4th ed., 82.

22 ⌐ἐδίδασκεν εἰς τὴν συναγωγήν⌐. καὶ ἐξεπλήσσοντο ἐπὶ τῇ διδαχῇ

21 εἰσελθὼν εἰς τὴν συναγωγὴν ἐδίδασκεν

the Jordan. Cf. Dalman, *SSW*, 128, 138; Rawlinson, 17; Sanday, *JTS*, Oct. 1903; Lagrange, 21; Schofield, 19; etc. Here can still be seen the remains of a synagogue which is not earlier than the second, or the beginning of the third, century, but which may have replaced an earlier building. Other scholars, with less probability, have identified Capernaum with *Khan Minyeh* two miles farther west. Cf. G. A. Smith, *HG*, 456; Sanday, *SSG*, 36 ff. It is strange that Capernaum is not mentioned until this point. Both Matthew (iv. 13) and Luke (iv. 31) mention it before the Call of the First Disciples. Mark's procedure is due to the fact that he found i. 16-20 as a self-contained story and the reference to Capernaum already connected with i. 21-39. This view is much to be preferred to the suggestion that the phrase forms the conclusion of the narrative of the Call (J. Weiss, *Die Schr.*² 76; Wendling, *Urmarkus*, 43). There is thus a gap between i. 16-20 and 21-39, and, in consequence, there is no need to raise the question whether Capernaum was entered on the first Sabbath after the call, as many commentators suggest, or on the same day.

In this verse εὐθύς appears to mean ' And so ' or ' Now '. σάββατον, 11 times and xvi. [19]*, is a Semitic word, which, although of the second declension, always has the third declension ending in the NT in the dat. plur. Successive Sabbaths are not meant, for the plur. is usual when feasts are mentioned; cf. xiv. 1, τὰ ἄζυμα, vi. 21, τὰ γενέσια, Jn. x. 22, τὰ ἐνκαίνια, but ' on the Sabbath day '.

The reading εἰσελθὼν εἰς τὴν συναγω-γὴν ἐδίδασκεν is very uncertain. The participle is omitted by א C L Δ fam. 13 28 565 837 892 and placed in brackets by WH. Moreover, the same MSS. and Origen (*Comm. Ioh.*) read ἐδίδασκεν εἰς τὴν συναγωγήν. This reading should probably be accepted. Cf.

Turner, *JTS*, xxvi. 15, xxviii. 153. In it εἰς = ἐν, as in i. 9, 39, x. 10, xiii. 9. εἰσελθών etc. is probably an Alexandrian grammatical correction.

Much emphasis is laid upon the teaching ministry in Mk; cf. ii. 13, iv. 1, vi. 2, 6, 34, etc. διδάσκω is used 17 times*. In these general statements it is usually vain to inquire what the theme may have been, but here in view of 24 (ἦλθες ἀπολέσαι ἡμᾶς) it is reasonable to infer that Jesus spoke of the Rule of God and the destruction of evil powers. συναγωγή, i. 23, 29, 39, iii. 1, vi. 2, xii. 39, xiii. 9*, originally ' a bringing together ', came to mean ' an assembly ' (cf. ἐκκλησία), especially a Jewish religious assembly, ' a synagogue '. Cf. Deissmann, 103 f.; *VGT*, 600 f. In Jas. ii. 2 it is used of a Christian assembly. The Gospels show that at first Jesus used the opportunities provided by the synagogue; cf. also iii. 1 and vi. 2. So later St. Paul; cf. Ac. ix. 20, xiii. 5, 14, xiv. 1. Even small towns and villages had their synagogues, where people gathered for worship, prayer, and the reading and exposition of the Law and the Prophets. Not only scribes and elders, but any member of the assembly might be invited by the President of the synagogue to expound the Law and teach. Cf. Abrahams, i. 1-17. The opportunity was great, but naturally it disappeared as the breach between Jesus and the Rabbis widened.

22. The effect produced is described by καὶ ἐξεπλήσσοντο ἐπὶ τῇ διδαχῇ αὐτοῦ. ἐκπλήσσομαι, vi. 2, vii. 37, x. 26, xi. 18*, pass. in the NT, is a strong word indicating amazement. The plur. is impersonal; *v*. Intr. 47 f., 62. Compare the use of *man* in German and *on* in French. ἐπί, ' at ', ' on the ground of '. διδαχή, i. 27, iv. 2, xi. 18, xii. 38*; Mt (3), Lk (1), Jn (3). Cf. Deissmann, 440 n.⁴. The reason for the astonishment is that He was teaching them with authority, and not as the scribes.

αὐτοῦ, ἦν γὰρ διδάσκων αὐτοὺς ὡς ἐξουσίαν ἔχων, οὐχ ὡς οἱ
γραμματεῖς. καὶ εὐθὺς ἦν ἐν τῇ συναγωγῇ αὐτῶν ἄνθρωπος ἐν 23

For the periphrastic imperf. ἦν . . . διδάσκων v. Intr. 45, 62 f.
ἐξουσία, i. 27, ii. 10, iii. 15, vi. 7, xi.
28 (bis), 29, 33, xiii. 34*, ‘authority’,
‘right’, ‘freedom’, ‘power’. From
the general idea of ‘power to act’
ἐξουσία in the LXX and NT expresses
the thought of ‘authority’ rather than
‘power’. Reitzenstein, Poimandres,
48 n.³, claims that in the NT the idea
of ‘knowledge’ is mingled with that of
‘power’. Cf. VGT, 225; Dodd, BG,
200; Barrett, 78-82. In i. 21 the idea
of authority is suggested by the contrast with the teaching of the scribes.
A direct inward assurance of truth,
based on a profound sense of divine
inspiration, is meant. The authority
is given (Mt. xxviii. 19) and is prophetic in character. The hearers were
astonished because the voice of prophecy had long been silent in Israel.
Cf. I Macc. iv. 46 and see W. Foerster,
KThW, ii. 566. ὡς . . . ἔχων indicates
the manner of the teaching.
οἱ γραμματεῖς, 21 times*. In Cl. Gk
the word means ‘a secretary’ or ‘re-
gistrar’; in the LXX a public officer
or ‘clerk of works’ (Ex. v. 6) or a subordinate military official who kept
records (Deut. xx. 5); in the papyri
a public official, town clerk, etc. (VGT,
131 f.). In the Gospels οἱ γραμματεῖς
are the scribes, the teachers of the Law.
Luke also describes them as νομικοί and
νομοδιδάσκαλοι. Most of the scribes
belonged to the party of the Pharisees
(v. ii. 16), but some were Sadducees
(v. xii. 18*). In their interpretations
of the Law their teaching lacked the
note of spontaneity, being based upon
tradition. Abrahams, i. 14 f., maintains that it would be improper to contrast the simplicity and directness of
Jesus with the scholasticism of the
Rabbis, since the Talmudic method
was a later development. Cf. Lohmeyer, 35. Even if this be conceded,
the difference must have been great.

The phrase οὐχ ὡς οἱ γραμματεῖς presents them in an unfavourable light,
but Mark also records the story of the
scribe to whom Jesus said, ‘Thou art
not far from the Kingdom of God’
(xii. 34). See further, Schürer, II. i.
306 ff.; Ed. Meyer, ii. 284 ff.; Swete,
18; Lightley, 12, 111, 127; Klostermann, 30 f.; Montefiore, i. 32 f.
καί before οὐχ should probably be
omitted with D Θ b c e ff. The asyndeton is characteristic of Mark's style
(v. Intr. 49 f., 58). So Turner, JTS,
xxviii. 153 f.
23. The story proper begins with the
interruption of the demoniac. It is
difficult to agree with Wellhausen, 10,
that εὐθύς (v. i. 10) is to be taken with
ἀνέκραξεν. None the less, when the
adv. is connected with ἦν, neither ‘immediately’ nor ‘so then’ is a satisfactory translation.¹ It is tempting to
regard it as a later insertion since it is
omitted in A C D W Δ Θ et al. fam. 13
22 28 118 565 700 1071 al. pler. it vg
sys pe hl geo aeth arm, and is wanting
in Lk. iv. 33. As, however, it is the
more difficult reading, it should probably be read with ℵ B L fam. 1 (exc.
118) 33 579 sa bo Or.
In ἐν πνεύματι ἀκαθάρτῳ the prep.
ἐν represents the Heb. בּ = ‘with’,
‘having’. Luke gives the sense in the
phrase ἔχων πνεῦμα δαιμονίου ἀκα-
θάρτου. Cf. Howard, ii. 464: ‘ἐν
πνεύματι ἀκαθάρτῳ is a Semitism of
thought which naturally employs this
possible construction in Greek’. That
ἐν is instrumental or indicative of
manner is less probable; cf. Blass,
131; Swete, 19. Mark uses πνεῦμα
ἀκάθαρτον 11 times, as often in fact
as he has δαιμόνιον (v. i. 34, etc.). Cf.
ix. 25: τὸ ἄλαλον καὶ κωφὸν πνεῦμα.
The adjectives may indicate different
manifestations of daemon possession,
but more probably ἀκάθαρτον represents a religious judgment on the part
of the Evangelist rather than a special

¹ But see Moffatt (‘Now’), RSV (‘immediately’), Bartlet, 108 (‘Then and there’).

24 πνεύματι ἀκαθάρτῳ, καὶ ἀνέκραξεν λέγων Τί ἡμῖν καὶ σοί,
Ἰησοῦ Ναζαρηνέ; ἦλθες ἀπολέσαι ἡμᾶς· ⌐οἶδά⌐ σε τίς εἶ, ὁ ἅγιος

24 οἴδαμέν

form of ceremonial impurity. In his view possession exposes men to a pollution which unfits them for worship and fellowship with God. Cf. F. Hauck, *KThW*, iii. 431 f. ἀνακράζω, vi. 49*, Lk. iv. 33, viii. 28, xxiii. 18**, ' to cry aloud ', ' shout '; a verb (Cl., LXX; cf. *VGT*, 34) indicating strong emotion. Elsewhere Mark has the simplex κράζω (*v*. iii. 11). He frequently mentions the loud cries of the possessed and often, as here, it is difficult, if not impossible, to say whether the cries are thought of as those of the sufferer or those of the unclean spirit. Here, apparently, the man identifies himself with the daemon and speaks in the name of the class to which it belongs.

24. The interjection ἔα (Ah!) is widely attested,[1] but is probably an assimilation to Lk. iv. 34. In Cl. Gk the question τί ἡμῖν καὶ σοί; would mean ' What have we in common? ', but here it probably corresponds to the Heb. מַה־לִּי וָלָךְ (Josh. xxii. 24, Judg. xi. 12, 1 Kgs. xvii. 18, etc.) with the meaning ' Why dost thou meddle with us? '. Cf. Rawlinson, 16; Lagrange, 22; and see Lk. iv. 34, Jn. ii. 4. By ἡμῖν the class is meant. Ναζαρηνός, x. 47, xiv. 67, xvi. 6*; Lk. iv. 34, xxiv. 19**. Mark does not use the form Ναζωραῖος found in Mt. ii. 23, xxvi. 71, Lk. xviii. 37, Jn. xviii. 5, 7, xix. 19, Ac (7)**. The meaning and derivation of these words are disputed. See the note on pp. 177-8.

The phrase ἦλθες ἀπολέσαι ἡμᾶς is frequently taken as a question (AV, RV, RSV; Swete, 19; Lagrange, 23; Plummer, 67), but it is better understood as a defiant assertion (cf. Rawlinson, 16; Klostermann, 20; E. R. Micklem, 51): ' Thou art come (into the world) to destroy us! '. The destruction of evil powers in the Messianic

Age was widely expected; cf. 1 En. lxix. 27, Lk. x. 18, Apoc. xx. 10. The possessed man is conscious of a sense of menace in the person and teaching of Jesus and implicitly recognizes Him as the Messiah. With the phrasing of the cry cf. 1 Kgs. xvii. 18, ' What have I to do with thee, O thou man of God? thou art come unto me to bring my sin to remembrance, and to slay my son! '

The abrupt change to the first person sing. in οἶδά σε τίς εἶ is very dramatic. οἴδαμεν is attested by ℵ L Δ 892 Iren Or Eus Bas Cyr. Alex. Turner, *JTS*, xxviii. 154, gives it a place in his margin, but thinks that it may have arisen out of assimilation to the preceding plurals. σε is redundant, but it produces a very vivid effect and is retained in Lk. iv. 34. ὁ ἅγιος τοῦ θεοῦ*, Lk. iv. 34, Jn. vi. 69**, is not a known Messianic title, but, as its record shows, neither is it a common primitive Christian designation. It has an Old Testament counterpart in the description of Aaron as ' the holy one of the Lord ' (τὸν ἅγιον κυρίου, Psa. cv. (cvi.) 16), and of Elisha as ' an holy man of God ' (ἄνθρωπος τοῦ θεοῦ ἅγιος, 4 Kgdms. iv. 9). In Isa. xl. 25, lvii. 15 God is ' the Holy One ', and ἅγιος is applied to Christ in Ac. iii. 14, iv. 27, 30, 1 Jn. ii. 20,[2] Apoc. iii. 7, and ὅσιος in Ac. ii. 27, xiii. 35. It is probable, therefore, that the demoniac uses ὁ ἅγιος τοῦ θεοῦ with Messianic significance, as expressing a sense of the presence of a supernatural person. J. Weiss, *Die Schr.*[2] 80, with much cogency, traces this discernment to the man's reaction to the preaching of Jesus concerning the inbreaking of the Kingdom of God and the end of Satan's might, but it is notable that in the fourth edition of his commentary (1929) edited by W. Bousset and W. Heitmüller the description of the man is traced to the

[1] By ℵᶜ A C L Δ *et al*. fam. 1 fam. 13 22 28 33 543 579 700 892 1071 *al. pler.* syʰˡ geo¹ geoᴬ Eus Or Cyr. Alex.

[2] In 1 Jn. ii. 20 the reference may be to the Father. Cf. A. E. Brooke, 56; C. H. Dodd, 53.

τοῦ θεοῦ. καὶ ἐπετίμησεν αὐτῷ ὁ Ἰησοῦς [λέγων] Φιμώθητι 25
καὶ ἔξελθε ἐξ αὐτοῦ. καὶ σπαράξαν αὐτὸν τὸ πνεῦμα τὸ ἀκάθαρ- 26
τον καὶ φωνῆσαν φωνῇ μεγάλῃ ἐξῆλθεν ἐξ αὐτοῦ. καὶ ἐθαμβή- 27

same stereotyped Markan representation which appears in i. 34, iii. 11, v. 7, where the possessed greet Jesus as ' the Son of God '. In this matter decision turns on how ' the Messianic Secret ' is interpreted; see Intr. 122-4. To the present writer Weiss's view seems sounder than that of his editors. See further, Lagrange, 22; Rawlinson, 16; O. Procksch, *KThW*, i. 102-4, who suggests that ὁ ἅγιος τοῦ θεοῦ designates Jesus as the bearer of the Spirit.

25. Jesus rebukes the unclean spirit, and charges it to be silent and come out of him. ἐπιτιμάω, iii. 12, iv. 39, viii. 30, 32 f., ix. 25, x. 13, 48*; c. ἵνα, iii. 12, viii. 30, x. 48. In Cl. Gk the verb means ' to honour ', ' raise in price ', and ' to censure '; in the NT ' to rebuke ', ' admonish ', ' charge strictly '; *v*. Moulton, ii. 312 f., *VGT*, 248; Allen, 117. The αὐτῷ refers to the spirit, as the command shows. The decisiveness of tone used by Jesus is part of the curative method, but it also marks His strong sense of indignation aroused by possession and His unwillingness to permit the testimony of the possessed. For the ' Messianic Secret ' *v*. Intr. 122-4. φιμόω, <φιμός, ' to muzzle ', 1 Cor. ix. 9, 1 Tim. v. 18; ' to silence ', here and iv. 39, Mt. xxii. 12, 34, Lk. iv. 35, 1 Pet. ii. 15**. The verb is one of a number the meaning of which is softened in Hellenistic Greek; cf. ἐμβριμάομαι i. 43, σκύλλω v. 35, χορτάζω vi. 42, ἐρεύγομαι Mt. xiii. 35, τρώγω Jn. vi. 54. Rohde, *Psyche*, ii. 124, maintains that φιμόω was used in Egypto-Syrian Greek to denote the *binding* of a person by means of a spell. This idea applies better to the situation in iv. 39 (The Storm on the Lake) than to the present passage, in which silencing followed by dismissal is the end desired. The command implies that Jesus shared the belief in daemon-possession so characteristic

of the age. Accommodation to the ideas of the possessed for curative purposes is nowhere indicated or suggested. Cf. v. 1-21, ix. 14-27.

ἐκ τοῦ ἀνθρώπου is read by D W Θ 330 565mg vg and many O. Lat. MSS., and Turner, *JTS*, xxviii. 154, gives it a place in his margin. λέγων (om. אׁ* A*) is fully in harmony with Mark's style and should be read. See Intr. 63.

26. The description of the exorcism follows. The unclean spirit convulses the man and crying with a loud voice comes out of him. σπαράσσω, ix. 26*, Lk. ix. 39**; Cl. ' to tear ', ' rend '. Swete, 21, suggests the meaning ' convulse ', pointing to the LXX rendering of the Heb. in 2 Sam. xxii. 8 (וַיָּ֫גַ, ' shake ', ' quake ') and in Dan. viii. 7 ([הָשְׁלֵךְ], ' cast down '; Theod. ἔριψεν). Cf. Lagrange, 25, *l'agita convulsivement*. Unfortunately, *VGT*, 582, gives only one uncertain example of the verb in the papyri. Lk. iv. 35 has ῥίψαν αὐτὸν τὸ δαιμόνιον εἰς τὸ μέσον . . . μηδὲν βλάψαν αὐτόν, which suggests convulsive movement rather than laceration. This appears to be Mark's meaning. Cf. Moffatt and RSV, ' convulsing him '; Torrey, ' racked '; Micklem, 53, who writes: ' The main symptom accompanying the cure is clear, and that is that the man fell down in a convulsion '. See the parallel use of συνσπαράσσω in ix. 20, Lk. ix. 42**. A loud cry during the paroxysm is described by φωνῆσαν φωνῇ μεγάλῃ; cf. v. 7, xv. 34, 37. κράξαν is very widely attested, but φωνῆσαν (א B L 33 579 892 1071 Or) must be read, for, as Turner observes, *JTS*, xxviii. 154, if κράξαν had stood in the text, no one would have altered it.

27. As often in Miracle-stories the effect on the bystanders is now described. θαμβέομαι, x. 24, 32** (all pass.), ' to be amazed '; a very strong word, found in the poets in Cl. Gk and occasionally in the LXX, which in

θησαν ἅπαντες, ὥστε συνζητεῖν ⌈αὐτοὺς⌉ λέγοντας Τί ἐστιν
τοῦτο; διδαχὴ καινή· κατ᾽ ἐξουσίαν καὶ τοῖς πνεύμασι τοῖς ἀκα-
28 θάρτοις ἐπιτάσσει, καὶ ὑπακούουσιν αὐτῷ. Καὶ ἐξῆλθεν ἡ ἀκοὴ

27 πρὸς ἑαυτοὺς

common speech was used to express
great astonishment. Cf. Lagrange,
24: *marque un extrême étonnement,
la stupeur, mais non pas toujours
l'effroi*; Moulton, ii. 387; *VGT*, 283.
The use of the verb is remarkable
since the Jews were not unfamiliar
with exorcisms; cf. Lk. xi. 19, Ac.
xix. 13. The astonishment is due to
the fact that Jesus casts out the unclean spirit with a word, without the
use of magical formulae, but it is
occasioned also by the teaching of
Jesus, as the comments of the crowd
show, above all by a sense of the uncanny, or supernatural, produced by
the personality of Jesus. In contrast
with Jewish and Greek stories, in the
Gospel narratives there are no cases
in which the reality of the exorcism is
proved by shattering a statue or over-
turning a bowl, nor is the daemon
drawn from the nose of the possessed
by means of a ring. ' In the case of
Jesus a word is enough . . . One will
seek in vain for magical manipulations
of the same kind in our NT stories ',
Fascher, 127 f. For parallel stories
v. Bultmann, 247; Josephus, *Ant.*
viii. 2. 5; Philostratus, *Vit. Apoll.*
iii. 38, iv. 20; cf. Fiebig, *Jüd. Wundergeschichten*, 25 f.
ἅπας, viii. 25, xi. 32, xvi. [15]*, is
very common in Lk-Ac. Luke recasts
the sentence in the form: καὶ ἐγένετο
θάμβος ἐπὶ πάντας. συνζητέω, viii. 11,
ix. 10, 14, 16, xii. 28*; rest of NT
(4)**, ' to discuss ', ' question '; cf.

*HS*², 13. ὥστε c. infin. indicating result (' so as to '), i. 45, ii. 2, 12, iii.
10, 20, iv. 1, 32, 37, ix. 26, xv. 5*;
c. indic. ii. 28, x. 8*. αὐτούς is correctly used and should probably be
read with א B b e ff, for, while πρὸς
ἑαυτούς is widely attested,[1] Mark uses
συνζητέω absolutely (viii. 11, ix. 10,
xii. 28) or of discussion with others
(ix. 14, 16).
For διδαχή and ἐξουσία v. i. 22.
καινός, ii. 21, xiv. 24 (?), 25, xvi. [17]*,
is ' new ' in respect of quality, as distinct from νέος, ' new ' as regards time.
Cf. ii. 21 f. The WH text takes κατ᾽
ἐξουσίαν with the following clause καὶ
τοῖς πνεύμασι τοῖς ἀκαθάρτοις ἐπιτάσσει . . ., ' With authority he commands
the unclean spirits and they obey him '.
So RV and RSV; Swete, 21; Torrey,
70; cf. Lk. iv. 36. In view, however,
of i. 22, ἦν γὰρ διδάσκων αὐτοὺς ὡς
ἐξουσίαν ἔχων, it is preferable to take
it with διδαχὴ καινή. So Lagrange, 24;
Wellhausen, 11; J. Weiss, *Die Schr.*⁴
85; Klostermann, 21; Gould, 24;
Blunt, 149. What arouses astonishment is not only the freshness of the
teaching, but also its note of authority.
Cf. Moffatt: ' It's new teaching with
authority behind it ! '. For κατά c. acc.
=' in the way of ' v. Rom. iv. 16, Phil.
ii. 3. The καί before τοῖς πνεύμασι τ. ἀ.
(=' even ') marks the climax of the
astonishment. ἐπιτάσσω, vi. 27, 39,
ix. 25*. ὑπακούω, c. dat., iv. 41*, is
used *ad sensum* in the plur.²
28. The effect is further described

¹ A C D W Θ *et al.* fam. 1 fam. 13 22 28 33 543 565 579 700 892 1071 *al. pler.* c d f vg syᵖᵉ.
² The textual problems of 27b are complicated. *V.* Legg. τί ἐστιν τοῦτο; is omitted by D W
b c e ff q syˢ geo aeth arm, and instead of διδαχὴ καινὴ κατ᾽ ἐξουσίαν καί (א B L, etc.), many MSS.
have τίς ἡ διδαχὴ αὕτη ὅτι κατ᾽ ἐξουσίαν with variations in the position of καινή, while D W
and other Western MSS. have also ἐκείνη in the manifestly conflate reading ἐκείνη ἡ καινὴ αὕτη.
Couchoud, *JTS*, xxxiv. 116, followed by Lohmeyer, 34, conjectures that the original text was τίς
ἐστιν ἡ διδαχὴ ἐκείνη;, attested by e in *quaenam esset doctrina haec*, on the ground that the parallel
in Lk. iv. 36, τίς ὁ λόγος οὗτος, has nothing corresponding to καινή, but has a parallel to
ἐκείνη in οὗτος. The existence of this text, he argues, explains the existing variants. This argument is not satisfactory. Confusion between ἡ καινή and ἐκείνη has undoubtedly taken place, but
exclusively in Western MSS., while καινή is attested in every quarter. Further, Lk. iv. 36 appears
to be a smoother version of the Markan text, and the same explanation accounts well for the
variants noted above. The rough א B L text invited modifications, and assimilation to Lk. iv. 36
has been a contributory factor.

αὐτοῦ εὐθὺς πανταχοῦ εἰς ὅλην τὴν περίχωρον τῆς Γαλιλαίας.

by a reference to the spread of the tidings. ἀκοή, vii. 35, xiii. 7*, ' hearing ', ' ears ' (in the plur. vii. 35), ' report '. Here the meaning is ' report ', ' fame ' (Moffatt, Torrey). The gen. αὐτοῦ is objective, ' the report about him ', as in the LXX in Nah. i. 12, Jer. vi. 24, xxvii. (l.) 43, xliv. (xxxvii.) 5. Lk. iv. 37 has καὶ ἐξεπορεύετο ἦχος περὶ αὐτοῦ. εὐθύς here means ' immediately ', ' forthwith '; it marks the immediacy with which the news about Jesus spread, just as πανταχοῦ describes its wide range. πανταχοῦ, xvi. [20]*; Lk. ix. 6, Ac. xvii. 30, xxiv. 3, xxviii. 22, 1 Cor. iv. 17**, ' everywhere ', is omitted by A D Δ et al. 22 157 1071 al. pler. f g² l vg sy pe hl. It is implied, however, by Luke's πάντα τόπον (iv. 37), and the redundancy is characteristic of Mark's style. It should therefore be read with ℵc B C L W fam. 13 b e. Cf. Turner, JTS, xxviii. 155.

The area described by ὅλην τὴν περίχωρον τῆς Γαλιλαίας might mean the country around Galilee (cf. Mt. iv. 24, εἰς ὅλην τὴν Συρίαν), or ' throughout Galilee ', the gen. being epexegetic (cf. Swete, 22). But it is more probable that Mark means all parts of Galilee in the neighbourhood of Capernaum; cf. Lk. iv. 37, εἰς πάντα τόπον τῆς περιχώρου. Cf. Moffatt, ' the whole of the surrounding country of Galilee '. περίχωρος*, Mt. iii. 5, xiv. 35, Lk (5), Ac (1)**, ' round about a place ', sc. γῆ, ' the country round about '; LXX (Gen. xiii. 10, etc.); VGT, 510. With the vague character of the geographical phrase cf. vii. 31. Mark's main interest is to suggest the deep impression made by Jesus upon the people, and probably the summary statement belongs to the story itself, since in it the narrative reaches a natural climax.

DETACHED NOTE ON Ναζαρηνός AND Ναζωραῖος [1]

Among modern discussions see Burkitt, The Syriac Forms of NT Proper Names, 28 f.; Moore, The Beginnings of Christianity, i. 426-32; Goguel, 191-8; Guignebert, Jesus, 88 f.; Moulton, ii. 107 f., 150; Bauer, 839. Suggested derivations include: (1) from Ναζαρέτ (-θ), Ναζαρά; cf. Moore; (2) from נֵצֶר ' shoot ', ' branch '; cf. Holtzmann, 194; (3) from נָזִיר ' consecrated ', ' holy '; cf. Burkitt; Loisy, i. 376; Guignebert; (4) from נוֹצְרִי, the Jewish name for the followers of Jeshu ha noṣri; v. Moore, i. 426. The suggestion of Goguel, who derives the words from Nasaraeans, the supposed name of the followers of the Baptist, is speculative. Cf. Loisy, The Origins of the NT (Eng. tr.), 34. Still more speculative is the assumption of the mythical school (cf. B. W. Smith, Der vorch. Jesus, 36, 42 ff.), that the words are to be traced to an alleged pre-Christian sect. Cf. J. W. Jack, The Historic Christ (1933), 92, 181 f. Against the second and the fourth of the derivations mentioned above it has been objected that almost invariably zeta represents the Heb. zain, while tsade is rendered by sigma; but there are exceptions to this rule. Moore, 427, points out that the reverse process is seen in the translation of Ναζαρέτ (naṣrat) and Ναζωραῖος (naṣraya) in the Old Syriac and Peshitta versions. It may well be that Matthew had in mind the ' shoot ' mentioned in Isa. xi. 1 when he wrote Ναζωραῖος κληθήσεται (ii. 23; but cf. McNeile, 21, Smith, 81), but otherwise there seems little to be said for this derivation. If the view that ὁ ἅγιος τοῦ θεοῦ (i. 24) is an interpretation of Ναζαρηνέ could be supported, there would be reason to trace the latter to

[1] This note merely summarizes points in the discussions of Moore and Goguel.

nazir ('consecrated'); but, in this case, the form Ναζιραῖος might be expected, and a further difficulty is that Jesus was not an ascetic (cf. Lk. vii. 33 f. = Mt. xi. 18 f.). *Noṣri*, and especially its Aramaic equivalent *neṣorai*, supplies a good explanation, and might be accepted if we could show how, from being a name for the followers of Jesus, it came to be a patrial adjective. As it is, Ac. xxiv. 5 ('the sect of the Nazarenes') is the only exception to the consistent NT use of the name as a designation of Jesus. On the whole, and in the present state of our knowledge, we must rest content with the conclusion of G. F. Moore, *op. cit.* 429, that 'there is no philological obstacle to deriving Ναζωραῖος, Ναζαρηνός, from the name of a town, Nazareth '.

| Mk. i. 29-31 | 7. THE HEALING OF PETER'S WIFE'S MOTHER | Cf. Mt. viii. 14 f. Lk. iv. 38 f. |

Like the previous narrative this Miracle-story (Bultmann, 226 f.) stands near the testimony of an eyewitness. The detail, which is not great, is significant, consisting, not so much of matters connected with the malady and its cure, as of unimportant features of interest to those concerned in the event. Thus, the house is said to be that of Peter and Andrew, and incidentally the presence of James and John is mentioned. The request for healing is implicit in the words, 'they tell him of her'. No sayings of Jesus are recorded, although it may reasonably be inferred that the cure was not accomplished in silence. The result is indicated in the simple statement, 'And the fever left her, and she attended upon them'. The parallel accounts in Mt and Lk heighten the miraculous element and omit details which seemed of secondary importance, although, in reality, it is these which give the story its life-like character. We have good reason to describe the narrative as Petrine. So J. Weiss, 147; Branscomb, 32; and many others. It is told from his standpoint and mentions things which must have been of interest to him. Zahn, ii. 496, points out how naturally the story can be turned into the first person : ' Immediately we betook ourselves out of the synagogue into our house and James and John also accompanied us within, and my wife's mother was lying down with a fever, and forthwith we spoke to him on behalf of the sick one '. Of the ' superfluous detail ' that Jesus is told of the sickness Weiss, 147, says : ' But Peter was wont to mention it, because to him it was unforgettable '. By no means all the Markan narratives are of this primitive character, and for this reason it is important to observe its peculiar features. Lohmeyer, 40, goes so far as to say that there is no other narrative in Mk with this distant and yet near sound of recollection.

29　Καὶ εὐθὺς ἐκ τῆς συναγωγῆς ⌜ἐξελθὼν ἦλθεν⌝ εἰς τὴν οἰκίαν

29 ἐξελθόντες ἦλθαν

29. The narrative is connected with the preceding story by the words : ' And straightway, when he came out of the synagogue, he came . . .'. The meaning of εὐθύς may be ' So then ', but it is also possible that the intention is to say that the first thing He did on leaving the synagogue was to enter the house of Simon and Andrew. So Moffatt : ' . . . they went straight to . . .'. For συναγωγή *v.* i. 21. WH and Ti read ἐξελθόντες ἦλθον with ℵ A

Σίμωνος καὶ ᾿Ανδρέου μετὰ ᾿Ιακώβου καὶ ᾿Ιωάνου. ἡ δὲ πεν- 30
θερὰ Σίμωνος κατέκειτο πυρέσσουσα, καὶ εὐθὺς λέγουσιν αὐτῷ
περὶ αὐτῆς. καὶ προσελθὼν ἤγειρεν αὐτὴν κρατήσας τῆς χειρός· 31
καὶ ἀφῆκεν αὐτὴν ὁ πυρετός, καὶ διηκόνει αὐτοῖς.

C L Δ *et al*. 28 33 118 892 1071 *al. pler*.
vg sy^pe bo geo¹ (with variations of
order), and Turner, *JTS*, xxviii. 115, in
accepting it says that the phrase is so
odd that change was tempting. But
there is strong support for the sing.
(WH^mg) ἐξελθὼν ἦλθεν (again with variations of order) in B D W Θ b c f ff vg
(4 MSS.) fam. 1 (exc. 118) fam. 13 22 543
565 579 700 sy^s (in part), and probably
this reading should be preferred, since
it accords with the central place occupied by Jesus in these narratives. Cf.
J. Weiss, 148 ; Swete, 23. Both οἰκία
and οἶκος (ii. 1) are frequently found
in Mk. The house is that of Simon
and Andrew who apparently live together. Matthew and Luke mention
Simon only (Mt, Peter) and Mark
alone alludes to the presence of James
and John. For these names *v*. i. 16, 19.
Simon's house appears to have been
a rendezvous of Jesus and His disciples at this period. Several commentators (J. Weiss, 148 n. ; Klostermann, 21 ; cf. Bultmann, 227) suggest
that the three names peculiar to Mk
are a later addition. Turner, 16, on
the contrary, says that the awkward
phrase becomes intelligible only when
it is put back into the mouth of Peter
' We came into our house with James
and John '.

30. πενθερά*, Mt. viii. 14, x. 35, Lk.
iv. 38, xii. 53**, ' mother-in-law '.
Peter, then, was a married man at the
time of his call. Cf. 1 Cor. ix. 5 from
which it appears that later his wife
accompanied him on his missionary
journeys. Cf. Clem. Alex. *Strom*. iii.
6. 52, vii. 11. 63, cited by Eusebius,
HE, iii. 30 (Bright, 91). κατάκειμαι,
ii. 4, 15, xiv. 3*, ' to lie down ', ' lie in
bed ' (here and ii. 4), ' recline at table '
(ii. 15, xiv. 3 ; Cl., LXX, Pap. (*VGT*,
326). πυρέσσω*, Mt. viii. 14**, ' to be
feverish', ' fall into a fever ', is a rare
word found in a few classical writers

(LS, 1556 ; Bauer, 1172), but not in
the LXX, and *VGT* cites no example
from the papyri. Matthew has βεβλημένην καὶ πυρέσσουσαν (viii. 14) and
Luke ἦν συνεχομένη πυρετῷ μεγάλῳ
(iv. 38). Whether the malady was
incipient or grave cannot be determined. Luke interprets it as a ' high
fever ', following the usage of ancient
physicians who distinguished fevers by
the terms μέγας and σμικρός. Cf.
Creed, xx, 71. Again Mark uses
εὐθύς, here undoubtedly with the meaning ' at once ', ' immediately '. To tell
Jesus of the sufferer was the first thing
they did. Turner, *JTS*, xxv. 378, suggests that λέγουσιν is used impersonally, ' He is told ', but it seems more
probable that οἱ περὶ τὸν Σίμωνα is the
subject understood ; cf. Swete, 23 ;
Lagrange, 25. It has been surmised
that the intention was to explain the
apparent want of hospitality in the
absence of the sick woman ; cf. J.
Weiss, 147. Lagrange makes the same
comment, but adds : *peut-être aussi
avec une espérance qu'ils osent à peine
s'avouer à eux-mêmes* (Loisy). On the
whole, it seems best to interpret ' and
straightway they tell him of her ' as
an artless request that He will use His
healing power on her. This is Luke's
interpretation : καὶ ἠρώτησαν αὐτὸν περὶ
αὐτῆς (iv. 38).

31. προσελθών, vi. 35, x. 2 (?), xii.
28, xiv. 35 (?), 45*, indicates either the
approach of Jesus to the sufferer, or
His entrance into the room where she
was ; cf. Lagrange, 25. D W b q read
or support ἐκτείνας τὴν χεῖρα. His
action is to raise her up, taking hold
of her hand. κρατήσας c. gen. (as in
v. 41, ix. 27) expresses concurrent
(Swete, 23) rather than antecedent
action (Burton, § 134), χειρός being
partitive gen. For κρατέω in the sense
of *laying hold of* or *arresting v*. iii.
21, etc. Luke almost personifies the

fever: καὶ ἐπιστὰς ἐπάνω αὐτῆς ἐπετίμησεν τῷ πυρετῷ (iv. 39). πυρετός*,
Mt. viii. 15, Lk. iv. 38 f., Jn. iv. 52,
Ac. xxviii. 8**. For the augment in
διηκόνει v. i. 13. The serving at the
evening meal is mentioned as the

sign of the cure. The careful use of
tenses, imperfects and aorists, is noteworthy. Matthew replaces αὐτοῖς by
αὐτῷ, thus representing the act of
service to all as an act of gratitude to
Jesus.

Mk. i. 32-4	8. HEALINGS IN THE	Cf. Mt. viii. 16 f.
	EVENING	Lk. iv. 40 f.

Although the narrative mentions healings and exorcisms, it is not a
Miracle-story, nor is it a summary statement like iii. 7-12. It is a Story
about Jesus connected with a particular time and place which records
things recalled at the close of a memorable day. The temporal statement
at the beginning and the tacit reference to Simon's house in 33 link the
narrative to the preceding stories in the group i. 21-39. In the light of
these stories the assembling of the crowds at the beginning, the bringing
of the sick and the possessed, and the sense of tension and excitement in
the account are fully credible, and with some confidence we may classify
it as Petrine. Matthew's version is briefer and more conventional, and
Mark's Semitic expression ' He healed many ' is made explicit in the
statement ' He healed all ' (viii. 16). Luke's account heightens the
miraculous element further in the statement that He laid His hands on
every one of them and healed them and in the description of the daemons
who, when exorcized, cried ' Thou art the Son of God ' (iv. 40 f., cf. Mk.
iii. 11). Compared with Mark's narrative, these versions are manifestly
secondary. Of outstanding interest in the Markan account is the statement that He would not permit the daemons to speak, because they knew
Him. Whether this detail belongs to the tradition or is a dogmatic construction on the part of Mark (cf. Lohmeyer, 41) depends on the view
which is taken of the ' Messianic Secret '.

32   Ὀψίας δὲ γενομένης, ὅτε ἔδυσεν ὁ ἥλιος, ἔφερον πρὸς αὐτὸν

32. ὄψιος, iv. 35, vi. 47, xiv. 17, xv.
42*. With ὥρα understood, it describes
the late afternoon, and in every instance in Mk it is used in the gen. abs.
construction. The phrase ὅτε ἔδυσεν ὁ
ἥλιος defines the time more precisely
as sunset. Thus, as is often the case
in Mk, the double phrase is not so
tautologous as it appears. Matthew
has a parallel to the first phrase only,
and Luke to the second, but it should
be noted that Matthew has not connected the previous story with the
Sabbath. In Mk it is made explicit
that it was when the Sabbath ended
that the crowds assembled bringing the
sick. Then only could the incidents
happen without a breach of the Law.

Mark's use of δέ is notable in view of
his strong preference for καί. V.
Intr. 48 f.
δύω (δύνω)*, Lk. iv. 40**, ' to enter
into ', ' plunge in ', ' sink ', ' set '.
ἔδυ, used in Cl. Gk in this sense, is read
by all MSS. except B D 28 349 517
which have ἔδυσεν. So WH, probably
rightly (cf. Turner, JTS, xxviii. 155)
and Nestle, while Ti and Souter read
ἔδυ. ἥλιος, iv. 6, xiii. 24, xvi. 2*. ἔφερον
is impersonal : ' People were bringing '.
Cf. Swete, 24 : ' Case after case
arrived '. Once more the imperf. is
used effectively; cf. i. 30 f. The idiomatic phrase οἱ κακῶς ἔχοντες, i. 34,
ii. 17, vi. 55*, describes sick people;
Mt (4), Lk (1)**. These are clearly

πάντας τοὺς κακῶς ἔχοντας καὶ τοὺς δαιμονιζομένους· καὶ ἦν ὅλη 33
ἡ πόλις ἐπισυνηγμένη πρὸς τὴν θύραν. καὶ ἐθεράπευσεν πολλοὺς 34
κακῶς ἔχοντας ποικίλαις νόσοις, καὶ δαιμόνια πολλὰ ἐξέβαλεν,
καὶ οὐκ ἤφιεν λαλεῖν τὰ δαιμόνια, ὅτι ᾔδεισαν αὐτόν.

distinguished from the possessed. δαι-
μονίζομαι, v. 15 f., 18*, Mt (7), Lk.
viii. 36, Jn. x. 21**, which belongs to
Hellenistic Gk, corresponds to the
classical δαιμονάω, 'to be under the
power of a δαίμων'; cf. VGT, 135.
See also E. C. E. Owen, JTS, xxxii.
133-53, 'Δαίμων and Cognate Words'.
For δαιμόνιον v. i. 34.

33. This descriptive passage, which
is peculiar to Mark's account, is fully
in keeping with his style. For this
reason we should be slow to agree to
the suggestion that because it is not
found in Mt and Lk is the work of
a redactor (J. Weiss, 148). For the
periphrastic construction ἦν . . . ἐπισυνηγμένη v. i. 6. The tense vividly
describes the growing crowds. Swete,
24 f. writes : ' the acc. dwells on the
thought of the flocking up to the door
which preceded, and the surging, moving, mass before it '. Cf. Plummer, 72 :
' Flocked towards the door and formed
a dense crowd there '. ἐπισυνάγω,
xiii. 27* ; Mt. xxiii. 37 (bis), xxiv. 31,
Lk. xii. 1, xiii. 34, xvii. 37**, belongs
to late Gk (cf. VGT, 247), and is a
strengthened form of συνάγω, ' to
gather together '. ὅλη ἡ πόλις is hyper-
bolical like πᾶσα ἡ Ἰουδαία χώρα in
i. 5. For πρός c. acc. in the sense of
' about ' or ' at ' v. also ii. 2 and xi. 4.
The ' door ' is the door of Peter's house.
This small point suggests that the section i. 21-39 is a unity, and that the story
is told from the standpoint of Peter.

34. For κακῶς ἔχοντας v. i. 32. θεραπεύω, iii. 2, 10, vi. 5, 13*, ' to do service ', ' serve ', ' treat medically '. The
classical meaning ' to treat medically '
is well illustrated in the papyri and
inscriptions (VGT, 289), and Ramsay
has effectively maintained that it is
used in this sense in Lk-Acts (cf. Luke
the Physician, 16 f.). Cf. Harnack,
Luke the Physician, 15 f. It is un-

likely, however, that Mark uses the
verb with this meaning or that Jesus
thought of Himself as ' treating ' sickness. ' Healed ', therefore, or ' cured '
(Moffatt) is the best translation. It is
often pointed out that Mark says Jesus
healed ' many ' (πολλούς), although
previously, in 32, he has used the word
' all ' (πάντας). It is doubtful, however, if Mark wishes to make any distinction (so now Lagrange, 26). Cf.
Swete, 25. Possibly the usage is a
Semitism ; cf. J. Jeremias, 91 f. ; Lohmeyer, 41. The later Evangelists remove the ambiguity : Mt. viii. 16
transposes πολλούς and πάντας, and
Lk. iv. 40b reads : ὁ δὲ ἑνὶ ἑκάστῳ
αὐτῶν τὰς χεῖρας ἐπιτιθεὶς ἐθεράπευσεν
αὐτούς. Luke also improves the order
by removing ποικίλαις νόσοις to the beginning of the story. ποικίλος*, originally ' many-coloured ', ' variegated ';
then, as here, ' various ', ' manifold '.
νόσος*, ' disease ', ' sickness '. δαιμόνιον, i. 34 (bis), 39, iii. 15, 22 (bis), vi.
13, vii. 26, 29 f., ix. 38, xvi. 9, [17]* ;
a substantive formed from the neut.
of the adj. δαιμόνιος, ' divine '; in
Cl. Gk ' the divine power ', ' a deity ';
later, as in NT, ' an evil spirit ', ' a
daemon '. Cf. VGT, 135. As in i. 32,
maladies and possession are distinguished and the reality of the latter is
tacitly assumed. Cf. ἄνθρωπος ἐν πνεύματι ἀκαθάρτῳ in i. 23.

The form ἤφιεν is derived from ἀφίω,
as if the verb were simplex (cf. xi. 16).
Cf. Moulton, ii. 189, 192, 202. For
ἀφίημι (ἀφίω) c. infin., ' to suffer ', see
v. 37, vii. 12, 27, x. 14 ; c. dir. obj.
only, v. 19, xi. 6, xiv. 6 ; c. subj. xi. 16,
xv. 36 (without ἵνα). Here ὅτι = ' because '. For the uncanny knowledge
of the possessed see the note on i. 24.
If, as is probable, Mark understood
the perception to be that Jesus was the
Messiah, he has exercised restraint in

not adding an interpretative statement. Luke adds τὸν Χριστόν . . . εἶναι (iv. 41), a reading to which the Markan text has been assimilated in many MSS. (אc B C L W Θ fam. 1 fam. 13 22 28 33 349 543 565 700 et al. vg (2 MSS.) syhl bo). It is omitted by א* A D Δ 157 579 1071 et al. a b c d e f ff q vg sys pe, and is enclosed by WH in square brackets. This passage and i. 25 are part of the data for the theory of W. Wrede, that the ' Messianic Secret ' is a doctrinal conception by which Mark has coloured the record of the Ministry. See Intr. 122-4.

Wellhausen, 12, draws attention to the text of D which conflates the ordinary text with a parallel reading καὶ ἐθεράπευσεν αὐτοὺς καὶ τοὺς δαιμόνια ἔχοντας ἐξέβαλεν αὐτὰ ἀπ' αὐτῶν. This reading includes an example of the casus pendens, τοὺς δαιμόνια ἔχοντας, followed·by the resumptive pronoun in ἀπ' αὐτῶν. There are several examples of this construction in Mk; cf. vi. 16, vii. 20, xii. 10, xiii. 11. V. Intr. 58. Wellhausen suspects that D preserves the original text, which perhaps was οἱ δαιμόνια ἔχοντες. . . . Cf. Howard, ii. 423 f.

Mk. i. 35-9   9. THE DEPARTURE TO A   Cf. Lk. iv. 42-4
                    LONELY PLACE

This Story about Jesus differs from many narratives in Mk in that it is not self-contained, but derives its significance from the three preceding stories. Primitive features include the unusually full and picturesque temporal statement at the beginning and the striking words and phrases κατεδίωξεν, Σίμων καὶ οἱ μετ' αὐτοῦ, Πάντες ζητοῦσίν σε, εἰς τὰς ἐχομένας κωμοπόλεις. Lohmeyer, 42, speaks of it as a Traditionsstück. In it is present ' something of the breath of an oriental morning ' (Wohlenberg, 66, cited by Schmidt, 58). For the most part Form Critics speak of it as a ' redactional formation ' or the summary account of a period in the activity of Jesus ; cf. Bultmann, 167 ; Sundwall, 10. Such descriptions stand opposed to the opinions of most commentators who see in the narrative a story drawn from life. Cf. J. Weiss, 149, who again quotes Zahn's claim that ' Simon and those with him ' represents an original ' We ' ; Schmidt, 58 ; Lagrange, 27 ; Bartlet, 117 ; Swete, 26 ; Grant, 132 f. Rawlinson, 19, suggests that the events depicted in i. 21-39 are ' typical ' scenes. This is true, but it does not exclude the view that the incidents are historical. The story ends with the word of Jesus : ' Let us go elsewhere into the neighbouring country towns, that I may preach there also, for to this end came I forth '. The statement in 39, that He was preaching in their synagogues in all Galilee and casting out daemons, is a summary passage which rounds off the section and prepares the way for what follows.

Matthew omits the story. Luke's stylistic and interpretative alterations are of much interest and are indicated in the Commentary.

35   Καὶ πρωὶ ἔννυχα λίαν ἀναστὰς ἐξῆλθεν [καὶ ἀπῆλθεν] εἰς ἔρη-

35. The temporal statement πρωὶ ἔννυχα λίαν, consisting of three adverbs, is almost without parallel in the Gospels. Cf. xvi. 2, καὶ λίαν πρωὶ τῇ μιᾷ τῶν σαββάτων, and Jn. xx. 1, πρωὶ σκοτίας ἔτι οὔσης. The meaning is : ' At an early hour, while it was still night '.

Cf. Moffatt, ' In the early morning, long before daylight '. Luke loses the vividness of Mark's rough phrase in his better Greek γενομένης δὲ ἡμέρας (iv. 42).

πρωί, xi. 20, xiii. 35, xv. 1, xvi. 2, [9]*, Mt. xx. 1, xxi. 18, Jn. xviii. 28,

μον τόπον κἀκεῖ προσηύχετο. καὶ κατεδίωξεν αὐτὸν Σίμων καὶ 36
οἱ μετ' αὐτοῦ, καὶ εὗρον αὐτὸν καὶ λέγουσιν αὐτῷ ὅτι Πάντες 37

xx. I, Ac. xxviii. 23**, ' early ', ' in the morning '. The adverbial phrase τὸ πρωί is common in the LXX (Gen. xl. 6, etc.) and is found in MGk (cf. *VGT*, 556). ἔννυχα** is the neut. pl. of ἔννυχος ' at night ' used as an adv. Cf. πάννυχα, ' the livelong night ', Soph. *Ajax* 929. λίαν, vi. 51, ix. 3, xvi. 2*, ' very ', ' exceedingly '. The strange temporal phrase appears to reflect the point of view of those within the house who discovered that Jesus was gone. Cf. J. Weiss, 148.

ἀναστὰς ἐξῆλθεν is the first of several examples of the use of the redundant participle followed by a verb of motion; cf. ii. 14, vii. 24, x. 1, and v. Intr. 63. The construction is Semitic, but not exclusively so. Lagrange, 193, cites Thuc. i. 87, cf. vii. 49, etc., and says that the usage *n'est pas une tournure seulement hébraïque*. Cf. Howard, ii. 453. καὶ ἀπῆλθεν is omitted by B 28* 56 235 565 bo, and ἐξῆλθεν καὶ by W 1071 b d e ff q vg (2 MSS.) syᵖᵉ. The former is enclosed by WH in square brackets, and some commentators (Swete, 26) explain the redundant words as a conflation, but the double phrase is ' very Marcan ' (Turner, *JTS*, xxviii. 155) and should be retained. The ἔρημον τόπον is not the desert, for the district around Capernaum was cultivated at the time, but a lonely and retired spot. κἀκεῖ προσ- ηύχετο, ' And there he continued in prayer ', is peculiar to Mark's account. Elsewhere he mentions the prayers of Jesus in vi. 46, xiv. 35, 39. It is strange that Luke, who speaks of this custom of Jesus much more frequently (iii. 21, v. 16, vi. 12, ix. 18, 28 f., xi. 1, xxii. 41, 44), omits this Markan reference. On this ground J. Weiss, 148, mentions the possibility that it may be the addition of a redactor, but this view does not appear to be necessary.

36. καταδιώκω**, the perfective of

διώκω, is frequently found in the LXX, generally in a hostile sense (cf. Gen. xxxi. 36, etc.), but also in a good sense (cf. Psa. xxii. (xxiii.) 6, xxxvii. (xxxviii.) 21)*; ' to pursue closely ', ' follow down ', ' track down '. Cf. Moulton, i. 116 (' hunt down '); Moffatt, ' hunted him out '. The sing. is read, probably correctly, by א B Θ *et al.* 28 700 vg and the plur. by A C D L W *et al.* fam. 1 fam. 13 22 33 543 579 892 1071 *al. pler.* a b c e f ff q vg syˢ ᵖᵉ ʰˡ. This descriptive verb seems to preserve the vivid recollection of an active search. For the frequent use of compound verbs in Mk v. Moulton, i. 111-18, 237; Hawkins, 174 f.[1] Σίμων καὶ οἱ μετ' αὐτοῦ*, i.e. the four disciples mentioned in i. 29. Apparently, they thought that Jesus was losing a great opportunity afforded by the healings and exorcisms at Capernaum. The freshness of the Markan original stands out when it is compared with Lk. iv. 42. Instead of ' Simon and those with him ' Luke has ' the multitudes ', and instead of the picturesque κατεδίωξεν he has ἐπεζήτουν αὐτόν, καὶ ἦλθον ἕως αὐτοῦ.

37. In place of εὗρον . . . καί (א B L 892 e bo (3 MSS.)), εὑρόντες is read by A C Δ Θ *et al.* minusc. *omn.* (exc. 892) bo, and καὶ ὅτε εὗρον αὐτὸν λέγουσιν by D a f ff l q rı.² vg syˢ ᵖᵉ ʰˡ sa geo¹ arm. Probably these readings are secondary, especially since καὶ εὗρον αὐτὸν καὶ λέ- γουσιν is so characteristically Markan. Cf. Turner, *JTS*, xxviii. 156. For the same reason it does not seem desirable or necessary to put a full stop after αὐτόν and connect the first three words with the preceding verse. For the historic present v. Intr. 46 f. As in i. 15, 40, it is followed by ὅτι recitativum. Nothing could be more natural than the simple words Πάντες ζητοῦσίν σε which witness to the deep impression made by the ministry in Capernaum

---

[1] The average of compound verbs per WH page is Lk 6, Mk 5·7, Mt 3·6, Jn 2·1 (Moulton, i. 237).

38 ζητοῦσίν σε. καὶ λέγει αὐτοῖς "Αγωμεν ἀλλαχοῦ εἰς τὰς ἐχομένας
39 κωμοπόλεις, ἵνα καὶ ἐκεῖ κηρύξω, εἰς τοῦτο γὰρ ἐξῆλθον. καὶ ἦν
κηρύσσων εἰς τὰς συναγωγὰς αὐτῶν εἰς ὅλην τὴν Γαλιλαίαν καὶ
τὰ δαιμόνια ἐκβάλλων.

and the desire of the people that Jesus should remain with them. Luke has καὶ κατεῖχον αὐτὸν τοῦ μὴ πορεύεσθαι ἀπ' αὐτῶν (iv. 42). Cf. Jn. vi. 26.

38. With the hortatory subj. ἄγωμεν cf. xiv. 42. ἀλλαχοῦ**, ' elsewhere ', = ἄλλοσε or ἀλλαχόσε, and is found in the papyri (VGT, 22). Cf. ἀλλαχόθεν, Jn. x. 1**. The adverb is read by ℵ B C* L 33 579 sa bo geo¹ aeth arm, but is omitted by very many MSS. because of its redundancy and perhaps also because it was regarded as uncouth (cf. LS, 68). The use of ὁ ἐχόμενος = ' the next ', ' neighbouring ', is common in the LXX, but rare in the NT ; cf. Lk. xiii. 33, Ac. xiii. 44, xx. 15, xxi. 26, Heb. vi. 9 (Moffatt, ICC, 83). κωμόπολις** is a small country town which has only the status of a village. Not found in the LXX, it is used by Strabo, 12. 2. 6, and Josephus, Ant. xi. 8. 6. D replaces the rare word by κώμας καὶ εἰς τὰς πόλεις, cf. castella et ciuitates in a b e, vicos et ciuitates in c f vg sys pe sa.

The words εἰς τοῦτο γὰρ ἐξῆλθον indicate that the desire for a wider preaching ministry was the motive for the departure from Capernaum. It does not follow that the verb means ' from Capernaum ', though this view is taken by many commentators ; cf. Gould, 29 ; Bartlet, 117 ; Turner, 16 ; Rawlinson, 19 (tentatively) ; Wood, 683. Others think that Luke has correctly interpreted his source when he writes ὅτι ἐπὶ τοῦτο ἀπεστάλην (iv. 43), and that ἐξῆλθον means ' I came forth from the Father ' ; cf. Swete, 27 ; Plummer, 74 ; Lagrange, 28 ; Klostermann, 23 ; Schmidt, 58. It seems doubtful if so dogmatic an idea is intended, and it is best to conclude that Mark has in mind the mission of Jesus in Galilee : ' It was for that purpose I undertook my mission '. The nar-

rative leaves the impression that He left Capernaum to escape the pressure of the healing ministry here, but Mark does not say this and i. 39 suggests the contrary. On the whole, the desire for uninterrupted communion with the Father and the need to preach elsewhere appear to be the determining motives. Although differently expressed, this thought is conveyed by Lk. iv. 43.

39. For κηρύσσω v. i. 4 ; συναγωγή i. 21 ; ὅλος i. 28 ; Γαλιλαία i. 9 ; δαιμόνιον i. 34 ; ἐκβάλλω i. 12. Both the vocabulary and style suggest that this summary statement was added by Mark either in composing the Gospel or at a still earlier stage. Cf. Schmidt, 59.

Probably, instead of ἦλθεν (ℵ B L Θ 892 sa bo) we ought to read ἦν (A C D W Δ et al. minusc. omn. (exc. 892) it vg sys pe hl arm). The periphrastic imperf. is characteristic of Mk and is found in the parallel passage Lk. iv. 44. Cf. Schmidt, 59 ; Klostermann, 23 ; Turner, JTS, xxviii. 156. Probably ἦλθεν is a grammatical correction suggested by εἰς which, in fact, is the equivalent of ἐν, as in i. 9 (cf. Mt. iv. 23).

As compared with i. 28 the ministry has now extended throughout the whole of Galilee. Instead of ' Galilee ' Luke has ' Judaea ' (iv. 44), which Creed, 73, describes as the best attested reading in that Gospel ; cf. Plummer, St. Lk, 141. Probably it is there used in an inclusive sense for Palestine. J. Weiss, 151, Wendling, 4, and others explain καὶ τὰ δαιμόνια ἐκβάλλων as the addition of a redactor, but it is better to infer that Mark wanted to give a summary account of the activity of Jesus which is loosely related to the immediate context. A similar reference to exorcism in vi. 13 suggests that the allusion is somewhat conventional. Matthew extends the summary considerably (iv. 23). His use of περιῆγεν can be claimed in support of ἦλθεν in Mk, but may also be interpreted as a substitute for the periphrastic imperfect, a construction which he has three times only. Cf. Howard, ii. 452.

Mk. i. 40-5   10. THE CURE OF A LEPER   Cf. Mt. viii. 1-4
                                                    Lk. v. 12-16

This narrative bridges the gap between i. 21-39 and ii. 1-iii. 6, two sections which apparently formed self-contained groups before the Gospel was compiled. The narrative is a Miracle-story, but it is not stereotyped in construction and can be reduced to the form described by Form Critics only by a series of cancellations. Thus, Bultmann, 227, ascribes 43, the words ' See thou say nothing to any man, but ' in 44, and the whole of 45, to the Evangelist, and Dibelius, 71, 73 f., takes the same view of 45, but classifies the narrative with the *Novellen*. These reconstructions are possible, but it is preferable, as in the case of the account of the Demoniac in the Synagogue (i. 21-8), to assign the narrative to the earliest tradition at a point before the process of oral attrition had reduced it to a rounded form. Personal and place names have already disappeared, but the narrative still preserves the rugged form of early testimony.

The Miracle-story proper seems to end with 42, followed perhaps by 45, and 43 f. has the appearance of a Pronouncement-story on the question of obedience to the Law, a matter of great interest to Jewish-Christian communities. It is, of course, possible that Mark has combined two versions of the same story (cf. J. Weiss, 153 n.), as apparently he has done in ii. 1-12, but there is more to be said for the alternative explanation that i. 40-5 is a group of cells in the primitive tradition in process of bifurcation. The section on the observance of the Law (43 f.) is still closely connected with the account of the cleansing (40-2, 45); but it is ready to be detached and to become like the five stories in ii. 1-iii. 6, in which the interest centres on questions of religious importance to the community connected with significant acts and words of Jesus. A later stage can be seen in the shorter narrative of Mt. viii. 2-4, in which primitive Markan details are omitted and the climax is reached in the command to conform to the injunctions of the Law. Cf. Schmidt, 67.

The earlier rationalists (e.g. Paulus) described the narrative as the later version of a story which originally told of a leper in the healing crisis who, instead of resorting to the priests as the Law required, sought from Jesus a declaration that he was clean. This explanation, favoured by J. Weiss, 152 f., was decisively countered by D. F. Strauss,[1] when he pointed out that the meaning of ' I will; be thou clean ' is determined by the words ' And he was cleansed ', which show that καθαρίζω is here used of actual cleansing (as in Mt. x. 8, xi. 5), and by ἅπτομαι in 41 which is used of a curative touch. The only support for the view that the incident was not a miracle of healing is the strangeness of the command to observe the Law and the fact that καθαρίζω can mean ' to declare clean ' as well as ' make clean '. These arguments are too slender to sustain the hypothesis, and all the more because the narrative contains bold primitive features, especially the references to anger and deep emotion which raised great difficulties in the minds of later Evangelists and copyists.

[1] *Life of Jesus*, Eng. Tr. by Geo. Eliot, 438.

Bartlet, 118, classifies the narrative as ' primary Apostolic tradition (Petrine) ' in contrast with ' distinctively Petrine matter ', and the distinction, though fine, is not without justification. On the other hand, J. Weiss, 152, conjectures that Peter was not present (during the period mentioned in i. 39), and that thus Petrine tradition offered Mark nothing at this point. It is manifest that the incident is loosely connected with its present context; it has even been suggested, in view of the command ' Go and show thyself to the priest ', that it happened in Judaea. It is significant, however, that Mark makes no attempt to supply local or temporal statements. In this respect he differs from Matthew who prefaces the story by the words : ' And when he was come down from the mountain, great multitudes followed him ' (viii. 1), and from Luke who says that the leper came while Jesus was ' in one of the cities ' (v. 12). These developments show that ' reconstructions ' have a long history behind them and that, in a sense, the later Evangelists are the first historical critics. Mark writes earlier, and in the present story shows no sign of these tendencies. Accordingly, unless more positive objections arise, he is entitled to be read with confidence when he locates the incident during the earlier Galilean Ministry.

The decisive questions are the healing itself and the command to observe silence. The hypothesis of a cure by suggestion is relevant up to a point, if, as is commonly believed, the disease was not leprosy as it is known to-day; but this explanation is not completely satisfactory, since presumably the healing is instantaneous. A decision, therefore, upon this matter depends on whether it is believed that Jesus was invested with a power to heal which transcends all known analogies. The command to observe silence is misunderstood if it is isolated from the charge ' Show thyself to the priest '. The man is to make this duty his first concern. On this interpretation no serious difficulty arises, but it may be questioned whether Mark understood the injunction in this way, and, in this case, the hypothesis of the ' Messianic Secret ' is over-stressed. Neither of these difficulties excludes the view that he is dependent upon good tradition, and if we bring into consideration the realism of the narrative, and especially the strong emphasis upon the emotional response of Jesus to the sufferer's need, we have good reason to think that ultimately the tradition is that of an eyewitness. Whether Mark derived the narrative from Peter remains a matter for conjecture, but the view that the eyewitness was Peter or someone known to him is fully credible.

40 Καὶ ἔρχεται πρὸς αὐτὸν λεπρὸς παρακαλῶν αὐτὸν καὶ γονυπετῶν

40. Once more the narrative begins with simple parataxis. The historic present ἔρχεται is characteristic of Mk; v. Intr. 46 f. λεπρός, xiv. 3*. Luke has ἀνὴρ πλήρης λέπρας (v. 12). The leprosy in question is probably not the tubercular or anaesthetic leprosy of to-day which manifests itself in paralysis, the rotting of fingers and toes, facial deformity, and the loss of feeling, but rather a distressing skin disease which, according to Lev. xiii. 1-59, was characterized by bright white spots or patches on the skin and white hair, the depression of the patches (' quick raw flesh '), and the spreading of the scab or scall. Cf. Micklem, 43-45 ; Lagrange, 29 ; C. Creighton, EB, iii, cols. 2763-8 ; E. W. G. Masterman, DCG, ii. 24-6. παρακαλέω, v. 10, 12, 17 f., 23, vi. 56, vii. 32, viii. 22*, ' to beseech ', ' entreat ', ' admonish ', ' com-

λέγων αὐτῷ ὅτι 'Εὰν θέλῃς δύνασαί με καθαρίσαι. καὶ ⌈ὀργισθεὶς⌉ 41
ἐκτείνας τὴν χεῖρα αὐτοῦ ἥψατο καὶ λέγει αὐτῷ   Θέλω, καθαρί-
41 σπλαγχνισθεὶς

fort'; Cl. and frequently found in a common formula in papyrus private letters with the meaning 'beseech' (*VGT*, 484; Deissmann, 189 n.¹⁴, 307 f.).

καὶ γονυπετῶν is enclosed by WH in square brackets and is omitted by B D W some minusc. a b c ff sa; but it is strongly attested by ℵ L Θ fam. 1 565 579 892 e f vg syʰˡ bo geo arm Aug, and + αὐτόν by A C *et al.* fam. 13 (exc. 124) 28 33 1071 *al. pler.* syˢ pe, and it should probably be read. Cf. Swete (with hesitation), 28; Turner, *JTS*, xxviii. 157; Klostermann, 23; Plummer, 75; Holtzmann, 118, and see Mt. viii. 2, προσεκύνει, and Lk. v. 12, πεσὼν ἐπὶ πρόσωπον. γονυπετέω, x. 17*, Mt. xvii. 14, xxvii. 29**, 'to fall on the knee', 'fall before one', a late word (Polybius xv. 29. 9, Cornutus, *ND*, 12), not in LXX, nor recorded in *VGT*. For the construction λέγω ὅτι see i. 15.

The presence of the name κύριε in B before ὅτι, and before ἐάν or after θέλῃς in C L W Θ 579 700 892 c e ff vg, raises an interesting question. This voc., common in Mt (19) and Lk (17), is found in Mk elsewhere only in vii. 28 and in some MSS. in x. 51. It is not, therefore, characteristic of Mk and may be an assimilation to Mt. viii. 2 or Lk. v. 12, but its attestation in Alexandrian, African, and Caesarean MSS. entitles it to serious consideration. Cf. Streeter, 309; Rawlinson, 22. The construction ἐάν c. subj., here followed by the pres. indicative δύνασαι, is common in Mk (cf. Robertson, 1400), usually with the future in the apodosis. Cf. ix. 22, εἴ τι δύνῃ, in which the variant form δύνῃ is used, as here in B (cf. Turner, *JTS*, xxviii. 157). In the present passage doubt is not expressed, but rather confidence if Jesus is willing to act. καθαρίζω, i. 41 f., vii. 19*, 'to cleanse'; Hellenistic, for the Attic καθαίρω, Jn. xv. 2**. In the inscriptions (Deissmann, *BS*, 216 f.), as in the

LXX (Lev. xiii, xiv, 4 Kgdms. v. 10, 12), the verb is used both of physical and ceremonial cleansing, of *declaring* clean as well as *making* clean, but there is no reason to find the former meaning in the present story.

41. ὀργισθείς*. The *v.l.* σπλαγχνισθείς, from σπλαγχνίζομαι, vi. 34, viii. 2, ix. 22*, 'to be moved with compassion', <σπλάγχνον, used in the plur. of the heart, the lungs, the liver. The verb was 'perhaps a coinage of the Jewish Dispersion' (Lightfoot on Phil. i. 8) and is used in the LXX (2 Macc. vi. 8) as the equivalent of σπλαγχνεύω. Cf. *VGT*, 584. Although found elsewhere in Mt (5) and Lk (3), it is not taken over in the parallel narratives in these Gospels. This fact supports the view, very probable in itself, that the original Markan reading was ὀργισθείς (D a ff r¹), for it is easy to see why 'being angry' was changed to 'being filled with compassion', but not easy to account for the alteration *vice versa*. So, e.g., Rawlinson, 21; Turner, 17; Branscomb, 39; Creed, 77; Moffatt, 233 f.; Cadoux, 44; Micklem, 46. Hort, 23, thinks the reading is perhaps suggested by 43 or is derived from an extraneous source; Plummer, 76, suggests a marginal gloss; and, in rejecting Ephraem's explanation (*Quia dixit: 'Si uis', iratus est*), Swete, 29, observes that at this stage in the story there is nothing to suggest anger. The balance of the argument is strongly in its favour, and it should, I think, be accepted.

ἐκτείνας τὴν χεῖρα αὐτοῦ is better explained as a historical detail than as merely a stylistic feature in a Miracle-story (cf. Bultmann, 227). As followed by ἥψατο, it is a distinctive element in the story which leads C. G. Montefiore, i. 39, to say: 'Here we begin to catch the new note in the ministry of Jesus: his intense compassion for the outcast, the sufferer,

42 σθητι· καὶ εὐθὺς ἀπῆλθεν ἀπ᾽ αὐτοῦ ἡ λέπρα, καὶ ἐκαθερίσθη.
43 καὶ ἐμβριμησάμενος αὐτῷ εὐθὺς ἐξέβαλεν αὐτόν, καὶ λέγει αὐτῷ
44

who, by his sin, or by his suffering, . . . had put himself outside respectable Jewish society'. Special interest is taken in Mk in the fact that Jesus touched sufferers, vii. 33, viii. 22 (cf. x 13), or that they touched Him, iii. 10, v. 27 f., 30 f., vi. 56. After ἥψατο both Mt. viii. 3 and Lk. v. 13 read αὐτοῦ, and this may well be the original Markan reading (A C D W Δ Θ all minusc. (exc. 435 892) a b c d e f ff l q r1.2 vg). See Streeter's interesting discussion, 309 f., and cf. Turner, JTS, xxviii. 157. καθαρίσθητι, followed in the next verse by ἐκαθερίσθη, suggests actual cleansing rather than a declaration (see above).

If ὀργισθείς is read, the anger is best explained, with E. Bevan, JTS, xxxiii. 186-8, as the reaction of Jesus to the disease (so Branscomb, 39 f.; Cadoux, 44) rather than indignation at the interruption of His preaching ministry or the leper's breach of the Law (cf. Rawlinson, 22, 256).

42. εὐθύς here is meant to indicate the instantaneous character of the cure. λέπρα*, Mt. viii. 3, Lk. v. 12 f.**. The change from αρ to ερ in the augmented and reduplicated forms of καθαρίζω is due to popular etymology, which interpreted καθ as κατά, and thus produced a second augment. Cf. Moulton, ii. 67, 242, and see διηκόνουν i. 13, and διηκόνει i. 31. See also the double augment in a true κατά compound in ἀπεκατεστάθη iii. 5. The verse illustrates the redundancy of expression common in Mark's style. V. Intr. 50-2. While the first part is used in Lk. v. 13, Mt. viii. 3 has simply : ' And straightway his leprosy was cleansed'. Note that Naaman was cleansed (καὶ ἐκαθαρίσθη), but not touched; cf. 4 Kgdms. v. 11, 14.

43. ἐμβριμάομαι, xiv. 5*, Mt. ix. 30, Jn. xi. 33, 38**, ' to be angry', ' express violent displeasure', ' groan', indicating strong feeling within oneself (Moulton, ii. 305), <βρίμη,

'strength'. The verb is rare in Cl. Gk (cf. Aesch. Theb. 461, where it is used of the snorting of horses) and in the LXX (Dan. xi. 30; cf. Lam. ii. 6), and no example is cited from the papyri in VGT, 206. In the present passage it is difficult to find a satisfactory English equivalent. In Jn. xi. 33, 38 ' groaned ' is the best rendering, but in Mk. i. 43, xiv. 5, and Mt. ix. 30 there is a personal object in the dative. Strong feeling which ' boils over ' and finds expression appears to be indicated. ' They murmured against her ' (the woman with the alabaster cruse) is too weak a translation in Mk. xiv. 5 ; ' growled at ' or ' upbraided ' (Moffatt) is better (cf. vg : fremebant in eam). In the present case we need something like ' crying out ' or an adverbial expression like ' with strong feeling ': ' menacing ' or ' roaring at ' and similar renderings are only a little too strong. Cf. it and vg, comminatus est. Many commentators follow Swete, 30, who suggests the paraphrase : ' He gave him a stern injunction '; cf. RVmg and RSV; Lagrange, 31, Et s'adressant à lui avec sévérité ; Moffatt, ' With the stern charge '; Plummer, 77 ; Bartlet, 119 ; Wood, 683 ; Gould, 31 ; but this meaning is not sufficiently attested and does not adequately give expression to the emotional tone of the narrative. Bernard's comment is excellent : ' It (ἐμβριμᾶσθαι) represents the inarticulate sounds which escape men when they are physically overwhelmed by a great wave of emotion. And Jesus, the Perfect Man, experienced this as He experienced all else that is human and not sinful. As he charged the leper and the blind whom He had relieved to tell nothing of what had been done for them, He stumbled over the words, the loud and harsh tone of His voice indicating His agitation. " He roared at them " would not exactly convey the sense, for that would suggest violence of speech or

"Ορα μηδενὶ μηδὲν εἴπῃς, ἀλλὰ ὕπαγε σεαυτὸν Δεῖξον τῷ ἱερεῖ

command. But it is nearer the primary meaning of ἐνεβριμήσατο than " strictly charged them " ' (*ICC*, *St. Jn*, 392 f.). Translations which suggest *anger*, although closely related to the meaning of the verb (cf. Klostermann, 24: ' *Und er fuhr ihn an* '; Holtzmann, 118: *zornig anfahren*), are not satisfactory, if they suggest that Jesus was angry with the man, for there is nothing to indicate this. Torrey, *FG*, 298, *TG*, 8, 42 f., makes the interesting suggestion that ἐμβριμησάμενος is a mistranslation of the Heb. and Aram. verb רגז which originally signified strong *agitation*, but in later usage became more and more exclusively used for *anger*. This suggestion, however, is speculative and appears to ignore the fact that the Greek verb has other meanings than *anger*. But he rightly stresses the idea of agitation, and possibly the best translation of i. 43 is: ' Moved by deep feeling towards him, immediately He drove him forth '.

In this context we are justified in rendering ἐξέβαλεν ' drove forth '. Swete, 30, understates the facts when he says that the original ' involves at least some pressure and urgency '. Many commentators take the verb (cf. ἐξελθών, i. 45) to imply expulsion from a house (so e.g. Wellhausen, 13; J. Weiss, *Die Schr.*[4] 88; Rawlinson, 22); others (e.g. B. Weiss, 28 f., cf. i. 39) suggest a synagogue; but neither inference is necessary, and the incident may have happened out of doors (cf. Schmidt, 64; Branscomb, 37; Plummer, 77). Cf. ἐκβάλλει in i. 12. Following Pallis, Couchoud, *JTS*, xxxiv. 116 f., conjectures that the original reading referred to the daemon of leprosy and ran καὶ ἐμβριμησάμενος εὐθὺς ἐξέβαλεν (cf. e, *et eiecit eum*).

It is not surprising that both Matthew and Luke omit the verse, which is also omitted by W b c and, except the last two words, by e. There can be no doubt of its genuineness and

primitive character. Only rarely in the Gospels are the emotions of Jesus described and His reaction to persons indicated. Cf. iii. 5, vi. 6, x. 14, 21, xiv. 33, and the implications of viii. 33. Whatever the obscurities of i. 43 may be, in this verse we stand near events as they happened.

44. ὁράω, viii. 15, 24, ix. 4, xiii. 26, xiv. 62, xvi. 7*. In the command ὅρα μηδενὶ μηδὲν εἴπῃς the pres. imper. ὅρα is followed by μή c. aor. subj. expressing a prohibition. Moulton, i. 124, suggests that the ὅρα is virtually a particle adding emphasis : ' See that you do not . . .'. Cf. *VGT*, 455. The use of the double negative is characteristic of Mark's usage; cf. Intr. 46. Both Matthew and Luke omit μηδέν, and important MSS. (א A D L W Δ fam. 13 minusc. *pler*. it vg sype sa bo) omit it in Mk, but there can be no doubt that it is original. The asyndetic construction in ὅρα μηδενὶ μηδὲν εἴπῃς, and again in ὕπαγε σεαυτὸν δεῖξον τῷ ἱερεῖ, is a feature of Mark's style, sometimes in narratives, but more frequently in sayings, and, as Lagrange, lxxi, says, in most cases the omission renders the style more rapid, and in consequence more expressive. Cf. *HS*[2], 137 f. The change from the pres. imperative to the two aorists, δεῖξον and προσένεγκε, illustrates once more Mark's facility in the use of tenses. ὑπάγω, 15 times*, ' to go away ', ' go '; Cl. trans. ' to lead ' as well as intrans.; rare in LXX, but common in the vernacular (*VGT*, 649 f.). ' The word is avoided by Luke, perhaps, as Abbott suggests, because of its variety of usage in the vernacular, meaning " go on " or " come on ", as well as " go back " ', *VGT*, 650.

The command to tell no one is another example (cf. i. 34) of the injunctions to secrecy which are characteristic of Mk. See Intr. 122-4. Here the command is naturally explained by the withdrawal of Jesus

καὶ προσένεγκε περὶ τοῦ καθαρισμοῦ σου ἃ προσέταξεν Μωυσῆς
45 εἰς μαρτύριον αὐτοῖς. ὁ δὲ ἐξελθὼν ἤρξατο κηρύσσειν πολλὰ καὶ

from Capernaum and His desire to devote Himself to a preaching ministry (i. 38). The idea of Messiahship is so much in the background that one thinks of it only in the light of the saying, not recorded by Mk, that the healing of lepers is one of the signs of Messianic activity (Lk. vii. 22 = Mt. xi. 5). The instruction, that the restored leper is to show himself to the priest, illustrates the recognition by Jesus of the validity of the Mosaic Law (Lev. xiii. 49) in cases where moral issues are not at stake. Cf. V. Taylor, *JHS*, 72 f.; C. J. Cadoux, 121, and see Lk. xvii. 14, Mt. v. 23 f. δείκνυμι, xiv. 15*. ἱερεύς, ii. 26*; the art. indicates the serving priest (cf. Klostermann, 24). προσφέρω, ' to offer '*, ' bring ', ii. 4, x. 13 (*bis*)*. καθαρισμός*, Lk. ii. 22, v. 14, Jn. ii. 6, iii. 25, Heb. i. 3, 2 Pet. i. 9**; ' cleansing ', here of actual cleansing (*nicht ' für deine Reinsprechung* ', Klostermann, 24). προστάσσω*. Μωυσῆς, vii. 10, ix. 4 f., x. 3 f., xii. 19, 26*. For the offerings in question see Lev. xiv. 4 ff.

εἰς μαρτύριον αὐτοῖς, vi. 11, xiii. 9*, i.e. for a testimony to the priests that the cure is complete. The suggestion of Swete, 31, that the testimony is to the presence of a Prophet amongst them, who might be suspected (cf. Mt. xi. 5) to be the Messiah, reads too much into the phrase. αὐτοῖς is dat. of advantage, without any suggestion of hostility. The agreement is *ad sensum*, whether the pronoun refers to the priests (Swete, 31 ; Plummer, 78 ; McNeile, 103), or, as many commentators think, to people in general (Klostermann, 24 ; Lagrange, 30 f. ; Creed, 77 ; Easton, 63 ; Luce, 130).

45. No change of subject is indicated, and it is a possible interpretation that ὁ δὲ ἐξελθών refers to Jesus, and that τὸν λόγον means ' the Gospel ' or ' the message of salvation ' (*Heilsbotschaft*). So Allen, 64 ; cf. Kloster-

mann, 24 f. But it is much more probable that Mark means that the healed leper went out and, disobeying the command of Jesus, began to publish his story (τὸν λόγον, Luther : *die Geschichte*) far and wide. Cf. Rawlinson, 22. Mark has the construction ἤρξα(ν)το c. infin. 26 times ; Intr. 48. Of these examples Matthew retains only six. Luke reduces them to two, but has the construction in 23 or 25 other cases, five in Markan contexts. For this probably Semitic construction see Intr. 63 f.

Mark's use of πολλά in an adverbial sense (= ' much ') is also probably due to the influence of Aramaic (שַׂגִּי). Cf. Howard, ii. 446 ; Lagrange, xcviii, who none the less observes that the usage is perfectly Greek at all times ; Allen, 64, *ET*, xiii. 330. Hawkins, *HS²*, 35, notes nine instances in Mk (here and iii. 12, v. 10, 23, 38, 43, vi. 20, ix. 26, xv. 3 ; Pl (4), Rest of NT (1)). ' In all other cases ', he says, ' πολλά is more probably an accusative.' διαφημίζω*, Mt. ix. 31, xxviii. 15**; ' to spread abroad ', ' make known ' ; a late verb, Josephus, *BJ*, i. 33. 3, Vettius Valens 250. 5, *VGT*, 157. For the constr. ὥστε c. acc. and infin. see i. 27. Schmidt, 66, is inclined to think that φανερῶς* was added by the Evangelist to his source, since there is an inner contradiction in the verse, in that, after the stress on ' openly ', one expects a statement to the effect that only secretly (λάθρα) could Jesus enter into a town. J. Weiss, 152, and Wrede, 126, 137 f., see a dogmatic motive in the verse connected with the idea of the ' Messianic Secret '. It may well be that Mark has over-emphasized the idea of secrecy, but Schmidt is surely right in holding that 45 belongs to the original story and that at most the clause ὥστε . . . ἦν is an addition. The statement that the leper proclaimed the great deed of Jesus and that people

διαφημίζειν τὸν λόγον, ὥστε μηκέτι αὐτὸν δύνασθαι ⌜φανερῶς
εἰς πόλιν⌝ εἰσελθεῖν, ἀλλὰ ἔξω ἐπ' ἐρήμοις τόποις [ἦν]· καὶ
ἤρχοντο πρὸς αὐτὸν πάντοθεν.

45 εἰς πόλιν φανερῶς

were coming to Him from every quarter, makes an excellent climax. ἤρχοντο is an impersonal plur. (Intr.	47). πάντοθεν*, 'from all sides' (LXX, VGT, 478). Inferior MSS. read the classical πανταχόθεν.

(b) Mk. ii. 1-iii. 6   CONFLICTS WITH THE
                                    SCRIBES

This topical section, which describes conflicts between Jesus and the Rabbis, is very different in content and construction from the group of narratives in i. 21-39. As it stands in Mk, it includes the following :

(11) ii. 1-12.   The Paralytic and Forgiveness.
(12) ii. 13 f.   The Call of Levi.
(13) ii. 15-17.   On Eating with Taxgatherers and Sinners.
(14) ii. 18-20.   On Fasting.
(15) ii. 21 f.   Sayings on Patches and Wineskins.
(16) ii. 23-6.   On the Sabbath (Cornfields).
(17) ii. 27 f.   Sayings on the Sabbath.
(18) iii. 1-6.   On the Sabbath (The Man with the Withered Hand).

For the discussion of the pre-Markan character of this complex see Intr. 91 f. where it is argued that it consists of a group of five Pronouncement stories in which the Call of Levi and the sayings in ii. 21 f. and 27 f. have been inserted for topical reasons.

Mk. ii. 1-12   11. THE PARALYTIC AND   Cf. Mt. ix. 1-8
                          FORGIVENESS   Lk. v. 17-26

The need for a double title for this narrative suggests that it may be composite. It is strange that Dibelius, 43, should classify it among eight Paradigms which ' represent the type in noteworthy purity '. Bultmann, 12-14, 227, shows a better understanding of its nature when he describes it as a combination of an Apothegm in 5b-10a and a Miracle-story in 1-5a, 10b-12. In support of the view that 5b-10a is an insertion he cites Wrede, Völter, Fridrichsen, Loisy, and Klostermann. Among English commentators Rawlinson, 25, while rejecting the view that 5b-10 is an interpolation, thinks that the episode was expanded in Christian preaching and that the controversial element ' came in as an echo of early Christian controversy with the synagogue '. It is interesting also to recall the suggestion of J. Weiss, 156, that Mark derived the narrative from ' the Apostolic Source ' (represented by Mt. ix. 1-8), but supplemented it by many details from his recollections of Peter's narratives. Some hypothesis of double origin seems necessary, and I adhere to the view set out in FGT, 66-8, which substantially is that of Bultmann mentioned above. A possibility in the story of the Leper, this hypothesis has stronger grounds in the present narrative.

Several considerations suggest compilation. (1) The vividness of 3-5a, 11 f., including the references to the breaking up of the roof, the crowds, and the house, suggests dependence on primitive tradition. (2) The controversial section, 5b-10a, is of another mould. (3) The phrases ' he saith to the paralytic ' in 5a and 10b have the appearance of editorial links. (4) 11 f. takes account only of the act of healing, and in the intention of the Evangelist ' all ' refers to the crowd, whereas, as the narrative stands, it is open to the erroneous interpretation that even the scribes are included. (5) Although lacking an introduction, 5b-10a has a strong resemblance in form and construction to the Pronouncement-stories in 16 f., 18-20, 23-6, iii. 1-6. It may be, of course, that, like i. 40-5, ii. 1-12 is an original and uneven unit out of which new elements are ready to evolve. Something of this process is illustrated in Mt. ix. 1-8, in which, with the miracle in the background, the foreground is occupied by the question of the forgiveness of sins. There is, however, better reason to take the view outlined above.

In 5b-10a names of persons, statements about time and place, and vivid details in the course of events, have disappeared. Everything is concentrated on the question of forgiveness. This interest must have been stimulated by the life and experience of the primitive community (cf. Jn. xx. 23, 1 Cor. v. 3-5, 2 Cor. ii. 5-11), which, in the presence of acute spiritual problems, recalled the example and authority of Jesus. It seems reasonable to suggest that historical testimony would be preferred to creative invention at a time when eyewitnesses still lived. This consideration suggests that the account is historical and not *Gemeindetheologie*.

II. 1   Καὶ εἰσελθὼν πάλιν εἰς Καφαρναοὺμ δι᾽ ἡμερῶν ἠκούσθη ὅτι

1. εἰσελθών is an example of anacoluthon or broken construction, a feature which Hawkins, 135, notes as ' particularly characteristic of Mark '. Naturally, the MS. tradition shows that attempts were made to improve the connexion by the introduction of a finite verb (v. Legg *in loc.*), but there can be no doubt that the text is correct.

δι᾽ ἡμερῶν, ' after some days '. Here διά c. gen. = ' after the lapse of ', describing the interval which has elapsed between two points of time. The construction is classical (LS, 389) and appears in the papyri (*VGT*, 146). Cf. Goodwin, 1206 ; Robertson, 581 ; Robertson and Davis, 343 (e), 359 ; Burton, *ICC*, *Gal.* 68. See Ac. xxiv. 17, δι᾽ ἐτῶν δὲ πλειόνων, and Gal. ii. 1, ἔπειτα διὰ δεκατεσσάρων ἐτῶν. Probably this note of time should be taken with εἰσελθών rather than with ἠκούσθη (cf. Swete, 32 ; Klostermann, 25 ; Lohmeyer, 50).

πάλιν, 28 times* (*HS²*, 13), is a favourite Markan word, originally meaning ' back ', which in later Gk came to be used in the sense of ' again '. It is also used as an inferential conjunction with the meaning ' further ', ' thereupon ' ; cf. Howard, ii. 446 ; *VGT*, 476 ; Souter, 187, and cf. xv. 13. It is claimed as a translation of *tubh* by Wellhausen, *Einl.*² 21, but Howard thinks that in many of the Markan instances the meaning is really iterative and that where it is inferential it is unnecessary to go back to Aramaic. Cf. Moffatt, *Exp.* VIII. xx. 141. Lagrange, xcviii, says that in Mk the meaning is always iterative. Here πάλιν points back to i. 21. The interval may have been a matter of days or even weeks. There is certainly a gap in Mk at this point. As in Jn. ix. 32, ἠκούσθη is impersonal, ' it was heard ' or ' reported ' (Moffatt). So Swete, 32 ; Lagrange, 32 ; Plummer, 80 ; Lohmeyer, 50. The ὅτι may be *recitativum* : ' People were heard to say,

Γἐν οἴκῳ ἐστίν⌉· καὶ συνήχθησαν πολλοὶ ὥστε μηκέτι χωρεῖν μηδὲ 2
τὰ πρὸς τὴν θύραν, καὶ ἐλάλει αὐτοῖς τὸν λόγον. καὶ ἔρχονται 3
φέροντες πρὸς αὐτὸν παραλυτικὸν αἰρόμενον ὑπὸ τεσσάρων. καὶ 4
μὴ δυνάμενοι προσενέγκαι αὐτῷ διὰ τὸν ὄχλον ἀπεστέγασαν τὴν

1 εἰς οἶκόν ἐστιν

"He is at home"' (Plummer, 80). If the speech is indirect (RV, RSV), the tense is that of the original utterance.

Moulton, i. 82, maintains that ἐν οἴκῳ is not 'in a house', and many commentators take the phrase to mean 'at home' (οἴκοι, *domi*). Cf. Lagrange, 32, who cites 1 Cor. xi. 34 and xiv. 35. Cf. also Pap. Lond. 42. 5, οἱ ἐν οἴκωι πάντες, Pap. Fay. 115. 12, *VGT*, 443. In view of this evidence Wellhausen's submission, 14, that the presence or absence of the article is without significance, is difficult to sustain. On the other hand, εἰς οἶκον in iii. 19b, vii. 17, ix. 28* appears to mean 'in a house'. This phrase is read here by A C Δ *et al.* fam. 1 fam. 13 22 28 543 565 579 700 *al. pler.* g¹, but ἐν οἴκῳ is much more strongly attested (אּ B D L W Θ 33 571 892 1071 it (exc. e) vg (*pler.*)). It is probable that Mark means Peter's house. J. Weiss, 155, sees in the undefined phrase Peter's mode of narration, 'who, just because it was his house, added no closer designation'. So Swete, 32; Plummer, 80; Lagrange, 32; Klostermann, 26; Bartlet, 122.

2. The description of the crowd gathering about the door recalls i. 33. For συνάγω *v.* i. 33; ὥστε c. acc. and infin. i. 27; the double neg. i. 44. χωρέω* can be intrans. and trans.; intrans. 'to make room', 'go forward', Mt. xv. 17, Jn. viii. 37, 2 Pet. iii. 9; trans. (as here) 'to have space for', 'hold', 'contain', Jn. ii. 6, xxi. 25, Mt. xix. 11 f., 2 Cor. vii. 2**; Cl., LXX, Pap. (*VGT*, 695). The acc. subj. τὰ πρὸς τὴν θύραν means the space about the door, probably in the open street. This humble house has no πυλών (Mt. xxvi. 71) or προαύλιον (Mk. xiv. 68). Here ὁ λόγος means 'the

Good News', as in iv. 14 ff., 33, xvi. [20]; elsewhere 'saying(s)', v. 36, vii. 29, viii. 32, 38, ix. 10, x. 22, 24, xiii. 31; 'matter' or 'story' i. 45; 'question' xi. 29; 'speech' xii. 13; 'petition' xiv. 39; 'word (of God)' vii. 13*. In Ac. iv. 29, 31, viii. 25, xi. 19, xiii. 46, etc. λαλεῖν τὸν λόγον is 'to proclaim the Christian Message', but there is no reason to find this meaning in Mk.

The summary statement in ii. 1 f. introduces the story of the Paralytic rather than the section as a whole. The impression we receive is that Mark is using a definite tradition. To what extent he modifies it for editorial purposes it is not easy to say. Schmidt, 78 f., suggests that εἰσελθὼν εἰς Καφαρναούμ, πάλιν, δι' ἡμερῶν, and ἠκούσθη are inserted by the Evangelist, and that the original story began: καὶ ἦν εἰς οἶκον (or ἐν οἴκῳ), followed by ii. 3.

3. The story begins with a reference to the bringing of the paralytic borne by four. For φέρω in Mk *v.* i. 32 ἔρχονται is impersonal and a historic present. For Mark's use of ἔρχεται *v.* i. 40. Lagrange, 33, conjectures that the parents are meant. παραλυτικός, ii. 4 f., 9 f.*, Mt. iv. 24, viii. 6, ix. 2 (*bis*), 6, Lk. v. 24 (WHᵐᵍ)**, 'a paralytic'; a late word, not Cl., nor in LXX. Luke prefers παραλελυμένος. The phrase αἰρόμενον ὑπὸ τεσσάρων is peculiar to Mk. It is unnecessary to explain it as a later addition (J. Weiss, 155). On the contrary, it is a detail remembered by an eyewitness. Weiss traces the story to Peter and speaks of ἔρχονται as used from the standpoint of the house.

4. προσφέρω (*v.* i. 44) is here used in the sense of 'bring to'. Swete, 33, suggests that the absence of a direct object (αὐτόν) may account for the *v.l.* προσεγγίσαι (A C D Δ *et al.* fam. 1

στέγην ὅπου ἦν, καὶ ἐξορύξαντες χαλῶσι τὸν κράβαττον ὅπου ὁ
5 παραλυτικὸς κατέκειτο. καὶ ἰδὼν ὁ Ἰησοῦς τὴν πίστιν αὐτῶν

fam. 13 22 28 565 579 700 1071 al.
pler. a b c e ff sypᵉ geo). Although the
presence of crowds has been indicated
in i. 5, 33, 45, Mark here uses ὁ ὄχλος
(37 times; pl. x. 1*) for the first time.
ἀποστεγάζω**, 'to uncover', 'unroof';
a rare word found in Strabo 4. 4. 6,
8. 3. 30, but not in the LXX (Symm.
in Jer. xxix. 11 (xlix. 10)). στέγη*, Mt.
viii. 8, Lk. vii. 6**, 'a roof'; Cl.,
LXX, Pap. (VGT, 587). A flat roof
covered with earth is implied. Luke
thinks of a tiled house, διὰ τῶν κεράμων
καθῆκαν αὐτόν (v. 19). Cf. Creed, 79.
The phrase ἀπεστέγασαν τὴν στέγην
anticipates the action described by ἐξορύξαντες and is redundant, but it may
be that Mark wishes to explain what
happened for the benefit of Gentile
readers (J. Weiss, 155). Wellhausen,
15, explains the phrase as a mistranslation of the Aramaic שְׁקְלוּהִי לְאִגָּרָא,
more correctly rendered, 'they brought
him to the roof'. This suggestion
is accepted by Wood, 684, and other
commentators, but it is conjectural, and
is not necessary. Schulthess, ZNTW,
xxi. 220, rejects the suggested translation, and maintains that the Aramaic would mean, 'to uncover the
roof'. See Howard, ii. 470.

ἐξορύσσω, Gal. iv. 15**, 'to dig
out'; Cl., LXX, Pap. (VGT, 225).
The participle ἐξορύξαντες, 'when
they had dug through it' (Lagrange,
35, ayant fait une ouverture), is very
vivid, and indicates the character of
the house. The roof was probably
formed by beams and rafters across
which matting, branches, and twigs,
covered by earth trodden hard, were
laid. To make an aperture large
enough for the bed would not be
difficult. Cf. Lagrange, 33 f.; S. A.
Cook, EB, col. 2132. The place where
Jesus was (ὅπου ἦν) may have been an
upper room, but is not likely to have
been a roofed gallery round the αὐλή
(Edersheim, i. 503). See Swete, 33 f.

The ascent to the roof, which Mark
does not mention (cf. Lk. v. 19, ἀνα-
βάντες ἐπὶ τὸ δῶμα), would be made by
means of an outside staircase (cf. xiii.
15). χαλάω*, Lk. v. 4 f. (of lowering
nets), Ac. ix. 25 (of the lowering of St.
Paul in a basket at Damascus), xxvii.
17, 30, 2 Cor. xi. 33 (as Ac. ix. 25)**,
'to loosen', 'lower', 'let down'; Cl.,
LXX, Pap. (VGT, 682).

ὁ κράβαττος (variously spelt in the
NT MSS., κράββατος, κράβαττος, κρά-
βακτος), ii. 9, 11 f., vi. 55*, Jn. v. 8 f.,
10 f., Ac. v. 15, ix. 33**, 'the poor
man's bed or mattress, and therefore
better suited to the narrative in Mk.
ii. 4 than κλίνη which Mt (ix. 2) and
Lk (v. 18) substitute', VGT, 357. In
v. 19, 24 Luke has κλινίδιον. Condemned as un-Attic, the word is said
to be of Macedonian origin (Moulton,
ii. 102), and from it comes the Latin
grabatus, a pallet or camp bed. For
ὅπου ὁ παραλυτικὸς κατέκειτο Luke has
εἰς τὸ μέσον ἔμπροσθεν τοῦ Ἰησοῦ (v.
19; cf. 25, ἐφ' ὁ κατέκειτο). For the
use of ὅπου in the vernacular see VGT,
453.

The description, it will be seen, is
full of local colour. Matthew omits
the verse and Luke recasts it, and
Western MSS. omit ἐξορύξαντες (D W
a b c e ff q) probably because it was
obscure to non-Palestinian readers.
All the greater, therefore, is our debt
to Mk in which the scene is visualized
on the basis of good tradition.

5. πίστις, iv. 40, v. 34, x. 52, xi. 22**,
'faith', is much less frequent in Mk
than πιστεύω (i. 15). It denotes a
confident trust in Jesus and in His
power to help. Victor and Ephraem
(cf. Swete, 34) explain τὴν πίστιν αὐτῶν
of the faith of the four bearers rather
than the paralytic, but most modern
commentators rightly include the faith
of the paralytic himself (e.g. Klostermann, 26; Lagrange, 35, Il (Jesus)
a compris la disposition de son âme;

λέγει τῷ παραλυτικῷ Τέκνον, ἀφίενταί σου αἱ ἁμαρτίαι. ἦσαν 6
δέ τινες τῶν γραμματέων ἐκεῖ καθήμενοι καὶ διαλογιζόμενοι ἐν
ταῖς καρδίαις αὐτῶν "Οτι οὗτος οὕτω λαλεῖ; βλασφημεῖ· τίς 7

Gould, 36; Bartlet, 123). τέκνον, vii.
27, x. 24, 29 f., xii. 19, xiii. 12 (bis)*,
is here used as an affectionate form of
address (x. 24*), ' my child ' (cf. Mt.
xxi. 28, Lk. ii. 48, xv. 31, xvi. 25, Jn.
xiii. 33 (τεκνία), I Cor. iv. 14, 17, Gal.
iv. 19). Compare the use of υἱέ in
Prov. i. 8, 10, ii. 1, etc. It is strange
that this tenderness is lost in Luke's
ἄνθρωπε (v. 20). ἀφίημι is used, as in
ii. 7, 9 f., iii. 28, iv. 12, xi. 25 (bis)*,
with the meaning ' to forgive ', more
particularly ' to remit ', that is, to set
aside sins and transgressions. While
the present is normally durative, ἀφίενται is here punctiliar (cf. Burton, § 13,
' aoristic present '; Moulton, i. 119),
with the meaning ' are this moment
forgiven '. The statement is an
authoritative declaration. This decisiveness of tone is lost by Luke's
perf. ἀφέωνται (v. 20), which, though
strongly supported in Mk (ℵ A C D
L W Θ fam. 1 579 700 892 b f q), is
the inferior reading (ἀφίενται, B 28 33
565).
The reference to forgiveness at a
point where one expects the word
of healing is abrupt. The inference
seems justified that Jesus traced the
man's plight to sin and believed that
his spiritual restoration was a primary
and indispensable condition to recovery. Jesus by no means believed
that sin was the sole cause of affliction
and calamity (cf. Jn. ix. 2, Lk. xiii.
1-5), but He could not fail to observe
how closely mental, spiritual, and
physical conditions are connected, in
this respect anticipating the conclusions of modern psychotherapy regarding hysterical forms of paralysis.
See Micklem, 88-91, who cites cases
of this kind in modern medical
practice; J. Weiss, 158 n. Whether
in the present case the paralysis was of
this kind must remain an inference,
but it is supported by the offer of

immediate forgiveness. It is even
possible that the declaratory word was
curative in intention.
There does not appear to be any
foundation for the view that the forgiveness of sins was a Messianic function. Cf. Billerbeck, i. 495, 1017.
Jesus has no authority to remit sins
because He is the Enochic Son of Man,
but because He is the Son of Man in
the sense in which He understood that
name, a sense, we must infer, based
upon the unique relationship in which
He believed Himself to stand toward
God and men.
6. For the periphrastic imperfect ἦ-
σαν ... καθήμενοι see Intr. 45, 62 f. κάθημαι, 11 times*, ' to sit '. κάθημαι, καθίζω, and καθέζομαι all take the augment
before the preposition, since the verbs
were not felt to be compounds. διαλογίζομαι, ii. 8 (bis), viii. 16 f., ix. 33, xi.
31*, ' to balance accounts ', ' debate ',
' reason '; Cl., LXX, Pap. In the
Egyptian documents the verb is used
to describe the conventus or judicial
' circuit ' of the Praefect (VGT, 151).
In the NT it is used of inward delibera-
tion or questioning. καρδία, ii. 8, iii.
5, vi. 52, vii. 6, 19, 21, viii. 17, xi. 23,
xii. 30, 33*. The expression is Hebraic. In accordance with OT thought
the heart is the centre of perception
and thought as well as affection. In
the narrative the scribes say nothing,
but their thoughts, visible in their
faces, are described (ii. 7).
7. Instead of τί WHmg has ὅτι with
B Θ 482. This use of ὅτι = τί ' why ? '
in a direct question is found elsewhere
in Mk (ii. 16, viii. 12 (C Or), ix. 11, 28).
Here, although the authorities for it
are few, they are excellent in quality,
and the reading has strong claims to
be accepted, since, as the MS. tradition shows, the tendency of scribes
was to replace ὅτι by τί or διὰ τί. οὗτος
appears to be contemptuous; cf. the

8 δύναται ἀφιέναι ἁμαρτίας εἰ μὴ εἷς ὁ θεός; καὶ εὐθὺς ἐπιγνοὺς
ὁ Ἰησοῦς τῷ πνεύματι αὐτοῦ ὅτι [οὕτως] διαλογίζονται ἐν ἑαυτοῖς

Latin *iste*. οὕτως, 10 times*. λαλεῖ here means ' talk ' (cf. Moffatt). βλασφημέω, iii. 28 f., xv. 29*, ' to speak profanely ', ' slander ', ' blaspheme '; Cl., LXX. Wellhausen, 15, explains λαλεῖ βλασφημεῖ as a misrendering of two Aramaic participles, the second of which should have been translated as a participle. Cf. Luke's use of the noun: λαλεῖ βλασφημίας (v. 21). Moulton, i. 231, ii. 16, rejects this suggestion and observes that the RV punctuation (stop and question mark after the first verb) is perfectly good Greek. Black, 47, 88, points out that the second Aramaic participle would actually be a participial present, and that therefore the literal meaning would be, ' What is this man thus saying, is blaspheming ? ', or more idiomatically, ' Why ! this fellow blasphemes ! '. εἷς ὁ θεός (cf. x. 18) is usually explained as meaning μόνος ὁ θεός (Lk. v. 21). E. F. F. Bishop, *ET*, xlix. 363-6 prefers to render the whole phrase ' except the one God ', and suggests that the original may have been, ' Who can forgive sins but the One ? ', ὁ θεός being a Markan comment.

It will be seen that Mark represents the scribes as mentally charging Jesus with blasphemy. Forgiveness is a prerogative of God in OT thought; cf. Ex. xxxiv. 6 f., Isa. xliii. 25, xliv. 22; and, in consequence, to usurp this right is to blaspheme Him. The penalty for blasphemy was stoning: cf. Lev. xxiv. 15 f., 1 Kings xxi. 13; cf. Jn. x. 33, Ac. vii. 58. This interpretation of the attitude of the scribes was doubtless traditional, being based partly on the words of Jesus in ii. 10 and ultimately on the impressions of eyewitnesses. It should be observed that the charge is still tentative; it is not actually made. In this fact the realism of events is preserved. Creative imagination, one may suspect, would not have been so discreet. Bartlet, 125 writes with much insight when he says

that the scribes showed a certain captious readiness to see in the words of Jesus an extravagant personal claim, ' going beyond that of delegated or prophetic " authority " to speak in God's name the Divine forgiveness of the man's sins '.

8. For διαλογίζομαι v. ii. 6. Here εὐθύς is either ' immediately ' (Moffatt : ' Conscious at once ') or ' forthwith '. ἐπιγινώσκω, v. 30, vi. 33, 54*, ' to observe ', ' perceive ', ' recognize '; Cl., LXX, Pap. See J. A. Robinson's careful study of the verb (*Eph.* 248 ff.). Dean Robinson concludes that the verb denotes, not so much fuller or more perfect knowledge, as knowing arrived at by the attention being directed to (ἐπί) a particular person or object. Moulton and Milligan say that on the whole this view is borne out by the evidence of the papyri (*VGT*, 236); and it is certainly illustrated in Mk. ii. 8 and v. 30, where the meaning is ' perceiving '. τῷ πνεύματι αὐτοῦ (cf. viii. 12*) is dative of sphere, ' in his spirit ', or, as we should say, ' in himself '. There is no reference to the Holy Spirit (cf. Swete, 36) nor is the knowledge supernatural in character. It is the result of a spiritual discernment man shares with God (cf. Psa. cxxxix. 2, Ac. xv. 8), which Jesus possessed to a pre-eminent degree (cf. x. 21, xi. 31 f., xii. 15, xiv. 20). Cf. Bartlet, 125 : ' His spirit read their minds " like a book " '. Cf. Mt. ix. 4, ἰδών . . . τὰς ἐνθυμήσεις αὐτῶν, Lk. v. 22, ἐπιγνούς . . . διαλογισμοὺς αὐτῶν. ἐν ἑαυτοῖς, ' in themselves ', has the same meaning as ἐν ταῖς καρδίαις αὐτῶν (ii. 6); cf. ἐν τ. κ. ὑμῶν in the present verse. Luke omits ταῦτα before διαλογίζεσθε (v. 22) and Matthew paraphrases his source, ἱνατί ἐνθυμεῖσθε πονηρὰ ἐν ταῖς καρδίαις ὑμῶν; (ix. 5). Jesus is more concerned about the men who reason in this way than He is about their objections.

9. εὐκοπώτερον, x. 25*, the com-

λέγει [αὐτοῖς] Τί ταῦτα διαλογίζεσθε ἐν ταῖς καρδίαις ὑμῶν; τί 9
ἐστιν εὐκοπώτερον, εἰπεῖν τῷ παραλυτικῷ 'Αφίενταί σου αἱ
ἁμαρτίαι, ἢ εἰπεῖν 'Εγείρου [καὶ] ἆρον τὸν κράβαττόν σου καὶ
περιπάτει; ἵνα δὲ εἰδῆτε ὅτι ἐξουσίαν ἔχει ὁ υἱὸς τοῦ ἀνθρώπου 10

parative of εὔκοπος, ' easy ', lit. ' with easy labour ' (κόπος). τί ... ἤ ...; is a popular variant for the classical πότερον ... ἤ;, ' whether . . . or ? '. For the tense of ἀφίενται v. ii. 6. ἀφέωνται is read by the authorities which support this variant in ii. 5, together with Θ and fam. 13. ἐγείρου (B L Θ 28) is probably a grammatical correction for the intrans. ἔγειρε, read by most MSS., while ἔγειραι is perhaps due to itacism. Cf. Lagrange, 36 f. D 33 a ff add ὕπαγε εἰς τὸν οἶκόν σου. περιπατέω, 8 times and xvi. [12]*.

Superficially, it is easier to declare sins forgiven ; for to say ' Arise, etc.' is to expose oneself to the test of success or failure, while to say ' Thy sins are forgiven ' is to declare what cannot be verified. So Swete, 36 ; Lagrange, 37 ; Montefiore, i. 52 ; Rawlinson, 26, and most commentators. To the factual test Jesus is prepared to subject Himself, as a proof that not without reason He has declared the man's sins forgiven. The healing, moreover, is a sign that the man's sins are in fact forgiven. The doctrinal question of blasphemy is ignored, but in the next verse Jesus indicates His authority to declare sins forgiven.

10. For ἐξουσία v. i. 22. The ἵνα clause probably depends on λέγω understood, or implied in σοι λέγω (ii. 11). C. J. Cadoux, *JTS*, xlii. 173, instances ἵνα δὲ εἰδῆτε as an example of the imperatival subjunctive, as in v. 23. So D. S. Sharp, *ET*, xxxviii (July, 1926), 428 f. Cf. Moulton, i. 177-9 ; Meecham, *JTS*, xliii. 179 f. ; George, *JTS*, xlv. 56-60. The passage may be an instance of this construction, but the final sense is more probable. The purpose of the action is that the scribes may know that the Son of Man has authority on earth to forgive sins.

ὁ υἱὸς τοῦ ἀνθρώπου, ii. 28, viii. 31, 38, ix. 9, 12, 31, x. 33, 45, xiii. 26, xiv. 21 (*bis*), 41, 62*. The origins of the title go back at least to Dan. vii. 13 in which ' one like unto a son of man ' comes ' with the clouds of heaven ' to ' the Ancient of Days ', representing the Jewish people, ' the saints of the Most High ' ; and to the Book of Enoch in which ' the Son of Man ' is a superhuman figure of great dignity and power ; cf. 1 En. xlvi. 1, 3, xlviii. 2 f., li. 3, lxii. 2, 6 f., lxix. 27-9. Earlier in Ezek. ii. 1, etc., and Psa. viii. 4, the term is a synonym for ' man '. The Greek phrase is an attempt to translate *bar nasha* (נָשָׁא בַּר or אֲנָשָׁא בַּר), an Aramaic periphrasis for ' man '. It has been held that the Aramaic phrase cannot mean anything more than ' man ' ; cf. Wellhausen, *Skizzen und Vorarbeiten*, vi. 187-215, and *Einl.*[2] 123-30, Lietzmann, *Der Menschensohn* (1896); but Dalman, *WJ*, 234 ff., has shown that it means, not ' man ' in the generic sense, but ' the Man ', and so could be used as a Messianic designation.

Among the principal interpretations of the phrase the following may be distinguished. (1) Many hold that Jesus was speaking of ' man ' in general. Cf. Wellhausen, 16 ; Klostermann, 27 ; Jackson and Lake, i. 375 ; T. W. Manson, 214 ; Branscomb, 43 f. ; McNeile, 116 f. ; C. J. Cadoux, 75, 96. (2) For those who accept a collective interpretation of the term, a possible view is that Jesus was thinking of the Elect Messianic Community of which He is Head. Cf. J. Drummond, *JTS*, 1901, ii. 539-71. (3) In various ways it is suggested that Jesus was referring to Himself either (*a*) as the Messiah, or (*b*) as the ' Ideal ' or ' Representative Man '. The latter interpretation is given by many of the Fathers (cf. Lagrange, 37, who cites Victor)

11 ⌜ἀφιέναι ἁμαρτίας ἐπὶ τῆς γῆς⌝—λέγει τῷ παραλυτικῷ Σοὶ λέγω,
12 ἔγειρε ἆρον τὸν κράβαττόν σου καὶ ὕπαγε εἰς τὸν οἶκόν σου. καὶ
ἠγέρθη καὶ εὐθὺς ἄρας τὸν κράβαττον ἐξῆλθεν ἔμπροσθεν πάντων,

10 ἐπὶ τῆς γῆς ἀφιέναι ἁμαρτίας

and by Driver, *HDB*, iv. 58, Swete, 37, and Bartlet, 129. (4) Another possibility is that Jesus was speaking of Himself without (expressly) claiming to be the Messiah, using the indeterminate form *bar nash* = τις, ' a certain man ', ' one ', ' I who speak '. Cf. Bultmann, 13 ; and for *bar nash* T. W. Manson, 217 f. Cf. also J. Y. Campbell, *JTS*, xlviii. 145-55, who suggests that the phrase used was *hahu bar nasha* which ought to have been rendered οὗτος (or ὅδε) ὁ υἱὸς τοῦ ἀνθρώπου, *hic homo*, ' this man ', ' a phrase which expressed and even emphasized His real humanity and His solidarity with mankind '. (5) Finally, a widely accepted view is that ' Son of Man ' in ii. 10 represents the theology of the primitive Christian community. Cf. Bultmann, 13 ; Bousset, 40 ; Branscomb, 43 f. It will be seen that some of these views are not mutually exclusive. On the whole, there is most to be said for the third view or possibly the fourth. See the detached Note at the end of the section.

The ἐξουσία (*v.* i. 22) of the Son of Man is His authority to remit sins. In the phrase ἐπὶ τῆς γῆς a contrast is suggested. Authority to remit sins *on earth* is set over against the divine prerogative exercised *in heaven*. The implication of the passage is that the authority is given, and that the Speaker possesses it because He is the Son of Man. The words λέγει τῷ παραλυτικῷ recall the same phrase in ii. 5 and may indicate the fusion of separate sources. See the introduction to the narrative.

11. σοὶ λέγω is emphatic, and, together with the asyndetic construction (cf. i. 44) gives the command a decisive, if not a peremptory, tone. For the intrans. ἔγειρε *v.* ii. 9. Here, too, ἔγειραι is read by a few MSS. (*v.* Legg).

It is probably from this passage that ὕπαγε εἰς τὸν οἶκόν σου has found its way into some MSS. in ii. 9. The phrase is taken by many commentators to imply that the man's home was in Capernaum.

12. There does not seem to be any special emphasis in εὐθύς, and it may well be rendered by ' thereupon '. Moffatt, however, has ' at once ' and RSV ' immediately '. ἔμπροσθεν, ix. 2*, ' in front of ', is very common in Mt, but Luke prefers ἐνώπιον. The former is used in good Greek, but its use in Mt. xi. 26 (= Lk. x. 21), xviii. 14, xxiii. 13 is said by Howard, ii. 465, to be undeniably Semitic. Swete, 38, appears to imply that it is Semitic here. For ὥστε c. acc. and infin. *v.* i. 27. ἐξίστημι, causal (in pres., imperf., fut., and 1 aor.), ' to displace ', ' amaze ' ; intrans. (in 2 aor., perf., pluperf., mid. and pass.), ' to be amazed ' (here and v. 42, vi. 51*), ' to be beside oneself ', ' mad ' (iii. 21*). ἐξίστασθαι πάντας indicates strong amazement. The later Evangelists paraphrase their source : Mt. ix. 8, ἰδόντες δὲ οἱ ὄχλοι ἐφοβήθησαν, Lk. v. 26, καὶ ἔκστασις ἔλαβεν ἅπαντας. δοξάζειν τὸν θεόν is common in Lk-Ac, but appears here only in Mk. In Cl. Gk δοξάζειν is ' to think ', ' praise ', but in the LXX, as here, it is used with the deeper meaning of δόξα (cf. Kittel, *KThW*, ii. 236 ff.), to express the idea of praising and glorifying, of ascribing to God the splendour due to His name. Matthew adds τὸν δόντα ἐξουσίαν τοιαύτην τοῖς ἀνθρώποις, which probably refers to the miracle.

Instead of λέγοντας D reads καὶ λέγειν, and B W b omit the participle ; but it should probably be read. The words οὕτως οὐδέποτε εἴδαμεν are colloquial and lifelike. Matthew omits them and Luke has εἴδαμεν παράδοξα σήμερον

ὥστε ἐξίστασθαι πάντας καὶ δοξάζειν τὸν θεὸν λέγοντας ὅτι
Οὕτως οὐδέποτε εἴδαμεν.

(v. 26). οὐδέποτε, ii. 25*. Often in the Koine εἴδαμεν (cf. ἦλθαν, i. 29) has the I aor. ending. As frequently in Miracle-stories, the effect on the bystanders is described. This description is vivid and contains words not otherwise common in Mk. The Evangelist is manifestly recording tradition. It is notable that the amazement centres exclusively on the miracle, not the forgiveness of sins, so that II f. is more closely related to I-5a than to 5b-10. This point bears on the meaning of πάντας, which, as it stands, appears to include the scribes; cf. Bartlet, 127. Luke has ἅπαντας, but Matthew οἱ ὄχλοι, and this may be the meaning intended by Mark.

DETACHED NOTE ON THE MEANING OF 'SON OF MAN' IN MK. II. 10

Still a *crux interpretum*, this problem is nearer solution in the sense that it is increasingly recognized that certain interpretations are not satisfactory and that the term must be understood in the light of the attitude of Jesus to the question of His Messiahship. For Mark himself, and in the tradition he received, ' Son of Man ' was a Messianic title. It is possible also that in certain circles of Judaism [1] the title had this significance during the Galilean Mission since its use in the Book of Enoch offered this interpretation, but it is doubtful if this view was widely current. We cannot assume, therefore, that, if the term was used by Jesus in His reply to the scribes, it would be immediately recognized that He was making a Messianic claim. It may also be doubted whether it was His intention at this early period to make the claim openly.

(1) Although widely accepted, the view that Jesus meant that *man* has authority on earth to forgive sins is losing ground, and, apart from the philological objections, this explanation is not probable in itself.[2] It is exposed to the fatal objection that it is alien to the mind of Judaism and of early Christianity.[3]

(2) The view that the Son of Man is the Elect Community is speculative, but cannot be foreclosed in interpreting some of the ' Son of Man sayings '. In ii. 10, however, there is nothing to suggest this view. The action of Jesus is alone in question. Whether it can be said that in 5b-10 the Palestinian community seeks to trace its right to exercise the forgiveness of sins to the example of Jesus, is a different issue. Bultmann, 13 f., supports this view by Mt. ix. 8, maintaining that the plural ' to men ' shows that ' the authority of Jesus to forgive sins has become the possession of the community ' (A. Schlatter, *Der Evglist. Matt.* 301). Smith, 116, also argues that Matthew is thinking of the Christian community ' to whom Jesus, invested with all authority in heaven and earth, has given the power to forgive sins in his name '. It is doubtful if this view is sound, since Mt. xxviii. 18 does not mention forgiveness. This development appears first in the re-interpretation of Mt. xvi. 19 and xviii. 18 in Jn. xx. 22 f., and it is open to question if it can be traced either to the Palestinian community or to the Hellenistic community in its early days. Even I Cor.

[1] Cf. Bousset, 13. See also Intr. 119 f.
[2] Cf. Rawlinson, 25 ; Creed, 79 f. ; Lagrange, 38 ; Bultmann, 13 ; Meyer, i. 104.
[3] Here the idea is firmly maintained that forgiveness is the prerogative of God. Cf. Abrahams, i. 140 ; Moore, i. 535.

v. 3-5 implies no more than the belief that the community can exercise discipline, and 2 Cor. ii. 10 speaks of forgiveness between men, not power to mediate the forgiveness of God. These considerations strengthen the opinion that in ii. 10 the authority is personal and not communal, and indeed Bultmann, 13, expressly says that in this saying ' Son of Man ' was originally a rendering of ' I '. In some sense, we must conclude, Jesus was speaking of Himself.

(3) The possibility that ' Son of Man ' was not a current Messianic term does not exclude the view that He used it in this sense of Himself. On the contrary, Lagrange, 39, is probably right in suggesting that it was precisely on this account that He used the name. *Jésus n'a pas choisi un titre messianique courant, précisément parce qu'il ne voulait pas prouver qu'il était le Messie tel qu'on l'attendait.* On this view Jesus uses *bar nasha* in ii. 10 in a sense which was Messianic to Himself, but non-Messianic, yet a challenge to reflection, in the hearing of His opponents. It ought not to be assumed that it was His purpose to be immediately understood, especially if in His own estimation, and not merely in the mind of Mark, He was *Messias absconditus*. It is in agreement with this suggestion that, after Caesarea Philippi, the term is interpreted further, in terms of Messianic suffering.

(4) Alternately, it may be held that Jesus used the indeterminate form *bar nash*, ' I who speak ', and that subsequently in Christian tradition it was replaced by *bar nasha*, ' Son of Man '. In this case, the tradition was only bringing out the implications of the simpler expression used by Jesus, since He spoke, not simply as a man, but with the undertone of His Messianic consciousness. While this view is possible, it seems more probable that He referred to Himself as *bar nasha*, ' Son of Man '.

(5) On the question whether ii. 10 reflects the beliefs of the Christian community opinions alone are possible. I see no reason to recognize this influence beyond the remote possibility noted above. The opinion of Branscomb, 44, that the saying ' contradicts what we can reconstruct of the beliefs and methods of Jesus ', seems to me without foundation. Only if it can be shown that in no sense did Jesus believe Himself to be the Messiah has it validity. If, on the contrary, as I believe, He had His own distinctive conception of Messiahship, the saying is fully in keeping with the reserve with which He put forward His Messianic claims. There is no need therefore to think of the theology of the community. The allusiveness of ii. 10 is characteristic of Jesus, but not of later Church doctrine. In these matters every reader of Mk must form his own conclusions.

(6) The Idea of Christ as the ' Ideal ' or ' Representative Man ' has a certain analogy with the communal aspect of the Son of Man, and only to that extent is it relevant in the interpretation of ii. 10.

DETACHED NOTE ON JESUS AND THE FORGIVENESS OF SINS

The authority to forgive sins mentioned in ii. 10 has been variously estimated, by some as the exercise of the divine prerogative, by others as an assurance to penitents that God had forgiven them. The former is the silent assumption of the scribes in ii. 7, but it is to be noted that Jesus does not say ' I forgive thee ' and that His authority is an authority

exercised ' on earth ' and as the Son of Man.   For this reason it is not
such a function as any man might fulfil.   The activity is prophetic and
not merely declaratory.   The Speaker speaks as One come from God and
endowed with divine *dynamis*.   On the other hand, the words ' Thy sins
are forgiven ' are not the language of Deity, but the utterance of One who
can speak with complete certainty and as commissioned to declare a
stupendous spiritual fact.   The truth is that there is no complete analogy
known to us in history, and this fact is enough in itself to show that the
narrative is historical, and not simply the precipitate of a believing community.   When Nathan says to David, ' The Lord hath put away thy sin '
(2 Sam. xii. 13), there is a similarity in that his words give the assurance
of a prophet of God, but not a complete parallel.   Nathan reverently names
the name of God with a full assurance of truth, but Jesus in His own
person says ' Thy sins are forgiven ' with the conviction of One who sees
the paralytic through the eyes of God.   Moreover, in His case it is not only
a matter of knowledge, but also of action.   Without implying that sin is
the universal cause of sickness, He sees that forgiveness is indispensable
to the cure, and feels Himself able to mediate forgiveness to the paralytic.
The action is divine rather than declaratory, but it does not invade the
prerogative of Almighty God.   If we have no word to describe action of
this kind, we should recognize that this is precisely the situation in which
we must find ourselves if we think of the spiritual functions of One who
is in truth the Son of God, but who took the form of a servant, being
found in the likeness of men.   It is, however, too naïve an explanation
of the narrative to suppose that it was devised simply to illustrate this
theological truth.   We must think of it rather as belonging to the historical
data out of which the doctrine of the Incarnation takes its rise.

Mk. ii. 13 f.   12. THE CALL OF LEVI   Cf. Mt. ix. 9
                                                              Lk. v. 27 f.

    Prefaced by an editorial statement in 13, this brief narrative closely
resembles i. 16-20.   It is a Story about Jesus, told and re-told until it has
been reduced to its barest essentials, the only vivid detail being the statement that Levi was sitting by the toll house when the summons ' Follow
me ' was given.   Bultmann, 26 f., describes it as a Biographical Apothegm,
since the interest lies in the incident and not only in a saying of Jesus.
His further description of i. 16-20 and ii. 13 f. as ' ideal scenes ' is justified
only in so far as the incidents are typical and describe the distinctive
Christian response.   In such a characterization nothing precludes the
view that the narratives are historical.   They tell what was remembered
and prized, and if i. 16-20 is traced to Peter's reminiscences, the same
must be said of ii. 13 f.   The position assigned to it in the Gospel and the
immediate circumstances are naturally less assured.   Mark believes that
the meal which followed was the occasion when the scribes raised the
objection, ' Why does he eat with taxgatherers and sinners ? ', and the
absence of such links elsewhere suggests that he is writing on the basis
of knowledge.   Such inferences, however, can be based only on grounds
of probability.   The same also must be said of the reference to lakeside
teaching in 13.   Although the passage is editorial, it shows good literary
judgment and probably describes the actual circumstances.   As the crowds

came and went and Jesus taught by the lake side, Levi had opportunities to hear His teaching and form a judgment. Thus, when the call came, his response was dramatic, but not unmotivated.

13 Καὶ ἐξῆλθεν πάλιν παρὰ τὴν θάλασσαν· καὶ πᾶς ὁ ὄχλος
14 ἤρχετο πρὸς αὐτόν, καὶ ἐδίδασκεν αὐτούς. Καὶ παράγων εἶδεν

13. For πάλιν v. ii. 1; θάλασσα i. 16; ὄχλος ii. 4; διδάσκω i. 21. The verse prepares the way for the story of the call. Matthew omits it and Luke has simply καὶ μετὰ ταῦτα ἐξῆλθεν (v. 27). Wellhausen, 17, suggests that πάλιν may only indicate a transition, ' further ', ' thereupon ' (cf. Plummer, 87), but most commentators think there is a backward reference to i. 16, 35, or 45 (e.g. Swete, 39; Lagrange, 40). The v.l. ἐξῆλθον (א*) and the insertion of ὁ Ἰησοῦς are probably due to the use of the section in public reading in the Church. Cf. Schmidt, 82. The two imperfects indicate the coming and going of successive groups of hearers. αὐτούς is used ad sensum, as in iii. 8, iv. 1 f., and xiv. 44.

14. For παράγω v. i. 16; κάθημαι ii. 6; ἀκολουθέω i. 18; ἀνίστημι i. 35. The account is closely parallel to the Call of the First Disciples (i. 16-20); cf. παράγων εἶδεν and ἠκολούθησεν αὐτῷ in the two narratives.

Levi (Λευείς, יִב, v.ll. Λευίς, Λευΐ, Λευεί, Λευής) is mentioned here and in Lk v. 27, 29 only. Matthew has ἄνθρωπον . . . Μαθθαῖον λεγόμενον (ix. 9). The problem is further complicated by the fact that in the list of the Twelve in iii. 16-19 Matthew is mentioned, but not Levi. The list includes ' James the son of Alphaeus ' and in the present passage this name is read instead of ' Levi the son of Alphaeus ' by D Θ fam. 13 (exc. 346) 543 565 a b c e ff g¹ r¹ and by Tatian, Ephraem, and Photius (cf. Swete, 39; Lagrange, 40; Klostermann, 29). Origen also, Contra Cels. i. 62, says that Levi the taxgatherer, who followed Jesus, ' was not of the number of His Apostles, except according to some of the manuscripts of the Gospel according to Mark '. Cf. WH, Notes, 24.

With the knowledge at our disposal no complete solution is possible, but the following points may be noted. (1) The identification of Levi with Matthew is widely accepted, but unfortunately we cannot be certain whether it is more than an early guess, since it is supported by neither Mark nor Luke. (2) The reading ' James the son of Alphaeus ', attested by Western, Caesarean, and Syrian authorities, is also an early hypothesis, as early possibly as the middle of the second century. Blass, Textkritische Bemerkungen zu Markus, 58, accepts the reading, and so strong is its attestation that one might be inclined to regard it favourably, if an explanation could be given of the name ' Levi ' in א B C L W 1 33 118 579 700 1071 et al. (3) That the same person bore the two names ' Levi ' and ' James ' is only a conjecture, open to the objection that Mark does not support it as he does in the case of Peter (iii. 16). (4) While Levi may not have been regarded as an Apostle by Mark, the contrary is suggested by the close similarity of ii. 14 and i. 16-20.

On the whole, the best solution to the problem is to be found in the uncertainty which prevailed in the period A.D. 60–100 as to the exact constitution of the Apostolic College. The lists in the Synoptic Gospels and in Ac. i. 13 are not capable of more than conjectural co-ordination, and the reason is probably that by the time Mk was written the special functions of the Twelve had long ceased to be operative. That they had become a distant memory is suggested by the fact that in the Pauline Epistles they are mentioned once only, in 1 Cor. xv. 5 (' then to the Twelve '), in a phrase which may be a later interpolation (cf. J.

Λευεὶν τὸν τοῦ Ἀλφαίου καθήμενον ἐπὶ τὸ τελώνιον, καὶ λέγει
αὐτῷ Ἀκολούθει μοι. καὶ ἀναστὰς ἠκολούθησεν αὐτῷ.

Weiss, *1 Cor.* 350) or a 'traditional formula' (Robertson and Plummer, *ICC*, *1 Cor.* 336). If this view is accepted, light is thrown on Mark's literary methods. Believing Levi to be an Apostle, and aware that his name is absent in the list used in iii. 16-19, he leaves the tradition as he finds it. If this inference is justified, caution is fitting when his positive statements are questioned, as well as freedom to ask if his interpretations are sound. τελώνιον*, Mt. ix. 9, Lk. v. 27**, 'custom office', 'toll house', the suffix -ιον denoting the place connected with the person; cf. Moulton, ii. 342. Found in the comic poet Posidippus 13 (iii/ B.C.), the word is illustrated in the papyri (*VGT*, 631) and in the form

τελωνεῖον is used in MGk (Kennedy, 154). *Tell Ḥûm* (*v.* i. 21) would be the first point of importance round the northern end of the lake for travellers from the territory of Herod Philip and from the Decapolis; cf. Lagrange, 41; Rawlinson, 27. Levi, therefore, must have been an official in the service of Herod Antipas. For ἐπί c. acc. with the meaning 'at' *v.* Blass, 136. Although εὐθύς is not used, the aor. ἠκολούθησεν marks an immediate response to the challenge Ἀκολούθει μοι. Commentators rightly point out that his renunciation was greater than that of the four disciples mentioned in i. 16-20, since on occasion they could return to their fishing. Levi's decision was once for all. For the redundant participle ἀναστάς *v.* i. 35 and Intr. 63.

Mk. ii. 15-17   **13. ON EATING WITH TAX-**   Cf. Mt. ix. 10-13
GATHERERS AND SINNERS   Lk. v. 29-32

This narrative consists of a Pronouncement-story, 16 f., with a narrative framework in 15. Dibelius, 43, classifies it as a Paradigm of a less pure type, in which 17b is a later addition; Bultmann, 16, as an Apothegm (or *Streitgespräch*) in which 17 was originally an isolated logion. This saying, he suggests, is a Christian formation shaped through controversy with Jewish opponents, and 15 f. owes its origin to the fact that καλεῖν was understood as an invitation to the table-fellowship greatly prized in the community for its symbolic importance. Thus we best explain an obscure scene which the later Evangelists sought to make somewhat more intelligible.

There can be no doubt that much is obscure. We do not know when and where the scribes appeared, how they made contact with the disciples, and when Jesus gave His answer. Cf. Wellhausen, 17; Schmidt, 85; Bultmann, 16 n.; J. Weiss, 159; Strauss, 322 f. Bultmann's reconstruction is not convincing. A narrator whose invention was uncontrolled by the tradition would hardly have left so many points open. The presumption is that at the time when Mark wrote, by a process of attrition due to constant repetition, the narrative had assumed its present form. Mark knew that the reproaches of the scribes were occasioned by a meal at which Jesus ate with taxgatherers and people who sat loose to Law, but he knew little more. The impression left by his narrative is his restraint. He does not say that the scribes were present, and, if αὐτοῖς is omitted (*v.* Comm.), he does not record that Jesus addressed them. It is, of course, conceivable that, without the support of tradition, he connected a saying about table-fellowship with a meal in the house of Levi. Such assertions can neither be proved nor disproved. We can assess them only in the light of a writer's practice as a whole, and, it seems to me that, judged by this test, Mark is a writer worthy of trust. He tells what he knows without attempting to answer further questions.

A further point in Bultmann's discussion is very suggestive. It was probably the interest taken in the question of table-fellowship in the primitive community which led to the preservation of the story ; cf. Ac. xi. 3, Gal. ii. 12. When ' certain came from James ', Peter ' drew back and separated himself, fearing them that were of the circumcision '. But what led him to eat with Gentiles in the first place ? Did he remember the reproach, ' Why eateth he with taxgatherers and sinners ? ', and the reply, ' They that are whole have no need of a physician, but they that are sick : I came not to call righteous men, but sinners ' ? We cannot prove that this suggestion is true, but it has greater justification than the hypothesis of creative invention.

15 Καὶ γίνεται κατακεῖσθαι αὐτὸν ἐν τῇ οἰκίᾳ αὐτοῦ, καὶ πολλοὶ

15. For the construction with γίνεται v. the note on i. 9. Here, as in ii. 23, the acc. and infin. follow. Matthew changes the historic present γίνεται into the more familiar ἐγένετο. This reading appears also in most MSS. in Mk, but probably γίνεται (‭א‬ B L W 33 565 700 892*) should be preferred. The sentence is ambiguous. Most commentators take αὐτόν and αὐτοῦ to refer to Levi and understand the meaning to be that Levi held a feast in his house, but some think that Jesus was the host and that it was in His house, or in that of Peter, that the meal was held. Cf. Allen, 68 ; Klostermann, 29, who recognizes, however, that in the present setting (13 f.) Levi is the host. Luke says expressly καὶ ἐποίησεν δοχὴν μεγάλην Λευεὶς αὐτῷ ἐν τῇ οἰκίᾳ αὐτοῦ (v. 29) and, although Matthew omits αὐτοῦ (ix. 10) he probably means the same. κατάκειμαι, used in i. 30 and ii. 4 of the sick, is here used, as in xiv. 3*, of reclining at meals upon the left elbow (cf. Bernard, ICC, St. Jn, 471). This custom, due to Hellenistic influences, although ultimately eastern in origin, was universal in the time of Jesus (cf. Lagrange, 42), but J. Jeremias, 22 f., maintains that, at ordinary meals, it was usual to sit at table. Other verbs used in Mk with the same meaning are ἀνάκειμαι (vi. 26, xiv. 18, xvi. [14]*), ἀνακλίνω (vi. 39*), ἀναπίπτω

(vi. 40, viii. 6*) and συνανάκειμαι (here and vi. 22*). All these verbs, except the last, are classical ; and appear to belong to the vernacular (VGT, 34, 37). Possibly συνανάκειμαι is a Markan coinage (cf. Jn. xii. 2, ἀνακειμένων σὺν αὐτῷ, ‭א‬ A B D L Θ, for which W reads συνανακειμένων αὐτῷ). In Cl. Gk κατάκειμαι is used both of being ill and of reclining at table (Bauer, 642 f.) ; but in VGT, 326, it is illustrated only in the former sense.

τελώνης, ii. 16 (bis)*, ' tax-gatherer ', corresponds to the Latin portitor rather than publicanus, which is used in the Vulgate and from which the rendering ' publican ' is derived. The publicani were those to whom the public revenues were farmed, while the portitores or τελῶναι collected the dues, often with exaction. Universally despised for their rapacity and low morals (cf. Herondas vi. 64, τοὺς γὰρ τελώνας πᾶσα νῦν θύρη φρίσσει, Lucian, Necyom. 11, μοιχοὶ καὶ πορνοβόσκοι καὶ τελῶναι καὶ κόλακες καὶ συκοφάνται, Cicero, De Off. i. 150 ; cf. also Billerbeck, i. 377 f.), the τελῶναι of the Gospels were scorned on political grounds and because their work involved contact with Gentiles. Levi may have been of higher rank. Cf. Lagrange, 43 : Mais Lévi — comme Zachée — n'était pas non plus un de ces employés très subalternes qui étaient souvent des esclaves

τελῶναι καὶ ἁμαρτωλοὶ συνανέκειντο τῷ Ἰησοῦ καὶ τοῖς μαθηταῖς
αὐτοῦ, ἦσαν γὰρ πολλοὶ καὶ ἠκολούθουν αὐτῷ. καὶ οἱ γραμμα- 16

ἁμαρτωλός, ii. 16 (bis), 17, viii. 38, xiv. 41*, adj., but always in Mk (exc. viii. 38) in the plur. as a subst., and so frequently in the rest of the NT. Apart from sporadic earlier instances the word is late (LXX, Gen. xiii. 13, etc., and frequently in the Psalms and Sirach), but its use in sepulchral inscriptions in warnings to grave-robbers (Deissmann, 114 f.; VGT, 25) shows that it was in common use, but without the religious colouring which it has in the Pauline Epistles (cf. Rom. v. 8, 19, Gal. ii. 17), where it denotes men separated from God and in conscious opposition to Him. See K. H. Rengstorf, KThW, i. 320-39. There are approaches to Pauline usage in the Synoptics, especially in Lk (cf. v. 8, xv. 7, 10, xviii. 13), and possibly also in Mk (cf. viii. 38 and xiv. 41, where, however, the primary meaning is 'the heathen' as in Gal. ii. 15). But in ii. 15 (and 16 f.) the word is used along with τελῶναι to denote people who neglect to observe the Law according to the Pharisaic ideal, 'the people of the land' (הָאָרֶץ עַם) described in Jn. vii. 49, ' This multitude which knoweth not the law are accursed '. Probably also people of immoral life, and not merely those defiled by Gentile practices, are meant (cf. Abrahams, i. 55) or included, as in Lk. vii. 37, 39. That Jesus consorted with such people, and ate with them, was to the scribes a deep ground of offence.

μαθητής, some 43 times*, is regularly used in the plur. for ' the disciples ' of Jesus. In Cl. Gk (Herodotus iv. 77, Plato, Prot. 315 A, etc.) the word is used of the pupils of philosophers and rhetoricians, although not in the circle of Socrates (Plato, Apol. 33 A). The word is not found in the LXX, except for the v.l. in Jer. xiii. 21, xx. 11, xxvi. (xlvi.) 9, and its Heb. equivalent תַּלְמִיד appears only in 1 Chron. xxv. 8, a surprising feature which is due to the character of the religion of Israel as a religion of revelation; cf. Rengstorf, KThW, iv. 432-4). The OT prophets have servants (1 Kgs. xviii. 43, 2 Kgs. iv. 12, etc.) but not disciples. It was in Rabbinic Judaism that the word was commonly employed, perhaps under Greek influence, to denote the disciples of notable Rabbis. In the papyri μαθητής is used of apprentices (VGT, 385). The distinguishing feature of the disciples of Jesus was their utter devotion to Him and not simply to His teaching. Er ist für sie kein Rabbi/ διδάσκαλος, sondern ihr Herr (Rengstorf, op. cit. iv. 459). Their task is to testify of Him. Within the wider circle of the disciples are the Apostles (v. vi. 30) and, as a smaller group, the Twelve (v. iii. 14), the smallest circle being that of the three disciples, Peter, James, and John (v. v. 37). The reference to the disciples in ii. 15 is abrupt, for thus far the call of five disciples only has been mentioned. They are introduced at this point as a body in preparation for 16 f. It is this fact which accounts for the summary phrase ἦσαν γὰρ πολλοὶ καὶ ἠκολούθουν αὐτῷ. It reveals the Evangelist's consciousness that he has not mentioned the large company of disciples earlier, and that he must do so now. Much less probable is the view that Mark means the publicans and sinners (cf. Swete, 41; Bartlet, 132) and that καὶ ἠκολούθουν αὐτῷ must be taken with καὶ οἱ γραμματεῖς τῶν Φαρισαίων (cf. Swete, 41; Gould, 42; Plummer, 89). In the Gospels ἀκολουθέω is used of disciples (cf. Kittel, KThW, i. 214), not enemies, and the presence of the scribes in the house of Levi is highly improbable (cf. Lagrange, 43; Klostermann, 29 f.). In accordance with Semitic parataxis the καί before ἠκολούθουν may be used in the sense of the relative pronoun οἱ (Wellhausen, 17; Ed. Meyer, i. 105; Rawlinson, 29), with the meaning: ' for there were (now) many who followed Him '

τεῖς τῶν Φαρισαίων ἰδόντες ὅτι ἐσθίει μετὰ τῶν ἁμαρτωλῶν καὶ
τελωνῶν ἔλεγον τοῖς μαθηταῖς αὐτοῦ "Ὅτι μετὰ τῶν τελωνῶν

(οἱ καί is read by D b f ff r² vg, and οἱ (om. καί) by Θ 565 a c e l q r¹). This incidental reference is in harmony with Mark's style; cf. vii. 19.

16. The phrase ' the scribes of the Pharisees ', found here only, means the scribes who belonged to the party of the Pharisees. Cf. Ac. xxiii. 9, τινὲς τῶν γραμματέων τοῦ μέρους τῶν Φαρισαίων. Matthew (ix. 11, οἱ Φαρισαῖοι) and Luke (v. 30, οἱ Φαρισαῖοι καὶ οἱ γραμματεῖς) simplify the expression, and in Mk the secondary variant καὶ οἱ γραμματεῖς καὶ οἱ Φαρισαῖοι is found in A C Θ al. pler. fam. 1 fam. 13 (exc. 124) 22 157 543 565 579 700 892 al. pler. f l q r vg (pler.) sype hl sa aeth arm. οἱ Φαρισαῖοι, ii. 18 (bis), 24, iii. 6, vii. 1, 3, 5, viii. 11, 15, ix. 11 (?, —WH), x. 2 (?), xii. 13*, ' the Pharisees '. Most of these passages belong to Petrine stories and there is none in the Passion Narrative. In general Mark prefers to speak of the scribes (21 times), the elders (7), and the chief priests (14).

The Pharisees were the spiritual descendants of the Ḥasidim (' pious ones ') who supported the Maccabees. Strongly devoted to the Law and to tradition, they believed, in contrast with the Sadducees (v. xii. 18*), in divine providence, a future life with its rewards and punishments, and in angels and daemons. Cf. Josephus, Ant. xiii. 10.6, xviii. 1. 3, BJ, ii. 8. 14; and among modern interpreters, Schürer, II. ii. 10-28; Billerbeck, iv. 344 ff.; Klostermann, 30 f.; Jackson and Lake, i. 110-14, 436-45; Herford, Pharisaism (1912), The Pharisees (1924); Lightley, Jewish Sects and Parties. The derivation of the name is obscure. Commonly it is derived from the Aramaic פְּרִישַׁיָא (Hebrew פְּרוּשִׁים), ' the separatists ', and it is explained as meaning those who, in their fidelity to the Law, separated themselves from uncleanness and especially from ' the people of the land ' (עַם הָאָרֶץ). Some scholars (Le-

szynsky and Oesterley) have supposed that the name means ' interpreters ' (cf. Oesterley, The Books of the Apocrypha (1915), 130-2) and others (Lauterbach and Box) that it suggests ' seceders ' or ' expelled ' (cf. Box, ERE, Art. ' Pharisees '). Ed. Meyer, ii. 284, thinks that the name ' separatists ' arose from the separation of the Ḥasidim from the partisans of Judas Maccabaeus in 163 B.C. Recently T. W. Manson, Bulletin of the John Rylands Library, vol. 22, No. 1, April, 1938, 153-9, has suggested that ' Φαρισαῖος is the Graecized form of the Aramaic פְּרְסָאָה Persian ', and that it was applied to their rivals as a nickname by the Sadducees in protest against the foreign element in Pharisaic beliefs. The Pharisees described themselves as Ḥaberim, חֲבֵרִים, ' associates ', but this, of course, is a descriptive name and not a party title.

Before ἰδόντες ℵ L Δ 33 b r¹ read καί, a variant which is of interest as indicating that some copyists connected καὶ ἠκολούθουν αὐτῷ (ii. 15) with καὶ οἱ γραμματεῖς τῶν Φαρισαίων (see above). The tense of ἐσθίει is that of the original perception. The order ' the sinners and publicans ' reverses that of ii. 15 and 16b. Swete, 42, suggests that it indicates that the charge of being in the company of sinners was foremost in the minds of the scribes, but in view of their words, ' He eateth with publicans and sinners ' (16b), the suggestion seems doubtful. ἔλεγον may indicate that the charge was made repeatedly. The second ὅτι (before μετά) may be recitativum, and in this case, the statement: ' He eateth with publicans and sinners ' (RV), is implicitly an accusation; but it is more probable that ὅτι (= τί ὅτι) is used interrogatively in the sense of τί, as in ix. 11, 28 (so Swete, 42; Gould, 43; Klostermann, 31; Lagrange, 44; Turner, JTS, xxvii. 58 (also ii. 7 and viii. 12)): ' Why eateth he with pub-

καὶ ἁμαρτωλῶν ἐσθίει ^T; καὶ ἀκούσας ὁ Ἰησοῦς λέγει [ὅτι] Οὐ 17
χρείαν ἔχουσιν οἱ ἰσχύοντες ἰατροῦ ἀλλ' οἱ κακῶς ἔχοντες· οὐκ
ἦλθον καλέσαι δικαίους ἀλλὰ ἁμαρτωλούς.

16 καὶ πίνει

licans and sinners?'. Matthew and Luke have διὰ τί. At the end of the verse, after ἐσθίει, most MSS. add καὶ πίνει,[1] but it should probably be omitted with ℵ B D W Θ 235 271 a b e ff r[1].

17. ἀκούσας indicates either that Jesus actually heard the scribes speak or that their words were reported to Him. The latter is the better interpretation, since it is not probable that the scribes were present at the meal (v. the note on ii. 15), and this inference is supported if we omit αὐτοῖς, with D W fam. 1 28 a b c ff g[1] q r[1]. The ὅτι, enclosed by WH in square brackets, is omitted by all MSS. except B Δ Θ 565 1071. χρεία, ii. 25, xi. 3, xiv. 63*. ἰσχύω, v. 4, ix. 18, xiv. 37*, <ἰσχύς, 'to be strong', 'be able', 'prevail'; Cl., LXX, Pap. Luke has οἱ ὑγιαίνοντες (v. 31), 'those in good health'. For the idiom οἱ κακῶς ἔχοντες v. i. 32. ἰατρός, v. 26.

The proverb about the physician and the sick was used by the Cynics and by representatives of other philosophical schools, but the comparison is so natural that there is no need to suggest borrowing. Swete, 42, cites Pausanias ap. Plutarch, Apophth. Lacon. 230 F, οὐδ' οἱ ἰατροί, ἔφη, παρὰ τοῖς ὑγιαίνουσιν ὅπου δὲ οἱ νοσοῦντες διατρίβειν εἰώθασιν, and Diogenes Laertius, Antisth. vi. 1. 6, οἱ ἰατροί, φησί, μετὰ τῶν νοσούντων εἰσὶν ἀλλ' οὐ πυρέττουσιν. Cf. also Lagrange, 44; Klostermann, 31.

Bultmann, 96, and Dibelius, 64, explain the final saying: 'I came not to call the righteous, but sinners', as a doctrinal expansion. The more than local sense of ἦλθον (cf. x. 45, and ἐξῆλθον, i. 38) and the use of the Pauline

word δίκαιος (vi. 20*) might seem to favour this view; but Mark's use of δικαίους points in the opposite direction. The word refers to the scribes and, despite the hesitation of Swete, 43, who quotes Theophylact, κατ' εἰρωνείαν γὰρ τοῦτό φησιν, appears to be used in irony (cf. Plummer, ICC, St. Lk, 161). Jesus has not come to call men like the scribes, who think themselves righteous, but sinners. The sense of the word is nearer that of the corresponding verb in Lk. xvi. 15, 'Ye are they which justify yourselves', than it is to Pauline usage. If καλέσαι is used with the meaning 'invite' (cf. Rawlinson, 29; Manson, Congr. Quarterly, xiii. 158 f.; Cadoux, 49), there is further reason to hesitate, but this interpretation implies that Jesus was the host at the feast (v. supra, ii. 15). On the whole, it is best to conclude that Jesus is speaking of the call to repentance. This is Luke's explanation, v. 32, εἰς μετάνοιαν, a gloss which is added, probably in dependence on Lk, in the Markan text in C fam. 13 a c and other MSS. Plummer, 90, points out the frequency of οὐ . . . ἀλλά in Mk, in iii. 26, 29, iv. 17, 22, v. 39, vii. 19, ix. 37, x. 8, all of which are sayings.

Larger considerations, however, determine the historical character of this saying. Its spirit is the spirit of Jesus. The saying is characteristic of Him, and distinctively so. 'He did not avoid sinners, but sought them out. They were still children of God. This was a new and sublime contribution to the development of religion and morality', Montefiore, i. 55. The story does not stand alone. Along with it go the Lukan stories of the Woman in

[1] So A C L Δ et al. fam. 1 fam. 13 22 28 33 157 543 579 892 1071 al. pler. c f l q r² sy[pe hl] sa bo aeth arm Aug.

the City (vii. 36-50) and Zacchaeus (xix. 1-10), and, above all, the saying preserved in Q : ' Behold, a gluttonous man, and a winebibber, a friend of taxgatherers and sinners ' (Lk. vii. 34 = Mt. xi. 19). Cf. Cadoux, 39-50.

Mk. ii. 18-20   **14. ON FASTING**   Cf. Mt. ix. 14 f.
Lk. v. 33-5

Again the narrative is a Pronouncement-story not connected with those which precede and follow it. Cf. Dibelius, 43 ; Bultmann, 17. In contrast, Luke relates the call of Levi, the feast, and the question about fasting in a single section.

There is no need to suppose that the story belongs to the earliest days of the Galilean Ministry. On the contrary, the fact that the disciples of Jesus are distinguished from those of John, and, if the phrase in ii. 18 is original, from the disciples of the Pharisees, suggests a more advanced period, possibly after the execution of the Baptist. Originally the tradition of an eyewitness, the story has lost in the course of transmission all notes of time, place, and circumstance beyond the general statement that the disciples of John and the Pharisees were fasting (18a). The story was told because it made known the mind of Jesus concerning fasting. Bultmann contends that, if 18a refers to a mere custom, the situation does not correspond to the style of the *Streitgespräch*, and that, if an actual fast is meant, it ought to be named. This dilemma does not exhaust the possibilities of the case. A definite fast is probably in question (*v*. Comm.), but its precise character may have been forgotten, since it is the absence of the custom of fasting which is challenged. To Bultmann's further objection, that the question concerns the disciples only, and not Jesus Himself, it may be replied that not infrequently in religious controversy the followers of a teacher are attacked before he himself is openly challenged. There is no reason to doubt, therefore, that the narrative reflects trustworthy tradition.

The original extent of the narrative is a separate question. That 19b, 20 is a later addition is widely held, but in the Commentary I have given reasons for the rejection of this view. A further question is whether 18a is the work of a redactor (cf. J. Weiss, 160) or an explanatory statement supplied by Mark. The former alternative has nothing in its favour beyond the fact that Matthew and Luke omit the reference to the circumstance that John's disciples and the Pharisees were fasting. That Mark added the statement is possible, and, so far as the allusion to the Pharisees is concerned, is probable (*v*. Comm.). As an impersonal plural ἔρχονται (18b) would make quite a good beginning to the narrative, the circumstances being described in the question which follows. From the standpoint of form, however, there can be no objection to the originality of the statement that the disciples of John were fasting, for Rabbinical stories begin in the same way. Cf. Fiebig, *Altjüdische Gleichnisse*, 20 ff. : ' Once disciples were celebrating a Sabbath at Joppa. But Rabbi Jehoshua did not celebrate the Sabbath there. And when at length his disciples came to him, he said. . . .'[1] Rabbinical stories in fact frequently connect sayings and similitudes with events.[2] In substance, therefore, we may conclude

---

[1] Cited by Bultmann, 17a, and Klostermann, 31.
[2] Cf. Fiebig, *Der Erzählungsstil der Evangelien*, 77 ff.

that Mark gives the story much as he found it, with a minimum of editorial expansion.

Καὶ ἦσαν οἱ μαθηταὶ ᾽Ιωάνου καὶ οἱ Φαρισαῖοι νηστεύοντες. 18
καὶ ἔρχονται καὶ λέγουσιν αὐτῷ Διὰ τί οἱ μαθηταὶ ᾽Ιωάνου
καὶ οἱ μαθηταὶ τῶν Φαρισαίων νηστεύουσιν, οἱ δὲ σοὶ [μαθηταὶ]

18. The ' disciples of John ', vi. 29*, are mentioned also in Lk. vii. 18 = Mt. xi. 2, Lk. xi. 1, Mt. xiv. 12, Jn. i. 35, 37, iii. 25. The reading οἱ τῶν Φαρισαίων in L fam. 1 a b *et al.* is an assimilation to 18b, and from the same cause οἱ Φαρισαῖοι is read in the latter in Θ 433 474 a ff *et al.* Some commentators suggest that the references to the Pharisees and to their disciples are redactional (cf. Lohmeyer, 59; Wellhausen, 18; Klostermann, 31 f.; Montefiore, i. 58; Rawlinson, 30) and that originally the question mentioned only the disciples of John. This suggestion can be no more than a conjecture, but it has the advantage that it strengthens the further inference that the fasting in question was ' an expression of mourning for their master ' (Rawlinson, 31). If, however, the usual text is read, this may still be the character of the fast, since the contrast suggested by 18 f. implies a fast of mourning. It is not necessary to suppose that John's disciples and those of the Pharisees were observing the same fast, although this view is usually assumed. In any case a definite fast (or definite fasts) is probably in question. The periphrastic imperfect ἦσαν. . . νηστεύοντες (v. Intr. 45) means ' were fasting ' (Swete, 43; Lagrange, 45; Klostermann, 32), not ' were used to fast ' (cf. Lk. v. 33, νηστεύουσιν πυκνὰ καὶ δεήσεις ποιοῦνται).

The only fast enjoined by the Law was that of the Day of Atonement (Lev. xvi. 29; cf. ἡ νηστεία in Ac. xxvii. 9), but additional fasts were observed by the Pharisees, twice in the week, on Mondays and Thursdays (cf. Lk. xviii. 12, νηστεύω δὶς τοῦ σαββάτου). Traditional fasts, commemorative of historical events (e.g. the Great Fast

of the 9th of Ab (August)), were also observed. It is impossible, however, to be certain what fast, or fasts, are in mind in 18a. For the conjectures of commentators v. Schmidt, 87 n.

The plural ἔρχονται is probably impersonal (Turner, 19; Lagrange, 46; Klostermann, 32). Swete, 43, suggests that the subject is the scribes, but the want of connexion in Mk between this story and ii. 15-17 is against this view. ' People come and say to him ' represents Mark's meaning. Luke has οἱ δὲ εἶπαν, i.e. the scribes and Pharisees (v. 33), and Matthew οἱ μαθηταὶ ᾽Ιωάνου, with the question in the first person, ' Why do we . . . ? ' (ix. 14), but these are not very successful attempts to give a more literary presentation to the Markan narrative, and reveal its more primitive character. The phrase οἱ μαθηταὶ τῶν Φαρισαίων** presents great difficulties, and is explained by several commentators as an addition (Bultmann, 17 n.; Wellhausen, 18; Lohmeyer, 59). The objections are formidable. A ' disciple ' stands in a close personal relation to a ' teacher ' (*Es gibt keinen* תַּלְמִיד *ohne Lehrer* (רַב), Rengstorf, *KThW*, iv. 437), and the Pharisees, except those who were also scribes, were not teachers. Further, we have no other evidence of ' the disciples of the Pharisees ' beyond Mt. xii. 27 (= Lk. xi. 19), ' your sons ', which is usually interpreted to mean ' fellow-Jews ' (cf. McNeile, 175; Easton, 181; Luce, 214), and Mt. xxii. 16, ' their disciples ', where the term appears to be used loosely. Rengstorf (*op. cit.* 445 f.) defends the phrase, but is not able to cite evidence beyond the passages noted above and the fact that the bounds between scribes and Pharisees were fleeting and that Pharisaic com-

19 οὐ νηστεύουσιν; καὶ εἶπεν αὐτοῖς ὁ Ἰησοῦς Μὴ δύνανται οἱ
υἱοὶ τοῦ νυμφῶνος ἐν ᾧ ὁ νυμφίος μετ᾽ αὐτῶν ἐστιν νηστεύειν;
ὅσον χρόνον ἔχουσιν τὸν νυμφίον μετ᾽ αὐτῶν οὐ δύνανται νη-

munities grouped themselves around leading scribes. In this case we should expect rather the phrase ' the disciples of the scribes '. On the whole, the conjecture noted above, that originally the narrative mentioned only ' the disciples of John ', receives support from the dubiety of the phrase under discussion. It would appear that ' the Pharisees ' and ' the disciples of the Pharisees ' are mentioned because, at a time earlier than the composition of Mk, the story was included in a group of ' Conflict-stories ' illustrative of the breach between Jesus and the Rabbis.

19. μή c. indic. suggests a negative answer. νυμφών*, ' a bride-chamber ', a rare word used in Tob. vi. 14, 17 ; v. VGT, 431. In Mt. xxii. 10 it is the room in which a marriage feast is celebrated ; cf. Lohmeyer, 59 n. οἱ υἱοὶ τοῦ νυμφῶνος, lit. ' the sons of the bride-chamber ', either ' the groomsmen ' (νυμφευταί) (cf. Swete, 44 ; Rawlinson, 31 ; Lagrange, 47 ; Dodd, 115 ; Easton, 70 f. ; Gould, 45), or ' the wedding guests ' (cf. RSV ; Rawlinson, 257 ; McNeile, 121 ; Smith, 118 ; Souter, 168). This use of υἱός (or τέκνον) c. gen. in a metaphorical expression is Hebraistic, but is not un-Greek (cf. Deissmann, BS, 161 ff. ; Howard, ii. 441 ; VGT, 649). Cf. υἱ. βροντῆς, iii. 19 ; υἱ. γεέννης, Mt. xxiii. 15 ; υἱ. εἰρήνης, Lk. x. 6, οἱ υἱ. τ. αἰῶνος τούτου, xvi. 8, xx. 34, υἱ. τ. ἀναστάσεως, xx. 36 ; 2 Kgs. xii. 5, 1 Macc. iv. 2. It is best regarded as ' translation-Greek ', tolerable Greek which stands close to Aramaic idiom. It is worthy of note that all the passages from the Gospels noted above are sayings of Jesus. νυμφίος, ii. 19 (bis), 20*, ' bridegroom '. Influenced by such OT passages as Hos. ii. 19, Isa. liv. 4 ff., lxii. 4 ff., Ezek. xvi. 7 ff., in which Yahweh is portrayed as the husband of His

covenant-people, the idea of the Bridegroom gained Messianic significance, and appears in the NT in Jn. iii. 29 (where νυμφίος is used) and in 2 Cor. xi. 2, Eph. v. 32, and Apoc. xix. 7, xxi. 2. Cf. Billerbeck, i. 969 f., ii. 393 ; J. Jeremias, Jesus als Weltvollender, 21-32. Among the Rabbis there is a parallel development when they speak of the Law as a marriage contract, of Moses as the best man, and of God as the Bridegroom of Israel His Bride. Cf. E. Stauffer, Art. on γαμέω, γάμος, KThW, i. 652.

By many commentators Jesus is here recognized as claiming to be the Messianic Bridegroom (cf. Bernard, ICC, St. Jn, 131 ; Swete, 44 ; Bartlet, 136). Lagrange, 47, questions this view. Ce qui est comparé à une noce, c'est la joie des disciples de posséder leur maître, non pas directement les temps messianiques. It is doubtful, however, if this objection can be sustained. Wellhausen, 18, finds allegory not only in 20, where it is freely recognized by those who regard the verse as a later Christian formation (e.g. Klostermann, 33), but also in 19, and, consistently with this view, rejects both verses. Es schimmert also schon in ii. 19 der allegorische Sinn durch . . . und man darf ii. 20 nicht davon abschneiden. In view of the wide rejection of 19b, 20 (see below) this opinion concerning 19a, which is generally accepted as a genuine saying, is important. But, apart from the weight of critical opinion, general considerations favour the opinion that νυμφίος is a Messianic expression. Is it likely that Jesus, to whom the OT background indicated above was familiar, would use the metaphor of the marriage feast, and apply to Himself the name ' bridegroom ', in a purely general sense ? The shade of Jülicher must not affright us from admitting allegory

στεύειν· ἐλεύσονται δὲ ἡμέραι ὅταν ἀπαρθῇ ἀπ' αὐτῶν ὁ νυμφίος,   20
καὶ τότε νηστεύσουσιν ἐν ἐκείνῃ τῇ ἡμέρᾳ.

when we see it. Of course, in 19a Jesus does not put forth a public claim to be the Messiah; He silently implies it, and the claim is for those who have ears to hear. The implication of the saying is that the Kingdom is already present, that He is its rightful Lord, and that it is incompatible with a situation so joyous that His groomsmen should mourn. A parallel situation may be the background of the Parable of the Ten Virgins (cf. Dodd, 171-4), although this parable, as it stands in Mt. xxv. 1-13, has an eschatological setting; nor is it excluded that, along with the conviction that the Kingdom was already present, Jesus should also speak of it as to come, and should anticipate the joy of the Messianic Feast (cf. xiv. 25).

The second half of the verse, 19b, has no parallel in Mt and Lk, and is omitted by D W fam. 1 (exc. 131) 33 700 a b e ff g¹ et al., but its redundancy may well account for its absence from the later Gospels, and homoioteleuton for the textual omission. As Wellhausen observes (p. 18), such repetitions are throughout in the style of the Gospels; and especially is this Semitic colouring characteristic of Mk. Cf. xii. 23, xiii. 19, and v. Howard, ii. 419. ὅσος, 14 times*. χρόνος, ix. 21*. The phrase ὅσον χρόνον is an acc. of duration of time, ' during the time that '; cf. Rom. vii. 1. Already in these words the taking away of the Bridegroom is implied by contrast. For the question of the genuineness of 19b v. the note on 20.

20. ἐλεύσονται δὲ ἡμέραι, ' But days will come ', cf. Lk. xvii. 22, xxi. 6, also xix. 43 (ἥξουσιν ἡμέραι) and xxiii. 29 (ἔρχονται ἡμέραι).

ἀπαίρω*, Mt. ix. 15, Lk. v. 35**, ' to take away ', ' remove '. Cf. Isa. liii. 8: αἴρεται ἀπὸ τῆς γῆς ἡ ζωὴ αὐτοῦ. In the opinion of some (cf. McNeile, 121; A. T. Cadoux, 72-4) a non-violent death is indicated, but this view is not

convincing, especially in the light of Isa. liii. 8. Cf. Lohmeyer, 60. This passage may be in mind in the Markan saying, and in any case it illustrates the use of the simplex verb with reference to a violent death. In this verse the allegorical use of νυμφίος is generally recognized. Indeed, this is one of the reasons why the genuineness of the verse is suspected, on the ground that in 19a ' while the bridegroom is with them ' means ' during the marriage festivities '. Cf. Wellhausen, 18; Dodd, 116 n.

Allegorization, we have contended, is present in both verses. It may be doubted, however, if this is the best word to use. The use by Jesus of νυμφίος corresponds to His use of the third person in speaking of Himself as ' the Son of Man '. Moreover, there is no allegory in ἀπαρθῇ ἀπ' αὐτῶν, nor indeed in the rest of the sentence. νηστεύσουσιν is the language of prophecy, but to take it as prophesying the future institution of fasting seems unnecessarily prosaic. The idea of mourning of which fasting is a sign is uppermost. The phrase ἐν ἐκείνῃ τῇ ἡμέρᾳ after τότε (surprisingly rare in Mk, 6 times*, of which 4 are in xiii) is formally redundant, but it adds a peculiar impressiveness to the forecast which is lost by its omission in Mt. ix. 15. Luke has ἐν ἐκείναις ταῖς ἡμέραις (v. 35).

The view that 19b, 20 is a later addition to 19a, meant to justify the practice of fasting in the later Christian community, is widely accepted. Cf. Wellhausen, 18 f.; Bultmann, 17; Bousset, 40 f.; Dibelius, 65; Branscomb, 53 f. (apparently the whole reply, 19 f.). The prophecy of the Passion, it is held, stands too early in Mk and is best explained as a vaticinium ex eventu; 20 is allegorical as compared with 19a; and the attitude to fasting in 20 is at variance with that reflected in the claim that groomsmen cannot fast. Criticism itself has weakened the force of the first of these objections, for it is now widely recognized that the incident may have happened later (cf. Menzies, 87; Bartlet, 136 f.; K. L. Schmidt, 86-9; Cadoux, 57), its present position in Mk being due to the Evangelist's use of a pre-Markan group. The dubious objection based upon the presence of allegory is discussed above. The argument based upon fasting rests too exclusively on 19a without taking into account other sayings of Jesus, e.g. Mt. vi. 16. Finally, the poetic structure of 19 f. renders the hypothesis of redaction precarious. 19a and b provide a good example of Semitic parallelism, and there is also a contrast between 19a and 20a and between 19b and 20b. Cf. Albertz, 8 f. In short, the critical hypothesis in question is not convincing, and fails to take account of the delicate allusiveness of 19 f.

Mk. ii. 21 f.   **15. SAYINGS ON PATCHES**   Cf. Mt. ix. 16 f.
AND WINESKINS   Lk. v. 36-8

The Evangelist may have found these sayings already attached to the story about fasting or may have added them himself from some existing sayings-collection. In any case they probably had an independent existence, since ii. 18-20 is a unity in itself, and because the principle implicit in them is more radical than a question about a pious custom would warrant. In what circumstances they were first uttered it is impossible to say. Like many parabolic sayings they may be remnants of Pronouncement-stories from which statements have fallen away in the process of transmission. The sentiments they express are revolutionary, since they affirm that a new message must find a fresh vehicle, if it is not to perish and to destroy existing institutions. In this respect the sayings recall New Testament passages in which the new stands in contrast with the old; cf. Rom. vii. 6, Eph. iv. 22 ff., Col. iii. 9 f., and Heb. viii. 13. It is not surprising that they are sometimes held to reflect Pauline influence; cf. Intr. 125-9. What is perhaps more surprising is the failure to consider rather whether they do not bear the stamp of originality and state principles which naturally and inevitably were developed in Pauline teaching.

21   Οὐδεὶς ἐπίβλημα ῥάκους ἀγνάφου ἐπιράπτει ἐπὶ ἱμάτιον παλαιόν· εἰ δὲ μή, αἴρει τὸ πλήρωμα ἀπ᾽ αὐτοῦ [τὸ καινὸν τοῦ

21. Here and Mt. ix. 16 and Lk. v. 36 (bis)** ἐπίβλημα is used with the meaning ' patch '. In Cl. Gk, in accordance with its derivation, it can mean a ' coverlet ', a ' bedspread ', ' tapestry ', or a ' bandage ', and in the LXX a ' mantle ' or ' covering ' (cf. Isa. iii. 22 ; Jos. ix. 5 (11), Symm.), as also in early inscriptions (VGT, 236). ῥάκος, here and Mt. ix. 16**, is used in later Gk, the LXX (Jer. xlv. (xxxviii.) 11), and the papyri (VGT, 563), with the meaning ' a piece of cloth ', ' rag ', or ' lint '. Its character is described by ἄγναφος (= Cl. ἄγναπτος)

' not fulled ' or ' carded ' (Pap. ' new ', VGT, 4), i.e. not treated by the fuller (γναφεύς). Thus, ἐπίβλημα ῥάκους ἀγνάφου is 'a patch of undressed cloth'. Matthew reproduces the phrase, but Luke simplifies it by the paraphrase ἐπίβλημα ἀπὸ ἱματίου καινοῦ σχίσας (v. 36), thus suggesting the spoiling of a new garment. ἐπιράπτω**, ' to sew ', a late verb, not illustrated in VGT. ἱμάτιον, an (outer) garment ' (ctr. χιτών), 12 times*. παλαιός, ' old ', 3 times in ii. 21 f.*.

Matthew and Luke agree in replacing ἐπιράπτει by ἐπιβάλλει. As

παλαιοῦ], καὶ χεῖρον σχίσμα γίνεται. καὶ οὐδεὶς βάλλει οἶνον 22
νέον εἰς ἀσκοὺς παλαιούς· εἰ δὲ μή, ῥήξει ὁ οἶνος τοὺς ἀσκούς,
καὶ ὁ οἶνος ἀπόλλυται καὶ οἱ ἀσκοί. [ἀλλὰ οἶνον νέον εἰς ἀσκοὺς
καινούς.]

Streeter, 310, observes, the noun ἐπίβλημα almost shouts out to an editor
to alter the verb to ἐπιβάλλει.

εἰ δὲ μή, ' otherwise ', a classical use
(LS, 481*b*) found also in the papyri
(*VGT*, 122*a*). The verb in the protasis is omitted. πλήρωμα, vi. 43, viii.
20*, ' that which fills ', ' the complement '. As against the passive meaning ' fullness ', for which Lightfoot,
Col. 257 ff. contends, see J. A. Robinson's note, *Eph.* 255 ff. See also W.
Lock, *HDB*, iv. 1 f. Like ἐπίβλημα,
the word might be rendered ' patch ';
cf. Rawlinson, 32; McNeile, 122;
Allen, 70; Smith, 118. Wellhausen,
19, thinks that it is an Aramaism, representing a word from the root מְלָא,
' to fill '. Cf. Black, 96. It is found,
however, in the vernacular, although
rarely, in the sense of ' company ',
' complement ' (*VGT*, 520). The
phrase τὸ καινὸν τοῦ παλαιοῦ, in apposition with τὸ πλήρωμα, appears to
mean ' the new part of the old garment ' (cf. Swete, 46), but although
implied in Lk. v. 36, τὸ ἀπὸ τοῦ καινοῦ,
it is probably an early explanatory
gloss; cf. Wellhausen, 19; Klostermann, 33; Bultmann, 79; Burney,
PL, 141. καὶ χεῖρον σχίσμα γίνεται,
' and a worse rent is the result ', Swete,
46; McNeile, 123; Black, 69.
The general sense of this saying is
the incompatibility of combining the
new with the old. The patch of undressed cloth shrinks, and so the old
garment is torn further. Many commentators take the saying as referring
either to the Pharisees or to the disciples of John. Cf. Swete, 45; B.
Weiss, 38 f.; Lagrange, 49-51. But
it seems more probable that the two
sayings in 21 f. were appended by
Mark to 18-20. ' We do not know —
and it is idle to guess — in what context they were originally spoken. They

are characteristic sayings of Jesus, unforgettable in their homely vividness
and power ', Rawlinson, 32.

22. This saying is connected in the
simplest possible way with 21 by καί,
and it is constructed in the same manner : first, a negative principle, and
then a statement of what follows if it is
not observed. The common verb βάλλω
is here used in a softened sense, with
the meaning ' to put ' or ' pour '. For
this meaning in the vernacular *v.*
VGT, 102. οἶνος, here 4 times and xv.
23*. Although the distinction between νέος*, ' new ', *recens*, in respect
of time, and καινός, ' fresh ', in quality,
is not emphasized in the papyri (*VGT*
314 f.), it is clearly marked in this saying.
The wine is newly made and must
not be put into old skins. ἀσκός, here
four times*, ' skin ', ' leathern bag or
bottle ', ' wineskin '; Cl., LXX, Pap.
Neglect of this rule means that the
fermenting wine bursts the skins and
both the wine and the skins are lost.
ῥήγνυμι* (cf. ix. 18), ' to rend ', ' break
asunder '; Cl., LXX, Pap. Matthew
and Luke agree in mentioning the loss
of the wine and the destruction of the
skins separately. The wine is spilled
(Lk. v. 37, ἐκχυθήσεται, Mt. ix. 17, ἐκ-
χεῖται). This agreement against Mk
disappears if, with Streeter, 311, ἐκ-
χεῖται in Mt, which D a k omit or
otherwise alter, is attributed to assimilation from Lk.
The words, ἀλλὰ οἶνον νέον εἰς ἀσκοὺς
καινούς, are omitted by D a b ff, and
enclosed by WH in square brackets.
Cf. Lk. v. 38, ἀλλὰ οἶνον νέον εἰς ἀσκοὺς
καινοὺς βλητέον, and Mt. ix. 17, ἀλλὰ
βάλλουσιν οἶνον νέον εἰς ἀσκοὺς καινούς,
καὶ ἀμφότεροι συντηροῦνται. The passage in Mk is frequently explained as
due to assimilation. But Streeter, 311,
points out that the line divisions in D
are such that, if the words stood in

that MS., ' the words οἶνος ἀσκός, separated by only a few letters, would have occurred in each of three successive lines '. The formation, he suggests, is one which invites accidental omission. He therefore retains the bracketed passage in Mk. If this view is accepted, it does not exclude the possibility that, while the clause may be original in the Markan text, it may have been added to the saying earlier as an exegetical comment. Turner, 19 (cf. *JTS*, xxvi. 147), points out that, if the preceding clause, εἰ δὲ μή . . . ἀσκοί, is read as a parenthesis, no such

insertion as ' they put ' (RV) is necessary. This is true, for in this way the saying takes the form of antithetic parallelism : ' No one puts new wine into old wineskins ; but new wine into fresh wineskins ' ; but it is doubtful if the clause is a parenthesis, since in 21 the very similar line is the second element in the two-lined strophe. The structural form of 21 f. is *a b a b*, and to this couplet 22c seems an addition. The gerundive βλητέον, read by אa A C L *et al.*, is clearly an assimilation to Lk, and καὶ ἀμφότεροι συντηροῦνται, 118mg e f, an assimilation to Mt.

Mk. ii. 23-6   16. CORNFIELDS AND THE   Cf. Mt. xii. 1-4
QUESTION OF THE SABBATH   Lk. vi. 1-4

In this Pronouncement-story, after a brief allusion to the circumstances, a question is put to Jesus to which He replies by a counter-question. Schmidt, 89, describes the narrative as a characteristic example of an isolated story without statements about place and time (*ein Musterbeispiel für eine örtlich und zeitlich nicht festgelegte Einzelerzählung*). Cf. Dibelius, 46 ; Bultmann, 14 f. ; Albertz, 9 f. The simplicity of the Markan narrative is well revealed by a comparison with the parallels in Lk and Mt, in which attempts are made to give the story a more literary form, in Lk by the insertion of the mysterious δευτεροπρώτῳ (cf. Hort, 58 ; *VGT*, 143), in Mt by the introductory phrase ἐν ἐκείνῳ τῷ καιρῷ, by the addition of further proofs from Scripture, and by bringing Mk. ii. 28 within the story in the culminating phrase : κύριος γάρ ἐστιν τοῦ σαββάτου ὁ υἱὸς τοῦ ἀνθρώπου (xii. 8). Simple, however, as the Markan narrative is, it has a colourful introduction in the picture of Jesus passing through the cornfields on the sabbath day, and of the disciples plucking the ears of corn as they go. But this detail is strictly subordinate to the question of eating on the Sabbath, which is the main point of the story, and nothing beyond what is necessary is told. The picturesque addition of Luke, ' rubbing them in their hands ', is wanting in Mk. The probability that the incident happened in the weeks from April to the beginning of June is not based on a temporal statement, but on the fact that the corn was ripe for eating. The narrative is a popular story current in the early Christian community and preserved because it dealt with the burning issue of the observance of the Sabbath.

How real this issue must have been is evident from the fact that it is raised in a second Markan story, the Man with the Withered Hand, in the Lukan stories of the Bent Woman (xiii. 10-17) and the Man with Dropsy (xiv. 1-6), and the Johannine narratives of the Impotent Man at Bethesda (v. 1-19) and the Man born Blind (ix. i-41). From an early date, in consequence of the Resurrection, the first day of the week was observed in early Christianity (cf. Apoc. i. 10, ἐν τῇ κυριακῇ ἡμέρᾳ; Ignatius, *Ad Magn.* ix. 1, the Gospel of Peter 9, the *Didache*, xiv. 1); and for this reason it is natural that conflict-stories on the question of the Sabbath were remembered and told.

These considerations, as well as the character of Mk. ii. 23-6, forbid the view that the narrative element in the Markan story is a mere framework designed as a setting for a proof from Scripture cited by Jesus (cf. Bultmann, 14). The free use of the story of David corresponds to the manner in which He uses the Old Testament elsewhere, and the broad humanity of the narrative is characteristic.

Καὶ ἐγένετο αὐτὸν ἐν τοῖς σάββασιν ⌜παραπορεύεσθαι⌝ διὰ τῶν 23
σπορίμων, καὶ οἱ μαθηταὶ αὐτοῦ ἤρξαντο ⌜ὁδὸν ποιεῖν⌝ τίλλοντες

23 διαπορεύεσθαι | ὁδοποιεῖν

23. Without personal names or any mention of time or place, beyond the reference to the cornfields and the growing corn, the narrative begins abruptly with the καὶ ἐγένετο c. acc. and infin. construction. For the syntax see i. 9. διαπορεύομαι*, Lk. vi. 1, xiii. 22, xviii. 36, Ac. xvi. 4, Rom. xv. 24**, ' to pass across ', ' go through '; Cl., LXX, Pap. The infin. is attested here by B C D c e ff r¹, but παραπορεύεσθαι, ' to pass by ', is read by almost all other uncials and minuscules. This widely attested reading is accepted in Nestle's text and WHᵐᵍ, and by K. L. Schmidt, 89, Lagrange, 51, Lohmeyer, 62, and other commentators. Cf. Moulton, i. 17 n. Two considerations strongly favour it: (1) the change to διαπορεύεσθαι can readily be explained as the substitution of a more exact expression and an assimilation to Lk. vi. 1, whereas there is no reason why διαπορεύεσθαι should be replaced by παραπορεύεσθαι; (2) if Mark wrote παραπορεύεσθαι (ix. 30, xi. 20, xv. 29*, Mt. xxvii. 39**), ἐπορεύθη in Mt. xii. 1, and διαπορεύεσθαι in Lk. vi. 1, are clearly meant as improvements. There is indeed much to be said for Moulton's suggestion, i. 17, that the isolated example of καὶ ἐγένετο c. infin. in this passage ' is perhaps a primitive assimilation to Lk. vi. 1 ', and that παραπορεύεσθαι ' may be a relic of Mk's original text '.

σπόριμος, ' sown ', ' fit for sowing '; τὰ σπόριμα*, Mt. xii. 1, Lk. vi. 1**,

' cornfields '; Cl., LXX, Pap. ὁδὸν ποιεῖν means, literally, ' to make (build) a way ', but it is probably used in the sense of *iter facere* = ὁδὸν ποιεῖσθαι ' to journey ', as in Jud. xvii. 8, τοῦ ποιῆσαι τὴν ὁδὸν αὐτοῦ. Cf. Moulton, i. 159, ii. 389; Souter, 171; Field, 25; *VGT*, 438. It would be possible to translate the Greek in the sense: ' they began to make a road by plucking the ears of corn ' (so Bacon, *BGS*, 30 f.), or, explaining ὁδὸν ποιεῖν as above, by the rendering: ' they began to advance by plucking . . .'. From the sequel, however, it appears that the disciples' offence is not that of working or of exceeding the limits of a Sabbath day's journey, but of gathering and eating food on the Sabbath. Mark, therefore, must mean that the disciples ' began, as they went, to pluck ' (RV; Swete, 47; Plummer, 94; Lagrange, 51; and most commentators). The main idea is expressed by the participle, the infin. being subordinate in force. As Wellhausen, 20, observes, better Greek to express this meaning would have been, ἤρξαντο ὁδοποιοῦντες τίλλειν. Matthew has ἤρξαντο τίλλειν (xii. 1), and Luke ἔτιλλον (vi. 1).

The MS. tradition shows how difficult copyists found Mark's words: B G H 1 209 565* 892 read ὁδοποιεῖν τίλλοντες, fam. 13 543 a ὁδοιποροῦντες τίλλοντες, and D W b c e ff ἤρξαντο τίλλειν. Klostermann, 35, suggests the influence of Aramaic. τίλλω, Mk. ii. 23 = Mt. xii. 1 = Lk. vi. 1**, Cl., LXX, Pap.

24 τοὺς στάχυας. καὶ οἱ Φαρισαῖοι ἔλεγον αὐτῷ ῎Ιδε τί ποιοῦσιν
25 τοῖς σάββασιν ὃ οὐκ ἔξεστιν; καὶ λέγει αὐτοῖς Οὐδέποτε ἀνέγνωτε τί ἐποίησεν Δαυεὶδ ὅτε χρείαν ἔσχεν καὶ ἐπείνασεν αὐτὸς
26 καὶ οἱ μετ' αὐτοῦ; [πῶς] εἰσῆλθεν εἰς τὸν οἶκον τοῦ θεοῦ ἐπὶ

στάχυς, iv. 28 (bis)*, Mt. xii. 1, Lk. vi. 1**, 'an ear of corn'. There are no signs of an old acc. pl. in -ῦς (cf. Thackeray, 147) in the NT (cf. Moulton, ii. 142). In the papyri the word appears in farm accounts (VGT, 587). This reference to growing corn is the only clear indication in the Synoptic Gospels (cf. vi. 39) that the Ministry covered at least a year. The incident must have happened in the few weeks after Passover, from April to the beginning of June. Cf. Lagrange, 52; Schmidt, 89-92. How much longer the Ministry lasted we do not know. In view of the gaps in the Synoptic outline, before Mk. i. 16, 21, and ii. 1, etc., it would be precarious to conclude that, in contrast with Jn, the Synoptic Gospels imply that it lasted a year only. See further, the note on vi. 39 ('the green grass').

24. The imperf. ἔλεγον appears to be used loosely for the aor. Mt and Lk have εἶπαν. ἴδε, iii. 34, xi. 21, xiii. 1, 21, xv. 4, 35, xvi. 6*, 'behold!'. Already, even in Attic Gk, the word had lost much of its imperatival force and had become little more than an interjection. ἔξεστιν, ii. 26, iii. 4, vi. 18, x. 2, xii. 14*, impers. verb, 'it is lawful', 'permitted'. It is used c. acc. and infin. in ii. 26 and Lk. vi. 4, xx. 22, and with the dat. in vi. 18 and x. 2. The breach of the Law did not consist in the act of gleaning in itself, which is permitted in Deut. xxiii. 24 f., but in what was regarded as reaping on the Sabbath (Ex. xxxiv. 21). Cf. Moore, ii. 29. The Rabbis enumerated 39 different kinds of work which were forbidden on the Sabbath and later distinguished six sub-classes under each. For the 39 classes v. Shab. vii. 2, Danby, 106. See also Schürer, II. ii. 97; Billerbeck, i. 615-18, 623-9. Exceptions were recognized, e.g. in the

case of duties at the Temple (Mt. xii. 5, cf. Numb. xxviii. 9 f.), the unloosing of cattle, and other actions in which life was at stake. Cf. Klostermann, 34 f.; Jackson and Lake, i. 436 f.; Abrahams, i. 129-35. 'Yet no Pharisee would consent to the conclusion that it was permissible to pluck corn on the Sabbath', Klausner, 278. Montefiore, i. 63 f., says it is a remarkable fact that, 'in spite of the many restrictions and regulations, the Sabbath was upon the whole a joy and a blessing to the immense majority of Jews throughout the Rabbinic period'. Christian scholars have fully recognized the truth of such claims (v. Manson, SJ, 189 f.), but it is also true that the Sabbath was hedged about by burdensome restrictions, as the Gospels attest.

25. ἀναγινώσκω, xii. 10, 26, xiii. 14*. This use of the counter-question with an appeal to the Scriptures is characteristic of Rabbinical arguments (cf. Fiebig, Der Erzählungsstil der Evangelien, 107-12) and is used effectively by Jesus in xii. 10, 'Have ye not read even this scripture . . . ?', and 26, 'Have ye not read in the book of Moses . . . ?'. Δαυείδ, x. 47 f., xi. 10, xii. 35 (bis), 37*. The incident of the request of David for bread is related in 1 Sam. xxi. 1-6. Rawlinson, 34, is justified in saying that it is over-subtle to see in the allusion a veiled Messianic claim. The story is cited for its broad humanity and because of the acknowledged greatness of David. The words χρείαν ἔσχεν καὶ ἐπείνασεν are an added inference after the manner of Haggada, χρείαν ἔσχεν being peculiar to Mark's account. πεινάω, xi. 12*. For οἱ μετ' αὐτοῦ v. i. 36. For the fut. and aor. stems of πεινάω and the disappearance of the -ήω verbs from the Koine v. Moulton, i. 54, ii. 253; Thackeray, i. 242.

26. πῶς is omitted by B D r¹ t and

'Αβιάθαρ ἀρχιερέως καὶ τοὺϲ ἄρτουϲ τῆϲ προθέϲεωϲ ἔφαγεν, οὓς οὐκ ἔξεστιν φαγεῖν εἰ μὴ τοὺς ἱερεῖς, καὶ ἔδωκεν καὶ τοῖς σὺν αὐτῷ οὖσιν;

a has *et*. It may be an assimilation to Mt. xii. 4 (Lk. vi. 4 has [ὡς]) Cf. Allen, 71. On the other hand it may be that Mt and Lk imply the presence of πῶς in their source. A confident decision is hardly possible.

'The house of God', ὁ οἶκος τοῦ θεοῦ, is the name used in the LXX (Jud. xviii. 31, cf. 1 Kgdms. i. 7, 24) for the tent or shrine in which the sacred ark was kept. In the phrase ἐπὶ 'Αβιάθαρ ἀρχιερέως, ἐπί c. gen. means 'in the days of' (cf. Lk. iii. 2, Ac. xi. 28), and the absence of the article indicates that Abiathar is regarded as the high priest. The statement is incorrect, since at the time Ahimelech, the father of Abiathar, held office (cf. 1 Sam. xxi. 1, xxii. 20). For attempts to meet this difficulty see Lagrange, 53 f.; cf. also J. W. Wenham, *JTS* (N.S.), i. 156. The insertion of τοῦ before ἀρχιερέως in A C Θ *et al.* 1 fam. 13 28 33 543 565 579 700 1071 *al. plur.*, which would imply that Abiathar was not necessarily high priest at the time, is probably also an indication that the historical difficulty was felt in the east. The statement about Abiathar is either a primitive error or a copyists's gloss occasioned by the fact that, in association with David, Abiathar was better known than his father. The absence of the phrase in D W 271 a b e ff i r¹ t sʸˢ and in Mt and Lk can support either explanation. That it is a gloss has been frequently suggested (cf. Stanton, ii. 145; Swete, 48; Bartlet, 140; Branscomb, 57; McNeile, 168), but there are no compelling reasons in favour of this view. The probability of a primitive error cannot, therefore, be excluded, especially as the Markan story varies in detail from the account in 1 Sam. The statement that David entered into the shrine and ate and gave the loaves to his companions is a free expansion of the original narrative (cf. 1 Sam. xxi. 6,

'So the priest gave him holy bread'). Some confusion in the tradition is apparent from the first if 1 Sam. xxii. 20 is compared with 2 Sam. viii. 17; cf. A. R. S. Kennedy, *1 and 2 Sam.* 233. There are many references to bread in Mk, ἄρτος being used no less than 21 times. In the phrase οἱ ἄρτοι τῆς προθέσεως the noun πρόθεσις*, elsewhere 'purpose', is used in the literal sense of 'setting forth'. In the LXX (1 Kgdms. xxi. 6, Ex. xl. 23, etc.) this phrase, along with other expressions (ἄρτοι τοῦ προσώπου, ἄρτοι τῆς προσφορᾶς, ἄρτοι ἐνώπιοι), corresponds to the Heb. הַפָּנִים לֶחֶם, lit. 'bread of the face', 'presence-bread' (RVᵐᵍ). It describes the twelve newly baked loaves, the 'shewbread', placed every Sabbath in two rows on a table before God in the Tabernacle and later eaten by the priests (cf. Lev. xxiv. 5-9). Deissmann, *BS*, 157, suggests a possibly parallel usage in Egyptian Saturn worship, and quotes Athen. iii. 110 b, 'Αλεξανδρεῖς τῷ Κρόνῳ ἀφιεροῦντες προτιθέασιν ἐσθίειν τῷ βουλομένῳ ἐν τῷ τοῦ Κρόνου ἱερῷ. See further G. B. Gray, *Sacrifice in the OT*, 9 f., 27; Moore, *EB*, cols. 4211 f.

Instead of τοὺς ἱερεῖς, acc. subj. to φαγεῖν (א B 892), which with ἔξεστιν is correct although rare (cf. Lagrange, 53), the dat. τοῖς ἱερεῦσιν is read by A C D W Θ *et al.* fam. 1 22 28 565 700 *al. pler.* a ff i vg sys pe hl bo. μόνοις is also read by many MSS., but this reading is probably an assimilation to Lk. vi. 4; cf. Streeter, 312. The statement, 'which it is not lawful to eat save for the priests', is based on Lev. xxiv. 9, 'And it shall be for Aaron and his sons', a passage which may belong to a period later than that represented by 1 Sam. xxi, when greater liberty was possible. Turner, 20, suggests that the Markan phrase may be editorial, but it seems probable that the pointed use of οὐκ ἔξεστιν, with its backward reference to ii. 24, may be original.

Mk. ii. 27 f.   17. SAYINGS ON THE SABBATH   Cf. Mt. xii. 8
                                                            Lk. vi. 5

While 27 f. is often held to belong to the story of Cornfields on the
Sabbath Day, recent discussion tends to regard these sayings as isolated
logia appended to the narrative for topical reasons. Cf. Bultmann, 14 f. ;
Dibelius, 64 f. ; Schmidt, 97 ; Albertz, 10 ; Rawlinson, 33. It is significant that Lagrange, 56, finds it necessary to suggest a small literary
pause at the beginning of 27. There can be little doubt that the sayings
have been added, either by Mark or an earlier compiler, from a sayings-
collection. In support of this view it may be noted that (1) 23-6 reaches
its natural climax in the question about David ; (2) the phrase καὶ ἔλεγεν
αὐτοῖς may be a formula of citation ; (3) while 27 agrees with the ideas
of 23-6 and 28 presupposes 27, the final saying about the Son of Man
appears awkwardly in its present setting and has occasioned the recastings
traceable in Mt, Lk, and Codex D ; and (4) the sayings are gnomic as
compared with the polemical utterances in 25 f. The process of compilation is like that illustrated in ii. 21 and may have antedated the
composition of the Gospel. See further, Intr. 91 f.

27   Καὶ ἔλεγεν αὐτοῖς Τὸ σάββατον διὰ τὸν ἄνθρωπον ἐγένετο

27. The phrase καὶ ἔλεγεν αὐτοῖς is
frequently used in Mk, apparently
here and in iv. 13, 21, 24, vi. 10, vii. 9,
and ix. 1 as a connecting-link (cf. also
iv. 11, vii. 14, 20, viii. 34). For parallels to διά c. acc. = ' for ', ' because
of ', ' for the sake of ', cf. 2 Macc. v. 19,
οὐ διὰ τὸν τόπον τὸ ἔθνος, ἀλλὰ διὰ τὸ
ἔθνος τὸν τόπον ὁ κύριος ἐξελέξατο, and
1 Cor. xi. 9, καὶ γὰρ οὐκ ἐκτίσθη ἀνὴρ
διὰ τὴν γυναῖκα, ἀλλὰ γυνὴ διὰ τὸν ἄνδρα.
The saying is not recorded in Mt and
Lk, and in Mk it is omitted by D a c e
ff i, while 27b is wanting in W and sys.
D and it read λέγω δὲ ὑμῖν + 28 and W
has λέγω δὲ ὑμῖν ὅτι + 27a, 28.[1]
In the light of this evidence it is
natural to explain 27 as a ' Western
non-interpolation ' (cf. Branscomb,
58), that is, an addition which has
affected all families except the Western,
and it might seem surprising that few
commentators (cf. Ed. Meyer, i. 106 n.)
have taken this view. But there are
strong reasons for hesitation. Matthew
may have omitted 27 because it was
a ' hard saying ' for Jewish Christians
(cf. Hawkins, 122), and because his

main purpose was to show that the
Christ, who is ' greater than the temple ',
is ' lord of the Sabbath ' (xii. 6-8). It
is less easy to explain its omission by
Luke. Schmidt, 98, suggests that he
omitted it because its ideas are illustrated in xiii. 10 ff. and xiv. 1 ff.
Further, the καί in Lk. vi. 5, omitted
in ℵ B and some versions because it
seemed superfluous, suggests that
Luke read Mk. ii. 27 in his source ;
cf. Schmidt, 98; Wellhausen, 21.[2]
We cannot agree then that the saying
is a later addition, especially as it seems
the necessary premiss for 28. Cf.
Bultmann, 14.[3]
The saying is usually interpreted
as referring to mankind. T. W. Manson, CN, xi. 138-46, has suggested
that it should be rendered : ' The Sabbath was made for the Son of Man,
and not the Son of Man for the Sabbath '. This rendering is based on
Rabbinic teaching to the effect that
the Sabbath was made for Israel only
(cf. the comment of R. Simeon b.
Menasya in the Mekilta on Ex. xxxi.
14, and Jub. ii. 31) and similar teaching

[1] The reading ἐκτίσθη (for ἐγένετο) found in W fam. 1 (exc. 118) 700 sy s pe aeth is secondary.
[2] Wellhausen points out that in Lk the καί stands in the same place as in Mk verräterischerweise.
[3] Ich halte es indessen für überwiegend wahrscheinlich, dass v. 27 zum ursprünglichen
Mk-text gehört (vgl. Wellhausen z. St.).

καὶ οὐχ ὁ ἄνθρωπος διὰ τὸ σάββατον· ὥστε κύριός ἐστιν ὁ υἱὸς 28
τοῦ ἀνθρώπου καὶ τοῦ σαββάτου.

regarding creation (*Assumpt. Mos.* i.
12, 4 Ezra vi. 55-9, vii. 11). Cf.
Hermas, *Vis.* I. i. 6, II. iv. 1, in which
it is said that the world was created
for the ' Church '. Manson argues:
(1) that in fact the Sabbath was made
for the Jews, not man in general; (2)
that if 27 is rendered as above, there
is no difficulty about the conclusion in
28; (3) that *bar nasha* could be misunderstood as meaning ' man ', when
' Son of Man ' was intended; (4) that,
in the context, it is the disciples, ' the
people of the saints of the Most High ',
who break the Sabbatic regulations;
and (5) that Jesus and His disciples
regard the exigencies of the service of
the Kingdom as cancelling out the
claims of Sabbath observance. This
view is of the greatest interest. Against
it may be urged the doubt whether 27 f.
can be connected closely with 23-6,
the possibility that Jesus took a wider
view of the Sabbath than the Jewish
claim that it was made for Israel alone,
and the want of evidence that He
taught that it was made for the Elect
Community. For the connexion of
27 and 28 see below.

All the commentators cite the
opinion of R. Simeon b. Menasya
mentioned above, ' The Sabbath is
delivered unto you, and ye are not delivered to the Sabbath ', with reference
to Ex. xxxi. 14: ' Ye shall keep the
Sabbath therefore; for it is holy unto
you '. For other parallels *v.* Billerbeck, ii. 5; Lagrange, 54 f.; Klostermann, 36; Abrahams, i. 129 f. It is
natural that Rabbinical teaching
should emphasize what was in fact a
distinctive Jewish institution (cf.
Moore, ii. 22), but the tendency is to
speak of it as a gift. It is doubtful if
we should explain ' man ' in 27 as
meaning ' mankind ' in an abstract
sense; it means man as man, as a
human being in his frailty. With
some exaggeration Abrahams, i. 129,
says of the epigram coined by Jesus:

' The Pharisees would have done, nay,
did do, the same '. Montefiore, i. 63 f.,
compares the attitude of Jesus with
that of liberal Judaism to-day: ' His
teaching is an excellent counterbalance
to that casuistic minuteness which is
the danger of legalism. It is emanci-
pating; it enables one to breathe
freely.' ·

28. ὥστε c. indic. x. 8*, ' so that ';
c. infin. *v.* i. 27. The phrase κύριος
τοῦ σαββάτου describes one who exercises authority over the use of the
Sabbath. The thought is that, since
the Sabbath was made for man, He
who is man's Lord and Representative
has authority to determine its laws and
use. ' I do not think that the argument
is *necessarily* illogical even if Jesus
did here use " Son of man ", or rather
" the Man ", to mean Himself as the
Messiah', Montefiore, i. 62. καί, ' also '
or ' even ', is closely related to τοῦ
σαββάτου, implying 27. For ὁ υἱὸς τοῦ
ἀνθρώπου see the note on ii. 10.

The opinion of Wellhausen, 20,
following that of Grotius, that the
Aramaic original means ' man ', has
been widely accepted, often with the
proviso that the alternative is to explain
28 as a later Christian formation. Cf.
Bultmann, 14 f.; Ed. Meyer, i. 106 n.;
Branscomb, 58 f.; McNeile, 170;
Creed, 84; Luce, 138; Cadoux, 75,
95. Manson (*v. supra*) has renounced
the view expressed in *TJ*, 24, 213 f.
Other scholars think that the passage
is a comment added by Mark (Klostermann, 36; Smith, 131) or an unknown hand (Rawlinson, 33; Bartlet,
140). The older commentators explain
' Son of Man ' as a Messianic self-
designation (cf. Lagrange, 56; Gould,
50) which carries with it the idea of the
Ideal and Representative Man (cf.
Swete, 50; Plummer, 97).

In spite of wide support, it is very
doubtful if Wellhausen's interpretation is correct. Rawlinson, 34, justly
says: ' Our Lord would not have been

likely to say that " man " was " lord of the Sabbath ", which had been instituted by God '. It is difficult also to think that a redactor would have added such a comment except in the most liberal Christian circles (cf. Rom. xiv. 5). That the claim is made of the Elect Community is much more probable, if Jesus speaks in His own name as its Head. Nevertheless, there are strong objections to the view that the saying is an original utterance. Nowhere else does Jesus claim personal lordship over the Sabbath (cf. Rawlin-

son, 34 ; Lohmeyer, 66) save in action (iii. 1-6). Moreover, the verse reads like a Christian comment. Burney, *PL*, 98 f., has claimed that the couplet followed by a comment is a genuine form used by Jesus (in addition to 27 f. cf. Lk. vi. 13, 43, 45, xi. 34), but it may be questioned if the argument is conclusive. On the whole, it seems best to conclude that Mark found 27 supplemented by a Christian comment expressing the conviction that Jesus is the Lord of all that belongs to man, including the Sabbath.

Mk. iii. 1-6   18. ON THE SABBATH (THE   Cf. Mt. xii. 9-14
                      MAN WITH THE WITHERED   Lk. vi. 6-11
                            HAND)

The form is that of the Pronouncement-story. Cf. Dibelius, 43 ; Bultmann, 9 ; Albertz, 11 f. Its purpose is to give the teaching of Jesus on the question of healing on the Sabbath. Unlike the three preceding stories, no direct question is put as in the story of the Paralytic, but a hostile attitude is indicated which is met by a counter-question indicating a point of view confirmed by the healing. The story is not a Miracle-story because the healing is subordinate in interest to the religious question at issue.

The narrative is self-contained. There is no introduction beyond the connecting-link in πάλιν. Bultmann maintains that οἱ δὲ ἐσιώπων in 4 and the account of the healing in 5 form an organic conclusion and that there is no ground for assuming that the saying in 4 was originally an isolated logion. Verse 6 is redactional, but otherwise the narrative is an organic Apothegm formulated in the Palestinian community. More, however, must be said than this. The picture of the silent watchers who have made up their minds and wait for an opportunity to accuse Jesus (ii. 2), His action in bringing the man into the midst, and His grief at the blindness of their hearts (3-5), suggest a tradition based on reminiscence. The narrative differs from 16 f., 18-20, and 23-6 in the amount of Petrine tradition still attached to it. It is an original narrative which, by its concentration on the issue of the Sabbath, is on its way to become a Pronouncement-story. Mt. xii. 9-14 illustrates a later stage whereby such forms came into being, although here the process is literary. Lk. vi. 6-11 is a redactional development of the Markan story.

Dibelius and Albertz agree with Bultmann that iii. 6 is a later addition which rounds off the group of conflict-stories in ii. 1-iii. 6. Schmidt, 100, on the contrary, while admitting that the narrative could end with 5, thinks that the absence from 6 of the customary phrase ' the Pharisees and scribes ' favours the view that it is original. This is probably the better view. Already in 2 the words ' that they might accuse him ' prepare the way for 6 which is the climax to the narrative. In this case, 6 determined the place of iii. 1-6 within the complex ii. 1-iii. 6. The narrative serves a double purpose : it reveals decisively the attitude of Jesus to the Sabbath, and it shows how this attitude led to a final breach with the Pharisees. See further, the note on iii. 6. The common objection that the passage appears too early in the Markan outline loses much of its force if ii. 1-iii. 6 is pre-Markan. See Intr. 91 f.

Καὶ εἰσῆλθεν πάλιν εἰς συναγωγήν, καὶ ἦν ἐκεῖ ἄνθρωπος 1 III
ἐξηραμμένην ἔχων τὴν χεῖρα· καὶ παρετήρουν αὐτὸν εἰ τοῖς σάβ- 2
βασιν θεραπεύσει αὐτόν, ἵνα κατηγορήσωσιν αὐτοῦ. καὶ λέγει 3

1. The phrase εἰς συναγωγήν is used as we should speak of 'going to Church'. The art. is read by all Greek MSS. except ℵ B, but it is probably an assimilation to Mt or Lk intended as a grammatical improvement. πάλιν (v. ii. 1) points back to i. 21 and is added by Mark. It is the only attempt he makes to establish a connexion with what goes before. Cf. Matthew's addition μεταβὰς ἐκεῖθεν (xii. 9) and Luke's insertion of ἑτέρῳ in ἐν ἑτέρῳ σαββάτῳ (vi. 6) which connect the narrative with its context and so give it a more literary form. The presence of ἐκεῖ suggests that ἦν . . . ἔχων is not a periphrastic tense and that the participle is descriptive. ξηραίνω, iv. 6, v. 29, ix. 18, xi. 20 f.*, 'to dry up', 'wither'; Cl., LXX, Pap. Cf. Hawkins, 13.

Some commentators (Swete, 50; Lagrange, 57 ; Plummer, 99) suggest that ἐξηραμμένην implies that the paralysis was not from birth (cf. Bengel, morbo aut verbere), a point lost in ξηρός (Mt, Lk), but it is not certain that the distinction is intended (cf. Klostermann, 37). τὴν χεῖρα is 'his hand'; Luke adds ἡ δεξιά (vi. 6). According to Jerome, the Gospel ad Hebraeos described the man as a mason, who said to Jesus, 'I was a mason seeking a livelihood with my hands : I pray thee, Jesu, to restore me mine health, that I may not beg meanly for my food' (M. R. James, 4 f.). The affliction seems to have been some form of paralysis. Dr. R. J. Ryle, HJ, v (April 1907), 581 f., suggests infantile paralysis. On the scanty evidence available in the narrative accurate diagnosis is not possible, and the case might be one of

functional paralysis (cf. E. R. Micklem, 96). Similarly Schniewind, 65. For an interesting parallel see the extract from the Journal of John Banks (1637-1710) given by Micklem, which relates how a paralysed hand and arm were cured by the prayer of George Fox.

2. παρατηρέω*, Lk. vi. 7, xiv. 1, xx. 20, Ac. ix. 24, Gal. iv. 10**, 'to watch closely', 'observe scrupulously' (of days, Gal. iv. 10); Cl., LXX, Pap. (VGT, 490, of keeping a careful eye upon criminals). The mid. is more frequent in this sense (Lk. vi. 7), but the act. is also so used. So Lk. xx. 20. The imperf. παρετήρουν ought not to be described as impersonal ; cf. Lagrange, 57. The meaning is not that Jesus was watched by people in general, but by His enemies. Luke takes this view when he adds οἱ γραμματεῖς καὶ οἱ Φαρισαῖοι (vi. 7). In Mk (and Mt) their identity is left to be understood, and only by implication is it disclosed in iii. 6. The indirect question εἰ . . . θεραπεύσει is correctly used (cf. Goodwin, 256 f.). Matthew replaces it by the direct form εἰ ἔξεστι . . . θεραπεύειν; (xii. 10), but thereby loses the suggestion of the Markan story that Jesus divined their intent. Mark leaves this to be understood, but Luke expressly says αὐτὸς δὲ ᾔδει τοὺς διαλογισμοὺς αὐτῶν (vi. 8). Instead of θεραπεύσει ℵ W Δ Σ 271 read the present (cf. Lk. vi. 7).

The principle admitted by the Rabbis was that relief might be given to a sufferer when life was in danger. Cf. Schürer, II. ii. 104. See M. Shab. xviii. 3, Yom. viii. 6 (Danby, 116, 172). The presence therefore of the man offered a test case whether Jesus would

τῷ ἀνθρώπῳ τῷ τὴν χεῖρα ἔχοντι ξηράν "Εγειρε εἰς τὸ μέσον.
4 καὶ λέγει αὐτοῖς "Εξεστιν τοῖς σάββασιν ἀγαθοποιῆσαι ἢ κακο-
5 ποιῆσαι, ψυχὴν σῶσαι ἢ ἀποκτεῖναι; οἱ δὲ ἐσιώπων. καὶ περι-

observe the Rabbinic rule. κατηγορέω, xv. 3 f.*; Cl., LXX, Pap.

3. In this verse the unspoken challenge is met and for this reason the man is summoned into the open. For the intrans. use of ἐγείρω v. ii. 9. In ἔγειρε εἰς τὸ μέσον the construction is pregnant ('Arise and come'). Luke completes the sense by inserting καὶ στῆθι and by adding καὶ ἀναστὰς ἔστη (vi. 8). ξηρός*, 'dry', 'withered'. With εἰς τὸ μέσον* cf. εἰς μέσον in xiv. 60, ἐν μέσῳ vi. 47, ix. 36, ἀνὰ μέσον vii. 31*. Mt omits the verse because after the direct question in xii. 10 a saying of Jesus follows from Q or some other collection, to which there is a parallel in Lk. xiv. 5 (the saying about the sheep (Lk, son or ox) falling into a pit). He then transforms the question of Jesus into a statement: 'Wherefore it is lawful to do good on the sabbath day', and, omitting the descriptive details in Mk. iii. 5a, reproduces the account of the cure in iii. 5b almost verbatim. Thus, in Mt the narrative assumes the form of a Pronouncement-story, whereas in Mk and Lk an un-spoken challenge is perceived and met by action and speech. Luke reproduces the Markan story more exactly, omitting some of the details (cf. Mk. iii. 4) and elucidating others.

4. ἀγαθοποιέω*, Lk. vi. 9, 33, 35, 1 Pet. ii. 15, 20, iii. 6, 17, 3 Jn. 11**, 'to do good', is used in the LXX and in later Gk, the classical equivalent being εὖ ποιέω.¹ For ἀγαθοποιός v. VGT, 1. The verb is formed on the analogy of κακοποιέω*, Lk. vi. 9, 1 Pet. iii. 17, 3 Jn. 11**, 'to do evil'; Cl., LXX, Pap. ψυχή, viii. 35 (bis), 36 f., x. 45, xii. 30, xiv. 34*, 'breath', 'life', 'the self'. σώζω, 13 times and xvi. [16]*. In many of these cases it is a question of saving life (iii. 4, xv. 30 f.) or of deliverance from maladies and afflictions (v. 23, 28, 34, vi. 56, x. 52);

in others of the saving of the self (viii. 35, x. 26) or of deliverance from the Messianic Judgment (xiii. 13, 20). xvi. [16]: 'He that believeth and is baptized shall be saved', discloses a later point of view.

The silent question is answered by an ironical counter-question, as in ii. 23-6. The question sets right doing over against wrong doing, but has also a pointed and particular reference. 'Was it unlawful on the Sabbath to rescue a life from incipient death (ψυχὴν σῶσαι), and yet lawful to watch for the life of another, as they were doing at the moment?' (Swete, 52; cf. Rawlinson, 36; Lohmeyer, 69). Turner, 20, and Bartlet, 143, think this exposition over-subtle, but it is difficult to agree, for those addressed are reduced to silence. Had only a general principle been announced, they might have replied that the healing could be postponed until the next day; cf. Montefiore, i. 82. σιωπάω, iv. 39, ix. 34, x. 48, xiv. 61*, 'to be (or 'keep') silent'; Cl., LXX, Pap. An alternative explanation, that failure to do a good action is in itself evil-doing (cf. Klostermann, 37) is less satisfactory (cf. Wood, 684).

5. περιβλέπω, iii. 34, v. 32, ix. 8, x. 23, xi. 11*, Lk. vi. 10**, 'to look around'; Cl., LXX, Pap. In the NT the verb is used only in the mid., in all cases (except ix. 8) of the swift searching glance of Jesus upon His friends or enemies. As its record shows, the word is Markan (v. HS, 13). This reference to the look of Jesus is in line with Mark's not in-frequent allusions to the human emotions of Jesus, for one must reject Lohmeyer's view that they are the emotions of the divine Son of Man as in Jn. xi. 33 f.; v. Lohmeyer, 69. Cf. μετ' ὀργῆς and συνλυπούμενος ἐπὶ τῇ πωρώσει τῆς καρδίας αὐτῶν in the

¹ In 1 Pet and 3 Jn 'to do right'. Cf. Meecham, Aristeas, 289.

βλεψάμενος αὐτοὺς μετ᾽ ὀργῆς, συνλυπούμενος ἐπὶ τῇ πωρώσει
τῆς καρδίας αὐτῶν, λέγει τῷ ἀνθρώπῳ ῎Εκτεινον τὴν ⌐χεῖρά
σου⌐· καὶ ἐξέτεινεν, καὶ ἀπεκατεστάθη ἡ χεὶρ αὐτοῦ. Καὶ ἐξ- 6
5 χεῖρα

present verse; also σπλαγχισθείς or
ὀργισθείς in i. 41; ἐμβριμησάμενος i. 43;
ἐστέναξεν vii. 34; ἀναστενάξας viii. 12;
ἠγανάκτησεν x. 14; and ἐμβλέψας αὐτῷ
ἠγάπησεν αὐτόν x. 21. The phrase μετ᾽
ὀργῆς* is omitted by Mt and Lk, probably from an unwillingness to ascribe
this emotion to Jesus. These Gospels
also omit συνλυπούμενος ἐπὶ τῇ πωρώσει
τῆς καρδίας αὐτῶν. The presence of
such details is a sign of the primitive
character of the Markan tradition.
Cf. Loisy, i. 517, *Que ces traits des-
criptifs soient adventices dans Marc
et n'y aient pas encore existé quand les
deux autres évangélistes y ont puisé ce
récit* (J. Weiss, 383), *on le croira diffi-
cilement* (cited by Lagrange, 59). The
anger, which has in it no element of
personal rancour, is such as may
justly be felt at the spectacle of men
whose fidelity to the Law is matched
by blindness to moral values. There
is no need, therefore, with C. C.
Torrey, *TG*, 7 f., to suppose that, owing
to its ambiguity, and in accordance
with its later meaning, the Aramaic
בְּרַגַז, 'in distress', has been mis-
rendered 'with anger'.

συνλυπέω*, 'to hurt (or 'mortify') together', pass. 'share in grief', 'sympathize', 'condole'; Cl., LXX. None
of these meanings suits the passage, in
which the sense of 'being grieved with'
is required. Moulton, ii. 325, asks if
the meaning can be perfective, i.e.
'utterly distressed'. Cf. Bultmann,
KThW, iv. 325. Unfortunately, no
other example of the verb with this
meaning is available. W. L. Knox,
6 n., points out that *contristari* in this
sense is good Latin as early as Seneca
(*Ep.* 85. 14) and observes that ' we
might have here an isolated instance
of a Latin influence on the *koine*, the
lack of parallels being due to chance'.

πώρωσις*, Rom. xi. 25, Eph. iv. 18**,

' hardness ', ' insensibility ', <πωρόω,
' to petrify ', ' harden ', <πῶρος, ' a
stone ', ' a callus '. The word is commonly explained as meaning ' hardness ', but in a detailed note J. A.
Robinson, *Eph.* 264-74, has shown
that in the NT ' obtuseness or intellectual blindness is the meaning indicated by the context; and this
meaning is as a rule assigned by the
ancient translators and commentators'.
Cf. *caecitas* a b e f q vg; *emortua* . . .
corda c (d) ff i r; νεκρώσει D sys;
' hardness ' sype; ' blindness ' arm.
' " Blindness of heart " comes nearer
to the meaning than " hardness of
heart " ', *op. cit.* 274. Cf. Rawlinson,
36; Turner, 20; Lagrange, 59; Lohmeyer, 70 n.; and see vi. 52, viii. 17.

The rest of the verse, closely followed
by Mt and Lk, tells how Jesus commanded the man to stretch out his
hand, and that, when he obeyed, his
hand was restored. ἀποκαθίστημι,
viii. 25* (ix. 12 ἀποκατιστάνει WH),
' to restore '; Cl., LXX, Pap. For
the double augment, a well-established
vernacular usage, *v.* Moulton, ii. 189;
Blass-Deb. 69. 3; *VGT*, 63. Cf. viii.
25, also i. 42. Micklem, 95, conjectures that in part the cure was already
performed when the man obeyed.
Although the healing is wrought in
reply to a challenge, it is none the less
an act of benevolence. Whether the
man asked to be healed we do not
know. Much has dropped out of the
story, in spite of striking details which
remain, because the main interest of
the narrative is in the Sabbath.

The story of the restoration of the
hand of Jeroboam by the altar at Bethel
has little in common with this story
beyond the use of ἐκτείνω and ξηραίνω
(3 Kgdms. xiii. 4).

6. The use of ἐξελθόντες (cf. i. 29, 35,
45, ii. 13) belongs to Mark's narrative

ἐλθόντες οἱ Φαρισαῖοι εὐθὺς μετὰ τῶν Ἡρῳδιανῶν συμβούλιον
⌜ἐδίδουν⌝ κατ᾽ αὐτοῦ ὅπως αὐτὸν ἀπολέσωσιν.

6 ἐποίησαν

style. The Pharisees are here mentioned for the first time in the story. Luke adds that they were filled with rage (ἐπλήσθησαν ἀνοίας, vi. 11). εὐθύς here means ' immediately '. Cf. Bartlet, 143, ' they lost no time in taking steps to scheme his ruin '; Moffatt, ' On this the Pharisees withdrew and at once joined the Herodians in a plot against him, to destroy him '. Ἡρῳδιανοί, xii. 13*, Mt. xxii. 16**. The Herodians were not a sect or party, but the friends and supporters of Herod Antipas. Cf. Josephus, Ant. xiv. 15. 10, τοὺς τὰ Ἡρῴδου φρονοῦντας. The objection that the Pharisees would not have entered into league with the recreant followers of Herod (Lohmeyer, 67) ignores the strange unions which a common hostility can create. For the view that the Herodians were men of standing and influence friendly to the Herodian rule see the detailed study of H. H. Rowley, JTS, xli. 14-27. Cf. also Lagrange, 60 ; Rawlinson, 36 ; Jackson and Lake, i. 119 f.; and on the negative side Cheyne, EB, col. 2043 ; Bacon, 75.

συμβούλιον, xv. 1*, Mt. xii. 14, xxii. 15, xxvii. 1, 7, xxviii. 12, Ac. xxv. 12**, ' council ' (=Cl. συμβουλία), ' consultation ', ' counsel '. The word is late. Plutarch, Rom. 14, explains that it is used in the sense of consilium κωνσίλιον γὰρ ἔτι νῦν τὸ συμβούλιον καλοῦσι. It is found once in the LXX in 4 Macc. xvii. 17 (v.l. συνέδριον) and in Theodotion's version in Prov. xv. 22 (LXX συνέδρια) where the Heb. is סוד ' counsel '. In the examples given in VGT, 597, the meaning is ' council ', as in 4 Macc. xvii. 17 and Ac. xxv. 12. Cf. Deissmann, BS, 238. W. L. Knox, 6 n. says that there is no parallel for the meaning ' counsel ' as against ' council ', and that in συμβούλιον the influence of Latin (consilium) upon vernacular Gk is to be seen (cf. συνλυπούμενος, 5). The phrase συμβούλιον

ἐδίδουν is also strange. Wellhausen suggests that it reflects Aramaic idiom ; cf. Lohmeyer, 70 n. In xv. 1 Mark has συμβούλιον ποιήσαντες (v.l. ἑτοιμάσαντες), and in the present passage ἐποίησαν is attested in ℵ C Δ* Θ 238 476 514 892ᵐᵍ 1071 bo and ἐποίουν by A et al. fam. 1 22 33 157 579 al. pler. it vg arm, while W has ἐποιοῦντο and D a have ποιοῦντες and facientes respectively. In contrast with ἐδίδουν (B L fam. 13 28 543 565 700 bo) these readings are secondary and show how strange σ. ἐδίδουν was felt to be. Luke never uses the construction and Matthew prefers συμβούλιον λαμβάνειν (five times). The lexical and textual data bear on the question of the early history of the Gospel. Knox, for example, maintains that ' two Latinisms, both hapax legomena in their sense, in one pericope suggests that the story has passed from Greek (or Aramaic) into Latin and back into Greek before it reached its place in Mark '.

Lohmeyer, 67, is ready to recognize the originality of 6, if the names, Pharisees and Herodians, were added by Mark. Names, however, seem necessary if a plot is to be described, and it is not Mark's manner to supply them. In any case, whether the names are added or not, a league between the religious leaders and influential laymen is probable. F. C. Burkitt, 80 f., maintains that in iii. 6 ' we have our Lord's definite breach with official Judaism '. ' He left the Synagogue, never to return again, save once at Nazareth, in His own town.' Cf. Rawlinson, 37 ; Bartlet, 144 ; Plummer, 102. If the narrative owes its position in Mk to the prior existence of a pre-Markan complex, the incident may have happened later. In Mk, however, it has dramatic appropriateness at so early a point. As a dark cloud the death of Jesus hangs over the further course of His ministry (J. Weiss, Die Schr.⁴ 100).

III

Mk. iii. 7-vi. 13   THE HEIGHT OF THE
GALILEAN MINISTRY

With iii. 7 a new division of the Gospel begins. At what point it ends is another matter. Every possible answer has been given : iv. 34, v. 43, vi. 6, vi. 13, vii. 23, viii. 26, ix. 50. The variety of these views suggests that the Evangelist's intentions cannot be determined, and, in consequence, the limits must be fixed by considerations of geography and the progress of the Story. From this standpoint the outside limit is best fixed at vi. 13. The Galilean Ministry is at its height and reaches a climax in the Mission of the Twelve (vi. 7-13).

The division begins with a summary description of the great crowds which attended the ministry of Jesus (iii. 7-12) and an account of the institution of the Twelve (iii. 13-19a). Then follow three sections : (a) Charges brought against Jesus (iii. 19b-35) ; (b) a composite section dealing mainly with Parables of the Kingdom (iv. 1-34) ; and (c) a group of Miracle-stories (iv. 35-v. 43). To these are appended the stories of the Rejection at Nazareth (vi. 1-6a) and the Mission of the Twelve (vi. 6b-13). A dividing line is suggested at this point by the fact that the next division opens with a kind of interlude in the stories of Herod's Fears (vi. 14-16) and the Death of John the Baptist (vi. 17-29).

Mk. iii. 7-12   19. SUMMARY STATEMENT :   Cf. Mt. xii. 15-21
CROWDS BY THE LAKE   Lk. vi. 17-19

Mk. iii. 7-12 is an editorial summary composed by the Evangelist himself ; the style and the vocabulary are his, the only unusual word being ἀνεχώρησεν (iii. 7). Certain distinctive features mark the passage. (1) It is much longer than i. 14 f., ii. 1 f., iv. 1 f., vii. 24, 31, etc., longer indeed than is immediately necessary. (2) There are no links backward except in matters of vocabulary and the use of ἀνεχώρησεν. Matthew supplies this lack by inserting γνούς and ἐκεῖθεν, thus implying that Jesus withdrew to the lake because of the Pharisees' plot. (3) The summary looks forward. By mentioning the crowds, the boat, and the demoniacs it prepares the way for iv. 1 ff., the account of the lakeside teaching, and the miracle-stories of iv. 35-v. 43, especially the Gerasene Demoniac. The reference to the desire of the crowds to touch Jesus (iii. 10) anticipates v. 28-31 and vi. 56, and the mastery over the daemons described in iii. 11 f. is a foil to the claim of Jesus, implicit in iii. 27, to have bound Satan, the Strong Man.

Whether Mark wrote the summary when compiling the Gospel, or at an earlier time, is a matter for conjecture. It may be that iii. 7-12, iv. 1-9, (26-34), 35-v. 43 was an original series, into which iii. 13-19a, 19b-35, and iv. 10-25 were subsequently inserted. Wellhausen, 24, conjectures that perhaps iii. 7-12 was originally intended to stand before iv. 1-9. Cf. J. Weiss, 166. On the other hand, the summary may have been composed in preparation for the later sections. ' He who wrote iii. 7 and iii. 9 looked forward to iv. 1 and prepared here for the later scene ', Weiss,

165. In any case, the summary was compiled from primitive testimony. As here, editorial summaries are not always mere imaginative sketches.

7 Καὶ ὁ Ἰησοῦς μετὰ τῶν μαθητῶν αὐτοῦ ἀνεχώρησεν εἰς τὴν θάλασσαν· καὶ πολὺς ὄχλος ἀπὸ τῆς Γαλιλαίας, ⌜καὶ ἀπὸ τῆς

7 f. The only important words in these verses not already found in Mk are ἀνεχώρησεν and πέραν. With πέραν c. gen., 'beyond', x. 1*, cf. εἰς τὸ πέραν, iv. 35, v. 1, 21, vi. 45, viii. 13*. ἀνα-χωρέω*, Mt (10), Jn (1), Ac (2)**, ' to withdraw ', is a classical word found in Homer (of withdrawing from battle, *Il.* xvii. 30), Plato (of retiring from public life, *Phd.* 83 A), and Polybius (of retiring from the world, xxix. 25. 5); also LXX and Pap. Moulton and Milligan (*VGT*, 40) say that the connotation of ' taking refuge ' from some peril (P. Tebt. i. 41. 14, of husbandmen on strike) ' will suit most of the NT passages remarkably well '. This statement is true, especially in Mt, but the idea of flight from peril is not always associated with the verb (cf. Mt. ix. 24, xxviii. 5, Ac. xxiii. 19, xxvi. 31), and may not be intended by Mark here. Copyists have followed Mt in adding γνούς [1] in Mk with reference to iii. 6, and some commentators have taken the same view; cf. Swete, 54; Plummer, 102; Turner, 21; Klostermann, 38. It seems probable that Mark means no more than that Jesus turned from towns and synagogues to continue His ministry in the open air by the lakeside among the crowds from Galilee and adjacent districts. Cf. Rawlinson, 37. Lagrange, 61, writes : *Mais il n'y a pas dans Mc. la moindre allusion à une fuite.*

The text as printed above differs from that of WH in reading εἰς (before τὴν θάλασσαν) instead of πρός, and πολὺς ὄχλος instead of πολὺ πλῆθος, and in omitting ἠκολούθησεν and reading [πλῆθος πολύ] in 8. The textual evidence may be summarized as follows :

εἰς (cf. vii. 31) is read by D H P 579 *et al.* (παρά by fam. 13 28 543 1071 *et al.*), and πολὺς ὄχλος by D 372 b c e f ff i r[1.2] vg. ἠκολούθησεν is omitted by D W 28 124 788 it (exc. f l) sy[s] bo geo[1], and the plur. is read in א C Δ *et al.* fam. 13 (exc. 124) 22 33 157 543 *al. pler.* 1 sy[pe hl] sa, while the verb follows Ἰουδαίας in א C Δ 238 1071 f l vg. In 8 πλῆθος πολύ is omitted by W a b c sys.[2]

The evidence suggests that the original text has suffered from the desire to distinguish two groups, one consisting of Galileans and the other of people from more distant parts. That two groups are meant is held by many commentators (cf. Lagrange, 61; Rawlinson, 38; Gould, 55; Plummer, 102 f.), and is implied by the text and punctuation of WH and by RV and RSV. Turner, 21, however, omits ' followed ' and says that ' the true text of Mark enumerates in a single group the constituent parts of the " great multitude " '. This is probably the better view. Mark's style can be prolix, but it is difficult to think that the phrases beginning with ἀπό can be separated,[3] or that he is responsible for πολὺ πλῆθος followed by πλῆθος πολύ. Elsewhere he never uses πλῆθος (Lk (8), Ac (17)), but always ὄχλος, and it may be that πλῆθος πολύ in 8 is an assimilation to Lk. vi 17. The omission of ἠκολούθησεν and of πλῆθος πολύ is strongly attested, and if the use of εἰς instead of πρός has less support, it has transcriptional probability in its favour. In sum, for the text thus obtained it may be claimed that it enables us to account for the texts of WH and Nestle. It

[1] It is read in 51 234 659 1071 1241.
[2] Among other (grammatical) corrections are ὁ δὲ Ἰησοῦς in D W it (exc. l) bo geo; ἀκούσαντες in A C D L Θ *et al.* 22 28 33 157 579 700 1071 *al. pler.*; and ἐποίει in א A C D W Δ Θ minusc. *pler.*
[3] The repetition of the preposition here and in iii. 8, vi. 56, xi. 1 is Semitic. Cf. Black, 83 ; Intr. 64.

'Ιουδαίας¹ καὶ ἀπὸ 'Ιεροσολύμων καὶ ἀπὸ τῆς 'Ιδουμαίας καὶ 8
πέραν τοῦ 'Ιορδάνου καὶ περὶ Τύρον καὶ ⌈Σιδῶνα,¹ [πλῆθος πολύ],
ἀκούοντες ὅσα ⌈ποιεῖ¹ ἦλθαν πρὸς αὐτόν. καὶ εἶπεν τοῖς μαθηταῖς 9
αὐτοῦ ἵνα πλοιάριον προσκαρτερῇ αὐτῷ διὰ τὸν ὄχλον ἵνα μὴ
θλίβωσιν αὐτόν· πολλοὺς γὰρ ἐθεράπευσεν, ὥστε ἐπιπίπτειν αὐτῷ 10

7 καὶ ἀπὸ τῆς 'Ιουδαίας ἠκολούθησεν
8 Σιδῶνα,— | ἐποίει

may also be argued that δέ instead of
καί at the beginning is meant to mark
the beginning of a new section. The
present tenses in ἀκούοντες . . . ποιεῖ
are certainly in harmony with the
Evangelist's style. ' In ποιεῖ we hear
the report as it passed from one to
another in the crowd', Swete, 55.
With ὅσα, ' how many things ', cf. iii.
28, v. 19, vi. 30, x. 21.

In 7 f. Mark's desire to describe an
extension of the ministry of Jesus is
manifest. Judaea (cf. i. 5) and Jerusalem are mentioned for the first time.
Farther south Idumaea, Jewish since
the time of John Hyrcanus (cf.
Josephus, *Ant.* xiii. 9. 1 ; G. A. Smith,
239 f.), is included, and to the east
between the Jabbok and the Arnon
the region of Peraea (cf. Josephus,
BJ, iii. 3. 3) here described as πέραν
τοῦ 'Ιορδάνου as in the LXX (Isa. ix.
1). North-west the country about
Tyre and Sidon, a district closely connected with northern Galilee (Smith,
425 f.), is named. Samaria is not
mentioned, and the Decapolis not
until v. 20. The crowd is attracted
by the miracles of Jesus. People hear
how many mighty works He is doing,
and for this reason they come to Him
from far and near. 'Ιεροσόλυμα, iii.
22, vii. 1, x. 32 f., xi. 1, 11, 15, 27, xv.
41* (Mark does not use the Semitic
form 'Ιερουσαλήμ); 'Ιδουμαία**; Τύρος,
vii. 24, 31 ; Σιδών, vii. 24 (?), 31*.

9. As frequently in the vernacular,
the construction ἵνα . . . προσκαρτερῇ
expresses, not purpose, but the substance of a command; cf. Moulton,
i. 206-9; *VGT*, 305. Of the suggestion that it is due to Latin influence
Moulton says : ' The usage was deeply
rooted in the vernacular, in fields which

Latin cannot have touched to the extent which so far-reaching a change
involves '. As a typical example cf.
Par. P. 51 (ii/ B.C.) : λέγω . . . ἵνα προσ-
κυνήσῃς αὐτόν.
πλοιάριον*, Lk. v. 2 (?), Jn. vi. 22,
23 (?), 24, xxi. 8**, ' a skiff ', ' boat ',
dimin. of πλοῖον ; Cl., not LXX, Pap.
(*VGT*, 521) ; vg *navicula*. Mark frequently uses diminutives, but not
always in their literal sense ; *v.* Intr.
45. It is doubtful therefore if the word
should be distinguished sharply from
πλοῖον (iv. 1, 36). προσκαρτερέω*, Ac.
i. 14, ii. 42, 46, vi. 4, viii. 13, x. 7, Rom.
xii. 12, xiii. 6, Col. iv. 2**, <καρτερός,
' strong ', ' stedfast ', ' staunch ' ; ' to
attend constantly ', ' continue sted-
fastly ', ' adhere firmly to ', ' wait for ' ;
Cl., LXX, Pap. (*VGT*, 548). The idea
is that the boat is at the disposal of
Jesus as a refuge from the pressure of
the crowd. For διὰ τὸν ὄχλον *v.* ii. 4.
The clause ἵνα μὴ θλίβωσιν αὐτόν is
final. θλίβω*, Mt. vii. 14, Pl (6),
1 Tim. v. 10, Heb. xi. 37**, ' to
squeeze ', ' compress ', ' oppress ' ; Cl.,
LXX, Pap. (*VGT*, 292). Mark alone
gives this vivid portraiture, for which
it is reasonable to suppose that he is
dependent on living memory.

10. This verse is even more graphic.
It presents a lifelike picture of people
falling upon Jesus in their eagerness
to touch Him. πολλοὺς ἐθεράπευσεν
recalls i. 34a. Neither there nor here
(nor again in x. 45) does Mark mean
by ' many ' ' some, but not all ', and
too much has been made of the fact
that Matthew changes πολλούς to
πάντας (xii. 15). Cf. Lk. vi. 19, ἰᾶτο
πάντας. None the less, the restraint of
Mark's description is as notable as its
vividness. For ὥστε c. infin. *v.* i. 27.

11 ἵνα αὐτοῦ ἅψωνται ὅσοι εἶχον μάστιγας. καὶ τὰ πνεύματα τὰ
ἀκάθαρτα, ὅταν αὐτὸν ἐθεώρουν, προσέπιπτον αὐτῷ καὶ ἔκραζον
12 ⌜λέγοντα⌝ ὅτι Σὺ εἶ ὁ υἱὸς τοῦ θεοῦ. καὶ πολλὰ ἐπετίμα αὐτοῖς
ἵνα μὴ αὐτὸν φανερὸν ποιήσωσιν.

11 λέγοντες

ἐπιπίπτω*, Lk. i. 12, xv. 20, Jn. xiii. 25 (?), Ac (6) and v.l. xxiii. 7, Rom. xv. 3, Apoc. xi. 11**, ' to fall upon '; Cl. (Field, 25, cites Thuc. vii. 84, ἐπέπιπτόν τε ἀλλήλοις καὶ κατεπάτουν), LXX (2 Kgdms. xvii. 9, Job vi. 16, etc.), Pap. Whereas in i. 41 we read of the touch of Jesus, here we see the anxiety of sufferers to touch Him (cf. v. 27 ff., vi. 56). Luke explains that power (δύναμις) went out from Him and that He healed all. Mark has the same idea in v. 30, τὴν ἐξ αὐτοῦ δύναμιν ἐξελθοῦσαν. The sick people are described as ὅσοι εἶχον μάστιγας. μάστιξ, v. 29, 34*, Lk. vii. 21, Ac xxii. 24, Heb. xi. 36**, ' whip ', ' scourge '. Here as in Cl. Gk the noun is used of sickness regarded as a divine chastisement. Cf. Hom. Il. xii. 37, xiii. 812, ἀλλὰ Διὸς μάστιγι κακῇ ἐδάμησεν Ἀχαιοί, Aesch. Prom. 682, μάστιγι θείᾳ . . . ἐλαύνομαι. Arising in the antique world the idea becomes conventional.

11. For πνεύματα ἀκάθαρτα v. i. 23. ὅταν, normally used with the subj., is here followed by the indic., as in xi. 19, 25. The usage illustrates ' the weakening of the connexion between compounds of ἄν and the subjunctive ' (Moulton, i. 167 f., 248). Cf. also in Apoc. iv. 9, viii. 1 and in the papyri (VGT, 462 f.) ; and ὅπου ἄν and ὅσοι ἄν in Mk. vi. 56, Apoc. xiv. 4 (WH), and ἐάν c. indic. in 1 Thess. iii. 8 and 1 Jn. v. 15. Although ὅταν c. indic. is used by Homer (v. LS, 1264), it is not found in classical prose. There is no need, with Swete, 56 (v. Robertson and Davis, 326 f.), to render the con-

junction ' whenever '.[1] The meaning is simply that when the unclean spirits beheld Jesus, they fell down before Him (cf. Moulton, op. cit. 168, Lagrange, 62). θεωρέω, v. 15, 38, xii. 41, xv. 40, 47, xvi. 4*. προσπίπτω, v. 33, vii. 25*, Mt (1), Lk (3), Ac (1)**, ' fall upon ', ' fall at one's feet ' (Mt. vii. 25); Cl., LXX, Pap. κράζω, 11 times*. Instead of λέγοντα ℵ D W 28 69 have λέγοντες. ὅτι is recitativum. The words Σὺ εἶ ὁ υἱὸς τοῦ θεοῦ are a Christianized version of the cries of the possessed; cf. i. 24, ὁ ἅγιος τοῦ θεοῦ and v. 7, Ἰησοῦ υἱὲ τοῦ θεοῦ τοῦ ὑψίστου; they are important as illustrating Mark's theology (cf. i. 1; v. Intr. 120-2). It is unsatisfactory to explain the phrase as a Messianic title; it expresses Mark's conviction that the personality of Jesus is superhuman. See further, xiv. 61, xv. 39.

12. For πολλά adverbial v. i. 45. The ἵνα μή clause is probably final, but the possibility cannot be excluded that it is a noun clause giving the substance of the strict injunction, ' not to make Him manifest '. Cf. Moffatt: ' not to make him known '. φανερός, iv. 22, vi. 14*. φανερὸν ποιεῖν, here and Mt. xii. 16**. For the charge to keep silence v. i. 25, 34, 44, etc. and Intr. 122-4. Jesus did not welcome the testimonies of the possessed and maintained and enjoined silence in public regarding His Messiahship. To this verse, which he follows closely, Matthew (xii. 17-21) finely adds a quotation from the Servant poem in Isa. xlii. 1-4 : ' Behold, my servant whom I have chosen . . .'.

[1] See, however, among modern translators, Moffatt, Goodspeed, Weymouth, RSV, Knox.

Mk. iii. 13-19a   20. THE APPOINTMENT OF   Cf. (Mt. x. 2-4)
                          THE TWELVE   (Lk. vi. 12-16)
                                                (Ac. i. 13)

This narrative appears to have been constructed *ad hoc* on the basis of existing tradition. *V.* Intr. 82-5. It is possible, as Schmidt, 110 f., suggests, that it already existed, but there are no positive reasons for this view except the probability that the list of the Twelve in 16-19a is traditional. The narrative lacks the vivid detail which suggests a use of the reminiscences of an eyewitness. The reference to the mountain, or the highlands, is vague, and it is not certain whether Jesus goes alone or whence the disciples are summoned. The narrative embodies the belief that Jesus separated twelve disciples for close asssociation with Himself and in order to commission them for the work of heralds and evangelists. There is good reason, however, to infer that the account is based on historical tradition. The functions of the Twelve differ from those exercised later by the Apostles and Elders at the Apostolic Council at Jerusalem (Ac. xv), and it is difficult to explain how Mark writes with such objectivity unless he is describing what happened. It is an understatement when Wellhausen, 24, says that the story is merely a list presented in narrative form, or when Weiss, 165, declares that it gives shape to a dogmatic idea. These characterizations are based on the view that the appointment is not historical, which is affirmed by Wellhausen and is held by Weiss largely because of the silence of the Epistles. This silence and the difficulties raised by the lists are capable of a better explanation, and other considerations, especially the simple and restrained character of the narrative, favour a more positive conclusion. The hypothesis of Ed. Meyer (*v.* Intr. 74 f.) may be too explicit in positing a fusion of two distinct sources, but it rightly assumes the use of older material. This estimate certainly applies to the list. A catalogue which includes proper names, a patronymic, surnames and bynames, which omits Levi, and contains terms like Boanerges and Iscariot, strange perhaps already to Mark himself, is hardly the kind of thing the Evangelist would have constructed if he had been writing freely. To a less degree also the estimate applies to the narrative. Not only does Mark use a traditional list, but he knows also why the Twelve were appointed, and gives reasons which suit the conditions of the Galilean Ministry. Further, in default of more precise information, he does not attempt to add imaginative touches in respect of details which only an eyewitness could have supplied. See further, Note B on the Twelve and the Apostles, pp. 619-27.

Καὶ ἀναβαίνει εἰς τὸ ὄρος καὶ προσκαλεῖται οὓς ἤθελεν αὐτός, 13

13. εἰς τὸ ὄρος, vi. 46, xiii. 14*. The phrase is quite indefinite, but the hill country to the north of the Lake may be meant (cf. Swete, 57; Lagrange, 63). Black, 96, thinks that ὄρος suggests the influence of *ṭura* which in Palestinian Aramaic can mean either ' mountain ' or the ' open country ', as contrasted with inhabited places.

ἀναβαίνει is the historic present as in i. 12, ii. 3, iii. 3, and frequently in Mk (*v.* Intr. 46 f.). The initiative is taken by Jesus; He calls to Him whom He wills to call. προσκαλέομαι is frequently used by Mark, either with reference to the disciples as here (cf. iii. 23, vi. 7, viii. 1, x. 42, xii. 43*) or to the multitudes (vii. 14, viii. 34*) or

14 καὶ ἀπῆλθον πρὸς αὐτόν. καὶ ἐποίησεν δώδεκα, ἵνα ὦσιν μετ᾽
15 αὐτοῦ καὶ ἵνα ἀποστέλλῃ αὐτοὺς κηρύσσειν καὶ ἔχειν ἐξουσίαν
16 ἐκβάλλειν τὰ δαιμόνια· πρῶτον Σίμωνα (καὶ ἐπέθηκεν ὄνομα τῷ

to the summoning of the centurion by Pilate (xv. 44). The response is immediate: καὶ ἀπῆλθον πρὸς αὐτόν (v. i. 17, 20). A larger company appears to be in mind than the twelve mentioned in iii. 14. Matthew has no parallel to this verse. Luke says that Jesus went into the mountain to pray and that He continued all night in prayer to God (vi. 12).

14 f. In καὶ ἐποίησεν δώδεκα the verb means ' to appoint ', a meaning which is not classical, but which is used in the LXX to translate עָשָׂה (' to do ', ' make ') when it is used of appointing priests (3 Kgdms. xii. 31, καὶ ἐποίησεν ἱερεῖς, xiii. 33, 2 Chron. ii. 18) and Moses and Aaron (1 Kgdms. xii. 6, Κύριος ὁ ποιήσας τὸν Μωϋσῆν καὶ τὸν Ἀαρών). Cf. Ac. ii. 36, Heb. iii. 2 (cf. Moffatt, *Heb.* 42), Apoc. v. 10. This use of ποιέω should be classified as an example of ' translation Greek ', influenced by the LXX (cf. Klostermann, 40, Rawlinson, 40). The difficulty of the Greek is illustrated by the Western reading in which δώδεκα follows ἵνα ὦσιν (D a c d ff i vg). The number ' twelve ' is selected with reference to the twelve tribes of Israel (cf. Mt. xix. 28, Lk. xxii. 30). Mark frequently refers to the Twelve in the phrase οἱ δώδεκα, iii. 16 (?), iv. 10, vi. 7, ix. 35, x. 32, xi. 11, xiv. 10, 17, 20, 43*. Cf. Mt (3), with οἱ δώδεκα ἀπόστολοι in x. 2, and οἱ δώδεκα μαθηταί in x. 1, xi. 1, xx. 17, xxvi. 20; Lk (6); Jn (4); Ac (1); and 1 Cor. xv. 5**. The Twelve are not identical with ' the disciples ' (v. ii. 15), nor with ' the Apostles ', who represent a circle wider than that of the Twelve. See the note on ἀπόστολος in vi. 30. See also Lightfoot, *Gal.* 92-101; Burton, *Gal.* 363-84; Rengstorf, *KThW*, i. 406-44, ii. 325-8 ; Flew, *JC*, 106-20.

The clause οὓς καὶ ἀποστόλους ὠνόμασεν (ℵ B C* Δ Θ W fam. 13 28 238 543

syʰˡ ᵐᵍ sa bo aeth geo¹) is omitted by A C² D L *et al.* fam. 1 33 565 579 700 892 1071 *al. pler.* it vg sys ᵖᵉ ʰˡ geo² arm, and is probably an assimilation to the text of Lk. vi. 13. Cf. Klostermann, 40; Turner, *CQR*, July 1920, p. 338, cited by Rawlinson, 39 ; Bartlet, 148 ; Lagrange, 64. Swete, 58, accepts the reading in view of the strength of the MSS. evidence in its favour, but this opinion does not do justice to the evidence as a whole.

The purpose of the appointment is twofold : (1) that the Twelve may enjoy close fellowship with Him, and (2) that He may send them forth to preach and to have authority to cast out daemons. The phrase θεραπεύειν τὰς νόσους καί after ἐξουσίαν is attested by A C² D W Θ *et al.* minusc. *pler.* it vg sys ᵖᵉ ʰˡ bo aeth arm, but it is probably an assimilation to Mt. x. 1. The commission to preach and exorcize is not fulfilled until vi. 7, Mark's intention being to suggest an interval during which the Twelve are in intimate contact with Jesus. Ed. Meyer, i. 135-8, thinks that the two purposes mentioned above are incompatible, and that their presence, together with the repetition of καὶ ἐποίησεν τοὺς δώδεκα in 16, indicates that Mark has combined two separate accounts of the institution, 13-14a from a ' disciple-source ' and 14b-19a from a ' twelve-source '. For this suggestion see Intr. 74 f. Here it may be said that a break after ἵνα ὦσιν μετ᾽ αὐτοῦ in 14a seems awkward and unnecessary, and that in the second reference to the appointment (16) the text is doubtful.

16. The phrase καὶ ἐποίησεν τοὺς δώδεκα (ℵ B C* Δ 565 579) is omitted by A C² D L W Θ *et al.* minusc. *omn.* (except 565 579) it vg sys ᵖᵉ ʰˡ sa bo geo aeth arm, and by the RV and RSV text. A. C. Clark, *The Primitive Text of the Gospels and Acts*, 108,

Σίμωνι Πέτρον), καὶ Ἰάκωβον τὸν τοῦ Ζεβεδαίου καὶ Ἰωάνην τὸν 17
ἀδελφὸν τοῦ Ἰακώβου (καὶ ἐπέθηκεν αὐτοῖς ⌜ὄνομα⌝ Βοανηργές,

17 ὀνόματα

speaks of it as 'a dittography of the most puerile description' (cf. iii. 14). Cf. Rawlinson, 40; Klostermann, 40. Those commentators who retain the phrase suggest that the repetition is due to the necessity of picking up the thread after ἵνα ὦσιν . . . τὰ δαιμόνια, and interpret it in the sense : 'and so He created the Twelve'; cf. Swete, 59; Plummer, 106. The article, it is said, is inserted because the Twelve have already been mentioned and because οἱ δώδεκα is normal in Mk; cf. Lagrange, 64. It is doubtful if we can press the grammatical argument. With the exception of 565 and 579, and the addition of W Θ sa bo aeth, the MSS. which omit the phrase are almost wholly those which also omit οὓς καὶ ἀποστόλους ὠνόμασεν, and it may be that the insertion of this clause in ℵ B, etc. occasioned, or at least increased the need for, the addition of καὶ ἐποίησεν τοὺς δώδεκα. It is best to omit both clauses and to recognize that the original text has suffered from subsequent corruption. This possibility arises also in the second half of the verse, for one expects a reference to Simon *before* the explanatory passage about the change of name, as in the case of James and John (iii. 17). In fact fam. 13 543 sa read πρῶτον Σίμωνα before καὶ ἐπέθηκεν. Of this reading H. G. Wood, 685, says : 'The text adopted in RV is certainly corrupt, and some previous mention of Simon is required. This reading is perhaps better than *mg*.'
ἐπιτίθημι ὄνομα, iii. 17**; cf. Herodotus v. 68, Plato, *Symp*. 205 B; LXX, 4 Kgdms. xxiv. 17, καὶ ἐπέθηκεν τὸ ὄνομα αὐτοῦ, Σεδεκιά. 'By a usage similar to that of the Heb. שֵׁם, ὄνομα comes in the NT to denote the *character, fame, authority* of the person indicated (cf. Phil. ii. 9 f., Heb. i. 4) ', *VGT*, 451. The construction is broken.

After ἐπέθηκεν c. dat., we expect καὶ τῷ Ἰακώβῳ . . . καὶ Ἰωάνῃ ἐπέθηκεν ὄνομα Βοανηργές, but the acc. is used as if Mark had previously written Σίμωνα ᾧ ἐπέθηκεν ὄνομα Πέτρον. WH treat the explanatory clauses as parentheses, but, as Swete, 58, observes, 'a parenthesis in such a context is almost intolerable'. Either the text is a glaring example of anacoluthon or we must read πρῶτον Σίμωνα.

Πέτρος (=Σίμων=Κηφᾶς) is here used for the first time in Mk (19 times*) and henceforward throughout the Gospel except in xiv. 37 (Σίμων). Πέτρος, 'a stone' (cf. πέτρα, 'a rock '), is the Greek equivalent of the Aramaic כֵּיפָא, Κηφᾶς (Jn. i. 42, 1 Cor. i. 12, iii. 22, ix. 5, xv. 5, Gal. i. 18, ii. 9, 11, 14**), a form which Mark does not use. According to Jn. i. 42 the name was conferred when Simon was first called. Taken by itself Mk. iii. 16 suggests that it was given at the time of the Appointment of the Twelve, but Augustine's view, *hoc recolendo dixit, non quod tum factum sit (De Cons.* 109), may be correct. The name is intended to describe Simon's character, not his office (but cf. Westcott, *St. Jn*, 25; Lagrange, 65; Klostermann, 40), but it points forward (cf. Mt. xvi. 18). Σίμων became Πέτρος at Pentecost.

17. With the accs. sc. ἐποίησεν. W b e q assign the name Boanerges to all the disciples. W reads κοινῶς δὲ αὐτοῖς ἐκάλεσεν βοανηργέ, and continues in 18 ἦσαν δὲ οὗτοι σίμων καὶ ἀνδρέας . . .; cf. *communiter autem uocauit eos (illos,* b) b e q. This reading is of much interest but is not likely to be original. Cf. Lagrange, 65.

Βοανηργές** is usually explained as a corrupt transliteration of a Hebrew or Aramaic name, the o or the a in the Greek being an intrusion or gloss. 565 reads Βανηρεγες, 700 Βανηρεγεζ, and sys pe hl *ĕnai regesh*. The first

18 ὅ ἐστιν Υἱοὶ Βροντῆς), καὶ 'Ανδρέαν καὶ Φίλιππον καὶ Βαρθο-

part of the word represents the Heb. בְּנֵי, 'sons of'. The second part raises problems which have not yet been solved. Dalman, *Gr.* 112 n., *WJ*, 49, traces it to רֹגֶז, 'agitation', 'excitement', 'raging', which is used in Job xxxvii. 2 of the rumbling of the storm (*BDB*, 919, '*rumbling of his voice* (i.e. thunder)'). The original reading, he suggests, may possibly have been בְּנֵי־רֹגֶז. This view still remains the best, but it is weakened by the fact that the ordinary Hebrew word for 'thunder' is רַעַם. Jerome (on Dan. i. 7) indeed conjectured the reading *Benereem* or *Baneraem* (בְּנֵי־רַעַם). Lagrange, 65, prefers to find the original in בְּנֵי רֶגֶשׁ. He recognizes that רגשׁ is not found in the sense of 'thunder' in the Hebrew or Aramaic texts, but points out that *radjas* has this meaning in Arabic, and suggests that it may have been current in popular usage. Cf. also C. C. Torrey, 298, who says that 'thunderstorm' would perhaps be a more accurate rendering of *regesh*, *rugsha*. For other discussions *v.* W. C. Allen, *DCG*, i. 216; H. W. Hogg, *EB*, col. 593 f.; Klostermann, 41.

All these theories are attempts to do justice to the explanatory phrase ὅ ἐστιν Υἱοὶ Βροντῆς, 'sons of thunder', a name which has a certain appropriateness in ix. 38 and Lk. ix. 54. It may be, however, that originally it had another significance, for J. Rendel Harris has shown that 'sons of thunder' is closely connected with the cult of twins. Were James and John given a symbolic name because they were twins (cf. H. G. Wood, 685) or intimate comrades (Schulthess, cited by Klostermann, 41)? If we could be reasonably sure that the name was applied to all the Twelve, as in the Western MSS. indicated above, it might even be inferred that they were called in couples (cf. J. A. Findlay, *Jesus as They saw Him*, 29), as later they were sent out 'two by two'. Beyond sug-

gestions and conjectures of this kind it is impossible to go, with the knowledge at our disposal, for it may well be that like Δαλμανουθά (viii. 10), Βοανηργές is a corruption to which Mark has attempted to give what explanation he could. The phrase ὅ ἐστιν, vii. 11, 34, xii. 42, xv. 16, 34, 42*, is characteristic of his style (cf. Hawkins, 34), the only other NT examples being Col. i. 24, Heb. vii. 2, and Apoc. xxi. 17. βροντή*, Jn. xii. 29, Apoc. (10)**. For the gen. in υἱοὶ βροντῆς *v.* Howard, ii. 441, and the note on ii. 19.

18. In Mk, as in Ac. i. 13, Andrew is mentioned after James and John; in Mt and Lk immediately after Peter. This is the order we should naturally expect in Mk (cf. i. 16). The same Markan order is followed in xiii. 3 and is based on the desire to give priority to the three principal disciples, Peter, James, and John (v. 37, ix. 2, xiv. 33). Both 'Ανδρέας (*v.* i. 16) and Φίλιππος* (Mt. x. 3, Lk. vi. 14, Jn. i. 44 f., 46 f., 49, vi. 5, 7, xii. 21, 22 (*bis*), xiv. 8 f., Ac. i. 13**) are purely Greek names. Apart from the frequent references in Jn, Philip is mentioned only in the lists of the Twelve in the Synoptic Gospels and the Acts. In the Acts a second Philip is named among the seven deacons (vi. 5), who is probably also the missionary to the Samaritans (viii. 5-40) and 'the Evangelist' of xxi. 8 (but *v.* Lake, iv. 267). The two are often confused by early writers.

Βαρθολομαῖος*, Mt. x. 3, Lk. vi. 14, Ac. i. 13**, a patronymic = בַּר־תַּלְמַי, 'son of Talmai'; cf. Βαρτίμαιος (x. 46) and Βαριωνᾶς (Mt. xvi. 17). The name Talmai appears in 2 Sam. iii. 3, xiii. 37, and Josephus, *Ant.* xx. 1. 1, gives it in the Gk form Θολομαῖος. Klostermann, 41, regards the identification of Talmai with Πτολεμαῖος (Wellhausen, 24) as doubtful. Not infrequently Bartholomew is identified with Nathaniel (Jn. i. 45, etc.), but

λομαῖον καὶ Μαθθαῖον καὶ Θωμᾶν καὶ Ἰάκωβον τὸν τοῦ
Ἀλφαίου καὶ Θαδδαῖον καὶ Σίμωνα τὸν Καναναῖον καὶ Ἰούδαν 19

this suggestion (cf. Swete, 60; Lagrange, 66; Westcott, 26) is conjectural.

Μαθθαῖος*, Mt. ix. 9, x. 3, Lk. vi. 15, Ac. i. 13**, is an abbreviated form of Ματταθίας (1 Chron. xv. 21 (A), 1 Macc. ii. 1), derived from מַתְּנָה, 'gift', not מַת, 'man'; cf. Lagrange, 66. Mt. x. 3 adds ὁ τελώνης, thus identifying the Apostle with Levi (cf. ix. 9), and in Mk (by assimilation to Mt) τὸν τελώνην is added in Θ fam. 13 50 61 330 543 565 700 1071. Had Mark identified the two, he would presumably have written Λευεὶν τὸν καλούμενον Μαθθαῖον (Klostermann, 41). See further, the note on ii. 14.

Θωμᾶς*, Mt. x. 3, Lk. vi. 15, Jn. xi. 16, xiv. 5, xx. 24, 26 f., 28, xxi. 2, Ac. i. 13**, is interpreted by Jn. xi. 16, xx. 24, xxi. 2 (ὁ λεγόμενος Δίδυμος) as meaning 'twin' (תְּאוֹם). The Acts of Thomas (M. R. James, 365) speaks of him as 'Judas Thomas', and in Jn. xiv. 22 ('Judas, not Iscariot') sys reads 'Thomas' and syᶜ 'Judas Thomas' (cf. Bernard, St. Jn, 549). The evidence suggests that Thomas, which is not a Gk name, was felt to be a surname, or even a nickname, although Lidzbarski (v. Klostermann, 41) holds that it was not necessarily so used.

Ἰάκωβος ὁ τοῦ Ἀλφαίου is so named to distinguish him from James the son of Zebedee. Mentioned here only in Mk, and in Mt. x. 3, Lk. vi. 15, Ac. i. 13**, he is sometimes identified with James the Less (v. xv. 40) or with Levi (v. ii. 14). He may be the brother of Levi; cf. Turner, 22. Ἀλφαῖος, ii. 14*, is presumably, but not necessarily, the father of Levi and James. He has frequently been identified with Κλωπᾶς (Jn. xix. 25) and Κλεόπας (Lk. xxiv. 18). Cf. Lightfoot, Gal. 267 n.; Swete, 61; Dalman, Gr, 142 n. The difficulty is that we should expect π in חַלְפִּי to be represented by ḥ or ch rather than k, and that the normal contraction of εο is ου or ευ, not ω;

cf. Moulton, ii. 91, 109. But Moulton, who finds the identification of the three names 'an extremely hard saying', concedes that 'some analogy beyond our reach might account for the variant form'. Cf. Lightfoot, 267 n.: 'A man, whose real Aramaic name was Clopas, might grecize the word and call himself Cleopas'.

Θαδδαῖος*, Mt. x. 3**, = Θευδᾶς, a shortened form of Θεοδόσιος, Θεόδοτος, or Θεόδωρος (cf. Dalman, 50; Lagrange, 67; VGT, 290). Of this disciple nothing certain is known. Tradition connects his ministry with Edessa. In Lk. vi. 15 and Ac. i. 13 Ἰούδας Ἰακώβου is substituted, and Λεββαῖον is read in Mk by D a b ff i q rⁱ. Λεββαῖος is also found in Mt. x. 3 in D 122 k Or. See also the conflate readings, Λ. ὁ ἐπικληθεὶς Θαδ. in C² et al. syᵖᵉ ʰˡ arm aeth, Θαδ. ὁ ἐπικλ. Λεβ. in 13 346 543, and iudas zelotes in a b h q. Late ecclesiastical writers identify Thaddaeus, Lebbaeos, and Judas of James, e.g. Origen, Praef. ad Rom., who explains that it was the custom of the Hebrews to use two or three names. In this disciple the confusion in the lists reaches its climax and only tentative opinions are possible. (1) The tendency to assimilation (cf. Streeter, 145) began very early, and, despite the opinion of Hort, 11, either Λεββαῖον (D a b, etc.) or Θαδδαῖον (א B c 124, etc.) may be the original reading in Mk. (2) On the whole it is not probable that Λεββαῖον is an early attempt to introduce the name of Levi into the list. We should expect rather Λευείν; cf. Allen, EB, col. 5032. (3) Θαδδαῖος and Λεββαῖος may be hypocoristic nouns (cf. Moulton, ii. 344), which describe the person mentioned by a comparison with something of like nature, Θαδδαῖος being formed from שַׁד (? Aram. תַּדְּיָא), 'breast-nipple', Λεββαῖος from לֵב, 'heart'. Cf. Lagrange, 67; Allen, op. cit.; but v. Dalman, 50. (4) In

'Ἰσκαριώθ, ὃς καὶ παρέδωκεν αὐτόν.

this case, ' Judas of James ' (Lk-Ac) may be the true name of the disciple, and the traditional identification, Thaddaeus = Lebbaeus = Judas of James, correct. Allen, *op. cit.*, ingeniously suggests that by corruption in Gk or Aramaic Θαδδαῖος represents יהׄ(ו)רׄ or יהׄ(ו)רא. Tedious and uncertain as such explanations are, they have an important bearing on the question of the origin and early history of the Twelve. See further, Note B, pp. 619-627.

Σίμων ὁ Καναναῖος*, Mt. x. 4**; cf. Lk. vi. 15, Σ. τ. καλούμενον ζηλωτήν, Ac. i. 13, Σ. ὁ ζηλωτής**. Καναναῖος represents קַנְאָנָא, ' Cananaean ', an adherent of the party later known as ' the Zealots ', and is correctly rendered by Luke ζηλωτής. The word does not mean ' Canaanite ' (כְּנַעֲנִי, Χαναναῖος, Mt. xv. 22**), nor ' inhabitant of Cana ' (Καναῖος). Cf. Burkitt, *Syriac Forms of NT Proper Names*, 5. κανανίτην (cf. AV) is read by A Θ *et al.* fam. 1 fam. 13 22 28 157 543 700 892 1071 *al. pler.* syhl sa arm. Although the Zealots belonged to a later time, being especially active in leading the people to armed revolt against the Romans (cf. Josephus, *BJ*, iv. 3. 9), they were preceded, from the time of Judas of Galilee onwards, by many, including Pharisees of the left wing, with strong nationalist tendencies ; and to such Simon may have belonged ; cf. Wellhausen, 23 ; A. Stumpff, *KThW*, ii. 886-9 ; Klostermann, 41 ; Wood, 685 ; Branscomb, 66 ; Bartlet, 151. The alternative, preferred by Swete, 62 ; Lagrange, 67 ; Jackson and Lake, i. 425 ; McNeile, 132 ; Smith, 120, is to regard the term as descriptive of Simon's strong religious zeal. The former is probably the view of the Evangelists and there is no good reason for rejecting it.

19a. Ἰούδας Ἰσκαριώθ, xiv. 10*, Lk. vi. 16**; Ἰσκαριώτης, xiv. 43 (?)*, Mt. x. 4, xxvi. 14, Lk. xxii. 3, Jn. vi.

71, xii. 4, xiii. 2, 26, xiv. 22**. In 19a Σκαριώθ is read by D supported by it vg sys. Ἰσκαριώθ is commonly explained as = קְרִיּוֹת אִישׁ, ' man of Kerioth ', just as Ἰστωβος (Jos. *Ant.* vii. 6. 1) = טוֹב אִישׁ, ' man of Tob ' and Kerioth is identified either with Kerioth-Hezron (Josh. xv. 25) twelve miles south of Hebron (Buhl, *Geogr.* 182) or with Kerioth in Moab (Jer. xlviii. 24, LXX Καριώθ). That a place name is in question is suggested by the interpretative reading ἀπὸ Καρυώτου given by א* Θ fam. 13 in Jn. vi. 71 and by D in Jn. xii. 4, xiii. 2, 26, xiv. 22. Wellhausen, 23, objects that אִישׁ was not in use in Aramaic in the time of Christ, but Dalman, 52, contends that Heb. or Aramaic surnames usually remained unaltered without regard to the language in use at the time. See also Dalman, *JJ*, 28 f. The very tentative suggestion, that the name may have originated in *sicarius* (' assassin '), has commended itself to few ; cf. Klostermann, 41 who mentions Wellhausen, Merx, and Schulthess ; Dalman, *op. cit.* ; and Lagrange, 68, who adds an exclamation mark. It is surprising that Mark leaves Ἰσκαριώθ unexplained. ' It is a very plausible conjecture that Ἰσκαριώθ was already unintelligible to the evangelist ', Dalman, *WJ*, 52.

The phrase ὃς καὶ παρέδωκεν αὐτόν, in which καί = ' also ' or ' in fact ', strikes a note which resounds in all the Gospels. Cf. Mk. xiv. 10, 43, Mt. x. 4, Lk. vi. 16, Jn. vi. 64; also Ac. i. 13, etc. It is a striking tribute to the historical fidelity of the Gospels that the presence of a traitor among the Twelve is so frankly disclosed. Cf. Lagrange, 68, *Ce trait marque la fidélité de la tradition évangélique* ; Ed. Meyer, i. 297, *Wie wäre es denkbar, dass die Christengemeinde den Verräter, den sie verabscheut, in den Kreis der auserwählten Vertrauten aufgenommen hätte, wenn er garnicht in denselben gehörte ?*

(a) Mk. iii. 19b-35   CHARGES BROUGHT
AGAINST JESUS

This complex of narratives and sayings is topically arranged to illustrate the general theme of Charges brought against Jesus. It consists of the following :

(21) iii. 19b-21. The Fears of the Family of Jesus.
(22) iii. 22-6. On Collusion with Satan.
(23) iii. 27-30. Sayings on the Strong Man and on Blasphemy.
(24) iii. 31-5. On the True Kindred of Jesus.

Introduced by the phrase, ' And he cometh into a house ', these narratives and sayings are loosely attached one to another, and the last is merely appended to the rest. Apparently, Mark had no information as to the time and circumstances of the incidents. The presence of the complex at this point in the outline raises the question whether it existed in substantially its present form before the Gospel was written. See Intr. 92 f. In describing the hostility which the ministry of Jesus aroused, iii. 19b-35 stands in striking contrast to iii. 7-12 and prepares the way for the Parable of the Sower (iv. 1-9). It is perhaps for these reasons that it appears in its present position in Mk.

Mk. iii. 19b-21   21. THE FEARS OF THE   No parallel in
FAMILY OF JESUS   Mt and Lk

This narrative also is a Markan construction, as the vocabulary, style, and want of vivid detail show. The narrative is based on the best historical tradition. No one has the hardihood to suggest that it is a creation of the community, for without the warrant of fact no early narrator would have alleged that the family at Nazareth thought that Jesus was beside Himself and went out to restrain Him. It is not surprising that both Matthew and Luke omit the story, nor is it at all likely that it was added in Mk by a redactor (cf. J. Weiss, 166). Bultmann, 28 f., suggests that originally 21 and 31-5 formed a single unit, or rather 21 and 35, 22-34 being inserted later. Formerly Dibelius also connected 20 f. with 31-5, but in the second edition of his *Formgeschichte des Evangeliums* (Eng. tr. *From Tradition to Gospel*, 47) he retracted this opinion and now holds that 20 f. was written by the Evangelist ' as an introduction preparatory to the story of iii. 31 ff. '. Schmidt, 122 f., also thinks that in the two passages it is a question of two different traditions. There can be little doubt that this is the better view. Introduced by the words, ' And he cometh into a house ', in 19b, the narrative is an independent fragment of early tradition.

Καὶ ἔρχεται εἰς οἶκον· καὶ συνέρχεται πάλιν [ὁ] ὄχλος, ὥστε 20

19b, 20. The use of the historic present ἔρχεται, of πάλιν, and of ὥστε c. acc. and infin. with the double negative, suggests that Mark is writing freely without the aid of a source. References to a house and to the

gathering of crowds are among the few simple aids he uses in describing events in the Story of Jesus. συνέρχομαι, vi. 33 (?), xiv. 53*, Mt. i. 18, Lk (2), Jn (2), Ac (17), 1 Cor (7)**, here in the sense of *assemble*; Hero-

21 μὴ δύνασθαι αὐτοὺς μηδὲ ἄρτον φαγεῖν. καὶ ἀκούσαντες οἱ παρ᾽
αὐτοῦ ἐξῆλθον κρατῆσαι αὐτόν, ἔλεγον γὰρ ὅτι ἐξέστη.

dotus i. 152. 3, LXX, Pap. πάλιν
points back to iii. 7 f. The phrase
ἄρτον φαγεῖν, ' to eat bread ', that is,
to take food of any kind, = אָכַל לֶחֶם
(Gen. iii. 19, etc.). Cf. vi. 31, καὶ οὐδὲ
φαγεῖν εὐκαίρουν. Although there is
no connecting link, other than πάλιν,
with the preceding narratives, it is
clear that the incident belongs to the
early Ministry during the full tide of
success. In Mt and Lk there is no
parallel to 19b-21, but there can be
no doubt that it is an original element
in Mk, omitted by the later Evangelists
because of its bold character.

21. In Cl. Gk οἱ παρ᾽ αὐτοῦ means
' envoys ' or ' ambassadors '. In the
LXX it denotes ' adherents ' or ' followers ' (1 Macc. ix. 44 (א V), xi. 73,
xii. 27, xiii. 52, xv. 15, xvi. 16, 2 Macc.
xi. 20), but also ' parents ' and other
' relatives ' (Prov. xxxi. 21, οἱ παρ᾽ αὐτῆς, Heb. ' all her house ', Sus. 33;
cf. Jos. Ant. i. 10. 5). In the papyri
the phrase is used freely to describe
' agents ', ' neighbours ', ' friends ',
and ' relatives ' (Field, 25 f.; VGT,
478 f.; Moulton, i. 106). Cf. P. Grenf.
ii. 36. 9 (95 B.C.), ἔρρωμαι δὲ καὶ αὐτὸς
καὶ Ἐσθλύτις . . . καὶ οἱ παρ᾽ ἡμῶν
πάντες, ' all our family '. This is the
meaning in Mk. Cf. vg, sui and sys,
' His brethren '. The family at
Nazareth, and not merely ' His friends '
(RV), are indicated. So Holtzmann,
126; Klostermann, 42; Lagrange,
69 f.; Gould, 61; Swete, 63; Rawlinson, 41; Bartlet, 152; Plummer,
110; Branscomb, 68; Wood, 685.
The disciples (cf. οἱ περὶ αὐτόν, iv. 10)
are in no way suggested, still less the
scribes (D W a b (c) f ff i q r¹, Victor
(v. Swete, 63)). The circumstances
in which members of the family came
(ἐξῆλθον) are indicated by ἀκούσαντες
and their purpose by κρατῆσαι αὐτόν.
What they heard is not stated, but
it would be wrong to limit the information to the neglect of Jesus to care for
His personal needs. κρατῆσαι αὐτόν is

a strong expression. The verb is used
in i. 31 (q.v.), v. 41, ix. 27 of taking
hold of the hand, and in vii. 3 f., 8 of
keeping a tradition, but in vi. 17, xii.
12, xiv. 1, 44, 46, 49, 51 of arresting
a person. This is the meaning here.
The family wanted to get hold (cf.
Moffatt) of Jesus, to take control of
His actions, and not merely, as Lagrange, 70, says le contraindre, avec
une violence affectueuse, à s'occuper de
sa personne. Deep personal concern
for Jesus is combined with a want of
sympathy for His aims and purposes.

It is natural to take οἱ παρ᾽ αὐτοῦ as
the subject of ἔλεγον, and this is the
view taken by most commentators:
cf. Holtzmann, 127; Klostermann,
42; Swete, 64; Gould, 61; Branscomb, 68; Bartlet, 152; Wood, 685.
Others, however, prefer to regard the
verb as impersonal, on disait, ' People
were saying '; so Turner, 23; Lagrange, 70; cf. Streeter, 189. On this
interpretation the charge ἐξέστη was a
popular verdict reported to the family
at Nazareth, not a judgment formed by
them. On the whole this view seems
doubtful. The impersonal use of the
imperfect is a well established Markan
usage (v. Intr. 47, 62), but this interpretation is dubious when, as here, a
subject is naturally suggested by the
context. Nor does this explanation free
the Holy Family from blame, for even if
they did not originate the charge, they
gave credence to it and acted upon it;
and it is difficult to believe that their
sole motive was tender solicitude for
Jesus in His neglect to take food. See
κρατῆσαι above. Streeter's suggestion,
FG, 189, that it is by no means likely
that Mark would have told the story
at all, if he had meant what he is
usually understood to mean, is not
well based; for realism and boldness
of statement are characteristic of him,
and the Fourth Evangelist says plainly
that ' even his brethren did not believe
on him ' (Jn. vii. 5). Moreover, the

story of the True Kindred of Jesus (iii. 31-5), which Mark has in mind in 19b-21, has an unmistakable atmosphere of tension, for which we account best if the family of Jesus shared the opinion expressed by ἐξέστη. We conclude therefore that the subject of ἔλεγον is οἱ παρ' αὐτοῦ.

ἐξέστη means ' He is beside Himself ', ' out of His mind ' (cf. Moffatt). The aor. is timeless and is best represented by the English perfect; cf. Moulton, i. 134; Burton, 47; Robertson, 842, 845. Cf. also the Latin renderings: exentiat d i q; exsentiat b ff; excutiat a; in furorem uersus est f l vg, and the explanatory comment of Euthymius, παρεφρόνησε. The same charge is brought against St. Paul by Festus in the words, Μαίνῃ, Παῦλε (Ac. xxvi. 24), and the Apostle uses the

same verb in 2 Cor. v. 13 of himself, εἴτε γὰρ ἐξέστημεν, θεῷ, in contrast with εἴτε σωφρονοῦμεν, ὑμῖν. Some commentators (e.g. Lagrange, 70; Plummer, 111) think that a rendering like ' mad ', and, in particular, that of the Vulgate, in furorem uersus est, is too strong; but the verb can have this meaning (VGT, 224; Souter, Lexicon, 87) and may have been used hyperbolically to describe a course of action like madness, as when we say, ' he is mad '. Loisy's comment, cited by Lagrange, 70 f., is excellent: Ils ne disent pas que Jésus ait perdu la raison . . . mais ils le croient dans un état d'exaltation mystique qui lui fait perdre le sens réel de la vie et de sa propre condition (i. 698). The only query to be added is whether they said more than they believed.

Mk. iii. 22-6   22. ON COLLUSION WITH   Cf. Mt. xii. 22-6
                 SATAN   Lk. xi. 14-18

In the oral period this Pronouncement-story (cf. Bultmann, 10-12; Albertz, 48-50; Redlich, 96) was preserved because it gave the reply of Jesus to the charge of exorcizing daemons by the power of Satan. Usually the story is called ' the Beelzebul Controversy ', but, as suggested in the Commentary, this usage may be due to the tendency to connect the story with the similar but different tradition that Jesus was possessed by an evil spirit, a tradition attested by Mk. iii. 21-2a, 28-30, by Mt. xii. 27 f. = Lk. xi. 19 f., and by Jn. vii. 20, viii. 48 f., 52, x. 20 f. The story found a place also in Q (cf. Mt. xii. 22-6 = Lk. xi. 14 f., 17 f.), and from the two accounts it is possible with some confidence to infer the history of the tradition. The Q form is more original in representing that the controversy arose in connexion with the exorcizing of a dumb daemon. Instead of this introduction Mark has the editorial passage iii. 22-3a, in which he attributes the charge to the scribes from Jerusalem. Like Matthew's reference to the Pharisees, this may be an attempt to give greater definiteness to the tradition (cf. Lk. xi. 15, ' Some of them '). Otherwise, Mark's account preserves the story with great fidelity, greater in some respects than that of Q (cf. iii. 24 f. and Lk. xi. 17). From a very early time the story became a nucleus to which similar sayings were drawn, iii. 27 in Mk and Mt. xii. 27-9 = Lk. xi. 19-21 in Q. Other attracted material in Q is probably to be seen in the saying: ' He that is not with me is against me ' (Mt. xii. 30 = Lk. xi. 23), and the parable of the Untenanted House (Mt. xii. 43-5 = Lk. xi. 24-6). In these additions the process in the tradition whereby an original Apothegm was expanded by sayings-material is clearly evident. Cf. Bultmann, 12.

The historical value of the narrative stands high. It is not the record of an eyewitness, but the residue of a very early tradition. It reveals the fierce opposition to which the ministry of Jesus was exposed and His strong consciousness of being at death-grips with Satan and all his powers.

22 Καὶ οἱ γραμματεῖς οἱ ἀπὸ Ἱεροσολύμων καταβάντες ἔλεγον ὅτι Βεεζεβοὺλ ἔχει, καὶ ὅτι ἐν τῷ ἄρχοντι τῶν δαιμονίων ἐκ-

22. As the vocabulary shows, this editorial passage is the work of Mark. He has no account of the cure of the dumb demoniac which in Q (Lk. xi. 14 = Mt. xii. 22 f.) preceded the controversy, and was probably the occasion of it. Instead of οἱ γραμματεῖς Mt has οἱ Φαρισαῖοι, and Lk τινὲς ἐξ αὐτῶν. καταβάντες ἀπό is here used, as in Lk. ii. 51, x. 30 f., Ac. viii. 26, of coming *down* from the principal city. Cf. ἀναβαίνω, *VGT*, 29 f. The two charges, repeatedly uttered (ἔλεγον), are distinct, and may have been made by different groups (cf. Lagrange, 71). The first, ' He hath Beelzebul ', means that He is possessed by an evil spirit (cf. iii. 30); the second, that His exorcisms are wrought by the power of ' the ruler of the daemons ', that is, Satan, ἐν being either instrumental (cf. Heb. ב) or = ' in the sphere of '. Mt and Lk combine the two charges, ἐν (τῷ) Βεελζεβοὺλ (τῷ) ἄρχοντι τῶν δαιμονίων, thus identifying Beelzebul with Satan. It seems more probable that the two are distinct; that in the first charge Beelzebul is the name of a particular evil spirit, not otherwise known to us, and that in the second the instrumentality of Satan, ὁ ἄρχων τῶν δαιμονίων, is alleged. For the descriptive name cf. ὁ τοῦ κόσμου ἄρχων (Jn. xiv. 30), ὁ ἄρχων τοῦ κόσμου τούτου (Jn. xvi. 11), ὁ ἄρχων τῆς ἐξουσίας τοῦ ἀέρος (Eph. ii. 2). Cf. G. Delling, *KThW*, i. 486-8.

The view mentioned above is, of course, a conjecture; the generally accepted identification Beelzebul = the ruler of the devils = Satan may be supported not only by Mt. xii. 24 = Lk. xi. 15, but also by the saying, ' If I by Beelzebul cast out devils, by whom do your sons cast them out? ' (Mt. xii. 27 = Lk. xi. 19). This pas-

sage, however, is not quite decisive, since the meaning Beelzebul = Satan is suggested only in the context in which it appears (i.e. as following Mt. xii. 26 = Lk. xi. 18). It may be an isolated saying inserted in this context by the compiler of Q. The strongest objection to the identification is that nowhere in Jewish literature is Satan called Beelzebul, although other names, Mastema, Sammael, Asmodaeus, Beliar are applied to him. If Beelzebul were the name of a subordinate evil spirit, want of reference to him is not difficult to understand in view of the welter of names applied to evil spirits in the Magical Papyri of the early Christian centuries (cf. Deissmann, 254-64).

Βεελζεβούλ*, Mt. x. 25, xii. 24, 27, Lk. xi. 15, 18 f.**. Both the spelling of the name and its derivation are uncertain. B has Βεεζεβούλ, which is read also by א and B in all cases in Mt and Lk (cf. Hort, *Notes*, 159). On this reading Moulton, ii. 105, observes : ' No explanation of this reading is suggested which would justify its originality : we must perhaps assume a kind of assimilation based on the abnormality of the combination λζ in Greek. If so, the corruption must go to swell the list of small errors which א and B share, proving their common origin.' The form *Beelzebub* is found in vg and sysᵖᵉ, but in no Greek MS. It is probably derived from זְבוּב בַּעַל in 2 Kgs. i. 2 (LXX ἐν τῷ (τῇ) Βάαλ μυῖαν, but Symm. Βεελζεβούβ), lit. ' Lord of flies ', also described as ' the god of Ekron '. Among many attempts to account for the form Βεελζεβούλ three may be mentioned : (1) the view that the second element is a derisive corruption of זְבוּב formed from the Talmudic זִבּוּל, from בָּל,

βάλλει τὰ δαιμόνια. καὶ προσκαλεσάμενος αὐτοὺς ἐν παραβολαῖς 23
ἔλεγεν αὐτοῖς Πῶς δύναται Σατανᾶς Σατανᾶν ἐκβάλλειν; καὶ 24

'dung', Beelzebul thus meaning 'Lord of dung'; (2) the suggestion that ζεβουλ is derived from זְבֻל, 'height', 'abode', 'dwelling', and that the name means 'Lord of the dwelling', with reference either to the air or to the possessed in whom he dwells; (3) the conjecture that the name is connected with the Aramaic בְּעֵל־דְּבָבָא, signifying 'the enemy' (cf. Lagrange, 71). Certainty is not attainable, but strong support for the second is afforded by Mt. x. 25, 'If they have called the master of the house Beelzebul . . .'.

See further, Nestle, *DCG*, i. 181 f.; Cheyne, *EB*, col. 514 f.; Foerster, *KThW*, i. 605 f.; Lagrange, 71; Swete, 64; McNeile, 143 f.

23. The opening phrase is editorial. For Mark's use of παρακαλέομαι *v.* iii. 13. παραβολή, iv. 2, 10 f., 13 (*bis*), 30, 33 f., vii. 17, xii. 1, 12, xiii. 28*, 'a parable', 'a maxim', 'a wise saying'; Cl., LXX. Cf. *VGT*, 480: 'Our sources throw no special light upon this word which in the NT is found only in the Synoptics = "parable", "similitude", and *bis* in Heb. (ix. 9, xi. 19) = "figure", "type"'. The Fourth Gospel uses παροιμία (x. 16, xvi. 25 (*bis*), 29*). Although παραβολή is used in Cl. Gk with the meanings 'comparison', 'illustration', 'analogy', its use in the Synoptic Gospels is to be traced through the LXX, to the Hebrew מָשָׁל which denotes gnomic utterances, proverbs, taunts, riddles, and illustrative stories (cf. Judg. ix. 8-15, 2 Sam. xii. 1-4). Cf. Oesterley, *GP*, 3-18; Smith, 11 f.; W. J. Moulton, *DCG*, ii. 312-17; McNeile, 185 f.; Hatch, *Essays*, 64 ff. For the various types in the Gospels see the note on iv. 1-9, and for the question of the use of allegory see iv. 13 and xii. 6. The phrase ἐν παραβολαῖς, used here and in iv. 11 and xii. 1, is adverbial, and may be rendered 'in similitudes'; cf. Moffatt: 'by way of parable'; it

describes the picturesque and allusive maxims which follow and by which the charge of acting under the power of the ruler of the daemons is rebutted. It is noteworthy that Jesus does not use the name Beelzebul, but that of Satan (*v.* the note on i. 13). There can be no doubt that He accepted the contemporary belief in the reality of Satan as lord of the kingdom of evil. This belief is implicit in the present saying, in which the acc. Σατανᾶν means not only Satan himself, but also those over whom he exercises his sway. His attitude is also illustrated by His belief in the reality of demoniacal possession, the story of the Temptation (i. 12 f.), the saying on the Strong Man (iii. 27), and the Lukan sayings x. 18, 'I beheld Satan fall from heaven', xiii. 16, 'This woman . . . whom Satan had bound', and xxii. 31, 'Simon, Simon, behold, Satan asked to have you, that he might sift you as wheat'. This belief cannot be explained as accommodation to popular ideas; it is part of the conditions necessary to a real Incarnation. The modern Christian is not bound to take the same view. His attitude to the doctrine of Satan will be determined by his philosophy of evil and his interpretation of the facts of life and religious experience. Cf. Cadoux, 67.

iii. 23 is peculiar to Mark's account of the controversy, but the saying, 'How can Satan cast out Satan?', is implied by Mt. xii. 26. Mark has no parallel to the statement in Q that Jesus knew the thoughts of His opponents; cf. Mt. xii. 25, εἰδὼς τὰς ἐνθυμήσεις αὐτῶν, Lk. xi. 17, αὐτῶν τὰ διανοήματα. But cf. ii. 8 in the story of the Paralytic.

24 f. The general principle that Satan cannot cast out Satan is illustrated by two hypothetical parallels, the divided kingdom and the divided house, introduced by the construction ἐάν *c.* subj. in a conditional clause, and,

ἐὰν βασιλεία ἐφ' ἑαυτὴν μερισθῇ, οὐ δύναται σταθῆναι ἡ βασιλεία
25 ἐκείνη· καὶ ἐὰν οἰκία ἐφ' ἑαυτὴν μερισθῇ, οὐ δυνήσεται ἡ οἰκία
26 ἐκείνη στῆναι· καὶ εἰ ὁ Σατανᾶς ἀνέστη ἐφ' ἑαυτὸν καὶ ἐμερίσθη,
οὐ δύναται στῆναι ἀλλὰ τέλος ἔχει.

in 26, by the actual circumstances presupposed, a divided Satan, expressed by εἰ c. indic. βασιλεία here has the meaning 'kingdom' or 'realm'. μερίζω, iii. 24 f., 26, vi. 41*. ἐφ' ἑαυτήν, 'in relation to itself', or 'against itself', in 24, 25, and 26, is found also in Lk. xi. 17 f., and in Mt. xii. 26, but is replaced in Mt. xii. 25 (bis) by καθ' ἑαυτῆς. There does not appear to be any difference of meaning between σταθῆναι and στῆναι. Both Matthew and Luke have ἐρημοῦται instead of οὐ δύναται σταθῆναι (cf. Mt. xii. 25 = Lk. xi. 17). This agreement is one of the smaller indications that an account of the controversy stood in Q as well as in Mk. In Luke's version the fate of the house is part of the destruction which comes upon the kingdom : ' house falleth upon house ' (RVmg). Manson, SJ, 86, thinks that this arrangement is more original, and that the second similitude in Mk and Mt (+πόλις) is an expansion of the first. The parallelism, however, is Semitic, and it seems more probable that Luke has reduced the two to one.

26. The argument reaches its climax by showing the actual implication of the charge. Hence the change of construction ; cf. 24 f. Instead of ἀνέστη . . . ἐμερίσθη Luke has διεμερίσθη and Matthew τὸν Σατανᾶν ἐκβάλλει, and following Q both have the apodosis in the form πῶς σταθήσεται ἡ βασιλεία αὐτοῦ;. Mark preserves the parallelism with 24 f., but, perhaps rightly, א* C* Δ f l vg increase the force of ἐμερίσθη by transferring it to the apodosis. His final word ἀλλὰ τέλος ἔχει strikes a note of doom. In these respects Mark's version seems more original than that of Q. τέλος, xiii. 7, 13*, cf. Lk. xxii. 37, is here used of death, as in Cl. Gk, e.g. Plato, Lg. 717 E, 801 E, Xenophon, Cyr. viii. 7. 6, vii. 3. 11, Herodotus i. 31, etc. With 26 the section ends, but 27 may have been appended at an early period. At this point Q contained the two sayings : ' If I by Beelzebul cast out devils . . .', and ' If I by the finger (Mt, ' Spirit ') of God cast out devils . . .' (Mt. xii. 27 f. = Lk. xi. 19 f.), and then a version of the saying on the Strong Man (Lk. xi. 21 f.), unless this comes from L. See further, the note on iii. 27. The redundancy manifest in iii. 26 is effective, and may be intentional.

Mk. iii. 27-30   23. SAYINGS ON THE   Cf. Mt. xii. 29, 31 f.
STRONG MAN AND ON   Lk. xi. 21 f., xii. 10
BLASPHEMY

Like ii. 21 f. and 27 f. these sayings have been taken from an early collection. The saying on the Strong Man appears to have been connected with iii. 22-6 at a very early date, since the same association is found both in Mk and Q. This arrangement is natural in view of the subject-matter, but is editorial, if iii. 22-6 is a unit in itself. The theme of iii. 27 is the same, but the argument is new. The implication is that the exorcisms prove that Satan has been bound by Jesus or by the power of God by which He worked. Originally eschatological, this expectation is given a present setting in the historical ministry, and thus stands in line with much that He taught concerning the Kingdom of God. Such sayings, tuned to the enthusiasm of the eschatological hope, are of the utmost importance for an understanding of the mind and purpose of Jesus. Bultmann, 110, sees in them something characteristic, something new, which goes beyond popular wisdom and piety, and yet is just as little specifically scribal and rabbinical or apocalyptic. ' Here if anywhere must the characteristic element in the preaching of Jesus be found.' [1]

Mk. iii. 28 f. is a separate saying from a different context, as the parallel in Q shows (cf. Lk. xii. 10). But Mark has rightly divined, or was guided by good tradition, in connecting it with the charge of possession by Beelzebul. In the form of a solemn warning against the danger of blasphemy against the Holy Spirit it is part of the defence of Jesus against that charge. There is no justification for describing it as ' a product of the apostolic age ' (Branscomb, 74), although the influence of later interests may be reflected in Lk. xii. 10 = Mt. xii. 32, that is, in Q.

’Αλλ’ οὐ δύναται οὐδεὶς εἰς τὴν οἰκίαν τοῦ ἰσχυροῦ εἰσελθὼν 27 τὰ σκεύη αὐτοῦ διαρπάσαι ἐὰν μὴ πρῶτον τὸν ἰσχυρὸν δήσῃ,

27. ὁ ἰσχυρός, ' the Strong Man ', here used as a name for Satan, reflects the influence of Isa. xlix. 24 f. : ' Even the captives of *the mighty* shall be taken away, and the prey of *the terrible* shall be delivered ' (LXX, γίγας), and perhaps also of Isa. liii. 12 : ' And he shall divide the spoil with the strong ' (LXX, καὶ τῶν ἰσχυρῶν μεριεῖ σκῦλα). It may therefore be correct to say that behind this saying lies the consciousness that Jesus is the victorious Servant of God. Cf. W. Grundmann, *KThW*, iii. 403. Apart, however, from these OT echoes, the conviction that Jesus is ὁ ἰσχυρότερος (cf. i. 7) is suggested by the saying itself. His exorcisms prove that He has penetrated into the house of the Strong Man, that He has bound him and plundered his goods. σκεῦος, xi. 16*, is regularly used in Cl. Gk to denote *vessels* or *implements* of any kind, and in the papyri (*VGT*, 577) to describe ' furniture ', ' movables ', ' utensils ', ' goods ', and even the ' tackle ' of a ship. In 2 Cor. iv. 7 and 1 Thess. iv. 4 it is used of ' the body ' as the vessel of the soul. It is natural in the present saying to think of τὰ σκεύη αὐτοῦ as ' the possessed ' enslaved by Satan, and many commentators take this

view (e.g. Victor, cited by Lagrange, 74 ; Swete, 67 ; Bartlet, 154 ; Turner, 23 ; McNeile, 177 ; Manson, *SJ*, 86). But while ὁ ἰσχυρός is a symbolic name it is doubtful if we need to allegorize τὰ σκεύη and οἰκία, which are used to complete the picture. The τὰ σκεύη αὐτοῦ are ' his goods ' ; cf. Lk. xi. 21, τὰ ὑπάρχοντα αὐτοῦ. διαρπάζω*, Mt. xii. 29**, ' to plunder ' ; Cl., LXX, Pap. For ἐὰν μή c. subj. *v*. iv. 22, vii. 3 f., x. 30, xii. 19*. Mark uses πρῶτον fairly freely ; cf. iv. 28, vii. 27, ix. 11 f., xiii. 10, xvi. [9]*.

δέω, v. 3 f., vi. 17, xi. 2, 4, xv. 1, 7*. The idea of the binding of evil powers is an eschatological conception, found in Isa. xxiv. 22 f., and, as regards Satan, illustrated in Apoc. xx. 2 f. The same idea appears in the Zend religion. Cf. Charles, ii. 142. For the Apocalyptic Literature *v*. 1 Enoch x. 11 f., liv. 4 f., Test. Levi xviii. 12. A parallel, and often associated, idea is that of the falling, or casting down, of Satan to earth ; cf. Apoc. xii. 9 (Charles, i. 324), Lk. x. 18, ἐθεώρουν τὸν Σατανᾶν ὡς ἀστραπὴν ἐκ τοῦ οὐρανοῦ πεσόντα, Jn. xii. 31. The one who binds may be God (cf. Creed, 161 ; Rawlinson, 44 ; Branscomb, 71), but is more probably Jesus Himself (cf.

[1] Among such sayings Bultmann, 110, includes : Mk. iii. 24-6, 27, vii. 15, viii. 35, x. 15, 23b, 25, 31 ; Lk. ix. 60a, 62, xiv. 11, xvi. 15 ; Mt. v. 39b-41, 44-8, vii. 13 f., xxii. 14.

28 καὶ τότε τὴν οἰκίαν αὐτοῦ διαρπάσει. 'Αμὴν λέγω ὑμῖν ὅτι

Manson, *SJ*, 86) armed with divine power (cf. Lk. xi. 20). The redundancy in the words, καὶ τότε τὴν οἰκίαν αὐτοῦ διαρπάσει, is Semitic. Matthew's version (xii. 29) closely resembles that of Mk and is based wholly upon it. Lk. xi. 21 f. differs considerably and is more picturesque. It appears in a Q context and is usually assigned to Q (cf. Moffatt, 197-202; Creed, lxv; Manson, *SJ*, 85 f.). It pictures the Strong Man in peace, until he is attacked and overcome by one stronger than he, who takes away his suit of armour (πανοπλία) and divides his spoils (τὰ σκῦλα αὐτοῦ). Cf. Isa. xlix. 24 f. Easton, 183, thinks it is nearer the original saying. The fact that both Mk and Q independently place this saying in close connexion with the story of the controversy about exorcism suggests that the association was traditional at a very early period. Cf. Manson, *SJ*, 85.

In Mk the saying appears to be conformed to those which precede it (cf. οὐ δύναται and the double negative as in i. 44). It is loosely connected with 26 by ἀλλά, which, however, is omitted by A D W *et al.* 565 *al. plur.* b c e f g² i l q r¹ vg sys pe hl. Lagrange, 73, thinks the substitution of καί or δέ may be due to the presence of ἀλλά two words before, but the fact which he notes, that with the omission we have another example of the asyndeton characteristic of Mark's style, tells rather the other way. These considerations tend to support the preference of Easton noted above.

28. The introductory phrase, 'Αμὴν (ןמֵאָ) λέγω ὑμῖν (σοι), ' truly I say unto you ', is found exclusively in the sayings of Jesus, in which it adds emphasis and solemnity to that which follows; cf. viii. 12, ix. 1, 41, x. 15, 29, xi. 23, xii. 43, xiii. 30, xiv. 9, 18, 25, 30*, Mt (30), Lk (6), Jn (ἀμὴν ἀμήν, 25). In the OT (1 Kgs. i. 36, Jer. xi. 5, Psa. xli. 14, etc.) it refers to that which goes before (LXX, γένοιτο). Cf. McNeile,

58; D. Daube, *JTS*, xlv. 27-31; H. Schlier, *KThW*, i. 339-42. Schlier goes so far as to say that in the phrase all Christology is contained *in nuce*.

τοῖς υἱοῖς τῶν ἀνθρώπων is an overliteral rendering of the Aramaic original; cf. Mt. xii. 31, τοῖς ἀνθρώποις. In Q the Son of Man is mentioned (Lk. xii. 10 = Mt. xii. 32). Probably the two versions are different translations of the same Aramaic phrase. Some scholars prefer the Q form (Bultmann, 138, who cites A. Fridrichsen and M. Goguel; cf. Easton, 199), but most, rightly, I think, prefer Mark's version (cf. Wellhausen, *Mt*, 62 f.; Bultmann, 138; Jackson and Lake, i. 380; Manson, *TJ*, 217, *SJ*, 110; Cadoux, 96; Dalman, 254). It has been conjectured, however, that in connecting τοῖς υἱοῖς τῶν ἀνθρώπων with ἀφεθήσεται Mark modifies the original saying, in which blasphemy or railing against men (cf. Rom. iii. 8, 1 Cor. x. 30) stood in contrast with blasphemy against the Holy Spirit; cf. McNeile, 178; Smith, 133. An alternative possibility is that Jesus used the singular, ' a son of man ', with reference to Himself, but not in a Messianic sense; cf. Rawlinson, 44 f. Blasphemy against a son of man may be forgiven, but not if it is spoken against the Holy Spirit. Cf. Lagrange, 76, who takes the meaning to be that it is excusable to a point to fail to recognize the dignity of the One who hides Himself under the humble appearance of a man, but not to disparage works manifestly salutary which reveal the action of the Divine Spirit. On this interpretation, which is supported by iii. 30, Mark has generalized the saying, while the compiler of Q has read it Messianically.

τὰ ἁμαρτήματα καὶ αἱ βλασφημίαι is explained by Wellhausen, 26, as an insertion from Mt. xii. 31, but it seems more probable that Matthew's smooth phrase πᾶσα ἁμαρτία καὶ βλασφημία is a correction of Mark's rough Greek,

πάντα ἀφεθήσεται τοῖς υἱοῖς τῶν ἀνθρώπων, τὰ ἁμαρτήματα
καὶ αἱ βλασφημίαι ὅσα ἐὰν βλασφημήσωσιν· ὃς δ᾽ ἂν βλασφη- 29
μήσῃ εἰς τὸ πνεῦμα τὸ ἅγιον, οὐκ ἔχει ἄφεσιν εἰς τὸν αἰῶνα,
ἀλλὰ ἔνοχός ἐστιν αἰωνίου ἁμαρτήματος. ὅτι ἔλεγον Πνεῦμα 30

in which ὅσα (=ὅσας, read by A C L
et al. fam. 1 28 33 565 700 892 1071
al. pler.) is to be construed ad sensum.
ἁμάρτημα, iii. 29*, Rom. iii. 25, 1 Cor.
vi. 18, 2 Pet. i. 9 (?)**, ' an act of sin ';
Cl., LXX, Pap.; v. the note on i. 4.
βλασφημία, vii. 22, xiv. 64*; Cl., LXX,
' a railing ', ' blasphemy '. The particle ἐάν is here used as the equivalent
of ἄν, a usage, common in the first and
second centuries A.D., which had
almost died away before the great
uncials were written. ' It seems that
in this small point the uncials faithfully reproduce originals written under
conditions long obsolete ', Moulton,
i. 43, cf. VGT, 29,
The point of outstanding importance
in the saying is the universality of
forgiveness apart from the exception
noted in the next verse. As always
when ἀφίημι is used, forgiveness is the
setting aside of obstacles to fellowship.
29. ὃς ἄν (or ἐάν) c. subj. is found
some 20 times in Mk; c. indic. in viii.
35b. For constructions with ἄν cf.
Moulton, i. 165-9; VGT, 29. With
βλασφημέω εἰς cf. Lk. xii. 10**; also Ac.
vi. 11, ῥήματα βλάσφημα εἰς Μωυσῆν.
Elsewhere the verb is used either absolutely (ii. 7, iii. 28) or c. acc. (xv. 29)*·
For τὸ πνεῦμα τὸ ἅγιον vii. 36, xiii.
11*, v. the note on i. 8. Cf. Mt. xii. 31,
ἡ δὲ τοῦ πνεύματος βλασφημία, xii. 32,
κατὰ τοῦ πνεύματος τοῦ ἁγίου, Lk. xii.
10, τῷ δὲ εἰς τὸ ἅγιον πνεῦμα βλασφη-
μήσαντι.
In Greek literature βλασφημέω is
used to express the ideas of slandering
men and of irreverence towards the
gods (v. LS, 317 f.). The ideas of
slandering and reviling are found also
in the LXX and the NT (Mk. xv. 29,
Ac. xviii. 6, Rom. xiv. 16, etc.), but,
influenced by the doctrine of God, the
verb (also βλασφημία and βλάσφημος)
is used especially of defiant hostility

to God, His name or word, in speech
which defies His power and majesty.
Cf. H. W. Beyer, KThW, i. 621 f.
Such language might be used against
His Holy Spirit (cf. the Zadokite Document, vii. 12, 'their holy spirit') as
in the present saying, and by a natural
transition the meaning of blasphemy
was extended to the claim to forgive
sins (ii. 7) and to be exalted to the right
hand of God (xiv. 64). In Christian
usage blasphemy is seen in persecution (Ac. xxvi. 11), the denial of
Christ's Messiahship (probably the
reviling in xv. 29 is to be interpreted
so), and even false teaching (2 Pet.
ii. 2). In iii. 29, as indicated by Mark
(iii. 30), the blasphemy is the act of
attributing beneficent acts of healing
wrought by the power of the Spirit
(Lk. xi. 20) to the agency of Beelzebul
(iii. 22a). Such a charge is a deliberate
denial of the power and greatness of
the Spirit of God.
He who so blasphemes, it is declared, οὐκ ἔχει ἄφεσιν εἰς τὸν αἰῶνα.
αἰών, iv. 19, x. 30, xi. 14*, is ' an age '
(or ' epoch '), often ' the present age '
(ὁ νῦν αἰών or ὁ αἰὼν οὗτος) as distinguished from ' the age to come '
(ὁ αἰὼν ὁ ἐρχόμενος, x. 30*). But εἰς
τὸν αἰῶνα c. neg. (cf. xi. 14*) means
' never ', à jamais (Lagrange, 75), and
is correctly interpreted in Mt. xii. 32,
οὔτε ἐν τούτῳ τῷ αἰῶνι οὔτε ἐν τῷ μέλ-
λοντι. The words ἀλλὰ ἔνοχός ἐστιν αἰωνίου ἁμαρτήματος, peculiar to Mk, are
not merely tautologous, but bring out
in a sonorous and impressive manner
the enormity of the sin. ἔνοχος, xiv.
64*,=ἐνεχόμενος, ' liable to ', ' guilty
of ' (Cl., LXX, Pap. (VGT, 217)) is used
c. dat. of the tribunal (Mt. v. 21 f.),
c. gen. of the punishment (xiv. 64), or
of the thing injured (1 Cor. xi. 27,
Jas. ii. 10), or of the offence. αἰώνιος,
x. 17, 30*, the adj. corresponding to

ἀκάθαρτον ἔχει.

αἰών, ' eternal ', *perpetuus* (*v. VGT*, 16). It describes the act of sin as a permanent barrier raised by the soul between itself and God. Black, 102 n., suggests that ἁμάρτημα probably corresponds to *ḥiyyubha, condemnatio*. Cf. J. T. Marshall, *Exp.* IV. iii. 282 f.; Allen, 77. In this case, the meaning is ' is liable to an eternal judgment '. Cf. the reading κρίσεως, A C² *et al.* fam. I 22 124 157 700 892mg 1071 *al. pler.* f vg sype hl.

Such is the meaning of the saying as it stands. Some commentators think that the language is that of strong hyperbole, as in Num. xv. 30 f., I Sam. iii. 14, and Isa. xxii. 14. According to this view Jesus ' meant, and would be understood to mean, no more than that blasphemy against the Holy Spirit, by whose power He worked, was a terrible sin — more terrible than blasphemy against man ' (McNeile, 179; cf. Luce, 228; Cadoux, 202 n., 213). It is tempting, but not easy, to be satisfied with this opinion, and it is

doubtful if the OT passages support it. For Rabbinic teaching *v.* Abrahams, i. 142 f.; Billerbeck, i. 637 f. Even less confidence can be placed on interpretations based on the omission of εἰς τὸν αἰῶνα by D W Θ I 28 565 700 a b e ff g¹ q r¹, and perhaps sys. Cf. Bartlet, 156 f. The omission has no exegetical importance unless ἀλλὰ ἔνοχός ἐστιν αἰωνίου ἁμαρτήματος is also omitted.

30. This elliptical passage is an explanatory Markan comment. Cf. iv. 33 f., vi. 12 f., vii. 3 f., vii. 19, καθαρίζων πάντα τὰ βρώματα. It is the Evangelist's way of saying, ' This is the reply of Jesus to the charge, " He hath Beelzebul " '. ἔλεγον is not impersonal (' People were saying '), but points back to iii. 22a. It suggests that the saying on blasphemy was a warning addressed to the scribes. If this interpretation is valid, the view that Beelzebul is the name of an evil spirit, rather than of Satan, is confirmed. For πνεῦμα ἀκάθαρτον *v.* i. 23.

DETACHED NOTE ON THE SIN AGAINST THE HOLY SPIRIT

The saying is one of the most challenging of the words of Jesus, and misapprehensions of its nature have caused untold degrees of suffering. The truth of the saying must not be weakened or explained away, but it must always be estimated in the light of the major truth of the Gospel, namely that where there is true repentance, or even the possibility of repentance, sin can be and is forgiven by God. The sin is not any sin against the Holy Spirit, not even a railing judgment uttered in anger or ignorance ; nor is it simply the deliberate rejection of better light, with full knowledge that it is light. It is a perversion of spirit which, in defiance of moral values, elects to call light darkness. To infer that the scribes had committed this sin, may not be justified ; it is sounder to interpret it as indicating a moral peril of which they stood in danger. Whether we admit the possibility of such ' a sin unto death ' (I Jn. v. 16) will depend on whether we believe that there are final limits to which human self-assertion and self-worship can go, on our knowledge of life and history, and most of all on our recognition of the fact that the warning is that of Jesus. Of all religious teachers no one was less inclined than He to minimize possibilities of forgiveness and amendment and the boundless resources of divine grace.

Mk. iii. 31-5   24. ON THE TRUE KINDRED   Cf. Mt. xii. 46-50
                          OF JESUS   Lk. viii. 19-21

This Pronouncement-story preserves the word of Jesus that His true kindred are those who do the will of God. The story is self-contained and from it everything has fallen away except the few details which lead on to the saying. Dibelius, 63 f., who describes the narrative as a Paradigm, thinks that originally it ended with the words, ' Behold, my mother and my brethren ', 35 being a later addition. Bultmann, 29, on the contrary, finds the original element in 35, 31-4 forming an ' ideal scene '. These suggestions are speculative, but that of Dibelius becomes of much interest when the similar story in Lk. xi. 27 f. is considered. Bultmann's analysis is unnecessarily radical. So far from the scene being ' ideal ', the reference to the glance of Jesus upon those who sat around and the words spoken arise naturally out of the circumstances briefly described in 31-3, and the whole leaves a strong impression of originality. A unit in itself, the story seems to have been attracted to its place in the group 19b-35 by 21 f. It is intended by Mark as a sequel to the earlier story and serves this purpose excellently, but long before he incorporated it into his Gospel (or the complex 19b-35) the narrative was current and gained its form in oral tradition. It is a rounded whole from which much has fallen away by a process of attrition determined by an interest in the question of the true kindred of Jesus.

It is from this point of view that we can explain best the parallel story on the Blessing of the Mother of Jesus in Lk. xi. 27 f. : 'Εγένετο δὲ ἐν τῷ λέγειν αὐτὸν ταῦτα ἐπάρασά τις φωνὴν γυνὴ ἐκ τοῦ ὄχλου εἶπεν αὐτῷ Μακαρία ἡ κοιλία ἡ βαστάσασά σε καὶ μαστοὶ οὓς ἐθήλασας. αὐτὸς δὲ εἶπεν Μενοῦν μακάριοι οἱ ἀκούοντες τὸν λόγον τοῦ θεοῦ καὶ φυλάσσοντες. The two narratives are not variants of the same story (Bultmann, 30), for in details, ideas, and vocabulary they differ. In Mk. iii. 31-5 a new spiritual estimate of kinship is expressed ; in Lk. xi. 27 f. a higher degree of blessedness than parentage. The agreement between the idea of doing the will of God (Mk. iii. 35) and that of hearing and keeping His word (Lk. xi. 28) may be held to support Dibelius' view that Mk. iii. 35 is a later addition, but it is also possible, and on the whole more probable, that similar ideas were expressed independently by Jesus on different occasions. Both stories may have originated in the recollections of eyewitnesses before they attained their present attenuated form.[1]

Καὶ ἔρχονται ἡ μήτηρ αὐτοῦ καὶ οἱ ἀδελφοὶ αὐτοῦ καὶ ἔξω 31
στήκοντες ἀπέστειλαν πρὸς αὐτὸν καλοῦντες αὐτόν. καὶ ἐκάθητο 32

31. For the historic present in Mk v. i. 12. The mother of Jesus appears here only in Mk (but v. vi. 3, ὁ υἱὸς τῆς Μαρίας). οἱ ἀδελφοὶ αὐτοῦ*, cf. vi. 3, ἀδελφὸς Ἰακώβου καὶ Ἰωσῆτος καὶ Ἰούδα καὶ Σίμωνος. The absence of a refer-

ence to Joseph here and in vi. 3 is generally understood to mean that he was dead. στήκω, xi. 25*, Jn (2), Pl (7), Apoc. xii. 4**, ' to stand '; a new present formed from the perfect ἕστηκα (LXX, 3 Kgdms. viii. 11). ἔξω

[1] With a query Weiss, 350, classifies Mk. iii. 31-5 as Petrine. *Die lebhafte rhetorische Frage Jesu, das hochgespannte Berufsbewusstsein, das Wort vom Tun des Willes Gottes — das alles macht einen höchst authentischen und lebendigen Eindruck*, 170. Dibelius, 162, describes Lk. xi. 27 f. as a *Chria*, in which we receive the impression that the account of the situation may have been handed down to the Evangelist and that only the pregnant style is due to him.

περὶ αὐτὸν ὄχλος, καὶ λέγουσιν αὐτῷ 'Ιδοὺ ἡ μήτηρ σου καὶ
33 οἱ ἀδελφοί σου ἔξω ζητοῦσίν σε. καὶ ἀποκριθεὶς αὐτοῖς λέγει
34 Τίς ἐστιν ἡ μήτηρ μου καὶ οἱ ἀδελφοί; καὶ περιβλεψάμενος
τοὺς περὶ αὐτὸν κύκλῳ καθημένους λέγει "Ιδε ἡ μήτηρ μου καὶ

does not necessarily refer to the house mentioned in 19, since the narrative is a self-contained unit; it may mean outside the crowd gathered around Jesus. The message sent, ἀπέστειλαν . . . καλοῦντες αὐτόν, is a request for an interview. Mark's arrangement (cf. 21) shows that he regards it as connected with the intention to lay hold of Jesus because He was beside Himself. In contrast with Mt. xii. 46, ἔτι αὐτοῦ λαλοῦντος, no connecting link is made with the preceding narratives. Cf. Schmidt, 122. Matthew alters ἔξω στήκοντες to εἱστήκεισαν ἔξω, and Luke adds the explanatory statement: ' they could not come at him for the crowd ' (viii. 19).

32. The crowd mentioned is not further characterized; it is not hostile and apparently (cf. 34) includes many disciples. The plur. λέγουσιν is perhaps impersonal. ' The message is passed from one to another till it reaches Jesus' (Swete, 69). The reading καὶ αἱ ἀδελφαί σου (A D et al. 22 124 238 240 241 700 al. pler. a b c f ff q syhl mg) is a copyist's addition influenced by 34 and vi. 3. The presence of the sisters is most unlikely. Cf. Swete, 69; Lagrange, 77.

33. The construction ἀποκριθεὶς εἶπεν (or λέγει) is very common in the Synoptic Gospels; Mk (15), Mt (45), Lk (38); cf. Ac. (5), Jn (0). Cf. Howard, ii. 453. John prefers ἀπεκρίθη καὶ εἶπεν. Its use in the Synoptics reflects the influence of the LXX. Cf. Lagrange, xciii, and for its use in Aramaic v. Intr. 63. The passive forms ἀποκριθείς and ἀπεκρίθη are normal in the LXX and the NT, but occasionally in the Gospels the classical aor. mid. ἀπεκρίνατο is found (Mk. xiv. 61, Mt. xxvii. 12, Lk. iii. 16, xxiii. 9, Jn. v. 17, 19). See further, the note on xiv. 61. VGT, 65, notes the

silence of the papyri in the use of ἀπεκρίθη after ii/ B.C. ' We are inclined to suggest that the word belongs only to early Hellenistic, whence it was taken by the LXX translators to render a common Hebrew phrase, passing thence into the narrative parts of NT as a definite " Septuagintalism ".' But cf. Black, JTS, xlix. 159.

The question ' Who are my mother and my brethren? ' is the pivot of the narrative, and because of it the story was remembered. It is difficult not to find a tone of disappointment in the question, the recognition of a want of sympathy on the part of the family at Nazareth. The fact that it is consistent with tender care for kinsmen (Swete, 70; Lagrange, 77) need not be doubted. The more important issue is whether the question and the attitude of the family are consistent with the Virgin Birth tradition. No one will wish to settle this issue on the basis of this narrative alone, but it can scarcely be denied that in it the historical and doctrinal objections to that tradition find support. The claim that Mary's presence reveals a mother's anxiety (Turner, 24), while true, is perilously near special pleading. The difficulty that Mark has no knowledge of the Virgin Birth tradition is nowhere relieved in his Gospel. See further, vi. 3.

34. For Mark's use of περιβλέπομαι with reference to the searching look of Jesus v. iii. 5. κύκλῳ, vi. 6, 36*, Lk. ix. 12, Rom. xv. 19, Apoc. iv. 6, v. 11, vii. 11**, is an adverbial use of the dat. of the noun with the meaning ' round about ', ' around '; Cl., LXX, Pap. τοὺς περὶ αὐτὸν κύκλῳ καθημένους describes the disciples (cf. iv. 10, οἱ περὶ αὐτόν), not necessarily the Twelve only, and perhaps as distinct from the rest of the crowd. Cf. Mt. xii. 49, καὶ ἐκ-

οἱ ἀδελφοί μου· ὃς ^T ἂν ποιήσῃ ⌜τὸ θέλημα⌝ τοῦ· θεοῦ, οὗτος 35
ἀδελφός μου καὶ ἀδελφὴ καὶ μήτηρ ἐστίν.

35 γὰρ | τὰ θελήματα

τείνας τὴν χεῖρα αὐτοῦ ἐπὶ τοὺς μαθητὰς
αὐτοῦ. Despite 32, there is no distinction between ἴδε and ἰδού (WM,
319) in Mark's usage. Cf. ii. 24.
35. The asyndeton at the beginning
of the saying is characteristic of Mark's
style; v. Intr. 49 f., 58. Matthew
inserts γάρ, and almost all MSS. do
the same in Mk except B b e bo. For
τὸ θέλημα τοῦ θεοῦ Mt. xii. 50 has τὸ θ.
τοῦ πατρός μου τοῦ ἐν οὐρανοῖς, and Lk.
viii. 21 τὸν λόγον τοῦ θεοῦ. The οὗτος
in Mk is resumptive (Mt, αὐτός). See
the similar saying in Mt. vii. 21. By
some MSS. μου is repeated after each
substantive, after ἀδελφή by C Π Φ 22
33 124 157 1071 al. plur. a g² l vg
sys pe hl sa bo geo aeth, after μήτηρ by
H* 1071 1278 al. plur. a l sys pe sa bo
geo aeth. This Semitic redundancy
may be original, especially as the
tendency would be to omit the pronoun.
The emphasis in the saying upon
'doing the will of God' sets family
relationships on a new plane in which
the ties of a common obedience to God
are superior to those of blood. It is

one of the more extreme examples of
Bultmann's exegesis, 154, 176, that
he describes this saying as ' a product
of the (Palestinian) community'. More
discerning is the opinion of Branscomb, 75, who says that it gives us
' a glimpse of the personal aspects of
Jesus' conception of the reign of God '.
' It was to be constituted by a number
of people whose spirit of mutual service and fellowship would make it a
social body with the ethical quality
and value of a family group.' ' The
early Church ', he adds, ' grew naturally out of this conception.' No
understanding of this saying is complete which does not mark its strong
emphasis on ' doing the will of God '.
Rawlinson, 46, points to Heb. ii. 11,
and Swete, 70, reminds us of the comment of SH on Rom. ii. 18. Cf.
Lagrange, 78, Faire la volonté de
Dieu, c'est, d'après les mystiques, la
racine et le sommet de la perfection.
Si Jésus choisit ce signe, c'est qu'il a
toujours donné comme sa mission de
faire la volonté de son Père.

DETACHED NOTE ON THE BRETHREN OF JESUS

The literature on this question is very extensive, including the writings
of Jerome, Adversus Helvidium, and Epiphanius, Adversus Antidico-
marianitas (Adversus Haereses, iii. 2), and, in modern times, the discussions of A. H. Blom, Schaf, Mill, Th. Zahn, W. Bauer, A. Meyer, and
H. von Soden (v. Klostermann, 63). Among English and French writers
may be mentioned in particular J. B. Lightfoot, Gal. 252-91 ; J. B. Mayor,
St. Jas, v-xxxvi ; C. Harris, DCG, i. 232-7 ; Dom Chapman, JTS, vii.
424 ff. ; Lagrange, 79-93. See also J. H. Ropes, ICC, St. James, 53-74,
and the article of P. W. Schmiedel on ' Clopas ', EB, cols. 849-53.
The three main hypotheses are the Helvidian (maintained by Helvidius,
c. A.D. 380), which claims that the ἀδελφοί were brothers by blood ; the
Epiphanian (Epiphanius, c. A.D. 382), which maintains that they were
the sons of Joseph by a former wife ; and the Hieronymian (Jerome,
c. A.D. 383), that they were cousins of Jesus, the sons of Mary the wife of
Clopas and sister of the Virgin.
Jerome's view was new, having no support in earlier Fathers, and was
advanced against the opinions of Helvidius. He maintained that James

was the son of Alphaeus and that his mother was Mary ' the mother of James the Less and Joses ' (xv. 40; cf. xv. 47, xvi. 1, Jn. xix. 25). He held that in Jn. xix. 25 [1] three women are mentioned and that Mary of Clopas was the Virgin's sister. He also argued that in Scripture ἀδελφός is used, not only of a blood relationship, but also of kinship, common nationality, and friendship. In later discussions the identity of Alphaeus and Clopas was claimed, and also that of Judas of James (Lk. vi. 16) and Simon the Cananaean (Mk. iii. 18) with Judas and Simon respectively who are mentioned in Mk. vi. 3.

The objections to Jerome's hypothesis are conclusive. (1) While ἀδελφός can be used in a wider sense,[2] it does not denote ' cousin ' in classical writers, and is not likely to have been used in the NT in this sense when ἀνεψιός (Col. iv. 10) lay ready to hand. Cf. Lightfoot, op. cit. 261 ; Harris, op. cit. 234 n. (2) The ἀδελφοί of iii. 31-5 were not members of the Twelve. They were opposed to Jesus and did not believe in Him ; cf. Mk. iii. 21 and Jn. vii. 5. (3) They are never associated with Mary of Clopas, but always with Mary the mother of Jesus and with Joseph. (4) In Jn. xix. 25 four women are mentioned and there is no reason to think that Mary of Clopas was the sister of the Virgin. Further, the identity of Alphaeus and Clopas is at best uncertain, and also that of James of Alphaeus and James the Less. Jerome's argument is strongly coloured by his belief in the perpetual virginity of Mary. For these reasons the Hieronymian solution is almost universally rejected, except by Roman Catholic scholars.

The Epiphanian can claim the support of antiquity, being held, as Lightfoot shows, by Clement of Alexandria, Origen, Eusebius, Hilary, ' Ambrosiaster ', Gregory of Nyssa, Epiphanius, Ambrose, and Cyril of Alexandria. It is also implied in the Gospel of Peter (v. M. R. James, 13) and the Protevangelium of James (viii. 3, ix. 2). Among modern scholars it is supported by Lightfoot, Harris, and Bernard. The hypothesis avoids the difficulties of the Hieronymian view, but the main arguments in its favour are doctrinal, especially the claim that Mary's virginity was perpetual. Against it may be urged the implications of Lk. ii. 7, ' She brought forth her firstborn son ', and Mt. i. 25, ' And he knew her not, until she brought forth a son '. In reply to these objections it is argued that πρωτότοκος is a technical term, with the meaning ' that which openeth the womb ' (Ex. xiii. 2, 12, 15, xxxiv. 19 ff., Lk. ii. 22 f.), and does not necessarily imply the birth of other children. Mt. i. 25, it is said, neither asserts nor implies any subsequent intercourse ; cf. Lightfoot, 271 ; Harris, 235.

The Helvidian view can also claim the support of antiquity, but not to the same degree. It was held by Tertullian, Helvidius, Bonosus, and Jovinianus, and others. Many modern scholars, including Mayor, Gould, Plummer, Goguel, Bartlet, Wood, Branscomb, and Creed, take this view. Lightfoot, 272, maintains as a fatal objection the argument that, according to Jn. xix. 26 f., Jesus commended His mother to the care of St. John, and not to His ' brothers '. Apart from critical objections, the objection underestimates the fact that the brothers opposed the claims of Jesus, and it inadequately describes John as a ' stranger '. Nor are the doctrinal

---

[1] ' His mother, and the sister of his mother, Mary of Clopas, and Mary Magdalene.'

[2] Cf. Gen. xiv. 14, 16, xxix. 15, Lev. x. 4, 1 Chron. xxiii. 21 f. ; also the use of the term ' brethren ' for Christians in Acts. Cf. Cadbury, *The Beginnings of Christianity*, v. 378 f.

arguments on one side alone. The fact that Jesus had blood brothers and sisters, it may be held, underlines the reality and completeness of the Incarnation. It may also be fairly argued, as Lightfoot, 271, concedes, that the expressions used in Lk. ii. 7 and Mt. i. 25 would have been avoided by writers who believed in the perpetual virginity of Mary. There can be little doubt that the Helvidian view stands as the simplest and most natural explanation of the references to the brothers of Jesus in the Gospels.

(*b*) Mk. iv. 1-34   PARABOLIC TEACHING

The character and the limits of this complex are clearly discernible. After a brief narrative introduction in 1 f., it contains the following sections :

(25) iv. 1-9.   The Parable of the Sower.
(26) iv. 10-12. The Purpose of Parables.
(27) iv. 13-20. An Interpretation of the Parable of the Sower.
(28) iv. 21-5. A Group of Sayings.
(29) iv. 26-9. The Parable of the Seed Growing Secretly.
(30) iv. 30-2. The Parable of the Mustard Seed.
(31) iv. 33 f. Summary statement on the Use of Parables.

The subject-matter is teaching material, but there is a narrative element in 1 f., 10, and 33 f. The character of the material varies, and among the questions which arise are the following : (1) Had Mark access to a collection of Parables ?, (2) How is the narrative element to be explained ?, (3) Did the Evangelist make use of an existing complex, and, if so, with what modifications has he adapted it in the process of writing his Gospel ? The existence of a pre-Markan collection of sayings is manifest in 21-5, and the use made of it must be considered. For the arrangement and topical character of the section *v*. Intr. 93 f.

DETACHED NOTE ON THE LITERARY FORM OF
THE PARABLE

For the terminology see the note on iii. 23. The basic idea is probably that of *comparison*. A metaphor or a story connected with the affairs of daily life is used as an illustration of moral and spiritual truths, on the assumption that what applies in the one sphere is relevant also in the other. Under the term are included : Similitudes, e.g. the sayings on Patches and Wineskins (ii. 21 f.) ; Parables proper, the Sower, the Seed Growing Secretly, the Mustard Seed, etc. ; and Illustrative Stories, the Good Samaritan, the Rich Fool, the Rich Man and Lazarus, the Pharisee and the Publican, the Friend at Midnight, and the Unjust Judge. The types are far from being fixed, as the classifications of commentators show.

In the main the parable is distinguished from the allegory by the fact that normally the details are not meant to be significant. Since the classical discussion of A. Jülicher in *Die Gleichnisreden Jesu* (1899) it has come to be generally accepted that the parable has one main point, and one only. As a controlling principle and a protest against idle attempts to find a hidden meaning in details, this position is sound ; but it ought not to be pressed to the point of ruling out the possibility of references to the immediate situation of Jesus, as for example, in the parables of the Sower and the Wicked Husbandmen. Sometimes parables are introduced by explanatory phrases, such as ' So is the kingdom of God ' (iv. 26), ' How shall we liken the kingdom of God ? ' (iv. 30), or ' The kingdom of heaven is like . . .' (Mt. xiii. 31); but often the original meaning is lost, and sometimes it is obscured by later additions (e.g. Mt. xiii. 49 f.). Interpretations, therefore, are sometimes conjectural. With much force A. T. Cadoux and C. H. Dodd have argued that explanations which take account of the historical situation created by the Ministry of Jesus are the most convincing.

The purpose of parabolic teaching is clear ; its aim is to elucidate truth, not to obscure it, still less to conceal an issue or to serve as a punishment. Nevertheless, it cannot be assumed that the original application was transparent. The parables were meant to stimulate thought, to provoke reflection, and to lead men to a decision. Explanations of parables may sometimes have been sought by the first hearers, and given by Jesus, as in Rabbinic teaching. For Jewish and Rabbinic parables see P. Fiebig, *Altjüdische Gleichnisreden und die Gleichnisse Jesu* (1904), *Die Gleichnisreden Jesu* (1912), *Der Erzählungsstil der Evangelien* (1925), and Billerbeck, i. 653-5, ii. 7-9 ; and for general discussions of the Gospel parables see Jülicher, *op. cit.* ; H. Weinel, *Die Gleichnisreden Jesu* (1929) ; Bultmann, 179-222 ; A. B. Bruce, *The Parabolic Teaching of Christ* (1882) ; W. J. Moulton, *DCG*, ii. 312-17 ; A. T. Cadoux ; C. H. Dodd ; B. T. D. Smith ; W. O. E. Oesterley ; T. W. Manson. See the Bibliography.

Mk. iv. 1-9	25. THE PARABLE OF THE SOWER	Cf. Mt. xiii. 1-9 Lk. viii. 4-8

A comparison of the Synoptic accounts reveals the greater originality of the Markan version. In it the parable has been recorded with great fidelity. Only in the explanatory phrase in 5, ' where it had not much earth ', does the possibility of an interpretative addition arise. Further, the presence in so small a compass of several Semitisms (καὶ ἐγένετο . . . ἔπεσεν, ἐν τῷ σπείρειν, καρπόν . . . ἔδωκεν, ἕν . . . ἕν . . . ἕν, and possibly ἀνέβησαν) suggests that the Greek stands near an Aramaic original. Black, 45, points to the greater frequency of the hypotactic participle in the parables, which, in this respect, on the whole are written in idiomatic Greek. In contrast, the Markan version of the Sower has not one instance of a hypotactic aorist participle. ' Here in Mark we may speak with confidence of a literal translation Greek version of a parable of Jesus.'

The interpretation of the parable takes various forms. (1) Many commentators interpret it broadly, e.g. as giving encouragement to the disciples (Oesterley, 41 ; Luce, 167), or as teaching the responsibility of hearers (Wood, 686 ; Turner, 24 ; Luce, 167 ; Rawlinson, 50), or again as showing whether the coming of the Kingdom depends on the repentance of Israel as a whole (Smith, 137). All these ideas are suggested by the parable, but it is doubtful if they state the main point at issue. (2) Many scholars see in the parable a reflection of the experience of Jesus Himself as a teacher and prophet (Wellhausen, 32 ; Menzies, 107 f. ; Rawlinson,

50; Bartlet, 160; McNeile, 187; Burkitt, 83 f.). This interpretation is sound, but the fact that commentators combine it with other explanations suggests that it is not the whole truth. (3) Probably the parable relates to the preaching of the Kingdom of God. The Kingdom, it is true, is not expressly mentioned, but it is almost certainly in mind, since this was the absorbing theme of the early Galilean Ministry and because other parables of growth illustrate some aspect of the Kingdom. (4) The eschatological interpretation of Schweitzer, 354 f., has this merit. It stresses the right point, the abundant harvest (iv. 8). There is nothing, however, in the parable which points to the speedy in-breaking of the Kingdom. It is better, therefore (with Dodd, 182 f.; A. T. Cadoux, 154-7; Smith, 126; C. J. Cadoux, 48), to find its significance in the immediate situation of Jesus. By it He illustrates His belief that, despite unresponsive hearers, the field is white unto harvest (cf. Jn. iv. 35). ' The crop is ripe : it is time to reap ' (Dodd). Falling into good ground, the seed is bearing fruit amazingly, thirtyfold, sixtyfold, a hundredfold. This is the main point, but it is not necessary to regard the birds, the thorns, and the rocky ground as simply ' the dramatic machinery of the story '. These references reflect the experience of Jesus and His sense of the importance of attentive hearing.

Καὶ πάλιν ἤρξατο διδάσκειν παρὰ τὴν θάλασσαν. καὶ συνά- 1 IV
γεται πρὸς αὐτὸν ὄχλος πλεῖστος, ὥστε αὐτὸν εἰς πλοῖον ἐμβάντα
καθῆσθαι ἐν τῇ θαλάσσῃ, καὶ πᾶς ὁ ὄχλος πρὸς τὴν θάλασσαν
ἐπὶ τῆς γῆς ἦσαν. καὶ ἐδίδασκεν αὐτοὺς ἐν παραβολαῖς πολλά, 2

1. Mark's vocabulary is clearly apparent in this verse. For πάλιν v. ii. 1; ἤρξατο c. infin. i. 45; διδάσκω i. 21; θάλασσα i. 16; συνάγω ii. 2; ὄχλος ii. 4; ὥστε c. infin. i. 27; κάθημαι ii. 6. The passage takes up the thread of narrative in iii. 7-12, after the interlude provided by the Appointment of the Twelve (iii. 13-19a) and the group of narratives and sayings which illustrate the hostility aroused by the ministry of Jesus (iii. 19b-35). πάλιν points back to ii. 13 or iii. 7. It is the only connecting-link and there is no statement of time (cf. Mt. xiii. 1, ἐν τῇ ἡμέρᾳ ἐκείνῃ). The passage is editorial, but the picture of the very great crowd, so large that Jesus is compelled to teach from a boat, may well be based on good tradition. Little imagination is required to visualize the scene.

ἐμβαίνω, v. 18, vi. 45, viii. 10, 13*. On Syriac evidence J. Rendel Harris, ET, xxvi. 248 ff., claims that ἐμβάντα καθῆσθαι is an Aramaism for ' to go aboard ' (VGT, 205). It is doubtful

if εἰς πλοῖον is meant to refer back to πλοιάριον in iii. 9, for the expression is quite general. MSS. which insert τό (A B² D W Δ et al. fam. 13 22 28 700 1071 al. pler. sys pe hl aeth) reflect a desire to establish the connexion. There is no suggestion of a flight. The purpose of Jesus is to address more easily the great crowd ranged in a rising circle on the beach (Mt, αἰγιαλόν). Cf. Swete, 71. Mt. xiii. 2 replaces ἦσαν by ἱστήκει. Luke's modifications (viii. 4) are greater. He transposes Mark's order, making the parable the beginning of a new section. Using the gen. abs. construction, he abbreviates Mk. iv. 1 f., mentioning that people ' of every city ' came to Jesus who spoke to them ' by a parable ', Συνιόντος δὲ ὄχλου πολλοῦ καὶ τῶν κατὰ πόλιν ἐπιπορευομένων πρὸς αὐτὸν εἶπεν διὰ παραβολῆς.

2. In this reference to teaching πολλά is not adverbial (v. i. 45), but is acc. meaning ' many things ' (Moffatt, ' lessons '). D and sa have the

3 καὶ ἔλεγεν αὐτοῖς ἐν τῇ διδαχῇ αὐτοῦ ᾽Ακούετε. ἰδοὺ ἐξῆλθεν
4 ὁ σπείρων σπεῖραι. καὶ ἐγένετο ἐν τῷ σπείρειν ὃ μὲν ἔπεσεν παρὰ
5 τὴν ὁδόν, καὶ ἦλθεν τὰ πετεινὰ καὶ κατέφαγεν αὐτό. καὶ ἄλλο
ἔπεσεν ἐπὶ τὸ πετρῶδες [καὶ] ὅπου οὐκ εἶχεν γῆν πολλήν, καὶ
6 εὐθὺς ἐξανέτειλεν διὰ τὸ μὴ ἔχειν βάθος γῆς· καὶ ὅτε ἀνέτειλεν ὁ

secondary reading πολλαῖς. ἐν παραβολαῖς may be 'by way of parable', or even 'using similitudes' (v. iii. 23), but the simplest rendering 'in parables' is best. ἐν τῇ διδαχῇ αὐτοῦ is 'in the course of his teaching'; cf. xii. 38. Probably the phrase is the equivalent of ἐν τῷ διδάσκειν αὐτόν (Swete, 71). Lagrange, 94, thinks this would be an intolerable pleonasm and translates, *selon sa manière d'enseigner*.

3. The imperative ᾽Ακούετε, 'Hearken', is peculiar to Mark's account. Cf. vii. 14, ᾽Ακούσατέ μοι πάντες καὶ σύνετε, and יִּשְׁמְעוּ in Deut. vi. 4 quoted in xii. 29. The word indicates a certain intensity of tone which is heightened in the closing words in 9, ῞Ος ἔχει ὦτα ἀκούειν ἀκουέτω. These expressions suggest that the parables were intended to provoke thought, and were not the transparent illustrations they are sometimes supposed to have been. The substantival phrase ὁ σπείρων indicates the typical sower. σπεῖραι is the infin. of purpose, which is used much more freely in the Koine than in Attic Greek. Cf. Moulton, i. 205. Both Matthew and Luke independently use the more classical τοῦ c. infin. In contrast with the pres. in 4, Mark's use of the aor. here seems deliberate; the action is seen as a whole.

4. For καὶ ἐγένετο followed by the indic. without καί v. i. 9. ὃ μέν is 'a part'. Matthew (xiii. 4) has ἃ μέν, 'some (seeds)'. μέν, so common in Cl. Gk, is surprisingly rare in Mk; ix. 12, xii. 5, xiv. 21, 38, xvi. [19]*. μέν . . . ἀλλά appears in ix. 12, and μέν . . . δέ in the remaining examples. Here the correlative is καί. The picture of the seed falling by the wayside and of the birds coming and devouring it is vividly sketched. It is probable that παρὰ τὴν ὁδόν misrenders

the Aramaic 'al 'urḥa, which is ambiguous and should have been rendered 'on the road'. Cf. Torrey, *TG*, 9; Black, 120. πετεινός, iv. 32*, 'flying', <πέτομαι, is used as a neut. substantive, 'bird', in late writers, LXX, and Pap. In κατεσθίω, xii. 40*, the prep. has perfective force, 'eat up', 'devour'; Cl., LXX, Pap. Cf. Moulton, i. 111. For instances of alliteration, assonance, and word-play when the Gk version of the parable is translated back into simple Palestinian Aramaic see Black, 119-22.

5. ἄλλο, 'another portion'. μέν (iv. 4) is no longer used in the rest of the parable. In Galilee the soil is sometimes thin, with rock below which in places breaks through the surface. Cf. Swete, 72 f.; Lagrange, 95. It is in this sense that ἐπὶ τὸ πετρῶδες is to be understood. πετρώδης, iv. 16*, Mt. xiii. 5, 20**, 'rocky', <πέτρα, εἶδος; Cl. Otherwise, and for the most part, the soil is rich and fertile. Cf. G. A. Smith, 420; Josephus, *BJ*, iii. 3. 2.

The explanatory clause καὶ ὅπου οὐκ εἶχεν γῆν πολλήν is omitted by b c e syˢ; ὅπου is replaced by ὅτι in D W ff i q r¹; and καί (B) is omitted by almost all uncials, all minuscules, and f l vg sype hl sa bo geo. The words, it would seem, are either a Markan addition (cf. Lagrange, 95) or a later gloss which anticipates διὰ τὸ μὴ ἔχειν βάθος γῆς. εὐθύς here is 'straightway'; the seeds sprouted because the soil was so thin. ἐξανατέλλω*, Mt. xiii. 5**, 'to spring up'; Cl., LXX. Usually trans., the verb here is intrans. LS cite Empedocles lxii. 4 and Moschus Bucolicus ii. 58. διὰ τό c. infin. iv. 6, v. 4*. For the articular infin. in Cl. and Hellenistic Gk v. Goodwin, 315; Moulton, i. 213-16. βάθος*. Matthew

ἥλιος ⌜ἐκαυματίσθη⌝ καὶ διὰ τὸ μὴ ἔχειν ῥίζαν ἐξηράνθη. καὶ 7
ἄλλο ἔπεσεν εἰς τὰς ἀκάνθας, καὶ ἀνέβησαν αἱ ἄκανθαι καὶ συν-
έπνιξαν αὐτό, καὶ καρπὸν οὐκ ἔδωκεν. καὶ ἄλλα ἔπεσεν εἰς τὴν 8
γῆν τὴν καλήν, καὶ ἐδίδου καρπὸν ἀναβαίνοντα καὶ αὐξανόμενα,

6 ἐκαυματίσθησαν

follows Mk closely, but has the plur. τὰ πετρώδη. Less descriptively Luke has ἐπὶ τὴν πέτραν.

6. The result is that the shoot withers away. For ξηραίνω v. iii. 1. ἀνατέλλω, xvi. 2*, intrans. ' to rise ', Mt. iv. 16, xiii. 6, Lk. xii. 54, Heb. vii. 4, Jas. i. 11, 2 Pet. i. 19**; trans., Mt. v. 45**; Cl., LXX, Inscr. (VGT, 38). Cf. xvi. 2, ἀνατείλαντος τοῦ ἡλίου, Jas. i. 11, ἀνέτειλεν γὰρ ὁ ἥλιος σὺν τῷ καύσωνι καὶ ἐξήρανεν τὸν χόρτον. καυματίζω*, Mt. xiii. 6, Apoc. xvi. 8 f.**, ' to burn ', ' scorch up '; late Gk, not in LXX nor listed in VGT. Cf. Swete, 73, ' " It felt the burning heat " (καῦμα) ', Moffatt and RSV, ' was scorched '. B D a e sa attest the plur. The withering is due to the inability of the plant to form its roots. D e sa bo (1 MS.) read ἐξηράνθησαν. Again Matthew follows his source closely, but uses the gen. abs. ἡλίου δὲ ἀνατείλαντος. Luke abbreviates, losing the reference to scorching and explaining that the plant had no moisture (ἱκμάδα), possibly under the influence of Jer. xvii. 8, ἐπὶ ἱκμάδα βαλεῖ ῥίζαν αὐτοῦ (cf. Swete, 73).

7. For ἄλλο v. iv. 5. ἄκανθα, iv. 18*, ' a thorn '. In Cl. Gk the word is used of any thorny or prickly plant, including thistles and broom. Cf. M'Lean, EB, col. 5059 f. ' The LXX have always translated the Hebrew ḳoṣ by ἄκανθαι, which must always be taken to refer to a troublesome field herb, especially thistles ', Dalman, SSW, 248. Apparently, the farmer, instead of removing the thorns, has merely cut them down or burnt them, with the result that they grow stronger than ever, overtopping the wheat before the ears can form. Cf. Lagrange, 96. The portion of seed (ἄλλο) fell into, or among, the thorns. Matthew alters

εἰς to ἐπί, and Luke to ἐν μέσῳ, but Mark's preposition is the more graphic. Some MSS. read ἐπί in Mk (C D W Θ 28 33 565 700 b sa bo), but εἰς is the original reading (א A B L et al. minusc. pler. it (exc. b) vg bo (3 MSS.) geo¹ et ᴬ).

ἀναβαίνω (v. i. 10) is used in the LXX (= עלה) of the springing up of vegetation (Gen. xli. 5, Deut. xxix. 23, Isa. v. 6, xxxii. 13), but it is also used in this sense in Cl. Gk (Xenophon, Oec. xix. 18; Theophrastus, Hist. Plantarum, viii. 3. 2). It, therefore, need not be, but probably is, a ' secondary Semitism ' in this context. συνπνίγω, iv. 19*, Mt. xiii. 22, Lk. viii. 14, 42**, ' to press closely ', ' choke '; Cl. (Theophr. De Causis Plant. vi. 11. 6, of trees closely pressed together, συμπνιγόμενα), not in the LXX. The strong word is very descriptive. Both Matthew and Luke have the more common verb ἀποπνίγω (Mt, v.l. ἔπνιξαν), but συνπνίγω in the interpretation of the parable (Mt. xiii. 22, Lk. viii. 14; cf. Mk. iv. 19). διδόναι καρπόν is a ' secondary Semitism ' used in the LXX to render נתן פרי, ' to yield fruit ', (cf. Lev. xxvi. 20, Psa. i. 3). Cf. the more common ποιεῖν καρπόν in Lk. iii. 8 (v. Creed, 51), viii. 8, which is also Semitic (cf. Gen. i. 11 f.), also συμβούλιον ἐδίδουν in Mk. iii. 6.

8. In this verse, in contrast with ἄλλο in 5 and 7, ἄλλα is used of the individual seeds. The land is τὴν καλήν, ' fair ' or ' fine land '. καλός, iv. 20, vii. 27, ix. 5, 42 f., 45, 47, 50, xiv. 6, 21*. Once more discrimination is shown in the tenses. The seeds fell (ἔπεσεν) into the good earth and continued to yield fruit (ἐδίδου), sprouting and increasing (ἀναβαίνοντα καὶ αὐξανόμενα), and providing an abundant

9 καὶ ἔφερεν ἕν τριάκοντα καὶ ἕν ἑξήκοντα καὶ ἕν ἑκατόν. Καὶ
ἔλεγεν Ὃς ἔχει ὦτα ἀκούειν ἀκουέτω.

harvest (ἔφερεν). ἀναβαίνοντα is nom.
neut. in agreement with ἄλλα, not acc.
masc. agreeing with καρπόν.
Several readings were current at a
very early period :
(1) ἄλλα, ℵ* B C L W Θ 28 33 124 892
e sa bo.
ἄλλο, ℵᶜ A D Δ *et al.* fam. 1 fam. 13
(exc. 124) 22 157 543 565 700
1071 *al. pler.* it (exc. e) vg sys pe hl
geo arm aeth.
(2) αὐξανόμενα, ℵ B 1071.
αὐξανόμενον, A D L W Δ 238 892.
αὐξάνοντα, C Θ *et al.* fam. 1 fam. 13
22 33 157 543 579 *al. pler.* it
pler. vg (*crescentem*).
Probably the WH text is to be preferred, not only because it is strongly
attested, but also because the variants
appear to be early modifications of
this text. It may be conjectured that
ἄλλα was first altered to ἄλλο by assimilation to iv. 5, 7, and that, in consequence, the participles were taken
with καρπόν, αὐξανόμενον or αὐξάνοντα
replacing αὐξανόμενα.
There is great confusion in the MS.
tradition as regards the prepositions
after ἔφερεν. εἰς ter, ἐν ter, ἕν ter are
all read, but εἰς ... ἐν ... ἐν is accepted
by WH on the authority of B L 1071.
ἐν c. dat. may be used =' amounting
to ' (Turner, 24, *JTS*, xxvi. 17), but
the change of prepositions is intolerable, and Allen, 79, *ET*, xiii. 30, is
probably right in tracing the readings
to the over-scrupulous translation of
חַד, the Aramaic numeral ' one '. He
compares Dan. iii. 19, חַד־שִׁבְעָה, ' seven

times ' and Gen. xxvi. 12 (Targ. Onk.)
עַל חַד מֵאָה, ' one hundredfold '. Black,
90, gives a further example in the
Elephantine Papyrus, i. 3, *ḥadh 'ᵃlaph*,
' a thousandfold '. Cf. Wellhausen,
30 ; Lagrange, 96 f. ; Howard, ii. 439.
This Semitism shows that the Greek
version of the parable in Mk stands
near to the Aramaic original. Matthew
neatly substitutes ὃ . . . ὃ . . . ὃ . . .
Luke has simply ἑκατονταπλασίονα
(viii. 8).
The point of the parable lies in this
verse. While portions of the seed are
lost in various ways, the rest, perhaps
the greater part, yields an amazing
harvest. Cf. Jn. iv. 35, ' Lift up your
eyes, and look on the fields, that they
are white already unto harvest '.
9. For ὃς ἔχει Matthew and Luke
substitute ὁ ἔχων. οὖς, iv. 23, vii. 33,
viii. 18*. For the infin. ἀκούειν to express purpose *v.* iv. 3. Cf. Deut. xxix.
4 (LXX). In slightly different forms
the formula ' He that hath ears '
appears frequently in the sayings of
Jesus ; cf. iv. 23, vii. 16, Mt. xi. 15,
xiii. 9, 43, Lk. viii. 8, xiv. 35 ; also
Apoc. ii. 7, 11, 17, 29, iii. 6, 13, 22,
xiii. 9 (the writer)**. It is clearly a
characteristic expression by which He
impressed on His hearers the need to
give close attention to His words.
Here, as following 8, it indicates that
the harvest is the key to the interpretation of the parable. It may also reflect His perception that His parables
were not always easy to understand.
D b ff gⁱ·² i add καὶ ὁ συνείων συνειέτο.

Mk. iv. 10-12　　26. THE PURPOSE OF　　Cf. Mt. xiii. 10-15
　　　　　　　　　　　PARABLES　　　　　　　　Lk. viii. 9 f.

This section is a Markan construction (*v.* Intr. 83), that is, a passage
put together by Mark himself on the basis of tradition. It has the appearance of a Pronouncement-story,[1] but is not a popular narrative current
in the community. Signs of compilation are present in σὺν τοῖς δώδεκα,
and 11 f., introduced by καὶ ἔλεγεν αὐτοῖς, appears to be an isolated saying.

¹ Cf. Taylor, *FGT*, 79 f.

Verse 10 may have originally belonged to 13-20, if we may conjecture that τὴν παραβολήν has been replaced by τὰς παραβολάς, which looks like an adaptation made to introduce 11 f. In the Commentary it is argued that originally the saying was related to the teaching ministry of Jesus, and that Mark, believing it to refer to the purpose of parables, has introduced it into its present context, thus creating a difficulty which has persisted until modern times. He has done this in consequence of his belief that Jesus used parables to conceal His meaning from ' those without ', whereas in fact, His purpose was to elucidate His message by prompting reflection.

Καὶ ὅτε ἐγένετο κατὰ μόνας, ἠρώτων αὐτὸν οἱ περὶ αὐτὸν 10
σὺν τοῖς δώδεκα τὰς παραβολάς. καὶ ἔλεγεν αὐτοῖς Ὑμῖν τὸ 11
μυστήριον δέδοται τῆς βασιλείας τοῦ θεοῦ· ἐκείνοις δὲ τοῖς ⌜ἔξω⌝

11 ἔξωθεν

10. This editorial passage prepares the way for the saying in 11 f. The adverbial phrase κατὰ μόνας (sc. χώρας or ὁδούς) is classical (cf. Thuc. i. 32, 37), and is used in the LXX (Gen. xxxii. 16 (17), Judg. vii. 5, etc.), with the meaning ' alone ', but is found only here and in Lk. ix. 18 in the NT. It indicates that Jesus is away from the crowd, either in a house or in the way. Cf. vii. 17, ix. 28, x. 10.

In contrast with οἱ παρ' αὐτοῦ in iii. 21, οἱ περὶ αὐτόν* are the disciples, from whom the Twelve are distinguished. The phrase σὺν τοῖς δώδεκα (v. iii. 14) is awkwardly introduced. Bultmann, 71, explains it as a Markan addition to his source, Ed. Meyer, 138 f., as due to the combination of a ' twelve-source ' (10b-12) with a ' disciple-source ' (v. Intr. 74 f.). ἐρωτάω, vii. 26, viii. 5*; Cl. ' to ask ', ' question '; in later Gk. (LXX, Pap.) ' to ask for ', ' beg ' (=αἰτέω). Cf. Milligan, New Testament Documents, 51; Moulton, i. 66 n.; VGT, 255; Field, 101 f.; Bernard, St. Jn, 385. Mark always has the imperf. of ἐρωτάω, and uses it here with two accusatives. Elsewhere περί c. gen. rei is common. With Mk cf. Mt. xiii. 10, διὰ τί ἐν παραβολαῖς λαλεῖς αὐτοῖς; ; Lk. viii. 9, τίς αὕτη εἴη ἡ παραβολή. The sing. τὴν παραβολήν, a manifest correction, is read in Mk by A and other MSS. The plur. suggests that 10-12 is a separate unit.

11. For the formula καὶ ἔλεγεν αὐτοῖς v. ii. 27. μυστήριον*, Mt. xiii. 11, Lk.

viii. 10, Pl (19), 1 Tim (2), Apoc (4)**, ' mystery ' ' secret ', <μυέω, ' to initiate '. For discussions of this important word v. J. A. Robinson, Eph. 234-40; E. Hatch, Essays, 57 ff.; H. A. A. Kennedy, St. Paul and the Mystery Religions, 123-30; VGT, 420; W. Bousset, 66 f., 164 ff. In Cl. Gk the word is used of a ' secret ' or ' mystery ' and especially in the plur. of ' the mysteries ' connected with the pagan Mystery-religions. In the LXX it is used eight times in Dan. ii, and in the OT Apocrypha, with the meaning ' secret '. In the NT, and especially in the Pauline Epp., it means an ' open secret ' made known by God, and is used of the Gospel, or the inclusion of the Gentiles. There is no case in which it connotes secret rites or esoteric knowledge communicated to ' initiates '. In the present passage and its parallels, it is used of a knowledge concerning the Kingdom of God which has been imparted to the disciples, but not to the people in general, ἐκεῖνοι οἱ ἔξω. This knowledge presumably relates to the Kingdom as the Rule of God, imminent and indeed already exercising its power. Mt and Lk have γνῶναι and the plur. τὰ μυστήρια, but in Lk τὸ μυστήριον is read by C k sys Clem Iren and may be original (cf. Creed, 115, Streeter, FG, 313). Lk softens ἐκείνοις δὲ τοῖς ἔξω to τοῖς δὲ λοιποῖς. Mt has ἐκείνοις δέ. These changes show that Mark's account is more original.

12 ἐν παραβολαῖς τὰ πάντα γίνεται, ἵνα

ΒλέΠοΝΤΕC ΒλέΠωCΙ ΚΑὶ ΜΗ ἴΔωCΙΝ,

ΚΑὶ ὀΚΟΎΟΝΤΕC ἀΚΟΎωCΙ ΚΑὶ ΜΗ CΥΝΊωCΙΝ,

ἐν παραβολαῖς is usually taken to mean ' in parables ' as in iii. 23 and iv. 2. In the present case, not only is a distinction drawn between the teaching methods adopted for disciples and ' outsiders ' respectively, but parables are spoken of in a tone of disparagement, and indeed, in iv. 12, as a means of concealing the truth. The phrase, however, can be rendered ' in riddles ', and the clause translated : ' Everything comes to be a riddle '. Cf. J. W. Hunkin, *JTS*, xvi. 372-91, Apr. 1915. The objection to this interpretation is that it requires παραβολή to be understood in two different senses. Cf. Smith, 137 ; Creed, 115. But this objection is by no means conclusive if, as is probable, iv. 10-12 is a separate unit of tradition which has been inserted in this context. Misled by ἐν παραβολαῖς, Mark, or an earlier compiler, has interpreted the passage as concerned with parables and has introduced it *ad vocem* (cf. ix. 33-50) at this point. A decision on this question depends on the interpretation of 10-12 as a whole. Certainly τὰ πάντα γίνεται is a strange expression to describe teaching, and it is not surprising that some MSS. have replaced the verb by λέγεται (D Θ 28 124 565 1071) or by *dicitur* (b c ff g¹ i r¹) or *dicuntur* (a q). The article is omitted by ℵ D W Θ *et al.* 28 565 *et al.*

12. This verse is a well known *crux interpretum*. The saying is based on Isa. vi. 9 f., which in the form of a command ironically describes what in fact would be *the result* of Isaiah's ministry : ' Go, and tell this people, Hear ye indeed, but understand not ; and see ye indeed, but perceive not. Make the heart of this people fat, and make their ears heavy, and shut their eyes ; lest they see with their eyes, and hear with their ears, and understand

with their heart, and turn again, and be healed.' This use of a command to express a result is typically Semitic. In the LXX the first part of the passage is translated, ἀκοῇ ἀκούσετε, καὶ οὐ μὴ συνῆτε, καὶ βλέποντες βλέψετε, καὶ οὐ μὴ ἴδητε, and the last clause by καὶ ἰάσομαι αὐτούς. It will be seen that, in addition to other differences, Mark's version (in contrast with Mt. xiii. 15) omits the strong statements in Isa. vi. 10 about making fat the heart of the people, etc., and departs both from the Heb. and the LXX in reading καὶ ἀφεθῇ αὐτοῖς, ' and it be forgiven them '. In this Mark agrees with the form found in the Targum ; cf. T. W. Manson, 77. Manson observes that this fact alone ' stamps the saying as Palestinian in origin and thus creates a strong presumption in favour of its authenticity '.

The construction in Mk, βλέποντες βλέπωσι . . . ἀκούοντες ἀκούωσι is a Semitism found in the NT only (apart from (?) Eph. v. 5) in quotations from the LXX ; cf. Mt. xiii. 14, Ac. vii. 34, Heb. vi. 14**. By this use of the participle and the finite verb the LXX translators sought to represent in Gk the infin. absolute with the finite verb in Heb. to express emphasis.[1] Cf. Thackeray, 48 f. ; Howard, ii. 444. Thus, the meaning is ' . . . indeed see . . . indeed hear . . .'. Cf. Moffatt, ' for all their seeing . . . for all their hearing . . .'. The distinction between βλέπω and οἶδα, that is, between seeing and perceiving, is manifest, as also that between ἀκούω and συνίημι. συνίημι, vi. 52, vii. 14, viii. 17, 21*.

μὴ ποτε, xiv. 2*, ' lest haply ', is probably final. Manson, 78 f., takes the clause to mean : ' For if they did, they would repent and receive forgiveness '. Alternatively the construction might be an example of μή

---

[1] Alternatively the dat. of the cognate noun was used with the fin. verb ; *v.* the LXX rendering of Isa. vi. 9 above, also Mk. v. 42, vii. 10 (LXX). *V.* Intr. 61.

μή ποτε ἐπιστρέψωσιν καὶ ὀφεθῇ αὐτοῖς.

c. subj. in a cautious assertion (cf.
Moulton, i. 188): ' Perhaps they may
yet repent and be forgiven '. These
are possibilities which may or may
not concern the original form of the
saying. As it stands in Mk the meaning of μή ποτε is conditioned by ἵνα,
and must therefore be ' lest haply '.
Mark's meaning must be that for
those who are not disciples the purpose
of the parables is to conceal the truth
and to prevent repentance and forgiveness. ἐπιστρέφω, v. 30, viii. 33,
xiii. 16*, ' to turn round ' or ' back ',
is here used in the moral sense ' to
repent ' (cf. Ac. iii. 19); Cl., LXX,
Pap. Cf. Field, 246-9. ἀφεθῇ is used
impersonally, as in Mt. xii. 32 and
Jas. v. 15. Cf. Mt. vii. 2, 7, xxv.
29, Lk. xiv. 14, Rom. x. 10, 1 Pet.
iv. 6.

This interpretation of the purpose of
parables is so intolerable that from the
earliest times it has been questioned.
Luke retains the Markan ἵνα, but
omits the μή ποτε clause (viii. 10).
Matthew has ὅτι instead of ἵνα, thus
suggesting the idea that Jesus speaks
in parables because of the dullness of
the people (xiii. 13). He then quotes
fully the prophecy of Isa., but according to the LXX, with καὶ ἰάσομαι αὐτούς instead of καὶ ἀφεθῇ αὐτοῖς.

Several attempts have been made
to show that the Markan ἵνα is a mistranslation. It is suggested (1) that
the ἵνα is used in the sense of ὅτι (cf.
Allen, 80; H. Pernot, Études sur la
langue des Évangiles (1927), 90 ff.),
or of ὅπως, de façon que, ' in such a
manner as ' (cf. Lagrange, 99); or (2)
that ἵνα misrenders the Aramaic particle ד, actually used in the Targum,
which ought to have been rendered
οἵ, ' who ' (cf. Manson, 78 f.; Torrey,
TG, 10 f.); or, again, (3) that ἵνα is
used imperatively in the sense ' let
them, etc.' (cf. C. J. Cadoux, JTS,

xlii. 173). All these suggestions are
possible,[1] but, whatever bearing they
may have on the original saying, it
may be doubted if they affect Mark's
meaning. Cf. Black, 155, ' Nothing
is more certain than that Mark wrote
and intended ἵνα . . . μή ποτε '. Both
are used with telic force.

It is not surprising that since the
famous discussion of Jülicher, i. 118 ff.,
134 f., 146 ff., it has been widely maintained that the saying is not authentic,
but represents later Christian belief
at a time when the interpretation of
the parables had become obscure,
when opinion was strongly influenced
by Pauline teaching in Rom. ix-xi on
the hardening and rejection of Israel.[2]
There can be little doubt that as the
passage now stands in iv. 11 f., it
represents the beliefs of Mark. How
far he is influenced by Pauline teaching is more open to question, for he
does not speak of the hardening of
Israel as he does of the blindness of
the disciples (vi. 52, viii. 17) and the
scribes (iii. 5), and Paul does not allude
to the use of parables. What Mark
does is to distinguish revelation to the
disciples and concealment from the
crowd, and for this view he has
warrant in the Q sayings in Lk. x.
21 = Mt. xi. 25 f. and Lk. x. 23 f. =
Mt. xiii. 16 f. It is the application of
this teaching to the use of parables,
and the rigour with which he presents
the quotation from Isa. vi. 9 f., which
create the difficulties in question. So
far from being a completely unauthentic saying, iv. 11 f. is best explained if it took its rise in something
Jesus actually said, and its strong
Palestinian flavour and the genuine
sayings mentioned above support this
conjecture. Mark has given an unauthentic version of a genuine saying.

The original form of the saying can
only be conjectured. Probably it had

[1] Less satisfactory is the view that ἵνα is a loose equivalent for the Matthaean formula ' that it
might be fulfilled, etc.' (cf. Lagrange, 99; Turner, 25).
[2] Cf. J. Weiss, 52-9, Die Schr.⁴ 111; Schweitzer, 336-48; Bultmann, 215, 351; Bousset, 66 f.;
Klostermann, 47 f.; Ed. Meyer, i. 139; Goguel, 293 f.; Rawlinson, 46-8; Smith, 136 f.; Dodd,
13-15; Luce, 166; R. H. Lightfoot, 194.

nothing to do with parables at all.
Mark may have been misled by the
enigmatic ἐν παραβολαῖς which can
mean ' in riddles ' (v. iii. 23). It is
possible that Jesus was impressed by
the similarity between the results of
His ministry and the experience of
Isaiah and that He made use of the
ironic words of Isa. vi. 9 f. (cf. Wood,
686 ; Bartlet, 165) after the failure of
the Mission of the Twelve and His own
fruitless activity in Chorazin, Bethsaida, and Capernaum (Mt. xi. 20-4

=Lk. x. 13-15). To the disciples it
had been given to know the secret of
the Kingdom, but to those without
everything happened in riddles ! Familiar as He was with the Semitic telic
idiom in Isa. vi. 10, there is no reason
why He should not have used it Himself, since it was the will of the Father
to hide the revelation from the wise and
prudent and reveal it unto babes. This
suggestion cannot be proved, but it is
in every way superior to the view that
iv. 11 f. is a Markan invention.

Mk. iv. 13-20   27. AN INTERPRETATION   Cf. Mt. xiii. 18-23
OF THE PARABLE OF THE   Lk. viii. 11-15
SOWER

This section appears to be a Christian interpretation of the parable.
' It is difficult not to think that what is here presented is rather the way
in which the parable was currently applied when Mk was written than
any authentic word of Jesus ', Rawlinson, 52 f. This view is widely held
among modern commentators. Cf. Wellhausen, 32, *Er ist später als die
Parabel und kann nicht von Jesus selber herrühren* ; J. Weiss, 171, *Die
Schr.*[4] 113 f. ; Bultmann, 202 f. ; Dibelius, 228 ; Luce, 167 ; Branscomb,
80 f. ; Dodd, 14 ; Smith, 138 ; C. J. Cadoux, 48. For more conservative
discussions cf. Swete, 77-81 ; Gould, 71-7 ; Lagrange, 106-12 ; Plummer,
124-8 ; Bruce, i. 195-9. Bruce, 199, suggests that it is intrinsically likely
that Jesus talked to His disciples about the various sorts of hearers, their
spiritual state, and what they resembled, but says that it is another question whether His interpretation has been exactly preserved by any of the
Synoptics.

The reasons which suggest that iv. 13-20 is secondary tradition are :
(1) the un-Hebraic character of the style ; (2) the vocabulary, which
includes several words found only in the Epistles ; (3) the impression conveyed of an existing Christian community ; (4) the concentration of the
interpretation on important details rather than the main point of the
parable. More serious is the loss of the perception that, despite failures,
the amazing harvest is the supreme lesson. It would be wrong, however,
to assume that the interpretation has completely lost touch with the
teaching of Jesus. We are not in the presence of pure allegory. The
person of the sower is not identified, and no attempt is made, as in later
times, to find a hidden significance in the terms ' thirtyfold ', ' sixtyfold ',
' a hundredfold '. In short, the explanation is a partial adaptation of the
teaching of Jesus to later conditions.

13   Καὶ λέγει αὐτοῖς Οὐκ οἴδατε τὴν παραβολὴν ταύτην, καὶ πῶς

13. γινώσκω, v. 29, 43, vi. 38, vii.
24, viii. 17, ix. 30, xii. 12, xiii. 28 f.,
xv. 10, 45*. The distinction between
οἶδα, to know by insight or intuition,

and γινώσκω, to come to know by
observation and experience, is here
clearly apparent. Cf. Swete, 77. All
English versions treat οὐκ οἴδατε as a

πάσας τὰς παραβολὰς γνώσεσθε; Ὁ σπείρων τὸν λόγον σπείρει. 14
οὗτοι δέ εἰσιν οἱ παρὰ τὴν ὁδὸν ὅπου σπείρεται ὁ λόγος, καὶ 15
ὅταν ἀκούσωσιν εὐθὺς ἔρχεται ὁ Σατανᾶς καὶ αἴρει τὸν λόγον
τὸν ἐσπαρμένον εἰς αὐτούς. καὶ οὗτοί εἰσιν ὁμοίως οἱ ἐπὶ τὰ 16

question implying blame (cf. viii. 17 f.), but Luther reads it as a statement (cf. Plummer, 124). Klostermann, 48, compares v. 31. Both Matthew and Luke omit the reproach. Matthew inserts from Q the saying, ' Blessed are your eyes . . .' (xiii. 16 f. = Lk. x. 23 f.), and continues, ' Hear then ye the parable of the sower '. Luke has, ' Now the parable is this ' (viii. 11). καὶ πῶς;, ' How then? ' (Lk. xx. 44, Jn. xii. 34), introduces the further question arising out of what is said. Cf. καὶ τίς; in x. 26, Lk. x. 29, xviii. 26, Jn. ix. 36. πάσας τὰς παραβολάς is ' all my parables ' (Plummer, 125) or ' the other parables ' (Moffatt).

14. From this point onwards the phrases used in the parable are taken up and explained in the manner of a commentary. This procedure explains the awkwardness of the Gk from 15 onwards, and it would be of advantage in translation to put the phrases quoted in inverted commas; e.g. ' " The sower " sows the word '. ὁ σπείρων is quite general; it means ' the sower mentioned in the parable ', and is identified neither with Christ nor with the Christian missionary. By τὸν λόγον the Christian message is probably meant (cf. 1 Thess. ii. 13), but the phrase may be used in the sense of ' the teaching ' or ' the good news '.

15. The second phrase taken up is οἱ παρὰ τὴν ὁδόν. Usually it is said that σπειρόμενοι or σπαρέντες is to be understood, but the same effect is gained by ' those by the wayside ' or ' on the road ' (v. iv. 4). The phrase is not employed in the parable, but in it there is a clear allusion to ὃ μὲν ἔπεσεν παρὰ τὴν ὁδόν. The view that in the parable different groups of seed and in the explanation different kinds of soil are mentioned may over-simplify

the issue. In the parable the description is naturally given from the point of view of the sower. To the hearer, however, what happens to each group sown suggests different types of people, ' those on the road ', ' those sown upon the rocky places ', etc. People represent the point of interest. Hence the involved sentence, ' And these are " they on the road " . . . and when they have heard . . .'. Strictly speaking, ὅπου σπείρεται ὁ λόγος is redundant, but it is characteristic of a teacher's methods. For ὁ λόγος v. iv. 14. A relative clause seems required after the introduction. We should therefore expect οἳ ὅταν. This is read by B, but is probably secondary.

Luke has simplified his source in the words, οἱ δὲ παρὰ τὴν ὁδόν εἰσιν οἱ ἀκούσαντες . . . (viii. 12). Matthew has recast the Markan sentence. Using the gen. abs. construction, he explains that the hearers failed to understand the word of the Kingdom. Both Evangelists agree in mentioning the heart, Matthew as the soil in which the seed has been sown, Luke as the place from which the Devil takes away the word. Luke adds ἵνα μὴ πιστεύσαντες σωθῶσιν.

These later variations emphasize the brevity of the Markan explanation. All that is said in Mk is that the word is sown and is immediately taken away by Satan. The implication is that it is not received (cf. 16, 18, 20). One is reminded of the Q parable of the Untenanted House which is invaded and possessed by seven devils (Lk. xi. 24-6 = Mt. xii. 43-5).

For ὁ Σατανᾶς see the notes on i. 13 and iii. 23, and for εἰς (B W fam. 1 (exc. 131) 13 28 69 543), replaced in many MSS. by ἐν, v. iv. 7.

16-17a. The interpretation now takes up the case of ' those sown upon

πετρώδη σπειρόμενοι, οἳ ὅταν ἀκούσωσιν τὸν λόγον εὐθὺς μετὰ
17 χαρᾶς λαμβάνουσιν αὐτόν, καὶ οὐκ ἔχουσιν ῥίζαν ἐν ἑαυτοῖς
ἀλλὰ πρόσκαιροί εἰσιν, εἶτα γενομένης θλίψεως ἢ διωγμοῦ διὰ
18 τὸν λόγον εὐθὺς σκανδαλίζονται. καὶ ἄλλοι εἰσὶν οἱ εἰς τὰς
19 ἀκάνθας σπειρόμενοι· οὗτοί εἰσιν οἱ τὸν λόγον ἀκούσαντες, καὶ
αἱ μέριμναι τοῦ αἰῶνος καὶ ἡ ἀπάτη τοῦ πλούτου καὶ αἱ περὶ τὰ

the rocky ground '. Swete, 78, understands ὁμοίως (xv. 31*) to mean, ' On
the same principle of interpretation '.
Wellhausen, 32, observes that it is
probably like ὡς in iv. 31, and that
ὅμοιοι τοῖς would have been better Gk.
These hearers at once (εὐθύς) receive
the word with joy (χαρά*). Unfortunately, they are like plants where
there is no depth of earth, and so have
no roots in themselves. Thus, they are
only ' for a time '. πρόσκαιρος*, Mt.
xiii. 21, 2 Cor. iv. 18, Heb. xi. 25**,
' occasional ', ' opportune ', is used in
the sense of ' temporary ', ' lasting for
a time ', in later Gk and the LXX
(4 Macc. xv. 2, 8, 23); v. VGT, 548.
Moffatt omits εὐθύς with D 579 et al.
c ff i q sys.
   Matthew follows Mk closely, but
uses the sing. throughout. Luke
abbreviates his source and makes
verbal changes.
   17b. From this point onwards the
experiences of the early Christian community are reflected. εἶτα, viii. 25*.
θλῖψις, xiii. 19, 24*, Mt (4), Jn (2), Ac
(5), Pl (24), Rest (7)**, ' pressure ';
in the LXX, the NT, and the papyri
(VGT, 292), ' tribulation ', ' affliction '.
διωγμός, x. 30*, Mt. xiii. 21, Ac (2),
Pl (3), 2 Tim. iii. 11 (bis)**, ' the
chase ', but in the NT and later prose
' persecution ', ' pursuit '. As the distribution shows, the words belong to
the vocabulary of primitive Christianity (cf. 2 Thess. i. 4, and v. Swete,
79). Cf. Rawlinson, 53.
   σκανδαλίζω, vi. 3, ix. 42 f., 45, 47,
xiv. 27, 29*, Mt (14), Lk (2), Jn (2),
Pl (3)**; ' to cause to stumble ', pass.
' to stumble '. The verb is not classical,
being found only in the LXX and the
NT. Derived from σκάνδαλον, the

later form of σκανδάληθρον, the bait
stick in a trap (but v. Moulton, ii. 361),
it means, not ' to offend ', but perhaps
' to snare ', ' set a trap for ', rather
than ' to put a stumbling-block in the
way '. Cf. A. Carr, Horae Biblicae,
58 ff.; Allen, 199 ff.; VGT, 576.
εὐθύς (v. i. 10) is omitted by fam. 1
(exc. 131) 235, but, without doubt,
should be read. The meaning ' they
are forthwith trapped ' suits the passage well, but, it must be admitted,
so does the translation ' they forthwith
stumble '. Less convincingly Moffatt
has ' they are repelled ', and Torrey
and RSV ' they fall away '. It would
be too subtle to take διὰ τὸν λόγον with
the verb, with the meaning ' the word
ensnares them ', i.e. reduces them to
impotence. The idea is that when
they are persecuted on account of the
word, they are trapped at once because
their faith is so feeble. Luke thinks
of apostasy, καὶ ἐν καιρῷ πειρασμοῦ
ἀφίστανται (viii. 13), but Matthew is
in almost verbatim agreement with
Mk.
   18 f. ' Those sown among the
thorns '. The aor. ἀκούσαντες emphasizes the fact that these hearers have
indeed heard the word. Unhappily,
the ' thorns ' continue to choke it
(συνπνίγουσιν). For συνπνίγω v. iv. 7 ;
τὸν λόγον iv. 14.
   The change of subject in 19 is abrupt
and the words are either hapax leg.
or belong mainly to the vocabulary of
the Epistles. The interpretation is
allegorical. μέριμνα*, Mt. xiii. 22,
Lk. viii. 14, xxi. 34, 2 Cor. xi. 28,
1 Pet. v. 7**, ' care ', ' anxiety '; Cl.,
LXX, Pap. (VGT, 397). By αἱ
μέριμναι τοῦ αἰῶνος is meant worldly
care, anxiety arising out of the times,

λοιπὰ ἐπιθυμίαι εἰσπορευόμεναι συνπνίγουσιν τὸν λόγον, καὶ
ἄκαρπος γίνεται. καὶ ἐκεῖνοί εἰσιν οἱ ἐπὶ τὴν γῆν τὴν καλὴν 20
σπαρέντες, οἵτινες ἀκούουσιν τὸν λόγον καὶ παραδέχονται καὶ
καρποφοροῦσιν ἓν τριάκοντα καὶ ἓν ἑξήκοντα καὶ ἓν ἑκατόν.

20 ἕν . . . [ἕν] . . . [ἕν]

worry. Cf. Selwyn, *1 Pet.* 236. ἀπάτη*, Mt. xiii. 22, Eph. iv. 22, Col. ii.
8, 2 Thess. ii. 10, Heb. iii. 13, 2 Pet.
ii. 13**, 'deceit', 'guile', 'treachery';
Cl., LXX, Pap. Deissmann thinks
that the meaning here, as in popular
Hellenistic Gk, is 'pleasure'; cf.
VGT, 54; Lk. viii. 14, ὑπὸ μεριμνῶν
καὶ πλούτου καὶ ἡδονῶν τοῦ βίου. πλοῦτος, ἐπιθυμία, and ἄκαρπος are also
found predominantly, although not
exclusively, in the Epistles. πλοῦτος*,
Mt. xiii. 22, Lk. viii. 14, appears 14
times in the Pauline Epistles and in
1 Tim. vi. 17, Heb. xi. 26, Jas. v. 2,
Apoc. v. 12, xviii. 16**. Cf. ἐπιθυμία*,
Lk. xxii. 15, Jn. viii. 44, Pl (13), Past.
Epp. (6), Rest (16)**; and ἄκαρπος*,
Mt. xiii. 22, 1 Cor. xiv. 14, Eph. v. 11,
1 Tim. iii. 14, 2 Pet. i. 8, Ju. 12**.

In ἐπιθυμία (<θυμός) ἐπί is directive,
'having one's θυμός towards'; Cl.,
LXX, Pap., 'desire', 'longing',
'lust'. Sometimes it has a good sense
(Lk. xxii. 15, Phil. i. 23, 1 Thess. ii.
17), but for the most part it is used of
evil passions and lusts. αἱ περὶ τὰ
λοιπὰ ἐπιθυμίαι is a very general expression and is intended to cover all objects
of desire other than riches. Peculiar
to Mark's version, the phrase is half
personified in εἰσπορευόμεναι. Cf.
λοιπός v. xiv. 41, xvi. [13]*. καὶ ἄκαρπος γίνεται is a smoother alternative to
καὶ καρπὸν οὐκ ἔδωκεν (iv. 7). Luke
has καὶ οὐ τελεσφοροῦσιν (viii. 14). Cf.
Creed, 116.

The vocabulary and subject-matter
of 17b-19 clearly reflect the interests
and experiences of a primitive Christian community. Anxious care, it is
true, belongs to no one period, but the
combination of 'the cares of the age',
'the deceitfulness of riches', and 'all
other passions', coupled with the references to affliction and persecution

'on account of the word' by which
men are ensnared, reveals a period
later than that of the Galilean Ministry.
Such a period is most naturally found
in the beginnings of the Neronian persecution at Rome. This interpretation
is far from robbing the section of value
and significance for the modern
reader, for in world history such
periods recur in cycles. In the Europe
of to-day every peril mentioned in the
section is fully illustrated.

20. Lastly, the explanation of the
parable takes up 'those who were
sown upon the good earth'. The
change to ἐκεῖνοι, after οὗτοι (15 f.) and
ἄλλοι (18), corresponding to ὃ μέν . . .
ἄλλο . . . ἄλλο . . . ἄλλα in the parable,
preserves at least a trace of the thought
that here is the main point. But the
climax is not emphasized and developed: the earlier stages have ab-
sorbed the commentator's attention.
All, therefore, that he has to say is
that the people in question hear the
word, welcome it, and, in the language
of the parable, bear fruit 'thirtyfold,
and sixtyfold, and a hundredfold'.
They are a mere foil to the discreditable types. So little is the parable
understood!

Swete, 80, explains the tense of οἱ
σπαρέντες as a direct reference to the
parable: 'those who in the parable
were represented as sown'. Lagrange,
108, accounts for the change from the
presents in 16 and 18 (σπειρόμενοι) by
the comment: *comme si l'action était
plus éloignée, puisque le fruit est déjà
produit.* οἵτινες, 'such as', ix. 1,
xii. 18, xv. 7*. Cf. Moulton, i. 91 f.,
ii. 179, who points out how rare its
oblique cases are in the Koine. παρα-
δέχομαι*, Ac. xv. 4, xvi. 21, xxii. 18,
1 Tim. v. 19, Heb. xii. 6**, 'to receive', 'admit'; Cl., LXX, Pap.

The verb is stronger than λαμβάνω and can express the idea of welcoming. Cf. *VGT*, 482. καρποφορέω, iv. 28*, Mt. xiii. 23, Lk. viii. 15, Rom. vii. 4 f., Col. i. 6, 10**, ' to bear fruit '; so in later Gk (Xenophon), LXX, Pap. For ἕν . . . ἕν . . . ἕν *v.* the note on iv. 8. The Semitic idiom is that of the parable and is merely taken over here. B omits

the second and third repetitions of the preposition and C the second. ἕν is read by late uncials fam. 1 fam. 13 33 349 543 700 892 1071 1278 *et al.* syhl, and is accepted by Blass, 146, and Lagrange, 108; *v.* WHmg. Luke has ἐν ὑπομονῇ (viii. 15), and Matthew ὅ . . . ὅ . . . ὅ with the numbers in reverse order (xiii. 23, as in 8).

Mk. iv. 21-5   28. A GROUP OF SAYINGS   Cf. Mt. xiii. 12
Lk. viii. 16-18

This group raises interesting questions regarding the origin and use of the sayings-tradition in Mk. It has frequently been maintained that the Evangelist drew them from Q, but with the disposition to recognize the existence of other collections besides Q, this hypothesis has lost ground. It is unsatisfactory because doublets of some of the sayings appear in other contexts in Mt and Lk which depend on Q. It is better, therefore, to infer that Mark derived them from an independent sayings-collection or from oral tradition. Of these alternatives the former is the better. Why should the sayings be grouped so artificially unless the Evangelist was hampered by an existing arrangement? In 21-5 a basic twofold structure can be discerned, a double arrangement of two sayings connected by γάρ and introduced by the citation formula καὶ ἔλεγεν αὐτοῖς.

1. And he said unto them :   (21)
     Is the lamp brought . . . ?
     For (γάρ) there is nothing hid, save that . . .   (22)
2. And he said unto them :   (24)
     With what measure . . . ?
     For (γάρ) he that hath . . .   (25)

It may be that originally 23, ' If any man hath ears to hear . . .', belonged to the first group; but it has rather the appearance of a connecting link relating the sayings to the parable of the Sower (cf. iv. 9). Verse 24a, ' Take care what you hear ', may be a suture, to introduce the two sayings in 24 f. which are better placed in Q and are less suitable for Mark's purpose. The presumption is that the Evangelist found them detached in his sayings-collection, and brought them together, with editorial supplements, in order to develop the theme of teaching by parables. Possibly he wished to mitigate the severity of 11 f. by citing other sayings of Jesus. The ultimate purpose of Jesus, he would say, is to make the secret of the Kingdom widely known, just as the function of a lamp is to give light : even when a thing is hidden, the hiding is the mercy of revelation ! Mark also wished to add warnings uttered by Jesus. God Himself measures men by their own measuring of truth. The man who has it receives more, while he who lacks it loses the light he has. Apparently, it was in the sense indicated that Mark read 24 f., and he could use the sayings in this way because they stood apart from an interpretative context. In the saying, ' He that hath ', he is surely not far from its original significance (cf. Mt. xxv. 29, Lk. xix. 26), but is less happy in

his use of the maxim, ' With what measure ', which was spoken by Jesus
with reference to judging others (cf. Mt. vii. 2, Lk. vi. 38).
Other Markan groups of sayings, notably ix. 35-50, are co-ordinated
by catchwords, and some scholars (e.g. Bultmann, 351 ; R. H. Lightfoot,
34) find in iv. 21-5 an admittedly less obvious example in the words μόδιος,
μέτρον, and μετρέω. This explanation is hardly necessary, but it is
possible that these words suggested the use of the sayings in a chapter
which treats of sowing. Mark was reminded of their cogency when he
attached 10-12 and 13-20 to the parable of the Sower.

Καὶ ἔλεγεν αὐτοῖς ὅτι Μήτι ἔρχεται ὁ λύχνος ἵνα ὑπὸ τὸν 21
μόδιον τεθῇ ἢ ὑπὸ τὴν κλίνην, οὐχ ἵνα †ἐπὶ† τὴν λυχνίαν τεθῇ;
οὐ ⌜γὰρ ἔστιν⌝ κρυπτὸν ἐὰν μὴ ἵνα φανερωθῇ, οὐδὲ ἐγένετο ἀπό- 22
κρυφον ἀλλ' ἵνα ἔλθῃ εἰς φανερόν. Εἴ τις ἔχει ὦτα ἀκούειν 23

21 MSS. ὑπὸ   22 γάρ ἐστίν τι

21. For μή c. indic. in questions v.
Moulton, i. 170 f. λύχνος*. μόδιος*,
Mt. v. 15, Lk. xi. 33**, is the Latin
modius, a dry measure containing
nearly two gallons. The def. art., as
also in ὁ λύχνος, τὴν κλίνην, and τὴν
λυχνίαν, suggests the well-known object
of the kind. κλίνη, vii. 30*. λυχνία*,
Mt. v. 15, Lk. viii. 16**.
Matthew omits the Markan version
of the saying. Luke smooths away
its awkwardness. He replaces μήτι
ἔρχεται ὁ λύχνος by οὐδεὶς δὲ λύχνον
ἅψας, and ἵνα ὑπὸ τὸν μόδιον τεθῇ by
καλύπτει αὐτὸν σκεύει (viii. 16). Influenced by Q he adds ἵνα οἱ εἰσπορευόμενοι βλέπωσιν τὸ φῶς (v. infra).
The parallel version in Q (Lk. xi. 33
= Mt. v. 15) agrees in substance with
the Markan form, but Matthew thinks
of the lamp as giving light to the
householders and Luke as it welcomes
strangers. Probably the Markan form
is nearer the original. Cf. Bultmann,
82 ; Manson, SJ, 92. The rough
question form and the use of the intrans. ἔρχεται instead of the normal
passive point in this direction ; it is
much less likely that ἔρχεται is a dogmatic expression (cf. x. 45) used of the
appearing of Christ upon earth (cf.
J. Weiss, 175). Allen, ET, xiii. 330,
explains the verb as a mistranslation
of the Aphel or Ittaphal of אתא ' bring '
or ' be brought ', and strengthens his
argument by a list of thirteen places
where Matthew has changed an act.

or a mid. verb in Mk into a pass. (St.
Mt, xxiii ; Howard, ii. 448). See also
Lagrange, civ. The D reading ἅπτεται
(cf. καίεται W fam. 13 346, accenditur
d e ff i, accendunt f sa bo) is a ' correction ' influenced by Lk or Mt.
The saying insists that it is the true
function of a lamp to give light. In
what connexion it was uttered it is
impossible to say. Mark introduces
it here because he holds it to be relevant to the ideas of the mystery of
the Kingdom and the hiding of the
revelation. The association of 22 with
21 is prompted by the possible objection : ' But what if, for Providential
reasons, the light is concealed ? '. This
connexion may well be original. Lohmeyer, 85, thinks that the sayings are
eschatological.

22. The γάρ implies a connexion
with 21. W reads οὐδὲν γάρ ἐστιν, and
700 has οὐχ ἔστιν (sic). Many MSS.
(v. Legg) read τι before κρυπτόν*. ἀπό-
κρυφος*, Lk. viii. 17, Col. ii. 3**, ' concealed ' ; Cl., LXX, Pap. Cf. Lightfoot, Col. 172. ἐὰν μὴ ἵνα , ' save that ',
and ἀλλ' ἵνα, ' but that ', practically
agree in meaning. Wellhausen, 33,
Einl.² 16, thinks that they correspond
with the Aramaic אלא which has both
exceptive and adversative meanings.
Cf. Howard, ii. 468. Swete, 82, on
the contrary, holds that there is a ' perceptible difference of meaning ' : ' except with a view to . . . but on the
contrary (ἀλλά) that it might pass into

ἀκουέτω.

24 Καὶ ἔλεγεν αὐτοῖς Βλέπετε τί ἀκούετε. ἐν ᾧ μέτρῳ μετρεῖτε
25 μετρηθήσεται ὑμῖν καὶ προστεθήσεται ὑμῖν. ὃς γὰρ ἔχει, δοθή-

the light of day '. The awkwardness of the Gk disappears in Luke's version, ὃ οὐ φανερὸν γενήσεται . . . ὃ οὐ μὴ γνωσθῇ καὶ εἰς φανερὸν ἔλθη (viii. 17), which is influenced by Q, ὃ οὐκ ἀποκαλυφθήσεται . . . ὃ οὐ γνωσθήσεται (Lk. xii. 2 = Mt. x. 26).

Burney, 75 f., following Wellhausen, traces the difference between Mk and Q to the ambiguity of the Aramaic particle ד. ' Except in order that it should be revealed ', he suggests, should have been rendered ' except that which shall be revealed ' (cf. Q). Black, 57 f., questions this suggestion, pointing out that the two versions, Mk and Q, are very different. He thinks it much more probable that Mark's version is not that of a translator, unless it is an error, but that of a Greek writer. Where experts differ it is rash to intervene, but it seems likely that Mark's Greek is so rough that it may well be nearer to the original than the smoother version of Q, and that, if the difference is not due to mistranslation, the error may lie on the side of Q.

Like 21, the Markan saying is intended to refer to the manifestation of the Kingdom of God, and this may be its original significance. If the Kingdom is a mystery, it will not always be so, and it is not meant to be so. Concealment is the wise method of divine providence. Cf. Dodd, 144. Such appears to be Mark's interpretation of the saying, and a reference backwards to iv. 11 f. seems unmistakable. In Q the saying appears to be read otherwise. In both Mt and Lk it stands in a context defined by the exhortation ' Fear not '. In Mt it is the basis of the injunction to make known what has been imparted privately (x. 27) ; in Lk it is the ground for the assurance that ' truth will out ' (xii. 3). Luke's version and setting are more original than Matthew's (cf. Easton, 198, Manson, SJ, 106 ; contra,

Creed, 170), and are closer to Mk. Moreover Lk. xii. 3 is preceded by the saying on the lamp (xi. 33), separated from it by sayings on light (xi. 34-6) and the ' Woes on the Pharisees and Lawyers ' (xi. 37-xii. 1), a section which may not belong to Q. These considerations strengthen the possibility that Mark found 21 and 22 already connected and that he has rightly interpreted them as addressed to the disciples.

23. Εἴ τις ἔχει ὦτα ἀκούειν ἀκουέτω. For this characteristic saying of Jesus see the note on iv. 9. Here the saying begins with εἴ τις ἔχει (iv. 9, ὃς ἔχει) and there is no parallel in Mt and Lk. Whether Mark has added it, or whether he found it already connected with 21 f., is an open question.

24. For καὶ ἔλεγεν αὐτοῖς v. ii. 27. Here it may indicate that 24 f. were not connected with 21 f. in the Markan sayings-source. βλέπω, here ' to look to ', ' take heed ', is used in the same sense with ἀπό in viii. 15, xii. 38, with μή c. subj. in xiii. 5, and absolutely in xiii. 23, 33. Plummer, 129, ' Look at it carefully ' ; Moffatt, ' Take care ' ; RSV, ' Take heed '. For similar injunctions to attend v. iv. 3, vii. 14. Luke has πῶς and adds οὖν (viii. 18), thereby changing slightly the meaning. What Jesus refers to is the object, not the manner of attention : ' Carefully consider what you hear '. The saying which follows, introduced without any connecting link (asyndeton) gives the reason. μέτρον*, μετρέω*, προστίθημι*. In this context there is no parallel in Mt and Lk, but there is a parallel in Lk. vi. 38 = Mt. vii. 2 connected with the words, ' Judge not, that ye be not judged '. The significance of the saying in Mk is obscure. Swete, 83, explains it as meaning : ' Your attention to the teaching will be the measure of the profit you will receive from it '. Cf. Lagrange, 114. This exegesis

σεται αὐτῷ· καὶ ὃς οὐκ ἔχει, καὶ ὃ ἔχει ἀρθήσεται ἀπ᾽ αὐτοῦ.

seems forced, and, accordingly, the difficulties call for one or other of two explanations. Either (1) the saying is a later addition in Mk (cf. H. A. A. Kennedy, *ET*, xxv. 304), or (2) Mark has taken it from a collection and brought it into an unnatural connexion. The second hypothesis seems preferable, since it accords with Mark's habit of appending sayings to narratives or other sayings. The saying in question is proverbial, and its original meaning is best gathered from Q (*v. supra*). In Mk its connexion with the exhortation ' Take heed what you hear ' seems secondary.

καὶ προστεθήσεται ὑμῖν is peculiar to Mk. iv. 24. In Mt there is a parallel in the saying ' Whosoever hath, to him shall be given ' (cf. καὶ περισσευθήσεται in xiii. 12 and xxv. 29) which is wanting in Mk. iv. 25. Apparently at some stage in the tradition conflation has taken place.

25. Both Matthew (xiii. 12) and Luke (viii. 18b) reproduce this saying, the only differences being that Matthew adds to Mk καὶ περισσευθήσεται and has ὅστις instead of ὅς, while Luke has

ὃς ἄν and ὃ δόκει ἔχειν in place of ὃ ἔχει. The two later Evangelists also give a second version of the saying, Matthew from M at the end of the parable of the Talents (xxv. 29), Luke from Q after the parable of the Pounds (xix. 26). If, as is possible, Mt. xx. 29 comes from M, the saying ' Whosoever hath ' is attested in three of our primary sources. The association of the saying with apparently different versions of the same parable suggests early tradition. Mark, it would seem, found it detached from this setting and, along with 24, has used it to illustrate the theme of teaching by parables.

The saying may be a popular proverb suggested by social conditions in oriental society (cf. Rawlinson, 55, and for Jewish parallels, Bultmann, 112). The rich man, powerful as he is, receives more, but the poor man is ' fleeced to the last farthing ' (Rawlinson). As used by Jesus, the observation is applied to spiritual things, and in this sense also it is true to the facts of life. Cf. Manson, *SJ*, 248; C. J. Cadoux, 212; Lagrange, 114 f.

Mk. iv. 26-9   29. THE PARABLE OF THE   (No parallel in
                SEED GROWING SECRETLY   Mt or Lk)

This parable is peculiar to Mark's Gospel. Luke omits it altogether and Matthew substitutes for it the parable of the Tares (xiii. 24-30) in the same context. There is no good reason to suppose, with B. W. Bacon, *SM*, 85, 97, that Matthew has rewritten the Markan parable, but his vocabulary in the parable of the Tares (cf. καθεύδω, βλαστάνω, πρῶτον, χόρτος, σῖτος, καρπός, θερισμός) shows that he was familiar with it.[1] Various interpretations of the parable have been given according as attention is directed primarily to the seed, the process of growth, or the harvest. In most cases it is held to refer to the Kingdom of God, and there can be little doubt that this view is sound even if originally it began with ὡς ἄνθρωπος βάλῃ (cf. xiii. 34, Mt. xxv. 14). Cf. Bultmann, 186 f. Among the main types of interpretation the following may be distinguished : (1) that the theme is the divine seed which Christ implants in the heart and in the Church ; (2) the view, characteristic of the nineteenth century, that the parable teaches the gradual evolution of the Kingdom in human society ; (3) the eschatological interpretation, that the emphasis lies on the harvest,

---

[1] So Sir John C. Hawkins; cf. Streeter, *Oxford Studies in the Synoptic Problem*, 432.

significant of the speedy in-breaking of the Kingdom ; (4) the view, maintained by C. H. Dodd, A. T. Cadoux, and others, that the parable is
related to the immediate situation of Jesus and implies that the Kingdom
is already present before the eyes of men.

J. Weiss, 177, held that the main purpose of the parable was to teach
the need for patience ; *nur Geduld, er wird schon aufgehen, die Ernte
kommt!* The sower, whether Jesus Himself or His disciples, must sow
and wait. Somewhat similarly Lagrange, 118, notes the appropriateness
of the parable to the character of the Galileans, *anxieux des événements,
et toujours prêts à intervenir avec violence pour établir le règne de Dieu.*
This more general significance the parable has, but its fundamental meaning must be found in one or other of the four views noted above. There
is least to be said for the first interpretation, for there is nothing in the
parable to suggest that Jesus is thinking of Himself or of the divine seed
which He sows. Nor does it seem probable that His aim was to describe
the slow maturing of the Kingdom. This opinion, however, ought not
to be pressed to the neglect of the idea of *growth*,[1] which appears, not only
in 28, but also in the parables of the Sower, the Mustard Seed, and the
Fig Tree. The eschatological interpretation, in the form in which
Schweitzer [2] presented it, goes beyond what is portrayed, for the parable
does not describe an *impending* event. But so far as this view insists that
the Kingdom is the work of God and not man,[3] its emphasis is sound,
provided it is not also inferred that man's part is purely passive.[4] After
all, the sower sows the seed and there is no emphasis upon his impotence.
The best interpretation is the fourth, which connects the parable with the
situation of Jesus. ' The parable in effect says, Can you not see that the
long history of God's dealings with His people has reached its climax ?
After the work of the Baptist only one thing remains : " Put ye in the
sickle, for the harvest is ripe " ', C. H. Dodd, 180. Here justice is done
to the idea of growth manifest in 28, and to the sense of crisis which can
be felt in 29. Schweitzer, 354, was not mistaken in identifying the sowing
with ' the movement of repentance evoked by the Baptist ', now intensified
by the preaching of Jesus, and both A. T. Cadoux [5] and C. H. Dodd [6]
rightly point to the significance of the Q saying : ' The harvest is plenteous,
but the labourers are few : pray ye therefore the Lord of the harvest, that
he send forth labourers into his harvest ' (Lk. x. 2 = Mt. ix. 37 f., cf.
Jn. iv. 35-7).

For the Aramaic basis of the parable and its poetic form *v.* Black, 121 f.

26   Καὶ ἔλεγεν Οὕτως ἐστὶν ἡ βασιλεία τοῦ θεοῦ ὡς ἄνθρωπος

26. ὁ σπόρος, iv. 27*, Lk. viii. 5, 11,
2 Cor. ix. 10**, ' sowing ', is used here
of the *seed* (Hippocrates Medicus,
Epid. vii. 65, v/ B.C.). In the papyri it
is used of sowing or seed-time and of
seed sown, ' crop ' (*VGT*, 584 f.). The
use of the subjunctive βάλῃ is unusual.

Moulton, i. 185 f., suggests that perhaps the *futuristic* meaning suits best :
' as a man *will* sow '. So also the four
pres. subjunctives in 27. The reading
ὡς ἐάν (A C) 'has all the signs of an
obvious correction ' (Moulton).
There is no reason to think of the

[1] So rightly C. J. Cadoux, 131.
[2] *Quest,* 355 : ' The harvest ripening upon earth is the last ! With it comes also the Kingdom
of God which brings in the new age.'
[3] Cf. Rawlinson, 56 ; Otto, 113 ; Smith, 120, 130.
[4] Cf. Bultmann, *Jesus and the Word*, 36, 38 (' supernatural ', ' superhistorical '). G. Gloege, 85.
[5] *The Theology of Jesus,* 36.
[6] *PK*, 179 ; cf. Otto, 123.

βάλῃ τὸν σπόρον ἐπὶ τῆς γῆς καὶ καθεύδῃ καὶ ἐγείρηται νύκτα 27
καὶ ἡμέραν, καὶ ὁ σπόρος βλαστᾷ καὶ μηκύνηται ὡς οὐκ οἶδεν
αὐτός. αὐτομάτη ἡ γῆ καρποφορεῖ, πρῶτον χόρτον, εἶτεν στάχυν, 28
εἶτεν πλήρης σῖτον ἐν τῷ στάχυϊ. ὅταν δὲ παραδοῖ ὁ καρπός, 29

man as Christ Himself. ἄνθρωπος is quite general, and the action of sowing is only part of the circumstances described. The man sows his seed, sleeps, and rises, and the seed springs up and grows. All these are part of the picture. Lagrange, 115, explains the change from the aor. to the pres. subjunctives in 27 as meaning that, once the grain is sown, the man continues his ordinary daily life (*sa vie tranquille*). Cf. Plummer, 131.

27. For the subjunctives *v.* the note on iv. 26. On the possibility of Semitic influence in the circumstantial clause introduced by καί in καὶ ὁ σπόρος βλαστᾷ, ' while the seed sprouts ' (Torrey, 76), *v.* Wellhausen, 34; Howard, ii. 423. καθεύδω, iv. 38, v. 39, xiii. 36, xiv. 37 (*bis*), 40 f.* The order in νύκτα καὶ ἡμέραν is unusual, and may be Semitic or due to the influence of καθεύδῃ. But cf. v. 5, Lk. ii. 37. βλαστάνω*, later βλαστέω, Mt. xiii. 26, Heb. ix. 4, Jas. v. 18**, ' to sprout ', ' make to grow up ' (Jas. v. 18). The form βλαστᾷ is probably subj. formed from βλαστάω by confusion between -άω and -έω verbs. Cf. Moulton, ii. 231; Robertson, 1213; WM, 101 n.; Bauer, 223. μηκύνω** (<μῆκος, 'length '), Cl., LXX (Isa. xliv. 14), is used here in the mid. of the *growing* of the plant. Plummer, 131, strongly prefers the reading μηκύνεται (D W *et al.* 124 238 346 349 484 517 700 *et al.*), but the evidence for the subj. (א A B C L Δ Θ *et al.* fam. 1 13 22 28 33 157 565 579 892 1071 *al. pler.*) is conclusive. ὡς, after verbs of saying, thinking, etc. =' how ' (*VGT*, 703), and not ' while ' as in it vg and early Eng. translations (cf. Swete, 84): ' he (αὐτός) knoweth not how '.

The picture is that of a sower who has accomplished his work in the sowing, and can then only follow his daily

round, unable to explain the mystery of life and growth.

28. The verse further emphasizes the mystery of growth, which is independent of man and is wrought by the power of God alone. It is on this aspect of the growth that the emphasis lies, but, of course, the importance of husbandry and of rain and sun is not denied. Cf. Bengel, quoted by Swete, 84: *non excluditur agricultura et caelestis pluvia solesque.* αὐτόματος*, Ac. xii. 10**, is used almost as an adverb, ' spontaneously ', ' of its own accord '; Cl., LXX, *v. VGT*, 93. The position of the word and the absence of a connecting-link add to its force. γάρ is added by many MSS., including W Δ Θ fam. 1 fam. 13 579 1071, but it is interpretative and not original. χόρτος, vi. 39*, ' grass ', is here the green shoot. The Ionic form εἶτεν** (א* B* L), condemned by Phrynichus (ἐσχάτως βάρβαρα), is not uncommon in the papyri (*VGT*, 189). Cf. Moulton, ii. 68. σῖτος*. The reading πλήρης σῖτον (C), in which the adj. is an indeclinable, is probably original; it accounts best for the variants πλῆρες σῖτος (B) and πλήρης ὁ σῖτος (D), and the common reading πλήρη σῖτον (א A C² L *et al.*). Cf. Hort, 24; Moulton, i. 50, ii. 162; Swete, 85. πλήρης, viii. 19*.

The description of the stages of growth invites comparison with 1 Clem. xxiii. 4: ' Ye fools, compare yourselves unto a tree; take a vine. First (πρῶτον μέν) it sheddeth its leaves, then (εἶτα) a shoot (βλαστός) cometh, then (εἶτα) a leaf, then (εἶτα) a flower, and after these things a sour berry, then (εἶτα) a full ripe grape (σταφυλὴ παρεστηκυῖα). Ye see that in a little time the fruit (ὁ καρπός) of the tree attaineth unto mellowness. Of a truth quickly and suddenly shall His will be accomplished, the scripture also

εὐθὺς ἀποστέλλει τὸ δρέπανον, ὅτι παρέστηκεν ὁ θερισμός.

bearing witness to it, saying : *He shall come quickly and shall not tarry; and the Lord shall come suddenly into His temple, even the Holy One, whom ye expect.*' The passage is not a quotation; it may have been suggested by Mk. iv. 26-9, but this inference is not very probable. The same similitude appears in 2 Clem. xi. 2 f. The application is eschatological and illustrates an exegetical tendency to which parables were exposed.

29. The δέ marks a strong contrast introducing the climax of the similitude. παραδίδωμι is here used in the sense of *permit*, a meaning which it has in Cl. Gk; cf. τοῦ θεοῦ παραδιδόντος, Herodotus vii. 18, τῆς ὥρας παραδιδούσης, Polybius xxi. 41. 9. Swete, 85, suggests ' permits ' or perhaps ' yields [itself] ', and compares 1 Pet. ii. 23. The form παραδοῖ is subj., a vernacular ending well illustrated in the papyri; cf. Moulton, ii. 211. Cf. also xiv. 10 f., δοῖ viii. 37, γνοῖ v. 43. ' Though a late form of the opt. coincides with it, there is not the slightest syntactical reason for doubt that in the NT it is always subj., as W. F. Moulton proved long ago (*WM*, 360 n.) ' (Moulton). εὐθύς is ' immediately ', ' forthwith '.

T. W. Manson, *JTS*, xxxviii. 399 f., has suggested that the Aramaic *yishlam*, ' is fully mature ', has been mistranslated *yishlem* (παραδοῖ), but M. Black, 121 f., prefers to presuppose the Aramaic *yᵉhibha 'ibba(h)*, ' (when) its crop is ready '. Couchoud, *JTS*, xxxiv. 119, suggests reading, with e, ὁ στάχυς ὅταν παραδῷ καρπούς (*spica cum tradideret fructus*), omitting ἐν τῷ στάχυϊ in 28.

The rest of the sentence is based on Joel iii. (iv.) 13, ἐξαποστείλατε δρέπανα ὅτι παρέστηκεν τρυγητός. The language and the idea are eschatological ; cf. Apoc. xiv. 15, πέμψον τὸ δρέπανόν σου . . . ὅτι ἐξηράνθη ὁ θερισμὸς τῆς γῆς (cf. R. H. Charles, *Rev.* ii. 22), but this fact does not necessarily determine the use of the parable made by Jesus. The somewhat unusual use of ἀποστέλλει (Moffatt, ' has put in ' ; Torrey, ' is put in ') is doubtless due to the use of the semi-quotation from the LXX. δρέπανον*, Apoc. (7)**, ' pruning-knife ', ' sickle '. παρίστημι, xiv. 47, 69 f., xv. 35 (?), 39*, trans. ' to place by ', intrans. ' to stand by ', ' be present ' ; here, as in Joel, in the sense of ' is ready ' (Swete, 85), or ' is ripe ' (Black, 122). θερισμός*.

Mk. iv. 30-2   30. THE PARABLE OF THE   Cf. Mt. xiii. 31 f.
MUSTARD SEED   (Lk. xiii. 18 f.)

This parable is found both in Mk and in Q. One of the best attested elements in the teaching of Jesus, it is especially important as revealing His view of the nature of the Kingdom. In the main interpretation has followed four lines, according as the point has been found in the ideas of (*a*) growth, (*b*) slow and gradual development, (*c*) the speedy and catastrophic in-breaking of the Kingdom, and (*d*) the Kingdom as relevant to the immediate situation of Jesus and including Gentiles within its scope. Of these views the best are the first and fourth, especially in combination. Most commentators rightly emphasize the idea of growth; it belongs essentially to the comparison with a tiny seed which springs up and becomes a plant capable of giving shelter. It may be doubted, however, if this is the main emphasis,[1] although it is stressed in Mk. iv. 31. Neither the idea of a slow long-continued evolution,[2] nor the extreme

[1] Cf. Dodd, 190; Manson, *SJ*, 123; Blunt, 171.
[2] Cf. Smith, *St. Mt*, 139, and Dodd, Manson, Blunt, *in loc.*

eschatological interpretation,[1] can be justified by what the parable states, although the eschatological view rightly dwells on the supernatural character of the Kingdom, as the gift and manifestation of the power of God. The best and most satisfying interpretations connect the parable with the situation of Jesus, who saw the Kingdom as a present reality, a Rule of God embracing within its sweep all peoples, both actually and in promise. Cf. Dodd, 191, ' We must suppose that in this parable Jesus is asserting that the time has come when the blessings of the Reign of God are available for all men. . . . The Kingdom of God is here: the birds are flocking to find shelter in the shade of the tree '; Manson, *SJ*, 122, ' The Kingdom has begun to come in the mission of Jesus; and it must now run its course to the final consummation '; Otto, 123, ' A future kingdom cannot grow and in no possible sense can it be compared with a growing thing. In the present case, Christ puts something before men's eyes which is already in action around himself and his hearers as a miraculous process which they ought to perceive and rightly understand as being such '; Wood, 687, ' We should note that all these parables imply that the kingdom is already present in germ through the activity of Jesus Himself'.[2]

As in iv. 1-9 and 26-9 Black, 123, traces the Greek version to an Aramaic original in poetic form.

Καὶ ἔλεγεν Πῶς ὁμοιώσωμεν τὴν βασιλείαν τοῦ θεοῦ, ἢ ἐν   30
τίνι αὐτὴν παραβολῇ θῶμεν; ὡς κόκκῳ σινάπεως, ὃς ὅταν   31
σπαρῇ ἐπὶ τῆς γῆς, μικρότερον ὂν πάντων τῶν σπερμάτων τῶν

30. It is generally recognized that Mt. xiii. 31 f. is a conflation of Mk and Q, and that Lk. xiii. 18 f. is derived from Q. Cf. Streeter, 246-8; Bultmann, 186. Both Mk and Q have the double question. Cf. Lk. xiii. 18, Τίνι ὁμοία ἐστίν . . . καὶ τίνι . . . ; Matthew has simply 'Ομοία ἐστὶν ἡ βασ. τ. οὐρανῶν (xiii. 31). While there is no departure from Gk idiom, the tautology in Mk and Q is Semitic. Cf. Wellhausen, 35, who cites Lk. vii. 31 and xiii. 18, and points out that there is no parallelism in Lk. xiii. 20 and Mt. xi. 16, xiii. 31. παραβολή (*v.* iii. 23) is used in the broad sense of *similitude* or *figure*; cf. Heb. xi. 19, ἐν παραβολῇ. The subjunctives are deliberative: ' How shall we . . . ? ', or ' How are we to . . . ? '; cf. vi. 24, 37, xii. 14. For θῶμεν A C² D Θ *et al.* 33 565 700 1071 *al. pler.* c ff i q vg syᵖᵉ ʰˡ read (or imply) παραβάλωμεν, which

Moulton, ii. 319, (419), describes as ' a plausible reading '.

Fiebig, 36, shows how thoroughly Jewish the opening of this parable is, and cites an interesting parallel from *Mek. Jethro*, 6, which tells of a controversy between Rabbi Gamaliel (*c.* A.D. 100) and a philosopher: ' He said to him, " I will compose for thee a similitude. To whom is the matter like? To a king of flesh and blood who marches out to war. . . ." '

31. With ὡς κόκκῳ sc. ὁμοιώσομεν or θήσομεν. Cf. the Jewish parable mentioned above. κόκκος*, Mt. xiii. 31, xvii. 20, Lk. xiii. 19, xvii. 6, Jn. xii. 24, 1 Cor. xv. 37**, ' a grain ', ' seed '. For the meaning ' scarlet ' (Cl., LXX) *v.* LS and Swete, 86, and cf. κόκκινος. σίναπι*, Mt. xiii. 31, xvii. 20, Lk. xiii. 19, xvii. 6**, a late Gk form = the Attic τὸ νᾶπυ, ' mustard ', *sinapis nigra*; both of Egyptian origin

[1] For the eschatological view *v.* Schweitzer, 354, and in criticism, A. T. Cadoux, *TJ*, 36; Plummer, 134; Blunt, 171; etc.
[2] For the reference to all nations see further, A. T. Cadoux, *TJ*, 36; Bartlet, 171; Rawlinson, 58; Easton, 218. J. Weiss, 177, suggests that in Mark's view the promise is to the disciples. C. J. Cadoux, 157, thinks that the universalism is uncertain, but that the interpretation is possible and even in some cases quite probable.

32 ἐπὶ τῆς γῆς—καὶ ὅταν . σπαρῇ, ἀναβαίνει καὶ γίνεται μεῖζον πάντων τῶν λαχάνων καὶ ποιεῖ κλάδους μεγάλους, ὥστε δύνασθαι ὑπὸ τὴν ϲκιὰν ἀγτογ τὰ πετεινὰ τογ ογρανογ καταϲκηνογν.

(*VGT*, 575). The explanatory parenthesis μικρότερον ὄν . . . ἐπὶ τῆς γῆς, in which, as is normal in the Koine, the comparative is used for the superlative, reads strangely. Lagrange, 119, explains it as a kind of acc. absol., but it is much better explained as an addition by Mark (cf. Dodd, 190 n.) or a redactor, emphasizing the thought of the very small beginnings of the Kingdom. There is also an error in fact, since the mustard-seed is not the smallest of the seeds, although proverbially it was mentioned in this sense in Palestine (cf. Lk. xvii. 6 = Mt. xvii. 20). The repetition of ἐπὶ τῆς γῆς and of ὅταν σπαρῇ may suggest that the text is not in its original form. Lohmeyer, 88, ingeniously conjectures that two separate versions of the parable have been telescoped. Black, 123, says the repetition destroys the antithetic parallelism. Torrey, *TG*, 123 f. (contr. *FG*, 299), suggests that the confused passage is due to the misreading of similar groups of words in the Aramaic original, which was simple and straightforward : ' (It is) like a grain of mustard seed, which is less (דְּזְעֵיר) than all the seeds ; but when it is sown (כְּדִי זְרִיעַ) upon the ground, it grows up and becomes greater than all the herbs '. This suggestion is very ingenious, but it rests upon a number of assumptions which cannot be proved. Moreover, it may not be necessary, in view of the possibility of an explanatory corruption mentioned above. σπέρμα, xii. 19 f., 21 f.*. The textual variants reveal how the difficulties of the Markan text were felt in ancient times. That Mark wrote . . . ὡς κόκκῳ . . . μικρότερον ὄν is shown, not only by the strong attestation of א B and D (D reads ἐστίν for ὄν), but also by Matthew's smoother version, . . . κόκκῳ . . . ὃ μικρότερον μέν ἐστιν. The textual variants κόκκον

(A C L W Θ fam. 1 fam. 13 (exc. 124) 28 33 579 700 892 1071 it (exc. d) vg), μικρότερος (A C D² W² fam. 1 fam. 13 (exc. 13) 565 d q vg (1 MS.), and ἐστίν (D M² it (exc. e) vg), may also be explained as attempts to amend Mark's broken construction.

32. ἀναβαίνει is a strange word to describe the growing of plants (*v.* the note on iv. 7) and may be an over-literal reading of the Aramaic original. It is replaced by αὔξει in W, but this reading may be a translation of the Latin *crescit* read by b e r¹. Cf. Burkitt, *JTS*, xvii. 5. λάχανον*, Mt. xiii. 32, Lk. xi. 42, Rom. xiv. 2**, mostly in the plur. of *garden-herbs, vegetables* ; Cl., LXX, Pap. Q (Lk. xiii. 19, Mt. xiii. 32) less accurately speaks of a tree (δένδρον). κλάδος, xiii. 28*. For ὥστε and the acc. and infin. constr. *v.* i. 27. σκιά*. κατασκηνόω*, Mt. xiii. 32, Lk. xiii. 19, Ac. ii. 26**, ' to take up one's quarters ', ' camp ', ' settle ' ; late Gk (Xen.), LXX. WH, § 410, support the ending in -οῖν, mainly because of the evidence of B, but probably -οῦν is more original ; cf. Blass, 48, Moulton, i. 53, ii. 197. In the Q form the birds perch on the branches ; in Mk they rest under its shadow. The plant ' has often been found growing to a height of 8 to 12 ft., and great numbers of small birds alight upon its stalks to pluck the seeds ' (*EB*, col. 3244). The imagery used is illustrated in the OT, in Dan. iv. 12, καὶ ἐν τοῖς κλάδοις αὐτοῦ κατῴκουν τὰ ὄρνεα τοῦ οὐρανοῦ, Ezek. xvii. 23 (of the cedar), καὶ ἀναπαύσεται ὑποκάτω αὐτοῦ πᾶν ὄρνεον, καὶ πᾶν πετεινὸν ὑπὸ τὴν σκιὰν αὐτοῦ ἀναπαύσεται, xxxi. 6. In these passages the tree symbolizes the protection given to subject peoples by a great empire. It is reasonable, therefore, to suppose that Jesus has Gentile nations in mind. Cf. Manson, *TJ*, 133 n. ; Dodd, 190 f. ; *per contra*, Smith, 28 f., 120 f.

Mk. iv. 33 f.   **31. SUMMARY STATEMENT**   Cf. Mt. xiii. 34 f.
                   ON THE USE OF PARABLES

This editorial passage rounds off the section iv. 1-34. As suggested
in the Commentary, there are signs that originally, perhaps in the source
used by Mark, 33 f. was more closely connected with 1-9. On this view
it is easier to give a satisfactory account of the composition of 1-34. It
may be that 34, especially the clause, ' but privately he expounded all
things to his own disciples', suggested to the Evangelist the insertion of
11 f. and the explanation of the parable of the Sower in 13-20. This
suggestion is better than the view that 34 is a redactional passage prompted
by 11 f., for 34 refers to the exposition of *parables*, not a different kind of
teaching. If this view is sound, the summary was preceded originally
by one parable, that of the Sower, which served as an example of many
(τοιαύταις παραβολαῖς). Further consideration of this point depends on
the view taken of the compilation of the complex iv. 1-34 as a whole.
See Intr. 93 f.

Καὶ τοιαύταις παραβολαῖς πολλαῖς ἐλάλει αὐτοῖς τὸν λόγον, 33
καθὼς ἠδύναντο ἀκούειν· χωρὶς δὲ παραβολῆς οὐκ ἐλάλει αὐτοῖς, 34
κατ' ἰδίαν δὲ τοῖς ἰδίοις μαθηταῖς ἐπέλυεν πάντα.

33 f. It is advantageous to take the
two verses together in order to see
the Semitic parallelism in them.
Luke omits the passage, but Matthew retains it, omitting καθὼς ἠδύναντο ἀκούειν
and κατ' ἰδίαν . . . πάντα and replacing
the first ἐλάλει by the aor. τοιοῦτος,
vi. 2, vii. 13, ix. 37, x. 14, xiii. 19*,
such parables, parables *of this kind*,
implying that a selection has been
made; cf. also πολλαῖς. Plummer,
134, points to the correct use of the
imperfects; cf. iv. 2, 10. αὐτοῖς apparently refers to the ὄχλος πλεῖστος mentioned in iv. 1. So Mt. xiii. 34, τοῖς
ὄχλοις. The use of the pronoun suggests the possibility that 33 f. may
have been connected originally with
1-9, all the more as 10-32 show obvious
signs of compilation. τὸν λόγον is the
good news of the Kingdom, as in ii. 2.
καθώς is ' just as ', ' in proportion as ';
for the idea cf. Jn. xvi. 12, 1 Cor. iii. 2
(οὔπω γὰρ ἐδύνασθε).

χωρίς . . . αὐτοῖς repeats in a negative
form the positive statement in 33, but
κατ' ἰδίαν . . . πάντα introduces a new
idea, namely, that it was the habit of
Jesus to explain His parables to His
disciples. There is no suggestion, as

in iv. 11, that the parables were spoken
only for the multitudes. So to think
is to press αὐτοῖς unduly. The suggestion, therefore, of Holtzmann, 133, and
Wellhausen, 36, that iv. 33 is original,
and 34 redactional (cf. Klostermann,
52, *Hier herrscht die gleiche Theorie
wie v. 11 f.*; cf. Rawlinson, 58 f.;
Branscomb, 86), appears to lack
sufficient warrant. All heard, but to the
disciples further teaching was given.

κατ' ἰδίαν, vi. 31 f., vii. 33, ix. 2, 28,
xiii. 3*, ' privately '. For the form
καθ' ἰδίαν v. Moulton, ii. 98; Hort,
145. ἴδιος, ' one's own '. While an ' exhausted ' ἴδιος, conveying little more
than the personal pronoun, is a feature
of Hellenistic Greek (cf. Deissmann,
BS, 123 f.), in the NT generally its
proper force is discernible (cf. Jn. i. 41,
1 Cor. iii. 8, Gal. vi. 5, Heb. vii. 27,
etc.). See the full discussion in
Moulton, i. 87-90, 237, 246; *VGT*,
298. In 34 very many MSS., but not
‫א‬ B C L Δ 892 1071, omit ἰδίοις and
add αὐτοῦ, thus indicating the sense
in which it was read. Its use here appears to be intentional in the sense of
' His *own* disciples ' (so Swete, 88;
Plummer, 134; RV and RSV;

Moffatt; Torrey). If so, there is a note of intimacy in the passage which harmonizes with iv. 1 f. ἐπιλύω*, Ac. xix. 39**, ' to loose ', ' untie '. The metaphorical meaning ' expound ', which it has in the NT, is found in late writers (Vet. Val. (ii/ A.D.) cclix. 4) and in Aq. and Th. (v. Abbott-Smith, 171). Cf. *VGT*, 241 ; Swete, 88; Bigg, *St. Pet. and St. Jude*, 269.

(c) Mk. iv. 35-v. 43   A GROUP OF MIRACLE STORIES

The group includes the following narratives :

(32)	iv. 35-41.	The Storm on the Lake.
(33)	v. 1-20.	The Gerasene Demoniac.
(34)	v. 21-4, 35-43.	The Raising of the Daughter of Jairus.
(35)	v. 25-34.	The Woman with the Issue of Blood.

These narratives are more vivid and picturesque than those of the group i. 21-39, and quite different in form from those of ii. 1-iii. 6 and iii. 19b-35. In the narratives now under review the stories are told for their own sake, with a wealth of detail, in order to portray Jesus as the doer of beneficent and wondrous deeds. Dibelius calls them *Novellen*, Tales, and traces them to the work of story-tellers in the primitive Christian community. It is better, with Bultmann, 223-60, to call them ' Miracle-stories '. How far they are to be ascribed to the reminiscences of an eyewitness, to what extent, if any, they have been coloured by popular *motifs*, and whether they stand in an original historical succession, are some of the questions to be considered.

Mk. iv. 35-41	32. THE STORM ON THE LAKE	Cf. Mt. viii. 23-7 Lk. viii. 22-5

The narrative is a Miracle-story. Whatever view is taken of the miraculous element in the story, there can be little doubt that the story belongs to the best tradition, probably that of an eyewitness, and presumably Peter.[1] The details, at once vivid and artless, point to this conclusion : the reference to the time, the statement that the disciples take Jesus ' as he was ', the allusion to ' other boats ', the mention of the cushion, the bold reproach of the disciples, the direct address to the elements, the sharp rebuke of the disciples. Attempts to trace the story to the influence of Psa. cvi. 9, ' He rebuked the Red Sea also, and it was dried up ' (cf. Strauss, *Life of Jesus*, Eng. tr. 498), or to Psa. lxxxix. 9, ' Thou rulest the pride of the sea : when the waves thereof arise, thou stillest them ', are very unconvincing. Not more satisfactory are the objections based on parallel narratives. Of these perhaps the best is the story, quoted by Bultmann, 249, of the Jewish boy through whose prayer a storm ceases, to the astonishment of the heathen who pay respect to his God ; but it is not a complete parallel. The story of Jonah may have been in the minds of the Evangelists and may have influenced their phrasing, but Wellhausen, 37, bluntly says that the Markan story is not an echo

---

[1] Cf. J. Weiss, 185, *So kann bereits Petrus erzählt haben von dem Mann, dem Wind und Meer gehorsam sind*; Lagrange, 125, *le reflet des souvenirs plus précis de Pierre*; Wood, 687; Bartlet, 173.

of that narrative; cf. also J. Weiss, 182 f. Strangely enough, the parallels with the story of Aeneas (v. Comm.) are quite as impressive; but had Mark read his Virgil?

These considerations are valid as regards the historical worth of the narrative, but not necessarily for the inference, ' Who is this, that even the wind and the sea obey him?'. As suggested in the Commentary, the disciples are rebuked for their lack of faith in God, not faith in the power of Jesus to control the forces of nature. We are justified in regarding their question as an inference immediately drawn and underlined in the later tradition, prompted by the sudden end of the storm and the words of Jesus. But what really happened? We have reason to question the view that, in the words ' Peace, be still ', Jesus addressed the disciples and not the wind; v. the note on iv. 39. It is difficult to think that the disciples could have been mistaken on this point. Moreover, the attitude of Jesus to nature as the vehicle of divine power made it as natural for Him, as it is difficult for us, to address the wind and the sea. His words are a command; but also the expression of utter and complete dependence upon His Father's will, sustained by the belief that ' his hour was not yet come '. The miracle was probably a miracle of divine providence. Jesus trusted in God and His trust was not deceived. We ought not to close our minds to the possibility that, just as in His sayings there are uprushes of divine illumination (cf. Lk. x. 21 f. = Mt. xi. 25-7), so in His works there may have been outflowings of divine power transcending the normal tenor of His conscious life. But this issue is theological; it depends on our interpretation of the *manner* of the Incarnation in its historical manifestation. Other explanations of the incident, including that outlined above, are also compatible with belief in One who, though in the form of God, emptied Himself, taking the form of a servant.

Καὶ λέγει αὐτοῖς ἐν ἐκείνῃ τῇ ἡμέρᾳ ὀψίας γενομένης Δι- 35
ἐλθωμεν εἰς τὸ πέραν. καὶ ἀφίουσιν τὸν ὄχλον καὶ παραλαμ- 36

35 f. The precision of the opening temporal statement, ἐν ἐκείνῃ τῇ ἡμέρᾳ ὀψίας γενομένης, recalls i. 32 and 35. Bultmann, 230, accepts the reference to the late hour as belonging to the original story in view of 38, but explains ἐν ἐκείνῃ τῇ ἡμέρᾳ as editorial; so Klostermann, 53. With much force, Schmidt, 135, maintains that additions of this kind are not characteristic of Mark, that both chronological notices belong to the tradition which the Evangelist has taken over, and that the same is true of the local details which follow. Bultmann admits this as regards the reference to the ' other boats ', and Wellhausen, 37, takes the same view. Both critics, however, question ὡς ἦν, which follows awkwardly after παραλαμβάνουσιν αὐτόν. A

simple and satisfactory explanation is that it means ' without going ashore ' (Swete, 88); there is no need to conjecture a form of the story in which the disciples take Him into the boat (cf. Lagrange, 123). Jesus Himself takes the initiative in the words, Διέλθωμεν εἰς τὸ πέραν, and the disciples, as the boatmen, take Him with them just as He was. Cf. 4 Kgdms. vii. 7, καὶ ἐνκατέλιπαν τὰς σκηνὰς αὐτῶν . . . ἐν τῇ παρεμβολῇ ὡς ἔστιν.

The historic presents, λέγει and παραλαμβάνουσιν, add to the vividness of the scene, and the hortatory subj. διέλθωμεν imparts a note of urgency. Why Jesus leaves the west shore can only be conjectured. Either it was because of the pressure of the crowd or to find a new sphere for His ministry,

βάνουσιν αὐτὸν ὡς ἦν ἐν τῷ πλοίῳ, καὶ ἄλλα πλοῖα ἦν μετ᾽ αὐτοῦ.
37 καὶ γίνεται λαῖλαψ μεγάλη ἀνέμου, καὶ τὰ κύματα ἐπέβαλλεν εἰς
38 τὸ πλοῖον, ὥστε ἤδη γεμίζεσθαι τὸ πλοῖον. καὶ αὐτὸς ἦν ἐν τῇ

and by analogy i. 35 suggests the latter. διέρχομαι, x. 25*, 'to go through', is used normally of a journey by land. Ramsay, *Exp.* v. i. 385 ff., holds that in the Acts, where it is used freely, it implies missionary travel. Here (cf. 1 Cor. x. 1) it is used of crossing the lake. The phrase εἰς τὸ πέραν, v. 1, 21, vi. 45 (?), viii. 13 (cf. iii. 8, x. 1)*, refers generally to the east side. Schmidt, 145, maintains that in the LXX and the NT it is used exclusively so, but this claim presses the phrase too far, for in Jn. vi. 17 πέραν τῆς θαλάσσης describes a journey to Capernaum.

In 36 ἀφίουσιν (D W Θ P⁴⁵ fam. 13 28 543 565 700 b c e ff i q r¹ syᵖᵉ sa geo) is much to be preferred to ἀφέντες (WH). παραλαμβάνω, v. 40, vii. 4, ix. 2, x. 32, xiv. 33*, 'to take', 'receive' (Cl., LXX, Pap.), is used in ix. 2, x. 32, xiv. 33 of the action of Jesus in taking His disciples along with Him, but here of the action of the disciples themselves. Lagrange, 123, cites Plato, *Apol.* 18 B, τοὺς πολλοὺς ἐκ παίδων παραλαμβάνοντες. The ἄλλα πλοῖα must have dispersed in the ensuing storm, for we hear no more of them. This detail, so unnecessary to the story, is probably a genuine reminiscence. Cf. Wellhausen, 37, *Die Angabe . . . trägt für den Zusammenhang nichts aus und könnte auf wirkliche Tradition hinweisen.* There is no ground for the conjecture of Pallis (cf. Couchoud, *JTS*, xxxiv. 119), ἄλλα δὲ πλοῖα οὐκ ἦν μετ᾽ αὐτῶν. Couchoud would read καὶ ἅμα πολλοὶ ἦσαν μετ᾽ αὐτοῦ (with W and e), but ἅμα suggests accompanying circumstances rather than the disciples (implied already in παραλαμβάνουσιν); cf. *simul naves* or *naves simul* read by b c ff i q r¹.

Mt. viii. 23 and Lk. viii. 22 reveal the greater originality of Mk. In Lk. ὀψίας γενομένης is omitted and ἐν

μιᾷ τῶν ἡμερῶν is read; in Mt both temporal statements are wanting. Further, both Gospels independently speak of Jesus boarding the boat and have οἱ μαθηταὶ αὐτοῦ. For these 'deceptive' agreements v. Streeter, 302. Again, both omit the reference to the 'other boats' and Lk has ἀνήχθησαν. These changes are explained by the new contexts in which the narrative is placed and the need for abbreviation.

37. λαῖλαψ*, Lk. viii. 23, 2 Pet. ii. 17**, 'a furious storm', 'hurricane', 'squall'; Cl., LXX. Mt. viii. 24 has σεισμὸς μέγας. ἄνεμος, iv. 39 (*bis*), 41, vi. 48, 51, xiii. 27*. The descriptive gen. ἀνέμου is a popular usage; cf. Lagrange, 123.

The lake is subject to sudden storms of wind which sweep down the valleys. 'The atmosphere, for the most part, hangs still and heavy, but the cold currents, as they pass from the west, are sucked down in vortices of air, or by the narrow gorges that break upon the lake. Then arise those sudden storms for which the region is notorious', G. A. Smith, 441 f. Cf. also Le Camus, quoted by Rawlinson, 61. Mark's γίνεται is very expressive, but even more Luke's κατέβη. The ὥστε clause describes the result. The waves were beating into the boat so that it was now filling.

κῦμα*, Mt. viii. 24, xiv. 24, Ju. 13**. The verb ἐπιβάλλω, xi. 7, xiv. 46, 72*, 'to throw upon', is here used intransitively with the meaning 'to go straight towards', and with εἰς c. acc. suggests waves breaking into the boat. Cf. Moffatt, 'splashed into the boat'. ἤδη, vi. 35 (*bis*), viii. 2, xi. 11, xiii. 28, xv. 42, 44*, is 'now', 'already', in a relative sense as compared with νῦν, 'now', 'at present', and ἄρτι, 'now', 'just now'. These distinctions are well represented in the NT and the papyri (*VGT, in loc.*). γεμίζω, xv.

πρύμνῃ ἐπὶ τὸ προσκεφάλαιον καθεύδων· καὶ ἐγείρουσιν αὐτὸν
καὶ λέγουσιν αὐτῷ Διδάσκαλε, οὐ μέλει σοι ὅτι ἀπολλύμεθα;
καὶ διεγερθεὶς ἐπετίμησεν τῷ ἀνέμῳ καὶ εἶπεν τῇ θαλάσσῃ 39

36*. Matthew has ὥστε τὸ πλοῖον
καλύπτεσθαι ὑπὸ τῶν κυμάτων (viii. 24),
and Luke καὶ συνεπληροῦντο καὶ ἐκινδύ-
νευον (viii. 23; cf. Jon. i. 4).

38. 38a is peculiar to Mk and probably rests on the testimony of an eyewitness. Cf. Mt. viii. 24, αὐτὸς δὲ
ἐκάθευδεν, and Lk. viii. 23, πλεόντων
δὲ αὐτῶν ἀφύπνωσεν. To assign 38a
to a redactor is without warrant, for
the picturesque statement is an integral
part of the story. There is perhaps a
certain emphasis or nuance in αὐτός,
an implicit contrast between Jesus and
His disciples. πρύμνα*, Ac. xxvii. 29,
41**, 'the stern'; Cl., Pap.; not
'the bow' (Torrey). Lagrange, 123,
explains that the place of honour is
the little bench at the back of the boat,
and cites Virgil, Aen. iv. 554, Aeneas
celsa in puppi, iam certus eundi, car-
pebat somnos. The steersman, he adds,
places himself on the edge at the very
back. προσκεφάλαιον**, 'a pillow' or
'cushion'; Cl., LXX, Pap.; probably the only one (τό) on board, and
presumably a rower's wooden or
leathern (Hesychius) seat used as a
head-rest (cf. J. Weiss, 181 n.). Cf.
Swete, 89. The periphrastic imperf. ἦν
. . . καθεύδων describes continued sleep.
The historic presents, ἐγείρουσιν and
λέγουσιν, vividly picture the scene
which follows. Mt and Lk have
προσελθόντες and the aor. διδάσκαλος,
v. 35, ix. 17, 38, x. 17, 20, 35, xii. 14,
19, 32, xiii. 1, xiv. 14*, 'teacher', is
the Gk equivalent for 'Ραββεί (v. ix. 5)
which Mark rarely uses. Matthew has
Κύριε and Luke Ἐπιστάτα ἐπιστάτα.
All commentators draw attention to
the softened versions of the disciples'
question in the later Gospels. Mt has
Κύριε, σῶσον, ἀπολλύμεθα, Lk Ἐπιστάτα ἐπιστάτα, ἀπολλύμεθα. The outstanding feature is the boldness of the
original, Διδάσκαλε, οὐ μέλει σοι ὅτι
ἀπολλύμεθα;, 'Teacher, don't you care

that we are perishing?'. Moffatt's
free paraphrase admirably brings out
the sense, 'Teacher, are we to drown,
for all you care?'. Cf. Torrey,
'Master, is it nothing to you that we
are perishing?'; RSV, 'Do you not
care if we perish?'. Even Lagrange,
124, observes that οὐ μέλει σοι contient
une nuance de reproche que Mt. et Lc.
n'ont pas reproduite, but this remark
is an understatement. So also Turner's
phrase, 26, 'naïve remonstrances',
and Bartlet's, 173, 'a touch of reproach'. The cry expresses indignation and fear. Following Holtzmann,
133, Lagrange, 124, quotes Virgil,
Aen. iv. 560, Nate dea, potes hoc sub
casu ducere somnos, nec quae te circum
stent deinde pericula cernis? So
Klostermann, 53. The disciples are
sure that death stares them in the face,
and they resent the fact that Jesus is
asleep, oblivious of their plight. Cf.
Swete, 89; Blunt, 172.

μέλει c. dat., xii. 14*, used impersonally, 'It is a care to . . .'; Cl., LXX,
Pap. Cf. Mt. xxii. 16, Lk. x. 40, Jn.
x. 13, xii. 6, Ac. xviii. 17, 1 Cor. vii. 21,
ix. 9, 1 Pet. v. 7**.

39. διεγείρω*, Lk. viii. 24 (bis), Jn.
vi. 18, 2 Pet. i. 13, iii. 1**, 'to arouse
completely', 'wake up'; Cl., LXX
(in later books, Judith i. 4, etc.), Pap.
(in a spell for the raising of a dead
body); VGT, 160. Lagrange, 125,
Et s'étant éveillé. The meaning is
that Jesus awoke, not that He stood
up. The wind is dramatically rebuked
as if it were a hostile power or even a
daemon. For other cases in which
Jesus addresses inanimate objects v.
xi. 14 (a fig tree) and 23, in a saying
about a mountain. It is perverse to
explain this language as a kind of
primitive animism; it reflects a recognition of nature as the vehicle of divine
power which is strange to the modern
man.

Σιώπα, πεφίμωσο. καὶ ἐκόπασεν ὁ ἄνεμος, καὶ ἐγένετο γαλήνη
40 μεγάλη. καὶ εἶπεν αὐτοῖς Τί οὕτως δειλοί ἐστε; οὔπω ἔχετε
41 πίστιν; καὶ ἐφοβήθησαν φόβον μέγαν, καὶ ἔλεγον πρὸς ἀλλήλους

Wellhausen, 37, thinks that τῇ θαλάσσῃ is an insertion, since it stands in another position in D (καὶ τῇ θαλάσσῃ καὶ εἶπεν, D W fam. 1 565 700 b c e ff i geo). φιμόω is used in the command to the demoniac in i. 25 (φιμώθητι); here in the rarer but more emphatic perf. imperative. Cf. Moulton, i. 176. Rohde, *Psyche*, ii (Eng. tr., 604), suggests that the verb was used in rude Egyptian-Syrian Gk to denote the *binding* of a person by a spell so as to make him powerless to harm, and examples of this magical use are found in the papyri (*VGT*, 672). The contrast between the violence of the storm and the sequel to the command is very marked. The wind ceased and there was a great calm. With unconscious artistry the long vowels of γαλήνη μεγάλη suggest an atmosphere of complete peace. κοπάζω, vi. 51*, Mt. xiv. 32**, 'to grow weary', 'abate', <κόπος; Herodotus vii. 191, LXX, MGk. γαλήνη*, Mt. viii. 26, Lk. viii. 24**, 'stillness', 'calm'; Cl., Psa. cvi. (cvii.) 29, Symm. (Swete, 90).

The conjecture that the words were addressed to the disciples, while not inadmissible, has no support in the narrative. On the contrary, the rebuke follows the calm. Moreover, it refers to faith in God, not to the power of Jesus. In estimating the historical basis of the story it should be allowed that Jesus did address the wind. It does not follow that the inference in 41 was justified. 'Who then is this, that the wind and the sea obey him?', is the surmise of the disciples, and, in harmony therewith, only the words, 'Peace, be still', have been preserved in the tradition. More may have been said. The determination of this question depends on the view taken of the narrative as a whole and of the question of the miraculous. See Intr. 140-5.

40. δειλός*, Mt. viii. 26, Apoc. xxi. 8**, 'cowardly', 'timid'. The πίστις (v. ii. 5) mentioned here is faith in God, the faith in His Father's care which Jesus displayed when He slept peacefully on the cushion. It is not confidence in the wonder-working power of Jesus, and there is nothing to suggest the inworking of later Christian ideas. Cf. Wellhausen, 37; Rawlinson, 62; Bartlet, 173; Lagrange, 124. Matthew adds ὀλιγόπιστοι to δειλοί, omitting οὔπω ἔχετε πίστιν;, and placing the reproach before the end of the storm (viii. 26), while Luke has simply Ποῦ ἡ πίστις ὑμῶν; (viii. 25). The greater originality of Mk is evident. The tone of the rebuke is sharp. It is the first of a series of reproaches addressed to the disciples for their want of faith or understanding; cf. vii. 18, viii. 17 f., 21, 32 f., ix. 19, xvi. [14]. οὔπω, viii. 17, 21, xi. 2, xiii. 7*; v. *HS²*, 13.

After ἐστέ, οὕτως is added by A C W *et al.* and many minusc., and it is found before δειλοί in P⁴⁵ fam. 1 (exc. 118) fam. 13 (exc. 124) 28 543 arm. It may well be original. Cf. Couchoud, *JTS*, xxxv. 4.

πῶς οὐκ, instead of οὔπω, is read by A C *et al.* many minusc. sype hl f, and οὔπω is omitted by W e q. These readings are probably inferior to those of WH text (ℵ B D L Θ).

41. The verse describes the effect produced on the disciples and the immediate inference they drew. φοβέω, v. 15, 33, 36, vi. 20, 50, ix. 32, x. 32, xi. 18, 32, xii. 12, xvi. 8*, 'to frighten', is here used, as always in the NT, as a passive deponent, 'to fear'. The acc. φόβον μέγαν is cognate, 'they feared a great fear'; cf. Lk. ii. 9, 1 Pet. iii. 14. Cf. also 1 Macc. x. 8 and Jon. i. 10, καὶ ἐφοβήθησαν οἱ ἄνδρες φόβον μέγαν, καὶ εἶπαν πρὸς αὐτόν, a passage which may have influenced the Markan

Τίς ἄρα οὗτός ἐστιν ὅτι καὶ ὁ ἄνεμος καὶ ἡ θάλασσα ὑπακούει αὐτῷ;

story. The meaning is that the disciples were filled with a feeling of reverential awe, a sense of the uncanny. The change to the imperf. is deliberate, 'they began to say one to another'. πρὸς ἀλλήλους, viii. 16, ix. 34, xv. 31, ἐν ἀλλήλοις, ix. 50*. ἄρα, xi. 33*, is illative, 'then'. The use of ὅτι, instead of the relative ᾧ, seems Semitic; cf. Howard, ii. 436, who cites Moulton, *Einl.* 332 n.; Lagrange, xcvi, who, however, points to Plato, *Euthyph.* 2 A, Τί νεώτερον, ὦ Σώκρατες, γέγονεν, ὅτι σύ . . . διατρίβεις. For the verb in the sing. with two subjects cf. Mt. v. 18, vi. 19, 1 Cor. xv. 50, Apoc. ix. 12. Black, 54, mentions the important variant in ff i q, *cui et ventus et mare*

obaudiunt, in support of the view that ὅτι is a misreading of the Aramaic ר. *V.* Intr. 58.

There can be little doubt that the inference that the wind and the sea were obedient to Jesus was drawn on the spot. Independently both Matthew and Luke interpret the fear by ἐθαύμασαν and both have the plur. verb ὑπακούουσιν. Matthew says that the men (οἱ ἄνθρωποι, cf. McNeile, 111) said 'What manner of man (ποταπός) is this?', and Luke makes explicit what is implied in his source in the words, 'He commandeth (ἐπιτάσσει) even the winds and the water (ὕδατι)' (viii. 25). The tendency of the tradition is to emphasize the inference.

Mk. v. 1-20 　　33. THE GERASENE 　　Cf. Mt. viii. 28-34
　　　　　　　　　　DEMONIAC 　　　　Lk. viii. 26-39

Bultmann, 224, points out that the narrative has the form characteristic of the Miracle-story (exorcism) in the account of the meeting with the demoniac, his dangerous character, his suspicion of the exorcist, the exorcism, the demonstration of the departure of the daemons, the impression made on the eyewitnesses. The story, he suggests, is in its original form, apart from the transitional phrases in 1 and the redactional verse 8. This opinion hardly does sufficient justice to the narrative. It is not yet reduced to the rounded form which Miracle-stories possess when they have been handed down through a succession of narrators, and stands appreciably nearer the record of an eyewitness. This view is suggested by the unevenness of the narrative. Verses 6 f., with their picture of the demoniac seeing Jesus from afar, running, and falling down before Him read almost like the beginning of a separate account, while 3-5 stand apart as the vivid statement of neighbours long familiar with the man's violence.[1] Verse 8 appears to reflect the Evangelist's embarrassment in coping with an excess of material. . These features are well explained if we infer that he had heard the story told more than once and was telescoping his recollections.

Another feature of the narrative is the arrangement in scenes in which the point of interest shifts from the man (1-10) to the herd of swine (11-13), then to the townspeople (14-17), and finally back again to the man by the lakeside (18-20). In a rudimentary form we have the beginnings of a little drama in four acts. And yet we do not receive the impression of imaginative artistic creation; the story is what it is because it describes

---

[1] See the comment of Lohmeyer mentioned in the note on 3-5 below. Lohmeyer's treatment of the narrative is unusually positive.

what happened. ' The most natural assumption always abides, that here we have a tradition of something which actually happened ', J. Weiss, 190. It is true that miracle-stories may incorporate *motifs* like that of the outwitted daemon (*v.* the note on 13), or the belief that daemons belong to the abyss (cf. Lk. viii. 31), but it does not follow that all narratives which illustrate these *motifs* are purely imaginative constructions. Least of all is this view credible of the present story. The many artless details, the picture of the man smashing his fetters and cutting himself with stones, the dialogue, the expulsion, the description of the man ' sitting, clothed, and in his right mind ', the attitude of the spectators, the kind of message the man proclaims in the Decapolis, are details taken from life. We have good reason to classify the narrative as Petrine in origin.

It is another question how we are to interpret what is told. The greatest difficulty is the account of the swine. If we reject mythical explanations, or the suggestion of Dibelius that a secular story has been incorporated (*v.* the note on 13), and if we accept a psychological explanation of possession, we must explain the panic of the swine, as Weiss explains it, as occasioned by the paroxysm of the man's cure.

V. 1   Καὶ ἦλθον εἰς τὸ πέραν τῆς θαλάσσης εἰς τὴν χώραν τῶν

1. Instead of ἦλθον the singular ἦλθεν is read, possibly rightly, by C L Δ Θ fam. 13 28 543 579 700 892 *al. mu.* q sys pe hl bo geo Epiph. Cf. Schmidt, 139. τῶν Γερασηνῶν*, so Lk. Matthew has Γαδαρηνῶν. In Mk Γερασηνῶν (‎אֲ* B D it vg Eus) is the original reading. Γεργεσηνῶν (אc L Δ Θ fam. 1 28 33 565 579 700 892 1071 *et al.* sys bo geo aeth arm Epiph Or) is a later Caesarean correction, and Γαδαρηνῶν (A C *et al.* fam. 13 543 *al. pler.* sype hl) an assimilation to the text of Mt. Cf. Swete, 91; Lagrange, 132-5; Turner, 27; Rawlinson, 64.

The textual variations are due to the fact that both Gerasa (30 miles to the S.E.) and Gadara (6 miles to the S.E.) are too far from the lake, and to the necessity of finding a site where the mountains run down steeply into the lake (*v.* 11, 13). There can be little doubt that Mark wrote : ' the country of the Gerasenes ', meaning thereby the district extending to the lake of which Gerasa is the principal town. In this he followed existing tradition, since it is not his habit of himself to introduce place names. Cf. Schmidt, 141; J. Weiss, 186.

Mark's description is vague, probably because he lacked precise knowledge about the place of landing. This is not surprising if he was a Jerusalemite, still less if he was a Roman Christian. Cf. Bacon, *Is Mark a Roman Gospel?*, 63; Rawlinson, 65. The landing place was on the east side of the lake, but its identity can only be conjectured. Origen, *In Ioan.* vi. 41, pointed out the unsuitability of both Gerasa and Gadara. Γέρασα δὲ τῆς Ἀραβίας ἐστὶ πόλις οὔτε θάλασσαν οὔτε λίμνην πλησίον ἔχουσα . . . Γάδαρα γὰρ πόλις μέν ἐστι τῆς Ἰουδαίας . . . λίμνη δὲ κρημνοῖς παρακειμένη οὐδαμῶς ἐστιν ἐν αὐτῇ ἢ θάλασσα. He suggested that the place was Gergesa, ' an ancient city . . . by the lake now called Tiberias, by which is a cliff overhanging the lake, from which they show that the swine were cast down by the devils '. ἀλλὰ Γέργεσα . . . πόλις ἀρχαία περὶ τὴν νῦν καλουμένην Τιβεριάδα λίμνην, περὶ ἣν κρημνὸς προσκείμενος τῇ λίμνῃ, ἀφ' οὗ δείκνυται τοὺς χοίρους ὑπὸ τῶν δαιμόνων καταβεβλῆσθαι. Cf. Jerome, *De situ*, 130. Modern scholars identify the place as *Kersa*, or *Kursa*, at the mouth of the *Wady es-Samak*. Cf. Dalman, *SSW*, 177-9; Lagrange, 136. Since, however, the shore at this point is level, Dalman, following an older suggestion of C. W. Wilson (*The*

Γερασηνῶν. καὶ ἐξελθόντος αὐτοῦ ἐκ τοῦ πλοίου [εὐθὺς] ὑπ- 2
ήντησεν αὐτῷ ἐκ τῶν μνημείων ἄνθρωπος ἐν πνεύματι ἀκαθάρτῳ,
ὃς τὴν κατοίκησιν εἶχεν ἐν τοῖς μνήμασιν, καὶ οὐδὲ ἁλύσει οὐκέτι 3
οὐδεὶς ἐδύνατο αὐτὸν δῆσαι διὰ τὸ αὐτὸν πολλάκις πέδαις καὶ 4
ἁλύσεσι δεδέσθαι καὶ διεσπάσθαι ὑπ' αὐτοῦ τὰς ἁλύσεις καὶ τὰς
πέδας συντετρίφθαι, καὶ οὐδεὶς ἴσχυεν αὐτὸν δαμάσαι· καὶ διὰ 5

Recovery of Jerusalem, 368 f.), thinks
that the landing was made two kilometres farther south, at *Moka'-'Edlo*,
where ' a fairly steep slope, 44 metres
high, of a projection of the headland
reaches to within 40 metres of the sea-
shore '. Cf. also Lagrange, 136, who
now takes the same view. It is admitted that there are no graves in the
vicinity. Lagrange says that there are
some, with the appearance of dwelling-
places, four or five kilometres distant.
   2. In ἐξελθόντος αὐτοῦ the gen. abs.,
as often in the NT, refers to a pronoun
in the sentence (αὐτῷ). This unclassical usage is common in Hellenistic
Greek. Cf. Moulton, i. 74. The
meeting with the demoniac takes place
apparently soon after the landing, but
not necessarily immediately, if, with
B W b c e f ff i sys pe arm, we omit
εὐθύς. The man is described as ' from
the tombs '. It was a popular belief
that cemeteries were haunted by daemons, and, according to 3, the man
has his dwelling-place there. In 2
ἐκ τῶν μνημείων is omitted by sys.
Wellhausen, 38, thinks the text doubtful, in view of the use of μνήματα in
3 and 5, but the objection does not
seem sufficiently strong. ὑπαντάω*,
Cl., LXX, Pap. μνημεῖον, vi. 29, xv.
46, xvi. 2, 3, 5, 8*. For ἐν πνεύματι
ἀκαθάρτῳ v. i. 23.
   The later Synoptists interpret the
Markan text. Luke says that Jesus
and the disciples sailed to, or ' put in
at ' (κατέπλευσαν), the land of the
Gerasenes, and explains that it was
ἀντίπερα τῆς Γαλιλαίας. He also
changes the gen. abs. to ἐξελθόντι αὐτῷ,
and says that the man ἔχων δαιμόνια
was ἐκ τῆς πόλεως (viii. 26 f.). Matthew
mentions two demoniacs (viii. 28 ; cf.

xx. 30, where he speaks of two blind
men).
   3-5. This pictorial passage may well
be taken as a whole because in large
measure it is peculiar to Mk. Matthew
merely gives the sense of the passage
in his description of the two demoniacs
as a public danger, χαλεποὶ λίαν ὥστε
μὴ ἰσχύειν τινὰ παρελθεῖν διὰ τῆς ὁδοῦ
ἐκείνης (viii. 28). Luke also shows his
knowledge of the Markan narrative,
but merely says here, καὶ χρόνῳ ἱκανῷ
οὐκ ἐνεδύσατο ἱμάτιον, καὶ ἐν οἰκίᾳ οὐκ
ἔμενεν ἀλλ' ἐν τοῖς μνήμασιν (viii. 27).
Later (viii. 29) he gives the substance
of 3-5. The three verses contain
several words which are found here
only in Mk, κατοίκησις, ἅλυσις, πέδη,
διασπάω, δαμάζω. It is not necessary
to find any special significance in the
association of the demoniac with the
tombs. Not infrequently tombs were
inhabited, and the violence of the man,
so realistically described, is enough to
explain why he had been compelled
to live in seclusion. Cf. Psa. lxvii. 7
(LXX), Isa. lxv. 4. Apparently,
attempts had been made to restrain
him, but he could no longer (οὐκέτι,
vii. 12, ix. 8, x. 8, xii. 34, xiv. 25, xv.
5*) be bound by a chain. For the
double negative v. i. 44.
   For διὰ τό c. infin., v. iv. 5. Here
the construction is used to indicate
past circumstances which explain the
present situation. Cf. Burton, § 408.
Many a time (πολλάκις, ix. 22*) he had
been bound with fetters and chains,
but he had torn the chains in two
(διεσπάσθαι) and had smashed the
fetters to pieces (συντετρίφθαι), and no
one could tame him. διασπάω*, Ac.
xxiii. 10** ; Cl., LXX. συντρίβω, xiv.
3*, Mt. xii. 20, Lk. ix. 39, Jn. xix. 36,

παντὸς νυκτὸς καὶ ἡμέρας ἐν τοῖς μνήμασιν καὶ ἐν τοῖς ὄρεσιν
6 ἦν κράζων καὶ κατακόπτων ἑαυτὸν λίθοις. καὶ ἰδὼν τὸν Ἰησοῦν
7 ἀπὸ μακρόθεν ἔδραμεν καὶ προσεκύνησεν αὐτόν, καὶ κράξας φωνῇ
μεγάλῃ λέγει Τί ἐμοὶ καὶ σοί, Ἰησοῦ υἱὲ τοῦ θεοῦ τοῦ ὑψίστου;
8 ὁρκίζω σε τὸν θεόν, μή με βασανίσῃς. ἔλεγεν γὰρ αὐτῷ Ἔξελθε

Rom. xvi. 20, Apoc. ii. 27**; Cl., LXX, Pap. δαμάζω*, Jas. iii. 7 f.**; Cl., LXX. Of the string of perfects Swete, 93, says, ' It is as if the writer's imagination had caught the words of the neighbours as they told the tale of their repeated failures (οὐ δυνάμεθα αὐτὸν δῆσαι, πολλάκις γὰρ δέδεται κτλ.), and he embodied them without a change of tense '. Cf. Lagrange, 127 ; Lohmeyer, 94. This suggestion is supported by the change of tense at the end where Mark returns to the imperfect as in 3.

The demoniac's present mode of life is described in 5. Continually among the tombs and the hills he was crying out (Moffatt, ' shrieked ') and cutting himself with stones. διὰ παντός*, ' common in papyri as in Bibl. Greek in place of the obsolescent ἀεί ' (VGT, 146). νυκτὸς καὶ ἡμέρας: at intervals during the night and the day ; cf. iv. 27. For the periphrastic imperfects in ἦν κράζων . . . κατακόπτων see Intr. 45, 62 f. κατακόπτω**; Cl., LXX, Pap. In a derived sense the verb can mean ' bruise ', ' beat ' (cf. Wycliffe, ' betynge hymsilf '). Cf. Field, 27 ; VGT, 327. But probably cutting or gashing (Moffatt) is the meaning here.
6 f. In these verses the story is resumed. It might seem that 6 f. belong to a different account of the incident, for in 1 f., even if we omit εὐθύς, the meeting takes place immediately the boat touches the shore. Here the demoniac sees Jesus from a distance, and runs and falls down before him. The want of harmony, however, may be no more than an unevenness in the narrative occasioned by the introduction of 3-5. ἀπὸ μακρόθεν, viii. 3, xi. 13, xiv. 54, xv. 40*; Mt (2), Lk (2), Apoc. (3)**, ' from afar '; Polyb. i.

65. 7, LXX. Cf. Hawkins, HS², 12. The preposition is redundant (WM, 753 f.) and μακρόθεν is a late equivalent for πόρρωθεν. τρέχω, xv. 36*. προσκυνέω, xv. 19*, ' to go down on the knees to ', elsewhere (Mt. ii. 2, Lk. iv. 7, etc.) ' to worship '; Cl., LXX, Pap. ; generally c. dat in NT.
Several features are common to Mark's earlier references to demoniacs in i. 23 f. and iii. 11, the references to shrieking with a loud voice, to prostration (cf. προσέπιπτον, iii. 11), the question, ' Why dost thou meddle with me ? ' (cf. i. 24), the confession of Jesus as ' Son of God Most High ' (cf. i. 24, ὁ ἅγιος τοῦ θεοῦ, iii. 11, ὁ υἱὸς τοῦ θεοῦ), the fear of torment (cf. i. 24, ἦλθες ἀπολέσαι ἡμᾶς). Foiled in his hope of appeasing the strange exorcist and rendering him powerless by the use of his name, the demoniac in his terror makes a frantic appeal, ' I adjure thee by God, torment me not '. The man fears that he is about to be punished. ὁρκίζω*, Ac. xix. 13**; in both cases with two accusatives ; Cl., LXX, Pap. (VGT, 457). For μή c. aor. subj. in a prohibition or entreaty relating to the future v. Moulton, i. 122-4. βασανίζω, vi. 48*, Mt. viii. 6, 29, xiv. 24, Lk. viii. 28, 2 Pet. ii. 8, Apoc. ix. 5, xi. 10, xii. 2, xiv. 10, xx. 10**, ' to examine ', ' torture ', <βάσανος, ' touchstone '; Cl., LXX, Pap. (VGT, 104). For the idea of punishment in contemporary apocalyptic v. Apoc. xviii. 7 f., xx. 1-3, 7-10.
Matthew omits 6, but Luke has ἰδὼν δὲ τὸν Ἰησοῦν. The latter part of 7 apparently raised difficulties by reason of its boldness. Matthew omits ὁρκίζω σε τὸν θεόν and gives the rest an eschatological form, ἦλθες ὧδε πρὸ καιροῦ βασανίσαι ἡμᾶς; (viii. 29). Luke

τὸ πνεῦμα τὸ ἀκάθαρτον ἐκ τοῦ ἀνθρώπου. καὶ ἐπηρώτα αὐτόν 9
Τί ὄνομά σοι; καὶ λέγει αὐτῷ Λεγιὼν ὄνομά ⌜μοι⌝, ὅτι πολλοί
ἐσμεν· καὶ παρεκάλει αὐτὸν πολλὰ ἵνα μὴ αὐτὰ ἀποστείλῃ ἔξω 10

9 μοί ἐστιν

softens his source in the rendering, 'I beseech thee (δέομαί σου), torment me not'. Again the greater originality of Mark is evident.

8. This passage is Mark's explanation of the demoniac's frenzied words. Cf. vi. 52, xvi. 8. It is almost the only addition which he has made to his source. Cf. Bultmann, 224 n., who thinks the view of O. Bauernfeind, that originally 8 preceded 7, perhaps instead of 6, too circumstantial. So Lohmeyer, 96 n. Probably this opinion is sound, for we cannot assume that originally the narrative had a more logical form. Bauernfeind's suggestion describes how a writer would have proceeded who was using the tradition with a free hand. The presumption is that Mark found 6 f. as a fixed unit which he decided to retain as such, and it is notable that the more accomplished writer, Luke, has followed Mark's lead, replacing ἔλεγεν by παρήγγελλεν and the direct speech by indirect, and appending the substance of Mark's description of the demoniac given earlier in 3-5.

Mark's ἔλεγεν is used in the sense of the pluperfect, 'He had been saying'; cf. v. 28, vi. 18, Mt. xiv. 4, Ac. ix. 39 (v. Lake, iv. 111): Burton, § 29. This explanation is preferable to the view that Mark means that Jesus was repeatedly saying 'Come forth . . .'. For the suggestion that ἔλεγεν is used in the Semitic sense of 'enjoin' v. Black, JTS, xlix. 162. The words recall those of i. 25, ἔξελθε ἐξ αὐτοῦ. Apparently a simple command was not enough; fuller treatment was necessary. Micklem, 55, infers that in the first place the daemon was ordered to come out unsuccessfully.

9. ἐπερωτάω (ἐρωτάω, iv. 10) appears here for the first time in Mk; in all 25 times; 'to consult', 'inquire of',

'ask'; Cl., LXX, Pap. λεγιών, v. 15*, Mt. xxvi. 53, Lk. viii. 30**, legio, 'legion'. The word found its way into Hellenistic Greek (Plutarch, Rom. xiii. 20) and Aramaic, and is abundantly represented in the papyri (VGT, 371). It survives in the modern place name Lejjun which is identified with the ancient Megiddo (G. A. Smith, 386). The ideas lying behind the question, 'What is thy name?', are connected with the ancient belief that knowledge of the name carries with it power over an adversary (cf. Gen. xxxii. 29) and over a daemon (cf. Deissmann, 261 n.). Wellhausen, 39, suggests that perhaps the daemon avoids giving its name, giving its number instead, but the more usual suggestion, that the sight of a legion, which normally consisted of upwards of 6000 men, may have occasioned the use of the name, seems adequate. Cf. Swete, 95; Lagrange, 129. 'In applying this name to himself the possessed man appealed to Christ's pity. It meant that he felt himself a mere congeries of unco-ordinated impulses and evil forces — lacking a moral unity of will, and so not one, but an aggregate of many', Bartlett, 176. The alteration from the singular to the plural in 9-13 strongly supports this view. It may be that in His compassion Jesus adapted Himself to the sufferer's situation, but there is no reason at all why He should not have shared contemporary beliefs about the efficacy of the name.

10. The subject of παρεκάλει can be either 'he' or 'they' (sc. τὰ δαιμόνια). RV and RSV take the former view; Moffatt, probably rightly, the latter. The point is not of much importance, for in any case the man is the speaker and, as in cases of multiple personality, he speaks now in his own name and

11 τῆς χώρας. Ἦν δὲ ἐκεῖ πρὸς τῷ ὄρει ἀγέλη χοίρων μεγάλη
12 βοσκομένη· καὶ παρεκάλεσαν αὐτὸν λέγοντες Πέμψον ἡμᾶς εἰς
13 τοὺς χοίρους, ἵνα εἰς αὐτοὺς εἰσέλθωμεν. καὶ ἐπέτρεψεν αὐτοῖς.
καὶ ἐξελθόντα τὰ πνεύματα τὰ ἀκάθαρτα εἰσῆλθον εἰς τοὺς χοίρους, καὶ ὥρμησεν ἡ ἀγέλη κατὰ τοῦ κρημνοῦ εἰς τὴν θάλασσαν,
14 ὡς δισχίλιοι, καὶ ἐπνίγοντο ἐν τῇ θαλάσσῃ. Καὶ οἱ βόσκοντες

now collectively in the name of the powers by whom he believes himself to be possessed. πολλά is adverbial, as in i. 45. ἵνα μή . . . c. subj. expresses, not purpose, but the substance of the request; cf. iii. 9. The idea implicit in ἔξω τῆς χώρας was widely held in the ancient world. Daemons, it was held, were specially associated with a particular locality from which they were loth to be removed. In Lk. xi. 24, for example, the expelled daemon seeks a dwelling place and is embarrassed because he cannot find it. Cf. Klostermann, 57; Bultmann, 239. Luke (viii. 31) replaces Mark's phrase by εἰς τὴν ἄβυσσον, taking the view that what the daemons fear is imprisonment pending their destruction (cf. Apoc. ix. 1, xx. 10). Cf. Creed, 121; Easton, 123, 125.

11 f. Ἦν δὲ . . . βοσκομένη: 'Now there was feeding there'. For the periphrastic impf. v. Intr. 45, 62 f. In these words a new stage in the narrative begins. πρός c. dat., 'close to', 'at', is rare in the NT, being found 'in the ratio of less than ·01 to πρός with acc.' (Moulton, i. 63, 106). There are only six examples (Mk (1), Lk (1), Jn (3), Apoc. (1)). Cf. Lk. xix. 37. The region is very mountainous and the precise spot can only be conjectured. ἀγέλη, v. 13*, Mt. viii. 30 f., 32, Lk. viii. 32 f.**; Cl., LXX, Pap. χοῖρος, v. 12 f., 16*; Cl., (LXX, ὗς), Pap. The presence of the herd shows that the region was mainly pagan. Cf. Billerbeck, i. 492. βόσκω, v. 14*, Mt. viii. 30, 33, Lk. viii. 32, 34, x. 15, Jn. xxi. 15, 17**, 'to feed', 'tend', pass. 'to graze'; Cl., LXX, Pap. In παρεκάλεσαν a specific request is indicated as distinct from the repeated

entreaty in παρεκάλει (v. 10). For the plur. v. the note on v. 10.

Verse 12 is almost intolerably redundant, even in a Gospel which contains many redundancies, and there is much to be said for the view that ἵνα εἰς αὐτοὺς εἰσέλθωμεν is an example of the imperatival use of ἵνα c. subj. Cf. H. G. Meecham, JTS, xliii. 180. Cf. v. 23, x. 51. For this construction v. Moulton, i. 177-9. On this view, the rendering is: 'Send us into the swine, let us enter into them' (so Torrey). In different ways Matthew and Luke avoid the redundancy. Cf. Mt. viii. 31, Εἰ ἐκβάλλεις ἡμᾶς, ἀπόστειλον ἡμᾶς εἰς τὴν ἀγέλην τῶν χοίρων, and Lk. viii. 32, ἵνα ἐπιτρέψῃ αὐτοῖς εἰς ἐκείνους εἰσελθεῖν.

13. ὁρμάω*, Mt. viii. 32, Lk. viii. 33, Ac. vii. 57, xix. 29**, 'to set in motion', 'rush'; Cl., LXX, Pap. In all NT cases it is used intransitively in the sense of rush. κρημνός*, Mt. viii. 32, Lk. viii. 33**; 'an overhanging bank', 'steep bank', 'crag'; Cl., LXX, Pap. ὡς δισχίλιοι**, 'about two thousand': this detail is peculiar to Mark's account. It is a round number and may be an exaggeration. πνίγω* (cf. συνπνίγω, iv. 7), Mt. xiii. 7 (v.l.), xviii. 28**, 'to choke'; Cl., LXX, Pap. Matthew and Luke agree with small variations. Matthew has καὶ ἀπέθανον ἐν τοῖς ὕδασιν (viii. 32).

In this verse, as J. Weiss, 188, observes, there are four details, two visible and two inferred: (a) Jesus permitted the spirits to go out, perhaps by a sign or gesture, (b) they went out, and (c) entered into the swine, (d) the swine ran into the lake. He adds, as many interpreters have held, that it was the paroxysm accompanying the

αὐτοὺς ἔφυγον καὶ ἀπήγγειλαν εἰς τὴν πόλιν καὶ εἰς τοὺς ἀγρούς·
καὶ ἦλθον ἰδεῖν τί ἐστιν τὸ γεγονός. καὶ ἔρχονται πρὸς τὸν 15
Ἰησοῦν, καὶ θεωροῦσιν τὸν δαιμονιζόμενον καθήμενον ἱματισμένον καὶ σωφρονοῦντα, τὸν ἐσχηκότα τὸν λεγιῶνα, καὶ ἐφο-

exorcism which set the herd in motion. The man hurled himself upon the swine, struck terror into them, and drove them down the steep. For long he had been overpowered by the idea that the daemons by whom he was possessed would like to enter into them, and he recognized the opportunity provided by the strange exorcist who asked him his name. What, asks Weiss, is there unthinkable in this explanation, and wherein is violence done to the narrative? It is common to describe such explanations as 'psychologizing', as if it were possible to interpret an ancient narrative without reading between lines! The alternatives, e.g. the view that the story illustrates the *motif* of the cheated daemon (cf. Wellhausen, 39), reversed in the suggestion that the daemons deceive Jesus (so Bauernfeind; *v.* Bultmann, 224 n.), or the suggestion that a story which told originally of a Jewish exorcist has been ascribed to Jesus (cf. Dibelius, 89, 101), are also examples of 'reading between the lines', more open to the charge of distortion than the sober interpretation of Weiss. Much discussion has been directed to the responsibility of Jesus for the destruction of the swine, generally with the assumption that it was foreseen.

14. A third stage in the narrative begins at this point. The swineherds take to their heels and tell the news in the city and the surrounding hamlets. φεύγω, xiii. 14, xiv. 50, 52, xvi. 8*. ἀπαγγέλλω, v. 19, vi. 30, xvi. [10, 13]*, 'to bring tidings', 'report'; Cl., LXX, Pap. Here, and in the parallel passage in Lk. viii. 34, is the verb followed by εἰς c. acc.; elsewhere c. dat. ἀγρός, vi. 36, 56, x. 29 f., xi. 8, xiii. 16, xv. 21, xvi. [12]*, Mt (16), Lk (9), Ac (1)**, 'a field', 'the country', 'ham-

lets' in the plur. The word is classical and is used freely in the LXX, but rarely in the papyri and is obsolete in MGk. Here and in vi. 36, 56 it denotes 'hamlets' (Lagrange, 131, *hameaux*) as distinct from 'cities' and 'villages'. The town (πόλις) is not named and its identity can only be conjectured. The unexpressed subject of ἦλθον (ἐξῆλθον, ℵ* C D W Δ Θ it vg sys pe *et al.*) is 'the people'. They came out to see what had happened (τὸ γεγονός). Luke (viii. 34 f.) follows Mk closely. Matthew supplies an object to ἀπήγγειλαν in the words πάντα καὶ τὰ τῶν δαιμονιζομένων (viii. 33).

15 f. A new beginning, with the historic present ἔρχονται (*v.* i. 12), marks the point of arrival: the people come to Jesus. It does not seem necessary, with Swete, 97, to infer that, finding all quiet again, they went down to the shore. The choice of θεωροῦσιν (cf. ἰδεῖν in 14) seems deliberate and τὸν δαιμονιζόμενον appears to be used from their point of view. Later, in 15b, Mark characterizes him as τὸν ἐσχηκότα τὸν λεγιῶνα, and in 18 as ὁ δαιμονισθείς. The three participles, καθήμενον, ἱματισμένον, and σωφρονοῦντα describe features which must immediately have struck the attention of the beholders; they see the man, sitting, clothed, and in his right mind. ἱματίζω*, Lk. viii. 35**. Although not found in the LXX, the frequent use of this verb in the papyri shows that it was in common use in the Koine; cf. *VGT*, 304; *LAE*, 82 f. σωφρονέω*, Lk. viii. 35, Rom. xii. 3, 2 Cor. v. 13, Tit. ii. 6, 1 Pet. iv. 7**, 'to be of sound mind', 'self-controlled'; Cl., not in LXX (*v. VGT*, 622). Luke repeats the three participles and describes the man sitting παρὰ τοὺς πόδας τοῦ Ἰησοῦ. The participle in τὸν ἐσχηκότα τὸν λεγιῶνα is an aoristic perfect: 'the

16 βήθησαν. καὶ διηγήσαντο αὐτοῖς οἱ ἰδόντες πῶς ἐγένετο τῷ
17 δαιμονιζομένῳ καὶ περὶ τῶν χοίρων. καὶ ἤρξαντο παρακαλεῖν
18 αὐτὸν ἀπελθεῖν ἀπὸ τῶν ὁρίων αὐτῶν. Καὶ ἐμβαίνοντος αὐτοῦ
εἰς τὸ πλοῖον παρεκάλει αὐτὸν ὁ δαιμονισθεὶς ἵνα μετ᾽ αὐτοῦ ᾖ.
19 καὶ οὐκ ἀφῆκεν αὐτόν, ἀλλὰ λέγει αὐτῷ Ὕπαγε εἰς τὸν οἶκόν
σου πρὸς τοὺς σούς, καὶ ⸀ἀπάγγειλον⸀ αὐτοῖς ὅσα ὁ κύριός σοι

19 διάγγειλον

man that had the legion'. Moulton, i. 145, explains it by the fact that 'ἔσχον is almost (if not quite) exclusively used for the ingressive *got*, *received*'. The phrase is omitted by D 17 27 it vg sys bo, but it is implied by Lk. viii. 35, τὸν ἄνθρωπον ἀφ᾽ οὗ τὰ δαιμόνια ἐξῆλθεν, and is original. The fear mentioned (ἐφοβήθησαν, *v.* iv. 41) is awe in the presence of the supernatural. This awe is induced before the eyewitnesses relate what had happened. διηγέομαι, ix. 9,* Lk. viii. 39, ix. 10, Ac. viii. 33, ix. 27, xii. 17, Heb. xi. 32**, 'to set out in detail', 're-late'; Cl., LXX, Pap.

17. For ἤρξαντο c. infin. *v.* i. 45. ὅριον, vii. 24, 31, x. 1*, Mt (6), Ac. xiii. 50**, always in plur. in NT, 'boundaries', i.e. 'territory', 'district' (cf. Lat. *fines*), <ὅρος, 'a boundary'; LXX, Pap. (*VGT*, 457). A change of attitude is suggested. While the people had been deeply impressed by the sight of the restored man, the tale of what had happened to the swine convinced them that Jesus was a public danger. Hence their desire for his departure. Cf. Swete, 99 ; Lagrange, 131 ; Bartlet, 178. Less probably Luke connects their petition with their fear, ὅτι φόβῳ μεγάλῳ συνείχοντο. Matthew severely compresses 15-17 into the statement, καὶ ἰδοὺ πᾶσα ἡ πόλις ἐξ-ῆλθεν εἰς ὑπάντησιν τῷ Ἰησοῦ, καὶ ἰδόν-τες αὐτὸν παρεκάλεσαν ὅπως μεταβῇ ἀπὸ τῶν ὁρίων αὐτῶν (viii. 34). With this unexplained request he ends the story.

18 f. The vocabulary and style are clearly Markan. For the use of the gen. abs. *v.* the note on v. 2. In contrast with 15, Mark here uses ὁ δαιμο-νισθείς to describe the man who had

been possessed of daemons (cf. 15, τὸν ἐσχηκότα τὸν λεγιῶνα). As in 10, ἵνα c. subj. is used after παρεκάλει to give the substance of the man's request. He desires to accompany Jesus and to be one of His disciples. Cf. the phrase ἵνα ὦσιν μετ᾽ αὐτοῦ in the story of the appointment of the Twelve (iii. 14). Jesus, however, refuses the man's request and bids him return home and relate what things the Lord has done for him and how He had mercy on him.

διάγγειλον, which is used of missionary activity in Lk. ix. 60, Ac. xxi. 26, Rom. ix. 17**, is attested here by D W P45 fam. 1 fam. 13 28 543 700. Since the man is bidden ' to be in fact a sort of missionary ' (Turner, 28) it is possible it should be read here. Cf. Couchoud, *JTS*, xxxv. 4. But the Caesarean evidence is divided. Θ joins with ℵ B C Δ 50 258 and 579 in reading ἀπάγγειλον (v. 14, vi. 30, xvi. [10, 13]*). It is hardly possible, therefore, to do more than place διάγγειλον in the margin.

With τοὺς σούς cf. τὸ σόν in Mt. xx. 14, and τὰ σά in Lk. vi. 30. In the papyri ὁ σός, 'thy household, agent, friend', is often found (*VGT*, 581). A circle wider than the man's family (εἰς τὸν οἶκόν σου) is indicated. So Lohmeyer, 98. ὅσα (iii. 8), 'how many things', is the direct object of πε-ποίηκεν, but must be taken adverbially (' how ') with ἠλέησεν. ἐλεέω, x. 47 f.*, 'to show mercy to', 'pity'; Cl., LXX, Pap. The change of tense from the perfect to the aorist is deliberate and shows that the distinction was preserved in the Koine. Cf. Moulton, i. 143. The man has received blessings which abide and a definite boon in his

πεποίηκεν καὶ ἠλέησέν σε. καὶ ἀπῆλθεν καὶ ἤρξατο κηρύσσειν 20
ἐν τῇ Δεκαπόλει ὅσα ἐποίησεν αὐτῷ ὁ Ἰησοῦς, καὶ πάντες
ἐθαύμαζον.

cure. As in i. 3, xi. 9, xii. 11, 29 f.,
36, xiii. 20, ὁ κύριος is used of God.
Cf. Lk. viii. 39, ὁ θεός. The command
to tell his story stands out in contrast
to the injunctions to silence in i. 25,
44, iii. 12, v. 43, vii. 36, etc., but is
credibly explained by the fact that the
district lay outside Galilee. Wrede's
suggestion, 140 f., that the publication
of the news throughout Decapolis
(v. 20) was contrary to the wish of
Jesus (cf. vii. 36), is not convincing.
Nor is there justification for the speculation that preaching is mentioned
merely to prepare the way for vii. 31.

Luke alters his source freely, but the
variations are merely verbal and
stylistic.

20. For ἤρξατο c. infin. v. i. 45. Δε-
κάπολις, vii. 31*, Mt. iv. 25**, Decapolis (here with the fem. art.). The
district was a loosely defined confedera-
tion of ten Greek cities all (except Scythopolis) east of the lake of Galilee.
Pliny, Hist. Nat. v. 18. 74, mentions

Damascus, Philadelphia, Raphana,
Scythopolis, Gadara, Hippos, Dios,
Pella, Gerasa, and Kathana; but the
lists as given by later writers differ. Cf.
G. A. Smith, 595-608; Dalman, SSW,
6; Swete, 100. Wrede's suggestion
of a contrast between Decapolis and
the household mentioned in 19 (v. the
note on this verse) is a possible interpretation, but it seems very doubtful
if it represents Mark's intention. The
reference to Jesus is a lifelike touch.
The man is commanded to tell what
God had done for him, but instead
he tells of the work of Jesus. Such a
distinction is very primitive and belongs to a time when the name ὁ κύριος
was not yet used of Jesus in the tradition Mark used. Cf. xi. 3. The effect
was general astonishment; all marvelled. θαυμάζω, vi. 6, xv. 5, 44*. Cf.
θαμβέομαι, i. 27, x. 24, 32**. Luke
(viii. 39) says that the man went away
preaching καθ᾽ ὅλην τὴν πόλιν and
makes no reference to the Decapolis.

Mk. v. 21-4, 35-43   34. THE RAISING OF   Cf. Mt. ix. 18 f., 23-6
                       THE DAUGHTER OF   Lk. viii. 40-2, 49-56
                       JAIRUS (v. 21-4)

The narrative is a Miracle-story (cf. Bultmann, 228-30). It is not,
however, a community-product, rounded by repetition, but a record based
on personal testimony. In this way only can we account for its distinctive
characteristics : the vivid portraiture of Jairus and his agonized cry for
aid, the incident of the woman on the way to his house, the sceptical attitude towards Jesus of the messengers, His refusal to be dissuaded, the
picture of the mourners, the saying ' The child is not dead, but sleepeth ',
the mockery thereby provoked, the command in Aramaic addressed to the
girl, the compassionate regard for her welfare shown by Jesus. We have
only to compare Mark's account with those of Mt and Lk to be impressed
with its greater originality.

What really happened is a much more difficult question to answer.
The later versions leave it in no doubt that the girl was dead. In Mt she
is dead when Jairus comes to Jesus (ix. 18); Luke explains that the
mourners knew she was dead (viii. 53), and he says expressly that ' her
spirit returned and she rose up immediately ' (viii. 55). In Mk the position is ambiguous. The messengers report that she is dead, the family

wail and lament her death, and the chosen witnesses ' were lost in utter amazement ' (Moffatt). This representation probably justifies us in inferring that Mark himself saw in the incident a case of resurrection from the dead. On the other hand, there are features in the narrative which are capable of another interpretation. First, Jesus ignores the tidings of death and bids Jairus fear nothing but only believe (36). This might mean that He intended to restore the dead girl to life, but it is also possible that He disbelieved the message and went to awake her from a trance-like sleep. Secondly, the saying, ' The child is not dead but is sleeping ', is ambiguous and, together with the command ' Damsel, arise ', does not require the hypothesis of resurrection, although it is not inconsistent with it. In these circumstances I do not think that a modern reader need feel disquieted if he finds himself inclined now to this opinion and now to that. Nor does an attitude of reserve towards the so-called ' nature-miracles ' settle the question, since in the present case a human personality hovering on the threshhold of death is in question. It is even possible that Jesus went to challenge death when, in fact, the child was not dead. The deciding factor, if one can be found, is the uncertain character of all the evidence, including the obscure narrative of the young man at Nain (Lk. vii. 11-17) and the didactic story of Lazarus (Jn. xi. 1-46). It is hard to resist the conclusion that the evidence that the historical Jesus raised the dead is far from being decisive.

21 Καὶ διαπεράσαντος τοῦ Ἰησοῦ εἰς τὸ πέραν πάλιν συνήχθη
22 ὄχλος πολὺς ἐπ᾽ αὐτόν, καὶ ἦν παρὰ τὴν θάλασσαν. Καὶ ᵀ ἔρχε-

22 [ἰδού]

21. Jesus now crosses to the west shore and a great multitude again assembles to meet Him. Whether the incident of Jairus's daughter takes place on the day of landing is not said ; it is represented as the next event of importance. No place name is mentioned. Most commentators think of the neighbourhood of Capernaum, but Schmidt, 146, suggests that the house of Jairus might just as easily have been at Bethsaida on the northeast shore. In this opinion, however, he is influenced by the doubtful view that εἰς τὸ πέραν (v. iv. 35) necessarily points to the east side. διαπεράω, vi. 53*, Mt. ix. 1, xiv. 34, Lk. xvi. 26, Ac. xxi. 2**, ' to go over ', ' cross '; Cl., LXX, Pap. For the gen. abs. see the note on v. 2.

In the phrases which follow there is considerable variation in the MS. tradition. The WH text reads καὶ διαπεράσαντος τοῦ Ἰησοῦ ἐν τῷ πλοίῳ πάλιν εἰς τὸ πέραν συνήχθη ὄχλος πολὺς

ἐπ᾽ αὐτόν. The reference to the boat, ἐν τῷ πλοίῳ, is placed before τοῦ Ἰησοῦ by W and is omitted by D Θ P⁴⁵ fam. 1 28 565 700 it syˢ arm. P⁴⁵ also omits εἰς τὸ πέραν, and πάλιν immediately precedes συνήχθη in ℵ* D 565 700 it syᵖᵉ. Probably ἐν τῷ πλοίῳ is an early scribal insertion. Lagrange, 138, reads πάλιν before συνήχθη (v. supra), and there is much to be said for this view. Couchoud, JTS, xxxv. 4 f., would go farther and omit also εἰς τὸ πέραν with P⁴⁵. This suggestion does not seem to be necessary and on the whole it seems best to read καὶ διαπεράσαντος τοῦ Ἰησοῦ εἰς τὸ πέραν πάλιν συνήχθη ὄ. π. The point is that after the crossing to the other side a great crowd once more assembles. The contrast with the attitude of the Gerasenes is very marked. Cf. Swete, 101 : ' it (the crowd) swarmed down upon Him'. ἐπί is used in a pregnant sense. πρός (D Θ fam. 13 28 543 565 579 700) is clearly secondary.

ται εἰς τῶν ἀρχισυναγώγων, [ὀνόματι Ἰάειρος], καὶ ἰδὼν αὐτὸν
πίπτει πρὸς τοὺς πόδας αὐτοῦ καὶ ⸢παρεκάλει⸣ αὐτὸν πολλὰ λέγων   23

23 παρακαλεῖ

In Mt the scenic details disappear, since the narrative follows the sayings on Patches and Wineskins, with no further introduction than ταῦτα αὐτοῦ λαλοῦντος αὐτοῖς (ix. 18). Luke generalizes Mark's statement by saying that, when Jesus returned, the multitude welcomed Him, for all were waiting for Him (viii. 40).

22. Mark now describes the coming of the suppliant. καὶ ἰδού is read by A C N W et al. P⁴⁵ minusc. omn. (exc. 892) c f syʰˡ geoⁱ ᵉᵗ ᴮ arm, and ἰδού is found also in Mt. ix. 18 and Lk viii. 41. The reading may be original, but it is difficult to decide whether it is implied in Mk by Mt and Lk, or whether it is a case of assimilation. Couchoud, JTS, xxxv. 5, accepts it, but against the strong support for the omission by ℵ B D L Δ Θ 892 it (exc. c f) vg sys pe sa bo geoᴬ aeth Aug, it is impossible to do more than place it in the margin in brackets.

The use of εἷς = τις may be a Semitism (cf. Blass, 144; Intr. 60) but the well established usage of the LXX (VGT, 187) shows that this view is not necessary unless it is otherwise supported in a given case. ἀρχισυνάγωγος, v. 35 f., 38*, Lk. viii. 49, xiii. 14, Ac. xiii. 15, xviii. 8, 17**, 'a leader of the synagogue', not necessarily the supervisor of the worship, but a prominent member. Cf. VGT, 82; Ramsay, The Church in the Rom. Emp. 68; Deissmann, 440.

Is the name 'Jairus' original in Mk? Cadbury, HTR, xvi (1923), 89 n., suggests that it may have crept in from Lk; cf. Bultmann, 230. Schmidt, 147, is inclined to think that it was an addition in the tradition but

that it lay before Mark in his source. Rawlinson, 66 f., suggests that its absence in Western MSS. may be accidental. The facts are as follows. ὀνόματι Ἰάειρος is wanting in D a e ff i rⁱ and in Mt. The only other person mentioned by Mark outside the Passion Narrative, apart from the disciples, is Bartimaeus (x. 46), and the name Jairus is not mentioned in 35 f., 38, 40. Moreover, the use of ὀνόματι is Lukan rather than Markan; elsewhere Mark uses ὄνομα c. dat. (iii. 16 f., v. 9). The absence of the name from Mt may be significant, and, on the whole, I am inclined to think that ὀνόματι Ἰάειρος is an early scribal addition or at least that it should be placed in brackets. Whether it was suggested by Lk. viii. 41 is uncertain, since here the phrase is ἀνὴρ ᾧ ὄνομα Ἰάειρος.[1]

Ἰάειρος = יָאִיר, 'he enlightens' (LXX Ἰαείρ, Numb. xxxii. 41, Judg. x. 3 f.). Some scholars (e.g. Cheyne, EB, col. 2316) derive the name from יָעִיר, 'he awakes', and explain it as symbolic. The appropriateness of the symbolism, however, is not obvious; it is the daughter who is awakened and not by Jairus. Cf. Klostermann, 58; Rawlinson, 67; Easton, 126; Plummer, 147; J. S. Clemens, DCG, i. 845. The portraiture is lifelike. In the greatness of his distress he casts aside his dignity and falls at the feet of Jesus; cf. προσπίπτω in iii. 11, v. 33, vii. 25, and προσκυνέω, v. 6, xv. 19.

The Matthaean parallel is very brief, ἰδοὺ ἄρχων [εἷς] προσελθὼν προσεκύνει αὐτῷ (ix. 18). Luke (viii. 41) describes Jairus as ἄρχων τῆς συναγωγῆς and omits καὶ ἰδών. Both have the aor. instead of the historic present ἔρχεται.

---

[1] In a letter which I am permitted to quote, Dr. T. W. Manson has reminded me of Cadbury's article mentioned above, and observes that the variant ᾧ ὄνομα Ἰάειρος in W Θ 565 700 suggests that the name was wanting (cf. Lk. viii. 41). P⁴⁵ has the name but we cannot tell if ὀνόματι or ᾧ ὄνομα preceded. With reference to Mark's method of introducing names (v. 9, xiv. 32, xv. 7, 21) Dr. Manson says, 'In general it may be said that Mk's practice is to introduce his proper names without any formula. It is, as it were, taken for granted that the persons and places are as familiar to the reader (originally hearer) as they are to the writer (speaker). This points to a primitive stage in the tradition.' For P⁴⁵ v. Burkitt, JTS, xxxiv. 366; Couchoud, JTS, xxxv. 5.

ὅτι Τὸ θυγάτριόν μου ἐσχάτως ἔχει, ἵνα ἐλθὼν ἐπιθῇς τὰς
24 χεῖρας αὐτῇ ἵνα σωθῇ καὶ ζήσῃ. καὶ ἀπῆλθεν μετ᾽ αὐτοῦ. Καὶ
ἠκολούθει αὐτῷ ὄχλος πολύς, καὶ συνέθλιβον αὐτόν.

23. The pres. παρακαλεῖ, read by the WH text with ℵ A C L 28 33 565 892 1071 et al., is probably a conformation to the tenses in 22, and the imperf. (WHmg) should be read with B W Δ Θ et al. fam. 1 fam. 13 543 579 700 al. pler. c f vg sys pe hl bo geo¹ et B. Jairus began to beseech, or kept on beseeching, Jesus on behalf of his daughter. For πολλά used adverbially v. i. 45. θυγάτριον, vii. 25**. Here the diminutive appears to be used as a term of affection, 'my little daughter', as in later Greek (Plutarch, Ant. 33), and as distinct from θυγάτηρ in 34 f. (cf. also vi. 22, vii. 26, 29*). ἐσχάτως** ἔχει, ' is at the point of death ' (Moffatt and Torrey, ' is dying '). Cf. τοὺς κακῶς ἔχοντας in i. 32. The phrase is condemned by Atticists; cf. VGT, 256; Swete, 101. Lagrange, 139, cites ἐσχάτως διακεῖσθαι in Polyb. i. 24. 2. The changes in the later Gospels are noteworthy: Luke, who gives the passage in narrative form, says, καὶ αὐτὴ ἀπέθνησκεν (viii. 42), while Matthew says outright, ἄρτι ἐτελεύ-τησεν, ' has just now died ' (ix. 18).

ἵνα ἐλθὼν ἐπιθῇς may be explained by understanding an ellipsis of παρα-καλῶ or θέλω (WM, 396; Swete, 101 f.) but is more probably an example of the imperatival use of ἵνα c. subj. Cf. Moulton, i. 177-9, and v. the notes on v. 12 and x. 51. The meaning is: ' Please come and lay thy hands on her '. Cf. Moffatt, ' Do come and lay your hands on her '; Torrey, ' I beg you to come and lay your hands on

her '; cf. RSV. For ἐπιτίθημι τ. χεῖρας v. vi. 5, vii. 32 (sing.), viii. 23, 25, xvi. [18]*. From the references to the action of Jesus in laying His hands on the sick (common in ancient stories of healing; cf. Bultmann, 237 f.) the later ecclesiastical rite took its rise. For σώζω used of healing v. the note on iii. 4. ζάω, xii. 27, xvi. [11]*. The use of the two verbs in ἵνα σωθῇ καὶ ζήσῃ is not quite a redun-dancy, since the ideas are distinct. Jairus wants his daughter to be saved and live. It is possible, of course, that the two verbs say the same thing, and Matthew has taken them in this way when he writes ζήσεται only, unless the desire for abbreviation is a sufficient explanation. Black, 53 n., is inclined to think that Mark may have found two renderings of the Aramaic in exist-ence since both σωθῇ and ζήσῃ go back to the Aramaic ḥaya. If, however, the verbs express slightly different ideas, the difference can have been expressed in Aramaic as well as in Gk.¹

24. The verse, with its reference to thronging multitudes, prepares the way for the story of the Woman with the Issue of Blood. No reply to the en-treaty is mentioned. The response of Jesus is action; He went with Jairus. Matthew does not mention the crowd, but says that Jesus arose and His disciples followed Him (ix. 19). συν-θλίβω, v. 31**, ' to press together ', ' hustle ' (Souter); Cl., LXX, cf. θλίβω in iii. 9. Luke has συνέπνιγον (viii. 42), and replaces καὶ ἀπῆλθεν μετ᾽ αὐτοῦ by ἐν δὲ τῷ ὑπάγειν αὐτόν.

¹ I am glad to have Dr. Black's confirmation of this suggestion : ' At Mk. v. 23 there are quite clearly two distinct ideas, which could be expressed in Aramaic, detithasai weteḥe, " that she be healed and live " ('asi, " to heal "). In Gk this would be literally ἵνα ἰαθῇ καὶ ζήσῃ, though it might be rendered ἵνα σωθῇ καὶ ζήσῃ. What makes me suspicious, however, of the combination is that σώζειν and ζῆν give two regular meanings of ḥⁿya. Cf. Adalbert Merx, Die vier kanon. Evangelien, Marcus, p. 48. The two Gk words look like two " translation-variants " embedded in the text. It may also be, however, that the translator, anxious that no possible meaning of the original should escape him, gave a paraphrase of the original ḥⁿya.'

Mk. v. 25-34   35. THE WOMAN WITH THE   Cf. Mt. ix. 20-2
ISSUE OF BLOOD   Lk. viii. 43-8

This narrative is unique in that it is interwoven into that of the Daughter of Jairus. The closing words of the first part of the story (v. 24), prepare the way for the account of the cure, and the thread is resumed in the second part in the words, ' While he yet spoke ' (v. 35). In view of the comparative absence of connecting-links of this kind in Mk, it is reasonable to infer that the connexion is historical, and not merely literary. Cf. Schmidt, 148 ; Dibelius, 219. Bultmann, 228 f., conjectures that originally the two stories may have existed separately, but Schmidt holds that the interweaving is due to historical recollection.[1] The case is somewhat different from iii. 22-6 and xiv. 3-9, which separate different sections or stories, and is hardly, therefore, an example of ' Mk's fondness for dove-tailing one story into another ' (Rawlinson, 42 f., 67). A story may be told to fill an interval (e.g. vi. 14-29), but the intercalation of narratives is not a feature of Mark's method.

That the story of the woman rests on excellent tradition is confirmed by the narrative itself. It is a Miracle-story, and has the characteristic features of such stories : the description of the sufferer, the failure of many physicians, the cure, and its public confirmation ; but it is far indeed from being an ideal scene composed on a traditional plan by the use of common *motifs*. On the contrary, the psychological realism of the account of the woman's fears and her courageous action, the rough question of the disciples, and the portrayal of Jesus, leave upon the mind a strong impression of verisimilitude.

Nevertheless, the story has been the object of reflection. Inferences are combined with the narration of the event, as, for example, in the suggestion that Jesus perceived that His healing virtue had been appropriated (v. 30), and the explanation Mark gives of the woman's thoughts (v. 28). The inferences, however, are primitive and might have been drawn at the time of the incident. No really adequate explanation can be given of the question, ' Who touched my garments ? ' (v. 30), but the somewhat querulous protest of the disciples makes the suggestion of invention unconvincing. Modern parallels from psychotherapy are given by E. R. Micklem, 122 f. Auto-suggestion is a facile description of the cure. The suggestion of the narrative, that the cure was due to faith energized by the personality of Jesus, is the best explanation of a story which cannot be completely rationalized.

Καὶ γυνὴ οὖσα ἐν ῥύσει αἵματος δώδεκα ἔτη καὶ πολλὰ πα-   25
θοῦσα ὑπὸ πολλῶν ἰατρῶν καὶ δαπανήσασα τὰ παρ' ⌜αὐτῆς⌝   26

26 ἑαυτῆς

25-7. This passage is remarkable as being one of the very few examples in Mk of a longer Gk period with subordinating participles, in contrast with the repeatedly used paratactic

construction : . . . παθοῦσα . . . δαπανή-σασα . . . ὠφεληθεῖσα . . . ἐλθοῦσα . . . ἀκούσασα . . . ἐλθοῦσα . . . ἥψατο. Cf. Wellhausen, *Einl.*[2] 13. See xiv. 67, xv. 43. The woman is described as

---

[1] *Hier hat die wirkliche Erinnerung einen geschichtlichen Tatbestand festgehalten: die Heilung der Frau hat sich auf dem Wege zum Hause des Jairus ereignet*, Schmidt, 148. So also J. Weiss, 195.

πάντα καὶ μηδὲν ὠφεληθεῖσα ἀλλὰ μᾶλλον εἰς τὸ χεῖρον ἐλθοῦσα,
27 ἀκούσασα τὰ περὶ τοῦ Ἰησοῦ, ἐλθοῦσα ἐν τῷ ὄχλῳ ὄπισθεν
28 ἥψατο τοῦ ἱματίου αὐτοῦ· ἔλεγεν γὰρ ὅτι Ἐὰν ἅψωμαι κἂν
29 τῶν ἱματίων αὐτοῦ σωθήσομαι. καὶ εὐθὺς ἐξηράνθη ἡ πηγὴ

οὖσα ἐν ῥύσει αἵματος, a description which has a Semitic ring; cf. ἐν πνεύματι ἀκαθάρτῳ (i. 23). Matthew neatly summarizes the expression in γυνὴ αἱμορροοῦσα (ix. 20). ῥύσις*, Lk. viii. 43 f.**; αἷμα, v. 29, xiv. 24*. The acc. of duration of time δώδεκα ἔτη, which corresponds with the age of the daughter of Jairus, may be a coincidence (Lagrange, 140), but is probably a round number to describe an affliction of long standing. ἔτος, x. 42*.

Not only had the woman long been ill, but she had suffered greatly at the hands of many physicians, and had spent her all without receiving any benefit, but rather the contrary. πάσχω, viii. 31, ix. 12*, is here used with ὑπό in the sense of ' at the hands of '; cf. ἀπό in Mt. xvi. 21. δαπανάω*, Lk. xv. 14, Ac. xxi. 24, 2 Cor. xii. 15, Jas. iv. 3**. With τὰ παρ' αὐτῆς πάντα cf. Lk. x. 7 and Phil. iv. 18; Field, 27. ἑαυτῆς, ℵ C Δ 1071 al. It is perhaps a refinement, with Swete, 103, to interpret μηδὲν ὠφεληθεῖσα ' as her experience told her '. ὠφελέω, vii. 11, viii. 36*. With εἰς τὸ χεῖρον cf. 2 Tim. iii. 13.

Lagrange, 140, points out that to this day it is a vexatious eastern custom to call in as many physicians as possible, with the result that their prescriptions cause suffering, cost much money, and make the malady worse. Matthew has no parallel to 26 in his brief reproduction of the story. Luke severely abbreviates the passage, for in viii. 43 ἰατροῖς προσαναλώσασα ὅλον τὸν βίον should probably be omitted with B D sys arm (so WH text; Creed, 123; Easton, 129). Instead of Mark's disparaging allusion to the physicians, he merely says that the woman ' could not be healed of any '.

With τὰ περὶ τοῦ Ἰησοῦ, ' the things

concerning Jesus ', cf. Lk. xxii. 37, xxiv. 19, 27, Ac. i. 3, xviii. 25. The reference is to the reports of His healing ministry. The woman comes in the crowd behind (ὄπισθεν*) and touches the garments of Jesus. Matthew says ' the tassel (τοῦ κρασπέδου) of his garment ' (cf. Numb. xv. 38 f., Deut. xxii. 12), referring to one of the four fringes or tassels which the Law required every Jew to attach to the corners of his outer coat. The action implies a belief in the healing virtues of contact, but the significant fact is the woman's faith. Cf. iii. 10, vi. 56. She comes secretly (ἐν τῷ ὄχλῳ ὄπισθεν) because the malady rendered her ceremonially unclean and would convey uncleanness to all who came in contact with her (cf. Lev. xv. 25).

28. For ἔλεγεν γάρ v. v. 8, and for ἐάν c. subj. i. 40. The explanation is added by Mark or in the tradition he followed. It indicates the woman's thoughts and is made more explicit in Matthew's addition ἐν ἑαυτῇ (ix. 21). Luke omits the verse. κἄν, vi. 56, xvi. [18]*, Mt. xxi. 21, xxvi. 35, Lk. xii. 38, etc., ' even ', ' at least ', ' even if '; by crasis for καὶ ἄν (ἐάν); Cl., Pap. Cf. Moulton, i. 167, 169; Robertson, 984, 1025. In ancient belief even handkerchiefs and aprons carried from the healer's person possessed healing virtue (cf. Ac. xix. 12), and also his shadow (Ac. v. 15). The person of the healer himself was regarded as potent, and his garments or shadow, as the case might be, were looked upon as extensions of his personality. In the story the woman wants to touch Jesus, and the expression ' at least his garments ' marks the intensity of her desire. Mt. ix. 21, ἐὰν μόνον ἅψωμαι.

29. The cure is immediate (εὐθύς); the hemorrhage ceased. Luke has ἔστη ἡ ῥύσις (viii. 44). For the phrase

τοῦ αἵματος αὐτῆς, καὶ ἔγνω τῷ σώματι ὅτι ἴαται ἀπὸ τῆς
μάστιγος. καὶ εὐθὺς ὁ Ἰησοῦς ἐπιγνοὺς ἐν ἑαυτῷ τὴν ἐξ αὐτοῦ 30
δύναμιν ἐξελθοῦσαν ἐπιστραφεὶς ἐν τῷ ὄχλῳ ἔλεγεν Τίς μου

ἡ πηγὴ τοῦ αἵματος v. Lev. xii. 7. τῷ σώματι is dat. of sphere. The correct use of tenses is notable, the aorists ἐξηράνθη and ἔγνω being used of definite past actions and the perfect ἴαται of abiding consequences. ἰάομαι*, ' to cure ', Cl., LXX, Pap. Elsewhere Mark uses θεραπεύω (5 times; v. i. 34). The statement regarding the woman's knowledge is peculiar to his account. Matthew omits the entire verse. γινώσκω ὅτι, xii. 12, xiii. 28 f., xv. 10*.

30. Again Mark stresses the immediacy of the action (εὐθύς). Jesus is conscious that power has gone from Him. With ἐπιγνοὺς ἐν ἑαυτῷ cf. ii. 8, ἐπιγνούς . . . τῷ πνεύματι αὐτοῦ. Cf. Jn. vi. 61, xi. 38. As following upon ἔγνω in 29, ἐπιγνούς appears to indicate a *perception* immediately gained from attention (ἐπί) to a fact. See the note on ii. 8. After the verb of perceiving the acc. with the participle is used (with ἐπιγινώσκω here only in the NT) in the sense of the acc. and infin. construction, ' perceiving that the power from him had gone forth ', or even ' has gone forth '; not ' the power . . . which had gone forth '. The usage is allied to that of εἶδον ὅτι (v. ii. 16), used of seeing external facts, with the difference that here an inward condition is perceived. It is closely parallel to ἐγὼ γὰρ ἔγνων δύναμιν ἐξεληλυθυῖαν ἀπ' ἐμοῦ, which Luke has later in the story (viii. 46). See also Ac. xxiv. 10 and Heb. xiii. 23.

δύναμις, vi. 2, 5, 14, ix. 1, 39, xii. 24, xiii. 25 f., xiv. 62*, ' power ', or concretely ' a power ', ' a mighty work '; Cl., LXX, Pap. In the latter sense it is used in vi. 2, 5, 14, ix. 39. In ix. 1 it is used of the power with which the Kingdom of God comes, in xiii. 25 of the heavenly bodies or the spirits which reside in them, in xiii. 26 of the Parousia of the Son of Man, and in xii. 24 and xiv. 62 as a periphrasis for God.

Cf. VGT, 171 f.; KThW (W. Grundmann), ii. 300-18; Ramsay, Recent Discovery, 118; Selwyn, St. Pet. 207 f. The word was ' one of the most common and characteristic terms in the language of pagan devotion. " Power " was what the devotees respected and worshipped; any exhibition of " power " must have its cause in something that was divine ' (Ramsay). In the New Testament, however, the meaning of δύναμις is determined by Biblical usage. Fundamentally *dynamis* is the power of the living personal God (cf. Grundmann, op. cit. ii. 292) or a ' mighty work ' which manifests His power. In the present passage τὴν ἐξ αὐτοῦ δύναμιν is the divine healing power which dwells in Jesus (cf. Lk. v. 17, καὶ δύναμις Κυρίου ἦν εἰς τὸ ἰᾶσθαι αὐτόν) and proceeds from Him (cf. Lk. vi. 19, ὅτι δύναμις παρ' αὐτοῦ ἐξήρχετο καὶ ἰᾶτο πάντας). In the Markan phrase ἐξ αὐτοῦ is adjectival, ' the power from Him ', and by this is meant the outgoing of a personal power which resides in Him and is available for healing. Cf. Swete, 104. The RV rendering, ' that the power proceeding from him had gone forth ', which Turner, 29, describes as ' pedantic ', exactly expresses this meaning. Doubtless the Markan phrase is awkward, but this appears to be what Mark intends to say, and the meaning is lost in smoother English translation (e.g. Moffatt, ' that some healing virtue had passed from him '; Torrey, ' that healing power had gone out from him '). If Mark had meant this it would have been easy to place ἐξ αὐτοῦ elsewhere, as in D it vg, τὴν δύναμιν (τὴν) ἐξελθοῦσαν ἀπ' αὐτοῦ, a reading which is plainly secondary. How Jesus was conscious of the appropriation of His power we do not know; it is part of the secret of His spiritual sensitiveness.

31 ἥψατο τῶν ἱματίων; καὶ ἔλεγον αὐτῷ οἱ μαθηταὶ αὐτοῦ Βλέ-
32 πεις τὸν ὄχλον συνθλίβοντά σε, καὶ λέγεις Τίς μου ἥψατο; καὶ
33 περιεβλέπετο ἰδεῖν τὴν τοῦτο ποιήσασαν. ἡ δὲ γυνὴ φοβηθεῖσα
   καὶ τρέμουσα, εἰδυῖα ὃ γέγονεν αὐτῇ, ἦλθεν καὶ προσέπεσεν
34 αὐτῷ καὶ εἶπεν αὐτῷ πᾶσαν τὴν ἀλήθειαν. ὁ δὲ εἶπεν αὐτῇ
   Θυγάτηρ, ἡ πίστις σου σέσωκέν σε· ὕπαγε εἰς εἰρήνην, καὶ ἴσθι

The question, 'Who touched my garments?', betrays, not supernatural knowledge, but rather the reverse, since an answer is *sought*. The fact that suppliants were wont to touch Him (iii. 10, vi. 56) may have suggested to Him the significance of the touch, especially if it coincided with the consciousness expressed by ἐπιγνοὺς ἐν ἑαυτῷ τὴν ἐξ αὐτοῦ δύναμιν ἐξελθοῦσαν, but such inferences are very speculative. It is possible indeed that Mark is giving expression to primitive Christian beliefs. It is pertinent, however, to add that the roughness of the disciples' comment in 31 renders it improbable that the question is an invention.

31 f. The somewhat curt remonstrance of the disciples (Lk, ὁ Πέτρος) is omitted by Matthew and softened by Luke in the form, 'Ἐπιστάτα, οἱ ὄχλοι συνέχουσίν σε καὶ ἀποθλίβουσιν (viii. 45). The difference illustrates the primitive character of the Markan account. Cf. Lagrange, 141, *La réflexion des disciples n'est pas très respectueuse pour Jésus; elle part d'un gros bon sens qui ne pénètre pas l'intention du Maître.* For Mark's reference to the looking around of Jesus *v.* the note on iii. 5. The imperfect indicates a long and penetrating look. Cf. Lohmeyer, 103. The feminine adjectival participle is written from the Evangelist's standpoint, and does not necessarily imply supernatural knowledge on the part of Jesus. Cf. Klostermann, 60. There is no need, with Bruce, 375, to conjecture that 'a woman's touch' was recognized. ἰδεῖν is infin. of purpose.

33. τρέμω*. Cf. the use of τρόμος καὶ ἔκστασις in xvi. 8, ἐν φόβῳ καὶ ἐν

τρόμῳ πολλῷ (1 Cor. ii. 3), μετὰ φόβου καὶ τρόμου (2 Cor. vii. 15, Eph. vi. 5, Phil. ii. 12). The woman is seized with a sense of fear and begins to tremble as she thinks of what has happened to her (εἰδυῖα ὃ γέγονεν αὐτῇ). Luke traces her subsequent action to her consciousness that she had been found out (ἰδοῦσα δὲ ἡ γυνὴ ὅτι οὐκ ἔλαθεν, viii. 47), but this motive is not suggested by Mark. Mark rather ascribes her action to the cure itself, and perhaps also, since he mentions the searching glance of Jesus, to her perception that He desires her to make herself known. Other suggested motives, e.g. the fact that she had rendered Jesus ceremonially unclean, or disquietude because she had acted secretly (διὸ πεποίηκεν λάθρα, D Θ 28 50 124 348 565 700 1071 a ff i r¹ geo arm), are more speculative. Whatever the reason, her action in coming and falling down before Him bespeaks courage and a sense of gratitude. Mark does not stress the publicity of her action, as Luke does (ἐνώπιον παντὸς τοῦ λαοῦ), but affirms that she told Him everything. The expression πᾶσαν τὴν ἀλήθειαν is classical; cf. Plato, *Apol.* 17 B; and 'Johannine' (Jn. xvi. 13). Luke particularizes the phrase by saying that she declared why she had touched Jesus and how she was healed immediately (viii. 47). W 1 fam. 13 (exc. 124) 28 543 sa geo² read πᾶσαν τὴν αἰτίαν αὐτῆς (om. 1 28), c has *quid factum est*, q *quod factum est*, and e *quod est facti*. It is more than likely that this is the original Markan reading, especially as Lk. viii. 47 has αἰτίαν in the clause δι' ἣν αἰτίαν ἥψατο αὐτοῦ.

34. θυγάτηρ, v. 35, vi. 22, vii. 26, 29*.

ὑγιὴς ἀπὸ τῆς μάστιγός σου.

is here used instead of the vocative, as in the parallel passage Lk. viii. 48. Cf. Jn. xii. 15. For πίστις v. ii. 5 and for σώζω iii. 4. Jesus attributes the woman's cure to her faith, as He does also in the case of Bartimaeus (x. 52). This explanation cannot be watered down to the hypothesis of auto-suggestion, since the consistent NT view of faith is that it derives its content and virtue from the object in which it rests. Faith in God (cf. xi. 22), for example, is not a purely subjective experience, but a spiritual experience which begins in a venture of spirit and is constituted and made effective by God Himself. There is an echo of this idea in the present story, all the more striking because it is artless, in the fact that

Jesus is conscious that His spiritual resources have been drawn upon by the woman's faith. The expression ὕπαγε εἰς εἰρήνην* corresponds to the Hebrew לְכִי לְשָׁלוֹם (1 Sam. i. 17, etc.) and is most naturally to be traced to the influence of the LXX; cf. Lk. vii. 50, viii. 48, Ac. xvi. 36, Jas. ii. 16**. The phrase is a formula of farewell, but like all such phrases is capable of bearing the meaning which the speaker puts into it. Cf. Lagrange, 142. There is no need to regard ἴσθι ὑγιής as an Aramaism; cf. Prov. iii. 5 (LXX) and for the papyri VGT, 184. See Moulton, i. 174, 226. ὑγιής*, Mt (2), Jn (6), Ac (1), Tit (1)**. A permanent cure is promised. Matthew adds ἀπὸ τῆς ὥρας ἐκείνης.

Mk. v. 35-43   34 (ctd.). THE RAISING OF   Cf. Mt. ix. 23-6
                     THE DAUGHTER OF JAIRUS   Lk. viii. 49-56
                              (v. 35-43)

For the first part of the story see the Introduction to v. 21-4. Lohmeyer, 104, distinguishes four stages in the narrative; By the lakeside (21-4); On the road (35-7); In the court of the house (38-40); In the maiden's chamber (41-3). Cf. the arrangement of the story of the Gerasene Demoniac (v. 1-20). Lohmeyer also points out the difference of language and style between 21-4, 35-43 and 25-34. Here are no Hellenisms, no indirect speech, no periods, hardly a participle, but paratactic constructions, Semitisms (22, 42), and an Aramaic phrase (41).

Ἔτι αὐτοῦ λαλοῦντος ἔρχονται ἀπὸ τοῦ ἀρχισυναγώγου λέ- 35
γοντες ὅτι Ἡ θυγάτηρ σου ἀπέθανεν· τί ἔτι σκύλλεις τὸν διδά-

35. While Jesus is still speaking to the woman, the message of death comes. As in i. 32 (ἔφερον), ii. 3, etc., ἔρχονται is the impersonal plur., ' people came '. Cf. Swete, 106. Luke has ἔρχεταί τις. The phrase ἀπὸ τοῦ ἀρχισυναγώγου is used loosely for ἀπὸ τῆς οἰκίας τ. ἀ. The change to θυγάτηρ (θυγάτριον, 23) may be influenced by 34, but is more probably explained by the fact that in 23 the father himself is speaking. Apparently, ἀπέθανεν is used as an aoristic perfect (cf. ἐξέστη,

iii. 21), with the meaning ' is dead ' rather than ' died '. Luke substitutes τέθνηκεν (viii. 49). σκύλλω*, Mt. ix. 36, Lk. vii. 6, viii. 49**, originally ' to flay ', is used in later Gk with the meaning ' to harass ', ' annoy ', ' trouble '; VGT, 580. For other verbs with a softened meaning in Hellenistic Gk cf. ἐμβριμάομαι (i. 43), φιμόω (i. 25), χορτάζω (vi. 42). The rough question implies the absence of an expectation that Jesus would raise the dead. For διδάσκαλος =

36 σκαλον; ὁ δὲ Ἰησοῦς παρακούσας τὸν λόγον λαλούμενον λέγει
37 τῷ ἀρχισυναγώγῳ Μὴ φοβοῦ, μόνον πίστευε. καὶ οὐκ ἀφῆκεν
   οὐδένα μετ' αὐτοῦ συνακολουθῆσαι εἰ μὴ τὸν Πέτρον καὶ Ἰάκωβον
38 καὶ Ἰωάνην τὸν ἀδελφὸν Ἰακώβου. καὶ ἔρχονται εἰς τὸν οἶκον
   τοῦ ἀρχισυναγώγου, καὶ θεωρεῖ θόρυβον καὶ κλαίοντας καὶ

'Rabbi' v. iv. 38. In this verse Luke follows Mk closely, but Matthew says nothing of the message and of the conversation which follows.

36. Did Jesus overhear the message or did He ignore it? This is the issue raised by παρακούσας* (Mt. xviii. 17 (bis)**). In Cl. Gk the verb is used of hearing accidentally or heedlessly; it can therefore mean 'to overhear' or 'to refuse to hear'. The latter is the meaning in all the seven examples in the LXX, in Mt. xviii. 17 ('And if he refuses to hear them'), and in the papyri (VGT, 486). So many commentators (Swete, 106 f.; Plummer, 151; Bartlet, 183; McNeile, 125; cf. RV, RSV, Moffatt), but many others prefer 'overhearing' (Klostermann, 61; Lagrange, 143; Rawlinson, 70; Turner, 29; Gould, 100; cf. RVmg, RSVmg) mainly because Jesus acts on what He hears. Cf. Turner, 'Our Lord did "heed the word spoken" and answered it'. Equally well, however, can it be argued that Jesus addressed Jairus just because He ignored the message: 'not heeding' may mean that He declined to take it at its face value. It seems better to adopt the RV rendering, and all the more because if we translate παρακούσας by 'overhearing', we must still infer that Jesus was not deterred by the message. It does not seem necessary, however, to accept the suggestion of Field, 28, 'pretending not to hear'. Μὴ φοβοῦ, as distinct from μή c. aor. subj., implies that the father is already afraid. Cf. Moulton, i. 124 f. Accordingly, Jesus bids him keep on believing. The suggestion that μὴ φοβοῦ belongs to the style of the epiphany (Lohmeyer, 105) is pointless in this context. μόνον, vi. 8*. Luke loses the freshness of Mk

by replacing πίστευε by the aor., and παρακούσας by ἀκούσας (read in Mk by very many MSS., but not by א* B L W Δ 892 e). Luke adds καὶ σωθήσεται (viii. 50). For πιστεύω v. i. 15.

37. In Mk Jesus allows only Peter, James, and John to accompany Him (συνακολουθέω, xiv. 51*, Lk. xxiii. 49**), but in Lk the crowd is presumably not dismissed until the house is reached, when only the three disciples are allowed to enter. This variation arises from compression, and it is for this reason that at this point Luke mentions, less naturally, the father and mother of the child. Mark, who mentions them later, gives the more original account. The three disciples are present also at the Transfiguration (ix. 2), in Gethsemane (xiv. 33), and, along with Andrew, on the Mount of Olives (xiii. 3). Mark always has the order, Peter, James, and John (so Lk. vi. 14), but in Lk. viii. 51, ix. 28, Ac. i. 13, Luke mentions John second in view of his importance in the early Church. The three form an inner ring in the apostolic band; it is doubtful, however, if the single article in Mk (Swete, 107) is intended to represent them as such (cf. ix. 2, xiv. 33). For the phrase τὸν ἀδελφὸν Ἰακώβου v. i. 19, and for the double negative, οὐκ . . . οὐδένα, v. i. 44. Matthew has no parallel to 35-7.

38. Once more the historic presents are notable. Mt and Lk have ἐλθών. The picture of Jesus beholding (θεωρεῖ) the stricken house is peculiar to Mark's account and recalls his frequent use of περιβλεψάμενος. The expression θόρυβον καὶ κλαίοντας . . . is strange and has been replaced in Mt. ix. 23 by τοὺς αὐλητὰς καὶ τὸν ὄχλον θορυβούμενον, and in Lk. viii. 52 by ἔκλαιον δὲ

ἀλαλάζοντας πολλά, καὶ εἰσελθὼν λέγει αὐτοῖς Τί θορυβεῖσθε 39
καὶ κλαίετε; τὸ παιδίον οὐκ ἀπέθανεν ἀλλὰ καθεύδει. καὶ 40

πάντες καὶ ἐκόπτοντο αὐτήν. In Mk D and a read κλαιόντων καὶ ἀλαλαζόντων which Wellhausen, 41, prefers. Probably the loose Markan text in WH is original, the καί being epexegetic (Swete, 107). θόρυβος, xiv. 2*; κλαίω v. 39, xiv. 72, xvi. [10]*. ἀλαλάζω*, 1 Cor. xiii. 1**, ' to shout '; Cl., LXX, with either joy (Psa. xlvi. 2) or grief (Jer. iv. 8). Many commentators think that professional mourners are meant (Swete, 108; Plummer, 152; Bartlet, 183) and Matthew has taken the same view (τοὺς αὐλητάς, ix. 23); but there may not have been time to make the necessary arrangements (cf. Lagrange, 143; Rawlinson, 71) and probably members of the household are to be understood. πολλά is adverbial (v. i. 45); RV, 'greatly', RSV, 'loudly'. The scene is most vividly depicted. Jesus beholds the utter confusion and the weeping and wailing people.

39. Into what does Jesus enter? Is it the court before the house (Swete, 108), or the house itself (Lk. viii. 51)? The point is important in view of the words spoken, but unfortunately Mark's account does not permit a decisive answer. θορυβέομαι*, Mt. ix. 23, Ac. xvii. 5, xx. 10**, ' to make a noise ' or ' uproar '; Cl., LXX, Pap.

In the saying the meaning of καθεύδει is a question of the greatest difficulty. The verb can be used of the sleep of death and is so used in the LXX (Psa. lxxxvii. 6, Dan. xii. 2) and in 1 Thess. v. 10. Cf. κοιμάομαι, 3 Kgdms. ii. 10, etc., Jn. xi. 11, etc. But this meaning is excluded here by οὐκ ἀπέθανεν. It is possible, therefore, that καθεύδει is used of natural sleep. Turner, 30, observes that, if we could read Mk without presuppositions from Mt and Lk, we should take the meaning to be coma; and Creed, 124, McNeile, 126,

and Plummer, 152, recognize this possibility. This interpretation, however, is open to objection. At the time of speaking Jesus had apparently not seen the child, although on this point the silence of the narrative cannot be pressed. Further, His words are not a diagnosis, and it is foreign to His manner to speak as a physician. Cf. Lohmeyer, 106 n. If, then, He means some form of sleep, we must infer that He has an intuition or conviction to this effect gained we know not how. On the other hand, it is possible that, while καθεύδει does not mean death as men use the word, it describes it as God sees it, namely, as a sleep from which there is to be a speedy awakening. Cf. Swete, 108. In this sense ' sleep ' is mentioned in a Rabbinic passage in Gen. R. 96 (60c) quoted by Billerbeck, i. 523. Here, with reference to Jacob (Gen. xlvii. 30), it is said: ' Thou shalt sleep, but thou shalt not die '.[1] If this is the meaning, Jesus enters the chamber believing that the dead girl will be restored to life. It is more difficult to think that He intended to restore her, for it cannot be shown that He was accustomed to raise the dead or why the raising of this maiden should be an exception. And, in any case, it would still remain an open question whether the restoration was a case of resurrection. It is clear that the saying is one of great ambiguity. If, as is probable, Mark himself regarded the incident as one of resurrection, he has related the story with great objectivity in that another interpretation is possible. Mt. ix. 18 and Lk. viii. 53, 55 leave a very different impression, and it is this difference as well as the ambiguity of the Markan saying which suggests that the case was one of apparent death.

---

[1] In a letter Dr. Matthew Black says that it is quite clear from the context that *shokheb* could not here mean ' sleep ' in the natural sense; it denotes a ' death ' which is not Death. Jacob will either ' rise from the dead ' on the Day of Judgment or ' stand before ' the Judgment Seat of God.

κατεγέλων αὐτοῦ. αὐτὸς δὲ ἐκβαλὼν πάντας παραλαμβάνει τὸν
πατέρα τοῦ παιδίου καὶ τὴν μητέρα καὶ τοὺς μετ' αὐτοῦ, καὶ
41 εἰσπορεύεται ὅπου ἦν τὸ παιδίον· καὶ κρατήσας τῆς χειρὸς τοῦ
παιδίου λέγει αὐτῇ Ταλειθά, κούμ, ὅ ἐστιν μεθερμηνευόμενον
42 Τὸ κοράσιον, σοὶ λέγω, ἔγειρε. καὶ εὐθὺς ἀνέστη τὸ κοράσιον

The diminutive παιδίον (Cl., LXX, Pap.) denotes a child from birth onwards (*VGT*, 474) and can be used affectionately (cf. Jn. xxi. 5). Luke omits the word here and Matthew has κοράσιον (cf. Mk. v. 41).

40. The people laugh Jesus to scorn, but, ejecting them, He takes the father and mother with Him and enters the place where the child was (ὅπου ἦν τὸ παιδίον). The agreement of the three Synoptists in using καὶ κατεγέλων αὐτοῦ is a clear sign of literary dependence since the expression is so bold and the verb is not used elsewhere in the NT. καταγελάω*, Mt. ix. 24, Lk. viii. 53**, 'to deride', 'jeer at' (the κατά has perfective force); Cl. (c. acc.), LXX (c. gen.), Pap. αὐτὸς δέ, 'But he', stands in contrast with κατεγέλων. For ἐκβάλλω v. i. 12. Here some degree of force is implied; cf. Moffatt, 'put them all outside' (so RSV). For the natural reference to the father and mother at this point see the note on 37 above. The three disciples are described as τοὺς μετ' αὐτοῦ (cf. i. 36). For εἰσπορεύομαι v. *HS²*, 12. In the OT narratives of the raising of the dead Elijah and Elisha are alone and in each case prayer is offered (1 Kgs. xvii. 19 f., 2 Kgs. iv. 33). In writing ὅπου ἦν τὸ παιδίον Mark probably means to indicate that Jesus enters the room for the first time.

Matthew does not mention those who accompanied Jesus, while Luke, as we have seen, refers to them earlier. Mark alone speaks of the chamber. Τὸ καὶ κατεγέλων αὐτοῦ Luke adds εἰδότες ὅτι ἀπέθανεν (viii. 53), thus emphasizing the fact that the child was dead.

41. As in i. 31 Jesus takes hold of the girl's hand (κρατέω, i. 31). αὐτῇ is fem. *ad sensum*. Ταλειθά, κούμ is

a transliteration of the Aramaic מְלִיתָא קוּם. Other examples of Aramaic words in Mk are found in iii. 17, vii. 11, 34, xi. 9 f., xiv. 36, xv. 22, 34. Of these Luke retains none, and Matthew has one only (xv. 22, 'Golgotha'). In all cases, except xi. 9 f., Mark translates the original for his Gentile readers. טְלִיתָא is the fem. of טְלֵי, 'lamb', 'youth' and קוּם is masc. imperative, 'arise'. Mark translates the noun by κοράσιον, v. 42, vi. 22, 28 (*bis*)*, Mt. ix. 24 f., xiv. 11** (the diminutive of the classical κόρη, 'girl'), which is used in the LXX (Ruth ii. 8, etc.) and survives in MGk (*VGT*, 355; Kennedy, 154). Lagrange, 144, suggests that the masc. impv. is used without reference to sex and compares the use of *debout*. It is not surprising that many MSS. (A D Δ Θ *et al.* fam. 13 22 28 565 579 700 1071 *al. pler.* it vg sype hl) read the fem. κουμί (קוּמִי), or variants of the same, but κούμ is clearly original. For the intrans. use of ἐγείρω v. ii. 9, iii. 3.

D has the curious reading ραββι· θαβιτα, which Wellhausen, 41, explains as a corruption of ραβιθα = *puella*, 'maiden', an Aramaic variant which has been replaced by the less dialectical form *talitha*. Cf. the readings *thabitha* (b c i vg) and *tabitha* (a ff l vg). Confusion with Ταβειθά in Ac. ix. 40 is probably the simplest explanation. Cf. Lagrange, 144.

The use of foreign words is part of the technique of ancient miracle-stories (cf. Bultmann, 238; Dibelius, 83 f.), but it is improbable that v. 41 or vii. 34 are examples of this, for in most cases where Mark cites Aramaic healings are not in question (iii. 17, vii. 11, xiv. 36, xv. 22, 34). Here, as in vii. 34, knowledge of what was actually said is a satisfactory explana-

καὶ περιεπάτει, ἦν γὰρ ἐτῶν δώδεκα.   καὶ ἐξέστησαν ἐκστάσει
μεγάλῃ.   καὶ διεστείλατο αὐτοῖς πολλὰ ἵνα μηδεὶς γνοῖ τοῦτο,   43
καὶ εἶπεν δοθῆναι αὐτῇ φαγεῖν.

tion. The retention of the Aramaic words, absent in Mt and Lk, shows the greater originality of Mk.

42. In response to the command the girl gets up and begins to walk, to the great amazement of the on-lookers. The emphasis on immediacy (εὐθύς) is manifest. Probably, however, the second εὐθύς after ἐξέστησαν in the WH text should be omitted with A D N W Θ Π Σ Φ P⁴⁵ minusc. *plur.* it vg syᵖᵉ ʰˡ sa geo arm. The tenses are carefully distinguished and should be given their full force : the child arose and continued walking. Her age, ἐτῶν δώδεκα, is added to explain the walking. ἀνέστη is ambiguous, but it is doubtful if more is meant than that she got up ; cf. Moffatt, ' got up at once ' (so RSV). Luke makes it clear that he thought the case was one of resurrection, καὶ ἐπέστρεψεν τὸ πνεῦμα αὐτῆς, καὶ ἀνέστη παραχρῆμα (viii. 55). Cf. ix. 25, καὶ ἠγέρθη τὸ κοράσιον. Mark's objective word ἀνέστη leaves the question open.

The amazement of the beholders (Lk, οἱ γονεῖς αὐτῆς) is strongly expressed by καὶ ἐξέστησαν ἐκστάσει μεγάλῃ. Here the use of the finite verb with the dat. of the cognate noun is a ' Septuagintalism ' representing the infin. absolute with the fin. verb in Hebrew (cf. Gen. ii. 16 f.). Cf. vii. 10 (LXX) and Lk. xxii. 15 ; Intr. 61. See also the similar use of the cognate acc. in iv. 41, ἐφοβήθησαν φόβον μέγαν, and for the grammatical question *v.* Howard, ii. 443-5. We are entitled to conclude that Mark is using a Palestinian source.

For ἐξέστησαν *v.* ii. 12. ἔκστασις, xvi. 8*, Lk. v. 26, Ac. iii. 10, x. 10, xi. 5, xxii. 17**, ' displacement ', ' astonishment ', ' bewilderment ', ' a trance ' (Ac. x. 10, xi. 5, xxii. 17) ; Cl., LXX, Pap. (*VGT*, 198 ; Kennedy, 121 f.). The very strong expression suggests something utterly unexpected which

was regarded by the eyewitnesses as restoration from death. Matthew has no parallel, but Luke has καὶ ἐξέστησαν οἱ γονεῖς αὐτῆς (viii. 56).

43. The story ends with an injunction to maintain silence and a command to give the child something to eat. διαστέλλομαι, vii. 36 (*bis*), viii. 15, ix. 9*, Mt. xvi. 20, Ac. xv. 24, Heb. xii. 20**, ' to command ', ' expressly charge ' ; Cl., LXX, Pap. (*VGT*, 154). The verb is one of Mark's characteristic words (*HS²*, 12). For πολλά adverbial (' strictly ', Moffatt, Torrey, RSV) *v.* i. 45, and for the form γνοῖ *v.* the note on παραδοῖ in iv. 29. ἵνα . . . γνοῖ expresses, not purpose, but the substance of the command, as in iii. 9, etc.

The command must be considered along with the other injunctions to keep silence in i. 25, 44, iii. 12, etc. It is frequently suggested that the present instance shows the artificiality of Mark's schematization, since the facts could not be concealed ; cf. Bousset, 66 ; Bultmann, 371 ; Klostermann, 62 ; Easton, 131 ; Branscomb, 96, etc. One might wonder if the possibility could not occur to Mark himself. It seems more probable that he is recording a tradition. In the Introduction (p. 123) it is argued that the ' Messianic Secret ' represents an intention of Jesus. Here it may be held that He sought for a time at least to avoid the embarrassments of publicity ; cf. Swete, 110 ; Lagrange, 145 ; Plummer, 153 ; Rawlinson, 72 ; Bartlet, 185. There would be an added reason for the charge if Jesus interpreted the incident differently from the onlookers.

Luke repeats the substance of Mark's account of the charge (viii. 56), but Matthew omits it and writes καὶ ἐξῆλθεν ἡ φήμη αὕτη εἰς ὅλην τὴν γῆν ἐκείνην (ix. 26).

In καὶ εἶπεν δοθῆναι αὐτῇ φαγεῖν, the verb εἶπεν is used in the sense of ' told ' or ' commanded '. Allen, 50, sees a Semitism here, corresponding to the late use of אֲמַר, 'to command' followed by לְ c. infin. (v. 1 Chron. xxi. 17, 2 Chron. i. 18, xiv. 3, etc.). Cf. viii. 7. The same usage is found in the papyri (VGT, 372) and in Cl. Gk the simple infin. is used in a jussive sense after λέγω and εἶπον (LS, 490, 1034). Cf. Howard, ii. 450. These considerations do not exclude the possibility that Semitic idiom is reflected, especially when several elements in the narrative

point in this direction. Cf. ἔλεγεν in v. 8 and Black's note, JTS, xlix. 162. The passive infin. δοθῆναι is used because the one who is to execute the order is not named; cf. Lagrange, 145; Blass, 230, 322. Cf. viii. 7, Lk. xii. 13. φαγεῖν virtually = βρῶμα. This detail is added, not merely as a matter of technique in order to confirm the reality of the restoration, but because the thoughtful compassion of Jesus was remembered. Cf. Swete, 110; Lagrange, 145, Pourquoi pas plutôt simplement par bonté? Luke records this charge, but not Matthew.

Mk. vi. 1-6a   36. THE REJECTION AT   Cf. Mt. xiii. 53-8
               NAZARETH   (Lk. iv. 16-30)

The narrative cannot be more exactly described than as a Story about Jesus. Bultmann, 30 f., classifies it as an Apothegm, and Dibelius, 43, as a Paradigm of a less pure type. Cf. also Redlich, 97. Bultmann, indeed, describes it as a model example (Musterbeispiel) of an ideal scene which has been constructed from the Oxyrhynchus saying, ' A prophet is not acceptable in his own country, and a physician effects no cures among those who know him ', a process completed in the mission-preaching of the Palestinian community before Mark wrote. Dibelius, 110, takes a similar view, but no longer believes that the whole story was developed from the saying. This hypothesis is surely a Musterbeispiel of subjective criticism. In it justice is not done to the realism of the the narrative : the naming of the brothers, the mention of the sisters, the reflection in the word ' kin ' on those who were subsequently prominent in the Church, the implication that Jesus could not heal in the absence of faith, His surprise at unbelief. These features mark genuine tradition. In referring to some of them Dibelius is compelled to observe : ' There is too much special material in the brief story for it to be possible as a mere filling out '. Branscomb, 97, thinks that the narrative is ' one of unique biographical value ', and with this estimate J. Weiss and Schmidt agree. Weiss, in fact, goes so far as to classify the narrative as Petrine,[1] but this estimate applies only to its broad outlines since there is a want of those artless details which appear in the stories of i. 21-39 and iv. 35-v. 43. A special point in the analysis of Schmidt, 155, is worthy of note. He suggests that two separate narratives (2a, 4 and 2b, 3c, 5, 6a) have been telescoped in the tradition which Mark used ; cf. Bultmann, 31 ; Wellhausen, 42. The astonishment of verse 2 is unaccountably followed by the indignation of 3. Is a sermon like that described in Lk. iv. 23-7 presupposed ? The position assigned to the narrative in Mk suggests that the period of synagogue preaching is ending and that new methods are felt to be necessary ; cf. vi. 6b-13.

[1] Einer Ableitung aus den Petruserzählungen steht nichts im Wege, p. 199.

Καὶ ἐξῆλθεν ἐκεῖθεν, καὶ ἔρχεται εἰς τὴν πατρίδα αὐτοῦ, καὶ 1 VI
ἀκολουθοῦσιν αὐτῷ οἱ μαθηταὶ αὐτοῦ. Καὶ γενομένου σαββάτου 2
ἤρξατο διδάσκειν ἐν τῇ συναγωγῇ· καὶ οἱ πολλοὶ ἀκούοντες
ἐξεπλήσσοντο λέγοντες Πόθεν τούτῳ ταῦτα, καὶ τίς ἡ σοφία ἡ
δοθεῖσα τούτῳ, καὶ αἱ δυνάμεις τοιαῦται διὰ τῶν χειρῶν αὐτοῦ
γινόμεναι; οὐχ οὗτός ἐστιν ⌜ὁ τέκτων, ὁ υἱὸς τῆς Μαρίας⌝ καὶ 3

3 ὁ τοῦ τέκτονος υἱὸς

1. Mark connects this narrative closely with the preceding story by ἐκεῖθεν (vi. 10 f., vii. 24, ix. 30, x. 1*). So rarely does he use this adverb as a connecting-link (vi. 10 f. are sayings) as compared with Matthew (11 times), that Schmidt, 153, infers that he found it already present in his source. But the geographical indications are vague; we have only the bare statement of v. 21 that Jesus was 'by the sea'. We can therefore infer no more than that the visit to Nazareth followed the incident mentioned last. The claim of Schmidt, that there is a gap between v. 43 and vi. 1, may well be correct. Other events can have intervened. πατρίς, vi. 4*, Mt. xiii. 54, 57, Lk. iv. 23 f., Jn. iv. 44, Ac. xviii. 27 (?), Heb. xi. 14**, 'one's fatherland', is used here, as in classical and later Gk, of a 'native place' or 'town' (VGT, 499; Field, 10). Cf. Swete, 110. The reference to the disciples suggests that the occasion was not a private visit to His family. 'He came as a Rabbi, surrounded by His scholars' (Swete, 111). For ἀκολουθέω v. i. 18 and for μαθητής ii. 15.

Matthew connects the narrative with his Parable section in Mt. xiii. Luke has an independent account which he sets as the prelude to the Galilean Ministry (iv. 16-30).

2. Here, as in i. 32, iv. 35, etc., and in contrast with v. 2, 21, xiii. 1, etc., the gen. abs. γενομένου σαββάτου is used correctly. When the Sabbath was come, he began to teach. It does not seem necessary to interpret ἤρξατο c. infin. (v. Intr. 48, 63 f.) as implying a new departure (Swete, 111). Again, as in i. 22, the hearers are astonished,

but here in οἱ πολλοί Mark indicates that 'there was an undercurrent of dissatisfaction which in the end prevailed' (Swete). Cf. Lagrange, 147; Rawlinson, 73. The questions, vividly narrated, concern the origin (πόθεν) of His teaching and the nature (τίς) of His wisdom (σοφία*), as well as the mighty works which are being done by Him. For αἱ δυνάμεις v. the note on v. 30. τοιαῦται (iv. 33) is emphatic: mighty works of such a kind; and διὰ τῶν χειρῶν αὐτοῦ either refers to His healing touch (i. 41, v. 23) or, more probably, is the common OT idiom indicating instrumental action. If the question is hostile, the kind of suspicion indicated by iii. 22 (the power of Satan) is present, but this inference is not necessary, and the description of the 'wisdom' as 'given' to Him, that is, by God, suggests the contrary.

Matthew severely abbreviates his source by omitting the reference to the Sabbath, ἤρξατο c. infin., οἱ πολλοί, and the fuller allusion to the mighty works done by Jesus. In his parallel story Luke vividly depicts the fixed attention of the hearers (iv. 20).

3. The tone of this verse is perceptibly different from that of 2, and the disparaging questions, culminating in the statement ἐσκανδαλίζοντο ἐν αὐτῷ, are not represented as a minority attitude. There is thus some ground for the opinion (Bultmann, 31; Schmidt, 155) that two stories, or traditions, have been fused. See the Note on the Narrative. The phrase ὁ υἱὸς τῆς Μαρίας has no parallel in the Gospels and Epistles and raises difficult historical questions. It is contrary to

ἀδελφὸς Ἰακώβου καὶ Ἰωσῆτος καὶ Ἰούδα καὶ Σίμωνος; καὶ
οὐκ εἰσὶν αἱ ἀδελφαὶ αὐτοῦ ὧδε πρὸς ἡμᾶς; καὶ ἐσκανδαλίζοντο

Jewish custom to describe a man as the son of his mother, even when the father is no longer living, except in insulting terms (cf. Judg. xi. 1 f.), and it is improbable that Mark, and still less the Nazarenes, were familiar with the Virgin Birth tradition.[1] These considerations raise the question whether the phrase belongs to the original text. In Matthew the text is quite different, οὐχ οὗτός ἐστιν ὁ τοῦ τέκτονος υἱός; οὐχ ἡ μήτηρ αὐτοῦ λέγεται Μαριὰμ καὶ οἱ ἀδελφοὶ αὐτοῦ Ἰάκωβος καὶ Ἰωσὴφ καὶ Σίμων καὶ Ἰούδας; (xiii. 55), and in his parallel narrative Luke has οὐχὶ υἱός ἐστιν Ἰωσὴφ οὗτος; (iv. 22, cf. Jn. vi. 42). ὁ τέκτων, ὁ υἱὸς τῆς Μαρίας is attested by all uncials, many minuscules, f ff l q vg (WW) sype hl sa bo geo¹, but many important MSS., including P⁴⁵, support a text akin to that of Mt. ὁ τοῦ τέκτονος υἱός[2] is supported by P⁴⁵ 10 fam. 13 33 472 543 565 579 700 a b c e i r² δ aur vg (plur.) bo (3 MSS.) aeth, and by Origen, Contra Celsum, vi. 36, who, in reply to Celsus, denies that Jesus is anywhere described as an artisan in the Gospels current in the Church.[3] Further, most of the MSS. mentioned (but not P⁴⁵) add either καὶ τῆς Μαρίας, or καὶ Μαρίας, or Μαρίας. Klostermann, 63, with Fritzsche and Merx, accepts ὁ τοῦ τέκτονος υἱὸς καὶ Μαρίας as the older reading. This reading bears signs of assimilation and conflation, but while it may be a conflation of Mt and Mk, it may also be a conflation of two different texts of Mk. The evidence of P⁴⁵ shows that ὁ τοῦ τέκτονος υἱός was read in Mk as early as the first half of the third century, and perhaps earlier still. Origen's testimony also points in the same direction, for Hort's explanation, Notes, 24, that Origen either forgot Mk. vi. 3 or did not hold Mark respons-

ible for the words of the Galileans, is not satisfactory. Lohmeyer, 110, thinks he read a text assimilated to Mt.

Matthew's text is commonly attributed to motives of reverence ; he did not like to think of Jesus as a carpenter (cf. Allen, St. Mt, 155 f. ; Rawlinson, 74) ; but, against this view, McNeile, 207, justly observes that he ' does not shrink from recording far more insulting taunts (cf. xi. 19, xii. 24) '. ' Son of Mary ' would have been a phrase congenial to his mind (cf. Mt. i, ii), and it is not easy to think that he would have used instead the words ' the son of the carpenter ' unless they already stood in Mk. On the evidence as a whole it seems best to conclude that Mark wrote ὁ τοῦ τέκτονος υἱός and that an early scribe replaced this reading by ὁ τέκτων and added ὁ υἱὸς τῆς Μαρίας. Cf. Stanton, ii. 142.

τέκτων*, Mt. xiii. 55**, ' a carpenter ', is also used of a craftsman in stone or metal (LXX, 1 Kgdms. xiii. 19), but is especially applied to a carpenter (VGT, 628), and probably so here. Justin Martyr, Dial. 88, speaks of Jesus as having made ploughs and yokes, τὰ τεκτονικὰ ἔργα ἠργάζετο ἐν ἀνθρώποις ὤν, ἄροτρα καὶ ζυγά. Hilary, on Mt. xiv, describes Him as a smith, Fabri erat filius ferrum igne vincentis, omnem saeculi virtutem iudicio decoquentis. Cf. Swete, 112.

Ἰάκωβος*, the Lord's brother, Mt. xiii. 55, Ac. xii. 17, xv. 13, xxi. 18, 1 Cor. xv. 7, Gal. i. 19, ii. 9, 12, Jas. i. 1 (?), Ju. 1 (?)**. Ἰωσῆς*, Mt. xiii. 55 (Ἰωσήφ)**. The Joses of xv. 40, 47 is a different person. Ἰούδας*, Mt. xiii. 55**. Σίμων*, Mt. xiii. 55**. For the brothers of Jesus see the detached note on iii. 31-5. From the description of the sisters as ὧδε πρὸς ἡμᾶς it has been inferred that Mary

---

[1] Cf. V. Taylor, The Historical Evidence for the Virgin Birth, 8-12.
[2] The article precedes υἱός in P⁴⁵ 13 124 346.
[3] οὐδαμοῦ τῶν ἐν ταῖς ἐκκλησίαις φερομένων εὐαγγελίων τέκτων αὐτὸς ὁ Ἰησοῦς ἀναγέγραπται.

ἐν αὐτῷ. καὶ ἔλεγεν αὐτοῖς ὁ Ἰησοῦς ὅτι Οὐκ ἔστιν προφήτης 4
ἄτιμος εἰ μὴ ἐν τῇ πατρίδι αὐτοῦ καὶ ἐν τοῖς συγγενεῦσιν αὐτοῦ
καὶ ἐν τῇ οἰκίᾳ αὐτοῦ. Καὶ οὐκ ἐδύνατο ἐκεῖ ποιῆσαι οὐδεμίαν 5
δύναμιν, εἰ μὴ ὀλίγοις ἀρρώστοις ἐπιθεὶς τὰς χεῖρας ἐθεράπευσεν·
καὶ ⌜ἐθαύμασεν⌝ διὰ τὴν ἀπιστίαν αὐτῶν.   6

6 ἐθαύμαζεν

and the brothers were not resident in Nazareth at this time (Schmidt, 154), but this inference is not necessary (Klostermann, 64). For σκανδαλίζω v. iv. 17. Here the meaning is ' took offence ' (Torrey, RSV) ; Moffatt has ' were repelled ', Lagrange, scandalisés à son sujet. The ἐν (cf. Mt. xi. 6, xiii. 57, xxvi. 31) corresponds to the use of ב in Hebrew and is found with σκανδαλίζω in Sir. ix. 5, xxiii. 8. Cf. Howard, ii. 464.

4. This common proverb is found, not only here and in Mt. xiii. 57, but also in the parallel story in Lk. iv. 24 and in Jn. iv. 44. Luke has it in the form οὐδεὶς προφήτης δεκτός ἐστιν ἐν τῇ πατρίδι αὐτοῦ. Numerous parallels have been collected by Wetstein. Cf. Bultmann, 30 n.; Billerbeck, i. 678. Mark alone has the reference to kinsmen, ἐν τοῖς συγγενεῦσιν αὐτοῦ. Cf. iii. 20 f., 31·5. For συγγενεῦσιν v. Moulton, ii. 138. Many MSS., but not B Θ fam. 1 fam. 13 et al., read συγγενέσιν. συγγενής*, ' a relative ', ' kinsman ' ; cf. VGT, 595. Implicitly Jesus accepts the title ' prophet ' ; cf. Lk. xiii. 33. That He was popularly regarded as such is clear from vi. 15, viii. 28, Mt. xxi. 11, Lk. vii. 16, 39. See also Lk. xxiv. 19, Jn. iv. 19, vi. 14, vii. 40, 52, ix. 17, Ac. iii. 22, vii. 37, and for the title ' the prophet ' Jn. vi. 14, vii. 40. In the primitive community these terms passed quickly out of use because of their inadequacy. ἄτιμος*, Mt. xiii. 57, 1 Cor. iv. 10, xii. 23**. For ὁ Ἰησοῦς v. i. 9 ; πατρίς vi. 1.

Bultmann, 30, cites a form of the saying from Pap. Oxy. i. 5, οὐκ ἔστιν

δεκτὸς προφήτης ἐν τῇ πατρίδι αὐτοῦ, οὐδὲ ἰατρὸς ποιεῖ θεραπείας εἰς τοὺς γινώσκοντας αὐτόν, which is independent of Mk, but from which he believes the story to have originated. See the Introduction to the narrative, p. 298.

5, 6a. This passage is one of the boldest statements in the Gospels, since it mentions something that Jesus could not do (cf. xiii. 32). There is no parallel to it in Lk. iv. 16-30 and Matthew recasts it in the form καὶ οὐκ ἐποίησεν ἐκεῖ δυνάμεις πολλὰς διὰ τὴν ἀπιστίαν αὐτῶν (xiii. 58). Wellhausen, 43, claims that 5b contradicts 5a, but this is an exaggeration. All that we can say is that 5b modifies the rigour of 5a by stating an exception. Cf. εἰ μή . . . οὐκ, viii. 14. For δύναμις v. v. 30. ἄρρωστος, vi. 13, xvi. [18]*, Mt. xiv. 14, 1 Cor. xi. 30**, ' weak ', ' sickly ', <a- neg., ῥώννυμι ; Cl., LXX, Pap. (VGT, 79). For the act of laying on hands v. the note on v. 23, and for θεραπεύω i. 34.

The astonishment of Jesus at the unbelief of the people is a realistic human touch. He appears to have thought of faith as a natural attitude, although in the story of the Centurion's Servant He is surprised and deeply moved by the strength of the centurion's faith : ' Verily I say unto you, I have not found so great faith, no, not in Israel ' (Mt. viii. 10). Matthew omits the reference to surprise in 6a. ἀπιστία, ix. 24, xvi. [14]*, Mt. xiii. 58, Rom. iii. 3, iv. 20, xi. 20, 23, 1 Tim. i. 13, Heb. iii. 12, 19**. Holtzmann, 136, comments on the deep impression of historical accuracy left by verse 5.

37. THE
         MISSION CHARGE TO
            THE TWELVE

This narrative appears to have been put together by the Evangelist himself; it is little more than a framework for the Mission Charge to the Twelve. The sayings are the historical kernel, and were derived either from oral tradition, or more probably from a primitive collection comparable to Q and M. The narrative itself is redactional. This hypothesis is suggested by the vocabulary and style in 7 and 12 f. (*v.* Comm.), in which nothing, except perhaps the references to anointing with oil, and to exorcisms, points beyond Mark himself. But perhaps the strongest evidence is the fact that Mark has no real appreciation of the immense importance of the event itself in the Story of Jesus. He reports sayings which, even in their brief Markan setting, are breathless with a sense of urgency, but he does not tell us what the issue is. He records that the Twelve went out to preach, but does not relate their message apart from the phrase ἵνα μετανοῶσιν, and he has only vague ideas concerning their experiences and the results of the Mission. As Mark relates it, the incident is merely an extension of the teaching ministry of Jesus.

Of the importance of the Mission there can be no question. The opinion of Wellhausen, 44, regarding its historical character, is entirely unconvincing. The section, he declares, ' contains no historical tradition '. ' The Twelve merely make an experiment and remain afterwards as lacking in independence and as passive as before, although the experiment succeeds. In truth Jesus instituted no experimental missionary journeys with his seminar. But as testimony for the nature of the oldest Christian mission in Palestine this instruction is of value.' Cf. Bultmann, 155 f., who describes the story as a product of the community in which the speaker is the Risen or Exalted Lord. In complete contrast stands the estimate of many other NT scholars. Creed's opinion is tepid : ' It may have been so. On the other hand there seems to be no conclusive reason why we should assume that Jesus did not at some period associate the Twelve with him in his work of preaching the advent of the kingdom ', *St. Lk,* 125 ; cf. Rawlinson, 76. More discerning is the forthright opinion of Manson, *SJ,* 73, who writes : ' The mission of the disciples is one of the best-attested facts in the life of Jesus ', and side by side with this view may be set that of Branscomb, 101, who says : ' The event described in these few verses is one of the most significant of all those which the Christian tradition has preserved of the active life of Jesus '.

It is the combined witness of Mk, Q, M, and L, which fixes the historical value of the event. According to Manson's analysis, the Q version is to be found in Lk. x. 2 f., 8-12, 13-16 (with parallels in Mt), the M account in Mt. x. 5-8, 9-16, 23-5, 40-xi. 1, and the L extract in Lk. x. 1, 4-7, 17-20. In these sources the note of urgency present in Mk. vi. 8-11 is still more evident. Like Gehazi of old on his mission of life and death (2 Kings iv. 29) the messengers are to salute no man on the way (Lk. x. 4) ; they are to regard eating and drinking as secondary matters, to proclaim the Kingdom, and to know that he who hears them hears also Jesus, and that he who rejects them rejects both Jesus and Him that sent Him (Lk. x. 16). The time is that of harvest, and they are to pray the

Lord of the harvest that he send forth labourers into his harvest (Lk.
x. 2). It is possible that criticism has not said its last word about Mt.
x. 23 : ' Ye shall not have gone through the cities of Israel, till the Son
of Man be come ', and that, in a different sense from the one understood
by Schweitzer, the messengers were to proclaim the advent of the Son of
Man.

A later period in the Galilean Ministry is implied. But the narrative is
loosely placed in its context ; it belongs to an unspecified point in the
ministry, and has no direct connexion with the story of Herod's Fears
which immediately follows.

Καὶ περιῆγεν τὰς κώμας κύκλῳ διδάσκων. Καὶ προσκαλεῖται 7
τοὺς δώδεκα, καὶ ἤρξατο αὐτοὺς ἀποστέλλειν δύο δύο, καὶ ἐδίδου
αὐτοῖς ἐξουσίαν τῶν πνευμάτων τῶν ἀκαθάρτων, καὶ παρήγ- 8

6b. Καὶ περιῆγεν τὰς κώμας κύκλῳ
διδάσκων. By most editors and commentators this passage is taken with
the present section, thus connecting the
Mission with a period during which
Jesus moved from village to village
in Galilee. Wellhausen, 42, and
Schmidt, 158-62, connect it with the
Rejection at Nazareth. In this case
it describes the results of the rejection.
Unable to teach in the synagogues
Jesus turned to the villages in the
surrounding country. Either of these
views is possible, but the former is
better, since the story of the Rejection
ends well with 6a, and no more than
a bare reference to the journey is made
in 6b. The short passage is an editorial summary comparable to i. 39 and
ii. 13, but it may be based on tradition
(cf. J. Weiss, 199). περιάγω*, Mt. iv.
23, ix. 35, xxiii. 15, Ac. xiii. 11, 1 Cor.
ix. 5**; Cl., LXX, Pap., trans. ' to
lead about ' (1 Cor. ix. 5), intrans.
(elsewhere in the NT) ' to go about '
or ' around ' (Demosth. xlii. 5). For
κύκλῳ v. iii. 34 ; διδάσκω i. 21. κώμη,
vi. 36, 56, viii. 23, 26 f., xi. 2*, ' a
village ' or unwalled country town ;
contrast ἀγροί, v. 14, vi. 36, 56, ' hamlets '. Luke omits the passage.
Matthew adds τὰς πόλεις πάσας and
repeats the substance of iv. 23b.

7. The vocabulary and style suggest
that this verse is composed by the
Evangelist as a framework for the
Mission Charge which follows : cf.

προσκαλεῖται (iii. 13), τοὺς δώδεκα (iii. 14,
16), ἤρξατο c. infin. (i. 45), ἀποστέλλειν (i. 2), ἐξουσίαν (i. 22), τῶν πνευμάτων τῶν ἀκαθάρτων (i. 23). The only
new element is δύο δύο, ' two by two '.
Cf. vi. 39 f., συμπόσια συμπόσια, πρασιαὶ
πρασιαί, xiv. 19, εἷς κατὰ εἷς, Lk. x. 1,
ἀνὰ δύο [δύο], Mt. xiii. 30 (Epiph.),
δεσμὰς δεσμάς (Blass, 145). For this repetition of the cardinal numeral or of
the noun as distributives v. Intr. 60 f.
The practice of travelling in pairs is
Jewish ; it was adopted by the Baptist's
disciples (cf. Lk. vii. 18, Jn. i. 37) and
in the early Church by Barnabas and
Paul and Paul and Silas, etc. The
tense of ἐδίδου may imply that the
authority was given to successive pairs,
but this inference is not certain. In
any case the statement about exorcism
is difficult, because in ix. 18 the disciples were not able to cast out a spirit,
and in Lk. x. 17 the seventy speak of
the casting out of daemons in the name
of Jesus as though it had been unexpected. Moreover, while M has δαιμόνια ἐκβάλλετε (Mt. x. 8), the Mission
Charges in Q and L do not mention
exorcism. It is possible, therefore,
that here and in 13 Mark is unconsciously anticipating later ideas and
practices.

For ' The Twelve ' v. Note B on
pp. 619-27, and for Ed. Meyer's view,
that vi. 7-13 (30) was derived from a
' Twelve-source ', v. Intr. 74 f.

Matthew and Luke follow Mk

γειλεν αὐτοῖς ἵνα μηδὲν αἴρωσιν εἰς ὁδὸν εἰ μὴ ῥάβδον μόνον,
9 μὴ ἄρτον, μὴ πήραν, μὴ εἰς τὴν ζώνην χαλκόν, ἀλλὰ ὑποδεδε-
10 μένους σανδάλια, καὶ ⌐μὴ ἐνδύσασθε⌐ δύο χιτῶνας. καὶ ἔλεγεν

9 Μὴ ἐνδύσησθε

closely, but both omit ἤρξατο and δύο δύο, change ἐδίδου to ἔδωκεν, and mention the healing of diseases.

8 f. The Mission Charge in Mk consists of two excerpts from a sayings-source, introduced by καὶ παρήγγειλεν αὐτοῖς in 8 and καὶ ἔλεγεν αὐτοῖς in 10. For παραγγέλλω v. viii. 6. The ἵνα clause is not telic, but as in iii. 9, v. 10, etc., gives the substance of the command. Peculiar to the Markan version is the exception made in the case of the staff, εἰ μὴ ῥάβδον*. In both Mt. x. 10 and Lk. ix. 3, probably influenced by Q, the staff is prohibited. In the first edition of his Commentary Wellhausen suggested that εἰ μή is a mistranslation, אלא being read instead of לא. Cf. Lohmeyer, 114 n. Lagrange, 151, dismisses this suggestion as peu vraisemblable, and probably rightly, for the permission of the staff must be considered along with the injunction to wear sandals in 9 (cf. Mt. x. 10, Lk. x. 4, μὴ ὑποδήματα), both being influenced by the fact that travelling barefoot and without a staff was strange to western readers. The more rigid prohibitions of Mt and Lk are doubtless more original. The same also applies to the command to take neither bread (omitted by Mt) nor money. μὴ εἰς τὴν ζώνην χαλκόν, ' not a copper for your girdle ' (Swete, 116). χαλκός, xii. 41*, Mt. x. 9, 1 Cor. xiii. 1, Apoc. xviii. 12**, ' copper ', ' bronze ', ' copper money '; Cl., LXX, Pap. (VGT, 683). Cf. Mt. x. 9, μὴ κτήσησθε χρυσὸν μηδὲ ἄργυρον μηδὲ χαλκὸν εἰς τὰς ζώνας ὑμῶν, Lk. ix. 3, μήτε ἀργύριον, Lk. x. 4, μὴ βαστάζετε βαλλάντιον, Lk. xxii. 35, ἄτερ βαλλαντίου. Ancient custom was to keep small change in the girdle (ζώνη, i. 6*). Cf. Billerbeck, i. 565, and the classical phrase εἰς ζώνην δεδόσθαι used of pin-money (LS, i. 759). The Markan phrase seems more primitive than

Luke's μή ... βαλλάντιον (x. 4). Even the wallet (πήρα) is forbidden. Deissmann, 108-10, thinks that ' begging-bag ', rather than ' provision-bag ', is meant. Cf. Lagrange, 152, il était inutile d'interdire une besace de provisions après avoir interdit le pain. πήρα*, Mt. x. 10, Lk. ix. 3, x. 4, xxii. 35 f.**.

All these negative commands imply that the Mission was one of extreme urgency. ' The natural inference is that the missionaries are to be like an invading army, and live on the country ' (Manson, SJ, 181). Quoting Berakoth ix. 5, where it is ordained that a man ' may not enter the Temple Mount with his staff or his sandal or his wallet ', Manson suggests that possibly the Mission is meant to be regarded as a specially sacred undertaking. The journey was not simply a preaching tour and healings can only have been a secondary interest. The pairs of disciples were sent out as heralds charged with the delivery of a proclamation. Mark gives no indication of its subject, apart from 12 (ἐκήρυξαν ἵνα μετανοῶσιν), but its substance can hardly have been other than the imminence of the Kingdom. Cf. Mt. x. 7, Lk. ix. 2, x. 9.

In 9 there is a double change of construction. Instead of παραγγέλλω ἵνα c. subj., we have the ordinary use of παραγγέλλω c. acc. and infin. in ὑποδεδεμένους σανδάλια, in which σανδάλια is an internal acc. (v. i. 6), and finally direct speech in μὴ ἐνδύσασθε δύο χιτῶνας. ὑποδέομαι*, Ac. xii. 8, Eph. vi. 15**, ' to bind under one's feet ', ' put on shoes '; Cl., LXX, Pap. σανδάλιον*, Ac. xii. 8**, mostly in plur., ' sandals ', dimin. of σάνδαλον; Herodotus ii. 91, LXX (Josh. ix. 5, Isa. xx. 2, Judith x. 4, xvi. 9, elsewhere ὑπόδημα), Pap. There is no difference

αὐτοῖς "Οπου ἐὰν εἰσέλθητε εἰς οἰκίαν, ἐκεῖ μένετε ἕως ἂν
ἐξέλθητε ἐκεῖθεν. καὶ ὃς ἂν τόπος μὴ δέξηται ὑμᾶς μηδὲ ἀκού- 11
σωσιν ὑμῶν, ἐκπορευόμενοι ἐκεῖθεν ἐκτινάξατε τὸν χοῦν τὸν
ὑποκάτω τῶν ποδῶν ὑμῶν εἰς μαρτύριον αὐτοῖς. Καὶ ἐξελθόντες 12

between σανδάλιον and ὑπόδημα. Swete, 117, suggests that it is used here to avoid ὑποδεδέσθαι ὑποδήματα. There is no need, with McNeile, 135, to suppose that the phrase is a scribal addition in Mk.

Although not widely attested μὴ ἐνδύσασθε (B* 33 59 62 122 435) is probably original, since it best explains the textual variants: ἐνδύσασθαι (B² S Π* Ω 124 892) and ἐνδύσησθε (-θαι, A D W Δ 28 118 209²) read by ℵ C Θ Π² et al. 1 22 13 69 209* 543 565 579 700 1071 al. pler. These variants appear to be grammatical corrections of the unusual μή and the aor. imperative. For ἐνδύω (-δύνω) v. i. 6. χιτών, xiv. 63*, is the inner garment worn next to the skin, ' the tunic ' or ' shirt ' (for ἱμάτιον v. ii. 21). Two shirts (cf. xiv. 63) are a luxury, unsuitable for travelling. In Lk. ix. 3 (μήτε δύο χιτῶνας ἔχειν) and Mt. x. 10 (μηδὲ δύο χιτῶνας) the possession of an extra shirt is forbidden.

10 f. The choice of the second excerpt from the Mission Charge is probably due to the importance hospitality assumed in connexion with the earliest missionary preaching. The commands of Jesus to the Twelve were taken as a standard. Cf. Didache, xi. 4 f., πᾶς δὲ ἀπόστολος ἐρχόμενος πρὸς ὑμᾶς δεχθήτω ὡς Κύριος· μενεῖ δὲ ἡμέραν μίαν, ἐὰν δὲ ᾖ χρεία, καὶ τὴν ἄλλην· τρεῖς δὲ ἐὰν μείνῃ, ψευδοπροφήτης ἐστίν. For καὶ ἔλεγεν αὐτοῖς as a quotation-formula v. ii. 27, iv. 21, 24, etc. ὅπου ἐάν c. subj., 'wheresoever', vi. 56 (c. indic.), ix. 18, xiv. 9, 14. Matthew has εἰς ἣν δ' ἂν πόλιν ἢ κώμην (x. 11, cf. Lk. ix. 4, εἰς ἣν ἂν οἰκίαν) and adds ἐξετάσατε τίς ἐν αὐτῇ ἄξιός ἐστιν. μένω, xiv. 34*. ἕως ἄν c. subj., ' until ', ix. 1, xii. 36* ; cf. ἕως c. indic., ' while ', vi. 45, c. subj., xiv. 32*. For ἐκεῖθεν v. vi. 1. The saying describes the action to

be taken when a place (τόπος, i. 35, 45) refuses them a hearing. The other Synoptists mention people, Mt ὃς ἄν, Lk ὅσοι ἄν. All have δέχομαι (ix. 37 (quater), x. 15*) which means not only ' to receive ', but ' to welcome ' (cf. Jn. iv. 45). For ἐκπορεύομαι v. i. 5 (HS², 12). The Twelve are to shake off the dust that cleaves to their feet. The action is symbolic ; it means that the place is to be regarded as heathen. ' The significance of the ritual of wiping the feet before leaving the city is that the city is reckoned as heathen, and its inhabitants as no part of the true Israel, even though it is a city of Israel and its people Jews by birth ', Manson, SJ, 76. Cf. Lagrange, 153 f. The action is in harmony with the view that the tour partakes of the nature of a sacred mission. Cf. Ac. xiii. 51 (Paul and Barnabas at Antioch), xviii. 6 (Paul at Corinth). ἐκτινάσσω*, Mt. x. 14, Ac. xiii. 51, xviii. 6**, ' to shake off ' ; in Lk. x. 11, in the parallel saying, Luke has ἀπομάσσομαι*, ' to wipe off '. χοῦς*, Apoc. xviii. 19**, is excavated or heaped earth, but is used of dust in the LXX (3 Kgdms. xviii. 38). Q has κονιορτός (Mt. x. 14 = Lk. x. 11 ; cf. Lk. ix. 5). The two words are probably translation variants. ὑποκάτω, vii. 28, xii. 36*, properly a compd. adv., is used in the NT as a preposition c. gen. (Cl., LXX, Pap.).

The shaking off of the dust is not an acted curse, but a testimony intended to provoke thought and to lead men to repentance. Cf. Swete, 118; Gould, 107 ; Plummer, 162. It is offered, not against them (as in Lk. ix. 5, ἐπ' αὐτούς), but for or to them. For the phrase εἰς μαρτύριον αὐτοῖς v. i. 44, and cf. Moffatt, ' as a warning to them '. At this point many uncials, minuscules, and versions add ἀμὴν λέγω ὑμῖν ἀνεκτότερον ἔσται Σοδόμοις ἢ

13 ἐκήρυξαν ἵνα μετανοῶσιν, καὶ δαιμόνια πολλὰ ἐξέβαλλον, καὶ
ἤλειφον ἐλαίῳ πολλοὺς ἀρρώστους καὶ ἐθεράπευον.

Γομόρροις ἐν ἡμέρᾳ κρίσεως ἢ τῇ πόλει
ἐκείνῃ, but the reading is clearly an
assimilation to Mt. x. 15.
The variations from Mk. vi. 11
shared by Mt and Lk, including ἐξ-
ερχόμενοι . . . τῆς πόλεως ἐκείνης, and
κονιορτόν (cf. Mt. x. 14 and Lk. ix. 5
(x. 10 f.)), show that in using Mk the
later Evangelists were influenced by
Q. Further, in Mt. x. 12 f. there are
additional sayings, to which there is
a parallel in Lk. x. 6 f., assigned by
Manson, SJ, 181, to M and L respectively. Mt. x. 12 f. gives the injunction
to greet the house on entering it, and
the assurance that, if it is worthy (Lk.
x. 6, 'if a son of peace be there '),
their peace will rest upon it, but, if not,
it will return to them. Lk. x. 7 adds
that they are to remain in the same
house, eating and drinking such things
as are given, for the labourer is worthy
of his hire. The evidence shows that
the Mission Charge was widely attested, and that Mark has given only
excerpts. The reason for this must be
the fragmentary records of the Charge
and the special interests under which
Mark wrote.

12 f. As in 7, the vocabulary, style,
and ideas, show that these verses were
composed by the Evangelist to provide
a narrative frame for the Mission
Charge. Words and constructions
used by him elsewhere, in some cases
frequently, include ἐξελθόντες (i. 29),
ἐκήρυξαν (i. 4), μετανοῶσιν (i. 15), δαιμόνια (i. 34), ἐξέβαλλον (i. 12), ἀρρώστους (vi. 5), ἐθεράπευον (i. 34), ἵνα c.
subj. in a noun clause, and καί paratactic. The new words are ἀλείφω,
xvi. 1*, and ἔλαιον*.
The medicinal use of oil was familiar
to the ancient world ; cf. Isa. i. 6, Lk.

x. 34, Josephus, BJ, i. 33. 5, and for
Rabbinic evidence v. Billerbeck, ii.
11 f. Mark, however, does not think
of it simply as an emollient ; in his view
it is an adjunct to miraculous healing.
The fact that anointing with oil is mentioned here and in Lk. x. 34 only in the
Gospels, and in the rest of the NT in
Jas. v. 15 alone, suggests that the allusion may reflect contemporary practice;
but it is also possible that Mark is
following an old tradition concerning
a symbolical use of oil by the disciples
before the practice arose of healing in
the name of Jesus. Cf. Schmidt, 163 ;
Lagrange, 154 f. See also the articles
on ' Oil ' in EB, col. 3470; DCG, ii.
264 f. ; DAC, ii. 107 f. ; Windisch,
Handbuch z. NT, Der Jakobusbrief,
33. For the connexion with the later ecclesiastical rite of extreme unction v.
Swete,119; Lagrange, 155. From the
change of tense in ἤλειφον Swete infers
the incidental character of the healing
miracles during the Mission. ' The
preaching is regarded as a whole, the
miracles are mentioned as occurring
from time to time during the course of
the preaching.' On the question of
exorcisms v. the notes on i. 23-8 and
v. 1-20.

ἵνα μετανοῶσιν is the sole reference
to the preaching. The connexion of
the verb with the preaching of the
Kingdom in i. 15 suggests that the
disciples proclaimed the speedy approach of the New Age. Cf. Lk. ix. 2,
κηρύσσειν τὴν βασιλείαν τοῦ θεοῦ, Mt.
x. 7, πορευόμενοι δὲ κηρύσσετε λέγοντες
ὅτι ἤγγικεν ἡ βασιλεία τῶν οὐρανῶν,
Lk. x. 9, ἤγγικεν ἐφ' ὑμᾶς ἡ βασιλεία
τοῦ θεοῦ, 11, ἤγγικεν ἡ βασιλεία τοῦ θεοῦ·
Cf. Mt. x. 23, ἕως ἔλθῃ ὁ υἱὸς τοῦ
ἀνθρώπου.

IV

Mk. vi. 14-viii. 26   THE MINISTRY
BEYOND GALILEE

A new division begins at vi. 14. Instead of a summary passage like
i. 14 f. and iii. 7-12, Mark relates the stories of Herod's Fears (vi. 14-16)
and the Death of John the Baptist (vi. 17-29) to form a kind of interlude
prefacing a section in which Jesus is almost continually outside Galilee,
apart from vi. 53-6 and viii. 11-13. In it there is no public teaching with
the exception of the topical section vii. 1-23. For the most part Jesus is
in retirement, especially during His sojourn in the borders of Tyre (vii.
24-30) and in Decapolis (vii. 31-7), and His attention is given mainly to
His disciples and to the people who respond to His teaching (vi. 30-44).
Works of healing have a secondary place in the record and they are
wrought in privacy and almost against His intention (cf. vii. 24-30, 31-7,
viii. 22-6). The further limit of the division appears to be viii. 26, for
in viii. 27 a new stage is reached at Caesarea Philippi. The contents of
the division are as follows : (a) The stories connected with Herod Antipas
(vi. 14-29), (b) The Feeding of the Five Thousand and its sequel (vi. 30-
vii. 37), (c) The Feeding of the Four Thousand and its sequel (viii. 1-26).

(a) Mk. vi. 14-29   AN INTERLUDE

This brief section fills in the gap between the Mission of the Twelve
(vi. 6b-13) and the Return of the Disciples (vi. 30-4) which leads on to the
story of the Feeding of the Five Thousand (vi. 35-44) and its sequel (vi.
45-vii. 37). Where Jesus was in the interval and what He was doing we
do not know. Apparently Mark was without information and he has
made no attempt to reconstruct the course of the ministry of Jesus at this
point. All that he does is to record a story which reveals the popular
opinions concerning Him and the views of Herod Antipas. The opinion
of the tetrarch that His ministry was a renewal of the work of the Baptist
leads the Evangelist to record a popular story about the death of John,
an event which apparently had happened some time previously.

The section includes :

(38) vi. 14-16. Herod's Fears.
(39) vi. 17-29. The Death of John the Baptist.

Mk. vi. 14-16   38. HEROD'S FEARS   Cf. Mt. xiv. 1 f.
Lk. ix. 7-9

Like vi. 6b-13, the narrative is composed by the Evangelist on the
basis of popular tradition. By some (e.g. Goguel, 354 f.) it is held that
the narrative is a softened form of an original story in which Herod's
attitude was more menacing. In fact, this was doubtless the attitude of
Herod, as Lk. xiii. 31 shows. The same explanation may also cover the
Markan account of the subsequent course of events, in which in the main
(but cf. vi. 53, viii. 10) Jesus avoids Galilee, travelling in the region of
Tyre (vii. 24), in Decapolis (vii. 31), in the dominions of Herod Philip

(viii. 27), hurrying through Galilee (ix. 30), and journeying to Jerusalem by a route east of the Jordan (x. 1). Cf. Burkitt, 89-101. But to say that vi. 14-16 is not in its original form is pure conjecture. Mark himself does not represent the movements of Jesus as a flight from Herod, and Lk. xiii. 31 shows that His attitude to Herod's threats was one of great courage. Other motives can be inferred from Mk, the desire for rest for Himself and the Twelve (vi. 30-4), and perhaps also the necessity of facing in solitude the problems raised by the probability of suffering and death. It is sounder to infer that vi. 14-16 does less than justice to Herod's hostility than conjecturally to reconstruct the narrative.

14 Καὶ ἤκουσεν ὁ βασιλεὺς Ἡρῴδης, φανερὸν γὰρ ἐγένετο τὸ ὄνομα αὐτοῦ, καὶ ⌐ἔλεγον⌐ ὅτι Ἰωάνης ὁ βαπτίζων ἐγήγερται ἐκ

14 ἔλεγεν

14. Ἡρῴδης, vi. 16 f., 18, 20 f., 22, viii. 15*, was the son of Herod the Great and Malthace, and received at his father's death the tetrarchy of Galilee and Peraea. His ambition to be king led to his banishment in A.D. 39 under Caligula. Both Matthew and Luke correctly call him ὁ τετραάρχης (Mt. xiv. 9 has ὁ βασιλεύς). Mark's use of ὁ βασιλεύς in this story and the next (vi. 22, 25 f., 27) is sometimes cited as an error (Bacon, 72), but the usage may reflect local custom; cf. Swete, 120; Lagrange, 155; Rawlinson, 79; Gould, 108; Goguel, 350; etc. For the form Ἡρῴδης v. Moulton, ii. 84.

What was it that Herod heard? The fact that 14-16 is concerned with Jesus alone shows that the Mission of the Twelve is not in question; it is the ministry and mighty works of Jesus throughout Galilee. Mt. xiv. 1 adds τὴν ἀκοὴν Ἰησοῦ, and Lk. ix. 7 τὰ γινόμενα πάντα. Matthew also dates the incident as happening ἐν ἐκείνῳ τῷ καιρῷ. There is, however, a gap between 13 and 14, and it is impossible to say when the incident happened.

φανερὸν γὰρ ἐγένετο τὸ ὄνομα αὐτοῦ is a parenthesis. The ' name ' is the personality of Jesus revealed in word and deed. Goguel, 351 n., suggests that the clause is an awkward attempt to conceal the absence of a complement which is indispensable. ' The original narrative must have reported what Herod had heard which decided him

to take measures against Jesus ', op. cit. 355. Against this suggestion is the fact that not infrequently in Mk explanatory comments, introduced·by γάρ (cf. i. 22, ii. 15, iii. 10, 22, v. 8, 28, vi. 17 f., 20, vii. 3, xi. 13, xvi. 8), are added by the Evangelist and are a feature of his style. Further, references to the ' name ' (ὄνομα) of Jesus appear in ix. 37 f., 39, 41, xiii. 6, 13, xvi. [17]*. At the same time Goguel is right in maintaining that the opposition of Herod was of much greater moment than Mark would lead us to suppose, although it is he who mentions the Herodians (iii. 6, xii. 13) and ' the leaven of Herod ' (viii. 15). For φανερός v. iii. 12.

The reading ἔλεγον (B D (ἐλόγοσαν) W 6 271 a b ff vg (2 MSS.) Aug), ' people were saying ', on disait, is probably correct against the singular ἔλεγεν read by most MSS. Cf. Wellhausen, 46; Klostermann, 67; Lagrange, 155; Swete, 120; Rawlinson, 79; Turner, 31 f.; Field, 28; Lohmeyer, 115 n. The plur. corresponds with ἄλλοι . . . ἄλλοι in 15, and Herod's opinion is given in 16. The sing. is probably a scribal conformation to ἤκουσεν. The καί before ἔλεγον may be used in the sense of ὅτι. Cf. Lohmeyer, 115 n.

Ἰωάνης ὁ βαπτίζων, v. i. 4 and pp. 157 f. ἐγείρειν is used here and in vi. 16, xii. 26, xiv. 28, xvi. 6, [14] of rising from the dead. With no perceptible difference of meaning ἀναστῆναι is em-

νεκρῶν, καὶ διὰ τοῦτο ἐνεργοῦσιν αἱ δυνάμεις ἐν αὐτῷ· ἄλλοι δὲ 15
ἔλεγον ὅτι ᾿Ηλείας ἐστίν· ἄλλοι δὲ ἔλεγον ὅτι προφήτης ὡς εἷς
τῶν προφητῶν. ἀκούσας δὲ ὁ ῾Ηρῴδης ἔλεγεν ῝Ον ἐγὼ ἀπεκε- 16
φάλισα ᾿Ιωάνην, οὗτος ἠγέρθη.

ployed in viii. 31, ix. 9 f., 31, x. 34, xii. 23, 25, xvi. [9]. Cf. Howard, *FG*, 257. The perfect describes the abiding fact in contrast with the act itself indicated in 16 by ἠγέρθη. ἐκ νεκρῶν, ix. 9 f., xii. 25, xvi. [14]*, is regularly used without the article.

The popular opinions which identified Jesus with the Baptist *redivivus* or with Elijah *redivivus*, or which compared Him with one of the prophets, are mentioned again in viii. 28, but in each case the reports are germane to the story. Peculiar to the present narrative is the inference καὶ διὰ τοῦτο ἐνεργοῦσιν αἱ δυνάμεις ἐν αὐτῷ, ' That's the reason why supernatural powers are at work in him '. Here αἱ δυνάμεις is used, not of miracles as in vi. 2, but more generally of miraculous powers as in 1 Cor. xii. 10, 28 f., Gal. iii. 5 (*v.* Lightfoot, *Gal.* 136). ἐνεργοῦσιν* is used intransitively and means ' are operative ', ' at work ', as in Gal. ii. 8, Eph. ii. 2, and Phil. ii. 13. For the trans. use, ' work ', ' effect ', *v.* 1 Cor. xii. 6, 11, Gal. iii. 5, Eph. i. 11, 20, and for the passive *v.* 2 Cor. i. 6, Eph. iii. 20, Col. i. 29. See the important Note of J. A. Robinson, *Eph.* 241-7, also *VGT*, 214. Lohmeyer, 116, agrees with Torrey, 81, 293, 299, in the rendering ' these wonders ', and in inferring that the Aramaic had the passive ' are wrought '.

The idea that, as risen from the dead, the Baptist is invested with new powers, is not inconsistent with the fact that in his lifetime he wrought no miracles (Jn. x. 41). Goguel, 352, thinks the statement is secondary, since no Jewish or pagan writer attests the belief that one who has been restored to life possesses supernatural powers, and he suggests that its origins should be sought in the cycle of beliefs

connected with the Resurrection of Jesus. Nevertheless, as Goguel admits, the idea is fairly easy to understand, and can have existed as a popular explanation of a unique phenomenon.

Matthew repeats the explanatory passage, confining his account to the inference regarding the Baptist which he ascribes directly to Herod himself, and replacing ὁ βαπτίζων by ὁ βαπτιστής. Luke omits διὰ τοῦτο, etc., and says that Herod was ' quite at a loss ' (διηπόρει) because of the popular rumours (διὰ τὸ λέγεσθαι ὑπό τινων . . . ὑπό τινων δέ . . . ἄλλων δέ . . .). His Greek ' is an elegant paraphrase of Mk ' (Creed, 127).

15 f. For the belief in the return of Elijah see Mal. iii. 1, iv. 5, and the notes on Mk. i. 6, ix. 9-13. In the latter passage Jesus identifies the Baptist with Elijah. How far these views were ' realistic ' it is difficult to say, but it is reasonably clear that by Herod himself the identification with John was interpreted symbolically (*v.* 16). The phrase προφήτης ὡς εἷς τῶν προφητῶν (Wellhausen, 46, *schwerlich griechisch*) means ' a prophet like one of the (old) prophets ' (cf. Judg. xvi. 7, 11, καὶ ἔσομαι ὡς εἷς τῶν ἀνθρώπων).[1] Luke interprets it to mean one of the ancient prophets restored to life : προφήτης τις τῶν ἀρχαίων ἀνέστη (ix. 8). When Herod hears of these reports, he fixes on the first, but his words probably mean ' It is John the Baptist all over aₕain '. Cf. Wellhausen, 46 ; Creed, 127 ; Rawlinson, 79. His attitude is hostile. ἀποκεφαλίζω, vi. 28*, Mt. xiv. 10, Lk. ix. 9**, =ἀπο(κόπτειν) τὴν κεφαλήν (*v.* ii. 288, 291) : Arrian, *Epict.* i. 1. 24 ; LXX. 16 is an example of the *casus pendens* with the resumptive pronoun ; cf. vii. 20, xiii. 11, *v.* Intr. 58. Luke

---

[1] Pallis, 18 f., conjectures προφήτης εἷς, ' a unique prophet '.

alters his source into a statement and question : 'Ιωάνην ἐγὼ ἀπεκεφάλισα· τίς δέ ἐστιν οὗτος περὶ οὗ ἀκούω τοιαῦτα ; (ix. 9), and adds καὶ ἐζήτει ἰδεῖν αὐτόν.

Goguel, 355, conjectures that the original Lukan statement was that Herod wanted to put Jesus to death (cf. Lk. xiii. 31). Cf. Wellhausen, 48.

Mk. vi. 17-29   39. THE DEATH OF THE   Cf. Mt. xiv. 3-12
                         BAPTIST   (Lk. iii. 19 f.)

This narrative stands apart from other narratives in Mk as being the only one which is not in some sense or other a story about Jesus. The most varied opinions have been held regarding its historical character. In a phrase often quoted, H. J. Holtzmann, 77, calls it the typical example of a legend (das Muster einer Legende). If this term is used in its true sense, of things told (legenda) about a great man, without prejudice to the historical basis of the story, there would be much to be said for its use. Unfortunately, most critics mean by this label an unhistorical tale, the product of religious fancy and imagination. Cf. Bultmann, 328 f., who treats it in an appendix, and thinks that Mark probably derived it from Hellenistic-Jewish tradition. Bacon, BGS, 72, speaks of it as ' in the highest degree inaccurate and legendary '. J. Weiss, 201-4, is inclined to attribute it to a later redactor, and is unwilling to trace it to a Petrine source.

The narrative has precisely the same colourful character as other Markan stories, notably that of the Gerasene Demoniac, and particularly in vi. 20, it reveals acute psychological insight into the character of Herod Antipas. Especially lifelike is the remorse of the king when he finds himself trapped by his drunken folly and the bond of his oaths.

The difficulties of the story are raised by the statements of Josephus and the public dancing of Salome. Against Josephus, Mark speaks of the first husband of Herodias as Philip, actually the husband of Salome ; he appears to locate the court scene at Tiberias, whereas Josephus says that John was imprisoned in the fortress of Machaerus ; and, if αὐτοῦ in vi. 22 is original, he describes the girl as the daughter of Antipas and names her Herodias. Further, he differs from Josephus in tracing the death of John to the implacable hostility of Herodias, whereas Josephus represents it as due to political motives. ' Herod, who feared lest the great influence John had over the people might put it into his power and inclination to raise a rebellion (for they seemed ready to do anything he should advise), thought it best, by putting him to death, to prevent any mischief he might cause, and not bring himself into difficulties, by sparing a man who might make him repent of it when it should be too late ' (Whiston). δείσας 'Ηρῴδης τὸ ἐπὶ τοσόνδε πιθανὸν αὐτοῦ τοῖς ἀνθρώποις μὴ ἐπὶ ἀποστάσει τινὶ φέροι (πάντα γὰρ ἐῴκεσαν συμβουλῇ τῇ ἐκείνου πράξοντες), πολὺ κρεῖττον ἡγεῖται, πρίν τι νεώτερον ἐξ αὐτοῦ γενέσθαι, προλαβὼν ἀνελεῖν τοῦ μεταβολῆς γενομένης εἰς πράγματα ἐμπεσὼν μετανοεῖν, Ant. xviii. 5. 2. Moreover, OT motifs are present reminiscent of the stories of Jezebel and of Esther.

This is a formidable case ; but much of it falls away when it is submitted to a cool appraisal. It is improbable that αὐτοῦ is original in 22 and that Mark thought that the girl was the daughter of Antipas and bore the same name as her mother. Mark is mistaken if he identified the first husband of Herodias with Philip the tetrarch, but no one can call the error serious, and, in a family in which the same names are used repeatedly, it has yet to be proved that the wronged husband resident at Rome was not called Philip. Equally unimportant is it if Mark places the court scene at Tiberias, but he does not actually name the place, and excellent commentators have not thought it impossible to locate the incident in the palace of Machaerus. Opinions on the solo dance will necessarily differ, but the explanation given by Rawlinson and Branscomb (*v.* the note on vi. 22a) is credible, while assertions about the advanced age of Salome have the slenderest foundation. The stronger point is the conflict in the representations of the cause of John's murder, but political ends and the anger of an insulted woman cannot be regarded as mutually exclusive; both accounts may be true. Rawlinson's judicial statement is cogent: ' Josephus's version will give facts as they presented themselves to an historian who wrote sixty years later, and who was concerned to trace the political causes of a war. The story in Mk will be an account, written with a certain amount of literary freedom, of what was being darkly whispered in the bazaars or market-places of Palestine at the time . . .', *op. cit.* 82. Cf. Branscomb, 108 f. Literary freedom will cover the traits which recall the stories of Jezebel and Esther, while creation on the basis of these stories is exposed to formidable difficulties. When to the considerations already outlined we add the fidelity of Mark's narrative to the shrewd but vacillating character of Herod, ' that fox ' (Lk. xiii. 31), and to the bold and outspoken John, there cannot be much doubt where judgment should fall. Whence Mark derived the story it is impossible to say. No adequate reasons can be given for regarding it as a later addition, for it is used by Matthew, and Bussmann's view, 30-4, that Luke's copy of Mk lacked the story, is inadequately based on his claim that Luke has no fear of doublets. The presence of many unusual words is accounted for by the subject-matter, and signs of the Markan style are not wanting.[1]

Αὐτὸς γὰρ ὁ Ἡρώδης ἀποστείλας ἐκράτησεν τὸν Ἰωάνην 17 καὶ ἔδησεν αὐτὸν ἐν φυλακῇ διὰ Ἡρῳδιάδα τὴν γυναῖκα Φιλίππου

17. Αὐτός is often connected with ἐγώ in 16 and translated ' himself ' (cf. Swete, 122; Plummer, 163); but the pronoun is unemphatic and redundant and should be left untranslated (RSV). Wellhausen, 46, thinks the usage is Aramaic and cites vi. 22, αὐτῆς τῆς Ἡρῳδιάδος (A C), and vi. 18, αὐτὴν γυναῖκα τοῦ ἀδελφοῦ σου (D). For the use of the proleptic pronoun in Aramaic anticipating a following noun *v.* Black, 70 f. See also Howard, ii. 431; Lagrange, xcv. Against Wellhausen, Lagrange says the usage

is perfectly Gk; cf. αὐτὸς ὁ βασιλεύς, ' the king himself ', or the use of ὁ αὐτός in the papyri with the meaning ' the aforesaid ' (*VGT*, 94). It seems more probable, however, that the pronoun is proleptic: literally, ' For he Herod '. *V.* Intr. 59 f.

The aorists of 17-19 are virtually pluperfects (cf. RV, RSV, Moffatt). The reference is to a point earlier than 14-16 and subsequent to i. 14. For ἀποστέλλω *v.* i. 2; κρατέω i. 31; δέω iii. 27. φυλακή, vi. 28, ' a prison ' (vi. 48, ' a watch ')*. According to

[1] Lohmeyer, 118, notes, in addition to the unusual words, the absence of the historical present, the numerous aorists and the imperfects, the temporal distinctions, the free use of participles and of the gen. abs., and claims that, in spite of its popular character, the narrative has a cultivated style through which an Aramaic basis can be traced. If this description is warranted, it may be inferred that Mark is using a source.

18 τοῦ ἀδελφοῦ αὐτοῦ, ὅτι αὐτὴν ἐγάμησεν· ἔλεγεν γὰρ ὁ Ἰωάνης
τῷ Ἡρῴδῃ ὅτι Οὐκ ἔξεστίν σοι ἔχειν τὴν γυναῖκα τοῦ ἀδελφοῦ
19 σου. ἡ δὲ Ἡρῳδιὰς ἐνεῖχεν αὐτῷ καὶ ἤθελεν αὐτὸν ἀποκτεῖναι,

Josephus, *Ant.* xviii. 5. 2, John was imprisoned and executed in the fortress of Machaerus, situated at the NE corner of the Dead Sea near the wilderness of Judaea. Mark's account appears to assume that the place of execution was Herod's court at Tiberias. Herodias (Ἡρῳδιάς, vi. 19, 22*, Mt. xiv. 3, 6, Lk. iii. 19**) was the daughter of Aristobulus, the son of Herod the Great and Mariamne, and therefore the niece of Antipas. The statement that she was the wife of Philip, the brother of Antipas, is apparently an error, if Mark means Philip the tetrarch who married Salome the daughter of Herodias (22). Josephus says that Herodias was married to Herod, the son of Herod the Great and Mariamne (II), the daughter of Simon the high priest, *Ant.* xviii. 5. 4. The view that this Herod also bore the name of Philip is not impossible (cf. Lagrange, 158), but it is not attested and looks like an attempt to reconcile the statements in Mk and Josephus. ' It is simplest to suppose that Mark or his informant confused Herodias's husband and son-in-law ', Turner, 32. γαμέω, x. 11 f., xii. 25*. The name ' Philip ' is omitted in Mt. xiv. 3 by D a c d ff k vg Aug, and it is wanting in Lk. iii. 19. It is also omitted in Mk by P⁴⁵ and 47. The omission may be a scribal correction, but it is also possible that the presence of the name is a scribal corruption. The classical distinction between γαμέω (of the husband) and γαμέομαι (of the wife) tended to fall into disuse in Hellenistic Gk (cf. Mk. x. 12, 1 Cor. vii. 28, 34). Cf. *VGT*, 121, however, where it is pointed out that it survives in the legal language of marriage-contracts. Josephus, *Ant.* xviii. 5. 1, relates that the wife of Antipas, learning of his intentions, withdrew to Machaerus, and from thence escaped to the protection of her father Aretas,

the king of Arabia, who waged war on Antipas and defeated his army (A.D. 36), an event which some interpreted as a punishment from God for the murder of the Baptist.

Matthew follows Mk closely, adding καὶ ἀπέθετο to ἔδησεν (xiv. 3). Luke says summarily (iii. 18-20) that Herod, being reproved by John for Herodias, his brother's wife, and all the evil things he had done ' added this to them all, that he shut up John in prison '.

18. Again, as in 14, 20, etc., Mark adds an explanatory note. ἔλεγεν appears to be used in the sense ' had said '. See the aorists in 17. Like Elijah of old (1 Kgs. xvii. f., 2 Kgs. i. 15), John may have made the accusation directly, but it is also possible that the words put in the second person were reported to Herod. For ἔξεστιν c. dat. and infin. *v.* ii. 24. The law in question is that of Lev. xviii. 16, xx. 21. Matthew abbreviates his source : οὐκ ἔξεστίν σοι ἔχειν αὐτήν (xiv. 4). D reads αὐτὴν γυναῖκα τοῦ ἀδελφοῦ σου. Here, as in 17, αὐτήν may represent the Aramaic proleptic pronoun which emphasizes the following noun. Cf. Black, 72 ; Howard, ii. 431. See also αὐτῆς in 22 (A C).

19. Like Jezebel (1 Kgs. xxi), Herodias is incensed against John and seeks an opportunity to destroy him. ἐνέχω*, Lk. xi. 53, Gal. v. 1, 2 Thess. i. 4 (?)**, ' to hold in '; Cl., LXX, Pap. Here, however, the meaning is ' to have a grudge against ' (Moffatt; Field, 28 f.; Sahidic, ' was angry with '; RSV). In this respect the RV rendering ' set herself against him ' is inferior to the AV, ' had a quarrel against him ', and still more to the AVᵐᵍ, ' an inward grudge '. Field observes that there is no example of this use of the word in classical writers, except Herodotus with the addition of χόλον. The ellipsis, he suggests, was forgotten, like that of

καὶ οὐκ ἠδύνατο· ὁ γὰρ Ἡρῴδης ἐφοβεῖτο τὸν Ἰωάνην, εἰδὼς 20
αὐτὸν ἄνδρα δίκαιον καὶ ἅγιον, καὶ συνετήρει αὐτόν, καὶ ἀκούσας
αὐτοῦ πολλὰ ἠπόρει, καὶ ἡδέως αὐτοῦ ἤκουεν.   Καὶ γενομένης 21

νοῦν after ἐπέχω (' to fix attention on ';
cf. Lk. xiv. 7, Ac. iii. 5), and compares
Gen. xlix. 23, καὶ ἐνεῖχον αὐτῷ (Joseph)
κύριοι τοξευμάτων. Cf. Lk. xi. 53, δεινῶς
ἐνέχειν, which the Sahidic renders ' to
provoke him '.   See further, Lagrange,
158 f.; VGT, 214. Creed, 169, cites
Herodotus i. 118, vi. 119, viii. 27, and
Swete, 123, mentions Plummer's suggestion, JTS, i. 619, ' to have it in
with (or ' for ') a man '. As in the use
of ἐνεῖχον, the durative force of ἤθελεν
and ἠδύνατο is manifest.

20. The verse explains why Herodias could not accomplish her design.
Herod feared, or (better) ' stood in awe
of ' (Moffatt), John, knowing that he
was a righteous and holy man, and
' protected ' (συνετήρει) him (against
Herodias; so Bengel).   Here alone
Mark has οἶδα c. acc. and infin. (c. ὅτι
and indic. in ii. 10, x. 42, xii. 14, 28)
and ἅγιος (i. 8) to describe a man. For
δίκαιος v. ii. 17*. συντηρέω*, Mt. ix.
17, Lk. ii. 19**, in later Gk., LXX,
Pap. ' to preserve ', ' keep safely ',
is the ' perfective ' of τηρέω (cf.
Moulton, i. 113, 116) and is used with
the idea of protecting (' kept him safe ',
RV, RSV, vg custodiebat) rather than
of observing (AV, but mg ' kept him '
or ' saved him '). Cf. Swete, 124;
Turner, 32; Lagrange, 159; etc.

Mark adds that, when he heard
him, Herod was much perplexed, but
(nevertheless) heard him gladly.   For
πολλά adverbial v. i. 45. ἀπορέω*,
Lk. xxiv. 4, Jn. xiii. 22, Ac. xxv. 20,
2 Cor. iv. 8, Gal. iv. 20**, ' to be at
a loss ', ' puzzled '. In Cl. Gk and
elsewhere in the NT the verb is used
in the mid., but in the act. in Wisd.
xi. 5, 17 (cf. διηπόρει, Lk. ix. 7) and
in the papyri (VGT, 67), and Plummer,
165, cites examples in Cl. Gk. Herod's
attitude is finely described by Swete,
123 : ' Herod was awed by the purity
of John's character, feared him as the
bad fear the good ', and cites Bengel,

venerabilem facit sanctitas . . . argu-
mentum verae religionis timor ma-
lorum. There is no contradiction in
the contrast, ' And (yet) he was glad
to hear him '. ἡδέως, xii. 37*, 2 Cor.
xi. 19, superl. 2 Cor. xii. 9, 15**,
' gladly '; Cl., LXX, Pap. As Bruce,
381, points out, the description corresponds exactly to the character of the
man, ' a δίψυχος ἀνήρ—drawn two
ways, by respect for goodness on the
one hand, by evil passions on the
other '.

A textual question, difficult to decide,
is raised by ἠπόρει (ℵ B L Θ W
(ἠπορεῖτο) bo), for ἐποίει is very widely
attested (A C D et pler. minusc. omn.
vers. pler.). Field, 29 f., who favours
this reading, takes it to mean that,
as opposed to unconditional surrender,
there was some concession which
Herod was unwilling to make, and
suggests that ἠπόρει is a correction
influenced by Lk. ix. 7 (διηπόρει). Cf.
also Burkitt, Texts and Studies, v. 5,
p. xix; Nestle, Textual Criticism of
the Gk Test. 264; Lohmeyer, 119 n.
Some scholars suggest that ἐποίει is
a too literal version or a misrendering
of a Semitic original. Cf. Wellhausen,
Einl.² 21. In his commentary, 46,
he accepts the usual reading, but
observes that ἐποίει is gut semitisch.
Torrey, TG, 155, modifies a conjecture
in FG, 299, and infers that a defective
Aramaic original has been slavishly
followed, the correct rendering being
' And he kept (in memory) many
things which he had heard from him '.
See the comment of Howard, ii. 446.
Of the two readings ἠπόρει should
probably be preferred. The strong
support of ℵ B L bo is now increased
by Θ and W, and πολλά, read as adverbial (' greatly '), is a feature of
Mark's style (v. i. 45). Moreover, the
psychological description of Herod's
attitude leaves a strong impression of
originality, which is weakened, prob-

ἡμέρας εὐκαίρου ὅτε Ἡρῴδης τοῖς γενεσίοις αὐτοῦ δεῖπνον
ἐποίησεν τοῖς μεγιστᾶσιν αὐτοῦ καὶ τοῖς χιλιάρχοις καὶ τοῖς
22 πρώτοις τῆς Γαλιλαίας, καὶ εἰσελθούσης τῆς θυγατρὸς αὐτῆς

ably through misunderstanding, by early scribes in ἐποίει. Cf. Swete, 124; Gould, 113; Lagrange, 159, who says that with ἐποίει what follows is *absolument banal*; Allen, 97; Plummer, 165; Bartlet, 195; Turner, 32.

The Matthaean parallel (xiv. 5), with its suggestion that Herod feared the people, has been attributed to a different source, but, although another view is taken, there is no necessary contradiction; cf. Smith, 143.

21-2a. The first gen. abs. is temporal and is further defined by ὅτε . . . δεῖπνον ἐποίησεν. The second, εἰσελθούσης τῆς θυγατρός, is circumstantial, and, as elsewhere in Mk (cf. v. 2), is used loosely, since the person mentioned is the subject of ἤρεσεν. εὔκαιρος*, Heb. iv. 16**, ' opportune ', ' timely ', ' suitable '; Cl., LXX, Pap. Pallis, 21, suggests the meaning ' empty ', that is, a day without work, a festal day, and *VGT*, 262, says that the rendering is supported from Byzantine (Sophocles *Lex.*) and modern Greek. Against this suggestion is the fact that the festal character of the day is indicated later by τοῖς γενεσίοις αὐτοῦ, and the meaning ' opportune ' is to be preferred. Cf. Lohmeyer, 119 n.

δεῖπνον, xii. 39*, ' a dinner ', is in later Gk an afternoon meal or supper; cf. *VGT*, 139; Deissmann, 225. In Cl. Gk τὰ γενέσια is a day kept in memory of the birthday of the dead, but it is used in Plato, *Leg.* 784 D, and in later Gk as the equivalent of τὰ γενέθλια, ' a birthday feast '; v. LS, i. 343; *VGT*, 123. The view that it was the anniversary of Herod's accession lacks adequate support; cf. McNeile, 209; Lagrange, 160. The guests included the king's friends, the chief military officials, and the leading men of Galilee.

μεγιστᾶν*, Apoc. vi. 15, xviii. 23**, ' a great one ', ' a courtier ', is a late Gk word, found generally in the plur.

in the later books of the LXX (Dan. v. 23) and in the papyri (*VGT*, 393). χιλίαρχος*, Jn. xviii. 12, Ac (17), Apoc. vi. 15, xix. 18**, ' a chiliarch ', the commander of a thousand men, corresponding to the Roman *tribunus militum*; more generally, as here, a high ranking military officer; Herodotus, *et al.* -χης, LXX, Pap. and inscr. (*VGT*, 688; *DCG*, i. 271). οἱ πρῶτοι τῆς Γαλιλαίας, ' the leading men of Galilee ' (RSV), ' the notables of G.' (Moffatt), ' *l'aristocratie du pays* ' (Lagrange); cf. Lk. xix. 47, Ac. xiii. 50, xxv. 2, xxviii. 7. While the presence of these guests at Machaerus is not impossible, they are more naturally associated with the court at Tiberias.

Salome married Philip the tetrarch (*ob.* A.D. 34) and later Aristobulus, to whom she bore three children; cf. Josephus, *Ant.* xviii. 5. 4. She is not likely, therefore, to have been more than about twenty years of age in A.D. 28-9. Cf. Rawlinson, 81. The reference to her in Mk raises difficult textual and historical questions. According to the WH text (αὐτοῦ) she is described as the daughter of Antipas and is named Herodias. This statement is obviously incorrect. Many MSS., however, read αὐτῆς and others omit the pronoun.

(1) αὐτοῦ, ℵ B D L Δ 238 565. This reading is attested by few but very important MSS. In fact, the girl was Herod's grand-niece (cf. Justin, *Dial.* 49), not his daughter, and her name was Salome (v. *supra*). In itself, this is not an insuperable objection, since Mark might have been misinformed about the complicated relationships of Herod's family (cf. Turner, 32), but the reading is out of harmony with the narrative, which does not suggest that the illicit union had been of long duration. Few commentators accept the WH reading, although it might be held to explain the origin of αὐτῆς.

Ἡρωδιάδος καὶ ὀρχησαμένης, ἤρεσεν τῷ Ἡρῴδη καὶ τοῖς συν-
ανακειμένοις. ὁ δὲ βασιλεὺς εἶπεν τῷ κορασίῳ Αἴτησόν με
ὃ ἐὰν θέλῃς, καὶ δώσω σοι· καὶ ὤμοσεν πολλὰ αὐτῇ ⌜"Ὅτι⌝ 23
⌜ἐάν με⌝ αἰτήσῃς δώσω σοι ἕως ἡμίσους τῆς βασιλείας μου. καὶ 24

23 ὅτι °Ο | ἐάν

(2) αὐτῆς (τῆς), A C W Θ et pler.
fam. 13 28 33 157 543 579 700 892 1071
al. pler. a d ff i l q r¹·² vg syʰˡ. Most
commentators accept αὐτῆς in the sense
of ' the daughter of Herodias herself '.
So Gould, 113; Swete, 125; Lagrange, 160; Plummer, 155, 166;
Bartlet, 195; and RV. For ' the said
Herodias ' (AV) the article would be
necessary before αὐτῆς. Black, 72, suggests that the pronoun may be proleptic; v. the note on 18.

(3) Om. fam. 1 22 131 b c f aur sysᵖᵉ
sa bo geo aeth arm. The omission is
accepted by Klostermann, 68; Blunt,
182; Moffatt, Torrey, and RSV. Cf.
Mt. xiv. 6. In agreement with Allen,
98, and Burney, 85 f., Torrey, 299,
thinks that this was the reading of the
original Aramaic, which was mechani-
cally rendered ' the daughter of her,
Herodias '. See Black's suggestion
above. On the whole, a too literal
rendering of Aramaic seems the best
explanation of the textual problem.

The greater difficulty is the improbability that a Herodian princess should
have danced before the court of
Antipas. J. Weiss, 203, says that the
dance before strange men is an impossibility. Merx, ii. 1, 228, declares
that it can be believed by those only
who have not seen an oriental solo
dance. Windisch, ZNT, xviii. 73 ff.,
has cited heathen parallels, but Bultmann, 329 n., rejects their force. So
Klostermann, 69 f. The difficulty is
real, and Bacon, BGS, 74 f., presses
it to the full when he says that the
kind of public dancing at a banquet
here meant, by a member of Herod's
family, ' would be the last thing to
" please the king " '. This claim,
however, is not conclusive. ' It (the
dance of Salome) is nevertheless not
wholly incredible, however outrageous,

to those who know anything of the
morals of Oriental courts, or of Herod's
family in particular ', Rawlinson, 82.
Cf. Branscomb, 109, to the same effect.
ὀρχέομαι*, Mt. xi. 17, xiv. 6, Lk. vii.
32**; Cl., LXX, Pap. (ὀρχηστής).
ἀρέσκω*.

Matthew abbreviates his source : γενεσίοις δὲ γενομένοις τοῦ Ἡρῴδου ὠρχή-
σατο ἡ θυγάτηρ τῆς Ἡρωδιάδος ἐν τῷ
μέσῳ καὶ ἤρεσεν τῷ Ἡρῴδη (xiv. 6).
22b-3. For κοράσιον v. v. 41. αἰτέω
(9 times). For the stronger mid. v.
vi. 24 f., x. 38, xi. 24, xv. 8, 43*, and
for relative + ἐάν v. vi. 23 (?), vii. 11,
viii. 35, 38, x. 35, xiii. 11*. The king's
words recall Esth. v. 3 f., καὶ εἶπεν ὁ
βασιλεύς Τί θέλεις, Ἐσθήρ; . . . ἕως τοῦ
ἡμίσους τῆς βασιλείας μου, καὶ ἔσται σοι,
and may be influenced by this story.
It is true that the offer of half one has
is a familiar expression (cf. 3 Kgdms.
xiii. 8, Lk. xix. 8), but there is also a
parallel to the statement that the girl
pleased the king in Esth. ii. 9, ἤρεσεν
αὐτῷ τὸ κοράσιον. There can be little
doubt, therefore, that the story of
Esther has exercised a formative influence on the present narrative, but
it does not follow that the latter is
purely legendary. The well-known
remark of Holtzmann, 78, that Antipas
had no kingdom to dispose of, treats
the king's offer (les propos d'un prince
échauffé probablement par le vin et la
luxure, Lagrange, 161) much too
seriously.

ὄμνυμι, xiv. 71*. πολλά, attested by
D Θ P⁴⁵ 565 700 a b ff i q vg (3 MSS.)
arm, is characteristic of Mark's usage
and should probably be read. ἥμισυς*
(Cl. gen. ἡμίσεος), Lk. xix. 8, Apoc.
xi. 9, 11, xii. 14**. For the Hellenistic
forms of ἥμισυς, normal in the NT
and the papyri (VGT, 280), v. Moulton,
ii. 10, 161, 176 f. After ὅτι B Δ P⁴⁵ 118

ἐξελθοῦσα εἶπεν τῇ μητρὶ αὐτῆς Τί αἰτήσωμαι; ἡ δὲ εἶπεν
25 Τὴν κεφαλὴν Ἰωάνου τοῦ βαπτίζοντος. καὶ εἰσελθοῦσα εὐθὺς
μετὰ σπουδῆς πρὸς τὸν βασιλέα ᾐτήσατο λέγουσα Θέλω ἵνα
ἐξαυτῆς δῷς μοι ἐπὶ πίνακι τὴν κεφαλὴν Ἰωάνου τοῦ βαπτιστοῦ.
26 καὶ περίλυπος γενόμενος ὁ βασιλεὺς διὰ τοὺς ὅρκους καὶ τοὺς
27 ἀνακειμένους οὐκ ἠθέλησεν ἀθετῆσαι αὐτήν· καὶ εὐθὺς ἀποστείλας

124 435 omit ὅ (so WH). Matthew
omits vi. 22b and summarizes 23.

24 f. In the question τί αἰτήσωμαι ;
the subj. is deliberative, 'What am
I to ask?'. An inferior reading gives
the future (v. Legg). The change
from the act. in 22 f. to the mid. in
24 f. is intentional and indicates the
urgency of the request. Moulton, i.
160 f., recalls the comment of Blass,
186 n., that ' the daughter of Herodias,
after the king's declaration, stands in
a kind of business relation to him'.
The answer of Herodias, ' The head of
John the Baptist', is so promptly given
as to suggest calculation. αἴτησε (sic)
is added by W and sa, and (apparently)
αἰτήσαι by P⁴⁵. For Ἰωάνου τοῦ βαπτίζοντος v. i. 4. A C D W al. pler.,
minusc. plur. it vg have βαπτιστοῦ
(cf. 25).

The girl at once (εὐθύς) returns to
the king and ' with haste ' (μετὰ
σπουδῆς*). Cf. Lk. i. 39. Lagrange,
161, translates the phrase by avec
empressement, ' eagerly ', since the
idea of speed is already expressed by
εὐθύς (cf. VGT, 585), and he adds that
she speaks with some impertinence due
to the knowledge that she has given
pleasure rather than to her hatred
of John. ' Give me right away ', she
says, ' the head of John the Baptist on
a dish.' (Cf. Moffatt : ' I want you
to give me this very moment . . .'.)
θέλω ἵνα c. subj. is here used in a quasi-
imperatival sense, as in x. 35, and
without ἵνα in x. 36, 51, xiv. 12, xv. 9*.
ἐξαυτῆς*, Ac. x. 33, xi. 11, xxii. 32,
xxiii. 30, Phil. ii. 23**,=ἐξ αὐτῆς τῆς
ὥρας, ' at once ', ' here and now ';
late Gk, Pap. (VGT, 222). πίναξ,
vi. 28*, Mt. xiv. 8, 11, Lk. xi. 39**,
was originally ' a board ' or ' plank ',

anything flat like a tablet or disc, and
later ' a dish ' (VGT, 513). Wellhausen, 46, thinks the phrase strange
here, while in place in vi. 28, but Rawlinson, 83, observes that apparently
the girl adds this gruesome witticism
of her own initiative. Cf. Lagrange,
162. βαπτιστής, viii. 28*, a late non-
classical word, found in Jos. Ant.
xviii. 5. 2, but not illustrated in VGT;
it is regularly used of John in Mt (7)
and in Lk (3)**.

Matthew's modifications of Mk are
verbal and interpretative. Thus, he
has δός μοι, φησίν, ὧδε and he describes
the girl as ' instructed ' (προβιβασθεῖσα)
by her mother (xiv. 8).

26-8. The grief of the king is in harmony with his attitude to John (vi.
20). περίλυπος, xiv. 34*, Mt. xx. 38,
Lk. xviii. 23**, ' very sad ', ' deeply
grieved '; Cl., LXX. Matthew's
parallel phrase, καὶ λυπηθείς (xiv. 9),
is of interest as indicating his dependence on Mk, particularly in view of
xiv. 5. In διὰ τοὺς ὅρκους* the plur.
suggests repeated oaths. ἀνάκειμαι,
xiv. 18, xvi. [14]*; in Cl. Gk ' to be
laid up ', but in later Gk (VGT, 34)
' to recline at table ', accumbere.
ἀθετέω c. acc. of the thing (vii. 9*) is
' to reject ', but here the meaning
seems to be ' to disappoint ' (cf.
Moffatt; RSV, ' he did not want to
break his word to her '). Field, 30,
cites Psa. xiv. (xv.) 4, ὁ ὀμνύων τῷ
πλησίον αὐτοῦ, καὶ οὐκ ἀθετῶν, and
refers to the Prayer-book translation,
' He that sweareth unto his neighbour,
and disappointeth him not '.

In 27 καὶ εὐθύς might mean ' And
so ' (v. i. 10), but ' immediately ' is
not impossible. ἀποστέλλω, v. i. 2.
σπεκουλάτωρ**=the Latin speculator,

ὁ βασιλεὺς σπεκουλάτορα ἐπέταξεν ἐνέγκαι τὴν κεφαλὴν αὐτοῦ.
καὶ ἀπελθὼν ἀπεκεφάλισεν αὐτὸν ἐν τῇ φυλακῇ καὶ ἤνεγκεν τὴν 28
κεφαλὴν αὐτοῦ ἐπὶ πίνακι καὶ ἔδωκεν αὐτὴν τῷ κορασίῳ, καὶ τὸ
κοράσιον ἔδωκεν αὐτὴν τῇ μητρὶ αὐτῆς. καὶ ἀκούσαντες οἱ 29
μαθηταὶ αὐτοῦ ἦλθαν καὶ ἦραν τὸ πτῶμα αὐτοῦ καὶ ἔθηκαν αὐτὸ
ἐν μνημείῳ.

'a scout', a military officer responsible for the look-out and the carrying of dispatches, and, arising out of this meaning, 'an executioner'. See Swete, 127; *VGT*, 582. For ἐπιτάσσω *v. i.* 27; ἀποκεφαλίζω vi. 16; φυλακή vi. 17. The implication of the narrative is that the order is executed on the spot. Apparently, the event took place at Machaerus. It is doubtful if this is intended by Mark (*v.* the note on 21), but both Swete, 124, 128, and Lagrange, 160, 164, incline to think Machaerus is meant, and point out that, according to Josephus, *BJ*, vii. 6. 2, Herod the Great had built a splendid palace there. For ἐνέγκαι (‎א B C Δ 892 sype hl sa bo) ἐνεχθῆναι is read by A D L W Θ *al. pler.* minusc. *pler.* it vg sys. Lagrange, 162, thinks the pass. has no *raison d'être* since the one who does the action is designated (ctr. *v.* 43). Cf. Blass, 230.

For πίναξ *v.* vi. 25; κοράσιον v. 41. The simplicity of the Markan style is especially notable in 28. Matthew follows his source closely, but replaces 27a by ἐκέλευσεν δοθῆναι, 'commanded it to be given', and uses passive verbs (ἠνέχθη, ἐδόθη) in the sequel (xiv. 9-

11). His use of ὁ βασιλεύς in 9 (cf. ὁ τετραάρχης in xiv. 1) betrays dependence on Mk. Altogether his account is secondary, Mark's phrase οὐκ ἠθέλησεν ἀθετῆσαι αὐτήν and his reference to the σπεκουλάτωρ being lost through abbreviation.

29. For the reference to the disciples of John *v.* ii. 18*. πτῶμα, xv. 45*, literally 'fall' (πίπτω), is the fallen body, 'the corpse', as always in the NT (LXX, Judg. xiv. 8; cf. *VGT*, 558). μνημεῖον, v. 2. Presumably the body was interred near Machaerus. For later traditions *v.* Swete, 128. Matthew, ἔθαψαν αὐτόν, adds that they went and told Jesus (xiv. 12), and that it was when He heard this that He withdrew to a lonely place apart. Thus, contrary to Mk, Matthew represents the death of John as having taken place immediately before His withdrawal and as constituting the motive for it. This link is artificial and is due to a misreading of Mk, but Matthew may have been following a tradition which associated the departure of Jesus with the hostility of Antipas. Cf. McNeile, 213; Smith, 143.

(*b*) Mk. vi. 30- THE FEEDING OF THE FIVE
vii. 37 THOUSAND AND ITS SEQUEL

For the groups in this section, vi. 30-56, vii. 1-23, and 24-37 *v.* Intr. 95-7. The first and last groups have a strong narrative interest and are closely articulated; the second is topical and consists of teaching. The section includes:

(40) vi. 30-4. The Return of the Disciples.
(41) vi. 35-44. The Feeding of the Five Thousand.
(42) vi. 45-52. The Crossing of the Lake.
(43) vi. 53-6. The Landing at Gennesaret.
(44) vii. 1-8. The Question of the Washing of Hands.

(45) vii. 9-13. The Question of Qorban.
(46) vii. 14-23. Sayings on Defilement.
(47) vii. 24-30. The Syro-Phoenician Woman.
(48) vii. 31-7. The Cure of the Deaf Mute.

For the relation of the section to the events described in viii. 1-26 *v.* Note C, pp. 628-32. See also L. H. Jenkins, *Studies in History and Religion* (ed. E. A. Payne, 1942), 87-111.

Mk. vi. 30-4   40. THE RETURN OF THE   Cf. Mt. xiv. 13 f.
                DISCIPLES AND THE   Lk. ix. 10 f.
                DEPARTURE TO A LONELY PLACE

The story is either part of the Feeding of the Five Thousand or an independent narrative introducing that narrative. On the whole the latter appears to be the case. The narrative is constructed by Mark as a prelude to the account of the breaking of bread in the wilderness. So far most commentators are agreed, and the only question at issue is whether the narrative is purely redactional. Wellhausen, 47 f., speaks of it as *eine redaktionelle Verknüpfungsarbeit*, and his view is accepted by many commentators. In order to effect the transition, it is said, the Apostles must be brought back and conveyed across the lake. For the Feeding-story the crowd is indispensable. So the people go round the lake and arrive at the unknown destination on foot, but more quickly than Jesus who makes the direct journey by boat. This representation, it is held, is artificial and the later Evangelists rightly attached no value to it. Cf. Bultmann, 259, 365 ; Branscomb, 112, who describes it as ' stage scenery ' ; Klostermann, 71.

Wellhausen's explanation is open to grave objection. Mark is not the kind of writer who invents details for literary ends. He may use ' traditional formulae ' in describing the people coming and going and the disciples without leisure even to eat (cf. iii. 20), but his narrative is everywhere credible. In particular, his portraiture of Jesus beholding the people as sheep without a shepherd is drawn from life. Doubtless, this opinion is also an impression, but it does greater justice to Mark's account than a hypothesis which moves the actors across the stage 'like puppets to provide a *mise en scène* for the story which follows.

30   Καὶ συνάγονται οἱ ἀπόστολοι πρὸς τὸν Ἰησοῦν, καὶ ἀπήγ-

30. This verse is transitional. It connects the stories in vi. 35-56 with the account of the Mission of the Twelve. The vocabulary suggests that it is a Markan construction, since all the words, except οἱ ἀπόστολοι, are common elsewhere in the Gospel: συνάγω ii. 2, ἀπαγγέλλω v. 14, ὅσα with ποιέω iii. 8, διδάσκω i. 21. The description of the report given by the Twelve has the vagueness which characterizes Mark's account of the Mission; he merely relates that the missionaries reported to Jesus all that they had done and taught. For the conjunction of ποιέω and διδάσκω *v.* Ac. i. 1. Since the death of John lies in the past, Mark has no connecting link with vi. 17-29, differing in this respect from Matthew who attributes the tidings of the murder to the disciples of John and says that when Jesus heard of it He withdrew to a desert place apart. Luke makes the con-nexion with the Mission explicit; cf. ὑποστρέψαντες and διηγήσαντο (ix. 10).

γειλον αὐτῷ πάντα ὅσα ἐποίησαν καὶ ὅσα ἐδίδαξαν. καὶ λέγει 31
αὐτοῖς Δεῦτε ὑμεῖς αὐτοὶ κατ' ἰδίαν εἰς ἔρημον τόπον καὶ ἀνα-
παύσασθε ὀλίγον. ἦσαν γὰρ οἱ ἐρχόμενοι καὶ οἱ ὑπάγοντες
πολλοί, καὶ οὐδὲ φαγεῖν εὐκαίρουν. καὶ ἀπῆλθον ⌜ἐν τῷ πλοίῳ 32

ἀπόστολος (? iii. 14)*, Mt. x. 2 (τῶν δὲ δώδεκα ἀποστόλων), Lk (6), Ac (28), Pl (29), Past. Epp. (5), Rest (8)**. In Mk the name is not an official title as in the Acts and the Pauline Epistles. It appears to mean ' the missionaries '; cf. Rawlinson, 83. Apparently Mark uses the name because he has just used οἱ μαθηταί of the disciples of John (vi. 29). He does not use it again of the disciples of Jesus, but continues to employ οἱ μαθηταί and οἱ δώδεκα. This usage illustrates the primitive character of Mk, for at the time when the Gospel was written οἱ ἀπόστολοι was in common use. Mk. vi. 30, however, is of great importance since it indicates the ideas which came to be associated with the title. Thus, it describes the disciples as commissioned and empowered by Jesus for the work of preaching and exorcism. These characteristics belong to the later use of οἱ ἀπόστολοι and are connected with the idea that in their missionary work the Apostles represent Jesus Himself (Mt. x. 40) and later are witnesses of the Resurrection. See further, Note B, pp. 619-27.

The textual tradition shows how early the want of connexion with vi. 29 was observed. A W and many uncials and minuscules insert καί between πάντα and ὅσα, thus introducing a reference to the death of John.

31 f. After the transitional passage in 30 the section begins with a summons to the disciples to seek rest in a lonely wilderness place. Except for ἀνα-παύομαι and εὐκαιρέω, all the words and phrases are familiar Markan expressions. For δεῦτε v. i. 17; κατ' ἰδίαν iv. 34; εἰς ἔρημον τόπον i. 35; ὀλίγον i. 19 (of space); ἦσαν γάρ i. 22; ὑπάγω i. 44; and for the statement that they had no leisure to eat cf. iii. 20. With the familiar ἐν τῷ πλοίῳ, 32 re-

peats the ideas of 31 in the third person. Cf. also iv. 35 f. The presumption is that Mark is writing freely. ἀναπαύο-μαι, xiv. 41*, ' to take rest ', ' enjoy leisure ', is rarely used in this sense in Cl. Gk, but is freely found in the papyri as ' a technical term of agriculture ' (VGT, 36) and with reference to death. εὐκαιρέω*, Ac. xvii. 21, 1 Cor. xvi. 12**, ' to have leisure ' or ' opportunity '; late Gk (Polybius), Pap., but not in LXX.

The suggestion (Schmidt, 187) of a suture between 31 and 32 because ἀπῆλθον refers to the disciples, rather than to Jesus and His disciples, is a refinement, for it is not unnatural that after the command in 31 Mark should have the disciples in mind. ὑμεῖς αὐτοί is ' ye yourselves ' or ' by yourselves ', not ' ye also '.

The position of the wilderness-place is identified by most commentators with the north-east side of the lake (J. Weiss, 205; Wellhausen, 47; Klostermann, 71). The north-west, north or even south of Tiberias are not excluded, and Schmidt, 187 f., advocates these possibilities because the people arrive first at the place of landing and because of the difficulty of the crossing of the Jordan. Dalman, SSW, 161, thinks this difficulty is not insuperable. ' On October 10, 1921, I saw that it was almost possible to cross over the Jordan dry-shod, just where it enters the lake. An absolutely dry bar lay before the mouth.' He suggests (p. 173) the lonely neighbourhood between Wady es-Samak and Wady-en-Nkeb. Certainty is not attainable, but since Jesus desired a particularly remote region, this suggestion is sound, especially if an unfavourable wind delayed the boat. Cf. Rawlinson, 86; Swete, 129; Lagrange, 166. Luke has εἰς πόλιν

33 εἰς ἔρημον τόπον⁷ κατ' ἰδίαν. καὶ εἶδαν αὐτοὺς ὑπάγοντας καὶ
⌜ἐπέγνωσαν⌝ πολλοί, καὶ πεζῇ ἀπὸ πασῶν τῶν πόλεων συνέδραμον
34 ἐκεῖ καὶ προῆλθον αὐτούς. Καὶ ἐξελθὼν εἶδεν πολὺν ὄχλον, καὶ
ἐσπλαγχνίσθη ἐπ' αὐτοὺς ὅτι ἦσαν ὡς πρόβατα μὴ ἔχοντα ποιμένα, καὶ ἤρξατο διδάσκειν αὐτοὺς πολλά.

32 εἰς ἔρημον τόπον τῷ πλοίῳ (Ti.)   33 ἔγνωσαν

καλουμένην Βηθσαιδά (ix. 10). Both later
Evangelists greatly abbreviate the Markan account, omitting the reference to
the many who were coming and going.
33. Probably εἶδαν is impersonal
(Turner, *JTS*, xxv. 381; Lagrange,
166), πολλοί being the subject of
ἔγνωσαν. Instead of ἔγνωσαν (B* D
fam. 1), ἐπέγνωσαν is read by all other
uncials and minuscules, and, as by
Nestle, it should probably be accepted.
The meaning is that people saw them
going and many recognized them.
Converging from many places, they
ran together and outwent them.
πεζῇ*, Mt. xiv. 13**, ' on foot ', but
more commonly ' by land ' (sc. ὁδῷ);
Cl., LXX (2 Kgdms. xv. 17, *v.l.* πεζοί),
Pap. Mark's loose use of πόλις is
seen in πασῶν τῶν πόλεων. συντρέχω*,
Ac. iii. 11, 1 Pet. iv. 4**, ' to run together ' (cf. ἐπισυντρέχω, ix. 25); Cl.,
LXX, Pap. προέρχομαι, xiv. 35*, ' to
go forward ', ' precede ', or, as here,
' go in advance ' (=φθάνω); Cl., LXX,
Pap. D (28) 565 (700) read καὶ
συνῆλθον αὐτοῦ (αὐτῷ 28 700). Mk.
vi. 33 is the first of the instances discussed by WH in which the *TR* is
a conflation (καὶ προῆλθον αὐτοὺς καὶ
συνῆλθον πρὸς αὐτόν) of the β and δ
texts. Cf. Hort, 95 ff.
    The vivid description, peculiar to
Mk, of the converging groups from
the lakeside towns who arrive in advance is characteristic of the Gospel.
By omitting these details Matthew and
Luke were compelled to make a
general reference to the multitudes
who followed Jesus, and it is not surprising that they agree in reading
οἱ ὄχλοι and ἠκολούθησαν αὐτῷ (Mt.
xiv. 13, Lk. ix. 11). Cf. Streeter, 314.
Luke also has γνόντες and Matthew
ἀκούσαντες and πεζοί. In Mk οἱ ὄχλοι

is read by W fam. 13 349 sa, probably
by assimilation to Mt or Lk. With the
possible exception of x. 1 Mark always
has ὄχλος in the singular (37 times).
    34. By Wellhausen, Klostermann,
and others this verse is taken as the
beginning of the story of the Feeding
of the Five Thousand, while Lagrange
sees the beginning of this story at 30
and Rawlinson at 33. The connexion
between 33 and 34 is close, so that if
30-4 is not regarded as a separate
narrative, it is better to take 30-44 as
a single unit. On this point see
further, 35.
    ἐξελθών: from the boat rather than
(with Hort, 99) from retirement. For
σπλαγχνίζομαι *v.* i. 41; πρόβατον, xiv.
27*; ποιμήν, xiv. 27*; ἤρξατο c. infin.
i. 45; διδάσκω i. 21. πολλά is not included by Hawkins (*HS²*, 35) in his
list of adverbial uses of the word, but
there is good reason to interpret it
adverbially; cf. Moffatt, ' at length ';
Lagrange, 167, *longuement* or even
avec chaleur. These renderings agree
with the references to the late hour
(35) and compassion (34).
    The words ὡς πρόβατα μὴ ἔχοντα
ποιμένα are strongly reminiscent of the
LXX: Numb. xxvii. 17, ὡσεὶ πρόβατα
οἷς οὐκ ἔστι ποιμήν, 3 Kgdms. xxii. 17,
ἑώρακα τὸν πάντα Ἰσραὴλ διεσπαρμένους
ἐν τοῖς ὄρεσιν ὡς ποίμνιον, ᾧ οὐκ ἔστι
ποιμήν, Ezek. xxxiv. 5, καὶ διεσπάρη τὰ
πρόβατά μου διὰ τὸ μὴ εἶναι ποιμένας,
2 Chron. xviii. 16, Judith xi. 19. Cf.
also 2 Baruch lxxvii. 16 (Charles,
ii. 521). The picture called to mind
is one of surpassing tenderness and
beauty. Neither Matthew nor Luke
retains the passage, but Matthew has
a parallel in another context (ix. 36).
Both speak of healing (Mt. xiv. 14,
Lk. ix. 11). Cf. Streeter, 314.

Mk. vi. 35-44   41. THE FEEDING OF THE   Cf. Mt. xiv. 15-21
                          FIVE THOUSAND   Lk. ix. 12-17

Bultmann, 231 f., 251, classifies the narrative as a Miracle-story. In view of its colour and broader treatment Dibelius, 71, includes it among his *Novellen* or Tales. It seems reasonably clear that the story was prized in the primitive community because it related one of the greatest of the mighty works of Jesus and for its symbolic relevance to the Eucharist. But, like many Markan narratives, it has not yet attained the rounded form of a Miracle-story proper and stands nearer the testimony of eye-witnesses. Mark knows the circumstances in which the event happened (cf. 30-4) and is able to tell the story with the detail furnished by a living tradition. To this conclusion we are pointed by the dialogue between Jesus and His disciples, the boldness of the querulous question, ' Are we to go and buy two hundred pennyworth of bread and give to them to eat ? ' (37), and the picturesque description of the people arranged in companies and in ranks upon the green grass (39 f.). The account of the blessing and the distribution of the loaves is modelled on that of the Last Supper (xiv. 22) and points to a custom of which the Supper was the last and crowning example. We are justified in classifying the story as Petrine, provided we do not mean a story narrated by him exactly as it now stands in Mk. The signs that it has been the subject of reflection, and its symbolism appreciated, are too clear to be denied, and still more evident is this if in the development of the tradition a secondary interpretation has been imposed on the narrative.

Whether the original incident was non-miraculous will be variously estimated. This question is not foreclosed by the primitive character of the narrative, nor by the fact that the story is told in all four Gospels and that of the Four Thousand in two, for if a miraculous interpretation has been superimposed, it happened before Mk was written. Nor again is the question decided by the enthusiasm implied in vi. 45 and described in Jn. vi. 15. The considerations which suggest that the incident was non-miraculous are : the absence of surprise at the multiplication of the loaves and fishes on the part of the disciples and the people ; the enhancement of the miraculous element in the later versions of the story ; the difficulty of accepting the view that Jesus was conscious of possessing creative power over natural processes and exercised them in the circumstances described, when we appreciate the degree to which His life was subjected to human limitations.

The view that the incident was an idyllic expression of good comradeship is too facile to account for the narrative and its preservation. The same also must be said of mythical explanations, although the influence of 2 Kgs. iv. 42-4 in vi. 43 is not improbable. Much the best hypothesis is that of Schweitzer, coupled with the suggestion of Wellhausen that the numbers are exaggerated. That Jesus should have anticipated the Messianic Feast is in harmony with His teaching concerning the Kingdom of God and with Jewish customs. As suggested in the Commentary (*v.* vi. 41), ' eschatological sacraments ' may well have preceded the Last Supper. If this view is accepted, the multiplication of bread is a materialization of the original tradition at a time when the true nature of the event had not unnaturally become obscure. For further discussion of the narrative from various standpoints see Lagrange, 170 f. ; McNeile, 215-17 ; Creed, 127 f. ; Luce, 181 ; Schweitzer, 374-8 ; Goguel, 365-77 ; Lohmeyer, 128-30.

35 Καὶ ἤδη ὥρας πολλῆς ⌜γενομένης⌝ προσελθόντες αὐτῷ οἱ μαθηταὶ αὐτοῦ ἔλεγον ὅτι Ἔρημός ἐστιν ὁ τόπος, καὶ ἤδη ὥρα 36 πολλή· ἀπόλυσον αὐτούς, ἵνα ἀπελθόντες εἰς τοὺς κύκλῳ ἀγροὺς 37 καὶ κώμας ἀγοράσωσιν ἑαυτοῖς τί φάγωσιν. ὁ δὲ ἀποκριθεὶς εἶπεν αὐτοῖς Δότε αὐτοῖς ὑμεῖς φαγεῖν. καὶ λέγουσιν αὐτῷ Ἀπελθόντες ἀγοράσωμεν δηναρίων διακοσίων ἄρτους καὶ δώ- 38 σωμεν αὐτοῖς φαγεῖν; ὁ δὲ λέγει αὐτοῖς Πόσους ἔχετε ἄρτους;

35 γινομένης

35 f. If the story circulated as a separate unit, it cannot have begun so abruptly, nor is this difficulty greatly eased if, with Schmidt and Bultmann, we find the beginning in 34. It is better to conclude either that the story began with 31 or that Mark has interwoven its beginning with 30-4. Bultmann, 259, suggests that a statement like v. 21b, καὶ [. . .] συνήχθη ὄχλος πολὺς ἐπ' αὐτόν, must have introduced the story.
For ἤδη v. iv. 37. The reference to the late hour, probably late afternoon, has been retained because it is essential to the story. For ὥρας πολλῆς Lagrange, 167, cites Polybius v. 8. 3 and Josephus, Ant. viii. 4. 4 (cf. Swete, 131), and observes that if the phase is a Latinism, it is not peculiar to Mk. Mt. xiv. 15 has ὀψίας δὲ γενομένης and Lk. ix. 12 ἡ δὲ ἡμέρα ἤρξατο κλίνειν. For further Markan references to ' the hour ' v. xi. 11, xiii. 11, 32, xiv. 35, 37, 41, xv. 25, 33 f.*. The gen. abs. is used correctly. ℵ and D read γινομένης. For οἱ μαθηταὶ αὐτοῦ v. ii. 15 ; ἔρημος i. 3 ; προσέρχομαι i. 31.
ἀπολύω is here used in the sense of 'dismiss ' (cf. Field, 9 f., on Mt. xiii. 36), as in vi. 45, viii. 3, 9. In x. 2, 4, 11 f. it is used of putting away or divorcing a wife (in x. 12 a husband), and in xv. 6, 9, 11, 15 with the meaning ' to release '. The imperative is retained by Matthew and Luke, who have also ἵνα ἀπελθόντες (Lk. πορευθέντες) c. subj. For ἀγοράσωσιν (Mk,

Mt) Luke has καταλύσωσιν καὶ εὕρωσιν ἐπισιτισμόν (ix. 12). Cf. Mt. xiv. 15, βρώματα. Both Evangelists took offence at Mark's τί φάγωσιν, in which τί is used in an indirect question. Cf. WM, 210. The subj. is used because the deliberative subj. is implied in the direct question. For κύκλῳ v. iii. 34. D has ἔγγιστα, cf. proximas it vg. For κώμη v. vi. 6 ; ἀγροί v. 14. Contrast πόλεων in vi. 33.
37 f. For the construction ὁ δὲ ἀποκριθεὶς εἶπεν v. Intr. 63. In δότε αὐτοῖς ὑμεῖς φαγεῖν the pronoun ὑμεῖς is emphatic. Matthew prefaces the command with οὐ χρείαν ἔχουσιν ἀπελθεῖν (xiv. 16). In the disciples' reply ἀγοράσωμεν is deliberative and δηναρίων διακοσίων gen. of price. δηνάριον, xii. 15, xiv. 5*, = the Lat. denarius, roughly the equivalent of the reading δραχμή, and worth in pre-War values about 9½d. Cf. Mt. xx. 2, Lk. x. 35. Although δώσομεν is attested by B L A Δ P45 65 569 it vg Aug, the reading δώσωμεν, ℵ D N fam. 13 33 543 565 892 et al. (δῶμεν, W Θ al. pler. fam. 1 28 579 700 1071 al. pler.) is probably correct, for a change to the simple fut. after the deliberative subj. would be improbable. But see Robertson, 876, 934 ; Couchoud, JTS, xxxv. 7. For the confusion between ω and o v. Moulton, ii. 73-5 ; Robertson, 200 f. πόσος, viii. 5, 19 f., ix. 21, xv. 4*.
ἵνα ἕκαστος (+αὐτῶν, W) βραχύ τι λάβῃ, read by (W) fam. 13 543 sa, and perhaps by P45 (ut vid. propter

ὑπάγετε ἴδετε. καὶ γνόντες λέγουσιν Πέντε, καὶ δύο ἰχθύας.
καὶ ἐπέταξεν αὐτοῖς ἀνακλῖναι πάντας συμπόσια συμπόσια ἐπὶ 39
τῷ χλωρῷ χόρτῳ. καὶ ἀνέπεσαν πρασιαὶ πρασιαὶ κατὰ ἑκατὸν 40

39 ἀνακλιθῆναι

spatium), is an addition from Jn. vi. 7. Couchoud, *op. cit.* 7, accepts the reading.

The tone of astonishment, amounting to reproof, in the question ' Are we to go and buy . . . and give . . . ? ', is characteristic of the boldness of Mark's narrative. Matthew has the sober statement, οὐκ ἔχομεν ὧδε εἰ μὴ πέντε ἄρτους καὶ δύο ἰχθύας (xiv. 17), and Luke smoothes away the roughness of the original in the qualifying observation, εἰ μήτι πορευθέντες ἡμεῖς ἀγοράσωμεν εἰς πάντα τὸν λαὸν τοῦτον βρώματα (ix. 13). In Jn the question Πόθεν ἀγοράσωμεν ἄρτους ἵνα φάγωσιν οὗτοι; is put by Jesus Himself, and the Evangelist's explanation, τοῦτο δὲ ἔλεγεν πειράζων αὐτόν, αὐτὸς γὰρ ᾔδει τί ἔμελλεν ποιεῖν, follows together with the answer of Philip, διακοσίων δηναρίων ἄρτοι οὐκ ἀρκοῦσιν αὐτοῖς ἵνα ἕκαστος βραχὺ λάβῃ (vi. 5-7). In this version the Markan realism disappears.

The asyndetic construction in Πόσους ἔχετε ἄρτους; ὑπάγετε ἴδετε is a common feature of Mark's style; cf. Lagrange, lxx-lxxii; Intr. 49 f., 58. Cf. i. 41, iv. 40, v. 36, viii. 17, ix. 19, x. 14, etc. The two imperatives have a very decisive tone. For ὑπάγω *v.* i. 44. ἰχθύς, vi. 41 (*bis*), 43*.

39 f. These unusually vivid verses describe the people arranged in groups of fifty and a hundred on the green grass, resembling garden beds in their bright colours. For ἐπιτάσσω *v.* i. 27. ἀνακλίνω*, Mt. viii. 11, xiv. 19, Lk. ii. 7, xii. 37, xiii. 29**, ' to lean upon ', ' make to recline ', pass. ' to recline ' ; Cl., LXX. *VGT*, 34, observes that the NT writers use this verb instead of the classical παρα- and κατα-κλίνεσθαι, in a way which suggests the usage of common speech, although the editors are unable to illustrate it. Instead of the pass. (א B* G Θ fam. 1 fam. 13 565

700 1071 *et al.*) the act. ἀνακλῖναι is read by A B² D L W Δ *al. pler.* P⁴⁵ 33 579 892 *al. pler.* Or, and should probably be read with WHmg, the pass. being an assimilation to Mt (Lagrange, 168).

For the use of συμπόσια συμπόσια and πρασιαὶ πρασιαί in a distributive sense (= ἀνά or κατὰ συμπόσια) see the note on in vi. 7. *VGT*, 598, says that the construction ' can no longer be regarded as Hebraistic '. Cf. Pallis, 22. It is certainly not exclusively Semitic, but it corresponds to Semitic usage, and should probably be so regarded here. *V.* Intr. 60 f.; Meecham, 85. συμπόσιον**, ' a drinking-party ', ' a company of guests ' ; Cl., LXX, Pap. The sense of the repetition is ' in companies '. χλωρός*. Many commentators suggest that the reference to the green grass points to the springtime, and thus to the Passover season; cf. Gould, 118; Swete, 133; Lagrange, 169; Plummer, 173; Allen, 100; Turner, 19; Bartlet, 200. The inference, while probable, is not certain since green grass might be found in sheltered places and near streams as late as July. Cf. Schmidt, 191. Dalman, *SSW*, 174 f., describes the grass, not as a grass-plot, but as the exuberant wild growth of herbs which, in the spring and throughout most of the rainy season, cover the uncultivated ground in the district about the lake and even in the mountains.

ἀναπίπτω, viii. 6*, Mt. xv. 35, Lk (4), Jn (5)**, ' to fall back ', in late Gk ' to recline at table ' (*VGT*, 37). πρασιά**, ' a garden plot ' ; Cl., LXX (Sir. xxiv. 31*), Pap. Here the meaning is ' in ranks '. *VGT*, 533, says the reference is to regularity of arrangement rather than to variety of colouring. For a Rabbinic explanation *v.*

41 καὶ κατὰ πεντήκοντα. καὶ λαβὼν τοὺς πέντε ἄρτους καὶ τοὺς δύο ἰχθύας ἀναβλέψας εἰς τὸν οὐρανὸν εὐλόγησεν καὶ κατέκλασεν τοὺς ἄρτους καὶ ἐδίδου τοῖς μαθηταῖς αὐτοῦ ἵνα παρατιθῶσιν 42 αὐτοῖς, καὶ τοὺς δύο ἰχθύας ἐμέρισεν πᾶσιν. καὶ ἔφαγον πάντες

Exp. VIII. vii. 89 f. Moffatt, ' in groups '; so RSV. In κατὰ ἑκατὸν καὶ κατὰ πεντήκοντα the phrases are used distributively, ' by hundreds and fifties '. P45 omits the phrase.

Matthew and Luke omit these vivid details, although Luke mentions groups of fifties; cf. Mt. xiv. 19, Lk. ix. 14 f. Jn. vi. 10 mentions the command to make the men sit down and the presence of much grass in the place.

41 f. Jesus breaks the loaves after looking up into heaven, and gives them to His disciples to distribute to the people, and divides the two fishes for all. ἀναβλέπω, ' to look up ', vii. 34, viii. 24, xvi. 4 ; ' to receive sight ', x. 51 f.*. As used here, the word denotes the act of prayer (cf. vii. 34, also ἦρεν τοὺς ὀφθαλμούς, Jn. xi. 41). From this passage comes the practice in the Roman Canon before the act of consecration : *et elevatis oculis in coelum* (cf. Lagrange, 169). εὐλογέω, viii. 7, xi. 9 f., xiv. 22*, ' to speak well of ', ' praise ', ' bless ' (of God or men) ; Cl., LXX, Pap. The act is one of thanksgiving to God. Cf. the Jewish blessing : ' Blessed art thou, O Lord our God, King of the world, who bringest forth bread from the earth '. Cf. Dalman, *JJ*, 133-40. In xiv. 22 εὐλογέω is used as here, but in the parallel narrative in viii. 6 (and in xiv. 23) εὐχαριστέω is found, a usage which W. L. Knox, 3·5, claims as Hellenistic and as a sign that the present narrative is Semitic, while viii. 1-9 is the Hellenized version. κατακλάω*, Lk. ix. 16**, ' to break in pieces '; Cl., LXX ; *Aristeas* 149 (Meecham, 255). Cf. Mk. xiv. 22, ἔκλασεν. The change to the imperf. in ἐδίδου seems intentional, suggesting successive distributions of bread. To τοῖς μαθηταῖς, αὐτοῦ is added by A D N

W Θ *al. pler.* P45 fam. 1 fam. 13 22 28 157 543 565 700 1071 *al. pler.* it vg sys pe hl aeth, probably rightly. Normally Mark speaks of ' his disciples ', rarely of ' the disciples ' (viii. 1, ix. 14, x. 10, 13, 24, xiv. 16). Cf. Turner, 33. παρατίθημι, viii. 6 (*bis*), 7*, ' to set before '; Cl., LXX, Pap. For ἄρτος *v*. ii. 26 ; ἰχθύς vi. 38 ; οὐρανός i. 10 ; μαθητής ii. 15 ; μερίζω iii. 24. D reads ἵνα παραθῶσι κατέναντι αὐτῶν. Cf. Black, 85.

Of outstanding interest is the agreement of 41 with xiv. 22: λαβών . . . ἄρτους . . . εὐλόγησεν . . . (κατ)έκλασεν . . . ἐδίδου . . . (ἔφαγον πάντες, k in xiv. 22 ; cf. Turner, 68, *JTS*, xxix. 10). Mark has conformed the vocabulary of the passage to that of the Supper in the belief that in some sense the fellowship meal in the wilderness was an anticipation of the Eucharist. J. Weiss, 217 : *Die Speisungen sind Anticipationen des Herrenmahls.* In the same way he has understood the Baptism of Jesus and the Transfiguration as pointing forward. In none of these cases does it follow that the narrative is a purely imaginative creation ; on the contrary, it is probable that the concrete facts are seen in the light of history to have a richer meaning. Even the Supper itself points forward to the Messianic Feast on high (cf. xiv. 25). We have no reason to suppose that these beliefs are merely the ideas of the Evangelist; they represent the mind and purpose of Jesus Himself. The meal in the wilderness belongs to the same cycle as the Last Supper, with the important exception that, for intelligible reasons, it lacks a reference to the death of Jesus ; it is a foreshadowing of Messianic Feast, and thus, of the perfecting of the Kingdom. Cf. Schweitzer, 374 f. ; Cadoux, 58 ; McNeile, 216 ; Raw-

καὶ ἐχορτάσθησαν· καὶ ἦραν κλάσματα δώδεκα κοφίνων πληρώ- 43

linson, 106; Dodd, *Mysterium Christi*, 60, *Christian Worship*, 73; Goguel, 368 f.

χορτάζω, vii. 27, viii. 4, 8*, ' to feed ', ' fatten ', originally of animals, but in colloquial Gk (mid.) of men, ' to eat ', ' satisfy '; cf. *VGT*, 690; Kennedy, 82, who observes that in NT times all distinction between ἐσθίειν and χορτάζεσθαι has vanished. See the note on φιμόω, i. 25. As, however, 42 shows, the verb means the full satisfaction of physical appetite, ἔφαγον . . . ἐχορτάσθησαν. For ἐσθίω v. i. 6. This verse shows clearly that, in the tradition Mark followed, the incident was interpreted as a miracle, and as such it has been generally understood until modern times. Wellhausen's view, that the miracle disappears with the numbers which suffer changes in oral tradition, has steadily gained ground (cf. W. Sanday, *Bishop Gore's Challenge to Criticism*, 1914); but it is far from being universally held; cf. Lagrange, 170 f. A point of special interest, which it is difficult to assess, is the influence which may have been exerted on the narrative by the story of Elisha who through his servant fed a hundred men with twenty loaves of barley. Cf. καὶ ἔφαγον, καὶ κατέλιπον κατὰ τὸ ῥῆμα Κυρίου (4 Kgdms. iv. 44). Cf. J. Weiss, *Die Schr.*⁴ 131; Sanday, *op. cit.* 25; Smith, 144; Wood, 688. Older and more persistent are attempts to see in the story a guest meal in which Jesus and the disciples encouraged the crowd to share their provisions one with another. This was the view of the older rationalists, including Paulus, and in part Keim. It finds a classic statement in the picture drawn by Wellhausen, 50, of ' a beautiful evening in a lonely spot by the sea ', when Jesus provides for the bodily wants of the people, after ministering to their spiritual needs, ' convinced that the provisions which have been brought for himself and his disciples will

suffice also for the unbidden guests '. Cf. Bacon, *BGS*, 83; Branscomb, 115; Menzies, 143 f.; Bartlet, 203 f. Less naïve and much more attractive is the interpretation of Schweitzer, 374 : ' With the morsel of bread which He gives His disciples to distribute to the people He consecrates them as partakers in the coming Messianic feast, and gives them the guarantee that they, who had shared His table in the time of His obscurity, would also share it in the time of His glory '. The older commentators generally agreed in seeing in the incident a miracle of creation, and many modern scholars who take the narrative as it stands make similar claims (cf. Gould, 119; Temple, *Readings*, 75) and explain the action as one of benevolence (Lagrange, 171). The inadequacies of rationalistic explanations are stressed and the congruity of the story with a revelation which is supernatural through and through. Cf. Richardson, 94 f. Lohmeyer, 128-30, suggests that the wonder is apparent only to Jesus and His disciples [1] and that, like the stories in the Fourth Gospel, it reveals Jesus in His glory as the eschatological Son of Man.

43 f. Twelve baskets of fragments are gathered. κλάσμα, viii. 8, 19 f.*, (κλάω), ' a broken piece '; late Gk, LXX, cf. *VGT*, 345. The word is used in *Didache*, ix. 3 f. of the broken bread of the Agape and the Eucharist. κόφινος, viii. 19*, Mt. xiv. 20, xvi. 9, Lk. ix. 17, Jn. vi. 13**, a wicker-work basket, in which the Jews carried food. Cf. Juvenal iii. 14, *Judaeis quorum cophinus faenumque supellex*, vi. 542. In viii. 1-9, σφυρίς (v. viii. 8), a basket capable of carrying a man (Ac. ix. 25), is used. For πλήρωμα v. ii. 21. δώδεκα κοφίνων πληρώματα, ' twelve basketfuls ', is in apposition to κλάσματα. The idea is so awkwardly expressed that it is not surprising that the later Evangelists alter their source,

---

[1] *Es bleibt der Menge wie verborgen und nur die Jünger sehen, was hier geschieht, op. cit.* 129.

44 ματα καὶ ἀπὸ τῶν ἰχθύων. καὶ ἦσαν οἱ φαγόντες τοὺς ἄρτους πεντακισχίλιοι ἄνδρες.

in partial agreement with one another. Cf. Mt. xiv. 20, τὸ περισσεῦον τῶν κλασμάτων δώδεκα κοφίνους πλήρεις, Lk. ix. 17, τὸ περισσεῦον αὐτοῖς κλασμάτων, κόφινοι δώδεκα, Jn. vi. 13, καὶ ἐγέμισαν δώδεκα κοφίνους κλασμάτων. Cf. Stanton, ii. 213; Streeter, 315. ἀπὸ τῶν ἰχθύων, which Mt and Lk omit, is an inelegant pendant, which has almost the appearance of an afterthought. It is possible to see here an echo of the Semitic use of מן, but the grammarians remind us that in the Koine ἀπό and ἐκ c. gen. had largely replaced the partitive gen. Cf. Moulton, i. 72, 102, 245, Howard, ii. 433. It may none the less be Semitic, especially as κλάσματα δώδεκα κοφίνων πληρώματα suggests translation-Gk. The purpose of the passage is to confirm the wonder of the miraculous

feeding. Cf. Bultmann, 231 f.; Dibelius, 90. Lagrange, 170, sees in the gathering of the food that remains over the regard of the East for bread, and he thinks that the mention of the twelve baskets, corresponding to the twelve disciples, is natural enough. It is doubtful, however, if these observations adequately cover the details of the narrative, especially the fact that more food remains than was present at the beginning. A degree of schematization is present in the number 'twelve', as well as in the number 'five thousand'. πεντακισχιλίοι, viii. 19*. Both Mt and Lk take the figure as a round number (ὡσεί), and Mt adds χωρὶς γυναικῶν καὶ παιδίων (xiv. 21), thus revealing a tendency to increase the numbers. Cf. Jn. vi. 10, ὡς πεντακισχίλιοι.

Mk. vi. 45-52   42. THE CROSSING OF   Cf. Mt. xiv. 22-33
                        THE LAKE

Dibelius, 71, classifies this narrative among his *Novellen* and traces its origin to 'narrators' who sought to give it a picturesque setting, but it is better described as a Miracle-story (Bultmann, 231) which attained its present form under the influences of preaching and teaching. Whether it was current as an isolated unit is very doubtful, for it is closely connected with the Feeding of the Five Thousand in Mk and Jn. Some commentators trace the narrative to a vision of the Risen Christ, others describe it as a symbolical story (Bacon, *BGS*, 83) or 'a pious legend' (Branscomb, 117), while others again explain it as the account of a natural incident which has been given a miraculous interpretation.

The description of the hurried departure of the disciples under the constraint of Jesus, the reference to Bethsaida, the picture of the rowers buffeted by a contrary wind, and their cry ' It's a ghost ' as they see the phantom form, suggest that the narrative has a factual basis, and is not merely a product of fancy and imagination. It may well be true that homiletical and doctrinal motives have left their mark in such details as the picture of Christ walking on the waters, the sudden dropping of the wind when He enters the boat, and the blindness of heart of the disciples, and it is possible that the first narrators found in the narrative a symbolism which pointed to the death, resurrection, and parousia of Jesus; but the basic assumption of actual events remembered and interpreted is fully justified.

For the modern reader the point of difficulty is the walking on the water. A not negligible objection is the fact that it cannot be said that the intervention of Jesus meets a desperate need. The disciples are distressed by the wind, but they are not in jeopardy of their lives. Cf. Lagrange, 173, *il n'est point question d'une tempête*, and contrast iv. 37, καὶ τὰ κύματα ἐπέβαλλεν ἐπὶ τὸ πλοῖον, ὥστε ἤδη γεμίζεσθαι τὸ πλοῖον. Further, the circumstances described, the dark hours before dawn, the rough weather, the ghost-like form, their fear, are precisely those in which actual facts can have been misinterpreted. Again, mysterious as the words ' He would have passed them by ' undoubtedly are, they are difficult to reconcile with the purpose of rescue or a desire to test their faith. Most difficult of all is the objection that a docetic view of the person of Christ appears to be implied. Not without justice Dibelius, 94 f., 100, 277 f., describes the walking on the water as an epiphany of a divine wonderworker, and Lohmeyer, 135, as the picture of the Lord of death. One can hardly fail to observe a generic difference in the portrayal of Jesus as compared with the healing stories of i. 21-39. In these circumstances we must conclude that homiletical and doctrinal interests have left their mark upon an original tradition coloured from the first, in which the action of Jesus in wading through the surf near the hidden shore was interpreted as a triumphant progress across the waters. The later Gospels of Matthew and John show the further development of a process which has already begun in the Markan narrative and is based on the Petrine tradition that Jesus came to His own in the fourth watch of the night.

Καὶ εὐθὺς ἠνάγκασεν τοὺς μαθητὰς αὐτοῦ ἐμβῆναι εἰς τὸ 45
πλοῖον καὶ προάγειν εἰς Βηθσαϊδάν, ἕως αὐτὸς ἀπολύει τὸν

45 f. This passage is closely connected with the preceding story and it suggests that Mark found the two connected in the primitive tradition. Schmidt, 193, argues that the dismissal of the crowd, the constraint put upon the disciples and the reference to the Feeding of the Five Thousand in vi. 52, all point to the fact that the connexion of events already lay before the Evangelist.[1] ἀναγκάζω*, 'to compel ', ' constrain '; Cl., LXX, Pap. In this connexion the verb suggests the tension of Messianic excitement. Cf. Jn. vi. 15. For μαθητής *v.* ii. 15; ἐμβαίνω iv. 1; πλοῖον i. 19; εἰς τὸ πέραν iii. 8. προάγω, x. 32, xi. 9, xiv. 28, xvi. 7*, ' to lead forward ', but also intrans. ' to go before ', as here; Cl., LXX, Pap. (*VGT*, 537).
Βηθσαϊδά, viii. 22*, Mt. xi. 21, Lk. ix. 10, x. 13, Jn. i. 44, v. 2 (?), xii. 21 (τῆς Γαλιλαίας)**. Probably Bethsaida Julias at the mouth of the Jordan, rebuilt by Herod Philip and named

after Julia, the daughter of Augustus, is meant (Josephus, *Ant.* xviii. 2. 1). Since Mark uses εἰς τὸ πέραν, older scholars (Swete, 136, mentions Reland, Stanley, Tristram) conjectured the existence of a Western Bethsaida (cf. Jn. xii. 21 and see vi. 17), but this view is now generally abandoned; cf. Sanday, *SSG*, 41 f.; Dalman, *SSW*, 176. For the arguments in favour of a Western Bethsaida *v.* R. L. Stewart, *DCG*, i. 198 f.; *per contra*, G. A. Smith, 457 f., *EB*, col. 565 f. The difficulties of the geography may account for the omission of εἰς τὸ πέραν by W P⁴⁵ fam. 1 q sy^s geo¹, but the opinion of Burkitt, *JTS*, xxxiv. 367, that it is a harmonistic addition made from Mt. xiv. 22, is hard to resist, especially if εἰς Βηθσαϊδάν is read. Couchoud, *JTS*, xxxv. 8 f., reverses this opinion and prefers to omit εἰς (or πρὸς) Βηθσαϊδάν. The proposal to read πρός in the sense of ' opposite to ', *en face de* (cf. Lagrange, 172, *S. Jean*, 168),

[1] *Dies alles spricht dafür, dass hier schon dem Evangelisten vorliegender Zusammenhang anzunehmen ist*, 193.

46 ὄχλον. καὶ ἀποταξάμενος αὐτοῖς ἀπῆλθεν εἰς τὸ ὄρος προσεύξα-
47 σθαι. καὶ ὀψίας γενομένης ἦν πάλαι τὸ πλοῖον ἐν μέσῳ τῆς
48 θαλάσσης, καὶ αὐτὸς μόνος ἐπὶ τῆς γῆς. καὶ ἰδὼν αὐτοὺς βα-

is doubtful, for while the preposition can be used in the sense of 'facing' or 'over against' (Herodotus vi. 22, ἀκτή . . . πρὸς δὲ Τυρσηνίην τετραμμένη) to describe the position of one place with reference to another, its meaning after a verb of motion (προάγειν) is 'to' or 'towards'. The most that can be said is that πρός is perhaps less precise than εἰς, cf. Moffatt: 'towards Bethsaida', meaning some place in the vicinity, perhaps the fishing village (cf. viii. 23, 26) at the mouth of the Jordan. εἰς, however, should probably be read with Θ 1 28 209 565 700 Or (so Burkitt). Place names are very rare in the Markan narratives, and εἰς Βηθσαιδάν is omitted here by Matthew. Luke refers to Bethsaida at the beginning of his account of the Feeding of the Five Thousand (ix. 10, ὑπεχώρησεν . . . εἰς πόλιν καλουμένην Βηθσαιδά), thus indicating a knowledge of the section Mk. vi. 45-viii. 26 which he omits (cf. Streeter, 176 f.).

While the disciples cast off, Jesus dismisses the multitude. For ἀπολύω v. vi. 36. The use of the indicative is regular; Matthew replaces it by the subjunctive (ἕως οὗ ἀπολύσῃ). αὐτός may be, but is not necessarily, emphatic; cf. Swete, 136, 'While He for His part'. D has αὐτὸς δὲ ἀπολύει . . . Cf. Black, 64.

ἀποτάσσω*, Lk. ix. 61, xiv. 33, Ac. xviii. 18, 21, 2 Cor. ii. 13**, 'to set apart', mid. in late Gk, Josephus, Ant. xi. 8. 6, NT, and Pap. 'to bid adieu ', ' take leave of '. Cf. VGT, 70. It is improbable that αὐτοῖς refers to the disciples rather than the multitude. The reference to 'the mountain' in εἰς τὸ ὄρος (v. iii. 13) is somewhat formal. In Jn. vi. 3, 15 it plays a greater part. Matthew adds κατ' ἰδίαν (xiv. 23). προσεύξασθαι (v. i. 35) is an infin. of purpose; cf. iv. 9. Swete, 137, explains it as an infin. of

aim or object and refers to Blass, 223. For other Markan references to the prayers of Jesus v. i. 35, xiv. 35, 39. Both Swete and Lagrange quote Euthymius, χρήσιμον γὰρ ταῖς προσευχαῖς καὶ τὸ ὄρος καὶ ἡ νὺξ καὶ ἡ μόνωσις.

47. Apparently the disciples started on their journey in broad daylight, for in the late afternoon (ὀψίας γενομένης, v. i. 32) they were well out in the lake. B. Weiss, 104, observes that ἐν μέσῳ is used, not in the geographical sense, but in contrast to the land on which Jesus remained alone. μέσος, iii. 3, ἐν μέσῳ c. gen., ix. 36*. Matthew has τὸ δὲ πλοῖον ἤδη σταδίους πολλοὺς ἀπὸ τῆς γῆς ἀπεῖχεν (xiv. 24). Cf. Jn. vi. 19, ὡς σταδίους εἴκοσι πέντε ἢ τριάκοντα, i.e. nearly four miles. D P45 fam. 1 22 28 251 697 add πάλαι, 'just now ', and a b d ff g² i read iam. It seems implied by Mt and should, I think, be read. Cf. Couchoud, JTS, xxxv. 9. The tendency of the textual tradition is to suggest that the boat was far from land, an inference which Mark's words do not necessarily warrant; cf. Bernard, 186. Lagrange, 173, exaggerates when he says : ἐν μέσῳ indique qu'on est à peu près au milieu du lac, et non pas seulement en pleine eau. Cf. Moffatt: 'in the middle of the sea '. More cautiously Swete, 137, takes the Markan phrase to mean 'well out to sea '; cf. RSV, 'out on the sea '. It is not necessary to suppose that the boat was far from the shore. For πλοῖον v. i. 19; θάλασσα i. 16.

Meantime Jesus is alone on the land. μόνος, iv. 10. Since the preposition in ἐπὶ τῆς γῆς means 'on ', it is difficult to suppose that ἐπὶ τῆς θαλάσσης in 48 means ' by the sea '. V. infra.

48. No indication is given where Jesus was when he saw the storm-tossed boat, but the natural inference is that the mountain of 46 is meant.

σανιζομένους ἐν τῷ ἐλαύνειν, ἦν γὰρ ὁ ἄνεμος ἐναντίος αὐτοῖς,
περὶ τετάρτην φυλακὴν τῆς νυκτὸς ἔρχεται πρὸς αὐτοὺς περι-
πατῶν ἐπὶ τῆς θαλάσσης· καὶ ἤθελεν παρελθεῖν αὐτούς.   οἱ δὲ 49

For βασανίζω v. v. 7. As used by Mark the participle describes the disciples ('distressed', Moffatt, 'buffeted'). Matthew applies it to the boat (xiv. 24). ἐλαύνω*, Lk. viii. 29, Jn. vi. 19, Jas. iii. 4, 2 Pet. ii. 17**, 'to drive', 'row'; Cl., LXX, Pap. For the ἐν τῷ c. infin. construction v. iv. 4 (cf. Moffatt, 'as they rowed'). The infin., however, may be here used as a verbal noun, 'in the rowing' or 'in rowing' (RSV). Cf. Blass, 237; Robertson, 1073. The clause containing γάρ explains that the wind was contrary to them. Presumably it blew from the north or north-east and drove them off their course. Dalman, SSW, 175 f., records a similar experience when he and his campanions desired to sail northward, but the wind made it impossible to land and drove them to Capernaum. For ἄνεμος v. iv. 37; ἐναντίος, xv. 39*, cf. Ac. xxvii. 4, διὰ τὸ τοὺς ἀνέμους εἶναι ἐναντίους. Lagrange, 173, suggests that the wind blew from the north-west, and says that this is often the case in this northern part of the lake, but observes that there is no question of a tempest. Instead of ἐν τῷ ἐλαύνειν, D, supported by Θ 565 700 a b d ff, reads ἐλαύνοντας, a reading which may be original; cf. Klostermann, 75. Matthew omits the reference to rowing.

περὶ τετάρτην φυλακήν (Mt, τετάρτη δὲ φυλακῇ) implies the Roman reckoning of four night watches, as in xiii. 35. The Jewish division was three periods; cf. Lk. xii. 38. φυλακή, vi. 17. The time would be about three o'clock in the morning. For Mark's use of the historic present ἔρχεται v. Intr. 46 f. Whatever explanation is given of περι-πατῶν ἐπὶ τῆς θαλάσσης, there is no doubt that Mark means 'walking on the sea'. Cf. the note on ἐπὶ τῆς γῆς in 47. Matthew has ἐπὶ τὴν θάλασσαν, 'over the sea' (xiv. 25), but in the following verse ἐπὶ τῆς θαλάσσης. It

is true that ἐπί c. gen. can mean 'by' (cf. Ex. xiv. 2, Jn. xxi. 1, Ac. v. 23), but probably not here. There are several OT parallels of divine action in walking upon the sea, and the question arises whether they have influenced the interpretation of the incident. Cf. Job ix. 8, ὁ τανύσας τὸν οὐρανὸν μόνος, περιπατῶν ὡς ἐπ' ἐδάφους ἐπὶ θαλάσ-σης, xxxviii. 16, ἦλθες δὲ ἐπὶ πηγὴν θαλάσσης, ἐν δὲ ἴχνεσιν ἀβύσσου περι-επάτησας; see also Sir. xxiv. 5 in which Wisdom says, καὶ ἐν βάθει ἀβύσσων περιεπάτησα.

καὶ ἤθελεν παρελθεῖν αὐτούς is peculiar to Mk. Literally it means 'He purposed to pass them by'; cf. RSV, 'He meant to pass by them'. Cf. vii. 24, οὐδένα ἤθελεν γνῶναι, 'and would not have any one know it'. Swete, 138, citing Burton, 12, and Plummer, 176, describe the imperfect as conative ('began to', 'tried to', 'on the point of'); cf. Mt. iii. 14, Lk. i. 59, Ac. xxvi. 11. Moffatt has 'He could have passed them by'; RV 'He would have passed them by'; Bartlet, 207, 'He made as though He would pass them'. This rendering would require either the aor. indic. with ἄν or a verb like προσποιέω in Lk. xxiv. 28. It is best to conclude that ἤθελεν is used as a quasi-auxiliary: 'He was going to pass by them'. Cf. Meecham, ET, xlvii. 284 f. If we take this view two explanations are possible: either (a) Jesus intended to overtake the disciples on foot and surprise them on the other side (Wellhausen, 52, following Strauss), or (b) He purposed to test their faith (Swete, 138) or their knowledge of His power (Lagrange, 174). These inferences, however, are speculative, and necessarily so, since only what the disciples saw is described. P45, supported by 565 (ἤθελεν, sic), reads ἦλθεν, which Couchoud, JTS, xxxv. 9 f., is inclined to accept as original.

49 f. οἱ δέ, 'but they', marks a con-

ἰδόντες αὐτὸν ἐπὶ τῆς θαλάσσης περιπατοῦντα ἔδοξαν ὅτι φάν-
50 τασμά ἐστιν καὶ ἀνέκραξαν, πάντες γὰρ αὐτὸν εἶδαν καὶ
ἐταράχθησαν. ὁ δὲ εὐθὺς ἐλάλησεν μετ᾽ αὐτῶν, καὶ λέγει αὐτοῖς
51 Θαρσεῖτε, ἐγώ εἰμι, μὴ φοβεῖσθε. καὶ ἀνέβη πρὸς αὐτοὺς εἰς
τὸ πλοῖον, καὶ ἐκόπασεν ὁ ἄνεμος. καὶ λίαν ἐν ἑαυτοῖς ἐξίσταντο,
52 οὐ γὰρ συνῆκαν ἐπὶ τοῖς ἄρτοις, ἀλλ᾽ ἦν αὐτῶν ἡ καρδία πεπω-
ρωμένη.

trast and ἰδόντες is temporal. δοκέω,
x. 42*, can be followed either by the
acc. and infin. or, as here, by ὅτι
c. indic., the tense being that of the
original thought. φάντασμα*, Mt.
xiv. 26**, = φάσμα, ' an apparition ',
' a ghost '; cf. Job xx. 8, Wisd. xvii.
14; VGT, 664. sy^s appears to have
read δαιμόνιον. For an account of
Jewish beliefs v. DCG, i. 111 f.
In the darkness the form of Jesus
was taken for a ghost. Klausner, 269,
thinks that they saw no more than an
apparition. With emphasis Mark adds
that all saw Him and were ' terrified '
(RSV and Moffatt). ταράσσω*, ' to
stir up ', ' trouble '. Cf. Lk. xxiv. 38,
1 Pet. iii. 14, which support the meaning terrify. In contrast (ὁ δέ) with
the terrified disciples Jesus at once
(εὐθύς) talks (λαλέω) with them and
says (λέγω), ' Take heart; it is I;
cease fearing '. Cf. Trench, Syn. 277.
θαρσέω, x. 49*, Mt. ix. 2, 22, xiv. 27,
Jn. xvi. 33, Ac. xxiii. 11**, ' to be of
good courage '; Cl. (θαρρέω in later
Attic), LXX, Pap. ' Θάρσει -εῖτε is
used exclusively (Evv., Ac), while for
the rest of the verb forms of θαρρέω
occur 2 Co quinquies and Heb. xiii. 6,
without variant ', Moulton ii. 103. For
μή and the pres. imperative v. v. 36;
φοβέω iv. 41.
Matthew slightly abbreviates Mk,
omitting ἔδοξαν and πάντες γὰρ αὐτὸν
εἶδαν, but after φοβεῖσθε he adds the account of Peter walking on the water:
ἀποκριθεὶς δὲ ὁ Πέτρος εἶπεν αὐτῷ
Κύριε, εἰ σὺ εἶ, κέλευσόν με ἐλθεῖν πρὸς
σὲ ἐπὶ τὰ ὕδατα· ὁ δὲ εἶπεν Ἐλθέ. καὶ
καταβὰς ἀπὸ τοῦ πλοίου Πέτρος περι-
επάτησεν ἐπὶ τὰ ὕδατα καὶ ἦλθεν πρὸς τὸν
Ἰησοῦν. βλέπων δὲ τὸν ἄνεμον ἐφοβήθη,

καὶ ἀρξάμενος καταποντίζεσθαι ἔκραξεν
λέγων Κύριε, σῶσόν με. εὐθέως δὲ ὁ
Ἰησοῦς ἐκτείνας τὴν χεῖρα ἐπελάβετο αὐτοῦ καὶ λέγει αὐτῷ Ὀλιγόπιστε, εἰς τί
ἐδίστασας; (xiv. 28-31). Most New
Testament scholars explain this passage as a homiletical expansion of
Mark's narrative, but it is less widely
recognized that the same motives have
been at work in shaping the original
Markan account.
51 f. ἀναβαίνω, i. 10; πλοῖον, i. 19;
κοπάζω, iv. 39; ἄνεμος, iv. 37. The
statement that the wind ceased is
present verbatim in iv. 39, but this fact
supplies only a slender basis for the
view that the narrative is a doublet of
the Storm on the Lake, for the original
motive in vi. 45-52 is the walking on
the water, not the storm-motive (cf.
Bultmann, 231). The repetition of
such phrases is a sign of popular composition. Cf. HS², 168-73. Usually
Mark has ἐμβαίνω of entering into a
boat (v. iv. 1). Swete's suggestion, 139,
that ἀνέβη depicts the climb from the
hollow of the wave over the side of the
boat, seems fanciful, but it accounts
for the use of the verb. The usage is
classical (Homer, Thuc. iv. 44, ἀναβάν-
τες ἐπὶ τὰς ναῦς). The impression
produced on the disciples is one of complete, but silent, astonishment: ' they
were utterly astounded ' (Moffatt, RSV).
λίαν, i. 35; ἐξίστημι, ii. 12; ἐν ἑαυτοῖς, ii.
8. Instead of καὶ λίαν D and 565 read
καὶ περισσῶς (cf. 700, καὶ περισσός and
28, καὶ ἐκ περισσοῦ), and καὶ λίαν ἐκ
περισσοῦ is read by A et al. fam. 13 33
118 579 1071 al. pler. it vg syhl.
Mark's explanation is given in 52.
The disciples had failed to grasp the
significance of the multiplication of

the loaves, and their minds (καρδία, ii. 6) were dull (cf. Moffatt). συνίημι, v. iv. 12. πωρόω, viii. 17*, Jn. xii. 40, Rom. xi. 7, 2 Cor. iii. 14**, pass. ' to become insensible ',' obtuse ',' blind '; Cl., LXX, cf. VGT, 561. See the note on πώρωσις in iii. 5; also J. A. Robinson, Eph. 264-74; Turner, 33. In Mk the same idea reappears in viii. 17, πεπωρωμένην ἔχετε τὴν καρδίαν ὑμῶν ;. A failure to perceive akin to moral blindness rather than wilful obstinacy seems to be in mind. Cf. the renderings of the versions : obcaecatum f l vg, obtusum a b d,' blinded ' sys,' stupid ' syᵖᵉ, ' stupefied ' arm. Without subscribing to the view that Mark is deeply influenced by ' Paulinism ', one may infer the influence of Pauline teaching in these passages. Cf. 2 Cor. iii. 14, ἀλλὰ ἐπωρώθη τὰ νοήματα αὐτῶν, Rom. xi. 7, οἱ δὲ λοιποὶ ἐπωρώθησαν, 25, πώρωσις ἀπὸ μέρους τῷ Ἰσραὴλ γέγονεν, Eph. iv. 18, διὰ τὴν πώρωσιν τῆς καρδίας αὐτῶν.

The explanation that the disciples had failed to understand ' in the matter of the loaves ' (ἐπὶ τοῖς ἄρτοις) because their minds were dull, is far from convincing to the modern reader, for if they had observed the multiplication of the loaves, they ought not to have been completely astounded by the walking on the water. Swete's suggestion that ' perhaps their administration of the food diverted their thoughts from the work wrought by

the Lord ' does not adequately meet this difficulty. Lagrange, 175, suggests that they still lacked a true appreciation of the person of Jesus. Possibly the explanation reveals an embarrassment on the part of the narrator. It ' deepens our impression that the matter of the Loaves was really rather other and less non-natural than is suggested by the traditional account ', Bartlet, 108.

Matthew's version illustrates the further development of the tradition. He follows 51 closely, using the plural ἀναβάντων αὐτῶν in consequence of the story of Peter, but departs radically from 52 by saying that those in the boat ' worshipped ' Jesus, declaring Him to be the Son of God, οἱ δὲ ἐν τῷ πλοίῳ προσεκύνησαν αὐτῷ λέγοντες Ἀληθῶς θεοῦ υἱὸς εἶ (xiv. 33). This alteration illustrates Matthew's desire to ' spare the Twelve ' and his tendency to embellish stories in the interests of doctrine. John says that the disciples wished to take Jesus into the boat and that immediately it came to the land to which they were going, ἤθελον οὖν λαβεῖν αὐτὸν εἰς τὸ πλοῖον, καὶ εὐθέως ἐγένετο τὸ πλοῖον ἐπὶ τῆς γῆς εἰς ἦν ὑπῆγον (vi. 21). J. H. Bernard, clxxvi, 184-7, holds that the Johannine version is ' wholly devoid of a miraculous element '; cf. Howard, FG, 190 f. Other commentators doubt if this view can be sustained ; cf. Macgregor, 135 ; Hoskyns, 328 ; Strachan, 182.

Mk. vi. 53-6   **43. THE LANDING AT GENNESARET**   Cf. Mt. xiv. 34-6

This section is a narrative composed by Mark on the basis of tradition. In this respect it resembles iii. 7-12. Cf. Dibelius, 224 ; Bultmann, 366. It is not, however, a purely literary and imaginative sketch. There are good reasons for this view. The connexion with the preceding story of the Crossing is good, and there is reason to believe that the Feeding of the Five Thousand, the Crossing, and the Landing, attested twice over by Mark (vi. 30-56 and viii. 1-10) and by John (vi. 1-25), formed a fixed series in the earliest tradition. See Note C, pp. 628-32. Again, the narrative vividly pictures the Galilean Ministry and is distinctive in that no teaching is mentioned, but a rapid and mysterious journeying from place to place. That the section is composed by Mark is shown by the vocabulary (v. Comm.), but the picture of the people running to and fro and carrying their sick on pallets to any place where rumour said Jesus was, and the description of what happened when He entered villages, cities, and hamlets, is best accounted for by tradition based upon knowledge. Loisy, i. 939, speaks of the section as un souvenir historique, and J. Weiss describes in similar terms the group to which it belongs.[1] Further characterizations are more speculative, but, in pointing to the limitations of the plain of Gennesaret, and the use of χώραν in 55, Lagrange, 178, is not without justification in suggesting that Mark may have sketched in an abbreviated form (en raccourci) what happened on the way from the shores of the lake to the region of Tyre (vii. 24). He quotes with approval Loisy's opinion that, in Mark's account, Jesus had not come to Gennesaret to preach. He had supposed that He would not be recognized, and, in consequence of the crowds, He continued His journey, as if He wished to reach at length a place where He Himself and His disciples might be at peace and security from the attentions of Antipas. Cf. Burkitt, 92; Goguel, 362-4. Mk, it must be confessed, contributes little to this reconstruction.

53 Καὶ διαπεράσαντες ἐπὶ τὴν γῆν ἦλθον εἰς Γεννησαρὲτ καὶ
54 προσωρμίσθησαν. καὶ ἐξελθόντων αὐτῶν ἐκ τοῦ πλοίου εὐθὺς
55 ἐπιγνόντες αὐτὸν περιέδραμον ὅλην τὴν χώραν ἐκείνην καὶ

53. διαπεράω, v. 21*. D and 45, supported by a b c ff q, add ἐκεῖθεν (i.e. from Bethsaida). See Allen, 103. This reading is probably an early attempt to explain how the boat came to land at Gennesaret when the disciples had set out for Bethsaida. The generally accepted opinion is that the wind prevented a landing at Bethsaida, and this view is probably correct; cf. Swete, 140; Turner, 33 f.

Γεννησαρέτ*, Mt. xiv. 34, Lk. v. 1**. Γεννησάρ is attested by D b c ff aur vg (2 MSS.) sys pe. Cf. 1 Macc. xi. 67, τὸ ὕδωρ τοῦ Γεννησάρ, Josephus, BJ, iii. 10. 7, τὴν Γεννησάρ, Ant. xiii. 5. 7, Γεννήσαρα ὕδατα, xviii. 2. 1, λίμνη Γεννησαρῖτις. Γεννησάρ is probably the more correct form (cf. Blass, 13; Holtzmann, 141; Klostermann, 76), but it is less certain that it is the original Markan reading; cf. Chase, Syro-Latin Text of the Gospels, 105; Burkitt, Syriac Forms of NT Proper Names, 15. Lagrange, 177, thinks that Gennesar is a place-name, a town or village to which the plain gave its

name; cf. also Wellhausen, 52; Dalman, SSW, 128, 130. Usually Gennesaret is said to be the fertile plain, three miles long and over a mile in breadth, to the south of Capernaum; cf. Josephus, BJ, iii. 10. 8; DCG, i. 640 f.

προσορμίζομαι**, 'to come to anchor near (a place)', <ὅρμος, 'an anchorage'; Cl. (Herodotus vi. 97). So προσορμέω in Pap. (VGT, 550). καὶ προσωρμίσθησαν is omitted by D W Θ 1 28 209 565 700 a b c ff i q r¹ aur sys pe geo arm. Burkitt, JTS, xvii. 19 f., thinks the words are genuine, but that they were dropped out by almost all texts in very early times and were restored by Origen.

54 f. The awkward break between the verses is due to the influence of the Vulgate: . . . cognouerunt eum; et percurrentes . . . In contrast with 56, which describes what happened when Jesus entered the various towns and villages of the land, these verses picture people following Him from place to place, as reports of His presence

[1] So ist diese Gruppe, die wir trotz des Speisungswunders aus den Petruserzählungen abzuleiten wagen, voll lebendiger Züge der Erinnerung, 223.

ἤρξαντο ἐπὶ τοῖς κραβάττοις τοὺς κακῶς ἔχοντας περιφέρειν ὅπου ἤκουον ὅτι ἔστιν. καὶ ὅπου ἂν εἰσεπορεύετο εἰς κώμας ἢ 56 εἰς πόλεις ἢ εἰς ἀγροὺς ἐν ταῖς ἀγοραῖς ἐτίθεσαν τοὺς ἀσθενοῦν- τας, καὶ παρεκάλουν αὐτὸν ἵνα κἂν τοῦ κρασπέδου τοῦ ἱματίου αὐτοῦ ἅψωνται· καὶ ὅσοι ἂν ἥψαντο αὐτοῦ ἐσώζοντο.

are received, and carrying about their sick upon pallets. Apart from περι- τρέχω and περιφέρω, an instance of *paronomasia* (cf. v. 26), the vocabulary consists of common Markan words : the gen. abs. ἐξελθόντων αὐτῶν, cf. v. 2 ; πλοῖον i. 19 ; εὐθύς i. 10 ; ἐπιγινώσκω ii. 8 ; ὅλος i. 28 ; χώρα i. 5 ; ἤρξαντο c. infin. i. 45 ; κράβαττος ii. 4 ; τοὺς κακῶς ἔχοντας i. 32 ; ὅπου c. indic. ii. 4. ἔστιν preserves the tense of the report. περιτρέχω**, ' to run round ' ; Cl., LXX, Pap. So περιφέρω*, 2 Cor. iv. 10, Eph. iv. 14**. περιέδραμον is impersonal. The passage is editorial, like i. 39, 45, and iii. 7-12, but it re- flects good tradition and is not merely imaginative. Cf. Schmidt, 195. No reference to preaching or teaching is made in the section, and there is no reason to suppose that Jesus has re- sumed the ministry broken off at vi. 31. Apparently He seeks retirement in vain. For the anomalous use of the article in ἐπὶ τοῖς κραβάττοις v. Intr. 59.

Matthew abbreviates the passage, omitting the reference to the leaving of the boat, the verb περιέδραμον, the ἤρξαντο construction, the mention of pallets, and ὅπου ἤκουον ὅτι ἔστιν. He simply says that ' the men of that place ' sent throughout that neighbour- hood and brought to Jesus ' all ' who were sick.

56. For ὅπου ἄν and ὅσοι ἄν c. indic., illustrating the weakening of the con- nexion between ἄν and the subjunctive, see the note on iii. 11 (Moulton, i. 167 f. ; Blass, 207). ἐάν, which greatly predominated over ἄν in the first and second centuries A.D., is read after ὅπου in a number of important MSS., including ℵ Δ 33 and 579, and the second ἄν, after ὅσοι, is omitted by ℵ D Δ fam. 1 (exc. 118) 579 *et al.* Moul- ton observes : ' It seems that in this small point the uncials faithfully re- produce originals written under con- ditions long obsolete ', *op. cit.* i. 43. As in 54 f., the vocabulary of the verse is Markan. For εἰσπορεύομαι v. *HS²*, 12, and for εἰς κώμας ἢ εἰς πόλεις ἢ εἰς ἀγρούς v. the notes on v. 14 and vi. 6, 36. The repetition of εἰς is note- worthy ; cf. Intr. 64. ἀγορά, vii. 4, xii. 38*, ' market-place ', is here used somewhat generally, since, strictly speaking, only larger towns would have their ἀγοραί. Several commen- tators suggest that in 56 the word includes open spaces and village greens. This opinion appears to lie behind the reading ἐν ταῖς πλατείαις in D 565 700 (cf. Ac. v. 15) and in *plataeis* in the Old Latin and the Vulgate. Pallis, 22, conjectures ἐν ταῖς ἀγυιαῖς, ' in the roads '. ἀσθενέω*, Mt. x. 8, xxv. 36, 39, Lk. iv. 40. For παρεκάλουν ἵνα c. subj., indicating the substance of the request, v. v. 10, and for κἂν τοῦ κρασπέδου* τοῦ ἱματίου αὐτοῦ ἅψωνται . . . ἐσώζοντο v. the notes on v. 27 f. See also for the practice of touching i. 41, iii. 10. Clearly 56, like 54 f., is the composi- tion of Mark himself. He writes on the basis of tradition, although whether all the details described belong to the present occasion is more open to ques- tion. Matthew omits the first half of 56 and leaves the impression that Jesus merely landed without touring the neighbourhood, a representation of the course of events which J. Weiss, 208, thinks is to be preferred. This view is doubtful if it means that 56a is the addition of a later redactor. Still less satisfactory is the suggestion that 53-5 is another version of iii. 10 f. (Bussmann, iii. 68). It is better to explain iii. 7-12 as anticipating events subsequently narrated in detail.

Mk. vii. 1-8   44. THE QUESTION OF   Cf. Mt. xv. 1 f., 7-9
                   THE WASHING OF HANDS

The narrative is a Pronouncement-story defining the attitude of Jesus to the scribal rules regarding the washing of hands. The binding character of Jewish oral tradition must have been a living issue in the first Christian decades, and it was because of its bearing on this problem that the story was preserved. Bultmann, 15 f., and Albertz, 36-9, describe it as a *Streitgespräch*. Like all stories of this kind, the narrative probably circulated as a separate unit of tradition, without any precise indication of time or circumstance. Albertz thinks that the original unit is contained in verses 5-8, but, alternatively, that this unit may have been 1 f., 5-8, verses 3 f. being the explanatory addition of the Evangelist or a later redactor. In the Commentary the second alternative is held to be more probable. The historical value of the story stands high, the only really doubtful point is whether the quotation in 6 f. has been assimilated to a reading nearer to that of the LXX. Bultmann traces the origin of the story to discussions within the Christian community (*Gemeindepolemik*), largely because no real answer is given to the question propounded, but he admits that the narrative comes from the Palestinian community and prefers to find the original unit in 1-8 rather than, with Dibelius and Arnold Meyer, in 1-5 + 15. Dibelius, 220-2, does not include the narrative in his *Paradigmen* and explains 5-23 as a collection of sayings on parallel themes. This explanation hardly does justice to the unity of 1-8. The important question is that of authenticity. Not only is corporate authorship a highly doubtful hypothesis, but the plea that no real answer is given to the question, ' Why walk not thy disciples according to the tradition of the elders, but eat their bread with defiled hands ? ', must be held to fail. A pointed quotation from Isaiah, introduced by the ironic comment ' Well did Isaiah prophesy of you hypocrites ! ', coupled with the charge, ' You abandon God's commandments, and hold men's precepts ', is a devastating answer, for, rightly ignoring the reference to the disciples, it comes to grips with the main issue and answers with a decisive ' No '.

VII. 1   Καὶ συνάγονται πρὸς αὐτὸν οἱ Φαρισαῖοι καί τινες τῶν γραμ-
2 ματέων ἐλθόντες ἀπὸ Ἱεροσολύμων καὶ ἰδόντες τινὰς τῶν μαθητῶν αὐτοῦ ὅτι κοιναῖς χερσίν, τοῦτ' ἔστιν ἀνίπτοις, ἐσθίουσιν

1 f. Unlike the three preceding stories, there is no link between this narrative and the rest, no temporal or local statement which tells us when and where the incident took place. In form also the narrative is completely different, and for a parallel we have to go back to ii. 1-iii. 6 and iii. 22-6. For συνάγω *v.* ii. 2 ; οἱ Φαρισαῖοι ii. 16 ; οἱ γραμματεῖς i. 22 ; Ἱεροσόλυμα iii. 8. The reference to certain of the scribes who came from Jerusalem (*v.* iii. 22) implies that the incident happened in

Galilee, and the Pharisees mentioned were probably resident there. The only circumstance mentioned, καὶ ἰδόντες τινὰς τῶν μαθητῶν αὐτοῦ ὅτι κοιναῖς χερσίν . . . ἐσθίουσιν . . ., is relevant to the question in 5, and it is mentioned because of this inquiry. In this clause two constructions may be combined, ἰδόντες τινὰς . . . ἐσθίοντας (cf. i. 10) and ἰδόντες ὅτι ἐσθίουσίν τινες (cf. ii. 16). But it is better to regard the text as an example of hyperbaton (cf. xi. 32, xii. 34). *V.* Intr. 58. For

τοὺς ἄρτους.—οἱ γὰρ Φαρισαῖοι καὶ πάντες οἱ Ἰουδαῖοι ἐὰν 3
μὴ πυγμῇ νίψωνται τὰς χεῖρας οὐκ ἐσθίουσιν, κρατοῦντες τὴν
παράδοσιν τῶν πρεσβυτέρων, καὶ ἀπ' ἀγορᾶς ἐὰν μὴ ῥαντί- 4

οἱ μαθηταὶ αὐτοῦ v. the note on ii. 15;
ἐσθίω i. 6; ἄρτος ii. 26. κοινός, vii.
5*, 'common', 'shared', is used in
the NT in the Hebraistic sense of
'profane', 'unclean', 'unhallowed'.
In the papyri it has various meanings,
e.g. τὰ κοινά, 'the customary formula',
τὰ πάντα κοινά, 'the universe', τὸ
κοινόν, 'society', 'guild', 'council';
cf. VGT, 350.

The explanatory phrase τοῦτ' ἔστιν
ἀνίπτοις is added by Mark for the
benefit of his Gentile readers. Cf.
Bacon, Is Mark a Roman Gospel?, 58;
Rawlinson, 93. τοῦτ' ἔστιν*. Mark's
usual expression is ὅ ἐστιν, iii. 17, vii.
11, 34, xii. 42, xv. 16, 42*. ἄνιπτος*,
Mt. xv. 2**. For the practice of ritual
washing v. the note on 3. Matthew
severely abbreviates his source, losing
the distinction between the scribes
from Jerusalem and the (local) Pharisees, and omitting the reference to
the circumstances in 2.

3. This verse and the next give
an explanation of Jewish ceremonial
washings for the Gentile readers of
the Gospel. Like τοῦτ' ἔστιν ἀνίπτοις
in 2, they were added to the original
narrative by Mark or a later redactor.
Explanatory passages introduced by
γάρ are in accordance with Mark's
style, and κρατέω and παράδοσις are
among his characteristic words (cf.
HS², 13), but the phrase πάντες οἱ
Ἰουδαῖοι reads strangely if it comes
from his pen, being found here only
in the Gospel apart from the title ὁ
βασιλεὺς τῶν Ἰουδαίων in xv. 2, 9, 12,
18, 26*. Some commentators think
that the phrase is used (as in Jn) to
describe the Jews of Jerusalem who
strictly observed the Law; cf. Swete,
143; or the customs of the Western
Dispersion; cf. Rawlinson, 94; but
there is nothing in Mk to suggest such
a limited reference; cf. Lagrange,

180, ce sens ne paraît nulle part dans
les synoptiques. The phrase would
be more intelligible on the part of a
Gentile, but it cannot be said to be
impossible from Mark's pen as used
from the Gentile-Christian point of
view. The tone is certainly hostile as
throughout the entire passage. For
οἱ Φαρισαῖοι v. ii. 16, and for the construction ἐὰν μή c. subj. v. iii. 27. νί-
πτω*, 'to wash' (a part of the body), is
a late form of νίζω; LXX; MGk νίβω.

πυγμή**, 'fist'. No satisfactory
explanation of this difficult word in
Mk can be given. The difficulty was
felt from the earliest times as the
textual variants show. It is omitted
by Δ sys sa, and is replaced by πυκνά
('often') by ℵ W, implied also by
crebro in Old Lat. MSS. and the
Vulgate, and by sype hl. πυγμῇ, which
must be read with A B et al. (D has
πύκμῃ), is variously rendered: 'diligently' (RV), 'up to the elbow'
(RVmg and Moffatt), 'with the fist'
(RVmg). RSV omits the word.
Torrey, TG, 93 f., conjectures a misreading of the original Aramaic,
ligmodh ('with the fist') being misread for ligmar ('at all'). With the
knowledge at our disposal it is best to
translate 'with the fist', meaning by
this the rubbing of a closed fist in
the palm of the hand or the pouring
of water over clenched fingers. Cf.
Swete, 143 f.; Plummer, 181 (or
'diligently'); Black, 8 f. On the
basis of a passage in Palladius, Hist.
Lausiaca, 55 (fourth century), Turner,
34, suggests that the word means the
hands in contrast with washing up
to the elbows; cf. JTS, vi. 353, xxix.
279. Cf. also Lagrange, 180 f.; Field,
30 f.; VGT, 559. Wellhausen, 94,
says bluntly, Was πυγμῇ heissen soll,
weiss man nicht.¹ Cf. Rawlinson, 94.

For κρατέω v. i. 31. παράδοσις, vii.

¹ Couchoud, JTS, xxxiv. 120, conjectures that πυγμῇ is a misreading of πρὶν ἤ, and ἐὰν μή a
correction. Pallis, 23, conjectures πυγῇ.

σωνται˥ οὐκ ἐσθίουσιν, καὶ ἄλλα πολλά ἐστιν ἃ παρέλαβον
5 κρατεῖν, βαπτισμοὺς ποτηρίων καὶ ξεστῶν καὶ χαλκίων.—καὶ
ἐπερωτῶσιν αὐτὸν οἱ Φαρισαῖοι καὶ οἱ γραμματεῖς λέγοντες Διὰ

4 βαπτίσωνται

5, 8 f., 13*, lit. ' a handing over ', then ' a tradition ' oral or written. πρεσβύτερος, vii. 5, viii. 31, xi. 27, xiv. 43, 53, xv. 1*, ' an elder ', is the comparative of πρέσβυς, ' an old man ', and is used in the LXX. In the Egyptian papyri it is used as an honorific title with reference to village or communal officers (VGT, 535), and in Asia Minor for ' the members of a corporation ' and of the priests of pagan temples; cf. Deissmann, BS, 156, 233 ff. Here it describes honoured Jewish teachers of the Law whose judgments were handed down and were considered as binding by the scribes and Pharisees. Elsewhere in Mk it denotes the religious leaders of the Jews (viii. 31, etc.).

For the historical and exegetical problems raised by this passage and the story as a whole, see the Detached Notes on Ritual Cleansing and Qorban, pp. 338-9 and 341-2.

4. This verse completes the explanatory parenthesis by giving examples of traditions concerning ritual cleansing, the washing of things brought from the market-place, and the cleansing of cups, jugs, and bronze vessels. In the catalogue a tone of irony is present.

ἀπ' ἀγορᾶς may be a pregnant phrase meaning ' when they come from the market-place ' (WM, 776), but it is also possible that it is an emphasizing hyperbaton and that ἀπό=מן in a partitive sense, ' anything from the market-place '. This suggestion (Black, 37) is strengthened if αὐτοῖς, read by D (illis, it (exc. a b) vg) after παρέλαβον, represents the Aramaic ethic dative (Intr. 60), ' which they received them to keep ' (Black, 76). ῥαντίζω*, Heb. ix. 13, 19, 21, x. 22, Apoc. xix. 13**, ' to sprinkle ',=Cl. ῥαίνω, LXX, v. VGT, 563. So ℵ B and a number of minuscules, but A D W Θ et al. and many minuscules read βαπτίσωνται

(i. 5). The less familiar word is probably the original reading, but several commentators prefer βαπτίσωνται (cf. Turner, 35; Bartlet, 214; RV, Moffatt, Torrey). Sprinkling or washing, rather than bathing, is probably meant, the latter being the practice of the Essenes and strict Pharisees. Justin, Dial. 46 and Tatian, Diat. xx. 20, suggest that the purifying of the food is meant. Cf. Holtzmann, 141 f.; Lagrange, 182; Moffatt: ' till they have washed it '.

For παραλαμβάνω v. iv. 36. The verb is regularly used of the receiving of a tradition; cf. 1 Cor. xv. 3. κρατεῖν (i. 31) is an epexegetic infin. βαπτισμός*, Heb. vi. 2, ix. 10**, ' dipping ', the act of immersion; Josephus, Ant. xviii. 5. 2. ποτήριον, ix. 41, x. 38 f., xiv. 23, 36*. ξέστης**, ' a pitcher ', ' jug '. The word is commonly said to be formed from the Latin sextarius, a Roman dry measure nearly equal to one pint (but cf. Moulton, ii. 155). Here it describes a pot or jug. χαλκίον**, a bronze or copper vessel, ' a kettle ', ' cauldron '; Cl., LXX, Pap. A D W Θ et al. and most minuscules and versions add καὶ κλινῶν.

5. In this verse the question, characteristic in Pronouncement-stories, is put. οἱ Φαρισαῖοι καὶ οἱ γραμματεῖς looks very much like a repetition of the parallel phrase in 1, caused by the insertion of the parenthesis 3 f. If so, the original narrative is 1 f.+5-8. For ἐπερωτάω v. v. 9; διὰ τί ii. 18; μαθητής ii. 15; τὴν παράδοσιν τῶν πρεσβυτέρων vii. 3; ἀλλὰ κοιναῖς χερσὶν ἐσθίουσιν τὸν ἄρτον vii. 2. Probably (after γραμματεῖς) λέγοντες should follow with D W Δ Θ P⁴⁵ fam. 13 28 543 565 700 a c ff i r¹ aur vg (aliq.) sa sys. While ostensibly the inquiry concerns the action of the disciples, in fact it

τί οὐ περιπατοῦσιν οἱ μαθηταί σου κατὰ τὴν παράδοσιν τῶν
πρεσβυτέρων, ἀλλὰ κοιναῖς χερσὶν ἐσθίουσιν τὸν ἄρτον; ὁ δὲ 6
εἶπεν αὐτοῖς Καλῶς ἐπροφήτευσεν Ἡσαίας περὶ ὑμῶν τῶν
ὑποκριτῶν, ὡς γέγραπται ὅτι

ⸯΟῦτοσ ὁ λαὸϲⸯ τοῖϲ χείλεϲίν με τιμᾷ,
ἡ δὲ καρδία αὐτῶν πόρρω ἀπέχει ἀπ᾽ ἐμοῦ·
μάτην δὲ ϲέβονταί με,   7
διδάϲκοντεϲ διδαϲκαλίαϲ ἐντάλματα ἀνθρώπων·

6 Ὁ λαὸς οὗτος

is aimed at Jesus Himself, since His
teaching on the validity of the oral
law is challenged, and, as such, He
accepts the challenge, no reference
being made in His reply to His disciples. The Palestinian origin of the
story is revealed by the use of περιπατέω
(ii. 9), used here only in the Synoptic
Gospels in the Hebraic sense of *living*
or conducting one's life (הָלַךְ), as in
2 Kgs. xx. 3, Prov. viii. 20, Eccl. xi. 9,
and frequently in Jn (viii. 12, etc.) and
the Pauline Epistles (Rom. viii. 4, etc.).
Cf. Bultmann, 16. The greater originality of Mark's account is thrown
into relief by Matthew's more prosaic
version (xv. 2). At this point Matthew
inserts Mk. vii. 9-13 (the saying on
Qorban) into the present story.

6 f. The reply of Jesus is given in
the words of Isa. xxix. 13 which are
directly applied to the scribes and
Pharisees in 8. καλῶς, ' well ',
' finely ', ' yes indeed ' (Moffatt) ; cf.
xii. 32, Jn. iv. 17, viii. 48, xiii. 13. The
augment in ἐπροφήτευσεν (xiv. 65*)
is rightly placed, as against the inferior reading προεφήτευσεν (A B²
et al.). Ἡσαίας, i. 2. ὑποκριτής*,
Mt (13), Lk (3)**, LXX, ' a hypocrite ',
in Attic Gk ' an actor ', a meaning
preserved in the papyri (*VGT*, 657).
Cf. Meecham, *LA*, 282. The epithet
appears abruptly in Mk because the
of Evangelist is using an isolated unit
tradition. For γέγραπται *v.* i. 2.

The quotation differs from the LXX
in two important respects : (1) The
parallel to the first line in the longer
text (in B) reads : ἐγγίζει μοι ὁ λαὸς
οὗτος ἐν τῷ στόματι αὐτοῦ, καὶ ἐν τοῖς

χείλεσιν αὐτῶν τιμῶσίν με, but the
shorter text (א A) omits ἐν τῷ στόματι
αὐτοῦ καί ; (2) The last line in the LXX
reads : διδάσκοντες ἐντάλματα ἀνθρώπων καὶ διδασκαλίας. Mark's version
corresponds with that of Paul in Col.
ii. 22, ἐντάλματα καὶ διδασκαλίας τῶν
ἀνθρώπων. Naturally, the question of
Pauline influence upon the Markan
text arises, but, as against Torrey,
Bacon, 266, thinks that it is ' more
reasonable not to insist upon direct
literary interrelation '. Probably Mark
(and perhaps Paul also) was dependent
on a form of the Greek text which
differed from the LXX, perhaps some
florilegium of Old Testament prophecies current at Rome. As might
be expected in a quotation, the vocabulary includes words not common in
Mk : λαός xiv. 2*, χεῖλος*, τιμάω, vii.
10, x. 19*, πόρρω*, ἀπέχω, xiv. 41*,
μάτην*, σέβομαι*, διδασκαλία*, ἔνταλμα*. μάτην, ' in vain ', ' to no purpose ',
Cl., LXX, Pap. διδασκαλία, ' instruction ', Cl., LXX, Pap., 15 times in the
Past. Epp. ἔνταλμα, ' precept ', LXX.
For καρδία *v.* ii. 6 ; διδάσκω i. 21.

The fact that the argument turns
upon the LXX text rather than the
Hebrew creates a difficulty. Rawlinson, 94, puts the point strongly : ' The
fact that it (the quotation) is not based
upon the Hebrew text, and that an
accurate rendering of the Hebrew
would not yield quite the same point,
is a reason for thinking that it is due
to the Evangelist, or to one of his
sources, rather than to our Lord '.
So also Blunt, 188. So far as the form
of text is concerned, this argument is

8 ἀφέντες τὴν ἐντολὴν τοῦ θεοῦ κρατεῖτε τὴν παράδοσιν τῶν ἀνθρώπων.

probably sound (see above), but it is less certain that the Hebrew does not provide a basis for the charge. The Hebrew reads : ' Because this people draws nigh with its mouth, and honours me with its lips, and keeps its heart far from me, and the worship which they give me is a command-ment learnt from men : therefore . . .' (F. Delitzsch). Here also the charge made is that the worship of Yahweh is in part ' conscious hypocrisy ' (De-litzsch). ' They have learnt their religion by rote (mg), but have no intelligent interest in it ' (A. S. Peake). Cf. Dillmann, 265 ; Duhm, 181 ; G. A. Smith, i. 216 f. ; Box, 132 ; Kissane, i. 331 ; Snaith, *Notes on Isa. xxviii-xxxii*, 32-4.

8. Here the charge is pressed re-solutely home. What God commands and what man ordains are set in radical opposition. The oral law, with its burdensome rules about ceremonial washings, contravenes the divine in-tention and even sets it at naught. For ἀφίημι v. i. 18. ἐντολή, vii. 9, x. 5, 19, xii. 28, 31*, Cl. (rare), LXX, Pap. (of royal and imperial ordinances, *VGT*, 218). Lagrange, 184, suggests that ἐντολή marks the unity of the divine Law in contrast with the in-dividual ἐντάλματα inferred by men. So Swete, 147 : ' the Torah as con-trasted with the Halachah '. For κρατέω v. i. 31 ; παράδοσις vii. 3. The verse, which is peculiar to Mk, is omitted by sys. Swete tentatively suggests that it is perhaps a doublet of 9. It is, however, the climax of 1-8, which must have circulated inde-pendently of 9-13.

DETACHED NOTE ON RITUAL CLEANSING

It has been objected (cf. A. Büchler, *ET*, xxi. 34-40) that the practice described in vii. 3 can only have been that of the priests, not lay Jews, and that, in consequence, the Jews mentioned must have been priests who had recently joined the ranks of the Pharisees and had adopted the strict rules of purification instituted by the Rabbis to safeguard the levitical purity of the priestly dues. In reply to this objection G. Margoliouth, *ET*, xxii. 261-3, argued that the Synoptic Gospels are at least as good an authority for the customs prevalent during the period A.D. 1–70 as the Talmud, and that even if full ceremonial cleanness was not required of laymen at the time in question, it might none the less have been observed with con-siderable strictness by pious Jews. ' The strict codification of an ordinance is very often merely the final step in a course of development ; and one has the right to assume that formal extension of these rules of purification to the laity would not have been introduced, if they had not already taken root in the consciences and the conduct of the more pious of the people ', Margoliouth, *op. cit.* 262. Margoliouth admits that πάντες in vii. 3 must not be pressed and suggests that the customs mentioned were no doubt general rather than universal. Bartlet, 212-14, points out that the argu-ment from silence is precarious, especially in the face of current Essene views of ritual purity, and Box, *St. Mt*, 244, draws attention to the dis-putes in Pharisaic circles and suggests that ' the pious ' were expected to follow the priests in this matter.

The question is discussed by C. G. Montefiore, i. 133-44, who thinks that the scholars mentioned above take Büchler's argument too lightly, but admits that if his argument is accepted, we should be compelled to declare that the Markan story could not have arisen till about A.D. 100 or after the death of Akiba (A.D. 130) and that ' such a conclusion would be absurd '. Montefiore explains that Büchler now thinks that some, or even many, Jews in the Diaspora devised and practised rules which in Palestine were unknown (cf. Judith xii. 7) and asks if the Markan story may not have arisen outside Palestine. For this view cf. Moffatt, 232 n. ; Lohmeyer, 139. Bultmann, 16, it should be noted, traces 1-8 and 9-13 to the Palestinian community, for which the question of the relation of the παράδοσις to the Law was a living issue. Montefiore himself admits that ' after all, there may have been some Rabbis in the age of Jesus of whose stricter tendencies and habits even the Talmud itself is ignorant or has left no record ', *op. cit.* 142, and suggests that, with a prophet's intuition, Jesus realized the truth that religious defilement is essentially moral and spiritual. It may be that, owing to a contemporary interest current at Rome, Mark's explanation in 3 f. is expressed with rigour, but there is little advantage in assigning the passage to a redactor (cf. Bacon, *BGS*, 86), since the challenge, ' Why do thy disciples . . . eat their bread with defiled hands ? ', appears in 5 and is fundamental to the story.

Mk. vii. 9-13   45. THE QUESTION OF QORBAN   Cf. Mt. xv. 3-6

The section appears to be an isolated saying attached in Mark's manner to vii. 1-8. Cf. Bultmann, 15 ; Dibelius, 220. This suggestion, however, is not wholly satisfactory. It is possible that the original *Streitgespräch* ended with 9-13 (cf. Albertz, 37), or that 9-13 is all that remains of a Pronouncement-story independent of, and parallel to, 1-8. The difficulty of this suggestion is that we do not know whether 9-13 is the reply to a question put to Jesus on the subject of Qorban or to a challenge addressed to Him to the scribes (cf. xii. 35-7). More important is the historical character of the saying discussed in the detached note on pp. 341 f. There can be no reasonable doubt that the words were spoken by Jesus and illustrate His attitude to the oral law. On this matter Mk, as an almost contemporary record, deserves greater credit than inferences based on the Mishnah.

Καὶ ἔλεγεν αὐτοῖς Καλῶς ἀθετεῖτε τὴν ἐντολὴν τοῦ θεοῦ, 9

9. Apart from ἀθετέω (vi. 26*) and τηρέω*, the verse repeats words already found in vii. 1-8. The variant reading στήσητε, ' establish ', is strongly attested by Western, Caesarean, and Antiochian MSS. (D W Θ 1 28 209 565 a b c f ff i q r¹ sys pe arm Cyp. Aug), and it may well be original. So Lagrange, 184. Klostermann, 78, reads the sentence as a question, but it is better, with Moffatt and RSV, to read it as an exclamation : ' You have a fine way . . . ! '. So read, the saying may well be original ; otherwise, it

has the appearance of an editorial link designed to introduce 10-13. The charge is put in an extreme form. The tradition is described as ' your tradition ', and the claim made is that, in order to establish it, God's commandment is being rejected. Whether the accusation is just depends on the interpretation of the difficult passage, 10-13, which follows.

The phrase καὶ ἔλεγεν αὐτοῖς is often a formula introducing sayings. A question to be considered is whether vii. 9-13 is an excerpt from the sayings-

10 ἵνα τὴν παράδοσιν ὑμῶν στήσητε· Μωυσῆς γὰρ εἶπεν Τίμα τὸν
ΠΑΤΈΡΑ ϹΟΥ ΚΑῚ ΤῊΝ ΜΗΤΈΡΑ ϹΟΥ, καί 'Ο ΚΑΚΟΛΟΓῶΝ ΠΑΤΈΡΑ ῍
11 ΜΗΤΈΡΑ ΘΑΝΆΤῼ ΤΕΛΕΓΤΆΤῼ· ὑμεῖς δὲ λέγετε 'Εὰν εἴπῃ ἄνθρωπος τῷ πατρὶ ἢ τῇ μητρί Κορβάν, ὅ ἐστιν Δῶρον, ὃ ἐὰν ἐξ

tradition, or whether it is the remnant of a Pronouncement-story parallel to 1-8. Matthew's version of 9 is different largely because he has inserted the whole section into the preceding story.

10. For Μωυσῆς v. i. 44. Matthew has ὁ γὰρ θεὸς εἶπεν (xv. 4). τιμάω, vii. 6. κακολογέω, ix. 39*, Mt. xv. 4, Ac. xix. 9**, ' to speak evil of ', ' re-vile ', ' abuse '; Cl. (rare), LXX, Pap. (VGT, 316). The quotations agree almost verbatim with the LXX text of Ex. xx. 12 (Deut. v. 16) and xxi. 16 (17). In the second passage the Heb. is מְקַלֵּל, ' he that curseth ' or ' he that makes contemptible '. Either of these meanings would make good sense in the light of what is said in 11 f. regarding Κορβάν. Billerbeck, i. 709 f., cites Rabbinic parallels for the render-ing ' he that curseth '. Lagrange, 185, also points out that the death penalty supposes an injury equivalent to a curse, and says that to-day in Palestine ' cursed be thy father ' and still more ' cursed be thy religion ' are personal insults. Can, however, ὁ κακολογῶν be used in this sense? AV and Moffatt translate it ' curseth ', but it is highly doubtful if it can be so rendered; we should expect rather ὁ καταρώμενος (W reads ἀθετῶν); and it is doubtless for this reason that RV, RSV, and Torrey translate ὁ κακολογῶν ' he who speaks evil of '. We require something like the AV rendering in order to make sense of 9-13, for the implication is that the parents are brought into con-tempt or cursed, not merely that they are reviled or abused, which the RV recognizes to be the meaning of the Greek. If this argument is sound, it would appear that the use of the LXX text is secondary, and that in the original saying a text more akin to the Hebrew must have been used by Jesus. Cf. vii. 6 f.

θάνατος, ix. 1, x. 33, xiii. 12, xiv. 34, 64*. τελευτάω, ix. 48* (also a quota-tion). For the construction θανάτῳ τελευτάτω, in which the fin. verb with the dat. represents the force of the Heb. infin. abs. (מוֹת יוּמָת), see the note on v. 42 and compare the use of the participle in iv. 12. The meaning is ' let him surely die ', v. Intr. 61.

A point of no small importance is that, while oral tradition is assailed by Jesus, the Law in the Decalogue is ac-cepted by Him as binding : what God said through Moses stands (cf. x. 3).

11 f. ὑμεῖς, in contrast with Μωυσῆς, is very emphatic and intentionally provocative. It is undesirable, with Wellhausen, 54, to omit λέγετε as an insertion, taking ὑμεῖς as the subject of ἀφίετε and so avoiding the anaco-luthon in ἐὰν εἴπῃ followed by the second person plural. Anacolutha are a feature of Mark's style; v. Intr. 50. Matthew supplies the natural apodosis in οὐ μὴ τιμήσει which he substitutes for the comment οὐκέτι ἀφίετε . . . in 12. For ἐάν c. subj. v. i. 40.

Κορβάν**, a transliteration of קָרְבָּן, ' an offering ', ' a gift devoted to God '. The word is not found in the LXX, but is used by Josephus, Ant. iv. 4. 4, Contra Apion. i. 167. Cf. ὁ κορβανᾶς, Mt. xxvii. 6**, ' the Temple treasury '. Mark adds ὅ ἐστιν δῶρον* for the benefit of his readers, but the Greek word does not adequately bring out the meaning of the original which denotes something banned or placed under a tabu. Perhaps it is for this reason that sys pe aeth omit the phrase.

The statement put into the lips of the scribes is hypothetical : ' If a man shall say ', but it is pointless unless there were actual cases of the kind. Rawlinson, 95, conjectures that ' there may have been some contemporary cause célèbre of this description, which

ἐμοῦ ὠφεληθῇς, οὐκέτι ἀφίετε αὐτὸν οὐδὲν ποιῆσαι τῷ πατρὶ ἢ 12
τῇ μητρί, ἀκυροῦντες τὸν λόγον τοῦ θεοῦ τῇ παραδόσει ὑμῶν ᾗ 13
παρεδώκατε· καὶ παρόμοια τοιαῦτα πολλὰ ποιεῖτε.

formed a subject of current talk in the bazaars of Galilee '.

ὠφελέω, v. 26. ὃ ἐὰν ἐξ ἐμοῦ ὠφεληθῇς is ' that wherewith thou shalt be profited of me '. This, however, is not what Mark means, and the translators rightly feel that a *potential* clause is intended, the suppressed protasis being, ' if it had not been a δῶρον'. Cf. AV, ' By whatsoever thou mightest be profited by me '; RV, ' That wherewith thou mightest have been profited by me '; RSV, ' What you would have gained from me '; Moffatt, ' This money might have been at your service '; Torrey, ' That which you would have received from me for your support'; cf. *in loc.* Gould, Lagrange, Plummer, Klostermann, etc. For this meaning we should expect the construction ἄν c. indic., and there is good reason to accept the ' convincing emendation ' (Moulton, ii. 85) independently suggested by Goodspeed, *ET*, xx. 471 f. and Blass, 320, ὃ ἄν (so D) ἐξ ἐμοῦ ὠφελήθης. For ἀφίημι c. infin. in the sense of *suffer, permit*, *v.* the note on i. 18, and for the double negative οὐκέτι . . . οὐδέν i. 44. On the question of Qorban see the detached Note, pp. 341-2.

13. In these words the charge is pressed home; the tradition the scribes have received renders void the word of God; and it is not an isolated example, but one of many. ἀκυρόω*, Mt. xv. 6, Gal. iii. 17**, ' to cancel ',

' revoke ', < κῦρος, ' authority ': Cl., LXX, Pap. (where it is frequently used of annulling wills and contracts, *VGT*, 20). τὸν λόγον τοῦ θεοῦ is the mind of God made known in His Law. The dat. τῇ παραδόσει is instrumental and the case of the relative pronoun which follows is assimilated to it. For the redundancy *v.* Intr. 52. D, supported by the O. Lat. (except f l r²), two Vulg. MSS., and syhl mg, adds τῇ μωρᾷ. The clause ᾗ παρεδώκατε (RV, ' which ye have delivered ') is awkwardly expressed and Moffatt (' which you keep up ') and RSV (' which you hand on ') give it a present sense. It is doubtful, however, if it can be so rendered. The phrase is wanting in sys and Mt. xv. 6. Lagrange, 186, explains it as an addition made by the Evangelist in order to complete the argument, and suggests that it may have been omitted because it appeared useless and perhaps difficult. This explanation does not seem satisfactory. As Plummer, 184, says, the aor. seems to be out of place; it looks like a primitive corruption influenced by the regular use of παραδίδωμι of the handing down of a tradition (cf. 1 Cor. xi. 2, 23, xv. 3). The sense requires παρελάβετε. καὶ παρόμοια τοιαῦτα πολλὰ ποιεῖτε is peculiar to Mark's narrative and may be a homiletical expansion, since the saying ends effectively with τῇ παραδόσει ὑμῶν. παρόμοιος**. τοιοῦτος, *v.* iv. 33.

DETACHED NOTE ON QORBAN

The exact nature of the point at issue and the extent to which the practice mentioned in 11 f. obtained are not easy to determine in consequence of our limited knowledge of existing conditions in the time of Christ. In the Mishnah the tractate *Nedarim* shows how prone the Jews were to use oaths including *Qorban*. Often substitutes, *qonam, qonah, qonas*, were used, but these were held to be equally binding (*Ned.* i. 1 f.). A man, for example, might say, ' *Qonam!* if I taste cooked food ' (*Ned.*

vi. 1), or, of a cow, ' *Qonam!* if I ever again plough my field with it '
(*Ned.* iv. 6), or again, ' *Qonam* be any benefit my wife has of me, for she
has stolen my purse ' (*Ned.* iii. 2). This evidence comes from the second
century and how far back it extends is uncertain.

In Mk the man declares that the support on which his parents might
have counted is *qorban* ; that is to say, it is dedicated to God, or it is the
subject of an oath uttered perhaps in a fit of passion. The ban may be
actual or hypothetical (' *Qorban!* if thou shalt be profited '), but, in either
case, despite the fifth commandment, in consequence of it the parents
have lost their hope of support. Montefiore, i. 149, maintains that ' the
annulling, not the maintenance, of vows was the work of (Rabbinic)
tradition ', and further that ' according to the Rabbinic law as codified
in the Mishnah, and commented on in the Talmud, the Rabbis are on
the side of Jesus, and take his very line '. With important qualifications,
this statement is true. In the Mishnah, for example (*v.* Danby, 275),
with reference to a case like that in Mk, Rabbi Eliezer says, ' They may
open for men the way (to repentance) by reason of the honour due to
father and mother '. ' But ', the statement continues, ' the Sages forbid
it ', and the contrary opinion of Rabbi Zadok is given. Finally, it is said,
' But the Sages agree with R. Eliezer that in a matter between a man
and his father and mother, the way may be opened to him by reason of the
honour due to his father and mother ', *Ned.* ix. 1. This evidence, however, is late, and it is possible that in the days of Jesus stricter views
prevailed. Cf. McNeile, 224 f. ; Lagrange, 185 f.

Mk. vii. 14-23   46. SAYINGS ON DEFILEMENT   Cf. Mt. xv.
                                                   10 f., 15-20

These sayings are attached to vii. 1-8, 9-13 by the method already
illustrated in ii. 21 f., 27 f., iii. 27-9, and iv. 21-5, according to which Mark
appends sayings on similar topics to Pronouncement-stories or Parables.
The arrangement is topical and the narrative element small. In vii. 14
it is limited to the statement καὶ προσκαλεσάμενος πάλιν τὸν ὄχλον ἔλεγεν
αὐτοῖς, which appears to be purely editorial, and in vii. 17 to καὶ ὅτε
εἰσῆλθεν εἰς τὸν οἶκον ἀπὸ τοῦ ὄχλου, which is also editorial but may rest on
a tradition that private instruction was given to the disciples. In vii. 20-3
only ἔλεγεν δέ is used. In vii. 14-16, the saying in 15 is unquestionably
genuine. In laying down the principle that uncleanness comes from within,
and not from without, it stated a truth, uncommon in contemporary
Judaism, which was destined to free Christianity from the bondage of
legalism. The form of the saying is that of Semitic antithetical parallelism
(cf. Burney, *PL*, 74) and the parabolic mode of expression is one calcu-
lated to provoke thought. This fact warns us not too hastily to dismiss
the possibility that the disciples asked questions concerning it and were
given further instruction. Still more likely is it that it led to discussion
and interpretation in the early Church. The explicitness of 18b-19 and
its crudity of expression suggest that this explanatory saying received
its form in a Gentile community, for we cannot account for the early
disputes at Jerusalem and Antioch if Jesus spoke so directly. The par-
ticularity, as well as the vocabulary, of 21 f., points to the same conclusion.
Interpretation, however, is not necessarily corruption ; on the contrary,

it may give expression to latent ideas. The two sayings are Christian targums which, in the Church for which they were formulated, brought out the true meaning of the teaching of Jesus and applied it to the existing situation. Our only surprise can be that a Church which received this catechetical instruction still needed the teaching of St. Paul in Rom. xiv. 2 f. on eating herbs. See further, Intr. 96.

Καὶ προσκαλεσάμενος πάντα τὸν ὄχλον ἔλεγεν αὐτοῖς ᾿Ακού- 14
σατέ μου πάντες καὶ σύνετε.   οὐδὲν ἔστιν ἔξωθεν τοῦ ἀνθρώπου 15
εἰσπορευόμενον εἰς αὐτὸν ὃ δύναται κοινῶσαι αὐτόν· ἀλλὰ τὰ ἐκ
τοῦ ἀνθρώπου ἐκπορευόμενά ἐστιν τὰ κοινοῦντα τὸν ἄνθρωπον.

14 f. The introduction to the section in 14a consists of common Markan words and is almost certainly the Evangelist's free composition: for προσκαλέομαι v. iii. 13; πάλιν ii. 1, ὄχλος ii. 4, συνίημι iv. 12. The use of προσκαλεσάμενος is especially characteristic of his style. The command to hearken recalls the introduction to the parable of the Sower, but here the aorists, as relating to a single saying, are more appropriate. Matthew has present imperatives. For the construction οὐδὲν ἔστιν . . . ὅ . . . v. ix. 39 and x. 29. ' The termination -θεν has become stereotyped and meaningless in most cases in the words ἔσωθεν (vii. 21, 23*), ἔξωθεν (vii. 18*) " within ", " without ", as is often the case even in Attic Gk ', Blass, 59. In 15-23 they have the meaning ' from within ', ' from without '. κοινόω, vii. 15 (bis), 18, 20, 23*, Mt (5), Ac. x. 15, xi. 9, xxi. 28, Heb. ix. 13**, which in Cl. Gk means ' to make common ', ' communicate ', ' share ', is used in the LXX and the NT with the meaning ' to defile ', ' profane ' (Ac. x. 15, xi. 9, ' to count as unclean '); cf. κοινός vii. 2. In its implications, the saying in 15 is revolutionary, but it is expressed in general terms in an enigmatical form described in 17 as a παραβολή, ' a parabolic saying ' or even ' riddle '. Matthew makes it explicit by adding εἰς τὸ στόμα and ἐκ τοῦ στόματος (xv. 11). It is possible also that in the Markan form the phrases εἰσπορευόμενον εἰς αὐτόν and ἐκπορευόμενα are explanatory additions, for they are detachable and are characteristic of Mark's vocabulary; cf. Hawkins, 12. In this case the original saying is more arresting. Ultimately, it implies the abrogation of the Law regarding clean and unclean meats (cf. vii. 19b); but this consequence is not expressly stated. Cf. Klostermann, 79. Nor is it likely that Jesus directly repudiated the food laws of Lev. xi = Deut. xiv, since otherwise the hesitations of the primitive Church on this issue (cf. Ac. x. 14, xv. 28 f., Gal. ii. 11-17, Rom. xiv. 14, Col. ii. 20-2) would be inexplicable. Cf. Swete, 150. Few religious principles, however, have proved so pregnant. There is no parallel to the saying in the Rabbinical writings (cf. Billerbeck, i. 719), but the principle is endorsed by modern liberal Jews. ' THINGS cannot be religiously either clean or unclean; only PERSONS. And persons cannot be defiled by things, they can only be defiled by themselves, by acting irreligiously ', Montefiore, i. 153. The ancient counterpart to the idea of a ' person ' is expressed by the use of ὁ ἄνθρωπος as in ii. 27.

Of the genuineness of the saying there can be no question. Bultmann, 158, is without hesitation in finding in it the words of Jesus (v. also p. 110). Cf. also Sundwall, 44; J. Weiss, 224; Montefiore, i. 132 f. Montefiore says that to doubt its authenticity ' seems scepticism run wild '. Mark may have derived the saying from a primitive Roman collection.

The editorial link in 14 is loose, and

16 εἴ τις ἔχει ὦτα ἀκούειν ἀκουέτω. Καὶ ὅτε εἰσῆλθεν εἰς οἶκον
17 ἀπὸ τοῦ ὄχλου, ἐπηρώτων αὐτὸν οἱ μαθηταὶ αὐτοῦ τὴν παρα-
18 βολήν. καὶ λέγει αὐτοῖς Οὕτως καὶ ὑμεῖς ἀσύνετοί ἐστε; οὐ
νοεῖτε ὅτι πᾶν τὸ ἔξωθεν εἰσπορευόμενον εἰς τὸν ἄνθρωπον οὐ
19 δύναται αὐτὸν κοινῶσαι, ὅτι οὐκ εἰσπορεύεται αὐτοῦ εἰς τὴν
καρδίαν ἀλλ᾽ εἰς τὴν κοιλίαν, καὶ εἰς τὸν ἀφεδρῶνα ἐκπορεύεται;
20 —καθαρίζων πάντα τὰ βρώματα. ἔλεγεν δὲ ὅτι Τὸ ἐκ τοῦ

still more so if, with A W Θ *et al.* fam. 1 fam. 13 22 28 33 700 1071 *al. pler.* f sys pe hl sa geo arm, we read πάντα instead of πάλιν (ℵ B D L Δ 892 a b ff vg syhl mg bo aeth Aug). In favour of this preference is the difficulty of saying to what πάλιν refers, its frequency in Mk, and the congruity of πάντα with πάντες which immediately follows. Probably also we should read εἰ τις ἔχει ὦτα ἀκούειν ἀκουέτω (16), with most MSS, against ℵ B L Δ* 28 bo geo¹. Cf. Lagrange, 188 f.; Allen, 106; Rawlinson, 96; Moffatt, AV, as against Ti, WH, RV, RSV; Plummer, 179; Bartlet, 223. The saying (cf. iv. 9) is especially appropriate here, as following upon a gnomic utterance intended to provoke thought.

At this point Matthew adds a question by the disciples : 'Do you know that the Pharisees were offended when they heard this saying ?', followed by a saying from M: 'Every plant which my heavenly Father has not planted will be rooted up. Let them alone ; they are blind guides. And if a blind man leads a blind man, both will fall into a pit' (xv. 12-14).

17-19. Judged by its vocabulary, style, and content, 17 was composed by the Evangelist in order to provide a setting for the explanation which follows. εἰς οἶκον, iii. 20, ix. 28*, is 'indoors'; cf. ἐν οἴκῳ, ii. 1. The suggestion that the house may have been that of Peter at Capernaum is mere speculation, especially if vii. 1-23 is a cycle of catechetical tradition formed before the Gospel was written. Here, as in xi. 29, ἐπερωτάω (v. 9) is used with two accusatives; cf. iv. 10. For παραβολή v. iii. 23. The use of this

word in the sense of 'dark saying' (*mashal*) is justified by the terms of vii. 15 and therefore the request for an explanation is natural ; but it is another question whether the explanation which follows is original. If it is not, 17-19 is an exegetical comment which arose in the course of catechetical praxis.

The question which follows tends to support this view. Cf. οὕτως καὶ ὑμεῖς ἀσύνετοί ἐστε ; with vi. 52, viii. 17. The Evangelist tends to over-emphasize the dullness of the disciples. οὕτως (ii. 7) is here *sicine*, 'Is it not so ?', rather than *tam* taken with ἀσύνετοι, and καὶ ὑμεῖς is emphatic, 'Then ye also'. Cf. vg, *Sic et uos imprudentes estis?* Matthew has ἀκμήν, 'even yet' (xv. 16). ἀσύνετος*, Mt. xv. 17**,=Cl. ἄφοδος or ἀπόπατος, 'a privy', vg *secessus*. D reads εἰς τὸν ὀχετόν, a reading which Wellhausen, 55, and Torrey, 84, accept, taking it with καθαρίζων, despite the breach of concord, and translating 'the bowel which purifies all foods'. This exegesis is unnecessary and improbable. There is no doubt, however, that from very early times καθαρίζων πάντα τὰ βρώματα was felt to be difficult. Matthew omits the words, D reads καθαρίζει, and some inferior MSS. have καθαρίζον. M. Black, 159, points out that sys implies a text in which βρῶμα ('ukhla) is the subject of a passive verb : 'all the food being cast out and

ἀνθρώπου ἐκπορευόμενον ἐκεῖνο κοινοῖ τὸν ἄνθρωπον· ἔσωθεν 21
γὰρ ἐκ τῆς καρδίας τῶν ἀνθρώπων οἱ διαλογισμοὶ οἱ κακοὶ
ἐκπορεύονται, πορνεῖαι, κλοπαί, φόνοι, μοιχεῖαι, πλεονεξίαι, 22

purged away'; and that 'ukhla is regularly used in Palestinian Aramaic in the sense of excrementum. The pass. of the last verb is generally not distinguished in form from the act., and he is inclined to think that καθαρίζων is a mistranslation or that the translator preferred to read an act. and connect it with the subject of λέγει. Cf. Pallis, 25.

On the whole, it seems best to explain the strongly attested καθαρίζων (א A B L W Δ Θ et al. fam. 1 fam. 13 28 543 565 579 892 1071 et al. it (exc. i r¹) vg sype sa bo) as the Evangelist's comment. Restoring the interpretation held by Origen, Chrysostom, and Gregory Thaumaturgus, Field, 31 f., argues that καθαρίζων depends on καὶ λέγει αὐτοῖς, ' This he said, cleansing all meats '. So RV against AV; cf. RSV and Moffatt, ' Thus he declared all foods clean '. In this way the implications of the teaching of Jesus are stated, but not what He actually said at the time.¹ Cf. B. T. D. Smith, 148; K. Lake, BC, iv. 115.

In addition to the modifications already noted, Matthew introduces the saying by a request of Peter, ' Explain to us the parable ' (xv. 15).

20-3. A further explanation follows in which 15b is repeated in the sing. in 20 and expounded in 21-3. Τὸ ἐκ τοῦ ἀνθρώπου ἐκπορευόμενον, casus pendens, is followed by the resumptive pronoun ἐκεῖνο. V. Intr. 58. From within (ἔσωθεν, v. the note on vii. 15), it is explained, from the centre of a man's personality, evil thoughts go forth, and a list without parallel in the sayings of Jesus is given.

διαλογισμός*, ' a balancing ', ' discussion ', in the LXX and NT ' a thought ', ' a cogitation '; Moffatt

' designs '. The διαλογισμοὶ οἱ κακοί are not merely evil thoughts, but evil devisings which issue in degraded acts and vices now mentioned. For similar lists see Gal. v. 19-21, Rom, i. 29-31, and 1 Pet. iv. 3. Cf. also Wisd. xiv. 25 f., which among other vices mentions φόνος, κλοπή, δόλος, μοιχεία, and ἀσέλγεια. Catalogues of virtues and vices were drawn up by the Greek philosophers, e.g. Aristotle, Eth. Nicom. II. vii; they appeared also in comedies and on the counters used in parlour games. See the discussion of the catalogue method in E. G. Selwyn's First Ep. of St. Peter, Essay II, 421 ff. Klostermann, 80 f., cites an interesting Buddhist example from The Sacred Books of the East, x. 2. 40: ' Destroying life, killing, cutting, binding, stealing, speaking lies, fraud and deceptions, worthless reading, intercourse with another's wife — this is defilement, but not the eating of flesh '.

Of the twelve nouns in the Markan list six are in the plur. indicating evil acts and six in the sing. describing the different vices. πορνεῖαι* are acts of sexual vice. Originally meaning fornication, the word (rare in Cl. Gk) came to denote barter or traffic in sexual vice, being a wider term than μοιχεία (VGT, 529). κλοπαί* are thefts, φόνοι (xv. 7*) murders, and μοιχεῖαι* adulteries. Cf. Hos. iv. 2, φόνος καὶ κλοπὴ καὶ μοιχεία κέχυται ἐπὶ τῆς γῆς. πλεονεξίαι* are acts of coveting, but may be lusts (cf. Moffatt), for sometimes, as here, the word is associated with terms describing sexual sins (cf. Eph. iv. 19, v. 3, Col. iii. 5, 2 Pet. ii. 3). This meaning is not found in Cl. Gk, but VGT, 518, cites an example from the papyri in which the word is connected with sins of the flesh. See

¹ It is possibly right to use the catechetical argument in support of the textual evidence for καθαρίζων. A catechetical interest is certainly reflected in 14-23, and the tendency of this interes is to make sayings more explicit. If, therefore, Dr. Black is right in referring to the underlying Aramaic, the second alternative he mentions should be preferred.

πονηρίαι, δόλος, ἀσέλγεια, ὀφθαλμὸς πονηρός, βλασφημία, ὑπερη-
23 φανία, ἀφροσύνη· πάντα ταῦτα τὰ πονηρὰ ἔσωθεν ἐκπορεύεται
καὶ κοινοῖ τὸν ἄνθρωπον.

further, W. B. Sedgwick, *ET*, xxxvi. 478 f. *VGT* refers to Bunyan who mentions as Beelzebub's friends, ' my old Lord Lechery, Sir Having Greedy, with the rest of our nobility '. πονηρίαι* is a general term denoting acts of wickedness, and corresponding to the broad term ἀφροσύνη* which stands at the end of the second half of the list. Moffatt has ' malice '.

The six vices are headed by δόλος (xiv. 1*) ' deceit ', followed by ἀσέλγεια* ' wantonness '. The history of ἀσέλγεια is unknown (Moulton, ii. 287), its connexion with θέλγω being dubious (*VGT*, 84). In Plato, *Rep.* 424 E, it is used with the meaning *impudence* and thus is akin to ὕβρις, but in late Gk it was associated with the idea of sensuality. ' Wantonness ', however, is a better rendering since the word suggests something open and shameless. ' A man may be ἀκάθαρτος and hide his sin ; he does not become ἀσελγής until he shocks public decency', Lightfoot, *Gal.* 210. ὀφθαλμὸς πονηρός** is ' an evil eye ', i.e. envying, or possibly a malignant glance which casts a spell upon men, an idea found the world over (cf. F. T. Elworthy, *ERE*, v. 608-15) and not impossible here if 20-3 is an interpretation of the teaching of Jesus. Most commentators take the former view, comparing Lk. xi. 34 = Mt. vi. 22 f. Cf. Deut. xv. 9,

Sir. xiv. 10, xxxiv. 13, Tob. iv. 7 (B). Quoting Mt. xx. 15, ' Is thine eye evil, because I am good ? ', C. Ryder Smith argues that Jesus revolutionized the idea of an Evil Eye, interpreting it of the evil motive which becomes a moral boomerang (cf. Mt. vi. 22 f.). See the interesting discussion in *ET*, liii. 181 f., 354 f. (C. J. Cadoux), liv. 26 f. Cf. also Lightfoot, *Gal.* 133 f.; Meecham, 145.

Here, and possibly in iii. 28, βλασφημία is ' slander ' rather than ' blasphemy ' (xiv. 64*). It is strange that ὑπερηφανία**, ' pride ', appears here only in the NT, though ὑπερήφανος is found in Lk. i. 51, Rom. i. 30, 2 Tim. iii. 2, Jas. iv. 6, 1 Pet. v. 5**. In Cl. Gk the word means ' arrogance ' and it is so rendered here by Moffatt and Torrey. In the LXX it is common ; cf. also *Aristeas* 262, 269 (*v.* Meecham, *LA*, 71). The more subtle idea of self-centredness is illustrated in the parable of the Rich Fool (Lk. xii. 16-21). The last vice mentioned is ἀφροσύνη*, ' foolishness ', or ' folly ' ; it is the stupidity of the man who lacks moral judgment. Moffatt has ' recklessness ', Torrey ' impiety ', RSV ' foolishness '.

On the question whether the list is interpretative the vocabulary has an important bearing. The facts are as follows :

	Mk	Mt	Lk	Jn	Ac	Pl	1 Pt	Apoc	Rest
πορνεία	1	3		1	3	10		7	
κλοπή	1	1							
φόνος	2	1	2		1	1		1	1
μοιχεία	1	1		1?					
πλεονεξία	1		1			6			2
πονηρία	1	1	1		1	3			
δόλος	2	1		1	1	3	3		
ἀσέλγεια	1					4	1		4
ὀφθαλμὸς πονηρός	1								
βλασφημία	3	4	1	1		2		5	2
ὑπερηφανία	1								
ἀφροσύνη	1					3			
	16	12	5	3	6	32	4	13	9

The table shows that the vocabulary is Pauline, especially as regards πορνεία, πλεονεξία, πονηρία, δόλος, ἀσέλγεια, and ἀφροσύνη. This fact, the absence of such lists from the sayings-tradition, the comment ' cleansing all meats ', and other signs of a catechetical interest in 1-23, suggest that 20-3 is an early Christian interpretation of vii. 15. Cf. Bultmann, 15 ; Bartlet, 225 ; Blunt, 190 ; Branscomb, 128 : ' One feels the cooler atmosphere of later exegesis ' ; Lohmeyer, 142. The interpretation brings out what is latent in the original saying. In Mt this process is carried farther. While omitting many of the items in Mark's list, the Evangelist adds ψευδομαρτυρίαι and brings his catalogue into closer agreement with the Decalogue (cf. Smith, 148). ' These are the things which defile the man ', he says, and then, connecting the whole with the dispute concerning the washing of hands, adds, ' but to eat with unwashed hands does not defile the man ' (xv. 20).

Mk. vii. 24-30   47. THE SYRO-PHOENICIAN   Cf. Mt. xv. 21-8
WOMAN

This narrative is more akin in form to the Pronouncement-story than to the Miracle-story. Bultmann, 38, treats it in an Appendix to the *Biographische Apophthegmata*. The main interest is the attitude of Jesus to the Gentiles. Nevertheless, the narrative has not yet assumed the form characteristic of the Pronouncement-story ; it is still a narrative proper containing details which stamp it as primitive. Among these details are the locating of the incident, the vain quest for privacy, the woman's witty reply, the pleasure it gave Jesus, the passing reference to the cure, and signs of Aramaic tradition reflected by the vocabulary and style. *V.* Comm. Mark has Gentile readers in mind in the saying ' Let the children *first* be fed ', but if so, in recording the words ' It is not good to take the children's bread and throw it to the dogs ', he has followed with fidelity an existing tradition.[1]

The relation between Mk and Mt is difficult to decide. Dibelius, 261, suggests the use of a common source belonging to the sayings-tradition, which contained only the speeches and assumed the cure, like the source presupposed by the story of the Centurion's Servant in Mt. viii. 5-13 = Lk. vii. 1-10. Other scholars suggest that Matthew has conflated two sources in Mk and M. Cf. Streeter, 260 ; T. W. Manson, *SJ*, 200 f. The latter is the better hypothesis, for the basic use of Mk is manifest, not only in Mt. xv. 21, 26 f., where the agreement is close, but also in the modifications of 26 and possibly of 28, while the insertion (from M) of 22-5, or at least of 24, is illustrated by other cases in which Matthew inserts sayings in the Markan framework (e.g. Mt. ix. 13, xii. 5-7, 11 f.). Mt. xv. 24, ' I was not sent save to the lost sheep of the house of Israel ', is in tone like x. 5 f., ' Go not into the way of the Gentiles, and enter not into a city of the Samaritans : but go rather to the lost sheep of the house of Israel ' ; and probably both owe their rigour to exploitation by Jewish Christians in controversies regarding the Gentile Mission. We shall more truly understand the attitude of Jesus to the Gentiles, and the process which gave rise to these sayings, from Mark's narrative. This view is supported by the secondary features in Matthew's account.

[1] Comparing the Synoptic narratives with parallel Rabbinic stories, P. Fiebig, *Der Erzählungsstil der Evangelien*, 115, observes that living oral tradition lies at the basis of both : *Alle diese Erscheinungen sind von den rabbinischen Anekdoten her geläufig. Bei diesen, wie bei den Überlieferungen von Jesus, liegt die lebendig formende mündliche Überlieferung zugrunde.*

By Mark the cure is assumed. No word or promise of healing is spoken, only the strong assurance that the daemon has gone out from the daughter. It may be that Mark regards the incident as a cure wrought from a distance, but he does not expressly record it as such, and serious difficulties are raised by this interpretation. The usual Markan tradition is that cures are wrought by contact (i. 31 f., iii. 10, v. 41, vi. 5, 56, etc.) or by a commanding word (i. 25, v. 8, ix. 25), and if the incident were one of direct healing, we should expect an account more like Matthew's. Moreover, there are strong reasons for thinking that the references to healing did not belong to the original form of the parallel story of the Centurion's Servant. Cf. Harnack, *The Sayings of Jesus*, 210 f. In Luke's version all that is said is that the centurion found his servant in good health. Parallels from psychotherapy are wanting, and alleged ancient examples of *Fernheilungen* (Bultmann, 248), as, for example the healing of the son of Gamaliel II through the prayer of Rabbi Ḥanina ben Dosa, are not cases of direct healing. One must recognize that in the healings of Jesus there is a unique element to which no exact parallel exists. Nevertheless, the arguments summarized above and the objective character of the Markan narrative suggest, as an alternative to the hypothesis of healing at a distance, the explanation of supernatural knowledge. This alternative is also miraculous, in the sense that it implies a knowledge transcending that of common experience, but it has strong advantages of its own. It gives Mark's account its most natural sense ; it is not exposed to the difficulties of the common interpretation, which in fact is based on Mt rather than Mk ; and it is in keeping with that intuitive knowledge which is part of the secret of Jesus (cf. Mk. ii. 8), and accordant with His unique knowledge of the mind of His Father (cf. Mt. xi. 25-7 = Lk. x. 21 f.). Of this knowledge all that we can say is that it is born of an incomparable sense of communion with God, sustained by prayer and made possible by an unmatched consciousness of Sonship. To those who think of Jesus so, it cannot be a matter of surprise that, with complete certainty, He should say to the woman, ' Because of this saying go, the daemon has gone out of thy daughter '.

24   Ἐκεῖθεν δὲ ἀναστὰς ἀπῆλθεν εἰς τὰ ὅρια Τύρου. Καὶ εἰσελθὼν εἰς οἰκίαν οὐδένα ἤθελεν γνῶναι, καὶ οὐκ ἠδυνάσθη λαθεῖν·

24. For Mark's use of ἐκεῖθεν v. vi. 1, and for the redundant ἀναστάς i. 35. A new turn in the story is indicated by the geographical statement and Mark's rare use of δέ (*v.* Intr. 49). So rarely does he use ἐκεῖθεν (5 times) that we are entitled to infer that it was present in his source. It appears to refer to the house mentioned in vii. 17, but more probably points back to the plain of Gennesaret (vi. 53-6). It may also have stood originally in connexion with another series of events ; cf. Schmidt, 198. τὰ ὅρια (v. 17) Τύρου (iii. 8), described as Φοινίκη in the

Acts (xi. 19) and Herodotus (i. 2), is the district extending to the borders of Galilee. How far Jesus penetrated into this pagan region is not stated, but there is no reason to think of a journey far across the border. καὶ Σιδῶνος (iii. 8), bracketed by WH, is omitted by D L W Δ Θ 28 565 a b ff i n r¹ sys Or, and is probably an assimilation to Mt. xv. 21 and Mk. vii. 31. Cf. Turner, 36.

The purpose of the retirement is not missionary; the disciples are not mentioned and there is no indication in Mark's account of a flight from the

ἀλλ' εὐθὺς ἀκούσασα γυνὴ περὶ αὐτοῦ, ἧς εἶχεν τὸ θυγάτριον 25
αὐτῆς πνεῦμα ἀκάθαρτον, ἐλθοῦσα προσέπεσεν πρὸς τοὺς πόδας
αὐτοῦ· ἡ δὲ γυνὴ ἦν Ἑλληνίς, ⌜Συροφοινίκισσα⌝ τῷ γένει· καὶ 26

26 Σύρα Φοινίκισσα

menace of Herod Antipas. The phrase εἰσελθὼν εἰς οἰκίαν οὐδένα ἤθελεν γνῶναι, ' and wanted no one to know of it ', shows that Jesus was seeking privacy, and, in the light of the story which follows, it may be conjectured that He desired to reflect upon the scope and course of His ministry. εἰς οἰκίαν is ' into a house '. Whose house it was is not stated. Privacy, however, was impossible : οὐκ ἠδυνάσθη λαθεῖν. It may be that, while stating a fact, Mark believed that it was impossible for Jesus to escape recognition. The frustrated purpose was probably due to the fact that the fame of Jesus had spread beyond Galilee and that people across the border had heard Him there. ἠδυνάσθη is an Ionic form (Moulton, ii. 234), found frequently in the LXX and several times in the papyri (VGT, 171), but in the NT here only and in Mt. xvii. 16 (B). λανθάνω*, Lk. viii. 47, Ac. xxvi. 26, Heb. xiii. 2, 2 Pet. iii. 5, 8**.

Matthew omits ἀναστάς and uses ἀνεχώρησεν (xv. 21). He has no parallel to 24b. In his version of the story it is doubtful if Jesus crosses the border (v. Mt. xv. 22), and it may be that he does not wish to say that there were things Jesus could not do. Cf. McNeile, 230 ; Smith, 148.

25 f. εὐθύς (v. i. 10) may here suggest that it was immediately the woman heard of Jesus that she came to Him (RV and RSV), but it is also possible that the adverb is used more generally in the sense of so then ; cf. Moffatt and Torrey who leave the word untranslated. What the woman heard is not stated ; either His fame or His presence, or both. For θυγάτριον v. v. 23 ; πνεῦμα ἀκάθαρτον i. 23 ; and for the use of the relative pronoun

with the redundant αὐτῆς v. Intr. 60. Several linguistic features suggest that the narrative reflects Aramaic tradition. This point is of importance in view of the possibility that Mark has adapted the story in the interests of Gentile readers.

προσέπεσεν recalls iii. 11 and v. 23. The prostration is a mark of the deepest respect as well as of grief. Matthew's account is much fuller. The woman addresses Jesus with the words, Ἐλέησόν με, κύριε υἱὸς Δαυείδ· ἡ θυγάτηρ μου κακῶς δαιμονίζεται, and the Evangelist adds, ὁ δὲ οὐκ ἀπεκρίθη αὐτῇ λόγον (xv. 22). The disciples say, Ἀπόλυσον αὐτήν, ὅτι κράζει ὄπισθεν ἡμῶν, and Jesus replies, Οὐκ ἀπεστάλην εἰ μὴ εἰς τὰ πρόβατα τὰ ἀπολωλότα οἴκου Ἰσραήλ (xv. 23 f.). Thus, the Matthaean narrative is more Jewish in tone, and by some is thought to be more original.

Mark describes the woman as ' a Greek ', Ἑλληνίς* (Ac. xvii. 12**), and since he further characterizes her as a Συροφοινίκισσα* τῷ γένει, it is probable that he means ' a pagan ' or ' Gentile ', a sign that he has Gentile readers in mind. τῷ γένει is a dat. of reference, and ' Syro-Phoenician ' is a term used in antithesis to ' Liby-Phoenician ' (Λιβυφοῖνιξ) or ' Carthaginian ' (Polybius iii. 33). For Συροφοῖνιξ v. Lucian, Deor. Conc. 4, cf. Juvenal viii. 159.[1] Mark, then, as most commentators note, describes the woman by her religion and her nationality. Cf. Windisch, KThW, ii. 506. Matthew uses the Biblical term Χαναναία (LXX, Gen. xii. 6), ' Canaanite ', and says that she came forth ἀπὸ τῶν ὁρίων ἐκείνων (xv. 22). This phrase can be taken to imply that Jesus is still in Galilee if ἀνεχώρησεν εἰς τὰ μέρη Τύρου καὶ Σιδῶνος (xv. 21) means that

---

[1] Swete, 156, prefers the reading Σύρα Φοινίκισσα (B and most MSS.), and Couchoud, JTS, xxxiv. 120, conjectures (cf. Pallis, 26) ἡ δὲ γυνὴ ἦν χήρα (syˢ) Φοινίκισσα. Cf. Lohmeyer, 146.

ἠρώτα αὐτὸν ἵνα τὸ δαιμόνιον ἐκβάλῃ ἐκ τῆς θυγατρὸς αὐτῆς.
27 καὶ ἔλεγεν αὐτῇ Ἄφες πρῶτον χορτασθῆναι τὰ τέκνα, οὐ γάρ
ἐστιν καλὸν λαβεῖν τὸν ἄρτον τῶν τέκνων καὶ τοῖς κυναρίοις
28 βαλεῖν. ἡ δὲ ἀπεκρίθη λέγουσα αὐτῷ Κύριε, καὶ τὰ κυνάρια

Jesus withdrew in the direction of the district of Tyre and Sidon. For the construction ἠρώτα αὐτὸν ἵνα . . . ἐκβάλῃ, indicating the substance of her request, see the notes on iii. 9 and v. 10; δαιμόνιον, i. 34.

27 f. For ἀφίημι v. i. 34; for χορτάζω vi. 42. τὰ τέκνα (ii. 5) is here used of the Jews; cf. Isa. i. 2, ' I have nourished and brought up children ', Lk. xv. 31, Rom. ix. 4. The suggestion (Lohmeyer, 147) that Jesus is the ' Father ' who in a ' Johannine ' sense gives His children bread, is remote from this kind of narrative.

It is frequently suggested that πρῶτον is a modification of the original story, introduced by Mark or a later redactor under the influence of Pauline teaching in Rom. i. 16 (' to the Jew first, and also to the Greek '), ii. 9 f.; cf. Bultmann, 38; Klostermann, 82; Holtzmann, 144; B. Weiss, 117; J. Weiss, 225. Bussmann, i. 49-52, assigns the whole story to a later edition of Mk. The absence of a parallel to 27a in Mt gives doubtful support to the redaction theory, for Matthew's view of the incident differs from that of Mark. From the standpoint of internal consistency there is good reason to think that 27a is original, for some encouragement must have been given to the woman to prompt her witty reply in 28, and for this purpose the forbidding words of 27b are not adequate. ' Let the children *first* be fed ', supplies just what is necessary. Moreover, this use of πρῶτον is fairly common in Mk; v. iii. 27.

(ἐστὶν) καλόν c. infin., ix. 5, 43, 45, 47, c. εἰ and indic. ix. 42, xiv. 21*. The frequent references to bread (ἄρτος, ii. 26) in the two narrative-cycles, vi. 30-vii. 37 and viii. 1-26, may indicate a catechetical interest in the Eucharist.

κυνάριον, vii. 28*, Mt. xv. 26 f.**, ' a little dog ', ' puppy ', dim. of κύων, of which κυνίδιον is also a diminutive and, according to Phryn. 157, is ' more correct ' (LS, 1010). For κυνάριον Sharp, 23, quotes Epictetus iv. 1. 111, ἐπὶ κυνάριον, ἐπὶ ἱππάριον, ἐπὶ ἀγρίδιον (VGT, 364). Gentiles are sometimes described as ' dogs ' by Jewish writers, generally with reference to their vices. Wellhausen, 56, quotes a saying of Rabbi Eliezer, ' He who eats with an idolator is like unto one who eats with a dog '; cf. Billerbeck, i. 724 f.; Abrahams, ii. 195 f.; Montefiore, i. 167 f. The apparent harshness of the saying of Jesus is softened by the fact that He speaks of κυνάρια, not κύνες. Turner, 37, warns us that Mark uses diminutives too regularly for us to lay very much stress on this; but the word is not the only indication of a gentler tone. 27a and the fact that the woman makes her witty reply, together with the reference to ' the children's bread ' and the phrase τὰ κυνάρια ὑποκάτω τῆς τραπέζης in 28, all show that He is speaking of household dogs. Cf. Origen, τὰ κυνίδια τῆς οἰκίας, Mt. tom. xi. 17; and see Tobit v. 17, ὁ κύων τοῦ παιδαρίου. It does not seem necessary, therefore, with T. R. Glover, The Conflict of Religions, 127 n., to suppose that the allusion to dogs has been thrown back into Jesus's words from the woman's reply. Nor is it sufficient to explain 27b as a half-facetious saying, intended to test the woman's faith. Faith, in fact, is not mentioned in Mark's account (contr. Mt. xv. 28). Rather must we recognize a tension in the mind of Jesus concerning the scope of His ministry, and that, in a sense, He is speaking to Himself as well as to the woman. Her reply shows that she is quick to perceive this.

ὑποκάτω τῆς τραπέζης ἐσθίουσιν ἀπὸ τῶν ψιχίων τῶν παιδίων.
καὶ εἶπεν αὐτῇ Διὰ τοῦτον τὸν λόγον ὕπαγε, ἐξελήλυθεν ἐκ τῆς 29
θυγατρός σου τὸ δαιμόνιον. καὶ ἀπελθοῦσα εἰς τὸν οἶκον αὐτῆς 30
εὗρεν τὸ παιδίον βεβλημένον ἐπὶ τὴν κλίνην καὶ τὸ δαιμόνιον
ἐξεληλυθός.

For ἀπεκρίθη λέγουσα v. iii. 33.[1] The woman agrees and draws a further inference : the house dogs under the table eat the children's crumbs. ναί*, ' yes ', ' even so ', is omitted by P45 D W Θ 13 69 543 565 700 b c ff i arm, probably rightly ; cf. Turner, 37, JTS, xxviii. 19 f., who traces it to Mt. xv. 27. Lagrange, 195, thinks it is original. The vocative κύριε, ' Sir ', appears here only in Mk unless read in i. 40 and x. 51, and is especially appropriate on the lips of the Gentile woman. καί should be rendered simply ' and ', rather than ' also ' or ' even ' ; the word of Jesus is not rejected, but carried a stage farther. ὑποκάτω, vi. 11. ψιχίον*, Mt. xv. 27**, dim. of ψίξ, ' a crumb ' ; not classical nor in LXX ; MGk ψίχα (VGT, 698). In replacing τῶν παιδίων by τῶν κυρίων αὐτῶν, Mt is secondary as compared with Mk, and more Jewish.

ἐσθίω ἀπό** may be due to the influence of the LXX (Gen. ii. 16, etc.), but is not necessarily a Semitism. Cf. Howard, ii. 461. It may, however, be Semitic in this context ; cf. Swete, 158 ; Lohmeyer, 147 n.

29 f. Jesus is pleased by the woman's wit and persistence. Because of her saying (λόγος, i. 45), He bids her depart (ὑπάγω, i. 44) assuring her that the daemon has gone out of her daughter. Matthew's account raises in an acute form the question how far he is using another source. Cf. Mt. xv. 28, Ὦ γύναι, μεγάλη σου ἡ πίστις· γενηθήτω σοι ὡς θέλεις. Here faith is emphasized and the cure is granted as a boon. The same note is struck in Ὕπαγε, ὡς ἐπίστευσας

γενηθήτω σοι in the story of the healing of the centurion's servant (Mt. viii. 13), and it may well be that Matthew is influenced by that story. He takes Mark's words to imply that a cure has been wrought by Jesus, and this inference is drawn by most commentators ; cf. Swete, 158 ; Lagrange, 196 ; Gould, 137 ; Plummer, 189 ; Turner, 37 ; Bartlet, 235 ; Blunt, 191. Probably this is Mark's meaning, but it is a striking feature of his narrative that the saying is capable of being interpreted to mean a telepathic awareness of what is happening at a distance (v. C. J. Cadoux, 73). Matthew says outright that she was healed from that hour, καὶ ἰάθη ἡ θυγάτηρ αὐτῆς ἀπὸ τῆς ὥρας ἐκείνης (xv. 28), as he does in the case of the centurion's servant, καὶ ἰάθη ὁ παῖς ἐν τῇ ὥρᾳ ἐκείνῃ (viii. 13). In contrast Mark's account is distinguished by its objectivity. The woman departs to her house and finds the child lying in bed and the daemon gone (RSV, cf. Moffatt), βεβλημένον ἐπὶ τὴν κλίνην καὶ τὸ δαιμόνιον ἐξεληλυθός. It is even possible that the meaning is that the girl is ' bedfast ', in accordance with the idiom בְּמִשְׁכָּב נָפַל, ' to take to one's bed ' (Ex. xxi. 18). Cf. R. H. Charles, ICC, Rev. 71 ; Wellhausen, 57 ; Field, 7 (with reference to Mt. viii. 14, βεβλημένην καὶ πυρέσσουσαν) ; Torrey, TG, 3. On this view she is prostrate and presumably exhausted. The paroxysms attributed to the daemon are past and she is on the way to recovery.

For οἶκος v. ii. 1, παιδίον v. 39, κλίνη iv. 21, δαιμόνιον i. 34.

---

[1] WH read καὶ λέγει, but λέγουσα is probably to be preferred with D W Θ P45 13 28 69 543 565 700 a f i n q sy⁸ sa arm. See p. 42.

Mk. vii. 31-7   48. THE CURE OF THE DEAF   Cf. Mt. xv. 29-31
MUTE

The form of the narrative is that of a Miracle-story. Cf. Bultmann, 227. Dibelius, 72, classifies it among the *Novellen* or ' Tales '. Both think that the original unit begins with 32 and that 36 (the command to keep silence) was added by Mark. Dibelius also thinks that 37 is an addition. So far as 31 is concerned, this analysis is probably correct, for the geographical statement is a link between this narrative and that of the Syro-Phoenician Woman. Whether 36 is Markan depends on our view of the ' Messianic Secret ' ; in the Commentary the command is taken as part of the original story. As regards 37, Dibelius is probably right ; it is ' rather the conclusion of a number of stories than the acclamation of the people to Jesus who is just passing by '. There can be little doubt that when the story was first told, the narrator had Isa. xxxv. 5 f. in mind, possibly also Isa. xxix. 18-23 and Psa. xxxvii. (xxxviii.) 14, and that he saw its relevance for Gentile hearers, but the recognition of a symbolic interest need not compromise the historical value of the narrative. On the contrary, the details of the story, the insertion of the fingers into the man's ears, the use of saliva, the touching of the tongue, the sighing, and the use of the word ' Ephphatha ', suggest that it is taken from life. The fact that the later Evangelists omit the narrative points in the same direction.

31   Καὶ πάλιν ἐξελθὼν ἐκ τῶν ὁρίων Τύρου ἦλθεν διὰ Σιδῶνος

31. The verse is an editorial passage connecting the narrative with that which follows. πάλιν points back to 24 apparently in the sense of ' thereupon ' (*v.* ii. 1) ; cf. RSV, ' Soon after this ' ; Torrey, ' Then '. For τῶν ὁρίων Τύρου *v.* 24 and for τὴν θάλασσαν τῆς Γαλιλαίας i. 16. The route described is circuitous and uncertain. Many commentators think that a journey is meant north to Sidon, then south-east across the Leontes, continuing south past Caesarea Philippi to the east of the Jordan through the northern part of the Decapolis. Cf. Swete, 159 f. ; Lagrange, 197 ; Burkitt, 92 n., *JTS*, xvii. 14. Burkitt suggests that the journey may have occupied eight months ; cf. McNeile, 232. Dalman, *SSW*, 201, thinks that from Caesarea Philippi the route ran south-east to the Golan, then south from el-Ḳuneṭra, joining the Damascus road at *Tell Tshochadar* and proceeding to the lake through the Hippos district. The phrase ' coming through

the midst of the district of Decapolis ', he says, ' is thus apparently geographically inexact, and should not be taken literally '. Recent commentators are more outspoken. Rawlinson, 101, compares the route to a journey from Cornwall to London *via* Manchester, a comparison which apart from the mileage is apt, and Blunt, 192, says frankly : ' The geography is impossible '. Cf. Bacon, *Is Mark a Roman Gospel?*, 64. The reason for this long detour is said to be either the hostility of Antipas (Burkitt, 93 ; Turner, 36 ; cf. Swete, 159) or the desire to give rest and instruction to the Twelve (Swete, 159 ; Plummer, 190). Neither suggestion is supported by the Markan narrative, and it is doubtful if the itinerary is thereby explained.

A point of special difficulty is διὰ Σιδῶνος, for Sidon stands on the coast some twenty miles north of Tyre. The reading καὶ Σιδῶνος (A W *et al.* P45 fam. 1 fam. 13 22 28 543 1071 *al. pler.*

εἰς τὴν θάλασσαν τῆς Γαλιλαίας ἀνὰ μέσον τῶν ὁρίων Δεκαπόλεως. Καὶ φέρουσιν αὐτῷ κωφὸν καὶ μογιλάλον, καὶ παρα- 32

q sys pe hl sa geo arm) is easier, but is probably a very early attempt to relieve the geographical difficulty. Schmidt, 200, suggests that perhaps Mark meant ' the region of Tyre and Sidon' and has expressed himself awkwardly. Bacon, 303 f., holds that he has a confused knowledge of the geography of Palestine. It is tempting to accept the brilliant conjecture of Wellhausen, 58, that διὰ Σιδῶνος is a mistranslation of בצידן, which should have been rendered εἰς Βησσαιδάν (so D in vi. 45), but it is difficult to see how it explains εἰς. This conjecture is accepted by Allen, 110,[1] but is rejected by many as ' unproved ' (Schmidt, 201 n.) or ' unnecessary ' (Howard, ii. 471; McNeile, 232; Wood, 690) or as implying that Mk was translated from Aramaic (Rawlinson, 101). The last named objection is not conclusive since mistranslation might lie far back in Aramaic oral tradition, but this possibility and the suggestions offered are so speculative that it is better to consider the itinerary in itself. The route suggested by Wellhausen — from the region of Tyre to Bethsaida — is very probable, for it eliminates the need for a long detour along the Tyrian coast and through northern Palestine. Jesus returns across the border through Bethsaida into the midst of Decapolis. From the historical point of view this itinerary has much in its favour and should probably be accepted. The hypothesis still leaves open the question of ' Mark's geography ', for, in fidelity to his source, he has accepted the reading διὰ Σιδῶνος, and this implies the circuitous northern journey described by commentators. This question cannot usefully be considered apart from the Markan geographical statements as a whole.

It remains to consider ἀνὰ μέσον τῶν ὁρίων Δεκαπόλεως. ἀνὰ μέσον*, Mt.

xiii. 25, 1 Cor. vi. 5, Apoc. vii. 17**, is a double preposition used with the gen. with the meaning ' in the midst ' (= ἐν μέσῳ). Rare in Cl. Gk, it is used in the LXX and is common in the papyri (VGT, 29), and in MGk in the form ἀνάμεσα. Cf. Moulton, i. 99; Blass, 122; Lagrange, 197. Frequently the Markan phrase is held to refer to the country east or north-east of the lake, and in close proximity to it (v. supra), in order to find a suitable scene for the Feeding of the Four Thousand and the subsequent crossing to Dalmanutha. In itself, the phrase more naturally suggests a point farther inland among the hills of Decapolis.

Matthew omits the references to Tyre, Sidon, and Decapolis, saying only that Jesus departed thence and came by the Sea of Galilee, but he adds that He went up into the mountain and sat there, καὶ ἀναβὰς εἰς τὸ ὄρος ἐκάθητο ἐκεῖ (xv. 29). Streeter, 413 f., argues from Mt. xv. 29 and Jn. vi. 3 that these words stood in Mk and were accidentally omitted by homoioteleuton.

32. These words introduce the story of the cure of the Deaf Mute which in itself contains no reference to time or place. By inserting it after 31 Mark shows that he connected the cure with a locality in Decapolis and in this opinion may have followed an existing tradition. As in ii. 3, the story begins with an impersonal plural φέρουσιν (cf. viii. 22): People bring the man to Jesus. κωφός, vii. 37, ix. 25*, ' blunt ', ' dull ', and (with reference to speech) ' dumb ' (or hearing) ' deaf ', the latter being the meaning here. μογιλάλος**, lit. ' speaking with difficulty ', <μόγις, λάλος, is found in the LXX in Isa. xxxv. 6, τρανὴ δὲ ἔσται γλῶσσα μογιλάλων, where it translates the Heb. אִלֵּם, ' dumb '. This meaning is suggested by ἀλάλους in 37, but

---

[1] Allen, 50, suggests as the original לבית צידא.

33 καλοῦσιν αὐτὸν ἵνα ἐπιθῇ αὐτῷ τὴν χεῖρα. καὶ ἀπολαβόμενος
αὐτὸν ἀπὸ τοῦ ὄχλου κατ᾽ ἰδίαν ἔβαλεν τοὺς δακτύλους αὐτοῦ
34 εἰς τὰ ὦτα αὐτοῦ καὶ πτύσας ἥψατο τῆς γλώσσης αὐτοῦ, καὶ

ἐλάλει ὀρθῶς (35) supports the meaning
'stammered' (Moffatt); cf. RV and
RSV, 'had an impediment in his
speech'. An alternative reading,
μογγιλάλον, describes the man as
'hoarse of speech', which cannot be
dismissed, with Blass, 24, as having
'no authority', since it is read by
B³ L W Δ et al. fam. 13 (exc. 124) 28
33 118 579 892 al. plur. Cf. Pallis, 2 f.
A real v.l. (Moulton, ii. 106), it adds
support to the view that the man was
not dumb. Cf. Swete, 160; Lagrange,
197; Micklem, 115. For the contrary
view see Rawlinson, 101; Turner,
37. παρακαλέω, i. 40, c. ἵνα and subj.
v. 10. The ἵνα clause gives the substance of the request; cf. iii. 9. τὴν
χεῖρα: Mark usually has the plur.,
cf. v. 23, vi. 5, viii. 23, etc.

Matthew has omitted the story but
shows obvious knowledge of it both
in the geographical statement of xv. 29
and in the summary account of many
cures and the enthusiastic response of
the crowd in 30 f.

33 f. The action of Jesus in taking
the man aside for private treatment
has a parallel in the Cure of the Blind
Man (viii. 22-6). The verb ἀπολαμ-
βάνομαι*, 'to draw aside', is used in
the same sense in the papyri of the
recluses in the Serapeum (P. Lond.
xlii. 12 ff., v. VGT, 65); cf. ἐπιλαβόμενος, viii. 23. κατ᾽ ἰδίαν, iv. 34;
ὄχλος, ii. 4. The reference to the crowd,
here mentioned for the first time, may
indicate that originally the story stood
in another context. The reasons for
the withdrawal can only be conjectured: the desire to escape the publicity occasioned by spectacular cures
and the use of manual actions are
reasonable suggestions. The putting
of the fingers into the man's ears, the
spitting, and the touching of the tongue

powerfully suggest to him the possibility of a cure. Such actions are
common to the technique of Greek and
Jewish healers (cf. Bultmann, 237;
Klostermann, 83; Dibelius, 83-90;
Billerbeck, ii. 15 ff.). A well-known
story connected with Vespasian (Tacitus, Hist. iv. 81, Suetonius, Vesp. 7)
records how he healed a man with
spittle. Its use by Jews with incanta-
tions was condemned by the Rabbis.
Only here, in the story of the Cure of
the Blind Man, and in the Johannine
narrative of the Man born Blind, is
Jesus recorded to have used spittle in
his healings. πτύω, viii. 23*, Jn. ix.
6**. So incidental is the reference
in the present narrative that we cannot
be wholly certain how it was used. In
various ways the MS. tradition illustrates the attempts that were made to
overcome this defect. πτύσας is placed
before ἔβαλεν by D a b c ff i q r¹ and
after it by Θ 565, while W fam. 13
(exc. 124) 28 543 sys geo put the participle before εἰς τὰ ὦτα αὐτοῦ, and 0131
reads ἔπτυσεν εἰς τοὺς δακτύλους αὐτοῦ
καὶ ἔβαλεν εἰς τὰ ὦτα τοῦ κωφοῦ καὶ
ἥψατο τῆς γλώσσης τοῦ μογγιλάλου.¹
Probably the WH text is original, the
meaning being that saliva was applied
to the lips or placed in the mouth to
facilitate speech. The variants include
the ears also. For ἥψατο v. i. 41.
γλῶσσα, vii. 35, xvi. [17]*. None of
these actions is, or need be regarded
as, magical; they resemble rather the
manipulations used in modern psychotherapy. Cf. the case of hysterical
aphonia described by E. R. Micklem,
119: 'The treatment is . . . by direct
persuasion, but it is often advisable to
perform simultaneously gentle manipulations with the fingers over the glottis,
giving verbal encouragement and
persuasion all the time'.

¹ P⁴⁵ has πτύσας καὶ ἥψατο instead of καὶ πτύσας ἥψατο (WH). Couchoud, JTS, xxxv. 12
thinks it preserves the original text.

ἀναβλέψας εἰς τὸν οὐρανὸν ἐστέναξεν, καὶ λέγει αὐτῷ Ἐφφαθά,
ὅ ἐστιν Διανοίχθητι· καὶ ἠνοίγησαν αὐτοῦ αἱ ἀκοαί, καὶ ἐλύθη 35
ὁ δεσμὸς τῆς γλώσσης αὐτοῦ, καὶ ἐλάλει ὀρθῶς· καὶ διεστείλατο 36
αὐτοῖς ἵνα μηδενὶ λέγωσιν· ὅσον δὲ αὐτοῖς διεστέλλετο, αὐτοὶ

In the story, besides putting His fingers into the man's ears and touching his tongue, Jesus gives ' verbal encouragement' in the command, spoken in Aramaic, Ἐφφαθά = פְּתַח (Kautzsch, Gr. 10; cf. Moulton, ii. 109), which Mark explains for his readers by Διανοίχθητι. Not unnaturally sys pe omit the explanatory phrase. For ὅ ἐστιν v. iii. 17. διανοίγω*, ' to open completely', Lk (4), Ac (3)**. The use of foreign words is characteristic of the Miracle-story (Bultmann, 238), but this fact has no significance here since Aramaic was the natural medium of address. No difficulty arises from the fact that the man was deaf, for either he was not completely deaf or was able to read the lips of Jesus. Cf. Plummer, 191.

Two features distinguish the narrative from ancient and modern stories of healing, the use, namely, of ἀναβλέψας and of ἐστέναξεν. Although sighing and groaning belong to the technique of mystical magic (Dibelius, 86), only a love for the bizarre rather than sober exegesis will find in the groaning of Jesus anything other than a sign of His deep feeling and compassion for the sufferer. Like ἐμβριμάομαι, the verb is an example of the boldness with which Mark delineates the depths of His emotions. στενάζω*, Rom. viii. 23, 2 Cor. v. 2, 4, Heb. xiii. 17, Jas. v. 9 (v. Mayor, in loc.). In viii. 12 Mark uses the still stronger word ἀναστενάζω. The use of ἀναβλέπω, ' to look up', vi. 41, viii. 24, xvi. 4 (ctr. x. 51 f.*), here and in vi. 41 (q.v.) indicates the act of prayer. These features, together with the personality of Jesus Himself, mark the distinctiveness of the works of healing in the Gospels.

For the use of Ephphatha and of saliva in the early Baptismal rite at Milan and Rome see Swete, 161; Klostermann, 84.

35 f. The results of the cure are described simply. The ears were opened, the tongue loosed, and the man spoke clearly. ἀνοίγω*. The late 2 aor. pass. ἠνοίγησαν is found also in Mt. xx. 33, Ac. xii. 10, Apoc. xi. 19, xv. 5. Cf. Hort, 170; VGT, 45. διηνοίγησαν and διηνοίχθησαν are read by Caesarean MSS. (v. Legg), and the latter by P45, but they are probably secondary readings suggested by διανοίχθητι in 34. Couchoud, JTS, xxxv. 13, thinks that P45, in διηνοίχθησαν and in reading εὐθέως before the verb (with A W Θ fam. 1 fam. 13 565 700), may represent the original text.

Deissmann, 304-8, maintains that ὁ δεσμὸς τῆς γλώσσης is a technical expression illustrating the ancient idea that a man can be bound by daemonic influences. Cf. Lk. xiii. 16, ταύτην δὲ θυγατέρα Ἀβραὰμ οὖσαν, ἣν ἔδησεν ὁ Σατανᾶς. There is, however, nothing to suggest a case of daemon possession (cf. Lohmeyer, 151), and it is best to regard the phrase as a figurative description of the cure. Cf. Lagrange, 200; Plummer, 191; Rawlinson, 102. ἀκοή, ' hearing', ' report', is used of the organs of hearing; in i. 28, xiii. 7*, with the meaning ' report'. ὀρθῶς*. ἐλάλει ὀρθῶς means that he began to speak correctly; cf. Moffatt; RV 'plain'; RSV 'plainly'. The adverb suggests that the case was one of defective speech rather than of dumbness. The change of tense is noteworthy.

For διαστέλλομαι v. v. 43; ἵνα c. subj. iii. 9. The charge to keep silence (cf. i. 25, 44, iii. 12, v. 43, viii. 26), perhaps repeated, seems strange, since the change could not be concealed; v. Intr. 122-4. Reluctance to have the fame of the cure noised abroad might be felt and expressed even if the in-

37 μᾶλλον περισσότερον ἐκήρυσσον. καὶ ὑπερπερισσῶς ἐξεπλήσσοντο λέγοντες Καλῶς πάντα πεποίηκεν, ᵀ καὶ τοὺς κωφοὺς
ποιεῖ ἀκούειν καὶ ἀλάλους λαλεῖν.

37 ὡς

junction was sure to be disobeyed. ὅσον δέ . . . μᾶλλον περισσότερον is pleonastic, unless μᾶλλον=potius (' rather ') as Plummer, 191, suggests. Cf. καθ' ὅσον . . . κατὰ τοσοῦτο (Heb. vii. 20-2, x. 25). For ὅσος v. ii. 19 ; περισσότερος xii. 23, 40* ; κηρύσσω i. 4. Repeated action is expressed by the imperfects ; the more He continued to charge them to be silent, the more eagerly they kept on proclaiming the cure.

37. The effect of the cure is that the people are astonished beyond measure. For ἐκπλήσσομαι v. i. 22. ὑπερπερισσῶς**, ' exceedingly ', ' in the extreme ' (Moffatt), is found here only in Gk literature, but ὑπερπερισσεύω is used in Rom. v. 20 and 2 Cor. vii. 4. Nowhere, even in Mk, is so great astonishment depicted. For καλῶς v. vii. 6. πάντα πεποίηκεν may suggest that originally the story belonged to a group ; cf. the plurals κωφούς and ἀλάλους. καί . . . καί is ' both . . . and '

(WM, 547). Turner, 37, says that the Gk, which has only one article, is really equivalent to ' the deaf and the dumb to hear and speak '. Cf. W 28 sys, which by omitting ἀλάλους bring the infins. together. Probably, Isa. xxxv. 5 f. is in mind, καὶ ὦτα κωφῶν ἀκούσονται . . . τρανὴ δὲ ἔσται γλῶσσα μογιλάλων. Cf. Bacon, BGS, 94 ; Lagrange, 200 ; Rawlinson, 101 ; Branscomb, 135 ; Blunt, 192. If this is so, Mark would appear to have elaborated the close of the story for homiletical purposes. See the introductory note on the narrative. There are further signs of this interest in the tense of ποιεῖ, possibly also in the paronomasia in ἀλάλους λαλεῖν. Still greater editorial activity is manifest in Mt. xv. 31, where it is said that the people marvelled and ' glorified the God of Israel ' ; cf. Isa. xxix. 23, καὶ τὸν θεὸν τοῦ Ἰσραὴλ φοβηθήσονται, Gen. i. 31, Sir. xxxix. 16.

(c) Mk. viii. 1-26   THE FOUR THOUSAND,
THE CROSSING TO DAL-
MANUTHA, AND THE RETURN
TO BETHSAIDA

For the third section in Division IV, especially its character and contents, v. Intr. 97 f., and for its relation to the events described in vi. 30-vii. 37 v. Note C. The section includes :

(49) viii. 1-10.   The Feeding of the Four Thousand.
(50) viii. 11-13.   The Demand for a Sign from Heaven.
(51) viii. 14-21.   The Mystery of the Loaves.
(52) viii. 22-6.   The Cure of the Blind Man.

The catechetical interest is noteworthy ; v. Comm.

Mk. viii. 1-10   49. THE FEEDING OF THE   Cf. Mt. xv. 32-9
FOUR THOUSAND

Like the Feeding of the Five Thousand, this narrative is a Miracle-story. Dibelius, 78 n., does not include it among the *Novellen* to which he assigns vi. 35-44, because he holds it to be ' completely lacking in such

marks of a story-teller's gift or pleasure '. This opinion is consistent with
his definition of the ' Tale ', but the classification of Bultmann, 232,
among the *Naturwunder*, is better inasmuch as the narrator's intention
is to relate one of the greatest of the mighty acts of Jesus. Other motives
are also implied. The story is told because it anticipates the Christian
Eucharist and because it is viewed as a sign to the Gentiles in contrast
with the Feeding of the Five Thousand which is a sign to Jews. Cf. Bacon,
162 ; Rawlinson, 86. How far this interest is historical is, of course,
another question.

The probability that a fellowship meal has been given a miraculous
interpretation is closely bound up with the significance of the Feeding
of the Five Thousand. Here it is enough to say that if this interpretation
is valid in the case of vi. 35-44, it is still more probable in viii. 1-10, in
which from the outset a miracle is presupposed. It is noteworthy that
no indication is given of the effect of the multiplication of the loaves upon
the disciples or the people, a fact which shows that the miracle itself is
not the only point in Mark's interest.

The narrative is loosely connected with vii. 24-37 by ἐν ἐκείναις ταῖς
ἡμέραις, a vague phrase which implies that the Evangelist lacked precise
information. It may reasonably be inferred that he intends to locate the
incident in the Decapolis and to associate it with Gentiles. He does not
expressly describe a Gentile Mission. Nevertheless, he tells the story in
such a way as to suggest that he has in mind the Gentile Church of his
day. This interest does not prevent him from treating the existing tradition with relative fidelity, for there are details in viii. 2, especially the
reference to ' three days ', which are not necessary to his purpose. In this
temporal allusion, and in the reference to the disciples (last mentioned
in vii. 17), there are signs that at an earlier stage in the tradition the story
stood in a fuller context which it is now impossible to recover.

’Εν ἐκείναις ταῖς ἡμέραις πάλιν πολλοῦ ὄχλου ὄντος καὶ μὴ   1 VIII
ἐχόντων τί φάγωσιν, προσκαλεσάμενος τοὺς μαθητὰς αὐτοῦ

1. For ἐν ἐκείναις ταῖς ἡμέραις v. i. 9,
xiii. 24. No place name is given, but
the position of the narrative, after vii.
31, suggests that Mark thinks of the
Gentile hill country north-east of the
lake. The presence of a large crowd
is indicated by πολλοῦ ὄχλου ὄντος, and
πάλιν points back to vii. 33 or vi. 34.
The second gen. abs., in which ἐχόντων
is used with αὐτῶν understood, particularizes the individuals in the crowd.
For τί φάγωσιν v. vi. 36.

In contrast with vi. 35, Jesus takes
the initiative by calling the disciples
to Him; cf. Jn. vi. 5, λέγει πρὸς
Φίλιππον. αὐτοῦ should probably be
added to τοὺς μαθητάς with A B W Θ
et al. fam. 13 22 33 118 543 565 579
1071 al. pler. sys pe sa; cf. Turner,

JTS, xxvi. 237. Mt. xv. 30 omits the
temporal statement. For προσκαλέομαι
v. iii. 13 ; μαθητής ii. 15.

The account begins without any
connecting particle, unless δέ is read
with D W Θ 28 700 it (exc. g² l)
sy(s) pe sa geo¹. Most commentators
think that παμπολλοῦ (A and many
MSS.) is due to a misreading of
ΠΑΛΙΝΠΟΛΛΟΥ, especially as the word
(Cl.) is not found elsewhere in the Gk
Bible. Cf. Swete, 163; Klostermann,
85. Were the attestation stronger,
this argument might be reversed;
πάλιν, it might be claimed, has replaced an unfamiliar and descriptive
word (' a very great multitude '). As
it is, the opening statement is quite
colourless. Bartlet, 238, suggests that

2 λέγει αὐτοῖς Σπλαγχνίζομαι ἐπὶ τὸν ὄχλον ὅτι ἤδη ⌜ἡμέραι
3 τρεῖς⌝ ⌜προσμένουσίν μοι⌝ καὶ οὐκ ἔχουσιν τί φάγωσιν· καὶ ἐὰν
ἀπολύσω αὐτοὺς νήστεις εἰς οἶκον αὐτῶν, ἐκλυθήσονται ἐν τῇ
4 ὁδῷ· καί τινες αὐτῶν ἀπὸ μακρόθεν ἥκασιν. καὶ ἀπεκρίθησαν
αὐτῷ οἱ μαθηταὶ αὐτοῦ ὅτι Πόθεν τούτους δυνήσεταί τις ὧδε
5 χορτάσαι ἄρτων ἐπ᾽ ἐρημίας; καὶ ἠρώτα αὐτοὺς Πόσους ἔχετε
6 ἄρτους; οἱ δὲ εἶπαν Ἑπτά. καὶ παραγγέλλει τῷ ὄχλῳ ἀνα-

2 ἡμέραις τρισὶν | προσμένουσιν

Mark is following a later non-Petrine form of the tradition; cf. Turner, 38.

2 f. For σπλαγχνίζομαι v. i. 41. The statement of vi. 34, καὶ ἐσπλαγχνίσθη ἐπ᾽ αὐτούς, is here expressed in direct speech. But the motive is different; there Jesus is moved with compassion because the people are as sheep without a shepherd; here because they have been three days without food. For ἤδη v. iv. 37.

ἡμέραι τρεῖς is a parenthetic nom. (nom. pendens); cf. τρία ἔτη (Lk. xiii. 7), δέκα καὶ ὀκτὼ ἔτη (Lk. xiii. 16). D has ἡμέραι τρεῖς εἰσίν, ἀπὸ πότε ὧδε εἰσίν, B ἡμέραις τρισίν, and Δ and many minuscules ἡμέρας τρεῖς. These readings are probably grammatical corrections. The parenthetic nom. appears frequently in the papyri and survives in MGk; cf. Moulton, i. 70; Howard, ii. 447; Meecham, 90 f.; Lagrange, 201. There is no need, therefore, with Wellhausen, 59, to explain the construction as a Semitism, or, with Swete, 163, to understand εἰσίν (cf. D supra) and treat προσμένουσιν and ἔχουσιν as participles in the dat. προσμένω*.

The reference to 'three days' is peculiar to the narrative, distinguishing it from vi. 35-44, in which the crossing, the meal, and the recrossing all take place on the same day. The temporal statement, which is incidental to the story, probably belongs to the tradition used by Mark. Another detail peculiar to viii. 1-10 is the fact that the idea of dismissing the multitude is rejected by Jesus forthwith, whereas in vi. 36 it is enjoined by the disciples. It is also implied, in καὶ τινες αὐτῶν ἀπὸ

μακρόθεν εἰσίν, that some members of the crowd at least are local inhabitants. All these points bear upon the question whether vi. 35-44 and viii. 1-10 are doublets. See Note C. For ἀπολύω v. vi. 36; ἀπὸ μακρόθεν v. 6.

νῆστις*, Mt. xv. 32**, is a classical word which later assumed the rare form νήστης (VGT, 426). εἰς οἶκον αὐτῶν is 'to their homes'; cf. ii. 1, viii. 26. ἐκλύομαι*, Mt. xv. 32, Gal. vi. 9, Heb. xiii. 3, 5**, 'to faint', 'grow weary'. ἐν τῇ ὁδῷ, viii. 27, ix. 33 f., x. 32, 52*; cf. εἰς ὁδόν, vi. 8, x. 17; εἰς τὴν ὁδόν, xi. 8. Instead of εἰσίν (B L Δ 892 bo) ἥκασιν is attested by ℵ A D N W Θ et al. fam. 1 28 33 69 124 565 579 700 1071 al. plur. it sys. It is rejected as 'Western' by Hort, 176, but is read by Ti, von Soden, Nestle (ed. ix), and Souter, but not by Lagrange. Moulton, i. 53, says, 'It is after all a form which we might expect in Mk, and equally expect to find removed by revisers, whether Alexandrian or Syrian'.

Matthew repeats 2 verbatim, but recasts 3 in the form, καὶ ἀπολῦσαι αὐτοὺς νήστεις οὐ θέλω, μή ποτε ἐκλυθῶσιν ἐν τῇ ὁδῷ (xv. 32).

4 f. For ἀπεκρίθησαν v. iii. 33; χορτάζω vi. 42; ἐρωτάω iv. 10. ἄρτων is gen. rei. ἐρημία*, Mt. xv. 33, 2 Cor. xi. 26, Heb. xi. 38**, 'wilderness'; Cl., LXX, Pap. Mark's usual phrases are ἡ ἔρημος and ἔρημος τόπος. The question πόσους ἔχετε ἄρτους; is in verbatim agreement with vi. 38. In the reply fishes are not mentioned, but Mark refers to them in 7. With ἑπτά cf. πέντε in vi. 38.

The fact that the disciples are in a

πεσεῖν ἐπὶ τῆς γῆς· καὶ λαβὼν τοὺς ἑπτὰ ἄρτους εὐχαριστήσας ἔκλασεν καὶ ἐδίδου τοῖς μαθηταῖς αὐτοῦ ἵνα παρατιθῶσιν καὶ παρέθηκαν τῷ ὄχλῳ. καὶ εἶχαν ἰχθύδια ὀλίγα· καὶ εὐλογήσας 7

state of perplexity, despite what is narrated in vi. 35-44, is one of the main reasons which lead many modern commentators to think that the two narratives are variant accounts of the same incident. Cf. J. Weiss, *Die Schr.*[4] 140; Klostermann, 71, 85; McNeile, 237 f.; Williams, *Studies in the Synoptic Problem* (ed. W. Sanday), 419; Turner, 37 f.; Stanton, ii. 159; Streeter, 173. Branscomb, 136, writes: ' Had the tradition meant to describe two separate incidents, the disciples would certainly not have been described as so astonished on the second occasion '. Cf. Williams: ' To suppose that they had forgotten the first incident seems to postulate an almost incredible dullness on the part of the disciples '. The point is put even more trenchantly by Gould, 142, who holds the two incidents to be historical: ' The objection is valid; the stupid repetition of the question is psychologically impossible '. In reply, Swete, 164, argues that in the first story it is a question of ' the want of means ' (vi. 37), in the second of ' the scarcity of food ' in a ' thinly populated region '; and further, that the alleged ' stupidity ' of the disciples is in accordance with all that we know of them at this period (cf. viii. 17 ff.). Lagrange, 202, suggests that, while it would be an exaggeration to say that they ask for the miracle, although timidly, their question insists less on the impossibility than on the embarrassment in which they find themselves. The first miracle had happened a long time ago, and there must have been many occasions of need when Jesus had not wrought one. Cf. Plummer, 195: ' They confess their own powerlessness and leave the solution to Him '. See also Allen, 113. These explanations, in which a sense of strain is evident, are not satisfactory, and the only reasonable

alternative to the theory of doublets is the suggestion of Gould, 142, that, in respect of the disciples' question, ' the accounts got mixed in this particular '. See further, Note C.

The secondary character of the Matthaean version is clear. λέγουσιν replaces ἀπεκρίθησαν. The disciples' question becomes πόθεν ἡμῖν . . . ἄρτοι τοσοῦτοι followed by ὥστε c. infin., and the words καὶ ὀλίγα ἰχθύδια are added.

6 f. For παραγγέλλω v. vi. 8; ὄχλος ii. 4. Jesus commands the people to recline (ἀναπίπτω, vi. 40); cf. vi. 39 f. There is no reference to the ' green grass ' or to ' companies ' and ' ranks ' ' by hundreds and by fifties '. In short, the account is bare and colourless. But the agreement of the two narratives in the account of the breaking and distribution of the bread is very close, the following words in 6 being common to vi. 41: καὶ λαβὼν τοὺς . . . ἄρτους . . . ἔκλασεν (vi. 41, κατέκλασεν) . . . καὶ ἐδίδου τοῖς μαθηταῖς . . . ἵνα παρατιθῶσιν. . . . Equally striking is the agreement with xiv. 22 f. (v. the note on vi. 41 f.) and even more so, since the narrative has εὐχαριστήσας as in xiv. 23*. For the claim of W. L. Knox that the presence of this word stamps the narrative as Hellenistic v. the note on vi. 41 f. Knox points out that εὐχαριστέω and its derivatives appear rather late in Gk literature ' with a rather formal connotation, often of a religious kind ', especially in Philo and Josephus, and he maintains that its presence in the present narrative shows that the miracle has been recognized as a type of the Eucharist as in the Fourth Gospel. Cf. Bacon, *BGS*, 95; Rawlinson, 104. The action of the disciples in distributing the bread (παρέθηκαν τῷ ὄχλῳ) is also in line with early eucharistic practice in which the deacons dis-

8 αὐτὰ εἶπεν καὶ ταῦτα παρατιθέναι. καὶ ἔφαγον καὶ ἐχορτάσθησαν, καὶ ἦραν περισσεύματα κλασμάτων ἑπτὰ σφυρίδας.
9 ἦσαν δὲ ὡς τετρακισχίλιοι. καὶ ἀπέλυσεν αὐτούς. Καὶ εὐθὺς
10 ἐμβὰς ᵀ εἰς τὸ πλοῖον μετὰ τῶν μαθητῶν αὐτοῦ ἦλθεν εἰς τὰ
μέρη Δαλμανουθά.

10 αὐτός

tributed the elements received from
the presiding bishop. Cf. Gregory
Dix, *The Shape of the Liturgy*, 135 f. ;
W. D. Maxwell, *An Outline of Christian Worship*, 12-14.

The reference to the fishes is awkwardly appended in 7. For the form
εἶχαν *v.* Moulton, ii. 194. ἰχθύδιον*,
Mt. xv. 34**, is described by Swete,
165, as here a true diminutive ; cf.
VGT, 309. εὐλογήσας (*v.* vi. 41), with
reference to the ἰχθύδια, does not
appear to be used with any difference
of meaning from εὐχαριστήσας. The
act is one of thanksgiving to God.
For εἶπεν c. acc. and infin. in the sense
of commanding *v.* v. 43, Intr. 62. The
verse is not necessarily a subsequent
addition, but is awkwardly expressed
because it no longer had a primary
significance in the liturgical interest
which shaped the narrative.

Matthew's modifications in xv. 35 f.
are stylistic. He replaces παραγγέλλει
by the participle, and introduces the
reference to the fishes at an earlier
point, as in the Feeding of the Five
Thousand (cf. Mk. vi. 41 = Mt. xiv.
19 = Lk. ix. 16).

8 f. Verse 8 agrees closely with
vi. 42 f., the only new words being
περισσεύματα instead of πληρώματα,
ἑπτά in place of δώδεκα, and σφυρίδας
corresponding to κοφίνων. πάντες and
ἀπὸ τῶν ἰχθύων are wanting and the
amount of food left over is more simply
expressed : ' the remainder of the
broken pieces, seven baskets '. For
χορτάζω *v.* vi. 42. περίσσευμα*, ' that
which is over and above ', ' surplus '
(2 Cor. viii. 13 f.), is a late word found
once in the LXX (Eccl. ii. 15, where
it may be an addition) ; in Lk. vi. 45 =
Mt. xii. 34** it has the meaning
' abundance ' ; *v.* Bauer, 1041.

σφυρίς, viii. 20*, Mt. xv. 37, xvi. 10,
Ac. ix. 25**, a mat-basket for provisions ; in Ac. ix. 25 it is large enough
to carry a man. The form σφυρίς
(instead of σπυρίς) is regular in the
papyri ; cf. Hort, 148 ; Moulton, i. 45 ;
VGT, 618. As compared with vi. 44
the number is more briefly expressed
(ἦσαν δὲ ὡς τετρακισχίλιοι, viii. 20*).
Finally, the brief statement of dismissal, καὶ ἀπέλυσεν αὐτούς, to which
there is a parallel in the story of the
Crossing in vi. 45, is added. A comparison of vi. 35-44 and viii. 1-9 leaves
the impression that in many respects
the second is an abbreviated version
of the first, and the words peculiar to
it, προσμένω, νῆστις, ἐκλύω, περίσσευμα,
ἐρημία, and σφυρίς, and the forms
εἶχαν and ἥκασιν suggest independent
compilation.

Matthew's version of 8 f. is somewhat fuller. He has πάντες as in the
story of the Five Thousand, replaces
περισσεύματα by τὸ περισσεῦον and adds
πλήρεις to ἑπτὰ σφυρίδας. Omitting
ὡς before τετρακισχίλιοι, he inserts
ἄνδρες and adds χωρὶς γυναικῶν καὶ
παιδίων (xv. 38 ; cf. xiv. 21). In these
respects the wonder of the miracle is
enhanced.

10. WH connect this verse with 1-9 ;
Swete and Lagrange with 11-13. In
vocabulary the passage agrees closely
with vi. 45 and is in fact a summary
parallel to vi. 45-52. For εὐθύς *v.* i. 10 ;
ἐμβαίνω iv. 1 ; εἰς τὸ πλοῖον iv. 1 ;
μαθητής ii. 15 ; μέρος*.

The identity of Δαλμανουθά** is unknown. Mt. xv. 39 reads Μαγαδάν,
with Μαγδαλά(ν) as a *v.l.* In Mk most
MSS., including all the uncials except
D, read Δαλμανουθά or some equivalent
form, but some have readings which
appear to be harmonizations with the

text of Mt, e.g. Μελεγαδά D, Μαγαιδά D¹, Μαγεδάν P⁴⁵ (apparently), *magedan* (or -*am*) a f ff i r¹ aur syˢ, *mageda* c k Aug. Cf. Μαγδαλά Θ fam. 1 fam. 13 271 347, Μαγεδά 565, Μεγεδάν 28. Augustine identifies the places mentioned by Mk and Mt, and Eusebius and Jerome speak of a Μαγαιδανή or Μεγεδανή in the neighbourhood of Gerasa; *v.* Legg. Naturally the strangeness of the name has invited conjectures. Independently, J. R. Harris, *A Study of Codex Bezae*, 178, and Nestle, *Philologica Sacra*, 17, *DCG*, i. 406 f., have suggested that the name arose from the inadvertent repetition of למנותא = εἰς τὰ μέρη. This suggestion is rejected by Dalman, 66 f., who earlier had conjectured Μαγδαλουθά. Cheyne's conjecture, *EB*, col. 1635, that the original name was *Migdal-nunia*, ' the tower of fish ', a suburb of Tiberias, is favourably mentioned by Burkitt in *GHT*, 94, but in *JTS*, xvii. 16, he suggests that τὰ μέρη Δαλμανουθά is a corruption of Τιβεριαδααμαθους, a combination of Τιβεριάδα with its older name *Am(m)athus*, the Hamath of 2 Kings xiv. 25. Couchoud, *JTS*,

xxxiv. 121 f. (cf. xxxv. 13), holds that Μαγεδά is primitive, that Μαγδαλά is a later correction, and that Δαλμανουθά arose from the failure of copyists to understand the correction.

Burkitt's conjecture is probably the best yet offered, but there is wisdom in the comment of Lagrange, 205, *En somme, le plus sûr est de conserver Dalmanoutha, en attendant une solution plus satisfaisante du problème.* See further Torrey, 301; Allen, 111; G. A. Smith, *EB*, col. 985 f.; Schmidt, 182 f.; Lohmeyer, 154 f. Whether or not the place of landing was Tiberias or an adjacent locality, it is probable that a place on the west shore of the lake is meant; cf. Turner, 39. If so, after both narratives of feeding the boat reaches approximately the same spot. Further, the obscurity of Dalmanutha may be a sign that Mark is using primitive tradition. Imagination would have suggested a familiar locality. Cf. Schmidt, 210, *Aber was für eine Tendenz sollte man bei der Nennung von Bethsaida (Bethanien), Dalmanutha, Magadan erkennen? Diese Namen kann der Evangelist nicht erfunden haben.*

Mk. viii. 11-13   50. THE DEMAND FOR A   Cf. Mt. xvi. 1-4
                        SIGN FROM HEAVEN

The purpose of this narrative is to illustrate the attitude of Jesus to the demand for signs. It may be a Pronouncement-story,[1] but is perhaps more probably a Story about Jesus constructed by the Evangelist himself. This view is suggested by the narrative framework (11, 13) and the shortened form of the saying in 12 (as compared with the version in Q), which reflects Mark's belief that the Gospel is hidden from hostile Jews. Bultmann, 357, speaks of the narrative as a form analogous to that of the Apothegm, and Dibelius, 159, classifies it with the sayings which need ' data as to the situation ' and are reminiscent of the Greek *Chriae*. As used by Mark, the story reflects sound tradition in that it records the refusal of Jesus to accept the test of signs as a proof of His commission and message, but it lacks the implication, present in the corresponding saying in Q (Lk. xi. 29 = Mt. xii. 39), that His mission like that of Jonah to the Ninevites is self-authenticating. The story appears to be introduced as a contrast to the sign of the loaves in the feeding of the multitude; and if so, like the Fourth Evangelist (Jn. vi. 14), Mark interprets this

[1] Cf. V. Taylor, *FGT*, 78 f.

incident as a ' sign ' to the disciples even though he does not so designate the story. If this inference is justified, a catechetical interest is manifest in the section and in the use of the stories it contains.

11 Καὶ ἐξῆλθον οἱ Φαρισαῖοι καὶ ἤρξαντο συνζητεῖν αὐτῷ, ζητοῦντες παρ' αὐτοῦ σημεῖον ἀπὸ τοῦ οὐρανοῦ, πειράζοντες αὐτόν.
12 καὶ ἀναστενάξας τῷ πνεύματι αὐτοῦ λέγει Τί ἡ γενεὰ αὕτη ζητεῖ σημεῖον; ἀμὴν λέγω ᵀ, εἰ δοθήσεται τῇ γενεᾷ ταύτῃ

12 ὑμῖν

11. For ' the Pharisees ' v. ii. 16. Mt. xvi. 1 adds καὶ Σαδδουκαῖοι. It is natural to infer that the Pharisees ' came forth ' from the ' parts of Dalmanutha ', but the narrative may be placed for topical reasons in its present setting. For ἤρξαντο c. infin. v. i. 45, Intr. 48, 63 f. ; συνζητέω i. 27. P⁴⁵ and Δ omit ζητοῦντες παρ' αὐτοῦ, and Couchoud, *JTS*, xxxv. 13, favours the omission, but the fuller text is more Markan. W P⁴⁵ fam. 13 read ἐκ.

σημεῖον, viii. 12 (*bis*), xiii. 4, 22, xvi. [17, 20]*, ' a sign ', is used in the papyri of a ' seal ' or ' outward distinguishing mark ' ; *VGT*, 572 f. In the NT, especially in Jn, it describes a miracle conceived as a significant act revealing the superhuman personality of Jesus. Cf. Bernard, *St. Jn*, clxxvi ; *v.* 1 Cor. i. 22. This is not the usual Markan estimate of the Gospel miracles, for of seven examples of σημεῖον in Mk two take up the word because it is used by the Pharisees here, two appear in the Apocalyptic Discourse, and two in the spurious ending. Even less primitive is τέρας, ' a portent ' (xiii. 22*). The basic Markan conception is that of δύναμις (*v.* v. 30), namely, the outgoing of divine power.

The σημεῖον ἀπὸ τοῦ οὐρανοῦ sought by the Pharisees is a display which in their view will accredit Jesus and His message. The comment πειράζοντες αὐτόν, which Mark has also in x. 2 (cf. xii. 15), rightly interprets their action as an attempt to put Him to the test. For πειράζω *v.* i. 13. They had ascribed His exorcisms to Beelzebul (iii. 22) and now ask for a heavenly sign which could leave His claims in

no doubt. Cf. Theophylact (cited by Swete, 168) : ἐνόμιζον γὰρ ὅτι οὐ δυνήσεται ἐξ οὐρανοῦ ποιῆσαι σημεῖον, οἷα δὴ ἐν τῷ Βεελζεβοὺλ δυνάμενος ποιεῖν τὰ ἐν τῇ γῇ μόνα σημεῖα. Theudas promised his followers that he would divide the Jordan and give them an easy passage over it ; cf. Josephus, *Ant*. xx. 5. 1. Jesus makes no such promises. From the standpoint of the Pharisees the demand creates a dilemma : if He tries to give a sign He will fail ; if He refuses He will lose popular support. For Jesus there is no such dilemma.

Matthew's alterations are stylistic (xvi. 1).

12 f. As elsewhere (iii. 5), Mark mentions the emotion of Jesus : indignant, He groaned in His spirit. ἀναστενάζω**, ' to sigh deeply ', is a classical word (Aesch. *Choeph*. 335 ; Herodotus i. 86, vi. 80), found also in the LXX (Sir. xxv. 18, Thren. i. 4, 2 Macc. vi. 30) ; cf. στενάζω, vii. 34. For τῷ πνεύματι αὐτοῦ v. ii. 8. αὐτοῦ is omitted by D M* W fam. 1 282 b i l r¹ vg syˢ, as also in ii. 8 by D W a b c e ff q r². ὅτι (=τί) is read by C Or ; *v.* Intr. 61. The meaning is ' how ', cf. Pallis, 27, Black, 89. The use of γενεά, viii. 38, ix. 19, xiii. 30*, appears to reflect such passages as Deut. xxxii. 5 and Psa. xciv. (xcv.) 10 ; cf. Swete, 168. For ἀμὴν λέγω v. iii. 28. P⁴⁵ W have ἀμήν only. Cf. Couchoud, *JTS*, xxxv. 13.

εἰ δοθήσεται is a strong negation (=οὐ δοθήσεται Mt. xvi. 4) in which εἰ=אם implying an imprecation (e.g., ' If I do such a thing, may I die ! '). The refusal is absolute. Cf. Lagrange,

σημεῖον. καὶ ἀφεὶς αὐτοὺς πάλιν ἐμβὰς ἀπῆλθεν εἰς τὸ πέραν. 13

207; Howard, ii. 468 f. Apart from quotations from the LXX (Psa. xciv. 11) in Heb. iii. 11, iv. 3, 5, this is the only example in the NT, though an apodosis is wanting in Lk. xiii. 9, xix. 42, 2 Thess. ii. 3 f. (cf. Meecham, 88). The parallel saying from Q, in Lk. xi. 29 = Mt. xii. 39, adds the important exception εἰ μὴ τὸ σημεῖον 'Ιωνᾶ, the implication being that the message of Jesus is self-authenticating; cf. Manson, *SJ*, 90. The eschatological interpretation of Bultmann, 124 (' So will the Son of Man come from heaven to this generation ') is much less probable. Mark's version is more blunt, and is probably influenced by his view that the Messiahship of Jesus is concealed from the people and their

religious leaders. For the interesting conjecture of J. H. Michael, *JTS*, xxi. 146-59, that originally Q referred to ' the sign of John ', *v.* Creed, 163, Bultmann, 124. Matthew's version of the Markan saying is secondary. He omits the reference to groaning in spirit, adds πονηρὰ καὶ μοιχαλίς (cf. Mk. viii. 38) to γενεά and εἰ μὴ τὸ σημεῖον 'Ιωνᾶ from Q. Cf. xvi. 4 and xii. 39.

In 13, if πάλιν (*v.* ii. 1) is taken with ἀφείς, it must mean ' thereupon ', but if it is read with ἐμβάς, which is more natural, it refers to a further embarkation and so means ' again ' (cf. 10). For ἐμβαίνω *v.* iv. 1; εἰς τὸ πέραν iv. 35. Matthew has simply καὶ καταλιπὼν αὐτοὺς ἀπῆλθεν.

Mk. viii. 14-21   51. THE MYSTERY OF THE   Cf. Mt. xvi. 5-12
                          LOAVES

The narrative is a Markan construction in which a saying regarding ' the leaven of the Pharisees and the leaven of Herod ' is connected with a strong rebuke of the disciples for their failure to understand the significance of the loaves in the stories of miraculous feeding. Klostermann, 87, maintains that it is not a unity, and distinguishes 14, 16 (in which 15 is inserted), apparently the beginning of a third feeding-story, and 17-21 in which the disciples are blamed for their inability to trust Jesus after the double proof of His power in vi. 35-44 and viii. 1-9. This hypothesis exaggerates the artificiality of the narrative and estimates too narrowly the Evangelist's intention. K. L. Schmidt, 204, speaks of its vivid character and traces its origin to popular tradition. Dibelius, 229, assigns it to Mark on the basis of traditional material. So far as 14 f. are concerned, this reference to tradition is justified by the connexion of the narrative with the crossing of the lake, the artless allusion to a want of food which the disciples might well remember, and the introduction in 15 which is not irrelevant to the situation. But after 16 the saying is ignored, attention is concentrated on the stupidity of the disciples, and the two feeding-stories are treated as separate and miraculous incidents. The severe words of Jesus may well have a traditional basis, but, in the form in which they are recorded, they are assimilated to vi. 43 and viii. 8, that is, to secondary versions of the events. It is necessary, therefore, to consider the circumstances in which the narrative has a credible *Sitz im Leben*.

The conditions which account for the form of the narrative are probably to be found in the same liturgical and catechetical interests which are reflected in 1-10 and 11-13. The Feeding of the Four Thousand is viewed as a sign to the disciples of the coming of the Kingdom and the Demand for a Sign as showing that to the Pharisees, the Jewish religious leaders, no sign had been given. The present narrative carried this scheme of thought a stage farther. Even the first disciples had failed to understand the σημεῖα given to them! They were prototypes of many Christians in the writer's day who, like those at Corinth, had no true understanding of the κυριακὸν δεῖπνον (1 Cor. xi. 20).

Regarded in this way, the peculiar features of the narrative find a ready explanation. Mark is writing didactic history with the special needs of the Church in mind. Accordingly, under the pressure of practical interests, the historical prelude fades away. The stupidity of the disciples is exaggerated and their failure to interpret the metaphorical allusion in ' the leaven of the Pharisees ' is left unexplained. The feeding-stories are mentioned from the standpoint from which they had come to be interpreted, and the narrative ends with the pointed question, ' Do ye not yet understand ? ', which is aimed at the readers and not merely the original disciples. The story illustrates the beginnings of a type of Gospel narrative found often in the Fourth Gospel and which has persisted in Christian teaching down to the present day. Touch with history is not lost, but catechetical interests supervene.

If it be asked why such an explanation is given to this narrative while others in Mk are accepted more objectively, the answer is that the data call for this kind of explanation and that it is mistaken to assume that Markan narratives are of one stamp. Further, narratives must be studied, not only in themselves, but in relation to the groups in which they appear, for the groups differ according as historical, topical, or doctrinal interests are uppermost.

14   Καὶ ἐπελάθοντο λαβεῖν ἄρτους, καὶ εἰ μὴ ἕνα ἄρτον οὐκ εἶχον

14. It is not certain whether the narrative begins with 14 (WH, Swete, Huck, etc.) or with 13 (Rawlinson, Klostermann). This uncertainty points to the close connexion between the two stories. Mark intends to suggest that it was after the refusal of Jesus to entertain the demand for a sign from heaven that the incident happened. The failure to provision the boat, important to the disciples, was remembered. ἐπιλανθάνομαι*. B has ἐπελάθεντο. For εἰ μή . . . οὐ v. v. 37, vi. 4, although in these passages the negative comes first. Lagrange, 207 f., cites Herodotus i. 200, οὐδὲν ἄλλο σιτέονται εἰ μὴ ἰχθῦς μοῦνον. Cf. VGT, 182.

The saying on the leaven of the Pharisees is commonly explained as a patchwork insertion on the part of the Evangelist; cf. Wellhausen, 61; Klostermann, 87. Turner, 39, JTS, xxvi. 150, speaks of it as ' an obtrusive reference ' which interrupts the otherwise straightforward development of the episode. ' A modern writer would have put it in a note at the foot of the page.' So Blunt, 194. The saying will be considered later. Meantime an alternative possibility must be mentioned, namely, that Mark gives the saying in its original context, and that the real question to be asked is why it is ignored in the rest of the narrative. If Field, 11, is right in translating ἐπελάθοντο ' they had forgotten ', an intention to locate the saying is suggested.

Matthew connects the incident with the other side of the lake (ἐλθόντες οἱ μαθηταὶ εἰς τὸ πέραν) and omits the statement that, with the exception of one loaf, they had no bread with them in the boat (xv. 5).

In 14b P⁴⁵ reads (ἕνα μόν)ον ἄρτον ἔχοντες with the support of W Θ fam. 1 fam. 13 565 700. Couchoud, JTS, xxxv. 14, accepts the reading. When εἰ μή is followed by a noun, he argues, Mark always puts εἰ μή after

μεθ' ἑαυτῶν ἐν τῷ πλοίῳ.   καὶ διεστέλλετο αὐτοῖς λέγων 15
'Ορᾶτε, βλέπετε ἀπὸ τῆς ζύμης τῶν Φαρισαίων καὶ τῆς ζύμης
'Ηρῴδου.   καὶ διελογίζοντο πρὸς ἀλλήλους ὅτι ἄρτους οὐκ ἔχουσιν. 16

the verb; cf. ii. 26, v. 37, vi. 4, 5, 8, ix. 8, 29, x. 18, xi. 13, xiii. 32. This is a strong argument, but against it may be urged that the smooth reading appears to be a simplification of a more difficult original.

15. For διαστέλλομαι, elsewhere in Mk c. ἵνα and the subj., v. v. 43, and for the redundant ὁρᾶτε v. i. 44. Moulton, ii. 31, neatly counters the claim that βλέπειν ἀπό is a Hebraism by citing BGU iv. 1079 (A.D. 41): ὡς ἂν πάντες καὶ σὺ βλέπε σατὸν ἀπὸ τῶν 'Ιουδαίων, with the comment, ' Surely it was no Jew who gave this warning to his friend!'. For οἱ Φαρισαῖοι v. ii. 16; 'Ηρῴδης vi. 14; ζύμη*. For βλέπετε Matthew has προσέχετε, and instead of καὶ τῆς ζύμης 'Ηρῴδου he has καὶ Σαδδουκαίων (xvi. 6). Later he interprets the leaven as ' the teaching of the Pharisees and Sadducees ' (xv. 12). Luke (xii. 1) has a parallel to the saying, perhaps derived from L (cf. Manson, SJ, 105, 270), which reads: Προσέχετε ἑαυτοῖς ἀπὸ τῆς ζύμης, ἥτις ἐστὶν ὑπόκρισις, τῶν Φαρισαίων. Probably the saying was current as an isolated logion. Bultmann, 139, tentatively includes it among the Gesetzesworte und Gemeinderegeln, observing that its original form and meaning can scarcely be determined. Cf. Bacon, Studies in Matthew, 511-17, who suggests that the saying was brought to mind in the primitive Church by the Judaistic controversy when liberty was threatened by ' false brethren privily brought in ' (Gal. ii. 4). Influences of this kind may account for the phrase ἥτις ἐστὶν ὑπόκρισις which has been added in the Lukan form of the saying. In the Matthaean form καὶ Σαδδουκαίων is secondary, but the explanation of the leaven as teaching is by no means wide of the mark. In the Markan version the phrase καὶ τῆς ζύμης 'Ηρῴδου may

possibly be an addition, influenced by iii. 6 and xii. 13, but this inference is not necessary, and probably in Mk we approach nearest to the original significance of the saying. Cf. Manson, SJ, 105.

Apart from the Parable of the Leaven (Lk. xiii. 20 f. = Mt. xiii. 33) ζύμη in the NT is used metaphorically in a bad sense; cf. 1 Cor. v. 6, 7, 8, Gal. v. 9. So also the Rabbis used it of the idea of the evil disposition in man. Cf. Billerbeck, i. 728 f.; Abrahams, i. 52 f. See the prayer of Rabbi Alexander, cited by Abrahams : ' It is revealed before thee that our will is to do thy will. And what hinders? The leaven that is in the dough and servitude to the Kingdoms. May it be thy will to deliver us from their hand.' Abrahams refers to the parallel between ' the leaven that is in the dough ' and ' the leaven of the Pharisees ' in Mk and between ' servitude to the Kingdoms ' and ' the leaven of Herod '.

Mark does not interpret the phrase, but undoubtedly the idea of an evil disposition harmonizes with his story. Previously, in vii. 1-23, he has shown how the scribes and Pharisees pervert the teaching of the Law and the Prophets, and in the Demand for a Sign (viii. 11-13) has illustrated their blindness to the true nature of the mission of Jesus. It is natural therefore that, as the boat begins to cross the lake, He says: ' Take heed and beware of the evil disposition of the Pharisees ', less likely that He was thinking of their ' hypocrisy ', and improbable that the allusion is an imaginative addition. Even the reference to ' the leaven of Herod ' is timely if the enigmatic Dalmanutha was on the west shore in the neighbourhood of Tiberias.

The saying is undoubtedly genuine. Current as an isolated logion in Q or L, it is preserved in its original setting

17 καὶ γνοὺς λέγει αὐτοῖς Τί διαλογίζεσθε ὅτι ἄρτους οὐκ ἔχετε;
οὔπω νοεῖτε οὐδὲ συνίετε; πεπωρωμένην ἔχετε τὴν καρδίαν ὑμῶν;

by Mark. In favour of this view is the fact that it is not Mark's habit to insert sayings into the body of a narrative, as Matthew does (cf. ix. 13a and xii. 5-7), but to append them at the end; cf. ii. 21 f., 27 f., iii. 27-9, etc. Some MSS., including G W Δ Θ P⁴⁵ fam. 1 fam. 13 (exc. 124) 22 28 60 251 565 679 i k vg (1 MS.) sa geo arm, read τῶν Ἡρῳδιανῶν, but this reading is clearly a correction influenced by iii. 6 and xii. 13.

16. For διαλογίζομαι v. ii. 6. When used with πρὸς ἀλλήλους (cf. ix. 33 f.) or πρὸς ἑαυτούς (xi. 31) the verb implies the exchange of differences of opinion and point of view. Here the bone of contention is that the disciples have no bread. Turner, JTS, xxvii. 59, suggests that ὅτι is used as an indirect interrogative (as also in xiv. 60): they discussed with one another why they had no loaves. Matthew inserts λέγοντες and so makes it ὅτι recitativum followed by the first person Ἄρτους οὐκ ἐλάβομεν. There is strong support for λέγοντες in Mk (A C L Δ Θ et al. fam. 13 22 33 118 157 579 892 1071 al. pler. f g² l r² vg sys pe hl bo aeth arm) and most of these MSS., with the addition of ℵ, attest ἔχομεν, but probably ἔχουσιν should be read with B W P⁴⁵ fam. 1 (exc. 118) 28 565 700 1342 c g² k, especially if εἶχαν (D a b d ff et al.) is a grammatical variant.¹ In this case ὅτι may be rendered 'that' introducing indirect speech (Lagrange, 209; Klostermann, 87; Goodspeed, 'their being without bread') or 'because' (RVmg; Gould, 146; Torrey) or 'why' (v. Turner, supra), but it cannot be recitativum.

The issue is important; it affects the interpretation of the narrative as a whole, not merely the exegesis of 16. Many commentators and translators take ὅτι as recitativum (Swete, 170; Plummer, 198; Moffatt; RV, RSV), with the result that they follow (in most cases) the reading ἔχομεν. Cf. RV, 'saying, We have no bread'; RSV similarly; Moffatt, '"Leaven?" they argued among themselves, "we have no bread at all!"' These renderings are very attractive, but are textually unsound. Moreover, they interpret Mk in the light of Mt rather than Mk in itself. Moffatt's rendering suggests a connexion with 15 for which there is no warrant in the Gk. The truth is that in Mk the saying on the leaven is ignored either because the disciples do not understand it or more probably because the writer's interest is to emphasize their failure to understand the sign of the loaves in the stories of miraculous feeding. If this is so, the rendering of ὅτι by 'because' is doubtful. What the disciples discuss is their want of provisions, whose responsibility it is, and what they must do. There is much therefore to be said for Turner's rendering, 'why they have no bread', in preference to the alternative 'that they have no bread'.

17. The knowledge of Jesus (γνούς, iv. 13) is neither intuitive nor supernatural, but arises from the dispute in the boat. For οὔπω v. iv. 40; νοέω vii. 18; συνίημι iv. 12; πωρόω vi. 52*; καρδία ii. 6. As in iii. 5 and vi. 52, a darkening of the understanding is meant rather than hardness of heart. 'Here the close connexion with "the unseeing eye" favours the interpretation "moral blindness". Indeed "hardness" suggests a wilful obstinacy, which could scarcely be in place either here or in vi. 52', J. A. Robinson, Eph. 266. D reads πεπηρωμένη ('incapacitated', 'blinded') ἐστιν ἡ καρδία ὑμῶν; cf. caecatum f l r² vg, obtusum a q, obtusa b c d ff i, 'blinded' sys, 'stupefied' arm. Mark does not attribute the severity of the rebuke to the failure of the disciples to understand the saying on the leaven of the

¹ Ti and Souter read ἔχομεν; WH, Nestle and Lagrange ἔχουσιν.

ὀφθαλμοὺς ἔχοντες οὐ Βλέπετε καὶ ὦτα ἔχοντες οὐκ ἀκούετε; 18
καὶ οὐ μνημονεύετε ὅτε τοὺς πέντε ἄρτους ἔκλασα εἰς τοὺς 19
πεντακισχιλίους, πόσους κοφίνους κλασμάτων πλήρεις ἤρατε;
λέγουσιν αὐτῷ Δώδεκα. ὅτε ᵀ τοὺς ἑπτὰ εἰς τοὺς τετρα- 20
κισχιλίους, πόσων σφυρίδων πληρώματα κλασμάτων ἤρατε; καὶ
λέγουσιν αὐτῷ Ἑπτά. καὶ ἔλεγεν αὐτοῖς Οὔπω συνίετε; 21

20 καὶ

Pharisees, but to their want of faith in the power of Jesus to supply their need.

After Τί διαλογίζεσθε the phrase ἐν ἑαυτοῖς ὀλιγόπιστοι is read by W P⁴⁵ fam. 13, and ἐν ταῖς καρδίαις ὀλιγόπιστοι by Θ Φ 28 124 565 700 syhl mg geo² arm. So much is the adjective in harmony with Mark's narrative that, in spite of the possibility of assimilation to Mt. xvi. 8, it deserves serious consideration. Cf. Couchoud, *JTS*, xxxv. 15. One must feel more uncertain about the prepositional phrases since the wrangling may well have been open. Apart from the phrase noted above Matthew gives a greatly abbreviated version of the saying of Jesus. The sharp condemnation of the disciples disappears in the more sober question οὔπω νοεῖτε οὐδὲ μνημονεύετε τοὺς πέντε ἄρτους . . .;. This modification reveals Matthew's anxiety to ' spare the Twelve '. Meantime, it remains to be considered whether the Markan strictures, if not overpressed, are misapplied.

18. The indignant question, ὀφθαλμοὺς ἔχοντες οὐ βλέπετε καὶ ὦτα ἔχοντες οὐκ ἀκούετε;, omitted in Mt, is expressed in the language of the LXX. Cf. Isa. vi. 9 f. (used in iv. 12), Jer. v. 21, Ezek. xii. 2. Lagrange, 209, refers to *Oxyrh. Logia*, iii. 8, πονεῖ ἡ ψυχή μου ἐπὶ τοῖς υἱοῖς τῶν ἀνθρώπων ὅτι τυφλοί εἰσιν τῇ καρδίᾳ αὐτῶν καὶ οὐ βλέπουσιν, and *Corp. Hermeticum* (Scott, ii. 182), ἵνα μήτε ἀκούῃς περὶ ὧν ἀκούειν σε δεῖ, μήτε βλέπῃς, περὶ ὧν βλέπειν σε δεῖ. The question καὶ οὐ μνημονεύετε; (μνημονεύω*) leads on to

the direct allusions to the stories of miraculous feeding in 19-21. Again Couchoud, *JTS*, xxxv. 16, follows Θ P⁴⁵ 565 in reading οὔπω νοεῖτε οὐδὲ μνημονεύετε, supported by οὐδὲ μνημονεύετε in D and οὔπω νοεῖτε in N Σ. Cf. Mt. xvi. 9.

19-21. By question and answer 19 recalls the Feeding of the Five Thousand (vi. 35-44) and 20 the Four Thousand (viii. 1-9). The numbers are precisely given and the κόφινοι of the one story (vi. 43) are distinguished from the σφυρίδες of the other (viii. 8). In 19 κοφίνους κλασμάτων πλήρεις¹ replaces κλάσματα . . . κοφίνων πληρώματα (vi. 43) and in 20 πληρώματα is used instead of περισσεύματα (viii. 8). Other points of interest are the asyndetic use of λέγουσιν² in 19, and εἰς c. acc. in 19 f. instead of the simple dat. as in the Koine; *VGT*, 187; Deissmann, *BS*, 118; Lagrange, 210. The correspondences show that the compiler of 1-26 distinguished two separate incidents and was familiar with the text of vi. 43. It follows therefore that if vi. 35-44 and viii. 1-9 are doublets (*v*. Note C), the form of the sayings in 19-21 is redactional. This is the view taken by many commentators, including Wellhausen, J. Weiss, Wendling, Loisy, Branscomb, and Turner. Turner, 39, indeed, goes so far as to say that Mark ' has tampered with our Lord's words '. We may doubt if ' tampered ' is the right word; it is more like Mark to record tradition as he finds it. But it is improbable that the sayings are in their original form. All too clearly

¹ πλήρεις (iv. 28*) is omitted by P⁴⁵ (apparently) fam. 13 a b d ff i¹·² q *et al.*, and replaced by the indeclinable πλήρης in A F G M *et al.*
² Cf. Black, 40, who also cites ἔφη in ix. 38, x. 29, xii. 24.

they have been adapted in the tradition under a homiletical impulse. It is possible, even if the two narratives are doublets, that more than one fellowship-meal was celebrated by Jesus and His disciples, and credible that He should have reminded them of past experiences. But if vi. 35-44 and viii. 1-9 are secondary accounts of the same incident, viii. 19-21 must be a debased form of the words of Jesus. The Matthaean version shows the sayings in a further stage of adaptation. Mark's version is first abbreviated and then supplemented. His pointed climax, οὔπω συνίετε;, is lost in Mt in a cloud of words: ' How is it that you do not understand that I

did not speak to you about loaves?' (xvi. 11). The warning against the leaven of the Pharisees (with the addition of ' Sadducees ') is repeated, and the sober explanation is added that Jesus did not tell the disciples to beware of actual leaven, but of (false) teaching. Here nothing is left to the imagination.

Our conclusion must be that in Mk we are nearer to the original tradition than in Mt, but nevertheless at a greater distance from it than is usual in Mk. The explanation must be found in the circumstances which guided the composition of the entire section, viii. 1-26, and the interests it was meant to serve.

Mk. viii. 22-6   52. THE CURE OF THE BLIND
MAN

This Miracle-story and the Cure of the Deaf Mute (vii. 32-7) form a pair peculiar to Mk with striking linguistic agreements. Thus, both cures are wrought in privacy or semi-privacy ; in each case spittle is used and the laying on of hands ; restoration is accomplished with some difficulty or in stages ; and, finally, in each instance a charge to maintain secrecy is imposed. There are, of course, important differences ; but the agreements are so many, so close, and so striking that it is not surprising that several critics regard the narratives as duplicate accounts of the same incident. Cf. Bultmann, 228 ; Wendling, 77. Linguistic agreement between different narratives has already been noticed as characteristic of Mk (v. viii. 1-10), but it is so remarkable in the two narratives in question (and in xi. 1-6 and xiv. 13-16) as to call for special notice. The agreements may be set out as follows :

THE CURE OF THE DEAF MUTE (vii. 32-7)	THE CURE OF THE BLIND MAN (viii. 22-6)
32. καὶ φέρουσιν αὐτῷ κωφὸν καὶ μογιλάλον, καὶ παρακαλοῦσιν αὐτὸν ἵνα ἐπιθῇ αὐτῷ τὴν χεῖρα.	22. καὶ φέρουσιν αὐτῷ τυφλὸν καὶ παρακαλοῦσιν αὐτὸν ἵνα αὐτοῦ ἅψηται.
33. καὶ ἀπολαβόμενος αὐτὸν ἀπὸ τοῦ ὄχλου κατ᾿ ἰδίαν ἔβαλεν τοὺς δακτύλους αὐτοῦ εἰς τὰ ὦτα αὐτοῦ καὶ πτύσας ἥψατο τῆς γλώσσης αὐτοῦ,	23. καὶ ἐπιλαβόμενος τῆς χειρὸς τοῦ τυφλοῦ ἐξήνεγκεν αὐτὸν ἔξω τῆς κώμης, καὶ πτύσας εἰς τὰ ὄμματα αὐτοῦ, ἐπιθεὶς τὰς χεῖρας αὐτῷ ἐπηρώτα αὐτὸν Εἴ τι βλέπεις;
34. καὶ ἀναβλέψας εἰς τὸν οὐρανὸν ἐστέναξεν,	24. καὶ ἀναβλέψας

καὶ λέγει αὐτῷ Ἐφφαθά,
ὅ ἐστιν Διανοίχθητι·
35. καὶ ἠνοίγησαν αὐτοῦ αἱ ἀκοαί,
καὶ ἐλύθη ὁ δεσμὸς τῆς γλώσσης
αὐτοῦ,
καὶ ἐλάλει ὀρθῶς·
36. καὶ διεστείλατο αὐτοῖς

ἵνα μηδενὶ λέγωσιν·
ὅσον δὲ αὐτοῖς διεστέλλετο,
αὐτοὶ μᾶλλον περισσότερον ἐκήρυσσον.
37. καὶ ὑπερπερισσῶς ἐξεπλήσσοντο λέγο-
οντες
Καλῶς πάντα πεποίηκεν,
καὶ τοὺς κωφοὺς ποιεῖ ἀκούειν
καὶ ἀλάλους λαλεῖν.

ἔλεγεν Βλέπω τοὺς ἀνθρώπους
ὅτι ὡς δένδρα ὁρῶ περιπατοῦντας.
25. εἶτα πάλιν ἔθηκεν τὰς χεῖρας
ἐπὶ τοὺς ὀφθαλμοὺς αὐτοῦ,
καὶ διέβλεψεν, καὶ ἀπεκατέστη,
καὶ ἐνέβλεπεν τηλαυγῶς ἅπαντα.
26. καὶ ἀπέστειλεν αὐτὸν
εἰς οἶκον αὐτοῦ λέγων
Μηδενὶ εἴπῃς εἰς τὴν κώμην.

It is clear that the doublet-hypothesis is a possible explanation. Apart from actual agreements, some of the variants are due to the fact that the one story is that of a deaf-mute and the other of a blind man. Moreover, there are agreements which are differently expressed : ἀπὸ τοῦ ὄχλου κατ' ἰδίαν corresponds to ἔξω τῆς κώμης and ὀρθῶς to τηλαυγῶς. Τὸ ἵνα μηδενὶ λέγωσιν there is also a parallel in μηδενὶ εἴπῃς εἰς τὴν κώμην. But, having said this, we must conclude that the hypothesis is very improbable in the light of the striking differences. In the one case ἀνα-βλέψας describes an attitude of prayer on the part of Jesus ; in the other the natural raising of the blind man's eyes when he is addressed. Further, in vii. 32-7 there is nothing to correspond to the striking observation : ' I see men ; but they look like trees, walking '. This is not the kind of variant which might arise in different accounts of the same story, but a highly distinctive detail which stamps the story as genuine. Moreover, the reference to a second laying on of hands in 25 is without parallel in the Gospels and is not likely to have been invented. The suggestion which the story makes of a cure wrought with great difficulty, or at least in stages, is a mark of historical truth, and its bold realism is probably the reason why both Matthew and Luke have omitted it. It is true that confusion about the nature of a particular ailment can easily arise in oral tradition. Evidence of this is provided by a comparison of Mt. xii. 22 f. (a blind and dumb demoniac) with Mt. ix. 32 f. (a dumb demoniac) and Lk. xi. 14 (a dumb demoniac). But in the two Markan stories the differences are far greater, so great in fact as to belong to different incidents.

To some extent the linguistic agreements may be explained by the admitted tendency of Mark to repeat himself and by the ease with which popular narratives assume fixed forms in oral tradition. Such a form is the use of the impersonal plural and the frequent use of φέρω in stories of healing (cf. i. 32, ii. 3, ix. 17, 19, 20). Equally true is this of expressions like ἐπιθεὶς τὰς χεῖρας αὐτῷ and of references to touching (ἵνα αὐτοῦ ἅψηται), to manipulative actions in general, and the use of spittle (cf. Jn. ix. 6). But neither of these suggestions, any more than the doublet-hypothesis, will furnish a complete explanation of the genesis of the narrative. Direct reference to vii. 32-7 on the part of the writer, guided by the same catechetical interests which have shaped viii. 1-10, 11-13, and 14-21, will alone account for the peculiar features of viii. 22-6. Anxious for the sake of his readers to insist that blindness prevented the disciples from receiving the sign of the loaves, he wished none the less to sound a note of hope. The blind could be made to see. Such a note resounded in the closing story of the older cycle, but vii. 32-7 did not supply precisely what was wanted since here it was a case of a deaf stammerer. The cure of the blind was the theme required. Tradition told of the hard won cure of the blind man near Bethsaida. The story itself warrants us in speaking of tradition, since its realism shows it to be anything but a product of invention. Moreover, in καλῶς πάντα πεποίηκεν in vii. 37 we have seen reason to think that a cycle, and not only a single story, was known to the narrator. Mark, therefore, or a predecessor, deliberately uses the framework supplied by vii. 32-7, but fits into it a new story suitable to his didactic purpose. By this bold hypothesis alone we do justice to the literary agreements between vii. 32-7 and viii. 22-6 and the no less striking differences between the two stories. Indeed, it is confirmation of the account given of viii. 1-26 as a whole that the same liturgical and catechetical interests account for each of the four narratives. The blind man saw all things clearly. So did the disciples and so would Mark's readers. See further, Intr. 97 f.

22 Καὶ ἔρχονται εἰς Βηθσαιδάν. Καὶ φέρουσιν αὐτῷ τυφλὸν καὶ
23 παρακαλοῦσιν αὐτὸν ἵνα αὐτοῦ ἅψηται. καὶ ἐπιλαβόμενος τῆς
χειρὸς τοῦ τυφλοῦ ἐξήνεγκεν αὐτὸν ἔξω τῆς κώμης, καὶ πτύσας
εἰς τὰ ὄμματα αὐτοῦ, ἐπιθεὶς τὰς χεῖρας αὐτῷ, ἐπηρώτα ⌐αὐτόν

22. A second case of the cure of blindness is the story of Bartimaeus (x. 46-52). For Βηθσαιδάν v. vi. 45. As in many Markan narratives, it is difficult to decide whether καὶ ἔρχονται εἰς Βηθσαιδάν belongs to this story or to viii. 14-21. Schmidt, 207 f., thinks it belongs to the present story and maintains that Mark probably found the name connected with it in the tradition. He leaves open the question whether the well attested ἔρχεται (ℵ* A al. pler. fam. 1 565 700 al. pler. sys pe hl) may not be original. The reading Βηθανίαν (D 262 a b d f ff i l q r¹) may be a scribal correction influenced by κώμη in 23 and 26.

The impersonal plural φέρουσιν and καὶ παρακαλοῦσιν αὐτὸν ἵνα c. subj. appear also in vii. 32. Along with other agreements in 23 they raise the question of the relationship between the two narratives. For παρακαλέω v. i. 40, c. subj. v. 10; ἅπτομαι i. 41. τυφλός, viii. 23, x. 46, 49, 51*.

23. κώμη, cf. vi. 6. The use of the word with reference to Bethsaida is not impossible if the older fishing village is meant; otherwise, the incident took place near an unknown village in Decapolis.

There are several striking agreements with vii. 33 in this verse. With καὶ ἐπιλαβόμενος cf. καὶ ἀπολαβόμενος. Note also the removal of the sufferer to a distance (ἔξω τῆς κώμης), the use of spittle (πτύσας), and the reference to the laying on of hands (ἐπιθεὶς τὰς χεῖρας αὐτῷ). See the introductory note. ἐπιλαμβάνομαι*, Mt. xiv. 31, Lk (5), Ac (7), 1 Tim (2), Heb (2)**, 'to lay hold of'; Cl., LXX, Pap. Blass, 101 n., says that the reading of D, λαβόμενος τὴν χεῖρα τοῦ τυφλοῦ, is 'in the style of neither classical nor NT Greek'. χειρός is partitive, 'by the hand'. ὄμμα*, Mt. xx. 34** is a common poetical word found also in the papyri; VGT, 448. For ἐπιτιθέναι τὰς χεῖρας v. v. 23, and for the similar use of κρατεῖν i. 31.

Distinctive of the story is the direct

Εἴ τι βλέπεις;¹ καὶ ἀναβλέψας ἔλεγεν Βλέπω τοὺς ἀνθρώπους 24
ὅτι ὡς δένδρα ὁρῶ περιπατοῦντας. εἶτα πάλιν ἔθηκεν τὰς χεῖρας 25

23 αὐτὸν εἴ τι βλέπει

question Εἴ τι βλέπεις;. This usage is
not classical but is found in the NT
in Mt. xii. 10, xix. 3, Ac. i. 6, vii. 1, etc.
Cf. Gen. xvii. 17, Εἰ τῷ ἑκατονταετεῖ
γενήσεται υἱός;. Lagrange, 212, suggests that it comes probably from the
LXX where it translates ךְ; cf. Blass,
260 n. The origin of the constr. is
traced by WM, 639, to an ellipse, 'I
should like to know'. In the NT it
has become equivalent to a direct interrogative and is frequent in Lk/Ac.
Cf. Robertson, 916; Souter, 72. In
Mk, viii. 23 is the sole example, for εἰ
ἔξεστιν in x. 2 is indirect. βλέπει is read
here by אֵ A D² L W al. pler. fam. 1
fam. 13 28 700 al. pler. it vg sype hl
geoᴮ arm, but preference must be given
to βλέπεις read by B C D* Δ Θ 565 579
1342 sys sa bo geo¹ et ᴬ aeth.

24. For ἀναβλέπω v. vi. 41. Here
the word is used of the involuntary
raising of the eyes (Swete, 174; Klostermann, 88) rather than, as in x. 51 f.,
of the recovery of sight (Lagrange,
213, Et ayant commencé à voir). In
any case, the man was not born blind,
for he can distinguish certain moving
objects like trees as men. In the
clause ὅτι ὡς δένδρα ὁρῶ περιπατοῦντας
read by most MSS., ὅτι and ὁρῶ are
omitted by C² D Mᵐg W Θ fam. 1 22
28 565 892 1071 al. plur. it vg sys pe hl
sa bo geo aeth Aug. In spite of its
wide attestation. this smooth reading
is probably a later simplification of the
original text, for it is difficult to see
why ὡς δένδρα περιπατοῦντας should
have been altered to the form found in
אֵ A B C* L Δ, etc. The awkwardness
of this reading has been traced to the
misrendering of the original Aramaic.
Thus, Allen, 116, ET, xiii. 330, suggests that ך ought to have been translated by the relative οὓς and not by ὅτι,
the original being, 'I see men whom
I see as trees walking'. So Torrey,
301. Black, 37, points out that this

is still an unusually complicated way
of saying, ' I see men like trees walking ', and suggests that, with emphatic
hyperbaton, the original Aramaic ran,
' I see men that like trees they are
walking ', and that a translator may
have taken the participial present as
a true participle and made it agree
with the acc. ' men ', adding a second
verb ὁρῶ. It may be that these suggestions are not necessary, for the
whole passage lends itself well to
arresting modern translations. Cf.
Goodspeed, ' I can see the people, for
they look to me like trees, only they
are moving about '; Moffatt, ' I can
make out people, for I see them as
large as trees moving '; RSV, ' I see
men; but they look like trees, walking '. These translations are free, but
they preserve the vivid character of
the Gk. For the distinction between
βλέπω and ὁράω v. the note on iv. 12.
The contrast is natural and may well
be original. Field, 32, compares the
proverbial expression οὐδὲ ἀνθρώπους
ἑώρων τοὺς ἀνθρώπους used of persons
suddenly thrown into a state of intense
excitement.

A striking Hellenistic parallel is
cited by Klostermann, 88, and Rawlinson, 108, with reference to a blind
man, Alcetas of Halice, who saw a
vision in which the god Asclepios
appeared to go over his eyes with his
fingers, with the result that ' the first
things he saw were the trees in the
temple precincts ' (Dittenberger, Syl-
loge Inscr. Graec.³ iii. 1168; v. VGT,
30). Such parallels do not prove that
the present story, and vii. 32 ff., ' were
developed, if not originated, in the
syncretistic atmosphere of the Hellenistic world ' (Branscomb, 142); they
merely illustrate how common features
tend to recur in stories of the kind,
e.g. that a round object like a tree is
a man and that the touch of a healer

ἐπὶ τοὺς ὀφθαλμοὺς αὐτοῦ, καὶ διέβλεψεν, καὶ ἀπεκατέστη, καὶ
26 ἐνέβλεπεν ⌜τηλαυγῶς⌝ ἅπαντα. καὶ ἀπέστειλεν αὐτὸν εἰς οἶκον
αὐτοῦ λέγων Μηδενὶ εἴπῃς εἰς τὴν κώμην.

25 δηλαυγῶς

is curative. For the story of how Vespasian cured a blind man by the use of spittle cf. Tacitus, *Hist.* iv. 81 ; Suetonius, *Vesp.* 7. See further, Bultmann, 237 n., 248 ; Dibelius, 86.

25. Instead of εἶτα (iv. 17*) καί is read by D b c ff i k q r¹ syˢ aeth, and εἶτα is omitted by syᵖᵉ sa arm. πάλιν, ' again ', points back to 23. The second laying on of hands implies that the first was not successful and that the cure was gradual. This fact alone probably accounts for the omission of the story by Matthew and Luke, and strongly supports the historical character of the incident. In spite of the distinctions which Swete, 174, draws between the three verbs διέβλεψεν, ἀπεκατέστη, and ἐνέβλεπεν, the description is tautologous and the existence of variant readings (*v. infra*) is not surprising. διαβλέπω*, Mt. vii. 5, Lk. vi. 42**, ' to see clearly '. The verb is not found in the LXX and is scantily attested in the papyri (*VGT*, 147). It is used by Plato (*Phaedo*, 86 D) in the sense of *looking fixedly*, but LS give two examples with the meaning ' to see clearly ' (cf. Lk. vi. 42 = Mt. vii. 5, καὶ τότε διαβλέψεις τὸ κάρφος). For the double augment in ἀπεκατέστη *v*. the note on iii. 5. ἐμβλέπω, x. 21, 27, xiv. 67*, Mt (2), Lk (2), Jn (2), Ac (1)**, ' to look at '; Cl., LXX, Pap. The rare adv. τηλαυγῶς**, <τῆλε ' afar ', αὐγή ' radiance ', is a poetical word found also in late prose which means ' clearly from afar '; *v. VGT*, 633 ; Moulton, ii. 283. The meaning is that the man sees everything clearly at a distance. The *v.l.* δηλαυγῶς (ℵ* C L Δ 579) has the same meaning. The masc. ἅπαντας, read by A C² 579, etc., is secondary, giving a cross reference to 24. The

point made is that the man can focus distant objects (ἅπαντα). The variants ἐποίησεν αὐτὸν ἀναβλέψαι (A N Θ *al. pler.* 22 33 118 124 565 700 1071 *al. pler.* a f q syʰˡ) and ἤρξατο ἀναβλέψαι (D b c ff i l r¹·² vg) are probably attempts to remove the tautology in καὶ διέβλεψεν καὶ ἀπεκατέστη. διέβλεψεν is very strongly attested (ℵ B C L W Δ fam. 1 (exc. 118) 28 579 1342 k) and should be read with WH. Cf. Swete, 174. In διέβλεψεν . . . ἐνέβλεπεν there is a careful distinction of tenses ; the man saw clearly and began to fix his eyes upon things. This is one of a number of cases in which Mark's prolixity is in the interests of objectivity ; *v.* Intr. 50-2.

26. The man is sent home (RV, RSV, Moffatt, Goodspeed) or to his house (Torrey). Cf. v. 19 and viii. 3, and for ἀποστέλλω *v.* i. 2. The command, μηδὲ εἰς τὴν κώμην εἰσέλθῃς (WH, Ti, Nestle, Souter), forbids him even to enter the village, but there is good reason to prefer μηδενὶ εἴπῃς εἰς τὴν κώμην, in which case he is forbidden to speak of his cure there. Cf. Turner, 39, *JTS*, xxvi. 18, xxix. 2, *The Study of the NT*, 59 ; Allen, 116 ; Rawlinson, 108 ; R. H. Lightfoot, 72 n. ; Couchoud, *JTS*, xxxiv. 122 f. ; Lohmeyer, 158 n.

The passage provides one of the examples of conflate readings on which Westcott and Hort, 99 f., base their claim for the superiority of the ' Neutral Text '. They hold that the late Antiochian text is a conflation of μηδὲ[1] εἰς τὴν κώμην εἰσέλθης (ℵ B L W fam. 1 (exc. 118) syˢ sa geo¹) and μηδενὶ εἴπῃς εἰς τὴν κώμην (D c q k), and that the former is the original text. But further investigation has shown that the reading μηδενὶ εἴπῃς μηδὲ ἐν τῇ κώμῃ was more widely

[1] μή ℵ* W.

current than they supposed and that its various forms [1] give further support to the Western reading. Pointing to the Markan use of εἰς for ἐν, Turner claims that the case for its originality is unanswerable. Secrecy, of course, could not be ensured. Here, therefore, as in vii. 36, we must infer either that the prohibition was temporary or, and perhaps more probably, that it is editorial, reflecting the Evangelist's interest in the idea of the Messianic secret. *V*. Intr. 122-4.

V

Mk. viii. 27-x. 52   CAESAREA PHILIPPI:
THE JOURNEY TO JERUSALEM

The fifth division begins with the events in the vicinity of Caesarea Philippi in the tetrarchy of Herod Philip, and thence by easy stages describes the journey to Jerusalem through Galilee, Peraea, and Judaea. The arrangement is loose and for the most part topical. Brief topographical statements in viii. 27, ix. 30, x. 1, and x. 32 introduce successive groups of material, but, as pointed out in the Introduction (pp. 98-100), it is clear that Mark has no detailed information at his command. The whole is dominated by the thought of the approaching Passion which finds powerful expression in the three predictions in viii. 31, ix. 31, and x. 33 f., and in other Passion sayings in viii. 34, ix. 12b, x. 38 f., and x. 45. The four main sections are: (*a*) Messiahship and Suffering (viii. 27-ix. 29); (*b*) The Journey through Galilee (ix. 30-50); (*c*) The Journey through Peraea and Judaea (x. 1-31); (*d*) The Approach to Jerusalem, (x. 32-52).

(*a*) Mk. viii. 27-ix. 29   MESSIAHSHIP AND
SUFFERING

For the general character of this group of narratives and sayings *v*. Intr. 98. In many respects it continues the account of the Ministry beyond Galilee, but in the Confession of Peter and the First Prophecy of the Passion the decisive steps are taken which lead inevitably to the journey to Jerusalem and the events of the Passion.

The section includes:

(53) viii. 27-33.   The Confession of Peter and the First Prophecy of the Passion.
(54) viii. 34-ix. 1.   Sayings on Crossbearing, Sacrifice, and the Coming of the Kingdom.
(55) ix. 2-8.   The Transfiguration.
(56) ix. 9-13.   The Descent from the Mount.
(57) ix. 14-29.   The Epileptic Lad.

---

[1] With variations ὕπαγε εἰς τὸν οἶκόν σου καὶ ἐὰν εἰς τὴν κώμην εἰσέλθῃς μηδενὶ εἴπῃς μηδὲ ἐν τῇ κώμῃ is attested by Θ Φ fam. 13 (exc. 124) 28 61 565 b f ff g² i l r² vg.   μηδὲ om. Θ Φ 565.   μηδὲν εἴπῃς τινί Φ.   μηδενὶ μηδὲν εἴπῃς 28 61.   ἐν τῇ κώμῃ om. it (exc. ff) vg.

Mk. viii. 27-33   53. THE CONFESSION OF   Cf. Mt. xvi. 13-23
                       PETER AND THE FIRST   Lk. ix. 18-22
                       PROPHECY OF THE PASSION

This narrative is a Story about Jesus. It cannot justly be regarded
as a ' Markan construction ' ; it is too personal and suggests too strongly
the use of a story given in the tradition. Both Dibelius, 115, and Bultmann, 275-8, classify it as a Legend, but this characterization fails to do
justice to the narrative and the impression it makes upon us. The perception that it rests upon testimony not far removed from the original
facts has led many scholars to describe it as a Petrine story ; cf. J. Weiss,
350, *Die Schr.*[4] 145-7 ; Ed. Meyer, i. 117 ; Bartlet, 247 (' Common
Apostolic Tradition ') ; etc. The points on which this estimate turns are
the natural reference to Caesarea Philippi, the lifelike picture of Peter
who speaks for the rest and remonstrates with Jesus, the fact that Jesus
does not forthwith confirm the truth of his confession, but sternly rebukes
him in the words, ' Get thee behind me, Satan : for thou mindest not the
things of God, but the things of men ' (viii. 33). The command to keep
silence does not forbid this hypothesis, and even if the prophecy of death
and resurrection is phrased in the light of events, it may be held in substance to voice the conviction of Jesus.

Bultmann's interpretation departs radically from this view. The
place-name, he holds, does not give to the narrative a historical character,
since it belongs to the preceding material corresponding to viii. 22a, while
ἐν τῇ ὁδῷ is a mere connecting link. The fact that Jesus puts the initial
question and its character show the secondary nature of the narrative,
since He must have been as familiar as the disciples with popular opinion
concerning Himself. The question is a Christian formation and the
answer represents the familiar Christian confession. The narrative is a
Glaubenslegende : faith in the Messiahship of Jesus is traced back to a
story of the Messianic confession of Peter. His Easter experience was
the hour in which the faith of the community is born. Further, the narrative is fragmentary ; a reaction of Jesus to the confession must originally
have been recounted. The primitive ending, retained in Mt. xvi. 17-19,
but itself unhistorical, has been replaced by a polemical passage directed
against the Jewish-Christian standpoint represented by Peter from the
point of view of Hellenistic Pauline Christianity. It is therefore unnecessary, Bultmann holds, to answer the question of Karl Holl : ' Who from
the primitive community would have dared to call the revered Kephas
Satan ? '.

There are too many assumptions and improbabilities in this view
to make it convincing. The reference to ' the villages of Caesarea Philippi '
by a writer who so rarely give place-names commands respect. While
it is usual for pupils to question a Rabbi, there is no good reason why
Jesus should not have questioned His disciples, especially as He had been
in retirement, and in any case as a step to the more direct question. Again,
sayings like Lk. xii. 50, Mk. ix. 12b, and Mk. ix. 31 support the view,
reasonable in itself, that Jesus foresaw His suffering. ' He possessed the
charisma of prophecy and exercised it with reference to Himself ', Otto,
363. Moreover, to explain the idea that ' the Son of Man must suffer '
as without warrant in His teaching, is more difficult than to accept the

view that He thought creatively about the issues of His ministry fore-shadowed in the fate of the prophets, the death of John, and the im-placable hostility of the Jewish hierarchy. Finally, Karl Holl's question stands, even when full justice has been done to the conflicts between Pauline Christianity and Jerusalem, which turned upon questions of circumcision and the eating of Jews with Gentiles rather than soteriology.

For these reasons the decisiveness of the confession of Peter and the teaching which followed claim recognition. Joseph Klausner, 300, recognizes their historical character, and goes so far as to say that ' to deny this would make the whole history of Christianity incomprehensible '. The story ought not to be interpreted as if no suspicion that Jesus might be the Messiah had ever dawned on the minds of the disciples before. Without some sense of His greatness and a hope that in Him ancient prophecies might be fulfilled, they are not likely to have forsaken all and followed Him, and first impressions must have been deepened by His subsequent words and deeds. The true significance of the confession is that what had been inchoate and provisional now became definite and irreversible. In the Markan plan the new teaching concerning Messianic suffering is more important than the confession. In viii. 31, ix. 12b, ix. 31, x. 33 f. the primary reference is to Jesus Himself, but it is not excluded that the Messianic community is also in mind.

Καὶ ἐξῆλθεν ὁ Ἰησοῦς καὶ οἱ μαθηταὶ αὐτοῦ εἰς τὰς κώμας 27
Καισαρίας τῆς Φιλίππου· καὶ ἐν τῇ ὁδῷ ἐπηρώτα τοὺς μαθητὰς

27. καὶ ἐξῆλθεν : Mt ἐξελθὼν δέ. Luke has the καὶ ἐγένετο c. infin. con-struction and, without mentioning Caesarea Philippi, says: ' as he was praying alone, the disciples were with him ' (ix. 18). Mark also mentions the disciples (οἱ μαθηταὶ αὐτοῦ, v. ii. 15) without any indication of when or how they rejoined Jesus. The refer-ence to the villages (κώμη, vi. 6) of a town (Mt, τὰ μέρη) is unusual. Prob-ably the neighbouring villages are meant or the villages of the region (*WM*, 234). Swete, 176, observes that the phrase is used repeatedly in the LXX of Josh. and 1 and 2 Chron. Καισαρία ἡ Φιλίππου*, Mt. xvi. 13**, was so named to distinguish it from Καισαρία (Ac, 15 times), the seat of Roman government on the coast (Καισαρία ἡ παράλιος, earlier Στράτωνος πύργος). Situated at the source of the Jordan on the slopes of Hermon, the town in ancient times was called Paneas (mod. Banias), so named from a grotto, τὸ πανεῖον, sacred to Pan. Near the grotto Herod the Great had

built a temple in honour of Augustus. Centuries earlier the place was associ-ated with the worship of the Baalim. The city was rebuilt by Herod Philip and named by him Caesarea. Cf. Josephus, *Ant.* xviii. 2. 1 : Φίλιππος δὲ Πανεάδα τὴν πρὸς ταῖς πηγαῖς τοῦ Ἰορδάνου κατασκευάσας ὀνομάζει Και-σάρειαν. Travellers and historians appear to vie one with another in de-scribing the beauty and fertility of the district. Stanley, *Sinai and Palestine*, 397, speaks of its ' park-like verdure ', its ' rush of waters through deep thickets ', its olive groves, its view over the distant plain, and describes it as ' almost a Syrian Tivoli '. Cf. G. A. Smith, 473 f. : ' Paneas lies scarcely an hour to the north of Tell-el-Kadi. From the latter you pass a well-watered meadow, covered with trees, and then a broad terrace, with oaks, like an English park, till you come to the edge of a deep gorge, through which there roars a headlong stream, half stifled by bush. . . . In the cliff is a cavern. Part of the upper

28 αὐτοῦ λέγων αὐτοῖς Τίνα με λέγουσιν οἱ ἄνθρωποι εἶναι; οἱ
δὲ εἶπαν αὐτῷ λέγοντες ὅτι Ἰωάνην τὸν βαπτιστήν, καὶ ἄλλοι
29 Ἠλείαν, ἄλλοι δὲ ὅτι εἷς τῶν προφητῶν. καὶ αὐτὸς ἐπηρώτα
αὐτούς Ὑμεῖς δὲ τίνα με λέγετε εἶναι; ἀποκριθεὶς ὁ Πέτρος
30 λέγει αὐτῷ Σὺ εἶ ὁ χριστός. καὶ ἐπετίμησεν αὐτοῖς ἵνα μηδενὶ

rock has fallen, and from the *débris* of boulders and shingle below there bursts and bubbles along a line of thirty feet a full-born river.' Caesarea Philippi lies some twenty-five miles north of Bethsaida. Presumably, but not certainly, Bethsaida was the starting point and the journey was made either along the east bank of the Jordan or through the hills. Mark does not say that Jesus entered the city, but He must have passed through it or its suburbs if the scene of the Transfiguration is Mount Hermon. The question is put ἐν τῇ ὁδῷ (v. viii. 3). For ἐπερωτάω v. v. 9. The inquiry prepares the way for the more personal question in 29, but it is asked for the sake of information since the disciples had been in touch with the people during the withdrawal in Tyre. For οἱ ἄνθρωποι Luke substitutes οἱ ὄχλοι (ix. 18), and instead of με Matthew has τὸν υἱὸν τοῦ ἀνθρώπου (xvi. 13).

28. The use of the redundant λέγοντες corresponds to the Heb. לֵאמֹר. Cf. Intr. 63. Cf. also xii. 26, πῶς εἶπεν αὐτῷ ὁ θεὸς λέγων. Here it is omitted by Matthew and replaced by ἀποκριθέντες by Luke. The variations in the constructions after ὅτι are of interest. With Ἰωάνην τὸν βαπτιστήν (so also Mt and Lk) λέγουσιν οἱ ἄνθρωποί σε εἶναι. On this the second ὅτι followed by the indic. depends. Matthew makes slight stylistic alterations (οἱ μέν . . . ἄλλοι δέ . . . ἕτεροι δέ) and adds Ἰερεμίαν. Cf. 4 Ezra ii. 18, *Mittam tibi adiutorium pueros meos Isaiam et Hieremiam.* For εἷς τῶν προφητῶν Luke has προφήτης τις τῶν ἀρχαίων ἀνέστη (ix. 19). Cf. Pallis, 27. As in vi. 25, Mark uses βαπτιστής (cf. i. 4). The account of the various opinions

recalls vi. 14 f., but it is not necessary to infer that the one passage is merely an echo of the other. It is remarkable that in both cases, despite i. 24, 34, iii. 11, v. 7, popular opinion does not hold Jesus to be the Messiah. In contrast with Jn. vii. 28-31, 41, ix. 22, the same representation is found also in Mt and Lk. For Ἠλείας v. vi. 15; προφήτης i. 2.

29 f. καὶ αὐτός, omitted by Mt and Lk, has no special emphasis (nor in iv. 38, vi. 47, xiv. 15, xv. 43*). Luke has εἶπεν δέ (ix. 20). For ἀποκριθείς . . . λέγει v. Intr. 63. ὁ Πέτρος has not been used since v. 37, but from this point onwards the name appears frequently; v. iii. 16.

The decisive question Ὑμεῖς δὲ τίνα με λέγετε εἶναι; is now put, ὑμεῖς being emphatic. Peter's reply is equally emphatic: ' *Thou* art the Christ ', Σὺ εἶ ὁ χριστός. All that such a confession implied cannot be known, but it certainly meant that Peter hailed Jesus as the One in whom the hopes of Israel would be fulfilled. Luke adds τοῦ θεοῦ (ix. 20), and Matthew ὁ υἱὸς τοῦ θεοῦ τοῦ ζῶντος (xvi. 16). By assimilation ὁ υἱὸς τοῦ θεοῦ is added in Mk in א L 157 syhier, and in addition τοῦ ζῶντος in W fam. 13 543 sype hier mg sa. The shorter text is undoubtedly original.

The verbal adjective χριστός is used in the LXX to render the Heb. מָשִׁיחַ ' anointed ' with reference to kings, priests, the patriarchs, the people, Cyrus, and the ideal king. In Psa. ii. 2 it was interpreted by Jews and Christians alike of the Davidic Messiah, as also in the Psalms of Solomon (xvii. 32), while in 1 Enoch xlviii. 10, lii. 4 the term is used of the superhuman Son of Man. While a personal Messiah is not expected in all the

λέγωσιν περὶ αὐτοῦ. Καὶ ἤρξατο διδάσκειν αὐτοὺς 31
ὅτι δεῖ τὸν υἱὸν τοῦ ἀνθρώπου πολλὰ παθεῖν καὶ ἀποδοκιμα-
σθῆναι ὑπὸ τῶν πρεσβυτέρων καὶ τῶν ἀρχιερέων καὶ τῶν γραμ-

Apocalyptic Writings, there can be no doubt, as the Markan passages show, that his coming was a widespread expectation. See the discussions in Dalman, 289-316; Foakes Jackson and Lake, *BC*, i. 346-68; O. C. Whitehouse, *DCG*, ii. 171-9.

At this point Matthew adds the account of the blessing pronounced by Jesus upon Peter because his confession is due to divine revelation, together with sayings concerning the rock on which the Ecclesia is built, the gift of the keys of the Kingdom of Heaven, and the authority to bind and loose (xvi. 17-19).

In 30 ἐπιτιμάω is used in the sense of *charging strictly* as in i. 25 (*q.v.*) and ἵνα μηδενὶ λέγωσιν περὶ αὐτοῦ gives the substance of the charge; *v.* iii. 12, v. 43, etc. The disciples are forbidden to make known that Jesus is the Messiah. Once more Wrede, 238 f., claims the passage as illustrating the Markan theory of the 'Messianic Secret'. The prohibition is more credibly explained as a counsel of prudence in view of the political repercussions of such a confession. Cf. J. Weiss, 236 f.: 'How easily could this attitude find an outlet in rash political undertakings, how easily could the disciples through the spreading of their thoughts set on fire a revolutionary movement among the people! That Jesus forbade them to speak of these things is deeply grounded in the situation and His personal attitude to the question of Messiahship; that He does so in an agitated manner one can fully appreciate. Who likes to see his innermost and most personal perceptions surrendered to the more or less undiscerning talk of even his best friends?' Both Matthew and Luke repeat the Markan statement with stylistic variations.

31-2a. The First Prophecy of the Passion follows, the second and third being ix. 31 and x. 33 f. It is possible to regard viii. 31 as the beginning of a narrative, or indeed a new section; cf. Turner, 40; Lagrange, 216, Ἤρξατο a ici toute sa valeur; c'est le début d'un enseignement nouveau. This is the view taken by Matthew, who inserts Ἀπὸ τότε, 'From that time', before ἤρξατο (xvi. 21). Luke, on the contrary, connects the passage with the prohibition by εἰπών, and this is probably the right view to take. For ἤρξατο c. infin. *v.* Intr. 48, 63 f. Many commentators regard the three predictions as variant forms of the same saying (cf. A. T. Cadoux, *SSG*, 25 f.); each, however, is distinctive in its narrative setting, and it is inherently probable that Jesus made several attempts to familiarize His disciples with the strange idea of Messianic suffering; cf. Wood, 694; Rawlinson, 143.

δεῖ, ix. 11, xiii. 7, 10, 14, xiv. 31*. In its simplest form the idea is expressed in the opening words δεῖ τὸν υἱὸν τοῦ ἀνθρώπου πολλὰ παθεῖν. To an extent which cannot now be measured details in the rest of the saying may have been conformed to the story of the Passion. In this there would be nothing unnatural or improbable, but only to this extent is the prophecy a *vaticinium post eventum*; no good reason can be given why Jesus rather than the later Christian community should not have been the first to give expression to this original conception. For ὁ υἱὸς τοῦ ἀνθρώπου, not used since ii. 28, *v.* the note on ii. 10. πολλά here is not adverbial (cf. i. 45) but the direct object of παθεῖν (*v.* v. 26). ἀποδοκιμάζω, xii. 10*, 'to reject' (Cl., LXX, Pap.), is derived from δόκιμος, 'tested', 'approved', an adjective used of the testing of metals; cf. Deissmann, *BS*, 259 ff., *VGT*, 167 f. For πρεσβύτερος *v.* vii. 3. Here the

μματέων καὶ ἀποκτανθῆναι καὶ μετὰ τρεῖς ἡμέρας ἀναστῆναι·

word describes the lay members of the Sanhedrin, as in xi. 27, xiv. 43, 53, xv. 1*. Only here are they mentioned first. οἱ ἀρχιερεῖς, as often, includes not only the ruling high priest Caiaphas, but also his father-in-law, Annas, and the members of the high-priestly families in Jerusalem. For οἱ γραμματεῖς v. i. 22. ἀποκτανθῆναι is a late 1 aor. (cf. 1 Macc. ii. 9) = Attic ἀποθανεῖν (Blass, 55). Note the absence of traces of this supposed common verb mentioned in VGT, 65, from popular sources, while it is common in the NT in various forms in the pres. stem.

The phrase μετὰ τρεῖς ἡμέρας appears also in ix. 31 and x. 34, but is replaced by τῇ τρίτῃ ἡμέρᾳ in Mt. xvi. 21, xvii. 22, xx. 19, and in Lk. ix. 22 (ix. 44 omits), and xviii. 33. The numerous examples cited by Field, 11-13, show that in the LXX and in late Greek writers the two phrases were identical in meaning; cf. Turner, 40. Thus, in Gen. xlii. 17 Joseph puts his brothers in prison ἡμέρας τρεῖς, but in 18 speaks to them τῇ ἡμέρᾳ τῇ τρίτῃ and sends them away. It may therefore be argued that μετὰ τρεῖς ἡμέρας, contrary to English idiom, can mean a period less than 72 hours. Nevertheless, τῇ τρίτῃ ἡμέρᾳ and τῇ ἡμέρᾳ τῇ τρίτῃ are so commonly used in early tradition of the Resurrection (cf. Mt. xxvii. 64, Lk. xxiv. 7, (21), 46, Ac. x. 40, 1 Cor. xv. 4) that the alteration of viii. 31 by Matthew and Luke may be influenced by the desire to sharpen the reference to the Resurrection. Can the same process have been at work in Mk? In other words, did Jesus refer so explicitly to His Resurrection? Many commentators and historians have doubted this; cf. Schmidt, 218; Ed. Meyer, i. 118; etc. How, they have asked, is the subsequent attitude of the disciples and of the women in xvi. 1 to be explained if Jesus spoke so clearly? It is pertinent to reply that so momentous an announcement

was not understood at the time, and this is Mark's explanation in ix. 32 : ' They understood not the saying, and were afraid to ask him '. It is difficult, however, to be entirely satisfied with this answer, especially when, as Mark relates, Jesus referred to His Resurrection several times; cf. viii. 31, ix. 9, 31, x. 34, xiv. 28. On the other hand, it is more difficult to suppose that He spoke of suffering and death without any reference to victory and resurrection. In these circumstances it is best to infer that He did speak of His rising again and exaltation, but in terms less explicit than those of viii. 31 and parallel passages. Cf. C. J. Cadoux, 297 f. It may be that He used the phrase τῇ ἡμέρᾳ τῇ τρίτῃ with the meaning ' after a short interval ' in the sense of Hos. vi. 2 : ὑγιάσει ἡμᾶς μετὰ δύο ἡμέρας· ἐν τῇ ἡμέρᾳ τῇ τρίτῃ καὶ ἀναστησόμεθα, καὶ ζησόμεθα ἐνώπιον αὐτοῦ. Cf. Bartlet, 250 f.; Rawlinson, 113; Taylor, JHS, 89. The subsequent sharpening of an originally less direct expression is the best explanation of the difficulty.

The teaching concerning Messianic suffering and death is bound up in the mind of Jesus with His sense of vocation. ' Jesus did not believe that he was the Messiah although he had to suffer; he believed that he was the Messiah because he had to suffer. This is the great paradox, the great originality, of his Gospel ', Goguel, 392. Cf. Otto, 249-61; Mackinnon, 194-8; Bowman, 127-36; Taylor, JHS, 85-91. The teaching is based on a unique combination of the idea of the Suffering Servant of Isa. liii with that of the Son of Man. For the communal interpretation, according to which Jesus and His followers share the destiny of the Son of Man, becoming the organ of God's redemptive purpose in the world, see Manson, 227-32; C. J. Cadoux, 100 f.

The fidelity of Matthew and Luke to their source is worthy of note.

καὶ παρρησίᾳ τὸν λόγον ἐλάλει. καὶ προσλαβόμενος ὁ Πέτρος 32
αὐτὸν ἤρξατο ἐπιτιμᾶν αὐτῷ. ὁ δὲ ἐπιστραφεὶς καὶ ἰδὼν τοὺς 33
μαθητὰς αὐτοῦ ἐπετίμησεν Πέτρῳ καὶ λέγει "Ὕπαγε ὀπίσω
μου, Σατανᾶ, ὅτι οὐ φρονεῖς τὰ τοῦ θεοῦ ἀλλὰ τὰ τῶν ἀνθρώπων.

Apart from the change to τῇ τρίτῃ ἡμέρᾳ, the use of ἐγερθῆναι instead of ἀναστῆναι, and the addition in Mt of αὐτὸν εἰς Ἱεροσόλυμα ἀπελθεῖν, their reproduction of viii. 31 is close. The same is true of ix. 31, but with severe abbreviation in Lk. ix. 44. Only in the third prediction, x. 33 f., are there notable expansions in καὶ ὑβρισθήσεται in Lk. xviii. 32 and σταυρῶσαι in Mt. xx. 19. This restraint suggests caution in too readily accepting the conjecture that these sayings have been greatly modified in transmission.

The statement (32a) that Jesus spoke the word plainly is a comment on what has just been said, suggesting the decisive character of the incident. Until now Jesus has said nothing about His Messiahship, and by injunctions of silence has prevented premature disclosures and confessions. He still charges His disciples not to make the secret known (30), but speaks to them quite openly about His Messianic destiny of suffering and death. This action is intelligible if His convictions had been deepened recently during His wanderings.

παρρησία*, Jn (9), Ac (5), Pl (7), 1 Tim (1), Heb (4), 1 Jn (4)**, ' confidence ', ' frankness ', ' boldness of speech ' (Cl., LXX, Pap.), is used adverbially in 32a (' plainly ', Goodspeed, RSV; ' quite freely ', Moffatt). τὸν λόγον is ' the saying ' (v. i. 45, ii. 2) or ' the message '. The MS. k reads the infin. loqui (λαλεῖν) and connects the phrase with the preceding infins. So Tatian and sy^s, implying λαλήσει. Couchoud, JTS, xxxiv. 123, accepts the reading of k : Après la résurrection seulement la Parole sera dite ouvertement.

32b-3. προσλαμβάνομαι*, Mt. xvi. 22, Ac (5), Pl (5)**, ' to take in addition ', ' to take to oneself '; Cl., LXX, Pap.

On the word McNeile, 245, observes : ' it may mean literally that Peter " drew Him to him ", with a gesture implying protection, if not superiority (cf. Ac. xviii. 26, Rom. xiv. 1, xv. 7, Philm. 17) '. ὁ Πέτρος, v. iii. 16 ; ἤρξατο c. infin. i. 45 ; ἐπιτιμάω i. 25. Matthew adds λέγων Ἵλεώς σοι, κύριε· οὐ μὴ ἔσται σοι τοῦτο (xvi. 22) : ' God bless you, Master ! that can never happen to you ' (Goodspeed), ' God forbid, Lord ! ' (Moffatt, RSV). Luke omits the incident entirely. Several Old Latin MSS. and sy^s contain readings resembling the Matthaean addition : c rogare ne cui haec diceret, k obsecrabat ne cui illa diceret, a b n vg (2 MSS.) + dicens, domine propitius esto: nam hoc non erit, sy^s ' Then Simon Kepha, as though he pitied him, said to him, Be it far from thee '. These readings may be assimilations to Mt, but it is easier to suppose that they represent the original Markan text, for, not only is the combination of a b sy^s strong, but the Matthaean reading is not the kind of addition we should expect to find in that Gospel, whereas it would be at home in Mk and accounts better for the rough reply of Jesus. Peter's attitude is presumptuous, if not patronizing (cf. i. 37), and, needless to say, is lifelike. Only original testimony can account for the story ; cf. Ed. Meyer, i. 117.

Swete, 180, describes the turning round (ἐπιστραφείς) of Jesus, as if to face the speaker, as ' a characteristic act ' and cites v. 30, Mt. ix. 22, Lk. vii. 9, 44, ix. 55, x. 23, xiv. 25, xxii. 61, xxiii. 28, Jn. i. 38. The additional phrase καὶ ἰδὼν τοὺς μαθητὰς αὐτοῦ (v. ii. 15) is peculiar to Mark's account ; the reproof which follows is for their benefit as well as Peter's. The words ὕπαγε ὀπίσω μου, Σατανᾶ recall Mt. iv. 10, ὕπαγε, Σατανᾶ and

suggest that Peter's interposition implies the same kind of temptation
which presented itself in the wilderness, that of accepting the popularly
expected Messianic role. F. Bussby,
ET, lxi. 159, suggests that the Aramaic
read ' behind thee ', with the meaning
' withdraw '. Cf. Torrey, 294. ὑπάγω,
v. ʾi. 44, ὀπίσω i. 7, Σατανᾶς i. 13.
Peter's counsel is that of minding
men's ways, not God's. φρονέω*, Mt.
xvi. 23, Ac. xxviii. 22, Pl (22), 1 Tim.
vi. 17**, ' to be minded ', LS, either
of reflection or purpose; Cl., LXX,
Pap. The verb keeps in view ' the
direction which thought (of a practical
kind) takes ', H. A. A. Kennedy,
EGT, iii. 420. Although the word is
Pauline, it is so common that there is
no need to suppose that Mark writes

under the influence of Rom. viii. 5 or
Col. iii. 2, especially as τὰ τῶν ἀνθρώπων
is a much simpler expression than τὰ
τῆς σαρκός or τὰ ἐπὶ τῆς γῆς. Cf. Lagrange, 219. J. Weiss, 63 : *Diese Nach-
richten stammen sämtlich aus Erin-
nerungen und Erzählungen des Petrus.*
After Σατανᾶ Matthew adds σκάνδαλον εἶ ἐμοῦ (xvi. 23). On this passage
Abbott, *Johannine Grammar*, 2566c,
makes the interesting suggestion that
the original may have been εἰμί σοι, ' I
am a stumbling-block (it seems) to
thee! '. Allen, *St. Mt*, 181, observes
that Σατανᾶ suggests that σκάνδαλον
is used of Peter. It is difficult to
think that Matthew would have added
the words without support in the tradition, but whether they stood originally
in Mk can be no more than a guess.

Mk. viii. 34-ix. 1   54. SAYINGS ON CROSS-   Cf. Mt. xvi. 24-8
         BEARING, SACRIFICE,   Lk. ix. 23-7
         AND THE COMING OF
         THE KINGDOM

The section consists of excerpts from a collection of sayings and is
inserted at this point for topical reasons. The phrases ' And calling unto
him the multitude with his disciples, he said unto them ' (34), and ' He
said unto them ' (ix. 1), are connecting links, either present already in
the collection or supplied by Mark himself. The common theme is
loyalty. The first four sayings (34-7) may have stood together in the
source. All have to do with the fidelity of the followers of Jesus in circumstances which call for courage and sacrifice, and their preservation is
intelligible if they come from a Church exposed to the fires of persecution.
In inserting them after the Confession of Peter and the First Prophecy
of the Passion Mark shows good editorial insight, for it is to such a period
that they naturally belong. ' He (Jesus) now asks for attachment to his
person, and not only for the acceptance of his message ', Goguel, 385.
The fifth saying (viii. 38) is attached to the rest because it illustrates the
same theme, but the reference to the eschatological Son of Man suggests
that it may belong to an earlier period. The same inference is justified
also in the case of the sixth saying (ix. 1) on the speedy coming of the
Kingdom; it is introduced because it provides a transition to the story
of the Transfiguration (ix. 2-8) but may have been spoken earlier in the
Galilean Ministry. All the sayings leave upon the mind a strong impression of originality.

34   Καὶ προσκαλεσάμενος τὸν ὄχλον σὺν τοῖς μαθηταῖς αὐτοῦ εἶπεν

34. The opening phrase καὶ προσκα-   τοῖς μαθηταῖς αὐτοῦ (ii. 15) is either
λεσάμενος (iii. 13) τὸν ὄχλον (ii. 4) σὺν   taken from a sayings-source or is an

αὐτοῖς Εἴ τις θέλει ὀπίσω μου ἐλθεῖν, ἀπαρνησάσθω ἑαυτὸν
καὶ ἀράτω τὸν σταυρὸν αὐτοῦ καὶ ἀκολουθείτω μοι. ὃς γὰρ ἐὰν 35
θέλῃ τὴν ψυχὴν αὐτοῦ σῶσαι ἀπολέσει αὐτήν· ὃς δ᾽ ἂν ἀπολέσει
τὴν ψυχὴν αὐτοῦ ἕνεκεν [ἐμοῦ καὶ] τοῦ εὐαγγελίου σώσει αὐτήν.

editorial link by which Mark connects
the six sayings which follow with
viii. 27-33. With much insight, and
perhaps on the basis of tradition, he
associates with the prophecy of Messianic suffering sayings which summon
the disciples to tread the way of sacrifice. Editorial action is suggested by
the reference to the crowd, which is
not mentioned in viii. 22-33, and
indeed not since viii. 6. Matthew
refers to the disciples only; Luke has
πρὸς πάντας.

In viii. 34 three conditions are laid
down which must be fulfilled by a loyal
follower of Jesus. Two are decisive
acts and the third is a continuous relationship. The first is self-denial;
ἀπαρνησάσθω ἑαυτόν. ἀπαρνέομαι, xiv.
30 f., 72*, 'to deny utterly', 'disown';
Cl., LXX (Isa. xxxi. 7). In the
Mimes of Herodas, iv. 74 (iii/ B.C.),
it has been suggested that ἀπηρνήθη
means 'failed to see' rather than 'was
denied'. 'Let him lose sight of himself' would give an attractive meaning
to ἀπαρνησάσθω ἑαυτόν, but Moulton
and Milligan point out that this involves a needless distinction from Mk.
xiv. 72, where the verb means 'disown' (*VGT*, 53). The second demand
is to accept the last consequences of
obedience, 'to take up the cross', καὶ
ἀράτω τὸν σταυρὸν αὐτοῦ. σταυρός, xv.
21, 30, 32*, 'a stake', 'the cross',
as an instrument of death. The
Markan references leave it in no doubt
that the latter is meant. The idea is
metaphorical, but not mystical as in
Gal. ii. 20; the last risk is to be taken.
It is by no means necessary to suppose
that the metaphor is 'Christian' in
the sense that the Crucifixion of
Christ is implied. If the idea of cross-
bearing is not found in the older
Rabbinic literature (cf. Billerbeck, i.
587), death by crucifixion under the

Romans was a sufficiently familiar
sight in Palestine to be the basis of the
saying (cf. Josephus, *BJ*, ii. 12. 6,
ii. 14. 9, v. 11. 1, *Ant.* xvii. 10. 10).
The third requirement is sustained
loyalty in discipleship, καὶ ἀκολουθείτω
μοι. For ἀκολουθέω v. i. 18. The
change to the pres. seems intentional.
Matthew repeats Mk almost verbatim. Luke adds καθ᾽ ἡμέραν after
ἀράτω τὸν σταυρὸν αὐτοῦ. All three
agree in the emphasis laid upon willing,
εἴ τις θέλει. It is only in the case of the
man who consciously wills discipleship
that the demands are relevant.

The readings ὅστις (A C² Θ *et al.*
22 118 157 *al. pler.* sys pe hl hier sa bo
geo aeth), comparatively rare in Mk,
and (after ὀπίσω μου) ἀκολουθεῖν (C* D
W Θ *et al.* P⁴⁵ fam. 1 22 28 157 565 700
al. plur. a b f ff i n q r² vg sa aeth Or)
may be assimilations to the Q form of
the saying in Lk. xiv. 27 and Mt. x. 38
respectively; but ἀκολουθεῖν is so well
attested that it may well be original and
ἐλθεῖν an assimilation to Mt. xvi. 24.
The corresponding saying in Q (Lk.
xiv. 27 = Mt. x. 38) is given in variant
forms which may be independent
renderings of the original Aramaic.

T. W. Manson, *SJ*, 131, observes:
'The implication of the words is that
Jesus is aware of an irreconcilable
hostility between the Kingdom for
which He stands and the Empire
represented by Pontius Pilate'.

35. In the text τὴν ψυχὴν αὐτοῦ (ℵ A
C D* L W Δ Θ *et al.* P⁴⁵ minusc. *omn.*
Bas) is read instead of τὴν ἑαυτοῦ
ψυχήν (B Or). So Swete. For ὃς ἐάν
c. subj. *v.* the note on vi. 22; ψυχὴν
σῶσαι iii. 4; ἀπόλλυμι i. 24; εὐαγγέλιον
i. 1; ἕνεκεν x. 7, 29, xiii. 9*. Both
Matthew and Luke omit καὶ τοῦ
εὐαγγελίου and replace ἀπολέσει in 35b
by the subjunctive; otherwise their
agreement is almost verbatim (cf. Mt.

36 τί γὰρ ⌜ὠφελεῖ ἄνθρωπον⌝ κερδῆσαι τὸν κόσμον ὅλον καὶ ζημιω-
37 θῆναι τὴν ψυχὴν αὐτοῦ; τί γὰρ δοῖ ἄνθρωπος ἀντάλλαγμα
38 τῆς ψυχῆς αὐτοῦ; ὃς γὰρ ἐὰν ἐπαισχυνθῇ με καὶ τοὺς ἐμοὺς

36 ὠφελήσει τὸν ἄνθρωπον

xvi. 25 and Lk. ix. 24). In Mk also the subjunctive ἀπολέσῃ is read by A L W *et al.* fam. I 22 33 69 124 565 700 892 1071 *al. pler.* Or, but this reading is almost certainly (as in Mt and Lk) a grammatical correction. The use of the future ἀπολέσει illustrates the weakening of the connexion of ἄν with the subj. in Hellenistic Gk; for parallel cases *v.* Lk. xvii. 33 (Q, *v. infra*), xii. 8, Ac. vii. 7, and in the LXX Judg. xi. 24 and Jer. xlix. (xlii.) 4. Cf. Blass, 217; Robertson, 956 f.

The phrase καὶ τοῦ εὐαγγελίου, found only in the Markan form, is an explanatory comment added by Mark. The words ἐμοῦ καί are wanting in D P⁴⁵ 28 700 a b i n sy^s aeth arm Or. It is possible, therefore, that the original Markan reading is ἕνεκεν τοῦ εὐαγγελίου, but the double expression is more in accordance with Mark's style. Cf. Couchoud, *JTS*, xxxv. 16.

Few sayings of Jesus are so well attested as this, for in addition to viii. 35 and its parallels, the saying stood in Q (Lk. xvii. 33 = Mt. x. 39) and is found also in Jn. xii. 25. Note also the successive sayings in Mk. viii. 34 f. and Mt. x. 38 f. (Q).

In the saying ψυχή (שׁ‍פֶשׁ) is used in a double sense, first of a man's ordinary human life and then of his true self or personality. The fact that the saying immediately follows one on taking the last risk (viii. 34) both in Mk and in Q (Mt. x. 38 f.) suggests that Jesus means that, even if death ensues, the disciple has preserved, or gained, his true self (cf. Lk. xvii. 33). Death is not loss, but gain. See further, T. W. Manson, *SJ*, 145.

36 f. These sayings carry the thought of the supreme value of the ψυχή farther : there is no greater gain (36) and no price can be put upon it (37). For ὠφελέω *v.* v. 26; κερδαίνω*.

κόσμος, xiv. 9, xvi. [15]*, is here used, not of the ordered world, but of the prizes of business and social life. ζημιόω*, Mt. xvi. 26, Lk. ix. 25, 1 Cor. iii. 15, 2 Cor. vii. 9, Phil. iii. 8**, ' to cause loss ', ' fine ' (Cl., LXX, Pap.), is used in the NT in the passive with the meaning ' to lose ', ' to suffer damage '. Cf. Field, 61. RV, Moffatt, and RSV have ' forfeit '. Both later Evangelists improve the Greek by using ὠφελέω in the passive and by avoiding the infinitive; Mt, ἐάν . . . κερδήσῃ, Lk, κερδήσας. Luke also interprets τὴν ψυχὴν αὐτοῦ by substituting ἑαυτόν.

In the second saying ἀντάλλαγμα* (Mt. xvi. 26**) is ' recompense ' or ' price '. Cf. Sir. xxvi. 14, οὐκ ἔστιν ἀντάλλαγμα πεπαιδευμένης ψυχῆς, ' nothing can buy a well-instructed soul '. Swete cites Euripides, *Orestes*, 1155 :

οὐκ ἔστιν οὐδὲν κρεῖσσον ἢ φίλος σαφής,
οὐ πλοῦτος, οὐ τυραννίς· ἀλόγιστον δέ τι
τὸ πλῆθος ἀντάλλαγμα γενναίου φίλου.

For the subj. δοῖ *v.* Moulton, ii. 210 f., ' an obviously vernacular form — as its papyrus record shows' ; cf. iv. 29, v. 43, xiv. 10 f. Mt. δώσει. Luke omits the saying.

38. Like the sayings in 35, 36, and 37, this saying is loosely connected with the rest by γάρ and has the same form, ὃς ἐάν c. subj. It is also concerned with the same general theme of loyalty. But otherwise, as Wellhausen, 67, observes, while it is of the same metal as 35, it is of another coinage. The Son of Man is not the Suffering Messiah of the present but the future Son of Man of popular eschatology, and, apparently, is distinguished by Jesus from Himself. The alternative is to suppose that Jesus is speaking of Himself as He is now and as He will be, in other

[λόγους] ἐν τῇ γενεᾷ ταύτῃ τῇ μοιχαλίδι καὶ ἁμαρτωλῷ, καὶ ὁ
υἱὸς τοῦ ἀνθρώπου ἐπαισχυνθήσεται αὐτὸν ὅταν ἔλθῃ ἐν τῇ δόξῃ
τοῦ πατρὸς αὐτοῦ μετὰ τῶν ἀγγέλων τῶν ἁγίων.

words, as the Son of Man *designatus.* So Matthew has understood the saying, for he boldly re-interprets it in the form, ' The Son of Man shall come in the glory of his Father with his angels . . .' (xvi. 27). The Lukan parallel (ix. 26) agrees closely with Mark's version, and the point for discussion is whether the apparent distinction between Jesus and the Son of Man is real, and, further, whether the Markan form of the saying has been overlaid with apocalyptic ideas. This question becomes still more burning when the Q version (Lk. xii. 8 f. = Mt. x. 32 f.) is compared with Mk.

The saying is concerned with the man who is ' ashamed ' of Jesus and His words (or followers). The vocabulary of the first part is not distinctively Markan : ἐπαισχύνομαι (*bis*)*, Cl., LXX ; ἐμός, x. 40*. W and k omit λόγους, and this omission is favoured by Turner, 41, *JTS*, xxix. 2, Manson, *SJ*, 109, and Cadoux, 78, with the resultant meaning ' and mine ', i.e. ' my followers '. The words ἐν τῇ γενεᾷ ταύτῃ τῇ μοιχαλίδι καὶ ἁμαρτωλῷ are peculiar to Mark's version, but the phrase γενεὰ πονηρὰ καὶ μοιχαλίς appears in the Matthaean form of the Q saying regarding the demand for a sign (xii. 39, Lk. xi. 29, γενεὰ πονηρά). μοιχαλίς*, Mt. xii. 39, xvi. 4, Rom. vii. 3 (*bis*), Jas. iv. 4, 2 Pet. ii. 14**, ' an adulteress ', used in Mk and Mt as an adj. ' adulterous '; late Gk, LXX. For ἁμαρτωλός v. ii. 15. The description of a community as ' adulterous ' and ' sinful ' is influenced by OT teaching ; cf. Hos. ii. 2 (4) ff., Isa. i. 4, Ezek. xvi. 32 ff. ; also Isa. i. 21, Jer. iii. 3. The phrase may be a homiletical expansion of the saying, but can be original.

For ὁ υἱὸς τοῦ ἀνθρώπου v. the note on ii. 10. δόξα, x. 37, xiii. 26*, is here used in its Biblical sense, correspon-

ding to the Heb. כָּבוֹד, of ' glory ', especially the glory of God as revealed in His creation and His mighty deeds, and in which angels and men are permitted to share. Cf. Kittel, *KThW.* ii. 245-55. 1 Enoch speaks of the Elect One placed by the Lord of Spirits ' on the throne of glory ' or ' His glory ' (lxi. 8, lxii. 2) from which He judges the righteous, kings, and mighty men. There is, however, no parallel to the use of the phrase τοῦ πατρὸς αὐτοῦ with reference to the Son of Man or the Elect One. The phrase appears here because in 38b (? in contrast with 38a) Jesus and the Son of Man are identified, so that the Sonship of Jesus is predicated of the Son of Man. The allusion to the angels, μετὰ τῶν ἀγγέλων τῶν ἁγίων, frequently accompanies references to the Son of Man ; cf. Mt. xiii. 41, xxv. 31, Jn. i. 51, 1 Enoch lxi. 10, etc. They are mentioned also by Paul when he speaks of the Parousia : ' at the revelation of the Lord Jesus from heaven with the angels of his power in flaming fire ' (2 Thess. i. 7).

Such is the Markan saying. Matthew adds : ' and then shall he render unto every man according to his deeds ' (xvi. 27). Luke follows Mk closely but has ἐν τῇ δόξῃ αὐτοῦ καὶ τοῦ πατρός, thus avoiding τοῦ πατρὸς αὐτοῦ. He also omits μετά before τῶν ἁγίων ἀγγέλων (ix. 26). In this manner the apocalyptic colouring is increased in Mt and reduced in Lk.

There is nothing in the Markan saying which could not have been said by Jesus ; but it is also possible that 38b is a later Christian adaptation under the influence of later beliefs concerning the Parousia (cf. Mt. xvi. 27 (above), 2 Thess. i. 7, etc.). Further points bearing upon this question are (1) other similar sayings in Mk, and (2) the parallel saying in Q (Lk. xii. 8 f. = Mt. x. 32 f.). Of these forms that of Lk (Manson, *SJ*, 109) is probably more original than that of Mt (Rawlinson, 116). If so, Q agrees with Mk in apparently distinguishing between Jesus and the Son of Man, but lacks the apocalyptic colouring of Mk. viii. 38b. The Q saying is eschatological, as the references to confession and denial ' in the presence of the angels of God ' show. It may be that Mk. viii. 38 is a third saying, rather than a parallel, in the series ' confessing ', ' denying ', ' being ashamed ' ; but, in any case, a comparison with Q suggests that it is less original in form.

This view is confirmed by other similar sayings in Mk : xiii. 26,

' coming in clouds with great power and glory ', and xiv. 62, ' coming with the clouds of heaven '. The former, from the Apocalyptic Discourse, does not invite confidence ; the latter lacks an apocalyptic element in Lk. xxii. 69. In the Trial scene it is probable that Jesus did refer to Dan. vii. 13 and its fulfilment in Himself, but the form of the three sayings, especially that of xiii. 26, suggests that the Markan tradition reflects current apocalyptic ideas still more visible in M sayings (Mt. xiii. 41, xix. 28, xxiv. 30, xxv. 31) but wanting in Q and L. We conclude, therefore, that viii. 38, while eschatological, lacked originally the apocalyptic colouring now present in 38b.

DETACHED NOTE ON MK. VIII. 38

The implications of viii. 38 are speculative and therefore need to be discussed separately. The apparent distinction between Jesus and the Son of Man in 38a is significant. In view of the tendencies of the Son of Man tradition the surprising thing is that this distinction still appears in both Mk and Q. If the saying is original, one of two possibilities must be true : either, at some point in His ministry, Jesus spoke of the coming of a supernatural Son of Man other than Himself, or by ' the Son of Man ' He meant the Elect Community of which He was to be the Head. Of these possibilities the former is highly doubtful ; the latter is sustained by not a little in His teaching and is not inconsistent with the view that He came to think of Himself as the Son of Man who ' must suffer ' (Mk. viii. 31, x. 45, etc.). If these conjectures have force, viii. 38 is out of place in its present setting ; it belongs to a period earlier than ' Caesarea Philippi ' (viii. 27). By it Jesus meant that people who confessed or rejected His claims, or were ' ashamed ' of Himself and His disciples, would be judged by the Elect Community shortly to be consummated at the coming of the Kingdom (cf. Mk. ix. 1). Such a view is in line with the saying, which cannot be precisely dated : ' Ye shall sit on thrones judging the twelve tribes of Israel ' (Lk. xxii. 30, cf. Mt. xix. 28), and it is illustrated by what happened in the Church at Corinth (1 Cor. v. 3-8, vi. 2-6). Cf. Manson, 263-70, *SJ*, 109.

IX. 1 Καὶ ἔλεγεν αὐτοῖς ᾿Αμὴν λέγω ὑμῖν ὅτι εἰσίν τινες ὧδε τῶν ἑστηκότων οἵτινες οὐ μὴ γεύσωνται θανάτου ἕως ἂν ἴδωσιν τὴν

1. For καὶ ἔλεγεν αὐτοῖς v. ii. 27 ; ἀμὴν λέγω ὑμῖν iii. 28. B D* read ὧδε τῶν ἑστηκότων (WH text), but almost all other MSS. have τῶν ὧδε ἑστηκότων (P⁴⁵ τῶν ἑστηκ. ὧδε). D adds μετ᾽ ἐμοῦ. Both Swete, 186, and Lagrange, 226, prefer the WH reading (RV, ' some

here '), since οἱ ἑστήκοτες by itself can mean ' the bystanders ' (cf. Mt. xxvi. 73, Jn. iii. 29, Ac. xxii. 25) and the widely attested reading is probably a correction. Cf. Klostermann, 96 f. ὅστις, iv. 20.

οὐ μή c. subj., ix. 41, x. 15, xiii. 2, 19,

βασιλείαν τοῦ θεοῦ ἐληλυθυῖαν ἐν δυνάμει.

30, 31 (?), xiv. 25, 31, xvi [18]*. In Cl. Gk (cf. Goodwin, 101-5, 389-97) οὐ μή expresses an emphatic negative, but this is by no means always the case in the LXX and the NT, especially when, as here, the clause amounts to a positive assertion (' some shall see '). The construction is very common in the LXX and the NT. In the Gospels most of the examples (57) are in sayings of Jesus, and in LXX quotations (13), i.e. nearly 90 per cent of the whole. Otherwise οὐ μή is as rare in the NT as in the papyri, where its force is emphatic. Cf. Moulton, i. 187-92; *VGT*, 464. Moulton suggests that the frequency of the construction in the quotations and sayings may be due to ' a feeling that inspired language was fitly rendered by words of a peculiarly decisive tone '. Apparently, it lost ' stress ' by overfamiliarity. Moulton refers to the parallel use of the double negative in uneducated speech, and Lagrange, xcix n., to the use of *pas* by foreigners when *ne* alone is adequate.

The metaphorical use of γεύομαι* is found in the LXX (Job xx. 18, Psa. xxxiii. (xxxiv.) 9, Prov. xxix. 36 (xxxi. 18), though not with reference to death. For parallels in the Talmud *v*. Billerbeck, i. 751. Cf. also Jn. viii. 52, Heb. ii. 9, 4 Ezra vi. 26.

ἕως ἄν c. subj., *v*. vi. 10. In Mk εἶδον is used with ὅτι and the indic. where the perception of a fact or situation is in question (cf. ii. 16, vii. 2, ix. 25, xii. 34, xv. 39), and, as here, with the acc. and the participle, to denote the object seen, the participle being an extension of the object (cf. i. 10, 16, ii. 14, vi. 33, 48 f., ix. 1, 14, 38, xi. 13, 20, xiii. 14, 29, xiv. 67, xvi. 5). So in all the Gospels with the possible exception of Jn. xix. 33, ὡς εἶδον ἤδη αὐτὸν τεθνηκότα, and so also when γινώσκω is used (except Lk. viii. 46, ἔγνων δύναμιν ἐξεληλυθυῖαν ἀπ' ἐμοῦ). The study of these usages is important in view of recent discussions of the

meaning of ἕως ἄν ἴδωσιν τὴν βασιλείαν τοῦ θεοῦ ἐληλυθυῖαν ἐν δυνάμει in the present passage.

C. H. Dodd, 53, translates : ' until they have seen that the Kingdom of God has come with power ', on the ground that the acc. and participle are used in the sense of the acc. and infin. construction with verbs *dicendi et sentiendi*. ' The bystanders are not promised that they shall see the Kingdom of God *coming*, but that they shall come to see that the Kingdom of God *had already come*, at some point before they became aware of it.' This view is rejected by J. Y. Campbell, *ET*, xlviii. 91-4, and in a reply Dodd, *ET*, xlviii. 141 f., points to Deut. xxxii. 36, εἶδε γὰρ παραλελυμένους αὐτούς, Psa. xlviii. (xlix.) 11, ὅταν ἴδῃ σοφοὺς ἀποθνήσκοντας, Jn. xix. 33, and Lk. viii. 46 (*v. supra*). Cf. also J. M. Creed, *ET*, xlviii. 184 f., who agrees with Campbell and argues that the context as well as the grammar points to a future event ; the participle means not ' coming ' but ' arrived and present '.

This discussion bears on the question whether Jesus taught a ' realized eschatology ' (cf. i. 15). There can be no doubt that He taught that in Himself and His mighty works the Kingdom was already present (cf. Lk. xi. 20), but to find this meaning in ix. 1 is to strain the meaning of the saying. It is much more probable that it means : ' until they see the Kingdom of God come ' ; that is to say, the Kingdom is not present at the moment of speaking, except proleptically in the mighty works, but it is imminent ; very shortly it will be seen to have come. Mark introduces the saying at this point because he sees at least a partial fulfilment in the Transfiguration (ix. 2-8), and this interpretation is given by many Patristic writers (Chrysostom, Theophylact, Euthymius) and by the Gnostic Theodotus (*Exc. Theod.* ap. Clem. Alex. 4).

Cf. Swete, 186; Lagrange, 227. Other interpreters have found the fulfilment of the prophecy in the Fall of Jerusalem, the gift of the Holy Spirit, or the spread of Christianity throughout the Roman Empire. All these are partial manifestations of the Kingdom, but none of them describes what Jesus had in mind in ix. 1. A visible manifestation of the Rule of God displayed in the life of an Elect Community is the most probable form of His expectation; but what this means cannot be described in detail because the hope was not fulfilled in the manner in which it presented itself to Him, although later it found expression in the life of the Church, as it still does in its life and its impact on human society. The Divine Rule was to come 'in power' (ἐν δυνάμει), that is, in the manifested power of God and not by human effort and ingenuity. Luke omits ἐληλυθυῖαν ἐν δυνάμει (ix.

27) and instead of the Markan clause Matthew substitutes ἕως ἂν ἴδωσιν τὸν υἱὸν τοῦ ἀνθρώπου ἐρχόμενον ἐν τῇ βασιλείᾳ αὐτοῦ (xvi. 28), undoubtedly with reference to the Second Advent. This is not the thought of Jesus in Mk. ix. 1, but, if 'the Son of Man' can be interpreted communally, the Matthaean form is a legitimate interpretation of Mk.

Both the content of the saying and the introductory formula indicate that ix. 1 does not stand in its original context. It is not in any way influenced by the teaching that the Son of Man 'must suffer' and for this reason probably belongs to an earlier stage of the Galilean Ministry. It voices the belief of Jesus at a time when He still looked for the speedy inbreaking of the Divine Rule of God, and may have been uttered at any point between the limits set by i. 15 and vi. 13. For ἡ βασιλεία τοῦ θεοῦ v. the note on i. 15.

Mk. ix. 2-8   55. THE TRANSFIGURATION   Cf. Mt. xvii. 1-8
Lk. ix. 28-36

The interpretation of the narrative presents a very difficult problem and few will claim that they can give an explanation which completely satisfies them. Among many hypotheses the following may be distinguished.

1. The historical character of the narrative is fully affirmed by those who hold that it records a factual experience in which the true μορφή of Jesus broke through the limitations of His humanity and was revealed to the three chosen disciples. Cf. Swete, 188, who cites Origen, In Mt. t. xiii. 36 ff., τὸν ἐν τοῖς εὐαγγελίοις Ἰησοῦν . . . θεολογούμενον . . . καὶ ἐν τῇ τοῦ θεοῦ μορφῇ κατὰ τὴν γνῶσιν αὐτῶν θεωρούμενον, and Lightfoot, Phil. 130 f. See the more recent presentation of this view by J. B. Bernardin, JBL, lii (1933), 181-9. This interpretation is doctrinal, and while it is not invalid on this account, its relevance is naturally determined by the view which is taken of the Person of Christ and its manifestation in the conditions of the Incarnation. Short of this hypothesis, a historical basis in the narrative is found by those who hold that it records a visionary experience of the disciples consequent on the confession of Peter at Caesarea Philippi. The special problems which arise are how the presence of Moses and Elijah, the cloud, and the voice, are to be explained, as well as the veridical character of the psychological experiences implied.

2. Visionary hypotheses are maintained by Ed. Meyer, i. 152-6, Harnack, Sitzungsberichte der preussischen Akademie der Wissenschaften (1922), 62-80, Schniewind, 122 f., E. Underhill, The Mystic Way, 114-23, Rawlinson, 118 f., Bartlet, 264-6, and others. Meyer traces the experience

to Peter and argues that events of this kind have happened at all times in religious circles and have even influenced political developments as in the case of Joan of Arc. He instances the effect of the vision of Joseph Smith in June 1829 upon the fortunes of the Mormons, and that of Muhammad's vision recorded in the Qoran (s. 53). Developing Meyer's argument, Harnack maintains that only Peter saw the vision and that it contributed to his subsequent vision of the Risen Christ.[1] Schniewind refers to the divine δόξα which manifested itself in Jesus (Jn. i. 14, ii. 11, vii. 39, xi. 4, 40, xii. 16, etc.) and to Paul's teaching (2 Cor. iii. 18, Rom. xii. 2), and he suggests that to Mark the experience was a prelude to the Resurrection. Miss Underhill gives examples of the luminous glory which transfigures the faces of the saints in ecstatic prayer. Bartlet suggests that an experience of Jesus Himself may have led the three disciples to feel more sure than ever that their Master was verily the Christ. H. G. Wood, 692, also speaks of the story as 'a record of the inner life of Jesus'. Naturally, in hypotheses of this kind the recognition of the basic historical element varies, but it is their peculiar merit that, if the psychological assumptions are conceded, they are able to give a worthy explanation of the several elements in the narrative.

3. In contrast with the views outlined above, many scholars interpret the narrative as a legend or a symbolic story. Many explain it as a Resurrection-story which has been read back into the earthly life of Jesus. Cf. Wellhausen, 68-71; Loisy, ii. 39; Bousset, 61, 268 n.; Bertram, *Festg. f. Ad. Deissmann* (1927), 189; Goetz, *Petrus als Gründer und Oberhaupt der Kirche* (1927), 76-89; Goguel, 343, *La Foi à la résurrection de Jésus* (1933), 317 ff.; Bultmann, 278-81. Mk. ix. 2-10, it is held, breaks the original sequence between ix. 1 and 11 ff. (*cf.* Klostermann, 98); the author of 2 Pet. i. 16-18 still knew the story as a resurrection-story; and in the Ethiopic *Apocalypse of Peter* and the *Pistis Sophia* the account of the transfiguration follows the death and resurrection of Jesus. Cf. Bultmann, 278 n. The standing objection to this hypothesis is its failure to account for the presence of Moses and Elijah in the story, the cloud, the voice, and Peter's words in ix. 5. So many details have to be deleted as accretions that little is left to sustain the hypothesis. Cf. G. H. Boobyer, *St. Mark and the Transfiguration Story*, 11-16.

4. The purely symbolic interpretation of the narrative is set forth by E. Lohmeyer in an article, *Die Verklärung Jesu nach dem Markusevangelium* (*ZNW*, 21 (1922), 185-215), in which two sources are distinguished: ix. 4 f., (6), 7 f., a legend based on Jewish eschatological speculations which presents Jesus as the Messiah, and ix. 3, which describes a metamorphosis of Jesus and is held to reflect Hellenistic Mystery ideas. In his Commentary (1937) Lohmeyer treats the story as a single unit, recognizing that the ideas of ix. 3 belong to Jewish apocalyptic (p. 175 n.). His suggestion is that to the three disciples, as the nucleus (*Keim und Kern*) of the eschatological community, Jesus is revealed as the heavenly Son of Man in the glory of His Parousia. The veil, which elsewhere in Mk lies over Him, is taken away by God and the secret of His future dignity is for a moment revealed. A point in favour of this interpretation

---

[1] Meyer speaks of the vision as the root of historical Christianity. *Aus der Verklärung sind die Auferstehung und die Erscheinungen des Auferstandenen erwachsen, sie ist die letzte Wurzel des Christentums, um ihretwillen sind die drei die ' Säulen' und die ersten Oberhäupter der sich bildenden Kirche, op. cit.* 156.

is that it takes into account Mark's theology and the needs of the Church for which he wrote ; its weakness is its failure to recognize any historical basis for the story. Even the ' six days ' of ix. 1 are traced to ' sacred tradition ' (Ex. xxiv. 16) and the narrative becomes a product of theological art. The view that the Transfiguration is ' a divine witness to Christ's Messiahship in the form of a forecast of the Parousia ' is developed further in G. H. Boobyer's valuable study mentioned above. The historical problem is left open since the aim of the investigation is to examine the meaning of the story for Mark, and its place and use in his Gospel. A. M. Ramsey, *GGTC*, 118 f., holds that, while the Transfiguration anticipates the Parousia, it also indicates that the messianic age is being realized.

This brief survey of critical opinion suggests that no one explanation can be accepted to the exclusion of the rest. The reference to the six days and the characteristic utterance of Peter point to actual experience and the allusions to Moses and Elijah, the cloud, and the divine voice suggest that it is visionary in character. It is probable, however, that in the interests of the primitive Christian apocalyptic hope imaginative details have been added, particularly in the references to metamorphosis and the cloud,[1] although whether these are exclusively eschatological calls for further consideration. Whether the essential form of Jesus was revealed is the challenge the story makes to us. In sum, we may say that, while it is impossible to say exactly what happened upon the mount, we may well believe that the confession of viii. 29 was deepened and confirmed in an incommunicable experience of prayer and religious insight.

2   Καὶ μετὰ ἡμέρας ἓξ παραλαμβάνει ὁ Ἰησοῦς τὸν Πέτρον καὶ τὸν Ἰάκωβον καὶ ᵀ Ἰωάνην, καὶ ἀναφέρει αὐτοὺς εἰς ὄρος ὑψηλὸν 3 κατ' ἰδίαν μόνους. καὶ μετεμορφώθη ἔμπροσθεν αὐτῶν, καὶ τὰ

2 τὸν

2. With μετὰ ἡμέρας ἕξ cf. μετὰ δύο ἡμέρας (xiv. 1). No other temporal statement in Mk outside the Passion Narrative is so precise. As it stands the reference is to Peter's confession. Luke has ὡσεὶ ἡμέραι ὀκτώ. For other temporal expressions in Mk *v.* i. 14, 21, 32, 35, ii. 1, 23, iv. 35, viii. 1, xiv. 1, 12, 17, xv. 1, 25, 33, 42, xvi. 1. For παραλαμβάνω *v.* iv. 36 ; ὁ Ἰησοῦς i. 9. As in the stories of Jairus' Daughter and of Gethsemane, Jesus takes with Him the three disciples, Peter, James, and John ; *v.* the note on v. 37. ἀναφέρω* ; ὑψηλός* ; κατ' ἰδίαν, iv. 34 ; μόνος, iv. 10. Reference is often made to the ' six days ' Moses tarried on ' the mount of God ' before the divine voice called to him from the cloud (cf. Lohmeyer, 173), but while Ex. xxiv.

15 f. may have coloured the narrative, the temporal statement is used differently.

From early times the ' high mountain ' was identified with Mount Tabor, ten miles south-west of the Sea of Galilee, but this hill is not more than 1000 feet high, and most modern commentators mention Mount Hermon, which rises to a height of 9200 feet and is about twelve miles to the north-east of Caesarea Philippi. So Swete, 187 ; Turner, 42 ; etc. Even this suggestion is conjectural. Dalman, *SSW*, 205, suggests that *Tell el-Aḥmar, Tell Abu en-Neda*, and *Tell esh-Shecha*, all to the south-east of Caesarea and each over 4000 feet high, ' may dispute among themselves for the honour of being the mount of Transfiguration '.

---

[1] A notable example of this view is the exegesis of J. Weiss, 242-9, *Die Schr.*[4] 155.

ἱμάτια αὐτοῦ ἐγένετο στίλβοντα λευκὰ λίαν οἷα γναφεὺς ἐπὶ τῆς
γῆς οὐ δύναται οὕτως λευκᾶναι.   καὶ ὤφθη αὐτοῖς Ἡλείας σὺν 4

'For him who would pray they afford the desired undisturbed solitude.' The desire for solitude is expressed by Mark in κατ' ἰδίαν μόνους. The reference to prayer is Luke's interpretative addition, προσεύξασθαι (ix. 28), to which ἐν τῷ προσεύχεσθαι αὐτούς, attested in Mk by W (Θ) P⁴⁵ fam. 13 (28) (565) Or (αὐτόν Θ 28 565), is an assimilation.

Wellhausen, 69, asserts that the mountain is that of Mt. xxviii. 16, but there is no warrant for this identification unless it can be shown that the narrative is a Resurrection story read back into the earthly life of Jesus. μεταμορφόω*, Mt. xvii. 2, Rom. xii. 2, 2 Cor. iii. 18**, 'to transform'; late Gk, Symm. in Psa. xxxiii. (xxxiv.) 1, Pap. The rendering 'transfigured', current from the time of Wycliffe, comes from the vg transfiguratus est. The idea recalls that of Ex. xxxiv. 29, in which the skin of the face of Moses is 'glorified' (δεδόξασται) while he talks with God, but the use of μεταμορφόω rather than δοξάζω has suggested the influence of 2 Cor. iii. 18. There is, however, no close dependence on Pauline thought since, in 2 Cor. iii. 12-iv. 6, Paul emphasizes the abiding glory of Christ (in contrast with that of Moses which was 'passing away'), whereas in Mk the transformation is temporary. Everything points to the independent use of the word by Mark and it cannot be assumed that the idea is exclusively Hellenistic. For Mark's rare use of ἔμπροσθεν v. ii. 12*.

Matthew also has μετεμορφώθη, but adds καὶ ἔλαμψεν τὸ πρόσωπον αὐτοῦ ὡς ὁ ἥλιος (xvii. 2). Luke avoids the verb (v. Creed, 134) and has καὶ ἐγένετο . . . τὸ εἶδος τοῦ προσώπου αὐτοῦ ἕτερον (ix. 29). For the surprising absence of πρόσωπον in Mk v. ix. 29.

3. The garments of Jesus are described as glistering with heavenly light. στίλβω**, 'to gleam', 'glitter',

is used in Cl. Gk of polished or bright surfaces (Homer, Il. xviii. 596, Od. vi. 237) and in the LXX (1 Esdras viii. 56, Nah. iii. 3) of burnished brass, gold, or steel. Cf. VGT, 590. λευκός, xvi. 5*, is similarly used with reference to the στολή of the young man at the tomb. For ἱμάτιον v. ii. 21; λίαν i. 35. Very many MSS. add ὡς χιών (Dan. vii. 9, Theod.), but it is rightly omitted with א B C L W Δ Θ P⁴⁵ fam. 1 (exc. 118) 892 1342 d k sa geo¹ aeth arm. The clause, οἷα γναφεὺς ἐπὶ τῆς γῆς οὐ δύναται οὕτως λευκᾶναι, is peculiar to Mk and is intended to indicate that the brightness is of heavenly origin. γναφεύς is the later form of κναφεύς, 'a fuller', <κνάπτω, 'to card (or) comb wool'; VGT, 128. For οἷος v. xiii. 19*; οὕτως ii. 7. λευκαίνω*, Apoc. vii. 14**, Cl., LXX (5 times). Matthew says that His garments became white as the light (ὡς τὸ φῶς, xvii. 2) and Luke that His raiment became dazzling white (λευκὸς ἐξαστράπτων, ix. 29).

The absence of a reference to the face of Jesus is strange (cf. Mt. xvii. 2, Lk. ix. 29), and there is much to be said for the conjecture of Streeter, 315 f., that the original Markan text may have been καὶ ἐγένετο στίλβον τὸ πρόσωπον, καὶ τὰ ἱμάτια αὐτοῦ λευκὰ λίαν. He points out that 1 etc. 346 k (candida) syˢ omit στίλβοντα, and that Θ and 565 transpose λευκά and στίλβοντα, 'a sign that one of these words was absent from their ancestor'. syˢ 'he became gleaming' (στίλβων). The variants may be attempts to amend an original text from which πρόσωπον had been accidentally omitted.

4. ὁράω (i. 44) is not used freely in Mk and this is the only place in which ὤφθη occurs. It is to be presumed that it is used, as elsewhere in the NT (cf. 1 Cor. xv. 5-8), of the sudden appearance of a heavenly form. According to Mark all three disciples see the heavenly visitors engaged in

5 Μωυσεῖ, καὶ ἦσαν συνλαλοῦντες τῷ ᾽Ιησοῦ. καὶ ἀποκριθεὶς ὁ
Πέτρος λέγει τῷ ᾽Ιησοῦ ῾Ραββεί, καλόν ἐστιν ἡμᾶς ὧδε εἶναι,
καὶ θέλεις ποιήσωμεν τρεῖς σκηνάς, σοὶ μίαν καὶ Μωυσεῖ μίαν

talking with Jesus. For the periphrastic impf. v. Intr. 45, 62 f.
Luke adds that they appeared ἐν δόξῃ, and
that they spoke of ' the departure (τὴν
ἔξοδον αὐτοῦ) which he was about to
accomplish at Jerusalem ' (ix. 31).
He also explains that the disciples
were ' heavy with sleep ' (βεβαρημένοι)
but that ' when they were fully awake '
(διαγρηγορήσαντες) they saw His glory
and the two men who stood with Him.
Like Mark, therefore, but with greater
emphasis, Luke implies the actual
presence of Moses and Elijah. Matthew
follows Mk closely but implies later
that what the disciples had seen was
a vision (ὅραμα, xvii. 9). For Μωυσῆς
v. i. 44; ᾽Ηλείας vi. 15; συνλαλέω*.

Moses and Elijah are the representatives of the Law and the Prophets
respectively. Their very presence
with Jesus is a sign that He is the
Messiah, and this is probably the
primary suggestion of the Markan
narrative. The fact that Moses and
Elijah are in no way connected with
the Resurrection is a strong objection
to the view that the story originally
described a Resurrection Appearance
of Jesus which has been read back
into His earthly life. Bultmann, 279,
suggests that originally the story told
of an appearance to Peter only, and
that the two heavenly forms were
those of angels or saints, subsequently
identified with Moses and Elijah.
There is more to be said for the view
that Moses and Elijah are eschatological figures and that therefore the
narrative points forward to the
Parousia of Jesus. This view was
certainly current with reference to
Elijah from the time of Mal. iv. 5 f.
onwards (cf. Mk. ix. 11), but the evidence as regards Moses is late and
uncertain. Boobyer, 70, admits that
it does not seem to appear until after
the first century A.D., but points out

that the Samaritans expected the
re-appearance of Moses as the Messiah
and argues that the general nature of
Jewish eschatology may point to a
belief in the return of Moses ' in spite
of the lack of specific evidence for it.'.
This interesting hypothesis depends
on the interpretation given to other
details in the narrative, the cloud and
the heavenly voice, and must be considered later. Meantime, the usual
interpretation of the presence of Moses
and Elijah seems adequate, although
it is strange that Elijah (᾽Ηλείας σὺν
Μωυσεῖ) is mentioned first.

5 f. For ἀποκριθεὶς . . . λέγει, in
which the participle is redundant, v.
Intr. 63, and for καλόν ἐστιν c. acc.
and infin. v. vii. 27. The presence of
the three is ' good ' either because the
experience is unique or because of
the opportunity of serving Jesus and
His heavenly visitors; probably the
former. ποιήσωμεν, hortatory subjunctive (Mk, Lk), is replaced in Mt
by εἰ θέλεις, ποιήσω. θέλεις ποιήσωμεν is read by D Θ fam. 13 565 b
ff i (ποιήσω D b ff i) and Turner, JTS,
xxix. 3, justly contends that the
balance is in its favour as giving a
good Markan construction (x. 36, 51,
xiv. 12, xv. 9, 12), improving the sense,
and accounting for the form given to
the sentence by Matthew.

σκηνή*, Mt. xvii. 4, Lk. ix. 33, xvi. 9
(αἱ αἰώνιοι σκηναί), Ac (3), Heb (10),
Apoc (3)**, ' a tent ', ' booth ',
' tabernacle '. The word is frequently
used of the dwelling place of a god
(Ac. vii. 43, ' the t. of Moloch '), and
in the LXX and NT of the Tabernacle
in the wilderness. The word is also
used with eschatological associations;
cf. Lk. xvi. 9 (supra), Apoc. xxi. 3, and
Paul's reference to the οἰκοδομὴ ἐκ
θεοῦ, the heavenly body in contrast
with ἡ ἐπίγειος ἡμῶν οἰκία τοῦ σκήνους
(2 Cor. v. 1). Lohmeyer and Boobyer

καὶ 'Ηλείᾳ μίαν ; οὐ γὰρ ᾔδει τί ἀποκριθῇ, ἔκφοβοι γὰρ ἐγένοντο. 6
καὶ ἐγένετο νεφέλη ἐπισκιάζουσα αὐτοῖς, καὶ ἐγένετο φωνὴ ἐκ 7
τῆς νεφέλης Οὗτός ἐστιν ὁ υἱός μου ὁ ἀγαπητός, ἀκούετε αὐτοῦ.

give to Peter's words an eschatological reference, but, apart from the fact that most of the passages cited have to do with the idea of God tabernacling with men (Ezek. xxxvii. 27, xliii. 7, 9, Joel iii. 21, Zech. ii. 10 f., viii. 3, 8, Tob. xiii. 10), there are no decisive reasons for this interpretation of Mk. ix. 5. It seems better to explain the word as used of a temporary dwelling-place like the ' booths ' made of interlacing branches at the Feast of Tabernacles (Lev. xxiii. 40-3). Peter wishes to prolong the blessed association perhaps in revolt against the idea of Messianic suffering. Cf. Lagrange, 230, *Il n'a toujours pas compris la leçon de la croix.*

'Ραββεί, x. 51 (WH, 'Ραββουνεί), xi. 21, xiv. 45*, Mt (4), Jn (8)**. It is strange to find Jesus addressed as ' Rabbi ' in such a narrative as this, and not surprising that Matthew substitutes κύριε and Luke ἐπιστάτα. The use of the word emphasizes the primitive character of Peter's words. Mark's explanation, οὐ γὰρ ᾔδει τί ἀποκριθῇ, ἔκφοβοι γὰρ ἐγένοντο, almost amounts to an apology, revealing his sense of the incongruousness of the remark (cf. xiv. 40, καὶ οὐκ ᾔδεισαν τί ἀποκρι-θῶσιν αὐτῷ). The direct interrogative is retained and the subjunctive (deliberative) of the direct question. Luke has μὴ εἰδὼς ὃ λέγει, and omits 6b ; Matthew omits the whole sentence.

Peter's words will always stand in the way of hypotheses which explain the story as a myth or a purely symbolic narrative ; their impulsive character is in keeping with his character and with the occasion. Rawlinson, 118, speaks of his remark as precisely the kind ' half-related to the supposed situation, semi-reasonable, and yet fundamentally foolish ', characteristic of a man in a dream or half-hypnotic condition. Cf. Wood, 691.

ἔκφοβος*, Heb. xii. 21**. Cf. xvi. 8. The fear is that of the three and is supernatural awe rather than fright ; cf. iv. 41, v. 15, 33, vi. 50. 7. The use of ἐγένετο with the participle twice in the same narrative (cf. 3) is notable ; *v.* the note on i. 4. Matthew and Luke have the finite verb. They agree also in using the gen. abs. (Mt, ἔτι αὐτοῦ λαλοῦντος, Lk, αὐτοῦ λέγοντος), and Streeter, 316, suggests that the former may have dropped out of Mark's account. νεφέλη, xiii. 26, xiv. 62*. ἐπισκιάζω*, Mt. xvii. 5, Lk. i. 35, ix. 34, Ac. v. 15**, is used in Ex. xl. 29 (35) of the cloud which rested upon the Tabernacle. A contrast appears to be suggested with the τρεῖς σκηναί of which Peter had spoken ; cf. Swete, 191, who cites Origen and Ephraem ; Lagrange, 230. In adding φωτινή, Matthew appears to be thinking of the *Shekinah,* ' the Presence (of God) ', and many commentators explain Mark's reference to the cloud in the same way ; cf. Rawlinson, 120 ; Montefiore, i. 208. Mark's thought may be simpler ; he appears to think of the cloud as the vehicle of God's presence (cf. Ex. xvi. 10, xix. 9, xxiv. 15 f., xxxiii. 9, Lev. xvi. 2, Num. xi. 25), the abode of His glory, from which He speaks (καὶ ἐγένετο φωνὴ ἐκ τῆς νεφέλης). Boobyer, *op. cit.* 84, 86, thinks that the whole scene is ' a representation of Jesus in the glory of his second advent ', but while both the cloud and the voice frequently appear in eschatological contexts (cf. Mk. xiii. 26, xiv. 62) and in apocalyptic writings (cf. Dan. vii. 13, 4 Ezra xiii. 3, Apoc. x. 1, etc.), there is no compelling reason to interpret these symbols in this manner in the present narrative. It is more natural to connect the Evangelist's thought with the passages from Exodus mentioned above. His in-

8 καὶ ἐξάπινα περιβλεψάμενοι οὐκέτι οὐδένα εἶδον ⌜μεθ᾽ ἑαυτῶν εἰ μὴ τὸν Ἰησοῦν μόνον⌝.

8 ἀλλὰ τὸν Ἰησοῦν μόνον μεθ᾽ ἑαυτῶν

terest centres in the message, Οὗτός ἐστιν ὁ υἱός μου ὁ ἀγαπητός, ἀκούετε αὐτοῦ. For ὁ ἀγαπητός v. i. 11. The message is a declaration of the Messianic Sonship of Jesus which points back to the Confession of Peter (viii. 29). What Peter confessed is now divinely affirmed. The command ἀκούετε αὐτοῦ refers to Christ's teaching, and possibly to His teaching concerning Messianic suffering (viii. 31). Mark has in mind Deut. xviii. 15, 'A prophet from the midst of thy brethren, like unto thee, shall the Lord thy God raise up unto thee ; him shall ye hear' (αὐτοῦ ἀκούσεσθε). A modern way of explaining the experience would be to say that on the mountain there came to the three disciples an overwhelming conviction that Jesus was indeed the Son of God. What form the experience took is less easy to describe. The testimony of Joan of Arc, George Fox, and the mystics generally is that such experiences can be auditory and sometimes visual : and there can be no objection in principle to the view that the disciples, or at least Peter, heard a voice which was believed to be the voice of God issuing from the cloud. The important thing is the revelation ; the details must remain matters of speculation.

A comparison with Mt and Lk reveals the greater originality of the Markan account. Matthew adds ἐν ᾧ εὐδόκησα (xvii. 5), thus conforming the message to that which he reports at the Baptism (iii. 17), but he retains the Markan ἀκούετε αὐτοῦ. Luke also has this command, but replaces ὁ ἀγαπητός by ὁ ἐκλελεγμένος (ix. 35). In two respects, however, the Lukan version is inferior : Peter's remark is made as the visitants were departing, and the religious fear of the disciples is connected with their entering into

the cloud. These details are either secondary modifications of Mk or come from a different source. In contrast with Mk and Lk, Matthew mentions the fear after the divine declaration. Jesus comes and touches the three disciples as they lie upon their faces, saying, ' Arise and fear not ' (xvii. 7). Here the fear is fright, and a legendary development of the story is manifest.

8. The story ends abruptly. Suddenly, looking around, the disciples see no one with them save Jesus only. ἐξάπινα** is a later form of ἐξαπίνης, ' suddenly ', found in Num. iv. 20 and in P. Giss. i. 68. 6 (VGT, 222). Cf. ἐξαίφνης (WH, ἐξέφνης) in xiii. 36. For περιβλεψάμενοι v. iii. 5 and for Mark's use of the double neg. v. i. 44. ὁ Ἰησοῦς, i. 9 ; μόνον, v. 36*. WHmg reads μεθ᾽ ἑαυτῶν with most MSS. after μόνον (after εἶδον B 33 579 c f aur sa), and instead of εἰ μή (א B D 33 579 892 vg sys) ἀλλά is read by many MSS., including A C L W Δ Θ fam. 1 fam. 13 28 565 700 1071 sa geo arm. If ἀλλά is read, the question raised by Wellhausen (Einl.² 16) arises, whether it is a misreading of the Aramaic אֽלא which may be exceptive (εἰ μή) or adversative (ἀλλά). Cf. iv. 22. See Moulton's discussion, i. 241 f., and his citation of Tb. P. 104, which shows a sense of ἀλλά very near to εἰ μή. Cf. also Lagrange, xcix. If in this case the evidence is not sufficient to point to an Aramaic original, the several cases where the question of Semitisms arises in 3-8, coupled with a relative infrequency of characteristic Markan words, suggest that the narrative is primitive and Palestinian in origin.

Matthew omits the double negative and adds ἐπάραντες τοὺς ὀφθαλμοὺς αὐτῶν. Luke has καὶ ἐν τῷ γενέσθαι τὴν φωνὴν εὑρέθη Ἰησοῦς μόνος.

Mk. ix. 9-13   56. THE DESCENT FROM   Cf. Mt. xvii. 9-13
                     THE MOUNT OF TRANSFIGURATION

This narrative is closely connected with the preceding story. It is not a popular narrative which circulated as a separate unit of tradition, and it cannot be classified on the basis of its form. The relevant questions are historical. R. H. Lightfoot, 92, tentatively suggests that in it ʲ we may perhaps see the church striving to construct some kind of a philosophy of history, in the light of its convictions about the person and office of its Master, and of his work and its results '. A similar view is taken by the Form Critics. Bultmann, 131 f., classifies 12 f. as an apocalyptic saying which originated in the theological discussions of the community in connexion with ix. 1, itself a ' community-formation '. The latter is a reassuring word (*Trostwort*) formulated in consequence of the delay of the Parousia : at least a few would live to see it ! ; and 12 f., connected therewith by 11, gives the Christian answer to the Jewish expectation that Elijah would come first. Similarly, Dibelius, 226 f., traces the origin of the story to theology and reflection. At the opposite remove from such estimates is the opinion of Burkitt : ' The passage Mark ix. 9-13, so abrupt, so unliterary, so obscure in detail, however clear may be the general meaning, reads to me like reminiscences of a real conversation ', *Christian Beginnings*, 33 f.

A decision depends on the impression which the narrative makes upon us, our view of ' community-sayings ', and our general estimate of the historical character of the Gospel. Judged by such tests the opinion of the Form Critics seems artificial and the estimate of Burkitt judicial.

Καὶ καταβαινόντων αὐτῶν ⌜ἐκ⌝ τοῦ ὄρους διεστείλατο αὐτοῖς 9
ἵνα μηδενὶ ἃ εἶδον διηγήσωνται, εἰ μὴ ὅταν ὁ υἱὸς τοῦ ἀνθρώπου

9 ἀπό

9 f. In view of the change of scene it is probable that 9-13 is a loosely connected whole. For the gen. abs. καταβαινόντων αὐτῶν *v.* the note on *v.* 2, and for διεστείλατο αὐτοῖς used with ἵνα c. subj. *v. v.* 43. For ἃ εἶδον Matthew has τὸ ὅραμα (xvii. 9) and for εἰ μὴ ὅταν he substitutes ἕως οὗ. In his view, and probably rightly, the experience was that of a vision.

The reference to the ' Son of Man ' (*v.* ii. 10) and to the Resurrection is abrupt, but is not out of place, for in ix. 2-8, not only is Peter's confession confirmed, but attention is directed to the teaching of Jesus in the words, ' Hear ye him '. In spite of much that has been said to the contrary, the injunction to maintain silence, ἵνα

μηδενὶ ἃ εἶδον διηγήσωνται, is natural, as it is in viii. 30, but the limit fixed by the Resurrection, given in Mark's summary statement, may have been expressed less explicitly. See the note on viii. 31. Lagrange, 234, takes the view that Jesus did not judge the nine to be ready to know the secret revealed to the three disciples. *N'eût-il pas été un nouvel obstacle à admettre les souffrances du Fils de l'homme ?* More radical critics also think that the secret is restricted to the three, but explain this representation as the Evangelist's attempt to explain why the story of the Transfiguration was not known in the earliest tradition. Cf. Loisy, ii. 40 ; Klostermann, 100 ; Branscomb, 163. For

10 ἐκ νεκρῶν ἀναστῇ. καὶ τὸν λόγον ἐκράτησαν πρὸς ἑαυτοὺς
11 συνζητοῦντες τί ἐστιν "Οταν ἀναστῇ ἐκ νεκρῶν. καὶ ἐπηρώτων
αὐτὸν λέγοντες "Οτι λέγουσιν οἱ γραμματεῖς ὅτι Ἠλείαν δεῖ
12 ἐλθεῖν πρῶτον; ὁ δὲ ἔφη αὐτοῖς Ἠλείας μὲν ἐλθὼν πρῶτον
ΓἀποκατιστάνειꞀ πάντα, καὶ πῶς γέγραπται ἐπὶ τὸν υἱὸν τοῦ ἀνθρώ-
13 που ἵνα πολλὰ πάθῃ καὶ ἐξουδενηθῇ; ἀλλὰ λέγω ὑμῖν ὅτι καὶ

12 ἀποκαταστάνει

ἐκ νεκρῶν v. vi. 14, and for Mark's use
of ἀναστῆναι with reference to the Resurrection v. the note on ἐγείρω in vi. 14.
Mark says that they kept the saying,
τὸν λόγον ἐκράτησαν, that is, they kept
it in mind and observed the charge.
πρὸς ἑαυτούς can be taken with ἐκρά
τησαν, with the meaning 'they kept the
matter to themselves' (RSV); but
it is better to read the phrase with
συνζητοῦντες (cf. ix. 14, 16): they discussed 'one with another' or 'among
themselves'. τὸ ἐκ νεκρῶν ἀναστῆναι,
read by most MSS., has a somewhat
formal ring, 'what the rising again
from the dead should mean' (RV),
and the reading "Οταν ἐκ νεκρῶν
ἀναστῇ should be preferred with D W
fam. I fam. 13 a b c f i r¹·² vg sys pe geo.
So Lagrange, 234. The meaning then
is, 'They discussed among themselves what " When he shall rise again
from the dead " means', a reading
which is concrete and might well give
rise to the widely accepted smoother
text.

Matthew omits 10; Luke, who omits
the whole section, shows his knowledge
of it in ix. 36, 'And they kept silence,
and told no man in those days any of
the things which they had seen'.

11-13. There is no good reason to
assume a break in the narrative at this
point. The question regarding the
coming of Elijah arises from his presence in the story of the Transfiguration. ἐπερωτάω, v. 9. The first ὅτι is
interrogative as in ii. 16 (q.v.). Cf.
Field, 33; Intr. 61. The opinion of
the scribes (οἱ γραμματεῖς, i. 22) was
based on Mal. iv. 4 (iii. 23), καὶ ἰδοὺ
ἐγὼ ἀποστέλλω ὑμῖν Ἠλίαν τὸν Θεσβίτην
πρὶν ἐλθεῖν ἡμέραν Κυρίου τὴν μεγάλην

καὶ ἐπιφανῆ, ὃς ἀποκαταστήσει . . . Cf.
Origen, Mt. t. xiii. 1, Justin Martyr,
Dial. 49. Ἠλείας, vi. 15; πρῶτον, iii. 27.
ἔφη, ix. 38, x. 20, 29, xii. 24, xiv.
29*. ἔφη is read by א B C L Δ Ψ 579
892 1342 sa bo, but most MSS. and
versions attest ὁ δὲ ἀποκριθεὶς εἶπεν.
μέν (v. iv. 4) is omitted by D L W Ψ
fam. I (exc. 118) 28 565 892 it vg
sys pe hl mg geo aeth arm; Torrey, TG,
57 f., thinks rightly. The form ἀπο
κατιστάνει (B* Ψ) is read by WH with
hesitation (Notes, 168); ἀποκαθιστάνει
is read by אc A B³ L W Δ fam. I 33,
but Moulton, ii. 99 f., thinks that the
true reading may be ἀποκαταστάνει
(א* D) and mentions MGk στάνω.

After conceding that Elijah must
come first, Jesus asks καὶ πῶς γέγραπται
ἐπὶ τὸν υἱὸν τοῦ ἀνθρώπου ἵνα πολλὰ
πάθῃ καὶ ἐξουδενηθῇ;. For ὁ υἱὸς τοῦ
ἀνθρώπου v. ii. 10. ἐπί = 'with reference to', as also in 13; cf. Swete, 194.
Swete thinks that the telic force need
not be excluded in ἵνα . . . πάθῃ . . .,
and cites WM, 577, but it is better to
read the words as a noun clause.
πάσχω, v. 26. ἐξουδενηθῇ* is variously
spelt in the MSS. (v. Legg). Moulton,
ii. 111, thinks that probably ἐξουδενωθῇ
(A C X Δ) should be read.

12b follows abruptly after 12a. Wellhausen, Mt, 87, thinks that the whole
verse should be read as a question,
as a rejection of the view that Elijah
must come first. So Torrey, TG, 56 f. :
'Does Elijah, coming first, restore all
things? How, then, is it written . . .?'
Turner, 43, suggests that 12a should
follow after 10; Allen, 124, after 11.
Such re-arrangements do not seem to
be necessary. Jesus draws attention to
a much more important matter which

'Ηλείας ἐλήλυθεν, καὶ ἐποίησαν αὐτῷ ὅσα ἤθελον, καθὼς γέγραπται ἐπ' αὐτόν.

precedes the Resurrection, namely, the suffering of the Son of Man. See the full discussion in *JHS*, 91-7. On the genuineness of the saying *v*. Otto, 250. Otto's views are in direct opposition to those which interpret 12b as a 'community saying'.

The saying in 13 implicitly identifies Elijah with John the Baptist. The statement that men did to him what they willed καθὼς γέγραπται ἐπ' αὐτόν is obscure.[1] 1 Kings xix. 2, 10 and traditions lying behind Apoc. xi. 3-13

may be in mind. John 'had found his Jezebel in Herodias', Swete, 194. Cf. Lagrange, 236 f.; Charles, *Rev*. i. 280-92. In Matthew's version (xvii. 11-13) Jesus says explicitly that Elijah comes first and establishes all things, and then that he has already come but was not recognized. A parallel is drawn in the case of the Son of Man, and it is explained that the disciples understood that Jesus was speaking of John. Thus, the obscurities of Mk are skilfully ironed out.

Mk. ix. 14-29   57. THE EPILEPTIC LAD   Cf. Mt. xvii. 14-21
Lk. ix. 37-43a

An unusual wealth of detail makes this Miracle-story distinctive even in Mk. Schmidt, 227, claims that the picture it gives 'can only go back to good tradition', and 'to actual recollection and history'. The same impression is made by it on the mind of J. Weiss, 249. Such details, he says, as the fact that the father has already brought the lad to the disciples who cannot heal him, and the coming of Jesus and the three to the crowd, would be in the highest degree artificial, and not in accordance with Mark's manner, if they were not very vivid recollections of the return from the Mount. He qualifies this opinion by suggesting that other details, such as the distinction between the disciples, the multitude, and the scribes, and the conversation with the father in 21-4, which is wanting in Mt and Lk, may be due to the work of a redactor. Bussmann, i. 169 f., also traces earlier and later stages in the formation of the narrative.

The description of the astonishment of the crowd in 15 is typically Markan and can well have been omitted independently by the later Evangelists. Equally the account of the conversation with the father (21-4) may have been omitted from the need for abbreviation. Rawlinson, 123, justly observes that these passages, as well as 25b, 26b, and 29, 'with their vivid description of symptoms and animated dialogue, have all the look of originality'. Whether the connexion with the story of the Transfiguration is as close as Mark represents depends in some measure on whether the singular, ἐλθών . . . εἶδεν, is read in 14. The textual evidence is far from being decisive, and the reading may be due to the influence of public reading in the early Church; but in any case it is not likely that Mark would have introduced the story at this point without the support of good tradition since its leading ideas, exorcism, faith, and prayer, are not vitally connected with the emphasis on Messiahship and suffering which is characteristic of viii. 27-x. 52.

Bultmann, 225 f., thinks that, together with redactional additions in 14 f. and 28 f., the narrative is a combination of two separate miracle-

---

[1] Couchoud, *JTS*, xxxiv. 123 f., accepts the interesting reading of k, *et fecit quanta oportebat illum facere* (καὶ ἐποίησεν ὅσα ἔδει αὐτὸν ποιῆσαι). The reading, however, appears to be secondary.

stories in 14-20 and 21-7. He points out that, whereas the disciples play a role only in 14-19, and then disappear, the father is the principal character in 21-7, but has only a secondary part in 17-19; that the sickness is described twice (18 and 21 f.); and that the people, already present in 14, stream forward in 25 apparently for the first time. In addition, whereas ' a dumb spirit ' is mentioned in 17, ' an unclean spirit ' both dumb and deaf is spoken of in 25, and there are two references to foaming (18 and 20). Probably, Sundwall's analysis in *Die Zusammensetzung des Markusevangeliums* (1934), 58 f., is simpler, for he distinguishes 20-7 from the rest and has only to add παιδίον ἔχοντα πνεῦμα ἄλαλον after ἤνεγκαν in 20 to obtain a simple and self-contained story. Better perhaps than either of these critical hypotheses is the suggestion that two narratives connected with the epileptic lad have been combined : 14-19 + 28 f., in which the main interest is the inability of the disciples to effect a cure by reason of their neglect of prayer ; and the miracle-story proper in 20-7, which has lost its original conclusion, imaginatively reproduced in Lk. ix. 43 which describes the astonishment of the people at ' the majesty of God '. It may well be that such refinements are not necessary. On the other hand, two considerations favour the analysis suggested above : (1) data within the narrative, and (2) the interest which different versions of the same story, one concerned mainly with prayer, and other with faith, may have had for the earliest Christian communities. For the catechetical and doctrinal interests of 14-29 see the discussion of Lohmeyer, 184-91.

14 Καὶ ἐλθόντες πρὸς τοὺς μαθητὰς εἶδαν ὄχλον πολὺν περὶ
15 αὐτοὺς καὶ γραμματεῖς συνζητοῦντας πρὸς αὐτούς. καὶ εὐθὺς
    πᾶς ὁ ὄχλος ἰδόντες αὐτὸν ἐξεθαμβήθησαν, καὶ προστρέχοντες
16 ἠσπάζοντο αὐτόν. καὶ ἐπηρώτησεν αὐτούς Τί συνζητεῖτε πρὸς

14 f. The reading ἐλθών . . . εἶδεν bears on the question whether the narrative is self-contained and so may have stood originally in another connexion. The sing. is well attested (A C D Θ *et al.* minusc. *plur.* it (exc. k) vg syᵖᵉ ʰˡ bo geo² aeth syˢ (=*cum uenisset . . . uiderunt*)), but probably the plur. (ℵ B L W Δ Ψ 892 1342 k sa arm) should be preferred with WH and Nestle. So Swete, 195 ; Lagrange, 236. Wellhausen, 72 f., reads the sing.

The vocabulary is Markan, though τοὺς μαθητάς without αὐτοῦ is unusual (it is read by Θ fam. 13 a c f vg sys *et al.*). For μαθητής *v.* ii. 16 ; ὄχλος ii. 4 ; οἱ γραμματεῖς i. 22 ; συνζητέω i. 27 ; εὐθύς i. 10. It is clear that for the most part Mark has himself supplied this introductory passage. ἐκθαμβέομαι, xiv. 33, xvi. 5, 6**, ' to be

amazed ', LXX (Sir. xxx. 9), can express amazement amounting to consternation; *v.* xiv. 33. Commentators have suggested that something of the glory of the transfiguration could still be seen upon the face of Jesus; cf. Turner, 43. This view is not necessary and the objections brought against it by Swete, 195, are strong. The situation is different from that described in Ex. xxxiv. 29 f. So Lagrange, 238. The amazement is due to the unexpected appearance of Jesus. προστρέχω, x. 17*, Acts viii. 30**. The reading of D προσχέροντες (for προσχαίροντες), supported by *gaudentes* in a b c d ff i k, harmonizes with this view, but it is probably an early scribal corruption. Cf. Swete, 195; Pallis, 31. ἀσπάζομαι, xv. 18*.

In the narrative it is nowhere said

αὐτούς; καὶ ἀπεκρίθη αὐτῷ εἷς ἐκ τοῦ ὄχλου Διδάσκαλε, 17
ἤνεγκα τὸν υἱόν μου πρὸς σέ, ἔχοντα πνεῦμα ἄλαλον· καὶ ὅπου 18
ἐὰν αὐτὸν καταλάβῃ ῥήσσει αὐτόν, καὶ ἀφρίζει καὶ τρίζει τοὺς

that the disciples are the nine, unless this is implied by the absence of αὐτοῦ. The presence of scribes in Gaulanitis seems improbable. The reference may be a conventional addition. Turner, 43, describes them as the local clergy, and it is just possible that the absence of the article, invariably present in Mk when the teachers of the Law are meant, indicates that an unfamiliar expression has been rendered by a rough equivalent. In the rest of the story they are not mentioned and there is no reference to a dispute with them. The scene is vividly sketched by Mark. Verses 14b-16 are peculiar to his account. All that Matthew has is καὶ ἐλθόντων πρὸς τὸν ὄχλον (xvii. 14) and Luke has little more, except that he says the incident happened on the next day (τῇ ἐξῆς ἡμέρᾳ, ix. 37).

16-18. A dialogue with the father follows in which the son's symptoms are described.

ἐπερωτάω v. v. 9. The ambiguity of 16 has occasioned secondary variants. Thus instead of the first αὐτούς, A C and many other uncials and minuscules read τοὺς γραμματεῖς, and instead of the second א A W *et al.* have ἑαυτούς, and read Θ 472 565 sa read ἀλλήλους, while D has ἐν ὑμῖν and most Lat. MSS. *inter vos.* Wellhausen, 73, interprets πρὸς αὐτούς reflexively and is inclined to prefer the Western reading. Probably the question is addressed to the crowd, for one from their number, the father, answers it. For ἀπεκρίθη v. the note on iii. 33, and for Mark's use of Διδάσκαλε iv. 38. As in v. 22 (*q.v.*), the numeral εἷς (= τις) is used as an indef. art. Cf. Mt, ἄνθρωπος, Lk, ἀνήρ. The father had brought his son (Lk, μονογενής) to Jesus. Matthew says that he fell upon his knees, γονυπετῶν αὐτόν, and both he and Luke introduce a direct request: Mt, ἐλέησόν μου τὸν υἱόν, Lk,

δέομαί σου ἐπιβλέψαι ἐπὶ τὸν υἱόν μου. In Mk the request comes later (22). The lad is described as 'having a dumb spirit', ἔχοντα πνεῦμα ἄλαλον (vii. 37) and his symptoms by four finite verbs. When the spirit takes hold of him (καταλαμβάνω*), it throws him down (ῥήσσω, v. *infra*), and he foams (ἀφρίζω, 20*) at the mouth, grinds (τρίζω**) his teeth, and wastes away (ξηραίνω, v. iii. 1) or is completely exhausted. The case is one of hysteria or epilepsy, afflictions which are difficult to distinguish; cf. Micklem, 58-60. Matthew (σεληνιάζεται, xvii. 15) appears to regard it as a case of epilepsy and summarizes the Markan detail in the phrase καὶ κακῶς ἔχει.

ῥήσσει is probably not from ῥήσσω, the later form of ῥήγνυμι, 'to rend' (ii. 22), although Luke, with a change of verb (σπαράσσει), appears to have understood it in this sense. It is either the Ionic form of ῥάσσω (LS), 'to strike or dash down', or an ancient error for ῥάσσει (D 565). *VGT*, 563, explains ῥάσσω as a form of ἀράσσω which has the same meaning. Cf. Moulton, ii. 71, 257, 403; Blass, 57; Turner, *JTS*, xxix. 3 f. This meaning suits the Markan context better: the lad is thrown violently to the ground. Cf. RV, 'dasheth him down' (mg, 'rendeth'); RSV, 'dashes him down'; Moffatt, 'throws him down'; Torrey, 'throws him to the ground'. The LXX illustrates the use of ῥάσσω and of variants arising from it: cf. Judith ix. 8, σὺ ῥάξον (συνράξον, א) αὐτῶν τὴν ἰσχύν, xvi. 10, ἐρράχθησαν, B א (ἐταράχθησαν, A אca). Cf. also Isa. ix. 11, xiii. 16; Jer. xxiii. 33, 39; Dan. viii. 10 f. Of the verbs which follow, ἀφρίζω is not found in the LXX and is not illustrated in *VGT*, but ἀφρός, 'foam', from which it is derived, is plentifully illustrated in medical writers (*VGT*, 99); cf. Lk. ix. 39.

ὀδόντας καὶ ξηραίνεται· καὶ εἶπα τοῖς μαθηταῖς σου ἵνα αὐτὸ
19 ἐκβάλωσιν, καὶ οὐκ ἴσχυσαν. καὶ ἀποκριθεὶς αὐτοῖς λέγει ˀΩ
γενεὰ ἄπιστος καὶ διεστραμμένη, ἕως πότε πρὸς ὑμᾶς ἔσομαι;
20 φέρετε αὐτὸν πρός με. καὶ ἤνεγκαν αὐτὸν πρὸς αὐτόν. καὶ
ἰδὼν αὐτὸν τὸ πνεῦμα εὐθὺς συνεσπάραξεν αὐτόν, καὶ πεσὼν ἐπὶ

τρίζω, used originally of the chirping of birds, describes the involuntary gnashing of the boy's teeth, and ξηραίνεται the pallor of complete exhaustion. Luke's account concentrates more on the malice of the daemon (πνεῦμα); it cries out and convulses the lad (κράζει καὶ σπαράσσει αὐτόν), so that he foams (μετὰ ἀφροῦ), and will hardly leave him, shattering him (καὶ μόλις ἀποχωρεῖ ἀπ' αὐτοῦ συντρῖβον αὐτόν). It is strange that the non-medical writer, Mark, should pay greater attention to the boy.

For ὅπου ἐάν c. subj. v. vi. 10. In this type of clause the aor. subj. has a future-perfect sense. Cf. Moulton, i. 186, ' wherever it *has* seized him '.

The father explains that he had asked the disciples of Jesus to cast out the daemon, but they were unable to do so. As often, the ἵνα clause gives the purport of the request ; v. iii. 9, v. 10, etc. ἰσχύω, ii. 17. Although the idea is not expressed by Mark, the failure of the disciples may be regarded by the father as a reflection on their Master. Cf. Lohmeyer, 186. In favour of this suggestion is the fact that the father's appeal to Jesus comes later after a paroxysm (22), and then with doubt and hesitation (εἰ δύνῃ).

19. For ἀποκριθεὶς . . . λέγει v. Intr. 63. Instead of ὁ δέ, καί should probably be read (D W Θ P45 fam. 1 fam. 13 28 565 it bo) ; cf. Turner, *JTS*, xxix. 4. The participle is not entirely redundant since it indicates the response of Jesus to the father's words in 17 f. For γενεά v. viii. 12 ; ἄπιστος* ; ἕως πότε ' how long ? ', Mt. xvii. 17, Lk. ix. 41, Jn. x. 24, Apoc. vi. 10**. For πρός = ' with ' (in πρὸς ὑμᾶς) v. the note on vi. 3. ἀνέχομαι*, Mt. xvii. 17, Lk. ix. 41, Ac. xviii. 14, Pl (9), 2 Tim. iv. 3, Heb. xiii. 22**, ' to endure ',

' put up with '. In Cl. Gk the verb is used mainly c. acc. ; in LXX c. gen. in Isa. xlvi. 4, lxiii. 15. *VGT*, 42, cites the Stoic formula ἀνέχου καὶ ἀπέχου.

The reference to an unbelieving generation is probably an echo of Deut. xxxii. 5, γενεὰ σκολιὰ καὶ διεστραμμένη (cf. Mt. xvii. 17, Lk. ix. 41). καὶ διεστραμμένη is also read in Mk in W P45 fam. 13 543 and a few other minuscules. With good reason Couchoud, *JTS*, xxxv. 17, accepts the reading. Matthew and Luke may independently have inserted the word from Deut., but it is more probable that they found it in the Markan text.

It is not necessary to suppose that the comment is made solely with reference to the father, or the disciples, or the crowd. Like viii. 12, it discloses what Jesus thought of the people amongst whom His ministry was exercised, especially His surprise at their want of faith (cf. vi. 6). In view of His expectation of death (viii. 31, etc.) it is relevant to the situation in which He found himself. It is therefore unnecessary to explain the saying as mythological or doctrinally inspired, as describing the life of one whose true home is the divine world, but who for a dark span is adrift in this generation, only to return again to that world. Cf. Lohmeyer, 187 ; Bultmann, 169 ; Dibelius, 278. The tone of the saying is much more convincingly described by Lagrange, 239, as *celui d'un maître fatigué de jouer un rôle ingrat, et déjà pénétré de la pensée de sa mort prochaine.*

20-2. The best way to explain the syntax of 20 is to regard ἰδών as being in agreement with τὸ πνεῦμα *ad sensum*, with a change of subject in πεσών . . . ἐκυλίετο ἀφρίζων. So Swete, 198;

τῆς γῆς ἐκυλίετο ἀφρίζων. καὶ ἐπηρώτησεν τὸν πατέρα αὐτοῦ 21
Πόσος χρόνος ἐστὶν ὡς τοῦτο γέγονεν αὐτῷ; ὁ δὲ εἶπεν Ἐκ
παιδιόθεν· καὶ πολλάκις καὶ εἰς πῦρ αὐτὸν ἔβαλεν καὶ εἰς ὕδατα 22
ἵνα ἀπολέσῃ αὐτόν· ἀλλ' εἴ τι δύνῃ, βοήθησον ἡμῖν σπλαγχνισθεὶς
ἐφ' ἡμᾶς. ὁ δὲ Ἰησοῦς εἶπεν αὐτῷ [Τό] Εἰ δύνῃ, πάντα δυνατὰ 23
τῷ πιστεύοντι. εὐθὺς κράξας ὁ πατὴρ τοῦ παιδίου ἔλεγεν 24
Πιστεύω· βοήθει μου τῇ ἀπιστίᾳ. ἰδὼν δὲ ὁ Ἰησοῦς ὅτι ἐπι- 25

23 τό

Lohmeyer, 187. The alternative is to treat τὸ πνεῦμα . . . αὐτόν as an anacoluthon; cf. Blass, 283; WM, 710; Lagrange, 240. Cf. Jn. xvi. 13 f., ἐκεῖνος, τὸ πνεῦμα . . . ἐκεῖνος. The attributing of the action now to the spirit and now to the lad is characteristic of these stories: cf. i. 24, v. 9 f. συνσπαράσσω*, Lk. ix. 42**, not found in Cl. Gk nor in the LXX, is a stronger form of σπαράσσω, with the meaning ' to convulse completely '. Luke (ix. 42) says that, while he was coming, the daemon ' tore him ' (ἔρρηξεν) and ' convulsed ' him (συνεσπάραξεν). κυλίομαι** (LXX) is a late form of κυλίνδω, ' to roll '.

A second conversation with the father follows in 21-4. Jesus asks how long it is since (ὡς) the affliction overtook the lad. ὡς = ἀφ' οὗ. In ἐκ παιδιόθεν**, the preposition is redundant, and is probably due to the weakening of the original force of the suffix -θεν; cf. Moulton, ii. 164, as in ἀπὸ μακρόθεν (v. 6) and ἐξ [οἴ]κόθεν in the papyri (VGT, 474). The sufferer is a youth. Often (πολλάκις, v. 4*), the father explains, the spirit has cast him into the fire and into the water, in order to destroy him. ' If you can do anything ', he says, ' help us.' δύνῃ is a late form derived from δύνομαι which is frequently found in the papyri; cf. Moulton, ii. 206; i. 40 (B), Lk. xvi. 2, Apoc. ii. 2, Dan. v. 16. The verb is used absolutely as in Lk. xii. 26 and 2 Cor. xiii. 8. For σπλαγχνίζομαι v. i. 41. βοηθέω, ix. 24*; Mt. xv. 25, Ac. xvi. 9, xxi. 8, 2 Cor. vi. 2, Heb. ii. 18, Apoc. xii. 16**, ' to come to aid ', ' help ', < βοή, θέω; Cl., LXX,

Pap. The verb is freely illustrated in petitions and references to divine help.

The father's words leave a very vivid impression; his doubt about the healer's power, his appeal for compassion and help, his identification of himself, and perhaps his family also, with the lad, shown in his use of the plural, ' Have pity on us and help us ', are lifelike to a degree. Cf. Mt. xv. 22. The whole of 21-4 is peculiar to Mk.

23 f. Jesus at once fixes upon the words εἰ δύνῃ. Many MSS. omit the τό (D Θ P⁴⁵ fam. 13 565 it vg sys pe et al.) or add πιστεῦσαι (v. Legg); cf. Torrey, 302; Couchoud, JTS, xxxv. 18. The article has the force of inverted commas or an exclamation mark: ' If thou canst!'; cf. Swete, 200; Turner, 44, ' That phrase of yours " if thou canst " '; Lagrange, 241, ' Si tu peux! cela n'est pas la question '. ' All things ', He says, ' are possible to him who believes.' δυνατός, x. 27, xiii. 22, xiv. 35 f.*; πιστεύω, i. 15. Once more is evident the emphasis Jesus laid upon faith; cf. i. 15, v. 36, xi. 23 f. Cf. C. E. B. Cranfield, Scottish Jl. of Theol. iii, No. 1, p. 64.

Forthwith (εὐθύς, i. 10) the father cries out (κράζω, iii. 11): ' I believe; help my unbelief '. The cry is natural and there is no need (with Lohmeyer, 188) to think of it as divinely inspired, as a sign not of human distress, but of divine help. ἀπιστία v. vi. 6. The phrase ' help my unbelief ' is a cry for aid to a faith in the pains of birth. Swete, 200, explains it as meaning

συντρέχει ὄχλος ἐπετίμησεν τῷ πνεύματι τῷ ἀκαθάρτῳ λέγων
αὐτῷ Τὸ ἄλαλον καὶ κωφὸν πνεῦμα, ἐγὼ ἐπιτάσσω σοι, ἔξελθε
26 ἐξ αὐτοῦ καὶ μηκέτι εἰσέλθῃς εἰς αὐτόν. καὶ κράξας καὶ πολλὰ
σπαράξας ἐξῆλθεν· καὶ ἐγένετο ὡσεὶ νεκρὸς ὥστε τοὺς πολλοὺς
27 λέγειν ὅτι ἀπέθανεν. ὁ δὲ Ἰησοῦς κρατήσας τῆς χειρὸς αὐτοῦ
28 ἤγειρεν αὐτόν, καὶ ἀνέστη. καὶ εἰσελθόντος αὐτοῦ εἰς οἶκον οἱ

' help my faith where it is ready to fail' and as nearly =μοι τῷ ἀπίστῳ. It is not the unbelief mentioned in vi. 6, but a half-faith encompassed with doubts and fears which needs power to bring it to life. Very many MSS. (v. Legg) add (after ἔλεγεν) [1] μετὰ δακρύων, but it is wanting in ℵ A* B C* L W Δ P⁴⁵ 28 700 syˢ sa geo aeth arm et al. and must be regarded as the addition of an early scribe who had entered into the spirit of the story.

25. Mark represents Jesus as taking action because He saw that a multitude was rapidly gathering, ἰδών . . . ὅτι ἐπισυντρέχει ὄχλος, literally, ' came running together ' (RV). ἐπισυντρέχω**. While many compound verbs and nouns are introduced by ἐπισυν-(ἐπισυνάγω, i. 33, ἐπισυναθροίζω ' to collect besides ', ἐπισυναντάω ' to meet at one point ', LS), no parallel to ἐπισυντρέχω has been cited in Cl. Gk or in the papyri. VGT, 247, cites ὁ ἐπιτρέχων as used of a village inspector, but this has no bearing on the present passage. There can be no doubt, however, about the meaning of the word ; it describes a crowd converging on a single point, perhaps from several directions. The reference is made as if there had been no earlier allusion to the crowd. If, then, the story is a unity, the crowd which now gathers must be different from that mentioned in 14 which ran (προστρέχοντες) to greet Jesus. So Lagrange, 241 ; Plummer, 220. Swete, 200, thinks that the original crowd, from which Jesus with the father and the lad had withdrawn, is meant. Bultmann, 225 f., suggests that two different narratives have been combined.

See the Introduction to the narrative, p. 396.

A different view of the incident is suggested if ἐπισυντρέχει represents the Aramaic rᵉhaṭ followed by ʿal, in the sense of ' to attack ' ; cf. Black, 85 n. In this case Jesus acts at once when he sees the crowd rushing upon the lad.

For ἐπιτιμάω v. i. 25 ; τὸ πνεῦμα τὸ ἀκάθαρτον i. 23 ; κωφός vii. 32 ; ἄλαλος vii. 37 ; ἐπιτάσσω i. 27. The vocabulary is clearly Markan. For the first time in the narrative the daemon is described as deaf and unclean ; cf. 17, πνεῦμα ἄλαλον. This difference may be significant, but in a popular narrative it is hardly of importance in itself. As compared with i. 25 and v. 8 the command is more peremptory, being expressed both positively and negatively. Matthew and Luke merely mention the rebuke.

26 f. Crying and convulsing him much (RSV, ' terribly '), the daemon came out. For πολλά adverbial v. Intr. 61 ; κράζω iii. 11 ; σπαράσσω i. 26. A less grievous convulsing does not appear to be implied, and as compared with 20 the omission of the preposition in σπαράσσω need not imply a weakened sense ; cf. Moulton, i. 115. For the masculine participles v. the note on 20. The youth looked like a corpse. ὡσεί*. So much so that most people (τοὺς πολλούς) said, ' He is dead '. For ὥστε c. infin. v. i. 27. The case of Eutychus (Ac. xx. 10) is similar and probably that of the daughter of Jairus (v. 39-42). As in the latter case, Jesus takes the youth by the hand and raises him, and with great simplicity it is said ' he arose '

[1] λέγει is read by D Θ 565 700 b d g¹ i aeth arm ; εἶπεν by W P⁴⁵ fam. 13 (exc. 124) 543 a f k q syˢ.

μαθηταὶ αὐτοῦ κατ᾽ ἰδίαν ἐπηρώτων αὐτόν "Οτι ἡμεῖς οὐκ
ἠδυνήθημεν ἐκβαλεῖν αὐτό; καὶ εἶπεν αὐτοῖς Τοῦτο τὸ γένος 29
ἐν οὐδενὶ δύναται ἐξελθεῖν εἰ μὴ ἐν προσευχῇ.

(ἀνέστη, cf. v. 42). It is remarkable that no statement describes the effect produced on the eyewitnesses. Luke says that Jesus gave him to his father (cf. Lk. vii. 15) and adds that all were astonished at the majesty of God (ix. 43). Matthew says that the boy (παῖς) was healed 'from that hour' (xvii. 18, cf. ix. 22, xv. 28). The more primitive character of the Markan narrative is manifest.

28 f. This passage is an appendix to the story unless originally it belonged to 14-19. See the Note on the narrative. Usually such additions in Mk are loosely appended; cf. ii. 21 f., 27 f., iii. 27-9, iv. 21-5; but these verses, as in x. 10-12, have a narrative form. When Jesus went indoors (εἰς οἶκον) (v. iii. 20, vii. 17), His disciples asked Him privately (κατ᾽ ἰδίαν, v. 34) why they could not cast out the daemon. Probably ὅτι is used interrogatively as in ii. 16 and ix. 11, Moffatt, RVmg, and RSV being correct as against RV. Cf. Turner, 44. The gen. abs. is used loosely as in v. 2, 18, x. 17, xiii. 3, etc.

Jesus replies that this kind (of daemon) cannot be driven out by anything but prayer (RSV). For γένος v. vii. 26; προσευχή, xi. 17*. ἐξελθεῖν is here used as the equivalent of the passive of ἐκβάλλω and should be translated accordingly. The exorcist

is to make use of prayer; he is to rely, not on his own powers but on the power of God. For other teaching on prayer in Mk v. xi. 24 f. Most MSS.[1] add καὶ νηστείᾳ, but this reading is wanting in ℵ* B k geo[1] Clem. Alex. In P45 there is a gap after ἐν προσευχῇ. WH and Nestle omit the phrase and most commentators agree. There is a similar gloss in Ac. x. 30 (νηστεύων D) and again in 1 Cor. vii. 5 (τῇ νηστείᾳ καί). For a defence of the reading in Mk v. Couchoud, JTS, xxxv. 18 f. See also J. Jeremias, JW, 30; C. J. Cadoux, 67 n.

Luke omits the passage. Matthew reproduces 28, but substitutes for 29 ὁ δὲ λέγει αὐτοῖς Διὰ τὴν ὀλιγοπιστίαν ὑμῶν, and then adds from Q the saying on faith as a grain of mustard seed (Mt. xvii. 20 = Lk. xvii. 6; cf. Mk. xi. 23). Later scribes have added Mk. ix. 29 + καὶ νηστείᾳ in Mt. xvii. 21 (omitted by WH, Nestle, and most editors).

Matthew (xvii. 19) says that the disciples came to Jesus (προσελθόντες), and in Mk προσῆλθον and καὶ ἐπηρώτησαν (ἠρώτησαν) αὐτὸν λέγοντες are read by W Θ P45 fam. 13 565 700 et al. Cf. Couchoud, JTS, xxxv. 18, who cites also Tatian. These readings are in the Markan style and would account for the text in Mt, but it is hardly possible to say more.[2]

(b) Mk. ix. 30-50   THE JOURNEY THROUGH GALILEE

The second group of narratives in V is introduced by the statement, 'And they went forth from thence, and passed through Galilee; and he would not that any man should know it'. It is evident that Mark has no detailed information about this part of the journey, and the greater

[1] Including ℵb A D W Θ fam. 1 fam. 13 565 700 it (exc. k) sy⁺ pᵉ arm.
[2] P45 also reads εἰσελθόντι αὐτῷ and apparently by inadvertence omits εἰς οἶκον, but the text is defective between προσῆλθον and καί.

part of the material consists of sayings.   The instruction of the disciples
is the main interest.   See further, Intr. 98 f.   The section includes :

(58) ix. 30-2.   The Second Prophecy of the Passion.
(59) ix. 33-7.   The Question concerning True Greatness.
(60) ix. 38-41. The Strange Exorcist.
(61) ix. 42-50. Sayings on Offences, Renunciation, and Salt.

Mk. ix. 30-2   58. THE SECOND PROPHECY   Cf. Mt. xvii. 22 f.
                  OF THE PASSION   Lk. ix. 43b-5

The narrative appears to have been constructed by Mark on the basis
of tradition.   Schmidt, 219, observes that, while a name like Dalmanutha
cannot have been invented by the Evangelist, to speak of Galilee requires
no special tradition.   This may be so, but Mark not only mentions Galilee,
but represents Jesus passing through it incognito and using the opportunity to instruct His disciples about the ' delivering up ' of the Son of
Man.   All his interest centres upon this theme.   In his intention the
incident is distinct from those described in viii. 31-3 and x. 32-4.   If the
prophecies are different versions of the same saying derived from different
sources, the saying is ' one of the best authenticated and most significant
of all his sayings ' (A. T. Cadoux, *SSG*, 168 f.) ; but, as they appear in
Mk, the three prophecies are sufficiently distinct to be regarded as separate
utterances.   The present narrative stands out by the emphasis it lays upon
the Son of Man being delivered (by God) into the hands of men.   J. Weiss
regards it as historically the first prediction.   R. Otto, 361 f., esteems it
the most original of the three, at least as regards 31a.   ' He thinks that
he will fall into the hands of excited fanatics.   And it is just as indubitable
that he was not thinking of crucifixion, but of stoning by a popular mob ',
op. cit. 361.   In 31b, he adds, ' the theology of the church is beginning
to press in '.   We may doubt if this qualification is justified since Jesus is
not likely to have spoken of His death without affirming the certainty of
His vindication in victory over death.   The triple conception of abandonment to the will of men, death, and resurrection is attributed with greater
reason to the creative mind of Jesus than to the theology of the primitive
Church.

30   Κἀκεῖθεν ἐξελθόντες ⌐παρεπορεύοντο⌐ διὰ τῆς Γαλιλαίας, καὶ
31   οὐκ ἤθελεν ἵνα τις γνοῖ· ἐδίδασκεν γὰρ τοὺς μαθητὰς αὐτοῦ καὶ

                          30 ἐπορεύοντο

30. The brief geographical statement says that they went out from
' thence ' (the scene of the Transfiguration and its sequel) and passed
secretly through Galilee.   For ἐκεῖθεν
v. vi. 1.   ἐπορεύοντο (WH) is read by
B D 1402 a c f goth aeth, but παρ-
επορεύοντο (Nestle) is strongly attested
(ℵ B³ A C W Θ P⁴⁵ fam. 1 fam. 13 565
700 b d k sysˢ *et al.*) and should probably be accepted.   Cf. Swete (' perhaps

genuine '), 203 ; Lagrange, 243 ; Couchoud, *JTS*, xxxv. 19 (*certainement
original*).   For the verb *v.* the note on
ii. 23.   For the form γνοῖ *v.* the notes
on iv. 29 and v. 43 ; ἵνα c. subj. vi. 25.
    The reason for the secret journey is
the desire to instruct the disciples concerning the delivering up of the Son
of Man (31 f.), but behind this motive
lies the fact that the public ministry in
Galilee is now ended.   The statement

ἔλεγεν [αὐτοῖς] ὅτι ʽΟ υἱὸς τοῦ ἀνθρώπου παραδίδοται εἰς χεῖρας
ἀνθρώπων, καὶ ἀποκτενοῦσιν αὐτόν, καὶ ἀποκτανθεὶς μετὰ τρεῖς
ἡμέρας ἀναστήσεται.   οἱ δὲ ἠγνόουν τὸ ῥῆμα, καὶ ἐφοβοῦντο 32
αὐτὸν ἐπερωτῆσαι.

covers the section as far as ix. 50.
Nothing is said of a desire to avoid the
attentions of Herod and there is no
need to assume this purpose. See
Note D on the journey to the region
of Tyre, pp. 632-6.

31 f. The imperf. ἐδίδασκεν (i. 21)
is practically the equivalent of ἤρξατο
διδάσκειν in viii. 31. The saying is
briefer than viii. 31 ; the references
to suffering and rejection are wanting,
and instead it is said that the Son
of Man (ὁ υἱὸς τ. ἀνθ., cf. ii. 10) is delivered up into the hands of men. παραδίδοται (i. 14) is a futuristic present
which conveys a note of assurance ; cf.
Moulton, i. 120; Blass, 189; Robertson, 870. Both Matthew and Luke
have replaced it by μέλλει παραδίδο-
σθαι. Many commentators see here a
reference to the betrayal by Judas,
but Lohmeyer, 192, thinks there is also
another and deeper meaning, a reference to all that happens in the Passion
under the eschatological point of view,
as part of the action of ʽ the world ʼ
over against God or the Son of Man.
Swete, 203, and Lagrange, 243, think
of the delivering up of the Son in the
counsels of God, as in Rom. viii. 32.

Cf. Klostermann, 105. Probably this,
rather than the action of Judas, is the
thought of Jesus. For the use of ἀποκτείνω, μετὰ τρεῖς ἡμέρας, and ἀνίστημι
v. viii. 31.

The disciples are represented as unable to understand the saying and as
afraid to ask Jesus about it. ἀγνοέω*,
Lk (1), Ac (2), Pl (14), 1 Tim (1), Heb
(1), 2 Pet (1)**. ῥῆμα, xiv. 72*. For
the reference to ʽ fear ʼ v. iv. 41, and
for ἐπερωτάω v. 9. There is no good
reason why this should not have been
their attitude and no justification for
regarding these sayings as Gemeinde-
bildungen (Bultmann, 163). Least of
all the prophecies of the Passion is
ix. 31 open to this interpretation.

Matthew reproduces 31 with only
verbal changes. Luke omits the references to killing and rising again, but
precedes the saying with the words,
θέσθε ὑμεῖς εἰς τὰ ὦτα ὑμῶν τοὺς λόγους
τούτους (ix. 44). He also adds, with
reference to τὸ ῥῆμα, the comment,
καὶ ἦν παρακεκαλυμμένον ἀπ' αὐτῶν ἵνα
μὴ αἴσθωνται αὐτό. These additions
suggest that he is following a tradition
independent of Mk ; cf. Easton, 149 ;
V. Taylor, BTG, 90 f.

Mk. ix. 33-7   59. THE QUESTION CON-   Cf. Mt. xviii. 1-5
CERNING TRUE GREATNESS   Lk. ix. 46-8

The narrative appears to have been compiled by Mark himself, but
a possible use of Petrine reminiscences is suggested in the opening verses ;
cf. J. Weiss, 257. Otherwise the story consists of fragments loosely connected at 35 and 36. The story begins a section which Weiss declares
to be the most obscure part of Mk. In no small part the obscurity is
occasioned by the fact that in 37-50 Mark makes use of an extract from
a collection of sayings strung together by catchwords, the first of which,
ἐπὶ τῷ ὀνόματί μου, appears in 37 (cf. 38, 39, 41) ; and it is difficult to decide
whether the story has suggested the use of the extract or vice versa. The
situation is not unlike that in ii. 1-iii. 6 and iv. 1-34, where at the beginning
material topically arranged is combined with tradition derived from
Peter's testimony.

How it comes about that, in xviii. 3, Matthew supplies a saying far more appropriate to the Markan narrative than Mk. ix. 37 we cannot tell, beyond the inference that Mark's knowledge of the incident was fragmentary. Sufficient consideration has not been given to the probability that, besides rounded stories and detached sayings from which the narrative element has disappeared, fragmentary stories existed because attention halted at a saying or a circumstance of sufficient interest in itself : ix. 33 f., 35 f., and 37 may be fragments of this kind. The genuineness of the traditions, and particularly that of the sayings, is not affected by this uncertainty. The teaching on true greatness (35), the indispensability of the attitude of childlike trust (Mt. xviii. 3), and the mind which esteems the lowly as in some sense Jesus Himself (37), are some of the most authentic and characteristic elements in His thoughts. Cf. Montefiore, i. 220, ' Who can measure or count the deeds of sacrifice and love to which this saying has prompted ? '.

33 Καὶ ἦλθον εἰς Καφαρναούμ. Καὶ ἐν τῇ οἰκίᾳ γενόμενος
34 ἐπηρώτα αὐτούς Τί ἐν τῇ ὁδῷ διελογίζεσθε; οἱ δὲ ἐσιώπων,
35 πρὸς ἀλλήλους γὰρ διελέχθησαν ἐν τῇ ὁδῷ τίς μείζων. καὶ
    καθίσας ἐφώνησεν τοὺς δώδεκα καὶ λέγει αὐτοῖς Εἴ τις θέλει
36 πρῶτος εἶναι ἔσται πάντων ἔσχατος καὶ πάντων διάκονος. καὶ

33 f. The absence of an expressed subject to ἦλθον is due to the fact that Mark has placed the story in the context of the journey through Galilee. For this reason he finds it unnecessary to say that he is speaking of Jesus and His disciples. For Καφαρναούμ v. i. 21. The house mentioned is presumably that of Peter as in i. 29. There Jesus asks His disciples what they had been discussing ' in the way '. For ἐπερωτάω v. v. 9 ; διαλογίζομαι ii. 6 ; ἐν τῇ ὁδῷ viii. 3. The disciples are silent (σιωπάω, iii. 4) and Mark explains that they had been discussing the question who was the greatest. In μείζων, as often in Hellenistic Gk, the comparative is used for the superlative. So simply is the story told that, if it ended at 35, we might almost suppose it to be a Pronouncement-story leading to the saying of Jesus on true greatness.

Matthew and Luke omit the reference to Capernaum and introduce the story differently. Matthew says the disciples came to Jesus ' in that hour ' and themselves put the question to Him, Τίς ἄρα μείζων ἐστὶν ἐν τῇ βασιλείᾳ τῶν οὐρανῶν; (xviii. 1). Luke says

simply that a discussion arose among them, and he puts the question in the indirect form using ἄν and the optative, τὸ τίς ἂν εἴη μείζων αὐτῶν (ix. 46). In contrast with Mk, he assumes that Jesus had an intuitive knowledge of the reasoning of their heart. In Mk He questions them and they are too ashamed to answer.

35. καθίζω, x. 37, 40, xi. 2, 7, xii. 41, xiv. 32, xvi. [19]*. The word describes the action of a teacher; cf. Mt. v. 1, xiii. 1, Lk. v. 3, Jn. viii. 2. It is strange that, when Jesus has already addressed His disciples, He should ' call ' (φωνέω, i. 26) ' the Twelve ' (οἱ δώδεκα, v. iii. 14), for it does not seem likely that Mark is drawing a distinction between them and the other disciples. It is preferable to assume the use of another source ; cf. Schmidt, 230. Ed. Meyer, i. 139-44, derives 33-50 from his ' Twelve-source '.

The saying which follows, Εἴ τις θέλει πρῶτος εἶναι ἔσται πάντων ἔσχατος καὶ πάντων διάκονος, appears to be an abbreviated variant of x. 43 f. διάκονος, x. 43*. In the latter saying there is a double contrast, μέγας . . .

λαβὼν παιδίον ἔστησεν αὐτὸ ἐν μέσῳ αὐτῶν καὶ ἐναγκαλισάμενος αὐτὸ εἶπεν αὐτοῖς "Ὃς ἂν [ἓν] τῶν τοιούτων παιδίων 37
δέξηται ἐπὶ τῷ ὀνόματί μου, ἐμὲ δέχεται· καὶ ὃς ἂν ἐμὲ δέχηται,
οὐκ ἐμὲ δέχεται ἀλλὰ τὸν ἀποστείλαντά με.

διάκονος and πρῶτος . . . δοῦλος, but here διάκονος has no parallel corresponding to πρῶτος . . . ἔσχατος. It is evident that the primitive communities preserved a lively recollection of the way in which Jesus rebuked personal ambition, for there is still another variant form of the saying (from M) in Mt. xxiii. 11, Ὁ δὲ μείζων ὑμῶν ἔσται ὑμῶν διάκονος, and probably another in Lk. ix. 48b, Ὁ γὰρ μικρό-τερος ἐν πᾶσιν ὑμῖν ὑπάρχων οὗτός ἐστιν μέγας[1] (cf. Easton, 151).

Matthew omits 35. So also does Luke, unless ix. 48b (v. supra) is a modification of the Markan saying. The omission of καὶ λέγει . . . διάκονος in D d k might suggest that the words did not belong to the original text (cf. T. F. Glasson, ET, lv. 181, lvii. 54), but this reading is more probably a further attempt, as in Mt and Lk, to improve the order of narrative.

36. A new stage, possibly a new beginning (Holtzmann, 153; Schmidt, 230), follows when Jesus takes a child (παιδίον, v. 39) and sets him in the midst (ἐν μέσῳ, vi. 47). ἐναγκαλίζομαι, x. 16**, 'to take into one's arms'; LXX, Prov. vi. 10, xxiv. 48 (33), Plutarch, Cam. 5, and an inscr. cited in VGT, 210. The presence of this rare verb suggests that there is a point of contact with x. 13-16, the Blessing of the Children. Black, ET, lix. 14 f., makes the fascinating suggestion that, since the Aramaic talya means ' child ' or ' servant ', the incident of the child in the midst may be a dramatized play on the word and is thus a true mashal.

37. By placing 37 at this point in the narrative Mark shows that he takes ἐν τῶν τοιούτων παιδίων to refer to children, but in view of ἕνα τῶν μικρῶν τούτων τῶν πιστευόντων in 42 (Mt + εἰς ἐμέ), it is doubtful if this is

the original meaning of the saying. It is more probable that the ' little ones ' are the weaker members of the community, ' those who have the greatest need of being served ' (Lagrange, 246). The use of δέχομαι in the sense of ' welcome ' (cf. vi. 11) and of ἐπὶ τῷ ὀνόματί μου, ' because of (or ' on the ground of ') my name ', points also in this direction, for it is implied that some natural reluctance might have to be overcome. To Loisy's suggestion, that Mark has Paul in mind, Lagrange rightly objects that, while Paul might speak of himself as the least of the Apostles, an admirer is not likely to have thought of him so. Cf. to the same effect, Rawlinson, 127. The situation is more like that presupposed in Rom. xiv. 1-xv. 13 (cf. Bacon, 263), though there is no need to presuppose the influence of that passage on Mark, since counsel to respect the lowly is fully credible in a genuine saying of Jesus.

The saying recalls the words in the Mission Charge about the welcome which the missionaries will receive as the representatives of Jesus. Cf. Lk. x. 16 (=Mt. x. 40, cf. Jn. xiii. 20):

Ὁ ἀκούων (Mt, δεχόμενος) ὑμῶν ἐμοῦ ἀκούει, καὶ ὁ ἀθετῶν ὑμᾶς ἐμὲ ἀθετεῖ· ὁ δὲ ἐμὲ ἀθετῶν ἀθετεῖ τὸν ἀποστείλαντά με. But here the situation is exactly the reverse of that contemplated in Mk. ix. 37, since it is no longer a question of an attitude which the disciples are to display, but of their reception by others. It is, of course, possible that 37b, with its reference to ' Him that sent me ', is influenced by the Q saying, but this inference is not necessary. The idea that the envoy of a man is as the man himself is fundamentally Jewish; cf. Billerbeck, i. 590, ii. 167, and the principle that

[1] μέγας may represent the Semitic use of the positive for the superlative. Cf. Black, 86.

to receive the lowly is to receive Jesus is independently attested in Mt. xxv. 40. On the whole, it is best to regard Mk. ix. 37 and Mt. x. 40=Lk. x. 16 as separate sayings.

But does Mk. ix. 37 belong to its present setting? It is not surprising that sayings relating to children and sayings about 'little ones', in the sense of the lowliest members of the community, should be confused in the tradition, or that, interpreting it of children, Mark should have placed it in its present context. Yet, even so, it may be doubted if it suits that context. It is an acute observation of Turner, 48, that it would suit the story of the Blessing of the Children better, and that x. 15 (receiving the Kingdom as a child) is more appro-

priate to the present story. Cf. Bartlet, 281. Matthew appears to have been of this opinion, for he omits Mk. x. 15, but has a parallel to it in his version of Mk. ix. 33-7. Cf. Mt. xviii. 3: Ἀμὴν λέγω ὑμῖν, ἐὰν μὴ στραφῆτε καὶ γένησθε ὡς τὰ παιδία, οὐ μὴ εἰσέλθητε εἰς τὴν βασιλείαν τῶν οὐρανῶν. It is difficult to regard this as a free adaptation of Mk. x. 15; it is better to suppose that Matthew knows a more authentic version of the story which told how Jesus rebuked the ambition of the disciples by insisting that without the trustfulness of a child they could have no place at all in the Kingdom of God. Mark's use of 37 is bound up with the question of the sayings-source in 38-50. For ἀποστέλλω in Mk v. i. 2.

Mk. ix. 38-41   60. THE STRANGE EXORCIST   Cf. Lk. ix. 49 f.

This Pronouncement-story was current in the earliest tradition because it defined the attitude of Jesus to helpers who were not disciples. Bultmann, 23 f., classifies it as an Apothegm; Dibelius, 160, with qualifications, as a Chria; Redlich, 99, as an Apothegm-story. It is possible that a story of this kind was quoted in support of the ministry of Paul, but there is no evidence of this, and the reference to exorcism does not lend itself well to such a purpose. Still less credible is the description of the story as a community-product (Bultmann, 23; Lohmeyer, 195). Against Wendling, 104 f., Bultmann declines to derive the narrative from Mt. vii. 22, and Lohmeyer, 195 n., rejects Bultmann's suggestion that it may have been influenced by Numb. xi. 26-9. In contrast with such views, Schmidt, 236, suggests that the abrupt beginning is 'a genuine pericope-introduction of the oldest tradition' which rests on a good knowledge of what happened, since otherwise we cannot see how John's name came to be attached to the story. The narrative contains no question, but is introduced by a statement which leads to the decisive word of Jesus. When this is spoken the story ends. For the question whether the primitive unit is 38 f. or 38-40, and whether the saying in 41 is appended, see the Commentary. A special problem concerns the place of the narrative in its present context. Did Mark find it in the primitive collection which he is using in 37-50? Did he insert it himself, or was it added by a redactor?

38   Ἔφη αὐτῷ ὁ Ἰωάνης Διδάσκαλε, εἴδαμέν τινα ἐν τῷ ὀνόματί σου ἐκβάλλοντα δαιμόνια ὃς οὐκ ἀκολουθεῖ ἡμῖν, καὶ ἐκωλύομεν

39   αὐτόν, [ὅτι οὐκ ἠκολούθει ἡμῖν]. ὁ δὲ Ἰησοῦς εἶπεν Μὴ κωλύετε

38. ἔφη is asyndeton as in x. 29 and xii. 24. For ὁ Ἰωάνης v. i. 19. This is the only story in Mk in which John

alone plays a leading part. For Διδάσκαλε v. iv. 38; ἐκβάλλω i. 12; δαιμόνιον i. 34; ἀκολουθέω i. 18. κωλύω,

αὐτόν, οὐδεὶς γὰρ ἔστιν ὃς ποιήσει δύναμιν ἐπὶ τῷ ὀνόματί μου
καὶ δυνήσεται ταχὺ κακολογῆσαί με· ὃς γὰρ οὐκ ἔστιν καθ' 40
ἡμῶν, ὑπὲρ ἡμῶν ἐστίν. Ὃς γὰρ ἂν ποτίσῃ ὑμᾶς ποτήριον 41

ix. 39, x. 14*. The imperfect ἐκωλύομεν
is conative, 'we sought to stop him'.
Cf. Moulton, i. 129.

The Western text omits ὅτι οὐκ ἠκολούθει ἡμῖν, and inserts ὃς οὐκ ἀκολουθεῖ ἡμῖν after δαιμόνια; so D W fam. 1
fam. 13 28 565 a b c ff i k arm (μεθ'
ἡμῶν D a k, ἠκολούθει W 565). This
reading should probably be preferred
to that of the WH text, in spite of its
strong support in ℵ B C L Δ Θ sys
et al., for the reading with ὅτι in 38b
may be an assimilation to the text
of Lk. ix. 49 which reads ὅτι οὐκ
ἀκολουθεῖ μεθ' ἡμῶν. So Turner, JTS,
xxix. 4; Lagrange, 246.

Black, 53, suggests that the variants
are due to the ambiguity of the Aramaic
dᵉ, which can be a relative or a conjunction, and to the Aramaic verb
which can be represented by either
a present or an imperfect. He is
inclined to think that Mark may have
found two renderings of the Aramaic
in existence and set them down in his
'conflate' text, and cites (as a parallel)
v. 23, ἵνα σωθῇ καὶ ζήσῃ, 'a combination impossible in Aramaic'. Mk.
iv. 41 and ix. 38, he suggests, point to
the use of an Aramaic sayings-source
or tradition, but he notes that both
passages are in reported speech (AA,
207). Coupled with the fact that the
sayings in 38-45 assume a poetic form,
marked by alliteration, assonance, and
paronomasia, when translated back
into Aramaic, this opinion is very
weighty.

39. To the implied question regarding the unauthorized exorcist Jesus
replied μὴ κωλύετε αὐτόν, adding the
explanation that no one who shall do
a mighty work in His name will be
able quickly to speak evil of Him.

For μή c. impv. v. v. 36; οὐδεὶς ἔστιν
ὅς x. 29; δύναμις v. 30; ἐπὶ τῷ ὀνόματί μου ix. 37; ταχύ*; κακολογέω
vii. 10*. It is tempting to regard the

change from ἐν to ἐπί in ἐπὶ τῷ ὀνόματί μου as deliberate, as implying that,
whereas the exorcist had been using
the name as a means or instrument (ἐν),
Jesus chose to explain his action more
charitably as wrought because of, or
on the ground of (ἐπί), His name.
It is doubtful, however, if any distinction can be drawn between ἐν and
ἐπί in these phrases; cf. S. New, The
Beginnings of Christianity, v. 123 f.;
Lohmeyer, 194. In ix. 41 ἐν ὀνόματι
ὅτι appears to mean 'because'. In
the present saying Jesus is speaking
of healing activity in which there is
a direct appeal to His authority. The
use of the name of Jesus in later times
by pagan exorcists (Ac. xix. 13) in no
way rules out the possibility of similar
instances in His lifetime. There is
no reason to suppose that the story has
been influenced by the account of El-
dad and Medad in Numb. xi. 26-9;
cf. Bultmann, 24.

Luke omits the explanatory passage
in 39b and ends the story with μὴ κωλύετε. Matthew omits the entire story,
perhaps because of Mt. vii. 22 or because in his day it might have been
misapplied; cf. Streeter, 171.

As in 37, Loisy, ii. 69 f., sees in 38 f.
a polemic directed against Paul. Cf.
J. Weiss, 258 f. Lagrange, 247, dismisses this view as fantastic and makes
an effective criticism when he asks
whether we can conceive a partisan
of Paul contenting himself with this
slender justification. Cf. Rawlinson,
129.

40 f. Possibly the story ends with
39 (so Bultmann, 23), but there is no
sufficient reason why Jesus should not
have added the saying ὃς γὰρ οὐκ ἔστιν
καθ' ἡμῶν, ὑπὲρ ἡμῶν ἐστίν in 40. The
tolerant spirit which it expresses is
fully in harmony with the rest of the
story. Wellhausen, 76, prefers the
reading ὑμῶν . . . ὑμῶν (A D it (exc. k)

ὕδατος ἐν ὀνόματι ὅτι [Χριστοῦ] ἐστέ, ἀμὴν λέγω ὑμῖν ὅτι οὐ
μὴ ἀπολέσῃ τὸν μισθὸν αὐτοῦ.

41 cj. ἐμοί, v. Comm.

vg sype hl), but the agreement of ℵ B C W Δ Θ Ψ fam. 1 (exc. 118) fam. 13 (exc. 124) 28 565 579 892 1071 k sys sa bo geo arm is decisively in favour of ἡμῶν . . . ἡμῶν. The similar saying in Q, ὁ μὴ ὢν μετ' ἐμοῦ κατ' ἐμοῦ ἐστίν, καὶ ὁ μὴ συνάγων μετ' ἐμοῦ σκορπίζει, found in Mt. xii. 30 and Lk. xi. 23, does not contradict Mk. ix. 40 since both statements are true.

In contrast with 40, the saying in 41 about giving a cup of water to the disciples is probably appended because of the phrase ἐν ὀνόματι ὅτι Χριστοῦ ἐστέ. It is omitted by Luke and is more suitably placed by Matthew in the Mission Charge (x. 42). For Mark's habit of appending sayings cf. ii. 21 f., 27 f., iii. 27-9, iv. 21-5, vii. 14-23, x. 10-12.

For ὃς ἄν c. subj. v. iii. 29; ἀμὴν λέγω ὑμῖν iii. 28. ποτίζω xv. 36*. For ποτήριον ὕδατος Matthew has π. ψυχροῦ. He has also ἕνα τῶν μικρῶν τούτων instead of ὑμᾶς.

The reading ἐν ὀνόματι ὅτι Χριστοῦ ἐστέ is remarkable. It is not surprising that ℵ* C³ W 118 124, etc. add μου, and that τῷ ὀνόματί μου is read by D Δ Θ fam. 13 (exc. 124) 28 565 700 it vg syhl sa bo aeth Or. Matthew has εἰς ὄνομα μαθητοῦ, which Swete, 208, thinks is 'perhaps nearer to the original'. Hawkins, 152, suggests that ὅτι Χριστοῦ ἐστέ was added by an editor, and Lagrange, 249, suggests the hand of a copyist. The idea

is Pauline; cf. Rom. viii. 9, 1 Cor. i. 12, iii. 23, 2 Cor. x. 7.

To suggest that the original reading was ἐπὶ τῷ ὀνόματί μου as 37 and 39, is too easy a solution of the textual problem. The parallel saying in Mt. x. 42 suggests that the gift of the cup of water is an act characteristic of a disciple. Did the original Markan text convey the same idea? ℵ* reads ὅτι ἐμόν ἐστε. Professor T. W. Manson has suggested to me that the obvious correction is ἐμοί and that ἐν ὀνόματι ὅτι ἐμοί ἐστε would give a perfectly good sense and account for Matthew's interpretation. Cf. Psa. Sol. ix. 16, ὅτι σοί ἐσμεν. He recalls that W. Heitmüller, Im Namen Jesu, 63, speaks of ἐν ὀνόματι ὅτι as durchaus griechisch. Cf. Deissmann, BS, 197 f.; Milligan, Selections from the Gk Papyri, 50, where P. Oxy. 37, i. 17 (A.D. 49) has ὀνόματι ἐλευθέρου, 'in virtue of its being freeborn', in a report of a lawsuit in which a nurse is sued for the recovery of a male foundling. If this conjecture is accepted, the meaning is 'on the ground that ye are mine'. Cf. τοὺς ἐμούς in viii. 38.

For οὐ μή c. subj. v. ix. 1. Here the tone is very emphatic. μισθός*. Cf. x. 21, 29 f., Mt. vi. 19 f. Bultmann, JW, 78 f., observes that the attitude of Jesus to the idea of rewards is paradoxical; 'He promises reward to those who are obedient without thought of reward'.

Mk. ix. 42-50　　　61. SAYINGS ON　　Cf. Mt. xviii. 6-9 (v. 13)
　　　　　　　OFFENCES, RENUNCIATION,　　(Lk. xvii. 1 f.,
　　　　　　　AND SALT　　　　　　　xiv. 34 f.)

The arrangement of these sayings raises a question of the greatest interest. Together with 37 and 38-41, they appear to have been compiled under a catechetical impulse by the aid of catchwords intended to assist the memory. It is true that in 43-7 phrases are used by Jesus intentionally in poetic parallelism, and that the same kind of arrangement is visible in the M version of these sayings in Mt. v. 29 f. It is impossible, however, to extend this explanation to the entire section, as the history of the inter-pretation of 33-50 abundantly shows. Not to speak of the variety of the sayings, the structure of the whole is artificial and must be set down to the work of a pre-Markan compiler who sought to assist catechumens in committing the sayings to memory. He appears to have taken his cue from the original parallelism in 43-7 and has selected for his purpose sayings which were of particular interest to the Roman community. In order to observe the structure it will be useful to print the whole of 37-50, with the connecting links in italics. Verses 44 and 46, which simply repeat 48, are omitted by most editors on textual grounds (*v. infra*).

37. Whosoever shall receive *one of such little children in my name*, receiveth me ; and whosoever receiveth me, receiveth not me, but him that sent me.

38. John said unto him, Master, we saw one casting out devils *in thy*
39. *name* : and we forbade him, because he followed not us. But Jesus said, Forbid him not : for there is no man which shall do a mighty
40. work *in my name*, and be able quickly to speak evil of me. For he that is not against us is for us.

41. For whosoever shall give you a cup of water to drink, because ye are Christ's (Gk., ' *in name* that ye are Christ's '), verily I say unto you, he shall in no wise lose his reward.

42. And whosoever shall *cause one of these little ones* that believe on me *to stumble*, it were better (Gk., ' it were *good* ') for him if a great millstone were hanged about his neck, and he were *cast* into the sea.

43. And if thy hand *cause* thee *to stumble*, cut it off : it is *good* for thee *to enter into life* maimed, rather than having thy two hands *to go into Gehenna*, into the unquenchable *fire*.

45. And if thy foot *cause* thee *to stumble*, cut it off : it is *good* for thee *to enter into life* halt, rather than having thy two feet *to be cast into Gehenna*.

47. And if thine eye *cause* thee *to stumble*, cast it out : it is *good* for thee *to enter* into the kingdom of God with one eye, rather than having
48. two eyes *to be cast into Gehenna* ; where their worm dieth not, and the *fire* is not quenched.

49. For everyone shall be *salted* with *fire*.

50. *Salt* is *good* : but if the *salt* have lost its saltness, wherewith will ye season it ?
Have *salt* in yourselves, and be at peace one with another.

It will be seen that 38-40 and 41 fall within this structural arrangement and that 37 and 42 are closely related. Further, the last part of 50 (50c) recalls the dispute of 33 f. These complex relationships are discussed in the Commentary. It is also clear that the group has been built around 43-8. The saying in 42, with which 37 is connected, has been attached to this section because of the catchwords ' cause to stumble ', ' good ', and ' cast ', while the phrase ' in my name ' in 37 accounts for the intro-duction of the story of the Strange Exorcist in 38-40 (cf. 38 f.) and the saying on giving a cup of water in 41. Further the word ' fire ' (43 and 48) has suggested the addition of the saying ' Everyone shall be salted with fire ' in 49, while the reference to salting in this verse has attracted to the group the three sayings on Salt in 50 in the first of which ' good ' reappears.

This explanation might be dismissed as fanciful if a satisfactory account could be given of the order of the several sayings, but only to a small degree is this possible in the case of adjacent sayings. After the saying on receiving little children (37) it is not surprising to find that about offending ' little ones ' (42). Nor is it strange that the saying on giving a cup of water (41) follows the story of the Strange Exorcist (38-40). But why does 38-40 separate 37 and 42 if its presence is not due to the phrases ' in thy name ' and ' in my name ', and what bond is there between 37-42, 43-48, 49, and 50 other than the catchwords ?

Distaste for such artificial methods of compilation is more than compensated for by the knowledge we gain of catechetical practices in the pre-Gospel period. Moreover, it is to these very methods that we are indebted for the preservation of the sayings. Further, behind the catchwords we see signs of poetical forms used by Jesus Himself which the compiler recognized and used.

42 Καὶ ὃς ἂν σκανδαλίσῃ ἕνα τῶν μικρῶν τούτων τῶν πιστευόντων ᵀ, καλόν ἐστιν αὐτῷ μᾶλλον εἰ περίκειται μύλος ὀνικὸς περὶ
43 τὸν τράχηλον αὐτοῦ καὶ βέβληται εἰς τὴν θάλασσαν. Καὶ ἐὰν

42 εἰς ἐμέ

42. It is not improbable that originally this saying formed a pair with 37. Matthew, who omits 38-40 and has 41 in the Mission Charge, brings the two together in xviii. 5 f. Both sayings begin with ὃς ἂν c. subj., ἕνα τῶν μικρῶν τούτων τῶν πιστευόντων corresponds with ἐν τῶν τοιούτων παιδίων in 37, and the idea of causing to stumble (σκανδαλίζω, iv. 17) stands in contrast with that of receiving. The ' little ones ' are the humblest members of the community. Cf. Swete, 209; Lagrange, 249, who cites Rom. xiv. 1, τὸν ἀσθενοῦντα τῇ πίστει, 1 Cor. viii. 10-12, ὁ ἀσθενῶν, ix. 22, τοῖς ἀσθενέσιν. The participle τῶν πιστευόντων defines their character as ' believers '. Mt. xviii. 6 adds εἰς ἐμέ, and this reading (omitted in ℵ Δ b ff i k) is very strongly attested in Mk (A B C² L W Θ et al. minusc. omn. c f l q r² vg sys pe hl sa bo geo aeth arm) and should probably be read (RV, RSV).

For καλόν ἐστιν v. vii. 27, and for the use of the positive followed by μᾶλλον to express the comparative (' it were better ') v. Ac. xx. 35 and Gal. iv. 27 (LXX). Matthew has συμφέρει αὐτῷ and Luke λυσιτελεῖ αὐτῷ. After καλόν we should expect ἦν, and after εἰ (xiv. 21*) περιέκειτο and ἐβλήθη (so

D W), since the sentence is hypothetical, but the pres. and perf. give greater vividness. Cf. Swete, 209. περίκειμαι*, τράχηλος*. Instead of καὶ βέβληται εἰς τὴν θάλασσαν (the lake; so Lk), Matthew thinks of the open sea, καὶ καταποντισθῇ ἐν τῷ πελάγει τῆς θαλάσσης (xviii. 6).

μύλος* ὀνικός* (Mt. xviii. 6**) is a millstone turned by an ass, in contrast with the hand mill served by a woman (cf. Lk. xvii. 35 = Mt. xxiv. 41). Formerly regarded as ' Biblical ' (Grimm), ὀνικός is now shown to have been in common use in the time of Christ (VGT, 450 f.). As illustrating Roman usage Ovid, Fast. vi. 318, quae pumiceas versat asella molas, is cited by many commentators. Cf. A. R. S. Kennedy, EB, col. 3093 f.; Swete, 209 f.; Lagrange, 249 f. The punishment of drowning was Roman; cf. Suetonius, Aug. 67, oneratis gravi pondere cervicibus praecipitavit in flumen; but Josephus, Ant. xiv. 15. 10, speaks of Galileans who rebelled and drowned the partisans of Herod in the lake, Γαλιλαῖοι . . . τοὺς τὰ Ἡρώδου φρονοῦντας ἐν τῇ λίμνῃ κατεπόντωσαν. Lk. xvii. 2 describes the stone as λίθος μυλικός.

Apparently the saying stood in both

⌜σκανδαλίσῃ⌝ σε ἡ χείρ σου, ἀπόκοψον αὐτήν· καλόν ἐστίν σε
κυλλὸν εἰσελθεῖν εἰς τὴν ζωὴν ἢ τὰς δύο χεῖρας ἔχοντα ἀπελθεῖν
εἰς τὴν γέενναν, εἰς τὸ πῦρ τὸ ἄσβεστον. καὶ ἐὰν ὁ πούς σου 45
                    43 σκανδαλίζῃ

the Markan collection and in Q. Luke
gives the Q version in xvii. 1 f. while
Matthew conflates Mk and Q in xviii.
6 f. Although there can be little doubt
that in the Markan collection the
saying described the attitude to be
taken to the lowliest members of the
community, it is much less certain
that this was its original form. Cf.
Manson, *SJ*, 138 : ' We should expect
the tendency of the tradition to be to
transfer sayings concerning " children " or " little ones " to the disciples '. Cf. Rawlinson, 130. In this
case it would appear that, while Mark
retains 42 in the secondary form in
which he found it, he makes a partial
return to the original form of the
teaching in 37, ἐν τῶν τοιούτων παιδίων.

43-8. These sayings on the necessity
of sacrificing any obstacle to ' entering
into life ', hand (43), foot (45), or eye
(47), were arranged in the Markan
collection *ad vocem*, with reference to
the catchword σκανδαλίζειν. In contrast with 42, the theme is no longer
that of causing others to stumble but
of ensnaring oneself. ' Better to live
under a sense of partial mutilation and
incompleteness than to perish in the
enjoyment of all one's powers ', Swete,
210. Actual mutilation is not coun-
selled, but in the strongest possible
manner the costliest sacrifice. This
teaching must have been greatly
esteemed in the Roman Church during
the days of the Neronian persecution.
    Along with the change of theme
goes a change of construction ; for
ἐάν c. subj. *v.* i. 40. In καλόν . . . ἤ the
use of the positive of the adjective for
the comparative is Semitic (cf. καλόν
. . . μᾶλλον in 42). Cf. Lagrange,
250 f. ; Black, 86. Black says that
there does not appear to be any parallel in Gk, but Lagrange, while claiming that the construction is Semitic,

cites Herodotus ix. 26. 7, οὕτω ὦν
δίκαιον ἡμέας ἔχειν τὸ ἕτερον κέρας ἤ
περ ᾿Αθηναίους. Cf. *Aristeas* 281. See
further, Howard, ii. 441 f. For LXX
usage *v.* Psa. cxvii. 8 f., Gen. xlix. 12.
    ἀποκόπτω, ix. 45*. κυλλός*,
' crooked ', ' crippled ', Mt. xv. 30 f. ;
here ' maimed ', Mt. xviii. 8**. ζωή,
ix. 45, x. 17, 30*, as distinct from βίος,
denotes in most cases in the NT the
higher life of the soul in fellowship
with God. Here the phrase εἰσελθεῖν
εἰς τὴν ζωήν, used again in 45, is the
equivalent of εἰσελθεῖν εἰς τὴν βασιλείαν
τοῦ θεοῦ in 47.
    γέεννα, גֵּי הִנֹּם, ' Gehenna ', ix. 45,
47*, Mt (7), Lk. xii. 5, Jas. iii. 6**, as
distinct from ᾅδης, ' Hades ', means
' Hell ' (RV, RSV), but in view of the
misleading associations of this rendering, it is better to transliterate the
word in the form ' Gehenna ' (so
Moffatt and Torrey). Originally the
name of a valley west of Jerusalem,
where infants were offered in sacrifice
to Moloch (4 Regn. xxiii. 10, Jer. vii.
31, xix. 5 f., xxxix. 35), and which
subsequently was desecrated by Josiah
and used for the burning of offal,
Gehenna came to be employed as a
symbolic name for the place of future
punishment. Cf. 1 Enoch xxvii. 2,
' This accursed valley is for those who
are accursed for ever ', xc. 24-6 ; 4
Ezra vii. 36, *clibanus gehennae osten-
detur, et contra eum iocunditatis para-
disus* ; Aboth i. 5, v. 19 f. Jesus used
an accepted idea of His time. He is
not to be credited with later ideas of
eternal punishment which are alien
to His teaching concerning God and
man, but, on the other hand, His words
must not be explained away as a
picturesque metaphor. By contrast
with the phrase ' to enter into life ' the
words ' to go into Gehenna ' indicate
spiritual ruin and perhaps destruction.

σκανδαλίζῃ σε, ἀπόκοψον αὐτόν· καλόν ἐστίν σε εἰσελθεῖν εἰς τὴν
ζωὴν χωλὸν ἢ τοὺς δύο πόδας ἔχοντα βληθῆναι εἰς τὴν γέενναν.
47 καὶ ἐὰν ὁ ὀφθαλμός σου σκανδαλίζῃ σε, ἔκβαλε αὐτόν· καλόν
σέ ἐστιν μονόφθαλμον εἰσελθεῖν εἰς τὴν βασιλείαν τοῦ θεοῦ ἢ
48 δύο ὀφθαλμοὺς ἔχοντα βληθῆναι εἰς ᵀ γέενναν, ὅπου ὁ ϲκώληξ

47 τὴν

The phrase εἰς τὸ πῦρ τὸ ἄσβεστον is best explained as a comment of Mark, based on Isa. lxvi. 24, καὶ τὸ πῦρ αὐτῶν οὐ σβεσθήσεται, for the benefit of his Gentile readers. ἄσβεστος*, Mt. iii. 12, Lk. iii. 17**, ' unquenchable'; Cl. (Homer), LXX. Mt, αἰώνιον.

Luke omits the whole passage. Matthew follows Mk closely, except that he combines the two sayings regarding the hand and the foot, with the necessary changes and assimilations to the parallel version from M used in v. 29 f.

For the omission of 44 and 46 v. infra.

Verses 45 and 47 repeat the statement of 43 with reference to the foot and the eye respectively. χωλός*. In each verse βληθῆναι replaces ἀπελθεῖν in 43. μονόφθαλμος*, Mt. xviii. 9**, is an Ionic word (Herodotus iii. 116, iv. 27), condemned by Atticists.

The phrase εἰσελθεῖν εἰς τὴν βασιλείαν τοῦ θεοῦ in 47 is found in Mk here and x. 15, 23 f., 25*; it implies that the Basileia is not only the Rule of God, but also the domain in which His sovereignty is exercised; cf. Otto, 53 f.; Flew, JC, 34 f. Even so, the phrase εἰσελθεῖν εἰς τὴν ζωήν in 43 and 45 implies that the emphasis is upon the kind of life which belongs to this domain, that is, the rule of God in human experience. See further, the note on i. 15, also x. 15.

Verse 48 is a quotation from Isa. lxvi. 24, slightly modified from the LXX, ὁ γὰρ σκώληξ αὐτῶν οὐ τελευτήσει (A, τελευτᾷ), καὶ τὸ πῦρ αὐτῶν οὐ σβεσθήσεται, καὶ ἔσονται εἰς ὅρασιν πάσῃ σαρκί. From this passage the use of σκώληξ* became common as a symbol of destruction; cf. Sir. vii. 17, Judith

xvi. 17. The quotation is omitted by Matthew and may have been added to the sayings by Mark or the original compiler. σβέννυμι*; τελευτάω, vii. 10*.

A marked feature of 38-48 is the poetical form revealed when the passage is translated into Aramaic. Black, 127 f., who calls attention to this fact, points out the repetition of hard sounds and gutturals which give a fitting expression for the utterances in the sayings-group. Even in the Greek the repetitions of kappa and chi are notable. The poetical form is given to the sayings by Jesus Himself. The relationship between 43-8 and the M version in Mt. v. 29 f. will doubtlessly be variously adjudged, but there is good reason to think that the latter is less original. The omission of the foot, the characterization of the eye and the hand as the 'right' eye and hand, the use of συμφέρει σοι, and the limitation of the sayings to warnings without the positive idea of entering into life seem to point in this direction. Lohmeyer, 196, it should be said, takes the opposite view, suggesting that the contrast is that between a Palestinian version (Mt) and a Roman (Mk). So far as 43c and 48 are concerned this opinion may be correct. The quotation in 48 is added in most MSS. in 44 and 46, but it is omitted in ℵ B C L W Δ Ψ fam. 1 22 28 565 892 et al. k sys sa bo geo (in 44) arm and in critical texts (WH and Nestle; so RV and RSV).

49. The T.R. of this verse is one of the instances of conflate readings on which the textual theory of WH is based. The short text, πᾶς γὰρ πυρὶ ἁλισθήσεται, accepted as original by

αγτῶν ογ τελεγτᾷ καὶ τὸ πγ̂ρ ογ cβέννγται· πᾶς γὰρ πυρὶ ἁλισθή- 49

WH, Nestle, and most critical editors, remains the best attested reading. The textual facts are as follows :

(1) πᾶς γὰρ πυρὶ ἁλισθήσεται :
א B L W Δ fam. 1 565 700 et al. sys sa bo geo arm.

(2) + καὶ πᾶσα θυσία ἁλὶ ἁλισθήσεται :
A C Θ al. pler. fam 13 28 892 1071 al. pler. f l q r vg sype hl aeth.

(3) πᾶσα γὰρ θυσία ἁλὶ ἁλισθήσεται :
D a b c d ff i k.

From this evidence WH conclude that the second reading is a conflation of the first and third, and that the first deserves preference over the third which is exclusively Western. MSS. more recently discovered do not shake this conclusion (W reads ἁλισγηθήσεται and Θ ἀναλωθήσεται (after πυρί), already read by Ψ' (after ἁλί)), but the exegetical difficulties have invited conjectures. Pallis, 34, suggests that we read ἁγνισθήσεται, ' shall be purified ', instead of ἁλισθήσεται, ' shall be salted ', but while this reading supplies a good meaning, it does not account for the textual variants. Couchoud, JTS, xxxiv. 124, advocates the Greek text implied by the MS. k, omnis autem substantia consumitur (amended to consumetur), πᾶσα δὲ οὐσία ἀναλω-θήσεται (Ψ) ; so also Lohmeyer, 197 n. The phrase then adds the conclusion to the quotation from Isa. lxvi. 24 in 48 : ' where their worm shall not die, nor their fire be quenched, and all (their) substance shall be destroyed '. This solution is attractive, but it is difficult to see how this rendering, dif-ferent from the LXX, could be obtained from the Hebrew which reads, ' and they shall become a horror to all flesh '. Some allusion to salt is necessary to account for the use of the sayings in 50. The WH text raises difficulties, but they are exegetical rather than textual, and it has a better claim to acceptance than any other reading. ἁλισθήσεται (ἁλίζω*, Mt. v. 13**) called to mind

Lev. ii. 13, καὶ πᾶν δῶρον θυσίας ὑμῶν ἁλὶ ἁλισθήσεται, and so gave rise to the D reading, while the Byzantine text combined both. See Turner's discussion of the variant readings in W, Θ, and k, JTS, xvii. 16-18.

The connexion of 49 with 48 is purely ad vocem. It is impossible, therefore, with Gould, 181, to infer that the object of the penal retribu-tions of Gehenna is to purify, and still less to agree with Lagrange, 254, that the fire preserves the sufferers of Gehenna and is thus the last word of the terrible description of the punish-ment. The fire of 49 has nothing to do with that of 48. The connexion effected by γάρ is the work of the com-piler. The saying may be eschato-logical. Burkitt, op. cit. 17, suggests that ' salted with fire ' may correspond to ' baptized with the Holy Ghost and with fire '. The combination of the metaphors of salt and of fire suggests the idea of purifying, and it is not improbable that Jesus meant that in the eschatological situation in which His disciples stood every man would be tried and purified by the fires of persecution and suffering. Evil would be destroyed and good preserved. Cf. Mal. iii. 2 f. ; 1 Cor. iii. 13-15. Many commentators have held that persecu-tion is meant ; cf. Wellhausen, 76 ; Klostermann, 109 ; Gould, 181 ; Turner, 46 ; Rawlinson, 131 ; Bartlet, 284 f. ; Branscomb, 174 ; but of a saying concerning which H. A. W. Meyer, 153-5, lists no less than four-teen explanations in addition to his own, no one will wish to speak with too much assurance. Torrey, 302, TG, suggests that the original Aramaic has been misunderstood, but, apart from the assumptions involved, the translation, ' Whatever would spoil, is salted ', seems prosaic. A challenging word on suffering is the most probable suggestion. It also has the merit that, on this interpreta-tion, its preservation in the teaching

50 σεται. Καλὸν τὸ ἅλας· ἐὰν δὲ τὸ ἅλας ἄναλον γένηται, ἐν τίνι
αὐτὸ ἀρτύσετε; ἔχετε ἐν ἑαυτοῖς ἅλα, καὶ εἰρηνεύετε ἐν ἀλλήλοις.

manual of a persecuted Church is fully intelligible.

50. τὸ ἅλας, ix. 50 (bis)*, Mt. v. 13, Lk. xiv. 34 (bis), Col. iv. 6**. This late form has replaced the older ἅλς in the NT, except for ἁλί in ix. 49 (D) and ἅλα in 50c. Cf. Moulton, ii. 132; VGT, 20 f. In the LXX ἅλς predominates, but ἅλας is found in 2 Esdr. vii. 22 and Sir. xxxix. 26 (A). It is strange that the two forms should appear in 50, and hard to think that the distinction is original. N. D. Coleman, JTS, xxiv. 387-96, ET, xlviii. 360-2, has suggested that ἅλας, as distinct from ἅλς, might mean ' salted fish ', but this rendering lacks support. Strictly speaking, salt cannot become ἄναλος**, but by combination with other substances it can lose the character, while retaining the appearance, of salt.

The parallel in Mt. v. 13 (perhaps from M) shares ἁλισθήσεται with 49, while the Q version in Lk. xiv. 34 shares καλόν . . . τὸ ἅλας with 50. Against Mk, Matthew and Luke agree in using μωραίνω, ' to make foolish ', and in describing the uselessness of the salt. Since בָּפֵל can signify both un-savoury and a fool, Black, 124, suggests that, if the word was used by Jesus, we can account for Mark's ἄναλον as the literal translation, especially as the presumed Aramaic original shows signs of word-play (taphel ' unsavoury ', tabbel ' salted '; 'ar'a ' ground ', re'a ' dung '). With Lagrange, St. Luc, 413 f., he is doubt-ful about the suggestion of Perles, ZNTW, xix. 96, that ' ground ' is a mistranslation for ' seasoning '. Be-hind these disagreements among ex-perts the growing conviction that Aramaic tradition accounts for the Synoptic variants is impressive, and it is significant that, as often, the question arises in sayings of Jesus. The artificiality of the link with 49

is manifest, for here in 50 the purpose of the salt is to season. Cf. Well-hausen, 76 f. No longer describing an experience to which the disciples are subject, salt is a quality to be used in daily life. Cf. Mt. v. 13, Ὑμεῖς ἐστε τὸ ἅλας τῆς γῆς.

Mark shares ἀρτύω, ' to season ' with Lk. xiv. 34 and Col. iv. 6**. In this later sense the verb is used in Cl. Gk and in the papyri (VGT, 80). For ἀρτύσετε Luke has ἀρτυθήσεται and Matthew ἁλισθήσεται. For an Aramaic parallel see the Babylonian Talmud, Bekhoroth, 8b: ' If the salt becomes insipid, wherewith shall it be salted ? '. Cf. Billerbeck, i. 236.

50c, ἔχετε ἐν ἑαυτοῖς ἅλα, καὶ εἰρη-νεύετε ἐν ἀλλήλοις, is probably a com-ment of the compiler which points back to the dispute mentioned in 33 f.; cf. Klostermann, 109; Turner, 47; Bartlet, 286. εἰρηνεύω*, Rom. xii. 18, 2 Cor. xiii. 11, 1 Thess. v. 13**, is a Pauline word. Cf. εἰρηνεύετε ἐν ἑαυτοῖς in 1 Thess. v. 13. As in Paul, the words are an exhortation. Lohmeyer, 197, suggests that the first part is a blessing to which the second forms an apodosis. The Greek appears to be an instance of two imperatives in conditional parataxis joined by the consecutives καί, with the meaning, ' Have salt in yourselves, then you will be at peace among yourselves '. Cf. Wellhausen, Einl.² 13, and see viii. 34 and Lk. vii. 7. But this con-struction is not distinctively Semitic, being found in fact in many languages. Cf. Howard, ii. 421. J. Rendel Har-ris, ET, xxxv. 403-5, xlviii. 185 f., suspects a Latinism in the reading salem in d, in which by word-play salem is mystically interpreted as=' peace '. Cf. Heb. vii. 2. This suggestion is in-genious and there is force in his ob-servation that in 50c we get behind Mark ' into somebody else's notebook '. Torrey's rendering is ' and pass it on to your fellows '. A declaration that the way to peace is a life seasoned as with the astringent qualities of salt, perhaps, as we should say, with common sense, appears to be the meaning of the passage.

(c) Mk. x. 1-31   THE JOURNEY THROUGH
PERAEA AND JUDAEA

The third section in V is introduced by the summary geographical statement in x. 1 and consists of the following narratives :

(62) x. 1-12.   On Adultery.
(63) x. 13-16. On Children.
(64) x. 17-22. The Rich Man and Eternal Life.
(65) x. 23-7.   The Conversation on Riches.
(66) x. 28-31. The Question of Rewards.

The arrangement is mainly topical. The first two stories probably existed as isolated narratives in the earliest tradition. There is no connecting link between the second and the third, but 64, 65, and 66 have a certain unity of theme which may point to their association before the time when Mark composed his Gospel. See further, Intr. 99 f.

Mk. x. 1-12   62. ON ADULTERY   Cf. Mt. xix. 1-9 (v. 32)
(Lk. xvi. 18)

The kernel of the section is the Pronouncement-story on the question of adultery in 2-9. To this narrative the sayings in 11 f. are appended, and the whole is preceded by the geographical statement in 1 which introduces x. 1-31. Cf. Bultmann, 25 f. ; Albertz, 39-41 ; Redlich, 99. The question whether it is right for a man to put away his wife is hostile and suggests that it was known or felt that on this issue the teaching of Jesus was distinctive. The Matthaean additions, κατὰ πᾶσαν αἰτίαν and μὴ ἐπὶ πορνείᾳ (xix. 3, 9), limit the discussion to the rival opinions of the schools of Hillel and Shammai and are secondary. The later character of the Matthaean version is shown also by the fact that it weaves the appended saying in Mk. x. 11 into the story.

In the Markan narrative the freshness of the original encounter is manifest. Jesus does not question the validity of Deut. xxiv. 1 but claims that it was written because of the hardness of men's hearts. He then lifts the issue to a higher plane by relating it to the purpose of God in creating man as indicated in Gen. i. 27 and ii. 24. This argument leads to the principle ὃ οὖν ὁ θεὸς συνέζευξεν ἄνθρωπος μὴ χωριζέτω, and when this is stated, without any reference to the effect produced, the story ends. Only in a community which believed that Jesus had forbidden divorce can it have been current.

Whether the statement that the disciples questioned Jesus further ' in the house ' is redactional or reflects knowledge, is capable of different answers. Dependence on tradition is suggested by the fact that in many sayings and narratives Mark could have imaginatively constructed a mise en scène if he had wished to do so. The saying regarding the husband in 11 transcends Jewish teaching and that in 12, as generally read, contradicts it. For the acute question here raised see the Commentary and the Note on 10-12.

X. 1   Καὶ ἐκεῖθεν ἀναστὰς ἔρχεται εἰς τὰ ὅρια τῆς 'Ιουδαίας καὶ
πέραν τοῦ 'Ιορδάνου, καὶ συνπορεύονται πάλιν ὄχλοι πρὸς αὐτόν,

1. For ἐκεῖθεν v. vi. 1 ; ὅριον v. 17 ;
πέραν iii. 8 ; and for the redundant
ἀναστάς v. Intr. 63. A new stage in
the journey is indicated by εἰς τὰ ὅρια
τῆς 'Ιουδαίας and πέραν τοῦ 'Ιορδάνου.
A textual problem of much interest and
importance is raised by the variant
forms of this statement. (1) Between
the two phrases καί is wanting in C²
D W Δ Θ fam. 1 fam. 13 28 565 579
et al. a b c d f ff i k l q r² aur vg sys pe
geo arm Aug. Cf. Mt. xix. 1. (2) καί
is read by ℵ B C* L Ψ 892 sa bo.
(3) διὰ τοῦ πέραν is attested by A et al.
157 569 575 700 al. pler. syhl aeth.
These readings affect Mark's account
of the journey.

(1) The reading without καί is
strongly attested by Western, Caesarean, and Antiochian authorities, and
is accepted by Wellhausen, 77, Burkitt, 96 n., and others. Manifestly it
has strong claims, but the omission
may be an assimilation to Mt. xix. 1.
Moreover, the expression ' Judaea
beyond Jordan ' is strange, and in the
opinion of Klostermann, 110, is
' against every known speech usage '.
Burkitt's view is that with James and
John, Jesus travelled through Samaria
in order to avoid Herod's dominion,
while Peter and the rest went through
Peraea, and that the expression in
question describes the west side from
Peter's standpoint. This hypothesis
is little more than a conjecture, as
Burkitt admits, and it is rejected by
Rawlinson, 132, Bartlet, 286, and
Blunt, 214. In view of the geographical obscurities in vii. 31 and viii. 10,
the possibility that it is the original
reading cannot be excluded, but only
if the reading with καί is inadmissible.

(2) The reading with καί is exclusively Alexandrian and might be regarded as a learned correction, but
it is somewhat against this suggestion
that Judaea is mentioned first. If it
is original, Mark's meaning may be
that Jesus went first through Judaea

and then crossed the Jordan into
Peraea. Cf. Swete, 214; Lagrange,
256. An advantage of this view would
be that, in this case, there is an ' undesigned coincidence ' with Lk. xvii. 11
and with Jn. vii. 10, x. 40, xi. 54. Cf.
Dodd, Exp. VIII. xxii, pp. 286 ff.;
Streeter, 400 n. Support is given to
it by the fact that x. 1 is a summary
statement which connects the two
sections, viii. 27-ix. 50 and x. 1-52,
and is not simply a local setting for
x. 2-9. Alternatively Mark's intention may be to describe a journey
through Peraea to Judaea. This view
cannot be ruled out on the ground that
' Judaea and beyond Jordan ' is a
careless inversion of the right order
(Klostermann, 110), for there is a
similar inversion in xi. 1, ' When they
drew nigh unto Jerusalem, unto Bethphage and Bethany ', where Jerusalem
is the place reached last (Holtzmann,
156). Nor is it a valid objection that
Jesus would have avoided Herod's
tetrarchy in Peraea, for, not to speak
of the doubtful theory of ' a flight from
Herod ', Jesus had already passed
through Galilee, albeit incognito.
There do not appear to be solid objections against the reading with καί, but,
on the contrary, it is in harmony with
Mark's usage.

(3) There can be little doubt that
the third reading (AV, ' into the coasts
of Judaea by the farther side of
Jordan ') is a scribal attempt to explain that Jesus journeyed via Peraea.
So Swete, 214; Klostermann, 110;
and most commentators. At the same
time it may be a ' correct gloss ' in the
sense that it explains Mark's meaning.
We do not know at what point Jesus
crossed the Jordan eastwards. See
further, Dalman, SSW, 236 f. The
choice lies between the first two readings and on the whole there is most
to be said for that with καί. Each is
difficult, but the first is so difficult as
to be without parallel, while the second

καὶ ὡς εἰώθει πάλιν ἐδίδασκεν αὐτούς. Καὶ ἐπηρώτων αὐτὸν 2
εἰ ἔξεστιν ἀνδρὶ γυναῖκα ἀπολῦσαι, πειράζοντες αὐτόν. ὁ δὲ 3
ἀποκριθεὶς εἶπεν αὐτοῖς Τί ὑμῖν ἐνετείλατο Μωυσῆς; οἱ 4

is only partially explicable as a correction and not unnatural in Mk. The resumption of the teaching ministry is indicated by the double use of πάλιν (v. ii. 1) which here means ' once more '. The second πάλιν is omitted by 348 k sys sa geo. The plural ὄχλοι is unusual in Mk, since everywhere else (36 times) the sing. is used. The singular is read by D W Θ fam. 13 (exc. 124) 28 565 700 et al. a b c d ff i k q r¹ sys sa geo², and is accepted by Turner, 47, *JTS*, xxix. 4 f., and R. H. Lightfoot, 39, 50. Most of these MSS. also read a sing. verb (συμπορεύεται or συνέρχεται) and by reading ὡς εἰώθει καί D b ff i take the meaning to be that the crowd as usual assembles. It is doubtful if any of these readings should be accepted. If x. 1 is a *Sammelbericht*, it is natural that ὄχλοι should be used, and much more probable that ὡς εἰώθει denotes the resumption (πάλιν) of the customary teaching ministry.

συνπορεύομαι*. εἴωθα*, Mt. xxvii. 15, Lk. iv. 16, Ac. xvii. 2**. For διδάσκω v. i. 21. Matthew introduces the passage by saying καὶ ἐγένετο ὅτε ἐτέλεσεν ὁ Ἰησοῦς τοὺς λόγους τούτους, μετῆρεν ἀπὸ τῆς Γαλιλαίας (xix. 1). He omits ἀναστάς, says that many multitudes followed Him, and adds καὶ ἐθεράπευσεν αὐτοὺς ἐκεῖ. Luke omits Mk. x. 1-12 but has a parallel saying on divorce from Q in xvi. 18.

2 f. προσελθόντες Φαρισαῖοι is omitted by D a b k sys and probably rightly; cf. Wellhausen, 78; Burkitt, 98; Turner, 47, *JTS*, xxix. 5. In this case ἐπηρώτων (v. v. 9) is an impersonal plur., ' People asked him ' or ' he was asked '; cf. x. 13. The question εἰ ἔξεστιν (ii. 24) is probably indirect (cf. Moffatt, Lagrange, 257), but is taken by RV and RSV as direct; v. the note on viii. 23. Here and in 4 and 11 ἀπολύω is used of the divorcing of a wife by her husband, the only kind of

divorce recognized by Jewish Law. For Jewish teaching v. Billerbeck, i. 312-20; Abrahams, i. 66-79; Moore, ii. 121-6. πειράζοντες αὐτόν indicates the intention to put Jesus to the test (cf. viii. 11, xii. 15) either by bringing Him into conflict with the Law or by compromising Him in the eyes of Herod (cf. vi. 17 f.). It may have been added by Mark or an early scribe (om. c).

Matthew adds κατὰ πᾶσαν αἰτίαν in harmony with μὴ ἐπὶ πορνείᾳ in xix. 9 (cf. παρεκτὸς λόγου πορνείας, v. 32). Some commentators (e.g. Bartlet, 287; Wood, 693; Creed, 208; cf. Charles, *The Teaching of the NT on Divorce*, 85 ff.; Streeter, 259) think that the addition more truly defines the actual issue since divorce for adultery was permitted by the Law in Deut. xxiv. 1 ('. . . because he hath found some unseemly thing in her . . .'). In this case the question turns upon the issue with which of the rabbinic schools Jesus agreed, that of Shammai who interpreted the ' unseemly thing ' as adultery or that of Hillel who permitted divorce for even trivial causes. It is much more probable that the question concerned divorce itself; cf. Swete, 215; Rawlinson, 134 f.; Branscomb, 177 f.; McNeile, 274; Smith, 164; Easton, 250; cf. Manson, 292 f.; Branscomb, *Jesus and the Law of Moses*, 149-56; Marshall, *The Challenge of NT Ethics*, 143-8.

Jesus asks what Moses had commanded. If the original question was hostile, the counter-question might have seemed to be playing into their hands, but the sequel proved otherwise. For ἀποκριθεὶς εἶπεν v. Intr. 63. ἐντέλλομαι, xiii. 34*, ' to enjoin '; Cl. LXX, Pap., mostly in mid. The question is not merely dialectical; Jesus accepted the Law of Moses, though He claimed the right to interpret it; cf. vii. 10. In Mt the reference to Moses appears later (xix. 7)

δὲ εἶπαν Ἐπέτρεψεν Μωυσῆς Βιβλίον ἀποστασίου γράψαι καὶ
5 ἀπολῦσαι. ὁ δὲ Ἰησοῦς εἶπεν αὐτοῖς Πρὸς τὴν σκληροκαρδίαν
6 ὑμῶν ἔγραψεν ὑμῖν τὴν ἐντολὴν ταύτην· ἀπὸ δὲ ἀρχῆς κτίσεως
7 ἄρσεν καὶ θῆλυ ἐποίησεν [αὐτούς]· ἕνεκεν τούτου καταλείψει
8 ἄνθρωπος τὸν πατέρα αὐτοῦ καὶ τὴν μητέρα, καὶ ἔσονται οἱ

as an argument used by the Pharisees.
For Μωυσῆς v. i. 44.

4 f. The allusion is to Deut. xxiv. 1b,
καὶ γράψει αὐτῇ βιβλίον ἀποστασίου, καὶ
δώσει εἰς τὰς χεῖρας αὐτῆς, καὶ ἐξαποστελεῖ αὐτὴν ἐκ τῆς οἰκίας αὐτοῦ. The
words assume the practice of divorce
and describe a right to which the wife
is entitled. She is to be given a
βιβλίον ἀποστασίου. The Gk phrase
renders ספר כריתת, ' a writ of cutting
off ' (cf. S. R. Driver, ICC, Deut., in
loc.). βιβλίον* is here used in the sense
of letter or document; cf. G. Schrenk,
KThW, i. 616. ἀποστάσιον*, Mt. v.
31, xix. 7**. In Cl. Gk the word
was used in the phrase ἀποστασίου
δίκη to describe an action against a
freedman for forsaking his προστάτης
and choosing another, Demosth. xxv.
65, cf. xxxv. 48. In the papyri ἀποστασίου συγγραφή means a deed of cession,
VGT, 69. ' The specializing of this
term for divorce is not paralleled in our
documents, but it was clearly the
nearest word to use to represent the
Hebrew phrase.' See further, Kennedy,
121. ἐπέτρεψεν (v. 13*) is suitably
used because the clause in Deut. is conditional. For γράψαι Matthew has δοῦναι.
ἀπολῦσαι (v. 2) in Mk and Mt brings
out the meaning of the LXX, καὶ
ἐξαποστελεῖ αὐτὴν ἐκ τῆς οἰκίας αὐτοῦ.

Jesus does not question the Law but
gives a new turn to the discussion by
declaring that Moses wrote this particular (ταύτην) commandment (ἐντολή,
vii. 8) having regard to (πρός) the
hardness of their hearts. σκληροκαρδία, xvi. [14]*, Mt. xix. 8**, ' hardheartedness ', is not a classical word;
it appears in the LXX in Deut. x. 16,
Jer. iv. 4, Sir. xvi. 10; cf. Ezek. iii. 7.
The implication is that the words
express a merciful concession for the
woman's sake.

6-9. The argument is carried farther
by an appeal to the divine intention
in the creation of man as shown in
Gen. i. 27 and ii. 24. The first quotation ἄρσεν* καὶ θῆλυ* ἐποίησεν αὐτούς
is introduced by ἀπὸ τῆς ἀρχῆς κτίσεως,
' from the beginning of the creation ',
an expression used again in xiii. 19.
Some MSS. (A Θ et al. a l q r² vg
sys pe hl geo¹ Aug) add ὁ θεός, and
others (D W 86 219 b f ff k r¹ aeth arm)
ὁ θεός without αὐτούς, and D 255 b d
ff vg omit κτίσεως. These readings are
explanatory. Wellhausen, 78, claims
that the opening words mean ' at the
beginning of his book ' or ' at the beginning of Genesis ', with ἔγραψεν
Μωυσῆς understood; cf. Klostermann,
111; Rawlinson, 135. Torrey, TG,
12, prefers the hypothesis of mistranslation for ' In the beginning the
Creator . . .'. Cf. Mt. xix. 4, ὁ κτίσας.
The use of ἀπό for מן is illustrated in
Psa. lxxvii. (lxxviii.) 2 and similar
prepositional phrases are found in
Mt. xiii. 35, xxiv. 21, Lk. xi. 50;
Rom. i. 20; 2 Pet. iii. 4. Cf. Dalman,
167. For the form ἄρσην v. Moulton, ii. 103 f. κτίσις, xiii. 19, xvi.
[15]*.

The second quotation from Gen. ii.
24 immediately follows. The words are
used of Adam and ἕνεκεν τούτου refers
to the woman's origin from his rib.
As freely used by Jesus the phrase
refers to the fact of creation; it is
because God made them male and
female that a man will leave his father
and mother and the two will become
one flesh. Virtually the words are
taken as those of God, or of Scripture;
cf. 1 Cor. vi. 16, Eph. v. 31. Probably
(as against McNeile, 272) this is what
Matthew means (xix. 5) when he
inserts καὶ εἶπεν, an addition made in
Mk. x. 7 in D W Θ et al. fam. 13 28

ΔΎΟ εἰς cάρκα μίαν· ὥστε οὐκέτι εἰσὶν δύο ἀλλὰ μία σάρξ· ὃ ὁ θεὸς συνέζευξεν ἄνθρωπος μὴ χωριζέτω. Καὶ εἰς τὴν οἰκίαν $^9_{10}$ πάλιν οἱ μαθηταὶ περὶ τούτου ἐπηρώτων αὐτόν. καὶ λέγει αὐτοῖς 11 ⸀Ὃς ἂν ἀπολύσῃ τὴν γυναῖκα αὐτοῦ καὶ γαμήσῃ ἄλλην μοιχᾶται ἐπ᾽ αὐτήν, καὶ ἐὰν ⸀γυνὴ ἐξέλθῃ ἀπὸ τοῦ ἀνδρὸς καὶ⸂ γαμήσῃ 12

12 αὐτὴ ἀπολύσασα τὸν ἄνδρα αὐτῆς

543 565 1071 *et al.* b c ff g² q r¹ vg geo arm.

In Mk (not in Mt) the words καὶ προσκολληθήσεται τῇ γυναικὶ αὐτοῦ (or πρὸς τ. γ.) are omitted by ℵ B Ψ 892 sys, perhaps by inadvertence (cf. Klostermann, 111 f.), though Lagrange, 259, judges otherwise. For ἕνεκεν *v.* viii. 35. καταλείπω, xii. 19, 21, xiv. 52*. The use of εἰς c. acc. for the predicative nom. in ἔσονται . . . εἰς σάρκα μίαν is taken over from the LXX where it is an over literal rendering of the Heb. use of ל. Moulton, i. 72, 76, points to the presence of this construction in the papyri (*VGT*, 186) where it appears to be an extension of the use of εἰς expressing destination. Cf. Howard, ii. 462. σάρξ, xiii. 20, xiv. 38*.

From this passage the deduction ὥστε οὐκέτι εἰσὶν δύο ἀλλὰ μία σάρξ is drawn, in which ὥστε c. indic. (*v.* i. 27) states a factual consequence. For οὐκέτι *v.* v. 3. The positive command then follows ὃ ¹ ὁ θεὸς συνέζευξεν ἄνθρωπος μὴ χωριζέτω. συνζεύγνυμι*, Mt. xix. 6**, is often used of the marriage relationship (*v.* LS); χωρίζω*, ' to separate ', Cl., LXX, Pap. *VGT*, 696, observes that the word has become almost a technical term for divorce. In 1 Cor. vii. 10 this saying of Jesus is cited. In ἄνθρωπος the reference is to the husband rather than to a judicial authority, for in Jewish practice divorce was effected by the husband himself. Behind the imagery Jesus has in mind personal relationships. It is folly to treat His saying as a legal prescription. His words are

spiritual, and therefore are the more binding, but their application is left to the enlightened Christian consciousness.

10-12. These sayings are appended to the narrative of 2-9 which is a unity in itself. In Mt the first saying, introduced by λέγω δὲ ὑμῖν, is made part of the story. As in vii. 17, Mark explains that in the house (οἰκία i. 29) the disciples again asked Jesus concerning this matter (περὶ τούτου). For πάλιν *v.* ii. 1 ; οἱ μαθηταί ii. 16 ; ἐπερωτάω *v.* 9. αὐτοῦ is added in A D W *et al.* fam. 1 fam. 13 543 565 700 *al.* *pler.* it vg sys pe hl sa geo aeth.

Introduced by καὶ λέγει αὐτοῖς, the first saying declares without qualification that a man who divorces his wife and marries another commits adultery against her. For ἀπολύω *v.* x. 2 ; γαμέω vi. 17. μοιχάομαι, x. 12*, Mt. v. 32, xix. 9 (?)**, = Cl. μοιχεύω, ' to commit adultery' ; LXX (Jer., Ezek.), Pap. (*VGT*, 416). ἐπ᾽ αὐτήν refers to the first wife and therefore goes beyond Jewish Law, in which a man can commit adultery against another married man but not against his own wife. Cf. Manson, *SJ*, 136. Matthew's addition μὴ ἐπὶ πορνείᾳ is secondary ; cf. McNeile, 274. So also his omission of ἐπ᾽ αὐτήν. For ὃς ἂν c. subj. *v.* iii. 29.

The second saying, which is peculiar to Mk, makes the same statement regarding the wife. If she divorces her husband and marries another, she commits adultery. This view is contrary to Jewish Law. Cf. Josephus, *Ant.* xv. 7. 10, who says of the action of Salome in divorcing her husband :

¹ οὖν, read by most MSS., is rightly omitted with D k Or ; *v.* Turner, *JTS*, xxix. 5. The particle is rarely found in Mk (Mt, nearly 60 times ; Lk, some 30 times ; Jn, nearly 200). It should also probably be omitted in Mk. xi. 31, thus leaving two examples (xiii. 35, xv. 12) and xvi. [19]* ; *v.* Turner, *JTS*, xxviii. 20 f.

ἄλλον μοιχᾶται.

' though this was not according to the Jewish laws; for with us it is lawful for a husband to do so; but a wife if she departs from her husband, cannot of herself be married to another, unless her former husband put her away '. In respect of impotence, denial of conjugal rights, and unreasonable restriction of movement, a wife could sue for divorce, but even so divorce was the husband's act. Cf. Moore, ii. 125. For the greater freedom in the Jewish community at Elephantine v. Aramaic Papyri of Fifth Century B.C., ed. Cowley, Nos. 9 and 15. In view of Jewish custom 12 has often been explained as a secondary addition or modification based on Roman Law; cf. H. A. W. Meyer, i. 162; B. Weiss, 160; J. Weiss, 253; Schmiedel, EB, col. 1851; Wellhausen, 78; Gould, 186; Bruce, i. 409; Bartlet, 290. Accepting the reading of sys, ' The woman that leaves her husband and becomes the wife of another commits adultery, and the man that leaves his wife and takes another commits adultery ', in which 11 and 12 are reversed,[1] Burkitt, 99-101, suggests that Jesus is referring to the well-known case of Herodias, and explains the saying as ' one of the really primitive features of the Gospel of Mark '.

Unfortunately, the exegetical question is complicated by textual considerations.

(1) The WH text, καὶ ἐὰν αὐτὴ ἀπολύσασα τὸν ἄνδρα αὐτῆς γαμήσῃ ἄλλον is attested by א B C L Δ Ψ 579 892 1342 sa bo aeth. The reading is exclusively Alexandrian and may be a stylistic and exegetical recast of an earlier text. It is somewhat ambiguous since the woman (αὐτή) may be the one in x. 11 who is divorced.

(2) ἐὰν γυνὴ ἀπολύσῃ τὸν ἄνδρα αὐτῆς καὶ γαμηθῇ ἄλλῳ is read by A et al. 22 118 1071 al. pler. f g² r² vg sype hl Aug (ἐαν ἀπολ. γ. W fam. 1 geo¹).[2] Here

the evidence is more widely distributed, but it is not impressive, perhaps because from early times Nos. 1 and 3 (v. infra) were serious competitors. The reading is accepted by Lagrange, 260 f., as accounting best for the textual variants.

(3) A third reading, γυνὴ ἐὰν (ἐὰν γ. D) ἐξέλθῃ ἀπὸ (τοῦ) ἀνδρὸς καὶ γαμήσῃ ἄλλον (γαμηθῇ ἄλλῳ), is attested by D Θ fam. 13 28 543 565 700 a b ff (k) q arm sys. This reading represents the text current at Antioch, Caesarea, Carthage, Italy and Gaul at least as early as c. 150 A.D. It is accepted as original by Wellhausen, 78 (Nur so kann Mc geschrieben haben) and Burkitt (v. supra), and is favoured by Allen, 133, Montefiore, i. 234, and Wood, 693. It is open to the objection that it is a modification of 1 or 2 to bring the text into agreement with Jewish marriage customs; but, as Lohmeyer, 202, observes, it is not in complete agreement since, without being divorced, the woman marries a second husband presumably while the first is still alive. This is precisely the situation to which Burkitt draws attention in the case of Herodias.

On the whole, there is most to be said for accepting No. 3. Between Nos. 1 and 2 it is very difficult to decide, and in itself this fact suggests that each is a modification of an earlier text. Both, moreover, can readily be explained as primitive attempts to transform No. 3 into a regulation concerning divorce in line with Gentile practice. Further, No. 3 is much nearer to what may be presumed to be the original form of the saying. Although Jesus can have commented on pagan customs, it is much more likely that He had a Jewish situation in mind, while it would not be strange if later His words were adapted to conditions which obtained at Rome. Again, the reading agrees with 1 Cor.

[1] Along with W 1 geo¹.
[2] Almost all the Latin texts read either nupserit or nubserit preceded by alio or alii. k has nubet and d alium duxerit.

vii. 10, in which Paul cites, as a word of the Lord, the command that a wife depart not (μὴ χωρισθῆναι) from her husband, nor is it likely to have been adapted under the influence of this passage since the vocabulary is different and in it no reference is made to adultery. The objection that, after x. 2-9, we should expect sayings on *divorce*, is not sustained by other appended sayings in ii. 21 f., 27 f., iii. 27-9, iv. 21-5, which introduce *allied* themes rather than the identical subject previously treated.

Can the key to the problem be found in the underlying Aramaic? Cf. Manson, *SJ*, 137. Torrey, 91, 302, *TG*, 94 f., suggests that a passive participle has been mistranslated as active, and that, in agreement with Lk. xvi. 18b, we should read, ' And if she who has been divorced by her husband marries another, he commits adultery '. For this suggestion little more can be said than that mistranslation is possible, but the harsh change of subject is unwarranted, while if we read 'she ',[1] the statement is contrary to Jewish teaching. Lk. xvi. 18b is best regarded as a different saying.

DETACHED NOTE ON THE TEACHING OF JESUS REGARDING MARRIAGE AND DIVORCE

From x. 2-12 it is clear that Jesus regarded marriage as an indissoluble union and that He placed husband and wife in a relationship of equality. In these respects His teaching went beyond Jewish and Pagan conceptions, giving to marriage a position of the highest dignity. This positive emphasis is His gift to the Church and the world. It is more difficult to apply His teaching to the problem of divorce in the modern world. For Christians His words are regulative, but in particular cases they need to be interpreted under the guidance of the Spirit (Jn. xvi. 13). It cannot be assumed that the question is settled by simply quoting His words ; for the record is limited to His reply to a hostile question and to detached sayings in Mk. x. 11 f., Mt. v. 32, and Lk. xvi. 18. Moreover, the trend of His teaching is against legalism. The exceptive clauses in Mt represent the first stage in a process by which His sayings have been treated as enactments, but in their original form they are operative principles all the more searching because they have this spiritual character. The individual Christian will not be left in doubt if he will observe them under the illumination of the Spirit in the Church and in his own understanding. For society at large the issue is more complex. Still less in this realm can the words of Jesus be treated as laws. Nevertheless, for its own protection and well-being, society will do well to be guided by His positive teaching in defining grounds for divorce which threaten personal and family life. In the social question the Church has a vital part to play. It is her duty to insist that Christ's emphasis on the sanctity of the marriage relationship is the over-riding principle by which grounds for divorce must be judged.

Mk. x. 13-16   **63. ON CHILDREN**   Cf. Mt. xix. 13-15
Lk. xviii. 15-17

This story circulated in the earliest Christian community because it showed the attitude of Jesus to children, and by continual repetition it has gained the rounded form of a Pronouncement-story. Cf. Bultmann, 32 ;

[1] Cf. F. C. Grant, *The Earliest Gospel*, 117.

Dibelius, 43 ; Redlich, 99. Details of time and place have disappeared, and of the original circumstances only as many are related as provide a setting for the words and actions of Jesus. In these its point lies. The arrangement is topical. After a story about marriage it seemed fitting to record an incident regarding children. It is therefore mistaken, with earlier commentators, to associate the children with the house mentioned in x. 10. Probably, an additional recommendation to the Evangelist was the fact that 15 speaks of the conditions under which men can enter into the Kingdom.

The beauty of the story is universally recognized. To a degree which leaves an indelible impression in the mind of all readers, the story shows that ' hardly anything is more characteristic of Jesus than His attitude to children ' (Bartlet, 292). It also reveals how He transmuted eschatological conceptions of the Kingdom and presented it as a gift of God and as an experience into which, if they have the receptiveness of a child, men may enter here and now. It is very fitting that since 1549 the story has been included in the English Baptismal Office in its Markan form. Cf. Swete, 222 ; Rawlinson, 137.

13   Καὶ προσέφερον αὐτῷ παιδία ἵνα αὐτῶν ἅψηται· οἱ δὲ μαθη-
14 ταὶ ἐπετίμησαν αὐτοῖς. ἰδὼν δὲ ὁ Ἰησοῦς ἠγανάκτησεν καὶ

13. The story begins without any statement of time or place and the circumstances are indicated in the barest possible manner. The sole connecting link is καί. προσέφερον is an impersonal plur. as in i. 32, etc., ' People were bringing . . .'. This impersonal use of the act. instead of the pass. is usual in Hebrew and Aramaic and is uncommon in Gk apart from λέγουσι and φασί; cf. Howard, ii. 447 f. Luke retains the construction (with δέ for καί), but Matthew replaces it by the passive, τότε προσηνέχθησαν αὐτῷ παιδία (xix. 13). For προσφέρω v. i. 44 ; παιδίον v. 39. The children may have been of any age from infancy to twelve years; it is from Luke that the idea of ' infants ' is derived ; cf. τὰ βρέφη, Lk. xviii. 15. Those who brought the children are not necessarily the mothers ; they may have been fathers or other‘children.

The purpose of the touching, which otherwise in Mk is used of the sick (cf. the note on ἅπτομαι in i. 41), is to obtain a blessing. Cf. Gen. xlviii. 14 where Jacob lays his hands on the heads of Ephraim and Manasseh, and for modern Jewish parallels v. Abra-

hams, i. 119 ; Billerbeck, i. 807 f. There is no need to regard so natural an action as magical. Matthew explains the Markan phrase by ἵνα τὰς χεῖρας ἐπιθῇ αὐτοῖς and adds καὶ προσεύξηται.

The intention of the disciples in rebuking (ἐπιτιμάω, i. 25) those who brought the children is to protect Jesus against apparently embarrassing attentions. The possible ambiguity of αὐτοῖς (ℵ B C L Δ Ψ 579 892 1342 c k bo) is explained by the substitution of τοῖς προσφέρουσιν or τοῖς φέρουσιν in most MSS. (v. Legg). In D Θ 565 700 a c f ff sys pe aeth αὐτοῦ is added to οἱ μαθηταί (cf. Mt. x. 10).

14. This verse describes the response of Jesus. It is because of this response, and the saying in which it is expressed, that the story was preserved. ἰδών recalls viii. 33 ; because of what He sees Jesus acts and speaks. ἀγανακτέω, x. 41, xiv. 4*, Mt. xx. 24, xxi. 15, xxvi. 8, Lk. xiii. 14**, ' to be vexed ', ' indignant ', <ἄγαν ' much ', ἄχομαι ' to grieve '; Cl., LXX, Pap. Here only in the Gospels is indignation ascribed to Jesus; in this narrative Matthew and Luke omit the word.

εἶπεν αὐτοῖς "Αφετε τὰ παιδία ἔρχεσθαι πρός με, μὴ κωλύετε
αὐτά, τῶν γὰρ τοιούτων ἐστὶν ἡ βασιλεία τοῦ θεοῦ. ἀμὴν λέγω 15
ὑμῖν, ὃς ἂν μὴ δέξηται τὴν βασιλείαν τοῦ θεοῦ ὡς παιδίον, οὐ

With it may be compared Mark's reference to anger in iii. 5 and to sighing
in viii. 12 and most of all his account
of the emotion of Jesus in Gethsemane
in xiv. 33 f. The object of a man's
indignation is always revealing; here
it is the disciples' rebuff to children.
The indignation felt affects the form
of the rebuke, for there is no connecting καί (as in Mt and Lk) between
ἄφετε τὰ παιδία ἔρχεσθαι πρός με and
μὴ κωλύετε αὐτά. For similar examples
of asyndeton v. i. 27, ii. 7, iv. 39 f., vi.
38, viii. 17 f., ix. 19. For ἀφίημι v.
i. 34; κωλύω ix. 38 f.*. In the story
ἔρχεσθαι πρός με means ' to approach
me ', but from such expressions the
idea of ' coming to Jesus ' took its
rise; cf. also i. 40, 45, ii. 3, 13, iii. 8,
v. 15, 22, 27, 33, vi. 31, x. 50.
The well-known words which follow
are somewhat ambiguous. The gen.
τῶν τοιούτων is possessive; cf. Plummer, 236; Gould, 188; and ἐστίν
means ' belongs ' (Moffatt, RSV, Goodspeed). Cf. Lagrange, 263, appartient.
The Kingdom belongs to such because
they receive it as a gift. The children
are not treated as symbolic; they
themselves possess the right spirit,
which is not merely humility but receptiveness. So Rawlinson, 137;
Branscomb, 180. Branscomb rightly
observes that in justification by faith
the same attitude is enjoined. For the
attitude of Jesus to children cf. Burkitt,
285 f.: ' Apart from the Gospels, I
cannot find that early Christian literature exhibits the slightest sympathy
towards the young '. For Jewish
teaching cf. Billerbeck, i. 786; Montefiore, Rabbinic Literature and Gospel
Teachings, 258 f., 270. ἡ βασιλεία τοῦ
θεοῦ (v. i. 15) is the gift of the divine
rule; cf. Mt. v. 3, ὅτι αὐτῶν ἐστιν ἡ
βασιλεία τῶν οὐρανῶν.
Of great interest and importance is
the concurrence of the statement that
the Kingdom belongs to children with

the command ἄφετε τὰ παιδία ἔρχεσθαι
πρός με. The implication is not far
distant that in a true sense Jesus Himself is the Kingdom; to use the word
of Origen, Comm. Mt. t. xiv. 7, He is
αὐτοβασιλεία. See the article of K. L.
Schmidt, βασιλεία, KThW, i. 590 f.
  15. For ἀμὴν λέγω ὑμῖν v. iii. 28;
ὃς ἂν c. subj. iii. 29; δέχομαι vi. 11.
The βασιλεία (i. 15) is here conceived
as a gift (of God) which a man receives
and welcomes ὡς παιδίον. This phrase
is most naturally taken to mean ' as
a child receives it ', that is, simply
and naturally, without making any
claims. Cf. Dodd, 41 f.; Branscomb,
180. It is possible, however, to read
παιδίον as an acc. with the meaning
' as one receives a little child '; so
W. K. L. Clarke, New Testament
Problems, 37 f.; cf. C. J. Cadoux,
230 f. But the parallel sayings in
Mt. xviii. 3 and Jn. iii. 3, 5 support
the former interpretation; cf. also
Mt. xi. 25 = Lk. x. 21. So Lohmeyer,
204 f.
  With strong emphasis Jesus says
that the man who does not so receive
the Kingdom shall not enter into it.
For οὐ μή c. subj. v. ix. 1 and for the
idea of ' entering into ' the Kingdom
v. the note on ix. 47. It may be that
two different ideas of the Kingdom
are combined: the present Kingdom is
received, the future Kingdom is entered. Cf. Cadoux, 230 n. In this
case the meaning of the saying is that
the man who does not now receive the
Kingdom as a gift, with the simplicity
of a child, will not enter into it when
it is finally established. J. Schneider,
KThW, ii. 674, speaks of the Synoptic
sayings which speak of entering into
the Kingdom as prophetisch-apokaly-
ptishe Worte. Cf. also Lohmeyer, 204.
  This reading of the saying may be
correct, but it is not easy to believe
that a distinction of this kind is intended. It is easier to suppose that

16 μὴ εἰσέλθῃ εἰς αὐτήν. καὶ ἐναγκαλισάμενος αὐτὰ κατευλόγει
τιθεὶς τὰς χεῖρας ἐπ᾽ αὐτά.

a single idea runs through the saying, namely, that men who do not receive the Kingdom as a gift cannot enter upon its blessings and responsibilities. Cf. the distinction in *Berakoth*, ii. 2 f. (Danby, 3) between taking upon oneself the yoke of the kingdom of heaven by reciting the *Shema*ʿ and afterwards taking the yoke of the commandments.

The verse is omitted by Matthew in consequence of his use of the parallel saying in xviii. 3; by Luke it is reproduced verbatim. Bultmann, 32, and A. Meyer, 45, explain it as a free logion which has been added to the original Apothegm which has its point in 14. If 15 is eschatological in meaning there is reason for this suggestion. We recall also the suggestion of Turner, 48, that 15 is more appropriate in the context of ix. 33-7. But opinions regarding the original form of the

story are necessarily speculative, and if 15 is explained as above it is harmonious with 14. There can be no question of the genuineness of the saying. Bultmann, 110, includes it in his (short) list of those which are characteristic of the preaching of Jesus. Cf. also *JW*, 206.

16. The action of Jesus is as significant as His words. He took the children in His arms and blessed them, laying His hands upon them. For ἐναγκαλίζομαι *v.* ix. 36*. κατευλογέω** is a strengthened form of εὐλογέω; Plutarch 2. 66 A, Tob. xi. 1, 17. Cf. Swete, 222; Rawlinson, 137. With τιθεὶς τὰς χεῖρας ἐπ᾽ αὐτά cf. viii. 25. Matthew omits 16a and adds ἐπορεύθη ἐκεῖθεν. Luke omits the whole verse. D c f ff q r¹ sysˢ read προσκαλεσάμενος. Many commentators quote Bengel, *Plus fecit, quam rogatus erat.*

Mk. x. 17-22   64. THE RICH MAN AND   Cf. Mt. xix. 16-21
ETERNAL LIFE   Lk. xviii. 18-23

Like the Blessing of the Children this narrative has the form of a Pronouncement-story; but it contains more detail than is usual in a narrative of this kind. Mark has information which enables him to weave x. 17-22, 23-7 and 28-31 into a whole. In substance this analysis agrees with those of Bultmann and Dibelius. Bultmann, 20, includes the whole of 17-31 among the Apothegms, but he finds the basic unit in 17-22, to which supplements are attached in 23-7, 28-30, and 31. Dibelius, 50, classifies 17 ff. as a Paradigm ' of a less pure type ' which, with its necessary details, is related for the sake of the phrase in 25 concerning the rich in the Kingdom of God, and together with its ' tempering interpretation ' in 27 has been worked up into a little dialogue. The contents of 17-22 show that Mark had a fuller knowledge of the incident than would have been supplied by a Pronouncement-story pure and simple. He relates that, as Jesus was going forth into the way, a man ran to Him and fell on his knees. The vividness of this account is lost in Mt. xix. 16 : ' And behold one came to him ', and in Lk. xviii. 18 : ' And a certain ruler asked him '. Matthew softens the question, ' Good Master, what shall I do that I may inherit eternal life ? ' (Mk and Lk), so that it becomes, ' Master, what good thing shall I do that I may have eternal life ? ' (xix. 16), and replaces the reply, ' Why callest thou me good ? none is good save one, even God ' (Mk and, substantially, Lk) with ' Why askest thou me concerning that which is good ? One there is who is good ' (xix. 17). The greater originality of the Markan narrative is manifest.   But this is not all.   When the man claims to have observed the commandments from his youth, Mark says that Jesus ' looking upon him loved him ' (x. 21), and that when he was challenged to sell all and follow Him, ' his face fell ' (x. 22), and explains that he had large estates.

The details are too deeply woven into the story to be regarded as amplifications.   Moreover, 23-7 and 28-31 are not self-contained narratives current in their own right, but incidents recorded because it was remembered that they were connected with the story of the Rich Man's Question.   It is much less probable that the connexion extends backwards to the Blessing of the Children and the house mentioned in x. 10.   Lagrange's suggestion (p. 264) that the man, hearing the Kingdom promised to children, asked if he himself possessed the necessary qualifications, is slenderly based.   The position would seem to be that while 17-31 forms a whole, 1-31 is topically determined by the Evangelist's interest in the Kingdom of God and in teaching about sacrifice and renunciation.   Of outstanding interest is the doctrinal issue raised by the question, ' Why callest thou me good ? ', and only second in importance is the approximation to Johannine teaching in the use of the expression ' eternal life ' as synonymous with ' the Kingdom of God '.

Καὶ ἐκπορευομένου αὐτοῦ εἰς ὁδὸν προσδραμὼν εἷς καὶ γονυ- 17
πετήσας αὐτὸν ἐπηρώτα αὐτόν   Διδάσκαλε ἀγαθέ, τί ποιήσω

17. Unlike 2-9 and 13-16 the present story is connected with the journey mentioned in 1 ʼby the gen. abs. ἐκπορευομένου αὐτοῦ and the phrase εἰς ὁδόν. The expressions are Markan (for ἐκπορεύομαι v. HS², 12 and for εἰς ὁδόν v. the notes on viii. 3, 27, xi. 8) and may be editorial (cf. Bultmann, 20; Klostermann, 114), but the absence of such links in 2-9 and 13-16 encourages the inference that Mark is following a tradition. For the free use of the gen. abs. v. the note on v. 2. The description of the man running to Jesus (προστρέχω, ix. 15*) and falling upon his knees (γονυπετέω, i. 40*) is vivid. Mt and Lk omit these details. It is all the more noteworthy that Mark has no characterization of the man himself save εἷς. Luke speaks of him as τις ἄρχων and Matthew ὁ νεανίσκος (cf. Mk. x. 20, ἐκ νεότητός μου). The Markan story implies that he is no longer in his first youth. Only at the end are we told that he was rich (v. 22). The familiar title ' Rich Young Ruler ' is thus a composite description, and apart from the reference to his wealth is probably misleading. For Mark's use of εἷς = τις v. Intr. 60. ἐπερωτάω, v. 9. The Gospel according to the Hebrews mentions two rich men.

The address διδάσκαλε ἀγαθέ is very rare in Jewish literature, but similar examples of the use of the adjective are common in Gk. Dalman, 337, and Billerbeck, ii. 24, cite a single Jewish example in the sense of ' kind master '. The reply of Jesus proves that the phrase was used. The address was flattering, but there is no need, with Dalman, to describe it as ' mere insolent flattery '. The rest of the story, and particularly v. 21a, sufficiently refutes such a suggestion. In the OT ἀγαθός is frequently applied to God, e.g. Psa. cxvii. (cxviii.) 1 f., 1 Chron. xvi. 34, 2 Chron. v. 13, 2 Esdr. iii. 11. The Jewish view is that God alone is good, and that in the sense that He is good no one else is ἀγαθός. Cf. W. Grundmann, KThW, i. 14-16. This idea is powerfully expressed in Rom. vii. 18: οἶδα γὰρ ὅτι οὐκ οἰκεῖ ἐν ἐμοί, τοῦτ' ἔστιν ἐν τῇ σαρκί

18 ἵνα ζωὴν αἰώνιον κληρονομήσω; ὁ δὲ 'Ιησοῦς εἶπεν αὐτῷ Τί
19 με λέγεις ἀγαθόν; οὐδεὶς ἀγαθὸς εἰ μὴ εἷς ὁ θεός. τὰς ἐντολὰς

μου, ἀγαθόν. Nevertheless, this usage
does not obliterate moral distinctions.
In a derivative sense created things
are good (Gen. i. 31, בוֹט, LXX καλὰ
λίαν). Paul speaks of the law and the
commandment as good (Rom. vii. 12,
16). Later Jewish writings speak of
the ἀγαθὸς ἀνήρ and the ἀγαθὴ καρδία;
v. the passages cited by Lohmeyer,
209 n.², Test. XII Patr., Sym. iv. 4, 7,
Dan i. 4, Asher iv. 1, etc. Jesus also
speaks of 'the evil and the good' on
whom God makes His sun to rise
(Mt. v. 45); cf. also Mt. xii. 35, Lk.
viii. 15. The distinguishing feature
would appear to be that man is not
good absolutely and apart from divine
grace. For διδάσκαλε v. iv. 38; ἀγαθός,
x. 18 (bis)*.

ζωὴ αἰώνιος, x. 30* (cf. ix. 43, 45),
is the LXX rendering of םלוֹע ייח, and
appears first in Dan. xii. 2 in connexion with the idea of the resurrection of the dead. Cf. also Psa. Sol.
iii. 16, 1 Enoch xxxvii. 4, xl. 9, lviii. 3,
2 Macc. vii. 9, 4 Macc. xv. 3. In
origin the conception is eschatological;
ζωὴ αἰώνιος is life in 'the coming age'
which man 'inherits' (κληρονομεῖν* as
here), 'receives' (λαμβάνειν, Mk. x.
30), 'gains' (περιποιεῖσθαι, Hermas,
Mand. iii. 5), 'enters into' (εἰσελθεῖν,
cf. Mk. ix. 43, 45). No mere equivalent of immortality, it is a gift which
a man receives from God in the resurrection. Cf. Dalman, 156-62; Bultmann, KThW, ii. 844-74. The richer
conception of eternal life as a present
possession (ἔχειν ζ. α., Jn. iii. 15)
naturally does not emerge in this
story.

The man asks concerning the conditions by which he may enter into the
inheritance of eternal life. It is to
press ποιήσω too much if it is taken
to mean 'How can I earn it?'. Evi-
dently he thinks that there are conditions over and above those in the Law.
Apart from the change to ποιήσας,
Luke reproduces the question closely.

Matthew's alterations go deeper. In
preparation for his version of the reply
of Jesus in xix. 17 he drops ἀγαθέ after
διδάσκαλε and gives the request in the
form τί ἀγαθὸν ποιήσω ἵνα σχῶ ζωὴν
αἰώνιον;. This form, and in particular
σχῶ (' get ', cf. xxi. 38), suggest a goal
reached by effort.

18. Jesus takes up the word ἀγαθός.
Why does the man use a word which
by right can be used of God alone?
τί με λέγεις ἀγαθόν; οὐδεὶς ἀγαθὸς εἰ μὴ
εἷς ὁ θεός. 'No one is good save God
alone.' E. F. F. Bishop, ET, xlix.
363-6, suggests the rendering: 'There
is none good save the One', and explains ὁ θεός as an interpretative
Markan addition; cf. ii. 7, xii. 29, 32.
Cf. Mt. xix. 17, εἷς ἐστιν ὁ ἀγαθός.
This view is more probable than the
suggestion of Torrey, TG, 20, that the
Aramaic original implied the neuter.

The implications of the question are
variously estimated. We may dismiss
simplifications which overstress the
fact that με is an enclitic; the use of
the question along with the statement
that God alone is good implies a contrast of some kind between Jesus and
God. (1) Some commentators see an
implicit acknowledgment of imper-
fection and sin; cf. G. Volkmar, Die
Evangelien (1870), 489; C. G. Montefiore, i. 239 f. This interpretation is
not only unnecessary in itself, but is
at variance with the entire Synoptic
portraiture of Jesus. (2) A second
view, held by many of the Fathers
(v. Swete, 223 f.; Lagrange, 264 f.),
is that the question was intended to
lead the man to a perception of His
divinity. Ambrose, for example, observes: 'What he (the man) does not
believe, Christ adds, that he may
believe in the Son of God, not as a
Good Master, but as the Good God',
De Fide, ii. 1. Among modern commentators Turner, 48, suggests that it
may not be fanciful to think that Jesus
had His disciples in mind, whom He

οἶδας Μὴ μοιχεγςηc, Μὴ πορνεγςηc, Μὴ κλέψηc, Μὴ ψεγδο-

was now trying to make realize that, because of His Sonship, He had in truth a right to the term ' good '. Of this type of interpretation one must entertain strong suspicions ; there does not appear to be any ground for such doctrinal refinements. (3) Some interpreters, of whom Warfield, *Christology and Criticism*, 139, may be cited as an example, have approached the question from this very angle, maintaining that Christ's concern is not to glorify Himself but God, not to give any instruction concerning His own person, but to point to the will of God as the only prescription for pleasing Him. There is much to be said for this view, but it is open to the charge of oversimplification ; it avoids the sense of contrast which pervades the saying. (4) The same must be said of yet another type of exposition, from very early times, according to which Jesus repudiates the predicate ' good ' from the questioner's point of view, and seeks to correct the man's flattery. Many of the Fathers, including Victor (cf. Lagrange, 265), have explained the question in this way, and among modern commentators Swete, 223 f., Bartlet, 293, Blunt, 217, Plummer, 238 f., Rawlinson, 139. So far as it goes, this interpretation is on right lines, but it needs to be combined with other views, as in the exegesis of Rawlinson and Plummer (*v. infra*). (5) The explanation that Jesus used ἀγαθός in the sense of ' gracious ' (*gütig*) needs only to be mentioned ; cf. Wellhausen, 80 ; Dalman, 337 ; Lagrange, 264 ; W. Wagner, *ZNTW* (1907), 143-61. P. W. Schmiedel, *HJSuppl.* (1909), 68, administered the *coup de grâce* to this view when he observed that its advocates ' do not reflect that Jesus cannot have justly regarded himself as morally good if he repudiated even the epithet " gracious " '.

The most complete explanations recognize (6) that, while the main interest of Jesus is the man himself

and his facile appreciation of goodness, His question implies a tacit contrast between the absolute goodness of God and His own goodness as subject to growth and trial in the circumstances of the Incarnation. Origen, *De Principiis*, I. ii. 3, carries this view into the relationships of the Persons of the Trinity, but most modern advocates of it think rather of the conditions of the Incarnate Life. Cf. H. A. W. Meyer, i. 164 f. ; Gould, 190 ; Plummer, *St. Lk*, 422 ; Wood, 693 ; Rawlinson, 139. H. R. Mackintosh, *The Doctr. of the Person of Christ*, 37, maintains that the words are not a veiled confession of moral delinquency, but a disclaimer of *God's* perfect goodness on the part of One who learned obedience by the things which He suffered, being tempted in all points like as we are (Heb. iv. 15, v. 8).

The secondary character of the Matthaean version of the question is generally recognized ; cf. W. C. Allen, *St. Mt*, 208 ; McNeile, 277 ; Lagrange, 264. Taking exception to the Markan form on doctrinal grounds Matthew has recast it so that it becomes, τί με ἐρωτᾷς περὶ τοῦ ἀγαθοῦ; εἷς ἐστιν ὁ ἀγαθός, and to this he adds εἰ δὲ θέλεις εἰς τὴν ζωὴν εἰσελθεῖν, τήρει τὰς ἐντολάς. The masc. εἷς following upon the neut. τοῦ ἀγαθοῦ shows that he is following the Markan text. Luke adheres to his source. The claim of F. C. Conybeare, *HJ*, i. 96-113, that the Marcionite reading in Lk. xviii. 19 μή με λέγε ἀγαθόν, εἷς ἐστιν ἀγαθὸς ὁ θεὸς ὁ πατήρ, found also in the Clementine Homilies (iii. 57, xvii. 4, xviii. 1, 3), is original, has not been sustained. Cf. Warfield, *op. cit.* 139-45 ; H. A. W. Meyer, ii. 266.

19. Jesus directs the man's attention to the Law, τὰς ἐντολὰς (vii. 8) οἶδας. Thereby He shows how highly He esteemed the Law as containing the norm of conduct. Cf. Branscomb, 182, *Jesus and the Law of Moses, passim*. Nevertheless, as the rest of the story shows,

μαρτγρήςμς, Μὴ ἀποστερήσῃς, Τίμα τὸν πατέρα coy καὶ τὴν
20 μητέρα. ὁ δὲ ἔφη αὐτῷ Διδάσκαλε, ταῦτα πάντα ἐφυλαξάμην
21 ἐκ νεότητός μου. ὁ δὲ Ἰησοῦς ἐμβλέψας αὐτῷ ἠγάπησεν αὐτὸν

He did not suppose that the Law would
supply the full answer to the man's
question. His words therefore are a
challenge.

The order of the commandments
quoted varies in the MSS. In the
WH text the order is vi-ix, (x), v. In
Mk and Lk the form is μή c. subj.,
in Mt οὐ c. fut. D k Iren omit μὴ
φονεύσῃς and add μὴ πορνεύσῃς which
is attested also by c. Turner, 49, suggests that the true text of Mk is likely
to be found in authorities which differ
from Mt and Lk. He points out that
in vii. 21 both 'adulteries' and 'for-
nications' are named and commends
the text attested by D k Iren μὴ μοιχεύ-
σῃς, μὴ πορνεύσῃς, μὴ κλέψῃς. Murder
was the sin least likely to be in question.
Cf. *JTS*, xxix. 5.

Of the verbs in the WH text φονεύω,
μοιχεύω, κλέπτω, and ἀποστερέω are
found here only in Mk ; ψευδομαρτυρέω,
xiv. 56 f.*. ἀποστερέω, I Cor. vi. 7 f.,
vii. 5, I Tim. vi. 5**, 'to deprive',
'defraud of'; Cl., LXX, Pap. Field,
33, points out that in the Gk Bible the
verb is appropriated to the act of *keeping back the wages* of an hireling,
whereas in Cl. Gk it is used of refusing
to return goods or money deposited
with another for safe keeping. Thus,
μὴ ἀποστερήσῃς may be a negative
form of the ninth commandment, μὴ
κλέψῃς. Most commentators see in
it a reference to the tenth commandment; cf. Swete, 224. For the OT
use of the verb cf. Ex. xxi. 10, Deut.
xxiv. 14 (A); *v.* also Sir. iv. 1 and
Jos. *Ant.* iv. 8. 38.

μὴ ἀποστερήσῃς is omitted by B* K
W Δ Π Σ Ψ fam. 1 28 69 579 700 sys
geo arm Clem, and is not found in Mt
and Lk. This is strong evidence for
regarding it as a scribal addition, but
the argument is not conclusive, for
the words might have been omitted
because they are not found in the
Decalogue. Turner, 49, describes it

as 'quite certainly genuine'; cf.
Bartlet, 294. McNeile, 278, thinks
that it may be a later addition. The
balance of the argument favours its
genuineness. It is read by ℵ A B² C
D Θ fam. 13 69mg 543 565 892 1071
al. pler. it vg sype hl sa bo aeth. The
originality of the citation of the fourth
commandment at the end of the list
is more open to question (cf. Bartlet,
294); its presence may be an illustration of the tendency towards expansion manifest in the addition in
Mt. xix. 19b, καὶ ἀγαπήσεις τὸν πλησίον
σου ὡς σεαυτόν. More important than
these details is the broad fact that the
questioner's attention is directed to
the part of Decalogue which deals
with human relationships (cf. Mk. xii.
28-34). In itself this fact indicates that
τὰς ἐντολὰς οἶδας is no mere paedagogic
device, but a positive part of the answer
to the question how ζωὴ αἰώνιος may
be inherited.

20 f. For ἔφη *v.* ix. 12 ; διδάσκαλε
iv. 38 ; φυλάσσω xv. 25 (?)* ; νεότης*.
Matthew and Luke independently
correct Mark's use of ἐφυλαξάμην,
which is not reflexive ; cf. Moulton,
i. 159 ; Lagrange, 266. In the LXX
the verb is frequently used of keeping
commandments and ordinances, in
the act. in Gen. xxvi. 5, Ex. xx. 6,
Deut. xxvi. 18, 3 Kgdms. ii. 3, in the
mid. in Lev. xviii. 4, Deut. iv. 2, I
Chron. xxviii. 7, Psa. cxviii. 4 ff.; ἐκ
νεότητος is also common, Gen. viii. 21,
I Kgdms. xii. 2, Psa. lxx. 17; cf.
Ac. xxvi. 4. Although the reply is
impulsive, Jesus does not condemn
the man ; on the contrary, fixing His
eyes upon Him, He loves him. ἐμβλέπω,
v. viii. 25 ; cf. the note on περιβλέπω,
iii. 5. ἀγαπάω, xii. 30 f., 33 (*bis*)*, in
the NT ' is purged of all coldness, and
is deeper than φιλέω, though the latter
remains more human ' (*VGT*, 2). Cf.
E. Stauffer, *KThW*, i. 34-55.

With hesitation Field, 34, suggests

καὶ εἶπεν αὐτῷ "Ἐν σε ὑστερεῖ· ὕπαγε ὅσα ἔχεις πώλησον καὶ
δὸς [τοῖς] πτωχοῖς, καὶ ἕξεις θησαυρὸν ἐν οὐρανῷ, καὶ δεῦρο
ἀκολούθει μοι. ὁ δὲ στυγνάσας ἐπὶ τῷ λόγῳ ἀπῆλθεν λυπού- 22

that ἠγάπησεν αὐτόν may be rendered
' caressed him ', citing Plutarch, *Vit.
Pericl.* I ; cf. Turner, 49 ; Dibelius,
50 n. ; W. Bauer, 7 ; Lohmeyer, 211 n.
The meaning is possible but most of
the authorities mentioned say little
more, and one must agree with J.
Moffatt, *Love in the NT,* 76, that here
the verb ' probably covers no more
than the inward impulse of admiring
affection '. ' Jesus felt instinctively
drawn to this clean, earnest character ',
ibid. Cf. Swete, 225. Even so, the
phrase, which Mt and Lk omit, is
highly distinctive ; it recalls the phrase
' the disciple whom Jesus loved ', Jn.
xiii. 23, etc.

In saying to the man ' One thing
thou lackest ', Jesus does not mean
that there is just one act to perform in
order that he may inherit eternal life,
for after the command to sell all that
he has He adds καὶ δεῦρο ἀκολούθει μοι.
It is this ' following ' which leads to
life ; the renunciation of riches and
gifts to the poor are actions which in
his case following entails. For the influence of this saying on St. Francis of
Assisi *v.* Sabatier, *Life of St. Francis,*
75, and for its effect upon St. Antony
v. Kirk, *The Vision of God,* 180.

ὑστερέω*, ' to come short of ', ' fail ',
' be lacking ' (Cl., LXX, Pap.). The
dat. σοι is read in Mk by A D *et al.*
fam. I fam. 13 565 700 1071 *al. pler.*
it vg, but is plainly a grammatical
correction of the acc. σε. The use of
σε is strange, and both Matthew and
Luke have avoided it : in Mt the man
asks τί ἔτι ὑστερῶ ; and the answer
given is Εἰ θέλεις τέλειος εἶναι . . . (xix.
20 f.) ; in Lk the statement becomes
Ἔτι ἕν σοι λείπει (xviii. 22). It may be
that Mark has in mind the LXX
rendering of Psa. xxiii. 1, καὶ οὐδέν με
ὑστερήσει, and has based *Ἐν σε ὑστερεῖ
upon it ; whereas nothing is lacking
to the Psalmist because God is his
Shepherd, the man lacks one all im-

portant thing supplied only by a
resolute sacrifice. He must sell all and
give to the poor.

For ὑπάγω *v.* i. 44 ; ὅσος ii. 19 ;
πωλέω xi. 15 (*bis*)* ; πτωχός xii. 42 f.,
xiv. 5, 7* ; θησαυρός* ; οὐρανός i. 10.
Commentators are right in saying that
Jesus does not demand the universal
renunciation of property, but gives
a command relative to a particular
case. Nevertheless, as Lohmeyer, 211,
points out, Jesus Himself appears to
have chosen a life of poverty ; He
wanders to and fro without a settled
home (i. 39, Lk. ix. 58), His disciples
are hungry (ii. 23, viii. 14), women
provide for His needs (Lk. viii. 3), and
His disciples can say Ἰδοὺ ἡμεῖς ἀφήκαμεν πάντα καὶ ἠκολουθήκαμεν σοι (Mk.
x. 28). In this respect His teaching
transcends that of Judaism in which
wealth is a mark of the divine favour
(as in Job). His standpoint is nearer
to that of the Rechabites and the
Essenes, but with important differences, and is in agreement with the
Rabbinic emphasis on the duty of
almsgiving (though not as a ground
of merit) and on the obligation to love
God rather than the body or life or
property. Cf. Billerbeck, i. 817, and
see further, x. 23, 25. Treasure in
heaven means treasure with God (cf.
Mt. vi. 19 f.) in the life of the Kingdom.

The command καὶ δεῦρο ἀκολούθει
μοι recalls i. 17 f., 20, ii. 14. δεῦρο*
is an adv. (' hither ') used as an imperative, ' Come ! ', to which δεῦτε (i.
17) forms the plur. ; Cl., LXX, Pap.
(*VGT,* 143 ; Moulton, i. 172). For ἀκολουθέω *v.* i. 18.

The Gospel according to the Hebrews
at this point declared that the second
of the two rich men ' began to scratch
his head ', being displeased, and that
the Lord said to him : ' How sayest
thou : I have kept the law and the
prophets ? For it is written in the law :
Thou shalt love thy neighbour as thy-

μενος, ἦν γὰρ ἔχων κτήματα πολλά.

self, and lo, many of thy brethren, sons of Abraham, are clad in filth, dying for hunger, and thine house is full of many good things, and nought at all goeth out of it unto them '; so the Latin version of Pseudo-Origen on Mt, cf. M. R. James, 6.

22. Gloom falls upon the man's face and he goes away sorrowful. στυγνάζω*, Mt. xvi. 3 (D it)**, ' to have a gloomy, lowering look '; late Gk, LXX, Pap. (VGT, 594). The adjective στυγνός is used of a gloomy night in Wisd. xvii. 5 (cf. Mt. xvi. 3) and the verb of the human face in Ezek. xxvii. 35, xxviii. 19 (A), xxxii. 10. Cf. also Isa. lvii. 17, καὶ ἐλυπήθη καὶ ἐπορεύθη στυγνός, Dan. ii. 12, στυγνὸς γενόμενος καὶ περίλυπος. RV and RSV, ' his countenance fell '; Moffatt and Torrey, ' his face fell ', ἐπὶ τῷ λόγῳ, ' at the saying '. His inner feeling is described by λυπούμενος (xiv. [19]*), his action by ἀπῆλθεν. The explanation given is

ἦν γὰρ ἔχων κτήματα πολλά. For the periphrastic imperfect v. Intr. 45, 62 f. κτῆμα*, Mt. xix. 22, Ac. ii. 45, v. 1**, ' a possession ', is used to describe ' a piece of landed property ' of any kind (VGT, 362), a farm or a field (Ac. v. 1), and in the plur. lands or estates. Only at this point in the Markan narrative do we learn that the man was a landed proprietor.[1] This is the only story in the Gospels in which the command of Jesus to follow Him is even tacitly refused. Mark makes no comment on the fact, but merely records what happened. Cf. Lagrange, 267 : l'évangéliste ne le blâme pas; qui ne le plaindrait? Mark alone has στυγνάσας ἐπὶ τῷ λόγῳ, but with the rest of the verse Matthew is in verbatim agreement (xix. 22). Luke has ὁ δὲ ἀκούσας ταῦτα περίλυπος ἐγενήθη, ἦν γὰρ πλούσιος σφόδρα (xviii. 23). As so often, the Markan account is the most objective.

Mk. x. 23-7   65. THE CONVERSATION ON   Cf. Mt. xix. 23-6
                            RICHES   Lk. xviii. 24-7

The account of the conversation is not an independent narrative, but a story closely connected in the tradition with the Rich Man's Question, so much so as to be almost part of it. Short as it is, and consisting mainly of sayings, the story is not without picturesque detail which is enhanced if 24 and 25 are reversed (v. Comm.). Looking round about upon His disciples, presumably after the departure of the rich man, Jesus observes how difficult it is for men with riches to enter into the Kingdom of God. The disciples are astonished, and still more when Jesus goes on to say that it is difficult for anyone to enter into the Kingdom. ' Who then can be saved ? ', they ask. Jesus declares that ' with men it is impossible, but not with God : for all things are possible with God '; and with these words the story ends. There can be little doubt that the story rests on authentic tradition, ultimately that of an eyewitness, for it is lifelike and contains teaching on wealth which transcends that of Judaism. Of the hyperbole concerning the camel Branscomb, 183, observes that it is ' quite in the style of one whose speech sparkled with picturesque comparisons and metaphors '. The story is also of interest on textual grounds and for its bearing on the teaching of Jesus concerning the Kingdom of God.

23   Καὶ περιβλεψάμενος ὁ 'Ιησοῦς λέγει τοῖς μαθηταῖς αὐτοῦ

23 f. For περιβλέπω v. iii. 5; οἱ   xix. 23, Lk. xviii. 24**, ' hardly ', μαθηταὶ αὐτοῦ ii. 15. δυσκόλως*, Mt.   ' with difficulty '. For the correspon-

---

[1] Turner, JTS, xxix. 6, thinks that the reading χρήματα, ' riches ' (D a b ff k sy Clem) is practically certain. It may, however, be an assimilation to x. 23. b k Clem add et agros.

Πῶς δυσκόλως οἱ τὰ χρήματα ἔχοντες εἰς τὴν βασιλείαν τοῦ θεοῦ
εἰσελεύσονται.   οἱ δὲ μαθηταὶ ἐθαμβοῦντο ἐπὶ τοῖς λόγοις 24
αὐτοῦ.   ὁ δὲ Ἰησοῦς πάλιν ἀποκριθεὶς λέγει αὐτοῖς Τέκνα,
πῶς δύσκολόν ἐστιν εἰς τὴν βασιλείαν τοῦ θεοῦ εἰσελθεῖν· εὐκο- 25
πώτερόν ἐστιν κάμηλον διὰ ⌜τρυμαλιᾶς⌝ ῥαφίδος διελθεῖν ἢ πλού-

25 τῆς τρυμαλιᾶς τῆς

ding adjective δύσκολος, literally ' hard to please with food ' (κόλον), v. 24. The presence of this rare adverb in all the Synoptics is a sign of their interdependence. χρῆμα, Lk. xviii. 24, Ac (4), ' a thing one uses ' (χράομαι), in the plur. ' wealth ', ' riches '. The expression is more general than κτήματα in 22. For the idea of ' entering into the kingdom of God ' see the notes on ix. 47 and x. 15 and for the teaching, strange to Judaism, concerning wealth as a barrier see x. 21.

It is not surprising that the disciples were amazed at these words. For θαμβέομαι v. i. 27. This astonishment is all the more intelligible if 24 and 25, as in the Western text, are reversed ; v. the note on 25. Jesus addresses them a second time (πάλιν ii. 1) with an affection expressed by the vocative τέκνα (ii. 5). Cf. the Johannine use of τεκνία (Jn. xiii. 33 ; 1 Jn. ii. 1, 12, 28, iii. 7 (mg. παιδία), 18, v. 21, used also in Gal. iv. 19**). His words are even stronger than before, for τοὺς πεποιθότας ἐπὶ τοῖς χρήμασιν must be omitted with ℵ B Δ Ψ k bo (some MSS.) aeth. So WH, Nestle, Ti, RVmg, RSV, Swete, 228 ; Lagrange, 269 ; Turner, 50 ; Rawlinson, 140 ; etc. It is particularly hard for a rich man, but hard indeed for anyone, to enter into the Kingdom of God. For ἀποκριθεὶς λέγει v. Intr. 63.

Both Matthew and Luke omit 24, but Matthew shows his knowledge of the verse by the phrase πάλιν δὲ λέγω ὑμῖν in xix. 24.

25. The difficulty of a rich man's entering into the Kingdom is emphasized by the metaphor of the camel and the needle's eye. For εὐκοπώτερον (here c. acc. and infin.) v. ii. 9 ; κάμηλος

i. 6 ; πλούσιος xii. 41*. τρυμαλία*, used by Mark for the eye of a needle, is a LXX word (Judg. xv. 8, Jer. xiii. 4, etc.) denoting a hole or perforation in a rock ; <τρύω, ' wear away '. Both Matthew (τρύπημα) and Luke (τρῆμα) avoid the word. Cf. Streeter, 317, who says that assimilation has run riot. For ῥαφίς*, Mt. xix. 24**, ' needle ', Luke has βελόνη (xviii. 25**). See Rutherford, New Phrynichus, 174 f.

Possibly the Kingdom (v. i. 15, ix. 47, x. 15, 24) is conceived eschatologically, but more probably it is thought of as present ; cf. Manson, 207.

Attempts to soften the rigour of the saying are to be deprecated, especially the exegetical fancy that there was a door in the walls of Jerusalem through which with difficulty a camel might perhaps squeeze, or the once popular interpretation of κάμηλος in the sense of κάμιλος, ' a cable ' (read by 13 28 543, etc.). So Theophylact, Euthymius ; cf. Lagrange, 269 f. The saying is a hyperbole, like those on the beam and splinter (Lk. vi 41 f.) and the gnat and the camel (Mt. xxiii. 24), to express what, humanly speaking, is impossible or absurd. Cf. C. J. Cadoux, ET, lii. 378-81. A Rabbinic parallel speaks of the impossibility of an elephant passing through the eye of a needle ; Ber. 55b, cf. O. Michel, KThW, iii. 598, Dalman, JJ, 230.

After the more general statement in 24 the return to the idea of the difficulty of a rich man's entering the Kingdom in 25 is strange. There is therefore much to be said for the reversal of the verses attested by D a b d ff r¹·², especially as in this case the intensification of the paradox accounts well for the second and stronger ex-

26 σιον εἰς τὴν βασιλείαν τοῦ θεοῦ εἰσελθεῖν. οἱ δὲ περισσῶς ἐξεπλήσσοντο λέγοντες πρὸς ἑαυτούς Καὶ τίς δύναται σωθῆναι;
27 ἐμβλέψας αὐτοῖς ὁ Ἰησοῦς λέγει Παρὰ ἀνθρώποις ἀδύνατον ἀλλ'
οὐ παρὰ θεῷ, πάντα γὰρ δυνατὰ παρὰ [τῷ] θεῷ.

pression of astonishment in 26. Cf. Wellhausen, 81; Rawlinson, 140. Lagrange, 269, prefers to think that the too logical order of D, etc. is suspicious. As an alternative explanation Wellhausen suggests the omission of ἢ πλούσιον . . . εἰσελθεῖν in 25, but there is no textual support for this view. Equally speculative is the suggestion of Bultmann, 21, and others, that Mark has added 24 and 26 f. to his source. Of these views the best is that the original order was 23, 25, 24, 26 f.

26 f. The astonishment of the disciples is greatly increased. For ἐκπλήσσομαι v. i. 22. περισσῶς, xv. 14*; cf. vi. 51. Instead of πρὸς αὐτόν (א B C Δ Ψ 892 sa bo) πρὸς ἑαυτούς is read by A D W Θ et al. minusc. pler. it (exc. k) sype hl Aug. Lagrange, 270, prefers this reading (cf. AV, RVmg, RSVmg), as also Nestle and Klostermann, 117. Turner, 50, says that it is the only reading which conforms to Mark's usage (i. 27, xi. 31, xii. 7, xvi. 3; cf. iv. 41, viii. 16, ix. 34), and Black, 77, thinks that it represents the Semitic ethic dat., ' were them saying '. Some confirmation is given by πρὸς ἀλλήλους in M* k, and on the whole the reading is to be preferred; πρὸς αὐτόν too exclusively Alexandrian and may be a correction. It is accepted by Swete, 230; Plummer, 242; but without discussion.

The question prompted is: ' Who then can be saved?'. καὶ τίς in Mk and Lk = τίς ἄρα in Mt; cf. Jn. ix. 36. σώζω (v. iii. 4) is here used as denoting entrance into the Kingdom, and in this sense here only in Mk. The idea of a residue, the elect who escape the eschatological judgment (Wellhausen, 81), reads much into the passage, but, as propounded by the disciples, the

question may be eschatological : ' Who will finally be found within the Basileia?'. Cf. Lohmeyer, 215. This interpretation would not be excluded even if the disciples had perceived the emphasis of Jesus upon the Kingdom as a present opportunity, but, in point of fact, there is nothing in the question to show whether its reference is present or future, and to raise the issue may not be relevant. The inquiry is restricted to the doubt whether anyone can be ' saved '.

The reply of Jesus is remarkable in its sole emphasis upon the power of God : with men it is impossible, but not with God, for with God all things are possible. The implied subject is τὸ σώζεσθαι: Mt τοῦτο, Lk τὰ ἀδύνατα. Nothing is said concerning ' works ' or faith, but Lagrange, 271, is justified in saying that the reply contains in germ the teaching of Paul. The reference to the look of Jesus (ἐμβλέψας, v. viii. 25, x. 21), which is peculiar to Mark's account, indicates the stress which He laid on the saying. ἀδύνατος*; δυνατός, ix. 23; παρά c. dat.* Both the thought and the language are illustrated by the LXX in Gen. xviii. 14, μὴ ἀδυνατεῖ παρὰ τῷ θεῷ ῥῆμα; Job x. 13, xlii. 2, Zech. viii. 6.

D 157 a ff (k) Clem omit ἀλλ' οὐ παρὰ θεῷ and read simply παρὰ δὲ (τῷ) θεῷ δυνατόν. The last phrase in the verse is omitted also by Δ Ψ fam. 1 (exc. 118) 69 579 et al. Wellhausen, 81, prefers the shorter text of D, etc., but it looks very much like an attempt to relate the saying to the circumstances of the story. Matthew follows Mk closely, but Luke paraphrases the saying, τὰ ἀδύνατα παρὰ ἀνθρώποις δυνατὰ παρὰ τῷ θεῷ ἐστιν (xviii. 27).

Mk. x. 28-31   66. THE QUESTION OF   Cf. Mt. xix. 27-30
                        REWARDS   Lk. xviii. 28-30

As it stands the story is closely connected with x. 17-27, but Mark does not supply a grammatical link. Swete, 230, observes that the conversation ' arose out of the previous incident '. Bultmann, 21, thinks that either 28 is redactional, or is the introduction to an old Apothegm in which the original saying (according to Loisy, Mt. xix. 28) has been replaced by 29 f. Such hypotheses are highly speculative and it is not safe to classify the story as more than a Story about Jesus. But is it ' Petrine ' and in what sense ? J. Weiss, 350, classifies it as such, but with a mark of interrogation. The fact that Mark assigns the opening remark to Peter indicates that he is following a tradition, and the remark itself, ' Lo, we have left all, and have followed thee ', is characteristic of Peter. Bartlet, 287-300, assigns the whole of x. 1-31 to ' primary Apostolic tradition (Petrine) '. There is much to commend this view. The story lacks those details of verisimilitude which belong to the Petrine stories of i. 21-39, iv. 35-v. 43, etc., but at some remove it may be derived from Peter's testimony. Much depends on how the saying in 29 f. is interpreted. In the Commentary it is suggested that, while the saying is coloured by later interests, it is in substance authentic. The saying on ' the first and the last ' in 31 is a Markan appendage derived from a primitive collection.

"Ηρξατο λέγειν ὁ Πέτρος αὐτῷ   'Ιδοὺ ἡμεῖς ἀφήκαμεν πάντα 28
καὶ ἠκολουθήκαμέν σοι. ἔφη ὁ 'Ιησοῦς 'Αμὴν λέγω ὑμῖν, οὐδεὶς 29
ἔστιν ὃς ἀφῆκεν οἰκίαν ἢ ἀδελφοὺς ἢ ἀδελφὰς ἢ μητέρα ἢ τέκνα
ἢ ἀγροὺς ἕνεκεν ἐμοῦ καὶ [ἕνεκεν] τοῦ εὐαγγελίου, ἐὰν μὴ λάβῃ 30

28 f. Without any connecting particle the narrative begins with ἤρξατο λέγειν ὁ Πέτρος αὐτῷ. For ἤρξατο c. infin., here manifestly a mere equivalent for the imperfect, v. Intr. 48, 63 f.; ὁ Πέτρος iii. 16; ἰδού i. 2. His words ἡμεῖς ἀφήκαμεν πάντα καὶ ἠκολουθήκαμέν σοι have a characteristic touch of exaggeration, for it is clear from i. 29, and perhaps also from the references to the boat in iii. 9, iv. 1, 36, etc., that his separation from home ties was not complete. The saying is a cross reference, rare in Mk, to i. 17 and ii. 14, and it recalls the invitation to the rich man, δεῦρο ἀκολούθει μοι (x. 21), and is perhaps prompted by it. The distinction of tenses in ἀφήκαμεν and ἠκολουθήκαμεν is noteworthy; the decisive renunciation in Peter's mind stood out against the permanent following. In Mt and Lk this detail is lost. Cf. Swete, 230. At this point

Matthew adds τί ἄρα ἔσται ἡμῖν; and inserts the saying on ' twelve thrones ' (cf. Lk. xxii. 28-30).

For the use of ἔφη asyndeton in 29 v. ix. 38; ἀμὴν λέγω ὑμῖν iii. 28; οὐδεὶς ἔστιν ὅς ix. 39. The reply of Jesus is remarkable for its detail in His references to the abandonment of home (οἰκίαν, cf. Turner, 50), or brothers, or sisters, or mother, or father, or children (τέκνα, v. ii. 5), or fields (ἀγρούς, v. 14). In contrast with 30, the nouns are separated by ἤ . . . ἤ . . ., whereas in 30 they are connected by καί. Bengel's comment is : Quae relinquuntur, disiunctive enumerantur: quae retribuuntur, copulative. Matthew is in close agreement, but Luke omits ἀδελφάς and ἀγρούς, adds ἢ γυναῖκα, and has γονεῖς instead of μητέρα ἢ πατέρα. The phrase ἢ πατέρα in Mk (om. D a ff k) is probably a scribal addition (so Turner, JTS, xxix. 6)

ἑκατονταπλασίονα νῦν ἐν τῷ καιρῷ τούτῳ οἰκίας καὶ ἀδελφοὺς
καὶ ἀδελφὰς καὶ ⌈μητέρας⌉ καὶ τέκνα καὶ ἀγροὺς μετὰ διωγμῶν,
31 καὶ ἐν τῷ αἰῶνι τῷ ἐρχομένῳ ζωὴν αἰώνιον. πολλοὶ δὲ ἔσονται

30 μητέρα

and ἢ γυναῖκα (A C *et al.* fam. 13 28 579 1071 *al. pler.* f q sype hl geo² aeth) is an assimilation to the text of Lk. For ἕνεκεν ἐμοῦ *v.* viii. 35 ; εὐαγγέλιον i. 1. The second ἕνεκεν is omitted by A B* S* 700 *al.* c k Bas, but is otherwise very strongly attested (cf. Legg). The phrase καὶ ἕνεκεν τοῦ εὐαγγελίου is editorial (cf. viii. 35), as many commentators recognize (Swete, 231 ; Plummer, 243 ; Rawlinson, 141 f. ; Klostermann, 117 ; cf. Hawkins, 152) ; but, together with the Synoptic variants, it is important as indicating an identification of Jesus Himself with the ' Gospel ' and the ' Kingdom ' in primitive Christian thought ; cf. K. L. Schmidt, *KThW*, i. 590 f. Cf. Mt. xix. 29, ἕνεκεν τοῦ ἐμοῦ ὀνόματος ; Lk. xviii. 29, εἵνεκεν τῆς βασιλείας τοῦ θεοῦ.

30. ἐὰν μὴ λάβῃ, lit. ' if he shall not receive ', more freely ' without receiving ' (Swete, 231). Swete compares the construction with iv. 22, but Lagrange, 272, thinks the case is different : there ἐὰν μή = εἰ μή, here ἐάν is used for ἄν, as often in the Koine. Luke simplifies by using ὃς οὐχὶ μὴ λάβῃ, and D by ὃς ἂν μή. Matthew recasts his source and has πᾶς ὅστις ἀφῆκεν . . . λήμψεται. The form ἑκατονταπλασίονα*, Lk. viii. 8 (cf. 2 Kgdms. xxiv. 3, 1 Chron. xxi. 3), is replaced by πολλαπλασίονα in Mt. xix. 29, and probably by ἑπταπλασίονα in Lk. xviii. 30 (so D it, cf. Streeter, 318). Apparently ' a hundredfold ' was thought excessive.

In Mk (and Lk) a distinction is drawn between the rewards received here and now and in the age to come. The phrase ἐν τῷ καιρῷ τούτῳ is unusual. Swete, 231, compares ὁ νῦν καιρός in Rom. iii. 26, viii. 18, xi. 5, 2 Cor. viii. 13. The more common phrase is ὁ αἰὼν οὗτος in contrast with

ὁ αἰὼν ὁ ἐρχόμενος or ὁ μέλλων (Mt. xii. 32). The list from οἰκίας to ἀγρούς is peculiar to Mk ; it is omitted by ℵ* 255 c k, and these authorities, except k, omit μετὰ διωγμῶν (*v.* iv. 17) which is also peculiar to Mk. μ. διωγμοῦ is read by D sys pe geo¹ aeth.

Some commentators regard οἰκίας . . . μετὰ διωγμῶν as an expansion of the original saying, suggested by the fellowship of the primitive Church and its experiences of persecution ; cf. Wellhausen, 81 f. ; Bultmann, 115 ; Klostermann, 118 ; Lohmeyer, 217 ; Smith, 167 ; Luce, 288 ; Branscomb, 184 f. Others think that at least μετὰ διωγμῶν is an addition, a caveat added in Christian teaching ; cf. Bartlet, 299 ; Rawlinson, 142 ; Hawkins, 152 ; McNeile, 282. Goguel, *Rev. d'hist. et phil. rel.*, ' Avec les persécutions ', 1928, pp. 264-77, limits the addition to καὶ ἐν τῷ αἰῶνι τῷ ἐρχομένῳ ζωὴν αἰώνιον (30c), explaining the preceding promise as an ironical reply to Peter's foolish question.

The objections to the authenticity of the saying are cogent, but only up to a point. (1) It is urged that 30 reflects the enriched sense of personal relationships characteristic of the primitive Church ; cf. Rom. xvi. 13, ' his mother and mine ', 1 Cor. iv. 13, ' not many fathers ', Phlm. 10, ' my child . . . Onesimus ', 1 Tim. v. 1 f. (cited by Victor), Jn. xix. 26 f. But Mk. iii. 35, ' the same is my brother, and sister, and mother ', shows that the impulse goes back to Jesus Himself. He could well have promised personal relationships richer a hundredfold than those renounced. (2) The reference to ' persecutions ' can represent a later interest, but no less the foresight of Jesus who certainly believed that His followers would be exposed to calamities and afflictions.

πρῶτοι ἔσχατοι καὶ [οἱ] ἔσχατοι πρῶτοι.

(3) The strongest objection is the linking of ' eternal life ' with ' the age to come '. Despite Lk. xvi. 8, xx. 34 f. and Mt. xiii. 22, 39, etc., Dalman, 148, claims that ' the ideas, " this age ", " the future age ", *if Jesus used them at all*, were not of importance in His vocabulary '. Cf. H. Sasse, *KThW*, i. 207, who says that, while the NT speaks of two ages, the αἰὼν μέλλων no longer lies only in the future. Cf. Gal. i. 4, Heb. vi. 5. This view is confirmed by the references to ' life ' in Mk. ix. 43, 45 and to the Kingdom of God in Mk. x. 15. On the whole, the best view to take is that substantially the saying is authentic, but that in the phrase ' and in the world to come eternal life ' it has been adapted to current views by the Evangelist or a predecessor (cf. Goguel, *supra*).

Particular interest belongs to the form in which Clement of Alexandria quotes the saying : ἀπολήψεται ἑκατονταπλασίονα. νῦν δὲ ἐν τῷ καιρῷ τούτῳ ἀγροὺς καὶ χρήματα καὶ οἰκίας καὶ ἀδελφοὺς ἔχειν μετὰ διωγμῶν εἰς ποῦ; ... ἐν δὲ τῷ ἐρχομένῳ ζωή ἐστιν αἰώνιος, *Quis Dives?* (*v*. Legg).[1] ' He shall receive in return a hundredfold. To what end (does he expect) to have now in this time fields and riches and houses and brothers with persecutions ? But in the coming age there is eternal life.' In these words the possibility of material awards is dismissed in comparison with the gift of eternal life in the world to come. Wellhausen, 81 f., is obviously attracted by this version ; cf. also C. J. Cadoux, 235. But attractive as it is, Clement's version [2] is probably an attempt to put a more spiritual interpretation on the saying, a recast which is not necessary since by wide

consent the items in 30 are not to be taken literally. The sneer of Julian the Apostate about the faithful receiving a hundred wives (cf. Swete, 232) was pointless, and equally invalid was the exploitation of the saying by the Millenarians (*Ex occasione huius sentientiae, quidam introducunt mille annos post resurrectionem*, Jerome, *in Mt.* xix. 29 f.). What Jesus promised was that, so far from suffering real loss, Hi disciples would be rewarded a hundredfold in a richer social and religious fellowship. The ' communism ' of the Early Church (Ac. ii. 44, iv. 32-7) and monasticism were partial fulfilments of what the life of the Ecclesia is meant to become.

31. The saying πολλοὶ δὲ ἔσονται πρῶτοι ἔσχατοι καὶ [οἱ] ἔσχατοι πρῶτοι is given here by Matthew but is omitted by Luke. Matthew has a doublet in xx. 16 after the Parable of the Labourers in the Vineyard and Luke has it in a group of sayings from Q in xiii. 30. In Mk the ' last ' who are to be ' first ' may be the disciples ; so Wellhausen, 82. But equally well the saying may be a warning to the disciples ; so Swete, 233 ; Turner, 50. Much depends on whether δέ=γάρ (237 259 sys geo¹ arm) or whether it is sharply adversative, a point which it is impossible to decide. Both Lagrange, 274, and Rawlinson, 142, rightly reject Loisy's view that Mark is championing the claims of Paul and others against the position of the Twelve. In view of Mark's editorial methods elsewhere (cf. ii. 21 f., 27 f., iii. 27-9, etc.) it is best to regard the saying as an appendage to the story. οἱ is omitted by ℵ A D L W Δ Θ fam. 1 28 565 579 700 1071 *al. plur.*

[1] This is the text quoted by Wellhausen, 82, from E. Schwartz, *Hermes* (1903), 87 ff., which I have not seen. It differs from the text of *De Divite Servando*, xxii, xxv, printed by G. Dindorf, *Clementis Alexandrini Opera* (1869), 400, 402. See further, P. M. Barnard, *Texts and Studies*, v, No. 5, p. 35.
[2] Or possibly comment.

(*d*) Mk. x. 32-52   STORIES CONNECTED WITH
THE FINAL STAGE OF THE
JOURNEY TO JERUSALEM

Once more the fourth section in V begins with a geographical and circumstantial statement, which serves as an introduction to the first narrative and as a heading for the whole.   The sub-section includes :

(67) x. 32-4.   The Third Prophecy of the Passion.
(68) x. 35-40.   The Request of James and John.
(69) x. 41-5.   The Rebuke of the Ten : Rank and Precedence.
(70) x. 46-52.   The Cure of the Blind Man at Jericho.

Of these narratives 67, 68, and 70 are self-contained stories, the last being connected with Jericho, but 68 and 69 are so closely related as almost to form a single story.

Mk. x. 32-4   67. THE THIRD PROPHECY   Cf. Mt. xx. 17-19
OF THE PASSION   Lk. xviii. 31-4

The introductory geographical and descriptive statement is discussed in the Commentary.

Like the second prophecy, the third is set in the context of the journey to Jerusalem.   The initial phrase, ' And he took again the twelve, and began to tell them the things that were to happen unto him ', is distinctive. The claim of Ed. Meyer, i. 144 f., that it comes from a ' Twelve Source ', from which x. 32b-45 has been derived, is uncertain ;   but it is of interest to recall that in 1903 J. Weiss, 265, suggested that it is not impossible that Mark owed the second prophecy to Peter, the third to the Sayings-source, and composed the first himself.   Such opinions can only be tentative, and it is more important to consider the historical character of x. 32-4 on more general grounds.   Two points call for notice.   (1) The third prophecy is connected with a definite historical situation which is described with great vividness (x. 32) ;   (2) The prophecy is much more detailed than the first (viii. 31) and second (ix. 31) and probably reflects knowledge of the events which subsequently happened.   The relationships between the three and the Passion Narrative may be illustrated as follows :

	First Prophecy	Second Prophecy	Third Prophecy	Passion Narrative
1. Handing over to the Chief Priests	—	(ix. 31)	x. 33	xiv. 53
2. Condemnation by the Chief Priests	(viii. 31)	—	x. 33	xiv. 64
3. Handing over to the Romans	—	—	x. 33	xv. 1
4. Mocking, Spitting, and Scourging	—	—	x. 34	xiv. 65, xv. 15, 16-20
5. Execution	viii. 31	ix. 31	x. 34	xv. 24, 37
6. Resurrection	viii. 31	ix. 31	x. 34	xvi. 1-8

The table shows the much greater detail of the third prophecy and its close correspondence with the Passion Narrative.   It also shows how misleading it may be to extend to the first and second prophecies inferences which may legitimately be drawn from the third. In its precision the third is a *vaticinium ex eventu*. Can we justly say this of viii. 31 and ix. 31 ? The agreement is even less close than the table might suggest. The first alone says that the Son of Man ' must suffer ' and speaks of rejection by the chief priests rather than condemnation ; the second mentions delivering up into the hands of men. Only in respect of the death and the resurrection is the agreement precise. None of the prophecies mentions crucifixion specifically ; σταυρόω appears for the first time in Mt. xx. 19. The Lukan version adds τελεσθήσεται πάντα τὰ γεγραμμένα διὰ τῶν προφητῶν and καὶ ὑβρισθήσεται (xviii. 31 f.).

Ἦσαν δὲ ἐν τῇ ὁδῷ ἀναβαίνοντες εἰς Ἱεροσόλυμα, καὶ ἦν 32 προάγων αὐτοὺς ὁ Ἰησοῦς, καὶ ἐθαμβοῦντο, οἱ δὲ ἀκολουθοῦντες ἐφοβοῦντο. καὶ παραλαβὼν πάλιν τοὺς δώδεκα ἤρξατο αὐτοῖς

32. With added solemnity, as compared with viii. 31 and ix. 31, this vivid passage describes the circumstances in which the third prophecy was uttered. For ἦσαν ἀναβαίνοντες and ἦν προάγων v. Intr. 45, 62 f. ἀναβαίνω (i. 10) is regularly used of going up to a city (*VGT*, 30) and is especially appropriate here because of the high ground on which Jerusalem stood. For ἐν τῇ ὁδῷ v. i. 2, viii. 3 ; Ἱεροσόλυμα iii. 8 ; προάγω vi. 45 ; θαμβέομαι i. 27 ; φοβέομαι iv. 41.

The distinction between those whom Jesus preceded (αὐτούς) and those who followed (οἱ ἀκολουθοῦντες) is strange ; xi. 9 is not a parallel. The strangeness is reflected in the textual tradition. οἱ δὲ ἀκολ. ἐφοβοῦντο is omitted by D K 28 700 *et al.* a b vg (1 MS.), οἱ δέ is replaced by καί in A *et al.* fam. 13 118 892 1071 *al. pler.* l q r vg syᵖᵉ ʰˡ geo, and syˢ and arm have the equivalent of *qui erant cum eo mirabantur timentes*. Blunt, 219, tentatively suggests the translation ' they as they followed ' (cf. AV), but it is more probable that two groups are distinguished. So Swete, 233 ; Lagrange, 275 ; Gould, 197 ; Plummer, 245 (cf. RV, RSV, Moffatt). Turner, 50 f., claims that the words in the immediate sequel, ' He took again the Twelve ', prove that the AV is right in mentioning a single group,

and conjectures that ἐθαμβεῖτο, ' He was overcome with consternation ', should be read, pointing out that a stronger compound of the same verb is used of the Agony (xiv. 33). The experience, he suggests, is ' a foretaste of that moment '. See further, Turner, *The Study of the NT* (1926), 62 ; Bartlet, 301. A similar view is maintained by C. C. Torrey, 302, *TG*, 152 f., who thinks that the plur. in the Gk came from *waw* in the Aramaic at the beginning of the next word, the original reading being ' And He was in deep distress, and they who followed were afraid '. If these suggestions are accepted, it is no longer necessary to distinguish two groups and to account for the amazement of the one and the fear of the other. The distress of Jesus at the imminence of His arrival at Jerusalem explains the fear, or awe, of the disciples.[1]

There is certainly a feeling of tension in the narrative. The action of Jesus in taking the lead (προάγω) corresponds to Rabbinic custom (G. Kittel, *KThW*, i. 213 f.), but more than a custom is suggested. The conscious acceptance of His Messianic destiny is depicted, and it is possible that, in the mind of Mark, ἀκολουθοῦντες implies a sharing of the disciples in the same,[2] albeit with fear. In a context full of religious

[1] Pallis, 36, conjectures that the words followed the prophecy in 34 in the form οἱ δὲ ἀκούοντες ἐθαμβοῦντο.

[2] For this meaning Kittel cites viii. 34.

33 λέγειν τὰ μέλλοντα αὐτῷ συμβαίνειν ὅτι Ἰδοὺ ἀναβαίνομεν εἰς
Ἱεροσόλυμα, καὶ ὁ υἱὸς τοῦ ἀνθρώπου παραδοθήσεται τοῖς
ἀρχιερεῦσιν καὶ τοῖς γραμματεῦσιν, καὶ κατακρινοῦσιν αὐτὸν
34 θανάτῳ καὶ παραδώσουσιν αὐτὸν τοῖς ἔθνεσιν καὶ ἐμπαίξουσιν
αὐτῷ καὶ ἐμπτύσουσιν αὐτῷ καὶ μαστιγώσουσιν αὐτὸν καὶ
ἀποκτενοῦσιν, καὶ μετὰ τρεῖς ἡμέρας ἀναστήσεται.

significance, in which ἀναβαίνοντες εἰς Ἱεροσόλυμα may have more than a geographical meaning (cf. J. Schneider, *KThW*, i. 517; Lohmeyer, 220), Turner's exegesis may be as relevant as it is fascinating, although, in default of textual support, his suggested reading must remain conjectural.

The statement that Jesus took again the Twelve reads like a new beginning (cf. ix. 35) and may point to the use of a source. In any case, it suggests that 32a is the introduction to the section x. 32-52. For παραλαμβάνω v. iv. 36; πάλιν ii. 1; οἱ δώδεκα iii. 14; ἤρξατο c. infin. i. 45; μέλλω c. infin. xiii. 4*; συμβαίνω*. The statement that Jesus began to tell the things that would happen to Him, which is peculiar to Mark's narrative, is biblical: LXX, Gen. xlii. 4, 29, xlv. 29, Job i. 22, Esth. vi. 13, 1 Macc. iv. 26; cf. Lk. xxiv. 14. Luke simply says that Jesus took the Twelve and spoke to them. Matthew mentions the ascent to Jerusalem and the way, and adds κατ᾽ ἰδίαν (xx. 17).

33 f. For ἰδού v. i. 2; ἀναβαίνομεν εἰς Ἱεροσόλυμα x. 32; ὁ υἱὸς τοῦ ἀνθρώπου ii. 10; παραδίδωμι i. 14; οἱ ἀρχιερεῖς ii. 26; οἱ γραμματεῖς i. 22; κατακρίνω, xiv. 64, xvi. 16*; θάνατος, vii. 10; ἔθνος, x. 42, xi. 17, xiii. 8 (*bis*), 10*. Many of these words and phrases

are common in Mk and on the whole it may be said that the vocabulary reveals the Evangelist's hand. The dat. in κατακρινοῦσιν αὐτὸν θανάτῳ is peculiar. D* reads θανάτου, and in Mt. xx. 18 ℵ has εἰς θάνατον. *WM*, 263, explains the dat. as one of direction, ' to sentence some one to death ', and observes that it is not found in Gk writers who use the acc. of the person and the acc. or gen. of the sentence. In xiv. 64 Mark has the acc. and infin. with ἔνοχον θανάτου. Blass, 111, cites the analogy of θανάτῳ ζημιοῦν and the Latin *capite damnare*, but Lagrange, 276 f., does not see why the influence of the latter should be admitted and says that to Frenchmen the dat. seems natural. Cf. Dan. iv. 34a (LXX); Hermas, *Sim.* viii. 11. 3.

The references to mocking (ἐμπαίζω, xv. 20, 31*), spitting (ἐμπτύω, xiv. 65, xv. 19*), and scourging (μαστιγόω*) are paralleled in the Passion Narrative, except that in xv. 15 Mark has φραγελλώσας (cf. Jn. xix. 1, ἐμαστίγωσεν). All these verbs are used in the LXX. For ἀποκτείνω v. iii. 5. As in viii. 31 and ix. 31, Mark has μετὰ τρεῖς ἡμέρας, and ἀναστήσεται, as in ix. 31 (ἀναστῆναι, viii. 31). The vocabulary, it will be seen, supports the view that the passage is a *vaticinium ex eventu*. See the introduction to the narrative.

Mk. x. 35-40   68. THE REQUEST OF JAMES   Cf. Mt. xx. 20-3
AND JOHN

The limits and the character of the narrative raise difficult questions. Dibelius, 43, 60, includes it among the Paradigms of ' a less pure type ', explains 38-40 as a prophecy after the event, and questions whether originally 41 or 42 ff. followed 37. Wendling, 133 f., finds the primitive unit in 35-7 + 41-4, with 45 loosely attached. Bultmann, 23, 72, 370, classifies the narrative as an Apothegm.   Like Dibelius, he regards 38 f. as secondary.   In his view 35-7 + 40 is a ' community-formation ' implying belief in Jesus as the Messiah, and 41-5 is a supplement parallel to Lk. xxii. 24-7 (True Greatness).

These reconstructions provide good examples of the effort to recover a basic unit in x. 35-45.   The narrative is stretched on the Procrustean bed of Form Criticism.   But not without qualifying statements.   Thus, Dibelius, 51, sees in the narrative a real interest in James and John, ' although ', he says, ' this interest is surely foreign to the Paradigm ', and Bultmann, 370, recognizes that the naming of the disciples is original (as in v. 37, ix. 38, and perhaps in xiii. 3).   The situation, it may be suggested, is one in which a Story about Jesus current in the primitive community has not yet attained by continual repetition the rounded form of a Pronouncement-story.   Cf. Intr. 78.   The ambitious request of James and John was remembered because of its bearing on the question of precedence in the Kingdom of God.   The narrative may well be a Petrine story (cf. J. Weiss, 350, 357).   To it 41-5 may have been the immediate sequel, although there are signs that it was appended by Mark.   See the next section, p. 442.

The tradition that James and John asked for the chief seats is in every way credible.   As Branscomb, 187, observes, the story does not seem to be a natural product of early Christian piety, since it is ' discreditable ' so far as the petitioners are concerned.   Rawlinson, 144, has justification for saying that it rests upon authentic reminiscence.   The more detailed treatment of 38 f. must be reserved for the Commentary.   Here it may be claimed that the reply of Jesus, ' You do not know what you are asking ', is natural, and equally so His challenging question, ' Can you drink the cup that I drink, or undergo the baptism with which I am baptized ? '. The assumption that martyrdom is prophesied accepts too readily the dubious Papias tradition regarding the death of James and John.   See the detached note on this question.   The declaration of Jesus that it is not for Him to assign precedence in the Kingdom of God (x. 40) places this saying in the same category as xiii. 32 (the day or the hour) which it is impossible to attribute to the creativeness of the Christian community.

Καὶ προσπορεύονται αὐτῷ Ἰάκωβος καὶ Ἰωάνης οἱ [δύο] 35
υἱοὶ Ζεβεδαίου λέγοντες αὐτῷ Διδάσκαλε, θέλομεν ἵνα ὃ ἐὰν
αἰτήσωμέν σε ποιήσῃς ἡμῖν.   ὁ δὲ εἶπεν αὐτοῖς Τί ⌐θέλετε⌐ 36

36 θέλετέ με

35 f. For Ἰάκωβος καὶ Ἰωάνης οἱ [δύο] υἱοὶ Ζεβεδαίου v. i. 19. δύο, read by B C 579 1342 sa bo aeth Aug, is wanting in most MSS.   The order suggests that James was the elder. προσπορεύομαι**, ' to come near ', ' approach ' (Cl., LXX, Pap.) illustrates Mark's preference for compounds of πορεύομαι.   For Διδάσκαλε v. iv. 38. The request is first put in the most

general terms, θέλομεν ἵνα ὃ ἐὰν αἰτήσωμέν σε ποιήσῃς ἡμῖν, where ἵνα c. subj. is used instead of the infin. ; v. the note on vi. 25.   For ὃ ἐάν c. subj. in the object clause v. vi. 22b, where αἰτέω is also used.   In Mt the suppliant is the mother of the sons of Zebedee and the request is not defined, καὶ αἰτοῦσά τι ἀπ' αὐτοῦ (xx. 20).

Jesus sympathetically replies, ' What

37 ποιήσω ὑμῖν; οἱ δὲ εἶπαν αὐτῷ   Δὸς ἡμῖν ἵνα εἷς σου ἐκ δεξιῶν
38 καὶ εἷς ἐξ ἀριστερῶν καθίσωμεν ἐν τῇ δόξῃ σου. ὁ δὲ Ἰησοῦς
εἶπεν αὐτοῖς Οὐκ οἴδατε τί αἰτεῖσθε· δύνασθε πιεῖν τὸ ποτήριον
ὃ ἐγὼ πίνω, ἢ τὸ βάπτισμα ὃ ἐγὼ βαπτίζομαι βαπτισθῆναι;

do you want me to do for you ? '. In Τί θέλετε ποιήσω ὑμῖν; אᶜ B Ψ arm insert με before ποιήσω. Commentators explain that Mark is mixing two constructions, τί θέλ. με ποιῆσαι and τί θέλ. ποιήσω; cf. Swete, 236; Lohmeyer, 220. The whole verse is omitted by k, and D omits τί θέλετε, thus giving the affirmative answer, ' I will do it for you ', Wellhausen, 83, prefers this reading, but the omissions are more probably grammatical or doctrinal. Howard, ii. 421, refers to Plummer's comment on the co-ordinate use of the subj. after θέλω, that in Cl. Gk the construction is more common with βούλομαι, and that ἵνα, which sometimes follows θέλω, is not inserted when the first verb is in the second person, and the second verb in the first (St. Lk, 264); cf. Mk. x. 51, xiv. 12, xv. 12, Lk. ix. 54, Mt. xiii. 28. Matthew has simply τί θέλεις;.

37. The request now made is for seats at the right hand and the left in Christ's glory. The object clause after δὸς ἡμῖν is expressed by ἵνα and the subj. as in verse 35, ἵνα . . . ποιήσῃς ἡμῖν. The place of honour is the seat on the right (ἐκ δεξιῶν, x. 40, xii. 36, xiv. 62, xv. 27, xvi. (5), [19]*); cf. 2 Kgdms. xvi. 6, Psa. cix. (cx.) 1, and next to it the seat on the left (ἐξ ἀριστερῶν); cf. Josephus, Ant. vi. 11. 9, ἐκ τῶν ἑτέρων. ἀριστερός*, Mt. vi. 3, Lk. xxiii. 33, 2 Cor. vi. 7** (Cl., LXX, Pap.), is used of that which is ominous or which bodes ill, because bad omens were thought to come from the left. Cf. εὐώνυμος, x. 40, xv. 27*. In contrast with εὐώνυμος, ἀριστερός is found freely in the papyri in personal descriptions of litigants in legal documents (VGT, 76). For καθίζω v. ix. 35. Here it is used of occupying a position of honour and authority; cf. Psa. cix. (cx.) 1.

For δόξα v. viii. 38. Here, in the thought of Mark, ἐν τῇ δόξῃ σου is used

of the Parousia, as in viii. 38 and xiii. 26; cf. Wellhausen, 84; Blunt, 220. The phrase reflects Mark's theology. It is remarkable that Matthew, despite his strong apocalyptic interests, has ἐν τῇ βασιλείᾳ σου (xx. 21, cf. xvi. 28). It may be that for Matthew the two expressions are synonymous, but it is also possible that he gives the original phrase (cf. Lohmeyer, 221). Probably the two disciples were thinking of the Kingdom of which Jesus had spoken and which they believed to be imminent; in it they desired places of eminence and authority; cf. Bartlet, 303; Wood, 694. If the saying about ' thrones ' (Lk. xxii. 30 = Mt. xix. 28) had already been spoken, they wanted the most important thrones. Alternatively, the reference may have been to the chief seats at the Messianic Feast. Cf. Branscomb, 187; Rawlinson, 144. It follows that they had entirely failed to apprehend the teaching concerning Messianic suffering; their minds still moved in the circle of contemporary beliefs.

38 f. In His reply Jesus tells them that they do not know what they are asking (for the mid. αἰτεῖσθε v. vi. 24 f.) and inquires whether they can face the cost of a share in His Messianic suffering. When they say that they can, He promises them that they shall drink his cup and partake in His baptism. Far more than martyrdom is meant.

For πίνω v. ii. 16; ποτήριον vii. 4; βάπτισμα and βαπτίζω i. 4. Here and in 39 the cognate acc. βάπτισμα and the relative ὅ are accusatives of inner content after the passive verb. Cf. Blass, 90; Robertson, 478; WM, 281 f. For the same constr. after a verb in the active v. Jn. xvii. 26 and Eph. ii. 4.

In the OT the cup is the symbol both of joy (Psa. xxii. (xxiii.) 5, cxv. 4 (cxvi. 13)) and of retribution and suf-

οἱ δὲ εἶπαν αὐτῷ Δυνάμεθα. ὁ δὲ Ἰησοῦς εἶπεν αὐτοῖς Τὸ 39
ποτήριον ὃ ἐγὼ πίνω πίεσθε καὶ τὸ βάπτισμα ὃ ἐγὼ βαπτίζομαι
βαπτισθήσεσθε, τὸ δὲ καθίσαι ἐκ δεξιῶν μου ἢ ἐξ εὐωνύμων οὐκ 40
ἔστιν ἐμὸν δοῦναι, ἀλλ' οἷς ἡτοίμασται.

fering (Psa. lxxiv. (lxxv.) 9, Isa. li. 17-22, Jer. xxxii. 1 (xxv. 15), Ezek. xxiii. 31-4). Here the idea is that of Messianic redemptive suffering (cf. viii. 31, etc.). The cup is one which Jesus Himself is drinking, ὃ ἐγὼ πίνω. The use of the pres. is distinctive, indicating an action already begun (cf. Plummer, 247), unless the case is one in which the original Aramaic would be rightly interpreted by a fut., as in Mt. xx. 22, ὃ ἐγὼ μέλλω πίνειν. Cf. McNeile, 287. The figure of baptism expresses the same idea. βάπτισμα is not used in this sense in the LXX, but the use of the symbolism of water for the idea of calamity is frequent in the OT; cf. Psa. xlii. 7, lxix. 2, 15, Isa. xliii. 2. In popular Gk βαπτίζεσθαι was used metaphorically to express the thought of being flooded or overwhelmed with calamities; cf. VGT, 102. Matthew omits this clause, but the saying has an important parallel in Lk. xii. 50, βάπτισμα δὲ ἔχω βαπτισθῆναι, and the symbolism of the cup is used at the Supper (xiv. 24) and in Gethsemane (xiv. 36). The relevancy of the sacraments of Baptism and the Eucharist may have been in the mind of Mark; cf. Bacon, BGS, 148; Rawlinson, 145; Lohmeyer, 223; but there is no reason to suppose that current sacramental practice has influenced the form of the saying. On the contrary, it is more justly interpreted as an original and creative utterance. Paul's statement, εἰς τὸν θάνατον αὐτοῦ ἐβαπτίσθημεν (Rom. vi. 3), may be a development and an application of the saying, or again it may be an independent formulation of what is involved in the union of the Christian with Christ in death and resurrection. The view of many commentators that 38 f. is a vaticinium ex eventu (cf. Wellhausen, 84; Klostermann, 121;

Bultmann, 23; Dibelius, 60; Branscomb, 189) fails to do justice to this striking saying. It accepts too readily the alleged Papias tradition regarding the death of James and John (v. infra) and too narrowly interprets the saying as a prophecy of martyrdom. If the exegesis outlined above is sound, Jesus prophesied that, like Himself, James and John should endure great tribulation and suffering. Although James was martyred, martyrdom is not exclusively meant, or even necessarily implied, for the NT does not use the imagery of baptism in this sense, and it is not found in Christian usage until the turn of the second century. Cf. Bernard, St. Jn, xlv, JTS, xxviii. 268-70; Lohmeyer, 223; A. Oepke, KThW, i. 536.

40. While promising to James and John a part in His Messianic sufferings, Jesus denies that He has the power to set men on His right or left. These positions are for those for whom they have been prepared. Cf. xiii. 32. For εὐώνυμος, xv. 27*, v. the note on 37. ἐμός, so frequent in Jn, is found in Mk here and in viii. 38 only. For ἑτοιμάζω v. i. 3. Matthew adds ὑπὸ τοῦ πατρός μου, and by assimilation this reading appears in Mk in א* Φ fam. 1 91 299 1071 1342. παρὰ τοῦ πατ. μ. is read by Θ 22 251 697 1278, and a patre meo by a syhl mg. These readings merely bring out what is implied.

More important is the reading ἄλλοις attested by 225 a b d ff k sa aeth and by sys syc (or ἄλλῳ). dare vobis is also read by c f g1.2 k (nobis) l r2 vg (not WW) aeth. The reading must have originated at a very early time in copying a MS. in which ΑΛΛΟΙΣ could be read either as ἀλλ' οἷς or ἄλλοις. Couchoud, JTS, xxxiv. 125, prefers the latter, but it is more probably of Marcionite origin. The introduction of vobis was probably made in opposition to the claims of Arians who used the passage to illustrate the subordination of the Son; it softens the boldness of the saying. Cf. Lagrange, 280. A similar objection may be brought against Turner's rendering, 'save to those for whom it hath been prepared'. See Moulton's discussion, i. 241. The text must be read as it stands, with the recognition that it 'implies a certain "subordination" of the Son (in His

incarnate manifestation) to the Father ' (Blunt, 220). ' Prepared ' does not necessarily carry with it the idea of ' predestination '; it means no more than that places of honour are of the Father's appointing according to His counsels. The note of reserve in the saying is in line with the refusal of Jesus to accept even the appearance of an arbitrary authority; cf. Lk. xii. 14. As such its authenticity is unquestionable.

DETACHED NOTE ON THE ALLEGED PAPIAS TRADITION REGARDING THE DEATH OF JAMES AND JOHN

On the question whether Papias (c. 140 A.D.) attests the martyrdom of James and John critical opinion is sharply divided. Among those who accept the tradition are Schwartz, Wellhausen, Schmiedel, Moffatt, Bacon, Burkitt, Charles, McNeile, Macgregor, and Ed. Meyer; among those who reject it are J. B. Lightfoot, Drummond, Zahn, Chapman, Harnack, Loofs, Clemen, J. A. Robinson, Bernard, Peake, Nolloth, Carpenter, Howard, and Dodd. For the arguments for and against see Charles, *Rev.* xlv-l, and Bernard, *St. Jn*, xxxvii-xlv. In favour of the tradition are : (1) A statement by a late epitomizer of the Chronicle of Philip of Side (c. A.D. 450) which reads : ' Papias in the second book says that John the divine (ὁ θεολόγος) and James his brother were killed by the Jews ' [1] ; (2) A repetition of this statement by Georgius Hamartolus (9th century) who finds in it a fulfilment of Mk. x. 39 ; (3) A Syriac martyrology (c. A.D. 411) which lists under Dec. 27th ' John and James, the apostles, at Jerusalem ' ; (4) The Calendar of Carthage (A.D. 505) which under the same date has ' *S. Iohannis Baptistae et Jacobi apostoli quem Herodes occidit*, the first name being probably a mistake for ' *S. Iohannis Evangelistae* '. Among the arguments against the tradition are : (1) The unreliability of Philip of Side as a historian and the doubt whether he or the epitomizer has correctly reported the Papias statement [2] ; (2) The probability that Georgius Hamartolus is dependent on Philip or the epitomizer ; (3) The doubtful value of the evidence based on the calendars [3] ; (4) The precarious character of the view that Mk. x. 39 predicts ' red ' martyrdom ; (5) The silence of Asian tradition regarding the martyrdom of John ; (6) The silence of Irenaeus and, in particular, of Eusebius who had read Papias ; (7) The strength of the tradition that John lived to a peaceful old age in Ephesus. On these grounds the alleged tradition ought to be dismissed. Cf. Howard, *FG*, 249-51 ; Dodd, 59 n. ; Strachan, *The Fourth Gospel*, 89 ; V. Taylor, *The Gospels*, 101 f.

Mk. x. 41-5   69. THE REBUKE OF THE   Cf. Mt. xx. 24-8
           TEN : RANK AND PRECEDENCE   (Lk. xxii. 24-7)

This narrative, which appears to be a Markan construction, consists mainly of sayings. It is connected with the story of James and John by

---

[1] Printed by De Boor, *Texte und Untersuchungen*, v. 2 (1888).
[2] Cf. Bernard, *St. Jn*, xl.   [3] Cf. Bernard, *op. cit.* xliv.

the words, ' And when the ten heard it, they began to be moved with
indignation concerning James and John ',·and the statement that Jesus
called them to Him.   To the sayings on rank and precedence (42b-4)
there is a parallel in ix. 35, but the more important parallel is Lk. xxii.
24-7 in the Lukan Passion Narrative.   Here too the narrative element
is small, consisting only of the words, ' And there arose also a contention
among them, which of them is accounted to be the greatest ' (cf. Mk.
ix. 34).   Probably teaching on true greatness was given on more occasions
than one, but Mk. x. 41-4 and Lk. xxii. 24-7 appear to be a doublet.   If
so, the question arises which setting is original.   Several considerations
favour that of Mk. x. 41-4.   The section is closely connected with x. 35-40
by the reference to ' the ten ', and it is not easy to account for it unless
Mark is following a tradition.   Again, in spite of what has been said
to the contrary, 41-4 follows well after 35-40: teaching on rank and
service is natural after a request for precedence.   Further, in this respect,
much less can be said for Lk. xxii. 24-7.   In a discourse after the Supper,
service (xxii. 27) is a fitting theme, but a dispute concerning the greatest
(xxii. 24) is difficult to credit.   Several scholars think that xxii. 24-6(7)
is inserted in its present context; cf. Bacon, 181-3; Manson, SJ, 338;
Otto, 270-7.

The ' ransom saying ' in 45 must be considered separately.   See the
detached note on pp. 445-6.   The view there taken is that it is not a
doctrinal modification of Lk. xxii. 27, but a genuine saying of Jesus
which is integral to Mk. x. 41-5.

Καὶ ἀκούσαντες οἱ δέκα ἤρξαντο ἀγανακτεῖν περὶ Ἰακώβου 41
καὶ Ἰωάνου. καὶ προσκαλεσάμενος αὐτοὺς ὁ Ἰησοῦς λέγει 42
αὐτοῖς Οἴδατε ὅτι οἱ δοκοῦντες ἄρχειν τῶν ἐθνῶν κατακυρι-
εύουσιν αὐτῶν καὶ οἱ μεγάλοι αὐτῶν κατεξουσιάζουσιν αὐτῶν.
οὐχ οὕτως δέ ἐστιν ἐν ὑμῖν· ἀλλ' ὃς ἂν θέλῃ μέγας γενέσθαι ἐν 43

41 f. ἀκούσαντες suggests that James
and John were not present.   Only here
do we read of ' the ten '.   For ἤρξαντο
c. infin. v. Intr. 48, 63 f.; ἀγανακτέω
x. 14; προσκαλέομαι iii. 13.   Matthew's
phrase περὶ τῶν δύο ἀδελφῶν reveals
dependence on Mk since previously he
attributes the request to their mother.
The first saying, which reminds the
ten that rulers lord it over their servants, is an example of synonymous
parallelism; cf. Burney, PL, 64.   For
οἴδατε ὅτι v. ii. 10; δοκέω vi. 49*.   οἱ
δοκοῦντες ἄρχειν carries with it a note
of irony; cf. Moffatt, ' the so-called
rulers '; RSV, ' those who are supposed to rule '.   Cf. Gal. ii. 2, 6, 9.
It is difficult to accept the view that οἱ
δοκοῦντες is used without irony (so
Lightfoot and Burton) in Gal.   In Mk

this tone seems evident and still more
in εὐεργέται καλοῦνται in Lk. xxii. 25.
Matthew has οἱ ἄρχοντες, Luke οἱ βα-
σιλεῖς.   οἱ μεγάλοι αὐτῶν, ' their great
men ' (cf. οἱ μεγιστᾶνες (vi. 21)) is
parallel to οἱ δοκοῦντες ἄρχειν.   κατα-
κυριεύω*, Mt. xx. 25, Ac. xix. 16,
1 Pet. v. 3**, is ' to exercise complete
dominion over '; LXX, Gen. i. 28,
ix. 1, Psa. ix. 26, 31, cix. 2.   κατεξου-
σιάζω*, Mt. xx. 25**.   No other example, except a late instance, is cited
by LS, but the simplex is used in Lk.
xxii. 25, etc.   Luke also has κυριεύουσιν.
43 f. A peremptory statement follows: οὐχ οὕτως δέ ἐστιν ἐν ὑμῖν.   In
xxii. 26 Luke has ὑμεῖς δὲ οὐχ οὕτως.
οὕτως, ii. 7.   The present tense ἐστιν
is distinctive, and it is not surprising
that it has been replaced by the fut.

44 ὑμῖν, ⌈ἔσται⌉ ὑμῶν διάκονος, καὶ ὃς ἂν θέλῃ ἐν ὑμῖν εἶναι πρῶτος,
45 ἔσται πάντων δοῦλος· καὶ γὰρ ὁ υἱὸς τοῦ ἀνθρώπου οὐκ ἦλθεν
διακονηθῆναι ἀλλὰ διακονῆσαι καὶ δοῦναι τὴν ψυχὴν αὐτοῦ λύτρον
ἀντὶ πολλῶν.

43 ἔστω

in A C³ many minuscules and versions;
it suggests a principle which is operative in the New Israel (cf. Swete, 239 f.).
Like 42 the sayings which follow
in 43 f. (and 45) have the form of
synonymous parallelism; cf. Burney,
PL, 64. The form is more perfect than
in the brief variant in ix. 35 (q.v.). The
same structure appears in Lk. xxii. 26,
but the vocabulary and syntax are different, pointing to independent translation from the Aramaic. For ὃς ἂν
c. subj. v. iii. 29; διάκονος ix. 35*;
δοῦλος xii. 2, 4, xiii. 34, xiv. 47*. How
deeply this idea of service penetrated
into primitive Christianity is shown by
such passages as 1 Cor. ix. 19, 2 Cor.
iv. 5, and Gal. v. 13. Swete cites Clem.
of Rome, 1 Cor. 48, and Lagrange,
281, the title of the Popes, servus ser-
vorum Dei. For the use of μέγας to
represent the superlative v. Lagrange,
281; Black, 86; v. Intr. 61.

45. This saying is one of the most
important in the Gospels. Its interpretation is discussed below. The
structure is that of Semitic synonymous
parallelism; cf. Burney, PL, 64. The
form οὐκ ἦλθεν διακονηθῆναι ἀλλὰ διακονῆσαι, in which the idea is expressed
first negatively and then positively,
is also Semitic, as also the associations
of δοῦναι τὴν ψυχὴν αὐτοῦ and λύτρον
ἀντὶ πολλῶν.

καὶ γάρ is either etenim or the more
emphatic nam etiam (WM, 560), probably the latter (vg, nam et): RV, ' For
verily'; Torrey, ' For indeed'; RSV,
' For'; Moffatt, ' For the S. of M.
himself '. For ὁ υἱὸς τοῦ ἀνθρώπου v.
ii. 10. ἦλθεν is used as in ii. 17, Mt.
xi. 18 f., etc. It could be used retro-
spectively (Mt. xi. 18), but there is no
reason why it could not also be used
by someone looking back from the
moment of speaking. διακονέω (v. i

13) is by no means limited to the action
of waiting at table (Wellhausen, 84 f.).
In the papyri it is used of a lad appren-
ticed by his father (VGT, 149); cf.
LS; H. W. Beyer, KThW, ii. 84 f.
For δοῦναι τὴν ψυχήν v. 1 Macc. ii. 50,
vi. 44, Thuc. ii. 43. 2, τὰ σώματα δι-
δόντες. F. Büchsel, KThW, ii. 168,
observes that among the Jews the expression is common for the death of
martyrs and among the Greeks for
the death of soldiers.

The most important word is λύτρον*,
Mt. xx. 28** (ἀντίλυτρον, 1 Tim. ii.
6**). In Cl. Gk the word is used,
generally in the plur., of the price of
the redemption of a captive; in the
papyri of the purchase-money for the
manumitting of slaves; cf. Deissmann,
327 ff.; VGT, 382 f. In the LXX it
denotes an equivalent and, with very
few exceptions, is always in the plural
(for כֹּפֶר, פִּדְיוֹן, גְּאֻלָּה, and מְחִיר). For
the idea in later Judaism cf. 2 Macc.
vii. 37 f., 4 Macc. i. 11, xvii. 22. The
prevailing notion behind the word is
that of deliverance by purchase. In
the saying it is used metaphorically
but forcibly to describe an act of redemption.

In ἀντὶ πολλῶν the preposition is used
with the meaning ' for' in the sense
of ' instead of' or ' in place of', its
commonest significance in the papyri
(VGT, 46 f.); cf. Büchsel, KThW, i.
373. Used here only in Mk, it is found
in the Gospels in Mt. ii. 22, v. 38, xvii.
27, xx. 28, Lk. i. 20, xi. 11, xii. 3, xix.
44, Jn. i. 16, and in the rest of the NT
11 times**. It should not be treated
as a synonym of ' the more colourless
ὑπέρ' (so Moulton, i. 105); it suggests
that in the act of deliverance the ' many'
not only benefit but receive what they
cannot effect. The use of πολλῶν recalls Isa. liii. 11 f.; it does not exclude

the meaning ' all ', but contrasts the sacrifice of the one with those for whom it is made; cf. xiv. 24. The phrase goes with λύτρον, not δοῦναι (Klostermann, 122); the self-giving is a means of deliverance which in themselves the ' many ' are not able to accomplish.

In view of the widespread assumption that the saying reflects Pauline influence, it is important to note that Paul does not use this terminology (cf.

1 Tim. ii. 6, Tit. ii. 14). His theology, as expressed in 1 Cor. vi. 20, vii. 23, Gal. i. 4, ii. 20, iii. 13, iv. 5, Rom. iii. 24, 25 f., etc., is in line with Mk. x. 45, but reveals its distinctiveness.

Apart from replacing καὶ γάρ by ὥσπερ, Matthew reproduces the saying verbatim. Luke's parallel version in xxii. 27 lacks λύτρον and ἀντὶ πολλῶν, and reads, τίς γὰρ μείζων, ὁ ἀνακείμενος ἢ ὁ διακονῶν; οὐχὶ ὁ ἀνακείμενος; ἐγὼ δὲ ἐν μέσῳ ὑμῶν εἰμι ὡς ὁ διακονῶν.

DETACHED NOTE ON THE INTERPRETATION OF MK. X. 45

Many writers question the genuineness of the saying and trace its form to Pauline influence. Wellhausen, 84 f., claims that it is out of harmony with its context. The change from the idea of service to that of the giving of life as a ransom, he argues, is a μετάβασις εἰς ἄλλο γένος, a transition from one class (of ideas) to another, and is derived from the tradition of the Last Supper where Jesus, with bread and wine, dispenses His flesh and blood. J. Weiss, *Die Schr.*[4] i. 174 f., maintains that in the saying the whole life and work of Jesus are seen in retrospect (ἦλθεν). λύτρον and the ideas suggested by it appear nowhere else in the preaching of Jesus and the original form of the saying is to be seen in Lk. xxii. 27 which says nothing of a redemptive death. While Jesus may have included His death in His work of service and of love for men, it is doubtful if He thought of it as sacrificial or as involving penal suffering, as, according to later interpretation, Isa. liii described it. ' We men of to-day, for whom the idea of an expiatory sacrifice presents many difficulties, may be thankful that we can be satisfied with the view that His death, no less than His whole life, was a true service for His brethren.' Both Bousset, 8, and Bultmann, 97, agree that the saying is a dogmatic recast of Lk. xxii. 27. Similarly, Loisy, ii. 241, thinks that the idea *appartient à un autre courant que celle du service* and claims that Mark has borrowed the theory of redemption, *étrangère à la pensée de Jésus*, from Paul.

Rashdall's treatment of the saying in *The Idea of the Atonement*, 49-56, is well known. The only doctrine of the Atonement, he holds, which can be traced to Jesus Himself is ' the simple doctrine that His death, like His life, was a piece of service or self-sacrifice for His followers, such as they themselves might very well make for one another ', *op. cit.* 37. Branscomb, 190 f., also thinks that x. 45 is a highly developed theological version of Lk. xxii. 27, influenced by Gal. iii. 13, Rom. iii. 24, and 1 Cor. vii. 23. He agrees that such explanations have been overstated, and that many of Paul's most characteristic ideas are wanting in Mk, but holds that ' the Gospel belongs undoubtedly to the Pauline school—that is, one which viewed Christianity essentially as a religion of redemption through the death of the Messiah '.

On the positive side Rawlinson, 146-8, thinks that the saying, despite its omission by Luke, is in all probability genuine and that the reference to ' the many ' is an echo of Isa. liii. 11 f. The ' ransom ' metaphor 'sums up the general thought of Isa. liii, and expresses the idea of a vicarious and voluntary giving up of life, with the thought also implied that the sacrifice was in some way mysteriously necessitated by sin '. In reply to Loisy, Lagrange, 281-3, points out that not only the redemptive death is known to Paul, but also the thought of service unto death (Phil. ii. 7 f.), and asks the pertinent question whether Jesus has furnished the theme for the Pauline developments or Mark has summarized in a word the theology of Paul in order to attribute it to Jesus. The former hypothesis, he holds, is the only one that is probable. Howard, *ET*, l. 107-10, finds the key to the saying in Isa. liii. The significant word, he observes, is not Pauline. In Pauline circles the form of the logion is most characteristically seen in 1 Tim. ii. 6 (' a ransom *for all* ') and Tit. ii. 14 (' *for us* '). The answers given in the Early Church to the questions provoked by the Cross ' are interpretations of the luminous hint which Jesus gave to His perplexed disciples in such sayings as Mk. x. 45 and xiv. 24 '. See also Turner, 52 ; Otto, 252 f., 256-61 ; Schniewind, 144 ; Büchsel, *KThW*, iv. 343-51.

The strength of the argument is on the affirmative side. Those who deny the genuineness of the saying too easily assume that its ideas are exclusively Pauline and do not sufficiently recognize that Paulinism is rooted in primitive Christianity. Adequate consideration is not given to the possibility that Lk. xxii. 27 is an independent saying. Again, notably in the case of J. Weiss, the rejection of Mk. x. 45 is influenced by the desire to avoid older doctrines of the Atonement which have found shelter under the saying and to obtain a purely general interpretation of its meaning. It is wise never to forget that λύτρον is used metaphorically, but it is equally wise to remember that a metaphor is used to convey an arresting thought. Jesus died to fulfil the Servant's destiny and His service is that of vicarious and representative suffering. We are ill-advised if we seek to erect a theory upon x. 45 alone, but equally so if we dismiss it as a product of later theological construction.

| Mk. x. 46-52 | 70. THE CURE OF THE BLIND MAN AT JERICHO | Cf. Mt. xx. 29-34 Lk. xviii. 35-43 |

The detail and vividness of this story are notable. The incident is precisely located at Jericho. Dibelius, 52, holds that the name belongs to the section as such : it is mentioned first by the Evangelist in the connecting sentence : ' And they come to Jericho ' (46a), and then in the section itself in the words : ' And as he went out from Jericho ' (46b). Again, the blind man is named. Some critics think that ' Bartimaeus ' is a later addition, in view of the tendency to add names in early tradition and because Mark alone gives the name ; cf. Bultmann, 228 ; Dibelius, 52. Mark, however, so rarely records names that his statement deserves credit. Further, the details of the story make a good impression : the beggar sitting by the wayside, his quickness to grasp the opportunity, his bold use of the title ' Son of David ', his refusal to be silenced, the alacrity with which he casts aside his garment and comes to Jesus, his confidence and subsequent following in the way. ' Apparently ', says Branscomb, 192, ' we have in this story an account which goes back, and owes its details to, the reminiscences of an eyewitness.' Cf. Rawlinson,

148. Turner, 52, suggests that, more perhaps than in any miracle recorded in Mk, the story is told from the point of view of the man healed. Very different is the opinion of the Form-critics. Bultmann, 228, thinks the narrative is secondary in character and that it is scarcely possible to perceive an original Miracle-story as its foundation. Dibelius 43, 115, includes it among the Paradigms of ' a less pure type ' and describes it as a legendary narrative which has grown out of a Paradigm. A better explanation is the one already suggested in other cases, that the report of an eyewitness has not yet attained the rounded form of a Miracle-story proper. As it stands, the story is hardly told as the account of a ' mighty work ' ; it is doubtful if it is correct to say with Dibelius, 87, that the healing reaches its ' high point ' in the proof and consequence of faith, although this is a feature to which Mark attaches great importance. It is more probable that he records it primarily because of its Messianic character as a preparation for the story of the Entry (xi. 1-11) and because it belongs to the last stage of the journey to Jerusalem. Whence he derived the story is impossible to say. It may be a Petrine story or more generally be drawn from good Jerusalem tradition.

Καὶ ἔρχονται εἰς Ἰερειχώ. Καὶ ἐκπορευομένου αὐτοῦ ἀπὸ 46 Ἰερειχὼ καὶ τῶν μαθητῶν αὐτοῦ καὶ ὄχλου ἱκανοῦ ὁ υἱὸς Τιμαίου Βαρτίμαιος τυφλὸς προσαίτης ἐκάθητο παρὰ τὴν ὁδόν.

46. For the historic present v. Intr. 46 f. The plur. is not impersonal; Jesus and His disciples are meant. ' He enters with a crowd of followers (Lk. xviii. 36), as a great Rabbi on His way to the Passover ; and His passage through the city bears the character of an ovation ', Swete, 241. Ἰερειχώ, x. 46b*, Mt. xx. 29, Lk. x. 30, xviii. 35, xix. 1, Heb. xi. 30**. For the accentuation v. Hort, 155. Now known as Eriḥa, Jericho is five miles west of the Jordan and fifteen miles north-east of Jerusalem. It was rebuilt by Herod the Great, who died there, and adorned by Archelaus. Later it was held by a Roman garrison ; Jos. BJ, ii. 18. 6. For descriptions of its former beauty and fertility v. G. A. Smith, 266-8 ; Dalman, SSW, 242-4.

The gen. abs. ἐκπορευομένου αὐτοῦ, used correctly and followed by τῶν μαθητῶν αὐτοῦ and ὄχλου ἱκανοῦ, de-scribes the circumstances in which the incident happened. For οἱ μαθηταὶ αὐτοῦ v. ii. 15. ἱκανός (v. i. 7) is used in the sense of ' considerable ' (VGT, 302). Here only in Mk is it used with the meaning of πολύς, but frequently in this sense in Lk (6) and Ac (16). The crowd (ὄχλος, ii. 4) consisted of people from Jericho or pilgrims on their way to the Feast, perhaps both. Luke places the incident before the arrival at Jericho, ἐγένετο δὲ ἐν τῷ ἐγγίζειν αὐτὸν εἰς Ἰερειχώ (xviii. 35), probably because of his use of the story of Zacchaeus in xix. 1-10; cf. Taylor, BTG, 93, 196 f.

A blind man sitting begging by the way side is a common sight in the east. προσαίτης*, Jn. ix. 8**, is a late word, not found in Cl. Gk or the LXX and not recorded in VGT. Many MSS. substitute προσαιτῶν for it after ὁδόν, including A C² W et al. fam. 1 fam. 13 28 700 al. pler. it (mendicans, exc. k) vg syhl sa geo¹. D Θ 565 have ἐπαιτῶν (cf. Lk. xviii. 35). For τυφλός v. viii. 22 ; κάθημαι ii. 6 ; ὁδός i. 2.

Only here and in the case of Jairus (v. 22) is a name given in Mk earlier than the Passion Narrative and apart from the disciples. The derivation of Βαρτίμαιος is unknown. It may be derived from the Greek name Τίμαιος, familiar in the Timaeus of Plato, but it is more likely to be a patronymic

47 καὶ ἀκούσας ὅτι Ἰησοῦς ⸀ὁ Ναζαρηνός ἐστιν⸌ ἤρξατο κράζειν καὶ
48 λέγειν Υἱὲ Δαυεὶδ Ἰησοῦ, ἐλέησόν με. καὶ ἐπετίμων αὐτῷ
πολλοὶ ἵνα σιωπήσῃ· ὁ δὲ πολλῷ μᾶλλον ἔκραζεν Υἱὲ Δαυείδ,
49 ἐλέησόν με. καὶ στὰς ὁ Ἰησοῦς εἶπεν Φωνήσατε αὐτόν. καὶ
φωνοῦσι τὸν τυφλὸν λέγοντες αὐτῷ Θάρσει, ἔγειρε, φωνεῖ σε.

47 ἐστὶν ὁ Ναζαρηνὸς

of Aramaic origin. Probably it represents בַּר טִמַי, 'son of Timai', or
'son of the unclean' (טָמֵא), prefer-
ably the former. Derivation from
samya, 'blind', is highly doubtful,
and Lagrange, 284 f., thinks that the
explanation assigned to Jerome in
words frequently quoted : Barsemia,
filius caecus, quod et ipsum conrupte
quidam Bartimaeum legunt (Liber
interpr. hebr. nom., ed. Lagarde, 66),
is the work of a copyist who drew it
from some Syrian author. The reading 'Timaeus, the son of Timaeus' in
sys pe looks like an attempt at simplification. See further, Schmiedel, EB,
col. 490 f.; Swete, 242 f.; Milligan,
DCG, i. 173 ; Lagrange, 284 f. The
explanatory phrase ὁ υἱὸς Τιμαίου preceding Βαρτίμαιος is not in accordance
with Mark's style, for usually after
the Aramaic word he adds ὅ ἐστιν
. . . (iii. 17, vii. 11, 34; cf. also xii. 42,
xv. 16, 42), although in x. 47 he has
υἱὲ Δαυεὶδ Ἰησοῦ. The phrase may be
a scribal gloss; cf. ⸀Lagrange, 284;
Schmiedel, EB, col. 490 n.; Branscomb, 192; Rawlinson, 149; Blunt,
223. The use of the name points to
special information, and perhaps to
the fact that Bartimaeus was known
in the Church at Jerusalem. Cf.
Bengel : Notus apostolorum tempore
Bartimaeus. The name is not found
in the later Gospels : Lk, τυφλός τις,
Mt, δύο τυφλοί (cf. viii. 28, ix. 27).

47 f. The blind man hears that Jesus
is near and appeals to Him for help.
After ἀκούσας, the clause ὅτι . . . ἐστιν
preserves the tense of the thought : it
is Jesus the Nazarene. For Ἰησοῦς
v. i. 9 ; Ναζαρηνός i. 24 ; ἤρξατο c. infin.
Intr. 48, 63 f.; Δαυείδ ii. 25 ; ἐλεέω
v. 19. For the order of the words in

Υἱὲ Δ. Ἰησοῦ v. the note on 46. Here
and in verse 48 alone in Mk is Jesus
addressed as 'the Son of David', although in xii. 35 He Himself mentions
the name ; cf. Mt (9), Lk (3). The
title is Messianic and implies the
nationalistic hopes which centred on
a Davidic king; cf. Psa. Sol. xvii. 21.
It is here used by an individual and
not by the crowd at large ; it expressed
a view which Bartimaeus had formed,
perhaps under the influence of Isa.
lxi. 1, ἔχρισέ με κύριος . . . κηρῦξαι
. . . τυφλοῖς ἀνάβλεψιν.

The man's importunity is unwelcome
to many in the company and they tell
him to be quiet (Moffatt). For ἐπιτιμάω
v. i. 25. As in iii. 12, the ἵνα clause is
either final or gives the purport of the
rebuke. Undeterred, the man re-
solutely repeats his cry. With πολλῷ
μᾶλλον, here only in Mk, cf. αὐτοὶ μᾶλλον περισσότερον ἐκήρυσσον in vii. 36.
For σιωπάω v. iii. 4; κράζω iii. 11.

Luke edits his source, replacing
Ναζαρηνός by Ναζωραῖος and ἐστιν by
παρέρχεται (Mt παράγει). Both Evangelists replace ἤρξατο c. infin. by a
finite verb (Mt ἔκραξαν, Lk ἐβόησεν)
and both particularize πολλοί (Mt ὁ
ὄχλος, Lk οἱ προάγοντες). All these
changes are editorial, and also Luke's
explanation that the blind man, hearing a crowd passing through, inquired
what was happening (τί εἴη τοῦτο) and
received the reply that Jesus the
Nazarene was passing by.

49 f. Jesus bids the people call the
blind man, and they do so, saying,
'Be of good cheer, arise, he calls thee'.
For θαρσέω v. vi. 50*; ἐγείρω ii. 9;
φωνέω i. 26. In Mt and Lk the direct
speech is omitted and the facts briefly
summarized : Mt. xx. 32, ἐφώνησεν

ὁ δὲ ἀποβαλὼν τὸ ἱμάτιον αὐτοῦ ἀναπηδήσας ἦλθεν πρὸς τὸν 50
Ἰησοῦν. καὶ ἀποκριθεὶς αὐτῷ ὁ Ἰησοῦς εἶπεν Τί σοι θέλεις 51
ποιήσω; ὁ δὲ τυφλὸς εἶπεν αὐτῷ Ῥαββουνεί, ἵνα ἀναβλέψω.
καὶ ὁ Ἰησοῦς εἶπεν αὐτῷ Ὕπαγε, ἡ πίστις σου σέσωκέν σε. 52
καὶ εὐθὺς ἀνέβλεψεν, καὶ ἠκολούθει αὐτῷ ἐν τῇ ὁδῷ.

αὐτούς, Lk. xviii. 40, ἐκέλευσεν αὐτὸν ἀχθῆναι πρὸς αὐτόν. Both Gospels also omit Mark's vivid picture of the man casting away his outer garment (ἱμάτιον, v. ii. 21), leaping up, and coming to Jesus. ἀποβάλλω*, Heb. x. 35**, 'throw off', 'let go'; Cl., LXX, Isa. i. 30, Pap. Cf. 4 Kgdms. vii. 15 (ἔρριψεν) and Heb. xii. 1, ὄγκον ἀποθέμενοι πάντα. Lohmeyer, 226, thinks that this use of the word is Hellenistic, and that ἐπιβαλών (sys 565) suits the circumstances better; cf. the references to girding in Jer. i. 17 and Ac. xii. 8. So also Pallis, 37. The man would not be wearing his garment, but using it spread out on the ground to receive alms. Even in this case, however, he could have thrown it aside, and indeed on this interpretation his action is more dramatic and decisive. In any case ἐπιβαλών is secondary. Swete, 244, calls it tame. Lagrange, 285, traces it to the influence of Jn. xxi. 7. Mrs. Lewis, *The Old Syriac Gospels*, xxii, prefers the reading because it agrees with oriental custom. ἀναπηδάω**, Cl., LXX, Pap. (Bauer⁴, 108). Cf. 1 Kgdms. xx. 34, xxv. 9, Esth. v. 1, Tob. (4). Only in Mk is the man's spirited action described. The fact that he is able to approach Jesus unaided suggests that his blindness is not total; cf. E. R. Micklem, 105 f.

51 f. For ἀποκριθεὶς . . . εἶπεν v. Intr. 63. The redundancy of the participle is manifest, for no question has been asked. For the subj. after θέλεις v. the note on x. 36. The man's plight is obvious, but the question is put in order that he may give expres-

sion to his need. 'The Lord will have the want specified', Swete, 245. Ῥαββουνεί*, Jn. xx. 16**, is a stronger word than Ῥαββεί and means 'My Lord'; cf. Swete, 245; Lagrange, 286; Schniewind, 145; Lohmeyer, 226 n.; Dalman, 324, 340. For its use in the Targums cf. Black, 21. It is replaced in Mt and Lk by Κύριε, which is read in Mk by 409 geoᴬ (D a b ff i sys, κύριε ῥαββεί). With ἵνα ἀναβλέψω sc. θέλω¹ and for the meaning of ἀναβλέπω (v. vi. 41), 'to recover sight', cf. Tob. xiv. 2, Mt. xi. 5, Jn. ix. 11, 15, 18; cf. also *VGT*, 30, Milligan, *Documents*, 154. Luke repeats the word (xviii. 41), but Matthew has the pass. ἀνοιγῶσιν (xx. 33).

It is remarkable that no action or healing word of Jesus is mentioned in Mk; Luke adds the command Ἀνάβλεψον and Matthew mentions the act of touching (ἥψατο τῶν ὀμμάτων αὐτῶν). All that Jesus says in Mk is Ὕπαγε, ἡ πίστις σου σέσωκέν σε. For πίστις v. ii. 5; σώζω iii. 4. As in v. 34 the faith in question is confident trust in God and in the power of Jesus to heal. Cf. Schniewind, 138. For ὑπάγω v. i. 44.

Mark adds that straightway (εὐθύς, i. 10) he received his sight and followed Him in the way. A literal following may be meant, but it is highly probable that Mark has in mind the personal attachment to Jesus described in i. 18 and ii. 14. The phrase ἐν τῇ ὁδῷ (v. viii. 3) connects the incident with the journey to Jerusalem and anticipates xi. 1-11. Matthew follows Mk closely, but Luke adds, δοξάζων τὸν θεόν. καὶ πᾶς ὁ λαὸς ἰδὼν ἔδωκεν αἶνον τῷ θεῷ (xviii. 23).

¹ Unless ἵνα ἀναβλέψω is imperatival. Cf. Meecham, *ET*, lii. 437, *JTS*, xliii. 180.

VI

Mk. xi. i-xiii. 37　　THE MINISTRY IN
JERUSALEM

The sixth division begins with the Entry into Jerusalem and continues to the end of the Apocalyptic Discourse in xiii. Its limits are determined by the fact that its contents are connected with the Ministry in Jerusalem and its neighbourhood previous to the Passion Narrative proper in xiv. 1-xvi. 8. Three separate sections may be distinguished: (a) The Events preceding the Ministry (xi. 1-25); (b) Teaching in Jerusalem (xi. 27-xii. 44); (c) The Apocalyptic Discourse (xiii. 1-37).

The structure of these sections is of much interest. In the first the narratives are set in a framework of three days (cf. xi. 1, 12, 19 f.) and apparently all that is recorded further in the second and third sections falls within this third day. Nowhere else in the Gospel, except in the Passion Narrative (cf. xiv. 1, 12, 17, xv. 1, 33, 42, xvi. 1 f.), have we a chronological scheme so precise. Nevertheless, the arrangement is plainly artificial. Not only is the third day overloaded, but the sections included in it are groups of narratives and sayings which probably existed as units of tradition before the Gospel was compiled. As Albertz, 16-39, has shown, the foundation of the second section is a collection of Controversy-stories, xi. 27-33, xii. 13-40 (perhaps originally preceded by xi. 15-17), comparable to ii. 1-iii. 6 and in like manner concerned with conflicts with the Jewish hierarchy. V. Intr. 101. Further, by general consent the third section (xiii. 1-37) is a compilation. It is manifest that the Evangelist has imposed on xi. 1-xiii. 37 a chronological scheme to bring it into harmony with the Passion Narrative in order to describe in detail the successive days of the last tragic week. He had no detailed knowledge of the Ministry in Jerusalem like that displayed in the Passion Narrative itself, and, in default of continuous tradition, was compelled to assemble in the best manner possible existing units of tradition which in some cases belonged to other periods in the Story of Jesus.

(a) Mk. xi. 1-25　　THE EVENTS PRECEDING
THE MINISTRY

The incidents and sayings included in this section include the following:

(71) xi. 1-11. The Entry into Jerusalem.
(72) xi. 12-14. The Cursing of the Fig Tree.
(73) xi. 15-19. The Cleansing of the Temple.
(74) xi. 20-5. The Withered Fig Tree and Sayings on Faith and Prayer.

As already observed, the material is set in a closely articulated chronological and topographical frame. The Entry is introduced by the words, ' And when they drew near to Jerusalem, to Bethphage and Bethany, at the Mount of Olives ' (xi. 1), and the narrative closes with the statement that, when Jesus had looked round at everything, it being now late, He went out to Bethany with the Twelve (xi. 11). The incident of the Fig Tree happens ' on the following day ' (xi. 12), and, presumably, on the same day Jerusalem is entered again and the Cleansing takes place (xi. 15-19). The narrative closes with the words, ' And when evening came they went out of the city ', and they see the fig tree withered away ' as they passed by in the morning ' (xi. 20). The saying, ' Have faith in God ', may belong to the story, but the remaining sayings on faith and prayer are loosely appended, as in ii. 21 f., 27 f., iii. 27-9, iv. 21-5, etc. The arrangement appears to be catechetical, but before this view can be accepted it will be necessary later to consider more closely the position assigned to the Cleansing.

| Mk. xi. 1-11 | 71. THE ENTRY INTO JERUSALEM | Cf. Mt. xxi. 1-17
Lk. xix. 28-38
Jn. xii. 12-19 |

Mk. xi. 1-11 includes two stories, the Sending for the Colt (1-6) and the Entry proper (7-11), but the two are so closely connected that they may be taken together. A third story is recorded by Luke, the account of the Pharisees who said, ' Master, rebuke thy disciples ' (xix. 39 f.). The later Evangelists, Matthew and John, expressly refer to Zech. ix. 9 :

> ' Tell ye the daughter of Zion,
> Behold, thy King cometh unto thee,
> Meek, and riding upon an ass,
> And upon a colt the foal of an ass ',

(Mt. xxi. 5, cf. Jn. xii. 15). It is probable that Mark also has this prophecy in mind (cf. xi. 2) and that it influenced the action of Jesus Himself.

Different views have been taken of the nature of the story. (1) Generally it has been held to have Messianic significance ; cf. Swete, 246-53 ; Lagrange, 287-92 ; Turner, 53 f. ; Rawlinson, 151 ; Dobschütz, *The Eschatology of the Gospels*, 175-7 ; Ed. Meyer, i. 162 f. (*Der Anspruch, der Messias zu sein, ist ganz unverkennbar*) ; Goguel, 410 ; Cadoux, 59 ; etc. Influenced by Mt, some commentators exaggerate this aspect, as if the one intention of Jesus was to assert Messiahship. On this matter the observation of Dobschütz is very much to the point : ' The manner He chose for His entrance was very fit for declaring His Messianic dignity to those who were able and inclined to understand and to conceal it from the others '. Wellhausen, 87, is justified in saying that the incident has no result ; neither the high priests nor the Romans took action. (2) Alternatively, it is held that a spontaneous outburst of enthusiasm on the part of the disciples and pilgrims was afterwards interpreted in a Messianic sense under the influence of Zech. ix. 9 ; cf. Wellhausen, 88 ; Dalman, 222 ; Bacon, *BGS*, 158 ; J. Weiss, *Die Schr.*⁴ 177 ; Otto, 224 ; Lohmeyer, 233 ; Branscomb, 198-200 ; etc. ' The acclamation ', says Otto, 224, ' is eschatological, but not specifically Messianic.' This view pays too little regard to the action of Jesus in sending for the colt, to the Messianic associations of the Mount of Olives and of the phrase ' he that cometh ' as interpreted by Matthew. (3) A third view is that the narrative is a ' Messianic legend ' (Bultmann, 281) or a ' cultus-legend ' (Dibelius, 122). In principle, this view does not differ greatly from the second, for Bultmann allows that the legend may be based on an account of the entry into Jerusalem by Jesus with a crowd of pilgrims full of joy and expectation, and Dibelius thinks of the form of the narrative rather than its historical content. (4) Recently it has been emphasized how much the story is influenced by the idea of the ' Messianic Secret ' ; cf. Lohmeyer, 232 ; Schniewind, 148 (*Das Messias-Geheimnis waltet über dem Ganzen*). This is a view which by no means rules out the historical character of the incident.

In favour of the historical worth of the narrative are the local expressions at the beginning, the vivid character of the account, including the instructions to the two disciples, the description of what happened, the restrained nature of the acclamation, and the strange manner in which the account breaks off without any suggestion of a ' triumphal entry ' (as in Mt). These characteristics suggest the eyewitness rather than the artist.

The key to the interpretation of the narrative is the strange combination within it of Messianic and non-Messianic elements. Schweitzer, 391 f., was justified when he affirmed that the Entry was Messianic for Jesus, but not Messianic for the people, although there is no evidence for his view that the people hailed Jesus as Elijah. Their cry is *almost* Messianic. In speaking of the Kingdom of their father, David, they imply that the Kingdom is near, but stop short of the use of the title ' Son of David '. Their words transcend what might be said of a famous Rabbi, but are not full-throated Messianic homage. The atmosphere is one of dangerous tension, but the tension breaks and dies away. Strictly speaking, there is no Messianic entry ; as in Lk. xix. 37-40, the story describes the rapturous exultation felt when the city comes in sight. When Jesus enters He is accompanied by His disciples only, and, when He has looked round at everything, He departs with the Twelve to Bethany. The contrast with Matthew's narrative is astonishing and bespeaks an earlier and superior tradition.

Despite the warning of Wellhausen, 87, a historical reconstruction of the original events is unavoidable. Jesus must have observed the growing Messianic tension among His disciples and have realized that His teaching about a Suffering Messiah had failed. The very stones were impregnated with political expectations (Lk. xix. 40). He therefore resorts to prophetic action, as at the feast in the wilderness and as He was to do at the Last Supper. By previous arrangement He sends two disciples for the colt, intending to fulfil Zechariah's prophecy.[1] Unable to deny that He is the promised Messiah, He seeks to show to His disciples and to the crowd the kind of Messiah He is, no man of war, but lowly, and riding upon an ass. The crowd is puzzled, but penetrates His meaning sufficiently to see that He is not to be the Messiah of their hopes. That is why later they turned against Him. Jesus wills just *this* Entry (cf. Schniewind, 147 f.). His purpose fails, but succeeds in its failure. So unique is the Markan narrative that we must conclude that it comes from the best tradition, with

---

[1] ' This correspondence with the prophecy does not prove that the narrative was forged, because Jesus may have been inspired by the passage in Zechariah to make his Messianic entry into Jerusalem in this manner ', Goguel, 410. That the Messianic interpretation of the prophecy is not strange to Judaism is shown by the saying of Rabbi Joshua ben Levi (*c.* A.D. 250) : ' Behold, the Son of Man comes " on the clouds of heaven ", and " lowly, and riding upon an ass ". If they (Israel) are worthy, " with the clouds of heaven " ; if they are not worthy, " lowly, and riding upon an ass " ', *Sanhedrin*, 98a. Cf. Moore, ii. 334 f.

embellishment only in the phrase concerning the colt : ' whereon no man
ever yet sat '. With good reason we may assign it to the Petrine tradition ;
cf. J. Weiss, 350.

Καὶ ὅτε ἐγγίζουσιν εἰς Ἱεροσόλυμα ⌜εἰς Βηθφαγὴ καὶ⌝ Βη- 1 XI
θανίαν πρὸς τὸ Ὄρος ⌜τῶν⌝ Ἐλαιῶν, ἀποστέλλει δύο τῶν μαθητῶν αὐτοῦ καὶ λέγει αὐτοῖς Ὑπάγετε εἰς τὴν κώμην τὴν κατέν- 2
αντι ὑμῶν, καὶ εὐθὺς εἰσπορευόμενοι εἰς αὐτὴν εὑρήσετε πῶλον

1 καὶ εἰς | τὸ

1 f. For Ἱεροσόλυμα v. iii. 8 ; ἐγγίζω
i. 15. The topographical passage belongs to the present story, but points
forward to the opening of the Ministry
in Jerusalem. Βηθφαγή*, Mt. xxi. 1,
Lk. xix. 29**, ' Bethphage ', lit. ' house
of figs ' (?), is omitted by D 700 ff g²
i k r¹·² vg Or, but is probably original ;
cf. Streeter, 318 ; Lagrange, 287 ;
Turner, 53 ; Rawlinson, 152 ; Branscomb, 196. Per contra v. Goguel, 409 ;
Lake, Beginnings, v. 475 ; Lohmeyer,
228. Streeter observes that ' Western
omissions are not always " non-interpolations " ', and apart from the
textual evidence, the inconspicuous
character of the place and the Lukan
text point to the presence of the name
in Mk.

Bethphage is frequently mentioned
in the rabbinic literature (cf. Dalman,
SSW, 252 f.). Apparently it was a
hamlet or suburb, or even a manor,
which in any case was quite near Jerusalem. Βηθανία, xi. 11 f., xiv. 3*, Mt.
xxi. 17, xxvi. 6, Lk. xix. 29, xxiv. 50,
Jn. i. 28 (' beyond Jordan '), xi. 1, 18,
xii. 1**, ' Bethany ', lit. ' house of
dates ' (?). It is usually identified with
the modern El Azariyeh, south-east
of Jerusalem, and 15 furlongs (Jn. xi.
18) from the city, on the road from
Jericho, but Lake, Beginnings, v. 475 f.
argues powerfully for a site higher up
on the eastern side of the Mount of
Olives, a view which would agree well
with Lk. xxi. 37. See further, Dalman,
SSW, 249-51. Ψ and sa omit Βηθανία
and Branscomb, 196, thinks that it is
a later addition.

Τὸ Ὄρος τῶν Ἐλαιῶν, xiii. 3, xiv.
26*. Mark does not use the noun

Ἐλαιών, ' Olive orchard ' (Lk. xix. 29,
xxi. 37, Ac. i. 12), though it appears
here in B k r. Cf. Deissmann, BS,
208-12. The hill, which rises to a
height of over 2600 feet, runs from
north to south on the east side of Jerusalem, and from it across the Kidron
the city can be clearly seen. From
ancient times a place of prayer (2 Sam.
xv. 32), the hill was the scene of
Ezekiel's vision of the glory of the
Lord (Ezek. xi. 23) and the place prophesied by Zechariah for the judgment
of the enemies of Israel (Zech. xiv. 4).
Later it was associated by the Rabbis
with the resurrection of the righteous
dead and the coming of the Messiah.
Cf. Lake, Beginnings, v. 22 ; Lohmeyer, 229 ; Billerbeck, i. 840. Cf.
Josephus, BJ, ii. 13. 5 ; Ant. xx. 8. 6.

The vocabulary of 1 f. contains
familiar Markan words. For ἀποστέλλω v. i. 2 ; οἱ μαθηταὶ αὐτοῦ ii. 15 ;
ὑπάγω i. 44 ; κώμη vi. 6 ; εὐθύς i. 10 ;
εἰσπορεύομαι i. 21 ; δέω iii. 27 ; οὔπω
iv. 40 ; καθίζω ix. 35. κατέναντι, xii.
41, xiii. 3*, ' opposite ', ' over against ',
belongs to late Gk : LXX (Ex. xix. 2,
Ezek. xi. 1), Pap. (VGT, 335). The
village is usually identified with Bethphage, but Bethany also is a possible
suggestion ; cf. Bartlet, 312 ; Lake,
op. cit. 475 f. ; Dalman, SSW, 254 f.
For the construction with καί after a
participle in D cf. Howard, ii. 420 ;
Black, 50.

πῶλος, xi. 4, 5, 7*, in Cl. Gk can be
used of the young of any animal, generally of the horse, but in the LXX
(Gen. xxxii. 15, etc.), as in the papyri
(VGT, 561), it is used of the ' colt ' or
' foal ' of an ass. Matthew mentions

δεδεμένον ἐφ᾽ ὃν οὐδεὶς οὔπω ἀνθρώπων ἐκάθισεν· λύσατε αὐτὸν
3 καὶ φέρετε. καὶ ἐάν τις ὑμῖν εἴπῃ Τί ποιεῖτε τοῦτο; εἴπατε Ὁ
κύριος αὐτοῦ χρείαν ἔχει· καὶ εὐθὺς ⌜αὐτὸν ἀποστέλλει πάλιν⌝
4 ὧδε. καὶ ἀπῆλθον καὶ εὗρον πῶλον δεδεμένον πρὸς θύραν ἔξω

3 ἀποστέλλει πάλιν αὐτὸν

both the ass (ὄνος) and the colt (πῶλος) in accordance with Zech. ix. 9. Mark also appears to have the prophecy in mind in ἐφ᾽ ὃν οὐδεὶς οὔπω ἀνθρώπων ἐκάθισεν (cf. Lk. xix. 30) omitted in Mt. Cf. Zech. ix. 9, πῶλον νέον. The phrase is probably an expansion of the saying; cf. Bartlet, 312; Gould, 206. *Per contra* Swete, 247. It characterizes the animal as in some sense sacred; cf. Numb. xix. 2, Deut. xxi. 3. The distinction of tenses in λύσατε and φέρετε is noteworthy. Both Matthew and Luke have λύσαντες.

The principal variants in Mt and Lk are manifestly secondary.[1] For the modern reader of Mk the main interests are historical and religious. Does the precise command to the two disciples imply a previous arrangement with the owner of the colt? Or is the story purely legendary? It is probable that Mark thought of the knowledge of Jesus as supernatural and that the description of the colt in 2b is a legendary trait; but this view does not exclude the possibility that an understanding was made with the owner. There is no evidence for this supposition, but it accounts best for the Markan story and its development in the tradition. Cf. Wood, 694; Bartlet, 312; Rawlinson, 152.

3 f. For ἐάν c. subj. *v.* i. 40; χρείαν ἔχω ii. 17, 25; εὐθύς i. 10; ἀποστέλλω i. 2; πάλιν ii. 1; ὧδε vi. 3; πῶλος

xi. 2; δέω iii. 27; θύρα i. 33. The message, which is intended to make it possible for the two disciples to bring back the colt, is somewhat obscure. Is ὁ κύριος Jesus, God, or the owner of the colt? And is καὶ εὐθὺς αὐτὸν ἀποστέλλει πάλιν ὧδε part of the message, or a statement of what will happen? If πάλιν is read, the words are an assurance: the colt will be sent back; but important MSS. omit the adverb and others read ἀποστελεῖ instead of ἀποστέλλει.

Couchoud, *JTS*, xxxiv. 125 f., concludes that the original Markan text was καὶ εὐθὺς αὐτὸν ἀποστελεῖ ὧδε, ʻ and straightway he will send it here ʼ. Cf. Field, 34 f.; Pallis, 38. It is very doubtful, however, if this view is justified. (1) ἀποστέλλει[2] is almost certainly original, not only because of its very strong attestation but because, as a futuristic present (ʻ is going to send ʼ), it invited assimilation to the Matthaean text. (2) On the whole πάλιν[3] must be judged to be original, in spite of its omission by important authorities. It disappeared because it was assumed by scribes that the passage described the effect of the message: the colt would be sent to Jesus. For the same reason it is omitted by Matthew. (3) The omission of ὧδε is of trifling importance; it could be understood to refer either to the village or the place where Jesus waited.

The greater difficulty is the meaning

[1] In Jn (xii. 12-16) the incident happens the day after Jesus has reached Bethany ʻ six days before the Passover ʼ (xii. 1). This is the origin of the Christian tradition regarding Palm Sunday. A crowd of pilgrims, hearing that Jesus is coming to Jerusalem, comes out from the city to greet Him. In contrast with Mk, John relates that Jesus finds an ass (ὀνάριον) and sits thereon. The Evangelist expressly cites Zech. ix. 9, and either he, or a later editor (cf. Bernard, 427), explains that ʻ when Jesus was glorified ʼ His disciples remembered that these things were written of Him and that they did these things to Him.

[2] ἀποστέλλει. ℵ A B C D L Δ Θ *et al.* fam. 13 28 118 543 565 579 892 *al. mu.* b c g¹ k vg (1 MS.) sy⁵ pe hl.
ἀποστελεῖ. G U W Π Φ Ψ fam. 1 (exc. 118) 22 506 569 700 1071 *al. plur.* a d f ff i q r² vg (*pler.*) sa bo geo. So also Mt.

[3] πάλιν. ℵ B C* D L Δ Θ 579 892 sa aeth. With variations of order. Om. A C² W *et al.* fam. 1 fam. 13 28 543 565 700 1071 *al. pler.* it (*pler.*) vg sy³ pe hl bo Or. So also Mt.
ὧδε. Om. c k vg (1 MS.).

ἐπὶ τοῦ ἀμφόδου, καὶ λύουσιν αὐτόν. καί τινες τῶν ἐκεῖ ἑστη- 5
κότων ἔλεγον αὐτοῖς Τί ποιεῖτε λύοντες τὸν πῶλον; οἱ δὲ εἶπαν 6
αὐτοῖς καθὼς εἶπεν ὁ Ἰησοῦς· καὶ ἀφῆκαν αὐτούς. καὶ φέρουσιν 7
τὸν πῶλον πρὸς τὸν Ἰησοῦν, καὶ ἐπιβάλλουσιν αὐτῷ τὰ ἱμάτια

of ὁ κύριος. By most commentators, but with a sense of embarrassment, it is held that Jesus is speaking of Himself. But, as a name for Jesus, ὁ κύριος, while common in Lk and in Jn (after the Resurrection; cf. Bernard, 132), is not used at all by Mark or Matthew, unless it be in this message. Lagrange, 289, takes the meaning to be *le Maître*; cf. Swete, 248; Bartlet, 313; Blunt, 224. Turner, 53, suggests that it is not unfitting that, on the occasion of His public entry, ' He should speak a new language and formulate in new terms His unique dignity '. Zahn even conjectures that the owner may have belonged to a circle in which Jesus was designated ' the Lord ' (Klostermann, 127). None of these suggestions is convincing. The difficulty of the usage led Allen, 142, to take the desperate expedient of maintaining that God is meant, as in v. 19. The better alternative is to explain the phrase as referring to the owner of the colt. Several considerations favour this view, as, for example, (1) Mark's usage (*v. supra*); (2) the fact that the message is not sent to the owner, but to anyone (τις) who happens to intervene; (3) the consideration that a message to the effect that the owner wanted his colt and would return it shortly would be likely to win the response described. We conclude then that ὁ κύριος is the owner and is also the subject of ἀποστέλλει. The difficulty is that we do not know where the owner was. Presumably he was not at home, and by inference we assume that he was with Jesus; but we are not told this, and the justification of the inference must be that, on this view, a satisfactory explanation is given of the message. The agreement, also, of the details mentioned in verse 4 with the instructions (*v.* 2) is natural.

The two disciples find the facts as they are described. The colt is tied at a door, and they loose him. A new detail, however, is added in ἐπὶ τοῦ ἀμφόδου, but it is far from certain what is meant. ἄμφοδον** (Ac. xix. 28 in D), ' street ', ' quarter '; Cf. Aristoph. *Fragm.* 327, Polybius xxxix. 3. 2, οὐ θύρᾳ . . . ἀλλ᾽ ἀμφόδῳ, ' not at the door, but in the street '; LXX (Jer. xvii. 27, xxx. 16 (xlix. 27)), Pap. (*VGT*, 28). RV renders ' in the open street ', and similarly Swete, Lagrange, Turner, RSV, Moffatt, Torrey. It is possible, however, that the meaning is ' at the cross roads ', Lat. *compitum* (Turner, 53); cf. AV, 'in a place where two ways met ', vg *bivium*. The suggestion of Couchoud, *JTS*, xxxiv. 126, that the original reading was ἀμπέλου, ' vineyard ' (cf. Justin, *1 Apol.* 32; Clem. of Alex. *Paed.* i. 5. 15) is attractive, but hardly convincing.

Matthew and Luke merely summarize Mk, omitting the precise details.

5-8. All falls out as anticipated. Some of the bystanders ask why they are loosing the colt, and the disciples reply as instructed. For τινες τῶν ἑστηκότων *v.* ix. 1, xv. 35; πῶλος xi. 2. Luke has οἱ κύριοι αὐτοῦ (xix. 33). Lagrange, 289, conjectures that the owner arrived and that, knowing Jesus, at least by hearsay, he consented readily to associate himself with His project. None of these assumptions is necessary and, in the absence of a reference to the owner, the presumption is that he is not present. Τί ποιεῖτε λύοντες τὸν πῶλον; = ' What do you mean by loosing the colt?'; cf. Plummer, 258; Moffatt.

Permission being given, they bring the colt to Jesus; they throw their outer garments upon him and He sits thereon. For ἐπιβάλλω *v.* iv. 37;

8 ⸢αὐτῶν⸣, καὶ ἐκάθισεν ἐπ᾽ αὐτόν. καὶ πολλοὶ τὰ ἱμάτια αὐτῶν
ἔστρωσαν εἰς τὴν ὁδόν, ἄλλοι δὲ στιβάδας κόψαντες ἐκ τῶν ἀγρῶν.
9 καὶ οἱ προάγοντες καὶ οἱ ἀκολουθοῦντες ἔκραζον

Ὡσαννά·

Εὐλογημένος ὁ ἐρχόμενος ἐν ὀνόματι Κυρίου·

10   Εὐλογημένη ἡ ἐρχομένη βασιλεία τοῦ πατρὸς ἡμῶν Δαυείδ·

7 ἑαυτῶν

ἱμάτιον ii. 21; καθίζω ix. 35. So in
4 Kgdms. ix. 13, when Jehu is saluted
as king. In Lk the idea of homage is
enhanced by the statement that they
set Jesus on the colt (ἐπιβιβάζω).
Matthew has ἐπεκάθισεν ἐπάνω αὐτῶν
(xxi. 7). From the crowd many spread
their garments on the road and others
rushes gathered from the fields. στρών-
νυμι, xiv. 15*; εἰς τὴν ὁδόν, cf. εἰς ὁδόν,
vi. 8, x. 17. Cf. the account of the
entering of Simon Maccabaeus into
Jerusalem ' with praise and palm
branches . . . and with hymns and with
songs ', 1 Macc. xiii. 51.

στιβάς**, a litter of straw, rushes,
or leaves; Cl., but not in LXX (Aq.,
Ezek. xlvi. 23). In Pap. Oxy. iii. 520.
10 it is used, as in Cl. Gk, of ' mat-
tresses '. For the form στοιβάς v.
Moulton, ii. 76, 375. The primitive
character of Mk is shown by the
parallel phrases in Mt. xxi. 8, κλάδους
ἀπὸ τῶν δένδρων, and Jn. xii. 13, τὰ
βαΐα τῶν φοινίκων. For ἀγρός v. v. 14;
κόπτω*.

9 f. οἱ προάγοντες and οἱ ἀκολουθοῦντες describe those who preceded
and followed Jesus. There is no suggestion of two crowds, one from Jerusalem and the other consisting of the
disciples and others already with Jesus,
as is implied by Jn. xii. 12 f. Cf.
Lagrange, 290; Turner, 54. Swete's
attempt, 250, to distinguish between
the Galileans who brought palm leaves
with them from Jerusalem and the
villagers who strewed the road with
garments and foliage is without foundation.

Ὡσαννά, xi. 10*, Mt. xxi. 9 (bis),
Jn. xii. 13**, is a transliteration of
נָא־הוֹשִׁיעָה in Psa. cxviii. 25, where the
cry to God means ' Save now '. In

2 Sam. xiv. 4 and 2 Kings vi. 26 the
word is used in addressing kings, and
in all these cases the LXX has σῶσον.
The psalm was used liturgically at the
Feasts of Tabernacles and the Passover. ' Hosanna ' could therefore be
used in addressing pilgrims or a famous
Rabbi, but as a greeting or acclamation rather than a cry for help. At
Tabernacles branches were carried
and waved and in popular speech were
known as ' hosannahs '. A similar
usage was connected with the Feast
of the Dedication, and Burkitt, JTS,
xvii. 139-49, has conjectured that the
Entry took place at the time of this
feast (December), the purpose being
to rededicate the Temple (cf. 2 Macc.
x. 8). It is possible that Mark thought
of Ὡσαννά as a cry of homage, a kingly
greeting rather than an appeal for
divine help, but Ὡσαννὰ ἐν τοῖς ὑψίστοις
in 10 suggests an invocation to God
for aid and blessing or even a cry of
thanksgiving. This uncertainty suggests the possibility that in liturgical
usage the original significance of the
word had been lost. One may compare the religious use of ' Hallelujah '
as an expression of intense joy rather
than in its original sense as an ascrip-
tion of praise to God. In most English
versions (RV, RSV, Moffatt) ' Hosanna! ' is left untranslated, but
Torrey's rendering, 94, TG, 21, ' God
save him! ' in 9 and ' God in heaven
save him! ' in 10, probably correctly
interprets the sense of the original.

Between the two phrases are two
lines which may have been chanted
antiphonally; cf. Lohmeyer, 231.
The first is a quotation from Psa.
xviii. 26, in agreement with the LXX,
Εὐλογημένος ὁ ἐρχόμενος ἐν ὀνόματι

'Ωcαννά ἐν τοῖς ὑψίστοις.

Καὶ εἰσῆλθεν εἰς Ἱεροσόλυμα εἰς τὸ ἱερόν· καὶ περιβλεψάμενος ΙΙ πάντα ⌈ὀψὲ ἤδη οὔσης τῆς ὥρας⌉ ἐξῆλθεν εἰς Βηθανίαν μετὰ τῶν δώδεκα.

11 ὀψίας ἤδη οὔσης [τῆς ὥρας]

Κυρίου. For εὐλογέω v. vi. 41 ; Κύριος i. 3. In the Psalm the words bespeak a blessing in the name of the Lord upon pilgrims who came to the feast. Whether ὁ ἐρχόμενος had a Messianic sense is uncertain ; Cadbury says that there is no evidence that it was a Jewish or Christian term (Beginnings, v. 373 f.). This judgment, however, needs to be qualified : the evidence of such passages as Mt. xi. 3 = Lk. vii. 19, Mt. xxiii. 39 = Lk. xiii. 35 (LXX), Jn. i. 15, 27, vi. 14, xi. 27, Ac. xix. 4, and Heb. x. 37 (LXX) appears to suggest that, influenced by Psa. cxviii. 26 and perhaps Dan. vii. 13, the phrase had a brief and restricted currency in Baptist and Christian circles. It is not likely that the Psalm was quoted by the crowd as a Messianic acclamation, especially as, in this case, the authorities would have been compelled to intervene : cf. Wellhausen, 87 f. ; Schniewind, 147. Moreover, even in Jn (xii. 16) it is only subsequently that the true nature of the incident is perceived by the disciples. Mark himself may have seen in the phrase an indication of the fact that, during His Mission, the Messiahship of Jesus remained concealed.

The second line, Εὐλογημένη ἡ ἐρχομένη βασιλεία τοῦ πατρὸς ἡμῶν Δαυείδ (10), appears to be a comment on the quotation. The reference to ' the Kingdom of our father David ' is strange ; only in the obscure passage Ac. iv. 25 (cf. Lake, Beginnings, iv. 46) is David called ' our father '. Usually the name is applied to the Patriarchs, and to Abraham, Isaac, and Jacob in particular ; cf. Moore, Judaism, i. 542. Moreover, preeminently the Kingdom is ' of God ' (v. i. 15), and when David is mentioned it is a question of the Kingdom coming

again, or being restored ; cf. Lohmeyer, 231. For these reasons it is tempting, with Lohmeyer, to regard the line as a subsequent addition, especially as it is wanting in Mt and Lk ; but against this view it may be argued that its omission by the later Evangelists is intelligible, that the content of an insertion might be expected to be more specifically Messianic, and that its restraint is in keeping with the Markan narrative as a whole. For Δαυείδ v. ii. 25.

The tendency of the variants in Mt and Lk is to make details more explicit and to represent the homage as Messianic. Matthew identifies οἱ προάγοντες as οἱ ὄχλοι, and adds τῷ υἱῷ Δαυείδ to the first 'Ωσαννά. Luke inserts ὁ βασιλεύς and has ἐν οὐρανῷ εἰρήνη καὶ δόξα ἐν ὑψίστοις. This reading appears as a variant in Mk. xi. 10 in Θ geo, and εἰρήνη ἐν τοῖς ὑψίστοις is read by W 28 700 sys.

11. In contrast with Mt and Lk, in which the Cleansing follows immediately after the Entry, a day intervenes in Mk. Jesus enters Jerusalem, looks around on all things in the Temple, and then with the Twelve leaves for Bethany. For Ἱεροσόλυμα v. iii. 8. Turner, 54, JTS, xxvi. 230, prefers to read εἰσῆλθον (Θ i k sys geo¹), but it is better, with Lagrange, 291, to read the well-attested sing. Mark's intention appears to be to concentrate attention upon the action of Jesus. ἱερόν, xi. 15 f., 27, xii. 35, xiii. 1, 3, xiv. 49*, describes the whole of the Temple precincts, including the sanctuary (ναός) and the various courts, but there is no reason to suppose that Jesus proceeded farther than the Court of Men. The comprehensiveness of His survey is indicated by περιβλεψάμενος (v. iii. 5) ; He looked around on all

that could be seen (πάντα). The opinion that His glance was that of a pilgrim visiting the Temple for the first time (Holtzmann, 161, *weil es ihm neu war*) lacks foundation; cf. Wellhausen, 88; Klostermann, 130; Loisy, ii. 268; Rawlinson, 153.

The reason for the departure is given by the gen. abs. ὀψὲ ἤδη οὔσης τῆς ὥρας : in the late afternoon it was impossible to do more. ὀψέ, xi. 19, xiii. 35*, is strongly attested by ℵ C L Δ 892 1342 Or. In other uncials and minuscules it is replaced by ὀψίας (*v.* i. 32), but it deserves the preference given to it by WH (mg, ὀψίας) and Nestle. In the papyri it is frequently construed with a partitive gen. as in Mt. xxviii. 1 ; *v.* *VGT*, 470. For Βηθανία *v.* xi. 1 ; οἱ δώδεκα iii. 14 ; ἤδη iv. 37 ; ὥρα vi. 35.

The allusion to ' the Twelve ' is abrupt. Meyer, i. 145, does not trace it to his ' Twelve Source ' in view of δύο τῶν μαθητῶν αὐτοῦ in xi. 1. It is best to regard 11 as an addition made by Mark on the basis of good tradition. One has only to compare the

development which the narrative has undergone in the Matthaean picture of all the city stirred and the children crying in the Temple, ' Hosanna to the Son of David ! ' (Mt. xxi. 10, 15), in order to perceive the greater worth of the Markan tradition. Presumably the crowds have melted away and Jesus is left alone with His disciples. A *dénouement* consisting of a survey of the Temple scene followed by a departure from the city is certainly not a product of imagination and invention. The one point of uncertainty is the reference to Bethany. J. Weiss, 268, prefers the special Lukan tradition that Jesus bivouacked on the Mount of Olives (Lk. xxi. 37) ; and it may be that Mark's reference to the village is prompted by the tradition which connected the story of the Fig Tree with the road from Bethany to Jerusalem. On the other hand, the two localities are sufficiently close to preclude the suggestion of contradiction, especially if Lake's identification of the village (*v.* the note on xi. 1) is accepted.

Mk. xi. 12-14   72. THE CURSING OF THE   Cf. Mt. xxi. 18-20
FIG TREE

The story, as Mark records it, is a Miracle-story intended to illustrate the divine power of Jesus. It is doubtful if he interpreted it symbolically (cf. J. Weiss, 268), but he may have regarded the incident as significant with reference to Jerusalem and Judaism. Bultmann, 232 f., thinks that originally 12-14 and 20 formed a whole and that the story of the Cleansing in 15-19 was inserted by Mark. Cf. Schmidt, 298-300, who thinks that τῇ ἐπαύριον is original, but that ἀπὸ Βηθανίας and the statement about the time of figs are secondary. It seems more probable that the Evangelist found the story of the Fig Tree associated in the tradition with the road from Bethany to Jerusalem and for this reason introduced it at this point in connexion with the Cleansing. Many modern commentators deny the historical character of the incident. The arguments used are not equally cogent. Thus, it is contended that it is not likely that Jesus would look for figs if there was no reasonable ground for expecting them at that season of the year. This argument probably assumes too much ; *v.* the note on 13. Again, it is pointed out that the incident is regarded as an example of faith in God (xi. 22) and a ground for perseverance in prayer (xi. 23 f.), whereas neither of these counsels is the natural suggestion of the narrative ; but this contention loses its force if, as is probable, the sayings are artificially attached. The strongest objection will always be that the action is not worthy to be assigned to Jesus, since an adequate motive is not supplied by the reference to hunger (cf. Mt. iv. 2-4). Among those who accept the historical character of the event some interpret it as a symbolical incident or an acted parable; *v.* the note on 13. Probably the best explanation of the narrative is that the parable of the Fig Tree in Lk. xiii. 6-9, or a similar parable, has been transformed into a story of fact, or that in primitive Christian tradition a popular legend came to be attached to a withered fig tree on the way to Jerusalem. The latter suggestion was first made by E. Schwartz, *ZNTW*, v (1904), pp. 80-4; cf. also Wellhausen, 106; J. Weiss, *Die Schr.*⁴ 178; Branscomb, 201 f.; Goguel, 241. These suggestions are conjectural, but either of them would give a good explanation of the genesis of the story. See further, Klostermann, 131; Bartlet, 316 f.; Rawlinson, 154 f.; Wood, 694.

Καὶ τῇ ἐπαύριον ἐξελθόντων αὐτῶν ἀπὸ Βηθανίας ἐπείνασεν. 12 καὶ ἰδὼν συκῆν ἀπὸ μακρόθεν ἔχουσαν φύλλα ἦλθεν εἰ ἄρα τι 13 εὑρήσει ἐν αὐτῇ, καὶ ἐλθὼν ἐπ᾿ αὐτὴν οὐδὲν εὗρεν εἰ μὴ φύλλα,

12 f. Mark may have found the story of the Fig Tree connected in respect of time and place with the preceding incident. It happened on the next day when Jesus and His disciples (ἐξελθόντων αὐτῶν) went out from Bethany. With τῇ ἐπαύριον sc. ἡμέρᾳ. ἐπαύριον*, Mt (1), Lk (0), Ac (10), Jn (5)**, 'on the morrow', is not a classical word, but is used in the LXX (Gen. xxx. 33, etc.) and in the papyri (*VGT*, 230). The statement that Jesus hungered (ἐπείνασεν, ii. 25*) prepares the way for the story, indicating that He sought to satisfy a physical need. Matthew substitutes πρωί, and omitting the gen. abs., says that it was as Jesus was returning (ἐπαναγωγών) to the city that He was hungry (xxi. 18).

ἰδών followed by the participle ἔχουσαν is explained by Blass, 246, as a case where the participle is somewhat distinct from the object φύλλα, presenting an additional clause, 'which had leaves', but probably the phrase is adequately rendered by 'in leaf' (Moffatt and RSV) or 'having leaves' (RV). For ἀπὸ μακρόθεν *v.* v. 6; συκῆ, xi. 20 f., xiii. 28*; φύλλον, xiii. 28*. Lagrange, 293, explains that leaves can be seen at the end of March or the beginning of April, especially on the east side of the Mount of Olives.

The suggestion that Jesus expected to find fruit of the previous season which had survived the winter has nothing to commend it; only early green figs could be expected at this time, and, although it has frequently been asserted that such figs are commonly eaten in Palestine, Lagrange says that they are disagreeable and are not normally eaten. Whether it is a gloss or not the explanation ὁ γὰρ καιρὸς οὐκ ἦν σύκων is correct, since figs are not ripe before June. Lagrange, therefore, concludes with Victor, Le Camus, and Knabenbauer that Jesus performed a symbolic action. Cf. B. Weiss, 177, who suggests that He saw in the tree a picture of the people of Israel; Gould, 211 f.

The suggestion that the incident was 'an acted parable' is out of harmony with ἐπείνασεν and εἰ ἄρα τι εὑρήσει ἐν αὐτῇ in Mark's narrative, and still more with the exhortation Ἔχετε πίστιν θεοῦ ir. xi. 22. Cf. Wood, 694. The inferential ἄρα (*v.* iv. 41*) means 'in these circumstances' and the vivid fut. εὑρήσει represents εὑρήσω in the implied direct question. Thus, the expectation of fruit to satisfy hunger is strongly suggested. Either this fact is an inconsistency within the narrative itself or the expectation

14 ὁ γὰρ καιρὸς οὐκ ἦν σύκων. καὶ ἀποκριθεὶς εἶπεν αὐτῇ Μηκέτι εἰς τὸν αἰῶνα ἐκ σοῦ μηδεὶς καρπὸν φάγοι. καὶ ἤκουον οἱ
μαθηταὶ αὐτοῦ.

is due to unusually favourable circumstances in the position of the tree.[1] Disappointment is probably implied by καὶ ἐλθὼν ἐπ᾽ αὐτὴν οὐδὲν εὗρεν εἰ μὴ φύλλα. For ἐπ᾽ αὐτήν to describe the goal v. v. 21 and xv. 22. Whatever the original facts may have been, Mark clearly intends to describe a miracle of power. Matthew's much briefer account merely mentions a fig tree (συκῆν μίαν) by the way side which Jesus saw and approached only to find nothing but leaves; ἀπὸ μακρόθεν and εἰ ἄρα, etc. are omitted.

The parenthesis ὁ γὰρ καιρὸς οὐκ ἦν συκῶν is best ascribed to Mark himself, since such explanations are in accordance with his style. For καιρός v. i. 15.

14. For ἀποκριθεὶς εἶπεν v. Intr. 63. The purely redundant character of the participle is manifest here, as in ix. 5, xii. 35, Mt. xi. 25, xii. 38, xvii. 4, xxviii. 5. Cf. Howard, ii. 453. For the double negative μηκέτι . . . μηδείς v. i. 44. The optative φάγοι expresses a prohibition; cf. Moulton, i. 165, 179. Many commentators deny that the words are a curse, despite xi. 21,

ἡ συκῆ ἦν κατηράσω. Lagrange, 294, for example, prefers to explain the opt. as the expression of an express wish. This distinction, however, seems rather fine. That the expression is strong is shown by the milder subjunctive used by Matthew, οὐ μηκέτι . . . γένηται (xxi. 19). As the sequel shows (cf. ἐξηραμμένην ἐκ ῥιζῶν in xi. 20), the words are the equivalent of a sentence of death upon the tree. For the habit of Jesus of addressing inanimate objects cf. iv. 39 and xi. 23.

The narrative ends with the statement that His disciples were hearing Him (ἤκουον). These words point forwards to xi. 20-5. This use of the imperfect is characteristic of Mark, and the change to the aor. in W 28 575 579 892 et al. k sys pe geo shows that it was felt to be unusual. For this reason it is likely to be original, and it is not necessary, with Pallis, 39, to conjecture that ἤκουον has taken the place of ἠπόρουν. Cf. Lohmeyer, 234. Matthew's substitution of καὶ ἐξηράνθη παραχρῆμα ἡ συκῆ enhances the miraculous element in the story. So also ἐθαύμασαν in xxi. 20.

Mk. xi. 15-19   73. THE CLEANSING OF THE   Cf. Mt. xxi. 12 f.
TEMPLE   Lk. xix. 45-8

The narrative is a Story about Jesus which may have been current as an isolated unit of tradition, although Mark connects it closely with the narrative of the Fig Tree. Bultmann, 36, 58 f., classifies it as a Biographical Apothegm, to which 15a ('And they come to Jerusalem') and 18 f. (The Priests' Plot) have been added. He also makes the interesting suggestion that 17 (the saying 'My house', etc.) may have replaced an older saying which Jn. ii. 16 has retained. Dibelius, 43, 45, includes 15-17 among his 'Paradigms of a less pure type', and also regards 18 as an addition. In this narrative, he says, 'we have to do, in fact, with the rare case that an event has been handed down in two different Paradigms, approximately of a similar kind and value', one or both of which once

[1] This possibility is shown by an original photograph of a fig tree with fruit sent to me by the Rev. Eric F. F. Bishop, M.A., Newman School of Missions, Thabor, Jerusalem and dated 'Good Friday 1936'.

stood in connexion with the story of the Passion. Cf. Redlich, 101. Probably, the original unit is 15b-17. Mark has added the short statement about entering into Jerusalem, and has appended the passage describing the reaction of the chief priests and scribes in 18, and the reference to the departure from the city (19). The story was told because it was held to describe the Messianic action of Jesus and His conflict with the Jewish authorities at Jerusalem.

The story is remarkably vivid. Cf. J. Weiss, 269; Ed. Meyer, i. 162-6. Branscomb, 202, describes it as ' one of the most important events in the life of Jesus '. How Jesus had driven out the buyers and sellers, and had overturned the tables of the money-changers and the seats of the sellers of doves, above all, how He had charged the priests with having turned the House of prayer into a den of robbers, was remembered and handed down in the tradition.

DETACHED NOTE ON THE DATE OF THE CLEANSING OF THE TEMPLE

Since the time of Holtzmann most scholars, including Bernard, Rawlinson, Bartlet, Macgregor, Branscomb and Hoskyns, have favoured the Markan date. In Mark's intention the Cleansing is a turning point in the story of the Passion. In consequence of it the priests plot to destroy Jesus (xi. 18). Moreover, the saying about the destruction of the Temple, although not included in Mark's narrative, is mentioned at the Trial (xiv. 58) and the Crucifixion (xv. 29 f.). Strong, however, as the Markan case is, it is open to formidable objections. (1) The events assigned by Mark to the last week require a longer period. (2) In particular, if Mark was to tell the story at all, no other context was available. (3) Further, the temporal links in 15 and 19 may belong rather to the story of the Fig Tree. The Cleansing fills in the interval between the two parts of this story, in this respect resembling Mark's use of the Beelzebul Question (iii. 22-6) and the account of the death of John (vi. 17-29). (4) Again, in Mk the Cleansing does not really describe a decisive action in the course of events, as by its position it seems intended to do. The reference to the priests is followed by a group of controversy-stories, and only after a second allusion to the hostility of the hierarchy (xiv. 1) does the action quicken. (5) The confused testimony of the witnesses at the Trial (xiv. 58) is more intelligible if the saying about the Temple had been spoken considerably earlier. (6) Similarly, the question, ' By what authority doest thou these things ? ', which refers to the Cleansing,.seems to belong to a time when the ministry of the Baptist had not long ended. (7) Lastly, as an act of reforming zeal, rather than a challenge to Judaism, the incident is more suited to an earlier period. Why is the protest delayed until the end of the Ministry ? We have, in fact, the paradoxical situation that the Markan story agrees better with the Johannine date and the Johannine account with the Markan setting.

The objections to the Markan date are so many arguments in favour of the Johannine setting, and the latter is preferred by many scholars, including J. Weiss, 268 ; Lagrange, S. Jean, 65 ; McNeile, 300 ; A. E. Brooke, Cambridge Bibl. Essays, 308 ; W. Sanday, The Criticism of the

FG, 149 f. Further, the L tradition does not appear to have connected the Cleansing with the Passion Story, for Lk. xix. 45 f. is derived from Mk. Cf. V. Taylor, *BTG*, 237 f.; Howard, *FG*, 152, 176. Nevertheless, the Johannine date is open to the strong objection that it reflects a doctrinal motive and a desire to set this crucial encounter at the beginning of the Gospel. A sense of this difficulty is apparent in the discussions of some who accept the Johannine setting and is at its maximum in the minds of those who prefer the Markan date. Cf. Bernard, 88 f.

Schmidt, 292, thinks that a third possibility is open ; *sed tertium datur*, he writes. In the Gospel tradition the time of this Jerusalem-story was not fixed. In this connexion Goguel's discussion, 412-19, 507-11, is of great interest. He attaches great value to the saying concerning the destruction of the Temple, in which Jesus expressed the feeling that there was nothing more to hope from Israel, and conjectures that it was uttered shortly before His withdrawal to Peraea (cf. Jn. x. 40) during a visit which preceded by some months His final return to the city. He regards the narrative of the Cleansing as an amplification of this saying. There is no sufficient reason for this estimate of the narrative, but it is a possible view that the Cleansing belongs to this period. Either this date, or the Johannine, seems preferable to the Markan setting.

15 Καὶ ἔρχονται εἰς Ἱεροσόλυμα. Καὶ εἰσελθὼν εἰς τὸ ἱερὸν ἤρξατο ἐκβάλλειν τοὺς πωλοῦντας καὶ τοὺς ἀγοράζοντας ἐν τῷ ἱερῷ, καὶ τὰς τραπέζας τῶν κολλυβιστῶν καὶ τὰς καθέδρας τῶν
16 πωλούντων τὰς περιστερὰς κατέστρεψεν καὶ οὐκ ἤφιεν ἵνα τις

15 f. ἔρχονται (v. *HS*², 13) is included by Turner, *JTS*, xxvi. 225-31, in his list of ' impersonal plurals ' which have replaced the first person plur. in Peter's Memoirs (cf. xi. 1, 11 (?), 12, 19 f., 27, xiv. 18, 22, 26, 32, etc.). It is difficult to decide whether the statement καὶ ἔρχονται εἰς Ἱεροσόλυμα is editorial, and is thus a sign that Mark has introduced the Cleansing into this context, or whether the connexion (cf. ἀπὸ Βηθανίας, xi. 12) was already given in the tradition.[1] For ἱερόν v. xi. 11 ; ἤρξατο c. infin. Intr. 48, 63 f. ; ἐκβάλλω i. 12. ' Those who sold ' (πωλέω, x. 21*) are the people who traded in victims for the Temple sacrifices and in wine, oil, and salt, and ' those who bought ' (ἀγοράζω, vi. 36) are the pilgrims who required such things for the needs of the cultus. The scene is probably the Court of the Gentiles. κολλυβιστής*, Mt. xxi. 12, Jn. ii. 15**, is a late word in popular use (*VGT*,

353) condemned by Atticists ; it is derived from κόλλυβος, a small coin or a rate of exchange, and thus means ' money-changer ' ; cf. τραπεζείτης, Mt. xxv. 27. These men sat at their tables (τράπεζα, vii. 28*) or ' banks ' (*VGT*, 639) for the purpose of changing the Greek or Roman money of the pilgrims into Jewish or Tyrian coinage in which alone the Temple dues could be paid ; cf. Ex. xxx. 13 ff., Mt. xvii. 24. Mark also mentions the seats (καθέδρα*, < ἕδρα) of those who sold doves (περιστερά, i. 10), the offerings of the poor for the purification of women (Lev. xii. 6, Lk. ii. 22-4), the cleansing of lepers (Lev. xiv. 22), and other purposes (Lev. xv. 14, 29). These seats Jesus overturned ; καταστρέφω*, Mt. xxi. 12, Ac. xv. 16 (LXX)** ; Cl., LXX. The word is omitted by D k sys and placed after κολλυβ. in א*.

The statement in 16 that Jesus allowed no one to carry a vessel

---

[1] The addition of πάλιν in N Σ 517 892 b f ff i r² aur and some lectionaries is probably an attempt to secure a firmer connexion between the narratives. Cf. Schmidt, 275 f.

διενέγκῃ σκεῦος διὰ τοῦ ἱεροῦ, καὶ ἐδίδασκεν καὶ ἔλεγεν ᵀ Οὐ 17
γέγραπται ὅτι Ὁ οἶκόс ΜΟΥ οἶκος προсεγχῆс κληθήcεται πᾶcιν
τοῖс ἔθνεcιν; ὑμεῖς δὲ πεποιήκατε αὐτὸν cπΗλαιον ληcτῶν.

17 αὐτοῖς

through the Temple is peculiar to Mk. For ἀφίημι ἵνα c. subj. v. Moulton, i. 176, and for the form ἤφιεν ii. 189. The subj. is used without ἵνα in xv. 36. For διαφέρω*, 'to carry through', cf. Ac. xiii. 49, xxvii. 27 (Lake, iv. 335, 'drift across'); elsewhere 'to differ' or 'excel'; Cl., LXX, Pap. (*VGT*, 156 f.). For σκεῦος v. iii. 27; ἱερόν xi. 11. The prohibition implies a respect for the holiness of the Temple and is thoroughly Jewish in spirit. Cf. *Berakoth*, ix. 5 (Danby, 10) where a man is prohibited from entering the Temple Mount with staff, sandal, or wallet, or with dust on his feet, and from making it a short by-path. Swete, 256, and Klostermann, 131, cite Josephus, *c. Ap.* ii. 7, but v. Lagrange, 295. Several commentators, e.g. Turner, 55, refer to the use of Old St. Paul's in London as a thoroughfare.

The action of Jesus is a spirited protest against injustice and the abuse of the Temple system. There is no doubt that pilgrims were fleeced by the traders, as in Mecca to-day (cf. Lagrange, 294), and that the Temple police and, above all, the priests were ultimately responsible. It has been objected (cf. Lohmeyer, 237) that, if Jesus acted in the way described, the Temple police or the Roman watch in the Tower of Antonia would have intervened, and that reference to the event would have been made in the Trial; but against this contention it may be justly urged that Jesus must have had public sympathy on His side, that His action was not revolutionary and, although the contrary has been claimed (v. Oesterley, *DCG*, ii. 713), was not an attack upon the sacrificial system.

For the Messianic aspect of the incident v. the note on 17.

Matthew follows Mk closely with πάντας before τοὺς πωλοῦντας καὶ ἀγορά-

ζοντας and the substitution of ἐξέβαλεν for ἤρξατο ἐκβάλλειν. Luke omits everything after τοὺς πωλοῦντας. In Jn additional details enhance the vividness of the scene. Thus, the Passover is near; oxen and sheep are mentioned and Jesus makes a scourge of cords, φραγέλλιον ἐκ σχοινίων (ii. 13-15).

17. καὶ ἐδίδασκεν καὶ ἔλεγεν is perhaps only a conventional Markan expression (cf. i. 21 f., ii. 13, ix. 31, etc.), but it may indicate continuous teaching, in which more was said than is recorded. Cf. Mt, καὶ λέγει αὐτοῖς; Lk, λέγων αὐτοῖς. For γέγραπται v. i. 2. Only Mark has the question form. The quotation agrees exactly with the LXX text of Isa. lvi. 7. Luke replaces the Semitic use of κληθήσεται by ἔσται, and both later Synoptists omit πᾶσιν τοῖς ἔθνεσιν. Lohmeyer, 236, sees in the use of the phrase 'a house of prayer' for the Temple the point of view of a Galilaean layman who reveres the Temple only as the principal synagogue. This is a possible explanation, but it is not very probable, for the name as applied to the Temple is old; cf. 3 Kgdms. viii. 29 in addition to Isa. lvi. 7 and lx. 7. It is unsatisfactory to see here the old prophetic antithesis of prayer and offering, especially as in the case of the prophets themselves the presence of this antithesis has been grossly exaggerated. For προσευχή v. ix. 29*; ἔθνος x. 33. The reference to the Gentiles will have commended itself to Mark in view of his readers, but it stands in the quotation itself and there is good reason to think that Jesus used it. Cf. Isa. ii. 1-4. The quotation has an eschatological colouring (Lohmeyer, 237); cf. συνάξω ἐπ᾽ αὐτὸν συναγωγήν in Isa. lvi. 8; also Psa. Sol. xvii. 30 f., where it is said that the expected Son of David will cleanse (καθα ιεῖ) Jerusalem and

18 καὶ ἤκουσαν οἱ ἀρχιερεῖς καὶ οἱ γραμματεῖς, καὶ ἐζήτουν πῶς
αὐτὸν ἀπολέσωσιν· ἐφοβοῦντο γὰρ αὐτόν, πᾶς γὰρ ὁ ὄχλος ἐξ-

nations will come from the ends of the earth to see his glory.

In contrast to the divine intention stands the charge ὑμεῖς δὲ πεποιήκατε αὐτὸν σπήλαιον λῃστῶν, which echoes the language of Jer. vii. 11, μὴ σπήλαιον λῃστῶν ὁ οἶκός μου . . . ἐνώπιον ὑμῶν;. σπήλαιον*, Mt. xxi. 13, Lk. xix. 46, Jn. xi. 38, Heb. xi. 38, Apoc. vi. 15**, ' a cave ', ' den ', ' cavern '; Cl., LXX, Pap. Cf. Souter, 239; VGT, 583. λῃστής, xiv. 48, xv. 27*, ' a robber ', ' brigand ', as distinct from κλέπτης, ' a thief '; Cl., LXX, Pap. The charge is addressed primarily to the crowd, but, as mainly responsible, the chief priests are included. For the question of the traffic in the Temple court cf. Edersheim, i. 114 f., 369-76; Abrahams, i. 82-9; Klausner, 311-16. πεποιήκατε illustrates Mark's use of tenses; Matthew has ποιεῖτε and Luke ἐποιήσατε.

In Jn the sayings are different: Ἄρατε ταῦτα ἐντεῦθεν, μὴ ποιεῖτε τὸν οἶκον τοῦ πατρός μου οἶκον ἐμπορίου (ii. 16), and Λύσατε τὸν ναὸν τοῦτον, καὶ ἐν τρισὶν ἡμέραις ἐγερῶ αὐτόν (ii. 19). That a genuine utterance lies behind ii. 19 is implied by the statement of the false witnesses in Mk. xiv. 58 and the taunts by the Cross (Mk. xv. 29 f.). Cf. Goguel, 415, 507-9. The original reference was probably to ' the " spiritual house " of Christian believers (1 Pet. ii. 5), who are collectively the Body of Christ (1 Cor. xii. 27) ', Bernard, 97. John relates it to the Resurrection. Jesus prophesied that after a brief interval the Temple would be replaced by a spiritual temple of believers in the Kingdom of God. Whether the saying was uttered in this context is, in the light of the Markan narrative, more open to question. Its presence in Jn. ii. 19 gives to the Cleansing the character of an attack upon the sacrificial system. Cf. Bernard, 87: ' A protest against the whole sacrificial system of the Temple ';

Hoskyns, 203: ' A sign that the end of animal sacrifice is at hand '. Cf. R. H. Kennett, The Church of Israel, 133. If this is the meaning of the Johannine story, it seems probable that the Markan account should be preferred.

Was the action of Jesus Messianic? From the time of Ezekiel (xl-xlviii) the renewing of the temple was expected in Messianic times. Cf. 1 Enoch xc. 28 f.; Psa. Sol. xvii. 30 f.; Apoc. xxi. 2-5; v. J. Jeremias, JW, 38-40. The action of Jesus is prophetic, but more than prophetic (cf. Schniewind, 150), and regarded in itself it is Messianic. It is another question, however, how far He intended to make a Messianic claim, except for those who had eyes to see. His ἐξουσία (xi. 28) was veiled and, in accordance with the consistent representation of Mark, remained His secret until His reply to the high priest's challenge (xiv. 61 f.).

18 f. These verses, which describe the hostility and plotting of the chief priests and the scribes, are added by Mark to explain why immediate action was not taken by them after the Cleansing. Jesus was still too popular with the multitude. For οἱ ἀρχιερεῖς v. viii. 31 and for οἱ γραμματεῖς i. 22. The two formed two of the principal groups in the Sanhedrin. Henceforward they are mentioned several times in conjunction; cf. xi. 27, xiv. 1, 43, 53. Once more the distinction between the aor. and the imperfects which follow is notable, as also the parataxis in καί . . . καί.

The priests and scribes began to seek how they might destroy Him. As often in the papyri, πῶς is used in an indirect sense, and the clause implies a deliberative question: ' How are we to destroy him? '. Cf. xiv. 1, 11. The reason is that they are afraid of Him. Mark frequently makes explanatory comments of this kind using γάρ. Cf. v. 8, xvi. 8, etc. For φοβέομαι

ἐπλήσσετο ἐπὶ τῇ διδαχῇ αὐτοῦ. Καὶ ὅταν ὀψὲ ἐγένετο, ⌜ἐξεπο- 19
ρεύετο⌝ ἔξω τῆς πόλεως.

19 ἐξεπορεύοντο

v. iv. 41. Fear, rather than awe, is meant, and the reason, expressed in a second clause containing γάρ, is the astonishment of the whole multitude at His teaching. For ἐκπλήσσομαι and διδαχή *v.* i. 22. Mark's intention is to indicate that Jesus made the same impression in Jerusalem as in Galilee. In 19 ὅταν c. indic., as in iii. 11, xi. 25, means 'when'; cf. Moffatt and RSV, as against RV, RVmg, and Torrey. Turner, 56, speaks of the RV rendering as a serious blunder, due to the assumption that Mark wrote classical Greek. Both the RV and WHmg read the sing., ἐξεπορεύετο, with ℵ C D Θ *et al.* fam. I fam. 13 (exc. 124) 22 33 543 579 892 *al. pler.* it vg sys hl bo geo² sa. So also Lagrange, 297; Moffatt; Rawlinson, 157. The plur. ἐξεπορεύοντο is strongly attested (A B W Δ *et al.* 28 124 565 700 1071 *et al.* c d aur sype hl mg geo¹ arm) and is read by WH (text), Nestle, Plummer, 255, RSV, Torrey. Probably the sing. should be read, since Jesus alone is mentioned in the narrative. The suggestion made by Plummer, 'but it (the plur.) may be a correction to harmonize with παραπορευόμενοι (*v.* 20)', describes what may well have happened. For ὀψέ *v.* xi. 11; πόλις i. 33, of Jerusalem xiv. 13, 16.

Matthew uses 18b later in xxii. 33; he has no parallel to 19. Whether Luke uses 18 f. is doubtful (cf. V. Taylor, *BTG*, 96 f.), but he is generally held to have done so (cf. Creed, 242 f.). If so, he precedes the passage by καὶ ἦν διδάσκων τὸ καθ᾽ ἡμέραν ἐν τῷ ἱερῷ, omits ἤκουσαν, and adds καὶ οἱ πρῶτοι τοῦ λαοῦ. He describes the priests' dilemma by saying καὶ οὐχ ηὕρισκον τὸ τί ποιήσωσιν, and adds ὁ λαὸς γὰρ ἅπας ἐξεκρέμετο αὐτοῦ ἀκούων, omitting 19 (xix. 47 f.).

Mk. xi. 20-5   74. THE WITHERED FIG   Cf. Mt. xxi. 20-2
                      TREE AND SAYINGS ON
                      FAITH AND PRAYER

The first three verses of this narrative form the second part of the story of the Fig Tree in xi. 12-14, and to it the sayings on faith and prayer in 23-5 are loosely attached. Similar examples of appended sayings have already been noticed in ii. 21 f., 27 f., iii. 27-9, ix. 37-50, x. 11 f. The division of a single story into parts is illustrated in the narrative of the Gerasene Demoniac (*v.* 1-20), and still better in the account of the healing of Jairus' Daughter (*v.* 21-4, 35-43). The vocabulary and diction of 20-2 suggest that the narrative was composed by Mark on the basis of current tradition, partly to describe the *dynamis* of Jesus and partly as an introduction to the sayings which follow. Thus the motives of composition are apologetic and catechetical. The catechetical interest is also apparent in the internal arrangement of the sayings, as will be seen in the Commentary. The sayings themselves are genuine utterances of Jesus, but the manner in which they are introduced is artificial. For the historical value of the narrative *v.* the introductory note on xi. 12-14.

Καὶ παραπορευόμενοι πρωὶ εἶδον τὴν συκῆν ἐξηραμμένην ἐκ 20

20 f. The second part of the story of the Fig Tree is set on the following day, although Mark does not expressly say this. It was early in the morning

21 ῥιζῶν. καὶ ἀναμνησθεὶς ὁ Πέτρος λέγει αὐτῷ 'Ραββεί, ἴδε ἡ
22 συκῆ ἣν κατηράσω ἐξήρανται. καὶ ἀποκριθεὶς ὁ 'Ιησοῦς λέγει
23 αὐτοῖς "Εχετε πίστιν θεοῦ· ἀμὴν λέγω ὑμῖν ὅτι ὃς ἂν εἴπῃ τῷ
ὄρει τούτῳ "Αρθητι καὶ βλήθητι εἰς τὴν θάλασσαν, καὶ μὴ διακριθῇ ἐν τῇ καρδίᾳ αὐτοῦ ἀλλὰ πιστεύῃ ὅτι ὃ λαλεῖ γίνεται, ἔσται

(πρωί, v. i. 35), as they passed by (παραπορευόμενοι, v. ii. 23), that they saw the
fig tree withered away (ξηραίνω, v. iii.
1) from its roots (ῥίζα, v. iv. 6). The
vocabulary is wholly Markan and suggests, so far as it goes, that the account
was composed by Mark himself. The
use of the perfect ἐξηραμμένην illustrates the precision with which he uses
this tense, as frequently elsewhere (cf.
iii. 1, v. 15, xi. 17, etc.), to describe
abiding results. The omission of πρωί
in 517 a c k is an early attempt to harmonize the two accounts. Complete
destruction is indicated by ἐκ ῥιζῶν as
in Plutarch, Pomp. 21 and in the LXX
in Job xxviii. 9, xxxi. 12, Ezek. xvii. 9.
Lohmeyer, 238 n., asks if the phrase
is an echo of ἐκριζώθητι in Lk. xvii. 6.
With the plur. εἶδον cf. xi. 1, 15, etc.

The statement that Peter remembered (ἀναμνησθείς) recalls the similar
passage in xiv. 72, καὶ ἀνεμνήσθη ὁ
Πέτρος τὸ ῥῆμα. It suggests that the
tradition contained statements about
what Peter recalled but does not ab-
solve us from the task of estimating
their historical value. ἀναμιμνήσκω,
xiv. 72*, 1 Cor. iv. 17, 2 Cor. vii. 15,
Heb. x. 32, 2 Tim. i. 6**, ' to remind ',
pass. ' to remember ' ; Cl₁, LXX, Pap.
(literary). For 'Ραββεί v. ix. 5. κατ-
αράομαι*, Mt. xxv. 41, Lk. vi. 28, Rom.
xii. 14, Jas. iii. 9**, ' to curse ' ; Cl.,
LXX, Pap. (κατάρατος). With 21 the
narrative element in the story ends ; it
appears to have been introduced for
the sake of the sayings which follow
in 23-5.

22 f. For ἀποκριθεὶς λέγει v. Intr. 63.
The sayings are introduced by the
exhortation to have faith in God. For
πίστις v. ii. 5. The variant reading
εἰ ἔχετε is well supported by א D Θ
fam. 13 28 33 61 543 565 700 1071 a b
d i r¹ sy^s geo¹ arm, but it is probably

an assimilation to Lk. xvii. 6 ; cf. Mt.
xvii. 20, xxi. 21. The phrase πίστις
θεοῦ (om. 28 a c k bo (1 MS.)) is found
nowhere else (Rom. iii. 3 is not a
parallel), but cf. 1 Thess. i. 8, πρὸς τὸν
θεόν, Heb. vi. 1, ἐπὶ θεόν, Jn. xiv. 1,
εἰς τὸν θεόν ; also Rom. iii. 22 (Χριστοῦ)
and 26 ('Ιησοῦ). The exhortation is
inappropriate in this context and reveals the artificial character of the
arrangement. The same is true also
of the three undoubtedly genuine
sayings which follow.

For ἀμὴν λέγω ὑμῖν in 23 v. iii. 28 ;
ὃς ἄν c. subj. iii. 29 ; ἐν τῇ καρδίᾳ (αὐτοῦ)
ii. 6 ; πιστεύω i. 15. διακρίνω*, ' to
separate ', ' discern ', ' decide ', ' con-
tend ' ; in NT, but not in LXX, mid.
and pass. ' to hesitate ', ' doubt ', as
here and in Ac. x. 20, Rom. iv. 20,
Jas. ii. 4. This reference to doubting
is wanting in the parallel Q form of
the saying and may be a homiletical
expansion. Matthew has ἐὰν ἔχητε
πίστιν καὶ μὴ διακριθῆτε (xxi. 21) and
γενήσεται instead of ἔσται. The objection that the saying must have been
uttered in Galilee is unsound, for the
Dead Sea can be seen from the Mount
of Olives.

The parallel versions in Mt. xvii. 20
and Lk. xvii. 6 are of great interest.
Streeter, 284, suggests that Luke gives
the Q version and that Matthew conflates Mk and Q. Cf. also 1 Cor. xiii.
2, κἂν ἔχω πᾶσαν τὴν πίστιν ὥστε ὄρη
μεθιστάνειν. The relationship between
these passages is obscure. Mark agrees
with Mt. xvii. 20 and 1 Cor. xiii. 2 in
speaking of the removal of a mountain
and with Lk. xvii. 6 in mentioning the
sea. Apparently the reference to the
smallness of the faith has dropped out
because the exhortation ἔχετε πίστιν
θεοῦ takes the place of εἰ ἔχετε πίστιν,
but to some extent the expansion καὶ

αὐτῷ. διὰ τοῦτο λέγω ὑμῖν, πάντα ὅσα προσεύχεσθε καὶ αἰτεῖσθε, 24
πιστεύετε ὅτι ἐλάβετε, καὶ ἔσται ὑμῖν. καὶ ὅταν στήκετε προσ- 25
ευχόμενοι, ἀφίετε εἴ τι ἔχετε κατά τινος, ἵνα καὶ ὁ πατὴρ ὑμῶν
ὁ ἐν τοῖς οὐρανοῖς ἀφῇ ὑμῖν τὰ παραπτώματα ὑμῶν.

μὴ διακριθῇ, etc. compensates for ὡς κόκκον σινάπεως. The main difference is that Mark, Matthew, and Paul speak of a mountain (or mountains), while Luke mentions a tree. This is strong evidence for thinking that Jesus spoke of a mountain, but it is possible, as Manson, *SJ*, 140, suggests, that Lk. xvii. 6 is an independent saying, although on the whole this view is doubtful. It goes without saying that Jesus is speaking figuratively. He wishes to say in the strongest manner possible that by faith men can do what seems absurd or impossible. This is brought out in the Markan form in the words ὃς ἄν . . . πιστεύῃ ὅτι ὃ λαλεῖ γίνεται, ἔσται αὐτῷ.

24 f. The second saying on prayer is similar in form to the first; cf. διὰ τοῦτο λέγω ὑμῖν and ἀμὴν λέγω ὑμῖν, πιστεύετε ὅτι and πιστεύῃ ὅτι, and ἔσται ὑμῖν and ἔσται αὐτῷ. So far as it goes, this conformation suggests the use of a collection and a catechetical interest; cf. ix. 37-50. With διὰ τοῦτο cf. xii. 24; πάντα ὅσα vi. 30, xii. 44; προσεύχομαι i. 35; αἰτέω vi. 22; and for the urgency expressed by the mid. vi. 24 f. προσεύχομαι is used of prayer to God or the gods, while αἰτέω is more general; cf. LS and *VGT*, 547. Burton, 110, takes the view that the imperative πιστεύετε is used in place of a protasis with εἰ or ἐάν in a supposition and instances i. 17. If so, greater emphasis is intended, in fact, an intentional exaggeration, for it is not true to say prayers are answered because we believe that we have received our request. ἐλάβετε points back to something that has already happened. Matthew substitutes the participle πιστεύοντες with λήμψεσθε (xxi. 22) and so loses the boldness of the Markan form. The same tendency is seen in the textual tradition, in λαμβάνετε read

by A *et al.* fam. 13 28 33 579 1071 *al. pler.* sys pe hl hier aeth arm, and λήμψεσθαι by D Θ fam. 1 22 565 700 it vg geo.

The third saying in 25 reflects a knowledge of the Lord's Prayer. Cf. Mt. vi. 14, ἐὰν γὰρ ἀφῆτε τοῖς ἀνθρώποις τὰ παραπτώματα αὐτῶν, ἀφήσει καὶ ὑμῖν ὁ πατὴρ ὑμῶν ὁ οὐράνιος. The Markan form is important because it suggests that the Prayer was already known in Rome before A.D. 60. Only here does Mark use the phrase ὁ πατὴρ ὑμῶν ὁ ἐν τοῖς οὐρανοῖς and the word παράπτωμα, 'a trespass' or 'transgression'. In Cl. Gk, as in the papyri (*VGT*, 489), it denotes 'a slip' or 'error', but in the NT, influenced by the LXX (cf. Ezek. xiv. 13, etc.) and Christian teaching, the word acquired a moral and religious content in respect of offences against God and man. Cf. Field, 160.

For ὅταν c. indic. *v.* the notes on iii. 11 and xi. 19. The custom of standing was common among the Jews (cf. 1 Kgs. viii. 14, 22, Neh. ix. 4, Psa. cxxxiv. 1, Mt. vi. 5, Lk. xviii. 11, 13), although kneeling was also practised (1 Kgs. viii. 54, Dan. vi. 10, Ac. vii. 60, xx. 36, xxi. 5, Eph. iii. 14). For στήκω *v.* iii. 31*; ἀφίημι i. 18, ii. 5. With εἴ τι ἔχετε κατά τινος cf. Col. iii. 13, ἐάν τις πρός τινα ἔχῃ μομφήν. The presence of the saying in this context is due to the key word προσευχόμενοι; cf. προσεύχεσθε in 24. Cf. the structure of ix. 37-50.

Verse 26, rightly omitted in RV and RSV, εἰ δὲ ὑμεῖς οὐκ ἀφίετε, οὐδὲ ὁ πατὴρ ὑμῶν ὁ ἐν τοῖς οὐρανοῖς ἀφήσει τὰ παραπτώματα ὑμῶν, as an addition from Mt. vi. 15, is found with small variants in A C D Θ *et al.* fam. 1 fam. 13 22 28 33 543 579 1071 *al. pler.* it vg sype hl aeth Cyp Aug. With other authorities it is omitted by ℵ B L W Δ Ψ 565 700 892 g² k l r² sys sa bo geo arm.

(*b*) Mk. xi. 27-   TEACHING IN JERUSALEM
xii. 44

The section includes :

    (75) xi. 27-33.   On Authority.
    (76) xii. 1-12.   The Parable of the Wicked Husbandmen.
    (77) xii. 13-17.   On Tribute to Caesar.
    (78) xii. 18-27.   On the Resurrection.
    (79) xii. 28-34.   On the First Commandment.
    (80) xii. 35-7a.   On David's Son.
    (81) xii. 37b-40.   A Warning against the Scribes.
    (82) xii. 41-4.   The Widow's Two Mites.

For the view that 75, 77-80, belonged to a pre-Markan complex of
' conflict-stories ' comparable to ii. 1-iii. 6 *v.* Albertz, 16-36 ; Intr. 101.
In both groups there is an absence of connecting-links between the several
narratives, and it cannot be said that the tension is stronger in one than
in the other. The only topographical reference is ' And they come again
to Jerusalem ' in xi. 27. The contrast with xi. 1-25, in which the narratives
are closely articulated, is striking. The five Pronouncement-stories are
set side by side. Almost the same is true of the three additions which
Mark has made in 76, 81, and 82. The Parable of the Wicked Husbandmen is attached by the general statement ' And he began to speak to them
in parables ' ; the sayings are introduced by the editorial phrase, ' And in
his teaching he said ' ; and the story of the Widow's Mites is appended
because of the reference to widows in xii. 40 and its connexion with the
Temple.

The section is a notable example of Mark's restraint in not introducing
statements of time, place, and circumstance, when they were not supplied
in the tradition. This restraint, which differs from the methods of the
later Evangelists, adds to the historical value of the Gospel even though
it raises problems which cannot be solved. It is possible, and even probable, that some of the incidents belong to earlier periods in the Ministry
of Jesus either in Jerusalem or in Galilee.

Mk. xi. 27-33   75. ON AUTHORITY   Cf. Mt. xxi. 23-7
                                                      Lk. xx. 1-8

The form of is that of a Pronouncement-story or Apothegm. Cf.
Bultmann, 18 f. ; Albertz, 23 (*Streitgespräch*). It is, as Albertz describes
it, a ' controversy-story ', but in the course of transmission the narrative
elements have fallen away almost entirely, and little more is left than the
pointed question : ' By what authority doest thou these things ? or who
gave thee this authority to do these things ? ', and the reply of Jesus. It
was for the sake of this reply that the story was preserved in the earliest
Christian community ; it enshrined the conviction of Jesus that His
ἐξουσία was from God. It may have been current as a self-contained story,
and in this case the references in 27 to Jerusalem and to walking in the
Temple, as well as the allusion to ' the chief priests, and the scribes, and
the elders ', may have been added by Mark ; cf. Bultmann, 18. But it
is also possible that ταῦτα refers to the Cleansing, and, in this case, from
the first the narrative reflected a rudimentary biographical interest ; it

told how Jesus answered a challenge arising out of His action in the Temple. This is probably the better view, for it is unlikely that the question put was purely general. In any case, it is arbitrary, with Bultmann, to limit the original story to 28-30, and to ascribe 31 f. to a Hellenist, perhaps Mark himself. There is no reason why Jesus should not have perceived the priests' dilemma nor why the situation should not have been remembered. Verse 33, in which the priests evade the issue and Jesus refuses to say by what authority He acts, strikes such an original note and is so much unlike invention that it is excessive scientific caution to ask whether 28-30 is a historical account or a formation of the community, especially if it is ' a genuine Palestinian Apothegm '.[1] The veiled reply is itself a claim and must have been recognized as such. It embodies the idea of a Messianic secret, but the phrasing is not a literary device of Mark but the actual reply of Jesus.[2]

Καὶ ἔρχονται πάλιν εἰς Ἱεροσόλυμα. Καὶ ἐν τῷ ἱερῷ περι- 27 πατοῦντος αὐτοῦ ἔρχονται πρὸς αὐτὸν οἱ ἀρχιερεῖς καὶ οἱ γραμματεῖς καὶ οἱ πρεσβύτεροι καὶ ἔλεγον αὐτῷ Ἐν ποίᾳ ἐξουσίᾳ 28 ταῦτα ποιεῖς; ἢ τίς σοι ἔδωκεν τὴν ἐξουσίαν ταύτην ἵνα ταῦτα

27 f. Once more in ἔρχονται we may have one of the ' impersonal plurals ' which Turner, *JTS*, xxvi. 225 f., thinks represent ' we ' in the oral tradition. For Ἱεροσόλυμα v. iii. 8.; ἱερόν xi. 11; πάλιν ii. 1. The details can be editorial, but they may also have belonged to the story from the first. D X 225 252mg 565 b c ff i k q aur bo (1 MS.) read the sing. ἔρχεται, which may be due to the influence of public reading rather than the tradition as Mark found it. Cf. Schmidt, 276. For the free use of the gen. abs. (περιπατοῦντος αὐτοῦ) v. v. 2; περιπατέω, ii. 9.

For οἱ ἀρχιερεῖς and οἱ πρεσβύτεροι v. viii. 31; οἱ γραμματεῖς i. 22. Only here and in viii. 31, xiv. 43, 53, xv. 1, with differences of order, are the three groups mentioned together. It is conceivable that the Sanhedrin is meant, and, if so, the compound phrase may be an expansion or addition, since it is improbable that a formal examination took place in public (cf. Lohmeyer, 240); but such an interpretation is neither necessary nor probable, since

elsewhere, when the Sanhedrin is meant, Mark adds expressions which leave his meaning in no doubt. Cf. πάντες in xiv. 53 and καὶ ὅλον τὸ συνέδριον in xv. 1. It is much more likely that in the present case Mark means representatives of the chief priests, scribes, and elders, and presumably only a few.

For the important word ἐξουσία v. the note on i. 22. Divine authority, and not legal or political right, is meant. Without questioning this meaning of ἐξουσία, D. Daube, *JTS*, xxxix. 45-59, suggests that, in the minds of the priests, the reference is to Rabbinical authority (רשׁות, רשׁוּתא). The tacit objection is that Jesus is not an ordained Rabbi. But here prophetic action rather than teaching is in question. Even if the two were not sharply separated in Jewish thought, the kind of reply which Jesus makes suggests that the issue is one of divine authority.

Most commentators take ταῦτα as a reference to the Cleansing. So Wellhausen, 92; Swete, 262; Lagrange, 302; Bacon, *BGS*, 164; Plummer,

---

[1] Cf. Bultmann, 19 : *ein echt palästinensisches Apophthegma . . . von dem nur fraglich sein kann, ob es ein geschichtlicher Bericht ist oder eine Bildung der Urgemeinde, die den Gegnern ihre Waffen aus der Hand winden will.*
[2] Cf. Albertz, 35, who says of the group xi. 27-33, xii. 13-37 : *Überall stehen hinter den Erzählungen wirklich gehaltene Gespräche.*

29 ποιῇς; ὁ δὲ Ἰησοῦς εἶπεν αὐτοῖς Ἐπερωτήσω ὑμᾶς ἕνα λόγον,
καὶ ἀποκρίθητέ μοι, καὶ ἐρῶ ὑμῖν ἐν ποίᾳ ἐξουσίᾳ ταῦτα ποιῶ·
30 τὸ βάπτισμα τὸ Ἰωάνου ἐξ οὐρανοῦ ἦν ἢ ἐξ ἀνθρώπων; ἀπο-
31 κρίθητέ μοι. καὶ διελογίζοντο πρὸς ἑαυτοὺς λέγοντες Τί εἴπω-

267; Lohmeyer, 240; Blunt, 228; though Swete and Plummer think that the whole career of Jesus is also in question. Others see a reference to the Entry (cf. Schlatter, with reference to Mt. xxi. 23). The connexion with the Cleansing, suggested by Mark and by Jn. ii. 18, seems the best view to take, although Luke appears to have had the teaching of Jesus in mind; cf. Creed, 243; Easton, 291; Luce, 307. Much depends upon whether the narrative was in circulation as an independent unit (cf. Bultmann, 18; Schniewind, 152), or whether, as seems more probable, a rudimentary biographical interest connected the question with the action of Jesus in the Temple.

The double form of the question is characteristically Jewish, but the second part (ἢ τίς, etc.) gives it a more personal form. The redundant ἵνα ταῦτα ποιῇς is omitted by Matthew and Luke. Both mention the teaching of Jesus, and Luke, as often, recasts the opening words. ποῖος, 'what sort of', xi. 29, 33, xii. 28*. Cf. Ac. iv. 7, ἐν ποίᾳ δυνάμει ἢ ἐν ποίῳ ὀνόματι ἐποιήσατε τοῦτο ὑμεῖς;.

29 f. As in x. 3, Jesus replies by a counter-question, a method common in Rabbinical discussions. For ἐπερωτάω v. v. 9. λόγος is used with the meaning 'matter' or 'point' (cf. Ac. i. 1, ' book ') and ἕνα = ' single '. With the imperative ἀποκρίθητε, used in a conditional sense, cf. πιστεύετε in 24. It is not necessary, with Baljon, to conjecture as the original κἂν ἀποκριθῆτέ μοι; cf. Swete, 263; Klostermann, 134; Lohmeyer, 241 n.; etc. For ἐξουσία v. i. 27, xi. 28; ἀποκρίνομαι iii. 33.

The question concerns the baptism of John: was it from God or from men? It is unsatisfactory to explain

this counter-question as a mere dialectical expedient; it implies that John's ἐξουσία came from God, and, more important still, a veiled claim that Jesus Himself is the Messiah. For βάπτισμα v. i. 4; Ἰωάνης (of the Baptist) i. 4. οὐρανός is a common Jewish periphrasis for God; cf. Dan. iv. 26, 1 Macc. iii. 18, Lk. xv. 18, 21, Jn. iii. 27, etc. Cf. Dalman, 219 f. τὸ βάπτισμα τὸ Ἰωάνου is not an example of casus pendens; the subject is placed first for emphasis; cf. Howard, ii. 423. Too much is claimed, if it is held that it is the baptism in particular which is in question (cf. Lohmeyer, 242 f.); John and his ministry are meant; cf. Ac. i. 22, xviii. 25. The imperative ἀποκρίθητε (om. in Mt and Lk) presses home the question.

Both later Evangelists agree in reading ἀποκριθείς at the beginning of the passage and κἀγώ after ὑμᾶς, and these readings are strongly attested in Mk: ἀποκριθείς by A D W Θ et al. fam. 1 fam. 13 28 565 700 1071 al. pler. it vg sys hl; κἀγώ by ℵ A D W Θ et al. P45 fam. 1 fam. 13 28 565 700 1071 al. pler. it (exc. k) vg sys pe hl. A good case can be stated for regarding these readings as original, and, if they are accepted, the agreements of Mt and Lk against Mk disappear; but Streeter, 319, thinks they should be rejected, ἀποκριθείς as too common to be significant, and κἀγώ because it is not found elsewhere in Mk. Bultmann's suggestion, 18 f., that the original Palestinian Apothegm ended at xi. 30, must, I think, be rejected, and still more that it may be a formation of the community. So Lohmeyer, 243, who observes that there is no later situation of the primitive community in which the ' authority ' of Jesus could have been based on the baptism of John.

μεν; ἐὰν εἴπωμεν Ἐξ οὐρανοῦ, ἐρεῖ Διὰ τί [οὖν] οὐκ ἐπιστεύ-
σατε αὐτῷ; ἀλλὰ εἴπωμεν Ἐξ ἀνθρώπων;—ἐφοβοῦντο τὸν ὄχλον, 32
ἅπαντες γὰρ ⌜εἶχον⌝ τὸν Ἰωάνην ὄντως ὅτι προφήτης ἦν. καὶ 33
ἀποκριθέντες τῷ Ἰησοῦ λέγουσιν Οὐκ οἴδαμεν. καὶ ὁ Ἰησοῦς
λέγει αὐτοῖς Οὐδὲ ἐγὼ λέγω ὑμῖν ἐν ποίᾳ ἐξουσίᾳ ταῦτα ποιῶ.

32 ᾔδεισαν

31-3. Jesus perceives the priests' dilemma. For διαλογίζομαι v. ii. 6; πρὸς ἑαυτούς, cf. viii. 16; πιστεύω, i. 15; φοβέομαι, iv. 41; προφήτης, i. 2; ὄχλος, ii 4. If they acknowledged (ἐάν c. subj., i. 40) John's ' authority ' to be divine (ἐξ οὐρανοῦ, xi. 30), they would expose themselves to the charge of unbelief. More, however, is involved than this; they would also be compelled to admit that the ἐξουσία of Jesus was from God.

Before the first conditional clause, Ἐὰν εἴπωμεν . . ., Τί εἴπωμεν; is attested, and should probably be read, with D Θ Φ fam. 13 28 565 700 a b c ff i k r. Turner, JTS, xxix. 6, observes that it seems so entirely to correspond to the style of the Gospel that it is difficult not to believe it genuine. Turner, JTS, xxviii. 20, omits οὖν after διὰ τί with A C* L W a b c d ff i k sys.

The second conditional sentence in 32 breaks off, the apodosis being replaced by the statement that they feared the people. All held John to be a prophet, and therefore inspired by the Holy Spirit. For ἅπας v. i. 27, and with the use of ἔχειν in the sense of ' to hold for ', cf. Lk. xiv. 18, Phil. ii. 29; Blass, 231. Blass explains the usage as a Latinism, but the constrn. is found in the papyri; v. VGT, 270; Bauer, 519; Lagrange, 303. ᾔδεισαν,[1] read by D W Θ 565 a b c ff i k arm, and οἴδασι 700, are probably secondary. Swete, 264, thinks that ὄντως* should be taken with εἶχον, ' all seriously held ', but it is drawn into the principal clause for emphasis in ℵc B C L Ψ

fam. 13 (exc. 124) 543 892, and should be read with the subordinate ὅτι clause, where it is found in A D (ἀληθῶς) W et al. 33 1071 al. pler. a b f ff i l q vg sype hl sa bo geo, ' John had been a real prophet '; cf. Klostermann, 134; Lagrange, 303; cf. Moffatt, Torrey, RSV.[2] ἦν is used in the sense of the pluperfect; cf. Blass, 192. ὄντως is omitted in ℵ* Θ fam. 1 28 124 565 579 700 et al. c k sys.

ἀποκριθέντες in 33, which is not redundant here, takes up the question of 30. Unable to answer, the priests say that they do not know, and pointedly referring to their negative reply, Jesus says Οὐδὲ ἐγὼ λέγω ὑμῖν ἐν ποίᾳ ἐξουσίᾳ ταῦτα ποιῶ. But He has already told them in His counter-question, and they can have been in no doubt about His veiled claim. For ποῖος v. xi. 28; ἐξουσία i. 22.

Matthew and Luke follow Mk closely with stylistic changes. Both have οἱ δέ before the verb in 31 (Lk, συνελογίσαντο) and both replace ἀλλά in 32 by ἐὰν δέ. Mark's broken sentence in 32 is made smooth by supplying an apodosis, Mt, φοβούμεθα τὸν ὄχλον, Lk, ὁ λαὸς ἅπας καταλιθάσει ἡμᾶς; and his roughly phrased explanation concerning John is recast, Mt, πάντες γὰρ ὡς προφήτην ἔχουσιν τὸν Ἰωάνην, Lk, πεπεισμένος γάρ ἐστιν Ἰωάνην προφήτην εἶναι. The direct speech in οὐκ οἴδαμεν is retained by Matthew, but is replaced by Luke with the infin. constrn. The historic presents in 33, λέγουσιν and λέγει, disappear in both Gospels. There can be no doubt whose is the primitive account.

---

[1] Turner, JTS, xxix. 7, reads ᾔδεισαν, pointing out that Mark does not use ἔχω in this sense while Matthew does so twice.
[2] For the similar Semitic use of hyperbaton v. Wellhausen, Einl.², 12; Black, 36; Intr. 58.

Mk. xii. 1-12   76. THE PARABLE OF THE   Cf.' Mt. xxi. 33-46
                     WICKED HUSBANDMEN   Lk. xx. 9-19

This Parable is controversial, resembling in this respect that of the
Two Sons by which it is preceded in Mt (xxi. 28-32). Since the publication of Jülicher's *Gleichnisreden Jesu* (2nd ed., 1910, ii. 385-406) it has
been widely regarded as an allegory constructed in the early Church with
reference to the death of Jesus. Cf. Bousset, 42 f. ; Bultmann, 191 ;
Klostermann, 135 ; Branscomb, 209-11 ; Loisy, ii. 306-19 ; Montefiore,
i. 273-5. Some who take this view, including Jülicher himself, think
that a nucleus within the parable in xii. 1, 9 may go back to Jesus ; cf.
Ed. Meyer, i. 167. There is no doubt that in part the parable is allegorical;
it is, as Lagrange, 311, describes it, a *parabole allégorique*. The owner is
God, the son is Jesus, the vineyard is Israel, the husbandmen are the
Jewish leaders or possibly the people as a whole, and the slaves are apparently the Old Testament prophets. But no allegorical significance belongs
to the hedge, the pit, the wine press, the tower, the other country, the fruit,
the exterior of the vineyard ; in short, the narrative is not pure allegory.
The details are necessary elements in the story. This consideration raises
the question whether the vineyard itself and the slaves are to be precisely
identified ; the only certain symbolic figures are the owner, the husbandmen, and the son. If this is so, no sufficient objection can be brought
against the parable on this ground, unless it is held that Jesus invariably
used parables to convey general truths and never as pointed weapons.

Other objections are based on improbabilities in the story, and above
all upon the fact that in it Jesus tacitly claims to be the Son of God and
refers to His death. The action of the owner is strange, it is said, if he is
God : he plants the vineyard, leases it to others, and departs expecting to
receive payment in kind. In spite of the treatment meted out to the slaves
he takes no action, and apparently does not foresee the fate of his son,
while the husbandmen stupidly suppose that by killing the heir they
will obtain the inheritance. The prophets are ill represented by slaves
who collect dues and the Jewish leaders are strangely conceived as tenants
rather than guardians. Pressed by Loisy and others, these objections
assume that the parable must be self-consistent and accurate in detail,
whereas its purpose is to describe the astounding patience and long-
suffering of God towards Israel and its leaders. Bizarre features are of
minor importance ; they appear, for example, in the parables of the Unjust
Judge, the Friend at Midnight, and the Labourers in the Vineyard. The
fact that Jesus alludes to His sonship and death in no way compels us to
think of the theology of the Christian community, if regard is paid to
viii. 31, x. 45, xiv. 24 f., and other prophecies of the Passion. On the
contrary, a representation which puts the death of the son on a level with
that of the slaves, differing only in its malignity and the dishonour done
to the body, and which does not mention the Resurrection,[1] is the reverse
of what might be expected in a community product. Lohmeyer, 249,
is fully justified in saying that the fundamental idea of the parable contains
nothing which contradicts the teaching of Jesus, and especially Lk. xi. 49
and xiii. 34.

----

[1] Cf. Burkitt, *Transactions of the Third International Congress for the History of Religion*,
ii. 321-8.

Whether the parable has undergone some degree of expansion is a matter for conjecture. Dodd, 127, 129, suggests that 4 (? 5) and 9b may be additions. Nothing is lost by their removal. Mark's literary practice elsewhere (cf. ii. 21 f., 27 f., xi. 23-5) supports the view that he has appended the quotation regarding the stone in 10 f. and the allusion to the priests in 12, but is no less consistent with the probability that he follows good tradition in making these additions.

For further discussions of the critical problems *v.* Lagrange, 305-12 ; Rawlinson, 161-4 ; Turner, 57 ; Bartlet, 325-9 ; Wood, 695.

Καὶ ἤρξατο αὐτοῖς ἐν παραβολαῖς λαλεῖν ᾿Αμπελῶνα ἄν- 1 XII
θρωπος ἐφύτεγσεν, καὶ περιέθηκεν φραγμὸν καὶ ὤργξεν ὑπολήνιον καὶ ᾠκοδόμησεν πύργον, καὶ ἐξέδετο αὐτὸν γεωργοῖς,
καὶ ἀπεδήμησεν. καὶ ἀπέστειλεν πρὸς τοὺς γεωργοὺς τῷ καιρῷ 2

1. The details are taken from the LXX text of Isa. v. 1 f., in which ἀμπε-λών, φυτεύω*, περιτίθημι, φραγμός*, ὀρύσσω*, ὑπολήνιον* (Isa., προλήνιον), οἰκοδομέω, and πύργος* also appear. For ἤρξατο c. infin. *v.* Intr. 48, 63 f. ; ἐν παραβολαῖς iii. 23. Mark is referring not to a series of parables, but to the manner of the teaching. Both Mt and Lk have the sing., and for ἄνθρωπος Mt has οἰκοδεσπότης. ἀμπελών, xi. 2, 8, 9 (*bis*)*, belongs to late Greek and is common in the papyri (*VGT*, 27 f.) and in the LXX. ἐφύτευσεν, Cl. Gk, LXX, Pap., is replaced in vg by *pastinauit*, 'dug and trenched'. περι-τίθημι, xv. 17, 36*. The ὑπολήνιον** (LXX, Isa. xvi. 10, Joel iii. (iv.) 13) was a vessel or trough into which the juice ran after the grapes had been squeezed in the προλήνιον above. The φραγμός gave protection from wild animals and the πύργος enabled a watch to be kept and provided shelter for the husbandmen. The description is true to methods of cultivating the vine in Palestine which have persisted until modern times; cf. Billerbeck, i. 867 f.; Lagrange, 305 ; Smith, *HG*, 82 f.

Thus far the parable is true to the traditional picture in Isa., in which the vine represents Israel, except that Mark has ἄνθρωπος instead of ὁ ἠγαπη-μένος. The various details have no allegorical importance (for Patristic interpretations *v.* Swete, 266), but

simply belong to the picture. At this point the parable deviates from Isa. v. i f. Nothing is said of a disappointing harvest of wild grapes. The man leases the vineyard to husbandmen and departs. ἐκδίδομαι*, Mt. xxi. 33, 41, Lk. xx. 9**, is used in Herodotus i. 68 and the NT in the mid. in the sense of ' to farm out ', ' let for advantage '; cf. the meaning ' apprentice ' in the papyri (*VGT*, 192). For the form ἐξέδετο *v.* Moulton, ii. 212. This vernacular form is replaced by ἐξέδοτο in B² D W Δ Ψ *et al.* fam. 1 fam. 13 (exc. 346) 28 33 565 700 892 1071 *al. pler.* ἀποδημέω*, Mt. xxi. 33, xv. 14 f., Lk. xv. 13, xx. 9**, ' to go (or ' be ') abroad '; Cl. Gk; LXX, Ezek. xix. 3*; Pap. The reference to the departure of the owner is necessary to the situation and there is no need to interpret it allegorically, e.g. with Origen, *in Mt., t.* xvii. 6, who refers to the withdrawal of the divine presence after God had led the Israelites through the wilderness by means of the cloud by day and the pillar of fire by night. Nor is it necessary, with Jerome, to see a gracious purpose in the departure; cf. Swete, 267. Luke adds that it was for a long time, χρόνους ἱκανούς. γεωργός, xii. 2 (*bis*), 7, 9*; used here of the Sanhedrists.

Of the later Synoptists Matthew follows Mk closely, using ληνός instead of ὑπολήνιον and altering the intro-ductory words to ἄλλην παραβολὴν

δοῦλον, ἵνα παρὰ τῶν γεωργῶν λάβῃ ἀπὸ τῶν καρπῶν τοῦ ἀμπε-
3 λῶνος· καὶ λαβόντες αὐτὸν ἔδειραν καὶ ἀπέστειλαν κενόν. καὶ
4
πάλιν ἀπέστειλεν πρὸς αὐτοὺς ἄλλον δοῦλον· κἀκεῖνον ἐκεφα-
5 λίωσαν καὶ ἠτίμασαν. καὶ ἄλλον ἀπέστειλεν· κἀκεῖνον ἀπέκτειναν, καὶ πολλοὺς ἄλλους, οὓς μὲν δέροντες οὓς δὲ ἀποκτεννύντες.

ἀκούσατε. Luke describes the parable
as addressed to the people, πρὸς τὸν
λαόν, and omits the details derived
from Isa. v. 1 f.

2-5. In succession three slaves are
sent to receive the produce of the vineyard. τῷ καιρῷ (i. 15) means 'at the
proper season ', ' when the time came ',
i.e. in the fifth year (cf. Lev. xix. 23-5).
For ἀποστέλλω v. i. 2. The term δοῦλος
Κυρίου is used of Moses (Jos. xiv. 7,
Psa. civ. (cv.) 26), Joshua (Jos. xxiv.
29), and David (2 Kgdms. iii. 18), and
then regularly of the prophets (Am.
iii. 7, Zech. i. 6, Jer. vii. 25, etc.). It
is natural, therefore, to think that in
the parable the prophets, as the fore-
runners of Jesus, are meant; but this
inference is not necessary, especially as
the function of the prophet is to declare
the will of God and not to gather His
dues. Possibly, then, the slaves merely
belong to the story.

A marked gradation is manifest in
the fortunes of the slaves. The first
is beaten and sent away empty; the
third is killed. This progressive malignity may help to solve some of the
problems connected with the fate of
the second servant; v. infra. δέρω,
xii. 5, xiii. 9*, was softened in meaning
in the Hellenistic period; v. the note
on φιμόω in i. 25. Originally meaning
' to skin ' or ' flay ' (so in the LXX),
it is found in Aristophanes, Vespae,
485, in the sense of ' beat ', as in the
NT and the papyri (VGT, 142).
κενός*.

The second slave (πάλιν, ii. 1) appears
to have been buffeted and treated
shamefully. Unfortunately, the text
is uncertain. Most MSS. read ἐκεφαλαίωσαν (A C D Δ Θ et al. fam. 13 22
33 157 543 1071 al. pler.), but κεφα-
λαιόω (<κεφάλαιον) means ' to sum
up ', and there is no example of the

verb with the meaning ' to wound in
the head '. A sense of the inadequacy
of the verb appears to be reflected by
the fact that very many MSS. which
read ἐκεφαλαίωσαν precede it by λιθοβο-
λήσαντες, ' stoning ' (v. Legg). An act
of violence is intended, as the renderings of Mt (ἐλιθοβόλησαν), Lk (τραυμα-
τίσαντες), and the Latin versions (in
capite uulnerauerunt, vg and many
O. Lat. MSS.; similarly sa bo), suggest. Either, then, Mark used κεφα-
λαιόω in a sense otherwise unknown,
or the reading is corrupt. ἐκεφαλίωσαν
is strongly attested by א B L Ψ 579
892, but this testimony is exclusively
Alexandrian, and, what is more serious,
κεφαλιόω is otherwise unknown, though
derivation from κεφάλιον, after the
analogy of γναθόω ' to hit on the
cheek ', has been conjectured (Lobeck,
Phryn. 95; cf. Swete, 268). In these
circumstances, unless ' something in
the Aramaic original suggested it '
(Allen, 148), there is much to be said
for Burkitt's view (AJT, 1911, 173 ff.),
that ἐκεφαλίωσαν may be a palaeo-
graphical blunder for ἐκολάφισαν, ' they
buffeted ' (cf. xiv. 65*). This conjecture, made earlier by Baljon, is
dismissed by Lagrange, 307, as banale
and as without textual support, but
it gives good sense and may account
for the textual variants. It must be
confessed, however, that Moffatt's
rendering ' knocked on the head '
gives the meaning required if it could
be adequately based. See further,
Moulton, ii. 395; VGT, 342; Field,
35 f.; Swete, 268; Lohmeyer, 245 f.

Not only was the slave beaten up,
he was also put to the utmost shame.
For ἀτιμάζω*, ' to dishonour ', ' insult '
(Cl., LXX, Pap.) v. 2 Kgdms. x. 5, Ac.
v. 41.

The brief reference to the murder of

ἔτι ἕνα εἶχεν, υἱὸν ἀγαπητόν· ἀπέστειλεν αὐτὸν ἔσχατον πρὸς 6
αὐτοὺς λέγων ὅτι 'Εντραπήσονται τὸν υἱόν μου. ἐκεῖνοι δὲ οἱ 7
γεωργοὶ πρὸς ἑαυτοὺς εἶπαν ὅτι Οὗτός ἐστιν ὁ κληρονόμος· δεῦτε
ἀποκτείνωμεν αὐτόν, καὶ ἡμῶν ἔσται ἡ κληρονομία. καὶ λα- 8
βόντες ἀπέκτειναν αὐτόν, καὶ ἐξέβαλον αὐτὸν ἔξω τοῦ ἀμπελῶνος.

the third slave is followed by a general statement καὶ πολλοὺς ἄλλους, οὓς μὲν δέροντες οὓς δὲ ἀποκτεννύντες. Dodd's suggestion, 129, that 5 is an addition, receives support from the rarity of μέν . . . δέ in Mk (xiv. 21, 38*) and the variant form ἀποκτεννύντες*, but the reference to three slaves (rather than two and the son) is more characteristic of the folk-tale, while 5b heightens the tension. ἀποκτεννύντες, read by B 892 and a few lectionaries, is more likely to be original than the widely attested ἀποκτέννοντες. Cf. Hort, 169; Moulton, ii. 245. For OT references to the fate of divine messengers v. 1 Kgs. xviii. 13, xxii. 27, 2 Chron. xxiv. 20 ff., xxxvi. 15 f., Neh. ix. 26, Jer. xliv. (xxxvii.) 15; cf. also Lk. vi. 23, xiii. 34, Ac. vii. 52, 1 Thess. ii. 15, Heb. xi. 36 ff., Apoc. xvi. 6.

6-8. The owner now puts the husbandmen to the supreme test by sending to them his only son. Probably a comma should be put after εἶχεν, ' He still had one, an only son '; the one son stands in contrast with the many slaves. For ἀγαπητός = μονογενής v. the note on i. 11. Cf. Gen. xxii. 2, Λάβε τὸν υἱόν σου τὸν ἀγαπητόν, Judg. xi. 34 (A), μονογενὴς ἀγαπητή, Tob. iii. 10 (ℵ), μία σοι ὑπῆρχεν θυγατὴρ ἀγαπητή. Cf. Turner, JTS, xxvii. 120; Creed, 58. In the NT and later Christian writings ὁ ἠγαπημένος (Eph. i. 6) and ὁ ἀγαπητός become Messianic designations, but it is doubtful if ἀγαπητός has this significance in the present passage, though it may well have this meaning in Lk. xx. 13, πέμψω τὸν υἱόν μου τὸν ἀγαπητόν. Matthew has τὸν υἱὸν αὐτοῦ (xxi. 37). Mark states with emphasis that the owner sent him last (ἔσχατος, ix. 35).[1] For ' Beloved ' as a Messianic

title v. J. A. Robinson, Eph. 229-233.

In Mk (and Mt) the owner's words are a conviction, ἐντραπήσονται τὸν υἱόν μου, in Lk a hope, ἴσως τοῦτον ἐντραπήσονται. ἐντρέπω*, ' to put to shame ', mid. or pass. ' to reverence '; Cl. (c. gen. of pers.), LXX, Pap. Cf. Moulton, i. 65. In 2 Thess. iii. 14, Tit. ii. 8 the meaning is ' to be ashamed ' (VGT, 219).

In the event things turn out differently. The husbandmen plot to kill the heir (ὁ κληρονόμος*) in order that the inheritance (ἡ κληρονομία*) may be theirs. ἐκεῖνοι (om. in Mt and Lk) has a tone of irony. For πρὸς ἑαυτούς v. xi. 31; δεῦτε i. 17. Cf. the words of Joseph's brothers in Gen. xxxvii. 20, νῦν οὖν δεῦτε ἀποκτείνωμεν αὐτόν. The plan seems foolish, but it has been held that, since leases were often long, the tenants might hope, if the heir died, to gain possession of the property; cf. Billerbeck, i. 871. More convincing is the explanation of Dodd, 125, who suggests that the parable reflects the disturbed conditions, partly due to economic causes, which existed in Palestine during the half century which preceded the revolt of A.D. 66. Cf. F. C. Grant, The Economic Background of the Gospels, Part II, ' The Economic Data '. The statement that they cast him out of the vineyard (ἐκβάλλω, i. 12; ἔξω, i. 45) implies that his body was left unburied. In Lk, but probably not in Mt (so D Θ a b c d e ff), the inversion by which the casting out is mentioned first may reflect a desire to bring the story into closer agreement with the tradition that Christ ' suffered without the gate ' (Heb. xiii. 12).

[1] Turner, JTS, xxix. 7, would omit πρὸς αὐτούς after ἔσχατον with D 1071 a ff i k.

9 τί ποιήσει ὁ κύριος τοῦ ἀμπελῶνος; ἐλεύσεται καὶ ἀπολέσει
10 τοὺς γεωργούς, καὶ δώσει τὸν ἀμπελῶνα ἄλλοις. Οὐδὲ τὴν
γραφὴν ταύτην ἀνέγνωτε

Λίθον ὃν ἀπεδοκίμασαν οἱ οἰκοδομοῦντες,
οὗτος ἐγενήθη εἰς κεφαλὴν γωνίας·
11 παρὰ Κυρίου ἐγένετο αὕτη,
καὶ ἔστιν θαυμαστὴ ἐν ὀφθαλμοῖς ἡμῶν;

9. Jesus gives point to the parable by the question τί ποιήσει ὁ κύριος τοῦ ἀμπελῶνος;. For κύριος v. i. 3; here of the owner or master of the vineyard. Luke inserts οὖν and adds αὐτοῖς, while Matthew prefixes ὅταν οὖν ἔλθῃ and adds τοῖς γεωργοῖς ἐκείνοις. Again Mk is simpler.

In Mk Jesus answers His own question: the owner will come and destroy the husbandmen and give the vineyard to others. The idea of the coming of God in judgment is fundamentally Jewish (cf. Psa. xcv. (xcvi.) 13, Amos v. 17, 1 Enoch i. 9, etc.), and the only question is whether the answer is a subsequent addition; cf. Dodd, 126 f. Its character favours this view, especially as in like situations Jesus leaves His questions unanswered; cf. Lk. xvii. 9, 'Doth he thank the servant because he did the things that were commanded?'. In Mt the answer is supplied by the hearers, and the 'others', to whom the vineyard is 'leased', are described as 'husbandmen, such as will give him the fruits in their seasons' (xxi. 41). Perhaps Matthew is thinking of the Apostles or the Christian Church (cf. xxi. 43, a nation producing the fruits of the Kingdom), but it is doubtful if Mark gives any precise connotation to ἄλλοις. Cf. Rawlinson, 164. Luke follows Mk closely, but adds that, when they heard, the hearers replied, μὴ γένοιτο. Whether 9b belongs to the parable is of secondary importance, since its ideas appear in the teaching of Jesus in Mt. viii. 11 = Lk. xiii. 28 f. and Mt. xxii. 13, and not only subsequently in Rom. xi. 17 ff.

10 f. The quotation is from Psa. cxvii. (cxviii.) 22 f. The question

arises whether it was added by Jesus or by the Evangelist (Bultmann, 191; Klostermann, 137). This question is not foreclosed by the parable form, since in Rabbinic parables Scripture quotations sometimes appear at the end; cf. P. Fiebig, Die Gleichnisreden Jesu, 78. With οὐδὲ τὴν γραφὴν ταύτην ἀνέγνωτε; cf. ii. 25. οὐδέ, ' not even ', implies that the prophecy was well known. Here only in Mk is the sing. ἡ γραφή used of a portion of Scripture; cf. Lk. iv. 21, Ac. i. 16, Jn. vii. 38, 42, xix. 37, 2 Tim. iii. 16, Jas. ii. 8, 23. Mk. xv. 28 is a scribal addition and in xii. 24, xiv. 49* the plur. is used. Normally Mark introduces quotations by using γέγραπται and sayings by καὶ ἔλεγεν αὐτοῖς. The introductory question, then, can hardly be called Markan.

The quotation agrees verbatim with the LXX. The casus pendens λίθον, taken up in οὗτος, is attracted to the case of the rel. pron., and is not affected by the Heb. Cf. Howard, ii. 423. εἰς κεφαλήν, instead of the predicative nom., while not contrary to Greek idiom, is used because it corresponds to ל; cf. x. 8 and v. Howard, i. 71 f.; Howard, ii. 462 f. In 11 αὕτη is an over literal rendering of the Heb. זאת, the fem. for the neut. These points of syntax concern the LXX, not Mark's style. For ἀποδοκιμάζω v. viii. 31; οἰκοδομέω xii. 1. In the passage the rejected stone becomes ' the head of the corner ' (κεφαλὴ γωνίας*), i.e. either the cornerstone which holds the walls of the building together or the keystone of the arch or gateway. Cf. ἀκρογωνιαῖος, 1 Pet. ii. 6, Eph. ii. 20**, and see VGT, 19; J. Jeremias, KThW, i. 792 f.; J. A. Robinson,

Καὶ ἐζήτουν αὐτὸν κρατῆσαι, καὶ ἐφοβήθησαν τὸν ὄχλον, ἔγνωσαν 12
γὰρ ὅτι πρὸς αὐτοὺς τὴν παραβολὴν εἶπεν. καὶ ἀφέντες αὐτὸν
ἀπῆλθαν.

Eph. 163 f.; E. G. Selwyn, *1 Pet.* 163
The second part of the quotation (xii.
11) describes the reversal as the work
of God and as marvellous in men's
eyes. θαυμαστός*; κύριος, i. 3.
In Rabbinic literature the stone is
identified with Abraham, David, and
perhaps even the Messiah; cf. Billerbeck, i. 875 f.; Cadbury, *BC*, v. 374;
Schniewind, 154 f.; and in primitive
Christianity it becomes a standing
designation of Jesus. Psa. cxvii.
(cxviii.) 22 is quoted in Ac. iv. 11 and
in 1 Pet. ii. 7. In 1 Pet. ii. 6, 8 two
other ' stone-prophecies ' are cited,
Isa. xxviii. 16 (' Behold, I lay in
Zion . . . ') and Isa. viii. 14 (' A stone
of stumbling . . . '), as also in Rom.
ix. 33. Similar groups are found in
Ep. Barn. vi. 2-4, in Cyprian, *Testimonia*, ii. 16 f., where the chapter
heading is *Quod idem et lapis dictus
est*, and in Aphraates, *Hom.* i. 6 f.,
while Justin Martyr twice speaks of
Christ as λίθος, *Dial. c. Trypho*, xxxiv.
2, xxxvi. 1. Cf. Lk. xx. 18. This
evidence points to the early existence
of collections of Messianic proof-texts
containing such passages (J. R. Harris,
Testimonies, i. 30 f.) and perhaps also
to their use in primitive Christian
hymns (Selwyn, *op. cit.* 273-7).
The facts have now been assembled
on the basis of which the question
raised at the outset may be considered.
It may be that Mark has appended
10 f., but there are no decisive arguments in favour of this view. On the
whole it is more probable that the
interest of primitive Christianity in
the thought of Christ as the λίθος rejected by men, but made by God the

cornerstone of a new Temple, is based
upon the memory that He used Psa.
cxviii. 22 f. in a devastating attack
upon the Jewish hierarchy.
The quotation is reproduced verbatim by Matthew, but he precedes it
by λέγει αὐτοῖς ὁ Ἰησοῦς, changes οὐδέ
to οὐδέποτε, and has ἐν ταῖς γραφαῖς.
More important is the addition,
peculiar to Mt, ' Therefore I say unto
you, the kingdom of God will be taken
away from you and given to a nation
producing the fruits thereof ' (xxi. 43).
Luke says that, before speaking, Jesus
looked on them (ἐμβλέψας), and introduces the quotation by τί οὖν ἐστιν τὸ
γεγραμμένον τοῦτο.   He omits the
second part of the quotation (Mk. xii.
11) and adds a saying which is also found
in many MSS. in Mt, πᾶς ὁ πεσὼν
ἐπ' ἐκεῖνον τὸν λίθον συνθλασθήσεται· ἐφ'
ὃν δ' ἂν πέσῃ, λικμήσει αὐτόν (xx. 18).
12. Mark makes a second reference
(cf. xi. 18) to the hostility of the Sanhedrists, using familiar words : ζητέω
(i. 37), here with the infin. of the object;
κρατῆσαι (i. 31); φοβέομαι (iv. 41);
ὄχλος (ii. 4); γινώσκω ὅτι c. indic.
(xiii. 28 f., xv. 10); παραβολή (iii. 23);
ἀφίημι (i. 18). With the redundant
ἀφέντες followed by the verb of departure cf. iv. 36, viii. 13, xiv. 50,
Howard, ii. 453. πρός = ' with reference to ', as in Lk. xii. 41, Heb. i. 7 f.,
xi. 18. Matthew recasts the sentence,
adding the explanation that the multitudes held Him to be a prophet (xxi.
46). Luke supplies a subject and a
temporal statement, substituting ἐπι-
βαλεῖν ἐπ' αὐτὸν τὰς χεῖρας for κρατῆσαι
(xx. 19). Both omit the reference to
the departure of the priests.

Mk. xii. 13-17   77. ON TRIBUTE TO   Cf. Mt. xxii. 15-22
                          CAESAR   Lk. xx. 20-6

As in xi. 27-33, the second of the five controversy-stories in this section
is a Pronouncement-story; cf. Bultmann, 25; Dibelius, 43; Albertz,
23 f. Everything in it is subordinated to the answer of Jesus to the burning

question whether it was lawful to pay tribute to Caesar, a question which was of the highest religious and practical importance at the time and also in the decades preceding the fall of Jerusalem. The narrative element is reduced to almost the barest essentials : the reference to the questioners and their hostile intentions, to Jesus's perception of their hypocrisy and His request for a *denarius*, and to their great astonishment at His answer. All the emphasis is upon what He said. His saying, ' Render unto Caesar the things that are Caesar's, and to God the things that are God's ', has deeply influenced all subsequent discussions of the complex relationships of Church and State ; and, while it does not solve that problem and does not expressly raise it, it enunciates the decisive principle relative to that discussion. Of its genuineness there can be no question. *An Gemeinde-bildung zu denken, liegt m.E. kein Grund vor*, Bultmann, 25.

13 Καὶ ἀποστέλλουσιν πρὸς αὐτόν τινας τῶν Φαρισαίων καὶ τῶν
14 Ἡρῳδιανῶν ἵνα αὐτὸν ἀγρεύσωσιν λόγῳ. καὶ ἐλθόντες λέγουσιν
αὐτῷ Διδάσκαλε, οἴδαμεν ὅτι ἀληθὴς εἶ καὶ οὐ μέλει σοι περὶ
οὐδενός, οὐ γὰρ βλέπεις εἰς πρόσωπον ἀνθρώπων, ἀλλ' ἐπ' ἀλη-

13. Without statement of time or place the story begins abruptly with a reference to a group of Pharisees and Herodians who are sent to Jesus to entrap Him in His talk. Probably the impersonal plur. ἀποστέλλουσιν (i. 2) is used instead of the pass., but it may be that Mark means that the San-hedrists sent them ; cf. Swete, 273 ; Lagrange, 312 ; Klostermann, 138. For οἱ Φαρισαῖοι v. ii. 16 ; οἱ Ἡρῳδιανοί iii. 6*. The reference to the court-party of Herod Antipas is strange in this context and may indicate that the story belongs to the Galilean period.¹ ἀγρεύω**, ' to take ' or ' catch ', by hunting or fishing. The verb is clas-sical (Euripides, *Ba.* 434 ; Herodotus ii. 95 ; Xenophon, *Cyn.* xii. 6) and is used in the LXX (Job x. 16, Prov. v. 22, vi. 25 f., Hos. v. 2*) and in the papyri. Matthew uses παγιδεύω and Luke ἐπιλαμβάνομαι. λόγῳ is a dat. of instrument or of manner. In addition to the change noted above, Matthew and Luke recast Mark's opening sentence. Matthew describes the Pharisees taking counsel and sending their disciples, together with the Herodians, to Jesus (xxii. 15 f.). Luke connects the story with the priests'

plot and describes them as sending spies who pretended to be upright and whose purpose was ' to deliver him up to the rule and authority of the governor ' (xx. 20). Manifestly, Mark's is the primitive account.

14 f. The question regarding tribute to Caesar is preceded by a fulsome compliment. Jesus is upright (ἀληθής*) and cares for no man, for He does not regard man's person (πρόσωπον, i. 2), but truly teaches the way of God. For διδάσκαλε v. iv. 38 ; οἴδαμεν ὅτι ii. 10 ; οὐ μέλει σοι iv. 38 ; and for the Semitic parallelism v. Black, 117 and xi. 28, xiii. 4, xv. 29.

While πρόσωπον is used in the Koine in the sense of ' person ' (*VGT*, 553), it is probable that οὐ . . . βλέπεις εἰς πρόσωπον ἀνθρώπων and οὐ λαμβάνεις πρόσωπον (Lk. xx. 21) reflect Hebraic idiom. ὁράω and λαμβάνω (but not βλέπω) are so used in the LXX : 1 Kgdms. xvi. 7, ὅτι ἄνθρωπος ὄψεται εἰς πρόσωπον, Psa. lxxxi. (lxxxii.) 2, ἕως πότε . . . πρόσωπα ἁμαρτωλῶν λαμ-βάνετε ;, cf. Lev. xix. 15, οὐδὲ θαυμάσεις πρόσωπον δυνάστου, etc. See also προσωπολημψία (Rom. ii. 11, Eph. vi. 9, Col. iii. 25), προσωπολήμπτης (Ac. x. 34), and προσωπολημπτέω (Jas. ii.

¹ At the same time the reference to the Herodians agrees well with the Lukan tradition that Antipas was present in Jerusalem at the Passover season (Lk. xxiii. 7).

θείας τὴν ὁδὸν τοῦ θεοῦ διδάσκεις· ἔξεστιν δοῦναι κῆνσον Καίσαρι
ἢ οὔ; δῶμεν ἢ μὴ δῶμεν; ὁ δὲ εἰδὼς αὐτῶν τὴν ὑπόκρισιν 15
εἶπεν αὐτοῖς Τί με πειράζετε; φέρετέ μοι δηνάριον ἵνα ἴδω.
οἱ δὲ ἤνεγκαν. καὶ λέγει αὐτοῖς Τίνος ἡ εἰκὼν αὕτη καὶ ἡ ἐπι- 16
γραφή; οἱ δὲ εἶπαν αὐτῷ Καίσαρος. ὁ δὲ Ἰησοῦς εἶπεν Τὰ 17
Καίσαρος ἀπόδοτε Καίσαρι καὶ τὰ τοῦ θεοῦ τῷ θεῷ. καὶ ἐξ-

9). The opposite attitude is described
by ἀλλ' ἐπ' ἀληθείας τὴν ὁδὸν τοῦ θεοῦ
διδάσκει. For ἀλήθεια v. v. 33 ; ἐπ' ἀληθείας, xii. 32*, means ' truly ', ' according to truth '. ἡ ὁδὸς τοῦ θεοῦ
is the kind of life God wills. The expression is Hebraic. Cf. BDB, 204,
Gen. vi. 12, Psa. i. 1, Jer. xxi. 8, Ac.
xviii. 25 f., and ἡ ὁδός in Ac. ix. 2,
xix. 9, 23, xxiv. 14, 22.

After the compliment the challenge
follows, ἔξεστιν δοῦναι κῆνσον Καίσαρι
ἢ οὔ;. For ἔξεστιν v. ii. 24 ; Καίσαρ,
xii. 16 f.*. The word κῆνσος*, Mt.
xvii. 25, xxii. 17, 19**, is a transliteration of the Latin census, ' poll-tax ';
VGT, 343. The tax in question was
paid direct into the Imperial fiscus and
was especially hateful to Jews as a
sign of subjection and because the
coinage (δηνάριον) bore the name and
image of Caesar. Thus, the question
δῶμεν ἢ μὴ δῶμεν ;, in which the subjunctives are deliberative, was skilfully
devised : He would be either discredited or imperilled. An affirmative
answer would disgust the people ; a
negative reply would bring Him into
collision with the Roman authorities.
The reading ἐπικεφάλαιον (Θ 124 565
1071 k sys pe) is probably an attempt
to replace κῆνσον. But see Turner,
JTS, xxix. 7 f.
The modifications in Mt and Lk are
of minor importance. Matthew re-
arranges 14 and adds εἰπὸν οὖν ἡμῖν,
τί σοι δοκεῖ;, omitting (with Lk) δῶμεν
ἢ μὴ δῶμεν;. Luke abbreviates his
source, replacing ἀληθής by ὀρθῶς
λέγεις καὶ διδάσκεις, and omitting οὐ
μέλει σοι περὶ οὐδενός. For his οὐ
λαμβάνεις πρόσωπον v. supra.
Mark says that Jesus knew (εἰδώς,
Mt γνούς, Lk κατανοήσας) their hypo-

crisy (ὑπόκρισις*, Mt πονηρία, Lk παν-
ουργία), and asked τί με πειράζετε ; (v.
i. 13). The command φέρετέ μοι δηνάριον ἵνα ἴδω implies that neither Jesus
nor His opponents had one, a point
lost in Luke's δείξατέ μοι δηνάριον (Mt
ἐπιδείξατε). ἵνα ἴδω is possibly imperatival. For δηνάριον v. vi. 37. Mt. xxii.
19, τὸ νόμισμα τοῦ κήνσου.
After Τί με πειράζετε F G N W Θ
Σ P⁴⁵ fam. 1 fam. 13 28 33 543 565 579
q syʰˡ sa geo arm attest ὑποκριταί,
which is in accord with Mark's style
(ὑπόκρισιν . . . ὑποκριταί, cf. vii. 13, 35,
xv. 4) and should probably be read.
Cf. Couchoud, JTS, xxxv. 19 f.
16 f. When the denarius is brought,
Jesus asks whose image and inscription it bears, and when the only possible reply, ' Caesar's ', is made, He
states a principle of the utmost importance for the relative claims of God and
the state which has led to much discussion. Cf. P. S. Watson, The State
as a Servant of God, 33 f. εἰκών*, Mt.
xxii. 20, Lk. xx. 24, Pl (9), Heb. x. 1,
Apoc (10)**, ' image ', ' likeness ',
Cl., LXX, Pap. (' description ', ' por-
trait ', ' statue '; VGT, 183). For the
doctrinal use of εἰκών v. Lightfoot, Col.
142 f. ἐπιγραφή, xv. 26*, Mt. xxii. 20,
Lk. xx. 24, xxiii. 38**, ' inscription ';
Cl., Pap. (' insertion ', ' impost ', ' as-
sessment '; VGT, 237). The Emperor
was Tiberius (A.D. 14–37) and extant
coins show the inscription to have been,
Ti[berius] Caesar Divi Aug[usti]
F[ilius] Augustus. Cf. Madden, Jewish Coinage, 247; HDB, iii. 424 f. ἀπο-
δίδωμι*; as Swete observes, 276, the
verb implies that the tribute is a debt;
cf. Rom. xiii. 7, Mt. v. 26. With τὰ
Καίσαρος v. Rom. xiv. 19, τὰ τῆς εἰρήνης, Lk. xxiv. 19 (etc.), τὰ περὶ Ἰησοῦ.

ἐθαύμαζον ἐπ' αὐτῷ.

Phil. i. 12, τὰ κατ' ἐμέ. Cf. Blass, 157. The amazement produced by the reply of Jesus is indicated by ἐκθαυμάζω**, a late compound which is found in *Aristeas*, 312, Sir. xxvii. 23 (c. ἐπί and gen.), xliii. 18 (c. acc.), 4 Macc. xvii. 17 (c. acc.), Philo, *de Somn.* ii. 70. Cf. Meecham, *The Letter of Aristeas*, 307. For similar compounds in Mk *v.* ἐκθαμβέομαι, ἐκπερισσῶς, ἔκφοβος.

The reply does not mean that the worlds of politics and religion are separate spheres, each with its own governing principles. Jesus held that the claims of God are all embracing (cf. Mk. xii. 29 f.), but He does recognize that obligations due to the State are within the divine order. In particular, the acceptance and use of Caesar's coinage implicitly acknowledge his authority and therefore the obligation to pay taxes; cf. Mt. xvii. 27. This duty is not in conflict with, nor merely parallel to, the requirement to pay back to God all that is due to Him. Quite different was the attitude of Judas of Galilee in A.D. 6 who at the

time of the enrolment carried out by Quirinius spoke of it as ' no better than an introduction to slavery ' and exhorted the nation to assert their liberty; cf. Josephus, *Ant.* xviii. I. I. In primitive Christianity the attitude to the State described in Rom. xiii. 7 and I Pet. ii. 13 f. is in close agreement with the teaching of Jesus, and was justified by the peace, justice, and toleration given to the world in the best days of the Empire. By the time the Apocalypse of St. John was written the situation had changed; cf. Apoc. xviii. I ff. See the important note of Turner, 58 f.; also Cadoux, 172 f., 273.

With the reference to the great amazement of the questioners the Markan story breaks off. As is not infrequent the later Synoptists expand the account. Matthew says that, when they heard, they marvelled (ἐθαύμασαν), left Him and departed (xxii. 22). Luke explains that they were not able to take hold of the saying before the people, and that marvelling (θαυμάσαντες) at His answer they were silent (xx. 26).

Mk. xii. 18-27   78. ON THE RESURREC-   Cf. Mt. xxii. 23-33
                            TION   Lk. xx. 27-40

The third Pronouncement-story is even more briefly introduced. Only as much is told of the Sadducees as is necessary to introduce their question, and at the end there is no narrative element at all. Cf. Bultmann, 25; Dibelius, 43, 56; Albertz, 24 f., 30 f. There is no real justification for Bultmann's view, echoed by Sundwall, 74, that 26 f. is a later addition. A new beginning is made at this point, but it is necessary because the original question requires a twofold answer, with reference to the *fact*, as well as the *manner*, of the resurrection. Nor is there ground for attributing the saying to a debate within the Christian community, since, as Lohmeyer, 257, points out, the ideas are purely Jewish and are in no way influenced by later Christian beliefs. On the contrary, as in xi. 27-33 and xii. 13-17, the story preserves genuine tradition of the most primitive kind. The method of discussion, by the use of Scripture and an illustrative story, and by counter-questions culminating in a positive statement, as well as the kind of exegesis illustrated, are typically Rabbinic, while the vigour of the debate, the grandeur of the statement concerning God (27), and the final deadly thrust are lifelike. Unobtrusive, but clearly discernible, are the moral elevation of Jesus, the spirituality of His outlook, and the force of His personality.

Καὶ ἔρχονται Σαδδουκαῖοι πρὸς αὐτόν, οἵτινες λέγουσιν ἀνά- 18
στασιν μὴ εἶναι, καὶ ἐπηρώτων αὐτὸν λέγοντες Διδάσκαλε, 19
Μωυσῆς ἔγραψεν ἡμῖν ὅτι ἐάν τινος ἀδελφὸς ἀποθάνη καὶ
καταλίπῃ γυναῖκα καὶ μὴ ἀφῇ τέκνον, ἵνα λάβῃ ὁ ἀδελφὸς
αὐτοῦ τὴν γυναῖκα καὶ ἐξαναστήσῃ σπέρμα τῷ ἀδελφῷ αὐτοῦ.

18. The Sadducees (Σαδδουκαῖοι*) are described as men who (οἵτινες, v. iv. 20) say that there is no resurrection. A priestly party, they belonged to the leading families of Jerusalem, and from their number the High Priest was appointed. Their name is commonly derived from that of Zadok (צָדוֹק) the priest, who lived in the days of David and Solomon (2 Sam. viii. 17, xv. 24, 1 Kgs. i. 8, etc.), and they are identified with ' the sons of Zadok' (Ezek. xl. 46). Another view finds their founder or principal representative in an otherwise unknown Zadok of the Greek period; cf. Ed. Meyer, ii. 291. These explanations are open to several objections, not least the doubled ד in the Hebrew or Aramaic original presumed by Σαδδουκαῖοι. T. W. Manson, *Bulletin of the John Rylands Library*, vol. 22, No. 1, Apr. 1938, p. 147, has suggested the derivation of the name from צָרוֹקי, apparently an Aramaic transliteration of the Greek σύνδικοι who from the fourth century B.C. in Athens defended laws against innovation or amendment. Be this as it may, the Sadducees were conservatives who took their stand on the Pentateuch, without necessarily denying the validity of other OT books, and questioned belief in immortality, angels and spirits, and in foreordination or fate. Cf. Ac. xxiii. 8, λέγουσιν μὴ εἶναι ἀνάστασιν μήτε ἄγγελον μήτε πνεῦμα, Josephus, *Ant.* xviii. 1. 4, *BJ*, ii. 8. 14. See further, Schürer, II. ii. 29 ff.; Moore, i. 68-70, 251 ff.; Branscomb, *Jesus and the Law of Moses*, 12 ff.; Lightley, *Jewish Sects and Parties*, 1-178.

The question (ἐπερωτάω, v. 9) naturally concerns the resurrection of the dead and is meant to disparage Jesus as a teacher. ἀνάστασις, xii. 23*, is

rarely used in Cl. Gk of *rising from the dead*; Aeschyl. *Eum.* 648; Luc. *Salt.* 45. In the LXX it is found in 2 Macc. vii. 14, xii. 43, Psa. lxv. (title), and freely in the NT; cf. *VGT*, 37 f.

The later Synoptists follow Mk closely, but Matthew adds a temporal phrase, ἐν ἐκείνῃ τῇ ἡμέρᾳ, and replaces ἔρχονται by προσῆλθον (cf. Lk, προσελθόντες). Luke has τινες τῶν Σαδδουκαίων.

19. As in the preceding story, Jesus is addressed as ' Teacher' (διδάσκαλε, v. iv. 38), but without the compliment paid by the Pharisees. Lohmeyer, 255, observes that, while the latter raise a political problem, the Sadducees put a scribal question. The question, which first appears in 23, is preceded in Rabbinic fashion by a quotation from the Law introduced by Μωυσῆς ἔγραψεν ἡμῖν. For Μωυσῆς v. i. 44; and for the more usual γέγραπται vii. 6. The quotation is a very free rendering of Deut. xxv. 5 f., excluding, in particular, the limiting clause ἐὰν κατοικῶσιν ἀδελφοὶ ἐπὶ τὸ αὐτό and the reference to leaving seed (σπέρμα), which shows that the main purpose of the ordinance is to maintain the possession of property within the family. For ἀποκτείνω v. iii. 4; καταλείπω x. 7; ἀφίημι i. 18. ἐξανίστημι*, Lk. xx. 18, Ac. xv. 5**, trans. ' to raise up ' intrans. tenses ' to rise'; Cl., LXX, Pap. For σπέρμα v. iv. 31. For the phrase v. Gen. xxxviii. 8.

The construction ὅτι . . . ἵνα . . . is best explained as a mixture of two constructions: ἔγραψεν ὅτι· ἐάν . . . ἀποθάνῃ . . . λήμψεται and ἔγραψεν ἵνα ἐὰν ἀποθάνῃ . . . λάβῃ. Cf. Swete, 278; Lohmeyer, 255 n. Both Matthew and Luke omit ὅτι. Matthew also omits the ἵνα and recasts the sentence in the smoother form ἐάν τις ἀποθάνῃ μὴ

20 ἑπτὰ ἀδελφοὶ ἦσαν· καὶ ὁ πρῶτος ἔλαβεν γυναῖκα, καὶ ἀποθνή-
21 σκων οὐκ ἀφῆκεν σπέρμα· καὶ ὁ δεύτερος ἔλαβεν αὐτήν, καὶ
22 ἀπέθανεν μὴ καταλιπὼν σπέρμα, καὶ ὁ τρίτος ὡσαύτως· καὶ οἱ
ἑπτὰ οὐκ ἀφῆκαν σπέρμα· ἔσχατον πάντων καὶ ἡ γυνὴ ἀπέθανεν.
23 ἐν τῇ ἀναστάσει, ὅταν ἀναστῶσιν, τίνος αὐτῶν ἔσται γυνή; οἱ
24 γὰρ ἑπτὰ ἔσχον αὐτὴν γυναῖκα. ἔφη αὐτοῖς ὁ Ἰησοῦς Οὐ διὰ
τοῦτο πλανᾶσθε μὴ εἰδότες τὰς γραφὰς μηδὲ τὴν δύναμιν τοῦ

ἔχων τέκνα, ἐπιγαμβρεύσει ὁ ἀδελφὸς
αὐτοῦ... Luke also simplifies, replacing καταλίπῃ γυναῖκα by ἔχων γυναῖκα
and καὶ μὴ ἀφῇ τέκνον by καὶ οὗτος
ἄτεκνος ᾖ.

20-3. Stories of the kind which
follows are fully in accordance with
Rabbinic methods; cf. Fiebig, 77-130.
The present story gives an example of
the literal fulfilment of the Law leading to the challenging question concerning the Resurrection in 23. Seven
brothers in succession take the same
wife and in each case there is no issue.
In the Resurrection whose wife will
she be? The intention is to show that
belief in the Resurrection leads to an
absurdity. As in popular stories, the
situation as it concerns the first three
brothers (πρῶτος, vi. 21 ; δεύτερος, xii.
31, xiv. 72* ; τρίτος, xv. 25*) is described with oriental repetitions, and
finally (ἔσχατον πάντων, cf. 1 Cor. xv.
8), it is said, the woman died. Matthew
and perhaps Luke (cf. Streeter, 320)
substitute ὕστερον. Note the stylistic
variations in ἀποθνήσκων οὐκ ἀφῆκεν
(20) and ἀπέθανεν μὴ καταλιπών (21).
The first participle means ' at his
death ' and ἀφίημι and καταλείπω are
used as synonyms. ὡσαύτως, xiv. 31*.

The tautology in ἐν τῇ ἀναστάσει,
ὅταν ἀναστῶσιν reflects Semitic idiom.
The second phrase is omitted by ℵ B
C D L W Δ Ψ 33 579 892 c k r¹ sype sa
bo, but it is in accord with Mark's style
(cf. xiii. 19 f.) and is probably original.¹
Semitic colouring is also suggested by
the asyndetic construction: Mt and
Lk add οὖν and the particle is added
in Mk in A C² D G W Θ Σ fam. 1 565
et al. a b ff et al. vg sys pe hl sa arm.

For other additions in c and k v. Hort,
26. With ἔχω followed by a second acc.
cf. Mt. iii. 9, Ac. xiii. 5, Phil. iii. 17.
The question is asked confidently.
The disbelief of the Sadducees is explained by the fact that belief in life
after death is reflected in the OT only
in late post-exilic passages, in Dan.
xii. 2, Isa. xxv. 8, xxvi. 19, Psa. lxxiii.
24 f., and perhaps Job xix. 25-7, probably under Persian influence, the
traditional belief being that after death
the soul shared a shadowy existence,
hardly worthy to be called life, in the
darkness and desolation of Sheol; cf.
Isa. xiv. 10, Job vii. 9 f., Psa. vi. 5,
cxv. 17, Sir. xvii. 27, etc. As conservatives in doctrine the Sadducees
held fast to older views, whereas the
Pharisees, with whom Jesus agreed,
believed in future resurrection. Cf.
Schniewind, 158; Abrahams, i. 168-
170; Barrett, 74 f.

The story is repeated in Mt and Lk,
but with abbreviations.

24 f. For ἔφη asyndeton v. ix. 38.
In reply to the Sadducees Jesus says
that they are in error because they
know neither the Scriptures nor the
power of God. πλανάω, xii. 27, xiii.
5 f.*, ' to lead astray ', ' deceive ',
pass.' to go astray ',' err '; Cl., LXX,
Pap. μὴ εἰδότες, ' because you do not
know ', indicates a present condition.
For the use of αἱ γραφαί with reference
to the Scriptures v. the note on xii. 10,
and for δύναμις v. v. 30. The unhappy
results of ignorance are stressed, not
only by Jesus, but by the New Testament generally; cf. i. 21, Jn. v. 37 f.,
1 Cor. xv. 34, Gal. iv. 8, etc. The
knowledge, however, is moral and

---

¹ So Turner, JTS, xxix. 8, with A Θ fam. 1 fam. 13 565 al. pler. a b ff i vg sys arm.

θεοῦ; ὅταν γὰρ ἐκ νεκρῶν ἀναστῶσιν, οὔτε γαμοῦσιν οὔτε γαμί- 25
ζονται, ἀλλ' εἰσὶν ὡς ⌜ἄγγελοι⌝ ἐν τοῖς οὐρανοῖς· περὶ δὲ τῶν 26
νεκρῶν ὅτι ἐγείρονται οὐκ ἀνέγνωτε ἐν τῇ βίβλῳ Μωυσέως ἐπὶ
τοῦ βάτου πῶς εἶπεν αὐτῷ ὁ θεὸς λέγων Ἐγὼ ὁ θεὸς Ἀβραὰμ

25 οἱ ἄγγελοι οἱ

experimental, and not only intellectual. The δύναμις of God is His power to overcome death and bestow the gift of life.

The question form in οὐ διὰ τοῦτο . . .; is replaced by a statement in Mt, but it is characteristic of such sayings; cf. ii. 25, xii. 10, 26. Probably διὰ τοῦτο points forward: ' Is not this the reason why you go wrong, that you know not, etc. ? '; cf. Swete, 280; Gould, 229. The phrase is omitted in Mt and Lk. For the very different text in Lk v. infra.

The Sadducees, Jesus contends, are mistaken about the nature of the resurrection life; they assume that present human relationships persist, whereas in that life people neither marry nor are given in marriage, but are as the angels in heaven. For ἐκ νεκρῶν v. vi. 14; γαμέω vi. 17. γαμίζω*, Mt. xxii. 30, xxiv. 38, Lk. xvii. 27, xx. 35 (?), 1 Cor. vii. 38 (bis)**, ' to give in marriage ', belongs to late Gk corresponding to the classical use of γαμέομαι. It may even mean ' to marry ' (cf. 1 Cor. vii. 38, VGT, 121), though not of course here. ἐν τοῖς οὐρανοῖς must be taken with ἄγγελοι. It is clear that Jesus is thinking only of the resurrection of the righteous.

This idea of a resurrection life comparable to that of angels has affinities with St. Paul's teaching in 1 Cor. xv. 35 ff. It corresponds with Jewish beliefs in this and in later times. Cf. 1 Enoch civ. 4: ' Ye shall have great joy as the angels of heaven '; Apoc. of Baruch li. 10, where it is said that the righteous ' shall be made like unto the angels, and be made equal to the stars '; Berakoth, 17a, cites a saying of Rab, a Babylonian teacher of the third century A.D., which declares that in the life to come there is no eating

and drinking, no begetting of children, no bargaining, jealousy, hatred, and strife, but that the righteous sit with crowns on their heads and are satisfied with the glory of God. Cf. Abrahams, i. 168 f.; Billerbeck, i. 888; Montefiore, i. 283; Klausner, 318 f.

Mt. xxii. 30 agrees closely with Mk, but with ἐν γὰρ τῇ ἀναστάσει at the beginning. Luke's version differs greatly in expression; cf. xx. 34-6. ' The sons of this age marry and are given in marriage.' ' Those who are accounted worthy to attain to that age and to the resurrection from the dead, neither marry nor are given in marriage ' and it is explained that they ' cannot die any more ' and are ' sons of God, being sons of the resurrection '. They are described as ἰσάγγελοι. Apparently Luke is following a parallel version; cf. V. Taylor, BTG, 100.

26 f. The answer now turns from the manner to the fact of the resurrection of the dead. ἐγείρονται (cf. vi. 14) is a gnomic present as in 1 Cor. xv. 16; cf. Burton, § 12; Swete, 281. The proof is based on Ex. iii. 6 (LXX), For οὐκ ἀνέγνωτε; cf. ii. 25, xii. 10. βίβλος* carries with it a connotation of sacredness and veneration (VGT, 111) and is used here with reference to the Law; cf. 2 Chron. xxxv. 12 (R), 1 Esdras v. 48, etc.; Lk. iii. 4, Ac. vii. 42. ἐπὶ τοῦ βάτου, ' at " the Bush " ', is a customary method of referring to the narrative of the burning bush; cf. Rom. xi. 2, ἐν Ἠλείᾳ. For the gender of βάτος* v. Moulton, ii. 123. It may be that πῶς εἶπεν αὐτῷ ὁ θεὸς λέγων is no more than a reference to what is said in the story, although undoubtedly Mark, as well as Jesus Himself, looked upon the Law as a divine authority. Matthew's variation (xxii. 31) τὸ ῥηθὲν

27 καὶ θεὸc ᾽Icaὰκ καὶ θεὸc ᾽Ιακώβ ; οὐκ ἔστιν ᵀ θεὸς νεκρῶν ἀλλὰ ζώντων· πολὺ πλανᾶσθε.

27 ὁ

ὑμῖν ὑπὸ τοῦ θεοῦ, leaves this point in no doubt; cf. Lk. xx. 37, ὡς λέγει κύριον τὸν θεὸν ᾽Αβρ. . . . For λέγων v. Intr. 63.

The argument that ᾽Εγὼ ὁ θεὸς ᾽Αβραὰμ καὶ ὁ θεὸς ᾽Ισαὰκ καὶ ὁ θεὸς ᾽Ιακώβ means that God is the God of the living, illustrates contemporary methods of exegesis. Cf. Klostermann, 141; Schniewind, 159; who cite Rabbinical interpretations of Deut. xi. 9 and Numb. xviii. 28. Strictly speaking, Ex. iii. 6 refers only to the God who had dealings with the patriarchs; the language used does not necessarily imply that they are alive. Yet, strangely enough, in a deeper sense the passage suggests the one consideration which above all others confirms the modern Christian in his belief in life after death; for to him this hope is based, not on Platonic arguments concerning the nature of the soul, but upon the experience of communion with God. It is this idea of fellowship with God that the Old Testament emphasizes in its nearest approaches to a doctrine o immortality; cf. Psa. xvi. 8-11, xlix. 15, lxxiii. 23 f. For later Jewish thought v. 4 Macc. vii. 19, xvi. 25.

Perfect expression is given to the thought when Jesus says: οὐκ ἔστιν θεὸς νεκρῶν ἀλλὰ ζώντων. The asyndeton adds force.

With the charge πολὺ πλανᾶσθε the Markan story ends. Matthew and Luke omit this phrase, preferring to suggest in different ways the effect produced by the words of Jesus. Matthew adds a reference to the astonishment of the multitudes at His teaching which he had omitted when describing the Cleansing of the Temple (cf. Mk. xi. 18b). Luke borrows material from the Markan story of the Great Commandment, which he otherwise omits because of the parallel version in Lk. x. 25-8. Some of the scribes, he says, answered and said, ' Teacher, you have spoken well ' (xx. 39, cf. Mk. xii. 32). ' For they no longer dared to ask him anything ', he adds (xx. 40, cf. Mk. xii. 34). Mark's conclusion: ' You are quite wrong ' (RSV), is impressive in its brevity; all the more after the redundancy at the beginning of 26: ' Concerning the dead, that they are raised '. Cf. Mt, ' Concerning the resurrection of the dead '; Lk, ' That the dead are raised '.

Mk. xii. 28-34   79. ON THE FIRST COM-   Cf. Mt. xxii. 34-40
MANDMENT   (Lk. x. 25-8)

The fourth Pronouncement-story gives the answer of Jesus to the question : ' Which commandment is the first of all ? '. In form it is a *Schulgespräch* (Bultmann, 21), i.e. a narrative which records a discussion between a teacher and a student, rather than a *Streitgespräch*, or controversy-story (Albertz, 25 f., 32 f.). It is interesting to observe that the parallel narrative in Q, which is preserved in Lk. x. 25-8 and which may have influenced Mt. xxii. 34-40, is of the latter type : the scribe, here called νομικός, seeks to put Jesus to the test and himself supplies the answer given in Mk by Jesus. This difference of form could easily arise during the oral period, and it is not of serious importance since even in Lk Jesus approves the answer (x. 28). Both Bultmann and Albertz think that the Markan form is the earlier, and with good reason. Easton, 169, and Branscomb, 220, take the opposite view, arguing that tradition would naturally tend to convert the approval of Jesus into an utterance of His. This view is not satisfactory, since the lawyer's quotation of Lev. xix. 18 in Lk may be adapted to prepare the way for the parable of the Good Samaritan (cf. Lagrange, 322), and because a controversy-story is more conventional than a story in which the attitude of the scribe is friendly. The greater detail in Mk supports this view, and especially the saying, ' Thou are not far from the kingdom of God ', which stands apart from the eschatological conception of the Kingdom which in the main dominates Mk. In its present setting in Mk the arrangement is topical ; it seemed desirable to the compiler to follow a story about Pharisees, and a second about Sadducees, with a third about a scribe, not, however, without some degree of artificiality since the scribes were not a third party. The content of the story would favour a Galilean setting for the incident. The reference to ' burnt-offerings and sacrifices ' is especially appropriate if the scene is the Temple courts, but otherwise there is no reason to connect the story with Jerusalem. Lohmeyer, 261, thinks that the tradition should be traced to the original community in Galilee, holding that the boldness of the question and of the answer of Jesus is more difficult to understand against the background of Pharisaic Judaism.

Καὶ προσελθὼν εἷς τῶν γραμματέων ἀκούσας αὐτῶν συνζη- 28 τούντων, ⌈ἰδὼν⌉ ὅτι καλῶς ἀπεκρίθη αὐτοῖς, ἐπηρώτησεν αὐτόν Ποία ἐστὶν ἐντολὴ πρώτη πάντων; ἀπεκρίθη ὁ Ἰησοῦς ὅτι 29

28 εἰδώς

28. The story is introduced by a sentence containing three participles, προσελθών . . . ἀκούσας . . . ἰδών, which connects it with the preceding narratives and anticipates v. 32. This multiplication of participles is a feature of Mark's style (cf. Swete, xlviii) and 28a is probably an editorial adaptation of a narrative which began καὶ προσελ- θὼν εἷς . . . ἐπηρώτησεν αὐτόν. Cf. Loh- meyer, 257. For οἱ γραμματεῖς v. i. 22 ; συνζητέω i. 27 ; καλῶς vii. 6. The friendly attitude of the scribe, more clearly evident in 32, is distinctive of the Markan story. In the parallel version in Q (Lk. x. 25-8) the attitude of the νομικός is hostile ; he seeks to put Jesus to the test : ἐκπειράζων αὐτόν, cf. Mt. xxii. 35. Such an attitude would have suited the Markan context well and the presumption is that Mark follows the better tradition.

ἰδών, read by א* C D L W Θ et al. fam. 1 fam. 13 (exc. 124) 28 543 565

700 1342 et al. a c ff sype hl geo¹ aeth arm, should probably be preferred to εἰδώς, for, as Turner says, 60, it is quite well supported, and makes better sense. So AV and RSV.

The question asked (ἐπερωτάω, v. 9) is : Ποία ἐστὶν ἐντολὴ πρώτη πάντων ;. In Q it is : Τί ποιήσας ζωὴν αἰώνιον κληρονομήσω; (Lk. x. 25). Again, pre- ference must be given to Mk, for the Lukan form appears to be influenced by the story of the Rich Man's Ques- tion (Mk. x. 17-22). ποία (xi. 28) may be used with the meaning ' what kind of ? ', but it is difficult to think, with Swete, 284, that Jesus is asked to specify a class of commandments, or one that is representative, and it is more probable that here ποία = τίς ; cf. VGT, 524 ; Moulton, i. 95 ; Blass, 176. For ἐντολή v. vii. 8. The reading πρώτη πάντων (Mt, μεγάλη), where πασῶν might have been expected, is undoubtedly original.[1] Alford ex-

---

[1] The omission of πάντων by D W Θ 565 et al. it sy⁸ sa arm geo, and the reading πασῶν (M* 1278 al. pauc.) in the TR, are grammatical corrections. Cf. Lagrange, 321 ; Lohmeyer, 258 n. Blass, 312, points out that in 29 Eusebius and some minuscules attest πάντων πρῶτον· ˈΑκουε ˈΙσραήλ.

Πρώτη ἐστίν ᵛΑκογε, 'Ιϲραήλ, Κγριοϲ ὁ θεὸϲ ⌜ἡμῶν κγριοϲ⌝ εἷϲ
30 ἐϲτίν, καὶ ἀγαπήϲειϲ Κγριον τὸν θεόν ϲογ ἐξ ὅληϲ ᵀ καρδίαϲ ϲογ
καὶ ἐξ ὅληϲ τῆϲ ψγχῆϲ ϲογ καὶ ἐξ ὅληϲ τῆϲ διανοίαϲ ϲογ καὶ ἐξ
31 ὅληϲ τῆϲ ἰϲχγοϲ ϲογ. δευτέρα αὕτη 'Αγαπήϲειϲ τὸν πληϲίον ϲογ

29 ἡμῶν, Κύριος 　　　　30 τῆς

plains it as a compound expression, 'first-of-all' (cf. Swete, 284); Blass, 108, as a stereotyped use of the neut. to intensify the superlative; cf. *WM*, 222. There is a parallel in Thuc. iv. 52, πόλεις . . . καὶ πάντων μάλιστα τὴν ᵛΑντανδρον. See further, Field, 36. It may be that the phrase is an example of translation Greek, to represent the Semitic use of the positive for the superlative more literally rendered by μεγάλη in Mt. Cf. Wellhausen, *Einl.*² 21; Black, 86 ; Howard, ii. 442.

Questions concerning the first commandment and light and easy commands were not infrequently discussed by the Rabbis, and various answers were given. See the notes on 29-31. The most famous reply is that of Hillel to a proselyte who desired to be instructed in the Law while standing on one leg : ' What thou hatest for thyself, do not to thy neighbour : this is the whole Law, the rest is commentary ; go and learn', *Shabb.* 31a. Cf. Abrahams, i. 21 f.; Billerbeck, i. 357.

29 f. In reply Jesus quotes the first part of the *Shema'* in Deut. vi. 4 f., which every pious Jew is bound to recite daily, and which, as Kittel, *KThW*, i. 41, observes, plays as great a role in late Jewish piety as in Rabbinic exegesis and theology. For Jewish teaching concerning the obligation of obedience and humble love to God see, in addition to Kittel's article, Montefiore, i. 284-6, *Rabbinic Literature and Gospel Teachings*, 312-16 ; A. Büchler, *Studies in Sin and Atonement*, 1-119 ; Snaith, *Distinctive Ideas of the OT*, 141 f. Of the Synoptists Mark alone includes the opening words, ᵛΑκουε, 'Ισραήλ, Κύριος ὁ θεὸς ἡμῶν κύριος εἷς ἐστιν. The connexion of these words with those that follow is vital ; for the command to love God

is not simply a duty; it is an obligation arising out of the fact that He is One, in comparison with whom the gods of the heathen are idols, and that He has chosen Israel in covenant-love (κύριος ὁ θεὸς ἡμῶν). Cf. Lohmeyer, 258 : *Liebe ist des Volkes Antwort auf Gottes erwählende und offenbarende Tat und ist damit dieses Einen Volkes Grundgesetz.*

The quotation is in close agreement with the LXX, reading καρδίας (A, διανοίας Bᵃ) and ψυχῆς, but substituting διανοίας for δυνάμεως, and adding καὶ ἐξ ὅλης τῆς ἰσχύος σου. Luke also has the same four nouns, with the last two in reverse order, while Matthew has καρδία, ψυχή, διάνοια. Matthew has ἐν c. dat., representing the Heb. ב, while Mk and Lk agree with the LXX in the better Gk. ἐκ c. gen. The Heb. reads : ' with all thine heart (לְבָבְךָ), and with all thy soul (נַפְשְׁךָ), and with all thy might (מְאֹדֶךָ) '. To some extent therefore the Markan reading is conflate. It reflects the desire to express the response fully. The love springs from the centre of personality, the heart and the soul, but no less from the understanding and the strength of a man's being. It is, however, not necessary to distinguish sharply these aspects of human personality, as in later discussions ; cf. Aquinas, *Summa*, II. ii, Qn. 44, Art. 5. The intention is not to distinguish faculties and powers, but to insist on a complete response.

For πρώτη v. the note on 28 ; Κύριος i. 3 ; ἀγαπάω x. 21 ; καρδία ii. 6 ; ψυχή iii. 4 ; 'Ισραήλ, xv. 32*. διάνοια*, ' the understanding ' or ' mind '; Cl., LXX, Pap. : *VGT*, ' a fair equivalent to the Latin *animus* ', 152. ἰσχύς, xii. 33*, ' strength ', ' might ', ' power '; Cl., LXX, Pap.

This passage, and Lk. xi. 42, are

ὡς ϲεαυτόν. μείζων τούτων ἄλλη ἐντολὴ οὐκ ἔστιν. ⌜Εἶπεν⌝ 32

32 Καὶ εἶπεν

the only passages in the Synoptic Gospels which speak of man's love for God. Similarly, there are only five Pauline passages which speak of this theme (Rom. viii. 28, 1 Cor. ii. 9, viii. 3, xvi. 22, Eph. vi. 24), a restraint which Moffatt, *Love in the NT*, 154-163, traces to the reticence of the NT writers in the use of love-language as addressed to God. Cf. J. Weiss, *HPC*, 509. The emphasis lies rather on God's love for man, and rightly so because it is from this love that love for God is derived and takes its character. As such, it is indeed ἀγάπη, pure self-giving, which looks neither for reward nor for satisfaction. Cf. A. Nygren, *Agape and Eros*, i, ii, *passim*. But it would be wrong to suppose that there can be no obedience to the command to love God until love is of this perfect character. At first man's love to God may be no more than φιλία, 'friendship', or akin to the Platonic ἔρως, needing to be cleansed from self-regarding motives, and to be fashioned by faith into ἀγάπη by the ἀγάπη of God in which it rests. See further, J. Burnaby, *Amor Dei*, 141-79, and the comments of P. S. Watson, *Let God be God*, 48-59.

31. Although the scribe's question is concerning the commandment which is πρώτη πάντων, Jesus adds a second (δευτέρα (xii. 21) αὕτη). Matthew feels that the statement is abrupt. He therefore follows the quotation from Deut. by the words, αὕτη ἐστὶν ἡ μεγάλη καὶ πρώτη ἐντολή, and then explains that the second is like (ὁμοία) to it (xxii. 38 f.). Luke simply connects the two by καί.

The passage quoted agrees verbatim with the LXX text of Lev. xix. 18, Ἀγαπήσεις τὸν πλησίον σου ὡς σεαυτόν. For ἀγαπάω v. the notes on x. 21 and xii. 30. The adverb πλησίον (xii. 33*), used with the article (as in Cl., LXX), translates the Heb. רֵעַ 'friend', 'fellow-citizen', 'the other man',

and, in view of the preceding clause, 'Thou shalt not take vengeance, nor bear any grudge against the children of thy people', refers, strictly speaking, to a fellow-Jew. But it would be wrong to suppose that the command was understood in this restricted sense in later times; the LXX rendering itself must have encouraged a wider connotation, and the enthusiasm with which it is quoted by the Rabbis and other Jewish writers makes this clear. See the comments of Montefiore, i. 285, *Rabbinic Literature and Gospel Teachings*, 319 f. Cf. the famous saying of Akiba : ' " Thou shalt love thy neighbour as thyself " ; this is the greatest general principle in the Torah ', *Sifra*, Lev. xix. 18 ; also the saying of Simon the Righteous : ' On three things stands the world : on the Law, on the worship, and on works of love ', *Aboth*, i. 2. Cf. also Philo, *de Spec. Leg.* ii. 63. 282. At least the command must have been held to cover ' the stranger in the land ', but that it was held to have a universal range is naturally more doubtful. See, however, Abrahams, i. 24 : above all the saying of Ben Azzai, which he quotes, in which a greater principle than that mentioned by Akiba (*v. supra*) is found in the creation of man : ' " This is the book of the generations of man " is a greater principle than the other '.

The question what it is to love one's neighbour as oneself is discussed at length in the writings of Clement of Alexandria, Augustine, Aquinas, Luther, and other great Christian teachers, and is variously explained. Sometimes it is held to be only another form of the love of God, sometimes as a higher form of self-love, sometimes as God's love for man received and redirected. Cf. Nygren, *Agape and Eros*, ii (tr. P. S. Watson), 149-52, 331-5, 425-7, 516-19. Such questions are inevitably raised, but in considering them it is necessary to begin with

αὐτῷ ὁ γραμματεὺς Καλῶς, διδάσκαλε, ἐπ' ἀληθείας εἶπες ὅτι
33 εἷς ἐστὶν καὶ οὐκ ἔστιν ἄλλος πλὴν αὐτοῦ· καὶ τὸ ἀγαπᾶν αὐτὸν
ἐξ ὅλης τ καρδίας καὶ ἐξ ὅλης τῆς συνέσεως καὶ ἐξ ὅλης τῆς ἰσχύος

33 τῆς

historical exegesis. In Leviticus the meaning of the command is determined by the parallelism in xix. 18. Loving one's neighbour there stands in contrast with taking vengeance and bearing ill-will and hatred against him ; it must therefore mean tender regard for him and the active promoting of his good, just as we should want to do in the case of ourselves. Cf. Butler, *Sermons*, xi, xii. Probably Jesus interpreted the command in this way, with the important qualification that for Him one's neighbour included the Samaritan (Lk. x. 29-37). As that parable teaches, it meant unselfishness, compassion, and succour. How deeply His teaching upon this question impressed the mind of primitive Christianity is reflected in Gal. v. 14, where Lev. xix. 18 is said to fulfil ' the whole law ', in Rom. xiii. 9 in which it sums up the second part of the Decalogue, and Jas. ii. 8 in which it is described as ' the royal law ', νόμου βασιλικόν. No less profound has been its creative influence in shaping the social consciousness of the Church throughout the centuries.

Distinctive of the narrative is the way in which Jesus brings together two widely separated commands; μείζων τούτων ἄλλη ἐντολὴ οὐκ ἔστιν. While love is warmly commended by the Rabbis, so far as is known no one save Jesus has brought them together as the two regulative principles which sum up man's duty. Even in Gal., Rom., and Jas. the second stands alone, but as Jesus presents them they form an indissoluble unity : love for man arises out of love for God. Cf. Abrahams, 28 : ' It does not seem that in any extant Rabbinic text, outside the *Testaments of the Twelve Patriarchs*, the *Shema* and the love of one's neighbour are associated '. Cf. *Test.*

Dan v. 3, *Test. Issach.* v. 2, vii. 6. Montefiore, *Rabbinic Literature and Gospel Teachings*, 316, points out that the combination is found in the *Didache*, and thinks there is a good deal of force in Kohler's argument that the combination was well known as far back as the age of Jesus, and that in a lost Jewish manual for the instruction of proselytes, we should have found it as in the *Didache*. Cf. *JE*, iv. 585 f.; *NT in the Apostolic Fathers*, 26.

32 f. At this point, in a section peculiar to Mk (32-4), the scribe intervenes commending the reply of Jesus and extending it by affirming the superiority of love to God and man over burnt-offerings and sacrifices. For γραμματεύς v. i. 22; καλῶς vii. 6; διδάσκαλε iv. 38 ; ἐπ' ἀληθείας xii. 14 ; and for the vocabulary of 33 v. 30 f. πλήν*.

The RV takes καλῶς with εἶπες, as in 28, regarding ἐπ' ἀληθείας as a further confirmation : ' Of a truth, Master, thou hast well said that . . .'; cf. Swete, 286 ; Plummer, 285 ; Klostermann, 143 ; Lohmeyer, 259 ; but the position of καλῶς makes this interpretation difficult, and it is better, with AV, RSV, Moffatt, to read it as an exclamation (cf. Euripides, *Orest.* 1216) : ' Right! Teacher, thou hast truly said that . . .'; cf. Wellhausen, 96 (*Recht so, Meister* . . .) ; Gould, 233 ; Turner, 60.

The omission of the divine name in εἷς ἐστίν agrees with Semitic usage. θεός is read by E F H W 1071 *al.*, and ὁ θεός by D G Θ fam. 13 28 565 700 it vg syˢ sa bo geo² arm Eus Hil, but these readings are secondary. The repetition of what Jesus has said is also Semitic. The agreement, however, is not complete ; the scribe substitutes σύνεσις for διάνοια and omits ψυχή. σύνεσις*, Lk. ii. 47, Pl (4), 2 Tim. ii.

καὶ τὸ ἀγαπᾶν τὸν πλησίον ὡς ἑαυτὸν περισσότερόν ἐστιν πάντων
τῶν ὁλοκαυτωμάτων καὶ θυσιῶν. καὶ ὁ Ἰησοῦς ἰδὼν αὐτὸν ὅτι 34
νουνεχῶς ἀπεκρίθη εἶπεν αὐτῷ Οὐ μακρὰν [εἶ] ἀπὸ τῆς βασιλείας τοῦ θεοῦ. Καὶ οὐδεὶς οὐκέτι ἐτόλμα αὐτὸν ἐπερωτῆσαι.

7**, 'intelligence', 'sagacity'; Cl.,
LXX, Pap. Cf. Abbott, *Col.* 202.
The use of the word harmonizes with
the glimpse we get of the man's disposition.

For περισσότερον v. vii. 36. ὁλο-
καύτωμα*, Heb. x. 6, 8**, is the *whole
burnt offering* (עֹלָה) and is taken from
the LXX; cf. Kennedy, 113 f. Cf.
Bengel, *nobilissima species sacrifici-
orum.* θυσίαι* (LXX, זְבָחִים) are the
OT sacrifices in general. It would be
mistaken to suppose that the scribe's
intention is to repudiate the sacrificial
system. He says no more than is
already said in 1 Kgdms. xv. 22 (ἰδοὺ
ἀκοὴ ὑπὲρ θυσίαν ἀγαθήν) and Hos. vi. 6
(διότι ἔλεος θέλω ἢ θυσίαν, καὶ ἐπίγνωσιν
θεοῦ ἢ ὁλοκαυτώματα), and may have
had these passages in mind. It is
difficult to agree with Lohmeyer, 261,
when he says that his view is strange
to Jewish thought: *ein wahrer Rabbi
kann nicht zwischen Wesentlichem
und Unwesentlichem unterscheiden.*
The scribe does not distinguish between the essential and the unessential:
what he does is to assert the supremacy
of love to God and man over the cultus.
Doubtless the significance of his words
is a question of tone, and this is difficult to estimate in a written narrative;
but it is fair to argue that the reply of
Jesus, 'Thou art not far from the
kingdom of God', implies that the
scribe had said something unusually
bold. Does, then, 32 f. transcend
Jewish teaching? Montefiore, *Rabbinic Literature and Gospel Teachings,*
315, asserts that the student of Rabbinic literature has nothing to learn
from the Gospels about the love of
God. Despite the moving passages [1]
which he cites, we must regard this
claim as exaggerated. The scribe's

words would have been more characteristically Jewish if he had set love
side by side with the Torah and with
sacrifice; cf. *Aboth*, i. 2, quoted in
the note on 31.

34. The reply of Jesus is preceded
by the statement ἰδὼν αὐτὸν ὅτι νουνεχῶς
ἀπεκρίθη. Cf. 28. νουνεχῶς**, 'sen-
sibly', 'discreetly'; Cl. (Aristotle,
Rhet. ad Alex. 1436b 33, Polybius
i. 83. 3, etc.), not in LXX; cf. *VGT*,
430 f. With the use of αὐτόν, which
anticipates the subject of the dependent
clause, cf. vii. 2, xi. 32, Lk. ix. 31 (D),
xxiv. 7, also viii. 24. The construction is found in Aramaic; cf. Wellhausen, *Einl.*[2] 12; Black, 36; but it
is not necessarily a 'Semitism'. Cf.
WM, 781. It is not strange that the
pronoun is omitted by a number of
MSS., including ℵ D L W Δ Θ fam. 1
28 33 565 579 892 it (exc. a) vg sys hl
geo aeth arm, and it should certainly
be read with A B *et al.* fam. 13 543
700 *al. pler.* a sype bo.

Simple though the reply of Jesus
appears to be, it raises difficult problems. μακράν*, acc. fem. of μακρός
used as an adv., 'far'; Cl., LXX,
Pap.; cf. οἱ μακράν, used of exiled
Jews in Isa. lvii. 19, and of Gentiles
in Eph. ii. 13. For ἡ βασιλεία τοῦ θεοῦ
v. the note on i. 15. Is the Kingdom
conceived as present or future? The
imagery is spatial, and the idea is that
of a domain in which God's will is done
and His rule supreme. Some scholars,
but with marked reserve, are inclined
to think that the idea is eschatological;
cf. Rawlinson, 172; Montefiore, i. 287;
Blunt, 233; but to take the meaning
to be that the man would be found
ready when the Kingdom arrived
seems strained, if not artificial (cf.
Schniewind, 162), and it is more prob-

---

[1] Lohmeyer, 259 n., cites *Aboth R. Nathan*, 4: 'From the beginning the world has been
created only through love: "I say: Love built up the world", Psa. lxxxix. 3'. Cf. also Billerbeck,
i. 499 f.; W. D. Davies, *Paul and Rabbinic Judaism*, 258.

able that the *Basileia* is 'within reach' (Dodd, 44). It is accessible, and the man stands on the threshold. Cf. Bartlet, 340. He is near the Kingdom in the sense that he recognizes the sovereignty of God and has the right moral and spiritual disposition as it is described in the Sermon on the Mount; cf. Mt. v. 7, 23 f., 41, 48, vii. 12. Of outstanding importance is the authority with which the statement is made. The speaker is the Lord, and not only the Teacher; cf. Lohmeyer, 260: *Hier spricht Einer, der weiss wer dem Königreich Gottes nahe und wer ihm fern ist.* Cf. also Schniewind, 162: *Nicht fern sein von der Gottes-Herr-*

schaft heisst: nicht fern sein von ihm. Behind the story Schniewind sees the Messianic secret.

As in 28, so in 34b Mark's hand is to be seen in the concluding statement, καὶ οὐδεὶς οὐκέτι ἐτόλμα αὐτὸν ἐπερωτῆσαι. For the double negative *v.* the note on i. 44; ἐπερωτάω v. 9. τολμάω, xv. 43*. It links together the four preceding controversy-stories, and marks a pause before the final member of the group in which Jesus Himself takes the initiative. Matthew transfers it to the end of this narrative (xxii. 46), while Luke, as already observed, places it after the account of the Sadducees' question (xx. 40).

Mk. xii. 35-7a   80. ON DAVID'S SON   Cf. Mt. xxii. 41-6
Lk. xx. 41-4

The narrative indicates, although obscurely, the mind of Jesus on the question of Messiahship. Albertz, 26, 34, classifies it as a *Streitgespräch*, but Bultmann, 54, points out that it attains this form in Mt. xxii. 41-6. In Mk the narrative is little more than a saying introduced by a brief statement : ' And Jesus answered and said, as he taught in the temple '. In Mt He asks, ' What think ye of the Christ? whose son is he ? ', and when the Pharisees reply, ' The son of David ', He then puts the question with which Mark's narrative begins. The statement that the people heard Him gladly (37b) is probably meant to introduce the following narrative, The Warning against the Scribes; cf. Swete, 289 ; Wellhausen, 97 ; Klostermann, 145. If so, the present narrative ends impressively with the pointed question, ' And how is he his son ? '. Mark may have found the reference to the Temple in the tradition, for already he has mentioned Jerusalem and the Temple in xi. 27 ; cf. Schmidt, 289. In any case, the content of the story and its linguistic features suggest that it was derived from Palestinian tradition. The view that it comes from the Hellenistic community (cf. Bousset, 78 n.) is much less probable. The saying is of great importance in its bearing on the true nature of ' the Messianic Secret '.

35   Καὶ ἀποκριθεὶς ὁ Ἰησοῦς ἔλεγεν διδάσκων ἐν τῷ ἱερῷ   Πῶς
36   λέγουσιν οἱ γραμματεῖς ὅτι ὁ χριστὸς υἱὸς Δαυεὶδ ἐστιν;   αὐτὸς

35. The redundancy of the participle in καὶ ἀποκριθεὶς . . . ἔλεγεν is manifest; *v.* Intr. 63. Here and in the use of αὐτός in 36 and 37 (*v. infra*) the question arises whether the narrative reflects Palestinian tradition. For διδάσκω v. i. 21 ; οἱ γραμματεῖς i. 22 ; ὁ Χριστός i. 1 ; Δαυεὶδ ii. 25 ; υἱὸς Δαυεὶδ x. 47 f.*. As the vocabulary and the

content of 35a show, the phrase is an editorial passage supplied by Mark, but on the basis of tradition rather than imaginatively, since no attempt is made to define the time or circumstances or to connect the narrative with 28-34. Contrast Matthew, who pictures the Pharisees gathered together (xxii. 41) and Jesus questioning

Δαυεὶδ εἶπεν ἐν τῷ πνεύματι τῷ ἁγίῳ

them. In Mk and Lk it is not said who are questioned. The problem arises in the course of teaching in the Temple (ἐν τῷ ἱερῷ, v. xi. 11); presumably the people are asked 'to consider one of the dicta of the Scribes' (Swete, 287), namely, that the Messiah is a descendant of David.

It is often maintained that the intention of Jesus is to contest the Davidic descent of the Messiah, and that the question implies that He did not believe Himself to be of David's lineage; but neither of these views is tenable. The Davidic descent of the Messiah is strongly attested in the OT, in Isa. ix. 2-7, xi. 1-9, Jer. xxiii. 5 f., xxxiii. 14-18, Ezek. xxxiv. 23 f., xxxvii. 24, Psa. lxxxix. 20 ff.; cf. Psa. Sol. xvii. 4 ff., 21 ff., Jn. vii. 42. In the face of this testimony it is impossible to believe that Jesus intended to attack this belief when there is no positive evidence to this effect. Cf. Lohmeyer, 262; Schniewind, 162 f. Such a denial on His part would have furnished a major ground for an attack against Him, but in disputes between the scribes and Himself there is no sign that on this issue any objection was taken to His teaching. It is therefore improbable that Jesus ever contested the Davidic descent of the Messiah. But, if so, the case for supposing that He knew that He was not of David's line disappears; for the only reason for this assumption is His alleged attack upon this doctrine. Had He known that He was not of David's lineage, He would have been compelled, in claiming to be the Messiah, to denounce scribal teaching and to reject the testimony of the OT mentioned above. The presumption therefore is that He believed Himself to be of David's house. This view is confirmed by primitive Christian belief in His Davidic sonship (cf. Rom. i. 3, 2 Tim. ii. 8, Mt. i. 1-17, Lk. iii. 23-38)

and by the use of the title 'Son of David' in the Gospels (Mk. x. 47 f.; Mt. ix. 27, xii. 23, xv. 22, xx. 30 f., xxi. 9, 15; Lk. xviii. 38 f., xx. 41). It may be that in some cases the descent was assumed, but it is unlikely that the belief was without foundation. See further, Lagrange, 325-7; Rawlinson, 173 f.; Bartlet, 341 f.; Turner, 60 f.; Allen, 153 f.; Menzies, 228. For the view that the passage reflects the beliefs of the Christian community see the note on 37.

36. Without any connecting particle the question is immediately followed by a reference to what David said under the inspiration of the Holy Spirit. αὐτός may be a proleptic pronoun anticipating the noun in accordance with Aramaic idiom; cf. Black, 71. In this case the translation is: 'He, David', or 'David'; so Lohmeyer, 262 n.; Klostermann, 144; Torrey, 98. Cf. Wellhausen, Einl.[2] 19, on Mt. iii. 4, and Mk. vi. 17; Moulton, i. 91; Howard, ii. 431. But these writers do not mention Mk. xii. 36 f., and the inference is not certain, since the pronoun, as commonly in Greek, may be used for emphasis: 'David himself' (RV, RSV, Moffatt). Nevertheless, the asyndetic construction in 36 f. and the use of ἀποκριθείς in 35, together with the character of the narrative, point to the use of Semitic tradition and possibly an Aramaic source.

For ἐν τῷ πνεύματι τῷ ἁγίῳ v. i. 8, 10, 12, iii. 29. The reference to the Holy Spirit shows that David is thought of as speaking as a prophet. Psa. cx, from which the quotation is taken, was not written by David, but by an unknown psalmist some 800 years later, probably during the Maccabaean period and with reference to Simon Maccabaeus, 'the high priest and friend of kings' (1 Macc. xiii. 36, xiv. 41), on whose name an acrostic is formed by the initial letters of the several lines in vv. 1-4.[1] Cf. R. H.

---

[1] So Duhm, Bickell, etc. Some commentators take the view that the date of the Psalm is pre-Deuteronomic and that David is the ruler addressed. Cf. C. A. Briggs, ICC, Psalms, ii. 374; W. E. Barnes, The Psalms, 534 f.

ΕἶπεΝ ΚΎριος τῷ κγρίῳ μογ ⌐Κάθογ⌐ ἐκ Δεξιῶν μογ
ἔως ἂΝ θῶ τοὺς ἐχθρούς σογ ὑποκάτω τῶΝ ποΔῶΝ σογ·
37 αὐτὸς Δαυεὶδ λέγει αὐτὸν κύριον, καὶ πόθεν αὐτοῦ ἐστὶν υἱός;
36 Κάθισον

Pfeiffer, *Introduction to the OT*, 630. At the time the Davidic authorship of the Psalm was universally assumed, and in this respect Jesus accepted the ideas of His day. The suggestion that David is mentioned as the reputed author (cf. Swete, 288) is not satisfactory, for the argument based on the quotation fails if David is not the speaker. The value of the saying is not thereby destroyed, since its main importance is the light it throws on the manner in which Jesus interpreted Messiahship; *v. infra*. Matthew also refers to the Spirit (ἐν πνεύματι), but Luke has ἐν Βίβλῳ Ψαλμῶν; cf. Lk. iii. 4. Here only in the sayings is the authority of the OT traced to the *afflatus* of the Holy Spirit, and it is introduced because of the nature of the argument. Cf. C. K. Barrett, 107-12.

The quotation follows the LXX version of Psa. cix. (cx.) 1, but before Κύριος Mark omits the article (so B D Ψ 472 579) and has ὑποκάτω (B D W Ψ 28 sys sa bo) instead of ὑποπόδιον. So Mt; Lk, ὑποπόδιον. It is possible, as Swete, 288, suggests, that it comes from a collection of *testimonia*; cf. Psa. viii. 7. For κάθου, which supplants κάθησο in the NT, *v.* Moulton, ii. 207; ἐκ δεξιῶν x. 37; ἕως ἄν c. subj. vi. 10; ἐχθρός*; ὑποκάτω, vi. 11*.

The quotation shows that the Psalm was interpreted Messianically by Jesus and by the Rabbis of His day. It is true that this interpretation is not found in Rabbinic literature until much later [1]; according to Billerbeck, iv. 1. 452-65, not until the second half of the third century. In Justin's *Dialogue with Trypho*, 32 f., 56, 83, for example, it is said that the Jews interpret the Psalm with reference to Hezekiah. Cf. Lohmeyer, 262 f. Billerbeck argues that the silence is due to anti-Christian polemic stimulated by the freedom with which the Psalm was quoted in the primitive Church; cf., in addition to Mk. xii. 36 and its parallels, Ac. ii. 34, Heb. i. 13, v. 6, vii. 17, 21, and other references in Mk. xiv. 62 and parallels, xvi. [19], Ac. vii. 56, Rom. viii. 34, 1 Cor. xv. 25, Eph. i. 20, Col. iii. 1, Heb. i. 3, viii. 1, x. 12 f., 1 Pet. iii. 22, Apoc. iii. 21. See also Clem. *1 Cor.* 36; Justin Martyr, *Apol.* i. 45.

37a. For αὐτός *v.* 36 and for λέγει = καλεῖ *v.* x. 18. πόθεν (vi. 2, viii. 4*) is used in the sense of πῶς, 'how?' (RSV, Moffatt, Torrey); cf. Mt, Lk. The question is ironical. Its point is not to deny the Davidic descent of the Messiah, but to suggest that a much higher view of his origin is necessary since David calls him 'lord'. Lohmeyer, 263, thinks that Jesus is taking His stand upon apocalyptic expectations concerning the Son of Man and is finding their basis in Scripture, but that He is not speaking of Himself, but of Another whose nature and origin are obscure. Schniewind, 163, agrees that the Messiah is conceived as a supernatural being, the World Ruler who is the Son of Man, and he thinks it is not inconceivable that preexistence is implied as in the Fourth Gospel. Such a suggestion may be thought to take us too far, but certainly a secret of Jesus concerning Himself is implied. His question is shaped by His estimate of Messiahship embodied in Himself. His purpose, however, is not to reveal this secret, which is and which remains His own, but to expose the futility of Messianic hopes which

---

[1] Cf. *Bereshith Rabba*, 85 (ed. Warsh., 153a) where it is said that the staff which Tamar received from Judah (Gen. xxxviii. 18) is King Messiah and mention is made of Isa. xi and Psa. cx. 2; Edersheim, ii. 721.

do not rise above the earthly and human plane.

Such an interpretation parts decisively with the widespread, and perhaps prevailing view, that the saying is a community-formation. The latter is the opinion of Bultmann, 145 f.; Bousset, 43; J. Weiss, *Die Schr.*⁴ i. 189; Klostermann, 144; Branscomb, 224 f.; and others. Bultmann's view is that either the saying expresses the mind of a circle in the primitive community, which held that the Messiah was the Son of Man rather than the Son of David (perhaps to meet the reproach that the Davidic origin of Jesus could not be proved) or, alternatively, that it comes from the Hellenistic community, and is motivated by the desire to prove that Jesus was more than David's Son, in fact, the Son of God. Enough is said above in refutation of the claim that xii. 35-7 is meant to deny the Davidic origin of the Messiah. The point therefore to be considered is whether the claim that Jesus is more than the Son of David must necessarily be assigned to the community, and not to Jesus Himself. The allusive character of the saying favours the view that it is an original utterance; it half conceals and half reveals the 'Messianic Secret'. It suggests, but does not state the claim, that Jesus is supernatural in dignity and origin and that His Sonship is no mere matter of human descent. It is difficult to think that the doctrinal beliefs of a community could be expressed in this allusive manner. The

intention in a doctrinal statement is that it should be understood, whereas the purpose of the saying is to challenge thought and decision. This is the very idiom of Jesus Himself, as His message to the Baptist shows (Lk. vii. 22 f.). But, demonstrably, it is not the tone or method of primitive Christianity. In the earliest preaching and teaching there is nothing tentative, tantalizing, or allusive. The conviction that Jesus is the Son of God exalted to His right hand rings out as with the tones of a bell in such passages as Ac. ii. 34-6, v. 31, x. 42 f., Rom. i. 3 f., etc. The one speaker to whom Mk. xii. 35-7 can be credibly assigned is Jesus Himself. His words led to the free use of Psa. cx. 1 in primitive Christianity. Cf. Albertz, 26; Lohmeyer, 263.¹ Bultmann rightly rejects the view that Jesus speaks of Himself as the Son of Man *designatus*. He speaks appreciatively of the view of Reitzenstein, that Jesus is conscious of being the divine envoy, who in lowliness walks the earth, restores the erring to God, and awaits his exaltation, but judges this interpretation inadmissible since the saying implies a consciousness of pre-existence which is Johannine in character. To this view it may be replied that there is indeed a Johannine tone or parallel in Mk. xii. 35-7, though not the definiteness of expression which we find in the Fourth Gospel, and that whether the Johannine interpretation is justified is the challenge which the Synoptic saying makes to us.

Mk. xii. 37b-40   81. A WARNING AGAINST   Cf. (Mt. xxiii)
                      THE SCRIBES   Lk. xx. 45-7 (xi. 37-53)

The narrative consists of sayings with a brief editorial introduction. The sayings themselves appear to be an extract, or a double extract (*v.* the note on 40), from a longer compilation comparable to Mt. xxiii (M and Q) and Lk. xi. 37-53 (Q). They are introduced at this point in the outline for topical reasons; just as the teaching of the scribes is attacked in xii. 35-7a, so here their practice is arraigned. This topical purpose

---

¹ *Nun hat die urchristliche Gemeinde das Psalmwort eindeutig auf Christus bezogen und damit die Dunkelheit beseitigt. Besteht sie aber hier noch, so kann dieser ganze Schriftbeweis nicht erst von ihr gebildet sein, sondern darf auf Jesus zurückgeführt werden.*

explains why only these sayings are given. Mark, or a predecessor, desired to show how completely Jesus had broken with the Rabbis. The selection of the sayings reveals the strong anti-Jewish temper of the Church at Rome, for Mark himself indicates that the relationships of Jesus with the scribes were not always hostile (cf. xii. 28-34). But this argument cannot be pressed to the extent of explaining away the sayings, for they undoubtedly point to a final clash with the scribes on the part of Jesus Himself. Independently, and with greater rigour, this breach is attested by the longer anti-Pharisaic discourses of Mt. xxiii and Lk. xi. When the sayings were uttered cannot be determined, but their decisiveness and the width of the opposition revealed suggest an advanced point in the Ministry best associated with Jerusalem.

38 Καὶ ὁ πολὺς ὄχλος ἤκουεν αὐτοῦ ἡδέως. Καὶ ἐν τῇ διδαχῇ αὐτοῦ ἔλεγεν Βλέπετε ἀπὸ τῶν γραμματέων τῶν θελόντων
39 ἐν στολαῖς περιπατεῖν καὶ ἀσπασμοὺς ἐν ταῖς ἀγοραῖς καὶ
πρωτοκαθεδρίας ἐν ταῖς συναγωγαῖς καὶ πρωτοκλισίας ἐν τοῖς

37b, 38 f. On the whole it is best to take 37b with the present narrative. If it goes with the preceding story, it suggests that the people marked the scribes' discomfiture with delight, whereas it seems more likely that Mark is making a general statement. The phrase ὁ πολὺς ὄχλος is unusual; it means ' the mass of the people ' (cf. Moffatt; Swete, 289). Cf. Jn. xii. 9, 12. Field, 37, supports the AV, ' the common people ', by Lev. iv. 27, and late Greek examples. With ἤκουεν αὐτοῦ ἡδέως cf. ἡδέως αὐτοῦ ἤκουεν, vi. 20*.

The two sayings which follow are introduced simply by the phrase καὶ ἐν τῇ διδαχῇ αὐτοῦ ἔλεγεν. Cf. iv. 2. Both Matthew and Luke add τοῖς μαθηταῖς. Matthew has a parallel to the first saying derived from M in xxiii. 6 f. which lacks the Markan reference to walking ἐν στολαῖς, but otherwise, apart from the omission of βλέπετε ἀπό, is in close agreement. Luke, with προσέχετε instead of βλέπετε, is in almost verbatim agreement, and has a parallel taken from Q in xi. 43. Cf. Manson, SJ, 98 f., 229.

For βλέπετε ἀπό v. viii. 15; οἱ γραμματεῖς i. 22; περιπατέω ii. 9; ἀγορά vi. 56; στολή, xvi. 5*; ἀσπασμός*. In τῶν θελόντων ἐν στολαῖς περιπατεῖν καὶ ἀσπασμούς, θέλω is used in the sense

of liking, as frequently in the papyri of a personal wish or desire (VGT, 286), and is followed, not only by the infin., as normally, but also by the acc. Luke improves the constr. by inserting φιλούντων before ἀσπασμούς (xx. 46). The reading ἐν στοαῖς,[1] ' in porticos ' (sys), is preferred by Lohmeyer, 263 n., as corresponding to ἐν ταῖς ἀγοραῖς, but it is more probably a scribal error: cf. Swete, 290; Wellhausen, 98; Rawlinson, 175; Klostermann, 145; Lagrange, 328. As suggestive of ostentation, ἐν στολαῖς is more in accord with the initial warning and with Mt. xxiii. 5, μεγαλύνουσιν τὰ κράσπεδα. From the meaning ' equipment ' στολή comes in later Greek to denote ' raiment ' or ' a robe '; cf. the LXX, Ex. xxxi. 10, Jon. iii. 6, Esth. viii. 15, I Macc. vi. 15; VGT, 591. The warning against the scribes (βλέπετε ἀπό) is peculiar to Mark's version; in Lk. xi. 43, οὐαὶ ὑμῖν τοῖς Φαρισαίοις . . ., the saying is addressed to them, and this form looks more original.

πρωτοκαθεδρία*, Mt. xxiii. 6, Lk. xi. 43, xx. 46**, is the bench before the ark containing the sacred rolls of the Law and the Prophets, a place of honour in the synagogue (συναγωγή, i. 21) facing the people; cf. Edersheim, i. 436. πρωτοκλισία*, Mt. xxiii. 6, Lk. xiv. 7 f., xx. 46**. The two

[1] So syᶜ in Lk. xx. 46; cf. Herodotus iii. 52. Cf. Pallis, 43.

Γδείπνοις, οἱ κατέσθοντες τὰς οἰκίας τῶν χηρῶν καὶ προφάσει 40
μακρὰ προσευχόμενοι·⌐ οὗτοι λήμψονται περισσότερον κρίμα.

39, 40 δείπνοις· οἱ . . . προσευχόμενοι,

words are found first in the Gospels.
For the former v. Hermas, *Mand*. xi.
12. For δεῖπνον v. vi. 21*. The picture
is that of men who expect the greatest
deference to be paid to them. No
qualification is made in the Markan
saying (nor in Mt. xxiii and Lk. xi),
but it would be wrong to suppose that
the characteristics censured applied
to all the Rabbis; cf. xii. 28-34.

40. The warning is continued in the
charge that the scribes devour widows'
houses and for a pretence make long
prayers. For κατεσθίω v. iv. 4*; χήρα,
xii. 42 f.*; πρόφασις*; προσεύχομαι
i. 35. If, as most commentators think,
the verse continues the description of
the scribes, the nom. οἱ κατεσθίοντες
(B, κατέσθοντες) is an anacoluthon (cf.
Hawkins, 136), the agreement with
θελόντων being *ad sensum*. Allen, 154,
suggests the careless translation of an
Aramaic participle. Luke corrects Mk,
using the relative and the indicative,
οἱ κατεσθίουσιν (xx. 47). The indic.
is also read in Mk by D fam. 1 91 299
it vg, and καί is omitted by D it (exc. e)
vg sys pe arm; but these readings, like
Luke's, are only grammatical corrections. Possibly the nom. is a *casus
pendens* followed by the resumptive
pronoun οὗτοι (cf. vii. 20, Lk. xiii. 4,
xxiii. 50-2, etc.). If so, the break after
προσευχόμενοι is avoided, and 40 may
be a separate extract from the sayings-
source attached to 38 f. for topical
reasons (cf. iii. 27-9, iv. 21-5, viii. 34-
ix. 1, ix. 37-50). Lohmeyer, 263,
suspects that two sayings have been
brought together on several grounds:
the change of construction in 40; the
association of unlimited avarice in 40
with mere vanity in 38 f.; the awkwardness of οὗτοι λήμψονται . . . ; the
want of a parallel to 40 in Lk. xi. 43.
He also conjectures that the original
form of 40 was: οὐαὶ (ὑμῖν) τοῖς
γραμματεῦσιν ὅτι κατεσθίουσιν (-ετε).
These conjectures are open to objec-

tion on the linguistic side, since anacolutha are common in Mk, but from the
standpoint of the subject-matter they
have much force. Grotius, Bengel,
Tischendorf, and others, take οἱ κατεσθ.
as the beginning of a new sentence.
Cf. Gould, 238.

The charge is one of exaction and
hypocrisy. The former, especially as
regards widows and orphans (D W
fam. 13 28 565 it (exc. e k) syhier add
καὶ ὀρφανῶν), is frequently condemned
in the OT (cf. Ex. xxii. 22, Isa. i. 17,
23, x. 2), generally in the case of the
wealthy and powerful. Cf. *Ass. Mos.*
vii. 6, and Psa. Sol. iv. 11, 13, 15, 23,
xii. 2-4. Josephus, *Ant.* xvii. 2. 4,
says that the Pharisees made men
believe that they were highly favoured
by God and that women were in-
veigled by them. Like Jesus (xiv. 3-9,
xv. 40 f., Lk. viii. 2 f., x. 38-42), the
Rabbis could look to women for support, and in all ages such generosity
has often led to abuse. There is,
therefore, reason to think that as regards some of the Rabbis, but by no
means all, the charge was not without foundation; cf. Branscomb, 226;
Montefiore, i. 292; Abrahams, i. 79-81.
Hypocrisy is prominent in the accusations of Mt. xxiii, and is the standing
peril of religious leaders, more especially in a religion based on legalism.
The real criticism to which 38-40 is
exposed is the sweeping character of
the charges and the absence of any
qualifications. A hostile attitude to
Judaism and to the Rabbis is reflected
in the choice and use of these sayings,
despite the probability that they represent actual utterances of Jesus.

μακρά*, Lk. xx. 47**, is an acc. neut.
pl. of the adj. used adverbially. For
περισσότερος v. vii. 36; κρίμα*. The
belief that these sins lie under the
condemnation of God is thoroughly
Jewish; cf. Rom. iii. 8, Gal. v 10,
1 Tim. v. 12, etc.

Mk. xii. 41-4   82. THE WIDOW'S TWO MITES   Cf. Lk. xxi. 1-4

The narrative is a Pronouncement-story similar in type to the True Kindred of Jesus (iii. 31-5) and the Blessing of the Children (x. 13-16). The story is told, not for its own sake, but because it leads to a significant saying of Jesus about almsgiving. Bultmann, 32 f., classifies it as a Biographical Apothegm ; Redlich, 102, as an Apothegm-story. Dibelius, 261, prefers to regard it as a narrative constructed by Mark on the basis of a saying of Jesus, and especially a parable. The position of the narrative is due to topical reasons. The reference to widows in xii. 40 and its connexion with the Temple account for its place in the Markan outline.

The genuineness of the story has been frequently questioned, partly because it is not apparent how Jesus knew that the woman had given her all (cf. Bultmann, 60 ; Lohmeyer, 265) and partly because there are parallels to it in Jewish tradition and in Indian and Buddhist literature. Lohmeyer, 266, for example, cites the Jewish story of a priest who rejected the offering of a handful of meal from a poor woman, and was commanded in a dream during the night : ' Despise her not ; it is as if she offered her life ' (Leviticus Rabba, iii. 107a). For further examples v. Billerbeck, ii. 46·; Abrahams, i. 81 f. That a story related by Jesus has been transformed into a story about Him, is, of course, a possibility, but the argument from parallels gives it dubious support. The story is not so distinctive that similar incidents, with differences, could not happen in the case of other teachers ; and it would be absurd to require that a lineal connexion must be found between them. Further, the story is in harmony with His teaching elsewhere (cf. ix. 41, Lk. xii. 15) and the use of ἀμὴν λέγω ὑμῖν is characteristic.

41   Καὶ καθίσας ⌜κατέναντι⌝ τοῦ γαζοφυλακίου ἐθεώρει πῶς ὁ ὄχλος βάλλει χαλκὸν εἰς τὸ γαζοφυλάκιον· καὶ πολλοὶ πλούσιοι
41 ἀπέναντι

41. Jesus is described watching the crowd casting their gifts into the Temple treasury. His position at the time is somewhat vaguely described as καθίσας κατέναντι τοῦ γαζοφυλακίου. With καθίσας cf. ix. 35 ; κατέναντι xi. 2, xiii. 3*. γαζοφυλάκιον (bis), xii. 43*, Lk. xxi. 1, Jn. viii. 20**, ' a treasury . (<γάζα, φυλακή), belongs to late Gk, Strabo vii. 6. 1 ; LXX, 4 Kgdms. xxiii. 11 ; inscr. (VGT, 120). Commentators explain the position of Jesus as facing thirteen trumpet-shaped chests placed round the walls of the Court of Women in which the people threw their offerings ; cf. Swete, 292 ; DCG, ii. 748 f. ; Edersheim, ii. 387. Billerbeck, ii. 37-45, thinks that the reference is to the treasury itself, and that donors had to declare the

amount of their gift and the purpose for which it was intended to the priest in charge, everything being visible and audible to the onlooker through the open door. We should not gather this from the narrative, which speaks only of beholding (ἐθεώρει), but it may be that through repetition the original details have disappeared, since the main interest is in what Jesus said.

D and q read καθεζόμενος ὁ Ἰησοῦς after γαζοφ., and W Θ fam. 1 (exc. 118) fam. 13 (exc. 124) 28 565 et al. sys hl mg hier arm geo Or have ἑστὼς ὁ Ἰησοῦς. Other MSS. also insert ὁ Ἰησοῦς ; v. Legg. By omitting βάλλει . . . πλούσιοι D gives a simpler reading, but the prolixity of the WH text is characteristic of Mark.

For χαλκός v. vi. 8* ; from 44 it is

XII. 44]   THE GOSPEL ACCORDING TO ST. MARK   497

ἔβαλλον πολλά· καὶ ἐλθοῦσα μία χήρα πτωχὴ ἔβαλεν λεπτὰ δύο, 42
ὅ ἐστιν κοδράντης. καὶ προσκαλεσάμενος τοὺς μαθητὰς αὐτοῦ 43
εἶπεν αὐτοῖς Ἀμὴν λέγω ὑμῖν ὅτι ἡ χήρα αὕτη ἡ πτωχὴ πλεῖον
πάντων [βέβληκεν] τῶν βαλλόντων εἰς τὸ γαζοφυλάκιον· πάντες 44
γὰρ ἐκ τοῦ περισσεύοντος αὐτοῖς ἔβαλον, αὕτη δὲ ἐκ τῆς ὑστερή-

clear that, as in the papyri (*VGT*, 683), it means ' money '. The reference to the rich (πλούσιος, x. 25*), which follows awkwardly, is necessary to the point of the story. In Luke's more elegant version the roughness of Mark's narrative disappears. This fact is a powerful reason for rejecting the suggestion that the narrative has been inserted in Mk from Lk. Cf. Lk. xxi. 1, ἀναβλέψας δὲ εἶδεν τοὺς βάλλοντας εἰς τὸ γαζοφυλάκιον τὰ δῶρα αὐτῶν πλουσίους.

42. For μία = τις *v.* Intr. 60, and for the ' redundant ' use of the participle ἐλθοῦσα *v.* Intr. 63. It is tempting to claim two possible Semitisms as a sign that the narrative is based on a Semitic original, but the use of the cardinal for τις is well attested in popular Gk and ἐλθοῦσα introduces a distinct idea (she came and cast). Moreover, the use of the pres., imperf., and aor. of βάλλω in 41 f., followed by the perf. in 43, indicates a careful use of tenses, while τὸ περισσεῦον and ἡ ὑστέρησις in 44 have a somewhat literary flavour. For πτωχός (om. D) *v.* x. 21 ; Luke has πενιχρός.

λεπτόν*, Lk. xii. 59, xxi. 2**, literally ' peeled ' (λέπω), was used in late Gk for the smallest coin in circulation (*VGT*, 374) ; AV and RV, ' mite '. Cf. Moffatt, ' two little coins amounting to a halfpenny ' ; RSV, ' two copper coins, which make a penny '. For the benefit of his Roman readers Mark computes the two in terms of Roman coinage, ὅ ἐστιν κοδράντης. κοδράντης is a transliteration of the Latin *quadrans* which was the fourth part of an *as* ; cf. Mt. v. 26**. For a lively discussion between W. M. Ramsay and F. Blass, in which the honours go to Ramsay in his submission that the *quadrans* was not in circulation in the east, and that therefore Zahn is justified in claiming that

the allusion points to Roman readers, cf. *ET*, x. 185·7, 232, 286 f., 336. The credibility of the story is in no way affected by the fact that Gk and Roman coins are mentioned (cf. Lohmeyer, 266) ; Mark's words no more imply that the narrative was first composed far away from Jerusalem than *zwei Scherflein, das ist ein Heller* suggests composition in Germany. For ὅ ἐστιν in Mk *v.* the note on iii. 17. Luke omits the explanation.

43 f. For Mark's use of προσκαλεσάμενος when Jesus addresses the disciples *v.* iii. 13, 23 ; οἱ μαθηταὶ αὐτοῦ ii. 15 ; ἀμὴν λέγω ὑμῖν iii. 28. The use of the phrase ἀμὴν ἤν, etc. indicates the earnestness with which Jesus spoke. This poor woman, He declared, cast in more than all. πλεῖον*. The aor. ἔβαλεν (WH) is very strongly attested (‍‍‍‍‍אc A B D L Δ Θ Σ 13 33 565 579 892 *al. mu.* Or), but the perf. βέβληκεν (W *et al.* fam. 1 fam. 13 (exc. 13) 28 700 1071 *al. pler.*) is perhaps more likely to be original ; so Ti and von Soden, cf. Moffatt and RSV, ' has put '. Luke omits τῶν βαλλόντων εἰς τὸ γαζοφυλάκιον, apparently judging it prolix. Turner, 62, suggests that the meaning is ' more than all of them put together '.

The reason is given in 44. In contrast with all who gave of their superfluity, she gave of her want all that she had, even her whole living. τὸ περισσεῦον* ; in viii. 8 Mark uses περίσσευμα*. ὑστέρησις*, Phil. iv. 11**, ' deficiency ', ' need ', is not illustrated by LS from the classical period, but is described as the equivalent of the more common ὑστέρημα, which is substituted by Luke (xxi. 4). The latter is found several times in the LXX (Judg. xviii. 10, xix. 19 f., Psa. xxxiii. (xxxiv.) 10, Eccl. i. 15, 2 Esdr. vi. 9), but ὑστέρησις appears only in Aquila's

σεως αὐτῆς πάντα ὅσα εἶχεν ἔβαλεν, ὅλον τὸν βίον αὐτῆς.

version in Job xxx. 3, and neither is illustrated in *VGT*. The NT record of ὑστέρημα is Lk (1), Pl (8)**. Klostermann, 147, compares the manner in which θέλησις-θέλημα and καύχησις-καύχημα pass over into one another; but this illustration is not entirely satisfactory since the one example of θέλησις in the NT is distinctive (cf. Heb. ii. 4, Moffatt, *ICC*, 20) and καύχημα often, though not always, means ' ground of glorying ' (cf. Rom. iv. 2, 1 Cor. ix. 15 f., 2 Cor. i. 14, Gal. vi. 4, cf. Burton, *ICC*, 333, Phil. i. 26, ii. 16). In view of the contrast with ἐκ τοῦ περισσεύοντος αὐτοῖς, we must suppose that by ἐκ τῆς ὑστερήσεως αὐτῆς Mark means ' out of her want '; cf. Moffatt, ' neediness ', RSV, ' poverty '. With πάντα ὅσα cf. vi. 30, xi. 24. βίος* ; for the common meaning ' livelihood ' *v. VGT*, 111. sys omits ὅλον τὸν βίον αὐτῆς, but the presence of the phrase

is implied by Luke's rearrangement, ἅπαντα τὸν βίον ὃν εἶχεν, is in accordance with Mark's style, and effectively describes the measure of the widow's generosity.

The fact that we do not know how Jesus knew exactly how much the widow had contributed to the treasury is not a valid objection to the historical value of the narrative ; for the account does not pretend to be a complete report : its main interest is in what Jesus said. It is easy to imagine circumstances in which He came to know what she had done ; *v.* the note on 41 ; but such explanations can be little more than conjectures. It is possible that the first Christians interpreted the knowledge of Jesus as supernatural, or at least uncanny ; but the narrative gives no ground for this view. On the contrary, it betrays no interest in the question.

(*c*) Mk. xiii. 1-37   THE APOCALYPTIC
                           DISCOURSE

Since the time of T. Colani [1] and W. Weiffenbach [2] the hypothesis that a small apocalypse lies at the basis of Mk. xiii has been widely accepted, so much so that Moffatt, 209, speaks of it as ' a *sententia recepta* of synoptic criticism '. To the full list of scholars who have accepted this hypothesis given by him may be added : McNeile, 343 f. ; Rawlinson, 180-2 ; Bultmann, 129 ; Ed. Meyer, i. 129 f. ; Branscomb, 231-3. The suggestion is that, in anticipation of the horrors of the siege of Jerusalem, some unknown Christian edited a small Jewish or Jewish-Christian apocalypse as a kind of fly-sheet to give encouragement and hope to the Christians of his day, and incorporated therewith eschatological sayings of Jesus. Using this primitive document and adding other sayings, Mark, it is held, built up the composite discourse in xiii. Not unnaturally, attempts to reconstruct the primitive apocalypse vary in detail. As examples may be mentioned : Wendt, 7-9a, 14-20, 24-7, 30 f. ; Weiffenbach and Pfleiderer, 7-9a, 14-20, 24-7 ; Loisy, 6-8, 14, 17-20, 24-31 ; Schmiedel, 7-9a, 14-20, 24-7, 30 ; Wellhausen, 7 f., 12, 14-22, 24-7 ; Holtzmann, 5-9, 14-20, 24-7.[3] Klostermann's list, 147, is 7 f., 12, 13b, 14-22, 24-7, (?) 30-2. In these conjectures it will be seen that the most constant element is 7 f., 14-20, 24-7. Here, if anywhere, the primitive core is to be found.

It is impossible here to describe the various subsequent modifications of this hypothesis. Rawlinson, 181, makes an important point in speaking

---

[1] *Jésus-Christ et les croyances messianiques de son temps*, 1864, pp. 201 f.
[2] *Der Wiederkunftsgedanke Jesu*, 1873, pp. 69 f., 135 f.
[3] Moffatt, 207 n.

of the author of the document as a Christian prophet who believed himself to be charged by the Spirit to convey to the Church an apocalyptic message in the name of the risen Jesus. In general, the tendency has been to think less of the picturesque suggestion of a ' fly-sheet ' and to stress more the influence of the doctrinal and catechetical interests of the Church of Mark's day. Schniewind, 166, doubts whether it is possible or necessary to pick out a Jewish apocalypse as the basis of the tradition. *V*. Intr. 13 n. Lohmeyer, 285, takes much the same view and maintains that the discourse consists of single sayings, or groups of sayings, which already lay before Mark in a fixed literary form. In these significant opinions we are witnessing a swing of the pendulum, although as long ago as 1903 J. Weiss, 281 f., renounced the hypothesis of a small Jewish apocalypse, to which he formerly had adhered, preferring to trace the discourse to the sayings-source, apart from Markan additions in 5b, 6b, 10, 15 f., 28 f., 32, 34-7.

Montefiore, i. 296, impatiently concluded that the discourse as a whole is unauthentic, and that it has a very slight interest for us to-day and little or no religious value. Many will be inclined to sympathize with the opinion, which in 1927 seemed not unreasonable ; but such an attitude is much less justifiable in the post-War world. And it must be recognized that exegetical progress has been made. It is now widely agreed that (1) the chapter is composite and that with reasonable certainty the last Markan modifications can be determined ; (2) that doctrinal and catechetical interests have affected the material which Mark used ; and (3) that genuine sayings of Jesus are embedded in it and adapted to later conditions. Less clearly perceived is (4) the importance of studying the bearing of Lk. xxi on the formation of Mk. xiii.

How far the tangled skein can be unravelled is the problem still with us. The problem is certainly far more than a mere critical puzzle. The relevant questions are of great importance. Why is the Apocalyptic Discourse preceded by the Prophecy of the Destruction of Jerusalem ? Why do *two* sections, 5 f. and 21-3, speak of deceivers ? Is the section on persecution, 9-13, of one piece with the rest ? Need the reference to ' the Abomination of Desolation ' in xiii. 14 be earlier than the allusion to Jerusalem in Lk. xxi. 20 ? In what relation do the Lukan and Markan discourses stand to each other, and possibly to a still earlier source ? Why is there no reference, as in apocalypses generally, to the casting down of Satan, to the Last Judgment, and to the destruction of evil ? How far is the picture of the Son of Man coming on the clouds harmonious with the teaching of Jesus ? Why is want of knowledge concerning the day mentioned in a discourse which insists that well-marked signs must precede the End ? What is the significance of the emphasis on watching ? These are not small and unimportant questions, and, *pace* Montefiore, have much religious and historical importance. In Note E, pp. 636-44, it is suggested that into the group A, 5-8 + 24-7, groups B, 9-13, and C, 14-23, have been inserted by the Evangelist, with small consequent editorial additions, and that D, 28-37, has been appended, the whole being preceded by 1 f. and 3 f. to form the existing discourse.

The several sections are as follows :

(83) xiii. 1 f. On the Destruction of the Temple.
(84) xiii. 3 f. The Question of the Four Disciples.

(85) xiii. 5-8.   Warnings against Deceivers, Wars, etc.
(86) xiii. 9-13. Sayings on Persecution.
(87) xiii. 14-20. The Abomination of Desolation.
(88) xiii. 21-3. Warnings against False Christs and Prophets.
(89) xiii. 24-7. A Prophecy of the Coming of the Son of Man.
(90) xiii. 28-37. Sayings and Parables on Watchfulness.

Mk. xiii. 1 f.   83. ON THE DESTRUCTION   Cf. Mt. xxiv. 1 f.
                     OF THE TEMPLE   Lk. xxi. 5 f.

The climax of the story is the prophecy that not one stone of the Temple will be left standing upon another; and to this saying the brief reference to the circumstances forms the necessary introduction. The narrative is a Pronouncement-story. Bultmann, 36, classifies it as a Biographical Apothegm and thinks the introduction is secondary; cf. Redlich, 102, who describes it as an Apothegm-story. Dibelius and Albertz do not treat the narrative.

Mark's hand may perhaps be seen in ἐκπορευομένου αὐτοῦ ἐκ τοῦ ἱεροῦ, but the cry of the unnamed disciple rings true to the situation of a Galilean disciple visiting the city. Matthew's account is a later version. Luke's narrative may be independent, for, if we allow for the presence of necessary words like ἱερόν and λίθοι, there is little linguistic agreement with Mk. On the other hand in Lk the story is no longer self-contained, and the question, ' When shall these things be . . . ? ', may indicate dependence. The story illustrates the insight of Jesus into the religious and political conditions of His day. Cf. C. J. Cadoux, 276.

XIII. 1   Καὶ ἐκπορευομένου αὐτοῦ ἐκ τοῦ ἱεροῦ λέγει αὐτῷ εἷς τῶν μαθητῶν αὐτοῦ Διδάσκαλε, ἴδε ποταποὶ λίθοι καὶ ποταπαὶ 2 οἰκοδομαί. καὶ ὁ Ἰησοῦς εἶπεν αὐτῷ Βλέπεις ταύτας τὰς με-γάλας οἰκοδομάς; οὐ μὴ ἀφεθῇ ὧδε λίθος ἐπὶ λίθον ὃς οὐ μὴ καταλυθῇ.

1 f. For ἐκπορεύομαι (HS², 12) v. i. 5; ἱερόν xi. 11. As frequently, the gen. abs. is used freely; v. v. 2. The whole phrase is a link by which Mark connects the story with xi. 27-xii. 44. His reference to an unnamed disciple is replaced in Mt by the conventional οἱ μαθηταὶ αὐτοῦ and in Lk by τινων λεγόντων. For διδάσκαλε v. iv. 38; ἴδε ii. 24. ποταπός*, Mt. viii. 27, Lk. i. 29, vii. 39, 2 Pet. iii. 11, 1 Jn. iii. 1**, ' of what sort ? ', is the Hellenistic form of ποδαπός, 'from what country ? ', and is here used in the sense of ποῖος; cf. Moulton, i. 95, ii. 375. Not found in the Gk OT, except in Dan. LXX. Su. 54, the word was in popular use; VGT, 530. The note of surprise,

easily intelligible in the Galilean disciple's words, is occasioned by the size of the stones and the magnificence of the buildings. Cf. Josephus, Ant. xv. 11. 3, who says that the white stones were 25 cubits in length, 8 in height, and 12 in breadth, and BJ, v. 5. 1-8, where the Temple is described in detail; cf. also Edersheim, Temple, 20 ff. οἰκοδομή, xiii. 2*, is late Gk for οἰκο-δόμησις and οἰκοδόμημα; LXX, Pap. (VGT, 442).

The reply of Jesus, Βλέπεις ταύτας τὰς μεγάλας οἰκοδομάς;, responds to the note of surprise in the disciple's exclamation. The distinctiveness of Mark's account is lost in Matthew's question, οὐ βλέπετε ταῦτα πάντα;.

Luke's version, ταῦτα ἃ θεωρεῖτε, ἐλεύσονται ἡμέραι . . ., is noteworthy because of the *casus pendens* ταῦτα and the Semitic tone of ἐλεύσονται ἡμέραι (cf. Mk. ii. 20), and may come from a different source; cf. Easton, 306 f.

The decisive tone of the prophecy is expressed in the double use of οὐ μή c. subj. (*v.* ix. 1) in which Lagrange, 332, sees an echo of the Aramaic spoken by Jesus. This suggestion is supported by the parallelism in οὐ μὴ ἀφεθῇ and οὐ μὴ καταλυθῇ and the repetition of the substantive in λίθος ἐπὶ λίθον. Swete, 296, accounts for the acc. by the idea of motion faintly present in οὐ μὴ ἀφεθῇ, but Lagrange, 332, sees in it only an instance of the decline of the dat. in the Koine. Luke has the dat. and agrees with Matthew in ὃς οὐ καταλυθήσεται (cf. Robertson, 960 f.). ὧδε is omitted by A *et al.* 22 69 157 *al. plur.* ff i l r¹·² vg (so Lk), but it is very strongly attested. It adds vividness to the saying, almost suggesting a gesture. All the indications point to the primitive character of the Markan form.

There is no good reason for regard-

ing the saying as a *vaticinium ex eventu*. In prophesying the destruction of the Temple Jesus stands in line with the prophets; cf. Mic. iii. 12 and Jer. xxvi. 6, 18. See further, Lagrange, 332 f.; Rawlinson, 182; Branscomb, 228-30; Lohmeyer, 268; Schniewind, 166. In point of fact the Temple was destroyed by fire (Jos. *BJ*, vi. 4. 5 ff.), and of this there is no hint in the saying, a difference which cannot lightly be dismissed (with Montefiore, i. 297). Of the destruction of the city Josephus says that 'there was left nothing to make those that came thither believe it had ever been inhabited', *BJ*, vii. 1. 1.

D W it (exc. l q r²) Cyp add καὶ διὰ τριῶν ἡμερῶν ἄλλος ἀναστήσεται ἄνευ χειρῶν. Cf. xiv. 58, to which (and Jn. ii. 19) Hort, 26, traces it. So Allen, 155; Plummer, 293; Lagrange, 333; and almost all commentators. Turner, 72, observes that, if Jesus was overheard, the words would account for the accusation of xiv. 58; but the reading is probably a Western interpolation, as Turner himself argues in *JTS*, xxix. 9. Cf. Burkitt, *JTS*, xvii. 18.

Mk. xiii. 3 f.　　84. THE QUESTION OF THE　　Cf. Mt. xxiv. 3
　　　　　　　　　FOUR DISCIPLES　　　　　　　Lk. xxi. 7

Unlike 1f., 3 f. is not a self-contained narrative, but an introduction to 5-37, possibly originally to 14-20, composed by Mark himself on the basis of tradition. For other passages of the kind *v.* iv. 10-13, vii. 17-23, ix. 11-13, 28 f., x. 10-12.

Seated on the Mount of Olives, in full view of the Temple, Jesus is asked privately by Peter, James, John, and Andrew when 'these things' will happen, and what is the sign when 'all these things' will come to pass. In contrast with its Matthaean form, the peculiarity of the question is that it appears to refer exclusively to the destruction of the Temple rather than to the Apocalyptic Discourse as a whole. This fact suggests that the phraseology may be due to a source or to a grouping of sayings earlier than the present discourse. If this is so, the disciples' question is part of the data which belong to the problem of the origin of Mk. xiii.

Καὶ καθημένου αὐτοῦ εἰς τὸ Ὄρος τῶν Ἐλαιῶν κατέναντι 3
τοῦ ἱεροῦ ἐπηρώτα αὐτὸν κατ' ἰδίαν Πέτρος καὶ Ἰάκωβος καὶ

3 f. The gen. abs. καθημένου αὐτοῦ ... αὐτόν is used freely as in 1b (*v. v.* 2)

and εἰς has the sense of 'on'. Every word in 3 is well represented in Mark's

4 Ἰωάνης καὶ Ἀνδρέας Εἰπὸν ἡμῖν πότε ταῦτα ἔσται, καὶ τί τὸ
σημεῖον ὅταν μέλλῃ ταῦτα συντελεῖσθαι πάντα.

vocabulary; for κάθημαι v. ii. 6; τὸ
Ὄρος τῶν Ἐλαιῶν xi. 1; κατέναντι
xi. 2; ἱερόν xi. 11; ἐπερωτάω v. 9; κατ'
ἰδίαν iv. 34. Similarly, in 4 the only
new word is συντελεῖσθαι; for σημεῖον
v. viii. 11; ὅταν c. subj. ii. 20; μέλλω
x. 32. συντελέω*, Lk. iv. 2, 13, Ac.
xxi. 27, Rom. ix. 28, Heb. viii. 8**,
is the ' perfective ' of τελέω, and means
' to complete ', ' bring to an end ' ;
Cl., LXX, Pap. (VGT, 613 f.).
The vocabulary suggests that 3 f.
is Mark's composition, but it is not a
mere literary setting for 5-37; it is
more probable that he is using oral
or written tradition. The four disciples are those whose call is described
in i. 16-20, Andrew being placed last
because of the close association of
Peter, James, and John in v. 37,
ix. 2, and xiv. 33. Cf Bultmann,
370.

ταῦτα points back to the prophecy
of the destruction of the Temple, and,
taken by itself, ταῦτα πάντα has the
same meaning. But, as the chapter
now stands, ταῦτα πάντα appears to
point forwards, and it is in this sense
that it is commonly interpreted. Cf.
Lagrange, 334; Klostermann, 148;
B. Weiss, 197; Gould, 242; etc. The
usage is strange, and controversy on this
point goes back to ancient times, as
the statement of Victor, Catenae Graec.
Pat., J. A. Cramer, i. 408, shows: οἱ
μὲν γὰρ περὶ τῆς συντελείας τοῦ αἰῶνος
εἰρῆσθαι ταῦτα ὑπολαμβάνουσιν, οἱ δὲ
περὶ τῆς ἐρημώσεως τῆς Ἰερουσαλήμ·
καὶ τῆς μὲν προτέρας δόξης Ἀπολινάριος

καὶ Θεόδωρος ὁ Μοψουεστίας, τῆς δὲ
δευτέρας Τίτος καὶ ὁ ἐν ἁγίοις Ἰωάννης
ὁ τῆς βασιλίδος ἐπίσκοπος. Matthew's
expansion, τί τὸ σημεῖον τῆς σῆς παρ-
ουσίας καὶ συντελείας τοῦ αἰῶνος;
(xxiv. 3), gives the sense required, but
it sharpens the question why Mark (cf.
Lk) has no more than ταῦτα πάντα.
The suggestion of Bartlet, 347, and
others, that Jesus may have previously
referred to other topics, is only a conjecture, and it is better to infer that
Mark is following a tradition which
dealt immediately with the destruction
of Jerusalem. Cf. Allen, 156. This
hypothesis is less strange than might
appear, when it is remembered that
5-37 is composite and contains material
from different sources.

The main point of interest in Mark's
statement is that the inquiry is private;
it is made by the four disciples and
apparently Peter is the speaker.
Matthew retains κατ' ἰδίαν, but attributes the question to the disciples
generally. In Lk nothing suggests a
private conversation; neither the disciples nor the four are mentioned and
τινων in 5 is quite indefinite. Like
Mark, Luke has ταῦτα without any
addition. Manson, SJ, 324, observes
that it is natural to suppose that
originally Lk. xxi. 5-7 was followed
immediately by xxi. 20-4, and that the
intervening passages have been inserted, probably at an earlier stage in
the tradition than the composition of
Lk. This suggestion applies equally
well to Mk. xiii. 1-4 and xiii. 14-20.

Mk. xiii. 5-8   85. WARNINGS AGAINST   Cf. Mt. xxiv. 4-8
              DECEIVERS AND OF WARS   Lk. xxi. 8-11
              AND RUMOURS OF WAR,
          EARTHQUAKES, AND FAMINES

This section consists of sayings introduced by the phrase, ὁ δὲ Ἰησοῦς
ἤρξατο λέγειν αὐτοῖς. The first part, 5 f., appears to be a doublet of 21-3,
and to 7 f. there is a parallel in the references to cosmic disturbances in

sun, moon, stars, and the heavenly powers, in 24 f. The parallels are as follows :

5 f.	21-3
Deceivers who come saying, ' I am he '.	False Christs and False Prophets.

7 f.	24 f.
Wars and Rumours of War.	The Darkening of Sun and Moon.
Nations and Kingdoms in Conflict.	Falling Stars.
Earthquakes. Famines.	The Shaking of the Heavenly Powers.

Questions to be considered are whether 21-3 belongs to 14-20, and, in this case, whether 24-7 followed 7 f. in a source or earlier grouping of sayings. The bearing of these questions on the origin and composition of the Apocalyptic Discourse is manifest.

'Ο δὲ 'Ιησοῦς ἤρξατο λέγειν αὐτοῖς Βλέπετε μή τις ὑμᾶς 5 πλανήσῃ· πολλοὶ ἐλεύσονται ἐπὶ τῷ ὀνόματί μου λέγοντες ὅτι 6 'Εγώ εἰμι, καὶ πολλοὺς πλανήσουσιν. ὅταν δὲ ⌐ἀκούσητε⌐ πολέ- 7

7 ἀκούητε

5. f. For ἤρξατο c. infin. v. Intr. 48, 63 f. Here, as compared with Mt (καὶ ἀποκριθείς . . . εἶπεν) and Lk (ὁ δὲ εἶπεν), the phrase has a more formal ring. βλέπειν μή* is a colloquial usage found in the papyri (VGT, 113) and in Mt. xxiv. 4, Lk. xxi. 8, Ac. xiii. 40, 1 Cor. viii. 9, x. 12, Gal. v. 15, Col. ii. 8 (c. fut.), Heb. iii. 12 (c. fut.), xii. 25, 2 Jn. 8 (ἵνα μή)**. Cf. ὁρᾶν μή (LS, 1245). The peril is that of being misled or deceived (πλανάω, v. xii. 24 ; Lk, πλανηθῆτε) and the warning is emphasized by the abrupt asyndeton in 6. γάρ is added in Mt and Lk, and in Mk by A D Θ et al. minusc. omn. vss. omn. For ἐπὶ τῷ ὀνόματί μου, ' in my name ', v. ix. 37, 39.

The meaning of λέγοντες ὅτι 'Εγώ εἰμι is obscure. Are the ' many ' false Messiahs or false teachers, or will they claim to be Jesus Himself ? The view that they are false Messiahs is suggested by Mt. xxiv. 5, 'Εγώ εἰμι ὁ χριστός. Cf. Swete, 298 ; Gould, 243 ; Lagrange, 336. Against it is the fact that the earliest known Messianic pretender is Bar Cochba (A.D. 132), for Judas of Galilee was a revolutionary and Theudas claimed to be a prophet (Josephus, Ant. xx. 5. 1 f.), while ' the

Egyptian ' mentioned in Ac. xxi. 38 was a rebel (BJ, ii. 13. 5 ; cf. Lake, iv. 276 f.). Nevertheless, it is true that in the first century A.D. false Messiahs might be expected at any time ; cf. Sanday, Life of Christ in Recent Research, 81. The stronger objection is that ἐπὶ τῷ ὀνόματί μου cannot mean ' claiming to be the Christ', but ' under my authority ' or ' in my name ' (ix. 39). If false Messiahs are meant, it would be necessary to explain this phrase as a secondary addition adapting the original source to the circumstances presupposed in Mk. xiii. This is a possibility which cannot be ignored, but it loses its force if another interpretation of the prophecy is preferable.

The view that the ' many ' are false teachers claiming to speak in Christ's name is strongly supported by ἐπὶ τῷ ὀνόματί μου, but it is less successful in giving a satisfactory meaning to 'Εγώ εἰμι. What, on this view, will the deceivers teach ? Two answers are possible : they will affirm either that the Messiah has come or that His Parousia is imminent. The former explanation takes 'Εγώ εἰμι to mean, in effect : ' The Christ is come, the Parousia has arrived ' ; cf. W. Manson,

μους καὶ ἀκοὰς πολέμων, μὴ θροεῖσθε· δεῖ γενέcθαι, ἀλλ' οὔ-
8 πω τὸ τέλος. ἐγερθήcεται [γὰρ] ἔθνοc ἐπ' ἔθνοc καὶ βαcιλεία ἐπὶ

JTS, xlviii. 139. The objection to this attractive suggestion is that in the Gospels and the Acts 'Εγώ εἰμι is almost always the speaker's affirmation, ' It is I ' or ' I am he ' (e.g. vi. 50, xiv. 62, and very frequently in Jn, even where there is a change of subject, as in viii. 24, 28). J. H. Bernard, *St. Jn*, cxvii-cxxi, argues that in Jn there are many sayings of Jesus in which the phrase is ' the style of Deity ', but in all cases the expressions are self-designations, not statements about another. The presumption is that the false teachers will make claims about themselves. The same criticisms may be advanced against the second explanation of the deceivers' message, namely, that the Parousia is imminent. Can 'Εγώ εἰμι mean this?

Luke's version bears on the two interpretations discussed above. In Lk. xxi. 8 the deceivers make the claim 'Εγώ εἰμι, but also say 'Ο καιρὸς ἤγγικεν, and, as in Q (Lk. xvii. 23 = Mt. xxiv. 26), the warning is added μὴ πορευθῆτε ὀπίσω αὐτῶν. If ἤγγικεν could be rendered ' has come ' (cf. Dodd, 44, with reference to Mk. i. 15) support would be given to W. Manson's interpretation (*v. supra*), but probably the imminence of the Parousia is predicted. Further, the difficulty of 'Εγώ εἰμι remains and is enhanced by the probability that in Lk two different versions (Mk and Q or L) have been combined.

The view that the deceivers are false prophets who will claim to be Jesus Himself returning from on high (cf. Turner, 63; Bartlet, 352; *v.* Rawlinson, 184) does justice to ἐπὶ τῷ ὀνόματί μου and 'Εγώ εἰμι, but we have no independent evidence of the existence of such teachers apart from the fact that Jesus Himself was supposed by some to be Elijah or John the Baptist raised from the dead (vi. 14 f., viii. 28). Cf. Wellhausen, 101; W. Manson, *op. cit.* 139.

From the foregoing discussion it appears that there is no explanation of the prophecy which is free from difficulty, but there is most to be said for those which interpret 'Εγώ εἰμι as a Messianic or quasi-Messianic claim. Cf. Schniewind, 167, who traces the expression to Ex. iii. 14, Isa. xliii. 10 f., lii. 6 f., and suggests that the 'Εγώ εἰμι, there used of Yahweh, is applied to the coming of the Messiah; and Lohmeyer, 270, who explains it as a traditional formula for the expected eschatological Deliverer (*Vollender*). It is a mysterious high-sounding expression comparable to (though different from) the terms in which Simon Magus described himself (Ac. viii. 9, λέγων εἶναί τινα ἑαυτὸν μέγαν). But if this is so, we are driven back (*v. supra*) upon the suggestion that ἐπὶ τῷ ὀνόματί μου is a ' Christian ' addition to a Jewish or Jewish-Christian source used in compiling the Apocalyptic Discourse. This conclusion is so far-reaching in its implications that it must be held in suspense in order to see whether other evidence points in this direction. See Note E, p. 639. In any case, 5 f. is not part of the original reply to the disciples' question in 3 f. It belongs to a group of sayings connected with the Parousia rather than the destruction of the Temple.

7 f. Besides deceivers, wars (πολέμους*), rumours of wars (ἀκοὰς (*v.* i. 28) πολέμων), the rising of nation against nation (ἔθνος, x. 33) and kingdom against kingdom (βασιλεία, i. 15) are predicted, together with earthquakes (σεισμοί*) and famines (λιμοί*). A W Δ Θ *et al.* minusc. *pler.* q sys pe hl geo Or.*int.* add ταραχαί, ' tumults '. Both Mt and Lk agree closely with Mk, but Lk has ἀκαταστασίας, ' revolutions ', and at the end λοιμοί, ' pestilences ', and φόβητρά τε καὶ ἀπ' οὐρανοῦ σημεῖα μεγάλα ἔσται, ' and there will be terrors and great signs from heaven ' (xxi. 11). With ὅταν ἀκούσητε cf. 11, 14.

Βαϲιλείαν, ἔσονται σεισμοὶ κατὰ τόπους, ἔσονται λιμοί· ἀρχὴ ὠδίνων ταῦτα.

The events and portents described are common apocalyptic expectations. Cf. Sib. Or. iii. 635, ' And king captures king . . ., and nations ravage nations '; 4 Ezra xiii. 31, *Et in alios alii cogitabunt bellare, ciuitates ciuitatem et locus locum et gens ad gentem et regnum aduersus regnum* ; 1 Enoch xcix. 4, ' In those days the nations shall be stirred up '; Apoc. Bar. xxvii. 7, lxx. 3, 8; Apoc. Jn. vi. 8, xi. 13, xvi. 18 (earthquake), xviii. 8 (famine, fire, etc.). So also in OT forecasts: Isa. viii. 21 (hunger), xiii. 13 (earthquakes), xiv. 30 (famine), xix. 2 (wars, ' city against city, kingdom against kingdom '); Jer. xxiii. 19; Ezek. v. 12; Hag. ii. 6; Zech. xiv. 4. Current historical events may be in mind: risings in Palestine, the Parthian invasion, the famine in the time of Claudius (Ac. xi. 28), the earthquakes at Laodicea (A.D. 61) and at Pompeii (A.D. 62) ; but, as the evidence cited above shows, the predictions may be quite general.

Amid all these upheavals, it is urged, there is no need for fear. Everything belongs to the divine plan; μὴ θροεῖσθε· δεῖ γενέσθαι. θροέω, ' to cry aloud ', is a classical word which in the LXX (Cant. v. 4) and in the NT is used in the pass. with the meaning ' to be alarmed ' or ' agitated ', Mt. xxiv. 6, Lk. xxiv. 37 (?), 2 Thess. ii. 2**. Cf. Kennedy, 126. Luke has μὴ πτοηθῆτε (*VGT*, 558). For δεῖ v. viii. 31. This insistence upon calm in the face of a divine purpose is also characteristic of eschatological forecasts, and it may be significant that

the only other NT instance of θροέομαι (apart from the parallel in Mt. xxiv. 6) is 2 Thess. ii. 2. Cf. Bacon, 88-98. There, too, Christians are warned εἰς τὸ μὴ ταχέως σαλευθῆναι ὑμᾶς ἀπὸ τοῦ νοὸς μηδὲ θροεῖσθαι, and receive the counsel, ' Let no one deceive you (ἐξαπατήσῃ) in any way '. The section on ' the Man of Sin ' then follows (2 Thess. ii. 3-10); cf. Mk. xiii. 14. It is manifestly a question for consideration whether the Pauline apocalypse has affected the arrangement of Mk. xiii and is in some way connected with it.

As it stands, the section breaks off with the statement that the calamities foretold are ' the beginning of woes ', ἀρχὴ ὠδίνων ταῦτα. ὠδίν*, Mt. xxiv. 8, Ac. ii. 24, 1 Thess. v. 3**, ' a pang ', ' throe ', especially in the plur. of the pangs of childbirth, is the Hellenistic form of ὠδίς. It calls to mind the later Rabbinical use of the phrase ' the birth-pangs of the Messiah ' which Billerbeck, i. 950, believes to have been a technical expression already current in the time of Christ. Cf. Schniewind, 168. Cf. Isa. xxvi. 17, Jer. xxii. 23, Hos. xiii. 13, Mic. iv. 9 f. The phrase, strengthened by πάντα, is repeated in Mt, but is omitted in Lk.

Two further examples of asyndeton are provided by 7b and 8b (cf. 6), and a third if γάρ is omitted in 8a (with W 245 247 sa geo¹, and b i k l q which have *autem* instead of *enim*). Together with the manifest presence of parallelism in 8 (cf. Burney, 66), these examples suggest the use of an Aramaic source in 5-8; cf. Black, 42.

Mk. xiii. 9-13   86. SAYINGS   Cf. Mt. xxiv. 9, 13 f.
ON PERSECUTION   (x. 17-22)
Lk. xxi. 12-19 (xii. 11 f.)

Introduced by ' But take heed to yourselves ', this section consists wholly of sayings : on being arraigned in courts, synagogues, and before governors and kings (9) ; on the guidance of the Holy Spirit when speaking in defence (11); on division within families (12); on being hated of all because of the Name (13a); on stedfastness to the end (13b). The sayings are arranged topically, and it is widely agreed that 10 (the preaching of the Gospel to all the nations) is inserted by Mark (v. Comm.). Lohmeyer, 270, sees signs of a poetical arrangement in the three strophes of four lines each, to which, he suggests, prose sentences have been attached in 10, 11b, and 13. The question whether the form of the sayings points to a Jewish or a Gentile environment calls for discussion, and also the place of the section in the structure of the discourse.

9   Βλέπετε δὲ ὑμεῖς ἑαυτούς· παραδώσουσιν ὑμᾶς εἰς συνέδρια καὶ εἰς συναγωγὰς δαρήσεσθε καὶ ἐπὶ ἡγεμόνων καὶ βασιλέων

9. The warning to take heed appears as in 5, 23, and 33, but here only is βλέπετε used c. acc.; cf 2 Jn. 8 where ἵνα μή c. subj. follows. In x. 17 Matthew has προσέχετε δὲ ἀπὸ τῶν ἀνθρώπων. For παραδίδωμι v. i. 14. There does not appear to be sufficient warrant for the view that παραδώσουσιν is here used absolutely as in i. 14 (cf. Turner, *JTS*, xxvi. 19) : ' They shall give you in charge, in sanhedrins and synagogues shall you be beaten . . .'; for in ix. 31, xiii. 12, and xiv. 41 it is used with εἰς. Nor is it desirable to take both εἰς συνέδρια and εἰς συναγωγάς with παραδώσουσιν (cf. Plummer, 296; Rawlinson, 185). On the whole, the parallelism preserved in the RV is to be preferred : ' They shall deliver you up to councils ; and in synagogues shall ye be beaten ; and before governors and kings shall ye stand . . .'; cf. Moffatt, Torrey, RSV. Certainly εἰς συναγωγὰς δαρήσεσθε reads strangely and it is not surprising that Matthew replaced it by ἐν ταῖς συναγωγαῖς αὐτῶν (x. 17). The construction has often been explained as pregnant: 'and ye shall be taken into synagogues and beaten '; cf. Swete, 300; Plummer, 296. But it may be due to assimilation to εἰς συνέδρια (Lagrange, 338), and, in any case, εἰς is freely used for ἐν in the Koine.

The συνέδρια (συνέδριον, xiv. 55, xv. 1*) are local Jewish councils, not meetings of the Great Sanhedrin at Jerusalem ; it must have been at the order of such courts that St. Paul five times received ' forty stripes save one '

(2 Cor. xi. 24). Cf. Lake, iv. 44, 57 f.; Moore, i. 260 f. In later Gk συνέδριον is used to denote a council or assembly of any kind (*VGT*, 604), but the use of the word here, in close connexion with συναγωγάς, suggests that Jewish courts of discipline are meant. For συναγωγή v. i. 21; δέρω xii. 3. The ἡγεμόνες* (Mt (10), Lk (2), Ac (6), 1 Pet. ii. 14**) are Roman provincial governors, procurators like Felix and Festus (Ac. xxiii. 24, xxiv. 27), and possibly also proconsuls like Sergius Paulus and Gallio, although for these Luke uses the term ἀνθύπατοι (Ac. xiii. 7 f., 12, xviii. 12, xix. 38**). Mark uses βασιλεύς freely, applying it to Herod Antipas (vi. 14), and it may be that by ἐπὶ . . . βασιλέων Antipas and Agrippa I (Ac. xxv. 13) are meant rather than the Emperor Nero. It is also possible that ἐπὶ ἡγεμόνων καὶ βασιλέων is used quite generally in the sense of Psa. cxviii. (cxix.) 46, καὶ ἐλάλουν ἐν τοῖς μαρτυρίοις σου ἐναντίον βασιλέων. There is thus no compelling reason to think that the historical horizon of the saying extends beyond Palestine, and, in fact, Wellhausen, 102, says explicitly, *Diese Instanzen führen nicht über Palästina hinaus.* So also Ed. Meyer, i. 130; Burkitt, *CB*, 147; Turner, 63; Allen, 157.

The view that the passage reflects the events of the Gentile Mission, and in particular the experiences of St. Paul, is supported by Bacon, *BGS*, 184; Streeter, *Oxford Studies*, 181; Bultmann, 129; Lohmeyer, 272; Bartlet, 353 f.; and other scholars.

σταθήσεσθε ἕνεκεν ἐμοῦ εἰς μαρτύριον αὐτοῖς. καὶ εἰς πάντα τὰ 10
ἔθνη πρῶτον δεῖ κηρυχθῆναι τὸ εὐαγγέλιον. καὶ ὅταν ἄγωσιν 11

This acute difference of opinion suggests that the interpretation is possible, but by no means certain. Current interests will account for the selection of these sayings, especially 13, and can have affected their form. In this case the prophecies of the Passion (x. 33 f.) would supply a parallel. But substantially the predictions of persecution are historical. Personal suffering anticipated by Jesus Himself, His knowledge of the fate of John and of many of the ancient prophets, and His forecasts of the fate of Jerusalem, not to speak of the opposition of the Jewish hierarchy, made it certain that His followers would be exposed to fierce persecution. And the sufferings would be for His sake (ἕνεκεν ἐμοῦ), i.e. not only because they belonged to His community, but as sharing in His Messianic task. With ἕνεκεν ἐμοῦ cf. viii. 35 and x. 29.

For εἰς μαρτύριον αὐτοῖς v. i. 44, vi. 11. The phrase is variously interpreted as meaning 'it will give you an opportunity to bear witness' (cf. Rawlinson, 185) and 'a testimony against them', that is, against the Jews (cf. Turner, 64). Important authorities connect the phrase with the following words καὶ εἰς πάντα τὰ ἔθνη: 'So you will be a testimony to Jews and to Gentiles' (Burkitt, CB, 147). So W Θ 108 124 127 131 157, and apparently c d ff g² i r¹ vg (1 MS.) sys bo geo arm, and most of these MSS. attest δέ after πρῶτον in 10. Burkitt is inclined to accept this reading,[1] but on doubtful grounds. After ἕνεκεν ἐμοῦ, the phrase εἰς μαρτύριον αὐτοῖς looks secondary and rather like an attempt to prepare the way for the insertion of 10. Cf. Burney, PL, 118 f.

Mt. xxiv. 9a, Τότε παραδώσουσιν ὑμᾶς εἰς θλῖψιν, merely summarizes Mk. xiii. 9, but Mt. x. 17 f. follows it closely.

Lk. xxi. 12 f. is probably taken from an independent source; cf. Taylor, BTG, 104; Manson, SJ, 327. Here ἀποβήσεται ὑμῖν εἰς μαρτύριον means, 'You will have an opportunity to bear testimony'.

10. This verse is widely regarded as an insertion made by Mark (or, less probably, a redactor) in his source; cf. J. Weiss, 276 f., Die Schr.⁴ 193; Burney, PL, 118 f.; Lohmeyer, 272; Blunt, 239. The case for this view is strong, and probably, if it were kept separate from that of the historical character of the saying, it would be accepted even more widely. The arguments are as follows: (1) The vocabulary is wholly and distinctively Markan: for τὰ ἔθνη v. x. 33; πρῶτον iii. 37; δεῖ viii. 31; κηρύσσω i. 4; εὐαγγέλιον i. 1; κ. τὸ εὐαγγέλιον i. 14, xiv. 9, xvi. [15]*; (2) 9 and 11 are very closely connected in thought and linked together by the catchword παραδίδωμι; (3) The prose sentence 10 interrupts the poetic arrangement visible in 9, 11-13; cf. Lohmeyer, 269 f.; Burney, PL, 118 f.²; (4) The introduction of 10 appears to be suggested by the subject-matter of 9 and 11. On these grounds the presumption is that Mark has added 10 to his source.

The right appraisal of 10 is another matter It appears as a saying, but it looks more like a comment expressing what Mark believed to be the mind of Jesus. The point at issue is the attitude of Jesus to the Gentile Mission. Any opinion we form on this question must take account of two apparently contradictory considerations. On the one hand, in view of the problem faced by the primitive Church over the question of the evangelization of the Gentiles, it is difficult to think that a saying so explicit as Mk. xiii. 10 was

[1] Couchoud, JTS, xxxiv. 126 f., also would put a stop after τὰ ἔθνη and then read (with the support of k and b) ἀλλὰ θαρσεῖτε, πρῶτον δεῖ . . .
[2] Burney suggests that the originality of εἰς μαρτύριον αὐτοῖς (9) and καὶ πατὴρ τέκνον (12) may be suspected as being merely half-lines and καὶ εἰς πάντα τὰ ἔθνη κτλ. (10) as having no parallel line.

ὑμᾶς παραδιδόντες, μὴ προμεριμνᾶτε τί λαλήσητε, ἀλλ' ὃ ἐὰν
δοθῇ ὑμῖν ἐν ἐκείνῃ τῇ ὥρᾳ τοῦτο λαλεῖτε, οὐ γάρ ἐστε ὑμεῖς
12 οἱ λαλοῦντες ἀλλὰ τὸ πνεῦμα τὸ ἅγιον. καὶ παραδώσει ἀδελφὸς

known. Cf. Cadoux, 142. On the other hand, and in spite of Mt. x. 5, 23, xv. 24, it is hard to believe that the vision of Jesus was narrower than that of the prophets (cf. Isa. xlix. 6, 12, lii. 10, lx. 6). So R. N. Flew, *JHC*, 85; Schniewind, 169, who cites Isa. lii. 7, lxi. 1, lx. 6, Psa. xcvi. 2 f. The resolution of this antithesis is the view that Mark truly represents the mind of Jesus (cf. vii. 27a) but does not give His *ipsissima verba*; and the deeper reason for His reserve must be found in His preoccupation with action, the fulfilment, namely, of His Messianic ministry of suffering, death, and resurrection. His reserve is a further consequence of His 'Messianic Secret'. Luke omits the saying. Matthew also omits it in x. 17-22, but recasts it in xxiv. 14. The Gospel is defined as that ' of the Kingdom '. With εἰς μαρτύριον he has πᾶσιν τοῖς ἔθνεσιν and to the saying he appends καὶ τότε ἥξει τὸ τέλος.

11. When put under arrest, they are to have no anxieties about their defence; the Holy Spirit will give them the right words to speak. With ὅταν ἄγωσιν cf. 7, 14; παραδίδωμι 9. προμεριμνάω**, ' to be anxious beforehand ', may be a Markan coinage; not Cl., nor in LXX, nor in Pap., and found only in later ecclesiastical writers. Matthew uses μεριμνάω, and Luke the classical προμελετάω, ' to practise beforehand '. What is prohibited is not thought, but anxious care; cf. Bengel (on Mt. x. 19), *Non omnis praeparatio ex eo nobis prohibetur*. They are not to ask, ' What am I to say ? '. The subj. λαλήσητε implies the deliberative subj. in the direct question.

The idea of testimony as something *given* lies far back in the OT; cf. Ex. iv. 1 ff.; Num. xxii. 35; Jer. i. 9, Ἰδοὺ δέδωκα τοὺς λόγους μου εἰς τὸ στόμα σου. In the saying this idea is

given prominence by ὃ ἐὰν δοθῇ ὑμῖν which forms a kind of *casus pendens* resumed later in τοῦτο. Cf. i. 34 (D), vi. 16, vii. 20; *v.* Lagrange, xcvi; Howard, ii. 424; Black, 36. With ἐν ἐκείνῃ τῇ ὥρᾳ in Mk cf. ἐν αὐτῇ τῇ ὥρᾳ in the Q form of the saying in Lk. xii. 12. For the possibility that the two phrases may be different renderings of the same Aramaic expression *v.* Black, 78-81. The initial position of the verb in οὐ γάρ ἐστε ὑμεῖς οἱ λαλοῦντες also suggests translation Greek (cf. Mt. x. 20, οὐ γὰρ ὑμεῖς ἐστε οἱ λαλοῦντες). This conjunction of Semitic ideas and points of syntax strongly suggests that an original saying spoken in Aramaic stands behind Mark's version; and this conclusion must stand whatever explanation is given of the difficulties which centre in the phrase τὸ πνεῦμα τὸ ἅγιον.

For the references to the Holy Spirit in Mk *v.* the notes on i. 8 and 10. The form τὸ πνεῦμα τὸ ἅγιον is found in iii. 29 and xii. 36*.

The question at issue is whether the reference to the Holy Spirit belongs to the original form of the saying or whether it is secondary, reflecting later Christian views. In this connexion the Synoptic variants are important. Mt. x. 20 has τὸ πνεῦμα τοῦ πατρὸς ὑμῶν τὸ λαλοῦν ἐν ὑμῖν. In the Q form Luke has τὸ ἅγιον πνεῦμα (xii. 12) and in the form parallel to Mk. xiii. 11 ἐγὼ γὰρ δώσω ὑμῖν στόμα καὶ σοφίαν (xxi. 15), probably from L. At first sight Lk. xxi. 15 invites confidence; it comes from a primitive Aramaic source, and, in view of Luke's special interest in the doctrine of the Spirit, it is difficult to think that he would have replaced a reference to the Spirit by ἐγὼ δώσω ὑμῖν . . . (*v.* xii. 12). Cf. C. K. Barrett, 131 f. The saying, then, was current at a very early time (at Caesarea) without a reference to the Spirit. It is difficult, however, to

ἀδελφὸν εἰς θάνατον καὶ πατὴρ τέκνον, καὶ ἐπαναϲτήϲονται
τέκνα ἐπὶ ΓΟΝΕῖϲ καὶ θανατώϲουϲιν αὐτούϲ· καὶ ἔϲεϲθε μιϲού- 13

accept this form as original. It has a distinctly Johannine ring and appears to reflect the doctrine of the Exalted Christ. But the Markan form has difficulties also. The Messianic Age was thought of as a time when the Spirit of God would be poured out freely (Isa. xi. 1 f., xlii. 1, lxi. 1, Joel ii. 28 f., etc.). Cf. Schniewind, 169 f. And the first Christians had the consciousness of speaking and acting in the power of the Spirit. But this fact can be interpreted in two ways, either as explaining the subsequent introduction of the reference to the Spirit into the saying, or as confirming its originality. The determining consideration is : when did Jesus believe the Messianic Age would have dawned for His disciples ?. In a true sense it had dawned already in His exorcisms and His works of healing, and in this dawning the disciples were privileged to share (cf. Lk. x. 23 f. = Mt. xiii. 16 f.) ; but the paucity of His references to the Holy Spirit,[1] and His concentration on His Messianic action and destiny, suggest that He thought of the New Age as dependent on His death and resurrection. Cf. Jn. vii. 39. The time of suffering and persecution belongs to the ' birth-pangs ' of the New Age. Cf. Mk. xiii. 8. This view does not mean that Jesus could not speak of the gift of the Spirit to His disciples in any sense before the fullness of the Messianic Age ; it suggests that the gift would be wholly exceptional. And this is the impression which xiii. 11 leaves. Not a universal outpouring of the Spirit is promised, but an endowment for a special situation (ἐν ἐκείνῃ τῇ ὥρᾳ). It is a gift for witness-bearing.

Of the terms used that of Matthew is more likely to be original. The phrases τὸ πνεῦμα τὸ ἅγιον and τὸ πνεῦμα are more reminiscent of the Epistles and the Acts ; τὸ πνεῦμα τοῦ πατρὸς ὑμῶν is more Jewish-Christian and is, in fact, unique in the NT ; cf. McNeile, 140. So closely does Matthew follow Mk in x. 19 f. that it must be presumed that the change to τὸ πνεῦμα τοῦ πατρὸς ὑμῶν τὸ λαλοῦν ἐν ὑμῖν is due to his knowledge of another version, probably Q, which preserved the original phrase.[2]

12 f. It can hardly be accidental that παραδίδωμι appears a third time in 12 (cf. 9, 11). The saying speaks of strife within families issuing in betrayal and death and is based on Mic. vii. 6, διότι υἱὸς ἀτιμάζει πατέρα, θυγάτηρ ἐπαναστήσεται ἐπὶ τὴν μητέρα αὐτῆς, νύμφη ἐπὶ τὴν πενθερὰν αὐτῆς, ἐχθροὶ πάντες ἀνδρὸς οἱ ἐν τῷ οἴκῳ αὐτοῦ. ἐπανίστημι*, Mt. x. 21**, mid. ' to rise up against ' ; Cl., LXX, VGT, 229 ; θανατόω, xiv. 55*, Mt. x. 21, Lk. xxi. 16, ' to doom to death ' ; Cl., LXX ; τέκνον, ii. 5 ; γονεύς*.

A parallel version in Q describes a crisis brought about by the ministry of Jesus when families are divided, three against two and two against three (Lk. xii. 52 f. = Mt. x. 35 f.). Of this saying Mk. xiii. 12 is a secondary form which appears to reflect the conditions which obtained during the Neronian persecution. One is strongly reminded of the *delatores* of later times who laid information against Christians before the imperial authorities. Cf. the reply of Trajen concerning those who were accused to Pliny as Christians (*qui Christiani ad te delati fuerant, Epp.* x. 96 f.). In any case, the saying conforms to common apocalyptic expectations. Cf. 4 Ezra v. 9, *Et amici omnes semetipsos expugnabunt*, vi. 24, *Et erit in illo tempore debellabunt amici amicos ut inimici*; Jubilees xxiii. 19; Apoc.

[1] Cf. E. F. Scott, *The Holy Spirit in the NT*, 77-80 ; V. Taylor, *The Holy Spirit* (Headingley Lectures, 1937), 53-5 ; Flew, *JHC*, 70 f. ; Barrett, 153-62.
[2] Probably τὸ ἅγιον πνεῦμα in Lk. xii. 12 is a Lukan variant.

μενοι ὑπὸ πάντων διὰ τὸ ὄνομά μου. ὁ δὲ ὑπομείνας εἰς τέλος οὗτος σωθήσεται.

Bar. lxx. 3; and in the Mishnah, Soṭah, ix. 15 (Danby, 306). Cf. Allen, 158; Manson, SJ, 120 f.

The view that 12 is a saying of Jesus which reflects the conditions of a later time is confirmed by the terms of 13a. Here it is prophesied that the disciples will be hated of all men (ἔσεσθε μισούμενοι ὑπὸ πάντων) because of their loyalty to Christ's name (διὰ τὸ ὄνομά μου, cf. vi. 14, ix. 37, etc.). Cf. Tacitus, Ann. xv. 44, quos per flagitia invisos vulgus Christianos appellabat; Justin, Apol. i. 4, ἐφ᾽ ἡμῶν τὸ ὄνομα ὡς ἔλεγχον λαμβάνετε; Tertullian, Apol. 2, Id solum expectatur quod odio publico necessarium est, confessio nominis; and the comments of Polycrates and Theophylact on 1 Pet. iv. 14, εἰ ὀνειδίζεσθε ἐν ὀνόματι Χριστοῦ, μακάριοι . . . (cf. Swete, 303). Doubtless this evidence belongs to a later period, when Christians suffered 'for the Name', but the idea is already present in Mk. xiii. 13a and the question to be answered is how far what Jesus said has been transposed into another key. That He foretold the persecution of His disciples is shown by 9, 11, and that He should have prophesied hatred as their portion is not in itself incredible. It is the prediction of universal hatred because of His name which suggests later interpretation rather than His actual words. Elsewhere, when He speaks of His name it is of action for His sake (ix. 37) or in reliance upon His authority (ix. 39) or in loyalty to Him (ix. 41) that He is thinking. Here it is a question of the hostile action of enemies provoked by His person (διὰ τὸ ὄνομά μου) against His disciples. The point of view is that of Mark himself when he accounts for the hostile interest of Antipas by saying φανερὸν γὰρ ἐγένετο τὸ ὄνομα αὐτοῦ (vi. 14).

13b is of the same tenor. It is some-times said that Luke paraphrases Mk in the saying ἐν τῇ ὑπομονῇ ὑμῶν κτήσεσθε τὰς ψυχὰς ὑμῶν (xxi. 19). So Swete, 303; Plummer, 297. It is far more just to say that Luke gives us the original utterance, and Mark a form adapted to contemporary apocalyptic. Cf. 4 Ezra vi. 25, Et erit omnis qui derelictus fuerit ex omnibus istis quibus praedixi tibi, ipse saluabitur et uidebit salutare meum et finem saeculi mei. The upshot of our inquiry is that we are near the actual words of Jesus in 9, 11, but a greater distance from them in 12 f.

For the periphrastic fut. v. Blass, 203 f.; WM, 438-40; cf. xiii. 25; μισέω*; ὑπομένω*. For σώζω v. iii. 4. Here the verb is used in an eschatological sense; cf. x. 26. It is improbable, however, that εἰς τέλος is used of 'the End', as in 7; it is used adverbially with the meaning 'finally', 'to the end', and describes an endurance which is complete. Cf. 1 Chron. xxviii. 9, 2 Chron. xxxi. 1, Psa. xlviii. (xlix.) 10, Job xx. 7; Lk. xviii. 5, Jn. xiii. 1, 1 Thess. ii. 16.

Matthew's reproduction of 12 f. in x. 21 f. and again of 13 in xxiv. 9b, 13, is almost verbatim, but his addition of τῶν ἐθνῶν to πάντων in xxiv. 9b illustrates the further development of the tradition. Luke inserts 12, 13a in his non-Markan source, Lk. xxi. 12-15, 18 f. and thereby alters its tone; for, while the atmosphere of Mk. xiii. 9-13 is one of foreboding, unrelieved except by the promise of eschatological salvation, Lk. xxi. 12-15, 18 f., presupposes a successful defence. Not a hair of their head will perish and in their endurance they will win their souls. Cf. V. Taylor, BTG, 105 f.; Manson, SJ, 327 f. This difference supports the view that, beginning with genuine logia of Jesus (9, 11), Mk. xiii. 9-13 is progressively coloured by apocalyptic expectations.

Mk. xiii. 14-20   87. THE ABOMINATION   Cf. Mt. xxiv. 15-22
                         OF DESOLATION   (Lk. xxi. 20-4)

This section introduces a new topic in the series of apocalyptic woes, namely the appearance of ' the Abomination of Desolation ', with the consequences that follow, the necessity of instant flight, unprecedented horrors for women and children, a tribulation shortened in the mercy of God for the sake of His Elect. What ' the Abomination of Desolation ' is, and whether the phrase originally belonged to the prophecy, are questions discussed in the Commentary. It must also be considered to what extent genuine sayings of Jesus are used, how far their original meaning can be inferred, whether they have been reinterpreted, and, above all whether the apocalyptic colouring in 19 f. is that of a later time. Matthew's version of the section is manifestly secondary. Lk. xxi. 20-4 is probably based on an independent non-Markan source, and in its present form contains extracts from Mk in 21a and 23a.

Ὅταν δὲ ἴδητε τὸ βΔέλυγμΑ τῆc ἐρΗΜώcεωc ἑστηκότα ὅπου 14
οὐ δεῖ, ὁ ἀναγινώσκων νοείτω, τότε οἱ ἐν τῇ Ἰουδαίᾳ φευγέτωσαν

14. For ὅταν ἴδητε v. 7, 11, 29. The phrase τὸ βδέλυγμα τῆς ἐρημώσεως comes from Dan. ix. 27, xi. 31, xii. 11, where it refers to the heathen altar which Antiochus Epiphanes built over the altar of the burnt offering in 168 B.C.; cf. 1 Macc. i. 54, ᾠκοδόμησαν βδέλυγμα ἐρημώσεως ἐπὶ τὸ θυσιαστήριον, 59, vi. 7. The original reference is to a profanation of the Temple rather then its destruction. Some commentators hold that in the source which Mark used the phrase referred to the attempt of the emperor Caligula in A.D. 40 to place his statue in the Temple, a profanation which was delayed by the proconsul Petronius, and averted by the assassination of the mad emperor in Jan. 41. So Bacon, 93, 99; Torrey, 262; Manson, SJ, 329 f. Cf. Josephus, Ant. xviii. 8. Against this view is the fact that the threat did not mature (cf. Goguel, 427 f., in reply to A. Piganiol) and the masc. participle ἑστηκότα which suggests a personal agent rather than a statue. Accordingly, most commentators see in 14a reference to Anti-Christ; e.g. Klostermann, 151; Loisy, ii. 420; Lohmeyer, 276; McNeile, 348; Streeter, 492; Branscomb, 237. Substantially, this view is correct, but the mysterious terms used, and parallel features shared

with 2 Thess. ii. 3-10, suggest that a manifestation of Anti-Christ in expected historical events is contemplated.

The intentional change from the neuter τὸ βδέλυγμα to the masc. ἑστηκότα, the vague local statement ὅπου οὐ δεῖ, the warning ὁ ἀναγινώσκων νοείτω, and the general atmosphere of reserve which marks the passage, must all be taken into account. And if ἐρημώσεως* is taken over with the phrase from Dan., it is possible that it is welcomed because it suggests more than the profanation of the Temple. Reconsideration must also be given to the Lukan parallel (xxi. 20) which definitely mentions the investing of Jerusalem by armed forces.

The crucial phrase is ὁ ἀναγινώσκων νοείτω. From the time of Colani onwards this phrase has often been explained as a warning taken from the apocalyptic fly-sheet which Mark is using; cf. Klostermann, 151; Ed. Meyer, i. 129; etc. Alternatively, and perhaps more probably, it is interpreted as a pointed allusion to the Book of Dan. made explicit in Mt. xxiv. 15, τὸ ῥηθὲν διὰ Δανιὴλ τοῦ προφήτου. Cf. McNeile, 348; Rawlinson, 188. But it is doubtful if even this explanation is complete. The paren-

15 εἰς τὰ ὄρη, ὁ ᵀ ἐπὶ τοῦ δώματος μὴ καταβάτω εἰς τὴν οἰκίαν
16 μηδὲ εἰσελθάτω τι ἆραι ἐκ τῆς οἰκίας αὐτοῦ, καὶ ὁ εἰς τὸν ἀγρὸν

15 δὲ

thesis reads more like a dark hint, a clue to Christian eyes but an enigma to others, presumably the imperial authorities. The situation is like that to which 2 Thess. ii. 6 f. and Apoc. xiii. 18 (the number of the beast) belong. But it is more tense. The Temple which could be named in 2 Thess. ii. 4 can now only be indicated by the cryptic phrase ὅπου οὐ δεῖ (Mt. xxiv. 15, ἐν τόπῳ ἁγίῳ). The explanation may well be that, in Rome during a time of persecution, when Christians were crucified and burnt (Tacitus, Ann. xv. 44), more precise language was politically dangerous. It is not improbable, therefore, that τὸ βδέλυγμα τῆς ἐρημώσεως and ὅπου οὐ δεῖ have replaced an original reference to armies surrounding Jerusalem and menacing the Temple comparable to Lk. xxi. 20, 24, or that, alternatively, both Mk. xiii. 14 and Lk. xxi. 20 are independent versions of the same prediction; cf. Manson, SJ, 330. The reference to the flight of the people of Judaea to the hills, τότε οἱ ἐν τῇ 'Ιουδαίᾳ φευγέτωσαν εἰς τὰ ὄρη (14b), and the warnings about the man on his house-top (15) and the labourer in the field (16), confirm this interpretation. These sayings suggest war-time conditions; they are not incompatible with the coming of Anti-Christ provided (as in 2 Thess. and the Apoc.) his parousia is manifest in history. For ἡ 'Ιουδαία v, i. 5; εἰς τὰ ὄρη iii. 13, vi. 46, etc. (sing.), v. 5 (plur.); φεύγω v. 14.

This explanation would be more readily accepted were it not that Lk. xxi. 20 has been so widely interpreted as an ex eventu recast of Mk. xiii. 14. But this exegesis needs reconsideration on two grounds: (1) Lk. xxi. 20 belongs to a non-Markan source, xxi. 20-36 (supplemented by Markan additions in 21a, 23a, 26b-7, 29-33), which is earlier than Mk. xiii (cf. A. M.

Perry, The Sources of Luke's Passion-Narrative (1920), 38; V. Taylor, BTG, 109-25; Manson, SJ, 328-37; Dodd, Jl. of Rom. Studies, xxxvii. 47-54); and (2) there is a greater readiness to recognize that Jesus did predict the destruction of Jerusalem and the Temple (cf. C. J. Cadoux, 266-79; M. Goguel, 428).

Eusebius, HE, iii. 5. 3, says that the Christians of Jerusalem were warned before the war by a prophetic revelation to leave the city and retire to Pella in Peraea. This tradition may be historical, but the 'revelation' cannot be identified with 14b.

15 f. These sayings vividly depict the crisis. Instant flight is necessary. The man on his housetop is to depart without entering into his house to take away any of his possessions (Lk. xvii. 31, τὰ σκεύη αὐτοῦ), and the field labourer is not even to turn back for his discarded outer garment. δῶμα* is the flat roof, to which men retire for sleep (1 Kgdms. ix. 25), for worship (Jer. xix. 13, Ac. x. 9), to watch (Isa. xxii. 1), or to proclaim tidings (Mt. x. 27). μὴ καταβάτω appears to suggest that the man is not to descend at all, and Torrey, 303, omits καταβάτω . . . μηδέ as an assimilation to Mt. xxiv. 17. But probably, as a Markan redundancy, εἰς τὴν οἰκίαν should be read with A D W Θ et al. fam. 1 fam. 13 28 565 579 700 1071 al. pler. a ff i l n q r¹·² aur vg sys hl aeth arm; cf. Turner, JTS, xxix. 9. Lagrange, 341, suggests that the μηδέ, which follows, is the equivalent of καί in a consecutive sense, and that the construction, while not unknown to MGk, has a Semitic flavour. This suggestion is supported by the asyndeton in 15a, if δέ is omitted with B F H 1342 c sa boc (καί is read by D Θ 565 700 et al. a ff i k sys pe aeth arm Aug), and by the parallelism in 15 f.

μὴ ἐπιστρεψάτω εἰς τὰ ὀπίσω ἆραι τὸ ἱμάτιον αὐτοῦ. οὐαὶ δὲ 17 ταῖς ἐν γαστρὶ ἐχούσαις καὶ ταῖς θηλαζούσαις ἐν ἐκείναις ταῖς ἡμέραις. προσεύχεσθε δὲ ἵνα μὴ γένηται χειμῶνος· ἔσονται γὰρ 18 19

ὁ εἰς τὸν ἀγρόν is the field labourer. Mt and Lk have ἐν c. dat. ἀγρός (v. v. 14) appears to have been a favourite word with translators from Hebrew or Aramaic; cf. VGT, 7. Again, εἰς τὰ ὀπίσω, Lk. ix. 62, xvii. 31, Jn. vi. 66, xviii. 6, xx. 14**, is frequently used in the LXX to render אַחֵר ' behind '. All these points, each small in itself, combine to suggest that 15 f. does not stand far removed from a Semitic original. For ἐπιστρέφω v. iv. 12; ἱμάτιον ii. 21.

As observed in the note on 14, the sayings appear to reflect war-time conditions. They seem also to be spoken from the standpoint of the countryside, for in Jerusalem it would have been more natural to speak of the townsman or the artisan rather than the farm labourer. Either, then, isolated sayings have been introduced into this context by a compiler (so Lohmeyer, 276) or the discourse belongs to an earlier period. The position of 15 f. in Lk (xvii. 31) is consistent with either suggestion. In Mk the Mount of Olives is indicated by xiii. 3, but it is not excluded that sayings from other situations have been included in the discourse, and 14b (' Then let those in Judaea . . .') suggests a locality outside Jerusalem. In Lk. xxi. 20-4 the sayings are omitted because they have been used earlier, but probably also because the L tradition did not connect them with Jerusalem. The further saying attached to them in Lk. xvii. 32, μνημονεύετε τῆς γυναικὸς Λώτ, strengthens the suggestion of hurried flight. Cf. Manson, SJ, 145; Cadoux, 274.

17 f. οὐαί, xiv. 21*, ' alas ! ', ' woe ! '. D and sa omit δέ, as in Lk. xxi. 23, v. the note on 15. The phrase ἐν γαστρὶ ἔχουσα is found in Herodotus (iii. 32) and in medical writers from Hippocrates onwards. Found also in the LXX, it appears in the NT in Mt. i. 18, 23, xxiv. 19, Lk. xxi. 23, 1 Thess. v. 3, Apoc. xii. 2**, and freely in the papyri (VGT, 121). θηλάζω*, Mt. xxi. 16, xxiv. 19, Lk. xi. 27, xxi. 23**, ' to suckle ' or ' suck ', can be used either of the mother or the child; Cl., LXX, Pap. (VGT, 291). Forgetfulness of this fact accounts for the reading θηλαζομέναις in D and 28. For ἐν ἐκείναις ταῖς ἡμέραις, here and in 24, v. i. 9.

In keeping with this cry of woe is the counsel to pray that the θλῖψις (18) may not happen (γένηται) in winter. The subj. may be final, but it is more probable that the clause gives the substance of the prayer as in xiv. 35, 38. Cf. the constr. εἶπεν ἵνα c. subj., iii. 9. χειμῶνος* is gen. of time; cf. Mt. ii. 14, Jn. iii. 2, Ac. ix. 24. The word (Cl., LXX, Pap.) can mean ' winter ' or ' stormy weather '. Matthew interprets the subject of γένηται as ἡ φυγὴ ὑμῶν, and this may be correct, but it is also possible that the circumstances as a whole, the θλῖψις, are in mind. Matthew also adds μηδὲ σαββάτῳ (xxiv. 20). Luke omits 18 but inserts 17 in his non-Markan source. Here the parallel is quite general, ὅτι ἡμέραι ἐκδικήσεως αὗταί εἰσιν τοῦ πλησθῆναι πάντα τὰ γεγραμμένα (xxi. 22).

The question whether 17 f. is an authentic saying or an apocalyptic development of the tradition is not easy to decide. The thought that the sufferings of the End Time fall heavily upon mothers and children is naturally common in apocalyptic forecasts. Cf. 4 Ezra vi. 21, Et annicula infantes loquentur uocibus suis, et praegnantes immaturos parient infantes trium et quattuor mensium et uiuent et scirtiabuntur. But in such forecasts, as here, the emphasis falls on the bizarre, and monstrous and untimely births are described. There is nothing of this kind in 17 f.; on the contrary, the

αἱ ἡμέραι ἐκεῖναι θλῖψιc οἷα ογ γέγονεν τοιαύτη ἀπ' ἀρχῆc
20 κτίcεωc ἣν ἔκτιcεν ὁ θεὸς ἕωc τογ νῦν καὶ οὐ μὴ γένηται. καὶ
εἰ μὴ ἐκολόβωσεν Κύριος τὰς ἡμέρας, οὐκ ἂν ἐσώθη πᾶσα σάρξ.

pathos is restrained and the description true to the conditions of war. Moreover, there is a parallel picture in Lk. xxiii. 29, ὅτι ἰδοὺ ἔρχονται ἡμέραι ἐν αἷς ἐροῦσιν· μακάριαι αἱ στεῖραι, καὶ αἱ κοιλίαι αἱ οὐκ ἐγέννησαν, καὶ μαστοὶ οἳ οὐκ ἔθρεψαν. On the whole, it must be said that the hypothesis of apocalyptic colouring is not made out so far as 17 f. is concerned. Whether this is true of 19 f. is another matter.

19 f. The opening words (ἔσονται γάρ) read like a homiletical comment on the preceding sayings; cf. the use of γάρ in i. 22b, v. 8, vi. 52, vii. 3, xvi. 8, etc. With direct reference to 17, αἱ ἡμέραι ἐκεῖναι are described as θλῖψις (v. iv. 17); cf. 24. The interpretation is suggested by Dan. xii. 1, ἐκείνη ἡ ἡμέρα θλίψεως οἵα οὐκ ἐγενήθη (Theodotion, γέγονεν) ἀφ' οὗ ἐγενήθησαν ἕως τῆς ἡμέρας ἐκείνης. The word is especially appropriate to describe the tribulations which were expected to precede the End, as its use in the Apoc. of St. Jn shows (i. 9, vii. 14). The θλῖψις is one of unparalleled ferocity. The position of τοιαύτη (v. iv. 33, HS², 13) is strange. Swete, 308, says that it is perhaps unique, and that the parallels suggested by Grimm-Thayer in 1 Cor. xv. 48 and 2 Cor. x. 11 are not exact. Possibly this word comes in as an afterthought after the use of the words οἵα οὐ γέγονεν suggested by Dan. Hawkins, HS², 134, points to the similar order in Gen. xli. 19, Ex. ix. 24, xi. 6, and to οἷα . . . οὕτως in the best texts of Mk. ix. 3. It is not necessary, therefore, with Torrey, 303, to see in τοιαύτη an indication of an Aramaic original (cf. Howard, ii. 435; Grant, EG, 118), though the Semitic colouring of the verse is unmistakable.

The tautology in ἀπ' ἀρχῆς κτίσεως ἣν ἔκτισεν ὁ θεός is Semitic, and is characteristic of Mark's style (cf. 20). Cf. also vii. 13, xii. 23, and for other examples of tautology ii. 19, iv. 30,

xi. 28, xii. 14. As is usual, Matthew simplifies his source, θλῖψις μεγάλη, οἷα οὐκ ἐγένετο ἀπ' ἀρχῆς κόσμου (xxiv. 21). With ἀπ' ἀρχῆς κτίσεως cf. x. 6; κτίζω*; ἕως τοῦ νῦν*. Cf. ἀπὸ τοῦ νῦν, Lk-Ac (6), Pl (1); ἄχρι τοῦ νῦν, Pl (2).

Not only is it emphasized that there has never been a θλῖψις of the kind, it is insisted that there never will be one (καὶ οὐ μὴ γένηται, v. xiii. 2). This assertion is much too emphatic for a siege; it is clear that the thought of 19 is eschatological. This is undoubtedly true of 20. Here the idea found in many apocalyptic writings, that in His mercy and for the sake of the elect God has shortened the period of tribulation for mankind (πᾶσα σάρξ), is strongly expressed. Cf. Dan. xii. 7, 1 Enoch lxxx. 2, 4 Ezra iv. 26, Apoc. Bar. xx. 1, Ep. Barn. iv. 3. Cf. Billerbeck, i. 953.

κολοβόω (bis)*, Mt. xxiv. 22 (bis)**, ' to curtail ', ' amputate '; Cl., LXX, Pap. For σώζω, here used eschatologically as in xiii. 13, v. iii. 4; σάρξ x. 8; ἐκλέγομαι*. By ' the Elect ' (οἱ ἐκλεκτοί, xiii. 22, 27*) the members of the Christian community are meant. The idea is rooted in the OT conception of God's choice of Israel to be His covenant people (Psa. civ. (cv.) 6, Isa. xliii. 20; cf. Isa. xlii. 1, lxv. 9). In 1 Enoch (i. 1, xxxviii. 2-4) the term is applied to ' the righteous ' who will inherit the Kingdom, and in the NT it describes members of the Christian community (Lk. xviii. 7, Rom. viii. 33, Col. iii. 12, 2 Tim. ii. 10, 1 Pet. i. 1, ii. 9) and in the sing. is used of Christ (Lk. xxiii. 35, Jn. i. 34 (אַ* e syᶜ)). With τοὺς ἐκλεκτοὺς οὓς ἐξελέξατο cf. ἀπ' ἀρχῆς κτίσεως ἣν ἔκτισεν ὁ θεός in 19. As before, Matthew avoids the redundancy; he also replaces the active (ἐκολόβωσεν) by the passive.

Luke's version is entirely different. He speaks of ἀνάγκη μεγάλη ἐπὶ τῆς γῆς καὶ ὀργὴ τῷ λαῷ τούτῳ, of massacre

ἀλλὰ διὰ τοὺς ἐκλεκτοὺς οὓς ἐξελέξατο ἐκολόβωσεν τὰς ἡμέρας.

and captivity, and the treading down of Jerusalem ἄχρι οὗ πληρωθῶσιν καιροὶ ἐθνῶν (xxi. 23b, 24; cf. Rom. xi. 25).

In respect of ideas and idiom the Semitic character of 20 is unmistakable. As already shown, the shortening of a divinely allotted span and the idea of the Elect are fundamentally Jewish conceptions, and the use of the anarthrous Κύριος is characteristic of OT quotations (cf. i. 3, xi. 9, xii. 11, 29 f., 36 f.) and appears freely in Lk. i. 5-ii. 52 (8 times).[1] Moreover, two Hebrew idioms are combined in οὐκ ἂν ἐσώθη πᾶσα σάρξ: οὐκ ... πᾶσα has the force of בֹּל ... לֹא = ' no one ' and πᾶσα σάρξ = כָּל-בָּשָׂר, ' all men '. Cf. Blass, 162, 178. The latter construction is not without analogies in Greek (cf. Moulton, ii. 22, 433 f.), but the coincidence with the other points men-

tioned is too striking to be ignored. Cf. Jer. xii. 12.

But, although Jewish in origin, 20 is not necessarily an authentic saying. On the contrary, like 19 (v. supra), it appears to be secondary; for, while Jesus uses eschatological ideas, He makes no use of apocalyptic speculations. Cf. Bultmann, JW, 39. The belief that God will shorten the tribulation for the Elect's sake is otherwise not found in His teaching, and probably represents the point of view of Mark himself or an earlier compiler. The use of οἱ ἐκλεκτοί for members of the Christian community supports this inference. It seems likely, therefore, that 19 f. is an early homiletical expansion of genuine logia in 15-18. What Jesus had said is interpreted in terms of contemporary apocalyptic.

Mk. xiii. 21-3   88. WARNINGS AGAINST   Cf. Mt. xxiv. 23-5
                           FALSE CHRISTS AND   (xxiv. 26)
                               PROPHETS   (Lk. xvii. 23)

In the introductory note to 85 it was suggested that 5 f. and 21-3 form a doublet. The presumption is that Mark has taken them from two different sources or groups. The present passage is fuller than 5 f., but is probably less original. The presence of the reference to ' the Elect ' suggests that it belongs to the source from which 14-20 has been derived (cf. also 27). That a saying of this kind goes back to Jesus is suggested by the parallel in Q (Lk. xvii. 23 = Mt. xxiv. 26), but in Mk (still more in Mt. xxiv. 23 f.) it is coloured by the same apocalyptic ideas which appear in 19 f. Whether 23 is added by the compiler needs to be considered in view of the direct address (cf. 5, 9, 33) and the use of the first person in προείρηκα. It is by this time clear that Mk. xiii is a compilation formed from different groups of sayings.

Καὶ τότε ἐάν τις ὑμῖν εἴπῃ ῎Ιδε ὧδε ὁ χριστός ῎Ιδε ἐκεῖ, 21
μὴ πιστεύετε· ἐγερθήσονται γὰρ [ψευδόχριστοι καὶ] ψευδοπρο- 22

21 f. Linked together by γάρ (δέ, א C), the two sayings differ completely in character and probably in origin: 21 is a genuine saying of Jesus attested by a parallel version in Q (Lk. xvii. 23 = Mt. xxiv. 26); 22 closely resembles the apocalyptic passage 19 f.

and, like that passage, is secondary and homiletical.

τότε (cf. 14, 26 f.) attaches the saying to its present context. For ἴδε v. ii. 24; ἐάν c. subj. i. 40; ὁ Χριστός i. 1; πιστεύω i. 15. The original significance of the saying is manifest in Q, where

[1] The past tenses also suggest a purpose already determined in the counsels of God.

φῆται καὶ Δώcoυcιν cημεῖα καὶ τέρατα πρὸς τὸ ἀποπλανᾶν εἰ
23 δυνατὸν τοὺς ἐκλεκτούς· ὑμεῖς δὲ βλέπετε· προείρηκα ὑμῖν
πάντα.

it is ' a command to observe strict
neutrality ' (Manson, *SJ*, 142) amidst
conflicting Messianic rumours, since
the coming of the Son of Man will
have the swiftness of lightning (Lk.
xvii. 24 = Mt. xxiv. 27). In part this
meaning is preserved in Mk, for the
cries ' Lo, here ! ', ' Lo, there ! ' are
attributed to ψευδοπροφῆται of whom
Jesus speaks in Mt. vii. 15 and Lk. vi.
26. But everything else in 22 suggests
a later point of view.

The vocabulary has a later ring.
ψευδοπροφῆται were a source of danger
to the early Christian communities
(cf. Ac. xiii. 6, 2 Pet. ii. 1, 1 Jn. iv. 1,
Didache, xi. 5) and are familiar figures
in apocalyptic forecasts (Apoc. xvi. 13,
xix. 20, xx. 10). Apparently ψευδό-
χριστος*, Mt. xxiv. 24**, is a Christian
coinage (cf. Swete, 309), but it may
not be original in Mk (om. D 124
i k). Cf. Turner, 64, *JTS*, xxix. 10.
Here only in Mk are τέρατα, 'wonders'
or ' portents ', mentioned, but σημεῖα
καὶ τέρατα is common in the Acts (cf.
ii. 19, 22, 43, iv. 30, v. 12, vi. 8, vii. 36,
xiv. 3, xv. 12) and not infrequent in
the Epistles (2 Thess. ii. 9, Rom. xv.
19, 2 Cor. xii. 12, Heb. ii. 4) and later
NT writings (Mt. xxiv. 24, Jn. iv.
48**). The use of δώσουσιν in the
sense of ‎נתן‎ also suggests an OT background, and it is not surprising that
important MSS. (D Θ fam. 13, etc.)
have replaced it by ποιήσουσιν. Only
here and in 1 Tim. vi. 10 is ἀποπλανάω,
' to cause to go astray ', found in the
NT, and the construction πρὸς τό
c. infin., indicating ' subjective purpose ', appears nowhere else in Mk.
For οἱ ἐκλεκτοί *v*. xiii. 20 ; εἰ δυνατόν,
xiv. 35*, Mt. xxiv. 24, xxvi. 39, Ac.
xx. 16, Rom. xii. 18, Gal. iv. 15**.

The distinctiveness of 22 extends
beyond matters of vocabulary. The
ideas are those of primitive Christianity. Especially significant is the
similarity of thought in 2 Thess. ii. 9,

οὗ ἐστὶν ἡ παρουσία κατ' ἐνέργειαν τοῦ
Σατανᾶ ἐν πάσῃ δυνάμει καὶ σημείοις καὶ
τέρασιν ψεύδους. Either this passage
has directly influenced 22 (cf. Bacon,
129-34) or it illustrates the doctrinal
and religious situation out of which
both have independently emerged.
Both reveal an apocalyptic outlook
which is strange to the mind of
Jesus.

22 follows naturally and impressively after 20. The shortening of the
days reveals the mercy of God because
the Elect are exposed to the lies and
spectacular works of false prophets.
This, we must suppose, was the original
order of the source into which the saying of Jesus in 21 has been inserted
by Mark or an earlier compiler. Of
these alternatives the latter is to be
preferred, for it is unlikely that after
using the sayings about being deceived
by men who say ' I am he ' (5 f.), Mark
would have inserted 21, while he
might well have reproduced that saying
if he found it in his source. The presumption is that he is using the work
of an earlier compiler.

23. This verse differs markedly from
those which precede it (14-22) in that
it is addressed directly to the four disciples mentioned in 3. Both ὑμεῖς and
ὑμῖν are emphatic. The second person
is used in 14 (ἴδητε) and in 21 (ὑμῖν),
but, apart from these sayings, 14-21
is expressed in the third. The force,
then, of 23 is : ' Do *you* take heed of
the things that have been said concerning the Elect '. With βλέπετε cf. 5,
9, 33. προείρηκα*, ' I have told you
beforehand ' (from an obsolete pres.),
is regularly used of prophetic announce-
ments ; cf. Ac. i. 16, Rom. ix. 29 ; and
of teaching previously given ; cf. 2 Cor.
vii. 3, xiii. 2, Ju. 17, etc. Cf. 3 Macc.
vi. 35 ; *VGT*, 539. πάντα covers far
more than the matters mentioned in
xiii. 4 ; it includes all that is mentioned
in the discourse to this point.

It is clear that 23 is editorial. Like ἀρχὴ ὠδίνων ταῦτα (9), it is one of the linchpins which hold the discourse together. Wellhausen, 104, speaks of it as ' Christian ' and as coming from

a time before the destruction of Jerusalem. Rawlinson, 189, attributes the 'passage to the Evangelist who here addresses himself to the Christian community.

Mk. xiii. 24-7

89. A PROPHECY OF THE COMING OF THE SON OF MAN

Cf. Mt. xxiv. 29-31
(Lk. xxi. 25-8)

It may well be that originally 5-8 and 24-7 formed a single unit which has been broken by the insertion of 9-13 and 14-23. See the introductory note to 85. If this view is sound, 24a must be editorial, but the hypothesis depends on the interpretation of 24b-7. The section describes portents in the heavens (24b, 25), the Parousia of the Son of Man (26), and the gathering of the Elect (27). Many questions are raised, in particular, whether the apocalyptic form and colouring reflect authentic tradition, and whether 5-8 + 24-7 comes from a Jewish or Jewish-Christian source and has been wrongly assigned to Jesus in the primitive tradition. In Lk. xxi. 25-8, 26b-7 appears to be a Markan addition from the present section to an independent version.

᾽Αλλὰ ἐν ἐκείναις ταῖς ἡμέραις μετὰ τὴν θλῖψιν ἐκείνην ὁ 24

24 f. 24a is part of the scenic directions in the apocalyptic drama. With ἐν ἐκείναις ταῖς ἡμέραις cf. 17 and the frequent references to ' days ' in xiii (17, 19, 20 (bis), 32). The phrase μετὰ τὴν θλῖψιν ἐκείνην is also prompted by the context (cf. 19). Moreover, it is at least strange and probably also artificial. Why should terrestrial troubles, wars, rumours of wars, earthquakes, and famines, precede and celestial signs, in sun, moon, and stars, follow the θλῖψις ? The explanation would appear to be that the latter are immediately connected with the appearance of the Son of Man on the clouds with great power and glory, which in the construction of the discourse is designedly held back as the climax of the whole. From this it would appear that the extract 14-22 (23) and the passage 9-13 have been inserted into another source in which 8 was immediately followed by 24b-26 (27). This suggestion is supported by the fact that in 24 ff. no more is heard of the ' Abomination of Desolation '. He still stands ' where he ought not '.

The presumption is that 24 ff. belong to a source which knew nothing of Anti-Christ, his menace, downfall, and destruction, but was concerned to depict the coming of the Son of Man after a period of wild rumour, wars, social disturbances, and earthly and heavenly portents. The scene is set for the descent of the Son of Man. The description is wholly pictorial. No room is left for men, and it is not clear how the Elect (27) can be gathered from ' the four winds '.

If μετὰ τὴν θλῖψιν is not editorial, it may be argued that the menace of Anti-Christ is past. Nevertheless, it is strange that nowhere in the discourse is the overthrow of evil or the Last Judgment mentioned.

Celestial portents are common features in apocalyptic writings. Derived in the first place from the OT, where they appear in symbolic pictures of divine judgments upon Babylon, Edom, and Egypt, they are interpreted more realistically in apocalyptic as signs of God's activity. Cf. Isa. xiii. 10, οἱ γὰρ ἀστέρες τοῦ οὐρανοῦ καὶ ὁ

25 ἥλιοc cκοτιcθήcεται, καὶ ἡ cελήνη οὐ δώcει τὸ φέγγοc αὐτῆc, καὶ
οἱ ἀcτέρεc ἔcονται ἐκ τοῦ οὐρανοῦ πίπτοντεc, καὶ αἱ δυνάμειc αἱ
26 ἐν τοῖc οὐρανοῖc cαλευθήcονται.   καὶ τότε ὄψονται τὸν υἱὸν τοῦ
ἀνθρώπου ἐρχόμενον ἐν νεφέλαιc μετὰ δυνάμεωc πολλῆc καὶ

'Ωρείων . . . τὸ φῶς οὐ δώσουσιν, καὶ
σκοτισθήσεται τοῦ ἡλίου ἀνατέλλοντος,
καὶ ἡ σελήνη οὐ δώσει τὸ φῶς αὐτῆς,
xxxiv. 4, Ezek. xxxii. 7 f., Amos viii.
9, Joel ii. 10; and in apocalyptic
books, 1 Enoch lxxx. 4-7, 'And the
moon shall alter her order, and not
appear at her time . . .', 4 Ezra v. 4,
Ass. Mos. x. 5, Apoc. St. Jn. vi. 12-14.
Cf. also 2 Pet. iii. 12. See further,
Billerbeck, i. 955. How far Mk. xiii.
24 f. is to be interpreted symbolically
(cf. Gould, 250; Plummer, 302;
Bartlet, 362) is difficult to decide. In
the light of 5 f. (wars, earthquakes,
famines) and 26 (the coming of the
Son of Man with clouds) it seems
probable that objective phenomena are
meant.

As the passage is without parallel
in Mk it is not surprising that the
vocabulary contains words not found
elsewhere in the Gospel: ἥλιος, v. i.
32; σκοτίζομαι*; σελήνη*; φέγγος*;
ἀστήρ*; σαλεύω*. The periphrastic
fut. (cf. 13), ἔσονται . . . πίπτοντες, may
be an Aramaism (cf. Lagrange, 346),
but is perhaps more probably a
vernacular variant which Matthew
(πεσοῦνται) has corrected (cf. Howard,
ii. 451). The expression αἱ δυνάμεις
αἱ ἐν τοῖς οὐρανοῖς denotes either the
heavenly bodies (in summary fashion)
or the elemental spirits which were
believed to inhabit or rule over the
stars (cf. Gal. iv. 3, Col. ii. 8, 20, 2 Pet.
iii. 10, 12). The use of σαλεύω (in the
LXX with reference to earthquakes;
cf. Psa. xvii. (xviii.) 8, etc.) supports
the former alternative.

Matthew's version, introduced by
εὐθέως, follows Mk closely, but the
parallel in Lk. xxi. 25 f. (apart from
26b = Mk. xiii. 25b) comes from an
independent source. After a passing
reference to signs in sun, moon, and
stars, Luke's account concentrates
on the distress of nations on the earth.

26 f. The celestial drama now
reaches its climax. The Son of Man
is seen coming in clouds with great
power and glory. For καὶ τότε v. 21,
27; ὁ υἱὸς τοῦ ἀνθρώπου ii. 10; νεφέλη
ix. 7; δύναμις v. 30; δόξα viii. 38. For
the impersonal use of ὄψονται in place
of the passive v. Intr. 47, 62. Matthew
heightens the effect by inserting before
26 the words : καὶ τότε φανήσεται τὸ
σημεῖον τοῦ υἱοῦ τοῦ ἀνθρώπου ἐν οὐρανῷ,
καὶ κόψονται πᾶσαι αἱ φυλαὶ τῆς γῆς
(xxiv. 30a).

The passage is based on Dan. vii. 13,
ἐθεώρουν ἐν ὁράματι τῆς νυκτός, καὶ
ἰδοὺ ἐπὶ τῶν νεφελῶν τοῦ οὐρανοῦ ὡς
υἱὸς ἀνθρώπου ἤρχετο. Whereas in
Dan. a symbolic figure resembling a
man is seen, in Mk the description is
that of a superhuman person invested
with divine authority (μετὰ δυνάμεως
πολλῆς) and clothed with heavenly
light (δόξης). His divine origin is
suggested by ἐν νεφέλαις, since in OT
thought the clouds are the vehicle of
God (v. the note on ix. 7). Cf. Dalman,
242.

27 implies that he has angels at his
command, and these are sent to gather
the Elect ' from the four winds '. For
ἄγγελος v. i. 2; ἐπισυνάγω i. 33; οἱ
ἐκλεκτοί xiii. 20; ἄνεμος iv. 37. The
expression ἐκ τῶν τεσσάρων ἀνέμων
comes from Zech. ii. 6 (10), ἐκ τῶν
τεσσάρων ἀνέμων τοῦ οὐρανοῦ συνάξω
ὑμᾶς. In Apoc. vii. 1 the four winds
execute the vengeance of God (cf.
Charles, 193), but here, as in Zech.,
the phrase denotes the four points of
the compass. The idea that the elect
people of God are scattered throughout
the earth and will be gathered together
by God is a familiar OT expectation
(Deut. xxx. 4, Isa. xi. 11, 16, xxvii. 12,
Ezek. xxxix. 27, Zech. ii. 6-11, Psa. cv.
(cvi.) 47, cxlvi. (cxlvii.) 2), prominent
also in the Apocrypha (Tob. xiii. 13,
xiv. 7 (א), Bar. v. 5-9, 2 Macc. ii. 7)

δόξης· καὶ τότε ἀποστελεῖ τοὺς ἀγγέλους καὶ ἐπισυνάξει τοὺς 27
ἐκλεκτοὺς [αὐτοῦ] ἐκ τῶν τεσσάρων ἀνέμων ἀπ' ἄκρου γῆς ἕως
ἄκρου οὐρανοῦ.

and the Pseudepigrapha (1 Enoch lvii, Psa. Sol. xi. 3, xvii. 26), and carried over into the NT (1 Thess. iv. 15-17, and 2 Thess. ii. 1, ἡμῶν ἐπισυναγωγῆς ἐπ' αὐτόν). The phrase ἀπ' ἄκρου γῆς ἕως ἄκρου οὐρανοῦ is peculiar. There is a parallel in a variant reading in 1 Enoch lvii. 2, 'the end of the earth to the end of the heaven', and Lohmeyer, 279, cites Philo, *Cherub*. 99, ἀπ' οὐρανοῦ περάτων μέχρι γῆς ἐσχάτων. The more common phrases are ἀπ' ἄκρου τῆς γῆς ἕως ἄκρου τῆς γῆς (Deut. xiii. 7, Jer. xii. 12) and ἀπ' ἄκρου τοῦ οὐρανοῦ ἕως ἄκρου τοῦ οὐρανοῦ (Deut. xxx. 4, Psa. xviii. (xix.) 7). Possibly Mark is thinking of the land to the east and the sea to the west; cf. Holtzmann, 169; Menzies, 240; Rawlinson, 190 f. The idea lying behind these phrases is that of the earth as a flat disc overarched by the vault of heaven. ἄκρον*.

Interpretations of 26 are necessarily subjective, but more objective considerations are provided by the character of the section 24-7 (+5-8) and the similar sayings in viii. 38 and xiv. 62. The section is fundamentally Jewish (Wellhausen, 105) and must be judged as an apocalyptic writing

rather than a spoken discourse. It is highly doubtful therefore if 26 can be regarded as an actual saying of Jesus. This view is supported by the fact that viii. 38 (*q.v.*) has an apocalyptic colouring which is wanting in the parallel saying in Q (Lk. xii. 8 f. = Mt. x. 32 f.), and, so far as it goes, by the absence of καὶ ἐρχόμενον μετὰ τῶν νεφελῶν τοῦ οὐρανοῦ (xiv. 62) from Lk. xxii. 69. This opinion may be held without prejudice to the possibility that Jesus used Dan. vii. 13 in His teaching concerning the Son of Man. In short, xiii. 26 may be a distorted echo of His words. The same interpretation accounts equally well for 24 f. and 27. Only a superficial resemblance exists between xiii. 27 and His saying about those who come from the north and south and east and west and sit down in the Kingdom of God (Lk. xiii. 28 f. = Mt. viii. 11 f.). The latter is an authentic saying, the former a traditional formulation. The presumption is that some early Christian teacher saw in 24-7 a sufficient resemblance to the teaching of Jesus to accept the section as authentic tradition, whereas, in reality, it is secondary and derivative.

Mk. xiii. 28-37   90. SAYINGS AND   Cf. Mt. xxiv. 32-6
PARABLES ON WATCH-   (42, xxv. 13-15)
FULNESS   Lk. xxi. 29-33 (34-6)

The discourse concludes with a series of sayings and parables, somewhat artificially compiled by the aid of catchwords, all dealing with the general theme of watchfulness in view of the Parousia. First comes the parable of the Fig Tree in Summer (28 f.), then two sayings on the certainty of the consummation (30 f.) and a third on the unknown day or hour (32), then an exhortation to be on the alert (33) followed by the parable of the Servants of the absent Householder and an application (34-6), and finally by an assurance that what is said applies to all and the command γρηγορεῖτε (37). The catchwords are visible in ταῦτα γινόμενα (29) and ταῦτα πάντα γένηται (30), παρέλθῃ (30) and παρελεύσονται (31), ἀγρυπνεῖτε (33) and γρηγορεῖτε (35 f.), ἐπὶ θύραις (29) and θυρωρῷ (34). The writer's interests are catechetical and practical. He uses authentic traditional material adapted to serve the needs of an overmastering motive, the desire to enjoin watchfulness. In particular, the two parables have been interpreted in the light of this purpose. How far their original meaning has been unconsciously modified thereby is a question to be considered in the Commentary. A second question is the bearing of the section on the composition of the whole.

28 Ἀπὸ δὲ τῆς συκῆς μάθετε τὴν παραβολήν· ὅταν ἤδη ὁ κλάδος αὐτῆς ἁπαλὸς γένηται καὶ ἐκφύῃ τὰ φύλλα, γινώσκετε ὅτι ἐγγὺς
29 τὸ θέρος ἐστίν· οὕτως καὶ ὑμεῖς, ὅταν ἴδητε ταῦτα γινόμενα,
30 γινώσκετε ὅτι ἐγγύς ἐστιν ἐπὶ θύραις. ἀμὴν λέγω ὑμῖν ὅτι οὐ

28 f. The phrase ἀπὸ δὲ τῆς συκῆς μάθετε τὴν παραβολήν adapts the parable to the situation presupposed by the discourse. Luke has καὶ εἶπεν παραβολὴν αὐτοῖς. Lohmeyer, 280, conjectures that the original introduction was ὁμοία ἐστὶν ἡ βασιλεία τοῦ θεοῦ δένδρῳ, and this suggestion gains in force so far as there is reason to think that the parable was uttered earlier and in different circumstances. The article is generic as in many parables; cf. ὁ σπείρων in iv. 3. There does not appear to be justification here for the suggestion of Ed. Schwartz that a well-known fig tree is meant; cf. the note on xi. 12-14, and v. Wellhausen, 106. So Ed. Meyer, i. 127 n. For συκῆ v. xi. 13; παραβολή iii. 23; μανθάνω*. παραβολή seems to be used in the sense of 'lesson': 'learn its lesson' (RSV), 'Heed the lesson of the fig tree' (Torrey, 100).

The fig tree is mentioned because in Palestine, where most trees are evergreens, the rising of the sap in its branches and the appearance of leaves is a sure sign that winter is past. Cf. Lagrange, 347. Luke's addition, καὶ πάντα τὰ δένδρα, is therefore unnecessary and misses the point. For ὅταν c. subj. v. ii. 20; κλάδος iv. 32*. ἁπαλός, Mt. xxiv. 32**, means 'tender', 'supple'; Cl., LXX (cf. Lev. ii. 14 (Aq.)), and ἐκφύω, Mt. xxiv. 32**, 'to generate', 'cause to grow', 'put forth'; Cl., Psa. ciii. (civ.) 14 (Symm.). It is difficult to decide whether the verb should be accented ἐκφύῃ, pres.

subj. act. ('and puts forth its leaves', RV, RSV) or ἐκφύῇ, 2 aor. subj. pass. ('and its leaves are put forth', Torrey). Moulton, ii. 60, 264, prefers the latter and points out that it cannot be 2nd aor. subj. act., since ἔφυν was obsolete and ἐφύην took its place. So also Field, 38. Swete, 314, prefers ἐκφύῃ, on the ground that there is no sufficient reason to suppose a change of subject. γινώσκετε is indic. and θέρος* is 'summer', not 'harvest'.

The similitude is applied to the circumstances of the disciples in οὕτως καὶ ὑμεῖς and again in ταῦτα γινόμενα. The latter phrase is awkward and is probably secondary, for it appears to refer to signs premonitory of the End rather than the Parousia and the gathering of the Elect mentioned in 26 f. The reference to ἐπὶ θύραις is also obscure, for it is not clear whether a person or an event, or even a series of events, is meant. These ambiguities strongly suggest that the parable is used by the compiler for a purpose for which it was not originally intended. Cf. B. T. D. Smith, 90 f.; Dodd, 137 n. The original meaning of the parable must remain a matter of conjecture, but it is reasonable to suppose that Jesus used it with reference to an existing situation relative to the Kingdom of God (so Smith and Dodd; v. Lohmeyer, supra), and perhaps early in the Galilean Ministry (cf. i. 15).

In 29 γινώσκετε is probably imperative, in contrast with the indic. in 28.

μὴ παρέλθῃ ἡ γενεὰ αὕτη μέχρις οὗ ταῦτα πάντα γένηται. ὁ 31
οὐρανὸς καὶ ἡ γῆ παρελεύσονται, οἱ δὲ λόγοι μου οὐ ᵀ παρελεύ-
31 μὴ

It is possible, however, that in 28 γινώσκεται (B² D L W Δ Θ 13 28 et al.)[1]
should be preferred ; cf. Klostermann,
154 ; Turner, 65. If read, γινώσκεται
is impersonal, ' it is known ', ' men
know '. This reading may be a case
of itacism (Swete, 314), but the argument can be reversed in favour of γινώσκεται, which as impersonal may
be the more difficult reading. Field,
37 f., rejects it because there is no
parallel in the NT or OT. For οὕτως
v. ii. 7 ; ἐγγύς* (v. Dalman, 106).

Matthew's version is almost verbatim, but with πάντα in addition to
ταῦτα in xxiv. 33. Luke summarizes
in the phrase ὅταν προβάλωσιν ἤδη.
Like Mt, he has γινώσκετε twice,
adding in xxi. 30 βλέποντες ἀφ' ἑαυτῶν
and omitting ἐπὶ θύραις in 31. More
notable is the subject ἡ βασιλεία τοῦ
θεοῦ which he supplies to ἐγγύς ἐστιν.

30 f. The two sayings which follow
declare that the events prophesied will
take place within the existing generation. They answer the question :
' When shall these things be ? ' (xiii.
4). For ἀμὴν λέγω ὑμῖν v. iii. 28 ; οὐ
μή c. subj. ix. 1 ; παρέρχομαι vi. 48 ;
γενεά viii. 12. Instead of μέχρις οὗ
c. subj.*, Mt and Lk have ἕως ἄν (cf.
Mk. vi. 10, ix. 1, xii. 36*). The ταῦτα
πάντα are all the events described in
5-27, including the Messianic woes,
the persecutions, the heavenly portents, the Parousia, and the gathering
of the Elect ; and accordingly some
commentators see in it the original
end of the discourse, in which 28 f. is
inserted ; cf. Bultmann, 132. In
any case, the form of the saying is
secondary ; ταῦτα πάντα has replaced a
reference to some definite event, probably the destruction of the Temple and
the fall of Jerusalem ; cf. Manson,
SJ, 333. A genuine saying has been
adapted in the interests of contemporary apocalyptic.

The same may be true of 31, but
here the process of adaptation has
gone farther. As the saying stands,
οἱ λόγοι μου refers to the preceding
prophecies ; its original meaning is
uncertain. Was it a claim made by
Jesus for His teaching as a whole ? If
so, it voices a superhuman authority
and is comparable to the Johannine
sayings ; cf. Lohmeyer, 282. Somewhat similar is the saying of Mt. v.
17 f. concerning the Torah which will
abide ἕως ἂν παρέλθῃ ὁ οὐρανὸς καὶ ἡ γῆ,
but in Mk it is said that Christ's words
will continue although the present
order ends. A more absolute claim is
made. The validity of this claim is not
the deciding issue in the question
whether the saying is authentic. The
issue is whether, having regard to the
sayings-tradition as a whole, we must
interpret the words as a doctrinal
adaptation of Mt. v. 17 f. So Bultmann, 130 ; Bartlet, 365. Even xiii.
32 and Lk. x. 22 = Mt. xi. 27 do not
stand upon quite the same plane, and
for like sayings we must turn rather
to Mt. xxviii. 18-20 and to Johannine
sayings which speak of the words
(τὰ ῥήματα) of Jesus (v. 47, vi. 63, 68,
xiv. 10, xv. 7, xvii. 8). Probability
favours the view that the Markan
saying is interpretative, but a decision
on this issue is so difficult that it is not
surprising that many commentators
leave the question open. The similar
phrase in viii. 38, τοὺς ἐμοὺς λόγους, is
not a parallel if, with W and k, λόγους
is omitted. The presence of the saying
in its present context is due to compilation, as παρέλθῃ (30) and παρελεύσονται (31) show, and therefore reflects
didactic interests.

The emphatic use of οὐ μή c. fut. is
without parallel in Mk. The omission,
therefore of μή, with B and D, as in
the WH text, is probably justified, as
an example of assimilation to Mt and

---

[1] In 29 γινώσκεται is read by A D L Δ 28.

32 σονται. Περὶ δὲ τῆς ἡμέρας ἐκείνης ἢ τῆς ὥρας οὐδεὶς οἶδεν,
33 οὐδὲ ⌜οἱ ἄγγελοι⌝ ἐν οὐρανῷ οὐδὲ ὁ υἱός, εἰ μὴ ὁ πατήρ. βλέπετε

32 ἄγγελος

Lk. Cf. Moulton, i. 190 f. Apart from the variations already mentioned, the agreement of Mt and Lk with Mk is very close.

32. The third saying is connected with 30 f. by δέ, but there is no reason to suppose that it was originally spoken in this connexion, with reference to the events prophesied in 5-37; it owes its position to the compiler. In these circumstances its meaning can be inferred only from its contents. That it is eschatological is clear. A statement so solemn and a denial so complete can hardly be intended to refer to an event like the destruction of Jerusalem. It must have been spoken with reference to the Last Judgment and the Parousia. Cf. Lohmeyer, 283, 'Jener Tag' ist bekanntlich der Tag des letzten Gerichtes; Swete, 316; Lagrange, 350. For the expression ἡ ἡμέρα ἐκείνη v. also xiv. 25, Lk. xxi. 34, 2 Thess. i. 10, 2 Tim. i. 12, 18, iv. 8. Cf. also ἡ ἡμέρα, Mt. xxv. 13, 1 Thess. v. 4; ἡ ἐσχάτη ἡμέρα, Jn. vi. 39, 40, 44, 54. All these phrases go back ultimately to the OT conception of ' the Day of the Lord ' (יוֹם יְהוָה), Amos v. 18 ff., Isa. ii. 12, Jer. xlvi. 10, Ezek. xiii. 5, Zeph. i. 7, Zech. xiv. 1, etc. Cf. G. von Rad, KThW, ii. 947-9. For the synonymous expression ἡ ὥρα v. Apoc. xviii. 10, ὅτι μιᾷ ὥρᾳ ἦλθεν ἡ κρίσις σου, also Lk. xvii. 22-30 and the use of ἡ ὥρα in Jn (ii. 4, etc.). The idea that the Day is known only to God is typically Jewish; cf. Zech. xiv. 7, Psa. Sol. xvii. 23. So also the belief that the knowledge of angels (ἄγγελος, i. 13) is limited; cf. Eph. iii. 10, 1 Pet. i. 12. The astonishing thing is the inclusion of the Son with men and angels who know not the day or the hour. Here alone is the title ὁ υἱός found in Mk (cf. Lk. x. 22 = Mt. xi. 27), although similar names, Son of God, My Beloved Son, Son of the Blessed, are also used; v. the note on

i. 1. For Mark's use of εἰ μή v. ii. 7; ὁ πατήρ viii. 38, xiv. 36*, cf. xi. 25. The challenge of the saying is manifest. The original text of Mt (xxiv. 36) probably omits οὐδὲ ὁ υἱός (om. אa L W Δ et al. minusc. pler. g1.2 l r2 vg (pler.) sys pe hl sa bo geoA), unless the omission is that of a later scribe, for doctrinal reasons. Cf. Allen, St. Mt, 260; McNeile, 356, Smith, 188; cf. Streeter, 594-6; Kenyon, TGB, 200. Luke omits the saying entirely, and in a similar passage in Ac. i. 7 makes no reference to the Son, Οὐχ ὑμῶν ἐστιν γνῶναι χρόνους ἢ καιροὺς οὓς ὁ πατὴρ ἔθετο ἐν τῇ ἰδίᾳ ἐξουσίᾳ. Even in Mk the ninth-century Codex Monacensis (X) and one Vulgate MS. omit the phrase.

With good reason Schmiedel included the saying in his list of nine passages which he called ' the foundation-pillars for a truly scientific life of Jesus ', EB, ii, col. 1881. Of its genuineness there can be no reasonable doubt. The suggestion that it is a Jewish saying to which later οὐδὲ ὁ υἱός, εἰ μὴ ὁ πατήρ was added by a Christian redactor (Buitmann, 130; Dalman, 194; cf. Bartlet, 366) is wholly improbable. Against this view the question, ' What Christians would have created the saying ? ', is decisive. Cf. Plummer, 306; Lagrange, 350; Blunt, 242; McNeile, 356; Smith, 188; Schniewind, 175; Lohmeyer, 283; Cadoux, 33; etc. Its offence seals its genuineness. In later times, in reaction to the Arian controversy, the saying raised the greatest difficulties. The phrase οὐδὲ ὁ υἱός was explained as an Arian interpolation (Ambrose, De Fide, v. 16), or the nescience of the Son was traced to the divine economy (Cyril of Alexandria, Adv. Anthr. xiv, σκήπτεται χρησίμως τὸ μὴ εἰδέναι, ' He usefully pretended not to know '), or the dependence of the Son on the Father's will was empha-

ἀγρυπνεῖτε, οὐκ οἴδατε γὰρ πότε ὁ καιρός [ἐστιν]· ὡς ἄνθρωπος 34
ἀπόδημος ἀφεὶς τὴν οἰκίαν αὐτοῦ καὶ δοὺς τοῖς δούλοις αὐτοῦ
τὴν ἐξουσίαν, ἑκάστῳ τὸ ἔργον αὐτοῦ, καὶ τῷ θυρωρῷ ἐνετείλατο
ἵνα γρηγορῇ. γρηγορεῖτε οὖν, οὐκ οἴδατε γὰρ πότε ὁ κύριος 35
τῆς οἰκίας ἔρχεται, ἢ ὀψὲ ἢ μεσονύκτιον ἢ ἀλεκτοροφωνίας ἢ

sized (Basil, *Ep.* ccxxxvi. 2, οὐδ' ἂν ὁ υἱὸς ἔγνω, εἰ μὴ ὁ πατήρ [cited by Swete]). See further, Gore, *Dissertations*, 111 ff., Bruce, *The Humiliation of Christ*, 65-75, 412-18. In modern times it is widely recognized that it is of the glory of the Incarnation that Christ accepted those limitations of knowledge which are inseparable from a true humanity.

The implications of the saying differ according as it is read in itself or in its present context. As used by Mark, it means that, while the Parousia is imminent, its precise time is not known; but, if it is read in itself, and with due regard to ἡ ἡμέρα ἐκείνη as the Day of the Divine Judgment, it reflects an attitude alien to apocalyptic speculation, with its emphasis on an orderly succession of events preceding the End. It is therefore out of harmony with the trend of 5-31. There is more to be said for Manson's suggestion that 32-7 is the original answer to the question of 4, *TJ*, 262 n., but it is more probable still that 32 is the answer to a question about the Judgment.

To ὁ πατήρ Matthew adds μόνος.

33-7. An exhortation follows, introducing the parable of the Absent Householder (34-6). The hearers are to be vigilant because they do not know when the time is. In its reference to the time (καιρός, i. 15) the exhortation echoes the ideas of 32; it also anticipates, and perhaps is suggested by, 35. For βλέπετε *v.* 5, 9, 23; cf. Lagrange, 351: *C'est la morale du discours.* ἀγρυπνέω*, Lk. xxi. 36, Eph. vi. 18, Heb. xiii. 17**, 'to be watchful'; Cl., LXX, Pap. The verb suggests the idea of chasing sleep away (<ἄγρα, ὕπνος). Cf. Moulton,

ii. 290. The asyndeton in 33 and the two imperatives add emphasis.[1]

The parable begins abruptly with ὡς, without a corresponding clause, as sometimes in Rabbinic parables; cf. Smith, 34. The καί before ἐνετείλατο (*v.* x. 3) reads strangely. We should expect either three participles, or ἔδωκεν instead of καὶ δούς, or ἐνετείλατο without καί. Together with the asyndeton in 34, these features suggest a Semitic original (for ὡς *v.* Wellhausen, 107; Plummer, 307); but it must be admitted that successive participles and imperfect constructions are not infrequent in Mk (cf. Swete, xlvi). ὡς = ' It is as when ' (RV) or ' It is like ' (Moffatt, RSV). Pallis, 44, suggests ' if '. The man has gone abroad (ἀπόδημος**, Cl., not in LXX, Inscr.), having given his slaves their tasks (ἑκάστῳ τὸ ἔργον αὐτοῦ) and charged the porter to watch. θυρωρός*, Jn. x. 3, xviii. 16 f.* (LXX, Pap.); γρηγορέω (formed from the perf. of ἐγείρω), xiii. 35, 37, xiv. 34, 37 f.**. For ἵνα c. subj. after a verb of commanding *v.* iii. 9. The description recalls the opening of the parable of Entrusted Wealth (the Talents); cf. Mt. xxv. 14, ὥσπερ γὰρ ἄνθρωπος ἀποδημῶν ἐκάλεσεν τοὺς ἰδίους δούλους καὶ παρέδωκεν αὐτοῖς τὰ ὑπάρχοντα αὐτοῦ. The difference is that in Mk the slaves are assigned duties and special reference is made to the porter.

In the application (35) the change from ἄνθρωπος to ὁ κύριος τῆς οἰκίας (i.e. to Christ Himself) reveals the standpoint of Mark's day. The Church is in daily expectation of the return of its Lord; cf. 1 Thess. v. 6, 1 Cor. xvi. 22, Rom. xiii. 11, Apoc. xxii. 20. Cf. also Mt. xxiv. 42, Lk. xii. 40 (the parable of the Thief). The

---

[1] Most MSS. and versions add καὶ προσεύχεσθε, but it is rightly omitted with B D 122 a c k.

$\overset{36}{\underset{37}{}}$ πρωί, μὴ ἐλθὼν ἐξέφνης εὕρῃ ὑμᾶς καθεύδοντας· ὃ δὲ ὑμῖν λέγω πᾶσιν λέγω, γρηγορεῖτε.

exhortation is enforced by the reference to the four watches of the night, which correspond with Roman usage (cf. vi. 48), and recall the three Jewish watches in the parable of the Waiting Servants (Lk. xii. 38). The temporal expressions in Mk are popular in character. For ὀψέ v. xi. 11 ; πρωί i. 35. μεσονύκτιον*, Lk. xi. 5, Ac. xvi. 25, xx. 7**, is an adj. used as a neut. substantive (acc.) adverbially, ' at midnight '. B and W read μεσανύκτιον (so D in Lk. xi. 5), and A D Θ Or, etc. have the gen. ἀλεκτοροφωνία*¹ is ' cock-crowing ', i.e. the third watch. Cf. Moulton, ii. 271. The μή clause (36) is better explained as final (RV, RSV) rather than as a warning (' in case . . .', Moffatt). For ἐξαίφνης*, ' suddenly ', Lk. ii. 13, ix. 39, Ac. ix. 3, xxii. 6**, v. the note on ἐξάπινα in ix. 38*. For καθεύδω v. iv. 27. Cf. Mt. xxv. 5, χρονίζοντος δὲ τοῦ

νυμφίου ἐνύσταξαν πᾶσαι καὶ ἐκάθευδον (the Ten Virgins). ἐξαίφνης is read by A B et al. fam. 1 22 69 700 1071 al. pler., but ἐξέφνης by א C D L W Δ Θ fam. 13 (exc. 69) 28 543 565 579 (WH). Cf. Hort, 151.

34-6 would seem to be a homiletical echo of several parables. This view accounts best for the reference to the porter, who is the central figure, suggested possibly by ἐπὶ θύραις in 29. The other slaves are mere lay figures. All the time Mark's attention is on the final injunction, γρηγορεῖτε. In 37 his readers are in mind : what is said to the four disciples (xiii. 4) applies to all.

Couchoud, JTS, xxxiv. 127 f., makes an interesting conjecture. Following k, which reads quod autem uni dixi omnibus vobis dico (without vigilate), but replacing dixi by dixit, he suggests that ὃ δὲ ἑνὶ ἔλεγεν πᾶσιν ὑμῖν λέγω be read before 35, and γρηγορεῖτε alone in 37.

VII

Mk. xiv. 1-xvi. 8   THE PASSION AND
(9-20)   RESURRECTION NARRATIVE

The last main division, the Passion and Resurrection Narrative, is the most closely articulated section in the Gospel. By general consent this circumstance is due to the fact that it was the first part of the Gospel tradition to be told as a continuous story, since, in order to solve the paradox of the Cross, it was necessary to relate the events as a whole. Cf. Dibelius, 178-217 ; Bultmann, 282-316 ; Schmidt, 303-6. It cannot be assumed, however, that Mark merely reproduces the earliest narrative ; on the contrary, it is probable that he has modified it and has incorporated additional material into it ; and one of the problems of interpretation is to determine, as far as is possible, what the additions are, and to estimate the importance and historical value of the whole. Naturally, critical estimates of the extent of the original *Grundstock* differ, but the amount of agreement is impressive, and the differences of opinion prompt further inquiry.

Without discussing the foundation narrative in detail, Dibelius includes the following among the Markan additions : the Anointing (xiv. 3-9), the Preparations for the Passover (xiv. 12-16), parts of the Gethsemane Story (xiv. 39 ff.) and of the Trial before the Priests (xiv. 59 ff.), and the narrative of the Empty Tomb (xvi. 1-8).

¹ G. Zuntz, JTS, l. 182 f., claims that πρὶν ἀλεκτοροφωνίας is the original reading in Mt. xxvi. 34 and 75.

Bultmann makes a much more detailed analysis.   An old account, he suggests, narrated quite briefly the Arrest, the Condemnation by the Sanhedrin and Pilate, the Departure to the Cross, the Crucifixion and Death of Jesus.   To this account Mark added a group of stories connected with Peter, the Journey to the High Priest's House, the Denial, and as an introduction to the latter the Prophecy of the Denial.   The Evangelist also used a complex of stories connected with the Last Supper, including the account of the Preparations (xiv. 12-16), the Prophecy of the Treachery of Judas (xiv. 17-21), and the Journey to Gethsemane, with its attendant prophecies (xiv. 27-31).   Into this complex, it is suggested, the Institution of the Supper (xiv. 22-5) was inserted, and the whole was preceded by the Priests' Plot (xiv. 1 f.) and the Treachery of Judas (xiv. 10 f.).   Other inserted stories include the Anointing (xiv. 3-9), Gethsemane (xiv. 32-42), the Trial before the Priests (xiv. 55-64), the Mocking by the Soldiers (xv. 16-20a), the Women at the Cross (xv. 40 f.), and the Burial (xv. 42-7).   Bultmann also explains many details within the stories as secondary formations which originated from the desire to solve the problem of a Crucified Messiah by the aid of Old Testament prophecies and in response to apologetic, parenetic, and legendary motives.[1]

Bultmann sees the influence of the cultus in the account of the Institution of the Supper, but to a fuller degree this question is treated by Bertram, who finds the influence of Christian worship reflected in every part of the Passion Story.   Bertram's radical criticism is based on a limited interpretation of the cult-motive, for he defines it as ' the inner relation of the believer to his cult-hero, which spontaneously comes to expression in his faith and life, and not only in divine worship ' (5).   What he really discusses is the effect of the primitive Christian religion on the Passion Narrative, with the assumption that it must be a distorting influence.   Bertram, indeed, believes that there never was a fixed tradition, and that the cult-motive was operative from the beginning.   In some of these discussions we receive the impression of an attempt to reach positive results upon a firm basis of critical despair by making bricks with a minimum of straw and sometimes without straw at all.   Nevertheless, the historical critic is debtor to these writers for many fearless and penetrating observations which challenge facile solutions and stimulate honest thinking.

A more sober note is struck by K. L. Schmidt, although unfortunately at this stage in his examination of the Markan framework his treatment is brief and incomplete.   He points out that single narratives satisfied the needs neither of the narrator, nor the worshipper, nor the apologist (304).   Many of them, he observes, have neither liturgical nor apologetic value;   only in their succession is this power perceptible (305).   The Passion Narrative, he affirms, is the oldest and most notable document in the garland of the acts of martyrs.   Hence the great agreement among the Synoptists, which extends even to the Fourth Gospel.   Herein also is explained the almost complete silence of Jesus in the records ; for the oldest community the story as it happened was defence enough.   He points to the sutures and seams in Mk and to additions such as the Priests' Plot (xiv. 1 f.), the Treachery of Judas (xiv. 10 f.), and the Anointing (xiv.

---

[1] More recently J. Jeremias, 54 f., has put forward a very similar view, distinguishing (1) the original Aramaic *kerygma* (1 Cor. xv. 3-5), (2) a short account of the Passion, beginning with the Arrest, (3) the ' long account ', from the Entry and including Petrine stories (xiv. 26-42, 53 f., 66-72), (4) the canonical form.

3-9); but in the main his attention is directed to the gaps which enabled the later Evangelists to insert new material; in Lk the Conversation after the Supper, the rearrangement of the Trial scene, and the story of Herod; in Mt the account of the frightful end of Judas and other material peculiar to the Gospel.

From the standpoint of the historian Ed. Meyer, i. 161-211, has a valuable chapter on the Passion Narrative, with special reference to the Treachery of Judas, the Supper, the Trial and Crucifixion, Caiaphas and Pilate. Earlier he discusses the Denial and the story of Gethsemane. Of these scenes he says that they, if any at all, bear the impress of complete authenticity, and that they can go back only to Peter himself on whom they made an indelible impression (149 f.). In contrast, he explains the Institution of the Supper as the aetiological justification of the primitive Christian fellowship-meal. The critical discussions of Goguel, to which reference is made in the Commentary, are also of great interest and importance.

In studying Mk the parallel versions in Mt, Lk, and Jn are illuminating in the highest degree. Matthew's Gospel shows how Mk was understood a decade or so later in response to the needs of worship, doctrine, and defence. Cf. G. D. Kilpatrick, *passim*. The Fourth Gospel shows the fidelity of Ephesus to the facts of the Passion Story and at the same time the Evangelist's interpretative and dramatic genius. Luke's Passion Story is of special interest because there is good reason to think that, apart from passages taken from Mk, it rests on an independent account. Cf. Perry, *The Sources of Luke's Passion-Narrative*; Streeter, 202 f.; V. Taylor, 33-75; Bultmann, 290, 292 f., 302 f.; *per contra*, Creed, 259 ff., *ET*, xlvi. 101 ff., 236 ff., 378 f. Cf. A. Barr, *ET*, lv. 227-31.

As the foregoing summary of critical opinion suggests, the Markan Narrative, while relatively a unity, contains material of different kinds and origin. Only tentatively can these be delimited and described. For convenience the following sections may be distinguished:

(*a*) xiv. 1-52.   The Events culminating in the Arrest.
(*b*) xiv. 53-xv. 47.   The Trials, the Crucifixion, and the Burial.
(*c*) xvi. 1-8 (9-20).   The Resurrection.

| (*a*) Mk. xiv. | THE EVENTS CULMINATING |
| 1-52 | IN THE ARREST |

In this section the high points of the Passion Narrative are the Priests' Plot, the Last Supper, and the Arrest, and around these incidents a certain grouping of the material can be observed. The several narratives are as follows:

(91) xiv. 1 f.   The Priests' Plot.
(92) xiv. 3-9.   The Anointing at Bethany.
(93) xiv. 10 f.   The Treachery of Judas.
(94) xiv. 12-16. The Preparations for the Passover.
(95) xiv. 17-21. The Prophecy of the Betrayal.
(96) xiv. 22-5.   The Last Supper.
(97) xiv. 26-31. The Prophecy of the Denial.
(98) xiv. 32-42. Gethsemane.
(99) xiv. 43-52. The Arrest.

Mk. xiv. 1 f.   91. THE PRIESTS' PLOT   Cf. Mt. xxvi. 1-5
Lk. xxii. 1 f.

This small section was composed to introduce the Passion Narrative. The date ' after two days was the feast of the Passover and the unleavened bread ' and the statement ' Not during the feast ' are points of outstanding interest. One question to be considered is whether the date is based on historical tradition or whether it belongs to the artificial scheme, illustrated from xi. 1 onwards, to bring the events of the Passion within the period of a week. This issue involves the further date in 12, ' On the first day of unleavened bread, when they sacrificed the Passover ', and the further question whether the Anointing (3-9), which Jn. xii. 1 dates ' six days before the Passover ', is rightly placed in Mk. The statement ' Not during the feast ' is closely connected with the problem whether the Last Supper was the Passover Meal or whether actually, as in Jn, it was celebrated a day earlier. In Mk the question is complicated by the variant reading, attested by D and the Old Latin version, ' lest haply there shall be a tumult of the people during the feast ' and by the emphasis which is to be put upon ' with guile ' in xiv. 1. Luke's shorter version avoids these difficulties. Matthew's more elaborate account begins with the formula which rounds off each of the five main groups of discourse material in his Gospel : ' And it came to pass, when Jesus had finished all these words '. It turns the Markan statement into direct speech, ' You know that after two days the Passover comes, and the Son of Man is delivered up to be crucified ' (xxvi. 2). The reference to the chief priests and scribes is expanded into the account of a formal gathering of the Sanhedrin in ' the court of the high priest, who was called Caiaphas ', and the statement ' Not during the feast ' is made more decisive by the use of ἵνα μή c. subj. The secondary and interpretative character of this version is manifest.

XIV. 1   ΗΝ ΔΕ ΤΟ ΠΑΣΧΑ καὶ τὰ ἄζυμα μετὰ δύο ἡμέρας. Καὶ

1. The phrase ἦν δέ looks back upon the events described. τὸ πάσχα (Aram. אחספ, Heb. פסח) is the form used in the NT and by Philo, and commonly in the LXX, where φάσεκ or φάσεχ is also found. Josephus uses πάσχα and φάσκα. The name is variously used of the Paschal lamb (xiv. 12 (bis), 14), the feast (here and in 16), or the whole festival (cf. Lk. xxii. 1, ἡ ἑορτὴ τῶν ἀζύμων ἡ λεγομένη πάσχα). The feast could be celebrated only in Jerusalem. On the late afternoon of Nisan 14 the lambs were slaughtered and offered in the Temple, and the meal followed on the evening of the same day, between sundown and midnight, according to our reckoning, but (since the Jewish day began at sunset) on Nisan 15 according to the Jewish calendar.

τὰ ἄζυμα, xiv. 12*, the Feast of Un-

leavened Bread (maççoth), or ἡ ἑορτὴ τῶν ἀζύμων (Ex. xxxiv. 18) as in Lk, was originally the feast of the barley harvest during which unleavened bread was eaten. Cf. N. H. Snaith, 23 f. In later times it was celebrated from the 15th to the 21st (22nd) of Nisan (Ex. xii. 1-20, cf. Josephus, Ant. iii. 10. 5). Occasionally the term covers the day of the Passover. The two are mentioned together in 2 Chron. xxxv. 17, but sometimes Josephus (Ant. ii. 15. 1, xiv. 2. 1, BJ, v. 3. 1) dates the Feast of Unleavened Bread from Nisan 14. For Rabbinic evidence v. Billerbeck, ii. 812-15, and the note on xiv. 12. Here, as in 2 Chron. xxxv. 17, the two phrases describe the whole eight days' festival. Matthew omits καὶ τὰ ἄζυμα, while Luke (xxii. 1, v. supra) combines the two expressions.

ἐζήτουν οἱ ἀρχιερεῖς καὶ οἱ γραμματεῖς πῶς αὐτὸν ἐν δόλῳ κρατή-
2 σαντες ἀποκτείνωσιν, ἔλεγον γάρ   Μὴ ἐν τῇ ἑορτῇ, μή ποτε

For the use of the neuter plural to denote festivals *v.* vi. 21, Jn. x. 22, τὰ
ἐνκαίνια.

μετὰ δύο ἡμέρας is ambiguous. Some
commentators think that two days are
meant (Klostermann, 156; Lagrange,
364; McNeile, 372; Smith, 192), but
others hold that, by Jewish reckoning,
the next day is indicated (Holtzmann,
171; Swete, 319; Turner, 66; Bartlet,
370), i.e. Wednesday, Nisan 13. While
simplicity favours the former view, the
latter is more probable, since μετὰ
τρεῖς ἡμέρας in viii. 31 = τῇ τρίτῃ ἡμέρᾳ.
For οἱ ἀρχιερεῖς *v.* ii. 26, viii. 31; οἱ
γραμματεῖς i. 22; κρατέω i. 31; ἀποκτείνω iii. 4; δόλος vii. 22*. Mark's
words do not imply a formal decision
of the Sanhedrin, but a purpose enter-
tained for some time (cf. the impf.
ἐζήτουν) by many of its leading members; cf. iii. 6, xi. 18, xii. 12. Their
intention was to proceed 'with subtilty' (ἐν δόλῳ). The phrase is wanting in D Δ Σ fam. 1 fam. 13 (exc. 124)
28 543 *al. pauc.*, but it is probably
original (cf. Mt, δόλῳ), especially if
ἔλεγον γάρ is read in 2 (*q.v.*). With the
subj. cf. xi. 18, xiv. 11.

2. ἔλεγον γάρ. Two questions arise :
the reading, and the identity of the
speakers. The widely attested δέ (A
C² Θ *et al.* minusc. (exc. 892 1342)
vg (*aliq.*) syʰˡ sa arm) is probably an
assimilation to Mt and preference
should be given to γάρ (א B C* D L Ψ
892 1342 it vg (*pler.*) sys ʰˡ ᵐᵍ bo),
which explains why the arrest must
be made 'with subtilty'. Turner, 66,
JTS, xxv. 384 f., distinguishes the
speakers from those previously mentioned, taking ἔλεγον as impersonal :
'(unnamed) people said'. The chief
priests 'so far deferred to the objection
that they proposed to make the arrest
privately'. This interpretation seems
to read too much into ἔλεγον, but it is
supported by the fact that a private
arrest calls for subtlety and a dangerous public arrest is deprecated (' Not

during the feast, lest haply there shall
be a tumult of the people '). The
situation, however, is not altered if the
chief priests are the speakers, and for
this reason Turner's suggestion is not
really necessary.

Μὴ ἐν τῇ ἑορτῇ. For μή used ellipti-
cally *v.* Blass, 294. Sc. κρατήσωμεν
αὐτόν. In μή ποτε (iv. 12*, c. subj.)
ἔσται the indic. represents the danger
' as real and imminent ' (Swete, 320).
ἑορτή, xv. 6* ; θόρυβος, *v.* v. 38*. The
suggestion, ' Not during the feast ',
is simplified if Μή ποτε ἐν τῇ ἑορτῇ ἔσται
θόρυβος κτλ. is read (D a (c) ff (k) i q).
Without any time designation, it explains the priests' purpose by the desire
to avoid a popular tumult (' Perhaps
there will be a tumult of the people ').
Even so, it may be argued, the reading
suggests an arrest *before* the Feast. In
any case, this exclusively Western
reading is a modification of Μὴ ἐν τῇ
ἑορτῇ, designed possibly to avoid the
suggestion of an arrest *after* the Feast.
For Μὴ ἐν τῇ ἑορτῇ is ambiguous. Does
it mean *before* (so most authorities,
including Wellhausen, 108 ; Klostermann, 157 ; Montefiore, i. 309 f. ; Goguel, 436 f. ; J. Jeremias, 40-2, cites
also Spitta, Bornhäuser, O. Holtzmann, Dibelius, Finegan ; Rawlinson,
195 ; Wood, 697) or *after* the Feast
(Holtzmann, 171 ; Zahn, with ref.
to Mt. xxvi. 5 ; Dalman, *JJ*, 98 ; A.
Schlatter, *Der Evangelist Matthäus*,
701) ? The objection to the former
view is that the interval was very short,
and that the crowds of pilgrims began
to gather before the Feast ; to the
latter, that no reference is made in Mk
to an unfulfilled plan (cf. Bultmann,
282). Some commentators think that
in the eyes of the priests either course
was open (Swete, 320 ; Plummer, 311 ;
Bartlet, 371) and that the offer of Judas
precipitated their action ; a tempting
solution which is exposed to both the
objections mentioned above. Equally
vulnerable is the suggestion that they

ἔσται θόρυβος τοῦ λαοῦ.

meant to arrest Jesus before the Feast and to kill Him afterwards (v. Schniewind, 177). Jeremias, 41 f., argues that all difficulties disappear if we take ἑορτή in the sense of the crowd at the Feast (*Festversammlung* or *Festmenge*), so that the phrase agrees with ἄτερ ὄχλου in Lk. xxii. 6. So also Bertram, 13, who cites Jn. ii. 23, vii. 11, and claims the support of Loisy, ii. 491. On this interpretation, Jeremias claims, Mk. xiv. 2 contains no temporal statement at all.

It is tempting to conclude that the problem is insoluble. The most prob-

able hypothesis is that, while Mark may have thought the priests intended to execute Jesus before the Feast, they themselves purposed to act subsequently, but were able to proceed almost at once ' with subtilty ' owing to the treachery of Judas. Objections based on the brevity of the interval and Mark's failure to indicate their change of plan lose their force on this interpretation. The least tenable view is that 1 f. is not historical, but was inferred from the events (Bultmann, 282; Bertram, 13 f.; Sundwall, 79). The passage is too obscure to be an invention.

Mk. xiv. 3-9   92. THE ANOINTING AT   Cf. Mt. xxvi. 6-13
BETHANY   (Lk. vii. 36-50)
Jn. xii. 1-8

In contrast with the bare reference to the Priests' Plot stands the vivid narrative of the Anointing which Mark has inserted between 1 f. and 10 f. The story is located at Bethany in the house of Simon the leper. The woman is not named and neither are those (τινες) who ask in their indignation, ' Why has this waste of the ointment been made ? '. The anointing of the head, a sign of royal dignity, is peculiar to Mk (and Mt); in Jn and Lk the feet are anointed. Only Mark records that the price of the ointment was 300 denarii, and that the onlookers spoke rudely (*Und sie fuhren sie an*, Klostermann). Jesus commends her lovely deed, rebukes her critics, and declares that she has anointed Him for burying (8). Finally the prophecy is added that, wherever the Good News is preached, what she has done will be told in memory of her (9).

The narrative is a Story about Jesus which is on its way to become a Pronouncement-story. Lohmeyer, 291, describes its form as between the *Streitgespräch* and the Biographical Anecdote; Bultmann, 37, as a Biographical Apothegm; Dibelius, 43, as a Paradigm. The story rests on good tradition. J. Weiss, 284-9, connects it and also 12-16 with a cycle of Bethany tradition (cf. xi. 11, 19). Cf. Lohmeyer, 292. The main interest lies in the sayings in 6-9. Both Bultmann and Dibelius think that the story ended originally with 7, or at most the words ' She hath done what she could ' in 8a. Bultmann, in particular, accepts the historical character of the story as thus constituted (*keine ideale Szene, sondern eine im engeren Sinn biographische*, p. 37) and its connexion with Bethany (*ebenso alt . . . wie das Stück selbst*, p. 69), and declines to agree with Bertram, 16-18, that 6 f. is secondary (*so gewinnt man eine pointelose Geschichte*, p. 283 n.). The burning question is whether 8b, ' she has anointed my body beforehand for burying ', was added by Mark. The Evangelist's hand may well be seen in 9 in the references to ' the gospel ' and ' the whole world '; yet it may be questioned whether anything more is to be seen here than the sharpening of a prophecy that the woman's deed would be held in memory continually. After this there is nothing more to be said ; the story has reached its natural climax.

The position of the story is another question. If it was inserted between 1 f. and 10 f., the incident may have happened earlier, and John is probably more correct in placing it before the Entry ' six days before the Passover ' (xii. 1). The variations in the later Gospels illustrate the development of the tradition. In Mt the ' some that had indignation ' are ' the disciples ' (xxvi. 8) and in Jn Judas is mentioned (xii. 4), while the unnamed woman of Mk. xiv. 3 is said to be Mary (xii. 3) who takes ' a pound ' of costly ointment and anoints the feet of Jesus and wipes them with her hair (xii. 3, cf. Lk. vii. 38). The relationships between the Markan story and that of the ' Woman in the City who was a Sinner ' (Lk. vii. 36-50) are more difficult to assess, especially if one does not accept the easy solution that the incidents are different. Matthew's version is manifestly secondary. It omits πιστικῆς (Mk. xiv. 3), the breaking of the vessel, the price of the ointment, the difficult phrase καὶ ἐνεβριμῶντο αὐτῇ, the words ' and whenever you will, you can do good to them ' and ' she has done what she could ', and recasts ' she has anointed my body beforehand for burying ' so that it becomes ' In pouring this ointment on my body she has done it to prepare me for burial ' (xxvi. 12). All these changes throw into relief the greater originality of Mk.

3   Καὶ ὄντος αὐτοῦ ἐν Βηθανίᾳ ἐν τῇ οἰκίᾳ Σίμωνος τοῦ λεπροῦ
κατακειμένου αὐτοῦ ἦλθεν γυνὴ ἔχουσα ἀλάβαστρον μύρου νάρδου
πιστικῆς ⌜πολυτελοῦς·⌝ συντρίψασα τὴν ἀλάβαστρον κατέχεεν αὐ-

3 πολυτελοῦς,—

3. For Βηθανία v. xi. 1. This precision, so rare in Mk, is notable. So also the allusion to the house of ' Simon the leper ', who must have been known to the circle from which the story comes. Torrey's picturesque suggestion, *TG*, 96, that ' Simon the leper ' is a mistranslation of the Aramaic *garabha*, ' jar-merchant ', is decisively rejected by Black, 9, on the ground that no noun of this meaning appears in any of the lexica. The use of two gen. absolutes, ὄντος αὐτοῦ and κατακειμένου αὐτοῦ, with the same subject repeated and no connecting link, is strange, and the suggestion of Lohmeyer, 292, that Mark inserted the first into a narrative which originally began (καὶ) κατακειμένου αὐτοῦ, is attractive. For κατάκειμαι v. i. 30 (*HS*², 12).

The woman (γυνή) is unnamed and nothing suggests that she is a sinner (cf. Lk. vii. 37). In Jn. xii. 3 she is Mary the sister of Martha and Lazarus.

The absence of the name is usual in a story in which the emphasis lies on the words of Jesus, but is strange in view of the prophecy that her deed will be remembered. For the tendency in the tradition to add names v. Bultmann, 72.

The ἀλάβαστρος, Mt. xxvi. 7, Lk. vii. 37**, is ' a globular vase without handles for holding perfumes, often made of alabaster ' (LS) ; Herodotus iii. 20. For the variations in gender, fem. in ℵc B C L Δ Ψ 579 1342, masc. in ℵ* A D 565 892, neut. in G M W Θ fam. 1 fam. 13, v. Moulton, ii. 122. μύρον, xiv. 4 f.*, ' ointment ', ' perfume '. νάρδος, Jn. xii. 3**, ' spikenard ', *Nardostachys Jatamansi*, the Indian plant from which it was prepared ; Cant. i. 12, iv. 13 f. ; Horace, *Od*. ii. 11, iv. 12. πολυτελής*, 1 Tim. ii. 9, 1 Pet. iii. 4**. Matthew has πολύτιμος.

The meaning and derivation of πιστικός (Jn. xii. 3**) are still un-

τοῦ τῆς κεφαλῆς. ἦσαν δέ τινες ἀγανακτοῦντες πρὸς ἑαυτούς T 4
Εἰς τί ἡ ἀπώλεια αὕτη τοῦ μύρου γέγονεν; ἠδύνατο γὰρ τοῦτο 5
τὸ μύρον πραθῆναι ἐπάνω ⌈δηναρίων τριακοσίων⌉ καὶ δοθῆναι τοῖς

4 καὶ λέγοντες   5 τριακοσίων δηναρίων

solved. The word may be derived from πιστός (<πείθω) with the meaning ' genuine '; less probably from πιστός (<πίνω)=ποτός, 'liquid'. Cf. Moulton, ii. 379 f. Several scholars have suggested that the word is a scribal corruption of σπικάτον, the name of an ointment (so Wetstein; cf. vg, *nardi spicati*), or of πιεστικῆς (<πιέζω) ' distilled ' (Pallis, 45), or again of τῆς στακτῆς, a particular kind of perfume (Couchoud, *JTS*, xxxiv. 128). There is more to be said for explaining πιστικός as the transliteration of an Aramaic word. Allen, 168, makes the complicated suggestion that the original was σπικάτον, transliterated into Aramaic, and then misread by the Greek translator. J. Lightfoot, *Hor. Heb.* ii. 446, and A. Merx, *Das Evang. Markus*, 148, conjecture that *pistaqa=balanus*, the ben nut, as the Aramaic original. ' Was it simply transliterated, and then taken into the sentence as an adjective πιστικῆς ? ', Black, 161. Cf. Klostermann, 159. Evidence cited by Lightfoot from Pliny (xiii. 1) shows that the oil or fluid ointment of the *balanus* (*myrobalanum*) was one of the ingredients of *nardinium*, the nard perfume. That πιστικός points to Aramaic tradition is supported by the asyndeton in 3b, συντρίψασα τὴν ἀλάβαστρον κατέχεεν αὐτοῦ τῆς κεφαλῆς.

4 f. The opening words, ἦσαν δέ τινες c. participle, recall ii. 6. It is noteworthy that Mark does not say who the people are. Matthew has οἱ μαθηταί (xxvi. 8), and οἱ δὲ μαθηταὶ αὐτοῦ appears as a *v.l.* in Mk in D Θ 565 a b ff i r¹, and τῶν μαθητῶν in W fam. 13 543 syᵖᵉ. Jn. xii. 4 mentions Judas only. For ἀγανακτέω *v.* x. 14; πρὸς·ἑαυτούς i. 27, ix. 10, xi. 31. Black, 77, suggests that πρὸς ἑαυτούς represents the use of the ethic dat. in

Aramaic : ' Some were *indeed* vexed '; cf. x. 26. Cf. Torrey, *TG*, 79. Usually the phrase is held to imply looks or remarks which they exchanged one with another (cf. Swete, 323), but it must be admitted that, in the absence of a verb of saying, this idea is at best obscurely expressed. Very many MSS. add καὶ λέγοντες or λέγοντες, and the absence of these phrases from ℵ B C* L Ψ 892* 1342 is not decisive. For the periphrastic imperf. ἦσαν . . . ἀγανακτοῦντες *v.* Intr. 45, 62 f. εἰς τί ;, ' to what end ? ', xv. 34*, Mt. xiv. 31, xxvi. 8, Ac. xix. 3, cf. Sir. xxxix. 17 (26), while classical, also corresponds to היל המל, and the asyndeton in the question, which gives it a certain roughness, is characteristic of Aramaic. Each of these points, taken by itself, can be accounted for as Greek, but the concurrence of several leaves the impression that a story told originally in Aramaic lies not far behind the narrative.

The weaker sense of ἀπώλεια*, ' waste ', is illustrated not only in Polybius vi. 59, 5 (opp. τήρησις), but also in the papyri (*VGT*, 73). With γέγονεν cf. v. 33, ix. 21. τοῦ μύρου: om. D fam. 1 63 64 a 1 syˢ geo¹; Klostermann, 159, says ' perhaps rightly '. Cf. Mt. xxvi. 8.

The reason alleged (in 5) is that the ointment might have been sold for a high price for the benefit of the poor. For the augment in ἠδύνατο *v.* Moulton, ii. 188. πιπράσκω*. δηναρίων τριακοσίων is gen. of price; cf. Jn. xii. 5; in pre-War values £10-12. Swete, 323, thinks ἐπάνω has no effect on the case; cf. *WM*, 313, Robertson, 511. Lagrange, 368, demurs (cf. Blass, 108), but cf. 1 Cor. xv. 6. G. D. Kilpatrick, *JTS*, xlii. 181, suggests that ἐπάνω* (om. 517 954 1675 c k syˢ geo¹) is a second-century addition which reflects

6 πτωχοῖς· καὶ ἐνεβριμῶντο αὐτῇ. ὁ δὲ Ἰησοῦς εἶπεν "Ἄφετε
αὐτήν· τί αὐτῇ κόπους παρέχετε; καλὸν ἔργον ἠργάσατο ἐν ἐμοί·
7 πάντοτε γὰρ τοὺς πτωχοὺς ἔχετε μεθ' ἑαυτῶν, καὶ ὅταν θέλητε
δύνασθε αὐτοῖς [πάντοτε] εὖ ποιῆσαι, ἐμὲ δὲ οὐ πάντοτε ἔχετε·
8 ὃ ἔσχεν ἐποίησεν, προέλαβεν μυρίσαι τὸ σῶμά μου εἰς τὸν ἐντα-

the depreciation of the currency after the time of Nero. For πτωχός v. x. 21. This interest in the poor is characteristic of the pious Jew. The possibility that the speakers are not the disciples, but other guests, is worth considering, for Mark shows no inclination to ' spare the Twelve ', and ἦσαν δέ τινες is used in ii. 6 of the scribes.

For ἐμβριμάομαι v. i. 43. Strong disapproval expressed in gesture and sound seems implied. Cf. vg, *fremebant in eam*. For the form of the verb v. Moulton, ii. 198.

6 f. With ἄφετε αὐτήν cf. x. 14. Here the meaning is ' Let her alone ' (RV, RSV). κόπους παρέχω c. dat., Mt. xxvi. 10, Lk. xi. 7, xviii. 5 (κόπον), Gal. vi. 17**, is illustrated in the papyri (*VGT*, 355); in Cl. Gk the use of πράγματα or πόνον is more common. καλὸν ἔργον is a fair or fine work; ' a beautiful thing ' (Moffatt and RSV). ἐργάζομαι*. The asyndeton in 6c (Mt, γάρ) is noteworthy, as compared with 6a and 6b where the absence of particles gives decisiveness of tone. ἐν ἐμοί, ' upon me ' (Mt, εἰς), corresponds to בִּי (cf. Swete, 324). But cf. Gal. i. 24.

The calmer tone of 7 is reflected in its form. The statement is not intended to assert that poverty is a permanent social factor (cf. Deut. xv. 11) but is the background to ἐμὲ δὲ οὐ πάντοτε ἔχετε. With the latter cf. Jn. xvi. 16, ' A little while, and ye behold me to more ', but the human aspect, with its suggestion of the fleeting opportunity for personal acts of devotion, is unique in the Markan saying. The first and third clauses are reproduced in Mt, but 7b, καὶ ὅταν θέλητε δύνασθε αὐτοῖς πάντοτε εὖ ποιῆσαι, is peculiar to Mk. There is no need to regard it as a gloss (cf. Klostermann, 159). The

second πάντοτε (א^c B L 892 1071 1342 sa bo) is omitted by most authorities, but it is well attested and the repetition may be intentional. εὖ ποιέω** (LXX, Ex. i. 20, Sir. xii. 1). αὐτοῖς is omitted by א* and αὐτούς (as in Cl. Gk) is read by A Θ *et al.* 28 700 892 1071 *al. pler.* Cf. Blass, 89.

8. ὃ ἔσχεν ἐποίησεν means ' she has done what she could '; sc. ποιῆσαι as in Lk. xii. 4 (cf. Mt. xviii. 25, Lk. vii. 42, xiv. 14, Jn. viii. 6, Ac. iv. 14, Heb. vi. 13). The situation is different in xii. 44, ὅσα εἶχεν ἔβαλεν. Here it is not a question of giving all she has, but of rendering the only service within her power. Kypke (cf. Swete, 325) cites Dion. Hal. *Ant.* vii, p. 467, οὐκ εἶχον δὲ ὅτι ἂν ἄλλο ποιῶσιν. See LS *s.v.* ἔχω, A III; Field, 14. Nevertheless, we should expect rather ἠδύνατο (cf. x. 38) or ἴσχυσεν (conjectured by Pallis, 46). The difficulty was felt from the first, as is shown by Matthew's recast, βαλοῦσα γὰρ αὕτη τὸ μύρον τοῦτο ἐπὶ τοῦ σώματός μου πρὸς τὸ ἐνταφιάσαι με ἐποίησεν (xxvi. 12) and by the textual variants. αὕτη is read before ἐποίησεν in A C D *et al.* 118 124 700 892 1071 *al. pler.* it (*pler.*) vg, and omitting ἐποίησεν, k reads *quod habuit haec praesumpsit et unguentavit meum corpus* (ὃ ἔσχεν αὕτη προέλαβεν καὶ ἐμύρισέν μου τὸ σῶμα). This last reading is accepted as original by Couchoud, *JTS*, xxxiv. 128 f., with the meaning *son bien celle-ci l'a prélevé* (or *l'a consommé*) *et a oint mon corps*, but several objections render it untenable. To represent the woman as having exhausted her resources in buying the ointment involves reading ὃ ἔσχεν in the light of xii. 44, interpreting προλαμβάνει in 1 Cor. xi. 21 in an impossible sense, and a highly conjectural account of the emergence of ἐποίησεν

φιασμόν.   ἀμὴν δὲ λέγω ὑμῖν, ὅπου ἐὰν κηρυχθῇ τὸ εὐαγγέ-   9
λιον εἰς ὅλον τὸν κόσμον, καὶ ὃ ἐποίησεν αὕτη λαληθήσεται εἰς
μνημόσυνον αὐτῆς.

as a copyist's error. It is better to read the accepted text and to interpret it in the sense already indicated.[1] Its peculiar character and the presence of asyndeton, not to speak of the phrase προέλαβεν μυρίσαι, suggest that the passage is ' translation-Greek '. προλαμβάνω*, 1 Cor. xi. 21, Gal. vi. 1**, ' to take beforehand ', ' anticipate ', ' overtake '; Cl., LXX (Wis. xvii. 11 (אca), 17), Pap. (VGT, 542). This use of προλαμβάνω c. infin. in the sense of anticipating has a parallel in φθάνω c. infin. Cf. Lagrange, 369, who cites Josephus, Ant. xviii. 9. 7, φθάσας ὑπαντιάζειν; Blass, 227; Robertson, 1120. But Lagrange observes that the resemblance to Aramaic is very striking and cites syˢ, קרמח בסמח. Allen, 169, says the constr. is unclassical and holds that Jos. Ant. vi. 13. 7, xviii. 5. 2, BJ, i. 20. 1, Ignat. Eph. iii. 2 are not exactly parallel. While admitting that the phrase is not impossible Gk, he thinks that it is probably a translation of the Aramaic root קרם. Cf. Wellhausen, Einl.² 21; Souter, 217; Klostermann, 160. It is doubtful if we can say more than that the ' Aramaism ' is a possibility, for the usage of Josephus suggests that the construction could be used in later Gk.² In any case, the meaning is not affected. The woman has anticipated the anointing of the body of Jesus. μυρίζω**; Cl., Pap. ἐνταφιασμός*, Jn. xii. 7**, means ' laying out ' according to Field, 98, or ' preparation for burial ' (VGT, 217), rather than ' burying ' (AV, RV, RSV), but the latter seems the sense required in Mk. It is not

necessary to interpret the word as meaning ' embalming ', although in Egyptian papyri the ἐνταφιαστής is a professional embalmer (Deissmann, BS, 120 f.).

Anointing for burial is not the woman's purpose, but the interpretation Jesus puts upon her action. The objection that the Jews did not anoint the dead cannot be sustained. Cf. Shabbath, xxiii. 5: ' They may make ready [on the Sabbath] all that is needful for the dead, and anoint it and wash it, provided that they do not move any member of it ' (Danby, 120). Neither is it necessary to explain the saying as an addition designed to explain that anointing, omitted at the burial (xv. 46) and frustrated by the resurrection (xvi. 1), was at least anticipated. On the contrary, if, as is probable, the incident happened shortly before the Passion, it is natural that Jesus should have interpreted the woman's action as the anointing of His body. Cf. Lohmeyer, 295: Dass solch ein Wort im Munde Jesu unmöglich ist, lässt sich kaum behaupten. The absence of a Passion saying in Lk. vii. 36-50 does not compromise the genuineness of Mk. xiv. 8; it may illustrate the different forms a common tradition assumes under catechetical and literary influences.

9. For ἀμὴν λέγω ὑμῖν v. iii. 28; ὅπου ἐάν vi. 10, 56; εὐαγγέλιον i. 1; κόσμος viii. 36. μνημόσυνον*, Mt. xxvi. 13, Ac. x. 4**, ' reminder ', ' memorial '; Cl., LXX. With εἰς ὅλον τὸν κόσμον cf. xiii. 10, εἰς πάντα τὰ ἔθνη.

The saying is widely regarded as an

---

[1] Wensinck compares Ḥagiga ii. 2, ' Thou, what is in thy power, do ' (אֶת כֹּה אִית בַּךְ עֲבַר).' Cf. Black, JTS, xlix. 161.

[2] The usage of Josephus is uncertain. In BJ, i. 20. 1, προλαβὼν ἐξετασθήσεσθαι ποταπὸς φίλος, οὐ τίνος, ἐγενόμην is translated by Whiston, ' and I desire that thou wilt first consider . . .', but it can be rendered quite literally, ' (I came) . . . anticipating that the question would be . . .', thus confirming the opinion of Allen (v. supra). On the other hand, Ant. vi. 13. 7, προέλαβες κατα-μειλίξασθαί μου τὸν θυμόν means ' thou (Abigail) hast seasonably mollified my anger ', thus averting David's purpose to destroy Nabal. Further, Ant. xviii. 5. 2, προλαβὼν ἀναιρεῖν, appears to mean ' by putting him (the Baptist) to death betimes ', thus excluding the possibility of a rebellion. In each case something happens first.

addition to the narrative on the ground that Jesus expected the immediate coming of the Kingdom and that the reference to the world-wide preaching of the Gospel represents a later point of view (cf. Loisy, ii. 497 ; Klostermann, 158 ; Bultmann, 37 ; Bertram, 17 ; McNeile, 375 f. ; etc.). Alternatively, the phrase ὅπου ἐὰν κηρυχθῇ τὸ εὐαγγέλιον εἰς ὅλον τὸν κόσμον is explained as illustrating the missionary vocabulary of the Gentile-Christian Church in a traditional saying of Jesus (cf. Bartlet, 375 ; Rawlinson, 198 ;

Blunt, 247). In view of ἀμὴν λέγω ὑμῖν, and the fitting character of the declaration that the woman's deed would be remembered, which forms the climax of the narrative, the latter hypothesis is preferable. The absence of the woman's name (cf. Wellhausen, 109 ; Montefiore, i. 318 f.) favours the genuineness of the saying, since the tendency of the later tradition is to supply names (cf. Jn. xii. 3), while the objection that no one is astonished at the reference to burial (cf. Wellhausen) asks too much from the narrative.

| Mk. xiv. 10 f. | 93. THE TREACHERY OF JUDAS | Cf. Mt. xxvi. 14-16 Lk. xxii. 3-6 |

This bald and somewhat colourless narrative belongs to the account broken off by the insertion of 3-9. It stands in the closest connexion with 1 f., giving the explanation of how the priests were able to arrest Jesus ' with guile '. No explanation is offered of the treachery. All that is told is that Judas went to the chief priests in order to deliver Jesus up to them, that they were delighted and promised him money, and that he sought how he might fulfil his purpose conveniently. Matthew follows his source closely, but expresses the traitor's purpose in direct speech : Τί θέλετέ μοι δοῦναι κἀγὼ ὑμῖν παραδώσω αὐτόν ;, and states the price paid. Luke explains that Satan entered into Judas (cf. Jn. xiii. 27). To the chief priests he adds the Temple officers (the στρατηγοί), and says that Judas accepted their offer and sought an opportunity to deliver Jesus up to them ἄτερ ὄχλου, that is, privately. Mark's sober account is clearly primary.

The historical value of Mark's account is beyond question. The earliest tradition would never have ascribed the betrayal of Jesus to ' one of the Twelve ' if the facts had been otherwise. Already in Lk, and still more in Mt and Jn, embarrassment is manifest in the endeavour to explain the act of Judas by avarice and Satanic inspiration. The true motives of his action can only be inferred. The supposition that he wanted to force the hand of Jesus lacks support, and it is more probable that he was the victim of disillusionment, doubt, and despair.

10   Καὶ Ἰούδας Ἰσκαριὼθ ὁ εἷς τῶν δώδεκα ἀπῆλθεν πρὸς τοὺς

10. For the form Ἰσκαριώθ v. iii. 19. Moulton and Milligan show that ὁ εἷς is paralleled in early papyri (VGT, 187). Cf. P. Par. xv. 50 (120 B.C.), τὸν ἕνα αὐτῶν Ὧρον, 54, τοῦ ἑνὸς τῶν ἐγκαλουμένων Νεχουθοῦ, and other examples cited. This evidence shows that the usage was popular, but it does not explain why the article is found here only in Mk and not in xiv. 20 and 43, unless it has completely lost its signi-

ficance. Lagrange, 370, thinks the article has no special importance and compares the use of l'un in French. That there is a backward reference to the list in iii. 16-19 is not likely, since cross references in Mk are so rare. Nor is it probable that Judas is distinguished from Judas the brother of Jesus (vi. 3), inasmuch as he is already characterized as Ἰσκαριώθ. Swete, 327, suggests that the meaning may

ἀρχιερεῖς ἵνα αὐτὸν παραδοῖ αὐτοῖς. οἱ δὲ ἀκούσαντες ἐχάρησαν 11
καὶ ἐπηγγείλαντο αὐτῷ ἀργύριον δοῦναι. καὶ ἐζήτει πῶς αὐτὸν
εὐκαίρως παραδοῖ.

be 'that one, the only one, of the
Twelve who proved a traitor', and A.
Wright, *JTS*, xviii. 32 f., has claimed
that the phrase means 'the first' or
'the chief' of the Twelve (cf. Jn. xii.
6). Better than either explanation is
Swete's further suggestion that the
reference is to the frequent designation εἰς τῶν δώδεκα (xiv. 20, 43, Mt.
xxvi. 47, Lk. xxii. 47), 'that One of
the Twelve', for this phrase may have
become current if the words of Jesus
in xiv. 20, Εἷς τῶν δώδεκα, ὁ ἐμβαπτόμενος μετ᾽ ἐμοῦ εἰς τὸ ἓν τρύβλιον, were
remembered with horror.

For παραδίδωμι, consistently used instead of προδίδωμι, v. i. 14; and for the
form παραδοῖ v. iv. 29; οἱ δώδεκα iii.
14. Ed. Meyer, i. 146, 172, assigns
10 f., with 1 f. and 17-24, to his
'Twelve-source'.

11. χαίρω, xv. 18*; ἐπαγγέλλομαι*;
ἀργύριον*. εὐκαίρως*, 2 Tim. iv. 2**,
'seasonably', 'opportunely'; Cl.,
LXX (Sir. xviii. 22*), Pap. Cf. vi. 21.
For παραδοῖ v. xiv. 10.

Mark merely records the priests'
promise to give Judas money, but
Matthew (xxvi. 15) assumes that a
sordid bargain was made, and says
that they paid Judas on the spot, οἱ δὲ
ἔστησαν αὐτῷ τριάκοντα ἀργύρια (cf.
Zech. xi. 12), a sum which in pre-War
values McNeile computes at £4: 16s.
Cf. Lk. xxii. 5, συνέθεντο, 'covenanted'.
John does not record any compact, but
has previously designated Judas as a
thief (xii. 6). These legendary developments provide slender ground
for the suggestion of Swete, 328, that
Judas went back 'with the price of
blood in his girdle'. Since Judas has
still to find his opportunity, no mention is made in the Markan narrative
of armed assistance, but xiv. 43 implies that in the interval some arrangement must have been made. The
detached and objective character of
1 f., 10 f., reflected in its vocabulary
and style, stands in notable contrast
with the vivid portraiture of 3-9 and
12-16.

Mk. xiv. 12-16   94. THE PREPARATIONS   Cf. Mt. xxvi. 17-19
                         FOR THE PASSOVER   Lk. xxii. 7-13

This picturesque narrative is introduced by two temporal statements
which have given rise to much discussion. The disciples' inquiry, where
they are to make ready for the Passover, suggests that the Last Supper
was the Passover Meal on the night of Nisan 15. The historical character
of the narrative is therefore particularly important. Two questions are
involved: (1) the similarity of part of the story with the sign given to Saul
in 1 Sam. x. 1 ff. of three men going up to Bethel, one carrying a wineskin; and (2) the close verbal parallels with the story of the Preparations
for the Entry (xi. 1-6). On these issues critical opinion is divided between
the view that the story is a legend (cf. Wellhausen, 110 f.; Bultmann,
283 f., 308; Bertram, 22-5; Ed. Meyer, i. 176; etc.) and the claim that
it records authentic tradition (cf. Lagrange, 371-5; Plummer, 316-19;
Bartlet, 378-80; Turner, 67; etc.). An important contributory question
is whether the precise instructions in 13-15 imply foreknowledge or an
arrangement previously made with the householder (xiv. 14). Another
question is why attention is limited to the large upper room, while nothing
is said of other preparations necessary to the Passover Meal. Does the
content of the story, as distinct from xiv. 12, suggest that the meal really

was the Passover ? The narrative cannot have been current as an isolated item of tradition ; its sequel must have been an account of the meal. Is the original sequel 17-21 or 22-5 ? These questions will be considered in the Commentary, but the parallels with xi. 1-6 may with advantage be examined here. These parallels are as follows :

xi. 1-6	xiv. 13-16
1. . . . ἀποστέλλει δύο τῶν	13. . . . ἀποστέλλει δύο τῶν
μαθητῶν αὐτοῦ	μαθητῶν αὐτοῦ
2. καὶ λέγει αὐτοῖς·	καὶ λέγει αὐτοῖς·
ὑπάγετε εἰς τὴν κώμην . . .	ὑπάγετε εἰς τὴν πόλιν . . .
καὶ . . . εὑρήσετε . . .	καὶ ἀπαντήσει ὑμῖν . . .
3. εἴπατε·	εἴπατε·
ὁ κύριος . . .	14. ὁ διδάσκαλος . . .
4. καὶ ἀπῆλθον	16. καὶ ἐξῆλθον . . .
καὶ εὗρον . . .	καὶ εὗρον
6. καθὼς εἶπεν ὁ Ἰησοῦς·	καθὼς εἶπεν αὐτοῖς·
καί . . .	καί . . .

These agreements show that the two stories are composed by the same writer, but they do not suggest that they are doublets. The parallelism is like that already noted in the narratives of the Deaf Mute (vii. 31-7) and the Blind Man at Bethsaida (viii. 22-6) and illustrates the tendency of Mark to repeat himself. Moreover, here the differences of subject-matter are greater, so great as to preclude the doublet-hypothesis. In the one story a colt is left ready in a definite place ; in the other a room is to be found in circumstances described. The water-carrier who guides the two disciples to the house is quite different from the bystanders who want to know why the colt is being loosed. The owner of the colt may be absent (v. the note on xi. 3), but the householder receives a message and permits the disciples to act upon it. The details in common (two unnamed disciples and, apparently, an arrangement previously made with friends) are natural in each case. The evidence suggests that each narrative is composed by Mark on the basis of tradition.

12   Καὶ τῇ πρώτῃ ἡμέρᾳ τῶν ἀζύμων, ὅτε τὸ πάσχα ἔθυον, λέγου-

12. The frequency of καί paratactic in 12-16 (11 times) is noteworthy. τῇ πρώτῃ ἡμέρᾳ τῶν ἀζύμων is ambiguous, since it usually means Nisan 15, but ὅτε τὸ πάσχα ἔθυον shows that Nisan 14 is meant. Cf. the numerous instances in Mk in which the second of two temporal expressions defines the first : i. 32, 35, iv. 35, xiii. 24, xiv. 30, xv. 42, xvi. 2. For this use of ' the first day of unleavened bread ' Billerbeck, ii. 813 f., cites *Mekh.* Ex. xii. 15, *b. Pes.*

36a, *b. Pes.* 5a, *j. Pes.* i. 27a, 27c. Jeremias, 11 n., disputes the first two passages, but, if the rest are conceded, it cannot be said (with Bultmann, 284) that for Jewish usage Mk. xiv. 12 is ' completely impossible '. It does not seem necessary, therefore, to explain πρώτῃ as a corruption for πρό (Allen, 172) or to explain the phrase as a misreading of the Aramaic which should have been rendered πρὸ μιᾶς τῶν ἀζύμων,[1] ' On the day before the feast of

---

[1] The Gospel of Peter (edn. J. A. Robinson, 17) has this phrase in the words of Herod, ' it is written in the law, that the sun go not down on him that is put to death, on the day before the unleavened bread which is their feast ' (πρὸ μιᾶς τῶν ἀζύμων τῆς ἑορτῆς αὐτῶν).

σιν αὐτῷ οἱ μαθηταὶ αὐτοῦ Ποῦ θέλεις ἀπελθόντες ἑτοιμάσωμεν
ἵνα φάγῃς τὸ πάσχα; καὶ ἀποστέλλει δύο τῶν μαθητῶν αὐτοῦ 13
καὶ λέγει αὐτοῖς Ὑπάγετε εἰς τὴν πόλιν, καὶ ἀπαντήσει ὑμῖν
ἄνθρωπος κεράμιον ὕδατος βαστάζων· ἀκολουθήσατε αὐτῷ, καὶ 14
ὅπου ἐὰν εἰσέλθῃ εἴπατε τῷ οἰκοδεσπότῃ ὅτι Ὁ διδάσκαλος

Unleavened Bread'; cf. Allen, *ibid.*, *St. Mt*, 272-4; Black, 100 n.; Jeremias, 12. It is, of course, another question whether in the pre-Markan tradition the preparations were made earlier, especially as the interval allowed by the Markan narrative is very short. In this case the possibility of the misunderstanding of an original Aramaic phrase would become relevant.

The imperfect ἔθυον denotes repeated action and τὸ πάσχα is used of the Paschal lamb; 'when it was customary to sacrifice the passover lamb' (Moffatt, RSV). Luke has ᾗ ἔδει θύεσθαι τὸ πάσχα (xxii. 7). θύω*, Mt. xxii. 4, Lk. xv. 23, 27, 30, xxii. 7, Jn. x. 10, Ac. x. 13, xi. 7, xiv. 13, 18, 1 Cor. v. 7, x. 20**, 'to offer sacrifice ', ' kill '; Cl., LXX, Pap. In most of these passages the meaning is ' to kill ', but in Ac. xiv. 13, 18 and 1 Cor. x. 20 it is used of pagan sacrifices and in 1 Cor. v. 7 of the Sacrifice of Christ. The phrase θύειν τὸ πάσχα is taken from the LXX; in Ex. xii. 21 it translates שחט, ' to slaughter', and in Deut. xvi. 2 זבח, ' to slaughter for sacrifice '. How far sacrificial ideas were associated with the Passover in the time of Christ it is difficult to say. The offering of the Paschal lamb certainly counted as a sacrifice and the meal which followed as a sacrificial meal, but the later tendency was to subordinate the sacrificial element in the meal and to regard it mainly as commemorative of God's redemptive acts at the Exodus from Egypt. Cf. G. B. Gray, *Sacrifice in the OT*, 376-82; R. H. Kennett, *The Church of Israel*, 135. This tendency does not mean that sacrificial ideas were absent from the mind of Jesus at the Last Supper; the words of institution (*v.* xiv. 22, 24) suggest the contrary.

In the narrative the initiative is taken by the disciples; they ask Jesus where He wants them to go and prepare the Passover meal. For θέλω c. subj. *v.* the note on vi. 25; ἑτοιμάζω i. 3; τὸ πάσχα xiv. 1. Matthew replaces ἵνα φάγῃς by the infin. Luke omits it.

13 f. Luke names the two disciples Peter and John (xxii. 8). The two are sent εἰς τὴν πόλιν because, in accordance with the rule founded on Deut. xvi. 7, it was held that the Passover must be celebrated in Jerusalem. Cf., e.g., *Sifré* on Num. ix. 10 (cited by Jeremias, 19 n.): ' What is the place in which it (the Passover lamb) must be eaten? Within the gate of Jerusalem.' Cf. also Dalman, *JJ*, 106. Matthew adds πρὸς τὸν δεῖνα, ' to such a one ' (xxvi. 18).

The sign given is that a man will meet them bearing a jar of water. ἀπαντάω*, Lk. xvii. 12**, ' to meet ', ' encounter ': Cl., LXX, Pap. κεράμιον*, Lk. xxii. 10**, a jar or jug. This fact in itself would make the man conspicuous, for Lagrange, 373, explains that men water-carriers carry leather-bottles and women only pitchers. βαστάζω*. The man is merely a guide and may have been unconscious of his task, unless ἀπαντάω implies a greeting. The disciples are to follow him to the house he enters and to give a message to the householder (οἰκοδεσπότης*). For ὅπου ἐάν c. subj. *v.* vi. 10. Cf. Moulton, i. 151, who suggests, ' wherever he *goes* in '. The fact that in His message Jesus merely describes Himself as ὁ διδάσκαλος (*v.* iv. 38) suggests a pre-arrangement. The same also must be said of the otherwise strange question, Ποῦ ἐστιν τὸ κατάλυμά μου ὅπου τὸ πάσχα μετὰ τῶν μαθητῶν μου φάγω;. It may be that Mark thought

λέγει Ποῦ ἐστιν τὸ κατάλυμά μου ὅπου τὸ πάσχα μετὰ τῶν
15 μαθητῶν μου φάγω; καὶ αὐτὸς ὑμῖν δείξει ἀνάγαιον μέγα
16 ἐστρωμένον ἕτοιμον· καὶ ἐκεῖ ἑτοιμάσατε ἡμῖν. καὶ ἐξῆλθον οἱ

of the incident as one of prophetic fore-knowledge, although he says nothing to indicate this. In any case it is highly improbable that what happened is so to be explained, for on this interpretation we have no answer to the question *why* the householder reacted in the way described to such a message, whereas, on the assumption of a previous arrangement, his action is entirely natural. Cf. Bartlet, 379 f. Lohmeyer, 299, hears the tone of a king in the question and even finds Johannine ideas at the basis of the narrative, but this acuteness of perception operates at the expense of the historical element.

κατάλυμα*, Lk. ii. 7, xxii. 11**, 'guest-room' as in 1 Kgdms. i. 18 rather than 'lodging-place' as in Lk. ii. 7. The word belongs to the Koine (*VGT*, 329). Blass, 217, explains ὅπου ... φάγω as an example of assimilation to sentences with ἵνα. Cf. Robertson and Davis, 322.

With a slight re-arrangement Luke follows Mk closely. Matthew omits the reference to the water-carrier and recasts the message in the form, 'Ο καιρός μου ἐγγύς ἐστιν· πρὸς σὲ ποιῶ τὸ πάσχα μετὰ τῶν μαθητῶν μου (xxvi. 18).

15. With καὶ αὐτός cf. iv. 38, but here the phrase is without emphasis as in viii. 29. It is possibly a 'secondary Semitism' (cf. Klostermann, 68) reflecting the anticipatory use of the Heb. אוה, but Lagrange, 215, rejects this view here and in viii. 29. ἀνάγαιον*, Lk. xxii. 12**, an 'upper room' (= ὑπερῷον, Ac. i. 13, etc.). The form belongs to the Koine (*VGT*, 30) and is well attested (א A B* C D, etc.), but numerous variants appear in the MSS. (*v.* Legg). Cf. Moulton, ii. 70, 76. Especially interesting is the reading of D, ἀνάγαιον οἶκον ... μέγαν, which Black, 180, thinks has probably arisen from confusion between רבחא 'large' and ביתא 'house'. Lagrange, 374, pictures a large guest room *fournie de*

tapis et de divans; cf. Swete, 330, 'perhaps provided with carpeted divans'; Bartlet, 380; Montefiore, i. 323; Rawlinson, 201; Lohmeyer, 299; etc. This interpretation is supported by the fact that στρωννύω is used to describe the covering of couches with carpets or rugs. Cf. Ezek. xxiii. 41, ἐκάθου ἐπὶ κλίνης ἐστρωμένης, Xen. *Cyrop.* viii. 2. 6, κλίνην στρώννυσι, τράπεζαν κοσμεῖ, and (cited by Field, 39) Aristoph. *Ach.* 1089, τὰ δ' ἄλλα πάντ' ἐστὶν παρεσκευασμένα, κλῖναι, τράπεζαι, προσκεφάλαια, στρώματα. Clearly στρωννύω can be used with this meaning, but it is also used of furnishing a ship and of saddling a horse (*VGT*, 594), and in Mk. xi. 8 of spreading garments and rushes in the way. It is possible therefore that the upper room may have been less pretentious than commentators have been wont to think. Was it a bare attic? To some extent preparations have already been made: ἐστρωμένον ἕτοιμον*; and the two disciples are to complete them: καὶ ἐκεῖ ἑτοιμάσατε ἡμῖν. For this plural, otherwise rare, *v.* x. 40; ἑτοιμάζω i. 3.

16. The narrative ends abruptly with the statement that the disciples went into the city and found things as Jesus had said, and that thereupon they prepared for the Passover Meal (τὸ πάσχα, *v.* xiv. 1). If the meal was actually the Passover feast, the preparations would include the killing and roasting of the lamb, and the providing of unleavened cakes (*Maҫҫoth*), wine, water, bitter herbs, sauce (*Ḥaroseth*), lamps, and divans. Nothing, however, is said of these details, and the exact nature of the preparations depends on the character of the meal. If it was eaten twenty-four hours earlier, it may still have had some of the features of a Passover Meal, but its precise nature must be a matter of speculation. For the question of the date *v.* Note K, pp. 664-7. The bearing of this issue

μαθηταὶ καὶ ἦλθον εἰς τὴν πόλιν καὶ εὗρον καθὼς εἶπεν αὐτοῖς,
καὶ ἡτοίμασαν τὸ πάσχα.

on the narrative is important. If the
Supper was not the Passover Meal,
the narrative describes what was originally intended, and Mark's chronological frame is broken. Everything
described, the preparations, the plotting of Judas, the time of the meal,
would have to be antedated, and a
change of plan inferred. It would be
necessary also to conclude that the
Markan tradition was mistaken in
supposing that the Supper was the
Passover Meal. Only in xiv. 1 f., 12-

16, it should be noted, is it clear that
Mark means the Passover Meal. Taken
by themselves, 17-21 and 22-5 leave the
question open, and even 12-16 implies
the Passover Meal only in 12 and 16b.
Matthew and Luke abbreviate 16,
but otherwise reproduce the reference
to the Passover Meal.
Here and in xi. 1-6 the indications
that Jesus has friends in Jerusalem and
its neighbourhood point to a longer
ministry in Jerusalem than Mark's
Gospel leads us to suppose.

Mk. xiv. 17-21   95. THE PROPHECY OF   Cf. Mt. xxvi. 20-5
                      THE BETRAYAL   (Lk. xxii. 14, 21-3)
                                            (Jn. xiii. 21-30)

The section is little more than a prophecy in a narrative setting. Only
the circumstances in which Jesus spoke are mentioned and the fact that
the disciples began to be sorrowful, and to say to Him one by one, ' Is
it I ? ' (19). The argument that the narrative belongs to a tradition which
knows nothing of the preparations described in 12-16, since the return of
the two disciples is not described (Lohmeyer, 300), may be too stringent,
but it is fair to say that after 12-16 one would expect a fuller account of
the Last Supper. Nor can it be claimed that 17-21 finds its true sequel
in 22-5, so that 17-25 forms a whole, for manifestly two separate units
are connected by καὶ ἀνακειμένων αὐτῶν καὶ ἐσθιόντων in 18 and καὶ ἐσθιόντων
αὐτῶν in 22. Bultmann, 285, is justified in maintaining that originally
17-21 and 22-5 did not stand side by side. He is equally convinced that
22-5 is not the original sequel to 12-16, holding (in opposition to Dalman,
Billerbeck, and Jeremias) that 22-5 is not the account of a Paschal Meal.
He therefore infers that 22-5 has driven out a section which described
such a meal as the natural sequel to 12-16. This contention has much
force, and it may well be that something has been omitted after 17 from
an earlier account to make room for the insertion of 22-5. See further,
the Note on that narrative.

The historical value of 17-21 is vindicated by the sayings it contains.
That Jesus should have read the mind of Judas and prophesied betrayal
is intelligible. His allusive words gave a last chance to the betrayer to
reflect, most of all the solemn warning in 21. It is remarkable that Judas
is not mentioned, still less denounced. It is not even apparent that the
other disciples are aware that he is meant. The position is the same in
the L tradition, in which the narrative ends with the statement that the
disciples began to question among themselves ' which of them it was that
should do this thing ' (Lk. xxii. 23). In Mt, however, a legendary development is manifest when Judas asks, ' Is it I, Rabbi ? ', and receives
the answer, ' Thou hast said ' (xxvi. 25), unless McNeile, 381, is warranted

in suggesting that the question and answer were spoken in whispers. In Jn the traitor is secretly indicated to the Beloved Disciple, and Jesus says to Judas, 'What thou doest, do quickly' (xiii. 27), but here it is expressly stated that no one at the table knew why Jesus spoke thus. In contrast with these later accounts the Markan narrative shows sober restraint and its interest in Judas is in line with 10 f. It is reasonable to conclude that it belongs to the same cycle as 1 f., 10 f., 12-16, sharing with 10 f. references to the Twelve (17 f.). Montefiore, i. 325, observes that, whatever the historic character of the scene may be, 'its solemnity and impressiveness cannot be denied'.

17
18 Καὶ ὀψίας γενομένης ἔρχεται μετὰ τῶν δώδεκα. καὶ ἀνακειμένων αὐτῶν καὶ ἐσθιόντων ὁ Ἰησοῦς εἶπεν Ἀμὴν λέγω
19 ὑμῖν ὅτι εἷς ἐξ ὑμῶν παραδώσει με Γὸ ἐϲθίωνⁿ μετ' ἐμοῦ. ἤρ-
20 ξαντο λυπεῖσθαι καὶ λέγειν αὐτῷ εἷς κατὰ εἷς Μήτι ἐγώ; ὁ

18 τῶν ἐσθιόντων

17 f. With ὀψίας γενομένης cf. i. 32. Since Mark is thinking of the Passover Meal, he means the period after sunset, the beginning of Nisan 15. Cf. Ex. xii. 8, καὶ φάγονται τὰ κρέα τῇ νυκτὶ ταύτῃ. For οἱ δώδεκα v. the notes on iii. 14 and 16. Either the term is used conventionally or Mark thinks that the two mentioned in 13 have returned. In the Passion Narrative the references to the Twelve are limited to xiv. 10, 17, 20, 43, in each case, except the present instance, in the phrase εἷς τῶν δώδεκα.

With the gen. abs. in 18 cf. 22, and for ἀνάκειμαι v. vi. 26. Whereas originally the Passover lamb was eaten standing (Ex. xii. 11), it had become customary to celebrate the feast reclining, as a sign that the people were no longer slaves, but free men. Cf. Dalman, JJ, 108. But it cannot be argued from the use of this verb that the Supper was the Passover Meal (cf. Jeremias, 22 f.), since reclining was also the custom at guest-meals (xii. 39, xiv. 3), feasts (ii. 15, Lk. v. 29), royal banquets (vi. 26), marriage feasts (Mt. xxii. 10 f., cf. Lk. xiv. 8, 10).

For ἀμὴν λέγω ὑμῖν v. iii. 28; παρα-δίδωμι i. 14. Peculiar to Mk is the additional phrase ὁ ἐσθίων μετ' ἐμοῦ, which apparently is based on Psa. xl. (xli.) 10, ὁ ἐσθίων ἄρτους μου, a passage

quoted in Jn. xiii. 18. The fact that the phrase is wanting in Mt and the v.ll. in Mk¹ suggests that it may be a gloss. Cf. McNeile, 380; Lohmeyer, 301. It is not certain, however, that the phrase is a quotation (cf. Lagrange, 376), and Matthew may not have thought of it as such; it does not point to Judas as the traitor, but voices horror at the idea of treachery associated with table-fellowship.

Luke's parallel is taken from his special source. He records that, when the hour was come, He reclined at table (ἀνέπεσεν) and the Apostles with Him. The prophecy of betrayal is quite differently expressed, πλὴν ἰδοὺ ἡ χεὶρ τοῦ παραδιδόντος με μετ' ἐμοῦ ἐπὶ τῆς τραπέζης (xxii. 21). Jn. xiii. 21 agrees with the Markan saying almost verbatim, but omits ὁ ἐσθίων μετ' ἐμοῦ.

19 f. The consternation and grief of the disciples are reflected in the asyndeton and the vocabulary of 19. For ἤρξαντο c. infin. v. Intr. 48, 63 f.; λυπέομαι x. 22*. Here, Lagrange, xciii, suggests, ἤρξαντο has its proper force. In εἷς κατὰ εἷς, κατά is used as an adv. distributively; cf. Moulton, i. 105; Howard, ii. 439. Citing Lev. xxv. 10, εἷς καθ' ἕκαστος (A), Deissmann, BS, 138, defends the usage against the charge of being a Semitism,

---

¹ It is read by sys pe sa bo before παραδώσει με, and is replaced in B sa bo by τῶν ἐσθιόντων μετ' ἐμοῦ.

δὲ εἶπεν αὐτοῖς Εἷς τῶν δώδεκα, ὁ ἐμβαπτόμενος μετ' ἐμοῦ εἰς
τὸ [ἓν] τρύβλιον· ὅτι ὁ μὲν υἱὸς τοῦ ἀνθρώπου ὑπάγει καθὼς 21
γέγραπται περὶ αὐτοῦ, οὐαὶ δὲ τῷ ἀνθρώπῳ ἐκείνῳ δι' οὗ ὁ υἱὸς

and certainly the analogous phrase τὸ
καθ' ἕν (' in detail ') is used in lists in
the papyri (VGT, 187). The alternative explanation is that εἰς κατὰ εἰς
represents a confusion between the
Aramaic חַד חַד and the vulgar Gk
καθεῖς (LXX, 3 Macc. v. 34). In cases
like the present, where the alternative
arguments are so nicely balanced, the
congruence of three possible Semitisms
in a single sentence is too remarkable
to be ignored, and we are entitled to
conclude that Aramaic tradition is
reflected in the rough Markan Greek.
Matthew retains the ἤρξαντο construction, but supplies καί and the participle,
and has εἰς ἕκαστος (xxvi. 22).

The answer Μήτι ἐγώ; is ' Surely
it is not I ' (cf. iv. 21). Too dumb-
founded to think of accusing anyone
else, each rebuts the accusation as it
concerns himself. D Θ et al. fam. 1
565 700 al. pler. it syhl mg geo arm Or
add καὶ ἄλλος μήτι ἐγώ ;. A has ῥαββεί
and 517 and 892 κύριε (so Mt). But
the abrupt shorter text is clearly to be
preferred. Lifelike, it is too subtle
to be the product of art.

The reply of Jesus repeats the charge
that it is one of the Twelve. ὁ ἐμβαπτόμενος μετ' ἐμοῦ εἰς τὸ ἓν τρύβλιον does
not specify an individual, but stresses
the enormity of the act. ἐμβάπτω*,
Mt. xxvi. 23**; Cl., but not found in
LXX nor cited in VGT. It is not
necessary, with Swete, 333, to explain
the participle as a present used to mark
a future event, as if Jesus were giving
a sign; cf. Lagrange, 376. This suggestion is made by Matthew, ὁ ἐμβάψας
μετ' ἐμοῦ τὴν χεῖρα ἐν τῷ τρυβλίῳ, οὗτός
με παραδώσει (xxvi. 23), but it is a
further development of the story, which
becomes explicit in Jn. xiii. 26, Ἐκεῖνός
ἐστιν ᾧ ἐγὼ βάψω τὸ ψωμίον καὶ δώσω
αὐτῷ, though still as a private word to
the Beloved Disciple. In Mk Judas
is not singled out. τρύβλιον*, Mt. xxvi.
23**, is a bowl rather than a dish;

Cl., LXX, Pap. (VGT, 643). εἰς τὸ
ἓν τρύβλιον emphasizes still further the
base character of the act; the traitor
is one who dips in the common bowl.
This point is lost in the mass of MSS.
which omit ἕν, and it is the merit of
B C* Θ 565 that they attest it. Cf.
Ruth ii. 14, καὶ βάψεις τὸν ψωμόν σου
[ἐν] τῷ ὄξει. Commentators identify
the contents of the bowl with the
Ḥaroseth, the sauce compounded of
dates, raisins, and vinegar used at the
Passover Meal (e.g. Swete, 333), but
this opinion depends on the view taken
of the character of the meal.

21. The narrative ends with a saying
concerning the Son of Man, who ' goes '
as it is written of Him, and a ' Woe '
pronounced upon the betrayer, culminating in the statement that it would
have been better for him if he had not
been born. For ὁ υἱὸς τοῦ ἀνθρώπου
v. ii. 10 ; ὑπάγω i. 44 ; καθὼς γέγραπται
i. 2 ; οὐαί xiii. 17 ; παραδίδωμι i. 14 ;
γεννάω*. Two points of special interest
are μέν . . . δέ, so rarely found in Mk
(v. xii. 5, xiv. 38, xvi. [19]*), and ὅτι
at the beginning (v. infra).

The saying draws a contrast between the ' going away ' of the Son
of Man and the action of the betrayer
(μέν . . . δέ). It suggests that, while
the death of the Son of Man is in accordance with the divine purpose (καθὼς
γέγραπται), the responsibility of Judas
remains. Behind the moral and religious issue stands the philosophical
problem of the relation of divine
causality to human activity, but it is
the former which more immediately
arises in the saying. The responsibility of Judas is affirmed because what
will befall Jesus is not remorseless fate
but a destiny willed by God, but freely
chosen and accepted by Jesus Himself.
As such, it finds its expression in a
course of historical events with which
the act of Judas is connected and for
which he is responsible in his own

τοῦ ἀνθρώπου παραδίδοται· καλὸν αὐτῷ εἰ οὐκ ἐγεννήθη ὁ ἄνθρωπος ἐκεῖνος.

degree. He is not the blind instrument of fate. Such appear to be the implications of the saying. The ' Woe ' pronounced over him is not a curse, but a cry of sorrow and of anguish : ' Alas ! for that man ', and the saying ' It were better, etc.' is not a threat, but a sad recognition of facts.

A particular interest belongs to the use of ὑπάγει, ' goes his way '. A typically Johannine expression (cf. viii. 14, 21 f., xiii. 3, 33, xiv. 4, 28), it is not compromised on the historical side on that account. On the contrary, it is better appraised as a mode of speech characteristic of Jesus, partly lost in Luke's more prosaic πορεύεται, and hardly credible as a ' community-formation ' (Gemeindebildung, cf. Bultmann, 163). It describes a voluntary act of ' homegoing ' on the part of the Son of Man in fulfilment of what ' stands written concerning him '.[1] There is no OT passage (except Dan. vii. 21) in which the suffering destiny of the Son of Man is affirmed. Only, therefore, in the mind of one who has identified the Son of Man with the Suffering Servant is the saying intelligible, and it is more intelligible if it is original than if it is secondary. Lohmeyer, 302, says that in a deeper sense the content of the narrative is historical even if its form is legendary, and the only doubtful element in this opinion is the qualification. Not only are the ideas Jewish, the vocabulary also has a Semitic tone. καλόν in 21b is used in the sense of the comparative, as in ix. 43, 45, 47, and in agreement with Aramaic idiom. Cf. Black, 86, and the notes on these passages.

Matthew reproduces Mk very closely, but adds ἦν after καλόν. Neither Evangelist has ἄν with ἐγεννήθη or the negative μή. The effect of these omissions is to increase the poignancy of the saying. For the omission of ἄν and for εἰ οὐ in ' unreal conditions ' v. Moulton, i. 171, 200. Luke's version, κατὰ τὸ ὡρισμένον πορεύεται, πλήν . . ., is plainly secondary (xxii. 22).

The use of ὅτι at the beginning of the saying (Mk and Lk ; Mt om.) is remarkable. It is not surprising that it is so widely omitted (A C D W Δ Θ et al. minusc. omn. exc. 579 892 a) or replaced by καί (291 544 1241 1342 it (exc. a f) vg sys pe hl aeth ; uerumtamen f arm) ; but the testimony of א B L Ψ 579 892 sa bo, although exclusively Alexandrian, is decisive by reason of its strangeness. We must suppose either that καὶ εἶπεν has dropped out or that the passage is added from a sayings-source.

Mk. xiv. 22-5   96. THE LAST SUPPER   Cf. Mt. xxvi. 26-9
[(Lk. xxii. 14-20
(1 Cor. xi. 23-5)

This narrative may be the original sequel to xiv. 12-16, but there are no decisive arguments in favour of this view, and it is more probable that it is an isolated unit of tradition derived from a primitive Christian liturgy. Cf. 1 Cor. xi. 23-5. That it is ' an aetiological cult legend ' (Eichhorn, Heitmüller, Bultmann, Bertram) formed in Hellenistic Pauline circles is improbable. Lohmeyer, 309, rightly says that the designation is without foundation and explains hardly anything (Die Bezeichnung ist unbegründet und erklärt kaum etwas). As will be shown in the Commentary, the vocabulary, style, and ideas are Jewish, and there are strong reasons for thinking that the narrative is of Palestinian origin. Moreover, the

---

[1] Black, JTS, xlix. 163, suggests the influence of the Aramaic 'ₐzal.

alleged influence of the Mystery-religions upon the tradition is highly doubtful, partly because these influences were operative later, and partly because references to sacred meals in the existing texts are very few. Cf. C. Clemen, *Primitive Christianity*, 266 ; H. A. A. Kennedy, *St. Paul and the Mystery Religions*, 69, 279 ; T. Wilson, *St. Paul and Paganism*, 183 ; N. P. Williams, *Essays Cath. and Crit.* 389 ; Rawlinson, *The NT Doctrine of the Christ*, 279 ; Goguel, 187. For the second-century parallel [1] to the phraseology of 1 Cor. x. 21 in Pap. Oxy. i. 110. 2 *v. VGT*, 365.

Apart from brief references to the circumstances and the significant actions of Jesus, the narrative consists of three sayings. The eschatological saying in 25 is loosely connected with the rest of the narrative, and, since it can hardly have been current as an isolated logion, it may be the residue of an independent narrative. The same also may be true of 24, for ἔπιον ἐξ αὐτοῦ πάντες in 23 reads like the end of a fragment.

The purpose of 22-5 is not to describe all that happened, but to relate what Jesus said and did, in the interests of faith and worship. It should not be assumed that such interests compromise the historical value of the tradition. On the contrary, this question remains open. The Palestinian origin of the tradition enhances its value, but a final decision depends on what can be learnt elsewhere of the mind of Jesus in relation to His death and upon His teaching as a whole.

The Matthaean narrative is an expanded version of Mk ; the Lukan account is probably independent, and so also is that of Paul. All the accounts agree that Jesus said : ' This is my Body ' and that He looked forward to the perfected fellowship of the Kingdom of God, and those of Mk, Mt, and Paul testify that He spoke of His Blood as covenant-blood. It is a mistake of method to content oneself with the lowest common denominator of the several narratives. Each is the deposit of an original tradition and its value must be appraised in relation to the rest. When this is done, the Markan narrative commends itself as one of the oldest, if not the most ancient, of the accounts which reveal the singularly original manner in which Jesus conceived the nature of His redemptive death and related the Eucharist thereto. Whether He commanded its continued observance depends on the interpretation of 1 Cor. xi. 24 f., but, important as this question is, it is secondary to the significance He gave to the Supper and to the fact that His followers continued to celebrate it from the first.

For the question whether the Supper was a Passover meal see Note K, pp. 664-7.

Καὶ ἐσθιόντων αὐτῶν λαβὼν ἄρτον εὐλογήσας ἔκλασεν καὶ 22

22. With καὶ ἐσθιόντων αὐτῶν cf. 18a. It seems reasonably clear that one of these expressions has been assimilated to the other, and that therefore 18-21 and 22-5 are separate items of tradition. That an account of the Last Supper could stand alone is proved by 1 Cor. xi. 23-6, although even here a link is provided by the words ἐν τῇ

νυκτὶ ᾗ παρεδίδετο. The frequent use of καί in Mark's narrative, to the total exclusion of δέ and γάρ, is one of several signs that the tradition is Palestinian in origin. The use of λαβών is claimed by Jeremias, 88 f., as an Aramaism (cf. Lk. xiii. 19, 21), but the participle is not redundant, but indicates a separate action, the taking of the loaf.

[1] ' Chaeremon requests your company at dinner at the table of the lord Sarapis in the Serapaeum to-morrow, the 15th, at 9 o'clock.'

ἔδωκεν αὐτοῖς καὶ εἶπεν Λάβετε, τοῦτό ἐστιν τὸ σῶμά μου.

As Jeremias shows, 34-7, ἄρτος can be used equally of leavened and of unleavened bread (cf. ii. 26). The use of this word therefore leaves open the question whether the Supper was the Passover Meal.

The Blessing (εὐλογήσας, v. vi. 41) is an act of thanksgiving to God, and, according to Jewish usage, would take the form : ' Praised be Thou, O Lord our God, King of the Universe, who bringest forth bread from the earth ', or, as Dalman, *JJ*, 135, suggests : ' Blessed art Thou, our Father in heaven, who givest us to-day the bread necessary for us '. Luke and Paul have εὐχαριστήσας (cf. Mk. viii. 6). κλάω is also used as in viii. 6 and 19*· Here, in contrast with vi. 41 and viii. 6, Jesus Himself gives the broken pieces to those present (Mt, τοῖς μαθηταῖς). To the command λάβετε Mt adds φάγετε, which by assimilation is added in Mk in later uncials fam. 13 28 118 543 1071 *al. pler.* ff bo (1 MS.). k adds *et manducaverunt ex illo omnes* (cf. xiv. 23) ; cf. Turner, 68, *JTS*, xxix. 10.

The ' words of institution ' appear in the shortest form in Mk and Mt, τοῦτό ἐστιν τὸ σῶμά μου. Paul adds τὸ ὑπὲρ ὑμῶν (1 Cor. xi. 24), and, in dependence on 1 Cor., Luke has διδόμενον (in the Western text). These additions are interpretative and are parallel to the explanatory phrase in Mk. xiv. 24, with reference to the wine, τὸ ἐκχυννόμενον ὑπὲρ πολλῶν. τοῦτο clearly refers to the broken bread, and τὸ σῶμά μου to Christ's body surrendered to death for men. The term ' body ' is used as a correlative to ' blood ' (in 24), but also because Jesus thinks of His death in terms of sacrificial ideas, as an offering for men. If, then, τὸ ὑπὲρ ὑμῶν (Pl and Lk) is an addition, it correctly brings out what is implied in τὸ σῶμά μου. It is not easy to find a satisfactory rendering for ἐστιν. In the Aramaic there would be no copula, but, of course, one is implied. To render it by ' is ' easily

suggests a relationship of identity, which there is no reason to assume, whereas the translation ' represents ' may convey only a purely figurative suggestion. On the whole, the least unsatisfactory translation is Moffatt's ' Take this, it means my body ', because it suggests a certain valuation which Jesus has given to the bread both by His words and by His prophetic action in breaking it. Cf. Isa. xx. 2, Jer. xix. 10, xxviii. 10, Ezek. iv. 3, 1 Kings xxii. 11, Ac. xxi. 11, and *v.* Otto, 299-309, Taylor, *JHS*, 118-25. Dalman, *JJ*, 141, thinks that the Gk corresponds to the Aramaic, *dēn hū gūphī*, which can be taken in the sense ' This is I myself ', but which, in view of early Christian usage and the reference in 24 to ' blood ', requires the translation ' My Body '.

The fact that the bread is to be taken and eaten (cf. Mt, φάγετε) confirms the view that the underlying ideas of the saying are sacrificial, for the eating of that which is offered to God is one of the oldest of man's religious practices. Portions of all the OT sacrifices, except the sin- and the guilt-offerings, were regularly eaten. In this way the worshipper shared in the sacrifice offered on his behalf and appropriated its blessings, although the degree to which he did this might vary from the mere unintelligent performance of a rite to the highest of spiritual exercises. These considerations suggest that, when Jesus took a loaf, gave thanks and broke it, and gave the broken pieces to His disciples, He meant their action to be a means whereby they might share in the power of His self-offering and the virtue of His approaching death. The substance of the bread is not changed, but by His will it receives a new value and becomes the vehicle of faith.

The absence of the words τοῦτο ποιεῖτε εἰς τὴν ἐμὴν ἀνάμνησιν (1 Cor. xi. 24 f., Lk. xxii. 19b, cf. Justin Martyr, *Apol.* i. 66. 3) leaves open the

καὶ λαβὼν ποτήριον εὐχαριστήσας ἔδωκεν αὐτοῖς, καὶ ἔπιον ἐξ 23
αὐτοῦ πάντες. καὶ εἶπεν αὐτοῖς Τοῦτό ἐστιν τὸ αῖμά μου τῆς 24
Διαθήκης τὸ ἐκχυννόμενον ὑπὲρ πολλῶν· ἀμὴν λέγω ὑμῖν ὅτι 25

question of their genuineness. Mark may have known of them and have taken the command for granted, or, alternatively, the words may express in direct speech a conviction of which Christians were conscious from the first (cf. Ac. ii. 42, 46, etc.). Jeremias, 115, cites P. Benoit, *RB*, 48 (1939), 386, *On ne récite pas une rubrique, on l'exécute*. Jeremias takes the meaning to be ' that God may remember me ' (*damit Gott meiner gedenke*), His remembrance being His action in establishing the Kingdom at the Parousia.

23. For the use of λαβών v. xiv. 22 ; εὐχαριστήσας, viii. 6*. There is no reason to identify the cup (ποτήριον, vii. 4) as the third cup known as the ' cup of blessing ' drunk at the Paschal feast (cf. Swete, 335), unless the occasion was that of the Passover Meal, nor does St. Paul's expression τὸ ποτήριον τῆς εὐλογίας (1 Cor. x. 16) necessarily presuppose this identification (cf. Robertson and Plummer, *ICC, 1 Cor.* 211 f.). It has indeed been argued that since, apparently, Mark speaks of a single common cup, the meal cannot have been the Passover, but must have been the *Kiddûsh* for the Sabbath (F. Spitta, G. H. Box, R. Otto) or for the Passover (W. O. E. Oesterley, G. H. C. Macgregor, F. Gavin, T. H. W. Maxfield); but the evidence for Passover usage in respect of cups in the first century A.D. (cf. Dalman, *JJ*, 153-5; Jeremias, *AJ*, 32 f.; Lagrange, 379) is too uncertain to sustain an argument either way.

The words καὶ ἔπιον ἐξ αὐτοῦ πάντες suggest that a single cup was passed round, but the more important question is why the statement is made at all. Cf. Mt : πίετε ἐξ αὐτοῦ πάντες (xxvi. 27). Either the solemnity of the fact was vividly remembered or (possibly) the statement is polemical in view of current diversities of practice. Harnack, *Texte und Untersuchungen*,

vii. 2, 115 ff., for example, maintains that in certain Jewish-Christian circles water was used instead of wine. Cf. Klostermann, 164 ; Otto, 280. The former view is more probable, for the presence of a polemical *motif* in Mk is very doubtful ; cf. the notes on ix. 37 and 39. The fact that the statement precedes the saying on the wine has no special significance.

ἔπιον ἐξ αὐτοῦ is not necessarily a Semitism (מִן), for while πίνω is used c. acc. or c. gen., the source or vessel (as here) is described by ἀπό or ἐκ c. gen. Cf. ἐκ κεράμων, Hom. *Il.* ix. 469 ; ἐκ τῆς χειρός, Herodotus iv. 172 ; ἐξ ἀργύρου ἢ χρυσοῦ, Plato, *Rep.* 417 A. Contrast xiv. 25, ἐκ τοῦ γενήματος τῆς ἀμπέλου.

24. With the phrase τὸ αἷμά μου τῆς διαθήκης cf. Ex. xxiv. 8, ᾽Ιδοὺ τὸ αἷμα τῆς διαθήκης ἧς διέθετο Κύριος πρὸς ὑμᾶς, and Zech. ix. 11, καὶ σὺ ἐν αἵματι διαθήκης σου ἐξαπέστειλας δεσμίους σου ἐκ λάκκου οὐκ ἔχοντος ὕδωρ. In Ex. xxiv. 8 the sprinkling of the dedicated blood means that the people now share in the blessings of the covenant made at Sinai. The saying of Jesus suggests reflection upon this passage ; it reflects the idea that ' as of old dedicated blood was applied in blessing to the people of Israel, so now His life, surrendered to God and accepted by Him, is offered to, and made available for men ', V. Taylor, *JHS*, 138. Cf. Lk. xxii. 29 f., 1 Cor. xi. 25. Of this life the wine is both the symbol and the means by which it is appropriated, in harmony with the words of Ex. xxiv. 11, ' and they beheld God, and did eat and drink '. For the possible influence of Zech. ix. 11 v. Jeremias, 107 n. The Targum on this passage connected the blood of the covenant with that of the Passover lamb at the time of the departure from Egypt, but Jewish exegesis also connected it with the blood of circumcision. Dalman,

οὐκέτι οὐ μὴ πίω ἐκ τοῦ γενήματος τῆς ἀμπέλου ἕως τῆς ἡμέρας

JJ, 167, thinks that, when administering the wine, Jesus did not think of this passage, but holds that Jewish ideas attached to it are valuable because they show what was understood by ' covenant-blood '.

διαθήκη*, Mt. xxvi. 28, Lk. i. 72, xxii. 20, Ac (2), Pl (9), Heb (17), Apoc. xi. 19**, ' covenant ', is used frequently in the LXX, nearly always for בְּרִית. In Cl. Gk it means ' testament ' or ' will ', as always in the papyri and inscrr., in Josephus and in Heb. ix. 15 ff.. But elsewhere in the NT, as in the LXX, it is used in the sense of ' covenant ', probably because the classical συνθήκη was felt to imply the idea of a ' compact' between equals, a meaning poles asunder from that of the Heb. *berith*. Cf. *VGT*, 148 f.; Milligan, *The NT Documents*, 75; J. Behm, *KThW*, ii. 132-7; contr. Deissmann, 337 f., who defends the meaning ' testament ' throughout. With justice Behm claims that the ' new covenant ' is a correlative idea to that of ' the kingdom of God ', and that διαθήκη owes its meaning to the OT. The ' covenant ' is that relationship of lordship and obedience which God establishes between Himself and men, and ' the blood of the covenant ' is the sign of its existence and the means by which it is effected. In the words of institution Jesus gives the wine that value and significance, clearly not in a material or mechanical sense, but as providing the opportunity and ensuring the means for man's entry into the covenant relationship with God. A conscious relationship to the older covenants of Israel is implied by the use of μου with αἷμα, ' *My* blood of the covenant '.

The atoning significance of the blood is further defined by τὸ ἐκχυννόμενον ὑπὲρ πολλῶν, which, like x. 45, is based on Isa. liii. 12, ἀνθ' ὧν παρεδόθη εἰς θάνατον ἡ ψυχὴ αὐτοῦ, καὶ ἐν τοῖς ἀνόμοις ἐλογίσθη, καὶ αὐτὸς ἁμαρτίας πολλῶν

ἀνήνεγκεν, καὶ διὰ τὰς ἀνομίας αὐτῶν παρεδόθη. ἐκχύννομαι*, Mt. xxiii. 35, xxvi. 28, Lk. v. 37, xi. 50, xxii. 20, Ac. i. 18, x. 45, xxii. 20, Rom. v. 5, Ju. 11**, ' to pour forth ', is a late form of ἐκχέω. The participle is used, as in Hebrew and Aramaic, in the sense of the future; cf. Jeremias, 91, Lohmeyer, 308. The use of πολλῶν is also Semitic; its meaning is not ' some, but not all ', but ' all in contrast with one '. Matthew adds εἰς ἄφεσιν ἁμαρτιῶν (xxvi. 28).[1] The addition is interpretation, but valid interpretation, for the connexion of forgiveness with the idea of the new covenant is distinctive of Jer. xxxviii. (xxxi.) 31-4; ὅτι ἵλεως ἔσομαι ταῖς ἀδικίαις αὐτῶν καὶ τῶν ἁμαρτιῶν αὐτῶν οὐ μὴ μνησθῶ ἔτι. The phrase is one of the clearest indications that Jesus thought of His death as a vicarious sacrifice for men. Peculiar to Mk and Mt, it is in harmony with τὸ ὑπὲρ ὑμῶν, used of the Body in 1 Cor. xi. 24, and τὸ ὑπὲρ ὑμῶν διδόμενον in Lk. xxii. 19b.

The Pauline counterpart in 1 Cor. xi. 25 mentions the Cup: Τοῦτο τὸ ποτήριον ἡ καινὴ διαθήκη ἐστὶν ἐν τῷ ἐμῷ αἵματι. Opinion on the relatively greater originality of the Pauline form (cf. Behm, *op. cit.* ii. 136; Flew, *JHC*, 99 f.) or the Markan (Jeremias, *op. cit.* 83-6; Lohmeyer, 306) is divided. If one must choose, greater originality, I think, should be assigned to the more difficult Markan form (*JHS*, 203-6); but, essentially, the meaning is the same, for τοῦτο τὸ ποτήριον means the content of the Cup. ' Mark and Matthew, as much as Paul and Luke, compare the wine with the blood by the shedding of which the New Covenant is established ', Jeremias, *op. cit.* 84. The distinctive feature of the Pauline form is the word καινή which recalls Jer. xxxi. 31. In Mk καινῆς is read by A Δ *et al.* fam. 1 fam. 13 *al. pler.* it (exc. k) vg sys pe hl geo²

---

[1] So also by assimilation to Mt in Mk (W 9 fam. 13 18 472 543 1071 a g² vg (1 MS.) bo). περί (A *et al.* fam. 1 22 28 700 1071 *al. pler.*) instead of ὑπέρ is a further assimilation to Mt.

ἐκείνης ὅταν αὐτὸ πίνω καινὸν ἐν τῇ βασιλείᾳ τοῦ θεοῦ.

aeth arm by assimilation to 1 Cor. xi. 24.

25. This eschatological saying is loosely attached. There are parallels in Mt and Lk, and in Paul the same eschatological interest appears in the words τὸν θάνατον τοῦ κυρίου καταγγέλλετε, ἄχρι οὗ ἔλθῃ (1 Cor. xi. 26). In the independent Lukan account there is also a parallel saying at the beginning of the narrative: λέγω γὰρ ὑμῖν ὅτι οὐ μὴ φάγω αὐτὸ ἕως ὅτου πληρωθῇ ἐν τῇ βασιλείᾳ τοῦ θεοῦ (xxii. 16); here with reference to eating the Passover. For ἀμὴν λέγω ὑμῖν v. iii. 28.

The ideas in the saying are typically Jewish and the vocabulary is Semitic. For the idea of the Messianic Banquet in the Kingdom of God v. Isa. xxv. 6, 1 Enoch lxii. 14, 2 Baruch xxix. 5 ff., 4 Ezra vi. 51 ff., Pirqe Aboth, iii. 20. Cf. also Mt. viii. 11, Lk. xiv. 15, xxii. 29 f., Apoc. xix. 9, and v. Billerbeck, i. 992, iv. 1154-65. Cf. also the use of ἀμήν, possibly of ἐκ, the phrase τὸ γένημα* τοῦ ἀμπέλου for ' wine ', and the expression ἕως τῆς ἡμέρας ἐκείνης. A clear Semitism is present if preference is given to the reading of D,[1] οὐ μὴ προσθῶ πεῖν (v. infra), for προσέθετο c. infin. is used freely in the LXX to render הוֹסִיף (c. infin.) = πάλιν. Cf. Thackeray, Gr. 52 f.; Howard, ii. 445. A further possibility (Black, 171 f.) is that καινόν (חדת) is a mistranslation of an Aramaic original, ' until I am renewed (אתחדתית) in the kingdom of God '. In the face of this evidence it requires some hardihood to claim that the saying was formed in Hellenistic circles; it belongs to Palestinian tradition. For the popular form γένημα*, Mt. xxvi. 29, Lk. xii. 18, xxii. 18, 2 Cor. ix. 10**, the ' fruits of the earth ', v. VGT, 123 f. Not classical,

the word is found in the LXX (Gen. xl. 17, al.) and the papyri, as distinct from γέννημα, ' offspring '. For καινός v. i. 27; πίνω ii. 16; ἡ βασιλεία τοῦ θεοῦ i. 15.

Matthew's form of the saying is fuller. He has οὐ μὴ πίω and ἀπ' ἄρτι (cf. ἀπὸ τοῦ νῦν, Lk. xxii. 18), speaks of ' this ' (τούτου) fruit of the vine, adds μεθ' ὑμῶν to πίνω, and has ἐν τῇ βασιλείᾳ τοῦ πατρός μου (xxvi. 29). Luke's shorter version ends with ἕως ὅτου ἡ βασιλεία τοῦ θεοῦ ἔλθῃ (xxii. 18). The saying shows that at the Supper Jesus looked forward, beyond death, to the perfect fellowship of the consummated Kingdom. The drinking of the cup is a present participation in that fellowship so far as it can exist here and now. Cf. Lohmeyer, 304, ein Stück gegenwärtiger Wirklichkeit einer ewigen Mahlgemeinschaft; Jeremias, JW, 75; Dalman, JJ, 182-4. In this sense there is no reason why Jesus should not have shared in the drinking of the cup, and, while certainty is not attainable, the probability is that the text implies this. Cf. Ed. Meyer, i. 179 n. Wellhausen, 118, is justified in acclaiming the authenticity of the saying (einen sehr altertümlichen Eindruck), but not in suggesting that Jesus is present only as a guest; His Messianic consciousness is manifest. See the interesting discussion of Montefiore, i. 335. This eschatological saying ought not to be isolated from the rest of the eucharistic sayings. Rawlinson, Mysterium Christi, 241, .rightly observes that it was the death upon Calvary, ' as the Last Supper interprets it and gives the clue to its meaning ', which constitutes our Lord's Sacrifice. ' It. was the Last Supper which afforded the clue ', ibid.

---

[1] The variant readings are as follows: οὐκέτι οὐ μὴ (πίω): A B Δ (Θ) et al. minusc. pler. b ff i l q r² vg sy³ pe hl sa geo (arm). οὐ μὴ πίω: אּ C (D) L W 471 892 1342 (a) c (f) k vg (1 MS.) bo aeth. οὐ μὴ προσθῶ(-ῶμεν Θ) πιεῖν (πεῖν D): D Θ 565 a f arm. There is much to be said for the view that the third reading is interpreted (correctly) in the first, and misunderstood in the second. What Jesus said is that He would not drink again of the fruit of the vine until the consummation of the Kingdom.

Mk. xiv. 26-31   97. THE PROPHECY OF   Cf. Mt. xxvi. 30-5
                          THE DENIAL   (Lk. xxii. 31-4, 39)
                                                     (Jn. xiii. 36-8)

Introduced by the statement that, when they had sung, they went forth
to the Mount of Olives, this narrative consists almost entirely of sayings :
the prophecy that all would be offended and a quotation from Zech. xiii. 7 ;
the promise to go before the disciples into Galilee (28) ; the protest of
Peter and the prophecy of the denial (29-31a). With the words, ' And in
like manner said they all ' (31b), the section ends. Like 17-21, it is a
' Markan construction ' (v. Intr. 83), which preserves a tradition of the
tragic circumstances in which Jesus spoke. With the possible exception
of 28, the narrative is a unity. A general prophecy of defection provokes
a characteristic reply of Peter and a vehement rejoinder, with which all
agree, follows. The psychological links give continuity to the story, and,
while such links can be the product of imagination, it is more probable
that they depend ultimately on Petrine testimony. This opinion is supported by the close connexion of the subject-matter with the narrative
of the Denial (xiv. 54, 66-72). The word ὑμνήσαντες is generally interpreted
as implying that the Supper was the Passover Meal, but this interpretation depends upon the connexion between 26-31 and 12-16 and 17-21.
Mark's intention is to record what was said after the Supper on the way
to the Mount of Olives. This representation is different from those of
Luke and John, who record the prophecy during the conversation in the
Upper Room (cf. Lk. xxii. 31-4, Jn. xiii. 36-8). In this matter Mark's
account deserves preference. Lk. xxii. 34 is loosely attached to 31-3, and
Jn. xiii. 36-8 also owes its position to editorial compilation.

26   Καὶ ὑμνήσαντες ἐξῆλθον εἰς τὸ Ὄρος τῶν Ἐλαιῶν.
27   Καὶ λέγει αὐτοῖς ὁ Ἰησοῦς ὅτι Πάντες σκανδαλισθήσεσθε, ὅτι
      γέγραπται Πατάξω τὸν ποιμένα καὶ τὰ πρόβατα διασκορπι-
28   σθήσονται· ἀλλὰ μετὰ τὸ ἐγερθῆναί με προάξω ὑμᾶς εἰς τὴν

26 f. ὑμνέω*, Mt. xxvi. 30, Ac. xvi.
25, Heb. ii. 12** ; Cl., LXX, Pap. It
is commonly held that the Psalms sung
at the end of the Paschal Meal, namely
the second part of the Hallel (Psa. cxv-
cxviii), are meant (cf. Swete, 337 ;
Lagrange, 382). For the view that
ἐξῆλθον reflects the use of the first pers.
pl. v. Turner, JTS, xxvi. 225 f., 231.
τὸ Ὄρος τῶν Ἐλαιῶν, xi. 1.
   In the quotation in 27 from Zech.
xiii. 7, both the Heb. and the LXX
have the imperative ' Smite '. The use
of the fut. in Mk may be due to early
Testimonia (cf. Swete, 338 ; McNeile,
387 ; Smith, 199 ; Blunt, 252) or to
Jesus Himself (cf. Lagrange, 383), and
may even be original in the Heb. (cf.
R. H. Kennett, Peake's Comm. 583).

To trace the quotation to later Christian reflection (cf. Bertram, 42 ; Branscomb, 265 ; Montefiore, i. 340) is unnecessary in view of the frequent use
by Jesus of imagery connected with
sheep and shepherds ; cf. vi. 34, Mt.
xv. 24, xxv. 31-46, Lk. xii. 32, xv. 3-7,
Jn. x. 11. Cf. J. Jeremias, JW, 32 f.
The saying shows that Jesus had reflected upon the effect which His death
would have on the disciples, the little
flock or community which belonged
to Him. Cf. Flew, JHC, 80. They
would ' fall away ' (RSV) or ' be made
to stumble '. For σκανδαλίζω v. iv. 17 ;
γέγραπται i. 2 ; πατάσσω*, ποιμήν, vi.
34*. διασκορπίζω*, ' scatter abroad ',
belongs to late Gk (LXX, Pap. (VGT,
153)).

Γαλιλαίαν.   ὁ δὲ Πέτρος ἔφη αὐτῷ   Εἰ καὶ πάντες σκανδα- 29
λισθήσονται, ἀλλ᾽ οὐκ ἐγώ.   καὶ λέγει αὐτῷ ὁ Ἰησοῦς   Ἀμὴν 30

28. For μετὰ τό c. infin. v. i. 14;
ἐγείρω vi. 14; προάγω vi. 45; Γαλιλαία
i. 9; and for other references to the
Resurrection v. viii. 31, ix. 9, 31, x. 34,
xvi. 6 f. Matthew reproduces the saying almost verbatim (with δέ instead
of ἀλλά). Luke omits it, perhaps because he follows the Jerusalem tradition of the Appearances. The saying
is also absent from the ancient Fayyum
Fragment in the Rainer papyri (i.
53 ff.), but it may have been omitted
because of its difficulty, and its evidence cannot be accepted against that
of the MSS. and versions. For the
text of the fragment v. Lake, v. 12.
The saying may have been inserted
by Mark to prepare the way for xvi. 7
(cf. xiii. 10). This view is supported
by the fact that there is an excellent
connexion between 27 and 29; cf.
Holtzmann, 174; Lohmeyer, 311. It
is strange, moreover, that in his reply
Peter makes no allusion to 28; cf.
R. H. Lightfoot, LDG, 52. On the
other side, however, it may be argued
that there is a good connexion between
28 and 27, provided προάξω is rendered
' I shall lead ' (v. infra). Is the meaning that, while the little flock will be
scattered in consequence of the smiting
of the shepherd, after His Resurrection
Jesus, the Shepherd, will reconstitute
His community and lead them to
Galilee? Cf. Jn. x. 4, ἔμπροσθεν αὐτῶν
πορεύεται, καὶ τὰ πρόβατα αὐτῷ ἀκολουθεῖ. Unfortunately, προάγω is ambiguous; in vi. 45 the verb means ' to
go before ', but in x. 32 ' to walk
ahead ' (cf. RSV) or ' take the lead '.
Clearly, the exegetical problem is
primary. The saying has been interpreted in three ways. (1) Commonly,
it is held to foreshadow the appearances
of the Risen Lord to the disciples in
Galilee: cf. Swete, 339; Lagrange,
384; Plummer, 324. (2) In Die Schr.²
i. 208 J. Weiss takes the meaning to

be that Jesus will lead His followers
to Galilee: ' I will place myself at your
head and lead you to Galilee '; cf.
also HPC, 18. As an unfulfilled prediction, Weiss contends, the saying has
strong claims to be considered genuine.¹
Cf. Klostermann, 166. (3) Lohmeyer,
312, thinks that the saying is to be
explained doctrinally, as reflecting the
point of view of the Markan tradition,
that Galilee is to be the scene of the
expected Parousia. Galiläa ist das
gelobte Land des Evangeliums und der
eschatologischen Gemeinde, in dem das
Werk der Auferstehung vollendet werden soll.
It is difficult to think that Lohmeyer's interpretation rests on any
more solid ground than the dominance
of the Galilean tradition in Mk.
Weiss's explanation is very attractive,
but it is excluded by the fact that in the
parallel in xvi. 7 προάγει cannot be
rendered ' I am leading ', but only by
' I am going before '. One must conclude that the saying anticipates the
Resurrection Appearances. The same
view is relevant if it is held to be a
later insertion; cf. Bartlet, 391; Blunt,
252; McNeile, 387; Cadoux, 294.
29 f. For ὁ Πέτρος v. iii. 16; ἔφη ix.
12; σκανδαλίζω iv. 17. The reply of
Peter fixes attention on the charge that
all will fall away. He does not venture
to repudiate it, but claims that there
is an exception: ἀλλ᾽ οὐκ ἐγώ. εἰ καί
introduces a supposition fulfilled or
likely to be fulfilled, whereas with καὶ
εἰ the supposition is regarded as improbable; v. Burton, § 281; Robertson, 1026; and cf. Lk. xviii. 4, 2 Cor.
iv. 3, 16, vii. 8, Phil. ii. 17, Col. ii. 5,
etc., and for καὶ εἰ, 1 Cor. viii. 5, καὶ
ἐάν, Gal. i. 8. καὶ εἰ is read in Mk by
A Δ et al. 28 157 al. pler., but the evidence for εἰ καί is decisive (א B C L W
Ψ fam. 1 fam. 13 (exc. 346) 22 543 579
892 1071 1342 arm). Matthew in-

¹ In Die Schr.⁴ 206, as revised by Bousset, the saying is treated as a formation of the community which presumes the Appearances in Galilee.

λέγω σοι ὅτι σὺ σήμερον ταύτῃ τῇ νυκτὶ πρὶν ἢ δὶς ἀλέκτορα
31 φωνῆσαι τρίς με ἀπαρνήσῃ. ὁ δὲ ἐκπερισσῶς ἐλάλει 'Εὰν δέῃ
με συναποθανεῖν σοι, οὐ μή σε ἀπαρνήσομαι. ὡσαύτως [δὲ] καὶ
πάντες ἔλεγον.

creases the emphasis, ἐγὼ οὐδέποτε σκανδαλισθήσομαι.

In reply Jesus explicitly foretells Peter's denial, using the solemn words, ἀμὴν λέγω σοι (v. iii. 28). The emphatic σύ is omitted by ℵ C D Δ Φ 22 330 al. it (exc. c k) geo[1], but appears to be intended : so far from being an exception, Peter will actually deny his Lord. The ' tautology ' in σήμερον and ταύτῃ τῇ νυκτί is only apparent. The former (om. in Mt) marks the Jewish day which began at sundown ; the latter (om. in Lk) the night of that day. If δίς is read, the precision is still greater. Either the threefold denial will take place before a cock crows twice, or, more probably, the reference is to the beginning of the fourth watch when the signal known as gallicinium (' cock-crowing ') was given by a bugle call. Cf. C. H. Mayo, JTS, xxii. 367 ff. Commentators frequently quote Aristophanes, Eccl. 390 f., ὅτε τὸ δεύτερον ἀλεκτρυὼν ἐφθέγγετ', Juvenal ix. 107 f., Quod tamen ad galli cantum facit ille secundi Proximus ante diem caupo sciet.

δίς is omitted by ℵ C* D W 238 it (exc. f l q r²) vg (3 MSS.) aeth arm, but it is probable that the omission is due to assimilation with Mt or Lk. Cf. Lagrange, 385 ; Rawlinson, 208 ; Turner, 69 ; per contra, Menzies, 256 ; Bartlet, 391 f. ; Branscomb, 266. If read, the whole expression means about 3 a.m. Precise as the statement is, it does not seem necessary to assume a supernatural knowledge. How Mark interpreted the prophecy is, of course, another question. Cf. xiv. 72.

For πρὶν (ἤ) c. infin. v. Moulton, i. 169. ἀλέκτωρ, xiv. 68, 72 (bis)*, (Cl., LXX, Pap.), is the poetical form of ἀλεκτρυών, which appears in the Fayyum Fragment mentioned in the note on 28, ὁ ἀλεκτρυὼν δὶς κοκ[κύξει]

(cf. VGT, 21) Here κοκκύζω replaces φωνέω which, although normally used of human speech, describes the cries of animals and birds in Aristotle, HA, 578 a 32, 593 a 14, and in Jer. xvii. 11 the call of the partridge. For ἀπαρνέομαι v. viii. 34. The main variants in Mt and Lk are mentioned above. Lk introduces the voc. Πέτρε and adds μὴ εἰδέναι after ἀπαρνήσῃ. The genuineness of the prophecy needs no defence ; Christian tradition would not have preserved it except on the highest testimony, namely that of Peter himself.

31. Peter's consternation is powerfully expressed by ὁ δὲ ἐκπερισσῶς ἐλάλει. ἐκπερισσῶς**, ' vehemently ' ; not Cl., nor in LXX, nor illustrated in VGT; cf. ὑπερπερισσῶς in vii. 37. L W Θ fam. 13 543 565 read περισσῶς and A N[uid] fam. 1 22 28 157 700 892 1071 al. pler. ἐκ περισσοῦ (cf. vi. 51). It is difficult to think that ἐκπερισσῶς is correct, but it may be a Markan coinage rendering the original Aramaic. In any case, a passionate and reiterated protest is described ; ' he began to say vehemently '. Cf. Swete, 340. In the saying ἐάν has the force of καὶ ἐάν, ' even if ' (Klostermann, 167). Matthew has κἄν. It is unnecessary to suppose that συναποθανεῖν* reflects Pauline influence (2 Cor. vii. 3, 2 Tim. ii. 11**). It describes sharing in the tragic fate of Jesus, in the sense of Jn. xi. 16, Ἄγωμεν καὶ ἡμεῖς ἵνα ἀποθάνωμεν μετ' αὐτοῦ. Cf. Sir. xix. 10, ἀκήκοας λόγον; συναποθανέτω σοι. For οὐ μή c. aor. subj. expressing an emphatic negative v. ix. 1. The effect of this bold statement on the rest is contagious : ὡσαύτως (xii. 21*) δὲ καὶ πάντες ἔλεγον. Matthew has ὁμοίως and adds οἱ μαθηταί to πάντες. Although omitted by B fam. 1 251 253 330 579 a c ff k sa geo arm, δέ should probably be read.

Mk. xiv. 32-42 98. GETHSEMANE Cf. Mt. xxvi. 36-46
(Lk. xxii. 40-6)

The narrative is one of the most vivid in the Passion Narrative and has strong claims to be regarded as Petrine. Only as dependent on the testimony of Peter himself is a story so damaging to his reputation and to that of all the disciples conceivable. Rawlinson's opinion, 210, that the basis of the story is ' certainly historical and beyond the reach of invention ', is widely shared. Bultmann, 288, it is true, speaks of its ' wholly legendary character ', and Goguel, 495, describes it as ' an admirable allegory ' ' which expresses what took place in the soul of Jesus ', but these views stand opposed to a consensus of opinion shared by radical and conservative critics alike. See the estimate of Ed. Meyer quoted on p. 526. Montefiore, i. 342, while sensitive to the danger of pressing its details, says that ' one cannot but marvel at the wonderful grace and beauty, the exquisite tact and discretion, which the narrative displays '. Klausner, 332, says that it bears ' the hallmark of human truth ' and that only a few details are dubious. ' The sorrow and sufferings of the solitary Son of Man, profound as they are, leave on every sympathetic heart, be it the heart of the believer or unbeliever, such an impression as may never be wiped out ', ibid.

Close study of the narrative confirms this estimate. Both in the descriptive element and in the words of Jesus, we receive the impression of standing very close to the original facts, by implications which carry us far beyond the record itself. Why, in contrast with the martyrs who faced death with serenity, is it said that Jesus ἤρξατο ἐκθαμβεῖσθαι καὶ ἀδημονεῖν ? Why does He take with Him Peter, James, and John ? Why does He say : ' My soul is exceeding sorrowful even unto death ' ? What is ' the cup ' which He prays may be removed from Him ? Why are the three bidden to watch and what is the πειρασμός into which they are to pray that they may not enter ? What is the meaning of ἀπέχει, and what is the significance of ' the Hour ' ? These are some of the questions raised by this astounding narrative. So far from reflecting later doctrinal interests, it may be questioned if many of its elements had not become obscure by the time that Mark wrote. If we are not able to illuminate them all by modern critical inquiry, the reason is that in the narrative we stand near the bedrock of primitive tradition, and in part our slowness to concede that Jesus had profound and creative ideas concerning His Passion.

Καὶ ἔρχονται εἰς χωρίον οὗ τὸ ὄνομα Γεθσημανεί, καὶ λέγει 32

32 f. For ἔρχονται· v. Turner, *JTS*, xxvi. 225 f. χωρίον*, Mt. xxvi. 36, Jn. iv. 5, Ac. i. 18 f., iv. 34, v. 3, 8, xxviii. 7**, ' a piece of land ', ' a field '; Cl., LXX, Pap. (*VGT*, 696). Γεθσημανεί*, Mt. xxvi. 36**, *Gethsemane*, from the Heb. *gat shemanim*, ' oilspress ' (Dalman, *SSW*, 321 f.). The scanty description suggests a (former) farmstead or country estate planted with olive trees. Jn. xviii. 1 f. speaks of a garden (κῆπος) on the farther side of the torrent Kidron, and explains that Jesus had often gathered there with His disciples. Apparently it stood at the foot, or on the lower slopes, of the Mount of Olives. Jerome, following the reading Γησαμανεί found in D, speaks of it as *uallis pinguissima* (v.l. *pinguedinum*), ' valley of fatness ' (cf. Isa. xxviii. 1, 4, *ge' shemanim*). Lu. Gautier, *EB*, col. 1713, says of the

33 τοῖς μαθηταῖς αὐτοῦ Καθίσατε ὧδε ἕως προσεύξωμαι. καὶ
παραλαμβάνει τὸν Πέτρον καὶ ⌜τὸν Ἰάκωβον καὶ τὸν⌝ Ἰωάνην
34 μετ᾽ αὐτοῦ, καὶ ἤρξατο ἐκθαμβεῖσθαι καὶ ἀδημονεῖν, καὶ λέγει
αὐτοῖς Περίλυπός ἐστιν ἡ ψυχή μου ἕως θανάτου· μείνατε ὧδε

33 Ἰάκωβον καὶ

traditional site that it is 'not demon-strable, but neither is it utterly im-possible'. From early times worship has been offered there, as the state-ments of Eusebius and Jerome (v. Swete, 341) show. For a picturesque description v. Dalman, *SSW*, 326.

At the entrance (presumably) Jesus bids His disciples sit while He prays (ἕως προσεύξωμαι) and takes with Him Peter, James, and John (cf. v. 37, ix. 2). For παραλαμβάνω v. iv. 36; καθίζω ix. 35; προσεύχομαι i. 35. For ἕως c. subj. v. vi. 10, ix. 1, xii. 36* (in these passages with ἄν). Cf. Gen. xxii. 5 (Abraham), Ex. xxiv. 14 (Moses). Why Jesus takes the three with Him is not indicated, except in so far as they are bidden to watch (34) and pray (38). More than the need for human fellowship must be inferred. Were they expected to share, in their measure, in His Messianic suffering? Cf. the sayings on drinking the cup (x. 39) and cross-bearing (viii. 34).

The phrase καὶ ἤρξατο ἐκθαμβεῖσθαι καὶ ἀδημονεῖν is one of the most im-portant statements in Mk. For ἤρξατο c. infin. v. Intr. 48, 63 f. Lagrange, xciii, suggests that here ἤρξατο has its proper force. Both infinitives express the strongest and deepest feeling. Cf. Lohmeyer, 314: 'The Gk words de-pict the utmost degree of unbounded horror and suffering' (*den äussersten Grad eines grenzenlosen Entsetzens und Leidens*). For θαμβέομαι v. i. 27 and the note on ix. 15. The verb is 'sug-gestive of shuddering awe' (Rawlin-son, 211). 'His first feeling was one of terrified surprise', Swete, 342. The difficulty of translation is manifest:

RV 'greatly amazed'; RSV 'greatly distressed'; Moffatt 'appalled'; Torrey 'deeply agitated'. ἀδημονέω*, Mt. xxvi. 37, Phil. ii. 26**, 'to be sorely troubled', 'in anguish'; Cl., Aquila in Job xviii. 20, Symm. in Psa. lx. (lxi.) 3, etc.; Pap. (*VGT*, 9).[1] Swete, 342, says the verb describes 'the distress which follows a great shock'. Cf. Lightfoot, *Phil.* 123: 'It describes the confused, restless, half-distracted state, which is produced by physical derangement, or by mental distress, as grief, shame, disappoint-ment, etc.'. Cf. Plato, *Phaedr.* 251 D, ἀδημονεῖ τε τῇ ἀτοπίᾳ τοῦ πάθους καὶ ἀποροῦσα λυττᾷ. RV translates 'sore troubled'; RSV 'troubled'; Moffatt 'agitated'; Torrey 'distressed'; Wey-mouth (both infins.) 'to be full of terror and distress'. The boldness of the phrase is its guarantee. It is absent from Luke's account and is weakened in Matthew's ἤρξατο λυπεῖσθαι καὶ ἀδη-μονεῖν (xxvi. 37). With every desire to avoid unwarranted psychological interpretations, it is impossible to do any kind of justice to Mark's words without seeing in them something of the astonishment of the Son of Man who knows that He is also the Suffering Servant of Isa. liii. It is too little observed that the description and the saying which follows belong to the brief interval before Jesus leaves His three disciples. The intensity of the anguish drives Him from them to seek peace before the face of His Father.

34 f. For περίλυπος v. vi. 26*; ψυχή ii. 4; θάνατος vii. 10. The saying re-flects the language of Psa. xli. (xlii.) 6, 12, xlii. (xliii.) 5, ἵνα τί περίλυπος εἶ, ἡ

---

[1] The derivation of ἀδημονέω is uncertain. To Buttmann's suggestion, that it is to be derived from ἄδημος 'away from home', Lightfoot objects that the form of the word is a serious obstacle. T. W. Allen, *CR*, xx. 5, traces it to ἀδήμων (from a presumed δήμων 'prudent', 'knowing'), but LS say that this adj. 'is itself of doubtful derivation'.

καὶ γρηγορεῖτε. καὶ ⌈προελθὼν⌉ μικρὸν ἔπιπτεν ἐπὶ τῆς γῆς, 35
καὶ προσηύχετο ἵνα εἰ δυνατόν ἐστιν παρέλθῃ ἀπ' αὐτοῦ ἡ ὥρα,
καὶ ἔλεγεν Ἀββά, ὁ πατήρ, πάντα δυνατά σοι· παρένεγκε τὸ 36

35 προσελθὼν

ψυχή, καὶ ἵνα τί συνταράσσεις με;, but whereas the Psalmist speaks in prayer to God, Jesus addresses the three disciples. Thus, the words are an echo rather than a quotation. The addition ἕως θανάτου denotes a sorrow which threatens life itself. Cf. Swete, 342, ' a sorrow that well-nigh kills '. Cf. Jon. iv. 9, σφόδρα λελύπημαι ἐγὼ ἕως θανάτου. The alternative, that death is a desired friend which delivers the soul from unutterable grief (Lohmeyer, 314), is less satisfactory. Cf. Klostermann, 168, who cites Judg. xvi. 16, 3 Kgdms. xix. 4, Sir. xxxvii. 2. The saying has a parallel in Jn. xii. 27, νῦν ἡ ψυχή μου τετάρακται, καὶ τί εἴπω;, and may be in mind in Heb. iv. 15, v. 7 f. In μείνατε (vi. 10*) and γρηγορεῖτε (xiii. 34) the tenses distinguish the definite act and the abiding attitude. For the idea of watching v. the note on 33. It is not fanciful to suppose that in recording this charge the narrator has in mind the Christians of his day; cf. xiii. 33-7. Matthew adds μετ' ἐμοῦ.

Jesus now separates Himself from the three, but not by a great distance (προελθὼν μικρόν). μικρόν is here used adverbially of distance; in xiv. 70 of time. For the attitude of prostration in prayer and supplication v. Gen. xvii. 3, 17, Lk. v. 12, xvii. 16, all c. ἐπὶ πρόσωπον as in Mt. In the Lukan parallel the attitude is one of kneeling (θεὶς τὰ γόνατα, xxii. 41). Swete, 343, suggests that the imperf. ἔπιπτεν describes the action as taking place under the eyes of the narrator; cf. Lagrange, 387. It is difficult to feel sure about this suggestion, but it is supported by WM, 336 f. and Robertson, 883; cf. Lk. x. 18, Ac. xvi. 22. For προσεύχομαι v. i. 35. In Luke's version Jesus is parted from His disciples a stone's throw (ἀπεσπάσθη ἀπ' αὐτῶν ὡσεὶ λίθου

βολήν, xxii. 41), a statement which agrees with προελθὼν μικρόν (Mk, Mt).

It is peculiar to Mark's account that he first gives the substance of the prayer in indirect speech (cf. viii. 31) and then (36) in the direct form. So the reader's attention is assured. With προσεύχομαι ἵνα . . . cf. xiii. 18; εἰ δυνατόν xiii. 22; παρέρχομαι vi. 48, xiii. 30, etc. Of outstanding interest is the idea of the appointed time, ' the Hour ' (ἡ ὥρα, xiv. 41*); cf. i. 15, xiii. 32. Eschatological in origin (cf. ὥρα (τῆς) συντελείας, Dan. xi. 40, 45), the idea is taken over by Jesus as appropriate to the fulfilment of His Messianic destiny. Cf. Jn. ii. 4, vii. 30, viii. 20, xii. 23, 27 (bis), xiii. 1, xvii. 1. Cf. also Lk. xxii. 14, 53.

36. Ἀββά*, Rom. viii. 15, Gal. iv. 6**, is the Aramaic word ' father '. Cf. Dalman, 191 f.; Kittel, KThW, i. 4-6; Black, 217 f. Mt has πάτερ μου, Lk πάτερ. The addition of ὁ πατήρ in Mk can hardly be an explanatory comment of Mark himself, since it is present also in Rom. and Gal., and must be either a primitive liturgical formula in a bilingual Church (cf. Lightfoot, Gal. 169) or the usage of Jesus Himself (cf. SH, Rom. 203). The claim that the three passages are emotional and that interpretation is out of place in a prayer (SH) tells against the Markan origin of the phrase, but loses much of its force if it is liturgical, and, on the whole, this is the best view to take, since Ἀββά ὁ πατήρ appears once only in Mk and never in Q, L, or M. The confident πάντα δυνατά σοι has an original ring as compared with the weaker versions of Mt (εἰ δυνατόν ἐστιν) and Lk (εἰ βούλει). Cf. x. 27.

The question raised in x. 38 f. regarding the nature of the cup is more pressing in xiv. 36, since Jesus prays that it may be removed. For παρένεγκε*

37 ποτήριον τοῦτο ἀπ' ἐμοῦ· ἀλλ' οὐ τί ἐγὼ θέλω ἀλλὰ τί σύ. καὶ
ἔρχεται καὶ εὑρίσκει αὐτοὺς καθεύδοντας, καὶ λέγει τῷ Πέτρῳ
38 Σίμων, καθεύδεις; οὐκ ἴσχυσας μίαν ὥραν γρηγορῆσαι; γρηγορεῖτε καὶ προσεύχεσθε, ἵνα μὴ ἔλθητε εἰς πειρασμόν· τὸ μὲν

in the sense of ' Turn aside, cause to pass by ' v. Field, 39. Cf. Lk. xxii. 42, Heb. xiii. 9, Ju. 12**; Cl., LXX, Pap. (VGT, 491). In the OT the metaphor describes punishment and divine retribution (cf. C. E. B. Cranfield, ET, lix. 137 f.), and it is natural to wish to restrict the meaning of xiv. 36 to suffering and death (cf. M. Black, ET, lix. 195). But the intensity of the prayer suggests that more is meant, and there is no need to exclude the thought of the divine judgment on sin, provided it is recognized that Jesus is not the personal object of wrath. His suffering is Messianic. He suffers as the Son of Man (viii. 31, x. 45, etc.) and therefore voluntarily exposes Himself to the judgment which rests upon His brethren. It is alien to the spirit of Jesus that He should ask for the cup to be taken away if it is no more than one of personal suffering and death, and the bewilderment and anguish of θαμβεῖσθαι καὶ ἀδημονεῖν show that it is more. The prayer suggests that Jesus had to school Himself to the necessity of redemptive suffering which involves the bearing of sin. The healthy fear of reading theology into His words may blind us to their true meaning; it may prevent us from finding in them a ' theology ' which is highly original and is not primitive Christian theology read back into His teaching.

In οὐ τί ἐγὼ θέλω the interrogative τί is used instead of the relative ὅ τι, as in the papyri and inscriptions (VGT, 636). Cf. Moulton, i. 93·5; Blass, 175; Robertson, 737. But possibly Swete, 344, is right in paraphrasing the clause : ' However, the question is not what is My will ', etc. Cf. Lagrange, 389. The negative οὐ shows that γενηθήτω must not be understood. This change is made in Lk. xxii. 42,

μὴ τὸ θέλημά μου ἀλλὰ τὸ σὸν γινέσθω, bringing the prayer into closer conformity with the Lord's Prayer. Mark's form is manifestly more original. In both Mt and Lk ἀλλά . . . ἀλλά becomes πλήν . . . ἀλλά. For the importance of the saying in the history of doctrine, as illustrating the reality of Christ's human will, v. H. R. Mackintosh, The Person of Jesus Christ, 220-222, 399, and for Patristic references v. Swete, 345.

37 f. In contrast with Jesus at prayer stands the picture of the sleeping disciples. For καθεύδω v. iv. 27. Luke explains that it was ἀπὸ τῆς λύπης. It is natural that Peter should be addressed in view of his confident boast (29, 31). Here only in Mk, apart from iii. 16, and with complete naturalness, is the name Σίμων used. ' For the time he is " Peter " no more ' (Swete, 345) ; cf. Jn. xxi. 15 ff. For ἰσχύω v. ii. 17. The meanings ' to have power ' and ' to be able ' are both illustrated by the papyri (VGT, 308), but of these the former seems more appropriate in this context : ' Hadst thou not strength ? ' (cf. Plummer, 328). He who was ready to die with Jesus lacked the will to watch for an hour. The obvious parenetic motif in no way compromises the tradition ; on the contrary, it was only because the facts were known that the example could be cited. For γρηγορέω v. xiii. 34 ; and for προσεύχομαι ἵνα xiii. 18, xiv. 35. Here the ἵνα clause may be final (Moffatt), but more probably gives the purport of the prayer (Meecham, JTS, xliii. 180) ; the imperatival use of ἵνα c. subj. (Cadoux, JTS, xlii. 172) is less likely.

πειρασμός* is frequently used of the proving of men by affliction ; cf. Sir. ii. 1, ἑτοίμασον τὴν ψυχήν σου εἰς πειρασμόν, Lk. xxii. 28, Ac. xx. 19, Gal. iv. 14, Jas. i. 2, 1 Pet. i. 6 ; πειράζω is also

πνεῦμα πρόθυμον, ἡ δὲ σὰρξ ἀσθενής. καὶ πάλιν ἀπελθὼν προσ- 39
ηύξατο [τὸν αὐτὸν λόγον εἰπών]. καὶ πάλιν ἐλθὼν εὗρεν αὐτοὺς 40
καθεύδοντας, ἦσαν γὰρ αὐτῶν οἱ ὀφθαλμοὶ καταβαρυνόμενοι, καὶ
οὐκ ᾔδεισαν τί ἀποκριθῶσιν αὐτῷ. καὶ ἔρχεται τὸ τρίτον 41

used of solicitations to evil, from lust (Jas. i. 13-15) and by Satan (Mk. i. 13). Neither meaning is relevant to the situation. A prayer to escape trial is the opposite of what is intended, and the idea of Satanic solicitation to evil is too general. A definite peril in which they may be overwhelmed appears to be in mind, and this is far more than the danger of sleep or of the impending Arrest. The origin of the foreboding may well be eschatological; cf. Apoc. iii. 10, κἀγώ σε τηρήσω ἐκ τῆς ὥρας τοῦ πειρασμοῦ τῆς μελλούσης ἔρχεσθαι . . . πειράσαι τοὺς κατοικοῦντας ἐπὶ τῆς γῆς. Cf. R. H. Charles, Rev. i. 90; Schweitzer, 387, 390; Lohmeyer, 317. This interpretation seems out of place in the present context; but the position is entirely different if ' realized eschatology' plays a part in the present experience of Jesus. Cf. Dodd, 166 n. The references to ' the Hour ' (35, 41), the description of the Agony (33), and the sayings in 34, 36, xv. 34, Lk. xxii. 53b, suggest that in one of its aspects the experience of Jesus was conceived as a conflict with Satanic powers; and, if this inference is justified, it is probable that He thought the three disciples were exposed to similar perils and therefore in need of the injunction ' Be vigilant, and pray '. These ideas are strange to the modern man, but not to the ancient world. It is possible, indeed, that the prayer had become strange to the early narrators. If so, its presence in the narrative is a sign of primitive tradition. Cf. Schniewind, 187. The frequent allusions of commentators to the Lord's Prayer are relevant only if in this prayer also the original ideas are eschatological.

The explanatory clause τὸ μὲν πνεῦμα πρόθυμον, ἡ δὲ σὰρξ ἀσθενής agrees well with the interpretation suggested above. There is no need to characterize

the words as ' Pauline ', as many commentators, including Wellhausen, 120; Menzies, 259; Lohmeyer, 317, recognize. The contrast (μέν . . . δέ, v. xiv. 21) is the common OT distinction between πνεῦμα and σάρξ, that is, between man as dependent upon the Spirit of God and as a frail creature subject to the limitations of his earthly nature; cf. Numb. xxvii. 16, Isa. xxxi. 3, Jn. iii. 6. Cf. Swete, 346 f.; Davidson, The Theology of the OT, 188-99. πρόθυμος*, Mt. xxvi. 41, Rom. i. 15**; ' ready ', ' eager '; Cl., LXX, Pap.; πνεῦμα i. 8; σάρξ x. 8.

With small additions the two vv. are closely reproduced in Mt. Luke's version is substantially independent, except perhaps in xxii. 46b. There is no parallel to Mk. xiv. 37b and 38b. 39 f. Jesus again departs and prays. For πάλιν v. ii. 1; ἀπέρχομαι i. 20; προσεύχομαι i. 35. The words τὸν αὐτὸν λόγον εἰπών are omitted by D a b c ff k and are bracketed by WH. The same MSS. omit πάλιν in 40. If read, λόγον has the meaning ' words' or ' prayer', but the phrase has every appearance of being a gloss. Cf. Allen, 177.

A second time Jesus comes and finds them sleeping. There is less reason to reject πάλιν here, since it corresponds to τὸ τρίτον in 41. For καθεύδω v. iv. 27. This time Mark gives the explanation that their eyes were weighed down and he repeats the phrase used of Peter in the story of the Transfiguration (ix. 6) καὶ οὐκ ᾔδεισαν τί ἀποκριθῶσιν αὐτῷ. καταβαρύνω** corresponds to the classical καταβαρέω. LS cite a single example from Theophrastus, Vert. 9 (iv/iii B.C.); the verb is found in the LXX (2 Kgdms. xiii. 25, xiv. 26, Jl. ii. 8, Sir. viii. 15*) but is not illustrated in VGT. For the periphrastic imperf. v. Intr. 45, 62 f., and with the use of the interrog. and the subj. in

καὶ λέγει αὐτοῖς Καθεύδετε. [τὸ] λοιπὸν καὶ ἀναπαύεσθε· ἀπ-
έχει· ἦλθεν ἡ ὥρα, ἰδοὺ παραδίδοται ὁ υἱὸς τοῦ ἀνθρώπου εἰς τὰς

the indirect question cf. ix. 6. Here the remark is much to the point; the three failed to understand the reference to the πειρασμός. 'The irresistible lethargy of the disciples was for Peter a shameful memory', J. Weiss, 301. Luke has no parallel to the rest of the Markan story after 38a. Matthew reproduces 39 f. closely, adding a second version of the prayer of Jesus, but omitting the statement that the disciples did not know what to answer Him.

41 f. τὸ τρίτον*. The first part of the saying is obscure, partly because of ἀπέχει and the reading τὸ τέλος, and partly because it is not clear whether the words are a command or a question. τὸ λοιπόν* (or λοιπόν), Mt. xxvi. 45, Ac. xxvii. 20, 1 Cor. i. 16, iv. 2, vii. 29, 2 Cor. xiii. 11, Phil. iii. 1, iv. 8, 1 Thess. iv. 1, 2 Thess. iii. 1, 2 Tim. iv. 8, Heb. x. 13**, is used in several senses: 'for the rest', 'henceforth', 'then', 'finally', 'therefore', 'so'. Cf. VGT, 380; Lightfoot, Notes, 51; H. G. Meecham, ET, xlviii. 331 f. For ἀνα-παύομαι vi. 31. There is not a little to be said for taking καθεύδετε τὸ λοιπὸν καὶ ἀναπαύεσθε as a question, 'Still asleep? Still resting?'; cf. Moffatt, RSV, Klostermann, 168, Schlaft ihr nun und ruht? The difficulty, as Torrey, TG, 58, observes, is the adverb. Even greater is the problem presented by ἀπέχει. Usually it is rendered 'It is enough' (RV, RSV, vg, sufficit), with reference either to sleep (Kloster-mann, 169; Rawlinson, 213) or to the ironical reproof (Swete, 348). This interpretation is possible, but the evi-dence for this impersonal use of ἀπέχει is scanty; cf. Pseud. Anacreon, Od. xxviii. 33, 'Απέχει· βλέπω γὰρ αὐτήν, also Cyr. Hag. ii. 9; cf. Field, 39. In each case the reading is uncertain; cf. Pallis, 47. J. de Zwaan, Exp. vi. xii. 452 ff., interprets the word in the com-mercial sense illustrated in the papyri and ostraca, where it is a technical

expression in a receipt (VGT, 58): 'He (Judas) did receive (the promised money)'. This suggestion is sup-ported by 41b, but it reads a great deal into ἀπέχει. It is tempting to suppose that the Gk is a misrendering of the original Aramaic, and this view is taken by Torrey, TG, 58 f., who suggests that kaddu 'already' has been given the Syriac meaning satis: 'Already the time has come'. To this suggestion Black, 161, objects that both in Palestinian Aramaic and in Syriac kaddu means iam, and, alter-natively, he suggests that ἀπέχει has arisen from the misreading by a trans-lator of a Dalath as a Rish, reḥeq 'is far away' instead of deḥeq 'is pres-sing'. D reads ἀπέχει τὸ τέλος καὶ ἡ ὥρα, and the original probably ran, 'The end and the hour are pressing', or 'The end is pressing, (and) the hour has come'. In ET, xlvi. 382, J. T. Hudson, accepting the reading τὸ τέλος, suggested that ἀπέχει τὸ τέλος should be read as a third ironical question, 'The end is far away?', followed by the cry, 'The hour has come!'.

Clearly the textual question is im-portant. τὸ τέλος is read by D W Θ Φ fam. 13 565 1071 et al. a c d f ff q r¹ sys pe hl, and there is good reason to think that it is original. It is attested by important Western, Caesarean, and Eastern authorities, and, as an eschato-logical term, is in line with the ideas which appear to underlie the narrative (v. xiv. 38). ἀπέχει presents a more difficult problem. It is omitted by Ψ 50 k bo, and while vg d q have sufficit, c f ff r¹ read adest (cf. consum-matus est finis in a) and sys pe hl appear to attest ἤγγικεν. Following K, Cou-choud, JTS, xxxiv. 129-31, explains ἀπ-έχει τὸ τέλος as a marginal note, and Pallis, 47-9, conjectures ἐπέστη. All these variants and conjectures appear to be simplifications. D also seems secondary in so far as it omits ἦλθεν.

χεῖρας τῶν ἁμαρτωλῶν. ἐγείρεσθε ἄγωμεν· ἰδοὺ ὁ παραδιδούς 42
με ἤγγικεν.

On the whole, therefore, there is most to be said for reading ἀπέχει τὸ τέλος, ἦλθεν ἡ ὥρα and for interpreting ἀπέχει as Black or Hudson suggest (v. supra).

Despite the difficulties of interpretation, it is possible to follow the drift of the saying, and details are studied best in the light of the whole. It is certainly much too drastic an operation to pass from ἀπέχει to ἐγείρεσθε, ἄγωμεν . . . in 42 and to treat 41b as secondary. So Wellhausen, 120 f. The reference to ' the hour ' is the heart of the saying, and ἰδοὺ παραδίδοται ὁ υἱὸς τοῦ ἀνθρώπου εἰς τὰς χεῖρας τῶν ἁμαρτωλῶν rightly explains what ' the hour ' means. For ἡ ὥρα v. xiv. 35 ; ἰδού i. 2 ; παραδίδωμι i. 14 ; ὁ υἱὸς τοῦ ἀνθρώπου ii. 10 ; ἁμαρτωλός ii. 15. It is quite inadequate to explain the hour as simply that of the arrest or the betrayal ; it is the hour when the Messianic ministry of Jesus

reaches its climax, in that He is delivered over into the hands of sinful men. Fortified by prayer, Jesus accepts His destiny. The approach of Judas (ἰδοὺ ὁ παραδιδούς με ἤγγικεν) is the human sign that the time is fulfilled. It is significant that, even after their failure, He says to the three ἐγείρεσθε, ἄγωμεν, ' Arise, let us be going '.

In the light of this vigorous climax to the saying it appears doubly doubtful that Jesus can have said to the three, ' Sleep on now, and take your rest ', adding sadly ' It is enough '. On this interpretation one is tempted to approve Wellhausen's use of the critical knife. Far more realistic is the rendering : ' Still asleep ? Still resting ? The End is far away ? The Hour has struck. Behold, the Son of Man is being delivered into the hands of sinners. Arise, let us be going. Behold, he who delivers me up is near.'

Mk. xiv. 43-52   99. THE ARREST   Cf. Mt. xxvi. 47-56
(Lk. xxii. 47-53)
(Jn. xviii. 2-11)

This narrative is very different from the vivid account of Gethsemane, with its several sayings. Sober and restrained, it contains no sayings apart from 48 f. Strictly speaking, the narrative ends at 46, in the statement that they arrested Jesus. Verses 47 (the wounding of the high priest's slave), 48-50 (the protest of Jesus), and 51 f. (the stranger who fled), are separate items of tradition which Mark has appended. With the exception of Jesus, no one is named. The crowd is not characterized. We do not learn who is the bold sympathizer who avenges the indignity of the arrest, nor the name of the stranger who follows when all have fled. All the interest is concentrated on the action of Judas and the arrest itself. Nevertheless, it cannot be said that the narrative is vague or diffuse. Painted with a few bold strokes, the scene is clear and impressive.

It is not surprising that the later Evangelists sought to embellish the sober Markan narrative for liturgical and catechetical ends. Thus, sayings are added (Mt, Lk, Jn), and dialogue is introduced ; the slave's ear is said to be the right ear (Lk, Jn), and both he and the bystander are named (Jn) ; and, finally, the incident of the stranger is suppressed. It is in these later versions that Bertram, 50-5, finds ground for his thesis that the account is a cult-narrative. Data for this view in 43-6 are harder to find, in the references to the traitor's kiss and to the fulfilling of Scripture, which may still be historical even if cited for an edifying purpose. Least of all is it necessary to question the narrative because it depicts for the reader ' the sufferings of Christ '. The narrative and its supplements contain good tradition, which ultimately may be Petrine.

The suggestion of Bultmann, 289, that 43-52 originally followed 27-31, is attractive, for the narrative records the fulfilling of the first part of the prophecy ' all shall be offended '. It may well be that 1 f., 10 f., 12-16, 17-21, 26-31, 43-52 belong to the narrative framework on which the Passion Narrative is built. The prominence of the figure of Judas in several of these stories is a primitive sign, for it reflects the horror which his deed aroused in the minds of the first narrators.

43 Καὶ εὐθὺς ἔτι αὐτοῦ λαλοῦντος παραγίνεται [ὁ] Ἰούδας εἷς
τῶν δώδεκα καὶ μετ' αὐτοῦ ὄχλος μετὰ μαχαιρῶν καὶ ξύλων
παρὰ τῶν ἀρχιερέων καὶ τῶν γραμματέων καὶ τῶν πρεσβυτέρων.
44 δεδώκει δὲ ὁ παραδιδοὺς αὐτὸν σύσσημον αὐτοῖς λέγων "Ον ἂν
45 φιλήσω αὐτός ἐστιν· κρατήσατε αὐτὸν καὶ ἀπάγετε ἀσφαλῶς. καὶ

43. Mark's hand is visible in εὐθύς (v. i. 10) and in ἔτι αὐτοῦ λαλοῦντος (v. v. 35) by which the story is linked with that of Gethsemane. παραγίνεται* may mark the use of a source; cf. also Ἰούδας (ὁ in A B alone) and εἰς τῶν δώδεκα as in xiv. 10, 20. The facts are narrated almost in note form, and it is not surprising that additions are made in the MS. tradition: ὁ Ἰσκαριώτης after Ἰούδας, ὤν after εἷς, πολύς following ὄχλος, and ἀπεσταλμένοι before παρά (v. Legg). The second μετά just after μετ' αὐτοῦ is harsh, although Matthew allows it to stand. The passage is like the summary accounts in xiv. 1 f. and 10 f., in contrast with the more detailed narratives of Gethsemane and the Denial.

Apparently, the arrest is made by a hired rabble. There is no mention of the Temple police (cf. Lk. xxii. 52) or of Roman soldiers (cf. Jn. xviii. 3, 12). In 47 a servant of the high priest is mentioned, and others may have been present, but substantially the description is that of a mob armed with the weapons of their trade. The μάχαιραι (xiv. 47 f.*) are short swords or possibly large knives (cf. Field, 76 f.) and the ξύλα (xiv. 48*) are cudgels. Originally meaning ' wood ', ξύλον came to be used of objects made of wood, e.g. ' staves ' (as here), stocks ' (Ac. xvi. 24), ' a gibbet '

(Moffatt, Ac. v. 30, x. 39, xiii. 29, Gal. iii. 13, 1 Pet. ii. 24), and later ' a (living) tree ' (Lk. xxiii. 31); cf. VGT, 434 f. The precision with which the three groups, ἀρχιερεῖς (v. ii. 26), γραμματεῖς (v. i. 22), πρεσβύτεροι (v. viii. 31), are mentioned recalls xiv. 1 (two groups) and apparently is meant to emphasize their joint guilt. Mt omits the γραμματεῖς and Lk substitutes στρατηγοὺς τοῦ ἱεροῦ in a verse (xxii. 52) which erroneously suggests that the members of the hierarchy were present.

44. This explanatory passage describes the arrangement which Judas had already made to distinguish Jesus in the garden. Cf. v. 8. For the dropping of the augment in the pluperfect v. Moulton, ii. 190. As in 42, Judas is designated as ὁ παραδιδοὺς αὐτόν. This phrase shows that in the most primitive period attention was concentrated on the horror and enormity of the act rather than upon the motives and character of Judas (ctr. Jn. xii. 6, Mt. xxvi. 15, xxvii. 3-10). σύσσημον**, ' a sign ' or ' signal '; a late Gk word condemned by Phrynichus; LXX (Ju. xx. 40, Isa. v. 26, etc.); Pap. (VGT, 617). Mt has σημεῖον. φιλέω* is found here and in Mt. xxvi. 48 and Lk. xxii. 47 in the sense of ' kiss '; Cl., Pap. (VGT, 670), LXX (Gen. xxvii. 26, etc.). The use of the kiss was customary among the

ἐλθὼν εὐθὺς προσελθὼν αὐτῷ λέγει 'Ραββεί, καὶ κατεφίλησεν
αὐτόν. οἱ δὲ ἐπέβαλαν τὰς χεῖρας αὐτῷ καὶ ἐκράτησαν αὐτόν. 46
εἰς δέ [τις] τῶν παρεστηκότων σπασάμενος τὴν μάχαιραν ἔπαισεν 47

Rabbis and their pupils; cf. Billerbeck, i. 996; Swete, 350. See also
Lk. vii. 45, xxii. 48 (φίλημα), and for
the custom in the primitive Church v.
Rom. xvi. 16, 1 Cor. xvi. 20, 2 Cor.
xiii. 12, 1 Thess. v. 26, 1 Pet. v. 14.
For ὅς ἄν c. subj. v. iii. 29; and for
αὐτός ἐστιν, ' He is the man ', v. Blass,
164; Robertson, 679. For κρατέω in
the sense of ' seize ', ' arrest ' v. iii. 21
and for ἀπάγω (xiv. 53, xv. 16*) with
the meaning ' carry off ', ' lead away '
v. LS and VGT, 51. ἀσφαλῶς*, Ac.
xvi. 23 (ii. 36, ' assuredly ')**, ' se-
curely ' (Cl., LXX), means that there
is to be no mistake; no chances are
to be taken. Mt omits the last three
words and Lk has no parallel to the
verse.

45 f For εὐθύς v. i. 10, and for the
redundant participle in ἐλθὼν προσελθών v. Howard, ii. 452; Lagrange,
xcii. Mt omits it. For 'Ραββεί v.
ix. 5. καταφιλέω*, Mt. xxvi. 49, Lk.
vii. 38, 45, xv. 20, Ac. xx. 37**, 'to
kiss ', ' caress '; Cl., LXX, Pap. Cf.
2 Kgdms. xx. 9. In recent discussions there is a marked tendency to question the meaning ' to kiss fervently '
in Hellenistic Gk illustrated in RVmg
' kissed him much '; cf. VGT, 334;
Sharp, 104; Turner, 71; v. also RV,
RSV, Moffatt, Torrey. Nevertheless,
the change from φιλέω in 44, the force
of the preposition in κατεφίλησεν and
Lk. vii. 38, 45, xv. 20, Ac. xx. 37
strongly support an added emphasis;
cf. Swete, 351, who cites Xen. Mem.
ii. 6. 33; Lagrange, 394; Gould, 274;
Bartlet, 399; Blunt, 254; Lohmeyer,
322. A simulated tender kiss agrees
with the manifest intention to effect
the arrest by surprise and as quickly
as possible. In the Markan narrative
no word of Jesus is recorded and the
arrest immediately follows. In Mt.
xxvi. 50 Jesus gives the familiar greeting 'Εταῖρε, ἐφ' ὃ πάρει ; (cf. Deissmann, 125-31), and in Lk. xxii. 48 asks,

'Ιούδα, φιλήματι τὸν υἱὸν τοῦ ἀνθρώπου
παραδίδως;. The phrase οἱ δὲ ἐπέβαλαν
τὰς χεῖρας corresponds to the use of
shalaḥ yad (Gen. xxii. 12, etc., cf.
Swete, 351), but need not be a Semitism
(cf. Lagrange, 394). It appears here
only in Mk; cf. Ac. iv. 3, etc. For the
ending in ἐπέβαλαν v. Blass, 45, and
for κρατέω v. iii. 21.

With 46 the narrative proper ends,
for 47-50 and 51 f. are appended. Its
sober and restrained character stands
in notable contrast to the Anointing,
Gethsemane, and the Denial.

47. The story of the bystander who
struck the high priest's slave is loosely
attached to the account. Mark has
several references to people who ' stood
by ' (xiv. 69 f., xv. 35, 39; v. iv. 29*).
The absence of names is characteristic
of Mk. Later, in Jn. xviii. 10, the
bystander is identified as Simon Peter
and the slave's name is said to be
Μάλχος. If Peter was the assailant,
it is difficult to explain why he was not
immediately arrested. Bernard, 589,
suggests that in the scuffle it was not
observed who had dealt the blow. It
is possible that it was the act of an unknown sympathizer (McNeile, 394),
but equally possible that the name was
withheld for prudential reasons. Lagrange, 394, thinks that εἷς τις indicates
that the narrator knows the name of
the assailant, and cites Sophocles, Oed.
Tyr. 118. If τις is omitted, with א A
L M Ψ 579 692 700 et al. f sype sa bo
aeth, it can be explained as a marginal
note or an assimilation to Lk. xxii. 50.
In this case εἷς is a further example
of the use of εἷς for τις as in v. 22 (q.v.).
But εἷς τις has the strong support of
B C Δ Θ et al. fam. 13 22 28 118 157 543
565 892 1071 al. pler. a l vg syhl, and,
if it is read, it gives force to the suggestion of Lagrange noted above (' A
certain man known to me '). Here
only in Mk do we find this expression,
for in xiv. 51 εἷς is much less strongly

48 τὸν δοῦλον τοῦ ἀρχιερέως καὶ ἀφεῖλεν αὐτοῦ τὸ ὠτάριον. καὶ
ἀποκριθεὶς ὁ Ἰησοῦς εἶπεν αὐτοῖς Ὡς ἐπὶ λῃστὴν ἐξήλθατε μετὰ
49 μαχαιρῶν καὶ ξύλων συλλαβεῖν με; καθ᾽ ἡμέραν ἤμην πρὸς ὑμᾶς
ἐν τῷ ἱερῷ διδάσκων καὶ οὐκ ⸀ἐκρατήσατέ⸀ με· ἀλλ᾽ ἵνα πληρω-

49 ἐκρατεῖτε

attested and is omitted by WH. Matthew has εἰς τῶν μετὰ Ἰησοῦ (xxvi. 51) and Luke (v. supra) εἷς τις. On the whole, it is probable that Mark knows that Peter struck the blow, and that, despite the later tendency to supply names, Jn. xviii. 10 in this matter is correct.

The bystander's act is impulsive; it is not a question of averting arrest, but of avenging the indignity done to Jesus. In Luke's version this suggestion is lost, and a desire for concerted action is expressed: ' Lord, shall we smite with the sword?' (xxii. 49). Lohmeyer, 322, endorses Rostovtzeff's suggestion, ZNTW (1934), 196-9, that the wounding was a symbolic act to show that the adversary was a despised person. It is certainly strange that Mark used ὠτάριον, which like ὠτίον, is a dimin. of οὖς, since elsewhere he has οὖς (iv. 9, 23, vii. 33, viii. 18*). It is improbable that he means ' a little ear '. It seems far more likely that he intends to describe a severe wound and the excision of the lobe of the ear.[1] This view harmonizes with Luke's independent statement that Jesus touched the ear (τὸ ὠτίον) and healed the man (ἰάσατο αὐτόν) in xxii. 51. John mentions excision explicitly, ἀπέκοψεν αὐτοῦ τὸ ὠτάριον, and, like Luke, says that it was the right ear (τὸ δεξιόν). In these respects an embellishing of the primary tradition seems probable. The narrative contains several words found here only in Mk: σπάω, παίω (Mt and Lk πατάσσω), ἀφαιρέω, and ὠτάριον (Jn. xviii. 10**). Mark also has the classical use of the middle in σπασάμενος τὴν μάχαιραν, which Matthew replaces by ἀπέσπασεν τὴν μάχαιραν αὐτοῦ. Cf. Blass, 184.

48-50. Like 47 and 51 f., 48-50 is an isolated piece of tradition which Mark has attached to the story of the Arrest. In support of this view one cannot argue that ἀποκριθείς implies a previous question, for the participle is redundant; v. Intr. 63. The opinion rests rather on the nature of the protest in 48 f. which appears to imply the presence of the priests; cf. Klostermann, 169. Lohmeyer, 323, argues that this contention makes too modern a demand on the technique of an ancient writer, but it is doubtful if this defence will serve. Certainly the later Synoptists felt the need for editorial adjustments. Matthew precedes the saying by ' in that hour ' and represents it as addressed ' to the multitudes ' (xxvi. 55), while Luke says that it was spoken to ' the chief priests and the captains of the Temple and the elders ' (xxii. 52). The presence of these men at the arrest is improbable, but the relevance of the saying in their hearing is manifest. Either, then, it was spoken later or it belongs to an imaginative recast of the scene. What Jesus condemns is the manner of the arrest; He is being treated like a bandit (λῃστής, v. xi. 17). Nowhere else does He protest against an indignity done to Himself. For μάχαιρα and ξύλον v. xiv. 43. With συλλαμβάνω*, ' to arrest ', cf. Jer. xliii. (xxxvi.) 26, xliv. (xxxvii.) 13, Jn. xviii. 12, Ac. i. 16, xii. 3.

For διδάσκω v. i. 21; ἱερόν xi. 11; κρατέω i. 31. The reference to daily (καθ᾽ ἡμέραν*) teaching in the Temple implies a longer Jerusalem ministry than the three days described by Mark, and is therefore in harmony with the Fourth Gospel; cf. also the implications of xi. 3 and xiv. 14. The language

[1] In the papyri ὠτάριον is used to describe the handle of a vessel; VGT, 704.

θῶσιν αἱ γραφαί. καὶ ἀφέντες αὐτὸν ἔφυγον πάντες. Καὶ νεανί- 50
σκος τις συνηκολούθει αὐτῷ περιβεβλημένος σινδόνα ᵀ, καὶ κρα- 51

51 ἐπὶ γυμνοῦ

suggests the Palestinian origin of the section; cf. ἀποκριθείς and the periphrastic imperf. ἤμην διδάσκων (v. Intr. 45, 62 f.). For the latter Matthew substitutes ἐκαθεζόμην διδάσκων and Luke has ὄντος μου μεθ' ὑμῶν. πρός c. acc. = ' with ' has also been claimed as a Semitism, but G. R. Driver regards the construction as ' an extension of many classical usages '; cf. Howard, ii. 467. In καὶ οὐκ ἐκρατήσατέ με the καί appears to have a quasi-adversative sense (' but '); cf. vii. 24.

The phrase ἀλλ' ἵνα πληρωθῶσιν αἱ γραφαί is difficult, and is not in Mark's manner (contrast Mt. xxvi. 56, τοῦτο δὲ ὅλον γέγονεν ἵνα κτλ.). It may be a scribal note, but it can also be explained as imperatival (' Let the Scriptures be fulfilled ! '). Cf. Holtzmann, 176; C. J. Cadoux, JTS, xlii. 168. More probably γέγονεν is to be understood. Isa. liii. 3, 12 may be in mind, or the reference may be quite general as in ix. 13 and xiv. 21. For αἱ γραφαί v. xii. 24. Matthew adds τῶν προφητῶν.

The statement that all forsook Him and fled refers to the disciples. ἀφέντες is not pleonastic (v. Intr. 63), but has its full meaning of forsaking. Mark does not mean that they fled to Galilee (cf. xiv. 54, xvi. 7) as the Gospel of Peter says (cf. M. R. James, 94). From his special source Luke adds: αὕτη ἐστὶν ὑμῶν ἡ ὥρα καὶ ἡ ἐξουσία τοῦ σκότους (xxii. 53b).

51 f. This short section is obviously appended. Suggestions that it is inspired by Gen. xxxix. 12 or Amos ii. 16 (Klostermann, 171; Montefiore, i. 350) are desperate in the extreme (cf. Lagrange, 397; Goguel, 500 f.; Bultmann, 290 n.). On the contrary, no good reason can be suggested for the recording of the incident unless it rests on a genuine reminiscence. After the statement that ' all fled ' the passage reads strangely and it is not sur-

prising that Matthew and Luke have omitted it. The reading νεανίσκος δέ τις (D it (exc. a) vg Aug) is an attempt to establish a better connexion, and καὶ εἶς τις νεανίσκος (A W Δ Θ et al. fam. 1 fam. 13 22 28 157 565 579 700 1071 al. pler. syhl geo) is also a scribal modification influenced by xiv. 47.

συνηκολούθει (v. v. 37*) may indicate that the young man had followed Jesus from the Upper Room, but it more naturally suggests an action continued after the disciples had fled. Apparently the stranger had been roused from sleep with time only to wrap a sheet about his body. Cf. Field, 40. With περιβεβλημένος cf. xvi. 5 where again a νεανίσκος is described clad in a white robe. σινδών, xiv. 52, xv. 46*, Mt. xxvii. 59, Lk. xxiii. 53**, is a fine linen cloth or a garment made of this material; Cl., LXX, Pap. (VGT, 575). It suggests that the young man belonged to a well-to-do family. Cf. Bengel, Locuples igitur erat.

With ἐπὶ γυμνοῦ it is usual to understand τοῦ σώματος, ' on his naked body ', but no parallel is cited either for the ellipse or the supplement; cf. Lohmeyer, 323. The phrase is omitted by W fam. 1 c k sys sa, probably correctly. Although ἐπὶ γυμνοῦ is strongly attested (B D al. pler. 22 28 124 157 579 700 892 1071 al. pler. it vg syhl bo arm), it may be a correction of the strange reading γυμνός (Θ fam. 13 (exc. 124) 543 565 sype aeth) which, apparently, was inserted inadvertently in 51 by an early scribe misled by σινδόνα γυμνός in 52. Cf. Couchoud, JTS, xxxiv. 131; Goguel, 500; Lohmeyer, 323. This suggestion is not only probable in itself, but is supported by the fact that the normal Gk expression for ' over his naked body ' is ἐπὶ χρωτός or ἐν χρῷ. No difference is made to the meaning if ἐπὶ γυμνοῦ is omitted. The common meaning of γυμνός is ' naked ', but it can also mean

52 τοῦσιν αὐτόν, ὁ δὲ καταλιπὼν τὴν σινδόνα γυμνὸς ἔφυγεν.

'lightly clad' (*v.* LS) or 'with a χιτών (under-garment) only' (*v. VGT*, 133). On this interpretation the σινδών replaces the ἱμάτιον. For κρατέω *v.* i. 31 ; καταλείπω x. 7 ; φεύγω v. 14. The reading οἱ νεανίσκοι (AV, *v.* Legg) is a scribal addition which supplies the impersonal plur. κρατοῦσιν with a subject.

The identity of the stranger can only be conjectured. Ancient opinion suggested St. John (Ambrose, Chrysostom, Bede) or James the Lord's brother (Epiphanius). Cf. Swete, 354 ; Lagrange, 397. Many modern commentators hold that he was Mark himself. Cf. Zahn, ii. 494 : ' He paints a small picture of himself in the corner of his work '; Holtzmann, 176. It is conjectured that the Last Supper was celebrated at the house of Mark's mother and that the young man accompanied Jesus and His disciples to Gethsemane. For various forms of this hypothesis see Zahn, *op. cit.* 490-2 ; Burkitt, *JTS*, xvii. 296 ; Plummer, 334 ; Rawlinson, 216 ; Allen, 178 ; Turner, 71 ; Bartlet, 401. J. M. C. Crum, *Roadmending on the Sacred*

Way, 42 f., further suggests that Mark, roused from sleep by the arrival of Judas and the armed band, rushed on ahead to warn Jesus, but arrived too late. These reconstructions read too much into the bare narrative. Lagrange, 397, pertinently asks why the young man should have followed in this dress and have exposed himself so long to the cold so keen at night at this season in Jerusalem. He thinks it can be a question only of one who lived at the villa of Gethsemane or a house quite near, and he may be Mark or some other person. Either supposition explains why the incident is mentioned, but two considerations favour the view that Mark is giving the account of an eyewitness known to him : (1) 43-52 is almost certainly a compilation, and (2) more detail might be expected if Mark was speaking of himself. Cf. Branscomb, 270 ; Ed. Meyer, i. 151 n., *Es ist der vortreffliche Bericht eines Augenzeugen, der hier vorliegt, aber keineswegs der des Schriftstellers selbst*; Bultmann, 290, *Wie v. 50, scheint v. 51 f. das Rudiment alter Tradition zu sein.*

(*b*) Mk. xiv. 53- xv. 47	THE TRIALS, THE CRUCI- FIXION, AND THE BURIAL

As previously explained (p. 526), the delimitation of this section is purely a matter of convenience. There is no real break at xiv. 52, except that 51 f. marks a certain pause in which the Evangelist appears to refer to one on whose testimony he depends, and 53 f. is introductory (and perhaps editorial) to the narratives which immediately follow. The contents of the section are as follows :

(100) xiv. 53-65. The Trial before the Priests.
(101) xiv. 66-72. The Denial.
(102) xv. 1-15. The Trial before Pilate.
(103) xv. 16-20. The Mockery by the Soldiers.
(104) xv. 21-41. The Crucifixion.
(105) xv. 42-7. The Burial.

Indications of compilation, consisting in the addition of smaller episodes to the main narratives and examples of intercalation, are visible. The former include the Mockery by the Priests (or the Attendants) in xiv. 65 which is attached to the account of the Trial, the Barabbas story

(xv. 6-15) which is fused with the story of the Trial before Pilate, and some of the various scenes which make up the account of the Crucifixion. The Crucifixion story is largely a string of such incidents, and one of the questions for consideration is whether an original and comparatively brief narrative has provided a nucleus for compilation both here and in the Trial before the Priests.

The examples of intercalation are more discernible, for they are preceded and followed by statements which read like doublets. This is notably the case in respect of the Trial before the Priests (cf. xiv. 54 and 67) and the Burial (cf. xv. 40 and 47). One point of importance needs to be observed. It does not follow that the distinction between an earlier account and the additions made by Mark can summarily be described as a difference of primary and secondary tradition more dubious in character. Some of the additions are primary tradition. Each case must be considered on its merits, with regard to the motives, liturgical, catechetical, and doctrinal, which appear to have affected its formation and use.

Mk. xiv. 53-65	100. THE TRIAL BEFORE	Cf. Mt. xxvi. 57-68
	THE PRIESTS	(Lk. xxii. 54 f.,
		67-71, 63-5)
		(Jn. xviii. 19-24)

This loosely constructed narrative includes the following : the priests' attempt to secure testimony against Jesus (55 f.), the witness of those who cited the saying of Jesus about the destruction of the Temple (57-9), the high priest's challenge and the reply of Jesus (60-2), and the verdict of guilt (63 f.). Verse 54 belongs to the story of the Denial and 65, the account of the mockery of the attendants, is appended to the whole. The narrative is of the kind which might be expected in the circumstances in question. No disciple was present at the trial, and for his information the Evangelist was dependent upon hearsay. This fact does not necessarily discredit the account, since knowledge of what happened, even if we allow for the absence of a biographical interest, must have been available ; but it explains the want of the artless details which are characteristic of the record of an eyewitness. Only in the description of the high priest rending his garments and crying, ' What further need have we of witnesses ? ', is there any approach to this kind of narrative. Almost wholly the story consists of sayings, questions, and answers. Clearly the narrative is not a Petrine story, but an account based on tradition.

A narrative so loosely constructed readily lends itself to partition hypotheses. Bultmann, 291, regards 57-9 as secondary in comparison with 56, and Wellhausen, 124 f., describes 61b-62 as an interpolation. These views are discussed in the Commentary. Here it may be said that the various items of tradition are by no means unrelated. The saying on the rebuilding of the Temple implies a claim to Messiahship and thus prompts the high priest's question, while this challenge evokes the explicit claim to be the Messiah which Jesus expresses in the language of Psa. cx. 1 and Dan. vii. 13. In general the narrative is historical, and there is no need to explain it as a secondary expansion of xv. 1 (Bultmann, 290). Most of the difficulties to which Montefiore, i. 352, refers arise from the time (during the night) to which Mark has assigned the narrative, and from the fact that he appears to regard the incident as a formal trial culminating in a verdict of guilt. Whether it was of this character, when it happened, and whether the procedure corresponded with Jewish usage, are discussed later in Note F, pp. 644-6. A special problem arises from the fact that Mark assigns to false witnesses the saying regarding the New Temple which many commentators, and Goguel, 507-11, in particular, believe to be genuine. The sayings in 58 and 62 form the backbone of the narrative, the point of which is to insist that His claim to be the Messiah was the real cause of the condemnation and death of Jesus. In this emphasis a doctrinal interest is manifest, as also in the details which recall the fate of the Suffering Servant [1]; but it does not follow that this interest clothes itself in the form of a legend, or that the story originated in the theology of a Church in want of precise information (cf. Lohmeyer, 330 f.; R. H. Lightfoot, 142), since Jesus Himself was conscious of the parallel between His situation and that of the Servant of Deutero-Isaiah. *V*. Intr. 120, also p. 378.

53   Καὶ ἀπήγαγον τὸν Ἰησοῦν πρὸς τὸν ἀρχιερέα, καὶ συνέρχονται
T   πάντες οἱ ἀρχιερεῖς καὶ οἱ πρεσβύτεροι καὶ οἱ γραμματεῖς.
54 καὶ ὁ Πέτρος ἀπὸ μακρόθεν ἠκολούθησεν αὐτῷ ἕως ἔσω εἰς τὴν
αὐλὴν τοῦ ἀρχιερέως, καὶ ἦν συνκαθήμενος μετὰ τῶν ὑπηρετῶν

53 αὐτῷ

53 f. This summary passage, which prepares the way for the Trial before the Priests (55-65) and the Denial (66-72), follows excellently after 46 and to this extent confirms the view that 47, 48-50, 51 f. are appended by Mark. Apprehended by those who accompanied Judas (46), Jesus is led away to the high priest (53). ἀπήγαγον recalls the command ἀπάγετε ἀσφαλῶς in 44. The high priest, who is not named, is Caiaphas (cf. Mt. xxvi. 57) who held office A.D. 18-36. Nothing is said by Mark of Annas, to whom according to Jn. xviii. 13 Jesus was brought first. For συνέρχομαι *v*. iii. 20*. The statement that all the high priests and the elders and the scribes (*v*. xiv. 43) come together unto him, that is, to the high priest (cf. Field, 40), reads strangely, especially if a full meeting of the Sanhedrin is meant, and the omission of αὐτῷ by ℵ D L W Δ Θ fam. 13 (exc. 124mg) 64 543 565 700 892 1342 it vg geo, and by Mt, is intelligible. The pronoun, however, should probably be read, with A B *et al*. 28 118 124mg

209 579 *al. pler.* sys pe hl sa geo¹ arm (C, πρὸς αὐτόν). In this case something less than a formal meeting may be meant; various members of the three groups make their way to the house of Caiaphas. Cf. xiv. 1.

54 may be the opening verse of the story of the Denial which is separated from 66-72 by the account of the Trial. Peter followed from afar until he came to the court of the high priest's house. For ὁ Πέτρος *v*. iii. 16; ἀπὸ μακρόθεν *v*. 6; ἀκολουθέω i. 18. The αὐλή is an open court around which rooms of the palace were built, and was approached through the προαύλιον (xiv. 68). αὐλή, xiv. 66, xv. 16*, *v*. VGT, 91 f. The expression ἕως ἔσω εἰς τὴν αὐλήν is peculiar and is not adequately explained by an appeal to the prolixity of Mark's style. Is it an over-literal rendering of the original Aramaic? ' Right inside ' appears to be the idea; cf. Moffatt, ' till he got inside the courtyard '; RSV, ' right into the courtyard '. If it may be so rendered, it is a very vivid touch. For

[1] With ῥάπισμα in 65 cf. Isa. l. 6, and with the allusion to the silence of Jesus in 60 f. cf. Isa. liii. 7. *V*. Comm.

καὶ θερμαινόμενος πρὸς τὸ φῶς. οἱ δὲ ἀρχιερεῖς καὶ ὅλον τὸ 55
συνέδριον ἐζήτουν κατὰ τοῦ Ἰησοῦ μαρτυρίαν εἰς τὸ θανατῶσαι
αὐτόν, καὶ οὐχ ηὕρισκον· πολλοὶ γὰρ ἐψευδομαρτύρουν κατ' αὐτοῦ, 56

ἦν συνκαθήμενος . . . καὶ θερμαινόμενος
v. Intr. 45, 62 f. How Peter succeeded
in entering the court is explained by
Jn. xviii. 15 f., but not by Mark, just
as subsequently he does not tell how
he was able to leave.

The ὑπηρέται (xiv. 65*) are the high
priest's attendants, possibly including
the temple police. Denoting literally
' an under-rower ', the word came to
be used of any kind of servant or
attendant, including those who dis-
charged religious duties; cf. VGT,
655; Plummer, St. Lk, 123. With
these men Peter was sitting and warming himself in the light of the fire.
συνκάθημαι*, Ac. xxvi. 30**, ' to sit
together with '; Cl., LXX (Psa. c.
(ci.) 6*), Pap. ; θερμαίνω, xiv. 67*, Jn.
xviii. 18 (bis), 25, Jas. ii. 16**, ' to
warm '; Cl., LXX. Moulton and
Milligan (VGT, 680) endorse the
opinion of Turner, 72, that πρὸς τὸ φῶς
should be translated with the AV ' at
the fire '; so Moffatt and RSV; cf.
Rawlinson, 221. But while in later Gk
φῶς is used in the sense of πῦρ (Xen.
Cyr. vii. 5. 27, 1 Macc. xii. 28 f.), it
carries with it the idea of illumination.
Cf. 1 Macc. xii. 29, ἔβλεπον γὰρ τὰ
φῶτα καιόμενα. Allen, 178, renders
πρὸς τὸ φῶς ' at the blaze '. Cf. Swete,
355; Lagrange, 398. The season
made the fire necessary.

Matthew follows Mk with almost
purely verbal changes. He simplifies
his source in ἕως τῆς αὐλῆς, but introduces ἔσω later in εἰσελθὼν ἔσω ἐκάθητο,
by which also he replaces the Markan
periphrastic imperfs. He omits πρὸς
τὸ φῶς and explains Peter's purpose
in the phrase ἰδεῖν τὸ τέλος (xxvi. 58).
Luke's version (xxii. 54 f.) is probably
from a different source; cf. Bultmann,
290.

55 f. With 55 the account of the
Trial begins. Οἱ δὲ ἀρχιερεῖς καὶ ὅλον
τὸ συνέδριον (v. xiii. 9) may be resumptive (v. 53), but is more probably the
beginning of a separate narrrative inserted between 54 and 66. For the
history and composition of the Sanhedrin v. Schürer, II. i. 163-95. Consisting of seventy-one members, under
the presidency of the high priest, it
included the heads of the great priestly
families (οἱ ἀρχιερεῖς), scribes (οἱ γραμματεῖς), and lay elders (οἱ πρεσβύτεροι).
How far the tractate Sanhedrin in the
Mishnah is an idealized account of the
functions of the Sanhedrin before the
Fall of Jerusalem, and whether the
court had the power to try capital
charges, are disputed questions. See
Note F on pp. 645 f. Apparently, Mark
thought of the meeting as a full session
of the Council, but whether it had this
character, especially if a night session
is in question, is doubtful. In Lk the
trial takes place on the following morning (xxii. 66-71), and this representation is inherently more probable (cf.
Burkitt, 136). No valid objection can
be brought against the historical character of the narrative because none of
the disciples was present. Knowledge
of what happened can have been given
by members of the Sanhedrin (Joseph
of Arimathaea or Nicodemus) or obtained through discussions between
Jews and Christians.

In Mark's account the attitude of
the Council is hostile. The chief
priests sought testimony against Jesus
in order to doom Him to death and
were baffled. The illegality of this procedure is manifest, but the action of
the priests agrees with what Mark
records in xiv. 1 f. and 10 f. and has
many parallels in history. μαρτυρία,
xiv. 56, 59*, ' testimony ', ' evidence ';
Cl., LXX, Pap. For θανατόω v. xiii.
12*; εὑρίσκω i. 37. εἰς τό c. infin.,
almost exclusively Pauline in the NT,
is used of remote or ultimate purpose,
and is found here only in Mk (Mt (3),
Lk (1), Ac (1)). Cf. Moulton, i. 218-20.
Matthew has ὅπως αὐτὸν θανατώσωσιν.

57 καὶ ἴσαι αἱ μαρτυρίαι οὐκ ἦσαν. καί τινες ἀναστάντες ἐψευδο-
58 μαρτύρουν κατ' αὐτοῦ λέγοντες ὅτι 'Ημεῖς ἠκούσαμεν αὐτοῦ
λέγοντος ὅτι 'Εγὼ καταλύσω τὸν ναὸν τοῦτον τὸν χειροποίητον
59 καὶ διὰ τριῶν ἡμερῶν ἄλλον ἀχειροποίητον οἰκοδομήσω· καὶ οὐδὲ

The explanation Mark gives is that, though many gave false witness against Jesus, their testimonies did not agree. For ψευδομαρτυρέω v. x. 19. D adds καὶ (om. D*) ἔλεγον. The point is that, according to Deut. xix. 15, the joint testimony of two witnesses was necessary. Cf. the Hist. of Susanna, 48-64. ἴσος, xiv. 59*, is 'equal' or 'the same' rather than 'adequate' (Erasmus, Grotius); cf. Swete, 356. καί is quasi-adversative; cf. xiv. 49. Matthew edits his source : καὶ οὐχ εὗρον πολλῶν προσελθόντων ψευδομαρτύρων (xxvi. 60a).

57-9. The repetition of ἐψευδομαρτύρουν κατ' αὐτοῦ in 57 (cf. 56a), and the parallel statement in 59 that 'not even so did their witness (μαρτυρία) agree (ἴση)' (cf. 56b), suggest that 55 f. and 57-9 may be different versions of the same tradition, stated generally in the former and particularized in the latter. This distinction disappears in Mt. xxvi. 60b, ὕστερον δὲ προσελθόντες δύο εἶπαν, where the better narrative form is manifestly secondary. As is usual in Mk, the speakers (τινες) are not named. For ἀναστάντες v. i. 35, Intr. 63.

The saying reported is that Jesus will destroy the sanctuary (τὸν ναὸν τοῦτον) and will rebuild it after three days. ναός, xv. 29, 38*, is the sanctuary as distinct from ἱερόν (xi. 11), the Temple precincts. χειροποίητον* (Ac. vii. 48, xvii. 24, Eph. ii. 11, Heb. ix. 11, 24**) and ἀχειροποίητον* (2 Cor. v. 1, Col. ii. 11**) are widely regarded as interpretative additions. The former is a classical word, used also in the LXX (with reference to idols) and in the papyri ; the latter is 'probably a coinage for the occasion in the earliest source' (VGT, 99). The distinction is only partially valid, for while the saying rightly speaks of the creation of a new spiritual system or community (ἀχειροποίητον), it refers, not merely to the destruction of a building (χειροποίητον), but also to the old order of which the Temple is the symbol and centre. For καταλύω v. xiii. 2, xv. 29*, and for διά with a temporal statement in the gen. v. the note on ii. 1. The phrase διὰ τριῶν ἡμερῶν means 'in the shortest possible time'. In itself it does not necessarily refer to the Resurrection, although this interpretation lies near to hand and is made in Jn. ii. 21 f.

With οἰκοδομήσω (v. xii. 1) cf. Mt. xvi. 18. D a c d ff k attest ἀναστήσω, and 579 sys Orint ποιήσω. Cf. Jn. ii. 19.

It is not clear why Mark represents the testimony as false. The suggestion that the disagreement was about the time and the occasion is not satisfactory. It is more probable that Mark reflects the uneasiness of primitive Christianity regarding the saying on the part of those who continued to observe the Temple worship (cf. Ac. ii. 46, iii. 1-10, v. 20 f., 42). Possibly the Matthaean form, 'I am able to destroy the temple of God' (xxvi. 61), and the absence of the saying from Lk, point in the same direction, as well as the interpretation in Jn. ii. 21 that Jesus spoke of the temple of His body, although the latter, if it means 'the "spiritual house"' of Christian believers' (Bernard, 97), is valid interpretation. Of the genuineness of the saying there can be little doubt; cf. Goguel, 509; Lohmeyer, 327; Wellhausen, 125; Rawlinson, 221; etc. In various ways its testimony is supported by xiii. 2 and xv. 29, by Jn. ii. 19, and by Ac. vi. 14. The original form of the saying is less certain. Montefiore, i. 357, thinks that it was nearer to xiii. 2, but the closer agree-

XIV. 62] THE GOSPEL ACCORDING TO ST. MARK 567

οὕτως ἴση ἦν ἡ μαρτυρία αὐτῶν. καὶ ἀναστὰς ὁ ἀρχιερεὺς εἰς 60
μέσον ἐπηρώτησεν τὸν Ἰησοῦν λέγων Οὐκ ἀποκρίνῃ οὐδέν; ⌜τί⌝
οὗτοί σου καταμαρτυροῦσιν; ὁ δὲ ἐσιώπα καὶ οὐκ ἀπεκρίνατο 61
οὐδέν. πάλιν ὁ ἀρχιερεὺς ἐπηρώτα αὐτὸν καὶ λέγει αὐτῷ Σὺ εἶ
ὁ χριστὸς ὁ υἱὸς τοῦ εὐλογητοῦ; ὁ δὲ Ἰησοῦς εἶπεν ⌜Ἐγώ εἰμι,⌝ 62

60 ὅτι   62 Σὺ εἶπας ὅτι ἐγώ εἰμι,

ment with xv. 29 and Jn. ii. 19 suggests rather that it was an independent saying in which Jesus made the Messianic claim that He would establish the new Temple (cf. 1 Enoch xc. 29, 4 Ezra ix. 38-x. 27, and the Targum on Isa. liii. 5). Cf. J. Jeremias, 37-40; Rawlinson, 221; Bartlet, 406; Billerbeck, 1004 f. If this view is taken, it becomes at once intelligible that the high priest presses Jesus for an answer.

60 f. The high priest now rises in the midst of the assembly and seeks to provoke Jesus to speak by a double question. For ἀναστάς v. i. 35; εἰς μέσον iii. 3; ἐπερωτάω v. 9; ἀποκρίνομαι iii. 33. For the double negative v. Intr. 46. καταμαρτυρέω*, Mt. xxvi. 62, xxvii. 13**, 'to bear witness against'; Cl., LXX, Pap.

The Vulgate (non respondes quicquam ad ea quae tibi obiciuntur ab his?) and several O. Lat. MSS. (a b c ff k l q r²), with bo and geo, render the two questions as one, but to this reading Blass, 331, objects that ἀποκρίνομαι would require a πρός (cf. Mt. xxvii. 14). Cf. Robertson, 738; Swete, 357; Lagrange, 400 f.; Klostermann, 173; Plummer, 336. The double question is more in accord with Mark's style (cf. viii. 17 f.) and its effect is vivid: first, an indignant query, 'Have you nothing to reply?', and then a demand, 'What is it that these testify against you?'. Here τί = τί ἐστιν ὅ.

Jesus, however, remains silent. Again the double statement (σιωπάω, v. iii. 4) is characteristic and effective, καὶ οὐκ ἀπεκρίνατο οὐδέν corresponding with οὐκ ἀποκρίνῃ οὐδέν;. The middle form ἀπεκρίνατο is found frequently in Cl. Gk and in the papyri, but is rare in the NT where passive forms predominate. The distribution of the

aor. mid. is as follows: LXX (5), Mt (1), Mk (1), Lk (2), Jn (2), Ac (1); cf. Swete, 358; Moulton, i. 39. In the similar passage in xv. 4 f. Mark has ἀπεκρίθη as elsewhere, and the difference may be due to the fact that xiv. 55-64 comes from a different source. VGT, 64, explains the aor. mid. form in a legal sense ('replied in a court of law'), as in the papyri.

In the circumstances and in defiance of justice the high priest puts the incriminating question, 'Art thou the Christ?'. This is one of the cases in which πάλιν (v. the note on ii. 1) might well mean 'thereupon'. For ὁ χριστός v. i. 1 and viii. 29. The σύ is emphatic and contemptuous. The expression ὁ υἱὸς τοῦ εὐλογητοῦ illustrates the Jewish tendency to avoid direct references to God. Dalman, 200, points out that usually the adjective appears as an appendix in the formula, 'The Holy One, Blessed is He', and says that 'the Blessed One', Ber. vii. 3, forms an exception. Cf. Billerbeck, ii. 51. Matthew recasts the phrase in the form 'the Son of God' (cf. Mk. iii. 11). How far the Messiah was regarded as the Son of God in the first century is a disputed question; v. the note on ii. 11. In any case, it cannot have been used in the later metaphysical sense, nor with the depth of meaning read into the phrase by the Evangelists. Swete, 358, suggests that the Messianic Sonship was perhaps not regarded as specifically different from the Sonship of Israel and refers to Schürer, II. ii. 158 ff.; v. HDB, iv. 570 ff. It may well be that the high priest has in mind echoes of the teaching of Jesus (cf. Mt. xi. 27 = Lk. x. 22) or the implications of the claim to be the Builder of the New Temple.

καὶ ὄψεςθε τὸν γἱὸν τοῦ ἀνθρώπογ ἐκ δεξιῶν καθήμενον τᾶς
63 δγνάμεως καὶ ἐρχόμενον μετὰ τῶν νεφελῶν τοῦ οὐρανοῦ. ὁ

Naturally, both here and in xv. 39, Mark reads a much deeper meaning into the title. εὐλογητός*, Lk. i. 68, Rom. i. 25, ix. 5, 2 Cor. i. 3, xi. 31, Eph. i. 3, 1 Pet. i. 3**, is used exclusively in the NT of God; v. H. W. Beyer, *KThW*, ii. 761 f. Matthew represents the high priest's question as put on oath: ' I adjure thee by the living God, tell us if thou art the Christ, the Son of God ' (xxvi. 63). Cf. Lk. xxii. 67, 70, ' Art thou the Christ ? ', ' Art thou the Son of God ? '.

62. Thus challenged, Jesus replies that He is the Christ and, using the language of Psa. cx. 1 and Dan. vii. 13, affirms that they will see the Son of Man seated at the right hand of God (' the Power ') and coming with the clouds of heaven. With ὄψεσθε cf. xiii. 26, xvi. 7, Lk. xiii. 28, Jn. i. 51, xvi. 16·19, Apoc. i. 7, xxii. 4. For ὁ υἱὸς τοῦ ἀνθρώπου v. ii. 10; ἐκ δεξιῶν x. 37; κάθημαι ii. 6; δύναμις v. 30; νεφέλη ix. 7; οὐρανός i. 10.

For ἐγώ εἰμι Mt. xxvi. 64 has σὺ εἶπας and Lk. xxii. 70 ὑμεῖς λέγετε ὅτι ἐγώ εἰμι. Cf. Mk. xv. 2 = Mt. xxvii. 11 = Lk. xxiii. 3, σὺ λέγεις (in reply to Pilate). There is good reason to think that in xiv. 62 Mark wrote σὺ εἶπας ὅτι ἐγώ εἰμι, for not only is this reading well attested (Θ fam. 13 472 543 565 700 1071 geo arm Or), but it would also account for the text of Mt and Lk, and it illustrates the note of reserve regarding Messiahship so frequently found in Mk. Cf. Streeter, 322; Lohmeyer, 328; V. Taylor, *ET*, lix. 150. The reply is affirmative (cf. xiv. 64), but it registers a difference of interpretation: ' The word is yours ', ' Yes, if you like '; as if to indicate that the Speaker has His own ideas about Messiahship. Cf. Moulton, i. 86; Blass, 260.

The phrase ὄψεσθε κτλ. does not necessarily describe a visible portent, but more probably indicates that the priests will see facts and circumstances which will show that Psa. cx. 1 and

Dan. vii. 13 are fulfilled in the person and work of Jesus. Again the agreement of Mt in using ἀπ' ἄρτι and Lk ἀπὸ τοῦ νῦν, with no corresponding phrase in Mk, is surprising. Here, as in xiv. 25, Debrunner, *CN*, xi. 45·9, conjectures that Matthew may have used a source earlier than Mk which read ἀπαρτί (' surely ') instead of ἀμήν in the phrase ἀμὴν λέγω ὑμῖν ὄψεσθε. Cf. Jn. i. 51.

The historical character of the saying has led to the liveliest discussion. While admitting that Jesus was crucified by Pilate as the Messiah, Wellhausen, 124, holds that the condemnation of the Sanhedrin must have had another basis, especially since the claim to be the Messiah was not blasphemy (v. 63 f.). The real ground for this charge was the claim of Jesus that He would destroy the Temple, implied by the testimony of the ' false ' witnesses, which Jesus confirmed by His silence. Thus, 61b (from πάλιν onwards) and 62 are a subsequent Christian insertion, and 63 is the original sequel to 61a. Meyer, i. 192, agrees that the saying regarding the Temple raises the claim to be the Messiah, but decisively rejects Wellhausen's view of the origin of 61b, 62. There can be no doubt, he thinks, that Jesus actually confessed Himself to be the Messiah before the Sanhedrin in reply to the high priest's question (*Es kann somit kein Zweifel sein, dass Jesus sich vor dem Synedrion auf die Frage des Hohenpriesters wirklich als der Messias bekannt hat, op. cit.* 194), though he holds the words taken from Dan. vii. 13 to be a later expansion as in xiii. 26 and viii. 38. Montefiore, i. 357, also dissents from Wellhausen's view. ' We must surely believe ', he says, ' that the Messiahship claim was at least ventilated, and that it was resolved that Jesus was to be denounced to Pilate upon that ground '. Cf. Klausner, 342 f., who says that ' the

δὲ ἀρχιερεὺς διαρήξας τοὺς χιτῶνας αὐτοῦ λέγει Τί ἔτι χρείαν
ἔχομεν μαρτύρων; ἠκούσατε τῆς βλασφημίας; τί ὑμῖν φαίνεται; 64

answer was perfectly in accord with Jesus' spirit and manner of speech '. There is indeed something forced in the suggestion that the action of the high priest in tearing his garments and crying, ' What further need have we of witnesses ? ', was prompted by the *silence* of Jesus. On the contrary, the submission that no further witnesses are necessary implies that by His own words Jesus claims to be the Messiah seated at the right hand of God and coming with the clouds.

It is precarious to argue that ' coming with the clouds ' is secondary because it is wanting in Lk. xxii. 69. Only if a visible descent of the Son of Man is meant can we apply to xiv. 62 the objections to which viii. 38 and xiii. 26 are exposed. Not to speak of the fact that Dan. vii. 13 does not describe a descent, but a coming to the Ancient of Days (cf. Glasson, 17, 64), the conjunction of Psa. cx. 1 and Dan. vii. 13 shows that a spectacular descent is not contemplated. What Jesus claims is that the glorious destiny which belongs to the Messiah, described in different ways by the Psalmist and the prophet, will be seen to be His. The emphasis lies on enthronement, and on enthronement as the symbol of triumph. Cf. Lagrange, 403, also *St. Mt, in loc.* It may be that, like viii. 38 and xiii. 26, also xiv. 62 reflects the apocalyptic hopes of the Church, but, as the foundation of this development, it is in every way probable that in reply to the high priest's challenge Jesus spoke of His triumph substantially as is recorded by Mark. The saying completes the prophecies of suffering and rejection in viii. 31, ix. 12b, 31, x. 33 f., Lk. xvii. 25, etc.

63 f. Mark now describes the response of the high priest. Whether the scene is imaginatively described it is impossible to determine. One can only say it is pictured most vividly and records what may well have hap-pened. The only serious difficulty is the closing statement, that all ' condemned ' Jesus to be worthy of death, since here the question presses whether the meeting was a formal gathering of the Sanhedrin, whether it had the powers suggested, and whether ' the decision ' was taken, or ' the sentence ' was pronounced, at night.

διαρήσσω*, Mt. xxvi. 65, Lk. v. 6, viii. 29, Ac. xiv. 14**, ' to break asunder ', ' rend '; a late form of διαρρήγνυμι, LXX, Pap. For χιτών v. vi. 9. Originally a sign of passionate grief (Gen. xxxvii. 29, 4 Kgdms. xviii. 37, Judith xiv. 19, Ep. Jer. 31, 2 Macc. iv. 38), the rending of clothes became, in the case of the high priest, a formal judicial act minutely regulated in the Talmud. Cf. Billerbeck, i. 1007 f. For the evidence of the Mishnah v. *Sanh.* vii. 5 (Danby, 392) : ' And the judges stand up on their feet and rend their garments, and they may not mend them again '.

For χρεία c. gen. v. ii. 17, ix. 3 ; μάρτυς*. Klostermann, 174, cites Plato, *Rep.* i. 340 A, Καὶ τί, ἔφη, δεῖται μάρτυρος ; αὐτὸς γὰρ Θρασύμαχος ὁμολογεῖ. The reply of Jesus is described as blasphemy (βλασφημία, iii. 28). Since the time of W. Brandt, *Die evangelische Geschichte* (1893), one of the strongest counts against the historical character of the Passion Narrative has been the claim that neither the confession of Messiahship nor the saying about the destruction of the Temple is blasphemy, for which a definite railing against the Divine Name is necessary (cf. Lev. xxiv. 10-23). At least two considerations render this objection untenable. First, there is good reason to think that the conception of blasphemy was broadened and made more inclusive ; cf. ii. 7, Jn. v. 18, x. 33. Cf. Billerbeck, i. 1008-19 ; J. Weiss, 318 f. ; Lohmeyer, 329. Secondly, Jesus not only claims to be the Messiah, but that He will sit at God's right

65 οἱ δὲ πάντες κατέκριναν αὐτὸν ἔνοχον εἶναι θανάτου. Καὶ ἤρξαντό
τινες ἐμπτύειν ⌈τῷ προσώπῳ αὐτοῦ⌉ καὶ κολαφίζειν αὐτὸν καὶ

65 αὐτῷ καὶ περικαλύπτειν αὐτοῦ τὸ πρόσωπον

hand and fulfil the vision of Daniel. *Nicht darin hat der Hohepriester die Gotteslästerung gefunden, dass Jesus die Frage, ob er der Messias sei, bejaht, sondern darin, dass Jesus von jetzt an im eigentlichen Sinn des Wortes seinen Platz einnehmen will zur Rechten der Allmacht,* Billerbeck, i. 1017. Cf. Montefiore, i. 359; Klausner, 343; McNeile, 403. It is not unfair to add that a Sadducean high priest, anxious to ensure the downfall of Jesus, would not be unwilling to put a damaging construction upon the claims of Jesus if His words provided an opportunity. His opinion is half insinuated and half expressed, ἠκούσατε τῆς βλασφημίας; τί ὑμῖν φαίνεται;, 'You have heard the blasphemy; what is your mind?', ' How does it strike you ' (cf. τί ὑμῖν δοκεῖ;, Mt. xxvi. 66). With φαίνεται* cf. the frequent use of the word in answers in the Platonic dialogues, *Rep.* 333 C, 383 A, etc.

For κατακρίνω v. x. 33; ἔνοχος iii. 29; θάνατος vii. 10. The judgment ἔνοχον εἶναι θανάτου appears to express a judicial opinion or verdict rather than a sentence (ctr. x. 33, κατακρινοῦσιν αὐτὸν θανάτῳ), probably because Mark is aware that the Sanhedrin was not able at this time to exact the penalty of death by stoning (Lev. xxiv. 16, 1 Kgs. xxi. 10). Nevertheless, a formal judgment is expressed, and this confirms the opinion that Mark looks upon the gathering as a judicial court. If this is so, his account is at variance with that of Lk. xxii. 66-71, where the ' trial ' takes place on the following morning. Neither account agrees with the rule laid down in *Sanh.* iv. 1, according to which in capital cases a verdict of conviction must not be reached until the following day (cf. Danby, 387). Most of the difficulties disappear if the meeting was informal (cf. Jn. xviii. 13) and had the nature of Grand Jury proceedings. Such may

have been its real character, although Mark's account does not suggest a meeting of this kind. Rawlinson, 220, justly observes that Mark has given the popular Christian version of what occurred, ' a version moreover which, however legally inaccurate, represents sufficiently the essential truth, viz. that the real cause of the death of Christ was the attitude of the leaders of the Jewish people, and that the charge upon which He was arraigned before Pilate was one which had first been trumped up for the purpose in the course of proceedings before the Sanhedrin '.

In addition to the changes noted above Matthew makes several alterations. The high priest explicitly says ἐβλασφήμησεν, ἠκούσατε is preceded by ἴδε νῦν, and the reply is introduced by ἀποκριθέντες εἶπαν. In Lk the rending is not mentioned, and the high priest makes no appeal to the Sanhedrists who themselves ask τί ἔτι ἔχομεν μαρτυρίας χρείαν;, adding αὐτοὶ γὰρ ἠκούσαμεν ἀπὸ τοῦ στόματος αὐτοῦ (xxii. 71).

65. This brief account of the ill usage done to Jesus is appended to the story of the Trial, and is manifestly a separate item of tradition. In Mark's account the τινες appear to be members of the Sanhedrin, but this representation is improbable in itself and is at variance with Lk. xxii. 63-5, in which the mockers are those who had effected the arrest, οἱ ἄνδρες οἱ συνέχοντες αὐτόν. The suggestion of a change of subject in Mk. xiv. 65 (Rawlinson, 223) is difficult to accept in view of the fact that later in the verse the τινες are distinguished from the ὑπηρέται. For ἤρξαντο c. infin. v. Intr. 48, 63 f.; ἐμπτύω x. 34; πρόσωπον i. 2; προφητεύω vii. 6. περικαλύπτω*, ' to cover all round ' (Cl., LXX), describes blindfolding. κολαφίζω, ' to slap ', ' buffet ' (not Cl. nor in LXX), is derived from κόλαφος the vernacular equivalent of κόνδυλοι ' knuckles '. Cf. Howard, ii. 407.

λέγειν αὐτῷ Προφήτευσον, καὶ οἱ ὑπηρέται ῥαπίσμασιν αὐτὸν
ἔλαβον.

The interpretation is complicated by textual problems. The question χριστέ, τίς ἐστιν ὁ παίσας σε;, although read by (Δ) Θ N U W X fam. 13 33 543 565 579 700 892 1071 *et al* syʰˡ bo geo aeth arm Aug, is probably an assimilation to the text of Lk or Mt. It is wanting in ℵ A B C D L *et al.* 28 157 1278 *et pler.* ff l q vg (*pler.*) syᵖᵉ. But if it is omitted, the reference to blindfolding becomes superfluous. It is therefore significant that καὶ περικαλύπτειν αὐτοῦ τὸ πρόσωπον is omitted by D a f syˢ, and is wanting in Mt, and, further, that τῷ προσώπῳ is read after ἐμπτύειν (instead of αὐτῷ) by D, and by Θ 565 700 a d f syᵖᵉ geo arm in addition to the ordinary reading. The presumption is that καὶ περικαλύπτειν κτλ. is also an addition suggested by περικαλύψαντες in Lk. xxii. 64. Cf. Turner, 73, *JTS*, xxix. 10 f.; Streeter, 325-8. ' In Mark the mockers spit on His face and slap Him and cry, " Play the prophet now ". In Luke they veil His eyes and then, striking Him, say, " Use your prophetic gift of second sight to tell the striker's name ". Each version paints a consistent picture ' (Streeter, 327).

65b is difficult. The ὑπηρέται (xiv. 54*) are presumably the high priest's attendants. ῥάπισμα*, Jn. xviii. 22, xix. 3**, is a slap on the cheek with the open hand rather than a blow with a rod. Cf. Field, 105 f., and see Isa. l. 6*, and for ῥαπίζω Hos. xi. 4; Mt. v. 39, xxvi. 67**. Reading ῥαπίσμασιν αὐτὸν ἔλαβον, Swete, 362, translates :

' caught Him with blows '; cf. Plummer, 339; RV and RSV ' received '; Moffatt ' treated '; Turner, 73, ' got him ' (in a colloquial sense). Blass, 118, describes the Gk phrase as a ' vulgarism ' and cites κονδύλοις ἔλαβεν in a first-century papyrus. Many commentators quote Cicero, *Tusc.* ii. 14 : *Spartae vero pueri ad aram sic verberibus accipiuntur, ut multus e visceribus sanguis exeat.* None of these renderings is completely satisfactory, and, in consequence, Field, 40 f., prefers the *v.ll.* ἔβαλον or ἔβαλλον. Either would give a good sense, but they are less strongly attested,[1] and, while βάλλειν ῥαπίσμασι may have appeared strange to a transcriber, it is more probable that ἔλαβον was interpreted by ἔβαλον. Probability, then, and its strong textual support, favour ἔλαβον. Accordingly, we are compelled to explain it as a rough translation taken from a source, possibly influenced by Latin; cf. B. Weiss, 227; Klostermann, 175.[2] The difference in detail from Luke's account (*v.* Streeter, *supra*) may be due to the prophetic saying in the Trial scene (cf. xiv. 56-9) and, possibly, to the influence of Isa. l. 6, τὰς δὲ σιάγονάς μου (ἔδωκα) εἰς ῥαπίσματα. The basis of the story is assured by the two independent narratives. Of these that of Luke stands nearer to the actual facts. Matthew's account is a secondary version of Mk. Turner and Streeter think that τίς ἐστιν κτλ. in Mt is an interpolation from Lk. Cf. Streeter, 327.

Mk. xiv. 66-72   101. THE DENIAL   Cf. Mt. xxvi. 69-75
(Lk. xxii. 54b-61)
(Jn. xviii. 15-18, 25-7)

The story of the Denial forms a unity in which the interest steadily rises to a particularly dramatic close. Montefiore, i. 368, says of it : ' The

---

[1] ἔβαλον, E M U X 0116 33 118 700 892 *et al.* it vg syˢ ᵖᵉ geo. ἔβαλλον, Η Σ 28 124 575 1071 *et al.* ἔλαβον, ℵ A B C L Δ *et al.* 1342 *et al.* ἐλάμβανον, D G W Θ 1 fam. 13 (exc. 124) 22 543 565 syʰˡ.
[2] H. Pernot, *ET*, xxxviii. 105, says it is a common colloquial expression in modern Gk=' to beat him '.

whole scene is indelibly fixed in the consciousness of the Western world. It is full of beauty, and yet awe-inspiring too. It tells its own lesson, and its moral need not be drawn out.' He also quotes the opinion of Loisy, who finds redactional elements [1] in the narrative, but nevertheless writes : ' If there is an actual reminiscence from Peter anywhere in the second Gospel it is most certainly in the story of the denial in the form in which it is found in Mark '. Compare, to the same effect, the opinion of Ed. Meyer, i. 149, cited on p. 526, also the views of scholars so different in standpoint as J. Weiss, 306-8, J. Schniewind, 193 (*v.* the note on 71), and G. Bertram, 61 f., who at the same time sees the story coloured by religious interests. The features which justify these estimates are the complete candour with which Peter's denials are related, the psychological appropriateness of his responses to the increasingly direct accusations, and the Semitisms in the narrative (*v.* Comm.). The religious and other interests which have shaped the story are naturally more difficult to assess. Preoccupation with these interests may account for the opinion of Bultmann, 290, that the narrative is legendary and literary, an estimate which in any case is too short and summary to be instructive. More surprising is the similar view of Goguel, 490-2, who accepts the genuineness of the prophecy of xiv. 30, but thinks that the story grew out of it. In part, this estimate is influenced by his belief that the Johannine narrative is more coherent and natural. Cf. also J. Weiss, 308, *Die Darstellung des Johannes ist ruhiger, natürlicher, die des Markus aufgeregt, gesteigert.*

Dibelius, 214, maintains that the story is told as a special example of a general backsliding of the disciples in accordance with scripture, that is, the will of God. Full and logically narrated, the whole composition is quite artistic, and it reflects the Church's interest in the event as in some way the presupposition of the Easter appearances. Such inferences are slenderly based. The desire to warn the primitive community of the perils of apostasy and to present vividly an authentic tradition accounts adequately for the narrative.

66 Καὶ ὄντος τοῦ Πέτρου κάτω ἐν τῇ αὐλῇ ἔρχεται μία τῶν παι-
67 δισκῶν τοῦ ἀρχιερέως, καὶ ἰδοῦσα τὸν Πέτρον θερμαινόμενον ἐμβλέψασα αὐτῷ λέγει Καὶ σὺ μετὰ τοῦ Ναζαρηνοῦ ἦσθα τοῦ

66 f. If 54 belongs to the story, καὶ ὄντος τοῦ Πέτρου κάτω ἐν τῇ αὐλῇ is Mark's editorial adjustment after inserting the story of the Trial. Cf. the use of the gen. abs. in the resumptive passage in v. 35. The phrase κάτω (xv. 38*) ἐν τῇ αὐλῇ (*v.* xiv. 54) suggests that the trial is taking place in one of the rooms above the court. For the use of ἔρχεται *v.* the note on i. 40, and for μία=τις *v.* v. 22. Although not necessarily a Semitism (*VGT*, 187), its presence in the narrative may be significant. παιδίσκη, xiv. 69*, the

dim. of παῖς, came to mean in later Gk a female slave; cf. *VGT*, 474, Kennedy, 40 f., Deissmann, 201 n. She may have been the ' portress ' (θυρωρός) mentioned in Jn. xviii. 16. Having seen Peter warming himself (θερμαινόμενον, xiv. 54) and looked closely at him (ἐμβλέψασα), she charges him with having been with the Nazarene, Jesus. For ἐμβλέπω *v.* viii. 25; Ναζαρηνός i. 24. The vividness of the description, the careful distinction between ἰδοῦσα and ἐμβλέψασα, the emphatic ' You too ' (cf. Jn. xviii. 15 f.),

[1] In 68b, ἰδοῦσα αὐτόν and πάλιν in 69, μετὰ μικρόν and πάλιν in 70, and the references to the prophecy and to Peter's grief in 72.

'Ιησοῦ· ὁ δὲ ἠρνήσατο λέγων Οὔτε οἶδα οὔτε ⌜ἐπίσταμαι σὺ τί 68
λέγεις,⌝ καὶ ἐξῆλθεν ἔξω εἰς τὸ προαύλιον. καὶ ἀλέκτωρ ἐφώ-

68 ἐπίσταμαι· σὺ τί λέγεις;

the contemptuous use of τοῦ Ναζαρηνοῦ before τοῦ 'Ιησοῦ are remarkable. Here undoubtedly is a scene from life. Cf. Swete, 362 f.: ' The order τοῦ Ναζαρηνοῦ . . . τοῦ 'Ιησοῦ suits an excited, hurried, utterance; "that Nazarene . . . Jesus"'. So also Lagrange, 406. In comparison the *v.ll.* which reverse the order (א sys pe and D Δ it vg syhl aeth arm) are manifestly secondary. ἦσθα is an old perf. form used in Attic for the genuine impf. ἦς of some other dialects. Moulton, ii. 203, says that, while both survive in the Koine, the latter is more common in the NT, ἦσθα being found here and in the parallel Mt. xxvi. 69 only, against seven instances of ἦς. ἦς is read in Mk by 1 13 209 543 565 700 Eus. Moulton asks, ' Is it possible that this ἦσθα started in Mt under LXX influence, and that the text of Mk was harmonised?'.

In Mt Mark's vividness is lost; in Lk it is reduced. Matthew says that Peter was seated (ἐκάθητο) without (ἔξω) in the court and that a maid (μία παιδίσκη) came (προσῆλθεν) to him. Luke retains ἰδοῦσα, but replaces ἐμβλέψασα by his favourite ἀτενίσασα and μία by τις. In Mt the charge becomes καὶ σὺ ἦσθα μετὰ 'Ιησοῦ τοῦ Γαλιλαίου (xxvi. 69) and in Lk καὶ οὗτος σὺν αὐτῷ ἦν (xxii. 56).

68. In ἠρνήσατο (xiv. 70*) Mark implies that Peter gave in substance a negative answer, but the actual reply is the confused utterance of a man taken suddenly at a loss. ἀρνέομαι (Cl., LXX, Pap.), ' to say "No"'', ' disown', ' to deny one's interest in something'. See the detailed discussion of H. Riesenfeld, *CN*, xi. 207-219. Mayor, *Jude*, 72, says that the use of the verb c. acc. of the person (' to disown ') is unclassical and seems to be confined to Christian literature (*VGT*, 78). For ἀπαρνέομαι, used in the same sense, *v*. viii. 34. All the

Synoptists have ὁ δὲ ἠρνήσατο . . . λέγων, but Matthew adds ἔμπροσθεν πάντων.

Peter's reply, οὔτε οἶδα οὔτε ἐπίσταμαι σὺ τί λέγεις, can be read in different ways. Cf. RV, ' I neither know, nor understand what thou sayest ' (RSV, ' what you mean '); RVmg, ' thou, what sayest thou? ' (cf. WHmg) ; Turner, 74, ' I neither know him, nor have I any idea what you can mean '. Blass, 265, thinks the use of οὔτε . . . οὔτε with ' the two perfectly synonymous words ' is inadmissible, and prefers the reading οὐκ . . . οὐδέ (A K M, *v.* Legg) ; cf. Klostermann, 175. But the best MSS. are against this reading, which looks like a grammatical correction, and whether οἶδα and ἐπίσταμαι* are synonymous is a point for discussion. Lagrange, 406, thinks it is difficult to distinguish them here ; Swete, 363, thinks they differ as *novi* and *scio*, though the Vulgate reverses the distinction. It may well be that to press such distinctions, or to object that the verbs are synonymous, is equally out of place in considering an unpremeditated reply from a speaker who is taken aback. Allen, 180, reminds us that the double expression is characteristic of Mark's style.

A new turn to the discussion is given by the claim of Torrey, 303, *TJ*, 16 f., that the Gk is ' pure nonsense ', that *yada'* lies behind οἶδα and *ḥakam* behind ἐπίσταμαι, and that *de* has been mistranslated ' that which ' instead of ' him of whom ', and that we ought to read : ' I am neither a companion of, nor do I know at all, him of whom you speak '. These are attractive conjectures, but the argument that Peter would be only *temporizing*, not *denying*, is less convincing. There is a temporizing that is in effect denial, though not yet outright. Black, 61, accepts Torrey's suggestion as regards the ambiguous *de*, but gives his own translation : ' I neither know nor am

69 νησεν. καὶ ἡ παιδίσκη ἰδοῦσα αὐτὸν ⌈ἤρξατο πάλιν λέγειν⌉ τοῖς
70 παρεστῶσιν ὅτι Οὗτος ἐξ αὐτῶν ἐστίν. ὁ δὲ πάλιν ἠρνεῖτο.
καὶ μετὰ μικρὸν πάλιν οἱ παρεστῶτες ἔλεγον τῷ Πέτρῳ 'Αλη-

69 εἶπεν

I acquainted with him of whom you speak ', adding that 'it is a curious statement for Peter to make, that he did not know nor understand what the serving-maid said '. The suggestion is possible, but, on the whole, an evasion seems more psychologically probable than a lie at this stage in the story. And *dᵉ* can mean ' that which '. On the whole, it seems probable that the RV or RVᵐᵍ (cf. Grant, *EG*, 120, ' I don't know nor understand! What is it you are saying ? ') is correct. The later Synoptists found the saying difficult and abbreviate it : Mt, οὐκ οἶδα τί λέγεις, Lk, οὐκ οἶδα αὐτόν, γύναι.

With the explanation given above the statement that Peter went out into the porch agrees. Anxious for his safety, he still cannot leave the scene. For ἔξω *v*. i. 45. The προαύλιον** (late Gk) is the ' vestibule ' leading from the gate (πυλών, Mt. 71) into the inner court (αὐλή) ; *v. VGT*, 537. Many MSS. add καὶ ἀλέκτωρ ἐφώνησεν (A C D Δ Θ *et al*. fam. 1 fam. 13 28 33 565 700 1071 *al. pler.* it (exc. c) vg syᵖᵉ ʰˡ geo² aeth arm Eus. But the MSS. which omit the phrase are very weighty (ℵ B L W Ψ 579 892 c syˢ sa bo geo¹), and the WH and Nestle texts, RSV, Torrey, and very many modern commentators (Swete, Plummer, Allen, Bartlet) reject it. Turner, 74 (with RV and Moffatt), accepts it on the ground that it is necessary to Mark's story, and explains its absence from very good MSS. by the influence of Mt on Mk. There is good reason to take this view, for both here, and in respect of δίς in 30 and 72 and ἐκ δευτέρου in 72, the authorities for omission are mainly Alexandrian with

partial Western support,[1] and seem to reflect desire to cancel the Markan allusions to two cockcrowings in favour of the one mentioned in Mt, Lk, and Jn. It is possible also that the correctors asked themselves how it was that, if Peter heard a cock crowing, he did not at once repent. If the clause is read there are two possible answers to this question. One is factual : Peter did not notice the crowing, or reflected that he had not yet formally denied his Lord ; cf. Lagrange, 407. The other is literary-critical : the clause is a legendary trait in an otherwise historical record, designed to emphasize the literal fulfilment of the prophecy of xiv. 30. The determining of this issue turns on the view taken of the Markan narrative in general and its reference to a double cock-crowing in particular. See further, the notes on ἐκ δευτέρου and δίς in 72.

69-70a. In Mk the maid-servant is the one who had first accosted Peter and it is the fact that he is now in the προαύλιον which suggests that she is the portress. Seeing him (ἰδοῦσα αὐτόν), she begins to say again to the bystanders, but more pointedly, Οὗτος ἐξ αὐτῶν ἐστίν. For ἤρξατο c. infin. *v*. Intr. 48, 63 f. ; πάλιν ii. 1 ; παιδίσκη xiv. 66 ; παρίστημι iv. 29. The strong participle παρεστώς is found in Mk here and in 70 only, as against παρεστηκώς in xiv. 47, xv. 35 (?), 39, but it would be precarious to base a literary argument upon this usage. Cf. Moulton, ii. 222.

Matthew (ἄλλη), Luke (ἔτερος), and John (εἶπον) assign the second charge to a different speaker or speakers. The

[1] In the four passages in question the authorities for omission are as follows :
xiv. 30, δίς: ℵ C* D W 238 it (exc. f l q r²) vg (3 MSS.) aeth arm.
xiv. 68, καὶ ἀλέκτωρ ἐφώνησεν : ℵ B L W Ψ 579 892 c syˢ sa bo geo¹.
xiv. 72, ἐκ δευτέρου: ℵ L 579 c vg (1 MS.).
xiv. 72, δίς: ℵ C* W Δ Σ 251 579 c ff g¹ l q geo aeth.

θῶς ἐξ αὐτῶν εἶ, καὶ γὰρ Γαλιλαῖος εἶ, [καὶ ἡ λαλιά σου ὁμοιάζει].
ὁ δὲ ἤρξατο ἀναθεματίζειν καὶ ὀμνύναι ὅτι Οὐκ οἶδα τὸν ἄνθρω- 71
πον τοῦτον ὃν λέγετε. καὶ εὐθὺς ἐκ δευτέρου ἀλέκτωρ ἐφώνησεν· 72

point is not important, but Mark's simpler account is to be preferred. Cf. the comments of Victor, οὐ γὰρ ἐξη-κρίβωται τοῦτο τῇ μνήμῃ τῶν γραψάντων, and Theophylact, οὐδὲν δὲ ἡμῖν τοῦτο πρὸς τὴν ἀλήθειαν τοῦ εὐαγγελίου, cited by Lagrange, 407, and Swete, 364. Lk. xxii. 58, μετὰ βραχύ, suggests a short interval of time and puts the accusation in the second person. Cf. Mt. xxvi. 71, Οὗτος ἦν μετὰ Ἰησοῦ τοῦ Ναζωραίου.

Mark's use of πάλιν in 70a shows that he regards both replies as denials and his change of tense in ἠρνεῖτο implies repeated denials. The later Synoptists make Peter's reply explicit, Mt, with the addition of μετὰ ὅρκου, has Οὐκ οἶδα τὸν ἄνθρωπον, Lk, Ἄνθρωπε, οὐκ εἰμί (cf. Jn. xviii. 17, 25, Οὐκ εἰμί).

70b-1. The third charge and the most explicit denial follows after a short interval (μικρόν, cf. xiv. 35). For πάλιν v. ii. 1; οἱ παρεστῶτες xiv. 69. Lk has διαστάσης ὡσεὶ ὥρας μιᾶς. This time it is the bystanders who begin to address (ἔλεγον) Peter. Cf. Mt. xxvi. 73, προσελθόντες οἱ ἐστῶτες εἶπον. In Lk. xxii. 59 'a certain other fellow' (ἄλλος τις) 'confidently affirms' (δι-ισχυρίζετο) his charge, and in Jn. xviii. 26 he is identified as one of the high priest's servants and a kinsman of Malchus.

The bystanders take up the maid-servant's words and apply them directly to Peter: ἀληθῶς (xv. 39*) ἐξ αὐτῶν εἶ, and add the explanation καὶ γὰρ Γαλιλαῖος εἶ, which Mt inter-prets in the words, καὶ γὰρ ἡ λαλιά σου δῆλόν σε ποιεῖ. Lk agrees in substance with Mk, but has the charge in the third person. The reference to Peter's dialect is very lifelike. καὶ ἡ λαλιά σου ὁμοιάζει appears also in Mk in A Δ Θ et al. fam. 13 28 543 579 892 1071 al. pler. q syᵖᵉ hl bo (3 MSS.) aeth arm (cf. δηλοῖ Ν Σ, δῆλόν σε ποιεῖ 579).

Usually this reading is explained as a case of assimilation to Mt, but when it is seen that ὁμοιάζει is read also in Mt by D a b c ff h n rⁱ syˢ, the question arises whether it is not original in Mk, with the further possibility that δῆλόν σε ποιεῖ and ὁμοιάζει may be different translations of the same Aramaic original. In any case the clause looks like an early comment, for Γαλιλαῖος itself refers to a peculiarity in Peter's dialect. That it has a doctrinal content, disclosing Mark's view that Galilee is the land of eschatological fulfilment (cf. Lohmeyer, 333; v. i. 15, xiv. 28, xvi. 7), seems very improbable.

Corresponding with the charge, the third denial is the most explicit. Peter calls down the wrath of God upon his head if what he says is not true. ἀναθε-ματίζω*, c. acc. Ac. xxiii. 12, 14, 21, 'to call oneself or another 'ana-thema' (ἀνάθεμα, ḥerem)'; LXX (Num. xxi. 2, 1 Kgdms. xv. 3, etc.), Pap. Although found in a i/ii A.D. lead tablet (Deissmann, 95 f.), the verb is best illustrated by such pas-sages as 1 Kgdms. xx. 13, τάδε ποιήσαι ὁ θεὸς τῷ Ἰωναθὰν καὶ τάδε προσθείη, 2 Kgdms. iii. 9, etc. See further, VGT, 33; SH, Rom. 228; Behm, KThW, i. 356 f. For ὀμνύω v. vi. 23. Lohmeyer, 333, thinks that the two verbs form a hendiadys, but it is more probable that they are distinct, the content of ὀμνύναι being found in the statement: 'I don't know this man of whom you speak'. ὃν λέγετε may represent the Aramaic dᵉ: cf. Black, 61. The acc. is similarly used with λέγω in Jn. vi. 71, viii. 27, and 1 Cor. x. 29. It is noteworthy that Peter still avoids the name of Jesus. Matthew uses τότε and καταθεματίζω, and omits τοῦτον ὃν λέγετε. Luke omits the reference to cursing and swearing and has Ἄνθρωπε, οὐκ οἶδα ὃ λέγεις (xxii. 60). The boldness of the account stands out at this point and justifies the comment of

καὶ ἀνεμνήσθη ὁ Πέτρος τὸ ῥῆμα ὡς εἶπεν αὐτῷ ὁ Ἰησοῦς ὅτι
Πρὶν ἀλέκτορα δὶς φωνῆσαι τρίς με ἀπαρνήσῃ, καὶ ἐπιβαλὼν
ἔκλαιεν.

Schniewind, 193, that it is completely unthinkable that the community would have originated a legend concerning its well-known leader which brought him so low, unless the facts were as stated.

72. Forthwith (εὐθύς, i. 10) a cock crows the second time. For the textual difficulties of ἐκ δευτέρου (= Cl. τὸ δεύτερον) and δίς v. the note on xiv. 68. Peter recalls the prophecy of Jesus (xiv. 30). For ἀναμιμνήσκω v. xi. 21 ; ῥῆμα ix. 32. The verb has the acc. as in 1 Cor. iv. 17, 2 Cor. vii. 15, Heb. x. 32. Cf. Blass, 104. The phrase ὡς εἶπεν αὐτῷ ὁ Ἰησοῦς is awkward and is replaced by ὃ εἶπεν in D Θ 565 it vg sys hl geo et al. (v. Legg) and in Mt by the use of the participle. With slight variations of order the prophecy of xiv. 30 is repeated. While it is right to say that the prophecy dominates the narrative (Lohmeyer, 333), it does not do this to the exclusion of other interests. The theme is the denial itself and it is told with a tension which reaches its climax in this final verse. From the first καὶ ἐπιβαλὼν ἔκλαιεν has proved difficult. Lk omits it (v. Streeter, 323 ; Creed, 277 ; Easton, 334 f.) and Mt has καὶ ἐξελθὼν ἔξω ἔκλαυσεν πικρῶς. Among commentators the utmost variety of opinion prevails. The AV and RV (text) renderings are ' And when he thought thereon ' (sc. τὴν διάνοιαν). Theophylact, as an alternative, suggests ' And covering his head ' (sc. τὴν κεφαλήν), and this view is strongly supported by Field, 41-3. Pallis, 53 f., modifies this suggestion by understanding τὸ ἱμάτιον ' And having drawn on his cloak '; cf. Rawlinson, 224. Turner, 74, favours the rendering, ' He cast himself on the ground and wept '. Swete, 366, thinks the word ' one of the unsolved enigmas of Mc's vocabulary '

and hesitates between the first view mentioned above and the idea that Peter answered by weeping. Plummer, 342, goes so far as to say that ' we must be content to share the ignorance of all the ages as to what Mk means by ἐπιβαλών '.

More solidly based is the suggestion of Moulton, i. 131 f., that ἐπιβαλών means ' setting to ', as in P. Tebt. i. 50. 12, ἐπιβαλὼν συνέχωσεν τὰ ἐν τῆι ἑαυτοῦ γῆι μέρη τοῦ σημαινομένου ὑδραγωγοῦ, ' he set to and dammed up ' (the part of the water-course in question). The aor. coincides with the first point of the linear ἔκλαιεν, and the compound phrase ' expresses with peculiar vividness both the initial paroxysm and its long continuance, which the easier but tamer word of the other evangelists fails to do '. Cf. the gloss of Euthymius ἀρξάμενος, and καὶ ἤρξατο κλαίειν in D Θ 565 it vg sys pe hl sa bo geo arm Aug. Allen, 181, explains ἐπιβαλών as due to confusion between ירו ' to begin ' and ירו ' to cast ', but Black, 178 f., rejects this explanation, preferring to trace the participle to 'aqla' used intransitively in the sense of ' dashing (out) ' (cf. ἐξῆλθεν in Mt). With Moulton's view cf. Bengel, prorupit in fletum ; Moffatt, ' he burst into tears '; RSV, ' he broke down and wept '.[1] Cf. also Bartlet, 413 ; Lohmeyer, 332 ; Schniewind, 190 ; Klostermann, 176. The conjecture of Couchoud, JTS, xxxiv. 131 f., that in a text which read καὶ ἤρξατο κλαίειν a copyist inserted the marginal note ἐπιβάλε (' add ') followed by the saying of Jesus, does not seem necessary.

Now that all the facts have been considered we may return to the question of the two cock-crowings. The persistence of this detail, despite the efforts of copyists to bring Mk into

[1] G. M. Lee, ET, lxi. 160, cites Diogenes Laertius vi. 27 in support of Moulton's rendering, but the reference has the infinitive, not the participle.

line with the other Gospels, shows it to be original. Foresight and coincidence may account for the precision, but it is more probable that δίς and ἐκ δευτέρου are due to a popular misunderstanding of the actual allusion ; v. the note on xiv. 30. The objection (Brandt, *Die evang. Geschichte*, 32-5)

that the rearing of cocks in Jerusalem was forbidden by the Rabbis (cf. Billerbeck, i. 992 f.) is effectively answered by J. Weiss, 306 n. and Bultmann, 290 n. Cf. also Dalman, *SSW*, 283 n., ' The Sadducees and the people were not likely to have bothered themselves much about such ordinances '.

Mk. xv. 1-15   102. THE TRIAL BEFORE   Cf. Mt. xxvii. 1-26
                         PILATE   (Lk. xxiii. 1-25)
                                               (Jn. xviii. 28-xix. 16)

While loosely constructed, Mark's narrative has a certain unity and is more than a mere compilation of separate items of tradition. Verse 1, which records a second meeting of the Sanhedrin (cf. xiv. 55-64) stands apart from the rest, and is used to introduce the Trial scene which follows. Verses 2 and 3-5 have been held to form a doublet by Loisy, who thinks that 2 (with 26) is secondary, and by Norden, who takes the same view of 3-5. Cf. Bultmann, 293 ; Klostermann, 177. Neither opinion is conclusive, but it is possible that Mark is using different accounts (cf. v. 6 f.). It is unlikely that the story of Barabbas ever existed as a separate item of tradition, for it is closely integrated with the story of the Trial as Mark tells it. The same ideas dominate the account from 2 to 15 : the emphasis on the silence of Jesus, the manifest intention of the chief priests to compass His death, the reluctance of Pilate to pass sentence, since he does not believe that the Prisoner is politically dangerous, and his subservience to expediency.

Very different opinions have been held of the historical character of the Barabbas story. Bultmann, 293, holds that it is manifestly a legendary development. Montefiore, i. 373, describes it as ' of a very doubtful historical character ', but at the same time says that the precise statements made ' suggest that some historical reminiscence is at the bottom of the tale '. Bertram, 67, says that the figure of Barabbas cannot be removed from the Gospel story, and writes : ' The story is drawn in rather thick colours, but it must have a historic kernel '. Cf. Branscomb, 289.

In the later Gospels the story of the Trial is developed and expanded. In addition to other modifications Matthew inserts the stories of Pilate's Wife's Dream (xxvii. 19) and of Pilate Washing his Hands (xxvii. 24 f.). Luke adds the narrative of the Examination before Herod Antipas (xxiii. 6-12). John gives a highly dramatic setting to the incident. Pilate confers with the priests without the Praetorium, and within it discusses the question of kingship with Jesus. He presents Jesus wearing the crown of thorns and the purple robe with the cry, ' Behold, the man ! ', and finally, after much hesitation, yields only to the cynical plea, ' If thou release this man, thou art not Caesar's friend ' (xix. 12). These developments reveal the growing importance which came to be attached to the story, and the desire to emphasize both the innocence of Jesus and the guilt of the Jews. In comparison, Mark's narrative has greater simplicity and realism. While not the narrative of an eyewitness, it rests probably on primitive testimony.

XV. 1   Καὶ εὐθὺς πρωὶ συμβούλιον ⌜ποιήσαντες⌝ οἱ ἀρχιερεῖς μετὰ
τῶν πρεσβυτέρων καὶ γραμματέων καὶ ὅλον τὸ συνέδριον δήσαντες
2   τὸν Ἰησοῦν ἀπήνεγκαν καὶ παρέδωκαν Πειλάτῳ. καὶ ἐπηρώτη-
1 ἑτοιμάσαντες

1. This passage is probably all that remains of the original reference to the action of the priests in the source into which Mark inserted xiv. 55-65. It is for this reason that it has the appearance of a ' Second Trial ' and to this cause that the difficulty of συμβούλιον ποιήσαντες (v.l. ἑτοιμάσαντες) is due. For συμβούλιον v. the note on iii. 6. Normally the word means ' council ' and with ποιέω it is difficult to see how the phrase can be translated otherwise than ' held a council ' or ' a consultation ' (so RV, Moffatt, RSV). Apart from xiv. 55-65 no problem arises. But when xv. 1 is read in the light of xiv. 55-65, one is conscious of a stop in the mind ; for a council has already been held and a decision reached, and nothing in xv. 1 suggests an adjourned meeting or indicates what happened. Matthew has perceived this difficulty. Accordingly, he omits κατέκριναν in Mk. xiv. 64 and in xxvii. 1 replaces the ποιήσαντες of Mk. xv. 1 by ἔλαβον, and by his use of συμβούλιον λαβεῖν elsewhere (xii. 14, xxii. 15, xxvii. 7, xxviii. 12) it is clear that he means ' took counsel '. This, of course, describes what happened (cf. xv. 2), but it is not what Mark says. The same story is told by the v.l. ἑτοιμάσαντες (א C L 892 1342), ' having prepared (a decision) ' which has every appearance of being a modification of the harder and more original reading ποιήσαντες (A B W Δ Σ Ψ minusc. pler. l r² vg arm Aug).[1] The suggestion of J. Weiss, 312, stands that xv. 1 records a tradition which contains nothing about the night session of the Sanhedrin and knows nothing about what happened in the morning. The elaboration of the phrase οἱ ἀρχιερεῖς μετὰ τῶν πρεσβυτέρων καὶ γραμματέων καὶ ὅλον τὸ συνέδριον may point in the same direction

even in the case of a writer whose style has many redundancies. For συνέδριον v. xiii. 9, 55*.

If the view outlined above is accepted, the fidelity of Mark to his sources is strikingly illustrated. As in the case of viii. 1-10, he records what he receives with little or no adaptation. For πρωί v. i. 35. εὐθύς ' forthwith ' marks the beginning of this period, i.e. 5-6 a.m. (cf. i. 10, 21). The temporal expression probably relates to all the events described. Here for the first time in the Markan Passion Narrative binding is mentioned (δέω, v. iii. 27). Contrast Jn. xviii. 12. ἀποφέρω* is used, as in P. Lille, i. 7. 17 (VGT, 39), of transference to another court. παραδίδωμι (v. i. 14), used 10 times in the Passion Narrative, may represent the point of view of one who sees behind the actions of men the fulfilment of the fate of the Suffering Servant.

Πειλᾶτος, xv. 2, 4, 5, 9, 12, 14, 15, 43, 44*, described only by his cognomen in Mk, is Pontius Pilate the procurator (ἐπίτροπος) provinciae Judaeae from A.D. 25/26 to 36 under the imperial legatus pro praetore Syriae. Cf. Tacitus, Ann. xv. 44, Christus Tiberio imperitante per procuratorem Pontium Pilatum supplicio adfectus erat. Matthew adds the general term ἡγεμών. Josephus, Ant. xviii. 2. 2, 3. 1 f., 4. 1 f., BJ, ii. 9. 2-4, describes his cruelty and oppression, and Philo, Leg. ad Gaium, 38, quotes a letter from Agrippa I to Caligula which speaks of him as ' inflexible, merciless, and obstinate ' and gives a terrible catalogue of his crimes and excesses. Cf. Lk. xiii. 1. Doubtless, to some extent, the passage is rhetorical and the picture overdrawn. Cf. Swete, 368 ; Rawlinson, 226 ; Lagrange, 411 ; Souter, DCG, ii. 364. The Gospels take a less unfavourable

[1] ἐποίησαν, D Θ 245 565 a c ff k q sy^s pe hl sa bo geo aeth Or.

σεν αὐτὸν ὁ Πειλᾶτος Σὺ εἶ ὁ βασιλεὺς τῶν Ἰουδαίων; ὁ δὲ
ἀποκριθεὶς αὐτῷ λέγει Σὺ ⌜λέγεις.⌝ καὶ κατηγόρουν αὐτοῦ οἱ 3
ἀρχιερεῖς πολλά. ὁ δὲ Πειλᾶτος πάλιν ἐπηρώτα αὐτὸν [λέγων] 4
Οὐκ ἀποκρίνῃ οὐδέν; ἴδε πόσα σου κατηγοροῦσιν. ὁ δὲ Ἰησοῦς 5

2 λέγεις;

view of him. Three times in Lk and Jn
he declares Jesus innocent, but yields
finally to popular clamour and political
expediency. In this representation the
intention is to lay the responsibility for
the death of Jesus upon the Jews.
Mark gives a more objective account,
not hiding the weakness of Pilate, but
showing plainly that he did not believe
the accusation of the priests to be valid.

The absence of any description of
Pilate, or of the place of trial, shows
that Mark wrote for readers well acquainted with the facts. Josephus,
BJ, ii. 14. 8, relates that Florus took
up his quarters in the palace of Herod
the Great, and it may be that this was
the residence of Pilate when he came
from Caesarea to Jerusalem at the time
of the Feast. Many scholars prefer
the view that he resided in the fortress
of Antonia on the north side of the
Temple court; cf. Westcott, in his
note on Jn. xviii. 28; Dalman, *SSW*,
335. For the former view *v.* Schürer,
I. ii. 48; Sanday, *SSG*, 53; Turner, 76.
No certain identification is possible.

The main modifications in Mt are
mentioned above. Luke's independent
account simply says that the whole
company of them arose and brought
Jesus before Pilate (xxiii. 1). Cf. Jn.
xviii. 28, ' They lead Jesus therefore
from Caiaphas into the praetorium '.

2-5. With no further description of
the circumstances Mark records that
Pilate put the question (ἐπηρώτησεν, *v.*
v. 9) : Σὺ εἶ ὁ βασιλεὺς τῶν Ἰουδαίων;.
From this question it is clear that the
Jewish hierarchy had decided to base
their charge on the political aspect of
the claim of Jesus to be the Messiah.
Probably the phrase used was ὁ βασιλεὺς Ἰσραήλ (cf. xv. 32). If so, there

may be a tone of irony in Ἰουδαίων.
The emphatic Σύ may also express surprise. All the Evangelists, including
John, give Pilate's question in this form.
For ἀποκριθείς . . . λέγει *v.* Intr. 63.
The question did not admit of a plain
' Yes ' or ' No ', and Σὺ λέγεις appears
to mean ' *You* say it '. Cf. Moulton,
i. 86; Blass, 260; Swete, 368; Klostermann, 177. It is an affirmation
which implies that the speaker would
put things differently; cf. Σὺ εἶπας
(Mt. xxvi. 64, *v.* the note on Mk. xiv.
62). Lohmeyer's suggestion, 335, that
the reply is a half-Yes, intelligible to
the believer who knows that Jesus is
the Christ, but mysterious to the unbeliever, seems unnecessarily subtle.

The reference to the accusations of
the chief priests is awkwardly introduced in *v.* 3. πολλά may be an adverbial acc. (*HS*², 35, *v.* i. 45), but it
is more probably the direct object of
κατηγόρουν (' many things ', RV, RSV,
or ' many accusations ', Moffatt). For
κατηγορέω *v.* iii. 2. The *v.l.* αὐτὸς δὲ
οὐδὲν ἀπεκρίνατο is rejected by WH and
Nestle and by many commentators as
an assimilation to Mt, but the addition
of W Θ 565 579 geo to the authorities
usually cited for the passage [1] leads one
to suspect that it may after all be original; all the more because Mt. xxvi.
12 looks like a recast of a loosely
constructed Markan sentence, while
Pilate's question in 4 implies the silence
of Jesus. The strongly attested omission may be due to the second reference
to silence in 5, a repetition not uncommon in Mark's style.

The imperf. ἐπηρώτα in 4 matches
κατηγόρουν in 3. The tenses suggest re-
iteration. But *v.* Meecham, *LA*, 111 f.
For ἴδε *v.* ii. 24; πόσος vi. 38. To Pilate

[1] *V.* Legg. It is read by N U W Δ Θ Σ Ψ fam. 13 33 543 565 579 1071 *et al.* a c vg (2 MSS.)
sy^s hl geo aeth arm, and omitted by ℵ A B C D *et al.* fam. 1 28 700 892 *al. pler.* it (exc. a c) vg sy^pe
sa bo.

6 οὐκέτι οὐδὲν ἀπεκρίθη, ὥστε θαυμάζειν τὸν Πειλᾶτον. Κατὰ δὲ
7 ἑορτὴν ἀπέλυεν αὐτοῖς ἕνα δέσμιον ὃν παρῃτοῦντο. ἦν δὲ ὁ

the continued silence is inexplicable. Emphatically Mark declares that Jesus no longer made any reply, so that Pilate marvelled. For Mark's use of ὥστε c. infin. *v.* i. 27; θαυμάζω v. 20. Once more it is impossible not to think of Isa. liii. 7 (cf. xiv. 61), but there is no need to think of the statement as unhistorical.

The loose structure in 2-5 is manifest. Matthew has sought to improve his source by prefacing the story with the words Ὁ δὲ Ἰησοῦς ἐστάθη ἔμπροσθεν τοῦ ἡγεμόνος, and by other small grammatical and linguistic additions. For Mt. xxvi. 12 *v. supra.* Pilate's second question is recast in the form οὐκ ἀκούεις πόσα σου καταμαρτυροῦσιν;. It is insisted that Jesus replied οὐδὲ ἓν ῥῆμα, and by the addition of λίαν stronger expression is given to the governor's surprise. Lk. xxiii. 2-5 is an independent account in which *v.* 3 (= Mk. xv. 2) has been inserted. A valuable historical statement of the charge brought against Jesus is contained in the words, τοῦτον εὕραμεν διαστρέφοντα τὸ ἔθνος ἡμῶν καὶ κωλύοντα φόρους Καίσαρι διδόναι καὶ λέγοντα ἑαυτὸν Χριστὸν βασιλέα εἶναι (xxiii. 2). Pilate declares that he finds no crime in Jesus, but the priests are ' more urgent ', alleging that He stirs up the people from Galilee to Jerusalem. John's account (xviii. 28-40) is much more dramatic. The priests decline to enter the praetorium ' that they might not be defiled '. Pilate asks the decisive question, ' Art thou the King of the Jews? ', but, so far from remaining silent, Jesus explains that His kingdom is not of this world and a dialogue between Him and Pilate follows. Again Pilate declares that he finds no crime in Him and offers the alternative ' Jesus or Barabbas '. The expansions of the tradition throw into relief the primitive character of Mark's story.

6 f. Mark now introduces the story of Barabbas mentioning Pilate's cus-

tom of releasing a prisoner at the time of the Feast. In spite of the absence of the article κατὰ ἑορτήν means ' at the feast of the Passover '. For ἀπολύω *v.* vi. 36; δέσμιος*. παραιτέομαι* (Cl., LXX, Pap.) means as here ' to beg of (or from) another ', but elsewhere ' to refuse ', ' avoid ' (1 Tim. iv. 7, v. 11, 2 Tim. ii. 23, Tit. iii. 10, Heb. xii. 25), c. neg. ' to entreat that not ' (Heb. xii. 19), and also ' to beg off ', ' ask to be excused ' (Lk. xiv. 18 f., Ac. xxi. 11)**. Field, 43, defends the reading ὅνπερ ᾐτοῦντο (א^c B² C N X Y *et al.* minusc. *pler.*), but ὅσπερ is not found elsewhere in the NT and ὅνπερ may well be a corruption of ὃν παρα . . . (א* A B), while ὅνπερ ἄν (Θ) and ὃν ἄν (D G fam. 13 543 565 it (exc. k) vg) are probably grammatical corrections, though the last is preferred by Blass, 36. Cf. Lagrange, 413; Plummer, 343; *VGT*, 484. Matthew has ὃν ἤθελον, and instead of ἀπέλυεν αὐτοῖς he has εἰώθει ὁ ἡγεμὼν ἀπολύειν . . . τῷ ὄχλῳ. Luke does not mention the custom, but John has a reference to it in the words of Pilate, ἔστιν δὲ συνήθεια ὑμῖν ἵνα ἕνα ἀπολύσω ὑμῖν ἐν τῷ πάσχα (xviii. 39).

The evidence for this custom is limited to the Gospels, but there are analogies in Livy's account of the *lectisternium*, the feast of the gods when chains were removed from the limbs of prisoners (*vinctis quoque demta in eos dies vincula*, v. 13), and in P. Flor. 61. 59 ff. (A.D. 85), cited by Deissmann, 269, in which the governor of Egypt, G. Septimus Vegetus, says to a certain Phibion, ' Thou hadst been worthy of scourging . . . but I will give thee to the people '. Moreover the *abolitio*, or suspension of a suit, though normally exercised by the ruling powers, appears in special conditions to have been applied by proconsuls and legates. Cf. Lagrange, 414, and Lohmeyer, 337, who quote Pliny the younger, *Erant tamen qui*

λεγόμενος Βαραββᾶς μετὰ τῶν στασιαστῶν δεδεμένος οἵτινες ἐν
τῇ στάσει φόνον πεποιήκεισαν. καὶ ἀναβὰς ὁ ὄχλος ἤρξατο 8

dicerent, deprecantes iussu procon-
sulum legatorumve dimissos, Ep. x.
40. (31).
Verse 7 is a parenthesis which could
follow 8 or 10. Cf. Lagrange, 414.
ἦν δὲ ὁ λεγόμενος Βαραββᾶς reads
strangely. Normally, ὁ λεγ. is preceded by a personal name and followed
by a descriptive title (cf. Mt. i. 16, iv.
18, x. 2, xxvii. 17, 22), but it can introduce a proper name (cf. Mt. ix. 9, Lk.
xxii. 47, Jn. ix. 11). Βαραββᾶς, *Bar
Abba*, ' Son of the father ', is a secondary epithet. In the Talmud Rabbis
are so named, e.g. R. Samuel Bar
Abba and R. Nathan Bar Abba. Cf.
Swete, 370; Billerbeck, i. 1031. In
Mt. xxvii. 16 f. ' Jesus Barabbas ' is
read by Θ fam. 1 241* 299** (1582)
sys hier arm geo². Origen, moreover,
who objected to the reading on theological grounds, says that he had
found it in very old MSS. There is
good reason, therefore, to think that
it is original in Mt: cf. Burkitt, *Ev-
angelion da-Mepharreshe*, ii. 277 f.;
McNeile, 411; Streeter, 87, 91 n., 101;
Rawlinson, 228; Smith, 206 ¹; and
to conjecture that it was read in Mk;
cf. Klostermann, *Mt*, 220; Deissmann, *Myst. Christi*, 22. Deissmann
observes: 'This text, just because it was
later felt to be an unbearable scandal
and was altered, mocks every hypothesis of the unhistoricity of Jesus of
Nazareth ', *op. cit.* 21. The alternative
derivation, Barabbas = *Bar Rabban* (cf.
Jerome, *Iste in euangelio quod scribitur
iuxta Hebraeos filius magistri eorum
interpretatur*), is not probable.
Barabbas is in prison with revolu-
tionaries. στασιαστής** (Josephus, *Ant.*
xiv. 1. 3) is late Gk, corresponding to
στασιώτης, ' a partisan ' or ' revolutionary '. στάσις*, Lk. xxiii. 19, 25,
Ac. xv. 2, xix. 40, xxiii. 7, 10, xxiv.
5, Heb. ix. 8**, ' a standing ', ' fac-
tion ' (Cl., LXX, Pap.), is used concretely of a ' dissension ' or ' revolt '.

The rebels are described as men who
(οἵτινες) had committed murder, presumably in a political fray. For the
pluperf. without the augment (cf. xiv.
44, xv. 10) *v.* Moulton, ii. 190. Mark
speaks of the circumstances as if they
were well known (' the insurrection '),
and, although the incident is not mentioned outside the Gospels, it is in no
way incredible; cf. Lk. xiii. 1, Ac. xxi.
38). Cf. Lk. xxiii. 19, διὰ στάσιν τινὰ
γενομένην ἐν τῇ πόλει καὶ φόνον βληθεὶς
ἐν τῇ φυλακῇ. Matthew does not mention the event, but speaks simply of Barabbas as a δέσμιος ἐπίσημος (xxvii. 16).

8-10. The crowd (ὄχλος, *v.* ii. 4),
now mentioned for the first time, goes
up (ἀναβαίνω, i. 10) to ask Pilate for
the usual amnesty. ἀναβάς suggests
an ascent to a higher point, possibly
the climbing of steps, and is much to
the point if Pilate's quarters were in
the Tower of Antonia. Most MSS.
read ἀναβοήσας*, but the strong testimony of ℵ* B D 892 it vg sa bo is
decisive for ἀναβάς (9 times in Mk).
Ed. Meyer, i. 195, thinks that the
people do not come to witness the trial
of Jesus, but are partisans of Barabbas
whose sympathies lay with the political
agitator rather than with Jesus, who
now appeared to be a convicted blasphemer. On this view, the amazing
change of attitude to Jesus can be explained; but, as Rawlinson, 227, says,
there is no reason to think that the
crowd of xv. 8 was at any time sympathetic to Jesus. Those who hailed
Him at the Entry were Galilean pilgrims. This argument is not entirely
satisfactory, since xii. 37 suggests that
the mass of the people heard Jesus
gladly. A change of attitude is therefore probable. Montefiore, i. 377,
thinks that Meyer's suggestion is not
very convincing, and this view is supported by the fact that Mark's frequent
use of ὄχλος is quite general. The
point that stands out is the main in-

---

¹ When Hort, 20, rejected this reading, sy⁸ and Θ were not known.

9 αἰτεῖσθαι καθὼς ἐποίει αὐτοῖς. ὁ δὲ Πειλᾶτος ἀπεκρίθη αὐτοῖς
10 λέγων Θέλετε ἀπολύσω ὑμῖν τὸν βασιλέα τῶν Ἰουδαίων; ἐγί-
νωσκεν γὰρ ὅτι διὰ φθόνον παραδεδώκεισαν αὐτὸν οἱ ἀρχιερεῖς.
11 οἱ δὲ ἀρχιερεῖς ἀνέσεισαν τὸν ὄχλον ἵνα μᾶλλον τὸν Βαραββᾶν
12 ἀπολύσῃ αὐτοῖς. ὁ δὲ Πειλᾶτος πάλιν ἀποκριθεὶς ἔλεγεν αὐτοῖς
13 Τί οὖν ποιήσω [ὃν λέγετε] τὸν βασιλέα τῶν Ἰουδαίων; οἱ δὲ

terest of the crowd in the release of
Barabbas. For ἤρξατο c. infin. v.
Intr. 48, 63 f. Lagrange, xciii, thinks
that here ἤρξατο has its proper force.
For the urgency expressed by the mid.
αἰτεῖσθαι v. vi. 24 f. ἐποίει is the imperfect of repeated action. Black, 92 n.,
raises the possibility that it is impersonal: 'just as one was wont to do
for them'. Couchoud's conjecture,
JTS, xxxiv. 132, that καὶ ἀναβὰς ὁ
ὄχλος is a corruption of καὶ πᾶς ὁ ὄχλος
(cf. k, *et tota turba rogabat illum*), is
hardly convincing.

Pilate's response is the alternative
θέλετε ἀπολύσω ὑμῖν τὸν βασιλέα τῶν
Ἰουδαίων;. For ἀπεκρίθη . . . λέγων v.
Intr. 63. With this instance of ἀπεκρίθη
c. partc. in Mk cf. vii. 28. For θέλω
c. subj. without ἵνα v. the notes on vi. 25
and x. 36. As in xv. 2, the phrase τὸν
βασιλέα τῶν Ἰουδαίων is contemptuous.
Mark adds the explanation that Pilate
knew that on account of envy (φθόνος*)
the chief priests had delivered up Jesus.
For the pluperfect without the augment v. xv. 7 and for παραδίδωμι i. 14.
It is not necessary to regard 10 as an
awkward addition (Lohmeyer, 337),
for such explanatory comments are
common in Mk. It is true that διὰ
φθόνον suggests a different motive
from the fear of the people mentioned
in xiv. 1, but the suggestion of 'envy'
may well represent the point of view
of Pilate. 'The pretence of loyalty
to the Emperor was too flimsy to
deceive a man of the world' (Swete,
371). The omission of οἱ ἀρχιερεῖς by
B 1 sys bo (cf. v. 11) is probably stylistic. Here Matthew adds the story
of Pilate's Wife's Dream (xxvii. 19).
The whole passage, 8-10, is remark-

ably vivid. It is wanting in Lk and is
severely abbreviated in Mt by the use
of the gen. abs. συνηγμένων αὐτῶν,
although here the alternative, Barabbas or Jesus, is more fully expressed.
In Jn. xviii. 39 Pilate himself mentions
the custom and offers the choice.

11 f. The chief priests now incite the
people to choose Barabbas. ἀνασείω*,
Lk. xxiii. 5**, 'to stir up', 'incite',
belongs to later Gk and is used by Aq.
and Symm. (but not in the LXX) and
in the papyri (*VGT*, 37). For political
reasons Barabbas may have been
popular, while, because He would not
resort to force, Jesus lost favour. D
565 a c d ff k r¹ aur sys sa arm attest
ἔπεισαν (cf. Mt. xxvii. 20). ἵνα ἀπολύσῃ indicates the end in view: 'to
get him to release' (Moffatt, cf. RSV).
Matthew simplifies his source by using
αἰτήσωνται and adding τὸν δὲ Ἰησοῦν
ἀπολέσωσιν (xxvii. 20). For ἀπολύω v.
vi. 36.

A second time Pilate seeks to influence the people. Probably πάλιν ¹
(v. ii. 1) bears this meaning, but it can
also be rendered 'thereupon' (cf. 13).
For ἀποκριθεὶς ἔλεγεν v. Intr. 63; cf.
xii. 35. Pilate's question is very weak:
'What, then, would you have me do
with the one you call the King of the
Jews?'; and even more so in the
variant form: 'What, then, am I to
do with the King of the Jews?'. The
textual evidence is conflicting. θέλετε
is omitted by ℵ B C W Δ Ψ 1 13 33 69
543 892 1342 sa bo geo, and ὃν (om. B)
λέγετε by A D W Θ fam. 1 13 69 543
565 700 it vg sys sa geo arm. On the
whole, it seems best to explain θέλετε
as an assimilation to xv. 9 (cf. WH,
RV, RSV, and Moffatt), and ὃν λέγετε

¹ Om. D W Γ 13 *et al.* ff k vg (2 MSS.) bo.

πάλιν ἔκραξαν Σταύρωσον αὐτόν. ὁ δὲ Πειλᾶτος ἔλεγεν αὐτοῖς 14
Τί γὰρ ἐποίησεν κακόν; οἱ δὲ περισσῶς ἔκραξαν Σταύρωσον
αὐτόν. ὁ δὲ Πειλᾶτος βουλόμενος τῷ ὄχλῳ τὸ ἱκανὸν ποιῆσαι 15

as a modification throwing the onus for the use of the title upon the Jews. Turner, 76, on the contrary, thinks the reading (cf. AV), ' What then do you want me to do ? ', a much more natural question for Pilate to put. So Lagrange, 417. For θέλω c. subj. v. vi. 25, x. 36, 51, xiv. 12, xv. 9, and for the construction ποιεῖν τινά τι, ' to do something with ', Blass, 91. D c ff k aur vg Aug read the more usual dat. (βασιλεῖ).

The question arises whether Pilate is likely to have spoken to the crowd in the manner described. Montefiore, i. 375, says his rejoinder is ' almost ludicrously inappropriate for a Roman governor '. A summary opinion of this kind is hasty. Pilate is interviewing people who are asking for an amnesty, possibly a deputation, though there is no evidence of this. He has put before them an alternative, Jesus or Barabbas. When, therefore, they choose Barabbas, there does not seem to be any good reason why he cannot have said, sarcastically, ' What, then am I to do with the King of the Jews ?'. Doubtless, the reply is weak, for he could legally have set Jesus free (cf. Lohmeyer, 338); but having grasped at a dubious expedient, he is reluctant to abandon it. Moreover, if primitive Christianity was anxious to lay the responsibility for the death of Jesus upon the Jews, the attitude of Pilate provided the opportunity.

In Matthew's version the alternative is put more clearly : τίνα θέλετε ἀπὸ τῶν δύο ἀπολύσω ὑμῖν;. The reply ' Barabbas ' is given, and Pilate's rejoinder is given as in Mk, except that its sting is lost in the conventional phrase ' Jesus who is called Christ '. Luke merely affirms Pilate's desire to release Jesus (xxiii. 20) and John dwells on the enormity of the choice (xviii. 40).

13 f. Incensed by Pilate's reference to ' the King of the Jews ', the crowd

cries ' Crucify him '. The change from ἤρξατο αἰτεῖσθαι in 8 to ἔκραξαν in 13 is very marked. For κράζω v. iii. 11. πάλιν is clearly ' thereupon '; v. ii. 1 and cf. Wellhausen, 129 ; Black, 82. σταυρόω, xv. 14 f., 20, 24 f., xvi. 6*, originally ' to fence with stakes ', has the meaning ' to crucify ' in Polybius i. 86. 4 and in the NT. Cf. Esth. vii. 9, where it renders talah ' to put to death by hanging '. Montefiore's claim, i. 376, that the cry is probably unhistoric is without justification, since the handing over of Jesus to Pilate and the rejection of the procurator's alternative entailed crucifixion. The cry indeed has been the cause of ' endless Jewish misery wrought by Christian hands ', but there can be no doubt that it was raised. Mt has σταυρωθήτω and Lk σταύρου σταύρου (xxiii. 21) but in 18 αἶρε τοῦτον. Cf. Jn. xix. 15, ἆρον ἆρον, σταύρωσον αὐτόν.

Pilate's reply is pitifully feeble, but it accords with the vacillating spirit he displays throughout. All the Synoptists record the question ' Why, what evil has he done ? ', and Luke adds ' I have found in him no crime deserving of death ' (xxiii. 22). Cf. Jn. xviii. 38, xix. 4. It is clear that increasing emphasis was laid in Christian tradition upon the innocence of Jesus. The effect of Pilate's question is to provoke a yet stronger outcry ; they cried ' all the more ' ' Crucify him '. For περισσῶς v. x. 26*. Cf. Lk. xxiii. 23, οἱ δὲ ἐπέκειντο φωναῖς μεγάλαις . . . καὶ κατίσχυον αἱ φωναὶ αὐτῶν. At this point Matthew adds the story of Pilate Washing His Hands (xxvii. 24 f.).

15. Anxious to pacify the crowd, Pilate releases Barabbas, and delivers up Jesus to be scourged and crucified. βούλομαι*, which is stronger than θέλω, expresses the exercise of volition ; cf. Swete, 373. τὸ ἱκανὸν ποιῆσαι, ' to satisfy ', is a Latinism (satis facere)

ἀπέλυσεν αὐτοῖς τὸν Βαραββᾶν, καὶ παρέδωκεν τὸν Ἰησοῦν φραγελλώσας ἵνα σταυρωθῇ.

found in Appian, Polybius, and Diogenes Laertius ; cf. Jer. xxxi. (xlviii.) 30, οὐχὶ τὸ ἱκανὸν αὐτῷ οὐχ οὕτως ἐποίησεν;, and Ac. xvii. 9, καὶ λαβόντες τὸ ἱκανόν. See Moulton, i. 20 f. ; *VGT*, 302 ; Robertson, 1385 ; Allen, 183 ; Turner, 76. A second Latinism appears in φραγελλώσας* (Mt. xxvii. 26**) which corresponds to *flagello*. Swete, 374, cites *Ev. Nicod.* 9, 16 and *Test. Benj.* ii. 3. The aor. is one of antecedent action. The punishment usually preceded crucifixion ; cf. Jos. *BJ*, ii. 14. 9, v. 11. 1 ; Livy xxxiii. 36, *alios verberatos crucibus adfixit*. This cruel punishment was inflicted with whips of leather (*flagella*) loaded with bone or metal, while the victim was sometimes bound to a pillar. It is a significant feature of the Gospel ac-

counts that it is described (Mk, Mt) in a single word. Lk and Jn do not mention it at this point. In Lk. xxiii. 16, 22 Pilate proposes it as an alternative to crucifixion ; in Jn. xix. 1 it takes place before the final condemnation.

All the Evangelists use παρέδωκεν, and only Luke expressly says that Pilate sentenced Jesus to death (ἐπέκρινεν, xxiii. 24). This fact is only partially explained by the Christian conviction that responsibility lay primarily with the Jews (cf. 1 Thess. ii. 15, Ac. ii. 23, Mk. x. 34), but rather, as the consistent use of παραδίδωμι shows, by the belief that, as the Suffering Servant, Jesus is ' delivered up by the determinate counsel and foreknowledge of God ' (Ac. ii. 23).

Mk. xv. 16-20   103. THE MOCKERY BY   Cf. Mt. xxvii. 27-31
                          THE SOLDIERS   Jn. xix. 2 f.

The narrative immediately follows the statement that, having scourged Jesus, Pilate delivered Him to be crucified. It is held by Wendling, 182, to be an insertion, since 20 goes back to the point already reached in 15. To this view Lohmeyer, 340 n., objects that 15 records only the command to crucify Jesus while 20 refers to the fulfilment of the command. As the Gospel now stands this claim is just, but the remarkable parallel between ἵνα σταυρώσωσιν in 20 and ἵνα σταυρωθῇ in 15 leaves ground for the suggestion that Mark is expanding an existing account of the Passion. Bultmann, 293 f., explains the narrative as a secondary elaboration of φραγελλώσας (xiv. 15) ; but to this view it is sufficient to reply that the scourging is not described, and that therefore we do not know in what sense it is an elaboration and why it is secondary ; cf. Lohmeyer, *ibid.* The truth is that 16-20 records a quite different incident.

The narrative has a parallel in Jn. xix. 2 f. which contains phrases which recall Mk. xiv. 16-20 ; but in Jn the Mockery precedes the condemnation and in comparison with the more detailed Markan story is secondary. More important are the parallels in the Lukan story of the examination of Jesus by Herod Antipas (Lk. xxiii. 11) and in the Markan account of the mishandling by the high priest's servants, especially the references to spitting and striking (Mk. xiv. 65). Possibly in the early tradition details have been carried over from one story to the other ; *v.* the note on xv. 19a. In any case the vivid and detailed story of Mark must be regarded as primary and as recording historical testimony, and this view is not in any way affected by the possibility that he is supplementing an earlier Passion Narrative.

This conclusion depends on the view taken of the several analogous stories familiar to English readers of J. G. Frazer's *Golden Bough*, iii. 138-200. These stories may show that the action of the soldiers has behind it a history of which they were barely conscious, unless they had in mind the excesses of the *Saturnalia*; but in no case is there any warrant for regarding the tradition as invention. See further, Note G, pp. 646-8.

Οἱ δὲ στρατιῶται ἀπήγαγον αὐτὸν ἔσω εἰς τὴν αὐλήν, ὅ ἐστιν 16
πραιτώριον, καὶ συνκαλοῦσιν ὅλην τὴν σπεῖραν. καὶ ἐνδιδύσκου- 17
σιν αὐτὸν πορφύραν καὶ περιτιθέασιν αὐτῷ πλέξαντες ἀκάνθινον

16 f. The στρατιῶται*, hitherto not mentioned by Mark, are provincials, recruited from Palestine and other parts of the Empire, under Pilate's command. For ἀπάγω v. xiv. 44, 53*; ἔσω xiv. 54*; αὐλή xiv. 54, 66*; ὅ ἐστιν iii. 17. πραιτώριον*, Mt. xxvii. 27, Jn. xviii. 28 (*bis*), 33, xix. 9, Ac. xxiii. 35, Phil. i. 13**, is a late word (not Cl. nor in LXX) which corresponds to the Latin *praetorium*. In the NT, as frequently in the papyri, it is used of the 'palace' or 'official residence' of a governor, probably (despite Lightfoot's note, *Phil*. 99-102) even in Phil. i. 13. Here it is either Herod's palace or the Tower of Antonia; v. the note on xv. 1. In either case a difficulty is raised by the explanatory phrase ὅ ἐστιν πραιτώριον, for here a court is apparently identified with a building. Swete, 374, suggests the most public part of the *praetorium* may have been known by the Latin name of the whole; cf. Lagrange, 419; but this distinction is not otherwise known. The explanation of ὅ ἐστιν π. as a gloss is too easy a solution of the difficulty. Citing the reading of c ff l vg, *in atrium praetorii*, Blass, *ET*, x. 186, conjectures that the original reading was ἔσω τῆς αὐλῆς τοῦ πραιτηρίου, but against this suggestion is the difficulty of explaining how in that case the current reading arose. It is probable that Blass is right in his tentative suggestion that the source of the confusion lies in the original Aramaic. As in xiv. 54, ἔσω εἰς τὴν αὐλήν is read by D P Θ fam. 1 22 fam. 13 (exc. 124) 59 506 543 565 679 700 1278 d vg (*plur.*)

geo arm Aug. This testimony is strong, and it may be that ὅ ἐστιν π. is an attempt to explain translation Gk, especially since occasionally αὐλή is used in the sense of 'palace' (cf. 1 Macc. xi. 46). Matthew's εἰς τὸ πραιτώριον is a better simplification.

The soldiers call together (συνκαλοῦσιν*) the whole cohort. σπεῖρα*, Mt. xxvii. 27, Jn. xviii. 3, 12, Ac. x. 1, xxi. 31, xxvii. 1**, originally meant 'a coil', but came to be used of a 'maniple' or 'cohort' of soldiers (*VGT*, 582), consisting of from 200 to 600 men. Cf. T. R. S. Broughton, *Beginnings of Christianity*, v. 427-55. The phrase is used loosely for those who were available at the time. Turner, 76, suggests a 'company' or 'platoon'.

The soldiers clothe Him with a purple robe, and having twisted a crown of thorns put it on Him. Here as in 16 the historic presents add to the vividness of the scene. ἐνδιδύσκω* is late Gk for ἐνδύω; LXX (2 Kgdms. i. 24), Lk. xvi. 19**, Josephus, *BJ*, vii. 2. 2. Cf. Deissmann, 82. As a verb of clothing it is followed by the ext. acc. (αὐτόν) and the inter. (πορφύραν). πορφύρα, xv. 20*, Lk. xvi. 19, Apoc. xviii. 12**, a purple fish, dye, or robe; Cl., LXX, Pap. (*VGT*, 529). Swete, 375, suggests that possibly a soldier's faded cloak which looked like royal purple is meant. Cf. Souter, *Lex*. 211 : '*a red-coloured cloak*, such as common soldiers wore'. Mt. xxvii. 28, χλαμύδα κοκκίνην.

περιτίθημι, v. xii. 1; πλέκω*, Mt. xxvii. 29, Jn. xix. 2**; ἀκάνθινος*, Jn. xix. 5 (Mt. xxvii. 29, ἐξ ἀκανθῶν)**;

18 στέφανον· καὶ ἤρξαντο ἀσπάζεσθαι αὐτόν Χαῖρε, βασιλεῦ τῶν
19 Ἰουδαίων· καὶ ἔτυπτον αὐτοῦ τὴν κεφαλὴν καλάμῳ καὶ ἐνέ-
20 πτυον αὐτῷ, καὶ τιθέντες τὰ γόνατα προσεκύνουν αὐτῷ. καὶ
ὅτε ἐνέπαιξαν αὐτῷ, ἐξέδυσαν αὐτὸν τὴν πορφύραν καὶ ἐνέδυσαν
αὐτὸν τὰ ἱμάτια αὐτοῦ.   Καὶ ἐξάγουσιν αὐτὸν ἵνα
σταυρώσωσιν αὐτόν.

στέφανος*. The *Zizyphus spina-Christi* or *nubk* tree and the *Calycotome villosa* have been suggested. The emperor's laurel wreath may have been in mind (Swete, 376), but Klostermann, 181, prefers the view that the crown symbolizes kingly dignity; cf. 1 Macc. x. 20, 2 Macc. xiv. 4. Otherwise the latter is expressed by the διάδημα (Isa. lxii. 3, etc.), which Mark does not mention. Cf. Mt. xxvii. 29, καὶ κάλαμον ἐν τῇ δεξιᾷ αὐτοῦ. Allen, 183 f., conjectures that a line has dropped out of Mk which mentioned a reed as in Mt (cf. Mk. xv. 19).

18-20. The soldiers now begin to greet Jesus with mock royal honours. For ἤρξαντο c. infin. *v.* Intr. 48, 63 f.; ἀσπάζομαι ix. 15*. χαῖρε, βασιλεῦ corresponds to the Latin greeting *Aue Caesar, uictor, imperator*. The voc., which admits the royal right (cf. Ac. xxvi. 7), is ' a note of the writer's imperfect sensibility to the more delicate shades of Greek idiom ', Moulton, i. 71. Mt. xxvii. 29 has the nom. ὁ βασιλεύς, ' you King ', in ℵ A L W *et al.* minusc. *pler.* Eus. The Gospel of Peter 3, καὶ ἐκάθισαν αὐτὸν ἐπὶ καθέδραν κρίσεως λέγοντες Δικαίως κρῖνε, βασιλεῦ τοῦ Ἰσραήλ, and Justin, *Apol.* i. 35, ἐκάθισαν ἐπὶ βήματος καὶ εἶπον Κρῖνον ἡμῖν, represent Him as sitting in judgment. In the former τοῦ Ἰσραήλ is more Jewish; τῶν Ἰουδαίων expresses contempt. In 19b Mark says that, falling upon their knees, they worshipped Him. It may be that no more than homage is meant; cf. RSV, ' they knelt down in homage to him '. Elsewhere, however, in the NT the phrase

τιθ(έντες) τὰ γόνατα is connected with prayer (cf. Lk. xxii. 41, Ac. vii. 60, ix. 40, xx. 36, xxi. 5**), and a mockery in terms of Caesar worship, or Oriental ideas of kingship, is probably meant.

Into this description Mark has introduced references to blows and spitting which recall the mishandling of Jesus by the high priests' attendants in xiv. 65. For ἐμπτύω *v.* x. 34, xiv. 65*; τύπτω*; κάλαμος, xv. 36*. Matthew so presents the story that all the signs of mockery (the scarlet robe, the crown, the reed, the kneeling, the homage) come first (xxvii. 29), and the references to violence (the spitting and striking) follow (xxvii. 30). This arrangement looks secondary. We must conclude that there was a combination of mimicry and abuse, as Mark records, or that the story has been influenced by xiv. 65. For the tendency of details to pass from one story to another *v.* V. Taylor, *FGT*, 154 f.

The account ends with the removal of the purple robe, the restoring of the garments, and the departure to the cross. ἐκδύω*; ἐνδύω, i. 6, vi. 9*; ἱμάτιον, ii. 21. B C Δ Ψ 1342 sype sa bo read τὰ ἱμάτια αὐτοῦ. Many MSS. add ἴδια (AV, Moffatt, RSV, ' his own clothes '; cf. Torrey); but the textual evidence [1] is too divided to afford confidence in amending the Gk text. ἐξάγω*, Lk. xxiv. 50, Jn. x. 3, Ac (8), Heb. viii. 9**; Cl. (generally c. gen. *loci*); LXX; Pap. (*VGT*, 220). With ἵνα σταυρώσωσιν[2] cf. ἵνα σταυρωθῇ in 15b, and see the intr. to the narrative. Matthew's modifications of 20 are purely stylistic.

[1] τὰ ἴδια ἱμάτια αὐτοῦ, ℵ Θ 115 282 472 (om. αὐτοῦ Θ 115 282); τὰ ἱμάτια, D ; τὰ ἱμάτια τὰ ἴδια, A N P X Π Σ *et al.* fam. 1 fam. 13 22 28 33 (565) 579 700 1071 *al. pler.* it vg syˢ ʰˡ geo¹.
[2] σταυρώσουσιν, A C D L N P Δ Θ Σ 33 69 122** 245 253 569. Cf. Moulton, ii. 75.

Mk. xv. 21-41　　　104. THE CRUCIFIXION　　Cf. Mt. xxvii. 32-56
(Lk. xxviii. 26-49)
(Jn. xix. 17-37)

The narrative consists of short separate scenes strung together in rapid succession. From it one gains the impression of a comparatively brief foundation story, which has attracted to itself various items of tradition, some historical and others legendary, out of which a kind of crucifixion drama has been compiled to meet the religious needs of a Gentile Church. The arrangement of the whole in three-hour periods, with an emphasis on the third, the sixth, and the ninth hours, and the account of three successive acts of railing, suggest this view. The references to the darkness and the rending of the Temple veil appear to be inserted, and the account of the watching women is added to prepare the way for the sequel in the Resurrection. There are two references to the act of crucifixion in 24 and 25, two taunt-sayings in 29 f. and 31 f., and two allusions to a loud cry of Jesus in 34 and 37. Further, the story concerning Simon of Cyrene, which may well reflect local knowledge, does not really enter into the structure of the narrative. Simon appears only to disappear, and we hear no more of him. All the interest is concentrated on the figure of Jesus. On these several points there is room for differences of opinion, but for the broad conclusion that the narrative shows marked signs of literary stratification there is very much to be said.

Attempts to distinguish stages in the process of compilation must necessarily be conjectural, for its history goes back into the oral period, and it is impossible to determine at what point a particular item of tradition was incorporated into the foundation narrative. In these circumstances the temptation to renounce the attempt to distinguish primary and secondary elements is strong, but this temptation ought to be resisted if progress is to be made. It must be emphasized that the terms ' primary ' and ' secondary ' relate to matters of structure, and do not necessarily denote ' historical ' and ' legendary ' material. The value of the added elements will vary. Some of them belong to the best tradition, others are inferior and even legendary; and, in consequence, each item must be considered separately. An attempt to tread this hazardous path is made in Note H, pp. 649-51. The Note is deferred until that point because it is conjectural and because the first essential is to study the narrative in detail in the Commentary. Here, for purposes of reference, it may be suggested that we are nearest to the foundation narrative in 21-4, 26, 29 f., 34-7, 39, and that the later elements in the Markan story are to be seen in 25, 27, 31 f., 33, 38, 40 f.

Καὶ ἀγγαρεύουσιν παράγοντά τινα Σίμωνα Κυρηναῖον ἐρ- 21

21. It was customary for the condemned man to carry his cross beam (*patibulum*). Cf. Plutarch, *De ser. num. vind.* 2, 554 A, τῶν κολαζομένων ἕκαστος τῶν κακούργων ἐκφέρει τὸν αὑτοῦ σταυρόν. It was therefore unusual that Simon of Cyrene was ' impressed ' to do this service. John omits this incident, possibly because it made no appeal to his mind (cf. Goguel, 532), possibly because Gnostics claimed that it was Simon and not Jesus who was crucified; cf. Irenaeus, *Adv. Haer.* i. 24. 4. It may well be that for a time Jesus carried the cross, but was unable to continue, although Mark does not say this. ἀγγαρεύω*, Mt. v. 41, xxvii. 32**, ' to impress ' into the public

χόμενον ἀπ᾽ ἀγροῦ, τὸν πατέρα ᾽Αλεξάνδρου καὶ ῾Ρούφου, ἵνα
22 ἄρῃ τὸν σταυρὸν αὐτοῦ. καὶ φέρουσιν αὐτὸν ἐπὶ τὸν Γολγοθᾶν τόπον, ὅ ἐστιν ⌜μεθερμηνευόμενος⌝ Κρανίου Τόπος.
23
24 καὶ ἐδίδουν αὐτῷ ἐσμυρνισμένον οἶνον, ὃς δὲ οὐκ ἔλαβεν. καὶ

22 μεθερμηνευόμενον

service. The word, which is found in the papyri and in MGk, is said to be of Persian origin. Cf. *VGT*, 2 f.; Deissmann, *BS*, 86 f. ℵ* B* read ἐγγαρεύουσιν. The name ' Simon ' is one of the very few proper names in Mk other than those of the disciples; cf. v. 22, x. 46. The adj. ' Cyrenean ' (Κυρηναῖος*, Mt. xxvii. 32, Lk. xxiii. 26, Ac. vi. 9, xi. 20, xiii. 1**) does not necessarily imply that he was a Gentile, nor do the references to Alexander and Rufus. He can have been a Gentile, but equally well a Jew returning to Jerusalem for the Passover from a country place or a farm near the city. For ἀγρός *v.* v. 14; παράγω i. 16. Torrey's conjecture, ' Simon, a farmer ', *TG*, 129, is very speculative; cf. Grant, *EG*, 120; and the bearing of ἐρχόμενον ἀπ᾽ ἀγροῦ on the date of the Crucifixion is uncertain. There is nothing to show that at the time Simon was a disciple or was in sympathy with Jesus; the probability is that he was a stranger.

The fact that Simon is described, without further explanation, as the father of Alexander and Rufus shows that all three, or at least the sons, were known to Mark and his readers. A Rufus is mentioned in Rom. xvi. 13; cf. SH, *Rom.* 426. He may be the Rufus to whom Mark refers, since the Gospel was almost certainly written in Rome. The Alexander mentioned is not likely to have been one of the antagonists of St Paul referred to in Ac. xix. 33, 1 Tim. i. 20, and 2 Tim. iv. 14. Of Simon it was remembered that he bore the cross of Jesus. Mark uses the language of viii. 34 in the clause ἵνα ἄρῃ τὸν σταυρὸν αὐτοῦ. Cf. Lohmeyer, 342, *Er ist der erste, der Ihm Sein Kreuz nachtrug*. The incident is undoubtedly historical. Goguel,

530 f., replies effectively to the objections of S. Reinach that the action would have been illegal and that the episode is only an illustration of viii. 34. ' No legal obligation ', he observes, ' can overrule a physical impossibility ', and he points out that in the saying everyone is summoned to bear his own cross willingly, and not under compulsion.

Matthew recasts the sentence and omits the allusion to Alexander and Rufus (xxvii. 32). So also Luke, who says that they laid (ἐπέθηκαν) the cross on Simon φέρειν ὄπισθεν τοῦ ᾽Ιησοῦ (xxiii. 26).

22 f. The use of the historic pres. is a striking feature of the Markan account of the crucifixion. In 21-7 there are five examples. There are also three imperfects in 23-32 apart from ἦν. In fact, there are only two aorists, ἔλαβεν in 23 to indicate a decided refusal, and ἐσταύρωσαν in 25, where it is required by the precise statement of time. This use of tenses gives great vividness to the scene; we see it before our eyes. For φέρουσιν v. Intr. 46 f. Γολγοθά(ν)*, Mt. xxvii. 33, Jn. xix. 17**, here an acc., otherwise indecl., is a transliteration of the Aramaic *golgoltha* (Heb. *gulgoleth*), ' a skull ', a hill so named from its shape or use. Legend connects it with the burial place of Adam's skull. Like many ancient places of execution, it stood without the gates of the city (cf. ἐξάγουσιν 20, Jn. xix. 20, Heb. xiii. 12), and from early times it was located within the site of the present Church of the Holy Sepulchre. Cf. Sanday, *SSG*, 67 ff.; Dalman, *SSW*, 346-56; Jeremias, *Golgatha*, 28 ff. Mark explains Γολγοθᾶν τόπον as Κρανίου Τόπος. For his use of ὅ ἐστιν v. iii. 17; μεθερμηνεύομαι v. 41, xv. 34**. Cf. Lk.

σταυροῦσιν αὐτὸν καὶ Διαμερίζονται τὰ ἱμάτια αὐτοῦ, βάλλον-
τες κλῆρον ἐπ' αὐτὰ τίς τί ἄρῃ.　ἦν δὲ ὥρα τρίτη καὶ ἐσταύ- 25

xxiii. 33 (which omits Γολγοθά) τὸν τόπον τὸν καλούμενον Κρανίον. The familiar name Calvary comes from the Vulgate rendering, *quod est interpretatum Calvariae locus.* In accordance with ancient Jewish custom, based on Prov. xxiv. 74 (xxxi. 6), wine drugged with myrrh was offered to Jesus, but He refused it, willing to die with an unclouded mind. Cf. *Sanh.* 43a and other Rabbinic evidence cited by Billerbeck, i. 1037 f. ἐδίδουν is probably a conative imperf., ' they sought to give '; cf. Swete, 379; Klostermann, 182. σμυρνίζω*, ' to drug with myrrh ' (intrans. ' to be like myrrh ', Diosc. i. 66), is *hapax leg.* Influenced by Psa. lxviii. (lxix.) 22, καὶ ἔδωκαν εἰς τὸ βρῶμά μου χολήν (cf. Lam. iii. 15), Matthew has οἶνον μετὰ χολῆς μεμιγμένον. He also expands Mark's abrupt ὃς δὲ οὐκ ἔλαβεν into καὶ γευσάμενος οὐκ ἠθέλησεν πιεῖν. ὃς δέ is replaced by ὁ δέ in A C L Δ Θ *et al.* fam. 13 22 28 157 543 565 700 892² 1071 *al. pler.* sype hl sa bo geo². For ὃς δέ without ὃς μέν *v.* Jn. v. 11; cf. Blass, 146, 331.

24. καὶ σταυροῦσιν αὐτόν. So, in the simplest possible terms, the dread act is recorded! No attempt is made to describe the harrowing details familiar enough in the ancient world. For σταυρόω *v.* xv. 13. Crucifixion was of eastern origin and from the time of the Punic wars was used by the Romans as a punishment for slaves. The shape of the cross varied. Sometimes it consisted of a single stake, to which the victim was fastened or on which he was impaled. Sometimes it consisted of two parts arranged diagonally or with an upright and a cross beam (*patibulum*) which might be set at the top (*crux commissa*) like a letter T, or a little lower (*crux immissa*). The traditional view is that the cross of Jesus was of the latter type, but it is not certain, since the superscription could be fixed equally well on the *crux*

commissa. The arms of the condemned were fastened to the cross beam with ropes or nails, and sometimes the feet were fastened in the same way, the body resting on a peg (*sedile*). In the case of Jesus nails are mentioned in Jn. xx. 25 (cf. 20), but not in the Synoptics. Albert Réville, *Jésus de Nazareth*, ii. 405 f., speaks of crucifixion as one of the most abominable forms of torture ever invented, and many commentators quote the phrase of Cicero, *crudelissimum taeterrimumque supplicium, In Verrem*, v. 64. Naked and unable to move, the victim was exposed to pain and insult, enduring thirst and finally, sometimes after days, dying from exhaustion, unless mercifully his sufferings were brought to an end by a spear-thrust or a shattering blow. Cf. D. Smith, *DCG*, i. 397-9; Goguel, 534-6; Klostermann, 183.

The garments of the condemned were the perquisites of the soldiers who guarded the cross. That they should have divided them by casting lots, using the dice by which they whiled away the time, is natural, and need not be regarded as a detail suggested by Psa. xxi. (xxii.) 19, διεμερίσαντο τὰ ἱμάτιά μου ἑαυτοῖς, καὶ ἐπὶ τὸν ἱματισμόν μου ἔβαλον κλῆρον. Mark's language shows that he has this passage in mind. Later it is quoted in Jn. xix. 24, and a distinction is made between the garments, which are divided into four parts, and the tunic for which they cast lots. Here, as in Mark's account of the crucifixion, the question arises how far events have recalled OT passages, and to what extent these have coloured the accounts.

διαμερίζω*, ' to distribute '; Cl., LXX, Pap. Mark has the mid. ' to divide among themselves ', as in the LXX (aor., *v. supra*), but not the redundant ἑαυτοῖς as in Jn. For ἱμάτιον *v.* ii. 21. κλῆρος*, ' a lot '; cf. LXX, ἔβαλον κλῆρον, also c. ἐπί and acc. τίς τί

26 ρωσαν αὐτόν. καὶ ἦν ἡ ἐπιγραφὴ τῆς αἰτίας αὐτοῦ ἐπι-
27 γεγραμμένη Ο ΒΑΣΙΛΕΥΣ ΤΩΝ ΙΟΥΔΑΙΩΝ. Καὶ σὺν
αὐτῷ σταυροῦσιν δύο λῃστάς, ἕνα ἐκ δεξιῶν καὶ ἕνα ἐξ εὐ-

ἄρη, ' what each should take ', lit. ' who should take what '; cf. Lk. xix. 15 (Α Δ Θ). The blending of the two interrogatives is classical; v. the examples from Plato, Xenophon, etc., quoted by Field, 43 f. ; also Blass, 177.

25 f. Precise statements of time are a feature of the Crucifixion narrative ; cf. 33 f., also 42 and xvi. 1. ὥρα τρίτη =9 a.m. Various dubious explanations have been offered to explain the disagreement with Jn. xix. 14 (ὥρα ἦν ὡς ἕκτη), e.g. that Mark followed the Roman reckoning (Westcott), that F has been confused with Γ (Ps. Jerome, cf. Swete, 381), or that the Jews really crucified Jesus when they cried, ' Crucify ' (Aug.). It is better to recognize that the two temporal statements belong to different traditions, and that Jn. xix. 14 is meant to be a correction ; cf. Bernard, St. Jn, 624. The reading ἕκτη in Mk in Θ 478** syhl mg aeth, Jer. Act. Pil. Catt.mosq. et oxon. is due to harmonization.

καί is usually explained as an example of co-ordination in place of subordination with the meaning ' that ' or ' when ' (Blass, 262 ; v. RSV), a usage sometimes found in Cl. Gk (Blass cites Plato, Symp. 220 c). The usage was formerly claimed as a Semitism by Wellhausen, but he retracts his claim in Einl.² 13 ; v. Howard, ii. 421. Black, 48, is not prepared to exclude altogether the possibility of Semitic influence. D ff k n r¹ sa read ἐφύλασσον, and this v.l. is strongly supported by Turner, 77, JTS, xxix. 11, Allen, 185, and Couchoud, JTS, xxxiv. 133; it appears to be implied by Mt. xxvii. 36, καὶ καθήμενοι ἐτήρουν αὐτὸν ἐκεῖ, and, if accepted, avoids an awkward repetition (cf. σταυροῦσιν in 24). These arguments are not entirely satisfactory, since the Western reading can be regarded as the correction of the Markan re-

petition. Bultmann, 295, regards the temporal statement as redactional and καὶ ἐσταύρωσαν αὐτόν as a doublet to 24; cf. J. Weiss, 335, who assigns it to the Bearbeiter who desired to complete the temporal scheme manifest in 1, 33, 35, 42. This suggestion is interesting, but there is no reason why Mark should not have made the addition himself. The three-hour periods, 6 a.m., 9 a.m., 12 p.m., 3 p.m., 6 p.m., may reflect the catechetical and liturgical interests of the Church at Rome.

The reference to the superscription is in accordance with Roman custom. Cf. Suetonius, Calig. 32, praecedente titulo qui causam poenae indicaret; Eus. Hist. Eccl. v. 1 (cf. Swete, 381). For ἐπιγραφή v. xii. 16*. ἐπιγράφω* (Cl., LXX, Pap.). αἰτία*, ' a cause ', is used forensically of 'an accusation' or ' charge ' (Cl., LXX, Pap.). All the Evangelists have the phrase ὁ βασιλεὺς τῶν Ἰουδαίων (v. xv. 2) which reflects Pilate's scorn. Lk. xxiii. 38 adds οὗτος and Mt. xxvii. 37 prefixes οὗτός ἐστιν, while Jn. xix. 19 has Ἰ. ὁ Ν. ὁ βασ. τ. Ἰουδαίων followed by the statement that the τίτλος was written in Hebrew, Latin and Greek. For the periphrastic tense v. Intr. 45 f., 62 f. Peculiar to Jn is the statement that, in reply to the remonstrance of the chief priests, Pilate replied Ὁ γέγραφα, γέγραφα (xix. 21).

27 f. After mentioning the superscription Mark relates that two bandits were crucified with Jesus. In Lk they are called κακοῦργοι earlier in the narrative (xxiii. 32). In Mk they appear to be mentioned in anticipation of the account of the railing and mockery which follows (29-32). For λῃστής v. xi. 17, xiv. 48* ; ἐκ δεξιῶν x. 37 ; ἐξ εὐωνύμων x. 40*. The use of ἕνα . . . ἕνα to express the idea of alter . . . alter may be Semitic (cf. x. 37 and Mt. xxiv. 40 f.), especially as in the same verse the plur. σταυροῦσιν is used imper-

ὠνύμων αὐτοῦ. Καὶ οἱ παραπορευόμενοι ἐβλασφήμουν αὐτὸν 29
κινοῦντεc τὰc κεφαλὰc αὐτῶν καὶ λέγοντες Οὐὰ ὁ καταλύων
τὸν ναὸν καὶ οἰκοδομῶν [ἐν] τρισὶν ἡμέραις, σῶσον σεαυτὸν 30
καταβὰς ἀπὸ τοῦ σταυροῦ. ὁμοίως καὶ οἱ ἀρχιερεῖς ἐμπαίζοντες 31
πρὸς ἀλλήλους μετὰ τῶν γραμματέων ἔλεγον ″Ἄλλους ἔσωσεν,

sonally instead of the passive (cf. Mt.
xxvii. 38, σταυροῦνται), as in vi. 14,
x. 13, xiii. 26. Cf. Intr. 47 f., 62.

Many MSS. and versions add in 28
καὶ ἐπληρώθη ἡ γραφὴ ἡ λέγουσα καὶ
μετὰ ἀνόμων ἐλογίσθη, but the omission
of the passage in ℵ A B C D X Y Ψ
27 71* 127* 157 471 474 476 478** 692
al. mu. k sy⁵ sa bo, as well as the
manner of citation, show that it has
been added from Lk. xxii. 37. Cf.
Swete, 382; Lagrange, 429; Hort,
27; etc. Later tradition named the
bandits: c has Zoathan and Cham-
matha; the Acts of Pilate Dysmas and
Gestas; the Arabic Gospel of the Infancy Titus and Dumachus; and l
Iothas and Maggatras. John says that
Jesus was crucified between them,
ἐσταύρωσαν . . . ἄλλους δύο ἐντεῦθεν καὶ
ἐντεῦθεν, μέσον δὲ τὸν Ἰησοῦν (xix. 18).

29 f. The section 29-32, which describes the railing and mockery of the
passers-by, the chief priests, and the
two bandits, raises acute historical problems. To what extent is the record
coloured by Lam. ii. 15 and Psa. xxi.
(xxii.) 8 f., and perhaps also Wis. ii.
17 f.? Is it historical, or partly or
wholly imaginative, the product of
Christian reflection?

For παραπορεύομαι v. ii. 23; βλασφημέω ii. 7; κινέω*. Those who pass by
are Jews from the city, not necessarily
members of a crowd. One would expect a phrase like τινες τῶν παρεστώτων
(xv. 35). The explanation can only
be that Mark is influenced by Lam.
ii. 15, πάντες οἱ παραπορευόμενοι ὁδόν
. . . ἐκίνησαν τὴν κεφαλὴν αὐτῶν, and
Psa. xxi. (xxii.) 8, πάντες οἱ θεωροῦντές
με ἐξεμυκτήρισάν με, ἐλάλησαν ἐν χείλεσιν, ἐκίνησαν κεφαλήν. From this fact
it does not follow that these passages
explain the origin of the tradition. It
may well be, as often happens, that

facts are related in appropriate Biblical
language. All depends on the view
taken of the saying in 29b, 30.

The first part of the taunt (29b) embodies the saying about the destruction
and renewal of the Temple, which
there is every reason to regard as fully
authentic (v. the note on xiv. 58). That
it should be repeated with derision
while the speaker hangs upon a cross
is not surprising. οὐά** is an interjection, ' Ah!' or ' Ha!', indicating
wonder real or assumed. Cf. Epictetus iii. 23 f., ἐπαίνεσόν με . . . εἰπέ μοι
' οὐά' καὶ ' θαυμαστῶς' (VGT, 464).
For ὁ καταλύων κτλ. v. xiv. 58. After
σῶσον σεαυτόν Matthew adds the taunt
εἰ υἱὸς εἶ τοῦ θεοῦ. The second part of
the invective arises out of the first. If
Jesus is the Messianic restorer of the
Temple, let Him save Himself and
come down from the cross! σώζω, iii.
4; καταβαίνω, i. 10; σταυρός, viii. 34.
To the mockers the logic of the challenge is irrefutable. Crucifixion is the
crowning proof of self-deception. All
this is realistically expressed, and there
is no good reason to regard the account
as other than historical. The only
question — and it is of minor importance — is whether the description of
the speakers is coloured by the OT
passages already cited. For a Christian teacher steeped in the ideas of
the OT the phrase about shaking the
head was a commonplace; v. further,
4 Kgdms. xix. 21, Job xvi. 5, Sir.
xiii. 7.

31 f. The railing of the chief priests
and scribes raises difficulties. Their
presence at the crucifixion, while not
impossible, excites surprise, and looks
like an attempt to find room for the
traditional opponents of Jesus. For
οἱ ἀρχιερεῖς v. ii. 26; οἱ γραμματεῖς i.
22; ὁμοίως iv. 16; ἐμπαίζω x. 34;

32 ἑαυτὸν οὐ δύναται σῶσαι· ὁ χριστὸς ὁ βασιλεὺς ᾿Ισραὴλ καταβάτω
νῦν ἀπὸ τοῦ σταυροῦ, ἵνα ἴδωμεν καὶ πιστεύσωμεν. καὶ οἱ συν-
εσταυρωμένοι σὺν αὐτῷ ὠνείδιζον αὐτόν.   Καὶ γενο-
33 μένης ὥρας ἕκτης σκότος ἐγένετο ἐφ᾿ ὅλην τὴν γῆν ἕως ὥρας
34 ἐνάτης. καὶ τῇ ἐνάτῃ ὥρᾳ ἐβόησεν ὁ ᾿Ιησοῦς φωνῇ μεγάλη ᴦ Ε λ ω ι

πρὸς ἀλλήλους iv. 41. The vocabulary,
it will be seen, consists of common
Markan words. At the same time a
certain art is manifest in the account.
The passers-by cry out in derision;
the priests and scribes exchange gibes
with one another, taking up and carrying farther what they have just heard.
Cf. Lagrange, 430; Rawlinson, 234.
The taunt "Αλλους ἔσωσεν, ἑαυτὸν οὐ
δύναται σῶσαι is one of the supreme
ironies of history. In contemptuous
words the popular cry is endorsed:
' Let the Messiah, the King of Israel,
come down *now* from the cross! ', and
to this is added the sceptical plea, ἵνα
ἴδωμεν καὶ πιστεύσωμεν (cf. Jn. vi. 30).
Elsewhere Mark's realism is based on
testimony, and it is hard to believe that
this speech is the product of creative
imagination. In it no false note is
struck. The religious assumption is
that of Wis. ii. 17 f., ἴδωμεν εἰ οἱ λόγοι
αὐτοῦ ἀληθεῖς, καὶ πειράσωμεν τὰ ἐν
ἐκβάσει αὐτοῦ. εἰ γάρ ἐστιν ὁ δίκαιος
υἱὸς θεοῦ, ἀντιλήμψεται αὐτοῦ, καὶ ῥύ-
σεται αὐτὸν ἐκ χειρὸς ἀνθεστηκότων. But
few would suggest dependence. Nor
is there any other passage which might
explain the genesis of the Markan
saying.[1] The case is different in Mt.
xxvii. 43. Here unquestionably Psa.
xxi. (xxii.) 9 has supplied the model:

Mt. xxvii. 43	Ps. xxi. (xxii.) 9
πέποιθεν ἐπὶ τὸν θεόν,	ἤλπισεν ἐπὶ κύριον,
ῥυσάσθω νῦν	ῥυσάσθω αὐτόν· σωσάτω αὐτόν,
εἰ θέλει αὐτόν.	ὅτι θέλει αὐτόν.

Mk, however, must not be read
through Matthaean spectacles, and
here ἑαυτόν . . . σῶσαι is the only
point of contact with the Psalm and
is a reminiscence at most. Brandt,

indeed, is driven to the suggestion that
the words are a sort of echo of taunts
often made in later days by opponents;
cf. Montefiore, i. 382. The account
of three successive acts of railing
may be catechetical, especially as no
words are assigned to the crucified
rebels; but substantially it is trustworthy. Several scholars have suggested that 29 f. and 31 f. are doublets;
the former is secondary in the opinion
of Wendling, 199 f., and Weiss, 336;
the latter according to Loisy, ii. 670,
Wellhausen, 131, and Bultmann, 295.

συνσταυροῦμαι* is manifestly not used
in its Pauline sense (Rom. vi. 6, Gal.
ii. 20) of being crucified with Christ;
in Mk, as in Mt. xxvii. 44 and Jn. xix.
32**, it describes those crucified at the
same time. Apparently the verb is not
found outside the NT and ecclesiastical
writings. ὀνειδίζω, xvi. [14]*, ' reproach ', ' revile '; Cl., LXX, Pap.
In Lk only one malefactor rails at
Jesus (xxiii. 39).

A point of linguistic interest arises
in ἔλεγον (31). In Mk k, and in Mt
D 273 569 ff g¹·² vg (*plur.*) syhl sa bo
aeth, read λέγοντες. If this reading is
original, it may be a Semitism, for the
use of the participle alone, while found
in Hellenistic Gk, is common in
Aramaic. Cf. Black, 95: ' WH read
ἔλεγον, but by making this the main
verb and subordinating ἐμπαίζοντες
to it, the natural emphasis is lost: the
chief priests and Pharisees were not
saying, mocking; they were mocking,
saying '.

33 f. The darkness (σκότος*) is described in simple and precise terms;
it begins with the sixth hour (γενομένης
ὥρας ἕκτης), i.e. at noon, and extends
over the whole land (ἐφ᾿ ὅλην τὴν γῆν)
until the ninth hour (ἕως ὥρας ἐνάτης),

---

[1] See Lagrange's criticism, 430, of the suggestion of Aytoun, *JTS*, xxi. 245 ff., that the saying
is a reminiscence of Psa. xxii. 29 (LXX, xxi. 30).

Ἐλωὶ λαμὰ cαβαχθανεί;[1] ὅ ἐστιν μεθερμηνευόμενον Ὁ θεόc
μου [ὁ θεόc μου], εἰc τί ἐγκατέλιπέc με; καί τινες τῶν ⌐παρεστη- 35
34 Ἠλεὶ Ἠλεὶ λαμὰ ζαφθανεί;

i.e. 3 p.m. By ὅλην τὴν γῆν probably
Judaea is described rather than the
whole earth; cf. Ex. x. 22. A natural
phenomenon may be meant; cf. Lagrange, 432, who mentions the possibility of a ' black sirocco ', and the
note of A. Parrot quoted by Goguel,
542 n. An eclipse is impossible at the
time of the full moon, as Origen
pointed out, and it is not necessarily
implied by Lk. xxiii. 45, τοῦ ἡλίου
ἐκλείποντος. Probably Mark thought
of the darkness as supernatural, and,
in this case, it is a legendary development of the kind commonly associated
with the death of great men. Cf.
Rawlinson, 235; Goguel, 541 f.; Lohmeyer, 345; etc. Cf. Virgil, *Georg.*
i. 463 ff. :

    Solem quis dicere falsum
Audeat? . . .
Ille etiam exstincto miseratus Caesare
    Romam
Cum caput obscura nitidum ferrugine
    texit
Impiaque aeternam timuerunt saecula
    noctem ;

Diog. Laer. iv. 64; Plutarch, *Pelop.*
295 A. See also Amos viii. 9, Jer. xv. 9,
Mk. xiii. 24; for Rabbinic parallels
Billerbeck, i. 1040-2; and for Patristic
interpretations Swete, 384 f. The
verse appears to be an addition to an
earlier account of the Passion, connected with the three-hour scheme in
which the Markan account is set.

The saying which follows (τῇ ἐνάτῃ
ὥρᾳ) is the only one recorded in Mk
and Mt. For βοάω v. i. 3*; φωνῇ
μεγάλῃ i. 26; cf. xv. 37. The cry
Ἐλωὶ ἐλωὶ λαμὰ σαβαχθανεί is a transliteration of a Hebraized Aramaic
original אֱלֹהִי אֱלֹהִי לָמָה שְׁבַקְתַּנִי. The
saying is a quotation from Psa. xxii. 1

which reads אֵלִי אֵלִי לָמָה עֲזַבְתָּנִי. Already
in Mk the Aramaic reflects the Hebrew,
in לְמָה (Aram. לְמָא)[1] and אֱלֹהִי (Aram.
אֱלָהִי) and this influence is more evident
still in the reading ζαφθανεί in D k.[2]
If Mark is using Palestinian tradition,
it is natural that he should give the
saying in an Aramaic form, but it is
more probable that the cry was uttered
in Hebrew, for the comment of the
bystanders, Ἴδε Ἠλείαν φωνεῖ (xv. 35),
is intelligible if Jesus cried ἠλεὶ ἠλεί or
ἠλὶ ἠλί rather than ἐλωί. In Mt. xxvii.
46 only א B 33 vg (*mu.*) sa bo aeth read
the latter; all other authorities have
either ἠλεί or ἠλί, forms which could
easily be confused with אֵלִיָּהוּ or אֵלִיָּה,
Elijah. Many scholars hold that Jesus
used the Hebrew form; cf. A. Resch,
Paralleltexte, 357 ff.; Dalman, *JJ*,
21, 204 f. (cf. *WJ*, 53 f.); Wellhausen,
132; Allen, 186; Turner, 78 f., *JTS*,
xxvi. 154 n.; Bartlet, 426; Kilpatrick,
105; others think He used an Aramaic
form; cf. Lagrange, 433; McNeile,
421; C. J. Cadoux, 258. Much depends on the view taken of the historical character of 35, 36b.

As frequently, Mark translates the
Aramaic for the benefit of his readers.
For ὅ ἐστιν v. iii. 17; μεθερμηνεύομαι
v. 41. ἐγκαταλείπω* (Cl., LXX, Pap.).
Mark's rendering is that of the LXX,
with the omission of πρόσχες μοι, and
with εἰς τί instead of ἵνα τί. The form
in the Gosp. of Pet. v. 19 is ἡ δύναμίς
μου, ἡ δύναμις, κατέλειψάς με. The
reading ὠνείδισάς με in D (cf. *expro-
basti me* c, *me in opprobrium dedisti* i,
maledixisti k), ' hast thou taunted me ',
may be due to a copyist who took
offence at ἐγκατέλιπές με, and intended
ζαφθανεί as a transliteration of עֲזַבְתָּנִי
(Aram. זְעִי, ' to storm ').[3]

---

[1] λεμά is read in Mk by א C L Δ Ψ 72 517 1342 c g² l bo and λιμά by A K M *et al.* fam. 13 33
118 700 *al. mu.* sy^hl.

[2] See the articles of König and Nestle, *ET*, xi. 237 f., 287 f., 334-6.

[3] Cf. Dalman, 54 n.; Nestle, *ET*, xi. 335 f.; Lagrange, 433; Harnack, *Studien* (1931), 98-103.
In the last named article, which I have not seen, Harnack argues that the Western reading is
original. Cf. Cadoux, 258. Cf. also Turner, *JTS*, xxix. 12, who prefers to read εἰς τί ὠνείδισάς με ;,
and Burkitt, *JTS*, i. 278 f.

36 κότων¹ ἀκούσαντες ἔλεγον "Ἴδε Ἠλείαν φωνεῖ. δραμὼν δέ τις
γεμίσας σπόγγον ὄξοϲ περιθεὶς καλάμῳ ἐπότιζεν αὐτόν, λέγων

35 ἑστηκότων

The saying has been explained as a secondary interpretation of the death cry mentioned in 37 in terms of OT prophecy; cf. Loisy, ii. 683; Bacon, *BGS*, 223; Bultmann, 295; Bertram, 83. Against this view must be set the great improbability that tradition would have assigned to Jesus such a saying except under the warrant of the best testimony. Its offence is manifest in the silence of Luke and John and in the textual tradition. Schmiedel, *EB*, col. 1881, included it among his nine 'foundation-pillars', and Arno Neumann described it as bearing unmistakably 'the stamp of genuineness' (*Jesus*, 162). Cf. also Klausner, 354; Goguel, 541; etc. Its meaning has been variously interpreted. The view maintained by Lutheran and Reformed theologians, and advocated by Dale (*The Atonement*, 61, 360), that Jesus, as a substitute for sinners, was forsaken by the Father, is inconsistent with the love of God and the oneness of purpose with the Father manifest in the atoning ministry of Jesus. The interpretation which sees in the Cry a final utterance of faith, in the light of Psa. xxii as a whole (M'Leod Campbell, *The Nature of the Atonement*, 240 f.; Carpenter, *The First Three Gospels*, 393; Menzies, 280 f.; A. T. Cadoux, *SSG*, 113; etc.), is a reaction from the traditional view which fails to take the saying seriously. The depths of the saying are too deep to be plumbed, but the least inadequate interpretations are those which find in it a sense of desolation in which Jesus felt the horror of sin so deeply that for a time the closeness of His communion with the Father was obscured. Glover writes: 'I have sometimes thought there never was an utterance that reveals more amazingly the distance

between feeling and fact', *The Jesus of History*, 192.

35 f. This little episode is more complex than might at first appear. The τινες τῶν παρεστηκότων ¹ who say ἴδε Ἠλείαν φωνεῖ are manifestly Jews, but the one who runs and fills a sponge with vinegar and tries to let Jesus drink may well be a soldier (cf. Jn. xix. 29). How, then, can he say ἄφετε ἴδωμεν εἰ ἔρχεται Ἠλείας καθελεῖν αὐτόν?

For παρίστημι v. iv. 29, and with τινες τῶν παρεστηκότων cf. xiv. 69. The action in ἔλεγον is probably continuous, 'were saying'. For the expectation of Elijah *redivivus* v. the notes on i. 2 and vi. 14; cf. also viii. 28 and xi. 11 f. Billerbeck, i. 1042, observes that in popular belief it was expected that Elijah would come to the rescue of the godly in time of need; cf. Edersheim, ii. 706-9. Many hold that the words were spoken in mockery; cf. Rawlinson, 237; Lohmeyer, 346. With the support of k, which reads *helion*, Turner, 79, conjectures that the bystanders were the soldiers who took 'Eli, Eli' to be an appeal to the sun-god. That they were Jews seems more likely.

The view that δραμὼν δέ τις is a soldier rests partly on the interpretation of ὄξος as *posca*, the sour wine drunk by labourers and soldiers (Plautus, *Mil.* iii. 2. 25, *Trucul.* ii. 7. 48; cf. Plutarch, *Cato maior*, 336) and partly on Jn. xix. 29, σκεῦος ἔκειτο ὄξους μεστόν· σπόγγον οὖν μεστὸν τοῦ ὄξους ὑσσώπῳ περιθέντες προσήνεγκαν αὐτοῦ τῷ στόματι, especially if ὑσσῷ, 'with a javelin', is read (Bernard, 640). For τρέχω v. v. 6 (cf. vi. 33, ix. 15, 25, x. 17); γεμίζω, iv. 37*; ὄξος*, Mt. xxvii. 48, Lk. xxiii. 36, Jn. xix. 29 f.**; περιτίθημι, xii. 1, xv. 17*; κάλαμος, xv. 19*. σπόγγος*, Mt. xxvii. 48, Jn. xix. 29**, 'a sponge'; Cl.,

---

¹ παρεστηκότων, C L N P Π Σ Ψ minusc. *pler.* παρεστώτων, א D U Θ 33 68 517 565 569. ἑστηκότων, B. ἐκεῖ ἑστηκότων, A sa aeth.

Ἄφετε ἴδωμεν εἰ ἔρχεται Ἡλείας καθελεῖν αὐτόν. ὁ δὲ Ἰησοῦς 37

Pap. (*VGT*, 584). For ποτίζω v. ix. 41*. Like ἐδίδουν in 23, ἐπότιζεν is a conative impf. The compound expression ἄφετε ἴδωμεν means 'Do let us see'. Cf. ἄφες c. subj. in Mt. vii. 4 = Lk. vi. 42 and ἄφετε c. infin. in Mk. x. 14. The imperative is not a mere auxiliary, but it is well on the way to becoming such. See Moulton's discussion, i. 175 f., also *VGT*, 97. The meaning is not 'Let him alone' (cf. xiv. 6), and 'Wait, let us see' (RSV) and 'Come on, let us see' (Moffatt) are perhaps too definite. It is very doubtful if there is any difference of meaning in Matthew's ἄφες ἴδωμεν, as Swete, 387, suggests, for it is not necessary to see a rebuke in ἄφετε. The conditional clause εἰ ἔρχεται Ἡλείας καθελεῖν αὐτόν expresses a doubtful expectation. In Mt the infin. is replaced by the fut. participle σώσων. καθαιρέω, xv. 46*, is the technical term for the removal of a crucified person; cf. Polybius i. 86. 6, Philo, *in Flacc.* 83, Josephus, *BJ*, iv. 5. 2, LXX, Pap. See Field, 44.

By whom are the words spoken? The differences between Mk and Mt are strange. In Mk the speaker is the man who offers the wine (cf. λέγων). In Mt he is one of the bystanders (εἷς ἐξ αὐτῶν), and yet the speakers are the rest (οἱ δὲ λοιποί). It cannot be said that a soldier could not confuse אֵלִי and אֵלִיָּה, or be entirely unfamiliar with Jewish expectations, since he may have been recruited from Sebaste (cf. Schürer, II. i. 65, 126); but it is much more probable that Jewish voices cried ἄφετε ἴδωμεν εἰ ἔρχεται Ἡλείας καθελεῖν αὐτόν. In this case, either Mark is mistaken in assigning the cry to the compassionate soldier, or, alternatively, the reading λέγων is not original. The latter may be argued from the fact that Matthew so explicitly writes οἱ δὲ λοιποὶ ἔλεγον. Can he have read λέγων in Mk? This doubt is increased by the fact that in Mk sys reads 'they say' and sype 'they said'.

Cf. Wellhausen, 132. The argument, however, is weakened by the isolation of these readings from the rest of the textual tradition, and by the possibility that they may be assimilations to the text of Mt. Moreover, the Matthaean text reads like a conscious correction of Mk. What need had Matthew to assign the cry to the rest if the giver of wine was one of their number? The answer must be that, holding the speakers to be Jews, he took exception to Mark's λέγων. We conclude, therefore, that in Mk λέγων is primary and incorrect. If we take that view, we must resort to conjecture; and the conjecture that does most justice to the facts is that in 35 f. Mark is combining two separate traditions: an account of the bystanders in 35, 36b who cried, 'Let us see if Elijah will come to take him down', and in 36a the story of a compassionate soldier who offered Jesus wine shortly before the end.

The view that 36a is a separate tradition from 35, 36b is suggested by Wellhausen, 132, Klostermann, 186, and others (cf. Bultmann, 295), and it has a parallel in Turner's suggestion (cf. Rawlinson, 237) that 36a is a Markan parenthesis. Such views do not necessarily carry with them the conclusion that one tradition is primary and the other secondary. Both may be historical. In particular, the opinion that 36a is inspired by Psa. lxviii. (lxix.) 22, καὶ εἰς τὴν δίψαν μου ἐπότισάν με ὄξος, is no more than surmise, and the contrary suggestion, that the incident drew the attention of Christians to the Psalm, which in turn influenced the vocabulary of 36a, is more probable. And, in any case, if 35 f. is a fusion of two traditions, 35, 36b is not dependent upon the Psalm. In Jn. xix. 28 the cry 'I thirst' is described as a fulfilment of scripture, and many commentators suspect the creative influence of Psa. lxviii. (lxix.) 22; but we cannot measure Mk by Jn. The

38 ἀφεὶς φωνὴν μεγάλην ἐξέπνευσεν. Καὶ τὸ καταπέτασμα τοῦ

soldier's act is fully credible, and an independent echo of it may be preserved in Lk. xxiii. 36, ὄξος προσφέροντες αὐτῷ, although here the act is conceived as mockery. No less credible is the taunt about Elijah. To dismiss the incident as apocryphal (Wellhausen, 132) or improbable (J. Weiss, 338) is unnecessary, and it is possible that Weiss, who finds a real difficulty in the vagueness of the subjects, τινες τῶν παρεστηκότων and δραμὼν δέ τις, might not have come to this conclusion if he had regarded 35, 36b and 36a as separate traditions. Goguel, 543 f., cites evidence for the belief that the death of a crucified person was hastened by drinking.

37 f. ' And, with a loud cry, Jesus expired.' For ἀφεὶς φωνήν v. Demosth. xviii. 218. ἐκπνέω, xv. 39, Lk. xxiii. 46**, v. Soph. Ajax, 1026 (with βίον), Aesch. Agam. 1493, Eur. Hel. 142 (with πνεῦμα), Eur. Orest. 1163; not in LXX nor cited in VGT. The vocabulary and the correct use of the aor. may suggest that the basic source of the Passion Narrative was drawn up in a Gentile Church. Mark describes a sudden violent death. For this reason renderings like ' breathed his last ' (RSV) or ' gave up the ghost ' (AV, RV) are too smooth. From a sense of something unusual in the death, all the Evangelists avoid verbs like ἀποθνήσκω and τελευτάω, and Mt. xxvii. 50, ἀφῆκεν τὸ πνεῦμα, and Jn. xix. 30, καὶ κλίνας τὴν κεφαλὴν παρέδωκεν τὸ πνεῦμα, describe a voluntary act. In the stark realism of Mark's account this suggestion is not made and no saying is recorded after xv. 34. Luke records the saying Πάτερ, εἰς χεῖράς σου παρατίθεμαι τὸ πνεῦμά μου (cf. Psa. xxx. (xxxi.) 6), and John the majestic Τετέλεσται. Intense spiritual suffering must have led to the embolism, if such it was, which was the immediate cause of death. Usually, crucified men lingered long in torment, dying in the end through exhaustion.

Both Pilate and the centurion marvelled that Jesus died so soon, and the centurion in particular was awed by the last loud cry.

The reference to the rending of the Temple veil appears to be a legendary addition doctrinal in origin. καταπέτασμα*, Mt. xxvii. 51, Lk. xxiii. 45, Heb. vi. 19, ix. 3, x. 20**, ' veil '; LXX, Pap. (LS), inscr. of a tablecover in a list of temple furniture (Deissmann, 102 f.). In the LXX τὸ καταπέτασμα (Heb. paroketh, maṣok) is the curtain between the Holy Place and the Holy of Holies (Ex. xxvi. 31-7, etc.), but the word is sometimes used of the veil which covered the entrance to the Holy Place, generally called τὸ κάλυμμα (Ex. xxvii. 16, etc.). See also Ep. Aristeas 86 (Meecham, 55); Philo, de Vit. Mos. ii. 148, de Gig. i. 270, τὸ ἐσώτατον καταπέτασμα; also Heb. vi. 19, ix. 3 (Westcott, Heb. 163) and the Christian interpolations in Test. Levi x. 3 f., Test. Benj. ix. 3 f. Many commentators think that Mark means the inner veil (B. Weiss, 238; Gould, 295; Swete, 388; Billerbeck, i. 1045; Turner, 79; Plummer, 360; Rawlinson, 238; Blunt, 263; etc.), but others the outer (Jerome and Aquinas (cf. Lagrange, 436); Dalman, 56, SSW, 306; Klostermann, 186; McNeile, 423; Smith, 209; Lohmeyer, 347; etc.). That a material veil is meant is not certain, and, on the whole, the former interpretation is to be preferred. The velum scissum symbolizes the opening of the way to God effected by the death of Christ, or alternatively, and perhaps at the same time, the end of the Temple system; less probably the destruction of the Temple (Goguel, 544; Schniewind, 201). G. Lindeskog, CN, xi. 132-7, suggests that the theological idea of the opening of the way to heaven has been dressed in a cultic pattern which is interpreted symbolically in Heb. and realistically in Mk.

Dubious historical support is sup-

ναοῦ ἐσχίσθη εἰς δύο ἀπ' ἄνωθεν ἕως κάτω. Ἰδὼν δὲ ὁ κεντυρίων 39
ὁ παρεστηκὼς ἐξ ἐναντίας αὐτοῦ ὅτι οὕτως κράξας ἐξέπνευσεν
εἶπεν Ἀληθῶς οὗτος ὁ ἄνθρωπος υἱὸς θεοῦ ἦν. Ἦσαν δὲ καὶ 40

plied by the prodigies reported by Josephus, *BJ*, vi. 5. 3, of a great light and the strange opening of its own accord of the eastern gate of the Temple, assigned by *j. Yoma*, vi. 43c, to a period forty years before its destruction (cf. Billerbeck, i. 1045), or by the tradition in the Gospel according to the Hebrews, that ' the lintel of the Temple, of marvellous size, fell down in fragments ', *legimus, non velum templi scissum, sed superliminare templi mirae magnitudinis corruisse* (Jerome, *Ep.* cxx. 8. 1), or again by the *prodigia* mentioned by Tacitus, *Hist.* v. 13. Matthew adds other legendary developments, the rending of the rocks, the opening of tombs, the rising of dead saints (xxvii. 51b-3).

For σχίζω v. i. 10*. With εἰς δύο sc. μέρη. The preposition in ἀπ' ἄνωθεν* ἕως κάτω (xiv. 66*) is redundant as in ἀπὸ μακρόθεν (v. 6). Cf. Blass, 59.

39. κεντυρίων, xv. 44 f.**, is a Latinism (*centurio*) found also in the Gospel of Peter, 8 ff., and in the papyri (*VGT*, 340 f.). Mt and Lk use ἑκατόνταρχος (-χης) which is found in later Gk, the LXX, and the papyri (*VGT*, 191), but not in Mk. His position by the cross is carefully described; he stands by over against Jesus. For ὁ παρεστηκὼς v. iv. 29, xiv. 47, 69 f., x., xv. 35*; ἐναντίος vi. 48*. The phrase ἐξ ἐναντίας is used in Thuc. iv. 33 and Herodotus vii. 225, and is common in the LXX; vg *ex adverso*. ' Being on duty, he stood facing the crosses, and nothing had escaped him ', Swete, 389.

Matthew adds καὶ οἱ μετ' αὐτοῦ and describes them watching Jesus and filled with awe when they saw the earthquake and what followed (xxvii. 54). Luke says that the centurion glorified God when he saw what had happened (xxiii. 47). In Mk the account is much simpler. The natural connexion of 39 is with ἐξέπνευσεν in

37 (so Lk); it was the spectacle of death and the loud cry of Jesus which moved the centurion to speak. This may not imply that 38 (the rending of the veil) is a later scribal addition; it suggests that it is a Markan supplement to the foundation narrative.

This situation has its bearing on οὕτως ἐξέπνευσεν (ℵ B L 892 sa), to which κράξας is added by A C Δ *et al.* minusc. *pler.* it vg sy^pe hl aeth Aug and without οὕτως by W Θ 565 sys geo arm Or^int.. 0112 and k attest ἔκραξεν and D reads αὐτὸν κράξαντα καί. So great a weight of attestation strongly suggests that the original text contained a reference to the loud crying. Couchoud, *JTS*, xxxiv. 133 f., argues that the text of D, οὕτως αὐτὸν κράξαντα καὶ ἐξέπνευσεν, which he calls *monstrueux*, gives the key to the initial fault, and the original reading was ὅτι οὕτως ἔκραξεν (cf. k *quia sic exclamavit*). Cf. Lohmeyer, 346 n.; Turner, 80, who says that the reading of AV and RV^mg, ' he so cried out and gave up the ghost ', gives a more natural sense.

The centurion's confession, Ἀληθῶς οὗτος ὁ ἄνθρωπος υἱὸς θεοῦ ἦν, may have been a spontaneous recognition of divinity in a man of outstanding greatness (cf. RV^mg, RSV, ' a son of God '), but Mark read much more into the words, regarding them as a parallel at the end of his Gospel to υἱὸς θεοῦ at the beginning (i. 1), i.e. as a confession of the deity of Jesus in the full Christian sense. Cf. J. Weiss, 46; Rawlinsón, 238; Bartlet, 430; etc. This is a possible view of the confession, but it is perhaps probable that Luke's version Ὄντως ὁ ἄνθρωπος οὗτος δίκαιος ἦν (xxiii. 47) is more primitive. Cf. Easton, 353. Plummer, *St. Lk*, 539, thinks there is not much difference in the two expressions. McNeile, 424, on the other hand, suggests that Luke seeks to avoid the idea of ' demigod ' with its heathen associations. Later

γυναῖκες ἀπὸ μακρόθεν θεωροῦσαι, ἐν αἷς καὶ Μαριὰμ ἡ Μαγδαληνὴ καὶ Μαρία ἡ Ἰακώβου τοῦ μικροῦ καὶ Ἰωσῆτος μήτηρ
41 καὶ Σαλώμη, αἳ ὅτε ἦν ἐν τῇ Γαλιλαίᾳ ἠκολούθουν αὐτῷ καὶ
διηκόνουν αὐτῷ, καὶ ἄλλαι πολλαὶ αἱ συναναβᾶσαι αὐτῷ εἰς
Ἰεροσόλυμα.

tradition gave the centurion a name, Longinus (Acts of Pilate, ed. Tisch. 288) or Petronius (Gospel of Peter, 8). For ἀληθῶς v. xiv. 70*. Lohmeyer, 347, observes that in Mk the confession surpasses that of Peter and asserts what to the high priest appears as blasphemy. The Evangelist, therefore, regards it as of the highest significance.

40 f. These verses are an addendum to the narrative preparatory to the accounts of the Burial and the Resurrection. The Crucifixion narrative reaches its climax in the centurion's confession. With ἦσαν δέ, which marks a new stage, cf. v. 11. Note also the more frequent use of δέ in vv. 36, 37, 39. For ἀπὸ μακρόθεν v. v. 6; θεωρέω iii. 11.

Probably three women are mentioned, but four if ἡ is read before Ἰωσῆτος μήτηρ with B Ψ 131. Μαριὰμ ἡ Μαγδαληνή is mentioned again in 47 and in xvi. 1 (Mt. xxvii. 56, 61, xxviii. 1, Lk. viii. 2, xxiv. 10, Jn. xix. 25, xx. 1, (11), (16), 18**), and in Lk. viii. 2 and also Mk. xvi. [9] it is said that seven devils had been cast out of her. The adj. describes her as belonging to Magdala (el-Mejdel) on the west side of the lake. Μαρία ἡ Ἰακώβου τοῦ μικροῦ καὶ Ἰωσῆτος μήτηρ (Mt, Ἰωσήφ) is referred to in 47 as ἡ Ἰωσῆτος (Mt, ἡ ἄλλη Μαρία) and in xvi. 1 as ἡ Ἰακώβου (Mt, ἡ ἄλλη M.). John speaks of her as M. ἡ τοῦ Κλωπᾶ (xix. 25). Apparently, she is the mother of James and Joses, for it is unlikely that sys is correct in speaking of her as the daughter of James (sype hl have 'mother'). Lagrange, 439, observes that for a woman to be known by the name of her son is common in Arabic usage and that in the Markan phrase Semitic influence may be conjectured (contrast ὁ υἱὸς τῆς Μαρίας in vi. 3). Presumably James and Joses were well known in

the primitive community (cf. the references to Simon, Alexander, and Rufus in xv. 21), but it is difficult to identify them. They are clearly not the brothers of Jesus (vi. 3), for Mark would not have designated Mary the Virgin in this roundabout manner. Much more probable is the view that James is 'the son of Alphaeus' (iii. 18). For the question whether Alphaeus = Clopas v. the note on iii. 18 and cf. Swete, 389, Bernard, 631 f. The designation τοῦ μικροῦ distinguishes him from some other James (perhaps the son of Zebedee) either in respect of stature or age (cf. Deissmann, BS, 144 f.). Of Joses (Joseph) nothing is known. Σαλώμη, xvi. 1*, is identified by Matthew as 'the mother of the sons of Zebedee' (xxvii. 56).

After ἐν αἷς most MSS. insert ἦν (as in Mt), but it is wanting in א B L 0112 482 892 1342 vg (pler. et WW), and is probably not original. Mark further describes the women as those who followed Him and ministered to Him when He was in Galilee, together with many other women who went up with Him to Jerusalem. For Γαλιλαία v. i. 9; ἀκολουθέω i. 18; διακονέω i. 13 (and for the augment); Ἰεροσόλυμα iii. 8. συναναβαίνω*, Ac. xiii. 31**, 'to go up with'; Herodotus vii. 6, Xenophon, An. v. 4. 16; LXX, Pap. The Gk of 40 f. is rough, and Matthew improves it by reversing 40b and 41. In particular, he replaces the ' translation Greek' of 41a, αἳ ὅτε ἦν ἐν τῇ Γαλιλαίᾳ ἠκολούθουν αὐτῷ καὶ διηκόνουν αὐτῷ, by the smoother passage αἵτινες ἠκολούθησαν τῷ Ἰησοῦ ἀπὸ τῆς Γαλιλαίας διακονοῦσαι αὐτῷ. In Lk. viii. 3, among many women who ministered to Jesus, Luke mentions Joanna the wife of Chuza, Herod's steward, and Susanna.

Mk. xv. 42-7 105. THE BURIAL Cf. Mt. xxvii. 57-61
Lk. xxiii. 50-6
Jn. xix. 38-42

The narrative belongs to the best tradition. Bultmann, 296, speaks of it as a historical account which, apart from 47 and 44 f., ' makes no legendary impression ' ; and, for a narrative which assigns the last offices to a pious Jew who was not a follower of Jesus, this estimate is a notable understatement. The account is detailed and full of movement. There is reason to think that it was compiled in a Gentile environment. The periphrastic imperfect in 43 might be held to reflect Palestinian tradition, but the construction θαυμάζω εἰ, the distinction of tenses in τέθνηκεν and ἀπέθανεν, the use of the words κεντυρίων, δωρέομαι, πτῶμα, καθαιρέω, and ἐνειλέω, and possibly the reference to buying a linen cloth in 46, favour the hypothesis of composition at Rome. The view that the story ends at 46 is probably sound, for the reference to the watching women in 47 seems appended. Much more open to question is the suggestion that 44 f. is an insertion. The surprise of Pilate at the speedy death of Jesus and the questioning of the centurion are easily credible, and the omission of these details by Luke, and in part by Matthew, is intelligible. In comparison with the later accounts Mark's narrative is manifestly primitive, and still more when it is compared with the version in the Gospel of Peter (edn. J. A. Robinson, 2, 6, 8). Here Joseph is ' the friend of Pilate and of the Lord '. Before the crucifixion he asks for the body for burial, and is supported by Herod's advice to Pilate, ' Even if no one had asked for Him, we should have buried Him ; since indeed the sabbath draweth on '. The nails are taken from the body while the earth quakes and the Jews give the body to Joseph, who washes it, wraps it in a linen cloth (καὶ εἴλησε σινδόνι), and brings it to his own tomb, ' the Garden of Joseph '. Finally, the elders and scribes roll a great stone and set it at the door of the sepulchre, sealing it with seven seals, and pitching a tent they keep watch. This account is based on Mk, Mt, and Jn, and carries farther the legendary development of the tradition already begun in Matthew's story of the Watch at the Grave (xxvii. 62-6).

Καὶ ἤδη ὀψίας γενομένης, ἐπεὶ ἦν παρασκευή, ὅ ἐστιν προ- 42
σάββατον, ἐλθὼν Ἰωσὴφ ᵀ ἀπὸ Ἀριμαθαίας εὐσχήμων βου- 43

43 ὁ

42 f. For ἤδη v. iv. 37 ; ὀψίας γενο-μένης iv. 35 ; ὅ ἐστιν iii. 17. The time is late afternoon, about 4 p.m. Mark explains that it was the day before the Sabbath, i.e. Friday, which ended at sunset. ἐπεί*. παρασκευή*, Mt. xxvii. 62, Lk. xxiii. 54, Jn. xix. 14, 31, 42**, ' preparation ', is here used technically of the day of preparation for a Sabbath or the Passover ; cf. Josephus, Ant. xvi. 6. 2, Didache, viii. 1. In ὅ ἐστιν προσάββατον Mark explains the word for his readers. προσάββατον**; LXX, Judith viii. 6, Psa. xci. (xcii.) tit. (א),

xcii. (xciii.) tit. (א B). Matthew omits the phrase, but Luke has Καὶ ἡμέρα ἦν παρασκευῆς, καὶ σάββατον ἐπέφωσκεν (xxiii. 54). The verse explains the urgency of the action of Joseph in interviewing Pilate ; there was no time to be lost. Cf. Jn. xix. 31. The coupling of this explanation with a description of Joseph himself and of his action overloads the long sentence in 42 f., and accordingly in Mt and Lk it is simplified and recast.
With Ἰωσὴφ ὁ ἀπὸ Ἀριμαθαίας cf. Εὐρυκλῆς ἀπὸ Λακεδαίμονος, Josephus,

λευτής, ὃς καὶ αὐτὸς ἦν προσδεχόμενος τὴν βασιλείαν τοῦ θεοῦ,
τολμήσας εἰσῆλθεν πρὸς τὸν Πειλᾶτον καὶ ᾐτήσατο τὸ ⌈πτῶμα⌉ τοῦ
44 Ἰησοῦ. ὁ δὲ Πειλᾶτος ἐθαύμασεν εἰ ἤδη τέθνηκεν, καὶ προσκαλεσάμενος τὸν κεντυρίωνα ἐπηρώτησεν αὐτὸν εἰ ⌈ἤδη⌉ ἀπέθανεν·

43 σῶμα   44 πάλαι

Ant. xvi. 10. 1, also Mt. xxi. 11, Jn. i.
44, 45, Ac. x. 38, etc. ὁ is omitted by
B D W** 0112 13 28 579 *et al.* it vg sy^s
bo aeth Aug. Joseph is not described
as having come from Arimathaea (see
Blass, 125), but the widely attested article more definitely characterizes him
as a native of the place. The precise
location is not known. Eusebius, *Ono-
mast.* 32, identifies Arimathaea with
the Ramathaim-zophim of 1 Sam. i. 1,
the Rentis of to-day, a few miles north
of Jerusalem (cf. Dalman, *SSW*, 226),
but he places it near Diospolis (Lydda).

Joseph is further described as εὐσχήμων βουλευτής, ' councillor of good
position ' (Moffatt). εὐσχήμων means
' graceful ' or ' comely ' in 1 Cor. vii.
35, xii. 24, but here and in Ac. xiii. 50,
xvii. 12** the meaning is ' noble ',
' influential ', ' wealthy '. Cf. Mt,
πλούσιος. Condemned by Phrynichus
(ed. Lobeck, 333), this meaning is
illustrated in Josephus, *Vit.* 9 and in
the papyri (*VGT*, 266). Cf. the Latin
honestus. βουλευτής*, Lk. xxiii. 50**,
' councillor ', ' senator ', though found
in Josephus, *BJ*, ii. 17. 1, was not a
technical expression current among
the Jews, and appears to be used in
Mk and Lk for Gentile readers to
describe a member of the Sanhedrin.
The clause ὃς καὶ αὐτὸς ἦν προσδεχόμενος τὴν βασιλείαν τοῦ θεοῦ (cf. Lk. ii.
25, 38), which may be Mark's addition
to his source, describes him as one of
those who looked for the fulfilment
of the Messianic hope of Israel. In
Mark's account he is not a disciple.
His action is dictated either by sympathy with Jesus or piety towards the
crucified and concern for ritual purity
(cf. Lohmeyer, 350). Matthew infers
that he is a disciple (xxvii. 57). Cf.
Jn. xix. 38. Luke speaks of him as
ἀγαθὸς καὶ δίκαιος and says that he had

not consented to the counsel and deed
of the Sanhedrin (xxiii. 50 f.). Once
more the primitive character of Mk is
manifest. For ἦν προσδεχόμενος *v.*
Intr. 45, 62 f.; ἡ βασιλεία τοῦ θεοῦ i. 15.
προσδέχομαι*, Lk (5), Ac (2), Pl (2),
Tit. ii. 13, Heb (2), Ju. 21**; Cl.,
LXX, Pap.

τολμήσας (xii. 34)*, used adverbially,
emphasizes the boldness of Joseph's
action. Cf. Turner, 81, ' screwed up
his courage ', RSV, ' took courage '.
For αἰτέομαι *v.* vi. 24 f.; Πειλᾶτος xv.
1; σῶμα *v.* 29. Usually the bodies of
the crucified were left to decay hanging
upon the crosses, but it was also customary to hand them over to friends
and relatives for burial if they sought
permission. That Joseph approaches
Pilate with boldness shows that he
sought a favour (cf. also ἐδωρήσατο in
45), but he makes his urgent request
(ᾐτήσατο) relying doubtless on his influential standing and impelled by the
law of Deut. xxi. 23 : ' His body shall
not remain all night upon the tree,
but thou shalt surely bury him the
same day '.

πτῶμα, read in 43 by D k sy^s geo²
and accepted by Turner, *JTS*, xxix.
13, although strongly attested, may be
a correction suggested by 45.

44 f. The questioning of the centurion is peculiar to Mark's account.
All that Matthew has is : ' Then Pilate
commanded it to be given up '. For
θαυμάζω *v. v.* 20; ἀποθνήσκω *v.* 35;
προσκαλέομαι iii. 13; κεντυρίων xv. 39;
ἐπερωτάω *v.* 9. Here and in 1 Jn. iii.
13 alone is the classical θαυμάζω εἰ
found in the NT. The careful distinction of tenses is also notable : the perf.
τέθνηκεν implies an existing condition ;
the aor. ἀπέθανεν, rightly used in the
question put to the centurion, describes
an observed event. Cf. Swete, 392 ;

καὶ γνοὺς ἀπὸ τοῦ κεντυρίωνος ἐδωρήσατο τὸ πτῶμα τῷ Ἰωσήφ. 45
καὶ ἀγοράσας σινδόνα καθελὼν αὐτὸν ἐνείλησεν τῇ σινδόνι καὶ 46
ἔθηκεν αὐτὸν ἐν μνήματι ὃ ἦν λελατομημένον ἐκ πέτρας, καὶ

Lagrange, 441. Both the surprise and the interrogation are natural, since crucified men often lingered two or three days in torment. The verse *porte en lui son cachet d'authenticité* (Lagrange). The second ἤδη (B D W Θ 472 1342 it vg syhier bo geo) is omitted in sys pe hl sa and is replaced, probably to avoid repetition, by πάλαι 'long ago' (cf. vi. 47) in ℵ A C L *et al.* minusc. *rell.* it vg.

δωρέομαι*, 2 Pet. i. 3 f.**, ' to present ', ' bestow '; Cl., LXX, Pap. The verb suggests a gracious act, as in Gen. xxx. 20, 1 Esdras i. 7, viii. 55, Esth. viii. 1. πτῶμα (vi. 29*), ' corpse ', is replaced by σῶμα in A C W *et al.*, but is manifestly original (ℵ B D L Θ 565 sys geo² aeth). Rawlinson, 241, well observes that the Gk may even possibly represent the official wording of the Governor's permission—*donavit cadaver*. Cf. Swete, 392.

46 f. Having received permission for the burial, Joseph buys a linen cloth. After taking down the body from the cross and wrapping it in the cloth, he lays it in a rock tomb and rolls a stone against the door. For ἀγοράζω *v.* vi. 36; σινδών xiv. 51. Only Mark mentions the act of buying. It has been argued that the purchase shows that the Passover Day had not yet begun; cf. Bruce, i. 452; Menzies, 284; Bartlet, 433; Rawlinson, 242, 263 f. The objections against this view seem strained. Thus, Dalman, *JJ*, 104 f., suggests that Mark was not perhaps aware of the prohibition concerning work on the first day of the Feast or was not quite certain when this day terminated. Billerbeck, ii. 833, suggests the possibility of mistranslation (' bought ' for ' took '), and Jeremias, 43 f., *JTS*, l. 5 f., appeals to Rabbinical decisions which softened the rigours of the Law in order to meet the necessities of daily life, provided that payments were made after the Festival-day; *v. Shab.* xxiii. 1 (Danby, 119 f.). It may be, as Lohmeyer says, 351, that Mark did not observe the difficulty or think it worth while to explain unusual circumstances in connexion with this death (*bei diesem vom Wunder umzitterten Tode*); but it is hard to agree that ἀγοράσας is not a confirmation of the Johannine chronology. See further, Burkitt, *JTS*, xvii. 291 ff.

The σινδών is a piece of new linen, not a garment; cf. Mt, σινδόνι καθαρᾷ. John thinks of the body as bound with strips of cloth, καὶ ἔδησαν αὐτὸ ὀθονίοις (xix. 40). For the technical word καθαιρέω *v.* the note on xv. 36. ἐνειλέω**, ' to wrap in ', is a late verb, found however in Dioscorides v. 72 and Aristotle, *Mu.* 396 a 14, and is used in the LXX (1 Kgdms. xxi. 9) of Goliath's sword (καὶ αὐτὴ ἐνειλημένη ἦν ἐν ἱματίῳ). In an important note Abbott, *Johannine Vocabulary*, 346, suggests that Matthew and Luke may have objected to ἐνείλησεν as being unseemly, because the verb is used of fettering prisoners, swathing children hand and foot, holding people fast in a net, entangling them in evil or in debt, and generally in a bad sense. In the papyri it is so used, but also colourlessly (*VGT*, 213). κατατίθημι* (Cl., LXX, Pap.): Mt, Lk, ἔθηκεν.

For μνῆμα *v.* v. 3; μνημεῖον v. 2. The tomb is described as hewn out of a rock. λατομέω*, Mt. xxvii. 60**, ' to quarry ', <λᾶς, τέμνω. The verb is late: Diod. Sic. v. 39; LXX (9 times) for חָצֵב and כָּרָה; Pap. (*VGT*, 371). Rock tombs were common in the neighbourhood of Jerusalem, sometimes containing chambers and sometimes a single room provided with a bench or shelf on which the body was placed, the entrance being closed by a large flat stone rolled or pushed into position. Cf. Dalman, *SSW*, 373 f.; Lagrange, 442, 445. Luke (ἐν μνήματι

47 προσεκύλισεν λίθον ἐπὶ τὴν θύραν τοῦ μνημείου. ʿΗ δὲ Μαρία ἡ
Μαγδαληνὴ καὶ Μαρία ἡ ᾿Ιωσῆτος ἐθεώρουν ποῦ τέθειται.

λαξευτῷ) probably thinks of a tomb
built of hewn stones; cf. Wellhausen,
Lk, in loc.; Lake, *HER*, 49 f.; Easton,
353 f.; *per contra*, Creed, 292; Lagrange, *S. Luc*, 596. Matthew says
the tomb was new (καινός), and Luke
writes to the same effect, οὗ οὐκ ἦν
οὐδεὶς οὔπω κείμενος, while John combines these statements and describes
the place as a garden (κῆπος). Mark
says simply that Joseph rolled a stone
against the door. Cf. Mt, λίθον μέγαν,
Mk. xvi. 4, ἦν γὰρ μέγας σφόδρα. προσκυλίω*, Mt. xxvii. 60**, ' to roll to ' or
' up '; late Gk (but Aristoph. *Vespae*, 202), not in LXX, nor cited in
VGT.

The task was too considerable for
Joseph to perform unaided; he must
have been helped by his servants. No
disciple was present to assist in the
offices for the dead and in them the
women took no part. Anointing is
not mentioned and in Mark's opinion
it was not carried out (cf. xvi. 1, cf.
also xiv. 8 and Lk. xxiii. 55 f.). According to Jn. xix. 39 f. Nicodemus
came bringing a mixture of myrrh
and aloes and these were placed in the

folds of the swathes of cloth ' as the
custom of the Jews is to bury '. Cf.
Billerbeck, ii. 53. There were thus
two traditions regarding the anointing,
the Markan according to which the
burial was carried out with the greatest
haste and without regard to Jewish
customs beyond the use of a linen cloth,
and the Johannine tradition in which
the familiar offices were fulfilled.

The reference to the women who
beheld where Jesus was laid (xv. 47)
is appended and does not belong to the
narrative proper; it may even be the
original introduction to the story of the
Empty Tomb (*v.* xvi. 1). In 47 there
are many textual variants: ᾿Ιωσῆτος
is read by אc B L Δ Ψ 0112 fam. 1
(exc. 118) fam. 13 (exc. 124) 543 565
k bo geo², ᾿Ιωσῆ by C W *et al.* 22 28 33
118 157 579 700 892 1071 *al. pler.*
sype hl sa aeth, ᾿Ιακώβου by D 472 1342
ff n q vg (2 MSS.) sys arm, ᾿Ιακώβου
καὶ ᾿Ιωσῆτος by Θ, cf. *iacobi et ioseph* c,
᾿Ιωσήφ by A Σ l aur. vg (*pler.*) Aug.
W fam. 13 543 add μήτηρ, and 472
adds καὶ Σαλώμη. sys has the equivalent
of *filia iacobi*, g² vg (2 MSS.) *maria
iacobi et maria ioseph.*

(*c*) Mk. xvi. 1-8   THE RESURRECTION
(9-20)

Although only 1-8 belongs to the original form of the Gospel, this
section must be considered separately in view of the new beginning manifestly made in xvi. 1. The detailed reference to the women in this verse
after the similar passages in xv. 40 and 47 shows that xvi. 1-8 stands apart
from the Passion Narrative proper, representing a different cycle of tradition; and this view is fully sustained by its character and contents. The
spurious addition in xvi. 9-20 also needs to be considered in its bearing
upon the composition of the Gospel, as well as the Shorter Addition found
in several MSS. and versions and the Freer Logion in the Washington
codex W.

Mk. xvi. 1-8   106. THE VISIT OF THE   Cf. Mt. xxviii. 1-10
WOMEN TO THE EMPTY   Lk. xxiv. 1-11
TOMB   Jn. xx. 1-10

The narrative is constructed by Mark himself on the basis of tradition,
although not that of an eyewitness. So far as one can see, the tradition

consists of little more than an early belief that the women had visited the tomb and found it empty, and the part of the *kerygma* which affirmed that Christ was buried and rose from the dead on the third day. This estimate of the narrative is confirmed by its vocabulary and its contents. Almost wholly its language consists of common Markan words; there are no signs of a Semitic source apart from the quasi-technical phrase ἡ μία τῶν σαββάτων. Several difficulties are treated in the Commentary: the purpose of anointing with which the women come, the question about the stone when two of them have already watched the burial, the form and appearance of the νεανίσκος on the right side, the verbal message which the women receive, especially the commission given to them in 7, and finally the statement that they said nothing to anyone because they were afraid. On the other side must be noted the dignity and restraint of the narrative, the absence of any attempt to describe the resurrection itself or to depict an appearance of the Risen Christ, features which stand out in relief when the narrative is compared with later accounts in the Gospels and the Gospel of Peter. The question for special consideration is how far Mark's account is a dramatic representation due to the exercise of reverent historical imagination, in this respect more like the Johannine narratives than those familiar to us in Mk. Special problems arise in the relation of 7 to the rest of the account, in the final words ἐφοβοῦντο γάρ, and the question whether Mark intended the Gospel to end in this manner.

Καὶ διαγενομένου τοῦ σαββάτου [ἡ] Μαρία ἡ Μαγδαληνὴ καὶ   1   XVI
Μαρία ἡ [τοῦ] Ἰακώβου καὶ Σαλώμη ἠγόρασαν ἀρώματα ἵνα
ἐλθοῦσαι ἀλείψωσιν αὐτόν. καὶ λίαν πρωὶ [τῇ] μιᾷ τῶν σαββάτων   2

1. Mark relates that the women bought spices when the Sabbath had ended, διαγενομένου τοῦ σαββάτου, i.e. during the evening after 6 o'clock. διαγίνομαι*, Ac. xxv. 13, xxvii. 9**, 'to go through', 'intervene', 'elapse'; Cl., LXX (2 Macc. xi. 26*), Pap. (*VGT*, 147). For ἀγοράζω v. vi. 36. The ἀρώματα* are probably perfumed oils (cf. ἀλείφω, vi. 13*) rather than aromatic herbs. Luke adds καὶ μύρα (xxiii. 56).

The three women are those named in xv. 40, two of whom are mentioned also in xv. 47. Here in xvi. 1 the second Mary is described as Μαρία ἡ (τοῦ) Ἰακώβου, whereas in xv. 40 she is Μαρία ἡ Ἰακώβου τοῦ μικροῦ καὶ Ἰωσῆτος μήτηρ and in xv. 47 Μαρία ἡ Ἰωσῆτος. In the light of xv. 40 she is the mother of James, but it is strange that in the preceding verse (xv. 47) she is described 'of Joses'. These perplexing designations are simplified if, with D d n, we omit καὶ διαγενομένου

to Σαλώμη in xvi. 1a, for, in this case, the two women mentioned in xv. 47 buy the ἀρώματα. Cf. k, which omits ἡ Μαρία to Σαλώμη, and q, which has *et abeuntes emerunt aromata ut eum unguerent*. Turner, 81 f., *JTS*, xxix. 13 f., and Bartlet, 434, accept the omission and connect xv. 47 with xvi. 1b. But the desire for simplification may have led to these changes, and in view of the strong attestation of ℵ A B C W Δ Θ (with minor variations), the WH text is to be preferred.

All the accounts mention Mary Magdalene, and she alone is named by John. Matthew adds ἡ ἄλλη Μαρία. Luke has Joanna instead of Salome and adds καὶ αἱ λοιπαὶ σὺν αὐταῖς (xxiv. 10). For these variations, and those in Mk. xv. 40, 47, and xvi. 1, v. Note I.

According to Mk the motive is that of anointing the body, ἵνα ἐλθοῦσαι ἀλείψωσιν αὐτόν. Cf. Lk. xxiv. 1, φέρουσαι ἃ ἡτοίμασαν ἀρώματα. In Mt the women go to see the tomb, θεωρῆσαι

3 ἔρχονται ἐπὶ τὸ μνημεῖον ⌜ἀνατείλαντος⌝ τοῦ ἡλίου. καὶ ἔλεγον

2 ἀνατέλλοντος

τὸν τάφον, a change due to the introduction of the story of the sealing and the guard, but, none the less, a point on which Matthew consciously deserts his source. No motive is mentioned by John. Presumably, in Jn as in Mt, Mary Magdalene comes to see the grave, since, according to xix. 40, spices had already been placed in the folds of the wrappings. It can be argued that the women sought to complete the last offices by adding perfumed oils. On the other hand, however, we should not gather from Jn that the binding with spices was merely provisional, and, in mentioning only a linen cloth, Mark's account suggests that the women went to perform offices which had been omitted and could only now be carried out. Moreover, the Markan account agrees closely with the saying, ' She hath anointed my body aforehand for the burying' (xiv. 8). There is, then, a difference difficult to reconcile between the narratives and, since the Markan account is contrary to what might be expected, there is reason to give it preference. But, in either case, whether the Johannine account is historical or not, it is hard to credit the women with the intention of going to anoint the body a day and two nights after death. Cf. Lohmeyer, 353; Montefiore, i. 401. Where the evidence is conflicting, no one will wish to speak with too much confidence. Cf. Branscomb, 306. But, on the whole, it seems more probable that the women went to see the grave (Mt, Jn) rather than to anoint the body (Mk, Lk). For Jewish practice in the matter of anointing v. the notes on xiv. 8 and xv. 46. Cf. also Ezek. xvi. 9, 2 Chron. xvi. 14, and see Billerbeck, ii. 53.

2. The temporal statement, which defines the time when the women came to the tomb, is difficult. λίαν πρωί suggests the earlier part of the period 3 to 6 a.m. (cf. πρωὶ ἔννυχα λίαν, i. 35), while ἀνατείλαντος τοῦ ἡλίου denotes sunrise. For ἀνατέλλω v. iv. 6. Lk. xxiv. 1 has ὄρθρου βαθέως, ' at first dawn ', and Jn. xx. 1 πρωὶ σκοτίας ἔτι οὔσης, ' early, while it was still dark '. Mt. xxviii. 1, ὀψὲ δὲ σαββάτων, τῇ ἐπιφωσκούσῃ εἰς μίαν σαββάτων, is ambiguous. Probably ὀψέ = ' after ',[1] and τῇ ἐπιφωσκούσῃ describes the beginning of the first day of the week[2]; either our Saturday evening,[3] say, 6-9 p.m. (if the Jewish reckoning is followed) or the next morning, say, 3-6 a.m. (if the Roman method is implied). If ἐπιφώσκω is used of actual dawn (Cl., Pap.), the time is about 6 a.m.

Lk and Jn, then, agree with Mk; possibly Mt also. But what must be said of ἀνατείλαντος τοῦ ἡλίου, which is contrary to what is related in Lk and Jn and is not consistent with λίαν πρωί in Mk? The textual tradition shows how early the difficulty was felt. ἀνατέλλοντος is read by D c ff n q Aug, λίαν πρωί is omitted by c, λίαν by D W k n sys pe hier arm, and πρωί by q. All these readings seek to relieve the disparity in the Markan text and are not original. Nevertheless, it is hard to think that Mark wrote ἀνατείλαντος τοῦ ἡλίου after λίαν πρωί. Swete, 395, explains that the women started just before daybreak and arrived just after sunrise, but this explanation is not satisfactory (cf. Klostermann, 190; Rawlinson, 244); the distance from Jerusalem is too short. Burkitt, *JTS*, xiv. 544, sees no incongruity between the two Gk expressions, and doubts if λίαν πρωί means more than ' as early as they possibly could '. Even so,

---

[1] ὀψέ means ' late ' (Moulton, i. 72, *VGT*, 470) or ' after ' (Blass, 97, 312); but, as followed by τῇ ἐπιφωσκούσῃ, the latter is the more appropriate. Cf. Billerbeck, i. 1051.
[2] Cf. Turner, *JTS*, xiv. 188-90; Burkitt, *JTS*, xiv. 538-46, xvi. 79; Black, 99. The Aramaic verb n⁺gah (Heb. 'or) can be used idiomatically of the beginning of the Jewish day at sunset.
[3] Cf. McNeile, 429; Allen, 189, *St. Mt*, 301; Smith, 211.

πρὸς ἑαυτάς Τίς ἀποκυλίσει ἡμῖν τὸν λίθον ἐκ τῆς θύρας τοῦ μνημείου; καὶ ἀναβλέψασαι θεωροῦσιν ὅτι ἀνακεκύλισται ὁ λίθος, 4

Plummer, 366, argues, the expression 'does not harmonize with "at sunrise"'. Turner, 82, finds it tempting to suppose that 'not yet' has dropped out of the text, and Torrey, *TG*, 70 f., puts a stop after μνημεῖον and connects the gen. abs. with *v.* 3, 'When the sun had risen, and they were saying . . .', deleting καί in 4 as a misrendering of a redundant וְ. Perhaps there is most to be said for regarding ἀνατείλαντος τοῦ ἡλίου as a primitive corruption, present in the pre-Markan tradition and arising from a misunderstanding of the Aramaic *nᵉgah*. Cf. Black, 100. Alternatively, the phrase may be a very early scribal gloss, arising from the same cause, but, although it has no parallel in Mt and Lk, there is no textual evidence to support this suggestion, which accordingly can be no more than a conjecture.

It remains to consider τῇ μιᾷ τῶν σαββάτων. This use of the cardinal numeral for the ordinal (contr. τῇ πρώτῃ ἡμέρᾳ τῶν ἀζύμων in xiv. 12) is frequently claimed as Semitic; cf. Blass, 144, Black, 90, and see Kautzsch, *Gr.* 122, Dalman, *Gr.* 131. For the argument to the contrary *v.* Moulton, i. 95 f., 237, ii. 174; *v.* also Howard, ii. 439. The phrase (Mt. xxviii. 1, Lk. xxiv. 1, Jn. xx. 1, 19, Ac. xx. 7, 1 Cor. xvi. 2**) may be quasi-technical. If so, its presence does not characterize the narrative which otherwise is not marked by Semitisms. See further, Swete, 395; Lagrange, 445; Klostermann, 190; Lohmeyer, 353.

3 f. At this point Matthew introduces a reference to a great earthquake and an account of the descent of an angel of the Lord from heaven who rolls away the stone and sits over against it. His appearance is as lightning and his raiment white as snow, and from fear the watchers tremble and become as dead men. Of this legend Mark knows nothing, and that

he has no knowledge of the sealing and the guard is shown by his account, peculiar to his Gospel, of the question of the women: 'Who will roll away for us the stone from the door of the tomb?'. The action in ἔλεγον is continuous, 'were saying'. For πρὸς ἑαυτάς *v.* ix. 10, xi. 31, xii. 7, xiv. 4. Like προσκυλίω, ἀποκυλίω*, Mt. xxviii. 2, Lk. xxiv. 2**, 'to roll away', belongs to late Gk (LXX, Gen. xxix. 3, 8, 10, Jdth. xiii. 9*). So also ἀνακυλίω in 4**, 'to roll up' or 'back', which is not found in the LXX, but appears in first- and second-century Gk writers. None of these verbs is illustrated in *VGT*. The women's question arises out of their purpose, and if this is held to be improbable (*v.* the note on xvi. 1), 3 must be dramatic and imaginative rather than historical. It may be that no other kind of narrative was possible in the sixties when Mark wrote, since for a generation attention had been concentrated on the Appearances of the Risen Lord (cf. 1 Cor. xv. 4-8) and the fact of the Resurrection itself (Ac. ii. 24, Rom. i. 4, etc.).

Mark makes no attempt to explain how the stone was rolled away; he may have thought of it as the act of the angel, but more probably as the work of God or of the Risen Christ Himself. Looking up, he says, the women see that the stone has been rolled away, and, he adds with great simplicity, it was very great. For ἀναβλέπω *v.* vi. 41; θεωρέω iii. 11; ὁ λίθος xv. 46. With the vivid use of the perf. ἀνακεκύλισται cf. xv. 44 and 47. In the Gospel of Peter, 9, the stone rolls away of itself, ἀφ' ἑαυτοῦ κυλισθεὶς ἐπεχώρησε παρὰ μέρος, after a great voice has sounded from heaven and two men have descended with a great light. k contains a remarkable gloss which mentions a sudden darkness over the whole earth and angels descending from the heavens and rising [1]

---

[1] 'And the Lord rising' is suggested as an emendation. Cf. Rawlinson, 244.

5 ἦν γὰρ μέγας σφόδρα. καὶ ⌜εἰσελθοῦσαι⌝ εἰς τὸ μνημεῖον εἶδον
νεανίσκον καθήμενον ἐν τοῖς δεξιοῖς περιβεβλημένον στολὴν λευ-
6 κήν, καὶ ἐξεθαμβήθησαν. ὁ δὲ λέγει αὐταῖς Μὴ ἐκθαμβεῖσθε·

5 ἐλθοῦσαι

in the glory of the living God, who
ascended with Him, when straightway
it was light, *Subito autem ad horam
tertiam diei tenebrae factae sunt per
totum orbem terrae, et descenderunt de
caelis angeli et surgentes in claritate
uiui dei simul ascenderunt cum eo, et
continuo lux facta est.*
It is often suggested that ἦν γὰρ
μέγας σφόδρα* should be transferred to
the end of *v.* 3, where it is read by D
Θ 565 c d ff n sys hier Eus, but delayed
explanatory clauses with γάρ are after
Mark's manner (*v.* v. 8). To Lk.
xxiii. 53 ὃν μόγις εἴκοσι ἐκύλιον is added
by D 0124 1071 c sa. The restraint
of the Markan narrative is astonishing.
It is implied that the tomb is empty,
but it is not stated. The dramatic
announcement is reserved until the
angel's words in *v.* 6, ἠγέρθη, οὐκ ἔστιν
ὧδε· ἴδε ὁ τόπος ὅπου ἔθηκαν αὐτόν.

5. Mark now relates that the women
entered into the tomb and saw a young
man sitting on the right side clothed
with a white robe. He describes their
amazement by the strong word ἐξεθαμβήθησαν which he alone among NT
writers uses (*v.* ix. 15). For μνημεῖον
v. v. 2; νεανίσκος xiv. 51*; κάθημαι
ii. 6; ἐν τοῖς δεξιοῖς x. 37; περιβάλλω
xiv. 51; στολή xii. 38*; λευκός ix. 3*.
Apparently, Mark is writing freely, for
every word belongs to his vocabulary.
B and 127 read ἐλθοῦσαι, and Lake,
HER, 62-5, is disposed to accept this
reading, with the meaning, ' when they
came to the tomb ', on the ground of
transcriptional probability and because
in Mt the angel is seated on the stone
which has been rolled away, that is,
outside the tomb. It is highly improbable, however, that the argument
from transcriptional probability can
stand against the overwhelming support of the MSS. for εἰσελθοῦσαι, and the
difference in Mt is due to the fact that

Matthew omits 3-5 in favour of another
tradition. The Markan account raises
in the most acute form the problem
of the Empty Tomb, but in appraising
the narrative it is desirable that the
wider issues should be kept distinct.
In view of the intimate connexion between the body and the soul or spirit
in Jewish thought there can be little
doubt that, when in the earliest preaching it was affirmed that God raised up
Jesus from the dead (Ac. ii. 24, 31 f.,
iii. 15, etc.), an empty tomb was implied, and, further, that the same
implication underlies the words of St.
Paul in 1 Cor. xv. 3-5 : ' Christ died
. . . he was buried . . . he hath been
raised . . . he appeared '. It is true
also that St. Paul thought of the resurrection body as a σῶμα πνευματικόν
(1 Cor. xv. 44), and must therefore
have believed that in some way the
Body laid in the tomb was transformed. But for Mark's narrative the
relevant issue is, granted that it attests
primitive belief in the Empty Tomb,
whether the account is based on direct
testimony or whether it is imaginatively constructed.

The description of the young man
suggests the latter. The claim of Lake,
HER, 190, 251 f., that a youth and
not an angel is meant, is inadmissible,
since in similar narratives terms like
νεανίσκος are used of angelic beings.
Cf. Lk. xxiv. 4, ἄνδρες δύο, Gospel of
Pet. 9, δύο ἄνδρες, 2 Macc. iii. 26,
ἕτεροι δὲ δύο ἐφάνησαν αὐτῷ νεανίαι, 33,
οἱ αὐτοὶ νεανίαι, Jos. *Ant.* v. 8. 2 (of
Manoah's wife), φάντασμα ἐπιφαίνεται,
ἄγγελος τοῦ θεοῦ, νεανίᾳ καλῷ παραπλή-
σιον καὶ μεγάλῳ. Moreover, περιβεβλημένος στολὴν λευκήν is the conventional
language in which such beings are
described ; cf. Apoc. vii. 9, 13, where
the blessed dead are said to be περι-
βεβλημένοι στολὰς λευκάς, x. 1, ἄλλον

Ἰησοῦν ζητεῖτε τὸν Ναζαρηνὸν τὸν ἐσταυρωμένον· ἠγέρθη, οὐκ
ἔστιν ὧδε· ἴδε ὁ τόπος ὅπου ἔθηκαν αὐτόν· ἀλλὰ ὑπάγετε εἴπατε   7
τοῖς μαθηταῖς αὐτοῦ καὶ τῷ Πέτρῳ ὅτι Προάγει ὑμᾶς εἰς τὴν

ἄγγελον . . . περιβεβλημένον νεφέλην, cf.
also the description of the transfigured
Christ in Mk. ix. 3. But, if so, without questioning the existence of supernatural beings, it is probable that
Mark's description is imaginative; he
picturesquely describes what he believes happened. This impression is
deepened when, in 6 f., the angel uses
human speech. Matthew speaks explicitly of an ἄγγελος κυρίου and describes his form as ὡς ἀστραπή and his
clothing as λευκὸν ὡς χιών. Cf. Lk,
ἐν ἐσθῆτι ἀστραπτούσῃ. For περιβάλ-
λομαι c. int. acc. v. the note on i. 6.

6. The angel bids the women cease
being amazed, declares that Jesus has
risen and points to the place where He
had been laid. Again the vocabulary
is Markan: for ζητέω v. i. 37; Ναζαρηνός i. 24; σταυρόω xv. 13; ἐγείρω
i. 31; τόπος i. 35; and with ὅπου
ἔθηκαν αὐτόν cf. xv. 46, καὶ ἔθηκεν αὐτόν,
and 47, ποῦ τέθειται.

The use of ἐσταυρωμένον corresponds
with Pauline usage in 1 Cor. i. 23, ii.
2, Gal. iii. 1. Along with Ἰησοῦν τὸν
Ναζαρηνόν it has a somewhat formal
ring, ' the Crucified '; cf. Turner, 82.
Possibly ζητεῖτε κτλ. is interrogative (so
Lk); cf. Klostermann, 190; Turner,
82. But, on the whole, it is more probable that a statement is intended (so
Mt); cf. Lagrange, 447; Lohmeyer,
354; Schniewind, 204. The sudden
change to the aor. in ἠγέρθη marks the
event as having just happened; cf.
Moulton, i. 135-7. Contrast ἐγήγερται
in 1 Cor. xv. 4, 20. ὁ τόπος is the shelf
on which the body had rested rather
than the tomb itself. The speech,
especially the asyndetic construction,
leaves the impression of rapid forceful
utterance.

Lake's interesting suggestion, *HER*,
68 f., 250-2, that the women approached
the wrong tomb, and were directed by
the young man to the right one, is
insufficiently based on the reading

attested by D W Θ 565 which inserts
ἐκεῖ before ὁ τόπος. Even if ἐκεῖ is
read, there is no reason to suppose that
it refers to the adjoining tomb. Lake's
interpretation proceeds on the assumption that the speaker is an unknown
stranger. The rejection, therefore, of
his view brings us face to face with
the question whether the account is a
dramatization or a narrative of things
heard. The probabilities of the case,
the description of the speaker, and
the Markan vocabulary, especially the
phrase Ἰησοῦν . . . τὸν Ναζαρηνὸν τὸν
ἐσταυρωμένον, strongly support the
former alternative.

In Mt the prohibition is more emphatic, μὴ φοβεῖσθε ὑμεῖς. Mark's τὸν
Ναζαρηνόν is omitted, and the statement
of the women's purpose is preceded by
the assurance οἶδα γὰρ ὅτι, which becomes the reason for the command.
The statements ἠγέρθη and οὐκ ἔστιν
ὧδε are reversed and καθὼς εἶπεν is
added. With added emphasis (δεῦτε
ἴδετε) the women are invited to see the
place, and the active ἔθηκαν is replaced
by ἔκειτο. Luke's parallel may be an
independent tradition. While the
women are afraid and bend their faces
to the earth, the two angels ask, ' Why
do you seek the living one among the
dead? ', and announce ' He is not
here, but has risen '. The announcement, however, is omitted by D a b e
ff l r, probably rightly.

7. The announcement breaks off
(ἀλλά, cf. ix. 22, xiv. 36) and gives
place to a message which the women
are to convey to the disciples and
Peter. For ὑπάγω v. i. 44; οἱ μαθηταὶ
αὐτοῦ ii. 15; Πέτρος iii. 16. Emphasis
is present in καὶ τῷ Πέτρῳ, and there
can be little doubt that the Denial is
in mind. Cf. Ac. i. 14, σὺν γυναιξὶν
καὶ Μαριάμ, 1 Cor. xv. 5, ὤφθη Κηφᾷ,
εἶτα τοῖς δώδεκα. There is no reason to
suppose that the disciples have already
fled to Galilee (Ed. Meyer, i. 18 f.);

8 Γαλιλαίαν· ἐκεῖ αὐτὸν ὄψεσθε, καθὼς εἶπεν ὑμῖν. καὶ ἐξελθοῦσαι

it is more probable that they are still in the neighbourhood of Jerusalem (Lohmeyer, 355). ὅτι is *recitativum*. The message takes up the prophecy of xiv. 28, changing the fut. προάξω into the pres. προάγει, and adding the promise that they shall see Him in Galilee, as He had said to them. The pres. is not a virtual fut., but gives the assurance that Jesus is on the way to Galilee *now*; when they arrive there, they will see Him. Since Jesus not told His disciples that they would see Him in Galilee, Turner, *JTS*, xxvi. 155 f., treats ἐκεῖ αὐτὸν ὄψεσθε as a parenthesis. It seems doubtful, however, that Mark could have intended so important a declaration to be read in this way, and it is better to recognize that καθὼς εἶπεν ὑμῖν is used loosely. If προάγει is a true pres., προάξω in xiv. 28 cannot mean ' I will lead you '; the meaning in both cases must be that of *going before*. Most commentators take the saying to refer to appearances of the Risen Christ to His disciples and to Peter, but Lohmeyer, 355 f., thinks that it speaks of the Parousia; cf. also R. H. Lightfoot, *LDG*, 52-65, 73-7. Were it a question only of Resurrection appearances, Lohmeyer argues, one cannot see why they must be connected with Galilee. The prophecy speaks of something which could happen only in Galilee, a land where that which begins with the Resurrection is completed. *Galiläa ist das Land der eschatologischen Vollendung.* ' To see Him ' is not the expression used of appearances in the Gospels and the Acts, but ὤφθη. Paul, it is true, uses ὁράω in 1 Cor. ix. 1 (οὐχὶ Ἰησοῦν τὸν κύριον ἡμῶν ἑόρακα;), and John three times in xx. 18 (Ἑώρακα τὸν κύριον), 25, and 29. But also in the Johannine writings (though not in Paul) ' Ye shall see Him ' is the fixed expression for the Parousia; cf. Jn. xvi. 16 f., 19, 1 Jn. iii. 2, Apoc. i. 7, xxii. 4. Cf. in particular, Mk. xiv. 62, ὄψεσθε τὸν υἱὸν τοῦ ἀνθρώπου . . ., and

xiii. 26. The exegesis is fascinating, but it is slenderly based. The question, Why must resurrection appearances be connected with Galilee ?, can be applied equally to the Parousia. Indeed, in *Test. Zeb.* ix. 8, to which Lohmeyer attaches importance (cf. Lightfoot, *op. cit.* 73), it is to happen in Jerusalem, καὶ ὑμεῖς ὄψεσθε αὐτὸν ἐν Ἱερουσαλήμ. The reference to Galilee is adequately explained by the commonly accepted view that Mark and Matthew (in contrast with Lk. xxiv and Jn. xx) know only of Galilean appearances, while the claim that Galilee is the land of eschatological fulfilment has no better support than the prominence of Galilee in Mk. Further, the attempt to claim ὄψεσθε as a technical term used of the Parousia fails because the verb is so common and, on Lohmeyer's showing, is used also of the Resurrection, and in ix. 1 of the kingdom (ἴδωσιν).

In Matthew's version the women are to go quickly (ταχύ), Peter is not mentioned, the message is recast in the form Ἠγέρθη ἀπὸ τῶν νεκρῶν, καὶ ἰδοὺ προάγει κτλ., the difficult καθὼς εἶπεν ὑμῖν is dropped, and ἰδοὺ εἶπον ὑμῖν is appended. In Lk a reference to the Galilean teaching about the suffering, crucifixion, and rising of the Son of Man is substituted apparently from another tradition.

Several scholars think that 7 is a secondary addition, either to the Ur-Markus (Wellhausen, 136), or made by Mark (Ed. Meyer, i. 20; Bultmann, 309; Klostermann, 191; Creed, *JTS*, xxxi. 180) in the interests of the appearances in Galilee. The latter is the better suggestion, but it is necessarily conjectural. Its advantage is that, if 7 is later, 8 refers to the announcement of the resurrection in 6. There is then no longer any need to ask why the message to the disciples and to Peter was not delivered, while the reference to the silence of the women is apologetic. Mark seeks to explain why

ἔφυγον ἀπὸ τοῦ μνημείου, εἶχεν γὰρ αὐτὰς τρόμος καὶ ἔκστασις·
καὶ οὐδενὶ οὐδὲν εἶπαν, ἐφοβοῦντο γάρ· * * * * * * *

the story was not known earlier. *Er (v. 8) soll auf die Frage Antwort geben, weshalb die Erzählung von der Frauen am leeren Grabe so lange unbekannt geblieben sei*, Bousset, 65. This suggestion, however, entails the consequence that Mark failed to perceive the difficulty created in 8. The view that 5-7 was inserted is more open to question since, while the Empty Tomb can evoke belief (Jn. xx. 8), the presence and words of the angel more naturally account for the quaking and amazement of the women. Cf. Lohmeyer, 357 n.

8. The effect of the message is to cause trembling and astonishment. τρόμος*, 1 Cor. ii. 3, 2 Cor. vii. 15, Eph. vi. 5, Phil. ii. 12**, ' trembling ', ' quaking ' (from fear); Cl., LXX, Pap. For ἔκστασις *v*. v. 42*. Swete, 398, comments : ' They turned and fled from the tomb, trembling and unable for the moment to collect their thoughts or control themselves '. Cf. Deissmann, *BS*, 293. Field, 44 f., says that εἶχεν is nearly the same as ἔλαβε, ' had taken hold ' (cf. Lk. v. 26, vii. 16), and is so used by the best Gk authors from Homer and Herodotus to Plutarch. For ἐξέρχομαι *v*. i. 25 ; φεύγω v. 14 ; μνημεῖον v. 2.

Mark adds that they said nothing to anyone, for they were afraid. For the double negative *v*. the note on i. 44 and for φοβέομαι *v*. iv. 41. With this abrupt statement the Gospel, as we know it, ends. To the later Evangelists this ending was intolerable : Matthew says that, with fear and great joy, they ran to tell His disciples ; Luke said that they told all these things to the Eleven and the rest. Several scholars hold that ἐφοβοῦντο γάρ is the original end of the Gospel. Cf. Wellhausen, 137 ; Ed. Meyer, i. 13-18 ; Creed, 314-18, *JTS*, xxxi. 175-80; R. R. Ottley, *JTS*, xxvii. 407-9; W. K. L. Clarke, *Theol.* xxix. 106 f. ; Lohmeyer, 356-60; R. H. Lightfoot,

LDG, 1-48, *GM*, 80-97, 106-16 ; J. Knox, 63 n. ; W. C. Allen, *JTS*, xlvii. 46-9 ; L. J. D. Richardson, *JTS*, xlix. 144 f. Lightfoot gives many examples of sentences ending with γάρ, from Homer, Aeschylus, Euripides, Plato, Aristotle, the LXX (Gen. xviii. 15, xlv. 3 (?), Isa. xvi. 10 (?), xxix. 11), Justin Martyr, and the Hermetic writings, and instances from the papyri cited by H. J. Cadbury (*JBL*, 1927). But none of the examples stands at the end of a book, and it is incredible that Mark intended such a conclusion. W. L. Knox, *HThR*, xxxv. 13-23, effectively argues that there is no parallel in the beginning of Mk, in the conclusion of any other Markan pericope, in Jn, despite the use of ' dramatic aposiopesis ' in that Gospel, or in Jewish and Hellenistic literature in general. The hypothesis implies that by pure accident Mark lighted on a conclusion which ' suits the technique of a highly sophisticated type of modern literature ' and credits him ' with a degree of originality which would invalidate the whole method of form-criticism ' (22 f.). To these considerations may be added the claim that 8 does not preclude a sequel and that no difference is made to the argument if ἐφοβοῦντο implies religious awe (cf. Allen, *JTS*, xlvii. 48, xlviii. 201-3) as in iv. 41 and ix. 6. It is highly doubtful that the ending is the equivalent of καὶ διὰ φόβον οὐδενὶ οὐδὲν εἶπαν or καὶ φοβηθεῖσαι οὐδενὶ οὐδὲν εἶπαν. On the contrary, ἐφοβοῦντο γάρ is the explanation of οὐδενὶ οὐδὲν εἶπαν. Cf. Bultmann, 309 n.

The view that ἐφοβοῦντο γάρ is not the intended ending stands. Cf. Hort, 46 ; Swete, ciii-cxiii ; Moffatt, 238 f. ; Burkitt, *Two Lectures on the Gospels*, 28 ; Bultmann, 309 n. ; Turner, 82 f. ; Streeter, 337 ; Branscomb, 310 ; Schniewind, 205 f. How the Gospel ended we do not know. The natural sequel to ἐφοβοῦντο γάρ would be a μή clause ('lest') referring to the Jews or to the charge of madness (Streeter, 337; Rawlinson, 268), followed by appearances to Peter and to all the disciples. How the original ending disappeared is equally obscure. The mutilation of the original papyrus MS., Mark's premature death, and deliberate suppression have been conjectured.

Mk. xvi. 9-20   THE LONGER ENDING

In view of the discussions of Hort, 28-51, Swete, ciii-cxiii, and Lagrange, 456-68,[1] it is unnecessary to examine in detail the almost universally held conclusion that xvi. 9-20 is not an original part of Mk. Both the external and the internal evidence are decisive. The passage is omitted by א B k sy⁵, and important MSS. of the Georgian, Armenian, and Aethiopic versions, and Eusebius and Jerome attest that it was wanting in almost all Gk MSS. known to them. It is also significantly combined with the 'Shorter Ending' in L and Ψ and in Sahidic, Syriac, and Aethiopic MSS. W inserts a third passage, the Freer Ending, after xvi. 14, and a tenth-century Armenian MS. contains the rubric Αριστωνος του πρεσβυτερου which by wide consent ascribes xvi. 9-20 to the Aristion mentioned by Papias [2] in the well-known quotation given by Eusebius in his *Historia Ecclesiastica*, iii. 39. 15. 'In the whole Greek Ante-Nicene literature', Hort, 37, writes, 'there are at most but two traces of *vv.* 9-20, and in the extant writings of Clem. al. and Origen they are wholly wanting.' The two exceptions are a possible allusion in Justin Martyr, *Apol.* i. 45, οἱ ἀπόστολοι αὐτοῦ ἐξελθόντες πανταχοῦ ἐκήρυξαν, and the express quotation of Irenaeus iii. 10. 6, *In fine autem euangelii ait Marcus: Et quidem Dominus Iesus, postquam locutus est eis, receptus est in caelos, et sedet* (v.l. *sedit*) *ad dextram patris.* With this evidence, the internal evidence, based on the vocabulary, style, and subject-matter of the section, is in complete agreement, as will be seen in the Commentary. The RSV is fully justified in placing the passage in the margin instead of, as in the RV, in the text after a wide space.

The passage consists of four sections:

xvi. 9-11.   The Appearance to Mary Magdalene;
xvi. 12 f.   The Appearance to Two Travellers;
xvi. 14-18.   The Appearance to the Eleven;
xvi. 19 f.   The Ascension and the Session on High.

9   [Ἀναστὰς δὲ πρωὶ πρώτῃ σαββάτου ἐφάνη πρῶτον Μαρίᾳ τῇ
10   Μαγδαληνῇ, παρ' ἧς ἐκβεβλήκει ἑπτὰ δαιμόνια. ἐκείνη πορευ-

xvi. 9-11: The Appearance to Mary Magdalene. The vocabulary and style of this section show clearly that it was not written by Mark, but is based on a knowledge of traditions found in Lk and Jn.

The section begins abruptly without a subject, as if Jesus (but not Mary) had been mentioned previously. The appearance to Mary is described by ἐφάνη (φαίνεται, xiv. 64) which is not found elsewhere in Mk, and she herself is characterized by παρ' ἧς ἐκβεβλήκει ἑπτὰ δαιμόνια (cf. Lk. viii. 2). The time is indicated by πρωί, which is frequently used in Mk (*v.* i. 35), but

[1] Cf. also Plummer, xlii-xlviii; Turner, 83-5; Streeter, 335-51. Lagrange affirms the canonicity of xvi. 9-20, but recognizes that the passage is a later appendix.
[2] But *v.* Streeter, 127; Turner, 84.

θεῖσα ἀπήγγειλεν τοῖς μετ᾽ αὐτοῦ γενομένοις πενθοῦσι καὶ κλαίου-
σιν· κἀκεῖνοι ἀκούσαντες ὅτι ζῇ καὶ ἐθεάθη ὑπ᾽ αὐτῆς ἠπίστησαν. 11
Μετὰ δὲ ταῦτα δυσὶν ἐξ αὐτῶν περιπατοῦσιν ἐφανερώθη ἐν ἑτέρᾳ 12
μορφῇ πορευομένοις εἰς ἀγρόν· κἀκεῖνοι ἀπελθόντες ἀπήγγειλαν 13
τοῖς λοιποῖς· οὐδὲ ἐκείνοις ἐπίστευσαν. Ὕστερον [δὲ] ἀνακει- 14
μένοις αὐτοῖς τοῖς ἕνδεκα ἐφανερώθη, καὶ ὠνείδισεν τὴν ἀπιστίαν
αὐτῶν καὶ σκληροκαρδίαν ὅτι τοῖς θεασαμένοις αὐτὸν ἐγηγερ-

also by πρώτη σαββάτου which differs
from τῇ μιᾷ τῶν σαββάτων in xvi. 2 (cf.
also xiv. 12). πρῶτον (xvi. 9) is a
common Markan word (v. iii. 27), but
ἐκβάλλειν παρά (xvi. 9) is not found
elsewhere in the NT. The account of
Mary's action in xvi. 10 recalls Jn. xx.
18, ἔρχεται . . . ἀγγέλλουσα τοῖς μαθηταῖς, but is colourless, while the reference to the disciples in τοῖς μετ᾽ αὐτοῦ
γενομένοις is not Markan. For κλαίω
v. v. 38 f., xiv. 72*; πενθέω*. πορεύομαι (xvi. 10, 12, 15) appears in Mk
once (ix. 30*), and κἀκεῖνος (xvi. 11,
13), although found in xii. 4 f.*, is not
used of the disciples. The Evangelist
has ζάω (xvi. 11) rarely (x. 23, xii.
27*), but θεάομαι (xvi. 11, 14), frequently found in Jn, never. Nor again
does he use ἀπιστέω (xvi. 11, 16*),
though the verb is common in Cl. Gk,
and appears in Lk. xxiv. 11, 14, Ac.
xxviii. 24, Rom. iii. 3, 2 Tim. ii. 13,
and 1 Pet. ii. 7**. Finally, the statement that the disciples disbelieved the
announcement agrees with Lk. xxiv.
11 and Mt. xxviii. 17b.

*xvi. 12 f.: The Appearance to Two
Travellers.* The narrative is a mere
summary stating that Jesus was
manifested (φανερόω, iv. 22, xvi. 12,
14*) to two (disciples) on their way
into the country ' in another form '.
It is obviously a distant echo of the
story of the two going to Emmaus
(Lk. xxiv. 13-35). Again, neither the
vocabulary nor style is Markan. μετὰ
ταῦτα is common in Jn, but is never
used by Mark. The same is true of
ἕτερος* and μορφή* in 12, but for
περιπατέω v. ii. 9 and for ἀγρός v. 14.
For πορεύομαι (12) and κἀκεῖνος (13)
v. xvi. 9-11; but for ἀπέρχομαι i. 20;
ἀπαγγέλλω v. 14; λοιπός iv. 19.

The phrase ἐν ἑτέρᾳ μορφῇ suggests
a form different from that in which
Jesus appeared to Mary, perhaps that
of a wayfarer (Swete, 402 ; Lohmeyer,
362) in contrast with that of a gardener
as in Jn. xx. 15. But it is also possible that the writer is thinking of the
manner in which the Risen Christ
appeared and disappeared in spite of
closed doors (Jn. xx. 19, 26 ; Lk. xxiv.
31). The statement that they told the
rest again recalls the Emmaus story,
but not the reference to disbelief (13)
which, as compared with Lk. xxiv. 34,
may represent a different tradition
(cf. Lohmeyer, 362). The use of
πιστεύω c. dat. in 13 f. is found in Mk
only in xi. 31. Once more, as in 9-11,
the writer is a compiler whose methods
and outlook are different from those
of Mark.

*xvi. 14-18: The Appearance to the
Eleven.* 14. Although longer, this
section has the same scanty narrative
element as 9-11 and 12 f., the greater
part consisting of late post-resurrection
sayings. The approach to a climax
is suggested by the series : ἐφάνη
πρῶτον (9), ἐφανερώθη ἐν ἑτέρᾳ μορφῇ
(12), and ὕστερον δέ (not elsewhere in
Mk) . . . ἐφανερώθη (14). No temporal statement is given and the circumstances are barely indicated in
ἀνακειμένοις (v. vi. 26) αὐτοῖς τοῖς
ἕνδεκα. Cf. Lk. xxiv. 41. The reproach (ὀνειδίζω, xv. 32*) is very
severe, more so than in viii. 14-21, and
includes words which in Mk are used
of men hostile to Jesus (ἀπιστία, vi. 6,
ix. 24*, and σκληροκαρδία, x. 5*). Cf.
Mt. xi. 20. So strong a rebuke can
be understood only by the supreme
importance attached to the Resurrection by the writer, who has in mind

15 μένον [ἐκ νεκρῶν] οὐκ ἐπίστευσαν. καὶ εἶπεν αὐτοῖς Πορευθέντες εἰς τὸν κόσμον ἅπαντα κηρύξατε τὸ εὐαγγέλιον πάσῃ τῇ
16 κτίσει. ὁ πιστεύσας καὶ βαπτισθεὶς σωθήσεται, ὁ δὲ ἀπιστήσας
17 κατακριθήσεται. σημεῖα δὲ τοῖς πιστεύσασιν ⸀ἀκολουθήσει
ταῦτα¹, ἐν τῷ ὀνόματί μου δαιμόνια ἐκβαλοῦσιν, γλώσσαις λαλή-
18 σουσιν ᵀ, [καὶ ἐν ταῖς χερσὶν] ὄφεις ἀροῦσιν κἂν θανάσιμόν τι

17 ταῦτα παρακολουθήσει | καιναῖς

the conditions of his day. For θεάομαι
v. 11* and with ἐγηγερμένον cf. xvi. 6
and 2 Tim. ii. 8. At this point Jerome,
c. Pelag. ii. 15, found a defence of the
disciples in some MSS.: *Et illi satis-
faciebant dicentes saeculum istud in-
iquitatis et incredulitatis substantia*
(v.l. *sub satana*) *est quae non sinit per
immundos spiritus ueram Dei apprehendi uirtutem. idcirco iam nunc re-
uela iustitiam tuam.* See the Freer
Ending *infra*.

15 f. After the harsh rebuke the
introduction of the sayings is very
abrupt. The commission to preach
the gospel to the whole creation is an
independent version of Mt. xxviii. 18 f.
Its universalism shows that it was
current in a Gentile Church. The
saying carries farther the ideas present
in germ in vii. 27 and more definitely
in xiii. 10. Admirably expressing the
spirit of Christianity, no more than
Mt. xxviii. 18 f. is it an actual saying
of Jesus; otherwise, the controversy
culminating in the Council of Jerusalem (Ac. xv) would not have been
possible. κηρύσσω (v. i. 4) and εὐαγγέλιον (v. i. 1) are common Markan
words, but κόσμος is found twice only
(viii. 36, xiv. 9), while κτίσις, used in
x. 6 and xiii. 19 in the phrase ἀπ᾽ ἀρχῆς
κτίσεως, here describes mankind (cf.
Col. i. 23; also Judith ix. 12, xvi. 14,
3 Macc. ii. 2, 7, vi. 2). Although the
content of the Gospel is not stated, the
Christian Message appears to be
meant. This view is supported by 16
which is the language of a later age.
Cf. Jn. iii. 17 f. John, however, uses
ὁ πιστεύων and the belief in question
is faith-union with Christ. Here ὁ
πιστεύσας points to an act, and probably, as καὶ βαπτισθείς suggests, a

confession made at baptism, while
baptism itself is a rite as part of an
established ecclesiastical order. Cf.
1 Pet. iii. 21, Tit. iii. 5. We are not
far, indeed, from the idea of baptism
as a seal which guarantees eschatological salvation (σωθήσεται). If so,
πιστεύω (v. i. 15) and βαπτίζω (v. i. 4)
are charged with post-Markan significance. For ἀπιστέω v. 11*. κατακρίνω (x. 33, xiv. 64*) is here used of
the Last Judgment.

17 f. The idea that signs (σημεῖον, v.
viii. 11) will follow believers (a strange
use of ἀκολουθέω (v. i. 18)) is Johannine; cf. Jn. xiv. 12, ὁ πιστεύων εἰς ἐμὲ
τὰ ἔργα ἃ ἐγὼ ποιῶ κἀκεῖνος ποιήσει.
But here again the Johannine note is
wanting. The signs are those recorded in the Synoptic Gospels and
the Acts; the casting out of daemons
in Christ's name (for ἐν τῷ ὀνόματί μου
v. ix. 37; δαιμόνια ἐκβάλλειν iii. 15),
speaking with tongues (Ac. ii. 3 f.,
x. 46, xix. 6, 1 Cor. xii. 28), taking
up serpents (cf. Lk. x. 19, Ac. xxviii.
3 f.; cf. Isa. xi. 8), the healing of the
sick (Mk. vi. 13). But once more the
point of view is later. Speaking
with tongues, for example, is not mentioned in the Gospels, and if καιναῖς
is read (A C² D W minusc. *omn.* it vg
syᶜ ᵖᵉ ʰˡ ʰⁱᵉʳ geo Ambr Aug), there is an
approximation to such phrases as καινὴ
διαθήκη and καινὸς ἄνθρωπος (cf. Swete,
406). While in vi. 13 anointing with
oil is mentioned, here the laying on
of hands is specified; and, while
Lk. x. 19 speaks of treading on serpents, here it is a question of taking
them up, and if καὶ ἐν ταῖς χερσίν is read
(C L Mᵐᵍ Δ Ψ 33 565 579 892 *et al.*
syᶜ ʰˡ sa bo geo²), in the hands. Further,
drinking of deadly poisons without

πίωσιν οὐ μὴ αὐτοὺς βλάψῃ, ἐπὶ ἀρρώστους χεῖρας ἐπιθήσουσιν
καὶ καλῶς ἕξουσιν. Ὁ μὲν οὖν κύριος ['Ιησοῦς] μετὰ τὸ λαλῆσαι 19
αὐτοῖς ἀνελήμφθη εἰς τὸν οὐρανὸν καὶ ἐκάθισεν ἐκ δεξιῶν τοῦ
θεοῦ. ἐκεῖνοι δὲ ἐξελθόντες ἐκήρυξαν πανταχοῦ, τοῦ κυρίου συνερ- 20
γοῦντος καὶ τὸν λόγον βεβαιοῦντος διὰ τῶν ἐπακολουθούντων
σημείων.⟧

20 Ἀμήν.

harm is not mentioned elsewhere in the NT, but mentioned by Papias (Eus. *HE*, iii. 39) of Barsabbas and in a well-known legend concerning St. John (Acts of Jn, cf. M. R. James, 263), and in many stories attested by Theophylact (*v.* Swete, 406) Here, without doubt, is the atmosphere of A.D. 100–40. θανάσιμος is a classical word not found in Bib. Gk. οὐ μὴ αὐτοὺς βλάψῃ recalls Lk. iv. 35. ἄρρωστος is used in Mk. vi. 5, 13*, but the classical καλῶς ἔχω here only in the NT.

xvi. 19 f.: The Ascension and the Session on High. In this final section the time and place are not indicated, but μετὰ τὸ λαλῆσαι αὐτοῖς more naturally suggests the meal referred to in 14 than the end of a series of Appearances (Swete, 407). ὁ μὲν οὖν . . . δέ is resumptive, but οὖν, rarely used in Mk (*v.* p. 419 n.) is omitted by C* L W 90* syᶜ ᵖᵉ ʰⁱᵉʳ sa arm aeth geo². For μέν . . . δέ *v.* xii. 5, xiv. 21, 38*. The effect is to distinguish the action of Jesus from that of the Eleven who, none the less, receive His help and confirmation through attendant signs. Manifestly a summary passage, the section both in vocabulary and ideas is post-Markan.

The name ὁ κύριος 'Ιησοῦς is used several times in the Acts and occasionally by St. Paul, but is not found elsewhere in the Gospels. Even if 'Ιησοῦς is omitted (with A C³ D Θ Ψ fam. 13 28 *al. plur.* geo²), ὁ κύριος, especially frequent in Lk, is not found in Mk apart from xi. 3 (*q.v.*). ἀνελήμφθη* describes the Ascension, as in Ac. i. 2, 11, 22 and 1 Tim. iii. 16; cf. 4 Kgdms. ii. 11 (the translation of Elijah). Swete, 407, points out that

the Creeds generally employ ἀναβαίνειν or ἀνέρχεσθαι, possibly because ἀνελήμφθη might admit of a docetic interpretation, although, as a matter of fact, the Ascension was known in the Greek Church as ἡ ἀνάληψις or ἡ ἑορτὴ τῆς ἀναλήψεως. After the Ascension mention is made of the *sessio ad dextram Dei* which occupied so prominent a place in primitive Christian belief (Ac. vii. 55 f., Rom. viii. 34, Eph. i. 20, Col. iii. 1, Heb. i. 3, viii. 1, x. 12, xii. 2, 1 Pet. iii. 22, Apoc. iii. 21). Swete, 407, and Lohmeyer, 363, think the language is credal. With καὶ ἐκάθισεν ἐκ δεξιῶν τοῦ θεοῦ cf. Psa. cx. 1, quoted in Mk. xii. 36.

The departure of the Eleven (ἐξελθόντες) is presumably from Jerusalem. If so, in contrast with Mark (cf. xiv. 28, xvi. 7), the writer follows the Jerusalem tradition of the Appearances. As Swete, 408, observes, ἐκήρυξαν πανταχοῦ (i. 28*) ' clearly does not belong to the earliest form of the Gospel-tradition '. For similar statements regarding the Apostles from Clement of Rome, Hermas, and Justin Martyr, see the quotations cited by Swete. In the gen. abs. with which the passage ends the three verbs are found only in the Epistles : συνεργέω (Rom. viii. 28, 1 Cor. xvi. 16, 2 Cor. vi. 1, Jas. ii. 22**) ; βεβαιόω (Rom. xv. 8, 1 Cor. i. 6, 8, 2 Cor. i. 21, Col. ii. 7, Heb. ii. 3, xiii. 9**) ; ἐπακολουθέω (1 Tim. v. 10, 24, 1 Pet. ii. 21**). The idea of the co-operation of the Exalted Christ with the disciple has a parallel in Heb. ii. 3 f., (σωτηρία) ὑπὸ τῶν ἀκουσάντων εἰς ἡμᾶς ἐβεβαιώθη, συνεπιμαρτυροῦντος τοῦ θεοῦ σημείοις . . . St. Paul thinks rather of the believer co-operating with others (Rom. xvi. 3, 9, 21) or with

God (1 Cor. iii. 9). But if ὁ θεός is read in Rom. viii. 28, he speaks of God co-operating in all things for good with those who love Him; cf. Dodd, *Rom.* 138. With reference to the signs which follow Swete closes his great commentary with the noble words of Bede: *sancta quippe ecclesia quotidie spiritaliter facit quod tunc per apostolos corporaliter faciebat . . . miracula tanto maiora sunt quanto magis spiritalia.*

THE SHORTER ENDING

The Shorter Ending is found in L Ψ 099 0112 274^mg 579 k sy^hl mg and in some MSS. of sa bo aeth. The text (with many *v.ll.*) is as follows :

πάντα δὲ παρηγγελμένα τοῖς περὶ τὸν Πέτρον συντόμως* ἐξήγγειλαν*. μετὰ δὲ ταῦτα καὶ αὐτὸς ὁ Ἰησοῦς ἐφάνη αὐτοῖς, καὶ ἀπὸ ἀνατολῆς* καὶ ἄχρι* δύσεως* ἐξαπέστειλεν* δι᾽ αὐτῶν τὸ ἱερὸν* καὶ ἄφθαρτον* κήρυγμα* τῆς αἰωνίου σωτηρίας*.

'And all that had been commanded them they made known briefly to those about Peter. And afterwards Jesus Himself appeared to them, and from the East as far as the West sent forth through them the sacred and incorruptible proclamation of eternal salvation.'

None of the words marked with an asterisk is found in Mk and the same is true of the phrases οἱ περὶ τὸν Πέτρον, μετὰ ταῦτα, τὸ ἱερὸν καὶ ἄφθαρτον κήρυγμα, and ἡ αἰώνιος σωτηρία. There can be no question of Markan origin. Like the Longer Ending, it witnesses to the belief of some early writer that ἐφοβοῦντο γάρ was not the original end of Mk. Swete, cviii, suggests that the pointed reference to the westward course of the Apostolic preaching is a sign of Roman origin; cf. Rawlinson, 248. Inevitably, and at an early date, it gave place to the superior and more detailed Longer Ending. See further, Hort, 38.

THE FREER LOGION

The so-called Freer Ending is really a gloss in Codex W added to xvi. 14, the beginning of which is quoted by Jerome (*v.* the note on this verse). The text of W is as follows :

κακεινοι απελογουντε λεγοντες οτι ο αιων ουτος της ανομιας και της απιστιας υπο τον σαταναν εστιν ο μη εων τα υπο των πνευματων ακαθαρτα την αληθειαν του θεου καταλαβεσθαι δυναμιν δια τουτο αποκαλυψον σου την δικαιοσυνην ηδη εκεινοι ελεγον τω χριστω και ο χριστος εκεινοις προσελεγεν οτι πεπληρωται ο ορος των ετων της εξουσιας του σατανα αλλα εγγιζει αλλα δινα και υπερ ων εγω αμαρτησαντων παρεδοθην εις θανατον ινα υποστρεψωσιν εις την αληθειαν και μηκετι αμαρτησωσιν· ινα την εν τω ουρανω πνευματικην και αφθαρτον της δικαιοσυνης δοξαν κληρονομησωσιν.

'And they replied [1] saying, This age of lawlessness and unbelief is under Satan, who by means of evil spirits does not permit the true power of God to be apprehended [2]; therefore reveal thy righteousness now. They were speaking to Christ, and Christ said to them in reply: The limit of the years of the authority of Satan has been fulfilled, but other terrible things draw near, even for the sinners on whose behalf I was delivered up to death, that they might turn to the truth and sin no more,

---

[1] Reading ἀπελογοῦντο.

[2] Following Jerome: *quae non sinit per immundos spiritus ueram Dei apprehendi uirtutem.*

in order that they may inherit the spiritual and incorruptible glory of righteousness which is in heaven.'

Apparently some early scribe desired to soften the severe condemnation of the Eleven in xvi. 14 and, with a view to the religious situation of his day, to add a current unwritten saying of Jesus. Bartlet, 450, thinks that the addition was made from some early second-century Christian writing, but it is better, with Rawlinson, 249, to suppose that it was composed *ad hoc*. Its date cannot be determined; the end of the second or the beginning of the third century may be suggested.

ADDITIONAL NOTES

A. THE BAPTISM OF JESUS

In the introduction to the narrative (p. 158) it was suggested that Mark's account and the experience of Jesus Himself ought to be treated separately. While all explanations must of necessity be tentative, it seems best to explain the experience as inner and spiritual. The Evangelist may have meant to describe objective phenomena seen by Jesus, for he gives no indication that he intends to record the story of a vision; and it is by no means excluded that for Jesus Himself the experience included auditory and visual elements. Mark's account may also reflect his view that the Messiahship of Jesus was a secret hidden from the people. These possibilities, however, do not preclude us from passing beyond the narrative to an explanation grounded in the inner life of Jesus.

Lk. x. 18, ' I beheld Satan fall as lightning from heaven ', and the experience described in the story of the Transfiguration (Mk. ix. 2-8), suggest that there were times when in a spirit of ecstasy Jesus saw truth in the form of visions and, like St. Paul, heard ' unspeakable words, which it is not lawful for a man to utter ' (2 Cor. xii. 4).[1] This possibility still obtains when the genesis of the story is traced to the belief of the primitive community, that dedication to the Messianic office implies the gift of the Spirit, and that baptism imparts the Spirit[2]; and it is not affected by the fact that, as a Pauline Christian, Mark uses the term ' the Spirit ' (v. p. 160), nor by the uncertainty whether Q contained an account of the Baptism.[3] In the Old Testament leaders of the people,

[1] For the view that Jesus was a ' pneumatic person' see Otto, 344 f., 379-81.

[2] Cf. Bultmann, 267 f.; Bousset, 55 f.; Branscomb, 19 f. Bultmann thinks that the story is to be traced to the Hellenistic community. Bousset hesitates between this view and that of an origin on Palestinian soil, with perhaps an inclination to the latter. Branscomb suggests that the narrative indicates what Christians came to think about Jesus.

[3] Cf. Bultmann, 268.

warriors, prophets, kings, and craftsmen are repeatedly described as endowed for special purposes by the *ruach-adonai*,[1] and it is natural that on the eve of His ministry Jesus should look for such an endowment. All the conditions for a vision significant of the divine call and empowering must have been present. The view that baptism imparts the Spirit is more credibly explained as an inference from the story of the Baptism of Jesus rather than, *vice versa*, as a belief which is responsible for the creation of the narrative. The occasion was one in which Jesus ' recognized His appointed hour '[2] and received the gift of the Spirit for His Mission. · To speak of it as the moment when He became the Messiah[3] puts the matter too crudely, unless Messiahship, as He interpreted it, was the flowering of His consciousness of Sonship, a Sonship rich and unique in character.[4]

The sense of Sonship and the anticipation of a Messianic destiny precede the crucial experience of baptism,[5] and they go far to explain why Jesus submitted to it at the hands of John. That He accepted baptism like other penitents is excluded by the entire absence of the consciousness of sin in His personality, as it is revealed in the Gospels. We must infer, therefore, that He came to be baptized as an act of self-dedication to His Mission and perhaps also of self-identification with sinful Israel in the fulfilment of righteousness.[6] In baptism He received the assurance that He was indeed God's Son and Servant. This view is suggested by the unique combination of ideas connected both with the Servant and the Messiah in the words of the Heavenly Voice and by His vision of the coming of the Spirit. It is not clear

---

[1] Othniel (Judg. iii. 10), Gideon (Judg. vi. 34), Jephthah (Judg. xi. 29), Samson (Judg. xiii. 25), Bezalel (Ex. xxxi. 3, xxxv. 31), Balaam (Num. xxiv. 2), Saul (1 Sam. x. 6, 10), also Isa. xi. 2 ff., xlii. 1. See Lagrange, 12; N. H. Snaith, *The Doctrine of the Holy Spirit* (Headingley Lectures), 11-37.

[2] Rawlinson, 253.

[3] *Mit ihr beginnt seine Messianität*, Wellhausen, 5.

[4] Cf. Holtzmann, *Theol.* i. 339, 352 f., 413-15; C. J. Cadoux, 35.

[5] Cf. Lagrange, 12, *Jésus n'est pas plus constitué Fils de Dieu au baptême qu'à la transfiguration* (ix. 7). H. G. Marsh, 104 f.

[6] Cf. Flemington, 27, ' For Jesus this acceptance of John's baptism need imply no consciousness of sin save in a corporate sense, but this identification of himself with the people of God was involved in the conception of Messiahship which we know our Lord found in Deutero-Isaiah '. Flemington cites A. Oepke, *KThW*, i. 536.

from the Markan account that at this point Jesus was conscious of being the Suffering Servant,[1] for the words quoted are from Isa. xlii, and not liii, but it is reasonable to infer that His sense of a suffering destiny is lineally connected with the initial experience of baptism   Cf. Lk. xii. 50.

B. THE TWELVE AND THE APOSTLES

The relationship between the Twelve and the Apostles is one of the outstanding problems of primitive Christianity, and it is of crucial importance in considering the allied questions of the Church and the Christian Ministry. In this Note the problem is considered mainly as it affects the Gospel of Mark, although in point of fact it is impossible to exclude the wider issues. The questions which claim attention are: the functions and significance of the Twelve in Mark's account; the further evidence supplied in the later Gospels and the Acts; the place of the Twelve in the primitive Church; and, finally, the relation of the Twelve to the Apostles.

(1) Mark's testimony is that the Twelve were appointed in order that, after a period of fellowship with Jesus, they might be sent forth to preach and to cast out daemons (iii. 14 f.), and that, subsequently, they went out two by two with authority over unclean spirits, commissioned to preach repentance (vi. 7, 12), presumably in view of the imminence of the Kingdom of God. After the Mission they are less prominent in Mk, but they are specially mentioned in connexion with the teaching which Jesus gave on His way to Jerusalem (x. 32) and at the Last Supper (xiv. 17). Peter, James, and John are present on important occasions, at the Raising of the Daughter of Jairus (v. 37), the Transfiguration (ix. 2), and Gethsemane (xiv. 33), and, together with Andrew, on the Mount of Olives (xiii. 3). Otherwise, the Twelve tend to be merged in the wider circle of 'the disciples', although it is possible that they are sometimes meant by this phrase and by 'His disciples'. Nowhere, according to Mark's account, are they appointed to exercise functions of rule and government in the primitive community. The general

---

[1] But see J. W. Bowman, 42 f.; O. Cullmann, *Baptism in the NT*, 16 f., *Urchristentum und Gottesdienst*, 64-7.

impression we receive is that, while the existence of the Twelve
and the nature of their original appointment were firmly
rooted in the tradition, apart from Peter, James, and John,
most of them had become a somewhat distant memory.

Two considerations deepen this impression. First, out
of nine references to the Twelve in Mk no less than seven
appear in ' Markan constructions ', that is, in narratives
compiled from fragmentary tradition (iv. 10, vi. 7, ix. 35,
x. 32, xiv. 10, 17, 20). Only xi. 11 (' with the Twelve ') and
xiv. 43 (' one of the Twelve ') belong to self-contained narratives, and even in these cases it is a matter of mere phrases,
as in iv. 10, xiv. 10, 17, 20. Secondly, iii. 16-19a is a mere
list. Of Philip, Bartholomew, Matthew, Thomas, James the
son of Alphaeus, and Simon the Cananaean the Evangelist
appears to know nothing. In default of further information,
it would be possible to infer from Mk that the original commission of the Twelve related only to the Galilean Mission
of vi. 6b-13, and that, after its failure, they were distinguished
from the rest of the disciples mainly in character and
ability.

(2) In view of the situation apparently implied by Mk,
it is necessary to widen the inquiry and to consider what
further data are supplied in the later Gospels, the Acts, the
Epistles, and the rest of the New Testament. The points to
consider are : the terms by which the Twelve are designated ;
the additional stories or traditions in Mt, Lk, and the Acts ;
and, most important of all, the sayings of Jesus which describe
the functions of the Twelve.

The names used are ' the Twelve ', ' the twelve disciples ',
' the twelve Apostles ', ' the twelve Apostles of the Lamb ',
and ' the Eleven '. It cannot be said that the later use of
these terms modifies the impressions we receive from Mk.
Including all these terms, the record is as follows : Mk (9),
Mt (9), Lk (8), Jn (4), Ac (3), Pl (1), Apoc. (1).[1] It is certainly remarkable that direct references to the Twelve are
not more frequent in the Acts, the Pauline Epistles, and the
Johannine writings, and are completely wanting in the
Catholic and the Pastoral Epistles. The three examples in

[1] In the Gospels the phrase ' the   x. 2 ; cf. Lk. vi. 13, ' twelve, whom
twelve Apostles ' is found only in Mt.   also he named apostles '

the Acts are probably explained by the fact that Luke identified the Twelve and the Apostles,[1] but this explanation will not account for the usage of the Fourth Gospel, nor for the single Pauline passage in 1 Cor. xv. 5. Again we receive the impression that, as a body, the Twelve are traditional figures of the past.

No clearer light is given by the lists in Mt. x. 2-4, Lk. vi. 14-16, and Ac. i. 13. Mt. x 2-4 is merely a second edition of Mark's list, with the characterization of Matthew as ' the tax-gatherer '. In both his lists Luke replaces Thaddaeus by Judas of James, but we know nothing of either. Indeed, unless Lk. vi. 12-16 comes from a non-Markan source, a view which is not widely held, there is but one primary list, namely that of Mark. The Fourth Gospel uses further traditions regarding Andrew (i. 40-2, 44, vi. 8, xii. 22), Philip (i. 43-5, 48, vi. 5-7, xii. 21 f., xiv. 8 f.), and Thomas (xi. 16, xiv. 5, xx. 24 f., 26-9); but, apart from the question of their historical character, these allusions only give colour to the personalities of these men and connect Thomas and his companions with the Risen Lord, without illuminating the problem of the Twelve. Ac. i. 15-26 records the reconstitution of the college of the Twelve, but it is difficult to feel much confidence in the historical value of this narrative. Of Matthias nothing further is known. Cf. Lake, *Beginnings*, v. 41-6.

Far more important are the sayings relative to the Twelve. Mt. x. 40 (cf. Lk. x. 16, Mk. ix. 37, Jn. xii. 44 f., xiii. 20), ' He that receiveth you receiveth me, and he that receiveth me receiveth him that sent me ', is an undoubtedly genuine saying, which enlarges our knowledge of the Mission Charge given in Mk. vi. 8-11. It embodies the Rabbinic principle that the emissary is as the one who sends him; *v.* the note on Mk. ix. 37. It gives to the Twelve a certain character which is relevant to, but need not be exhausted in, the circumstances of the Mission (cf. Jn. xiii. 20). It would be difficult to maintain that it describes them exclusively, and impossible to prove that, as *sheluḥim*, they possess an

---

[1] ' The Apostles ' are mentioned 28 times in the Acts and 12 times in the Pauline Epistles. For the rest the record is: Mk (1), Mt (1), Lk (4), Jn (0), Heb (0), Past. Epp. (0), Cath. Epp. (2), Apoc (2).

authority which they can transmit.[1] The saying underlines the great importance which Jesus attached to the Galilean Mission.

Lk. xxii. 30, ' Ye shall sit on thrones judging the twelve tribes of Israel ', is also a genuine saying addressed to the Twelve, even though the phrase ' twelve thrones ' belongs to the less authentic form of the saying in Mt. xix. 28. It can hardly have been addressed to a wider circle, since it speaks of functions of judging or ruling, or be a Christian formation subsequent to the defection of Judas. Unfortunately, its meaning is obscure. The saying is eschatological and it is usually taken to refer to the Parousia. In this case, it does not describe a power exercised by the Twelve in the course of history, but the rule of the saints which belongs to the End Time. It is possible, however, that the eschatology is ' realized eschatology ', and, on this interpretation, two views are possible. It may have been spoken to the Twelve at the time when Jesus sent them forth on their historic Mission to the cities of Galilee (Mk. vi. 6b-13); that is to say, it describes a rule which they were to exercise in the expected community of the Son of Man. Alternatively, it was addressed to the Twelve late in the Ministry of Jesus (cf. Lk. xxii. 28-30) and with reference to the interval before the Parousia. Against this view the objections are formidable. We have no other information concerning such a commission, and the place occupied by the Twelve in the primitive Church renders the interpretation improbable, unless the Twelve are the Apostles (*v. infra*). The former explanation of the saying is better. To it the position assigned to the saying in Mt and Lk offers no final objection, since its place in these Gospels is probably purely editorial. Nevertheless, to assign the prophecy to the time of the Galilean Mission is highly conjectural. It may be suggested, however, that the conjecture is not unreasonable in itself and is preferable to the view that the rule belongs to the world beyond time and space.

The remaining sayings, Mt. xvi. 17-19, xviii. 18, xxviii.

[1] For the meaning of *shaliah* v. K. H. Rengstorf, *KThW*, i. 413-44; T. W. Manson, *The Church's Ministry*, 31-52; also the articles of J. W. Hunkin, G. Dix, and H. St. J. Hart in *Theology*, li. 166-70, 249-56, 341-3, lii. 385 f.

18-20, Lk. xxiv. 46-9, Jn. xx. 23, xxi. 15-23, are not only obscure, but by wide consent are coloured with later Christian beliefs. In particular, Mt. xvi. 17-19 reflects a strong polemical interest in Peter [1] and its authenticity is much disputed. In any case, the pointed reference to Peter is adequately illustrated in the part he fulfilled after Pentecost in the building of the primitive Jerusalem community. The phrase 'the keys of the kingdom of heaven' does not describe the power to admit men to, or to exclude them from, the Church, but the imparting of that spiritual insight by which alone men can enter the Kingdom; and the power to 'bind' and to 'loose' has to do with the practical questions of conduct, and belongs to the Christian community as such (cf. Mt. xviii. 18).[2] Of this saying Jn. xx. 23 is almost certainly a later doctrinal expansion. Mt. xxviii. 18-20 [3] and Lk. xxiv. 46-9 are post-Resurrection sayings, and, as the early conflicts concerning the Gentile Mission prove, are much more explicit than original sayings on world evangelization and baptism are likely to have been. Moreover, the authority in question is moral and spiritual, as it is also in Jn. xxi. 15-23, and is not the exclusive prerogative of the Eleven.

In sum, we may say that, while the barer outlines of Mark's account of the Twelve are filled out in the later Gospels, the picture remains fundamentally the same. The Twelve are chosen disciples commissioned to undertake the work of evangelization and teaching in the name and under the authority of Christ Himself. They are especially prominent in the Galilean Mission when they are sent out as Christ's emissaries (sheluḥim). Subsequently, they retain the standing of men so commissioned, and it is with them that the Last Supper is celebrated and to them that the Risen Christ reveals Himself. There is, however, a tendency for the three disciples, Peter, James, and John, to stand out above the rest of whom we know so little. Of hierarchical powers possessed by the Twelve and of a commission which they can impart to others there is no authentic sign in the Gospels, although, in the sayings, there is manifest a tendency to enhance their importance and standing. How far this

---

[1] Cf. Streeter, 515.   [2] Cf. R. N. Flew, *JHC*, 123-38.
[3] Cf. G. D. Kilpatrick, 49.

estimate of the Twelve is confirmed by our knowledge of the
post-Resurrection period is the question to be considered
next.

(3) Our ability to determine the place occupied by the
Twelve in the primitive Church is largely conditioned by
the answer we give to the question of the relation of the Twelve
to the Apostles. To some degree, however, the two problems
can be isolated, for we know that at least Peter, James, and
John were Apostles, and unless we dismiss Lk. vi. 13 as an
anachronism, that Jesus did speak of the Twelve as 'apostles',
that is, as men commissioned and sent. Moreover, in the
early chapters of the Acts there are passages in which by
'the Apostles' the Twelve are designated. General considerations also bear upon the problem. It is highly improbable
that men who during the Ministry had been designated as
' the Twelve ', and to whom the Risen Lord had appeared,
can have disappeared as a body before Pentecost or even
immediately after it. Other things being equal, it is natural
to suppose that in the days which followed the Resurrection
the Christian community of some one hundred and twenty
members would look to the Twelve for leadership and direction. If it should prove to be that Luke has too summarily
identified the Twelve and the Apostles there must have been
some factual justification for this step. The passages in the
Acts in which ' the Apostles ' are ' the Twelve ' cannot be
precisely identified, but they are most probably to be found
in Ac. i-v. After this point it becomes increasingly difficult
to identify the two groups; it is impossible in xiv. 4, where
Barnabas and Saul are meant, and in xv and xvi, where the
Apostles include James, the Lord's brother, and are mentioned along with the Elders. Ac. i-v is a spirited and
inspiring account of apostolic devotion, courage, and leadership, possibly to some extent idealized, but, apart from the
list in i. 13, only Peter and John are expressly named. In
these chapters reference is made to the appearances of the
Risen Lord to the Eleven throughout forty days, and to the
command to await at Jerusalem the gift of the Holy Spirit.
Stories are told of the Ascension, the choice of Matthias,
Pentecost, the boldness of Peter's preaching, the healing of
a lame man by Peter and John, their arrest, arraignment,

and release, Ananias and Sapphira, the examination of Peter and John, the speech of Gamaliel, and the dismissal of the accused, after being beaten, with an injunction not to speak in the name of Jesus. Ac. vi. 2 is the last explicit reference to ' the Twelve ' in this writing, but it is important because it shows that until the appointment of the Seven responsibility for the care of the poor had rested upon their shoulders, in addition to preaching, as is also implied in iv. 36 and v. 2. The leading place which they occupied in the primitive community is also shown in the statement that the first believers devoted themselves to the Apostles' teaching and fellowship, to the breaking of bread and the prayers (ii. 42), and to the fact that they laid hands upon the Seven (vi. 6). On the other side, there is nothing to show that they had anything to do with the dominating place which James the Lord's brother came to occupy in the Church at Jerusalem, and apparently no attempt was made to fill the place left vacant after the martyrdom of James the son of Zebedee (Ac. xii. 2). The presumption is that by a process in which death played its part, members of the Twelve disappeared from the primitive community, and that leadership passed to a wider circle which included Peter, John, James the Lord's brother, and others.

(4) If to the evidence supplied by the Acts we add that of the Pauline Epistles, it is clear that it is impossible to equate the Twelve with the Apostles. In the course of time, in addition to those mentioned above, the Apostles came to include Paul (Gal. i. 1, 1 Cor. i. 1, iv. 9, ix. 1, 2 Cor. i. 1, Rom. i. 1, etc.), Barnabas (Ac. xiv. 4, 14), Andronicus and Junias (Rom. xvi. 7), and perhaps Silvanus (1 Thess. ii. 6 f.) and others whose names we do not know. There is no sign that any of these received a commission from the Twelve.

The actual part played by these Apostles in the primitive Church is obscure. Paul and Barnabas had nothing to do with the ordering and government of the Church at Jerusalem. In the records they represent the Church at Antioch. It is during worship and fasting at Antioch that the Holy Spirit enjoins the prophets and teachers of that Church to set them apart for the work of the Gentile Mission, and their

colleagues lay hands on them and send them on their way
(Ac. xiii. 1-3); and it is to the Church at Antioch that they
return and make their report (Ac. xiv. 26-8). It is that
Church which appoints them to go to Jerusalem, to the
Apostles and Elders there, after emissaries from Judaea have
raised the demand for circumcision (Ac. xv. 1 f.). The
natural inference to draw is that the Apostles at Jerusalem
and Antioch were distinct groups, a view which is supported
by the phrase οἱ ἐν Ἱεροσολύμοις ἀπόστολοι in Ac. viii. 14, and
by the references to ' the Apostles and Elders ' in Ac. xv. 2,
4, 6, 22 f. These phrases distinguish from the rest Barnabas
and Paul, who none the less are described as ' the Apostles'
in Ac. xiv. 14. The situation as regards Silvanus, Andronicus,
and Junias is still more obscure. They are described as
' Apostles ', but we are not told that they had seen the Risen
Lord, and they are not connected with the Church at Jerusalem. They are Apostles to the Gentiles commissioned for
service in respect of evangelization. In the same way Timothy
and Titus, who are not Apostles, have special duties in
preaching, teaching, and oversight.

Combining these inferences, we receive the impression
of the existence of four groups : (1) the Apostles at Jerusalem,
including James the Lord's brother, Peter, James, and John,
and other members of the Twelve; (2) the Apostles at
Antioch, Barnabas, Paul, and presumably Silvanus, who
are missionary Apostles, with oversight over the Gentile
Churches; (3) the Apostles Andronicus and Junias, with
more local functions among the Gentiles; (4) Timothy and
Titus, who exercise a similar ministry.[1] These four groups
foreshadow later developments in the Church. The Jerusalem Apostles who belonged to the Twelve had the prestige
of those who had been commissioned by Christ for the Galilean
Mission, and had been promised seats of authority in the
Elect Community of the Son of Man. No one else could
make such a claim. They had seen the Risen Lord, but with
the exception of Paul, to whom a special revelation had been
given, the other Apostles, so far as we know, had not seen
Him, but were witnesses to the Resurrection as part of the

---

[1] Cf. also 2 Cor. viii. 23, where ἀδελφοί, who are ἀπόστολοι ἐκκλησιῶν, are
mentioned.

kerygma. Nevertheless, the authority of these Apostles was spontaneously recognized, and, with the exception of that of Paul, appears to have been unchallenged. The basis of their authority can only be inferred. Undoubtedly, they must have been conscious of an inner call from Christ, to which the Holy Spirit bore unmistakable testimony, and their call, it may be presumed, was recognized and endorsed by the Church. The author of the Pastoral Epistles speaks of ' the spiritual gift ' which was imparted to Timothy through prophecy ' with the laying on of the hands of the presbytery ' (1 Tim. iv. 14), and he represents Paul as reminding him to rekindle ' the gift of God ' which is in him ' through the laying on of my hands ' (2 Tim. i. 6) ; and, although this evidence is late, it points to an early, but not necessarily an invariable, practice. ' Elders ' also are described as ' chosen ' or ' appointed ' for the Churches of Galatia by Barnabas and Paul with prayer and fasting (Ac. xiv. 23) ; but the evidence is far indeed from sustaining the idea of an unbroken succession from the original Apostles. Both the Acts and the Epistles suggest that the Jerusalem Apostles, together with Paul, stand apart from all other Apostles in dignity and authority, in virtue of the fact that they had ' seen the Lord ' and that most of them were members of the Twelve. As such they had not, and could not have, successors comparable to themselves. Apostolicity, however, became increasingly the mark of the Church itself, which had recognized the Apostolic character of Apostles other than the Twelve in the work of evangelization, liturgy, and government. In the course of time Apostles ceased to exist, but every consideration of probability suggests that those who were conscious of a like call to fulfil the same duties received a similar recognition in the Church.

It does not fall within the purpose of this Note to discuss further the origins of the Christian Ministry and the succession of Bishops and Elders in the Church. All that can be said here is that no conception of that Ministry is adequate or worthy which does not claim that it is a continuation of the essential ministry of Christ Himself, inspired by the Holy Spirit, and authorized by the Church through representatives who embody its tradition and share in its life.

C. THE RELATIONSHIP BETWEEN Mk. vi. 30-
vii. 37 AND viii. 1-26

The parallelism between these sections has long been noticed, and it has frequently been interpreted as indicating the use of duplicate accounts of the same incidents. Cf. J. Weiss, 204-26; C. H. Dodd, *Exp.* viii. xxii. 273-91; Ed. Meyer, i. 130-2; Klostermann, 84 f.; Rawlinson, 103 f.; Goguel, 359 f. The agreement is striking, especially when it is described in its simplest terms. Thus, it is frequently indicated as follows:

1. The Feeding of the Five Thousand.	1. The Feeding of the Four Thousand.
2. The Crossing and Landing.	2. The Crossing and Landing.
3. The Controversy with the Pharisees about Defilement.	3. The Controversy with the Pharisees about Signs.
4. The Syro - Phoenician Woman (The Children's Bread).	4. The Mystery of the Loaves (The Leaven of the Pharisees).
5. The Healing of the Deaf Mute.	5. The Healing of the Blind Man.

Even in this summary it is clear that the parallelism is not complete. There is close agreement only in Nos. 1, 2, and 5; and in 5 the incidents are different. In No. 3 the controversies are not the same, and the narratives in 4 have nothing in common apart from the references to bread. Further, the table does not disclose the fact that in the first series 4 and 5 are connected with a journey beyond the confines of Galilee, a complex introduced by 3 and to which the whole of viii. 1-26 belongs. A more detailed table is clearly needed.

Set out more fully the relationship of vi. 30-vii. 37 to viii. 1-26 is as follows:

A	B
1. The Return of the Twelve and the Departure to a Lonely Place.	—
2. The Feeding of the Five Thousand.	2. The Feeding of the Four Thousand.

A	B
3. The Crossing, the Storm, and the statement that the disciples did not understand concerning the loaves because their heart was blinded.	3. } The Crossing and Landing at Dalmanutha.
4. The Landing at Gennesaret including a summary statement regarding the healing ministry.	4. }
5. The Controversy with the Pharisees about Defilement, inserted as an introduction to the journey into the region of Tyre.	5. The Controversy with the Pharisees about Signs.
6. The journey into the region of Tyre and the story of the Syro-Phoenician Woman (The Children's Bread).	6. The Recrossing of the Lake (to Bethsaida) and the story of the failure to understand the mystery of the loaves and the leaven of the Pharisees.
7. The journey continued and the Healing of the Deaf Mute.	7. The Healing of the Blind Man.

This table shows the greater detail of the first series (A), which includes the introduction to the Feeding of the Five Thousand, a fuller account of the Crossing and the Landing, the journey into the region of Tyre with the story of the Syro-Phoenician Woman, and in A3 the reference to the dullness of the disciples. Parallelism is manifest, but so no less are important differences, especially in A5 and B5, A6 and B6, and A7 and B7.

The Narratives of the Feeding, Crossing, and Landing

There can be little doubt that A2-4 and B2-4 form a literary doublet.

(1) Both sections contain very similar stories of miraculous feeding. In each case the incident takes place in the wilderness (vi. 35, viii. 4). The same question, ' How many loaves have ye ? ', is asked (vi. 38, viii. 5), and the same command to recline is given (vi. 39, viii. 6). The same words are used

of the loaves : ' took ', ' gave thanks ' (εὐλόγησεν in vi. 41, εὐχαριστήσας in viii. 6), ' brake ', ' gave ', ' set before ' ; and the same statement follows : ' And they (' all ', vi. 42) did eat and were filled ' (vi. 42, viii. 8). Each narrative mentions the gathering of the broken pieces and gives the numbers present (vi. 43 f., viii. 8 f.), and in each case the dismissal of the crowd and a journey by boat follow (vi. 45-52, viii. 9 f.). These agreements strongly suggest that the narratives are doublets, and this inference is raised to a virtual certainty by the fact that, in spite of what is related in vi. 35-44, the disciples are in a state of complete perplexity in viii. 4 ; v. Comm. Editorial assimilation, the common effect of liturgical and catechetical interests, and the miraculous interpretation given to each narrative will account in part for the linguistic agreements, but the similarity is too great to be explained in this way.

(2) The differences between the two narratives do not rule out the doublet-hypothesis. The vivid character of vi. 35-44 and the more colourless form of viii. 1-10, the differences in the numbers, the fact that in viii. 1-9 the crowd has been with Jesus three days (contrast vi. 35-44), and the impression given of a more remote locality (contrast vi. 36) are modifications of the tradition in the course of transmission. Over against these differences the feature which more than anything else points to a common series of events behind the two sections is the order, feeding, crossing, and landing, which is found also in Jn. vi. 1-21

The Two Groups, A 5-7 and B 5-7

These groups raise more difficult problems. The controversies (A5 and B5) and the healings (A7 and B7) are quite different, and A6 and B6 have nothing in common beyond references to bread. The basic movement of events behind the two series has been obscured by the catechetical interests which have shaped viii. 1-26. In these circumstances conjecture alone is possible.

The best hypothesis is that of J. Weiss, 204-26, *Die Schr.*[4] 140 f., who points out that, if we include the Confession of Peter (viii. 27-33), the same succession of events lies also at the basis of Jn. vi. Cf. C. H. Dodd, *op. cit.* 284-91. The

controversy, Weiss holds, which followed the Landing at
Gennesaret (Mk. vi. 53-6) was the Demand for a Sign (viii.
11-13). After His refusal Jesus crosses over to Bethsaida
(viii. 22), as we should expect after the forced landing on the
west shore, since the original intention, frustrated by the
contrary wind, had been to go to this very place (vi. 45).
This fascinating hypothesis is oversimplified by Weiss, who
assigns the two cures, vii. 32-7 and viii. 22-6, to the hand of
the redactor, and it does not take sufficient account of the
two geographical statements, vii. 24 and 31, which describe
a withdrawal of Jesus to the region of Tyre and a return
to the Sea of Galilee and Decapolis. The strong point in
his reconstruction is the claim that the Galilean Ministry is
at an end.[1] The elimination of vii. 32-7 and viii. 26 simplifies
his hypothesis, but it is not warranted in view of the primitive
character of these narratives. The withdrawal across the
Galilean border (vii. 24) is a special problem in itself, which
is examined in Note D. Here it concerns us only in so far
as the introductory section, vii. 1-23, is concerned. This complex, which Weiss rightly omits from his reconstruction, is
loosely connected with its present context and was probably
compiled independently; v. Intr. 96. Its introduction into A,
as a preface to the Gentile sojourn, may have been prompted
by the position of the Demand for a Sign in B, for it can
hardly be accidental that a controversy with the Pharisees,
although different in each series, occupies relatively the same
position. Without prejudice to the historical character of the
sayings in vii. 1-23, Weiss is justified in giving preference to
viii. 11-13 in the original succession of events.

Recognizing the conjectural character of historical reconstructions, we may say that the original order of events in
vi. 30-viii. 26 is vi. 30-56, viii. 11-22a, vii. 24-37, viii. 22b-6,
or stated with reference to the foregoing table, A1-4, B5-6,
A6-7, B7, with uncertainty, yet to be discussed, concerning
the original order of vii. 24-37 and viii. 11-22a, that is of
A6-7 and B5-6. Our investigation suggests that vi. 30-vii. 37
and viii. 1-26 do contain duplicate accounts of the same

---

[1] *Mit dieser Erzählung* [viii. 11-13] *immer den Rücken. Galiläa ist im
ist das letzte Band zerschnitten, das grossen und ganzen verlorenes Land
Jesus und die galiläische Bevölkerung für ihn, Die Schr.*[4] 142. Cf. Dodd,
verbindet: jetzt wendet er ihr für op. cit. 278.

incidents, but not that the whole of one section is a doublet of the other. The actual situation is far too complex to be covered by so simple a hypothesis. The worship and teaching of the primitive community at Rome, as well as the editorial activity of Mark, have left their imprint on the two complexes, to a greater degree in viii. 1-26, but also in the more vivid section, vi. 30-vii. 37. Happily, the imprint can be read with sufficient clarity to afford reasonable grounds for tracing the course of events in a decisive episode in the Story of Jesus. The fact that light, although refracted, is thrown on the circumstances which attended the close of the Galilean Ministry by two different Markan complexes, and in part by Jn. vi,[1] is some assurance that the reconstruction is not without objectivity.

D. THE JOURNEY OF JESUS TO THE REGION OF TYRE

The geographical statements, vii. 24 and 31, and the contents of vii. 24-viii. 26 give reason to think that Mark thought of the section as suggesting a ministry of Jesus outside Galilee. In vii. 24-30 He converses with the Syro-Phoenician woman, in vii. 32-7 He cures the deaf mute in Decapolis, in viii. 1-9 He feeds the four thousand presumably in the same region, and in viii. 22-6 He cures the blind man near Bethsaida, probably also in Gentile territory. Only in viii. 10, 11-13, and for a brief period, does He return to Galilee, where He is met with the demand for a sign. With this exception throughout the section He is in contact with Gentiles or half-Jewish people. There is a similar situation in viii. 27-ix. 29, where Jesus is in the territory of Herod Philip, but here new interests appear, and for the most part Jesus is concerned with instructing His disciples concerning Messianic suffering and death. In vii. 24-viii. 26 four questions arise : (1) Does

---

[1] Jn. vi does not reflect the tradition of a withdrawal to Gentile territory, but as C. H. Dodd has observed, it is rather curious that in Jn. vii. 35 the Jews speculate on the possibility that Jesus might leave Palestine and go ' to the Dispersion of the Greeks '.

' Can it be that this remark betrays the author's knowledge that Jesus had actually made some slight and tentative advance into non-Jewish territory, such as is implied in the Marcan narrative?', *op. cit.* 287.

it describe a Ministry to Gentiles ? ; (2) What is the historical basis of the account ? ; (3) Did the journey precede or follow viii. 11-13 ? ; (4) What was the purpose of the withdrawal ?

(1) It is safe to infer that vii. 24-viii. 26 was planned to meet the needs of Gentile readers. The Evangelist wanted to show that the interest of Jesus was not confined to Jews, but extended to non-Jewish peoples beyond the confines of Galilee. Interest in this theme is shown earlier in the story of the Gerasene demoniac (v. 1-20), but here, in the request of the Gerasenes that Jesus should depart from their borders, it is suggested that the time for the Gentile Mission has not yet come. In vii. 24-viii. 26 it is implied that the time has arrived or at least is prefigured. The complex, vii. 1-23, by which it is preceded, shows how decisively Jesus had broken with Jewish customs regarding defilement, and had declared that nothing from without can defile a man (vii. 15). Mark himself had made the comment, ' making all meats clean ' (vii. 19). In the narrative of the Syro-Phoenician Woman the place of Gentiles in the mission of Jesus is adumbrated in the words, ' Let the children *first* be filled '. The feeding of the Four Thousand is a sign to Gentiles in contrast with the Feeding of the Five Thousand which is a sign to Jews. Healings are wrought in or near the Decapolis. In all these features the challenge raised by the Gentile Mission is unmistakably in mind.

Nevertheless, the limitations imposed by the tradition are not less apparent. No preaching or teaching to Gentiles is recorded because the tradition had no knowledge of it, and, although the disciples suddenly reappear in viii. 1-21, in the region of Tyre Jesus is alone. No mission to Gentiles is recorded ; only intimations of such a ministry. The section is a defeated attempt to represent what would have been welcomed if the tradition could have supplied the evidence. Mark truly divined the universalism implicit in the teaching of Jesus, but he could find little that suggested that His mission had extended beyond Israel, and it is to his credit as an Evangelist that he does not force the tradition to yield more than it will bear.

(2) The second question concerns the historical character of the section. In considering this issue vii. 24 and 31 deserve

serious attention, since it is not Mark's habit to invent geographical statements of the kind. We must infer that, from
a place which it may not be possible to name with certainty,
Jesus ' went away into the borders of Tyre ', and that subsequently He returned through Sidon (or Bethsaida) to the Sea
of Galilee and to the Decapolis. The only point on which
there is uncertainty is the strange phrase, ' through the midst
of the borders of Decapolis ' (vii. 31), which may have been
added to find room for vii. 32-7 and viii. 22-6, traditionally
connected with this region. The firm core of the section is the
account of the withdrawal beyond the border into Tyrian
country with the intention of securing privacy : ' He entered
into a house, and would have no man know it ' (vii. 24). The
intention of Jesus was not to undertake a mission, but to
retire for a while into obscurity apart from the people and
apart even from His disciples.

(3) At what point in the course of events did Jesus undertake this journey ? To this question alternative answers can
be given. In Note C we have found reason to think that the
historical sequence is A 1-4 followed by B5 ; in other words,
that the controversy with the Pharisees which followed the
landing at Gennesaret was the Demand for a Sign. Does
the withdrawal to the region of Tyre precede or follow this
controversy ?

(i) If the withdrawal preceded the demand for a sign,
it happened at the point where Mark places it, that is, immediately after the landing and stay at Gennesaret (vi. 53-6). The
difficulty is the reference to the Decapolis in vii. 31, for this
reference makes necessary the second crossing to the west
shore (to Dalmanutha), where the demand for a sign was made.

(ii) If the journey follows the demand, this duplication
of crossing and recrossing the lake becomes unnecessary,
since the controversy took place at the close of the stay at
Gennesaret. In other words, vi. 53-6 and viii. 11-13 describe
different incidents during one visit to the west shore. In this
case, the journey to the region of Tyre follows the return to
Bethsaida (viii. 22a) and Jesus returns approximately to the
same point, and thence passes into the Decapolis (vii. 31).

Either alternative involves a certain amount of recasting
of the Markan narrative, but there can be no objection to

this in principle if the view maintained in Note C is sound, namely that vi. 30-56 and viii. 1-10 form a doublet. If the first hypothesis is accepted, the phrase ' through the midst of the borders of Decapolis ' must be regarded as redactional and mistaken. On the second view this necessity does not exist, but a difficulty arises in the phrase ' from thence ' (ἐκεῖθεν) in vii. 24. In Mk as it stands, the reference is to Gennesaret. This meaning, however, is merely suggested by the context, and the adverb may belong to the section vii. 24-30, and so originally to another context ; v. Comm.

On the whole, the view that vii. 24-37 should follow viii. 22a is much to be preferred. After the demand for a sign all the elements are present which suggest a withdrawal from Galilee—the result of the Galilean Mission and the desire for retirement (vi. 30-4), the Messianic tension created by the meal in the wilderness (vi. 35-44), the forced landing at Gennesaret (vi. 45-52), the popular interest of the crowd in Jesus as a healer (vi. 53-6), the demand of the Pharisees for a decisive sign (viii. 11-13). It is natural that Jesus should cross the lake to Bethsaida (viii. 22a), from which the boat had been driven by the storm (vi. 45), and that from this locality He should withdraw northwards alone. Here, on the return journey, He could meet the disciples again and pass with them into the borders of the Decapolis (vii. 31-7, viii. 22-6). We conclude, therefore, that in terms of the Table printed in Note C the order of events is A1-4, B5-6, A6-7 together with B7, regarding B1-4 as a doublet of A1-4 and omitting A5 as a Markan insertion.

(4) The final question to be considered is the purpose of the withdrawal. Many commentators describe the journey as a ' flight '. Jesus, it is said, withdrew to escape the hostility of Herod Antipas. It must be allowed that there is little in Mk to sustain this hypothesis. The Herodians, it is true, are in league with the Pharisees to destroy Jesus in iii. 6 ; in vi. 14-16 Herod himself betrays a hostile interest in Him, menacing indeed, as the account of the fate of John shows (vi. 17-29) ; and in viii. 15 Jesus warns His disciples of the disruptive ' leaven of Herod '. Of the hostility of Herod, then, there can be no doubt, and it is a reasonable conjecture that Jesus may have felt that His Ministry might involve a

clash with the tetrarch and stir the people to armed revolt. But the idea of a flight is another matter. The picture of Jesus stealing away into Tyrian country, and haunting the Decapolis and the villages of Caesarea Philippi, in order to escape the attentions of Antipas, is not only gratuitous in itself, but is out of accord with the courage of Him who spoke of Herod as ' that fox ' and declined to turn from His appointed path until His destiny was consummated at Jerusalem (cf. Lk. xiii. 31-3). If, however, we reject the hypothesis of flight, only one explanation remains. Jesus withdrew because the Galilean Mission had failed ; the Kingdom of God had not come and the community of the Son of Man had not been established. Even the disciples had failed to understand the meaning of the eucharistic meal in the wilderness. The crowd cherished materialistic Messianic ideals, and were content that Jesus should heal their sick. The Pharisees looked for an authenticating sign. In these circumstances Jesus felt the need for time and opportunity to consider the nature of His work and the tragic fate which apparently awaited Him. One must not ignore the indications which point to this conclusion from fear of the charge of ' psychologizing ' or of reading history through the eyes of dogma. In its importance for Jesus the withdrawal into the region of Tyre is comparable to His departure into the wilderness of Judaea at the outset of His ministry and His stay beyond the Jordan and near the town called Ephraim at the end (Jn. x. 40-2, xi. 54 : cf. Goguel, 405-25).

E. THE COMPILATION OF THE APOCALYPTIC DISCOURSE

This Note discusses the suggestion concerning the composition of the Apocalyptic Discourse indicated at the end of the introduction to the section in the Commentary. It suggests that the Evangelist has combined several groups of sayings, some of which contained apocalyptic elements, and has not simply edited a Jewish-Christian apocalypse which can be traced in xiii. 7 f., 14-20, 24-7, 30 f.

1. Against the various forms of Colani's hypothesis at least two objections can be urged. First, only a very frag-

mentary apocalypse is suggested as the basis of the discourse.
It can hardly be called an apocalypse, since it lacks such
characteristic ideas as the casting down of Satan, the Last
Judgment, the punishment of sinners, and the blessedness
of the righteous. Secondly, the sayings usually cited as belonging to this apocalypse appear to be derived from different
groups of sayings. It would appear preferable to suppose
that Mark, or an earlier compiler, has formed these existing
groups into the Apocalyptic Discourse, adding editorial
phrases and extracts from his sayings-source. How far it may
be possible to describe the process of compilation will be
variously estimated. The data are the ideas which dominate
the chapter, our knowledge of Mark's literary methods, and
the linguistic characteristics of the sayings.

2. The determinative ideas of Mk xiii are manifest.
Mark, and the Church for which he wrote, eagerly expected
the Advent of Christ. Within a generation Christ would
come with clouds, invested with divine glory, and would
gather His Elect from the four winds (26 f., 30 f.). This
situation explains the repeated exhortations, ' Take heed '
(5, 9, 23, 33), ' Be vigilant ' (33), ' Watch ' (35, 37). It is
often said that Mark writes to check this Advent Hope, and
to show that it will not be fulfilled until certain events have
happened. Wars, rumours of wars, earthquakes, famines,
persecutions, the menace of Anti-Christ, heavenly portents
will precede the Day when the Son of Man comes with great
power and glory. All this is true ; but there is no reason
to suppose that Mark expects a long interval. The sayings
usually cited do not support this view. The Gospel is to be
preached first ' unto all the nations ' (10) ; but Mark is not
thinking of centuries of evangelization, but of the world of
his day. When, further, he quotes the saying of Jesus that
' the day ' is known neither to men, nor to angels, nor to
Himself, but to the Father only (32), it is not the historical
meaning of the saying, with its discouragement of apocalyptic
forecasts, which governs his thinking ; else, he would not
have compiled Mk. xiii. What he understands the saying
to mean is that within a short time the End will come, but
just when only God knows. Mark fervently shares the Advent
Hope of primitive Christianity.

The Evangelist's methods show that he uses his material with relative fidelity. The whole Gospel witnesses to this fact, and, in particular, Mk. xiii itself. Incoherences and inconsistencies in the chapter would have been removed if Mark had been writing freely. Only the use of disparate tradition will account for the references to an Anti-Christ who appears only to disappear, and to a Son of Man who does no more than send His angels to gather His Elect ; only so can we explain the use of the saying, ' Of that day or that hour knoweth no one ', which threatens the whole apocalyptic edifice, and the presence of parables which retain traces of their original and different meaning. This fidelity of Mark to his sources gives hope to the investigator. Had he worked with a masterful hand, we should know nothing of earlier stages in the tradition and it would not be possible to judge its historical value.

The linguistic data are difficult to assess. None the less, there is a difference between Mark's normal vocabulary and style and the words and expressions characteristic of the second generation of Christianity. ' Semitisms ', moreover, and their distribution in the chapter, may distinguish sayings and groups of sayings when they are present in some and not in others. In some cases they will merely point to the Aramaic background in genuine sayings of Jesus, but in other cases they may reveal the influence of the Jewish-Christian milieu in which His teaching had been interpreted. To distinguish different groupings of material and editorial passages is a delicate operation, but it can be controlled by the history of interpretation and accepted canons of exegesis. The primary task is to distinguish the separate groups of sayings in Mk. xiii. When this has been done, the original form of the material and the use Mark has made of it must be considered.

3. The discourse consists of four groups of sayings : (A) Signs preceding the Parousia (5-8, 24-7); (B) Sayings on Persecution (9-13); (C) The Abomination of Desolation (14-23); (D) Sayings and Parables on Watchfulness (28-37).

(A) *Signs Preceding the Parousia* (5-8, 24-7). The section has characteristic apocalyptic features ; it describes signs and portents leading up to the Parousia. As it now stands, the section is broken into two parts, 5-8 and 24-7, by the insertion of B and C, and editorial passages appear to have been added in 5a, ' Jesus began to say ', possibly in 6 in the phrase ' in my name ', in 8c, ' These things are the beginning of travail ', and in 24a, ' But in those days, after that tribulation '. Originally, it may be suggested, A read as follows :

5. ' Take heed that no man lead you astray.
6. Many shall come (in my name), saying, " I am he " ;
And shall lead many astray.
7. And when you hear of wars and rumours of wars,
Be not troubled :
These things must needs come to pass ;
But the End is not yet.
8. For nation shall rise against nation,
And kingdom against kingdom :
There shall be earthquakes in divers places ;
There shall be famines.
24. The sun shall be darkened,
And the moon shall not give her light,
25. And the stars shall be falling from heaven,
And the powers in the heavens shall be shaken.
26. And then shall they see the Son of Man coming in
clouds,
With great power and glory.
27. And then shall he send forth the angels,
And shall gather together his Elect from the four
winds,
From the uttermost part of the earth
To the uttermost part of heaven.'

With the exception of the phrase ' in my name ', and possibly the Son of Man saying in 26 (cf. xiv. 62), the section contains nothing which could not belong to a Jewish-Christian apocalypse or to a liturgical poem or early Christian sermon. Further, as is suggested in the note on xiii. 5 f., ' in my name ' has the appearance of an addition. Apparently, it is an attempt to explain A as a prophecy of Jesus, and its incoherence suggests that originally A was of another origin. If this is the character of A, it is possible to give a credible account of the compilation of the entire discourse. Mark was committed to the difficult task of combining different streams of tradition serviceable to the exhortation ' Be on the alert ! Watch ! '

(B) *Sayings on Persecution* (9-13). In this group of sayings there can be little doubt that 10 is added by Mark (*v.* Comm.), and that the primitive unit is 9, 11-13. The group appears to have been compiled in the Church at Rome at a time when the danger of a clash with the Imperial authorities grew nearer daily. Its purpose was to enhearten Christians by the assurance that their perils had been foreseen and by the promise of eschatological salvation. A certain poetic structure, which may go back to Jesus Himself, is manifest in the section. It may be that the opening exhortation, ' But take heed to yourselves ' (9a), is editorial, and that the basic unit is as follows [1] :

> 9. ' They shall deliver you up to councils ;
>   And in synagogues shall you be beaten ;
>   And before governors and kings
>   Shall you stand for my sake
>   (For a witness unto them).
> 11   And when they arrest you,
>   And deliver you up,
>   Be not anxious beforehand,
>   What you shall speak.
>   But what is given you in that hour,
>   That speak you ;
>   For it is not you that speak,
>   But the Holy Spirit.
> 12.   And brother shall deliver up
>   Brother to death (and father son) ;
>   And children shall rise up
>   Against parents and doom them to death
> 13.   And you shall be hated of all men
>   For my name's sake :
>   But he that endureth to the end,
>   The same shall be saved.'

The group, it will be seen, forms a unit. The sayings in 9 and 11 are preserved with relative fidelity, while those in 12 f. appear to reflect the ' killing times '. The tone is grim. That it is attuned to a later situation is suggested by the parallel in Lk. xxi. 12-19, which, apart from the Markan insertion in 16 f., is more resonant and confident, although less rhythmical in form, especially in the saying peculiar to this version, ' And not a hair of your head shall perish. In

---

[1] Cf. C. F. Burney, *PL*, 118 f. The passages in brackets, and *v.* 10, are explained by him as subsequent modifications.

your endurance you shall win your souls ' (18 f.). Not unnaturally, B reflects the circumstances of Neronic times.

(C) *The Abomination of Desolation* (14-23). This section
is quite different in form and subject-matter from B. It
appears to be a Palestinian group of sayings connected with
Jerusalem. So, at least, we should judge from 14 and the
Semitic character of 19 f. and 22. Verse 23 may be editorial,
since it repeats the warning ' Take heed ', which is characteristic of the discourse, while the saying in 21, ' Lo, here is the
Christ ' or ' Lo, there ', may have been inserted to give point
to the prophecy about false prophets in 22. The section is
as follows :

14.   ' But when you see the Abomination of Desolation
        standing where he ought not (let him that readeth
        understand), then let them that are in Judaea flee unto
15.   the mountains : and let him that is on the housetop
      not go down, nor enter into the house, to take any-
16.   thing out of his house : and let him that is in the field
17.   not return back to take his cloak. But woe unto them
18.   that are with child and to them that give suck in those
19.   days ! And pray that it be not in the winter. For
      those days shall be tribulation, such as there hath not
      been the like from the beginning of the creation which
20.   God created until now, and never shall be. And
      except the Lord had shortened the days, no flesh
      would have been saved : but for the Elect's sake,
21.   whom he chose, he shortened the days. (And then
      if any man shall say unto you, " Lo, here is the
22.   Christ ", or, " Lo, there " ; believe it not) : for there
      shall arise false Christs and false prophets, and shall
      show signs and wonders, that they may lead astray,
23.   if possible, the Elect. (But take you heed : behold,
      I have told you all things beforehand.) '

If 21 belongs to the section, it may be an indication that
C is distinct from A, for there is a very similar saying in 5 f.
A further difference is that C is concerned with a single event
and its consequences, whereas A mentions a series of signs.
Again, C lacks the poetic form of A and B, and, like B, may
not originally have been apocalyptic in character.

The original theme appears to have been the military
investment of Jerusalem (cf. Lk. xxi. 20-4). The phrase ' the
Abomination of Desolation ' may be used as a description

of Rome, comparable to the use of ' Babylon ' in 1 Pet. v. 13
and Apoc. xviii. 2 and ' the Man of Sin ' in 2 Thess. ii. 3,
with the suggestion that Roman might embodies Satanic
power and is Anti-Christ. The sayings about the man on
his housetop (15) and the field labourer (16) depict hurried
flight in time of war. The counsel to take to the hills (14b)
and the reference to pregnant women and infants (17), and
the hope that the tribulation may not happen in winter (18)
are all consistent with this interpretation and lose force if the
' Abomination ' is not Satanic power let loose in war. Even
the reference to the shortening of the days is not out of harmony with the situation. Nevertheless, this reference to
shortening, the allusion to unparalleled tribulation in 19, and
the prophecy that false prophets will arise with signs and
wonders capable of deceiving the Elect Community, all
suggest that an apocalyptic interpretation has been superimposed on the tradition. What Jesus had said is seen
through an apocalyptic haze. If this be so, Lk. xxi. 20-4,
or a source lying behind this passage and Mk. xiii. 14-23,
is the answer of Jesus to the question of Mk. xiii. 4.[1]

(D) *Sayings and Parables on Watchfulness* (28-37). In
the manner described in the introduction to the section in
the Commentary, the fourth group consisting of sayings and
parables has been compiled by Mark for purposes of exhortation and teaching in order to encourage an attitude of vigilance
in view of the Advent Hope. The key-note is struck in 33,
' Take heed, watch : for you know not when the time is '.

4. The final question to be considered is whether a convincing explanation can be given of the genesis of Mk. xiii
on the assumption of the prior existence of A, B, C, and the
addition of D.

If the sources are those indicated, there can be no doubt
that the Evangelist has accomplished a difficult editorial task
with no little skill and in a relatively conservative spirit. He
was obviously attracted by A, which expressed his own convictions, and which he regarded as genuine prophecy, as
indeed in substance it may be. What course, then, was more

---

[1] Cf. T. W. Manson, *SJ*, 329 f. The
view that Mk. xiii. 14 has been rewritten in the light of the design of
Caligula in A.D. 40 to set up his statue
in the Temple seems to me less probable than the explanation given above.

desirable than to expand A in line with its apocalyptic character ; to insert within it at suitable points B and C, in the
interests of the prevailing belief that definite signs would
precede the End, and to add the eschatological sayings and
parables in D ? The breaking of A into two parts, 5-8 and
24-7, is in every way intelligible. Group A mentioned signs
leading up to the Parousia ; but was there not also the sign
of persecution traditionally connected with the period of the
' Messianic Woes ' ? Accordingly, B was inserted after 8,
at the point where A mentioned wars, earthquakes, and
famines, and before it went on to speak of celestial portents
preceding the Parousia (24-7). It was natural also to insert
C at the same point, but after B. Whether the phrase ' the
Abomination of Desolation ' is a designedly obscure reference
to Rome or not, there can be no doubt that it describes
Satanic power let loose in war, and is thus a form of the Anti-
Christ conception.[1] Its presence, therefore, in C, together
with the subsequent references to the ' tribulation ', the
shortening of the days, and the rise of false prophets with
lying signs, gave to the complex an apocalyptic character
which rendered it suitable for insertion at the place where it
now stands. Was it not believed that the apostasy would
come first, and the Man of Sin be revealed, ' the son of per-
dition, he that opposeth and exalteth himself against all that
is called God or is the object of worship ; so that he sitteth
in the temple of God, setting himself forth as God ' (2 Thess.
ii. 3 f.) ?

Various editorial links were needed to assemble the
material : the declaration preceding B, ' These things are
the beginning of travail ' (8c), together with the warning,
' But take heed to yourselves ' (9a), and after C the resumptive
caption, ' But in those days, after that tribulation ' (24a). It
was necessary also to extend the relevance of the discourse
beyond the four disciples, Peter, James, John, and Andrew,
to Christians now living in Rome. The sayings-collection
supplied this need in D. Sayings and parables were available
which spoke of the coming of the Parousia within the limits
of a generation (30), but denied knowledge of the precise
time (32), and parables already interpreted eschatologically

[1] *V.* Comm. *in loc.*

(28 f., 34-6), so much so that in the second parable the figure of the porter stands in the centre of the picture. Thus, in the catechetical teaching of the Church at Rome, the way had been prepared for the reiterated injunction to watch, and for the assurance that what was said to the disciples was said to all (37).

The implication, that not a little in xiii is secondary tradition, is inescapable on any valid interpretation of the chapter. Genuine sayings are not explained away, but recognized where they exist or where traces of them lie beneath the surface, and the tradition is freed from overgrowths which hide the thought and teaching of Jesus. We gain also a revealing picture of the thought of the Church at Rome about the period A.D. 65. We are far from robbing the teaching of Jesus of its essentially eschatological content, which is unmistakably present in many sayings, but which, for the most part, describes hopes fulfilled in His Person and in the events of His historic ministry. What we detach from His shoulders is the glittering apocalyptic robe with which primitive Christianity clothed Him, and with which He is still draped in popular Christian expectation.

F. THE EXAMINATION BEFORE THE PRIESTS

The historical and legal problems connected with this incident have led to much discussion.[1] In Mk the trial takes place at night and there is a second session the next morning (so Mt); in Lk it is held in the morning (xxii. 66-71); in Jn the time is not stated, but is presumably the evening (xviii. 19-23). Mark appears to describe a formal gathering of the Sanhedrin (xiv. 55), but it is to be noted that, while Jesus is condemned (κατέκριναν, xiv. 64), the verdict is the judgment

---

[1] Cf. A. Taylor Innes, *The Trial of Jesus Christ* (1899); J. Weiss, 308-22; Moffatt, *DCG*, ii. 749-59; J. Juster, *Les Juifs dans l'empire romain* (1914), ii. 132-42; R. W. Husband, *The Prosecution of Jesus* (1916); S. Liberty, *The Political Relations of Christ's Ministry* (1916), 141-57; Ed. Meyer, i. 187-94; Rawlinson, 217-23; Montefiore, i. 350-66; Lagrange, 399, 404 f.; H. Danby, *JTS*, xxi. 51-76; Billerbeck, i. 1020-5; Abrahams, ii. 129-37; Dalman, *JJ*, 98-100; Lietzmann, *Der Prozess Jesu* (1931); Goguel, 502-12; R. H. Lightfoot, 142-51. Goguel cites the articles of Dibelius, Büchsel, Lietzmann, and himself in *ZNTW*, xxx. 193-201, 202-10, 211-15, xxxi. 74-84, 289-301.

that He is worthy of death (ἔνοχον εἶναι θανάτου) rather than a judicial sentence. It is in these circumstances that He is led away to appear before Pilate.

In various ways the Gospel narratives are at variance with the rules laid down in the Mishnah, in *Sanhedrin* iv-vii. Cf. Danby, 386-93. In this tractate it is held that in capital cases the charge must be decided by a quorum of twenty-three judges. The case must be begun with reasons for acquittal and a conviction decided by a majority of at least two; the trial must be conducted in the day time, but a verdict of conviction must not be reached until the following day. A trial, therefore, cannot be held on the eve of a Sabbath or a Festival-day (*Sanh.* iv. 1). Witnesses, it is stated, must be admonished and warned against supposition and mere hearsay (*Sanh.* iv. 5), and it is insisted that the more a judge tests the evidence the better is he deserving of praise (*Sanh.* v. 2). For blasphemy the penalty is stoning, but the blasphemer is not culpable unless he pronounces the Name itself (*Sanh.* vii. 4 f.). How far these regulations obtained in the first century A.D. is disputed; and also the claim made by Juster and Lietzmann that the Jews had the right to condemn men to death on religious grounds.

The problems which arise have been solved in various ways. (1) A. Taylor Innes, 58 f., powerfully argued that the process ' had neither the form nor the fairness of a judicial trial'. As Moffatt, *DCG*, ii. 749, observes, ' this (view) needs to be qualified, but substantially it seems accurate'. Montefiore, i. 351, says that, although the trial violates Jewish law in many important points, it does not follow that the account cannot be true, and adds: ' There have been illegal trials at all times, and even the flimsiest legal forms have sufficed to get rid of an enemy'.

(2) A second explanation, widely accepted and maintained by Husband and Danby, is that the provisions of the tractate *Sanhedrin* are theoretical and ' ideal', and that the so-called ' trial' was rather of the nature of ' Grand Jury proceedings'. Although Danby's statements are criticized in certain respects by Abrahams, the latter admits that the Mishnaic picture is ' idealized in parts'. Rawlinson, 219, thinks that the Sanhedrists had certain powers of initiative

in criminal cases, including the right of arrest, the taking of evidence, and a preliminary examination in preparation for a formal trial before the Roman procurator. It is probable that the later Rabbinic regulations were based on precedents followed in such examinations, but we know too little about the conditions which obtained in the first century to speak with confidence upon this point.

(3) The view maintained by Juster and Lietzmann, and supported by Lightfoot, 147 f., that in this period the San-hedrin had power to condemn men to death on religious grounds, cannot be said to have established itself, in spite of the story of Stephen, the well-known Temple inscription found in 1871 (cf. Robinson, *Eph.* 59 f., 160), and the acts of violence described by Josephus (*Ant.* xx. 9. 1), especially if credence is given to the statement of Jn. xviii. 31 f., ' It is not lawful for us to put any man to death '.

(4) For the view that the trial took place in the morning see the note on xiv. 55. Mark may have placed the trial during the night because he distinguished the account from that mentioned in xv. 1 (πρωί), his tendency being to interpret doublets as separate incidents (cf. vi. 35-44 and viii. 1-9). It is possible also that he knew the tradition concerning a private inquiry immediately after the arrest; cf. Jn. xviii. 13, ' to Annas first '. It is to be noted that only the context of xiv. 55-64 suggests a night session; in the narrative itself there is no temporal statement. In all the circumstances, while there may have been an earlier inquiry, the Lukan date is to be preferred; cf. J. Weiss, 320 f.; Burkitt, 138-8.

G. PARALLELS TO THE STORY OF THE MOCKERY BY THE SOLDIERS

As early as Hugo Grotius (*d.* 1645) attention was drawn to an interesting parallel in the account given by Philo, *In Flacc.* vi. (36-39), of a *mimus* staged to mock Agrippa I on the occasion of his entry into Alexandria on his return from Rome after receiving the kingship of Judaea from Caligula. The people crowned an imbecile named Carabas with a paper crown, clothed him with a mat for a robe, and put a papyrus reed in his hand. The young men formed themselves into a bodyguard, and, while he was seated in a public place, some of them saluted him as king, and others addressed him on matters of state, while the populace hailed him as *Marin*, or Lord. On the basis of this passage S. Reinach, *Orpheus* (Eng. Tr.), 229 f., and J. G. Frazer, *The Golden Bough*², iii. 192 f., have suggested that Carabas is a corruption for Barabbas, a character in a ritual drama analogous to the rites connected with the Roman *Saturnalia* or the Babylonian festival of the *Sacaea*, and it is claimed (e.g. by Loisy, ii. 653 f.) that Jesus was crucified ' in the character of ' or ' in the place of ' Barabbas. Of this view Montefiore, i. 379, observes that it is ' unlikely and needlessly sceptical '.

A closer parallel is supplied by the *Saturnalia* mentioned above. This festival, observed in ancient Rome from the 17th to the 23rd of December, was a season of feasting and revelry, presided over by a mock king, and during which great licence was permitted to slaves. A narrative of the martyrdom of St. Dasius, published by Professor F. Cumont of Ghent, *Analecta Bollandiana*, xvi (1897), 5-16, shows how the feast was celebrated by Roman soldiers on the Danube in the third century A.D. According to custom the Christian soldier Dasius was chosen by lot to play the part of Saturn, with power to indulge in licence and pleasure for thirty days, coupled with the necessity of suicide on the altar of the god after a short but merry reign. When Dasius refused he was beheaded. Frazer, *op. cit.* iii. 142, thinks that the martyrologist's account of the custom of putting a mock king to death as a representative of a god points back to a universal practice in ancient Italy, and P. Wendland, *Hermes*, xxxiii. 175 ff., sees in Mk. xv. 16-20 an attempt to treat Jesus as the Saturnalian king. Against this suggestion are the notable differences of the Markan narrative, as well as the disparity of date (Dec.), which by various conjectures Frazer seeks to overcome (*op. cit.* 144-6).

Alternatively a parallel is sought in the Babylonian festival, the *Sacaea*, celebrated in Western Asia in connexion with the worship of the Persian goddess Anaitis, when a condemned prisoner was arrayed in royal attire, suffered the use of the king's concubines, along with unrestrained feasting and debauchery, only in the end to be stripped of his robes,

scourged, and hanged (or, crucified). Cf. the passage from
Dio Chrysostom, *De Regno*, iv. 66, quoted by Lagrange,
421 f.: Λαβόντες, ἔφη, τῶν δεσμωτῶν ἕνα τῶν ἐπὶ θανάτῳ
καθίζουσιν εἰς τὸν θρόνον τὸν τοῦ βασιλέως, καὶ τὴν ἐσθῆτα
διδόασιν αὐτῷ τὴν βασιλικήν, καὶ προστάττειν ἐῶσι καὶ πίνειν
καὶ τρυφᾶν καὶ ταῖς παλλακαῖς χρῆσθαι τὰς ἡμέρας ἐκείνας ταῖς
βασιλέως, καὶ οὐδεὶς οὐδὲν αὐτὸν κωλύει ποιεῖν ὧν βούλεται. μετὰ
δὲ ταῦτα ἀποδύσαντες καὶ μαστιγώσαντες ἐκρέμασαν. Provided
we pass quickly over the references to the concubines and the
licentiousness, the parallelism lies in external features, the
kingly rôle assigned to a condemned prisoner and the royal
vesture, followed by a complete reversal of fortune seen in
disrobing, scourging, and death. But neither in this, nor
in any of the parallels cited, does the victim put forward
personal claims, nor is he condemned for lese-majesty; nor
again is there any suggestion of the moral and spiritual
dignity manifest even in the silence of Jesus. The same must
be said in respect of Frazer's identification of Purim with the
Sacaea, and his suggestion that Jesus was the Haman of
the year, while Barabbas played the part of the Mordecai,
a view in which conjecture is added to conjecture, and into
which he admits that he has perhaps been led by the interest
and importance of the subject ' somewhat deeper than the
evidence warrants ' (*op. cit.* iii. 195). The industry with which
parallels are gathered is not commensurate with the value
of the results gained. The conclusion actually suggested is
that, like many games, the action of the soldiers, their jesting
and buffoonery, has a long history behind it, on which
analogous stories alike depend, such a story, for example,
as that to which Field, 21 f., refers, in which Plutarch (*Pomp.*
xxiv) tells of Mediterranean pirates who made game of a
captured Roman citizen, but in the end pushed him from
the deck and drowned him. If it were necessary, one might
argue from the ' parallels ' that the soldiers' horseplay is not
strange or inconceivable; but the story is not in need of
defence. Ed. Meyer, i. 187, goes so far as to say that mis-
placed erudition which appeals to the Saturnalia and the
Sacaea only spoils the scene. See further, J. Moffatt, *DCG*,
ii. 756 f.; Lagrange, 421-3; Rawlinson, 229 f.; and the
works cited by Klostermann, 180, and Bultmann, 294 n.

H. THE LITERARY STRUCTURE OF THE CRUCIFIXION NARRATIVE

This Note takes up the points raised in the Introduction to the Crucifixion narrative and discussed in the Commentary. It seeks to ascertain to what extent stages can be distinguished in the construction of the account in xv. 21-41.

For purposes of discussion one cannot do better than begin with the analysis of Bultmann, 294-302, although some elements which he accepts as basic have been questioned by other scholars. Bultmann finds the original narrative in 20b-4a (καὶ ἐξάγουσιν to καὶ σταυροῦσιν αὐτόν), and possibly 27 (?) and 37 (the death cry). Thus, in his view, the original narrative told how Jesus was led out to be crucified, how Simon of Cyrene was impressed to carry the cross and Jesus was brought to Golgotha, how He was offered drugged wine which He refused, was crucified along with two bandits, and finally expired with a loud cry. All the rest is secondary tradition : the dividing of the garments, the taunt-sayings, and the cry ' Eloi ' are traced to the influence of Old Testament passages ; the temporal statements are redactional ; the darkness, the rending of the veil, and the centurion's confession are legendary. The added material is 24b, 25, 26 (a parallel to 2), 29-32, 33, 34-6, 38-41, although possibly 36a (the reference to the compassionate soldier) may be original. It is surprising that 23 (the drugged wine) is not questioned, since this detail has often been traced to Psa. lxix. 21 and is so explained by J. Weiss, 334-9. Weiss finds the original nucleus in 15b, 20b-2, 24a, 27, 31 f., 37, 39, 40-1a.

The core, 20b-4a, (27), 37, accepted by Bultmann, is a stable minimum ; but far too much is treated as secondary. An initial objection is the abrupt transition from the circumstances of the crucifixion to the death cry. All the taunts of the spectators disappear, leaving a break only partially filled by the reference to the soldier's act (36a), the originality of which is left an open question. It is reasonable to urge that any reconstruction which leaves the death cry isolated is fragile. The references to the miraculous darkness (33) and the rending of the Temple veil (38) are rightly described as legendary, for this opinion is widely shared (v. Comm.). The darkness is connected with the secondary scheme (' the third hour ', ' the sixth hour ', ' until the ninth hour ') and the rending interrupts the excellent connexion between 37 and 39. The account of the centurion (39) is not legendary, for it is recorded naturally without any overgrowth of suspicious detail, and if Mark reads too much into his confession, the cry ' a son of the gods ', or (as in Lk) ' truly a righteous man ', is readily intelligible. The temporal scheme (25, 33, 34) is probably superimposed, but the reference to ' the ninth hour ' may be original, since the time of the cry ' Eloi ', so near the end, can easily have been remembered, and may have suggested the extension of the three-hour scheme to the whole. This scheme is deliberately corrected in Jn. xix. 14, ' Now . . . it was about the sixth hour '. The relation of the superscription (26) to xv. 2, ' Art thou the King of the Jews ? ', is no good ground for claiming it as an addition, and the fact that Luke introduces it later (xxiii. 38) does not prove that originally it was wanting in Mk. Some degree of uncertainty must attach to the statement about the two bandits (27), for it may have been added to prepare the way for the account of the railings in 29-32.

The claim that 29 f. and 31 f. are doublets is persistent in critical discussions and is not without foundation ; cf. 30, σῶσον σεαυτὸν καταβὰς ἀπὸ τοῦ σταυροῦ, and 31b-2, Ἄλλους ἔσωσεν, ἑαυτὸν οὐ δύναται σῶσαι . . . καταβάτω νῦν ἀπὸ τοῦ σταυροῦ. A second difficulty is the presence of the chief priests and scribes at the crucifixion. While not impossible, this representation seems imaginative. The intention appears to be to obtain a series of three classes of revilers, although no speech is put into the lips of the bandits (32b). Moreover, the account of the robbers is at variance with Lk. xxiii. 39-43. If we have to choose between 29 f. and 31 f., it may be held that greater originality belongs to 29 f., which repeats the bitter charge regarding the destruction of the Temple (cf. xiv. 58).

The most important question is the presence of the cry ' Eloi ' (34) in the basic narrative. Even if it is inserted, the arguments set out in the Commentary point to its genuineness ; but probably it belongs to the bedrock of the narrative. This view carries with it the originality of 36 f. (the comment

of the bystanders), in which 36a was already fused by Mark
or an earlier compiler. F. C. Grant, *EG*, 179, justly observes
that 34-7 are ' too lifelike, too non-Hellenistic, and set too
many problems for Christian explanation to be anything
but original '.

The originality of 37 (the death cry) needs no discussion,
but consideration must be given to the claim that 34 and 37
form a doublet. It is very doubtful if this claim can be sustained. 37 refers to a loud but speechless death cry, 34 to
a saying spoken in a loud voice; and the two are not the
same. If the challenging cry, ' My God, my God, why hast
thou forsaken me ? ', is original, the use in rapid succession
of $\phi\omega\nu\hat{\eta}$ $\mu\epsilon\gamma\acute{a}\lambda\eta$ (34) and $\phi\omega\nu\grave{\eta}\nu$ $\mu\epsilon\gamma\acute{a}\lambda\eta\nu$ (37) is merely the
diction of an unskilled writer. The basic narrative must
have ended with the centurion's confession, and to this, in
accordance with Mark's methods, 40 f. (the reference to the
women) is appended.

From the above discussion it seems probable that the
primary narrative consisted of 21-4, 26, 29 f., 34-7, 39, and
that the (structurally) secondary passages are 25, (27), 31 f.,
33, 38, 40 f. If this result seems unduly conjectural, confirmation is supplied by the fact that the ' secondary ' passages contain possible Semitisms, and that the ' primary '
narrative contains few or none. See the Commentary. The
facts can be seen in the following table in which verses containing Semitisms are underlined :

A.	21-4		26		29 f.		34-7		39	
B.		25		(27)		31 f.	33		38		40 f.

This coincidence of literary, historical, and linguistic considerations is too striking to be accidental.

I. THE WOMEN AT THE CROSS AND THE
EMPTY TOMB

The references to the women in xv. 40 f., 47, and xvi. 1
reflect a desire to connect the death, burial, and resurrection
of Jesus with accredited witnesses. Nevertheless, they cannot
be regarded as inventions, for otherwise they would agree
more closely

The existing variations and obscurities have arisen from early traditions which identified the witnesses with the Galilean women who ministered to Jesus and His disciples and accompanied them to Jerusalem (cf. Lk. viii. 3, xxiii. 49, 55, Mk. xv. 41). Apparently the party consisted of several women, possibly as many as six or even more. Naturally, at different centres of Palestinian Christianity the lists would differ. All agreed that Mary of Magdala was one of the number, but at one centre the names of local women would be remembered and at another centre those of others. Luke's (Caesarean) tradition preserved the names of Joanna and Susanna, Mark's (Jerusalem) tradition a second Mary and Salome. In these circumstances the absence of Salome from Luke's list and that of Joanna and Susanna from Mark's is not surprising. The greater problem is why Salome is mentioned in xv. 40 and xvi. 1, but not in xv. 47, and why the second Mary is described ' of James ' in xvi. 1, ' of Joses ' in xv. 47, and ' the mother of James the less and Joses ' in xv. 40.

The most natural explanation is that Mark was familiar with two different traditions (xv. 47 and xvi. 1) which he has assimilated in xv. 40. The tradition followed in xv. 47 mentioned Mary Magdalene and ' Mary of Joses ', while that contained in xvi. 1 mentioned Mary Magdalene, ' Mary of James ', and Salome. Knowing that several women were present at the crucifixion, Mark has felt justified in combining the two lists. He knew, or assumed, that ' Mary of Joses ' and ' Mary of James ' were one and the same person and therefore used the cumbrous designation found in xv. 40, ' Mary the mother of James the less and Joses ', adding the names of Mary Magdalene (xv. 47, xvi. 1) and Salome (xvi. 1).

C. H. Turner, 81 f., takes a different view. He suggests that originally Mk. xvi. 1 mentioned no names and that xv. 47-xvi. 1 read : ' And Mary the Magdalene and Mary the mother of Joses beheld where he was laid, and when the Sabbath was past bought spices to come and anoint him '. Matthew, he suggests, who reproduces xv. 47 in xxvii. 61, after inserting the story of the sealing of the tomb in xxvii. 62-6, returns at xxviii. 1 to follow Mk, and therefore repeats the names of the women ; and it is in consequence of this fact that subsequently the names were added in Mk. xvi. 1. The difficulties of this view are considerable. First, textually it follows D d k n (q), which in whole or in part omit the names in xvi. 1, but against the rest of the textual tradition. Secondly, Mt. xxviii. 1 does not mention Salome. Thirdly, on the view suggested, ' the other Mary ' of Mt. xxviii. 1 is replaced by ' Mary of James ' in Mk. xvi. 1, in spite of the fact that the previous verse, Mk. xv. 47, has ' Mary of Joses ', where the parallel verse in Mt. xxvii. 61 also has ' the other Mary '. Fourthly, no good reason can be given why the text of Mk should have been altered, if originally it read as Turner suggests. Bartlet, 434, conjectures that the names may have been inserted when the text of Mk was divided into lections for reading in church ; but, if the names were wanting in xvi. 1, the lection could have been begun at xv. 47. Fifthly, if, as is probable, Mk. xvi. 1-8 is a piece of self-contained tradition, it is not surprising that the names are given in xvi. 1. Lastly, the alternative explanation offered above is simpler.

For these reasons the view that Mark has fused xv. 47 and xvi. 1 in xv. 40 is preferable. This explanation is strengthened by the conclusion, independently reached, that xv. 40 f. was appended by Mark to the account of the burial ; *v.* Comm. *in loc.*

J. THE CONSTRUCTION OF THE PASSION AND RESURRECTION NARRATIVE

Since it has frequently been suggested in recent discussions that xiv. 1-xvi. 8 is based on a shorter and more summary narrative (*v.* pp. 524 f.), it is desirable to examine the grounds on which this hypothesis rests and the extent to which it can be sustained.

(1) There are undoubtedly narratives which appear to be intercalated into the body of the account, as earlier in the Gospel in iii. 20-30 and v. 25-34. The Anointing (xiv. 3-9) is the clearest example. Other cases of the kind are the story of Gethsemane (xiv. 32-42), the Trial before the Priests (xiv. 55-64), the Denial (xiv. 54, 66-72), and the Mockery by the Soldiers (xv. 16-20).

(2) Further, as earlier in the Gospel (ii. 21 f., 27 f., iv. 21-5, ix. 28 f., x. 10-12), shorter passages are appended to,

or inserted in, narratives : e.g. xiv. 28 (?), 47, 48-50, 51 f., 65, xv. 25, 33, 38, 40 f., 47.

(3) Again, along with the more vivid and detailed narratives, there are short summary passages, written in better Greek, which have a certain continuity and give an outline to the story, although broken and incomplete : e.g. xiv. 1 f., 10 f., 26, 43b-6, 53a, xv. 1, 15, 22-4, 37, 39. If there is reason to presuppose a foundation source, these passages will probably belong to it.

(4) Finally, of the intercalated narratives mentioned above the Anointing, Gethsemane, the Denial, the Mockery, together with the Prophecy of the Betrayal (xiv. 17-21), the Last Supper (xiv. 22-5), and, in addition, very many of the shorter passages which appear to be appended to, or inserted in, narratives, contain Semitisms or, if the expression be preferred, apparent Semitisms, while these are wanting, or almost wanting, in the Priests' Plot (xiv. 1 f.), the Treachery of Judas (xiv. 10 f.), the Preparations for the Passover (xiv. 12-16), the Prophecy of the Denial (xiv. 26-31), the Arrest (xiv. 43-6), the Trial before the Priests (xiv. 53, 55-64), the Trial before Pilate (xv. 1-15, apart from 2, 8, 12), the Crucifixion (xv. 21-4, 26, 29 f., 34-7, 39), the Burial (xv. 42-6), and the Empty Tomb (xvi. 1-8). Semitisms are found in all the ' appended ' passages, except xiv. 28, xv. 33, 38.

These facts are too remarkable to be dismissed as fanciful. They supply a strong *prima facie* case for regarding the Passion Narrative as a composite section, in which ' primary ' and ' secondary ' elements (using the terms in a strictly structural sense, and without prejudice to historical considerations) can be distinguished. It is probable that a simple distinction between two groups is much too facile ; the construction of the narrative is likely to be much more complex. But it is by first isolating two stages, A and B, that progress is likely to be made. It is necessary also to consider if a credible account can be given of the process by which the existing narrative came into being. It is not necessary to be able to explain everything, to leave no ' loose ends ' and to avoid tantalizing alternatives ; it is enough if a comprehensive hypothesis covers the available data, in spite of points where the literary and historical facts are obscure.

The linguistic details are summarized below. It is fully recognized that several of the alleged ' Semitisms ' are still *sub judice*, but it is claimed that a ' Semitism ' need not be impossible as Greek, and that it is significant if two or more possible examples can be cited in a single verse, and several, or none, in a particular narrative.

1. *The Priests' Plot* (xiv. 1 f.). No Semitisms.

2. *The Anointing* (xiv. 3-9). Semitisms : ἦσαν ἀγανα-κτοῦντες (4) and πρὸς ἑαυτούς (4) ; possibly also πιστικῆς (3) and ἐν ἐμοί (6) ; in ὃ ἔσχεν ἐποίησεν (8) and προέλαβεν μυρί-σαι (8). Note also καλὸν ἔργον (6) in the technical Rabbinic sense of ' good work ' ; cf. D. Daube, *ATR*, xxxii. 3, 188. Asyndeta in 3b, 6c, and 8.

3. *The Treachery of Judas* (xiv. 10 f.). No Semitisms.

4. *The Preparations for the Passover* (xiv. 12-16). καί paratactic is used frequently and there is a possible Semitism in καὶ αὐτός (15) but otherwise the style is not Semitic. Contrast τῇ πρώτῃ ἡμέρᾳ τῶν ἀζύμων (12) and τῇ μιᾷ τῶν σαβ-βάτων (xvi. 2).

5. *The Prophecy of the Betrayal* (xiv. 17-21). Semitisms : ἤρξαντο c. infin. (19) ; εἷς κατὰ εἷς (19) ; καλόν (21) ; asyn-deton in 19.

6. *The Last Supper* (xiv. 22-5). Semitisms : ἐκχυννόμενον with a future sense (24) ; ὑπὲρ πολλῶν (24) ; ἀμὴν λέγω ὑμῖν (25) ; if read, οὐ μὴ προσθῶ πεῖν (25). Cf. also Black, 171 f., on καινόν (25) ; and Jeremias, 88-94. Καὶ ἐσθιόντων αὐτῶν (22) repeats 18a. For πίνω ἐκ (23, 25) v. Comm. The con-struction is not necessarily Semitic, but may be so in this context. The sayings are full of OT ideas ; ' blood ', ' covenant ', ' the fruit of the vine ', ' that day '.

7. *The Prophecy of the Denial* (xiv. 26-31). No Semitisms, apart from Ἀμὴν λέγω σοι in the saying in 30. δέ is used twice and probably three times.

8. *Gethsemane* (xiv. 32-42). Semitisms : ἔρχονται used first and without a subject (32) ; the name Γεθσημανεί (32) ; ἤρξατο c. infin. (33) ; Ἀββά (36), πάλιν (39 f.), ἦσαν κατα-βαρυνόμενοι (40) ; and possibly ἀπέχει (41), cf. Black, 161 f.

9. *The Arrest* (xiv. 43-52). No Semitisms in 43-6, for ἐλθών (45) is not quite redundant. Καὶ εὐθὺς ἔτι λαλοῦντος αὐτοῦ is editorial (cf. v. 35). In the appended passages in 47-52 there are several Semitisms : εἷς (47) ; ἀποκριθεὶς εἶπεν (48) ; ἤμην διδάσκων (49) ; κρατοῦσιν (51).

10. *The Trial before the Priests* (xiv. 53-65). No Semitisms in the narrative proper, 53a, 55-64. The Greek is easy and flowing. δέ is used five times, and the only Markan example of the aor. mid. ἀπεκρίνατο appears in 61. πάλιν (61) may mean ' thereupon ', but one will hesitate to trace it to the Aramaic *tubh* in this context. The impression left by 53b, 54 and 65 is quite different. In 53b the verb precedes the subject, and in 54 ἕως ἔσω εἰς reads like an over literal rendering of an Aramaic original. Cf. also ἦν συνκαθήμενος . . . καὶ θερμαινόμενος (54) ; ἤρξαντο c. infin. (65). 54 is taken up again in 66 by the repetition of θερμαινόμενον, and 53b and xv. 1 may be a doublet.

11. *The Denial* (xiv. 66-72). In contrast with 55-64 the presence of several possible Semitisms in this narrative is noteworthy. Cf. μία (66) ; ἤρξατο c. infin. twice in 69 and 71 ; Οὔτε οἶδα οὔτε ἐπίσταμαι σὺ τί λέγεις in 68 (Torrey, *TG*, 16 f. ; Black, 61) ; ὃν λέγετε (representing *dᵉ*) in 71 ; and ἐπιβαλών in 72, unless Moulton's excellent rendering ' set to ' is accepted. Note also the possibility that Matthew's δῆλόν σε ποιεῖ and (if read) Mark's ὁμοιάζει (70) may be translation variants, and the remarkable frequency of καί paratactic.

12. *The Trial before Pilate* (xv. 1-15). The linguistic features are peculiar. On the one hand, δέ appears no less than 12 times and there are ' Latinisms ' in τὸ ἱκανὸν ποιῆσαι and φραγελλώσας in 15. On the other hand, there are possible Semitisms in ἀποκριθεὶς λέγει (2), ἤρξατο c. infin. (8), and ἀποκριθεὶς ἔλεγεν (12). Possibly in 12 and probably in 13 πάλιν means ' thereupon '. Cf. also Black, 86, 92 n., who suggests that the problem of ' the intrusive πρός ' in Mt. xxvii. 14 may be solved by rendering 5 into Aramaic, and that ἐποίει in 8 may be impersonal. While a confident opinion is not possible, the possibility that 2 and 6-14 have been inserted into 1, 3-5, 15 (less the reference to Barabbas) cannot be ignored.

13. *The Mockery* (xv. 16-20). Cf. (if read) ἔσω εἰς (16);
ἤρξαντο c. infin. (18); also the unskilled use of the voc. in
βασιλεῦ (18) and the phrase τιθέντες τὰ γόνατα (19), not found
in the LXX and for which there are few classical parallels.[1]
That ἵνα σταυρωθῇ (15) and ἵνα σταυρώσωσιν (20) suggest that
16-20 is inserted, has often been suggested.

14. *The Crucifixion* (xv. 21-41). See Note H. The
narrative illustrates the features found in the Passion Narrative as a whole. In the verses which appear to belong to
the foundation narrative (21-4, 26, 29 f., 34-7, 39) there are
no Semitisms, apart from the quotation in 34, while, on the
contrary, in many of the ' insertions ' (25, 27, 31 f., 33, 38,
40 f.) possible Semitisms are found. Cf. καί (25); ἕνα . . .
ἕνα (27); the reading λέγοντες (k in 31); ἦσαν θεωροῦσαι
(40); the translation Gk of 41a.

15. *The Burial* (xv. 42-7). The only possible Semitism
is ἦν προσδεχόμενος (43), which may be inserted. Otherwise,
the vocabulary and constructions suggest composition in a
Gentile environment; *v.* Comm.

16. *The Empty Tomb* (xvi. 1-8). The only features which
might be claimed as Semitic are τῇ μιᾷ τῶν σαββάτων (2),
which may be quasi-technical, and the asyndeta in 6. The
presumption is that the narrative is non-Semitic.

If, as in Note H, we combine the literary and historical
conjectures with the evidence supplied by possible Semitisms,
the results are remarkable. In the following table A contains
the sections which have a certain continuity, in which Semitisms are almost non-existent, while classical words and
' Latinisms ' are not infrequent. Cf. συμβούλιον in the sense
of *consilium* (xv. 1), τὸ ἱκανὸν ποιῆσαι (xv. 15), φραγελλόω
(xv. 15), ἐκπνέω (xv. 37), κεντυρίων (xv. 39, 44 f.), ἐξ ἐναντίας
(xv. 39), τέθνηκεν as distinct from ἀπέθανεν (xv. 44), δωρέομαι
and πτῶμα (xv. 45). In addition may be mentioned the
custom described by ἀγγαρεύουσιν (xv. 21), the allusion to

---

[1] Many scholars explain the Gk
phrase as a Latinism; cf. W. Bauer,
1305; H. Schlier, *KThW*, i. 739;
Bl. Debrunner, § 5. 3b; Plummer, *St.
Lk*, 508. Schlier cites *genua ponere*
(Curtius viii. 7. 13; Quintil. ix. 4. 11),
also *genua submittere* (Ovid, *Fast.* iv.
317; Plin. *Hist. Nat.* viii. 1. 3) and
genua inclinare(Pseud.-Vergil,*Anthol.*
172. 10b; etc.). The evidence seems
too slight to account for the Gk phrase.
Cf. Eur. *Tro.* 1307, γόνυ τίθημι γαίᾳ.

Alexander and Rufus (xv. 21), and the translations of Aramaic and Jewish technical phrases (xv. 22, 34, 42), which may suggest Roman provenance. B contains the narratives and shorter passages which appear to be intercalated or appended, and which *at the same time* are full of possible Semitisms (underlined).

A. xiv. 1 f.	10 f. (12-16).	17-21.		26-31.	
B.	xiv. 3-9.		22-5.		32-42.
A. 43-6.	(53, 55-64.)		xv. 1, 3-5, 15.		
B.	47-52. 54.	65. 66-72.	xv. 2, 6-14.		16-20.
A. 21-4, 26, 29 f., 34-7, 39.			42-6.		(xvi. 1-8.)
B. 25, 27, 31 f., 33, 38, 40 f.			47.		

Note. xiv. 12-16 may have stood in A, but its detail and its use of the term ' disciples ' suggest that it is a later addition to A. Possibly xiv. 17-21 belongs to B, but its interest in the betrayal, which is characteristic of A, suggests that it should be classified as above. The Semitisms in 21, as also in xv. 34, appear in a saying, and xv. 34a is an OT quotation.

The evidence suggests that the Markan Passion Narrative came into existence in at least two main stages represented by A and B. A was non-Semitic and of a summary character. It was a simple straightforward narrative such as might well have been compiled for the needs of the Christian community at Rome. Its unity, continuity, and stark realism mark it as a primitive complex. B, on the contrary, had a strong Semitic flavour, and consisted of vivid self-contained narratives and of striking supplementary details derived from the reminiscences of Peter. It contained a richer tradition which could readily be inserted in the existing basic account. The hypothesis suggested is that Mark found an account of the Passion in Rome and expanded it by the aid of Petrine tradition. This hypothesis is the reverse of what *a priori* might be expected. A purely theoretical construction would suggest that the basic narrative contained Petrine reminiscences, and that, if it was expanded, the additions would be non-Semitic and less historical. The fact that the evidence compels a reversal of this not unnatural expectation is an encouragement to believe that the hypothesis stated above is objective.

It is possible that A is composite. It will be recalled that Bultmann, with whom Jeremias is in general agreement (*v.* p. 525), finds the nucleus of the Passion Narrative in an old account of the Arrest, the Condemnation, the Departure to the Cross, and the Crucifixion. To this Mark added a complex of narratives connected with the Last Supper, the Trial before the Priests, and the Burial, and preceded the whole with the Priests' Plot and the Treachery of Judas. He also added other narratives assigned above to B. It may be doubted, however, if A was so brief. The Priests' Plot and the Treachery of Judas are in line with the story of the Arrest, and the connexion of the Supper with the betrayal belongs to the earliest tradition (cf. 1 Cor. xi. 23). Whatever may be true of xiv. 22-5, it is at least probable that xiv. 17-21 stood in A ; for, although it does not describe the Passover Meal which xiv. 12-16 leads us to expect, its preoccupation with the prophecy of the betrayal is intelligible in a Passion Narrative which reflects so deep an interest in this theme. It is probable also that A included the story of the Burial, for the statement that Jesus ' was buried ' was intentionally included in the primitive *kerygma* (cf. 1 Cor. xv. 4). For the same reason the basic account must have ended in an account of the Resurrection (cf. 1 Cor. xv. 4-7). This account may have been xvi. 1-8, but this narrative is so late and legendary in character that it is more probably a late addition to A, and may have been preceded by some statement regarding the Resurrection and the appearance of Jesus to Peter, to the Twelve, and to other witnesses.

In some respects the most problematical element in A is the Trial before the Priests. It is conceivable that originally the account followed xv. 1a and was transferred to its present position at the time when A and B were combined. But, if xiv. 53b and xv. 1a form a doublet, it is more probable that, although xiv. 55-64 is a fuller account of the summary statement in xv. 1, it was regarded as the record of a separate trial, and accordingly stood in its present position in A. See pp. 565, 646. In view of this uncertainty xiv. 53, 55-64, as well as xvi. 1-8, is enclosed in brackets in the Table.

Tentatively, and for purposes of reference, the text of A may be set out as follows :

xiv. 1 f.	Now after two days was the Passover and the Feast of Unleavened Bread. And the chief priests and the scribes were seeking how they might arrest him by guile and kill him, for they said, ' Not at the Feast, lest haply
xiv. 10 f.	there be a tumult of the people '. And Judas Iscariot, who was one of the Twelve, went away to the chief priests in order to deliver him up to them. And when they heard it they rejoiced, and promised to give him money. And he sought how he might deliver him up conveniently.
xiv. 17-21.	And (on the first day of Unleavened Bread),[1] when evening was come, he cometh with the Twelve. And as they sat and were eating, Jesus said, ' Truly I tell you, One of you shall deliver me up, even he that eateth with me '. And they began to be sorrowful, and to say unto him one by one, ' Is it I ? '. And he said unto them, ' It is one of the Twelve, he that dippeth with me in the one dish. For the Son of Man goeth, even as it is written of him : but alas for that man through whom the Son of Man is delivered up ! it were better for that man if he had not been born.'
xiv. 26-31.	And when they had sung a hymn, they went out unto the mount of Olives. And Jesus saith unto them, ' All ye shall be ensnared : for it is written, " I will smite the shepherd, and the sheep shall be scattered abroad ". Howbeit, after I am raised up, I will lead you into Galilee.' But Peter said, ' Although all shall be ensnared, yet will not I '. And Jesus saith unto him, ' Truly I tell thee, that thou to-day, even this night, before the cock crow twice, shalt deny me thrice '. But he spoke exceeding vehemently, ' If I must die with thee, I will not deny thee '. And in like manner also said they all.
xiv. 43-6.	And straightway [2] Judas came, one of the Twelve, and with him a crowd with knives

---

[1] The inclusion of this phrase at this point is a pure guess. It is correct in this context, but not where it stands in xiv. 12.

[2] Omitting the editorial phrase, ' while he was yet speaking '. Cf. v. 35.

and cudgels, from the chief priests and the
scribes and the elders. Now he who was
delivering him up had given them a sign,
saying, ' The one I shall kiss is he ; seize him
and lead him away without any mistake '.
And when he came, he went up to him at once,
and said ' Rabbi '. And he kissed him fervently. And they laid hands on him, and
seized him.

xiv. 53a.   And they led Jesus away to the high priest.[1]

xv. 1, 3-5, 15.   And straightway in the morning the chief
priests with the elders and scribes, and the
whole council, held a consultation, and bound
Jesus, and carried him away, and delivered
him up to Pilate. And the chief priests
accused him of many things. And Pilate
asked[2] him, 'Answerest thou nothing? Behold
how many things they accuse thee of.' But
Jesus no more answered anything, so that
Pilate marvelled. And Pilate, wishing to
content the crowd,[3] delivered up Jesus, when
he had scourged him, to be crucified.

xv. 21-4, 26,   And they compel one passing by, Simon
29 f., 34-7,   of Cyrene, coming from the country, the
39.   father of Alexander and Rufus, to carry his
cross. And they bring him to the place Gol-
gotha, which is, being interpreted, The place
of a skull. And they sought to give him wine
mingled with myrrh, but he did not receive it.
And they crucify him, and distribute his garments among them, casting lots what each
should take. And the inscription of his
accusation was written, ' The King of the
Jews '. And the passers-by railed at him,
shaking their heads, and saying, ' Ha! thou
that destroyest the Temple, and buildest it
in three days, save thyself, and come down
from the cross '. And at the ninth hour Jesus
cried with a loud voice, ' Eloi, Eloi, lama
sabachthani ? ', which is, being interpreted,
' My God, my God, why hast thou forsaken
me ? '. And some of the bystanders, when
they heard it, said, ' Behold, he is calling for

---

[1] At this point the account of the
Trial before the Priests may have been
added to A.

[2] Omitting πάλιν, which, however,

with οὐκέτι in 5, may indicate that xv.
2 belongs to A.

[3] Omitting ' released to them Barabbas '.

Elijah '. And one ran and filled a sponge
with vinegar, and putting it on a reed sought
to give him to drink. And they said,[1] ' Do
let us see if Elijah comes to take him down '
And with a loud cry Jesus expired. And when
the centurion, who stood facing him, saw that
he so cried out [2] and expired, he said, ' Truly,
this man was the Son of God '.

xv. 42-6   And when evening was now come, since
it was the Preparation, that is, the day before
the Sabbath, there came Joseph of Arimathaea, a councillor of good position (who also
was looking for the kingdom of God), and,
taking courage, he went in to Pilate and asked
for the body of Jesus. And Pilate marvelled
that he was already dead, and summoning the
centurion, he asked him if he had died already.
And when he knew it from the centurion, he
granted the corpse to Joseph. And he bought
a linen cloth, and taking him down, wrapped
him in the linen cloth, and laid him in a tomb
which had been hewn out of the rock, and
rolled a stone against the door of the tomb.

*   *   *   *   *   *   *

Such is A, the Passion Story of the Roman community,
so far as we can recover it. It certainly has unity and distinctiveness. In addition to the linguistic features already
noticed, it is characterized by its emphasis on the guilt of the
hierarchy, the shame of the betrayal, the divinity of Jesus,
the reality of the death, burial, and resurrection, its frequent
use of $\pi\alpha\rho\alpha\delta\acute{\iota}\delta\omega\mu\iota$ (xiv. 10 f., 44, xv. 1, 15), and its allusions
to the Twelve (xiv. 10, 17, 20, 43). As Jeremias, 54, suggests,
the account is built on the outline illustrated in the prophecies
of the Passion (viii. 31, ix. 31, x. 33 f.) and the early Christian
creed in 1 Cor. xv. 3-5, and may have been current earlier
in a shorter form; but, at the time when Mark wrote, it
appears to have attained relative fixity.

In contrast with A, the group B had no continuity, but
consisted of separate narratives and traditions. It is necessary
to ask whether, by presuming the framework supplied by
A, a credible explanation can be given of the disposal of B
material in the Passion Narrative.

---

[1] Mark has $\lambda\acute{\epsilon}\gamma\omega\nu$.   V. Comm.   [2] V. Comm.

The insertion of the Anointing (xiv. 3-9) was determined by its connexion, in the form familiar to Mark, with the Passion. In particular, the statement that the woman had anticipated the anointing of the body of Jesus prepared the way for the account of a burial without anointing and with no other provision for the last offices save a linen shroud. Unless it had already been inserted in A, the narrative of the Preparations for the Passover (xiv. 12-16) was introduced to give greater detail to the account of the Supper, and the deficiencies of xiv. 17-21 were made good by the insertion of the narrative of the Institution of the Supper (xiv. 22-5), which appears to be a liturgical account derived from an early Palestinian source. Representing the best tradition, the Gethsemane story (xiv. 32-42) was naturally placed immediately before the arrest. It gave greater precision to the reference to the departure to the Mount of Olives (xiv. 26), since Gethsemane was probably located on the lower slopes of the hill. How little the B tradition is ' secondary ' in the historical sense is obvious from this narrative of incomparable poignancy. The appended passages, 47 (the incident of the sword), 48-50 (the saying about daily teaching in the Temple), and 51 f. (the story of the young man who fled naked), enriched the grim story of the arrest with ancillary traditions. The Denial (xiv. 54, 66-72), connected in all the accounts with the night of the arrest, was dovetailed into the story of the Trial (xiv. 53, 55-64), and to the latter the story of the mockery of the high priest's attendants was appended (xiv. 65). The narrative of the Trial before Pilate (xv. 1-15) was expanded, possibly by 2, in some sense a doublet of 3-5, and by the story of Barabbas (6-14), and after the sentence the account of the Mockery by the Soldiers (xv. 16-20) was appended. The supplements to the Crucifixion narrative are due to various motives, the desire to extend the temporal scheme suggested by the reference in xv. 34 to ' the ninth hour ' (xv. 25, 33), and to find room for legendary and doctrinal developments of the primitive tradition (xv. 33, 38). Finally, the allusions to the women in xv. 40 f., and 47 were inserted to prepare the way for the account of the Empty Tomb in xvi. 1-8.

In this way, we may presume, the Roman story of the

Cross was expanded by the aid of Petrine tradition and the necessary editorial supplements. If imaginative reconstruction were the only course available, the hypothesis would be extremely speculative and precarious ; but the fact that it is based on observable examples of addition and intercalation Semitic in character in a non-Semitic and continuous narrative, which is marked by distinctive historical and theological interests, goes far to give it an objective character. Allowing for uncertainty in respect of details, we are entitled to claim that Mark's Passion Narrative is the last stage in a process not unlike the building of an ancient church or cathedral. This inference is of far more than literary and critical importance. It implies that almost at once primitive Christianity began to tell the story of the Cross in the interests of worship, teaching, defence, and doctrine, and that before Mark wrote the account had attained a written form. By the aid of his special tradition the Evangelist carried forward a process which had already begun. No better illustration can be given of the immense importance which primitive Christianity gave to the Passion. St. Paul was not the first who could say, ' I decided to know nothing among you save Jesus Christ and him crucified ' (1 Cor. ii. 2).

K. THE DATE OF THE LAST SUPPER

Although this question emerges in xiv. 12-25, its discussion is deferred until this point because many of the relevant issues arise in the Passion Narrative as a whole.

Whether the Last Supper coincided with the Passover Meal is still a disputed question, as the very long list of authorities on both sides given by J. Jeremias in the second edition of his *Die Abendmahlsworte Jesu* (1949) shows.

In the discussion considerable interest has been taken, but without much agreement, in the attempts to show that both the Synoptics and Jn are in the right. D. Chwolson, *Das letzte Passamahl Christi und der Tag seines Todes* (2nd ed., 1908) maintains that, since in the year of the Crucifixion the 15th of Nisan fell on a Sabbath, Jesus, in agreement with the Pharisees, celebrated the Passover on the 14th, while the Sadducees observed the usual day, the 15th

To this hypothesis it is objected that, in the circumstance described, the slaughter of the Passover lambs was put forward four to six hours, not twenty-four, and that the Sadducees are not likely to have allowed a day to elapse before eating the Passover Meal. Alternatively, Billerbeck, ii. 847-53, contends that the Pharisees and the Sadducees disagreed about the day on which the month of Nisan began, and that the Synoptists agreed with the Pharisees and John with the Sadducees. Jeremias, 15, argues that, while it is a possible view, this theory is a pure construction and that there is no proof that the Passover lambs were slaughtered on two different days.

Of greater interest are the attempts to show that the Last Supper was either the *Kiddûsh* for the Sabbath (F. Spitta, G. H. Box, and others) or the *Kiddûsh* for the Passover (W. O. E. Oesterley, G. H. Macgregor, F. Gavin, T. H. W. Maxfield), but F. C. Burkitt, *JTS*, xvii. 294, points out that ' Kiddûsh immediately precedes the actual celebration of the day, e.g. kiddûsh for Sabbath is done on what we call Friday evening, not twenty-four hours earlier '. More recently it has been suggested that the Last Supper was not the Passover Meal, but a gathering of friends to celebrate a religious meal, like the *Ḥaburoth* of the Pharisees (H. Lietzmann, R. Otto, and others); but against this view it is objected that these meals were associated with the laws of marriage, circumcision, burial, and other legal observances. Cf. R. T. Herford, *The Pharisees*, 31; S. Mendelsohn, *JE*, vi. 123 f.; C. W. Dugmore, *JTS*, xlvii. 108 f.

Two outstanding attempts to prove that the Supper was the Passover Meal have been made by G. Dalman, *JJ*, 86-184, and by J. Jeremias, *op. cit.* 18-46. The latter bases his claim on ten points : (1) the fact that the Supper was celebrated in Jerusalem ; (2) during the night ; (3) with the Twelve ; (4) reclining ; (5) with bread eaten during the meal ; (6) and red wine ; (7) with remembrance of the poor ; (8) and with songs of thanksgiving ; (9) that it was followed by a journey within the limits of the city ; and (10) that interpretative words were spoken concerning the bread and the wine. These facts prove that the Supper shared the characteristic features of the Passover Meal ; but they leave open the vital

question of the time. The supper might still have had this
character, if it had been found necessary to celebrate it a day
earlier, especially if it was for the Passover that the upper
room had been prepared (xiv. 12-16).

Two considerations have been held to show that the
Supper was held earlier : (1) the explicit statement of Jn.
xviii. 28b (cf. xix. 31) that the priests did not enter the
Praetorium ' that they might not be defiled, but might eat
the Passover ' ; and (2) a number of facts in the Synoptic
Passion Narrative which are held to be inconsistent with a
date on the 15th of Nisan. The first objection can be turned
only by contending that the Johannine account is determined
by doctrinal ideas. But, although it is suggested that Jesus
is the Paschal Lamb of which no bone may be broken, it
cannot be said, with Jeremias, *JTS*, l. 6 f., that the comparison
with the Paschal Lamb is ' of great importance in the fourth
gospel '. Jn. i. 29, for example, which speaks of Jesus as
' the lamb which taketh away the sin of the world ', cannot
be interpreted by a simple reference to the Paschal Lamb.
On the contrary, the saying probably represents a synthesis
of Old Testament sacrificial ideas, including that of the
Suffering Servant. The Johannine tradition regarding the
date of the Supper commands respect.

Of the inconsistences alleged in the Synoptic Gospels
Jeremias collects ten : (1) The journey to Gethsemane ;
(2) The carrying of arms ; (3) The meeting of the Sanhedrin
and the condemnation to death ; (4) The rending of the high
priest's garments ; (5) The participation of the Jews in the
Roman trial ; (6) The coming of Simon of Cyrene ἀπ' ἀγροῦ ;
(7) The execution ; (8) The purchase of the linen ; (9) The
taking down of the body, the burial, and the rolling of the
stone against the door of the tomb ; (10) The preparation
of spices and ointments. No one has ever advanced all these
objections together and they are not all convincing. Jeremias
is justified in saying that No. 1 is erroneous, that 6 is based
on arbitrary assumptions, and that 5 and 7 concern Roman
ordinances ; but it is doubtful if he can claim more. Nos.
2, 4, 9, 10 are defended as exceptional circumstances or necessities of life covered by Rabbinical decisions. It is, of course,
a moot point how far these later decisions were valid in the

time of Christ; and the same uncertainty arises when Rabbinic evidence is held to dispose of Nos. 3 and 8 (*zwei ernst zu nehmende Einwände*). It is not said that the linen cloth was obtained by a fictitious purchase, and, as previously maintained (p. 570), it is doubtful if the examination before the priests was an official session with a verdict amounting to a condemnation. Later Rabbinical decisions about the trial of a ' false prophet ' on a feast day, in the presence of ' the whole people ', may therefore not be relevant. But there is a more pertinent objection. We may recognize a certain force when this or that ' irregularity ' is defended by an appeal to later Rabbinical decisions, but when this argument is repeated six times over, it wears thin. That arms might be borne by the mob and by the disciples on the day of the Passover, that a session of the Sanhedrin might be held on this day, followed by a condemnation and the rending of the high priest's garments, that the burial can be fitted into rules which, while permitting necessary preparations, enjoined that the limbs of the corpse must not be moved (*Shab.* xxiii. 5 ; Danby, 120), not to speak of the uncertain tradition concerning spices and ointments (Mk. xvi. 1, Jn. xix. 39 f.) — all this is such a remarkable collection of things to be explained, that it is simpler to believe that the Supper preceded the Passover. Jeremias, 34-7, answers Wellhausen's objection that ἄρτος is used in xiv. 22, and too much may be made of the fact that the lamb and bitter herbs are not mentioned, but it is difficult to concede that he is right in interpreting Μὴ ἐν τῇ ἑορτῇ in xiv. 2 as meaning ' Not in the presence of the festival crowd ', a possible rendering of ἑορτή, but one doubtfully supported by Jn. ii. 23 and vii. 11. While, therefore, it is right to say that the question is not finally settled,[1] probably most British scholars are justified in holding that the Last Supper and the Crucifixion preceded the Passover.

[1] Cf. G. Dix, *The Shape of the Liturgy*, 50 n.

INDEX OF GREEK WORDS USED IN
THE GOSPEL

An asterisk denotes that the word is not used elsewhere in the N.T.

ἀββά xiv. 36
*Ἀβιαθάρ ii. 26
Ἀβραάμ xii. 26 (LXX)
ἀγαθοποιεῖν iii. 4
ἀγαθός x. 17, 18 bis
ἀγανακτεῖν x. 14, 41, xiv. 4
ἀγαπᾶν x. 21, xii. 30-1 bis (LXX), 33 bis
ἀγαπητός i. 11, ix. 7, xii. 6
ἀγγαρεύειν xv. 21
ἄγγελος i. 2 (LXX), 13, viii. 38, xii. 25, xiii. 27, 32
ἄγειν i. 38, xiii. 11, xiv. 42
ἀγέλη v. 11, 13
ἅγιος i. 8, 24, iii. 29, vi. 20, viii. 38, xii. 36, xiii. 11
ἄγναφος ii. 21
ἀγνοεῖν ix. 32
ἀγορά vi. 56, vii. 4, xii. 38
ἀγοράζειν vi. 36, 37, xi. 15, xv. 46, xvi. 1
*ἀγρεύειν xii. 13
ἄγριος i. 6
ἀγρός v. 14, vi. 36, 56, x. 29, 30, xi. 8, xiii. 16, xv. 21, xvi. 12
ἀγρυπνεῖν xiii. 33
ἀδελφή iii. 35, vi. 3, x. 29, 30
ἀδελφός i. 16, 19, iii. 17, 31, 32, 33, 34, 35, v. 37, vi. 3, 17, 18, x. 29, 30, xii. 19 ter, 20, xiii. 12 bis
ἀδημονεῖν xiv. 33
ἀδύνατος x. 27
ἄζυμος xiv. 1, 12
ἀθετεῖν vi. 26, vii. 9
αἷμα v. 25, 29, xiv 24
αἴρειν ii. 3, 9, 11, 12, 21, iv. 15, 25, vi. 8, 29, 43, viii. 8, 19, 20, 34, xi. 23, xiii. 15, 16, xv. 21, 24, xvi. 18
αἰτεῖν vi. 22, 23, 24, 25, x. 35, 38, xi. 24, xv. 8, 43
αἰτία xv. 26
αἰών iii. 29, iv. 19, x. 30, xi. 14
αἰώνιος iii. 29, x. 17, 30
ἀκάθαρτος i. 23, 26, 27, iii. 11, 30, v. 2, 8, 13, vi. 7, vii. 25, ix. 25
ἄκανθα iv. 7 bis, 18
ἀκάνθινος xv. 17
ἄκαρπος iv. 19
ἀκοή i. 28, vii. 35, xiii. 7
ἀκολουθεῖν i. 18, ii. 14 bis, 15, v. 24, vi. 1, viii. 34 bis, ix. 38 bis, x. 21, 28, 32, 52, xi. 9, xiv. 13, 54, xv. 41, xvi. 17

ἀκούειν ii. 1, 17, iii. 8, 21, iv. 3, 9, 12, 15, 16, 18, 20, 23, 24, 33, v. 27, vi. 2, 11, 14, 16, 20 bis, 29, 55, vii. 14, 16 bis, 25, 37, viii. 18, ix. 7, x. 41, 47, xi. 14, 18, xii. 28, 29 (LXX), 37, xiii. 7, xiv. 11, 58, 64, xv. 35, xvi. 11
ἀκρίς i. 6
ἄκρον xiii. 27
ἀκυροῦν vii. 13
ἀλάβαστρος, ἡ xiv. 3 bis
ἀλαλάζειν v. 38
*ἄλαλος vii. 37, ix. 17, 25
ἅλας ix. 50 ter
ἀλεεύς i. 16, 17
ἀλείφειν vi. 13, xvi. 1
ἀλεκτοροφωνία xiii. 35
ἀλέκτωρ xiv. 30, 68, 72 bis
Ἀλέξανδρος xv. 21
ἀλήθεια v. 33, xii. 14, 32
ἀληθής xii. 14
ἀληθῶς xiv. 70, xv. 39
ἀλίζεσθαι ix. 49
ἀλλά i. 44, 45, ii. 17 bis, 22, iii. 26, 27, 29, iv. 17, 22, v. 19, 26, 39, vi. 9, 52, vii. 5, 15, 19, 25, viii. 33, ix. 13, 22, 37, x. 8, 27, 40, 43, 45, xi. 23, 32, xii. 14, 25, 27, xiii. 7, 11 bis, 20, 24, xiv. 28, 29, 36, 49, xvi. 7
*ἀλλαχοῦ i. 38
ἀλλήλων iv. 41, viii. 16, ix. 34, 50, xv. 31
ἄλλος iv. 5, 7, 8, 18, 36, vi. 15, vii. 4, viii. 28, x. 11, 12, xi. 8, xii. 4, 5, 9, 31, 32, xiv. 58, xv. 31, 41
ἅλυσις v. 3, 4 bis
Ἀλφαῖος ii. 14, iii. 18
ἁμάρτημα iii. 28, 29
ἁμαρτία i. 4, 5, ii. 5, 7, 9, 10
ἁμαρτωλός ii. 15, 16 bis, 17, viii. 38, xiv. 41
ἀμήν iii. 28, viii. 12, ix. 1, 41, x. 15, 29, xi. 23, xii. 43, xiii. 30, xiv. 9, 18, 25, 30
ἄμπελος xiv. 25
ἀμπελών xii. 1, 2, 8, 9 bis
*ἀμφιβάλλειν i. 16
*ἄμφοδον xi. 4
ἄν iii. 29, 35, v. 28, vi. 10, 11, 56 bis, viii. 35, ix. 1, 37 bis, 41, 42, x. 11, 15, 43, 44, xi. 23, xii. 36 (LXX), xiii. 20, xiv. 44, xvi. 18

669

27, xiv. 1, 10, 43, 47, 53, 54, 55, 60, 61, 63, 66, xv. 1, 3, 10, 11, 31
ἀρχισυνάγωγος v. 22, 35, 36, 38
ἄρχων iii. 22
ἄρωμα xvi. 1
ἄσβεστος ix. 43
ἀσέλγεια vii. 22
ἀσθενεῖν vi. 56
ἀσθενής xiv. 38
ἀσκός ii. 22 quater
ἀσπάζεσθαι ix. 15, xv. 18
ἀσπασμός xii. 38
ἀστήρ xiii. 25
ἀσύνετος vii. 18
ἀσφαλῶς xiv. 44
ἀτιμάζειν xii. 4
ἄτιμος vi. 4
αὐλή xiv. 54, 66, xv. 16
αὐξάνεσθαι iv. 8
αὐτόματος iv. 28
αὐτός passim ; nom. i. 8, ii. 25, iii. 13, iv. 27, 38, v. 40, vi. 17, 45, 47, viii. 29, x. 12, xii. 36, 37, xiv. 15, 44, xv. 43
ἀφαιρεῖν xiv. 47
ἀφεδρών vii. 19
ἄφεσις i. 4, iii. 29
ἀφίειν i. 34, xi. 16
ἀφιέναι i. 18, 20, 31, ii. 5, 7, 9, 10 bis, iii. 28, iv. 12 (LXX), 36, v. 19, 37, vii. 8, 12, 27, viii. 13, x. 14, 28, 29, xi. 6, 25 bis, xii. 12, 19, 20, 22, xiii. 2, 34, xiv. 6, 50, xv. 36, 37
*ἀφρίζειν ix. 18, 20
ἀφροσύνη vii. 22
ἀχειροποίητος xiv. 58

βάθος iv. 5
βάλλειν ii. 22, iv. 26, vii. 27, 30, 33, ix. 22, 42, 45, 47, xi. 23, xii. 41 bis, 42, 43 bis, 44 bis, xv. 24
βαπτίζειν i. 4, 5, 8 bis, 9, vi. 14, 24, x. 38 bis, 39 bis, xvi. 16
βάπτισμα i. 4, x. 38, 39, xi. 30
βαπτισμός vii. 4
βαπτιστής vi. 25, viii. 28
Βαραββᾶς xv. 7, 11, 15
Βαρθολομαῖος iii. 18
*Βαρτιμαῖος x. 46
βασανίζειν v. 7, vi. 48
βασιλεία i. 15, iii. 24 bis, iv. 11, 26, 30, vi. 23, ix. 1, 47, x. 14, 15, 23, 24, 25, xi. 10, xii. 34, xiii. 8, xiv. 25, xv. 43
βασιλεύς vi. 14, 22, 25, 26, 27, xiii. 9, xv. 2, 9, 12, 18, 26, 32
βαστάζειν xiv. 13
βάτος (ὁ) xii. 26
βδέλυγμα xiii. 14 (LXX, Th.)
βεβαιοῦν xvi. 20
Βεελζεβούλ iii. 22
Βηθανία xi. 1, 11, 12, xiv. 3
Βηθσαιδά[ν] vi. 45, viii. 22
Βηθφαγή xi. 1
βιβλίον x. 4 (LXX)

βίβλος xii. 26
βίος xii. 44
βλάπτειν xvi. 18
βλαστάνειν iv. 27
βλασφημεῖν ii. 7, iii. 28, 29, xv. 29
βλασφημία iii. 28, vii. 22, xiv. 64
βλέπειν iv. 12 bis (LXX), 24, v. 31, viii. 15, 18, 23, 24, xii. 14, 38, xiii. 2, 5, 9, 23, 33
βοᾶν i. 3, xv. 34
*Βοανηργές iii. 17
βοηθεῖν ix. 22, 24
βόσκειν v. 11, 14
βούλεσθαι xv. 15
βουλευτής xv. 43
βροντή iii. 17
βρῶμα vii. 19

γαζοφυλάκιον xii. 41 bis, 43
Γαλιλαία i. 9, 14, 16, 28, 39, iii. 7, vi. 21, vii. 31, ix. 30, xiv. 28, xv. 41, xvi. 7
Γαλιλαῖος xiv. 70
γαλήνη iv. 39
γαμεῖν vi. 17, x. 11, 12, xii. 25
γαμίζεσθαι xii. 25
γάρ i. 16, 22, 38, ii. 15, iii. 10, 21, iv. 22, 25, v. 8, 28, 42, vi. 14, 17, 18, 20, 31, 48, 50, 52, vii. 3, 10, 21, 27, viii. 35, 36, 37, 38, ix. 6 bis, 31, 34, 39, 40, 41, 49, x. 14, 22, 27, 45, xi. 13, 18 bis, 32, xii. 12, 14, 23, 25, 44, xiii. 8, 11, 19, 22, 33, 35, xiv. 2, 5, 7, 40, 56, 70, xv. 10, 14, xvi. 4, 8 bis
γαστήρ xiii. 17
γέεννα ix. 43, 45, 47
Γεθσημανεί xiv. 32
γεμίζειν iv. 37, xv. 36
γενεά viii. 12 bis, 38, ix. 19, xiii. 30
γενέσια vi. 21
γένημα xiv. 25
γεννᾶσθαι xiv. 21
Γεννησαρέτ vi. 53
γένος vii. 26, ix. 29
Γερασηνός v. 1
γεύεσθαι ix. 1
γεωργός xii. 1, 2 bis, 7, 9
γῆ ii. 10, iv. 1, 5 bis, 8, 20, 26, 28, 31 bis, vi. 47, 53, viii. 6, ix. 3, 20, xiii. 27, 31, xiv. 35, xv. 33
γίνεσθαι i. 4, 9, 11, 17, 32, ii. 15, 21, 23, 27, iv. 10, 11, 17, 19, 22, 32, 35, 37, 39, v. 14, 16, 33, vi. 2 bis, 14, 21, 26, 35, 47, ix. 3, 6, 7, 21, 26, 33, 50, x. 43, xi. 19, 23, xii. 10 (LXX), 11 (LXX), xiii. 7, 18, 19 bis, 28, 29, 30, xiv. 4, 17, vii. 33, 42, xvi. 10
γινώσκειν iv. 13, v. 29, 43, vi. 38, vii. 24, viii. 17, ix. 30, xii. 12, xiii. 28, 29, xv. 10, 45
γλῶσσα vii. 33, 35, xvi. 17
*γναφεύς ix. 3
Γολγοθᾶ[ν] xv. 22

INDEX OF PROPER NAMES

INDEX OF SUBJECTS

Thornapple Commentaries